July 24-26, 2017
Washington, DC, USA

Association for
Computing Machinery

Advancing Computing as a Science & Profession

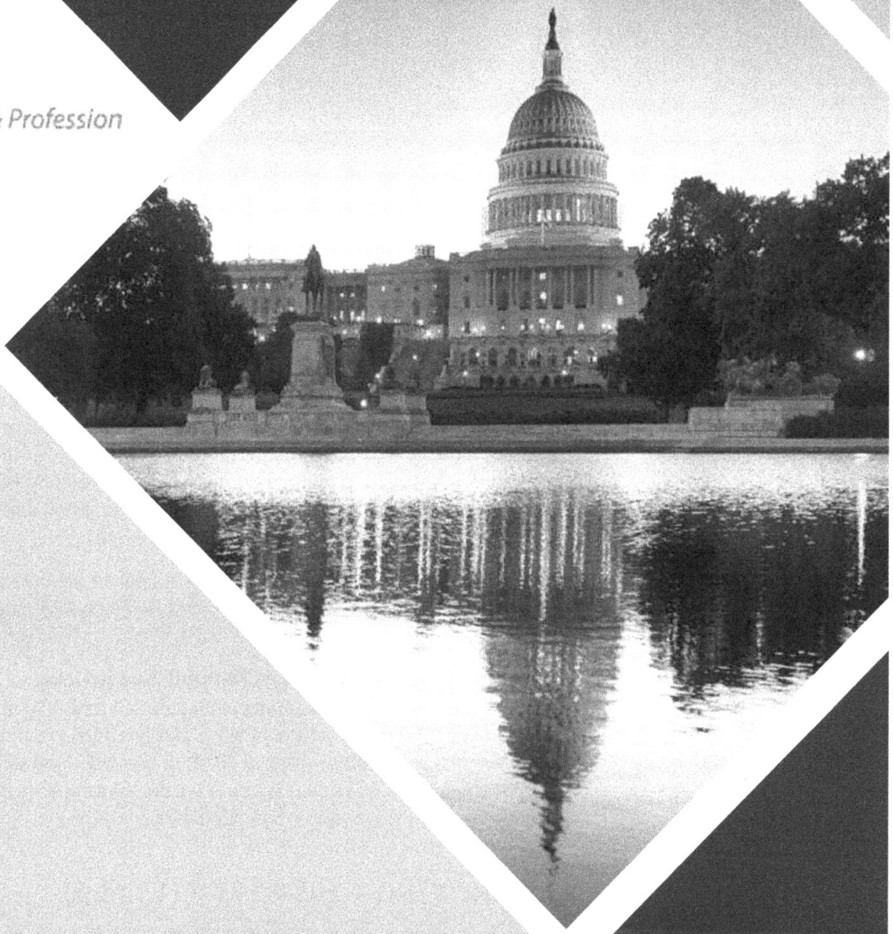

SPAA'17

Proceedings of the 29th ACM Symposium on
Parallelism in Algorithms and Architectures

Sponsored by:

ACM SIGACT & ACM SIGARCH

Supported by:

Akamai & Oracle Labs

Association for
Computing Machinery

Advancing Computing as a Science & Profession

The Association for Computing Machinery
2 Penn Plaza, Suite 701
New York, New York 10121-0701

Notice to Past Authors of ACM-Published Articles
ACM intends to create a complete electronic archive of all articles and/or other material previously published by ACM. If you have written a work that has been previously published by ACM in any journal or conference proceedings prior to 1978, or any SIG Newsletter at any time, and you do NOT want this work to appear in the ACM Digital Library, please inform permissions@acm.org, stating the title of the work, the author(s), and where and when published.

ISBN: 978-1-4503-4593-4 (Digital)

ISBN: 978-1-4503-5667-1 (Print)

Additional copies may be ordered prepaid from:

ACM Order Department
PO Box 30777
New York, NY 10087-0777, USA

Phone: 1-800-342-6626 (USA and Canada)
+1-212-626-0500 (Global)
Fax: +1-212-944-1318
E-mail: acmhelp@acm.org
Hours of Operation: 8:30 am – 4:30 pm ET

Foreword

It is our great pleasure to welcome you to the *29th ACM Symposium on Parallelism in Algorithms and Architectures – SPAA 2017.* The goal of SPAA is to develop a deeper understanding of parallelism in all its forms, bringing together the theory and practice of parallel computing. Over the last several years, the study of parallelism has significantly extended the state of the art in traditional areas of parallel computing but has also expanded to include various new models of parallel computation, new architectures, new techniques for managing parallelism, and new types of parallel systems – in particular Spark, Hadoop, as well as MapReduce and its extension Flume. These increasingly important topics are also represented at SPAA this year.

The call for papers attracted 127 submissions. Out of these submissions, the program committee accepted 31 as regular papers (an acceptance rate of only 25%) and 14 as brief announcements (an acceptance rate of only 11%). The committee's decisions in accepting brief announcements were based on the perceived interest of these contributions, with the hope that extended versions of these announcements will be published later in other conferences or journals.

The keynote talks are given by Guy Blelloch (jointly with PODC) and Piotr Indyk.

The best paper award for SPAA 2017 is awarded to:

- Sepehr Assadi and Sanjeev Khanna: Randomized Composable Coresets for Matching and Vertex Cover
- Sudipto Guha, Yi Li and Qin Zhang: Distributed Partial Clustering

Assadi and Khanna consider the problems of finding maximum cardinality matchings and minimum vertex covers over randomized distributed inputs and achieve a constant approximation factor for maximum matching and an $O(\log n)$-approximation factor for vertex cover. Guha, Li, and Zhang consider several fundamental and partial clustering problems such as k-center, k-median, and k-means with outliers in a distributed model, and provide algorithms with commu-nication sublinear of the input size.

The program committee would like to thank all who submitted papers and who helped the committee in the review process. The names of the external reviewers appear later in the proceedings. We would very much like to thank the program committee for their hard work during the paper selection process. The authors, the external reviewers, and the program committee together made it possible to come up with a great collection of papers for the conference.

Mohammad Hajiaghayi
SPAA 2017 Program Chair
University of Maryland at College Park, USA

Christian Scheideler
SPAA 2017 General Chair
Paderborn University, Germany

Table of Contents

KEYNOTE LECTURE 2

Session Chair: Mohammad Hajiaghayi *(University of Maryland, College Park)*

SESSION 4

Session Chair: Susanne Albers *(Technical University of Munich)*

SESSION 5

Session Chair: Keren Censor-Hillel *(Technion)*

SESSION 6

Session Chair: Frank Dehne *(Carleton University)*

SESSION 7

Session Chair: Mohsen Ghaffari *(ETH Zurich)*

SESSION 8

Session Chair: Boaz Patt-Shamir *(Tel Aviv University)*

SPAA 2017 Symposium Organization

General Chair: Christian Scheideler *(Paderborn University, Germany)*

Program Chair: Mohammad Hajiaghayi *(University of Maryland at College Park, USA)*

Local Arrangements Chairs: Jeremy Fineman *(Georgetown University, USA)*
Calvin Newport *(Georgetown University, USA)*

Publicity Chair: Nodari Sitchinava *(University of Hawaii at Manoa, USA)*

Treasurer: David Bunde *(Knox College, USA)*

Secretary: Jeremy Fineman *(Georgetown University, USA)*

Steering Committee: Guy Blelloch *(Carnegie Mellon University, USA)*
Thomas H. Cormen *(Dartmouth College, USA)*
David Culler *(University of California at Berkeley, USA)*
Frank Dehne *(Carleton University, Canada)*
Pierre Fraigniaud *(University of Paris-Sud, France)*
Phillip B. Gibbons *(Intel Research, USA)*
Maurice Herlihy *(Brown University, USA)*
Tom Leighton *(MIT and Akamai Technologies, USA)*
Charles Leiserson *(Massachusetts Institute of Technology, USA)*
Fabrizio Luccio *(University of Pisa, Italy)*
Friedhelm Meyer auf der Heide *(University of Paderborn, Germany)*
Gary Miller *(CMU and Akamai Technologies, USA)*
Burkhard Monien *(University of Paderborn, Germany)*
Franco Preparata *(Brown University, USA)*
Vijaya Ramachandran *(University of Texas at Austin, USA)*
Arnold Rosenberg *(University of Massachusetts at Amherst, USA)*
Paul Spirakis *(Computer Technology Institute, Greece)*
Uzi Vishkin *(UMIACS, University of Maryland, USA)*
Vijay Atluri *(Rutgers Institute, USA)*
Baisa Buxtino *(CERIAS, Purdue Institute, USA)*
David Fessaiolo *(NIST, USA)*
Trent Jaeger *(IBM Research, USA)*

Program Committee:

Umut Acar *(Carnegie Mellon University, USA)*
Susanne Albers *(TU München, Germany)*
Hossein Asadi *(Sharif University of Technology, Iran)*
Nikhil Bansal *(Eindhoven University of Technology, The Netherlands)*
Hossein Bateni *(Google Research, USA)*
Petra Berenbrink *(Simon Fraser University, Canada)*
Keren Censor-Hillel *(Technion, Israel)*
Hubert Chan *(The University of Hong Kong, China)*
Rajesh Chitnis *(Weizmann Institute of Science, Israel)*
Frank Dehne *(Carleton University, Canada)*
Martin Farach-Colton *(Rutgers University, USA)*
Pierre Fraigniaud *(CNRS and University Paris Diderot, France)*
Mohsen Ghaffari *(ETH Zurich, Switzerland)*
Michael Goodrich *(University of California at Irvine, USA)*
Fabrizio Grandoni *(IDSIA, Switzerland)*
Martin Hoefer *(MPI Informatik, Saarbrücken, Germany)*
Samir Khuller *(University of Maryland at College Park, USA)*
Ravi Kumar *(Google Research, USA)*
Silvio Lattanzi *(Google Research, Switzerland)*
Aleksander Mądry *(MIT, USA)*
Friedhelm Meyer auf der Heide *(Paderborn University, Germany)*
Vahab Mirrokni *(Google Research, USA)*
Morteza Monemizadeh *(Rutgers University, USA)*
Seffi Naor *(Technion, Israel)*
Boaz Patt-Shamir *(Tel Aviv University, Israel)*
Richard Peng *(Georgia Institute of Technology, USA)*
Giuseppe Persiano *(Università di Salerno, Italy)*
Cynthia A. Phillips *(Sandia National Laboratories, USA)*
Yuval Rabani *(The Hebrew University of Jerusalem, Israel)*
Rachid Guerraoui *(EPFL, Switzerland)*
Harald Räcke *(TU München, Germany)*
Rajmohan Rajaraman *(Northeastern University, USA)*
Mauricio Resende *(Amazon, USA)*
Laura Sanità (University of Waterloo, Canada)
Alex Slivkins *(Microsoft Research, USA)*
Peter Varman *(Rice University, USA)*
Roger Wattenhofer *(ETH Zurich, Switzerland)*
Ryan Williams *(Stanford University and MIT, USA)*
David Woodruff *(IBM Almaden Research Center, USA)*

Additional reviewers:

Mohammad Ali Abam
Amir Abboud
Jaume Abella
Saba Ahmadi
Dan Alistarh
Josh Alman
Carlos Eduardo de Andrade
Per Austrin
Hillel Avni
Kyriakos Axiotis
Michael Axtmann
Grey Ballard
Leonid Barenboim
Luca Becchetti
Soheil Behnezhad
Naama Ben-David
Ioana Bercea
Vladimir Boginski
Trevor Brown
Luciana Buriol
Sergiy Butenko
Karthik C. S.
Irina Calciu
Bernadette Charron-Bost
Lin Chen
Ashish Chiplunkar
Zeshan Chishti
Bogdan Chlebus
Florin Ciucu
Graham Cormode
Michel Dagenais
Tudor David
Laxman Dhulipala
Dimitar Dimitrov
Michael Dinitz
Michael Elkin
Alessandro Epasto
Hossein Esfandiari
Yoav Etsion
Guy Even
Björn Feldkord
Jeremy Fineman
Manuela Fischer
Matthias Fischer
Dimitris Fotakis
Waldo Galvez
Kristen Gardner
Rati Gelashvili
Loukas Georgiadis
Yiannis Giannakopoulos
Ellis Giles
Emmanuel Godard
Olga Goussevskaia
Vincent Gramoli
Ofer Grossman
Sudipto Guha
Shalmoli Gupta
Manoj Gupta
Sandy Heydrich
Qiang-Sheng Hua
David Ilcinkas
Sungjin Im
Hamidreza Jahanjou
Jeremy Jones
Daniel Jung
Shahin Kamali
Haim Kaplan
David Kempe
Thomas Kesselheim
Arindam Khan
Seri Khoury
Bojana Kodric
Frederic Koehler
Alex Kogan
Alex Kogan
Justin Kopinsky
Madhukar Korupolu
Sebastian Krinninger
Janardhan Kulkarni
Orna Kupferman
Konstantin Kutzkov
Leon Ladewig
Christoph Lenzen
Yossi Lev
Jian Li
Mehraneh Liaee
Vahid Liaghat
Zhiyu Liu
José M. Abuín
Alexander Mäcker

Additional reviewers (continued):

Sepideh Mahabadi
Tobias Maier
Kostya Makarychev
Konstantin Makarychev
Manuel Malatyali
Christine Markarian
Euripides Markou
Moti Medina
Henning Meyerhenke
Maged Michael
Phil Miller
Flavio K. Miyazawa
Benjamin Moseley
Cameron Musco
Judit Nagy-György
Paresh Nakhe
Danupon Nanongkai
Emanuele Natale
Amir Nayyeri
Thomas Nowak
Francesco Orciuoli
Rasmus Pagh
Roberto Palmieri
Debmalya Panigrahi
Kunsoo Park
Merav Parter
Francesco Pasquale
Ami Paz
Paolo Penna
Mor Perry
Vamsi Potluru
Aleksandar Prokopec
Oleg Prokopyev
Fabio Protti
Kirk Pruhs
Manish Purohit
Andrew Putnam
Mike Rainey
Vijaya Ramachandran
Sören Riechers
Heiko Röglin
Will Rosenbaum
Sushant Sachdeva
Barna Saha
Peter Sanders
Tao Schardl
Kevin Schewior
Warren Schudy
Christian Schulz
Gregory Schwartzman
Chris Schwiegelshohn
Saeed Seddighin
Udaya Shankar
Dimitrios Siakavaras
Michael Spear
Jochen Speck
Jukka Suomela
Omer Tamuz
Kanat Tangwongsan
Veerle Timmermans
Andrew Tinka
Dimitris Tsipras
Jara Uitto
Rob van Stee
Virginia Vassilevska Williams
Yadu Vasudev
Adrian Vladu
Adrian Vladu
Jonathan Walpole
Rolf Wanka
Justin Ward
Renato Werneck
Sam Westrick
John Wickerson
Anthony Wirth
Prudence W.H. Wong
Sheng Yang
Jonathan Yaniv
Grigory Yaroslavtsev
Huacheng Yu
Samson Zhou
Xiaotong Zhuang

SPAA 2017 Sponsors & Supporters

Sponsors: SIGACT SIGARCH

Supporters: Akamai Oracle Labs

Beyond P vs. NP: Quadratic-Time Hardness for Big Data Problems

Piotr Indyk
CSAIL, MIT
indyk@mit.edu

ABSTRACT

The theory of NP-hardness has been very successful in identifying problems that are unlikely to be solvable in polynomial time. However, many other important problems do have polynomial time algorithms, but large exponents in their time bounds can make them run for days, weeks or more. For example, quadratic time algorithms, although practical on moderately sized inputs, can become inefficient on big data problems that involve gigabytes or more of data. Although for many problems no sub-quadratic time algorithms are known, any evidence of quadratic-time hardness has remained elusive.

In this talk I will give an overview of recent research that aims to remedy this situation. In particular, I will describe hardness results for problems in string processing (e.g., edit distance computation or regular expression matching) and machine learning (e.g., Support Vector Machines or gradient computation in neural networks). All of them have polynomial time algorithms, but despite extensive amount of research, no near-linear time algorithms have been found for many variants of these problems. I will show that, under a natural complexity-theoretic conjecture, such algorithms do not exist. I will also describe how this framework has led to the development of new algorithms.

CCS Concepts
Theory of computation

Author Keywords
Edit Distance; Regular Expression Matching; Support Vector Machines; Neural Networks; Fine-grained Complexity

BIOGRAPHY

Piotr Indyk is a Professor of Electrical Engineering and Computer Science at MIT. He joined MIT in 2000, after earning PhD from Stanford University. Earlier, he received Magister degree from Uniwersytet Warszawski in 1995. Piotr's research interests lie in the design and analysis of efficient algorithms. Specific interests include high-dimensional computational geometry, streaming and sub-linear algorithms, sparse recovery and machine learning. He is an ACM Fellow. His work on Sparse Fourier Transform has been named to Technology Review "TR10" in 2012, while his work on locality-sensitive hashing has received the 2012 Kanellakis Theory and Practice Award..

REFERENCES

1. A. Backurs, P. Indyk, "Edit distance cannot be computed in strongly sub-quadratic time (unless SETH is false)", STOC 2015.
2. A. Backurs, P. Indyk, "Which Regular Expression Patterns are Hard to Match?", FOCS 2016.
3. A. Backurs, P. Indyk, L. Schmidt, "On the Fine-Grained Complexity of Empirical Risk Minimization: Kernel Methods and Neural Networks", arXiv:1704.02958, 2017.

SPAA'17, July 24-26, 2017, Washington, DC, USA.

ACM ISBN 978-1-4503-4593-4/17/07.
DOI: http://dx.doi.org/10.1145/3087556.3087603

Randomized Composable Coresets for Matching and Vertex Cover

Sepehr Assadi
Department of Computer and Information Sciences
University of Pennsylvania
Philadelphia, PA, USA

Sanjeev Khanna
Department of Computer and Information Sciences
University of Pennsylvania
Philadelphia, PA, USA

ABSTRACT

A common approach for designing scalable algorithms for massive data sets is to distribute the computation across, say k, machines and process the data using limited communication between them. A particularly appealing framework here is the simultaneous communication model whereby each machine constructs a small representative summary of its own data and one obtains an approximate/exact solution from the union of the representative summaries. If the representative summaries needed for a problem are small, then this results in a *communication-efficient* and *round-optimal* (requiring essentially no interaction between the machines) protocol. Some well-known examples of techniques for creating summaries include sampling, linear sketching, and composable coresets. These techniques have been successfully used to design communication efficient solutions for many fundamental graph problems. However, two prominent problems are notably absent from the list of successes, namely, the *maximum matching* problem and the *minimum vertex cover* problem. Indeed, it was shown recently that for both these problems, even achieving a modest approximation factor of polylog(n) requires using representative summaries of size $\widetilde{\Omega}(n^2)$ i.e. essentially no better summary exists than each machine simply sending its entire input graph.

The main insight of our work is that the intractability of matching and vertex cover in the simultaneous communication model is inherently connected to an *adversarial* partitioning of the underlying graph across machines. We show that when the underlying graph is randomly partitioned across machines, both these problems admit *randomized composable coresets* of size $\widetilde{O}(n)$ that yield an $\widetilde{O}(1)$-approximate solution[1]. In other words, a small *subgraph* of the input graph at each machine can be identified as its representative summary and the final answer then is obtained by simply running any maximum matching or minimum vertex cover algorithm on these combined subgraphs. This results in an $\widetilde{O}(1)$-approximation *simultaneous* protocol for these problems with $\widetilde{O}(nk)$ total communication when the input is randomly partitioned across k machines. We also prove our results are optimal in a very strong sense: we not only rule out existence of smaller randomized composable coresets for these problems but in fact show that our $\widetilde{O}(nk)$ bound for total communication is optimal for *any* simultaneous communication protocol (i.e. not only for randomized coresets) for these two problems. Finally, by a standard application of composable coresets, our results also imply MapReduce algorithms with the same approximation guarantee in one or two rounds of communication, improving the previous best known round complexity for these problems.

[1]Here and throughout the paper, we use $\widetilde{O}(\cdot)$ notation to suppress polylog(n) factors, where n is the number of vertices in the graph.

Supported in part by National Science Foundation grants CCF-1552909, CCF-1617851, and IIS-1447470.
A full version of this paper is available as an online preprint at [9].

SPAA '17, July 24-26, 2017, Washington DC, USA

ACM ISBN 978-1-4503-4593-4/17/07...$15.00
https://doi.org/10.1145/3087556.3087581

1 INTRODUCTION

Recent years have witnessed tremendous algorithmic advances for efficient processing of massive data sets. A common approach for designing scalable algorithms for massive data sets is to distribute the computation across machines that are interconnected via a communication network. These machines can then jointly compute a function on the union of their inputs by exchanging messages. Two main measures of efficiency in this setting are the *communication cost* and the *round complexity*; we shall formally define these terms in details later in the paper but for the purpose of this section, communication cost measures the total number of bits exchanged by all machines and round complexity measures the number of rounds of interaction between them.

An important and widely studied framework here is the *simultaneous* communication model whereby each machine constructs a small representative summary of its own data and one obtains a solution for the desired problem from the union of the representative summary of combined pieces. The appeal of this framework lies in the simple fact that the *simultaneous protocols* are inherently *round-optimal*; they perform in only one round of interaction. The only measure that remains to be optimized is the communication cost – this is now determined by the size of the summary created by each machine. An understanding of the communication cost for a problem in the simultaneous model turns out to have value in other models of computation as well. For instance, a lower bound on the maximum communication needed by any machine implies a matching lower bound on the space complexity of the same problem in dynamic streams [7, 45].

Two particularly successful techniques for designing small summaries for simultaneous protocols are *linear sketches* and *composable coresets*. Linear sketching technique corresponds to taking a linear projection of the input data as its representative summary. The "linearity" of the sketches is then used to obtain a sketch of the combined pieces from which the final solution can be extracted. There has been a considerable amount of work in designing linear sketches for graph problems in recent years [5, 6, 11, 17, 18, 20, 38, 39, 48]. Coresets are subgraphs (in general, subsets of the input) that suitably preserve properties of a given graph, and they are said to be composable if the union of coresets for a collection of graphs yields a coreset for the union of the graphs. Composable coresets have also been studied extensively recently [12, 13, 15, 34, 50, 51], and indeed several graph problems admit natural composable coresets; for instance, connectivity, cut sparsifiers, and spanners (see [47], Section 2.2; the "merge and reduce" approach). Successful applications of these two techniques has yielded $\widetilde{O}(n)$ size summaries for many graph problems (see further related work in Section 1.3). However, two prominent problems are notably absent from the list of successes, namely, the *maximum matching* problem and the *minimum vertex cover* problem. Indeed, it was shown recently [11] that both matching and vertex cover require summaries of size $n^{2-o(1)}$ for even computing a polylog(n)-approximate solution[2].

This state-of-affairs is the starting point for our work, namely, intractability of matching and vertex cover in the simultaneous communication model. Our main insight is that a natural *data oblivious partitioning scheme* completely alters this landscape: both problems admit $\widetilde{O}(1)$-approximate composable coresets of size $\widetilde{O}(n)$ provided the edges of the graph are randomly partitioned across the machines. The idea that random partitioning of data can help in distributed computation was nicely illustrated in the recent work of [50] on maximizing submodular functions. Our work can be seen as the first illustration of this idea in the domain of graph algorithms. The applicability of this idea to graph theoretic problems has been cast as an open problem in [50].

Randomized Composable Coresets. We follow the notation of [50] with a slight modification to adapt to our application in graphs. Let E be an edge-set of a graph $G(V, E)$; we say that a partition $\left\{E^{(1)}, \ldots, E^{(k)}\right\}$ of the edges E is a *random k-partitioning* iff the sets are constructed by assigning each edge in E independently to a set $E^{(i)}$ chosen uniformly at random. A random partitioning of the edges naturally defines partitioning the graph $G(V, E)$ into k graphs $G^{(1)}, \ldots, G^{(k)}$ whereby $G^{(i)} := G(V, E^{(i)})$ for any $i \in [k]$, and hence we use random partitioning for both the edge-set and the input graph interchangeably.

Definition (Randomized Composable Coresets [50]). *For a graph-theoretic problem P, consider an algorithm* ALG *that given any graph $G(V, E)$, outputs a subgraph* ALG$(G) \subseteq G$ *with at most s edges. Let $G^{(1)}, \ldots, G^{(k)}$ be a* random k-partitioning *of a graph G. We say that* ALG *outputs an* α-approximation randomized composable core-set *of* size *s for P if P* $\left(\text{ALG}(G^{(1)}) \cup \ldots \cup \text{ALG}(G^{(k)})\right)$ *is an α-approximation for P(G) w.h.p., where the probability is taken over the random choice of the k-partitioning. For brevity, we use randomized coresets to refer to randomized composable coresets.*

We further augment this definition by allowing the coresets to also contain a *fixed solution* to be *directly* added to the final solution of the composed coresets. In this case, size of the coreset is measured both in the number of edges in the output subgraph plus the number of vertices and edges picked by the fixed solution (this is mostly relevant for our coreset for the vertex cover problem).

1.1 Our Results

We show existence of randomized composable coresets for matching and vertex cover.

Result 1. *There exist randomized coresets of size $\widetilde{O}(n)$ that w.h.p. give an $O(1)$-approximation for maximum matching, and an $O(\log n)$-approximation for minimum vertex cover.*

Result 1 is formalized in Section 3. In contrast to Result 1, when the graph is *adversarially* partitioned, the results of [11] show that the best approximation ratio conceivable for these problems in $\widetilde{O}(n)$ space is only $\Theta(n^{1/3})$. We further remark that Result 1 can also be extended to the weighted version of the problems. Using the Crouch-Stubbs technique [22] one can extend our result to achieve a coreset for weighted matching (with a factor 2 loss in approximation and extra $O(\log n)$ term in the space). Similar ideas of "grouping by weight" of edges can also be used to extend our coreset for weighted vertex cover with an $O(\log n)$ factor loss in approximation and space.

The $\widetilde{O}(n)$ space bound achieved by our coresets above is considered a "sweet spot" for graph streaming algorithms [28, 52] as many fundamental problems are provably intractable in $o(n)$ space (sometimes not enough to even store the answer) while admit efficient solutions in $\widetilde{O}(n)$ space. However, in the simultaneous model, these considerations imply only that the total size of all k coresets must be $\Omega(n)$, leaving open the possibility that coreset output by each machine may be as small as $\widetilde{O}(n/k)$ in size (similar in spirit to coresets of [50]). Our next result rules out this possibility and proves the optimality of our coresets size.

Result 2. *Any α-approximation randomized coreset for the maximum matching problem must have size $\Omega(n/\alpha^2)$, and any α-approximation randomized coreset for the vertex cover problem must have size $\Omega(n/\alpha)$.*

Result 2 is formalized in Section 4. We now elaborate on some applications of our results.

Distributed Computation. We use the following distributed computation model in this paper, referred to as the *coordinator model* (see [59]). The input is distributed across k machines. There is also an additional party called the *coordinator* who receives no input. The machines are allowed to only communicate with the coordinator, not with each other. A protocol in this model is called a *simultaneous* protocol iff the machines simultaneously send a message to the coordinator and the coordinator then outputs the answer with no further interaction. *Communication cost* of a protocol in this model is the total number of bits communicated by all parties.

Result 1 can also be used to design simultaneous protocols for matching and vertex cover with $\widetilde{O}(nk)$ total communication and the same approximation guarantee stated in Result 1 in the case the input is partitioned randomly across k machines. Indeed, each machine only needs to compute a coreset of its input, sends it to the coordinator, and coordinator computes an exact maximum matching or a 2-approximate minimum vertex cover on the union

[2]The authors in [11] only showed the inapproximability result for the matching problem. However, a simple modification of their result proves an identical lower bound for the vertex cover problem as well.

of the coresets. We further prove that the communication cost of theses protocols are essentially optimal.

Result 3. *Any α-approximation simultaneous protocol for the maximum matching problem, resp. the vertex cover problem, requires total communication of $\Omega(nk/\alpha^2)$ bits, resp. $\Omega(nk/\alpha)$ bits, even when the input is partitioned randomly across the machines.*

Proof of Result 3 is deferred to the full version of the paper [9]. We point out that Result 3 is in fact a strengthening of Result 2; it rules out *any* representative summary (not necessarily a randomized coreset) of size $o(n/\alpha^2)$ (resp. $o(n/\alpha)$) that can be used for α-approximation of matching (resp. vertex cover) when the input is partitioned randomly.

For the matching problem, it was shown previously in [33] that when the input is adversarially partitioned in the coordinator model, any protocol (not necessarily simultaneous) requires $\Omega(nk/\alpha^2)$ bits of communication to achieve an α-approximation of the maximum matching. Result 3 extends this to the case of *randomly partitioned* inputs albeit only for simultaneous protocols.

MapReduce Framework. We show how to use our randomized coresets to obtain improved MapReduce algorithms for matching and vertex cover in the MapReduce computation model formally introduced in [40, 44]. Let $k = \sqrt{n}$ be the number of machines, each with a memory of $\widetilde{O}(n\sqrt{n})$; we show that *two* rounds of MapReduce suffice to obtain an $O(1)$-approximation for matching and $O(\log n)$-approximation for vertex cover. In the first round, each machine randomly partitions the edges assigned to it across the k machines; this results in a random k-partitioning of the graph across the machines. In the second round, each machine sends a randomized composable coreset of its input to a designated central machine M; as there are $k = \sqrt{n}$ machines and each machine is sending $\widetilde{O}(n)$ size coreset, the input received by M is of size $\widetilde{O}(n\sqrt{n})$ and hence can be stored entirely on that machine. Finally, M computes the answer by combining the coresets (similar to the case in the coordinator model). Note that if the input was distributed randomly in the first place, we could have implemented this algorithm in only one round of MapReduce (see [50] for details on when this assumption applies).

Our MapReduce algorithm outperforms the previous algorithms of [44] for matching and vertex cover in terms of the number of rounds it uses, albeit with a larger approximation guarantee. In particular, [44] achieved a 2-approximation to both matching and vertex cover in 6 rounds of MapReduce when using similar space as ours on each machine (the number of rounds of this algorithm is always at least 3 even if we allow $\widetilde{O}(n^{5/3})$ space per each machine). The improvement on the number of rounds is significant in this context; the transition between different rounds in a MapReduce computation is usually the dominant cost of the computation [44] and hence, minimizing the number of rounds is an important goal in the MapReduce framework.

1.2 Our Techniques

Randomized Coreset for Matching. Greedy and Local search algorithms are the typical choices for composable coresets (see, e.g., [34, 50]). It is then natural to consider the greedy algorithm for the maximum matching problem as a randomized coreset: the one that computes a *maximal matching*. However, one can easily show that this choice of coreset performs poorly in general; there are simple instances in which choosing arbitrary maximal matching in the graph $G^{(i)}$ results only in an $\Omega(k)$-approximation.

Somewhat surprisingly, we show that a simple change in strategy results in an efficient randomized coreset: *any maximum matching* of the graph $G^{(i)}$ can be used as an $O(1)$-approximate randomized coreset for the maximum matching problem. Unlike the previous work in [34, 50] that relied on analyzing a specific algorithm (or a specific family of algorithms) for constructing a coreset, we prove this result by exploiting structural properties of the maximum matching (i.e., the optimal solution) directly, independent of the algorithm that computes it. As a consequence, our coreset construction requires no prior coordination (such as consistent tie-breaking rules used in [50]) between the machines and in fact each machine can use a different algorithm for computing the maximum matching required by the coreset.

Randomized Coreset for Vertex Cover. In the light of our coreset for the matching problem, one might wonder whether a minimum vertex cover of a graph can also be used as its randomized coreset. However, it is easy to show that the answer is negative here – there are simple instances (e.g., a star on k vertices) on which this leads to an $\Omega(k)$ approximation ratio. Indeed, the *feasibility constraint* in the vertex cover problem depends heavily on the input graph as a whole and not only the coreset computed by each machine, unlike the case for matching and in fact most problems that admit a composable coreset [13, 34, 50]. This suggests the necessity of using edges in the coreset to *certify* the feasibility of the answer. On the other hand, only sending edges seems too restrictive: a vertex of degree $n-1$ can safely be assumed to be in an optimal vertex cover, but to certify this, one needs to essentially communicate $\Omega(n)$ edges. This naturally motivates a slightly more general notion of coresets – the coreset contains both subsets of vertices (to be always included in the final vertex cover) and edges (to guide the choice of additional vertices in the vertex cover).

To obtain a randomized coreset for vertex cover, we employ an iterative "peeling" process where we remove the vertices with the highest residual degree in each iteration (and add them to the final vertex cover) and continue until the residual graph is sufficiently sparse, in which case we can return this subgraph as the coreset. The process itself is a modification of the algorithm by Parnas and Ron [57]; we point out that other modifications of this algorithm has also been used previously for matching and vertex cover [16, 36, 56].

However, to employ this algorithm as a coreset we need to argue that the set of vertices peeled across different machines is not too large as these vertices are added directly to the final vertex cover. The intuition behind this is that random partitioning of edges in the graph should result in vertices to have essentially the same degree across the machines and hence each machine should peel the same set of vertices in each iteration. But this intuition runs into a technical difficulty: the peeling process is quite sensitive to the exact degree of vertices and even slight changes in degree results in moving vertices between different iterations that potentially leads to a cascading effect. To address this, we design a *hypothetical* peeling process (which is aware of the actual minimum vertex cover in G) and show that the our actual peeling process is in fact "sandwiched" between two application of this peeling process with different degree threshold for peeling vertices. We then use this to argue that the set of all vertices peeled across the machines are always contained in the solution of the hypothetical peeling process which in turn can be shown to be a relatively small set.

Lower Bounds for Randomized Coresets. Our lower bound results for randomized coresets for matching are based on the following simple distribution: the input graph consists of union of two bipartite graphs, one of which is a random k-regular graph G_1 with $n/2\alpha$ vertices on each side while the other graph G_2 is a perfect matching of size $n - n/2\alpha$. Thus the input graph almost certainly contains a matching of size $n - o(n)$ and any α-approximate solution must collect $\Omega(n/\alpha)$ edges from G_2 overall i.e. $\Omega(n/\alpha k)$ edges from G_2 from each machine on average. After random partitioning, the input given to each machine is essentially a matching of size $n/2\alpha$ from G_1 and a matching of size roughly n/k from G_2. The local information at each machine is not sufficient to differentiate between edges of G_1 and G_2, and thus any coreset that aims to include $\Omega(n/\alpha k)$ edges from G_2, can not reduce the input size by more than a factor of α. Somewhat similar ideas can also be shown to work for the vertex cover problem.

Communication Complexity Lower Bounds. We briefly highlight the ideas used in obtaining the lower bounds described in Result 3. We will focus on the vertex cover problem to describe our techniques. Our lower bound result is based on analyzing (a variant of) the following distribution: the input graph $G(L, R, E)$ consists of a bipartite graph G_1 plus a single edge $e^\star$. G_1 is a graph on $n/2\alpha$ vertices $L_1 \subseteq L$, each connected to k random neighbors in R, and $e^\star$ is an edge chosen uniformly at random between $L \setminus L_1$ and R. This way G admits a minimum vertex cover of size at most $n/2\alpha + 1$. However, when this graph is randomly partitioned, the input to each machine is essentially a matching of size $n/2\alpha$ chosen from the graph G_1 with possibly one more edge $e^\star$ (in exactly one machine chosen uniformly at random). The local information at the machine receiving the edge $e^\star$ is not sufficient to differentiate between the edges of G_1 and $e^\star$ and thus if the message sent by this machine is much smaller than its input size (i.e., $o(n/\alpha)$ bits), it most likely does not "convey enough information" to the coordinator about the identity of $e^\star$. This in turn forces the coordinator to use more than $n/2$ vertices in order to cover $e^\star$, resulting in an approximation factor larger than α.

Making this intuition precise is complicated by the fact that the input across the players are highly correlated, and hence the message sent by one player, can also reveal extra information about the input of another (e.g. a relatively small communication from the players is enough for the coordinator to know the identity of entire L_1). To overcome this, we show that by conditioning on proper parts of the input, we can limit the correlation in the input of players and then use the *symmetrization* technique of [59] to reduce the simultaneous k-player vertex cover problem to a one-way two-player problem named the *hidden vertex problem* (HVP). Loosely speaking, in HVP, Alice and Bob are given two sets $S, T \subseteq [n]$, each of size n/α, with the promise that $|S \setminus T| = 1$ and their goal is to find a set C of size $o(n)$ which contains the single element in $S \setminus T$. We prove a lower bound of $\Omega(n/\alpha)$ bits for this problem using a subtle

reduction from the well-known set disjointness problem. In this reduction, Alice and Bob use the protocol for HVP on "non-legal" instances (i.e., the ones for which HVP is not well-defined) to reduce the original disjointness instance between sets A, B on a universe $[N]$ to a lopsided disjointness instance (A, B') whereby $|B'| = o(N)$, and then solve this new instance in $o(N)$ communication (using the Håstad-Wigderson protocol [32]), contradicting the $\Omega(N)$ lower bound on the communication complexity of disjointness.

The lower bound for the matching problem is also proven along similar lines (over the hard distribution mentioned earlier for this problem) using a careful combinatorial argument instead of the reduction from the disjointness problem.

1.3 Further Related Work

Maximum matching and minimum vertex cover are among the most studied problems in the context of massive graphs including, in dynamic graphs [14, 53, 56, 60], sub-linear algorithms [31, 54, 55, 57, 62], streaming algorithms [3–6, 10, 11, 20–22, 24–30, 35, 36, 41, 42, 46, 47, 49, 58], MapReduce computation [5, 44], and different distributed computation models [8, 23, 30, 33]. Most relevant to our work are the linear sketches of [20] for computing an *exact* minimum vertex cover or maximum matching in $O(\text{opt}^2)$ space (opt is the size of the solution), and linear sketches of [11, 20] for α-approximating maximum matching in $\widetilde{O}(n^2/\alpha^3)$ space. These results are proven to be tight by [21], and [11], respectively. Finally, [11] also studied the simultaneous communication complexity of bipartite matching in the vertex-partition model and proved that obtaining better than an $O(\sqrt{k})$-approximation in this model requires strictly more than $\widetilde{O}(n)$ communication from each player.

Coresets, composable coresets, and randomized composable coresets are respectively introduced in [2], [34], and [50]. Composable coresets have been used previously in the context of nearest neighbor search [1], diversity maximization [34], clustering [13, 15], and submodular maximization [12, 34, 50]. Moreover, while not particularly termed a composable coreset, the "merge and reduce" technique in the graph streaming literature (see [47], Section 2.2) is identical to composable coresets. Similar ideas as randomized coreset for optimization problems has also been used in random arrival streams [36, 42]. Moreover, communication complexity lower bounds have also been studied previously under the random partitioning of the input [19, 37].

2 PRELIMINARIES

Notation. For any integer m, $[m] := \{1, \ldots, m\}$. Let $G(V, E)$ be a graph; $MM(G)$ denotes the maximum matching size in G and $VC(G)$ denotes the minimum vertex cover size. We assume that these quantities are $\omega(k \log n)^3$. For a set $S \subseteq V$ and $v \in V$, $N_S(v) \subseteq S$ denotes the neighbors of v in the set S. For an edge set $E' \subseteq E$, we use $V(E')$ to refer to vertices incident on E'.

Communication Complexity. We prove our lower bounds for distributed protocols using the framework of communication complexity, and in particular in the *multi-party simultaneous communication model* and the *two-player one-way communication model* (see, e.g., [43]).

---

[3]Otherwise, we can use the algorithm of [20] to obtain *exact* coresets of size $\widetilde{O}(k^2)$ as mentioned in Section 1.3.

Formally, in the multi-party simultaneous communication model, the input is partitioned across k players $P^{(1)}, \ldots, P^{(k)}$. All players have access to an infinite shared string of random bits, referred to as *public randomness* (or *public coins*). The goal is for the players to compute a specific function of the input by simultaneously sending a message to a central party called the coordinator (or the referee). The coordinator then needs to output the answer using the messages received by the players. We refer to the case when the input is partitioned randomly as the *random partition* model.

In the two-player one-way communication model, the input is partitioned across two players, namely Alice and Bob. The players again have access to public randomness, and the goal is for Alice to send a single message to Bob, so that Bob can compute a function of the joint input. The *communication cost* of a protocol in both models is the total length of the messages sent by the players.

3 RANDOMIZED CORESETS FOR MATCHING AND VERTEX COVER

We present our randomized composable coresets for matching and vertex cover in this section, formalizing Result 1.

3.1 A Randomized Coreset for Matching

The following theorem formalizes Result 1 for matching.

THEOREM 1. *Any* maximum matching *of a graph $G(V, E)$ is an $O(1)$-approximation randomized composable coreset of size $O(n)$ for the maximum matching problem.*

We remark that our main interest in Theorem 1 is to achieve *some* constant approximation factor for randomized composable coresets of the matching problem and as such we did not optimize the constant in the approximation ratio. Nevertheless, our result already shows that the approximation ratio of this coreset is *at most* 9 (with more care, we can reduce this factor down to 8; however, as this is not the main contribution of this paper, we omit the details).

Let $G(V, E)$ be any graph and $G^{(1)}, \ldots, G^{(k)}$ be a random k-partitioning of G. To prove Theorem 1, we describe a simple process for combining the maximum matchings (i.e., the coresets) of $G^{(i)}$'s, and prove that this process results in a constant factor approximation of the maximum matching of G; this process is only required for the analysis, i.e., to show that there exists a large matching in the union of coresets; in principle, any (approximation) algorithm for computing a maximum matching can be applied to obtain a large matching from the coresets.

Consider the following greedy process for computing an approximate matching in $G(V, E)$:

GreedyMatch(G):

(1) Let $M^{(0)} := \emptyset$. For $i = 1$ to k:
(2) Let $M^{(i)}$ be a *maximal matching* obtained by adding to $M^{(i-1)}$ the edges in an *arbitrary maximum matching* of $G^{(i)}$ that do not violate the matching property.
(3) return $M := M^{(k)}$.

LEMMA 3.1. GreedyMatch *is an $O(1)$-approximation algorithm for the maximum matching problem w.h.p (over the randomness of the edge partitioning).*

Before proving Lemma 3.1, we show that Theorem 1 easily follows from this lemma.

PROOF OF THEOREM 1. Let ALG be any algorithm that given a graph $G(V, E)$, ALG(G) outputs an arbitrary maximum matching of G. It is immediate to see that to implement GreedyMatch, we only need to compute a maximal matching on the output of ALG on each graph $G^{(i)}$ where $G^{(i)}$'s form a random k-partitioning of G. Consequently, since GreedyMatch outputs an $O(1)$-approximate matching (by Lemma 3.1), the graph $H := G^{(1)} \cup \ldots \cup G^{(k)}$ should contain an $O(1)$-approximate matching as well. We emphasize here that the use of GreedyMatch for finding a large matching in H is *only* for the purpose of analysis. □

In the rest of this section, we prove Lemma 3.1. Recall that MM(G) denotes the maximum matching size in the input graph G. Let $c > 0$ be a small constant to be determined later. To prove Lemma 3.1, we will show that $\left|M^{(k)}\right| \geq c \cdot \text{MM}(G)$ w.h.p, where $M^{(k)}$ is the output of GreedyMatch. Notice that the matchings $M^{(i)}$ (for $i \in [k]$) constructed by GreedyMatch are random variables depending on the random k-partitioning.

Our general approach for the proof of Lemma 3.1 is as follows. Suppose at the beginning of the i-th step of GreedyMatch, the matching $M^{(i-1)}$ is of size $o(\text{MM}(G))$. It is easy to see that in this case, there is a matching of size $\Omega(\text{MM}(G))$ in G that is entirely incident on vertices of G that are not matched by $M^{(i-1)}$. We can further show that in fact $\Omega(\text{MM}(G)/k)$ edges of this matching are appearing in $G^{(i)}$, *even* when we condition on the assignment of the edges in the first $(i-1)$ graphs. The next step is then to argue that the existence of these edges forces *any* maximum matching of $G^{(i)}$ to match $\Omega(\text{MM}(G)/k)$ edges in $G^{(i)}$ between the vertices that are not matched by $M^{(i-1)}$; these edges can always be added to the matching $M^{(i-1)}$ to form $M^{(i)}$. This ensures that while the maximal matching in GreedyMatch is of size $o(\text{MM}(G))$, we can increase its size by $\Omega(\text{MM}(G)/k)$ edges in each of the first $k/3$ steps, hence obtaining a matching of size $\Omega(\text{MM}(G))$ at the end. The following key lemma formalizes this argument.

LEMMA 3.2. *For any $i \in [k/3]$, if $\left|M^{(i-1)}\right| \leq c \cdot \text{MM}(G)$, then, w.p. $1 - O(1/n)$,*

$$\left|M^{(i)}\right| \geq \left|M^{(i-1)}\right| + \left(\frac{1 - 6c - o(1)}{k}\right) \cdot \text{MM}(G)$$

To continue we define some notation. Let $M^{\star}$ be an arbitrary maximum matching of G. For any $i \in [k]$, we define $M^{\star<i}$ as the part of $M^{\star}$ assigned to the first $i-1$ graphs in the random k-partitioning, i.e., the graphs $G^{(1)}, \ldots, G^{(i-1)}$. We have the following simple concentration result (the proof is deferred to the full version [9]).

CLAIM 3.3. *W.p. $1 - O(1/n)$, for any $i \in [k]$,*

$$\left|M^{\star<i}\right| \leq \left(\frac{i - 1 + o(i)}{k}\right) \cdot \text{MM}(G).$$

We now prove Lemma 3.2.

Proof of Lemma 3.2. Fix an $i \in [k/3]$ and the set of edges for $E^{(1)}, \ldots, E^{(i-1)}$; this also fixes the matching $M^{(i-1)}$ while the set of edges in $E^{(i)}, \ldots, E^{(k)}$ together with the matching $M^{(i)}$ are still random variables. We further assume that after fixing the edges in $E^{(1)}, \ldots, E^{(i-1)}$, $\left|M^{\star<i}\right| \leq \frac{i-1+o(i)}{k} \cdot \mathsf{MM}(G)$ which happens w.p. $1-O(1/n)$ by Claim 3.3.

We first define some notation. Let V_{old} be the set of vertices incident on $M^{(i-1)}$ and V_{new} be the remaining vertices. Let $E^{\geq i}$ be the set of edges in $E \setminus \left(E^{(1)} \cup \ldots \cup E^{(i-1)}\right)$. We partition $E^{\geq i}$ into two parts: (i) E_{old}: the set of edges with *at least one endpoint* in V_{old}, and (ii) E_{new}: the set of edges *incident entirely* on V_{new}. Our goal is to show that w.h.p. *any* maximum matching of $G^{(i)}$ matches $\Omega(\mathsf{MM}(G)/k)$ vertices in V_{new} to each other by using the edges in E_{new}; the lemma then follows easily from this.

Notice that the edges in the graph $G^{(i)}$ are chosen by independently assigning each edge in $E^{\geq i}$ to $G^{(i)}$ w.p. $1/(k-i+1)$[4]. This independence allows us to treat the edges in E_{old} and E_{new} separately; we can fix the set of sampled edges of $G^{(i)}$ in E_{old} denoted by E^i_{old} without changing the distribution of edges in $G^{(i)}$ chosen from E_{new}. Let $\mu_{\text{old}} := \mathsf{MM}(G(V, E^i_{\text{old}}))$, i.e., the maximum number of edges that can be matched in $G^{(i)}$ using only the edges in E^i_{old}. In the following, we show that w.h.p., there exists a matching of size $\mu_{\text{old}} + \Omega(\mathsf{MM}(G)/k)$ in $G^{(i)}$; by the definition of μ_{old}, this implies that *any* maximum matching of $G^{(i)}$ has to use at least $\Omega(\mathsf{MM}(G)/k)$ edges in E_{new}, proving the lemma.

Let M_{old} be any arbitrary maximum matching of size μ_{old} in $G(V, E^i_{\text{old}})$. Let $V_{\text{new}}(M_{\text{old}})$ be the set of vertices in V_{new} that are incident on M_{old}. We show that there is a large matching in $G(V, E_{\text{new}})$ that avoids $V_{\text{new}}(M_{\text{old}})$.

Claim 3.4. *There exists a matching in* $G(V, E_{\text{new}})$ *of size*

$$\left(\frac{k-i+1-o(i)}{k} - 4c\right) \cdot \mathsf{MM}(G)$$

that avoids the vertices of $V_{\text{new}}(M_{\text{old}})$.

Proof. We first bound the size of $V_{\text{new}}(M_{\text{old}})$. Since any edge in M_{old} has at least one endpoint in V_{old}, we have $|V_{\text{new}}(M_{\text{old}})| \leq |M_{\text{old}}| \leq |V_{\text{old}}|$. By the assertion of the lemma, $\left|M^{(i-1)}\right| < c \cdot \mathsf{MM}(G)$, and hence $|V_{\text{new}}(M_{\text{old}})| \leq |V_{\text{old}}| < 2c \cdot \mathsf{MM}(G)$.

Moreover, by the assumption that $\left|M^{\star<i}\right| \leq \frac{i-1+o(i)}{k} \cdot \mathsf{MM}(G)$, there is a matching M of size $\frac{k-i+1-o(i)}{k} \cdot \mathsf{MM}(G)$ in the graph $G(V, E^{\geq i})$. By removing the edges in M that are either incident on V_{old} or $V_{\text{new}}(M_{\text{old}})$, at most $4c \cdot \mathsf{MM}(G)$ edges are removed from M. Now the remaining matching is entirely contained in E_{new} and also avoids $V_{\text{new}}(M_{\text{old}})$, hence proving the claim. □

We are now ready to finalize the proof. Let M_{new} be the matching guaranteed by Claim 3.4. Each edge in this matching is chosen in $G^{(i)}$ w.p. $1/(k-i+1)$ independent of the other edges; hence, by Chernoff bound (and the assumption that $\mathsf{MM}(G) = \omega(k \log n)$), there is a matching of size

$$(1-o(1)) \cdot \left(\frac{1}{k} - \frac{o(i)}{k(k-i+1)} - \frac{4c}{k-i+1}\right) \cdot \mathsf{MM}(G)$$

$$\geq \left(\frac{1-6c-o(1)}{k}\right) \cdot \mathsf{MM}(G) \quad (i \leq k/3)$$

in the edges of M_{new} that appear in $G^{(i)}$. This matching can be directly added to the matching M_{old}, implying the existence of a matching of size $\mu_{\text{old}} + \left(\frac{1-6c-o(1)}{k}\right) \cdot \mathsf{MM}(G)$ in $G^{(i)}$. As argued before, this ensures that any maximum matching of $G^{(i)}$ contains at least $\left(\frac{1-6c-o(1)}{k}\right) \cdot \mathsf{MM}(G)$ edges in E_{new}. These edges can always be added to $M^{(i-1)}$ to form $M^{(i)}$, hence proving the lemma. □

[4] This is true even when we condition on the size of $\left|M^{\star<i}\right|$ since this event does not depend on the choice of edges in $E^{\geq i}$.

Proof of Lemma 3.1. Recall that $M := M^{(k)}$ is the output matching of GreedyMatch. For the first $k/3$ steps of GreedyMatch, if at any step we obtained a matching of size $c \cdot \mathsf{MM}(G)$, then we are already done. Otherwise, at each step, by Lemma 3.2, w.p. $1-O(1/n)$, we increase the size of the maximal matching by $\left(\frac{1-6c-o(1)}{k}\right) \cdot \mathsf{MM}(G)$ edges; consequently, by taking a union bound on the $k/3$ steps, w.p. $1-o(1)$, the size of the maximal matching would be $\left(\frac{1-6c-o(1)}{3}\right) \cdot \mathsf{MM}(G)$. By picking $c = 1/9$, we ensure that in either case, the matching computed by GreedyMatch is of size at least $\mathsf{MM}(G)/9 - o(\mathsf{MM}(G))$, proving the lemma. □

3.2 A Randomized Coreset for Vertex Cover

The following theorem formalizes Result 1 for vertex cover.

Theorem 2. *There exists an* $O(\log n)$*-approximation randomized composable coreset of size* $O(n \log n)$ *for the vertex cover problem.*

Let $G(V, E)$ be a graph and $G^{(1)}, \ldots, G^{(k)}$ be a random k-partitioning of G; we propose the following coreset for computing an approximate vertex cover of G. This coreset construction is a modification of the algorithm for vertex cover first proposed by [57].

> VC-Coreset($G^{(i)}$). An algorithm for computing a composable coreset of each $G^{(i)}$.
>
> (1) Let Δ be the smallest integer such that $n/(k \cdot 2^{\Delta}) \leq 4 \log n$ and define $G^{(i)}_1 := G^{(i)}$.
>
> (2) For $j = 1$ to $\Delta - 1$, let:
>
> $V^{(i)}_j := \left\{\text{vertices of degree} \geq n/(k \cdot 2^{j+1}) \text{ in } G^{(i)}_j\right\}$
>
> $G^{(i)}_{j+1} := G^{(i)}_j \setminus V^{(i)}_j$.
>
> (3) Return $V^{(i)}_{cs} := \bigcup_{j=1}^{\Delta-1} V^{(i)}_j$ as a *fixed solution* plus the graph $G^{(i)}_{\Delta}$ as the coreset.

In VC-Coreset we allow the coreset to, in addition to returning a subgraph, identify a set of vertices (i.e., $V^{(i)}_{cs}$) to be added directly to the final vertex cover. In other words, to compute a vertex cover of the graph G, we compute a vertex cover of the graph $\bigcup_{i=1}^{k} G^{(i)}_{\Delta}$ and return it together with the vertices $\bigcup_{i=1}^{k} V^{(i)}_{cs}$. It is easy to see that this set of vertices indeed forms a vertex cover of G: any edge in G that belongs to $G^{(i)}$ is either incident on some $V^{(i)}_j$, and hence is covered by $V_j^{(i)}$, or is present in $G_\Delta^{(i)}$, and hence is covered by the vertex cover of $G_\Delta^{(i)}$.

In the rest of this section, we bound the approximation ratio of this coreset. To do this, we need to prove that $\left|\bigcup_{i=1}^k V_{\text{cs}}^{(i)}\right| = O(\log n) \cdot \text{VC}(G)$. The bound on the ratio then follows as the vertex cover of $\bigcup_{i=1}^k G_\Delta^{(i)}$ can be computed to within a factor of 2.

It is easy to prove (and follows from [57]) that the set of vertices $V_{\text{cs}}^{(i)}$ is of size $O(\log n) \cdot \text{VC}(G)$; however, using this fact directly to bound the size of $\bigcup_{i=1}^k V_{\text{cs}}^{(i)}$ only implies an approximation ratio of $O(k \log n)$ which is far worse than our goal of achieving an $O(\log n)$-approximation. In order to obtain the $O(\log n)$ bound, we need to argue that not only each set $V_{\text{cs}}^{(i)}$ is relatively small, but also that these sets are all intersecting in many vertices. In order to do so, we introduce a hypothetical algorithm (similar to VC-Coreset) on the graph G and argue that the set $V_{\text{cs}}^{(i)}$ output by VC-Coreset($G^{(i)}$) is, with high probability, a subset of the output of this hypothetical algorithm. This allows us to then bound the size of the union of the sets $V_{\text{cs}}^{(i)}$ for $i \in [k]$.

Let $O^\star$ denote the set of vertices in an arbitrary optimum vertex cover of G and $\overline{O^\star} := V \setminus O^\star$. Consider the following process on the original graph G (defined only for analysis):

(1) Let G_1 be the bipartite graph obtained from G by removing edges between vertices in $O^\star$.
(2) For $j = 1$ to $t := \lceil \log n \rceil$, let:

$$O_j := \left\{\text{vertices in } O^\star \text{ of degree} \geq n/2^j \text{ in } G_j\right\}$$
$$\overline{O}_j := \left\{\text{vertices in } \overline{O^\star} \text{ of degree} \geq n/2^{j+2} \text{ in } G_j\right\}$$
$$G_{j+1} := G_j \setminus (O_j \cup \overline{O}_j).$$

We first prove that the sets O_j's and $\overline{O}_j$'s in this process form an $O(\log n)$ approximation of the minimum vertex cover of G and then show that VC-Coreset($G^{(i)}$) (for any $i \in [k]$) is *mimicking* this hypothetical process in a sense that the set $V_{\text{cs}}^{(i)}$ is essentially *contained* in the union of the sets O_j's and $\overline{O}_j$'s.

Lemma 3.5. $\left|\bigcup_{j=1}^t O_j \cup \overline{O}_j\right| = O(\log n) \cdot \text{VC}(G)$.

Proof. Fix any $j \in [t]$; we prove that $\overline{O}_j \leq 8 \cdot \text{VC}(G)$. The lemma follows from this since there are at most $O(\log n)$ different sets $\overline{O}_j$ and the union of the sets O_j's is a subset of $O^\star$ (with size VC(G)).

Consider the graph G_j. The maximum degree in this graph is at most $n/2^{j-1}$ by the definition of the process. Since all the edges in the graph are incident on at least one vertex of $O^\star$, there can be at most $\left|O^\star\right| \cdot n/2^{j-1}$ edges between the remaining vertices in $O^\star$ and $\overline{O^\star}$ in G_j. Moreover, any vertex in $\overline{O}_j$ has degree at least $n/2^{j+2}$ by definition and hence there can be at most $\left(\left|O^\star\right| \cdot n/2^{j-1}\right) / \left(n/2^{j+2}\right) \leq 8\left|O^\star\right| = 8 \cdot \text{VC}(G)$ vertices in $\overline{O}_j$, proving the claim. □

We now prove the main relation between the sets O_j's and $\overline{O}_j$'s defined above and the intermediate sets $V_j^{(i)}$'s computed by VC-Coreset($G^{(i)}$). The following lemma is the heart of the proof.

Lemma 3.6. *Fix an $i \in [k]$, and let $A_j = V_j^{(i)} \cap O^\star$ and $B_j = V_j^{(i)} \cap \overline{O^\star}$. With probability $1 - O(1/n)$, for any $t \in [\Delta]$:*

(1) $\bigcup_{j=1}^t A_j \supseteq \bigcup_{j=1}^t O_j$.
(2) $\bigcup_{j=1}^t B_j \subseteq \bigcup_{j=1}^t \overline{O}_j$.

Proof. To simplify the notation, for any $t \in [\Delta]$, we let $A_{<t} = \bigcup_{j=1}^{t-1} A_j$ and $A_{\geq t} = \bigcup_{j=t}^{\Delta} A_j$ (and similarly for B_j's, O_j's, and $\overline{O}_j$'s). We also use $N_S(v)$ to denote the neighbor-set of the vertex v in the set $S \subseteq V$.

Note that the vertex-sets of the graphs G and $G^{(i)}$ are the same and we can "project" the sets O_j's and $\overline{O}_j$'s on graph $G^{(i)}$ as well. In other words, we can say a vertex v in $G^{(i)}$ belongs to O_j iff $v \in O_j$ in the original graph G. In the following claim, we crucially use the fact that the graph $G^{(i)}$ is obtained from G by sampling each edge w.p. $1/k$ to prove that the degree of vertices across different sets O_j's (and $\overline{O}_j$'s) in $G^{(i)}$ are essentially the same as in G (up to the scaling factor of $1/k$).

Claim 3.7. *For any $j \in [\Delta]$:*

- *For any vertex $v \in O_j$, $\left|N_{\overline{O}_{\geq j}}(v)\right| \geq n/(k \cdot 2^{j+1})$ in the graph $G^{(i)}$ w.p. $1 - O(1/n^2)$.*
- *For any vertex $v \in \overline{O}_{\geq j+1}$, $\left|N_{O_{\geq j}}(v)\right| < n/(k \cdot 2^{j+1})$ in the graph $G^{(i)}$ w.p. $1 - O(1/n^2)$.*

We defer the proof of Claim 3.7 to the full version of the paper [9]. By a union bound on the n vertices in G, the statements in Claim 3.7 hold for all vertices of G w.p. $1 - O(1/n)$; in the following we condition on this event. We now prove Lemma 3.6 by induction.

Let v be a vertex that belongs to O_1; we prove that v belongs to the set $V_1^{(i)}$ of VC-Coreset, i.e., $v \in A_1$. By Claim 3.7 (for $j = 1$), the degree of v in $G_1^{(i)}$ is at least $n/4k$. Note that in $G_1^{(i)}$, v may also have edges to other vertices in $O^\star$ but this can only increase the degree of v. This implies that v also belongs to A_1 by the threshold chosen in VC-Coreset. Similarly, let u be a vertex in $\overline{O}_{\geq 2}$ (i.e., *not* in $\overline{O}_1$); we show that u is not chosen in $V_1^{(i)}$, implying that B_1 can only contain vertices in $\overline{O}_1$. By Claim 3.7, degree of u in $G_1^{(i)}$ is less than $n/4k$. This implies that u does not belong to B_1. In summary, we have $O_1 \subseteq A_1$ and $B_1 \subseteq \overline{O}_1$.

Now consider some $t > 1$ and let v be a vertex in O_t. By induction, $B_{<t} \subseteq \overline{O}_{<t}$. This implies that the degree of v to $B_{\geq t}$ is at least as large as its degree to $O_{\geq t}$. Consequently, by Claim 3.7 (for $j = t$), degree of v in the graph $G_t^{(i)}$ is at least $n/(k \cdot 2^{t+1})$ and hence v also belongs to A_t. Similarly, fix a vertex u in $\overline{O}_{\geq t+1}$. By induction, $A_{<t} \supseteq O_{<t}$ and hence the degree of u to $A_{\geq t}$ is at most as large as its degree to $O_{\geq t}$; note that since $O^\star$ is a vertex cover, u does not have any other edge in $G_t^{(i)}$ except for the ones to $A_{\geq t}$. We can now argue as before that u does not belong to B_t. □

Proof of Theorem 2. The bound on the coreset size follows immediately from the fact that the graph $G_\Delta^{(i)}$ contains at most $O(n \log n)$ edges and size of $V_{\text{cs}}^{(i)}$ is at most n. As argued before, to prove the bound on the approximation ratio, we only need to show that $\bigcup_{i=1}^k V_{\text{cs}}^{(i)}$ is of size $O(\log n) \cdot \text{VC}(G)$. Let $A^{(i)} = V_{\text{cs}}^{(i)} \cap O^\star$

and $B^{(i)} = V_{cs}^{(i)} \cap \overline{O^\star}$; clearly, each $A^{(i)} \subsetneq O^\star$ and moreover, by Lemma 3.6 (for $t = \Delta$), each $B^{(i)} \subsetneq \cup_{j=1}^{\Delta} \overline{O}_j$. Consequently, $\left|\cup_{i=1}^{k} V_{cs}^{(i)}\right| \leq \left|O^\star\right| + \left|\cup_{j=1}^{\Delta} \overline{O}_j\right| \leq O(\log n) \cdot \mathrm{VC}(G)$, where the last inequality is by Lemma 3.5. □

4 LOWER BOUNDS

We formalize Result 2 in this section. As argued earlier, Result 2 is a special case of Result 3 and hence follows directly from that result; however, as the proof of Result 3 is rather technical and complicated, we instead provide a self-contained proof of Result 2 that is easier to present and conveys some of the main ideas behind Result 3, and postpone the proof of Result 3 to the full version [9].

4.1 A Lower Bound for Randomized Composable Coresets of Matching

The following theorem formalizes Result 2 for matching.

THEOREM 3. *For any $k = o(n/\log n)$ and $\alpha = o(\min\{n/k, k\})$, any α-approximation randomized composable coreset of the maximum matching problem is of size $\Omega(n/\alpha^2)$.*

By Yao's minimax principle [61], to prove the lower bound in Theorem 3, it suffices to analyze the performance of deterministic algorithms over a fixed (hard) distribution. We propose the following distribution for this task. For simplicity of exposition, in the following, we prove a lower bound for $(\alpha/4)$-approximation algorithms; a straightforward scaling of the parameters proves the lower bound for α-approximation.

Distribution $\mathcal{D}_{\mathsf{Matching}}$.

- Let $G(L, R, E)$ (with $|L| = |R| = n$) be constructed as follows:
  1. Pick $A \subsetneq L$ and $B \subsetneq R$, each of size n/α, uniformly at random.
  2. Define E_{AB} as a set of edges between A and B, chosen by picking each edge in $A \times B$ w.p. $k \cdot \alpha/n$.
  3. Define $E_{\overline{AB}}$ as a *random* perfect matching between $\overline{A}$ and $\overline{B}$.
  4. Let $E := E_{AB} \cup E_{\overline{AB}}$.
- Let $E^{(1)}, \ldots, E^{(k)}$ be a *random k-partitioning* of E and let the input to player $P^{(i)}$ be the graph $G^{(i)}(L, R, E^{(i)})$.

Let G be a graph sampled from the distribution $\mathcal{D}_{\mathsf{Matching}}$. Notice first that the graph G always has a matching of size at least $n - n/\alpha \geq n/2$, i.e., the matching $E_{\overline{AB}}$. Additionally, it is easy to see that any matching of size more than $2n/\alpha$ in G uses at least n/α edges from $E_{\overline{AB}}$: the edges in E_{AB} can only form a matching of size n/α by construction. This implies that any $(\alpha/4)$-approximate solution requires recovering at least n/α edges from $E_{\overline{AB}}$. In the following, we prove that this is only possible if the coresets of the players are sufficiently large.

For any $i \in [k]$, define the *induced matching* $M^{(i)}$ as the unique matching in $G^{(i)}$ that is incident on *vertices of degree exactly one*, i.e., both end-points of each edge in $M^{(i)}$ have degree one in $G^{(i)}$. We emphasize that the notion of induced matching is with respect to the entire graph and not only with respect to the vertices included in the induced matching. We have the following crucial lemma on the size of $M^{(i)}$. The proof appears in the full version of the paper [9].

LEMMA 4.1. *W.p. $1 - O(1/n)$, for all $i \in [k]$, $\left|M^{(i)}\right| = \Theta(n/\alpha)$.*

PROOF OF THEOREM 3. Fix any randomized composable coreset for the matching problem that has size $o(n/\alpha^2)$. We show that such a coreset cannot achieve a better than $(\alpha/4)$-approximation over the distribution $\mathcal{D}_{\mathsf{Matching}}$. As argued earlier, to prove this, we need to show that this coreset only contains $o(n/\alpha)$ edges from $E_{\overline{AB}}$ in expectation.

Fix any player $i \in [k]$, and let $M^{\star(i)}$ be the subset of the matching $E_{\overline{AB}}$ assigned to $P^{(i)}$. It is clear that $M^{\star(i)} \subsetneq M^{(i)}$ by the definition of $M^{(i)}$. Moreover, define X_i as the random variable denoting the number of edges from $M^{\star(i)}$ that belong to the coreset sent by player $P^{(i)}$. Notice that X_i is clearly an upper bound on the number of edges of $E_{\overline{AB}}$ that are in the final matching of coordinator and also belong to the input graph of player $P^{(i)}$. In the following, we show that $\mathbb{E}[X_i] = o\left(\frac{n}{k \cdot \alpha}\right)$. Having proved this, we have that the expected size of the output matching by the coordinator is at most $n/\alpha + \sum_{i=1}^{k} \mathbb{E}[X_i] = n/\alpha + o(n/\alpha) < (\alpha/4) \cdot \mathsf{MM}(G)$, a contradiction.

We now prove $\mathbb{E}[X_i] = o\left(\frac{n}{k \cdot \alpha}\right)$. In the following, we condition on the event that $\left|M^{\star(i)}\right| = \Theta(n/k)$ and $\left|M^{(i)}\right| = \Theta(n/\alpha)$; by Chernoff bound (for the first part, since $n/k = \omega(\log n)$) and Lemma 4.1 (for the second part), this event happens with probability $1 - O(1/n)$. As such, this conditioning can only change $\mathbb{E}[X_i]$ by an additive factor of $O(1)$ which we ignore in the following.

A crucial property of the distribution $\mathcal{D}_{\mathsf{Matching}}$ is that the edges in $M^{\star(i)}$ and the remaining edges in $M^{(i)}$ are indistinguishable in $G^{(i)}$. More formally, for any edge $e \in G^{(i)}$,

$$\Pr\left(e \in M^{\star(i)} \mid e \in M^{(i)}\right) = \frac{\left|M^{\star(i)}\right|}{\left|M^{(i)}\right|} = \Theta(\alpha/k)$$

On the other hand, for a fixed input $M^{(i)}$ to player $P^{(i)}$, the computed coreset C_i is always the same (as the coreset is a deterministic function of the player input). Hence,

$$\begin{aligned}\mathbb{E}[X_i] &= \sum_{e \in C_i} \Pr\left(e \in M_i^\star \mid e \in M^{(i)}\right) \\ &= |C_i| \cdot \Theta(\alpha/k) = o(n/\alpha^2) \cdot \Theta(\alpha/k) = o\left(n/(\alpha \cdot k)\right)\end{aligned}$$

where the second last equality is by the assumption that the size of the coreset, i.e., $|C_i|$, is $o(n/\alpha^2)$. This finalizes the proof. □

4.2 A Lower Bound for Randomized Composable Coresets of Vertex Cover

The following is a formal statement of Result 2 for vertex cover.

THEOREM 4. *For any $k = o(n/\log n)$ and $\alpha = o(\min\{n/k, k\})$, any α-approximation randomized composable coreset of the minimum vertex cover problem is of size $\Omega(n/\alpha)$.*

By Yao's minimax principle [61], to prove the lower bound in Theorem 4, it suffices to analyze the performance of deterministic algorithms over a fixed (hard) distribution. We propose the following distribution for this task. For simplicity of exposition, in the following, we prove a lower bound for $(c \cdot \alpha)$-approximation algorithms (for some constant $c > 0$); a straightforward scaling of the parameters proves the lower bound for α-approximation.

Distribution $\mathcal{D}_{\mathrm{VC}}$.

- Construct $G(L, R, E)$ (with $|L| = |R| = n$) as follows:
  (1) Pick $A \subseteq L$ of size n/α uniformly at random.
  (2) Let E_A be a set of edges chosen by picking each edge in $A \times R$ w.p. $k/2n$.
  (3) Pick a single vertex $v^\star$ uniformly at random from $\overline{A}$ and let $e^\star$ be an edge incident on $v^\star$ chosen uniformly at random.
  (4) Let $E := E_A \cup \{e^\star\}$.
- Let $E^{(1)}, \ldots, E^{(k)}$ be a *random k-partitioning* of E and let the input to player $P^{(i)}$ be the graph $G^{(i)}(L, R, E^{(i)})$.

For any $i \in [k]$, we define L_i^1 as the set of vertices in L with degree *exactly one* in $G^{(i)}$. We further define R_i^1 as the set of neighbors of vertices in L_i^1 (note that vertices in R_i^1 do not *not* necessarily have degree exactly one). We have (the proof is deferred to the full version of the paper [9]),

Lemma 4.2. *For any $i \in [k]$, $\left|L_i^1\right| = \Theta(n/\alpha)$ and $\left|R_i^1\right| = \Theta(n/\alpha)$ w.p. $1 - o(1)$.*

Proof of Theorem 4. Let i be the index of the player $P^{(i)}$ that the edge $e^\star$ is given to. We argue that if the coreset sent by player $P^{(i)}$ is of size $o(n/\alpha)$, then the coordinator cannot obtain a vertex cover of size $o(n)$. As the graph G admits a vertex cover of size $(n/\alpha + 1)$ (pick A and $v^\star$), this proves the theorem.

By Lemma 4.2, the set of vertices in L with degree exactly one in $G^{(i)}$ and the set of their neighbors in R, i.e., the sets L_i^1 and R_i^1, are of size $\Theta(n/\alpha)$ w.p. $1 - o(1)$. In the following, we condition on this event. As the algorithm used by $P^{(i)}$ to create the coreset is deterministic, given a fixed input, it always creates the same coreset. However, a crucial property of the distribution $\mathcal{D}_{\mathrm{VC}}$ is that, conditioned on a fixed assignment to L_i^1, the vertex $v^\star$ is chosen uniformly at random from L_i^1. This implies that if the coreset of player $P^{(i)}$ contains $o(n/\alpha)$ edges, then w.p. $1 - o(1)$, $e^\star$ is not part of the coreset ($e^\star$ is chosen uniformly at random from the set of all edges incident on L_i^1). Similarly, if the coreset fixes $o(n/\alpha)$ vertices to be added to the final solution, w.p. $1 - o(1)$, no end point of $e^\star$ is added to this fixed set ($v^\star$ is chosen uniformly at random from L_i^1 of size $\Theta(n/\alpha)$, and the other end point of $e^\star$ is chosen uniformly at random from R_i^1 of size $\Theta(n/\alpha)$). Finally, the coresets of other players are all independent of the edge $e^\star$ and hence as long as the total number of fixed vertices sent by the players is $o(n)$, w.p. $1 - o(1)$, no end points of $e^\star$ are present in the fixed solution. Conditioned on these three events, w.p. $1 - o(1)$, the output of the algorithm does not cover the edge $e^\star$ and hence is not a feasible vertex cover.

We remark that this argument holds even if we are allowed to add extra vertices to the final vertex cover (other than the ones fixed by the players or computed as a vertex cover of the edges in the coresets), since conditioned on $e^\star$ not being present in any coreset, the end point of this edge are chosen uniformly at random from all vertices in $L \setminus A$ and R and hence a solution of size $o(n)$ would not contain either of them w.p. $1 - o(1)$. □

Acknowledgements

The first author would like to thank Sepideh Mahabadi and Ali Vakilian for many helpful discussions in the earlier stages of this work. The authors are grateful to the anonymous reviewers of SPAA 2017 for many insightful comments and suggestions.

REFERENCES

[1] S. Abbar, S. Amer-Yahia, P. Indyk, S. Mahabadi, and K. R. Varadarajan. Diverse near neighbor problem. In *Symposuim on Computational Geometry 2013, SoCG '13, Rio de Janeiro, Brazil, June 17-20, 2013*, pages 207–214, 2013.
[2] P. K. Agarwal, S. Har-Peled, and K. R. Varadarajan. Approximating extent measures of points. *J. ACM*, 51(4):606–635, 2004.
[3] K. J. Ahn and S. Guha. Linear programming in the semi-streaming model with application to the maximum matching problem. *Inf. Comput.*, 222:59–79, 2013.
[4] K. J. Ahn and S. Guha. Access to data and number of iterations: Dual primal algorithms for maximum matching under resource constraints. In *Proceedings of the 27th ACM on Symposium on Parallelism in Algorithms and Architectures, SPAA 2015, Portland, OR, USA, June 13-15, 2015*, pages 202–211, 2015.
[5] K. J. Ahn, S. Guha, and A. McGregor. Analyzing graph structure via linear measurements. In *Proceedings of the Twenty-third Annual ACM-SIAM Symposium on Discrete Algorithms*, SODA '12, pages 459–467. SIAM, 2012.
[6] K. J. Ahn, S. Guha, and A. McGregor. Graph sketches: sparsification, spanners, and subgraphs. In *Proceedings of the 31st ACM SIGMOD-SIGACT-SIGART Symposium on Principles of Database Systems, PODS 2012, Scottsdale, AZ, USA, May 20-24, 2012*, pages 5–14, 2012.
[7] Y. Ai, W. Hu, Y. Li, and D. P. Woodruff. New characterizations in turnstile streams with applications. In *31st Conference on Computational Complexity, CCC 2016, May 29 to June 1, 2016, Tokyo, Japan*, pages 20:1–20:22, 2016.
[8] N. Alon, N. Nisan, R. Raz, and O. Weinstein. Welfare maximization with limited interaction. In *IEEE 56th Annual Symposium on Foundations of Computer Science, FOCS 2015, Berkeley, CA, USA, 17-20 October, 2015*, pages 1499–1512, 2015.
[9] S. Assadi and S. Khanna. Randomized composable coresets for matching and vertex cover. *CoRR*, abs/1705.08242, 2017.
[10] S. Assadi, S. Khanna, and Y. Li. On estimating maximum matching size in graph streams. In *Proceedings of the Twenty-Eighth Annual ACM-SIAM Symposium on Discrete Algorithms, SODA 2017, Barcelona, Spain, Hotel Porta Fira, January 16-19*, pages 1723–1742, 2017.
[11] S. Assadi, S. Khanna, Y. Li, and G. Yaroslavtsev. Maximum matchings in dynamic graph streams and the simultaneous communication model. In *Proceedings of the Twenty-Seventh Annual ACM-SIAM Symposium on Discrete Algorithms, SODA 2016, Arlington, VA, USA, January 10-12, 2016*, pages 1345–1364, 2016.
[12] A. Badanidiyuru, B. Mirzasoleiman, A. Karbasi, and A. Krause. Streaming submodular maximization: massive data summarization on the fly. In *The 20th ACM SIGKDD International Conference on Knowledge Discovery and Data Mining, KDD '14, New York, NY, USA - August 24 - 27, 2014*, pages 671–680, 2014.
[13] M. Balcan, S. Ehrlich, and Y. Liang. Distributed k-means and k-median clustering on general communication topologies. In *Advances in Neural Information Processing Systems 26: 27th Annual Conference on Neural Information Processing Systems 2013. Proceedings of a meeting held December 5-8, 2013, Lake Tahoe, Nevada, United States.*, pages 1995–2003, 2013.
[14] S. Baswana, M. Gupta, and S. Sen. Fully dynamic maximal matching in o(log n) update time. *SIAM J. Comput.*, 44(1):88–113, 2015.
[15] M. Bateni, A. Bhaskara, S. Lattanzi, and V. S. Mirrokni. Distributed balanced clustering via mapping coresets. In *Advances in Neural Information Processing Systems 27: Annual Conference on Neural Information Processing Systems 2014, December 8-13 2014, Montreal, Quebec, Canada*, pages 2591–2599, 2014.
[16] S. Bhattacharya, M. Henzinger, and G. F. Italiano. Deterministic fully dynamic data structures for vertex cover and matching. In *Proceedings of the Twenty-Sixth Annual ACM-SIAM Symposium on Discrete Algorithms, SODA 2015, San Diego, CA, USA, January 4-6, 2015*, pages 785–804, 2015.
[17] S. Bhattacharya, M. Henzinger, D. Nanongkai, and C. E. Tsourakakis. Space- and time-efficient algorithm for maintaining dense subgraphs on one-pass dynamic streams. In *Proceedings of the Forty-Seventh Annual ACM on Symposium on Theory of Computing, STOC 2015, Portland, OR, USA, June 14-17, 2015*, pages 173–182, 2015.
[18] L. Bulteau, V. Froese, K. Kutzkov, and R. Pagh. Triangle counting in dynamic graph streams. *Algorithmica*, 76(1):259–278, 2016.

[19] A. Chakrabarti, G. Cormode, and A. McGregor. Robust lower bounds for communication and stream computation. In *Proceedings of the 40th Annual ACM Symposium on Theory of Computing, Victoria, British Columbia, Canada, May 17-20, 2008*, pages 641–650, 2008.

[20] R. Chitnis, G. Cormode, H. Esfandiari, M. Hajiaghayi, A. McGregor, M. Monemizadeh, and S. Vorotnikova. Kernelization via sampling with applications to finding matchings and related problems in dynamic graph streams. In *Proceedings of the Twenty-Seventh Annual ACM-SIAM Symposium on Discrete Algorithms, SODA 2016, Arlington, VA, USA, January 10-12, 2016*, pages 1326–1344, 2016.

[21] R. H. Chitnis, G. Cormode, M. T. Hajiaghayi, and M. Monemizadeh. Parameterized streaming: Maximal matching and vertex cover. In *Proceedings of the Twenty-Sixth Annual ACM-SIAM Symposium on Discrete Algorithms, SODA 2015, San Diego, CA, USA, January 4-6, 2015*, pages 1234–1251, 2015.

[22] M. Crouch and D. S. Stubbs. Improved streaming algorithms for weighted matching, via unweighted matching. In *Approximation, Randomization, and Combinatorial Optimization. Algorithms and Techniques, APPROX/RANDOM 2014, September 4-6, 2014, Barcelona, Spain*, pages 96–104, 2014.

[23] S. Dobzinski, N. Nisan, and S. Oren. Economic efficiency requires interaction. In *Symposium on Theory of Computing, STOC 2014, New York, NY, USA, May 31 - June 03, 2014*, pages 233–242, 2014.

[24] S. Eggert, L. Kliemann, and A. Srivastav. Bipartite graph matchings in the semi-streaming model. In *Algorithms - ESA 2009, 17th Annual European Symposium, Copenhagen, Denmark, September 7-9, 2009. Proceedings*, pages 492–503, 2009.

[25] L. Epstein, A. Levin, J. Mestre, and D. Segev. Improved approximation guarantees for weighted matching in the semi-streaming model. *SIAM J. Discrete Math.*, 25(3):1251–1265, 2011.

[26] H. Esfandiari, M. Hajiaghayi, and M. Monemizadeh. Finding large matchings in semi-streaming. In *IEEE International Conference on Data Mining Workshops, ICDM Workshops 2016, December 12-15, 2016, Barcelona, Spain.*, pages 608–614, 2016.

[27] H. Esfandiari, M. T. Hajiaghayi, V. Liaghat, M. Monemizadeh, and K. Onak. Streaming algorithms for estimating the matching size in planar graphs and beyond. In *Proceedings of the Twenty-Sixth Annual ACM-SIAM Symposium on Discrete Algorithms, SODA 2015, San Diego, CA, USA, January 4-6, 2015*, pages 1217–1233, 2015.

[28] J. Feigenbaum, S. Kannan, A. McGregor, S. Suri, and J. Zhang. On graph problems in a semi-streaming model. *Theor. Comput. Sci.*, 348(2-3):207–216, 2005.

[29] A. Goel, M. Kapralov, and S. Khanna. On the communication and streaming complexity of maximum bipartite matching. In *Proceedings of the Twenty-third Annual ACM-SIAM Symposium on Discrete Algorithms*, SODA '12, pages 468–485. SIAM, 2012.

[30] V. Guruswami and K. Onak. Superlinear lower bounds for multipass graph processing. In *Proceedings of the 28th Conference on Computational Complexity, CCC 2013, K.lo Alto, California, USA, 5-7 June, 2013*, pages 287–298, 2013.

[31] A. Hassidim, J. A. Kelner, H. N. Nguyen, and K. Onak. Local graph partitions for approximation and testing. In *50th Annual IEEE Symposium on Foundations of Computer Science, FOCS 2009, October 25-27, 2009, Atlanta, Georgia, USA*, pages 22–31, 2009.

[32] J. Håstad and A. Wigderson. The randomized communication complexity of set disjointness. *Theory of Computing*, 3(1):211–219, 2007.

[33] Z. Huang, B. Radunovic, M. Vojnovic, and Q. Zhang. Communication complexity of approximate matching in distributed graphs. In *32nd International Symposium on Theoretical Aspects of Computer Science, STACS 2015, March 4-7, 2015, Garching, Germany*, pages 460–473, 2015.

[34] P. Indyk, S. Mahabadi, M. Mahdian, and V. S. Mirrokni. Composable core-sets for diversity and coverage maximization. In *Proceedings of the 33rd ACM SIGMOD-SIGACT-SIGART Symposium on Principles of Database Systems, PODS'14, Snowbird, UT, USA, June 22-27, 2014*, pages 100–108, 2014.

[35] M. Kapralov. Better bounds for matchings in the streaming model. In *Proceedings of the Twenty-Fourth Annual ACM-SIAM Symposium on Discrete Algorithms, SODA 2013, New Orleans, Louisiana, USA, January 6-8, 2013*, pages 1679–1697, 2013.

[36] M. Kapralov, S. Khanna, and M. Sudan. Approximating matching size from random streams. In *Proceedings of the Twenty-Fifth Annual ACM-SIAM Symposium on Discrete Algorithms, SODA 2014, Portland, Oregon, USA, January 5-7, 2014*, pages 734–751, 2014.

[37] M. Kapralov, S. Khanna, and M. Sudan. Streaming lower bounds for approximating MAX-CUT. In *SODA*, 2015.

[38] M. Kapralov, Y. T. Lee, C. Musco, C. Musco, and A. Sidford. Single pass spectral sparsification in dynamic streams. In *55th IEEE Annual Symposium on Foundations of Computer Science, FOCS 2014, Philadelphia, PA, USA, October 18-21, 2014*, pages 561–570, 2014.

[39] M. Kapralov and D. Woodruff. Spanners and sparsifiers in dynamic streams. *PODC*, 2014.

[40] H. J. Karloff, S. Suri, and S. Vassilvitskii. A model of computation for mapreduce. In *Proceedings of the Twenty-First Annual ACM-SIAM Symposium on Discrete Algorithms, SODA 2010, Austin, Texas, USA, January 17-19, 2010*, pages 938–948, 2010.

[41] C. Konrad. Maximum matching in turnstile streams. In *Algorithms - ESA 2015 - 23rd Annual European Symposium, Patras, Greece, September 14-16, 2015, Proceedings*, pages 840–852, 2015.

[42] C. Konrad, F. Magniez, and C. Mathieu. Maximum matching in semi-streaming with few passes. In *Approximation, Randomization, and Combinatorial Optimization. Algorithms and Techniques - 15th International Workshop, APPROX 2012, and 16th International Workshop, RANDOM 2012, Cambridge, MA, USA, August 15-17, 2012. Proceedings*, pages 231–242, 2012.

[43] E. Kushilevitz and N. Nisan. *Communication complexity*. Cambridge University Press, 1997.

[44] S. Lattanzi, B. Moseley, S. Suri, and S. Vassilvitskii. Filtering: a method for solving graph problems in mapreduce. In *SPAA 2011: Proceedings of the 23rd Annual ACM Symposium on Parallelism in Algorithms and Architectures, San Jose, CA, USA, June 4-6, 2011 (Co-located with FCRC 2011)*, pages 85–94, 2011.

[45] Y. Li, H. L. Nguyen, and D. P. Woodruff. Turnstile streaming algorithms might as well be linear sketches. In *Symposium on Theory of Computing, STOC 2014, New York, NY, USA, May 31 - June 03, 2014*, pages 174–183, 2014.

[46] A. McGregor. Finding graph matchings in data streams. In *Approximation, Randomization and Combinatorial Optimization, Algorithms and Techniques, 8th International Workshop on Approximation Algorithms for Combinatorial Optimization Problems, APPROX 2005 and 9th InternationalWorkshop on Randomization and Computation, RANDOM 2005, Berkeley, CA, USA, August 22-24, 2005, Proceedings*, pages 170–181, 2005.

[47] A. McGregor. Graph stream algorithms: a survey. *SIGMOD Record*, 43(1):9–20, 2014.

[48] A. McGregor, D. Tench, S. Vorotnikova, and H. T. Vu. Densest subgraph in dynamic graph streams. In *Mathematical Foundations of Computer Science 2015 - 40th International Symposium, MFCS 2015, Milan, Italy, August 24-28, 2015, Proceedings, Part II*, pages 472–482, 2015.

[49] A. McGregor and S. Vorotnikova. Planar matching in streams revisited. In *Approximation, Randomization, and Combinatorial Optimization. Algorithms and Techniques, APPROX/RANDOM 2016, September 7-9, 2016, Paris, France*, pages 17:1–17:12, 2016.

[50] V. S. Mirrokni and M. Zadimoghaddam. Randomized composable core-sets for distributed submodular maximization. In *Proceedings of the Forty-Seventh Annual ACM on Symposium on Theory of Computing, STOC 2015, Portland, OR, USA, June 14-17, 2015*, pages 153–162, 2015.

[51] B. Mirzasoleiman, A. Karbasi, R. Sarkar, and A. Krause. Distributed submodular maximization: Identifying representative elements in massive data. In *Advances in Neural Information Processing Systems 26: 27th Annual Conference on Neural Information Processing Systems 2013. Proceedings of a meeting held December 5-8, 2013, Lake Tahoe, Nevada, United States.*, pages 2049–2057, 2013.

[52] S. Muthukrishnan. *Data streams: Algorithms and applications*. Now Publishers Inc, 2005.

[53] O. Neiman and S. Solomon. Simple deterministic algorithms for fully dynamic maximal matching. In *Symposium on Theory of Computing Conference, STOC'13, Palo Alto, CA, USA, June 1-4, 2013*, pages 745–754, 2013.

[54] H. N. Nguyen and K. Onak. Constant-time approximation algorithms via local improvements. In *49th Annual IEEE Symposium on Foundations of Computer Science, FOCS 2008, October 25-28, 2008, Philadelphia, PA, USA*, pages 327–336, 2008.

[55] K. Onak, D. Ron, M. Rosen, and R. Rubinfeld. A near-optimal sublinear-time algorithm for approximating the minimum vertex cover size. In *Proceedings of the Twenty-Third Annual ACM-SIAM Symposium on Discrete Algorithms, SODA 2012, Kyoto, Japan, January 17-19, 2012*, pages 1123–1131, 2012.

[56] K. Onak and R. Rubinfeld. Maintaining a large matching and a small vertex cover. In *Proceedings of the 42nd ACM Symposium on Theory of Computing, STOC 2010, Cambridge, Massachusetts, USA, 5-8 June 2010*, pages 457–464, 2010.

[57] M. Parnas and D. Ron. Approximating the minimum vertex cover in sublinear time and a connection to distributed algorithms. *Theor. Comput. Sci.*, 381(1-3):183–196, 2007.

[58] A. Paz and G. Schwartzman. A $(2 + \varepsilon)$-approximation for maximum weight matching in the semi-streaming model. In *Proceedings of the Twenty-Eighth Annual ACM-SIAM Symposium on Discrete Algorithms, SODA 2017, Barcelona, Spain, Hotel Porta Fira, January 16-19*, pages 2153–2161, 2017.

[59] J. M. Phillips, E. Verbin, and Q. Zhang. Lower bounds for number-in-hand multiparty communication complexity, made easy. In *Proceedings of the Twenty-Third Annual ACM-SIAM Symposium on Discrete Algorithms, SODA 2012, Kyoto, Japan, January 17-19, 2012*, pages 486–501, 2012.

[60] S. Solomon. Fully dynamic maximal matching in constant update time. In *IEEE 57th Annual Symposium on Foundations of Computer Science, FOCS 2016, 9-11 October 2016, Hyatt Regency, New Brunswick, New Jersey, USA*, pages 325–334, 2016.

[61] A. C. Yao. Lower bounds to randomized algorithms for graph properties (extended abstract). In *28th Annual Symposium on Foundations of Computer Science, Los Angeles, California, USA, 27-29 October 1987*, pages 393–400, 1987.

[62] Y. Yoshida, M. Yamamoto, and H. Ito. Improved constant-time approximation algorithms for maximum matchings and other optimization problems. *SIAM J. Comput.*, 41(4):1074–1093, 2012.

Almost Optimal Streaming Algorithms for Coverage Problems

MohammadHossein Bateni
Google Research

Hossein Esfandiari
University of Maryland

Vahab Mirrokni
Google Research

ABSTRACT

Maximum coverage and minimum set cover problems—here collectively called coverage problems—have been studied extensively in streaming models. However, previous research not only achieves suboptimal approximation factors and space complexities but also study a restricted set-arrival model which makes an explicit or implicit assumption on oracle access to the sets, ignoring the complexity of reading and storing the whole set at once. In this paper, we address the above shortcomings and present algorithms with improved approximation factor and improved space complexity, and prove that our results are almost tight. Moreover, unlike most of the previous work, our results hold in a more general edge-arrival model.

More specifically, consider an instance with n sets, together covering m elements. Information arrives in the form of "edges" from sets to elements (denoting membership) in arbitrary order.

(1) We present (almost) optimal approximation algorithms for maximum coverage and minimum set cover problems in the streaming model with an (almost) optimal space complexity of $\tilde{O}(n)$; i.e., the space is *independent of the size of the sets or the size of the ground set of elements.* These results not only improve the best known algorithms for the set-arrival model, but also are the first such algorithms for the more powerful *edge-arrival* model.
(2) In order to achieve the above results, we introduce a new general sketching technique for coverage functions: One can apply this sketching scheme to convert an α-approximation algorithm for a coverage problem to a $(1-\varepsilon)\alpha$-approximation algorithm for the same problem in streaming model.
(3) We show the significance of our sketching technique by ruling out the possibility of solving coverage problems via accessing (as a black box) a $(1 \pm \varepsilon)$-approximate oracle (e.g., a sketch function) that estimates the coverage function on any subfamily of the sets. Finally, we show that our streaming algorithms achieve an almost optimal space complexity.

1 INTRODUCTION

Maximum coverage and minimum set cover problems—here collectively called *coverage problems*—are among the most fundamental problems in optimization and computer science. Coverage problems have a variety of machine-learning and data-mining applications (for examples in data summarization and web mining, see [1, 9, 12, 14, 38]). Solving such problems has become increasingly important for various real-world large-scale data-mining applications where due to the sheer amount of data, either the computation has to be done in a distributed manner [11, 14, 17, 27, 35, 37, 38], or the data is presented and needs to be analyzed in a stream [6, 9, 13, 19, 41, 44].

These problems have been explored extensively in the literature, but despite development of several scalable algorithms, the existing approaches still suffer from a few shortcomings. First of all, most previously studied models make an explicit or implicit assumption on having oracle access to each set in its entirety. This assumption, in particular, ignores the computational complexity of reading the whole set, or computing the marginal impact of adding a subset to the solution (i.e., computing union and intersection of family of subsets). For instance, in the streaming setting, this assumption is implied in the extensively studied set-arrival model [13, 18, 19, 44]. Such models are less realistic since all the information of each set need to be gathered together. The set-arrival setting directly translates to the vertex-arrival setting in graph streaming[1], which is less interesting than the popular edge-arrival setting [4, 5, 7, 15, 21, 30, 31]. Secondly, current streaming algorithms often achieve suboptimal approximation guarantees compared to the offline optimum or do not have the best space complexities in terms of the number of sets in the input.[2]

In this paper, we aim to address the above issues. We develop streaming algorithms that achieve optimal approximation guarantees as well as optimal space complexities for coverage problems without any oracle-access assumptions. Moreover, our algorithm works in the (more general) edge-arrival streaming model. At the core of our analysis lies a simple, yet subtle sketching technique. In order to demonstrate the power of this technique, we show why natural sketching approaches do not work well. We also demonstrate that oracle access to a noisy estimator for the coverage function is not sufficient. We first present more formal definitions before elaborating on these results.

1.1 Preliminaries

Coverage Problems. We study three related *coverage* problems. The setting includes a ground set $\mathcal{E}$ of m elements, and a family $\mathcal{S} \subseteq 2^{\mathcal{E}}$ of n subsets of the elements (i.e., $n = |\mathcal{S}|$ and $m = |\mathcal{E}|$).[3] *The coverage function* C *is defined as* $C(S) = |\cup_{U \in S} U|$ for any subfamily $S \subseteq \mathcal{S}$ of subsets. In the *k-cover* problem, given a parameter k, the goal is to find k sets in $\mathcal{S}$ with the largest union size. We sometimes use Opt_k to denote the size of the union for the optimum solution.

SPAA '17, July 24-26, 2017, Washington DC, USA

ACM ISBN 978-1-4503-4593-4/17/07.
http://dx.doi.org/10.1145/3087556.3087585

[1] Modeled as a bipartite graph where vertices on one side corresponds to the sets and vertices on the other side corresponds to elements. See Preliminaries for a formal definition.
[2] We focus on the regime where the number of the element (i.e., the size of the ground set) is significantly larger than the number of sets, hence the importance of having bounds in terms of the number of sets rather than elements.
[3] There are two separate series of work in this area. We use the convension of the submodular/welfare maximization formulation [8], whereas the hypergraph-based formulation [44] typically uses n, m in the opposite way.

In the *set cover* problem, the goal is to pick the minimum number of sets from $\mathcal{S}$ such that all elements in $\mathcal{E}$ are covered. We also study a third problem: In the *set cover with λ outliers* problem[4], the goal is to find the minimum number of sets covering at least a $1 - \lambda$ fraction of the elements in $\mathcal{E}$.

Coverage problems may be modeled as a bipartite graph G, where $\mathcal{S}$ corresponds to one part of the vertices, and $\mathcal{E}$ corresponds to the other part. A vertex representing the set $S \in \mathcal{S}$ has $|S|$ edges in G, one to each element $i \in S$. For simplicity, we assume that there is no isolated vertex in $\mathcal{E}$. For a subset S of vertices in a graph G, let $\Gamma(G, S)$ denote the set of neighbors of S. When G is the graph corresponding to the original coverage instance, we have $C(S) = |\Gamma(G, S)|$ if S is a subfamily of the sets $\mathcal{S}$.

In the offline setting, a simple greedy algorithm achieves $1 - \frac{1}{e}$ approximation for k-cover and $\log m$ approximation algorithm for the set cover problem.[5] Moreover, improving these approximation factors are impossible unless NP has slightly superpolynomial time algorithm [22].

Streaming models. In the *streaming* model, we focus on the so-called *edge-arrival* model as opposed to the more studied *set-arrival* (aka *vertex-arrival*) model. In the former, edges arrive one by one, so we get to know about the set-element membership relations one at a time, whereas in the latter, sets arrive and bring with them a list of their elements. The number of passes allowed for processing the data is crucial and may change the nature of the problem.

The $(1 \pm \varepsilon)$-approximate oracle. We say C_ε is a *$(1 \pm \varepsilon)$-approximate oracle* to coverage function C if, given a subfamily of sets, it gives us an estimate of their union size within $1 \pm \varepsilon$ precision. In other words, C_ε estimates the coverage function C on any subfamily of the sets as a black box; i.e., for any subset $S \subseteq \mathcal{S}$, we have

$$(1 - \epsilon)C_\epsilon(S) \le C(S) \le (1 + \epsilon)C_\epsilon(S).$$

1.2 Related work

Coverage problems have been studied extensively in the context of set-arrival models [6, 13, 19, 41, 44]. Most of these give suboptimal approximation guarantees. In particular, Saha and Getoor [44] provide a $\frac{1}{4}$-approximation algorithm for k-cover in one pass using $\tilde{O}(m)$ space. The same technique gives a $\Theta(\log m)$ approximation algorithm for set cover in $\Theta(\log m)$ passes, using $\tilde{O}(m)$ space. On the hardness side, interestingly, Assadi et al. [6] show that there is no α-approximation one-pass streaming algorithm for set cover using $o(nm/\alpha)$ space. Demaine et al. [18] provide (for any positive integer r) a $4^r \log m$-approximation algorithm for the set cover problem in 4^r passes using $\tilde{O}(nm^{1/r} + m)$ space[6]. Recently, Har-Peled et al. improves this result and provide a p-pass $O(p \log m)$-approximation algorithm in $\tilde{O}(nm^{O(1/p)} + m)$ space[6]. Indeed, all the above results hold only for the set-arrival model.

Often in the graph streaming problems, while the size of the input is $\tilde{O}(|E|)$ for a graph $G(V, E)$, the solution size may be as large as $\Omega(|V|)$. The best hope then is to find the solution in $\tilde{O}(|V|)$ space.

[4]This is sometimes called the $(1 - \lambda)$-partial cover problem in the literature.

[5]Unless otherwise specified, we use the wide-spread convension for approximation ratios: factors larger than one for minimization problems and factors smaller than one for maximization problems.

[6] The space bounds claimed in [18, 25] assume $m = O(n)$, hence stated differently.

Algorithms fitting this description are called *semi-streaming* [39], and many graph problems have been studied in this setting [2, 3, 20, 23, 24, 32–34]. On the other hand, the extensive work on edge-arrival streaming [4, 5, 7, 15, 21, 30, 31] had not (prior to our owrk) studied coverage problems.

1.3 Results and techniques

As our main result, we address the aforementioned shortcomings of existing algorithms for coverage problems. These results are summarized in Table 1. This paper is *the first to study the problem in the edge-arrival model,* and present tight results for these problems.

1.3.1 Streaming results. We present almost tight streaming algorithms for coverage problems. The following theorem states our main results formally.

THEOREM 1.1. *In the edge-arrival streaming model, for any arbitrary $\varepsilon \in (0, 1]$, there exist*

- *(See Thm 3.1) a single-pass $(1 - \frac{1}{e} - \varepsilon)$-approximation algorithm for k-cover using $\tilde{O}(n)$ space;*
- *(See Thm 3.3) a single-pass $(1 + \varepsilon) \log \frac{1}{\lambda}$-approximation algorithm for set cover with λ outliers using $\tilde{O}_\lambda(n)$ space; and*
- *(See Thm 3.4) a p-pass $(1 + \varepsilon) \log m$-approximation algorithm for set cover using $\tilde{O}(nm^{O(\frac{1}{p})} + m)$ space.*

The above are the first such results for coverage problems in the streaming edge-arrival model. Moreover, they improve the approximation factor of previously known results for the set-arrival model [13, 19, 41, 44]. (However, in certain cases, the space complexities may be incomparable, say, $\tilde{O}(n)$ versus $\tilde{O}(m)$.[7]) In fact, our result for streaming set cover gives an exponential improvement over Demaine et al. [18] on both approximation factor and number of rounds given the same space. See Table 1 for comparison to previous work. Recently, Har-Peled et al. (Theorem 2.6 in [25]) provide a p-pass $O(p \log m)$-approximation algorithm in $\tilde{O}(nm^{O(1/p)} + m)$ space in the set-arrival model. Notice that our results for streaming set cover provide a better approximation factor—i.e., $(1 + \varepsilon) \log m$ versus $O(p \log m)$—in the same space and number of passes, while handling the more general edge-arrival model.

On the hardness side, we show that any $\frac{1}{2} + \varepsilon$-approximation streaming algorithm for k-cover requires $\Omega(n)$ space. This holds even for streaming algorithms with several passes.

THEOREM 1.2. *Any $\frac{1}{2} + \varepsilon$-approximation multi-pass streaming algorithm for k-cover requires $\Omega(n)$ space in total.*

In a simultaneous and independent work, McGregor and Vu [36] present a single-pass $1 - 1/e - \epsilon$ approximation algorithm for the k-cover problem in the streaming setting with $\tilde{O}(n)$ space, using a different approach: They directly analyze the behavior of the greedy algorithm on a specific noisy sketch, while we provide a sketch that translates any α-approximation algorithm for k-cover to an $(\alpha - \epsilon)$-approximation streaming algorithm using $\tilde{O}(n)$ space. In fact they require $\tilde{O}(nk)$ space to find an exponential time $1 - \epsilon$ approximate solution.

[7]Indeed, either m or n may be larger in practice [16]. See also Footnotes 2 and 6.

Problem	Credit	# passes	Approximation	Space	Arrival
k-cover	[44]	1	$1/4$	$\tilde{O}(m)$	set
k-cover	[9]	1	$1/2$	$\tilde{O}(n+m)$	set
k-cover	Here	1	$1-1/e-\varepsilon$	$\tilde{O}(n)$	edge
Set cover w. outliers	[13, 19]	p	$O(\min(n^{\frac{1}{p+1}}, e^{-\frac{1}{p}}))$	$\tilde{O}(m)$	set
Set cover w. outliers	Here	1	$(1+\varepsilon)\log\frac{1}{\lambda}$	$\tilde{O}_\lambda(n)$	edge
Set cover	[13, 44]	p	$(p+1)m^{\frac{1}{p+1}}$	$\tilde{O}(m)$	set
Set cover	[18]	4^r	$4^r \log m$	$\tilde{O}(nm^{\frac{1}{r}}+m)$	set
Set cover	[25]	p	$O(p\log m)$	$\tilde{O}(nm^{O(\frac{1}{p})}+m)$	set
Set cover	Here	p	$(1+\varepsilon)\log m$	$\tilde{O}(nm^{O(\frac{1}{p})}+m)$	edge

Table 1: Comparison of results in streaming models. Note that all our results for edge arrival model also hold for the set arrival model.

1.3.2 Sketching technique. The main technique at the heart of our results is a powerful sketching to summarize coverage functions. As its main property, we show that any α-approximate solution to k-cover on this sketch is an $(\alpha-\varepsilon)$-approximate solution to k-cover on the original input with high probability; see Theorem 2.7. Interestingly, this sketch requires only $\tilde{O}(n)$ space. Our sketch is fairly similar to ℓ_0 sketches [16], which are essentially defined to estimate the value of coverage functions. Indeed, one may maintain n instances of the ℓ_0 sketch, and estimate the value of the coverage function of a single feasible solution of size k with high probability. However, having $\binom{n}{k}$ different choices for a solution of size k leads to a huge blow-up on the failure probability of at least one such solution. In the full version, we show a straightforward analysis to approximate k-cover using ℓ_0 sketches with $\tilde{O}(nk)$ space, which is quite larger than our sketch.

All the algorithms presented here construct $\tilde{O}(1)$ independent instances of the sketch and then solve the problem without any other direct access to the input. The simplicity of our sketch enables its efficient construction and fast implementation of the resulting algorithms. Interestingly, this technique provides almost tight approximation guarantees. We remark that all the algorithms presented in this work have success probabilities $1-\frac{1}{n}$; i.e., they may fail to produce the claimed solution with probability $\frac{1}{n}$. For simplicity we do not repeat this condition elsewhere.

Finally, in an accompanied paper, we also show how to apply this to distributed models, and design scalable distributed algorithms for covering problems. There we also confirm the effectiveness of this algorithm empirically on real data sets [10].[8]

1.3.3 A $(1\pm\varepsilon)$-approximate oracle is not sufficient. There are several sampling or sketching techniques that can be used to develop a $(1\pm\varepsilon)$-approximate oracle C_ε to the coverage function. One might hope that a black-box access to such an oracle could be used as a subroutine in developing approximation algorithms with good approximation guarantees. Here, we show that this is not possible.

THEOREM 1.3. *Any α-approximation algorithm for k-cover via oracle C_ε requires* $\exp\left(\Omega(n\varepsilon^2\alpha^2-\log n)\right)$ *queries to the oracle.*

[8]We decided to remove this part of the paper due to space constraints, and focus on the streaming applications.

In particular, for any constant $\varepsilon>0$, there is no polynomial-time $n^{-0.49}$ approximation algorithm for k-cover given a $(1\pm\varepsilon)$-approximate oracle C_ε. This improves upon a similar hardness result for submodular functions [26][9]. Our proof technique here might be of independent interest.

In order to prove Theorem 1.3, first we define a problem called *k-purification* for which we show that any randomized algorithm requires $\delta\exp\left(\Omega(\frac{\varepsilon^2k^2}{n})\right)$ oracle queries to succeed with probability δ. In a k-purification problem instance, we are given a random permutation of n items, with k gold and $n-k$ brass items. The types of individual items are not known to us. We merely have access to an oracle $\mathsf{Pure}_\varepsilon(S)$ for $S\subsetneq[1,n]$ defined as

$$\begin{cases} 0 & \text{if } \frac{k|S|}{n}-\varepsilon\left(\frac{k|S|}{n}+\frac{k^2}{n}\right)\le \mathsf{Gold}(S)\le\frac{k|S|}{n}+\varepsilon\left(\frac{k|S|}{n}+\frac{k^2}{n}\right),\\ 1 & \text{otherwise,}\end{cases}$$

where $\mathsf{Gold}(S)$ is the number of gold items in S. The goal in this problem is to find a set S such that $\mathsf{Pure}_\varepsilon(S)=1$. The hardness proof is then based on a reduction between k-purification and k-cover.

2 SKETCHING FOR COVERAGE PROBLEMS

In this section we present a sketch $H_{\le n}$ to approximate k-cover. Specifically, we show that any α-approximate solution to k-cover on $H_{\le n}$ is an $\alpha-O(\varepsilon)$-approximate solution on the input graph, with high probability (see Theorem 2.7). Crucially $H_{\le n}$ uses only $\tilde{O}(n)$ space. In order to define and prove the properties of $H_{\le n}$, we introduce two intermediary sketches H_p and H'_p, where $p\in[0,1]$ is a parameter to be fixed later on.

In this section, we define the sketch in mathematical terms and establish its desirable properties. Then in the following section, we discuss the intricacies of building and using it in the streaming model.

Let h be a hash function mapping elements $\mathcal{E}$ to real numbers in $[0,1]$. First we throw away from the bipartite graph G any element whose hash value exceeds p. This constructs H_p. In Lemma 2.3 we show that, for sufficiently large p, any α-approximate solution to k-cover on H_p is an $\alpha-O(\varepsilon)$-approximate solution on G, with high probability. Unfortunately, the number of edges in H_p may be $\Omega(nk)$.

[9]Independently, they later extend their results to coverage functions.

Next we enforce an upper bound (defined below in terms of n, k, ε) on the degree of elements in H_p, by arbitrarily removing edges as necessary. This constructs H'_p. Again for a sufficiently large choice of p, any α-approximate solution to k-cover on H'_p is an $\alpha - O(\varepsilon)$-approximate solution on G, with high probability. Interestingly, if we select p wisely, H'_p requires only $\tilde{O}(n)$ space. However, this p depends on the value of the optimum solution and may not be accessible to the algorithm while constructing the sketch. To resolve this issue, we define $H_{\leq n}$ with a similar structure as H'_p, such that it always has $\tilde{O}(n)$ edges (see Definition 2.1). We remark that this conceptual description can be turned into efficient implementations in several computational frameworks. Next comes the formal definitions of our sketch.

Let us overload the notation $h(.)$ such that $h(e)$, for an edge e, denotes the value of h on the endpoint of e in $\mathcal{E}$. For a fixed parameter p, we define H_p to be the subgraph of G induced by all vertices in $\mathcal{S}$ and the vertices in $\mathcal{E}$ with h less than p. In other words, H_p contains an edge e if and only if $h(e) \leq p$. Let H'_p be a maximal subgraph of H_p such that the degree of the vertices of H'_p in part $\mathcal{E}$ is at most $\frac{n \log(1/\varepsilon)}{\varepsilon k}$; as necessary we throw away edges arbitrarily. Below we define $H_{\leq n}(k, \varepsilon, \delta'')$ based on H'_p. The former is the sketch used in all our algorithms.

Definition 2.1. For simplicity of notation, we set $\delta = \delta'' \log\log_{\frac{1}{1-\varepsilon}} m$. Let p^* be the smallest value such that the number of edges in H'_{p^*} is at least $\frac{24 n \delta \log(1/\varepsilon) \log n}{(1-\varepsilon)\varepsilon^3}$. Notice that p^* is a function of the randomness in the hash function. Remark that the number of edges in H'_{p^*} is at most $\frac{24 n \delta \log(1/\varepsilon) \log n}{(1-\varepsilon)\varepsilon^3} + n \in \tilde{O}(n)$. We denote H'_{p^*} by $H_{\leq n}(k, \varepsilon, \delta'')$, and drop the parameters from $H_{\leq n}(k, \varepsilon, \delta'')$ when it is clear from the context. See Algorithm 1.

We argue that, for sufficiently large p, the quantity $\frac{1}{p}|\Gamma(H_p, S)|$ is a good estimate for $C(S)$. This is formalized below.

Lemma 2.2. *Pick $\frac{6\delta'}{\varepsilon^2 Opt_k} \leq p \leq 1$, and let S be an arbitrarily subset of $\mathcal{S}$ such that $|S| \leq k$. With probability $1 - e^{-\delta'}$ we have*

$$\left|\frac{1}{p}|\Gamma(H_p, S)| - C(S)\right| \leq \varepsilon Opt_k. \tag{1}$$

In the following lemma we relate the approximate solutions on H_p and G.

Lemma 2.3. *Pick $\frac{6k\delta \log n}{\varepsilon^2 Opt_k} \leq p \leq 1$. All α-approximate solutions on H_p are $(\alpha - 2\varepsilon)$-approximate solutions to the k-cover problem on G with probability $1 - e^{-\delta}$. Simultaneously for any set $S \subseteq \mathcal{S}$ such that $|S| = k$, we have $\left|\frac{1}{p}|\Gamma(H_p, S)| - C(S)\right| \leq \varepsilon Opt_k$.*

Proof. Set $\delta' = k\delta \log n$. Lemma 2.2 states that for an arbitrary $S \subseteq \mathcal{S}$ of size at most k, we have with probability $1 - e^{-k\delta \log n}$,

$$\left|\frac{1}{p}|\Gamma(H_p, S)| - C(S)\right| \leq \varepsilon \mathrm{Opt}_k.$$

Note that there are $\binom{n}{k}$ different sets S of size k. By the union bound, with probability $1 - \binom{n}{k} e^{-k\delta \log n} \geq 1 - n^k e^{-k\delta \log n} = 1 - e^{-\delta}$, we have for all such choices

$$\left|\frac{1}{p}|\Gamma(H_p, S)| - C(S)\right| \leq \varepsilon \mathrm{Opt}_k. \tag{2}$$

Let Opt_k be the optimum solution on G and let S be the solution obtained from the α-approximation algorithm Alg when run on H_p. Applying Inequality (2) to Opt_k and S, we simultaneously have

$$\left|\frac{1}{p}|\Gamma(H_p, \mathrm{Opt}_k)| - \mathrm{Opt}_k\right| \leq \varepsilon \mathrm{Opt}_k \tag{3}$$

and

$$\left|\frac{1}{p}|\Gamma(H_p, S)| - C(S)\right| \leq \varepsilon \mathrm{Opt}_k. \tag{4}$$

In addition, since S is an α-approximate solution on H_p we have

$$|\Gamma(H_p, \mathrm{Opt}_k)| \leq \frac{1}{\alpha}|\Gamma(H_p, S)|. \tag{5}$$

Inequalities (5) and (3) together ensure with probability $1 - e^{-\delta}$ that

$$\alpha \mathrm{Opt}_k - \frac{1}{p}|\Gamma(H_p, S)| \leq \alpha\varepsilon \mathrm{Opt}_k.$$

Combining the above with Inequality (4), we obtain

$$\alpha \mathrm{Opt}_k - C(S) \leq \alpha\varepsilon \mathrm{Opt}_k + \varepsilon \mathrm{Opt}_k \leq 2\varepsilon \mathrm{Opt}_k.$$

This means that S is an $(\alpha - 2\varepsilon)$-approximation to k-cover on G as desired.

□

The following lemma relates the solutions on H'_p and H_p.

Lemma 2.4. *Pick arbitrary $0 \leq p \leq 1$ and $1 \leq k \leq n$. Any α-approximate solution of k-cover on H'_p is an $\alpha(1-\varepsilon)$-approximate solution on H_p.*

Proof. Let Opt_H and $\mathrm{Opt}_{H'}$ be subsets of $\mathcal{S}$ with size k that maximize $|\Gamma(H_p, \mathrm{Opt}_H)|$ and $|\Gamma(H'_p, \mathrm{Opt}_{H'})|$, respectively. Remark that H'_p is a subgraph of H_p, hence $|\Gamma(H'_p, S)| \leq |\Gamma(H_p, S)|$ for any $S \subseteq \mathcal{S}$. Later we show that there exists a set R of size k such that $|\Gamma(H'_p, R)| \geq (1-\varepsilon)|\Gamma(H_p, \mathrm{Opt}_H)|$. Thus, for an α-approximate solution S on H'_p, we have

$$\begin{aligned}
|\Gamma(H_p, S)| &\geq |\Gamma(H'_p, S)| && H'_p \subseteq H_p, \\
&\geq \alpha|\Gamma(H'_p, \mathrm{Opt}_{H'})| && S \text{ is } \alpha\text{-approximate}, \\
&\geq \alpha|\Gamma(H'_p, R)| && \text{definition of } \mathrm{Opt}_{H'}, \\
&\geq \alpha(1-\varepsilon)|\Gamma(H_p, \mathrm{Opt}_H)|.
\end{aligned}$$

To prove the existence of a suitable R, we follow a probabilistic argument, producing a randomized set R^* of size k such that $\mathrm{E}[|\Gamma(H'_p, R^*)|] \geq (1-\varepsilon)|\Gamma(H_p, \mathrm{Opt}_H)|$.

We construct R^* by removing εk sets from Opt_H uniformly at random, and adding εk sets from $\mathcal{S}$ uniformly at random. Note that each element in $\Gamma(H_p, \mathrm{Opt}_H)$ with degree at most $\frac{n \log(1/\varepsilon)}{\varepsilon k}$ in H_p appears in $\Gamma(H_p, R^*)$ with probability $1-\varepsilon$, hence in $\Gamma(H'_p, R^*)$. Now let us consider a high-degree element u—one with degree at least $\frac{n \log(1/\varepsilon)}{\varepsilon k}$ in H_p, i.e., degree exactly $\frac{n \log(1/\varepsilon)}{\varepsilon k}$ in H'_p. The probability that u is not included in any of the εk randomly added sets is at

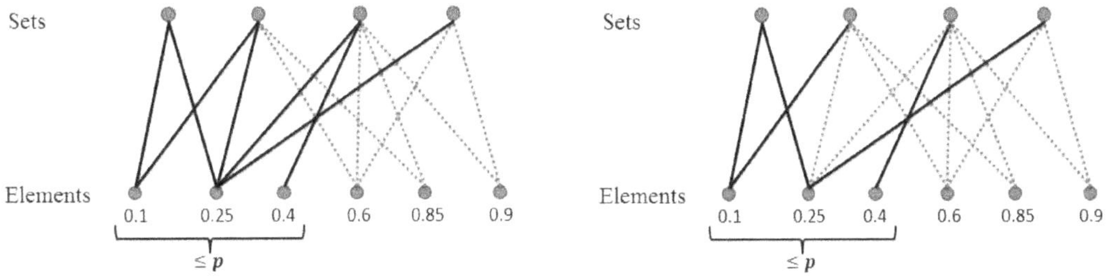

Figure 1: Left figure is an example of H_p and the right figure is an example of H'_p. In both figures, we have $p = 0.5$. The number below each vertex is its hashed value. Solid edges are those included in the sketch and dotted edges are the rest of the edges in the graph.

Algorithm 1 $H_{\leq n}(k, \varepsilon, \delta'')$

Input: An input graph G, k, $\varepsilon \in (0, 1]$, and δ''.
Output: Sketch $H_{\leq n}(k, \varepsilon, \delta'')$.

Set $\delta = \delta'' \log\log_{\frac{1}{1-\varepsilon}} m$.
Let h be an arbitrary hash function that uniformly and independently maps $\mathcal{E}$ in G to $[0, 1]$.
Initialize $H_{\leq n}(k, \varepsilon, \delta'')$ with vertices $\mathcal{S}$ of G, and no edge.
while number of edges in $H_{\leq n}(k, \varepsilon, \delta'')$ is less than $\frac{24n\delta \log(1/\varepsilon) \log n}{(1-\varepsilon)\varepsilon^3}$ **do**
  Pick $v \in \mathcal{E}$ of minimum $h(v)$ that is still not in $H_{\leq n}(k, \varepsilon, \delta'')$.
  if degree of v in G is less than $\frac{n \log(1/\varepsilon)}{\varepsilon k}$ **then**
    Add v along with all its edges to $H_{\leq n}(k, \varepsilon, \delta'')$.
  else
    Add v along with $\frac{n \log(1/\varepsilon)}{\varepsilon k}$ of its edges, chosen arbitrary, to $H_{\leq n}(k, \varepsilon, \delta'')$.

---

most

$$\left(1 - \frac{\frac{n\log(1/\varepsilon)}{\varepsilon k}}{n}\right)^{\varepsilon k} = \left(1 - \frac{\log(1/\varepsilon)}{\varepsilon k}\right)^{\varepsilon k} = \left(1 - \frac{\log(1/\varepsilon)}{\varepsilon k}\right)^{\frac{\varepsilon k}{\log(1/\varepsilon)} \log \frac{1}{\varepsilon}}$$
$$\leq \left(\frac{1}{e}\right)^{\log \frac{1}{\varepsilon}} = \varepsilon.$$

Therefore, each vertex in $\Gamma(H_p, \mathrm{Opt}_H)$ exists in $\Gamma(H'_p, R^*)$ with probability at least $1 - \varepsilon$, proving the claim $\mathrm{E}[|\Gamma(H'_p, R^*)|] \geq (1 - \varepsilon)|\Gamma(H_p, \mathrm{Opt}_H)|$. □

We prove the following two lemmas to argue that maintaining the solution in the reduced-degree subgraph H'_p does not require too much memory.

Lemma 2.5. *Pick arbitrary $C \geq 1$ and let $p = \frac{6Ck\delta \log n}{\varepsilon^2 Opt_k}$. With probability at least $1 - e^{\delta}$, we have*

$$\max_{S \subseteq \mathcal{S}: |S| = k} |\Gamma(H'_p, S)| \leq \frac{12Ck\delta \log n}{\varepsilon^2}.$$

Lemma 2.6. *Pick arbitrary $0 \leq p \leq 1$ and $1 \leq k \leq n$, and let m'_p denote the number of edges in H'_p. We have*

$$m'_p \frac{\varepsilon k}{2n \log(1/\varepsilon)} \leq |\Gamma(H'_p, Opt_{H'})|.$$

Proof. Let $\mathrm{Opt}_{H'} = \arg\max_S |\Gamma(H'_p, S)|$. There is a set $v \in \mathrm{Opt}_{H'}$ such that $|\Gamma(H'_p, \mathrm{Opt}_{H'})| - |\Gamma(H'_p, \mathrm{Opt}_{H'} - v)| \leq \frac{|\Gamma(H'_p, \mathrm{Opt}_{H'})|}{k}$, i.e., the marginal effect of v is at most a $\frac{1}{k}$ fraction of the total value of $|\Gamma(H'_p, \mathrm{Opt}_{H'})|$. Notice that by optimality of $\mathrm{Opt}_{H'}$, replacing v with any other set does not increase the union size. Thus, for any vertex $v' \in \mathcal{S}$ the number of neighbors of v' in $\mathcal{E} \setminus \Gamma(H'_p, \mathrm{Opt}_{H'})$ is at most $\frac{|\Gamma(H'_p, \mathrm{Opt}_{H'})|}{k}$. Therefore, the number of edges between $\mathcal{S}$ and $\mathcal{E} \setminus \Gamma(H'_p, \mathrm{Opt}_{H'})$ does not exceed $n\frac{|\Gamma(H'_p, \mathrm{Opt}_{H'})|}{k}$.

On the other hand, the degree of the elements in $\Gamma(H'_p, \mathrm{Opt}_{H'})$ is at most $\frac{\log(1/\varepsilon)n}{\varepsilon k}$, hence the number of edges between $\mathcal{S}$ and $\Gamma(H'_p, \mathrm{Opt}_{H'})$ does not exceed $|\Gamma(H'_p, \mathrm{Opt}_{H'})|\frac{n\log(1/\varepsilon)}{\varepsilon k}$. Therefore, one can bound the total number of edges in H'_p as follows.

$$m'_p \leq n\frac{|\Gamma(H'_p, \mathrm{Opt}_{H'})|}{k} + |\Gamma(H'_p, \mathrm{Opt}_{H'})|\frac{n\log(1/\varepsilon)}{\varepsilon k}$$
$$\leq \left|\Gamma(H'_p, \mathrm{Opt}_{H'})\right| \cdot \frac{n}{k}\left(1 + \frac{\log(1/\varepsilon)}{\varepsilon}\right)$$
$$\leq \left|\Gamma(H'_p, \mathrm{Opt}_{H'})\right| \cdot \frac{n}{k} \cdot \frac{2\log(1/\varepsilon)}{\varepsilon}.$$

We obtain by reordering

$$m'_p \frac{\varepsilon k}{2n\log(1/\varepsilon)} \leq |\Gamma(H'_p, \mathrm{Opt}_{H'})|.$$ □

The following theorem relates the approximate solutions on $H_{\leq n}$ and G.

Theorem 2.7. *Let $\delta'' \in [1, \infty)$ and $k \in [1, n]$ be two arbitrary numbers. Any α-approximate solution to k-cover on $H_{\leq n}$ is an $\alpha - 12\epsilon$ approximation solution on G, with probability $1 - 3e^{-\delta''}$.*

Proof. Pick $p \geq \frac{6k\delta \log n}{\varepsilon^2 \mathrm{Opt}_k}$. By Lemma 2.4, any α-approximate solution on H'_p is an $(\alpha - \varepsilon)$-approximate solution on H_p with probability $1 - e^{-\delta}$. Moreover, we know from Lemma 2.3 that any $(\alpha - \varepsilon)$-approximate solution on H_p is an $(\alpha - 3\varepsilon)$-approximate solution on G with probability $1 - e^{-\delta}$. Therefore, any α-approximate solution on H'_p is an $(\alpha - 3\varepsilon)$-approximate solution on G with probability $1 - 2e^{-\delta}$.

Let us set $p' = \frac{6k\delta \log n}{\varepsilon^2 \mathrm{Opt}_k}$ and $p_0 = \frac{1}{m}, p_1 = \frac{1}{m(1-\varepsilon)}, p_2 = \frac{1}{m(1-\varepsilon)^2}, \ldots, p_\mu = 1$, where $\mu = O(\log m)$. Indeed, there is some i such that $p' \leq p_i \leq \frac{1}{1-\varepsilon} p'$. Remark that we set $\delta = \log(\log_{1-\varepsilon} m)\delta''$. We may assume without loss of generality that Lemmas 2.3, 2.4 and 2.5 all hold for every p_j with $j \geq i$ since union bound ensures this outcome happens with probability at least

$$\begin{aligned}1 - 3\log_{1-\varepsilon} m \cdot e^{\delta} &= 1 - 3\log_{1-\varepsilon} m \exp[\log(\log_{1-\varepsilon} m)\delta''] \\ &= 1 - 3e^{\delta''}.\end{aligned}$$

Let p^* be (a random number) such that $p^* \geq \frac{1}{1-\varepsilon} \frac{6k\delta \log n}{\varepsilon^2 \mathrm{Opt}_k}$. Remark that, since $p^* \geq \frac{1}{1-\varepsilon} p'$, there is some (random number) j such that $p' \leq p_j \leq p^* \leq p_{j+1} = \frac{p_j}{1-\varepsilon}$. Thus,

$$\left|\mathrm{Opt}_k - \frac{1}{p_j}\mathrm{Opt}(H'_{p_j})\right| \leq 3\varepsilon \mathrm{Opt}_k, \tag{6}$$

and similarly,

$$\begin{aligned}3\varepsilon\mathrm{Opt}_k &\geq \left|\mathrm{Opt}_k - \frac{1}{p_{j+1}}\mathrm{Opt}(H'_{p_{j+1}})\right| \\ &= \left|\mathrm{Opt}_k - \frac{1-\varepsilon}{p_j}\mathrm{Opt}(H'_{p_{j+1}})\right| \\ &\geq (1-\varepsilon)\left|\mathrm{Opt}_k - \frac{1}{p_j}\mathrm{Opt}(H'_{p_{j+1}})\right| - \varepsilon\mathrm{Opt}_k,\end{aligned}$$

which, assuming $\varepsilon \leq \frac{1}{5}$, gives

$$5\varepsilon\mathrm{Opt}_k \geq \left|\mathrm{Opt}_k - \frac{1}{p_j}\mathrm{Opt}(H'_{p_{j+1}})\right|. \tag{7}$$

Combining (6) and (7) yields

$$\left|\frac{1}{p_j}\mathrm{Opt}(H'_{p_{j+1}}) - \frac{1}{p_j}\mathrm{Opt}(H'_{p_j})\right| \leq 8\varepsilon\mathrm{Opt}_k. \tag{8}$$

The inequalities $p_j \leq p^* \leq p_{j+1}$ implies $H'_{p_j} \subseteq H'_{p^*} \subseteq H'_{p_{j+1}}$, hence

$$\Gamma(H'_{p_j}, S) \leq \Gamma(H'_{p^*}, S) \leq \Gamma(H'_{p_{j+1}}, S) \quad \text{for any set } S, \tag{9}$$

and in turn,

$$\mathrm{Opt}(H'_{p_j}) \leq \mathrm{Opt}(H'_{p^*}) \leq \mathrm{Opt}(H'_{p_{j+1}}). \tag{10}$$

Combining (8) and (10) gives

$$\frac{1}{p_j}\mathrm{Opt}(H'_{p_{j+1}}) - \frac{1}{p_j}\mathrm{Opt}(H'_{p^*}) \leq 8\varepsilon\mathrm{Opt}_k. \tag{11}$$

Now suppose S is an α-approximate solution on H'_{p^*}. We have

$$\begin{aligned}
&C(S) + \varepsilon\mathrm{Opt}_k \\
&\geq \frac{1}{p_{j+1}}|\Gamma(H_{p_{j+1}}, S)| && \text{Lemma 2.3,} \\
&\geq \frac{1}{p_{j+1}}|\Gamma(H'_{p_{j+1}}, S)| && H'_{p_{j+1}} \subseteq H_{p_{j+1}}, \\
&\geq \frac{1}{p_{j+1}}|\Gamma(H'_{p^*}, S)| && \text{by (9),} \\
&\geq \alpha\frac{1}{p_{j+1}}\mathrm{Opt}(H'_{p^*}) && \text{definition of } S, \\
&= \alpha(1-\varepsilon)\frac{1}{p_j}\mathrm{Opt}(H'_{p^*}) \\
&\geq \alpha(1-\varepsilon)[\frac{1}{p_j}\mathrm{Opt}(H'_{p_{j+1}}) - 8\varepsilon\mathrm{Opt}_k] && \text{from (11),} \\
&\geq \alpha\frac{1}{p_{j+1}}\mathrm{Opt}(H'_{p_{j+1}}) - \alpha 8\varepsilon(1-\varepsilon)\mathrm{Opt}_k \\
&\geq \alpha\frac{1}{p_{j+1}}\mathrm{Opt}(H'_{p_{j+1}}) - \alpha 8\varepsilon\mathrm{Opt}_k \\
&\geq \alpha\frac{1}{p_{j+1}}\mathrm{Opt}(H'_{p_{j+1}}) - 8\varepsilon\mathrm{Opt}_k && \text{since } \alpha \leq 1, \\
&\geq \alpha\mathrm{Opt}_k - 11\varepsilon\mathrm{Opt}_k \\
&= (\alpha - 11\varepsilon)\mathrm{Opt}_k,
\end{aligned}$$

that is, any α-approximate solution on H'_{p^*} is an $(\alpha - 12\varepsilon)$-approximate solution on G.

Finally we argue that $p^* \geq \frac{1}{1-\varepsilon}\frac{6k\delta \log n}{\varepsilon^2 \mathrm{Opt}_k}$ for $H'_{p^*} = H_{\leq n}$. We set $C = \frac{1}{1-\varepsilon}$ in Lemma 2.5 to obtain $\max_{S \subseteq \mathcal{S}:|S|=k} |\Gamma(H'_{p''}, S)| \leq \frac{\frac{12k\delta}{1-\varepsilon}\log n}{\varepsilon^2}$, where $p'' = \frac{1}{1-\varepsilon}\frac{6k\delta \log n}{\varepsilon^2 \mathrm{Opt}_k}$. Thus, H'_{p^*} contains $H'_{p''}$ if $\max_{S \subseteq \mathcal{S}:|S|=k} |\Gamma(H'_{p^*}, S)| \geq \frac{\frac{12k\delta}{1-\varepsilon}\log n}{\varepsilon^2}$. On the other hand if we set $m'_{p^*} \geq \frac{24n\delta \log(1/\varepsilon)\log n}{(1-\varepsilon)\varepsilon^3}$ in Lemma 2.6, we get

$$\begin{aligned}|\Gamma(H'_{p^*}, \mathrm{Opt}_{H'})| &\geq m'_{p^*}\frac{\varepsilon k}{2n\log(1/\varepsilon)} \\ &\geq \frac{24n\delta\log(1/\varepsilon)\log n}{(1-\varepsilon)\varepsilon^3} \cdot \frac{\varepsilon k}{2n\log(1/\varepsilon)} \\ &= \frac{\frac{12k\delta}{1-\varepsilon}\log n}{\varepsilon^2}.\end{aligned}$$ □

The following lemma provides a bicriteria bound on the coverage of solutions in $H_{\leq n}$, where $k' \leq k$ is the size of the set cover on G. This lemma will be useful in obtaining results for set cover and set cover with outliers.

Lemma 2.8. *Let k' be the size of the minimum set cover on the input graph G, and let $k = \xi k'$. There exists a solution of size k' on $H_{\leq n}(k, \varepsilon, 1)$ that covers at least $1 - \xi\varepsilon$ fraction of the elements in $H_{\leq n}(k, \varepsilon, 1)$.*

3 THE STREAMING SETTING

Indeed, with no time constraint, one can use ℓ_0 sketches and give a $1 - \varepsilon$ approximation streaming algorithm for k-cover in $\tilde{O}(nk)$ space. This simple streaming algorithm constructs a $(1 \pm \varepsilon)$-approximate oracle to the value of the coverage function, using $\tilde{O}(nk)$ space. One can use this algorithm and try all solutions of size k to find a $1 - 2\varepsilon$ approximate solution of k-cover. However, as Theorem 1.3 states, using this oracle and without any further assumptions, there is no polynomial time $n^{-0.5+\varepsilon}$-approximation algorithm for k-cover. In addition, the space used by this algorithm may be quite large for large values of k.

In this section, we give a $1 - \frac{1}{e} - \varepsilon$-approximation one-pass streaming algorithm for k-cover, using $\tilde{O}(n)$ space. This is done by first constructing $H_{\leq n}$ in the streaming setting and then providing efficient algorithms that only access the sketch $H_{\leq n}$. Using the same technique, we give a $(1+\varepsilon) \log \frac{1}{\lambda}$ approximation one-pass streaming algorithm for set cover with outliers, using $\tilde{O}_\lambda(n)$ space. Besides, for any arbitrary $r \in [1, \log m]$, we give a $(1 + \varepsilon) \log m$ approximation r-pass streaming algorithm for set cover, using $\tilde{O}(nm^{O(1/r)} + m)$ space. Interestingly, the update times of all our algorithms are $\tilde{O}(1)$.

On the hardness side we show that any $\frac{1}{2} + \varepsilon$ approximation streaming algorithm for the k-cover problem requires $\Omega(n)$ space. We proof this hardness result in the full version. This hardness result rules out the existence of $\frac{1}{2} + \varepsilon$ approximation parametrized streaming algorithms for the k-cover problem and shows that the space of our algorithm is tight up to a logarithmic factor.

Next we show how to construct $H_{\leq n}$ in the streaming setting. Note that to define $H_{\leq n}$ we map (via a hash function) each element to a number in $[0, 1]$ independently. Such a mapping requires $\tilde{O}(m)$ random bits. However, we use a simple equivalent random process to construct $H_{\leq n}$ using $\tilde{O}(|H_{\leq n}|)$ random bits, where $|H_{\leq n}|$ is the number of edges in $H_{\leq n}$.

Let p^* be the probability corresponding to $H_{\leq n}$. Remark that the number of elements v with $h(v) \leq p^*$ is at most $|H_{\leq n}|$, i.e., at most equal to the number of edges in $H_{\leq n}$. Note that, if we know that the hash value of an element is greater than p^*, we can simply remove that element. Thus, at the beginning we iteratively sample $|H_{\leq n}|$ elements without replacement, and assume that this sequence is indeed that of the first $|H_{\leq n}|$ elements ordered by their hashed value. This process requires only $\tilde{O}(|H_{\leq n}|)$ random bits.

Next we describe how to use the sketch to solve each of the three problems: k-cover, set cover, and set cover with outliers. As a result, we provide tight and almost tight streaming algorithms for k-cover, set cover, and set cover with outliers.

The greedy algorithm for k-cover iteratively selects a vertex that increases the valuation function f the most and adds it to the solution. Let $Greedy(k, G)$ denote the set of k vertices picked by the greedy algorithm when run on input graph G. It is known that the Greedy is a $1 - \frac{1}{e}$ approximation algorithm [40]. In addition, we know that $C(Greedy(k \log \frac{1}{\lambda}, G)) \geq (1 - \lambda)Opt_k(G)$.

THEOREM 3.1. *For any $\varepsilon \in (0, 1]$ and any graph G, Algorithm 3 produces a $(1 - \frac{1}{e} - \varepsilon)$-approximate solution to k-cover on G with probability $1 - \frac{1}{n}$. The number of edges in the sketch used by this algorithm is $\tilde{O}(n)$.*

LEMMA 3.2. *For arbitrary $k', \varepsilon' \in (0, 1], \lambda' \in (0, \frac{1}{e}], C' \in [1, \infty)$, and graph G, Algorithm 4 returns false only if the size of the minimum set cover of G is greater than k'. Otherwise, the algorithm returns a solution of size $k' \log \frac{1}{\lambda'}$ that covers $1 - \lambda' - \varepsilon'$ fraction of $\mathcal{E}$ in G*

with probability $1 - \frac{1}{C'n}$. The number of edges in the sketch used by this algorithm is $O(\frac{n \log^2 n \log^6 m \log C'}{\varepsilon'^3})$.

THEOREM 3.3. *Given $\varepsilon \in (0, 1], C \geq 1$ and a graph G, Algorithm 5 returns a $(1+\varepsilon) \log \frac{1}{\lambda}$ approximate solution to set cover with λ outliers on G with probability $1 - \frac{1}{n}$. The total number of edges in the sketches used by this algorithm is $\tilde{O}(n/\lambda^3) \subseteq \tilde{O}_\lambda(n)$.*

PROOF. Remark that each iteration of the loop in Algorithm 5 increases k' by a factor of $1 + \frac{\varepsilon}{3}$, and we always keep $k' \leq n$. Thus, we run at most $\log_{1+\frac{\varepsilon}{3}} n$ instances of Algorithm 4. Lemma 3.2 holds for each of these instances with probability $\frac{1}{Cn \log_{1+\frac{\varepsilon}{3}} n}$. They all hold with probability $1 - \frac{1}{Cn}$ by the union bound. We prove the statement of the theorem assuming this.

Let k^* be the size of the minimum set cover in G, and let k' be the final value of this variable after run of Algorithm 5. Indeed Algorithm 4 returns false for $\frac{k'}{1+\varepsilon/3}$, hence $k' \leq (1 + \varepsilon/3)k^*$. Note that, the size of the set returned by Algorithm 5 is

$$
\begin{aligned}
k' \log \frac{1}{\lambda'} &= k' \log \frac{1}{\lambda e^{-\varepsilon/2}} \\
&= k' \left[\log \frac{1}{\lambda} + \frac{\varepsilon}{2} \right] \\
&\leq \left[\log \frac{1}{\lambda} + \frac{\varepsilon}{2} \right] \cdot \left[1 + \frac{\varepsilon}{3} \right] \cdot k^* \\
&= k^* \left[\log \frac{1}{\lambda} + \frac{\varepsilon}{2} + \frac{\varepsilon}{3} \log \frac{1}{\lambda} + \frac{\varepsilon^2}{6} \right] \\
&\leq (1 + \varepsilon)k^* \log \frac{1}{\lambda}.
\end{aligned}
$$

On the other hand, this solution covers at least

$$1 - \lambda' - \varepsilon' = 1 - \lambda e^{-\varepsilon/2} - \lambda(1 - e^{-\varepsilon/2}) = 1 - \lambda$$

fraction of the vertices in G, as claimed.

Lemma 3.2 bounds the number of edges in the sketch used by each instance of Algorithm 4 as

$$
O\left(\frac{n \log^2 n \log^6 m \log C'}{\varepsilon'^3} \right) = O\left(\frac{n \log^2 n \log^6 m \log C \log_{1+\frac{\varepsilon}{3}} n}{[\lambda(1 - e^{-\varepsilon/2})]^3} \right)
$$

$$
\subseteq \tilde{O}(n/\lambda^3) \subseteq \tilde{O}_\lambda(n).
$$

With $\log_{1+\varepsilon/3} n$ runs of Algorithm 4, the total number of edges in all the sketches used in this algorithm is $\tilde{O}(n/\lambda^3) \subseteq \tilde{O}_\lambda(n)$. □

We implement each iteration of Algorithm 6 in two streaming passes. In the first pass of each iteration we simply mark covered elements to virtually construct G_i, whereas in the second pass, we construct $H_{\leq n}$. After all $r - 1$ iterations, we utilize one extra pass to keep all edges to construct G_r. Hence, the following theorem proves the third statement of Theorem 1.1

THEOREM 3.4. *Given $\varepsilon \in (0, 1]$ and a graph G, Algorithm 6 finds a $(1 + \varepsilon) \log m$ approximate solution to set cover on G with probability $1 - \frac{1}{n}$. The total number of edges in the sketches used by this algorithm plus the number of edges in G_r is at most $\tilde{O}(nm^{\frac{3}{2+r}}) \subseteq \tilde{O}(nm^{O(1/r)})$.*

Algorithm 2 Streaming algorithm to compute $H_{\leq n}(k, \varepsilon, \delta'')$

Input: An input graph G, k, $\varepsilon \in (0, 1]$, and δ''.
Output: Sketch $H_{\leq n}(k, \varepsilon, \delta'')$.
Initialization:

Set $\delta = \delta'' \log\log_{\frac{1}{1-\varepsilon}} m$.
Pick $\frac{24n\delta \log(1/\varepsilon)\log n}{(1-\varepsilon)\varepsilon^3} + \frac{n\log(1/\varepsilon)}{\varepsilon k}$ element from $\mathcal{E}$ uniformly at random and let Π be a random permutation over these elements.
Initialize $H_{\leq n}(k, \varepsilon, \delta'')$ with vertices $\mathcal{S}$ of G, and no edge.

Update edge (u, v):

if v is not sampled in Π **then**
    Discard (u, v).
else if degree of v in G is $\frac{n\log(1/\varepsilon)}{\varepsilon k}$ **then**
    Discard (u, v).
else
    Add (u, v) to $H_{\leq n}(k, \varepsilon, \delta'')$.
while number of edges in $H_{\leq n}(k, \varepsilon, \delta'')$ is more than $\frac{24n\delta \log(1/\varepsilon)\log n}{(1-\varepsilon)\varepsilon^3} + \frac{n\log(1/\varepsilon)}{\varepsilon k}$ **do**
    Let w be the last element in Π.
    Remove w from Π.
    Remove w from $H_{\leq n}(k, \varepsilon, \delta'')$.

Algorithm 3 k-cover

Input: An input graph G, k, and $\varepsilon \in (0, 1]$.
Output: A $1 - \frac{1}{e} - \varepsilon$ approximate solution to k-cover on G with probability $1 - \frac{1}{n}$.

Set $\delta'' = 2 + \log n$ and $\varepsilon' = \frac{1}{12}\varepsilon$.
Construct sketch $H_{\leq n}(k, \varepsilon', \delta'')$. *// Compute this over the stream.*
Run the greedy algorithm (or any $1 - \frac{1}{e}$ approximation algorithm) on this sketch and report Greedy$(k, H_{\leq n}(k, \varepsilon', \delta''))$.

Algorithm 4 A submodule to solve set cover

Input: Parameters k', $\varepsilon' \in (0, 1]$, $\lambda' \in (0, \frac{1}{e}]$, and $C' \in [1, \infty)$, as well as a graph G promised to have a set cover of size k'.
Output: A solution of size $k' \log \frac{1}{\lambda'}$ covering $1 - \lambda' - \varepsilon'$ fraction of $\mathcal{E}$ in G with probability $1 - \frac{1}{C'n}$.

Set $\delta'' = \log_{1+\varepsilon} n[\log(C'n) + 2]$ and $\varepsilon = \frac{\varepsilon'}{13 \log \frac{1}{\lambda'}}$.
Construct sketch $H_{\leq n}(k' \log \frac{1}{\lambda'}, \varepsilon, \delta'')$. *// Compute this over the stream.*
Run the greedy algorithm on this sketch to get solution S = Greedy$(k' \log \frac{1}{\lambda'}, H_{\leq n})$
if S covers at least $1 - \lambda' - \varepsilon \log \frac{1}{\lambda'}$ fraction of $\mathcal{E}$ in $H_{\leq n}$ **then**
    return S
else
    return false

Algorithm 5 Set cover with λ outliers

Input: A graph G and parameters $\varepsilon \in [0, 1]$, $\lambda \in (0, \frac{1}{e}]$, and $C \geq 1$.
Output: A $(1 + \varepsilon) \log \frac{1}{\lambda}$ approximate solution to set cover with λ outliers on G with probability $1 - \frac{1}{Cn}$.

Set $\varepsilon' = \lambda(1 - e^{-\varepsilon/2})$, and $\lambda' = \lambda e^{-\varepsilon/2}$, and $C' = C \log_{1+\frac{\varepsilon}{3}} n$, and $k' = 1$.
repeat
    $k' \leftarrow (1 + \frac{\varepsilon}{3})k'$
    Run Algorithm 4 on $(k', \varepsilon', \lambda', C', G)$ and let S be the outcome. *// Run these in parallel.*
until S is not false or $k' = n$
return S

Algorithm 6 Set cover in r iterations

Input: A graph G as well as $\varepsilon \in (0, 1]$, $C \geq 1$, and $r \in [1, \log m]$.
Output: A $(1 + \varepsilon) \log m$ approximate solution to set cover of G with probability $1 - \frac{1}{Cn}$.

1: Let $G_1 = G$, $\lambda = m^{-\frac{1}{2+r}}$, $C' = (r-1)C$, $S = \emptyset$.
2: **for** $i = 1$ **to** $r - 1$ **do**
3:     Run Algorithm 5 on $(G_i, \varepsilon, \lambda, C')$ and let S_i to be the outcome.   // i-th streaming pass.
4:     Add S_i to S
5:     Remove from G_i the elements covered by S_i and call the new graph G_{i+1}.
6: Run the greedy algorithm to find a set cover of G_r and let S^{Greedy} to be the result.
7: Add S^{Greedy} to S.
8: **return** S

PROOF. The algorithm runs $r-1$ instances of Algorithm 5. Theorem 3.3 holds for each with probability $1 - \frac{1}{C'n} = 1 - \frac{1}{(r-1)Cn}$, hence for all simultaneously with probability $1 - (r-1)\frac{1}{(r-1)Cn} = 1 - \frac{1}{Cn}$. We assume these hold when proving the statement of the theorem.

Let k' be the size of the minimum set cover in G. Note that for any $i \in [1, r]$, G_i is an induced subgraph of G that contains all sets in G. Thus, any set cover of G is a set cover of G_i as well. This means that the size of the set cover of G_i is at most k'. Therefore, Theorem 3.3 bounds the number of sets chosen by each run of Algorithm 5 by $(1 + \varepsilon) \log \frac{1}{\lambda} k' = (1 + \varepsilon) \log m^{\frac{1}{2+r}} k'$. Also, each run of Algorithm 5 covers $1 - \lambda$ fraction of the remaining uncovered elements. Therefore, the number of uncovered elements in G_i is at most $m\lambda^{i-1}$, and in particular this is $m\lambda^{r-1} = m^{\frac{3}{2+r}}$ for G_r. Therefore, the total size of the set cover obtained by this algorithm is at most

$$(r-1)(1+\varepsilon)k' \log m^{\frac{1}{2+r}} + k' \log m^{\frac{3}{2+r}}$$
$$\leq (1+\varepsilon)k' \left[(r-1) \log m^{\frac{1}{2+r}} + \log m^{\frac{3}{2+r}} \right]$$
$$= (1+\varepsilon)k' \left[(r-1)\frac{1}{2+r} + \frac{3}{2+r} \right] \log m$$
$$= (1+\varepsilon)k' \log m.$$

Remark that the total number of edges in the sketches used by Algorithm 5 is $\tilde{O}(n/\lambda^3)$. With $r \leq \log m$ such runs, the total number of edges in all the sketches is $\tilde{O}(n/\lambda^3) = \tilde{O}(nm^{\frac{3}{2+r}})$. On the other hand, the number uncovered elements in G_r is $m\lambda^{r-1} = m^{\frac{3}{2+r}}$. Thus, the number of edges in G_r is at most $nm^{\frac{3}{2+r}}$. Therefore, the total number of edges in the sketches plus the number of edges in G_r is $\tilde{O}(nm^{\frac{3}{2+r}}) \subseteq \tilde{O}(nm^{O(1/r)})$. □

4 HARDNESS OF STREAMING PROBLEMS

Here, we give a lower bound on the space required to solve k-cover in the streaming setting. To establish this lower bound, we present a reduction from the set-disjointness problem. In the set disjointness problem, two parties, namely Alice and Bob, each holds a subset of $1, 2, \ldots, n$. The goal is to determine whether the sets are disjoint or not. Razborov [43] and Kalyanasundaram and Schintger [29] provide a lower bound of $\Omega(n)$ even when allowing randomization.

PROOF OF THEOREM 1.2. Let A be the set that Alice holds, and let B be the set that Bob holds. In our hard k cover instance we have two vertices (namely a and b) in $\mathcal{E}$ and n vertices in S. Vertex a has

an edge to the i-th vertex in $\mathcal{E}$ if and only if i exists in A. Similarly, b has an edge to the i-th vertex in $\mathcal{E}$ if and only if i exists in B. In the input stream first we see the edges of a (which contains the information Alice holds) and then the edges of b (which contains the information Bob holds).

In this example, if the sets A and B are disjoint, each of the vertices in S covers at most one of a and b, and thus, the value of an optimum solution to 1-cover on this graph is 1. Otherwise, there is a vertex i which has edge to both a and b, and thus, the value of an optimum solution to 1-cover on this graph is 2. Therefore, distinguishing between the case that the value of the optimum solution to 1-cover is 1 and the case that this value is 2 requires $\Omega(n)$ space in total. □

5 THE K-COVER PROBLEM VIA $(1 \pm \varepsilon)$-APPROXIMATE ORACLE

In this section we consider the approximability of k-cover using the $(1 \pm \varepsilon)$-approximate oracle, and prove Theorem 1.3 by showing that any α-approximation algorithm via oracle C_ε requires at least $\exp\left(\Omega(n\varepsilon^2\alpha^2 - \log n)\right)$ oracle queries.

Theorem 5.2 states the hardness of the k-purification problem. Its proof uses the following generalization of the Chernoff bound.

LEMMA 5.1. *Let X be the sum of several negatively correlated binary random variables. We have*

$$\Pr\left(|X - E[X]| > \gamma\right) \leq 2\exp\left(-\frac{\gamma^2}{3E[X]}\right).$$

PROOF. Panconesi and Srinivasan [42] show that if X is the sum of certain negatively correlated binary random variables, we have $\Pr\left(|X - E[X]| > \varepsilon E[X]\right) \leq 2\exp\left(-\frac{\varepsilon^2 E[X]}{3}\right)$. Setting $\gamma = \varepsilon E[X]$ yields

$$\Pr\left(|X - E[X]| > \gamma\right) \leq 2\exp\left(-\frac{\left(\frac{\gamma}{E[X]}\right)^2 \cdot E[X]}{3}\right) = 2\exp\left(-\frac{\gamma^2}{3E[X]}\right)$$

as desired. □

THEOREM 5.2. *Any randomized algorithm that solves k-purification with probability at least δ requires at least $\delta \exp\left(\Omega(\frac{\varepsilon^2 k^2}{n})\right)$ oracle queries.*

Proof. By Yao's principle we can restrict our analysis to deterministic algorithms. Let Alg be a deterministic algorithm for k-purification. Suppose that after q queries, algorithm Alg finds with probability δ a set S such that $\mathsf{Pure}_\varepsilon(S) = 1$. Let $S_1, S_2, \ldots, S_q$ be the q subsets queried by Alg. Definition of δ and the union bound give

$$\delta \leq \sum_{i=1}^{q} \mathbf{Pr}\big(\mathsf{Pure}_\varepsilon(S_i) = 1\big). \tag{12}$$

Now, we provide an upper bound to $\mathbf{Pr}\big(\mathsf{Pure}_\varepsilon(S) = 1\big)$ for an arbitrary subset S. Let X_i be a random variable that indicates whether the i-th item in S is gold. Let $X = \sum_{i=1}^{|S|} X_i$. Indeed, X_i variables are negatively correlated [28]. We set $\gamma = \varepsilon(\frac{k|S|}{n} + \frac{k^2}{n})$ in Lemma 5.1 to obtain

$$\begin{aligned}\mathbf{Pr}\big(\mathsf{Pure}_\varepsilon(S) = 1\big) &= \mathbf{Pr}\left(|X - \mathbf{E}[X]| > \varepsilon\left(\frac{k|S|}{n} + \frac{k^2}{n}\right)\right)\\ &\leq 2\exp\left(-\frac{\varepsilon^2(\frac{k|S|}{n} + \frac{k^2}{n})^2}{3\mathbf{E}[X]}\right)\\ &\leq 2\exp\left(-\frac{\varepsilon^2(\frac{k|S|}{n} + \frac{k^2}{n})^2}{3\frac{k|S|}{n}}\right)\\ &\leq 2\exp\left(-\frac{\varepsilon^2 k(|S| + k)^2}{3n|S|}\right)\\ &\leq 2\exp\left(-\frac{\varepsilon^2 k^2}{3n}\right).\end{aligned}$$

Coupled with Inequality (12) the above implies that $\delta \leq \sum_{i=1}^{q} \mathbf{Pr}\big(\mathsf{Pure}_\varepsilon(S_i) = 1\big) \leq 2q\exp\left(-\frac{\varepsilon^2k^2}{3n}\right)$, which means $q \geq \frac{\delta}{2}\exp\left(\frac{\varepsilon^2k^2}{3n}\right)$, as desired. □

Proof of Theorem 1.3. Given an instance of the k-purification problem we construct a k-cover instance with a $(1\pm\varepsilon')$-approximate oracle as follows. We associate one set for each gold or brass item in the original instance in such a way that the value of the coverage function (for nonempty S) is $C(S) = k + \frac{n}{k}\mathsf{Gold}(S)$; i.e., there are k elements common between all gold and brass *sets*, and in addition, each gold set contains $\frac{n}{k}$ additional exclusive elements. The optimum solution consists of all gold sets, hence

$$\mathsf{Opt} = k + \frac{n}{k}k = k + n > n. \tag{13}$$

We define

$$C_{\varepsilon'}(S) = \begin{cases} k + |S| & \text{if } \mathsf{Pure}_\varepsilon(S) = 0\\ C(S) & \text{otherwise.}\end{cases}$$

We claim that $C_{\varepsilon'}$ is a $(1\pm\varepsilon')$-approximate oracle to f for $\varepsilon' = 2\varepsilon$. We set $\varepsilon' = 2\varepsilon$. Notice that for $\mathsf{Pure}_\varepsilon(S) = 1$, the estimate $C_{\varepsilon'}(S)$ is clearly within the $1\pm\varepsilon'$ factor of $C(S)$. Moreover when $\mathsf{Pure}_\varepsilon(S) = 0$, we have $\frac{k|S|}{n} - \varepsilon(\frac{k|S|}{n} + \frac{k^2}{n}) \leq \mathsf{Gold}(S) \leq \frac{k|S|}{n} + \varepsilon(\frac{k|S|}{n} + \frac{k^2}{n})$. Thus we have

$$\begin{aligned}(1 - \varepsilon')C(S) &\leq \frac{1}{1+\varepsilon}C(S)\\ &= \frac{1}{1+\varepsilon}\left[k + \frac{n}{k}\mathsf{Gold}(S)\right]\\ &\leq \frac{1}{1+\varepsilon}\left[k + \frac{n}{k}\left(\frac{k|S|}{n} + \varepsilon\left(\frac{k|S|}{n} + \frac{k^2}{n}\right)\right)\right]\\ &= \frac{1}{1+\varepsilon}\left[k + |S| + \varepsilon(|S| + k)\right]\\ &= k + |S| = C_{\varepsilon'}(S).\end{aligned}$$

Similarly we have

$$\begin{aligned}(1 + \varepsilon')C(S) &\geq \frac{1}{1-\varepsilon}C(S)\\ &= \frac{1}{1-\varepsilon}\left[k + \frac{n}{k}\mathsf{Gold}(S)\right]\\ &\geq \frac{1}{1-\varepsilon}\left[k + \frac{n}{k}\left(\frac{k|S|}{n} - \varepsilon\left(\frac{k|S|}{n} + \frac{k^2}{n}\right)\right)\right]\\ &= \frac{1}{1-\varepsilon}\left[k + |S| - \varepsilon(|S| + k)\right]\\ &= k + |S| = C_{\varepsilon'}(S).\end{aligned}$$

Therefore, $C_{\varepsilon'}$ is a $(1 \pm \varepsilon')$-approximate oracle to C.

For an arbitrary subset S of size k with $\mathsf{Pure}_\varepsilon(S) = 0$, we have

$$\begin{aligned}\frac{C(S)}{\mathsf{Opt}} &< \frac{k + \frac{n}{k}\mathsf{Gold}(S)}{n}\\ &\leq \frac{k + \frac{n}{k}\left[\frac{k|S|}{n} + \varepsilon\left(\frac{k|S|}{n} + \frac{k^2}{n}\right)\right]}{n}\\ &\leq \frac{k + \frac{n}{k}\left[\frac{k^2}{n} + \varepsilon\left(\frac{k^2}{n} + \frac{k^2}{n}\right)\right]}{n}\\ &= \frac{(2k + 2\varepsilon k)}{n} \leq \frac{4k}{n}.\end{aligned}$$

Thus, if S is a $\frac{4k}{n}$-approximate solution to the k-cover instance, we have $\mathsf{Pure}_\varepsilon(S) = 1$. Therefore, any $\frac{6k}{n}$-approximation algorithm returns a set S such that $\mathsf{Pure}_\varepsilon(S) = 1$ with probability at least $\frac{6k/n - 4k/n}{\mathsf{Opt}} = \frac{2k/n}{n+k} = \frac{2k}{n^2+kn} \geq \frac{1}{n^2}$.

Recall that for any subset S given that $\mathsf{Pure}_\varepsilon(S) = 0$, the value of $C_{\varepsilon'}(S)$ is predetermined, and can be computed independent of the actual value of $C(S)$. Thus, using a $\frac{6k}{n}$-approximation algorithm for the k-cover problem with ε'-error oracle, with probability $\frac{1}{n^2}$, one can find a set S such that $\mathsf{Pure}_\varepsilon(S) = 1$, using the same number of queries. Theorem 5.2 states that the number of queries is not less than

$$\begin{aligned}\frac{1}{n^2}\exp\left(\Omega\left(\frac{\varepsilon'^2k^2}{n}\right)\right) &= \frac{1}{n^2}\exp\left(\Omega\left(\frac{\varepsilon^2k^2}{n}\right)\right)\\ &\in \exp\left(\Omega\left(\frac{\varepsilon^2k^2}{n} - \log n\right)\right)\\ &= \exp\left(\Omega\left(n\varepsilon^2\alpha^2 - \log n\right)\right).\end{aligned}$$

□

6 CONCLUSION

In this paper, we presented a simple, yet powerful sketching technique for coverage problems, and showed how to construct this sketch in streaming model. The streaming results improve the state of the art in three dimensions: approximation ratio, space complexity, and streaming arrival model (i.e., from set-arrival to element- or edge-arrival model). In an accompanied paper, we also applied this sketching idea for distributed computation models (such as MapReduce), and show how it improves the best known results in that area as well. More notably, we also performed an extensive empirical evaluation of resulting distributed algorithms and show the effectiveness of applying this sketching technique for analyzing massive data sets in practice [10]. As noted earlier, this sketch and the distributed and streaming algorithms based on it work very well in instances in which the size of the subsets is large. Notably, all the other techniques (e.g., based on composable core-sets) fail in these regimes. As future research, we hope this technique can be applied to other computation models and other problems.

REFERENCES

[1] Z. Abbassi, V. S. Mirrokni, and M. Thakur. Diversity maximization under matroid constraints. In *KDD*, pages 32–40, 2013.

[2] K. J. Ahn and S. Guha. Graph sparsification in the semi-streaming model. In *ICALP (2)*, pages 328–338, 2009.

[3] K. J. Ahn and S. Guha. Laminar families and metric embeddings: Non-bipartite maximum matching problem in the semi-streaming model. *Manuscript, available at http://arxiv.org/abs/1104.4058*, 2011.

[4] K. J. Ahn, S. Guha, and A. McGregor. Spectral sparsification in dynamic graph streams. In *Approximation, Randomization, and Combinatorial Optimization. Algorithms and Techniques*, pages 1–10. Springer, 2013.

[5] A. Andoni, A. Gupta, and R. Krauthgamer. Towards (1+ ε)-approximate flow sparsifiers. In *SODA*, pages 279–293. SIAM, 2014.

[6] S. Assadi, S. Khanna, and Y. Li. Tight bounds for single-pass streaming complexity of the set cover problem. In *STOC*, pages 698–711. ACM, 2016.

[7] S. Assadi, S. Khanna, Y. Li, and G. Yaroslavtsev. Maximum matchings in dynamic graph streams and the simultaneous communication model. In *SODA*, pages 1345–1364. SIAM, 2016.

[8] A. Badanidiyuru, S. Dobzinski, H. Fu, R. Kleinberg, N. Nisan, and T. Roughgarden. Sketching valuation functions. In *Proceedings of the twenty-third annual ACM-SIAM symposium on Discrete Algorithms*, pages 1025–1035. SIAM, 2012.

[9] A. Badanidiyuru, B. Mirzasoleiman, A. Karbasi, and A. Krause. Streaming submodular maximization: Massive data summarization on the fly. In *KDD*, 2014.

[10] M. Bateni, H. Esfandiari, and V. Mirrokni. Distributed coverage maximization via sketching. *arXiv preprint arXiv:1612.02327*, 2016.

[11] G. E. Blelloch, H. V. Simhadri, and K. Tangwongsan. Parallel and I/O efficient set covering algorithms. In *SPAA*, pages 82–90, 2012.

[12] A. Borodin, H. C. Lee, and Y. Ye. Max-sum diversification, monotone submodular functions and dynamic updates. In *PODS*, pages 155–166, 2012.

[13] A. Chakrabarti and A. Wirth. Incidence geometries and the pass complexity of semi-streaming set cover. In *Proceedings of the Twenty-Seventh Annual ACM-SIAM Symposium on Discrete Algorithms*, pages 1365–1373. SIAM, 2016.

[14] F. Chierichetti, R. Kumar, and A. Tomkins. Max-Cover in Map-Reduce. In *WWW*, pages 231–240, 2010.

[15] R. Chitnis, G. Cormode, H. Esfandiari, M. Hajiaghayi, A. McGregor, M. Monemizadeh, and S. Vorotnikova. Kernelization via sampling with applications to finding matchings and related problems in dynamic graph streams. In *SODA*, pages 1326–1344. SIAM, 2016.

[16] G. Cormode, M. Datar, P. Indyk, and S. Muthukrishnan. Comparing data streams using hamming norms (how to zero in). *Knowledge and Data Engineering, IEEE Transactions on*, 15(3):529–540, 2003.

[17] G. Cormode, H. J. Karloff, and A. Wirth. Set cover algorithms for very large datasets. In *CIKM*, pages 479–488, 2010.

[18] E. D. Demaine, P. Indyk, S. Mahabadi, and A. Vakilian. On streaming and communication complexity of the set cover problem. In *DISC*, pages 484–498. Springer, 2014.

[19] Y. Emek and A. Rosén. Semi-streaming set cover. In *Automata, Languages, and Programming*, pages 453–464. Springer, 2014.

[20] L. Epstein, A. Levin, J. Mestre, and D. Segev. Improved approximation guarantees for weighted matching in the semi-streaming model. *SIAM J. Discrete Math.*, 25(3):1251–1265, 2011.

[21] H. Esfandiari, M. T. Hajiaghayi, V. Liaghat, M. Monemizadeh, and K. Onak. Streaming algorithms for estimating the matching size in planar graphs and beyond. In *SODA*, pages 1217–1233. SIAM, 2015.

[22] U. Feige. A threshold of ln n for approximating set cover. *Journal of the ACM (JACM)*, 45(4):634–652, 1998.

[23] J. Feigenbaum, S. Kannan, A. McGregor, S. Suri, and J. Zhang. On graph problems in a semi-streaming model. *Theor. Comput. Sci.*, 348(2):207–216, 2005.

[24] J. Feigenbaum, S. Kannan, A. McGregor, S. Suri, and J. Zhang. On graph problems in a semi-streaming model. *Theoretical Computer Science*, 348(2):207–216, 2005.

[25] S. Har-Peled, P. Indyk, S. Mahabadi, and A. Vakilian. Towards tight bounds for the streaming set cover problem. In *PODS*, 2016.

[26] A. Hassidim and Y. Singer. Submodular optimization under noise. *arXiv preprint arXiv:1601.03095*, 2016.

[27] P. Indyk, S. Mahabadi, M. Mahdian, and V. Mirrokni. Composable core-sets for diversity and coverage maximization. In *ACM PODS*, 2014.

[28] K. Joag-Dev and F. Proschan. Negative association of random variables with applications. *The Annals of Statistics*, pages 286–295, 1983.

[29] B. Kalyanasundaram and G. Schintger. The probabilistic communication complexity of set intersection. *SIAM Journal on Discrete Mathematics*, 5(4):545–557, 1992.

[30] M. Kapralov, S. Khanna, and M. Sudan. Approximating matching size from random streams. In *SODA*, pages 734–751. SIAM, 2014.

[31] M. Kapralov, S. Khanna, and M. Sudan. Streaming lower bounds for approximating MAX-CUT. In *SODA*, pages 1263–1282. SIAM, 2015.

[32] J. A. Kelner and A. Levin. Spectral sparsification in the semi-streaming setting. In *STACS*, pages 440–451, 2011.

[33] C. Konrad, F. Magniez, and C. Mathieu. Maximum matching in semi-streaming with few passes. In *APPROX-RANDOM*, pages 231–242, 2012.

[34] C. Konrad and A. Rosén. Approximating semi-matchings in streaming and in two-party communication. In *ICALP*, pages 637–649, 2013.

[35] R. Kumar, B. Moseley, S. Vassilvitskii, and A. Vattani. Fast greedy algorithms in MapReduce and streaming. In *SPAA*, pages 1–10, 2013.

[36] A. McGregor and H. T. Vu. Better streaming algorithms for the maximum coverage problem. *arXiv preprint arXiv:1610.06199*, 2016.

[37] V. S. Mirrokni and M. Zadimoghaddam. Randomized composable core-sets for distributed submodular maximization. In *STOC*, pages 153–162, 2015.

[38] B. Mirzasoleiman, A. Karbasi, R. Sarkar, and A. Krause. Distributed submodular maximization: Identifying representative elements in massive data. In *NIPS*, pages 2049–2057, 2013.

[39] S. Muthukrishnan. *Data streams: Algorithms and applications*. Now Publishers Inc, 2005.

[40] G. L. Nemhauser, L. A. Wolsey, and M. L. Fisher. An analysis of approximations for maximizing submodular set functionsâĂŤi. *Mathematical Programming*, 14(1):265–294, 1978.

[41] N. Nisan. The communication complexity of approximate set packing and covering. In *Automata, Languages and Programming*, pages 868–875. Springer, 2002.

[42] A. Panconesi and A. Srinivasan. Randomized distributed edge coloring via an extension of the Chernoff-Hoeffding bounds. *SIAM Journal on Computing*, 26(2):350–368, 1997.

[43] A. A. Razborov. On the distributional complexity of disjointness. *Theoretical Computer Science*, 106(2):385–390, 1992.

[44] B. Saha and L. Getoor. On maximum coverage in the streaming model & application to multi-topic blog-watch. In *SDM*, volume 9, pages 697–708. SIAM, 2009.

Bicriteria Distributed Submodular Maximization in a Few Rounds

Alessandro Epasto
Google, New York, NY, USA
aepasto@google.com

Vahab Mirrokni
Google, New York, NY, USA
mirrokni@google.com

Morteza Zadimoghaddam
Google, New York, NY, USA
zadim@google.com

ABSTRACT

We study the problem of efficiently optimizing submodular functions under cardinality constraints in distributed setting. Recently, several distributed algorithms for this problem have been introduced which either achieve a sub-optimal solution or they run in super-constant number of rounds of computation. Unlike previous work, we aim to design distributed algorithms in multiple rounds with almost optimal approximation guarantees at the cost of outputting a larger number of elements. Toward this goal, we present a distributed algorithm that, for any $\epsilon > 0$ and any constant r, outputs a set S of $O(rk/\epsilon^{\frac{1}{r}})$ items in r rounds, and achieves a $(1-\epsilon)$-approximation of the value of the optimum set with k items. This is the first distributed algorithm that achieves an approximation factor of $(1-\epsilon)$ running in less than $\log \frac{1}{\epsilon}$ number of rounds. We also prove a hardness result showing that the output of any $1-\epsilon$ approximation distributed algorithm limited to one distributed round should have at least $\Omega(k/\epsilon)$ items. In light of this hardness result, our distributed algorithm in one round, $r = 1$, is asymptotically tight in terms of the output size. We support the theoretical guarantees with an extensive empirical study of our algorithm showing that achieving almost optimum solutions is indeed possible in a few rounds for large-scale real datasets.

1 INTRODUCTION

As a prominent problem in machine learning and data mining applications, submodular maximization have attracted a great amount of research in the past decade. A set function $f : 2^{\mathbb{N}} \to R$ on a ground set $\mathbb{N}$ is *submodular* if for any two sets A and B, $f(A) + f(B) \geq f(A \cap B) + f(A \cup B)$, or equivalently, it satisfies the following diminishing return property, for any two sets $A \subseteq B$ and an element x, $f(A \cup \{x\}) - f(A) \geq f(B \cup \{x\}) - f(B)$. Several machine learning and data mining applications can be formalized as a submodular maximization problem. In the majority of such applications, the goal is to select a subset of representatives in a universe of elements and optimize some objective function. Some of those machine learning applications include exemplar based clustering [13], coverage problems [2], document summarization [20], and active set selection for non-parametric learning [15], and feature selection for training complex models [20]. More recently, motivated by several large-scale applications, various techniques have been developed for solving this problem in a distributed manner [5, 6, 21, 23]. These distributed algorithms, however, either achieve a sub-optimal solution for the submodular maximization problem, or they run in super-constant[1] number of rounds of computation (which make them less appealing in distributed frameworks like MapReduce). In this paper, we aim to present distributed algorithms addressing the above issues achieving asymptotically optimal approximation guarantees in a constant number of rounds of computation by allowing to output more items.

More specifically, we focus on submodular maximization problem subject to a cardinality constraint: given a cardinality constraint k, and a submodular function f defined on subsets of $\mathbb{N}$ ($|\mathbb{N}| = n$), the goal is to find a set S of at most k items with maximum value $f(S)$. Let OPT be the set of k items that achieves the maximum value, i.e. $\text{OPT} = \arg\max_{S \subseteq \mathbb{N} \& |S| \leq k} f(S)$. In the rest of the paper, we focus on non-negative monotone submodular functions since for non-monotone submodular functions it is impossible to get better than 1/2-approximation factor using sub-exponential number of evaluations of function f even without any cardinality constraint [12]. For monotone submodular functions, it is computationally hard to approximate this problem within a factor better than $1 - 1/e \approx 63\%$ [11]. The best approximation guarantees for maximizing a general monotone submodular function in a scalable manner in two rounds is a 54%-approximation proposed by [21]; they also show that even if machines have unbounded computational power achieving an approximation factor better than $1 - 1/e$ is impossible in distributed settings (an information-theoretic hardness result). Other approximation algorithms developed for this problem achieve $1 - 1/e$-approximation, but they run in super-constant number of rounds of computation, e.g. logarithmic or $1/\epsilon$ rounds to achieve $1 - 1/e - \epsilon$. In practice, however, it is desirable to achieve an almost optimum solution, i.e., $(1-\epsilon)$-approximation. While such an approximation factor is not achievable even on a single machine when limiting the output size to k elements, a naive approach of getting $(1-\epsilon)$-approximation in a centralized way is to repeatedly run the greedy algorithm on the data, and output $O(k \ln(1/\epsilon))$ elements. In order to achieve such an approximation factor in a distributed manner, a naive idea is to run distributed constant-factor approximation algorithms for submodular maximization [5, 21, 23], and get to $(1-\epsilon)$-approximation in $O(\ln(1/\epsilon))$ rounds. In the distributed setting, even if some $(1-\epsilon)$-approximation algorithms are used by the distributed and central machines to select items, the overall distributed approximation factor will not be more than 1/2 based on Theorem 5 of [5]. Therefore still $\log(1/\epsilon)$ rounds are needed to achieve a $(1-\epsilon)$ approximation factor. We show these naive greedy approaches in Table 1. The main issue with these

[1] The number of rounds of other methods is some function of $1/\epsilon$ which increases as we aim for better approximation guarantees, i.e. smaller ϵ. For a constant ϵ, the other methods also give constant (but possibly large) number of rounds.

SPAA '17, July 24-26, 2017, Washington DC, USA

ACM ISBN 978-1-4503-4593-4/17/07.
https://doi.org/10.1145/3087556.3087574

Algorithm	Rounds	Size of output $\|S\|$	Approximation
GreedyScaling [18]	$O(\log(\Delta)/\epsilon)$	k	$1 - 1/e - \epsilon$
GreeDi [23]	1	k	$1/\min\{m, k\} \geq 1/n^{1/3}$
PseudoGreedy [21]	1	k	0.54
RandGreedi [5]	1	k	0.316
ParallelAlg [6]	$O(1/\epsilon)$	k	$1 - 1/e - \epsilon$
Naive Distributed Greedy	$O(\log(1/\epsilon))$	$k\log(1/\epsilon)$	$1-\epsilon$
BicriteriaGreedy*,	r	$O(rk\ln^2(1/\epsilon^{1/r})/\epsilon^{2/r})$	$1-\epsilon$
BicriteriaGreedy with multiplicity*	r	$O(rk\ln(1/\epsilon^{1/r})/\epsilon^{1/r})$	$1-\epsilon$
HybridAlg*	r	$O(rk/\epsilon^{1/r})$	$1-\epsilon$

Table 1: Summary of our results and the state of the art. The number of rounds shows the number of times the central algorithm interacts with the distributed machines. The results with * are the new results of this paper. The main advantage of our methods are achieving almost optimal solutions for any number of rounds $r > 0$.

approaches is the number of rounds which is a major bottleneck in making these algorithms scalable. This leaves open the problem of defining greedy-based algorithms in distributed settings with limited number of rounds. We propose the distributed Algorithm BicriteriaGreedy with pseudo-code as Algorithm 1 that outputs a set S of more than k items, and achieves the $1-\epsilon$ times the value of the optimum set for a given $\epsilon > 0$. The number of selected items, $|S|$, depends on k and ϵ as expected, and the dependence on ϵ can be reduced exponentially by increasing the number of rounds. So one can choose a small number of rounds (two or three), and still have a good guarantee on the number of selected items without sacrificing the scalability of the algorithm. We also prove that the polynomial dependence of the output size on $1/\epsilon$ is necessary by providing a hardness result that also shows our results are asymptotically tight when the algorithm has to perform in one distributed round[2]. In addition to the mathematical analysis of our algorithm, we support the theoretical guarantees with an extensive empirical study of our algorithm, and show that achieving almost optimum solutions are indeed possible in a few rounds. We highlight that our main contribution is not to introduce a new algorithmic technique for submodular maximization (we build on the well-known greedy algorithm). We explore theoretically and experimentally the trade-offs between outputting more items and number of rounds when we aim for a $1-\epsilon$ approximation guarantee.

Our Contributions. We provide the first distributed algorithm that achieves an approximation factor of $(1-\epsilon)$ running in less than $\log\frac{1}{\epsilon}$ number of rounds. We use the same distributed framework of [21, 23]. A central machine partitions the ground set randomly among a set of distributed machines (workers). Each machine runs the greedy algorithm to select a subset of its items, and return them to the central machine. Among all returned items, a final output set will be selected. We generalize the proof techniques of [21] and present algorithm BicriteriaGreedy that outputs a solution with value arbitrarily close to optimum. In particular for any $\alpha > 1$, we show that an approximation factor of $1 - 1/\alpha$ is achieved if each distributed machine greedily returns $O(\alpha k)$ items to the central machine, and then $\tilde{O}(\alpha^2 k)$ of these returned items are greedily selected as the final solution. We note that [21] provides a 0.54-approximation factor by outputting k items, and here we analyse the effect of growing the output size beyond k on the approximation factor and how fast we converge to an almost optimum solution. Using the simple trick of sending each item to $\alpha\ln(\alpha)$ random machines instead of a random partitioning of ground set, we can show that outputting $\tilde{O}(\alpha k)$ items as the final solution suffices to achieve an approximation factor of $1 - 1/\alpha$. We call this $\alpha\ln(\alpha)$ term the multiplicity factor as it is the number of machines we send each item to. By selecting a larger α, one can achieve better approximation guarantees while outputting more items. We further improve our results by presenting algorithm HybridAlg that outputs $O(\alpha k)$ items while having the $1 - 1/\alpha$ approximation (this gets rid of the extra log factor in the size upper bound).

So far, we have described our methods using one distributed round of computation. A major contribution of our work is to get the same approximation factors with outputting much fewer items when more number of rounds is allowed. We start with $S = \emptyset$, and we want to reduce the gap $f(\text{OPT}) - f(S)$ to at most $\epsilon f(\text{OPT})$ (equivalent of getting a $1-\epsilon$ approximation). At the beginning this gap is equal to $f(\text{OPT})$, and therefore in r rounds we want to reduce it by a total multiplicative factor of ϵ. This can be achieved by reducing the gap by a factor of $\epsilon^{1/r}$ in each round. Our proof techniques are of independent interest as they resemble some of the ideas of the *egg dropping puzzle* [14]. By setting $\alpha = O(1/\epsilon^{1/r})$, we can get a $1-\epsilon^{1/r}$ approximation in each round which is equivalent of reducing the gap by $\epsilon^{1/r}$. Therefore after r rounds, we have a $(1-\epsilon)$ approximation factor using $O(r\alpha k)$ items in HybridAlg, $\tilde{O}(r\alpha k)$ items in BicriteriaGreedy with multiplicity $\alpha\ln(\alpha)$, and $\tilde{O}(r\alpha^2 k)$ items in BicriteriaGreedy with just a random partitioning (multiplicity one).

Furthermore, we show that for a distributed algorithm that achieves a $1-\epsilon$ approximation guarantee in one distributed round, the algorithm needs to have an output size of at least $\Omega(k/\epsilon)$. This hardness result proves the tightness of our algorithmic result for $r = 1$, and also provides an insight on why the output size should have a polynomial dependence on $1/\epsilon$ in distributed setting versus the logarithmic dependence in centralized single machine setting.

[2]Having only one distributed round is an important case specially in time-sensitive applications in which the algorithm should process the data very fast and provide a solution instantly.

1.1 Related Work.

Submodular maximization in a distributed manner have attracted a significant amount of research over the last few years [4–6, 8–10, 18, 19, 21, 23]. From a theoretical point of view, for the coverage maximization problem, [9] present a $(1 - 1/e)$-approximation algorithm in polylogarithmic number of MapReduce rounds, and [8] improved this result and achieved $\log^2 n$ number of rounds. Recently, [18] present a $(1 - 1/e)$-approximation algorithm using a logarithmic number of rounds of MapReduce. They also derive $(1/2 - \epsilon)$-approximation algorithm that runs in $O(\frac{1}{\delta})$ number of rounds of MapReduce (for a constant δ), but this algorithm needs a $\log n$ blowup in the communication complexity, and number of rounds could become large for small δ. [6] present a distributed $1-1/e-\epsilon$ approximation algorithm that runs in $O(1/\epsilon)$ rounds, and their space requirement also grows linearly with $1/\epsilon$. As observed in various empirical studies [17], the communication complexity and the number of MapReduce rounds are important factors in determining the performance of a MapReduce-based algorithm and a $\log n$ blowup in the communication complexity can play a crucial role in applicability of the algorithm in practice. Our algorithm on the other hand runs only in a constant number of rounds. Recently, distributed approximation algorithms have been developed for this problem that run in two rounds [5, 21, 23], however, they do not achieve optimal approximation factor of $1 - 1/e$ for this problem, or they do not achieve a general result for all submodular functions. [23] shows the effectiveness of applying algorithm Greedy over a random partitioning empirically for several machine learning applications. The authors also prove theoretical guarantees for algorithm Greedy for special classes of submodular functions satisfying a certain Lipschitz condition [23].

2 ALGORITHM BICRITERIAGREEDY

We present Algorithm BicriteriaGreedy depicted as Algorithm 1 which uses the Greedy algorithm described as Algorithm 2 as a subroutine and achieves approximation guarantee of $1 - \epsilon$. Algorithm BicriteriaGreedy receives in the input the ground set $\mathbb{N}$, as the number of rounds r, approximation error ϵ, the number of machines m, and cardinality constraint k. The algorithm works for any $r > 0$, and the upper bound on the number of selected items improves as r grows. However one should be careful with setting r to a large number as the number of rounds directly influences the scalability of the algorithm. The algorithm also works for any number of machines $m > 0$ but for the sake of analysis we need $m \geq \alpha \ln(\alpha)$ for $\alpha = 3/\epsilon^{1/r}$. Increasing m reduces the workload on each of the distributed m machines, however it increases the number of items the central machine should process[3].

BicriteriaGreedy constructs output set S by starting with $S = \emptyset$, and adding items to S as follows. In each of the r rounds (lines 6–11), it partitions the items randomly between m machines, giving set T_i to machine i. This random partitioning in each round might seem an overhead, but since the running times of each machine is super-linear in the number of items it receives, repartitioning does not become a bottleneck both in terms of the asymptotic complexity, and also the running times of our experiments in Section 4. Every machine i runs Algorithm 2 (Greedy) to select a subset $S_i \subset T_i$. In both Algorithms 1 and 2, we use notation $\Delta(x, A)$ to denote the marginal value of adding item x to A, i.e. $\Delta(x, A) = f(\{x\} \cup A) - f(A)$. The selected items ($\cup_{i=1}^m S_i$) are sent to a central machine which does another filtering and selects a subset $A \subseteq \cup_{i=1}^m S_i$, and adds A to set S. This extra filtering corresponds to lines 9 – 11 in Algorithm 1. Parameter ϵ determines how much suboptimal we are allowed to be compared to the optimum solution.

The for loop in lines 7 – 8 of Algorithm 1 is parallelized, and machine i runs the subroutine $Greedy(\alpha k, S, T_i)$ described as Algorithm 2 for each $1 \leq i \leq m$. In lines 9 – 11 of Algorithm 1, the central machine gathers all selected items $\cup_{i=1}^m S_i$, and in each of the $(\alpha^2 \ln^2(\alpha) + \ln(\alpha))k$ iterations, chooses the item with maximum marginal gain among the selected items to add to S. To summarize, Algorithm 1 selects $(\alpha^2 \ln^2(\alpha) + \ln(\alpha))k$ items in each round.

1 **Input:** $\mathbb{N}$, r, ϵ, m, and k.
2 **Output:** Set $S \subset \mathbb{N}$ with $f(S) \geq (1 - \epsilon)f(\text{OPT})$.
3 $\alpha \leftarrow 3/(\epsilon^{1/r})$;
4 $S \leftarrow \emptyset$;
5 **forall the** $1 \leq \ell \leq r$ **do**
6   Send each item in $\mathbb{N}$ independently into one of $\{T_i\}_{i=1}^m$ uniformly at random;
7   **forall the** $1 \leq i \leq m$ **do**
8         $S_i \leftarrow Greedy(\alpha k, S, T_i)$;
9   **forall the** $1 \leq j \leq (\alpha^2 \ln^2(\alpha) + \ln(\alpha))k$ **do**
10         $x^* \leftarrow max_{x \in \cup_{i=1}^m S_i} \Delta(x, S)$;
11         $S \leftarrow S \cup \{x^*\}$;
12 Return S;

Algorithm 1: Algorithm BicriteriaGreedy

Input: k', S, and T_i.
Output: Set $S_i \subset T_i$ with $|S_i| \leq k'$.
$S_i \leftarrow \emptyset$;
forall the $1 \leq i \leq k'$ **do**
    $x^* \leftarrow max_{x \in T_i} \Delta(x, S_i \cup S)$;
    $S_i \leftarrow S_i \cup \{x^*\}$;
Return S_i;

Algorithm 2: Algorithm Greedy

2.1 Analysis

We start by proving that Algorithm BicriteriaGreedy returns a solution with $\mathbb{E}[f(S)] \geq (1 - \epsilon)f(\text{OPT})$ and $|S| \leq r(\alpha^2 \ln^2(\alpha) + \ln(\alpha))k$. In Subsection 2.2, we show that it is possible to reduce the number of selected items ($|S|$) by some slight changes while maintaining the $1 - \epsilon$ approximation guarantee. In Algorithm 1, we iteratively run the for loop in lines 6 – 11 for r consecutive times. We call each of these r executions a round. The high level proof plan is to show that at each round $f(S)$ is increased by at least $(1 - \epsilon^{1/r})(f(\text{OPT}) - f(S))$. In other words, the gap $f(\text{OPT}) - f(S)$

[3]Setting $m = \sqrt{n/k'}$ makes sure that the number of items each distributed machine processes, and the central machine processes are the same where k' is the number of items each distributed machine returns in line 8 of the algorithm.

is reduced by a multiplicative factor of $\epsilon^{1/r}$ in each round, and therefore after r rounds this gap is at most $\epsilon f(\text{OPT})$ which implies that $f(S) \geq (1-\epsilon)f(\text{OPT})$. We will formalize and elaborate this argument in the proofs. To avoid confusion, we define A_ℓ to be the set of selected items (set S) in the first ℓ rounds for any $0 \leq \ell \leq r$. At the beginning set S is equal to $A_0 = \emptyset$, and the final output is A_r. We start by showing that at each round, we get at least $1-\epsilon^{1/r}$ closer to OPT. We provide most of the proofs in the supplemental material, and include a high level intuition.

Lemma 2.1. *The expected value of* $\mathbb{E}[f(A_\ell)] - f(A_{\ell-1})$ *(increase in value of S at round ℓ) is at least* $(1-\epsilon^{1/r})(f(OPT) - f(A_{\ell-1}))$ *for any* $1 \leq \ell \leq r$, *and set* $A_{\ell-1}$.

We first prove that Lemma 2.1 is sufficient to achieve the $1-\epsilon$ approximation guarantee.

Theorem 2.2. *Algorithm BicriteriaGreedy returns a set S with expected value at least* $(1-\epsilon)f(OPT)$ *and at most* $r(\alpha^2\ln^2(\alpha) + \ln(\alpha))k$ *items where* α *is* $\frac{3}{\epsilon^{1/r}}$.

Proof. Algorithm 1 has r rounds and in each round, $(\alpha^2\ln^2(\alpha) + \ln(\alpha))k$ items are added to S. Therefore size of S can not be more than $r(\alpha^2\ln^2(\alpha) + \ln(\alpha))k$. To lower bound the value of final set $S = A_r$, we define a_ℓ to be $\mathbb{E}[A_\ell]$. Using Lemma 2.1, we know that $a_\ell - a_{\ell-1}$ is at least $(1-\epsilon^{1/r})(f(\text{OPT}) - a_{\ell-1})$. In other words, $f(\text{OPT}) - a_\ell$ is at most $\epsilon^{1/r}(f(\text{OPT}) - a_{\ell-1})$. By combining all these lower bounds for different values of $1 \leq \ell \leq r$, we have $f(\text{OPT}) - a_r \leq (\epsilon^{1/r})^r(f(\text{OPT}) - f(A_0)) = \epsilon f(\text{OPT})$, and therefore $\mathbb{E}[f(S)] = \mathbb{E}[f(A_r)] = a_r \geq (1-\epsilon)f(\text{OPT})$. □

To complete the analysis, we provide the main ideas of the proof of Lemma 2.1, and include the formal proof after that. We need to borrow some notations from [21], and use some of the techniques developed there for our analysis. Let OPT^S be the part of OPT that is selected by the machines, i.e. $\text{OPT}^S = \text{OPT} \cap (\cup_{i=1}^m S_i)$. Let OPT^{NS} be $\text{OPT} \setminus \text{OPT}^S$.

We will also borrow the following notations which are going to be used in the proof of Lemma 2.1. Therefore we can refer to set $A_{\ell-1}$ which is mentioned in the statement of Lemma 2.1 without any confusion. For every machine i, we define a partition of optimum set OPT into two sets OPT_i^S and OPT_i^{NS}. Set OPT_i^S consists of optimum items that if they were sent to machine i, they would be selected. Formally, OPT_i^S is defined as $\{x | x \in \text{OPT AND } x \in Greedy(k', A_{\ell-1}, T_i \cup \{x\})\}$ where $Greedy(k', S, T)$ is the output of Algorithm Greedy (depicted as Algorithm 2) with inputs k', S, and T. In other words, if we send an item $x \in \text{OPT}$ along with set T_i to machine i in round ℓ and machine i selects item x as part of its output, we will put x in set OPT_i^S. Any other optimum item is put in set $\text{OPT}_i^{NS} = \text{OPT} \setminus \text{OPT}_i^S$. Formally, OPT_i^{NS} is defined as $\{x | x \in \text{OPT AND } x \notin Greedy(k', A_{\ell-1}, T_i \cup \{x\})\}$. We also fix an arbitrary permutation of items in OPT, and for every $x \in \text{OPT}$, we define OPT^x to be the items in OPT that appear before x in the fixed permutation.

We focus on the claim of Lemma 2.1 for the first round and a similar argument works for the rest. We show there exists a small set B^* of selected items $\{S_i\}_{i=1}^m$ with value almost as large as $f(\text{OPT})$. Define $B^* = \text{OPT}^S \cup S_1 \cup S_2 \cdots S_C$ where $C = \alpha\ln(\alpha)$. By submodularity of f, we have $f(\text{OPT}) - f(B^*) \leq \sum_{x \in \text{OPT}} \Delta(x, B^*)$, and we show that the marginal values $\Delta(x, B^*)$ are all small in expectation. Optimum items that are selected, OPT^S, are already in B^* and therefore have zero marginal value to B^*. If some item x would not be selected by some machine $1 \leq i \leq C$ if x were sent to i, we can say that machine i would have preferred other αk items in S_i, and therefore $\Delta(x, S_i)$ is less than the average marginal values of selected items $f(S_i)/(\alpha k)$ which suffices to show $\Delta(x, B^*)$ is small. For any other optimum item x, we know all these C machines would have picked x, if it was sent to any of them, but apparently x was sent to some other machine that did not pick it. Similar to Lemma 3.2 of [21], we can prove that this happens with only a small probability of $1/\alpha$ with our choice of C. We conclude that expected marginal value $\Delta(x, B^*)$ is small for every $x \in \text{OPT}$, and therefore $f(B^*)$ should be almost as large as $f(\text{OPT})$. To see the rest of the proof, we note that all items of B^* are available to be chosen by the central machine in lines 9 – 11 of Algorithm 1. Using the classic analysis of algorithm Greedy, choosing $|B^*|\ln(1/\epsilon)$ items at this step suffices to have $f(S) \geq (1-\epsilon)f(B^*)$ which completes the proof. We are ready to formalize all these main ideas as the proof of Lemma 2.1.

Proof of Lemma 2.1 We first define set function $g(B)$ to be $f(B \cup A_{\ell-1}) - f(A_{\ell-1})$ for any subset of items B. Submodularity of f implies that g is also submodular. It suffices to show that $\mathbb{E}[g(A_\ell)]$ is at least $(1-\epsilon^{1/r})\mathbb{E}[g(\text{OPT})]$. We also note that Greedy returns the same solution when it maximizes g instead of f. In other words, proving the claim for every round ℓ is equivalent of proving it for the first round in which f and g are the same. First of all we show that among the selected items of all machines $\cup_{i=1}^m S_i$, there exists a set B^* with expected g value at least $(1-\frac{2}{\alpha})g(\text{OPT})$, and size at most $(1+\alpha^2\ln(\alpha))k$. Then we can show that running greedy on the set of all selected items, and choosing $|B^*|\ln(\alpha)$ items yields a final solution S with $g(S) \geq (1-\frac{1}{\alpha})g(B^*)$ which completes the proof.

We claim that for set $B^* = \text{OPT}^S \cup (\cup_{i=1}^{\alpha\ln(\alpha)} S_i)$, we have that $\mathbb{E}[g(B^*)] \geq (1-\frac{2}{\alpha})g(\text{OPT})$. It is important to note that we are lower bounding the expected value of $g(B^*)$. By definition, we have $\sum_{x \in \text{OPT}} \Delta(x, B^* \cup \text{OPT}^x)$ is equal to $g(B^* \cup \text{OPT}) - g(B^*)$ which is at least $g(\text{OPT}) - g(B^*)$. At this point, we only need to show that the expected value of $\sum_{x \in \text{OPT}} \Delta(x, B^* \cup \text{OPT}^x)$ is at most $\frac{2}{\alpha}g(\text{OPT})$. Since the expected value of a sum is equal to the sum of the expected value of summands, we can focus on upper bounding expected value of $\Delta(x, B^* \cup \text{OPT}^x)$ for each $x \in \text{OPT}$. Each $x \in \text{OPT}$ belongs to one of the following three categories:

- $x \in \text{OPT}^S$: In this case, x is also in B^*, and therefore $\Delta(x, B^* \cup \text{OPT}^x)$ is zero.
- $x \in \text{OPT}_i^{NS}$ for some $1 \leq i \leq \alpha\ln(\alpha)$: Item x was not chosen as one of the αk items in S_i. Therefore the marginal value of each item added to S_i was higher than the marginal value of adding x at that moment. Let δ_j be how much the value S_i increased when its jth item was added to it. So we have $g(S_i) = \sum_{j=1}^{\alpha k} \delta_j$. Since f is submodular, the marginal values to set S_i decrease as we add more items to S_i. So $\Delta(x, S_i)$ (at the end when S_i has all its αk items) is less than δ_j for each $1 \leq j \leq \alpha k$. We conclude

that $\Delta(x, S_i) \le g(S_i)/(\alpha k)$. If $g(S_i)$ is at least $g(\text{OPT})$, the claim is proved because we know $S_i \subset B^*$, and therefore $g(B^*) \ge g(S_i) \ge g(\text{OPT})$ in this case. Otherwise, $\Delta(x, S_i)$ is less than $\frac{g(\text{OPT})}{\alpha k}$. Therefore for every $x \in \cup_{i=1}^{\alpha \ln(\alpha)} \text{OPT}_i^{NS}$, we have $\Delta(x, B^* \cup \text{OPT}^x) \le \Delta(x, S_i) < \frac{g(\text{OPT})}{\alpha k}$ where the first inequality holds by definition of submodularity, and i is chosen such that $x \in \text{OPT}_i^{NS}$.

- The last case is when x is not in any of the sets OPT^S, and $\{\text{OPT}_i^{NS}\}_{i=1}^{\alpha \ln(\alpha)}$ in which we upper bound $\mathbb{E}[\Delta(x, B^* \cup \text{OPT}^x)]$ as follows.

We show that for any item $x \in \text{OPT}$, the probability of x being outside all these sets is at most $1/\alpha$. We also know by submodularity that $\Delta(x, B^* \cup \text{OPT}^x) \le \Delta(x, \text{OPT}^x)$. Therefore the expected value of $\Delta(x, B^* \cup \text{OPT}^x)$ cannot be more than $\Delta(x, \text{OPT}^x)/\alpha$ in this case.

Intuitively, the probability of selecting an item x ($Pr[x \in \cup_{i=1}^m S_i]$) is the same as $Pr[x \in \text{OPT}_i^S]$ for any arbitrary machine i. The event that item $x \in \text{OPT}$ is not selected ($\notin \text{OPT}^S$), and it also is not part of any of the $\alpha \ln(\alpha)$ sets $\{\text{OPT}_i^{NS}\}_{i=1}^{\alpha \ln(\alpha)}$ is equivalent of saying that among $\alpha \ln(\alpha)$ randomly chosen machines $(1, 2, \cdots, \alpha \ln(\alpha))$, they all select x if it is sent to them. But x is in fact sent to some other machine that did not select x. This is a very unlikely event as follows. If the probability x being selected (event $x \in \text{OPT}^S$) is higher than $1 - \frac{1}{\alpha}$, the above event has probability less than $\frac{1}{\alpha}$. Otherwise, assuming the sets $\{\text{OPT}_i^{NS}\}_{i=1}^{\alpha \ln(\alpha)}$ are independent, the probability that x is in none of them is at most $(1 - \frac{1}{\alpha})^{\alpha \ln(\alpha)} \le \frac{1}{\alpha}$ which concludes the proof. This part of the proof and how to deal with the dependencies are formalized in Lemma 3.2 of [21].

We conclude that the total $\mathbb{E}[\sum_{x \in \text{OPT}} \Delta(x, B^* \cup \text{OPT}^x)]$ is upper bounded by $\sum_{x \in \text{OPT}} \frac{g(\text{OPT})}{\alpha k} + \frac{\Delta(x, \text{OPT}^x)}{\alpha}$ which is at most $\frac{2g(\text{OPT})}{\alpha}$ because there are at most k items in OPT, and we know that the sum $\sum_{x \in \text{OPT}} \Delta(x, \text{OPT}^x)$ is equal to $g(\text{OPT})$ by definition of Δ values and OPT^x. This means that set B^* has expected value at least $(1 - \frac{2}{\alpha})g(\text{OPT})$.

We note that items of B^* are among the selected items $\cup_{i=1}^m S_i$, and Algorithm1 has the option of adding them to set S in lines 10 – 11. For $\alpha^2 \ln^2(\alpha) = |B^*| \ln(\alpha)$ times, the maximum marginal item is greedily chosen and added to S. Using the classic analysis of Greedy algorithm [24], we know that $g(S)$ should be at least $(1 - \frac{1}{|B^*|})^{|B^*| \ln(\alpha)} g(B^*) \ge (1 - \frac{1}{\alpha})g(B^*)$. We note that we showed $g(S) \ge (1 - \frac{1}{\alpha})g(B^*)$ not in expectation but in any case which is a stronger claim. This way we can combine it with the lower bound on expected value of $g(B^*)$. We conclude that $\mathbb{E}[g(S)]$ is at least $(1 - \frac{1}{\alpha})(1 - \frac{2}{\alpha})g(\text{OPT}) \ge (1 - \frac{3}{\alpha})g(\text{OPT}) = (1 - \epsilon^{1/r})g(\text{OPT})$ which completes the proof. □

2.2 Improving the Solution Size by Multiplicity

BicriteriaGreedy returns a set S with $\mathbb{E}[f(S)] \ge (1 - \epsilon)f(\text{OPT})$ and $\tilde{O}(\frac{k}{\epsilon^{2/r}})$ items in r rounds. Although one can choose the right number of rounds r to reduce the number of selected items, we propose the following simple trick that improves this upper bound to around $\tilde{O}(\frac{k}{\epsilon^{1/r}})$. In line 6, instead of just a random partitioning of items, we send each item to $C = \alpha \ln(\alpha)$ (multiplicity factor) randomly chosen machines which is similar to the multiplicity idea of [21]. With multiplicity C, we prove that we can achieve the same approximation guarantees as before while selecting much fewer items in lines 9 – 11. In line 9, we will select only $(\alpha \ln^2(\alpha) + \ln(\alpha))k$ items instead of $(\alpha^2 \ln^2(\alpha) + \ln(\alpha))k$ in the new algorithm.

Theorem 2.3. *The new Algorithm 1 with multiplicity $C = \alpha \ln(\alpha)$ also returns a set S with expected value at least $(1 - \epsilon)f(OPT)$, and size at most $r(\alpha \ln(\alpha) + \ln(\alpha))k$ items where $\alpha = \frac{3}{\epsilon^{1/r}}$.*

Proof. The changes in the number of selected items in line 11 are reflected in the new upper bound on size of S. We should show that expected value of S is still at least $(1 - \epsilon)f(\text{OPT})$. Similar to Theorem 2.2, we use Lemma 2.1 to lower bound the marginal value gained at each round. The only part that changes in the proof of Lemma 2.1 is the definition of B^*. We no longer need to include $C = \alpha \ln(\alpha)$ sets $\{S_i\}_{i=1}^C$ in B^* because sending each item to C random sets incorporates that idea automatically. We define B^* to be $\text{OPT}^S \cup S_1$. The number of items we select in line 10 of the new algorithm is $(\alpha \ln^2(\alpha) + \ln(\alpha))k$ which is equal to $|B^*| \ln(\alpha)$ as expected. To lower bound the value of B^*, we still need to upper bound $\Delta(x, B^* \cup \text{OPT}^x)$. The first two cases we considered for x are proved the same way. We just need to show that for each item $x \in \text{OPT}$, the probability that x is not in OPT^S nor in OPT_1^{NS} is at most $\frac{1}{\alpha}$. Since each item is sent to C random machines, this event is equivalent of saying that a random machine (machine 1) wants to select x, but none of the the other C random machines that we actually send x to does not want to select x. We have upper bounded this probability in proof of Lemma 2.1 by $\frac{1}{\alpha}$. The rest of the proof remains the same. □

We provide Algorithm HybridAlg with slight changes to improve solution size. In addition to the multiplicity factor $C = \alpha \ln(\alpha)$, we change the second selection procedure in lines 9 – 11 as follows. After the machines select sets $S_1, S_2, \cdots, S_m$, algorithm HybridAlg adds set S_1 to S, and then for $\ln(\alpha)k$ iterations, greedily chooses the item with maximum marginal value to S among items in $\cup_{i=2}^m S_i$, and adds it to S.

Theorem 2.4. *Algorithm HybridAlg returns a set S with expected value at least $(1 - \epsilon)f(OPT)$, and size at most $r(\alpha + \ln(\alpha))k$ items where $\alpha = \frac{3}{\epsilon^{1/r}}$.*

Proof. The proof is very similar to the proofs of Theorems 2.2 and 2.3, and crucially uses Lemma 2.1. In the proof of Theorem 2.3, we show that in each round $g(S_1 \cup \text{OPT}^S)$ has expected value at least $(1 - \frac{2}{\alpha})g(\text{OPT})$. By adding S_1 to S, we increase the value of S by $g(S_1)$. We need to show that the remaining items gain most of the remaining marginal value $g(S_1 \cup \text{OPT}^S) - g(S_1)$. Since there are at most k items in OPT^S, and we greedily insert $k \ln(\alpha)$ items to S. The extra marginal value we achieve is at least $(1 - \frac{1}{\alpha})(g(S_1 \cup \text{OPT}^S) - g(S_1))$. We conclude that in total the expected marginal value added in a round is at least $(1 - \frac{1}{\alpha})g(S_1 \cup \text{OPT}^S)$. The rest of the proof remains the same. □

3 HARDNESS RESULTS

A centralized greedy algorithm achieves a $1 - \epsilon$ approximation guarantee by outputting only $k \ln(1/\epsilon)$ items. Note that the dependence on $1/\epsilon$ is logarithmic when the algorithm has access to the whole dataset (all items). The number of items our distributed algorithms return have polynomial dependence on ϵ, i.e. $1/\epsilon^{1/r}$ for r rounds. In this section, we provide some evidence that why this polynomial dependence is necessary. In particular, we prove achieving an approximation factor of $1-\epsilon$ in one round requires outputting $\Omega(k/\epsilon)$ items which matches our positive algorithmic bounds as well. Here by one round, we mean distributing the data either randomly or worst case among distributed machines, then gathering the selected items of all machines in one place and choosing a final solution among them. The result focuses on distributed algorithms that perform in one distributed round which consists of a) partitioning the items among m machines either randomly or in a worst case partitioning, b) each machine outputs a summary of the data it has received (e.g. a subset of its items) and finally c) a central machine puts together all summaries and outputs a final solution based on the union.

Theorem 3.1. *For any $k > 0$, there exists some n, m and an instance of submodular maximization with n items, m machines and cardinality constraint k such that any distributed algorithm with approximation guarantee $1-\epsilon$ in one distributed round should output at least $\Omega(k/\epsilon)$ items as the final solution.*

Proof. We construct a coverage maximization instance in which each item is a subset of a large ground set of L elements, and the submodular value of a collection of these subsets (items) is defined to be the number of elements that their union covers (among the L elements). In this instance, suppose $L \gg n$, and $n, m \gg k$. There three categories of items:

- A collection of $k/2$ equal size disjoint subsets (items) $\mathbb{A} = \{S_1, S_2, \cdots, S_{k/2}\}$ that cover $1-2\epsilon$ fraction of the universe altogether. In particular, each set S_i has size $\frac{1-2\epsilon}{k/2}L$ since they are all disjoint. Assume that L is chosen such that $\frac{1-2\epsilon}{k/2}L$ is an integer.
- A collection of $k/2$ equal size disjoint subsets (items) $\mathbb{B} = \{T_1, T_2, \cdots, T_{k/2}\}$ that cover the other 2ϵ fraction of the universe. So each set T_i has size $\frac{2\epsilon}{k/2}L$ since they are all disjoint. Assume that L is chosen such that $\frac{2\epsilon}{k/2}L$ is also an integer. So far all these $k/2 + k/2 = k$ sets in families $\mathbb{A}$ and $\mathbb{B}$ are disjoint and cover the whole universe. So the optimum solution consists of these k subsets and has value L.
- A collection $\mathbb{C}$ of $n-k$ subsets each with size $\frac{2\epsilon}{k/2}L$ which is equal to the sets in collection $\mathbb{B}$. Each set in $\mathbb{C}$ is a random subset of the ground set with $\frac{2\epsilon}{k/2}L$ elements, and these sets are chosen independent of each other. So unlike families $\mathbb{A}$ and $\mathbb{B}$, sets in family $\mathbb{C}$ are not disjoint and can potentially intersect with each other and all other sets.

All n sets (items) are distributed randomly between the m distributed machines. Since m is chosen to be much larger than k, with high probability, the k sets in $\mathbb{A}\cup\mathbb{B}$ end up in different machines. We focus on set $T_i \in \mathbb{B}$ that has been sent to some machine $1 \le \ell \le m$. The machine ℓ does not receive any other set in $\mathbb{A}\cup\mathbb{B}$, instead it may receive many sets from $\mathbb{C}$. In the absence of other members of $\mathbb{A}\cup\mathbb{B}$, it is information theoretically impossible to distinguish set T_i from the other sets sent to machine ℓ. Note that they all have the same size and they are random sets. So the probability that set T_i is chosen for the next round is proportional to the core-set size k', i.e. $\frac{k'}{n/m}$. Limitations on memory enforces this probability to be very low, i.e. for instance less than ϵ for some choices of $n \gg mk'$. Therefore at most ϵ fraction of sets in $\mathbb{B}$ are selected for the next round.

Even if all sets in $\mathbb{A}$ are chosen, given only $\frac{\epsilon k}{2}$ sets in $\mathbb{B}$ are chosen, one needs to output many sets in C to achieve an approximation factor of $1-\epsilon$. Formally, the selected sets of $\mathbb{A}\cup\mathbb{B}$ cover up to $1-2\epsilon+\epsilon\times 2\epsilon$ fraction of the ground set. To compensate for the remaining gap of $(1-\epsilon)-(1-2\epsilon+\epsilon\times 2\epsilon) = \epsilon - 2\epsilon^2 > \epsilon/2$ (for $\epsilon > 1/4$), the final output set needs to have at least $\frac{k}{10\epsilon}$ sets (items) from $\mathbb{C}$ which completes the proof. This is true because each set in $\mathbb{C}$ covers $\frac{2\epsilon}{k/2} \times 2\epsilon L$ elements that were supposed to be covered by sets of $\mathbb{B}$, and using concentration bounds this number does not exceed $\frac{5\epsilon^2}{k}L$. □

4 EMPIRICAL EVALUATION

In this section we empirically confirm the theoretical findings of our paper by evaluating the algorithms described before over several large-scale real-world and synthetic datasets. Recall that the focus of this paper is not to introduce a new algorithmic technique for submodular maximization (we use the well-known greedy algorithm) but instead to explore theoretically and experimentally the trade-offs between the number of items output, the number of rounds used and the objective value obtained by the greedy distributed algorithm for maximizing submodular functions. Notice that no previous work has explored the problem of outputting more items to improve the solution. For this reason in this section our comparison is done using the standard greedy distributed algorithm and evaluating different output sizes and number of rounds using multiple real and artificial datasets. All real datasets used are publicly available. In this section we experiment with two different instantiations of monotone submodular maximization: coverage maximization and exemplar-based clustering.

4.1 Coverage maximization

First we evaluate the greedy distributed algorithm on the coverage problem. In a coverage instance we are given a family $\mathbb{N} \subseteq 2^U$ of sets over a ground set U and we want to find k sets from $\mathbb{N}$ with maximum size of their union. We first present our real datasets for coverage maximization. We consider datasets: **DBLP co-authorship** has $\sim 300k$ sets over $\sim 300k$ elements for a total sum of sizes of all sets of $1.0m$ elements; **LiveJournal friendship** [27] has $4m$ sets over $4m$ elements for a total size of $34m$. For the previous datasets the sets represent neighborhoods of nodes. Finally we used **Gutenberg bi-grams** with $41k$ sets over $99m$ elements for a total size of more than $1b$. Here sets represent bi-grams in books. We will elaborate on these coverage datasets and the experimental setup as follows.

Experimental setup DBLP co-authorship We extracted a dataset from a DBLP snapshot [27] by creating a set for each author representing the coauthors of that author. The ground set is the set of all authors in DBLP. There are $\sim$ 300 thousands sets over $\sim$ 300 thousands elements for a total sum of sizes of all sets of 1.0 million.

LiveJournal friendship Here we create one set for each LiveJournal user in a snapshot of the graph [27] where each set consists of the friends of the user. The ground set is the set of all users. There are about 4 millions sets over 4 millions elements for a total size of 34 millions.

Gutenberg bi-grams This dataset is obtained from the Gutenberg project [1, 7]. Each set represents an English text and contains all the bi-grams of the text. There are 41 thousands sets over 99 millions elements for a total size of more than 1 billion.

Synthetic instance We constructed a synthetic coverage instance which is designed to be hard for the greedy algorithm. We fix the ground set U of size n and we create an optimal solution for size K covering all n items in the following way: We create K disjoint sets by partitioning U in K equal parts of size $\frac{n}{K}$.[4] All these sets are added to the input family $\mathbb{N}$. We also add to $\mathbb{N}$ other t random sets, each consisting of $s = \lceil \frac{n}{k}(1+\epsilon_1) \rceil$ randomly picked items w/o replacement.

Experimental setup We first describe the implementation details of the distributed algorithm BicriteriaGreedy for coverage; the one for exemplar-based clustering is similar and will be sketched in the next section. The input of the algorithm is a dataset of n sets, a fixed size k of elements to output and number of rounds r. The algorithm outputs $k' = \lfloor \frac{k}{r} \rfloor$ sets at each round except in the last round where $k' = \lfloor \frac{k}{r} \rfloor + (k \mod r)$ sets are output (for a total of exactly k sets). Each round of the algorithm obtains k' sets in two steps. In the first step of each round the dataset is divided randomly in m blocks of data. Each set is assigned u.a.r. to a single block T_i from the m blocks $T_1, \ldots T_m$. We use multiplicity 1 as our experiments shows it is sufficient to achieve very good experiment results. We always fix m to be $\lceil \sqrt{n/k'} \rceil$. Then each block of data is analyzed independently executing the greedy max coverage algorithm to select k' sets. This is done in parallel by distributing the blocks across multiple machines. In the second step of each round, the mk' sets returned by the machines are gathered in a master machine and the same greedy algorithm is run to obtain the final k' set of the round. In this section we compare various outputting $k = K$ items and $k > K$ items for this algorithm as well as outputting uniformly at random sets.

Upperbound Since it is infeasible to compute exactly the optimum value even for small k values so we compare the algorithms with an upper-bound on the optimum solution value. One simple upperbound is given by the maximum value of the objective function (for coverage it is $|U|$). We also obtain a more sophisticated upperbound by post-processing the output of our algorithms as follows. Let $|S| = t$ be a solution obtained by our algorithm for size $t \geq k$. It can be show that $f(S)$ plus the sum of the top k marginal gains $\Delta(x, S)$ for any $x \in \mathbb{N}$ is a provable upperbound to the optimal value for any solution of size k. We report the results based on the best upperbound achieved for all (dataset, k) pairs.

Results on synthetic instances In this experiment we set the size of universe in the synthetic instance to $|U| = 10{,}000$, the optimal solution size to $K = 100$, the number of random sets to $t = 100{,}000$ and $\epsilon_1 = 0.2$. The results are shown in Figure 1(a). It is possible to make the following observations.

First notice that consistent with our theoretical analysis, outputting $k \geq K$ items allows to converge to the optimal value for K with few additional items. In this experiment we get 95% and 99% of optimum for $K = 100$ outputting $k = 1.5K$ and $k = 2K$

[4]For simplicity we assume n multiple of K

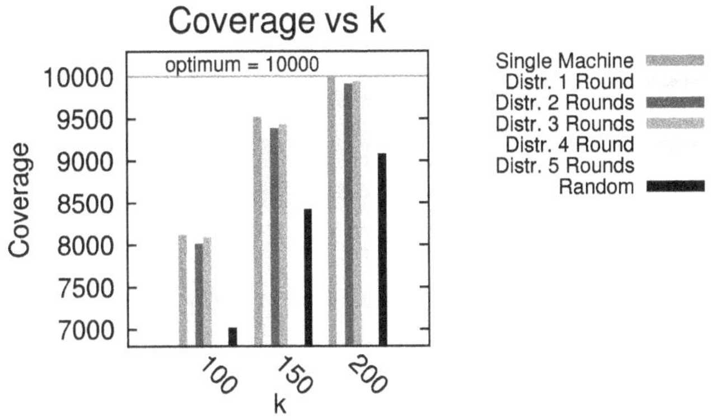

(a) Synthetic dataset

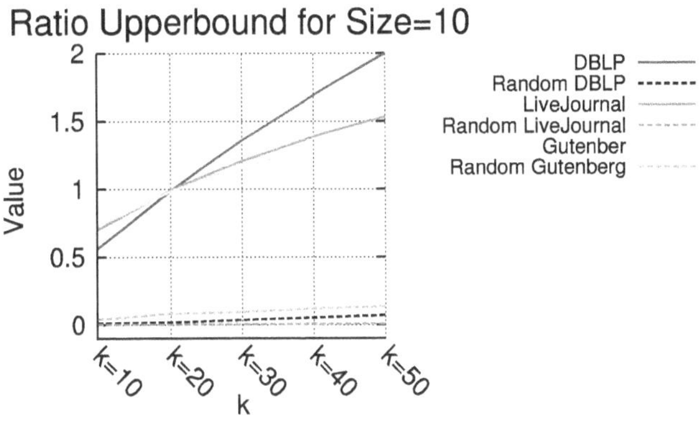

(b) Real datasets

Figure 1: Coverage maximization

respectively. This confirm the main theoretical contribution of our paper. Second, it is possible to see that for hard instances the use of multiple rounds improves the solution w.r.t. the single round algorithm. Notice also that a small number of rounds is sufficient in practice to achieve results very close to the greedy algorithm ran on a single machine. After 5 rounds we see no significant difference (81% of upperbound with 5 rounds vs 81.2% for the single machine algorithm with $k = K = 100$). Similar results holds for other k and K values. This confirms our theoretical finding that the use of multiple rounds improves the solution in hard instances. Finally, as expected the greedy algorithm is always significantly better than a random output.

Results on real datasets We also ran the algorithms on our real datasets as shown in Figure 1(b). In this experiment, we fix a target solution size $K = 10$ and run the algorithms with different values of $k \geq K$. The figure shows the ratio of the value of the solution obtained by the distributed algorithm and the random baseline for different $k \geq K$'s sizes over the upper-bound we computed for the solution with size $K = 10$. We report the results for the distributed algorithm using a single round ($r = 1$) and $m = \sqrt{n/k}$. It is possible to notice that as expected outputting more items increases the value of the objective function. It is interesting to observe that in real instances the algorithm significantly exceeds the worst case guarantees. With just $k = 2K$, we already obtain $> 98\%$, $> 99\%$, $> 98\%$ of our upperbound for the DBLP, LiveJournal, Gutenberg dataset respectively. We also ran the same experiments with more rounds and the results are very similar showing that for real instances algorithm already converges in one round.

4.2 Exemplar-based clustering

Exemplar-based clustering is a popular [22] way to identify k representative points from set of points with a notion of distance between them. In exemplar-based clustering we are given a set $\mathbb{N}$ of points and an arbitrary non-negative *distance* function (dist) over pairs of points.[5] For a set $S \subseteq \mathbb{N}$ we define the cost $c(S)$ of set S as $c(S) = \sum_{v \in \mathbb{N}} \min_{s \in S} \text{dist}(v, s)$. The cost $c(S)$ represent the sum of the minimum distances from every point in $\mathbb{N}$ to the nearest in S. Fix an point p_0 such that $\forall u, v \in \mathbb{N}$, $\text{dist}(u, v) \leq \text{dist}(u, p_0)$. We can now define the exemplar-based clustering as maximizing the following monotone submodular objective function $f(S) = c(\{p_0\}) - c(S \cup \{p_0\})$ for S of size k. Notice that this is equivalent to minimizing the cost of $c(S \cup \{p_0\})$.

We focus on the following datasets for exemplar-based clustering: **Wikipedia** has 3.8 millions vectors of 100 dimensions representing Wikipedia pages and **TinyImages** [26] has 80 millions vectors with 3072 dimensions representing images. We normalized all vectors in the datasets to have a unit L2 norm. We use as distance function the squared L2 distance, the maximum distance is 2 in all datasets, and we fix p_0 as a vector at distance 2 from any point in the dataset. We provide a more detailed overview on these datasets:

English Wikipedia dataset This is a dataset obtained from a snapshot of the entire English Wikipedia[6] with approximately 3.8 million articles. From each article we obtained a vector as follows: we extracted the text (discarding HTML tags, hyperlinks, removed stop words, etc) and then we ran Latent Dirichlet Allocation [16] with 100 topics using the `gensim` package [25]. The result is a probability distribution vector for each page of 100 dimensions.

TinyImages dataset This dataset [26], contains about 80 millions RGB images of size 32x32 obtained by an Internet crawl. Each image is represented as a $3072 = 3 \times 32 \times 32$ dimensional vector (one dimension for each pixel-color entry). From each image we obtain a 3072 dimensional vector by subtracting to each entry the average value of the entries in the vector. In the experiments involving the TinyImages dataset, to speed up the computation, we use a standard dimensionality reduction technique (i.e., Johnson Lindenstrauss random projection as in Achilopitas [3]) to convert the 3072-dimensional vectors to 300 dimensions before processing them. Notice that all objective function values shown are always computed on the original (unmodified) vectors.

Experimental setup The implementation details of the exemplar-based clustering algorithm are similar to that of the coverage one. We now highlight only the main differences. For this section we use a lazy variation of the greedy algorithm [22]. When analyzing a block of size N' of data to obtain k' elements we iterate over the block for k' times each time selecting a new element with maximum marginal gain. Here however the iteration evaluates only a independent u.a.r. subset of size $c\frac{N'}{k'}$ of the elements in the block as

[5]The function need not to respect the distance properties.

[6]https://meta.wikimedia.org/wiki/Data_dumps

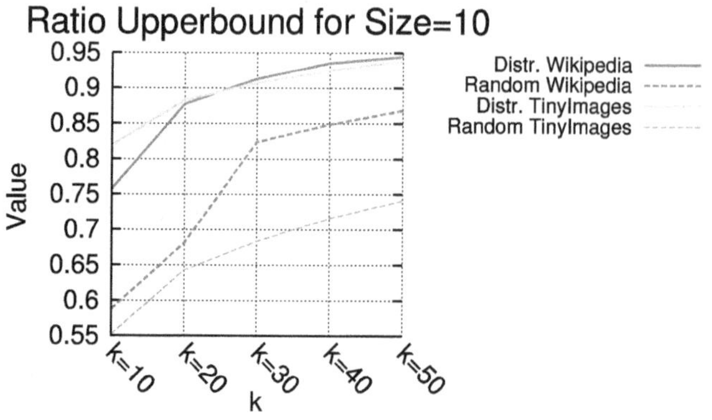

Figure 2: Exemplar-based clustering results.

in [22]. We fix $c = 3$, i.e. each element is evaluated in expectation 3 times over the iterations. Moreover, in this section, the objective function $f(S)$ in the greedy algorithm is estimated it by computing the distance of each element in S only to a u.a.r. sample V' of 500 elements from V (each machine receives an independent sample). Notice that when we report the values of the objective function for the solutions of the algorithm we do not use any estimation and we compute the exact value.

We will use similar techniques of the coverage case to compute an upperbound. The marginal gain in this case will be again estimated from a random sample of 500.

Results The results using a single round for the distributed algorithm are reported in Figure 2. Similarly to the coverage case we fix a target solution size $K = 10$ and run the algorithms with different $k \geq K$ values. The figure shows again the ratio of the value of the solution obtained for different $k \geq K$'s over the upper-bound for $K = 10$. It is possible to notice that the 1-round algorithm outputting more items increases the value objective significantly w.r.t to the outputing k items. Consistent with our theoretical analysis the algorithm approaches close to optimal value for the size $K = 10$ sets for $k \geq K$'s values (for $k = 2K$ we already obtain $> 87\%$, 88%, of our upperbound for Wikipedia and TinyImages, respectively). Similarly to the coverage case we observe strong convergence in just 1 round and great gap with a random baseline.

Speed-ups of the distributed framework We evaluated the gain obtained by the use of the distributed algorithm by comparing it to the lazy greedy algorithm ran in a single machine. Even for small datasets the centralized algorithm can take numerous hours to complete in a single machine even for small k values. Moreover, the distributed algorithm allows to analyze larger datasets as each machine need to store only a fraction $1/m$ of the dataset. Running the centralized algorithm on TinyImages would requires at least 200 GB of main memory.[7] We ran our framework fixing k and $m = \sqrt{N/k}$ and compared it with the centralized algorithm where a single machine is assigned the entire dataset. The speedup for the Wikipedia dataset using $k = 10$ and $k = 20$ was > 32 and > 37.

[7]While 200 GB memory machines are available, distributed computing with standard nodes (such as in MapReduce) is a more scalable approach widely used in practice. The algorithm could also be implemented using external memory and many passes, but this would increase even more the computational time.

Notice that we achieve substantial speedups even for such small datasets. The speedup for larger dataset are significantly larger however running the centralized algorithm on the larger dataset is simply infeasible (or expensive) for the memory requirement time required to run the experiment.

The centralized algorithm did not complete after many hours using larger k's or any other dataset. We also compared the solution obtained by the one round algorithm with the centralized one. The results shows that the distributed algorithm obtains $> 99.6\%$, $> 99.7\%$ of the value of the centralized one for $k = 10$ and $k = 20$ respectively.

5 CONCLUSIONS

We addressed the problem of submodular optimization under cardinality constraints in distributed setting. We analyzed an efficient constant-round distributed algorithm that can achieves the $1 - \epsilon$ approximation of the optimum for size k for $\epsilon > 0$ by allowing to output more than k items. We conductance an extensive empirical evaluation showing that almost optimum solutions can be obtained in few rounds in large-scale real dataset while outputting few more items.

Acknowledgements

We thank MohammadHossein Bateni for his comments and for sharing the datasets.

REFERENCES

[1] Gutenberg. search project gutenberg. https://www.gutenberg.org/ebooks/, 2016.
[2] Z. Abbassi, V. S. Mirrokni, and M. Thakur. Diversity maximization under matroid constraints. In *KDD*, KDD '13, pages 32–40, New York, NY, USA, 2013. ACM.
[3] D. Achlioptas. Database-friendly random projections: Johnson-lindenstrauss with binary coins. *J. of computer and System Sciences*, 2003.
[4] A. Badanidiyuru, B. Mirzasoleiman, A. Karbasi, and A. Krause. Streaming submodular maximization: Massive data summarization on the fly. In *KDD*, 2014.
[5] R. Barbosa, A. Ene, H. L. Nguyen, and J. Ward. The power of randomization: Distributed submodular maximization on massive datasets. In *ICML*, pages 1236–1244, 2015.
[6] R. Barbosa, A. Ene, H. L. Nguyen, and J. Ward. A new framework for distributed submodular maximization, 2016.
[7] M. Bateni, H. Esfandiari, and V. S. Mirrokni. Distributed coverage maximization via sketching. *CoRR*, abs/1612.02327, 2016.
[8] G. E. Blelloch, H. V. Simhadri, and K. Tangwongsan. Parallel and i/o efficient set covering algorithms. In *SPAA*, pages 82–90, 2012.
[9] F. Chierichetti, R. Kumar, and A. Tomkins. Max-cover in map-reduce. In *WWW*, pages 231–240, 2010.
[10] G. Cormode, H. J. Karloff, and A. Wirth. Set cover algorithms for very large datasets. In *CIKM*, pages 479–488, 2010.
[11] U. Feige. A threshold of ln n for approximating set cover. *J. ACM*, 45(4):634–652, July 1998.
[12] U. Feige, V. S. Mirrokni, and J. Vondrak. Maximizing non-monotone submodular functions. *SIAM Journal on Computing*, 40(4):1133–1153, 2011.
[13] B. J. Frey and D. Dueck. Mixture modeling by affinity propagation. In *NIPS*, pages 379–386, 2005.
[14] W. Gasarch and S. Fletcher. The egg game. http://www.cs.umd.edu/~gasarch/BLOGPAPERS/egg.pdf.
[15] A. Guillory and J. A. Bilmes. Active semi-supervised learning using submodular functions. *arXiv preprint arXiv:1202.3726*, 2012.
[16] M. Hoffman, F. R. Bach, and D. M. Blei. Online learning for latent dirichlet allocation. In *NIPS*, 2010.
[17] R. kiveris, S. Lattanzi, V. Mirrokni, V. Rastogi, and S. Vasilvitski. Connected components in mapreduce and beyond. In *ACM SOCC*, 2014.
[18] R. Kumar, B. Moseley, S. Vassilvitskii, and A. Vattani. Fast greedy algorithms in mapreduce and streaming. In *SPAA*, pages 1–10, 2013.
[19] S. Lattanzi, B. Moseley, S. Suri, and S. Vassilvitskii. Filtering: a method for solving graph problems in mapreduce. In *SPAA*, pages 85–94, 2011.
[20] H. Lin and J. A. Bilmes. A class of submodular functions for document summarization. In *HLT*, pages 510–520, 2011.
[21] V. S. Mirrokni and M. Zadimoghaddam. Randomized composable core-sets for distributed submodular maximization. In *STOC*, pages 153–162, 2015.
[22] B. Mirzasoleiman, A. Badanidiyuru, A. Karbasi, J. Vondrák, and A. Krause. Lazier than lazy greedy. In *AAAI*, pages 1812–1818, 2015.
[23] B. Mirzasoleiman, A. Karbasi, R. Sarkar, and A. Krause. Distributed submodular maximization: Identifying representative elements in massive data. In *NIPS*, pages 2049–2057, 2013.
[24] G. L. Nemhauser, L. A. Wolsey, and M. L. Fisher. An analysis of approximations for maximizing submodular set functionsâĂŤi. *Mathematical Programming*, 14(1):265–294, 1978.
[25] R. Řehůřek and P. Sojka. Software Framework for Topic Modelling with Large Corpora. In *LREC*, Valletta, Malta, 2010.
[26] A. Torralba, R. Fergus, and W. T. Freeman. 80 million tiny images: A large data set for nonparametric object and scene recognition. *IEEE TPAMI*, 2008.
[27] J. Yang and J. Leskovec. Defining and evaluating network communities based on ground-truth. *Knowledge and Information Systems*, 42(1):181–213, 2015.

On Energy Conservation in Data Centers

Extended Abstract

Susanne Albers*
Technical University of Munich
85748 Garching, Germany
albers@in.tum.de

ABSTRACT

We formulate and study an optimization problem that arises in the energy management of data centers and, more generally, multiprocessor environments. Data centers host a large number of heterogeneous servers. Each server has an active state and several standby/sleep states with individual power consumption rates. The demand for computing capacity varies over time. Idle servers may be transitioned to low-power modes so as to rightsize the pool of active servers. The goal is to find a state transition schedule for the servers that minimizes the total energy consumed. On a small scale the same problem arises in multi-core architectures with heterogeneous processors on a chip. One has to determine active and idle periods for the cores so as to guarantee a certain service and minimize the consumed energy.

For this power/capacity management problem, we develop two main results. We use the terminology of the data center setting. First, we investigate the scenario that each server has two states, i.e. an active state and a sleep state. We show that an optimal solution, minimizing energy consumption, can be computed in polynomial time by a combinatorial algorithm. The algorithm resorts to a single-commodity min-cost flow computation. Second, we study the general scenario that each server has an active state and multiple standby/sleep states. We devise a τ-approximation algorithm that relies on a two-commodity min-cost flow computation. Here τ is the number of different server types. A data center has a large collection of machines but only a relatively small number of different server architectures. Moreover, in the optimization one can assign servers with comparable energy consumption to the same class. Technically, both of our algorithms involve non-trivial flow modification procedures. In particular, given a fractional two-commodity flow, our algorithm executes advanced rounding and flow packing routines.

KEYWORDS

Heterogeneous machines; efficient algorithms; approximation algorithms; minimum-cost flow.

*Work supported by the European Research Council, Grant Agreement No. 691672.

SPAA '17, July 24–26, 2017, Washington, DC, USA

978-1-4503-4593-4/17/07.
DOI: http://dx.doi.org/10.1145/3087556.3087560

1 INTRODUCTION

We define and investigate an optimization problem with the objective of energy conservation in multiprocessor environments. We focus on two particularly timely settings.

Data centers. Energy management is a key issue in data center operations [7]. Electricity costs are a dominant and rapidly growing expense in such centers; about 30-50% of their budget is invested into energy. Data centers use about 1.5% of the total electricity worldwide [12]. This corresponds to the energy consumption of more than 90 million households [8]. Surprisingly, the servers of a data center are only utilized 20–40% of the time on average [3, 6]. When idle and in active mode, they consume about half of their peak power. Hence a fruitful approach for energy conservation and capacity management is to transition idle servers into standby and sleep states. Servers have a number of low-power states [1]. However state transitions, and in particular power-up operations, incur energy/cost. Therefore, dynamically matching the varying demand for computing capacity with the number of active servers is a challenging problem.

Multi-core architectures. Multi-core processors are architectures with multiple, often heterogeneous processing units on a single die. Originally, heterogeneous platforms contained several processor types, i.e. CPUs and GPUs. Modern platforms are also equipped with identical CPUs that have different micro-architectures leading to various levels of energy consumption [13]. To exploit such platforms effective power management strategies are needed. The optimization problem is identical to that described in the last paragraph, except that we have a small number of processing units here.

In Section 2 we formally define an optimization problem *Dynamic Power Management (DPM)* that captures the above scenarios. In short, there are m heterogeneous servers (processors). Each server has several states with associated power consumption rates. State transitions incur energy. The planning horizon contains times $t_1 < t_2 < \ldots < t_n$ at which the demand changes. During interval $[t_k, t_{k+1})$ at least d_k servers must be active and available for utilization, $1 \le k \le n-1$. The goal is to find a state transition schedule for the servers minimizing the total energy consumption.

Previous Work. Irani et al. [4] and Augustine et al. [14] study power-down strategies for a single device that is equipped with an active state and several low-power states. The goal is to minimize the energy consumed in an idle period. Our problem DPM is a generalization with multiple, parallel devices and time-dependent demand. The two articles [4, 14] develop online algorithms that achieve optimal competitive ratios. Dynamic power management for a single device with two states is equivalent to the ski-rental problem, a famous rent-or-buy problem [15, 16, 19, 21]. No generalization with several required resources has been examined. Azar et al. [5] study a capital investment problem where machines for manufacturing a product may be purchased over time. The machines differ in the capital and production costs.

Khuller et al. [17] and Li and Khuller [18] introduce machine activation problems that are also motivated by energy conservation in data centers. In [17] the authors assume that there is an activation cost budget, and jobs have to be scheduled on the selected, activated machines so as to minimize the makespan. They present algorithms that simultaneously approximate the budget and the makespan. The second paper [18] considers a generalization where the activation cost of a machine is a non-decreasing function of the load.

In the more applied computer science literature power management strategies and the value of sleep states have been studied extensively. The papers mostly focus on experimental evaluations. Articles that also present analytic results include [9–11, 22]. Ghandi et al. [10] model a server farm with setup costs as an $M/M/m$ queuing system. Lin et al. [22] study a dynamic rightsizing of data centers with homogeneous servers having one sleep state. The operating cost of a server is a convex function of the workload.

Our Contribution. We present an algorithmic study of an important capacity management problem in data centers. Our problem DPM dynamically rightsizes the pool of servers with the objective to minimize the energy consumed. Compared to previous work the new, essential aspects are that we consider (a) a time horizon with varying demand for computing capacity and (b) power-heterogeneous servers. In fact, with homogeneous servers the problem is easy to solve. In DPM the demand for computing capacity is specified by the number of servers needed at any time. In data centers it is common practice that a number of required servers is determined as a function of the current total workload, ignoring specific jobs. DPM focuses on energy conservation instead of individual job placement.

We investigate DPM as an offline problem, i.e. the varying computing demands are known in advance. From an algorithmic point of view it is important to explore the tractability and approximability of the problem. The offline setting is also relevant in practice. Data centers usually analyze past workload traces to identify long-term patterns. The findings are used to specify demands in future time windows.

In Section 3 we study DPM in the scenario that each server has two states, an active state and one sleep state. This is a basic setting that, in a first step, abstracts away the full spectrum of low-power modes. Most of the more applied literature on power management strategies assumes the existence of a single sleep state. We show that DPM can be solved in polynomial time by a combinatorial algorithm. We devise an algorithm that resorts to a single-commodity minimum-cost flow computation. In the corresponding network there is a component for each server. Such a component contains an upper path and a lower path, representing the server's active state and sleep state, respectively. Unfortunately, an arbitrary minimum-cost flow does not correspond to a feasible schedule. Our algorithm modifies flow so that an optimal schedule can be derived.

In Section 4 we investigate DPM in the general scenario that each server has multiple sleep states. We extend our approach based on flow computations. We develop a second algorithm that works with a more complex network in which each component has several lower paths, representing the various low-power states of a server. Furthermore, we need a second commodity to ensure that computing demands are met. With only a single commodity, flow units could switch between lower paths at no cost, and infeasible schedules would result. Given a fractional two-commodity minimum-cost flow, our algorithm executes advanced flow rounding and packing procedures. First, by repeatedly traversing components, the algorithm modifies flow so it becomes integral on the upper paths. Then flow on the lower paths is packed. The final integral flow allows the constructing of a schedule for DPM. Our algorithm achieves an approximation factor of τ, where τ is the number of server types in the problem instance. The servers can be partitioned into τ classes such that, within each class, the servers are identical. Of course, the servers of a class are independent and not synchronized. In practice, a data center has a large collection of machines but a relatively small number of different server architectures. Furthermore, in the optimization, machines with comparable energy consumption characteristics can be assigned to the same server class.

We note that our algorithms can handle the problem extension that the power consumption rates are time-dependent. This can model e.g. scenarios in which servers are temporarily unavailable due to maintenance or because they are reserved for other tasks.

Due to space constraints the proofs of lemmas and propositions are presented in the full version of this paper.

2 PRELIMINARIES

2.1 Problem Definition

We define the optimization problem *Dynamic Power Management (DPM)*. A problem instance $\mathcal{I} = (\mathcal{S}, \mathcal{D})$ is specified by a set of servers and varying computing demands over a time horizon. Let $\mathcal{S} = \{S_1, \ldots, S_m\}$ be a set of *heterogeneous servers*. Each server S_i, $1 \le i \le m$, has an active state as well as one or several standby/sleep states. The states of S_i are denoted by $s_{i,0}, \ldots, s_{i,\sigma_i}$. Here $s_{i,0}$ is the active state and $s_{i,1}, \ldots, s_{i,\sigma_i}$ are the low-power states. The modes have individual power consumption rates. Let $r_{i,j}$ be the power consumption rate of $s_{i,j}$, i.e. $r_{i,j}$ energy units are consumed per time unit while S_i resides in $s_{i,j}$. The states are numbered in order of decreasing rates such that $r_{i,0} > \ldots > r_{i,\sigma_i} \ge 0$. A server can transition between its states. Let $\Delta_{i,j,j'}$ be the non-negative energy needed to move S_i from state $s_{i,j}$ to state $s_{i,j'}$, for any pair $1 \le j, j' \le \sigma_i$. The transition energies satisfy the triangle inequality, i.e. the energy to move directly from $s_{i,j}$ to $s_{i,j'}$ is upper bounded by that of visiting an intermediate state $s_{i,k}$. Formally, $\Delta_{i,j,j'} \le \Delta_{i,j,k} + \Delta_{i,k,j'}$, for any j, j', k.

Over a time horizon the computing demands are given by a *demand profile* $\mathcal{D} = (T, D)$. Tuple $T = (t_1, \ldots, t_n)$ contains the points in time when the computing demands change. There holds $t_1 < t_2 < \ldots < t_n$ so that the time horizon is $[t_1, t_n)$. Tuple $D = (d_1, \ldots, d_{n-1})$ specifies the demands. More precisely, $d_k \in \mathbb{N}_0$ servers are required for computing during interval $[t_k, t_{k+1})$, for any $1 \le k \le n-1$. Thus at least d_k servers must reside in the active state during $[t_k, t_{k+1})$. We have $d_k \le m$, for any $1 \le k \le n-1$, so that the requirements can be met.

Given $\mathcal{I} = (\mathcal{S}, \mathcal{D})$, a *schedule* Σ specifies, for each S_i and any $t \in [t_1, t_n)$, in which state server S_i resides at time t. Schedule Σ is *feasible* if during any interval $[t_k, t_{k+1})$ at least d_k servers are in the active state, $1 \le k \le n-1$. The energy $E(\Sigma)$ incurred by Σ is the total energy consumed by all the m servers. Whenever server S_i, $1 \le i \le m$, resides in state $s_{i,j}$ it consumes energy at a rate of $r_{i,j}$. Whenever the server transitions from state $s_{i,j}$ to state $s_{i,j'}$, the incurred energy is $\Delta_{i,j,j'}$. The goal is to find an *optimal schedule*, i.e. a feasible schedule Σ that minimizes $E(\Sigma)$. We assume that initially, immediately before t_1, and at time t_n all servers reside in the deepest sleep state, i.e. S_i is in s_{i,σ_i}, $1 \le i \le m$. Our algorithms and results can be adapted easily if each server initially/finally takes arbitrary desired states.

2.2 Properties of Optimal Schedules

Given a problem instance $\mathcal{I}$, we characterize optimal schedules. Proposition 2.1 implies that there exists an optimal schedule in which a server never changes state while being in low-power mode. Of course the low-power states may vary for the various intervals in which a server is not active. Proposition 2.2 states that there exists an optimal schedule executing state transitions only when the computing demands change. A server *powers up* if it transitions from a low-power state to the active state. A server *powers down* if it moves from the active state to a low-power state.

PROPOSITION 2.1. *There exists an optimal schedule with the following property. Suppose that S_i powers down at time t and next powers up at time t'. Then between t and t' S_i resides in a single state $s_{i,j}$, where $j > 0$. At time t S_i transitions directly from $s_{i,0}$ to $s_{i,j}$. At time t' it moves directly from $s_{i,j}$ to $s_{i,0}$.*

PROPOSITION 2.2. *There exists an optimal schedule that satisfies the property of Proposition 2.1 and performs state transitions only at the times of T.*

We finally argue that w.l.o.g. the power-down energies $\Delta_{i,0,j}$ are equal to 0, $1 \le i \le m$ and $1 \le j \le \sigma_i$. We will always focus on optimal schedules with the property given in Proposition 2.1. At times t_1 and t_n every server is in its deepest sleep state. The first time server S_i moves to the active state, the least energy is consumed if it transitions directly from s_{i,σ_i} to $s_{i,0}$. The last time S_i powers down, the best option is to move directly from $s_{i,0}$ to s_{i,σ_i}. Hence, every server S_i performs the same number of transitions from $s_{i,0}$ to $s_{i,j}$ as from $s_{i,j}$ to $s_{i,0}$, for any $1 \le j \le \sigma_i$. For any server S_i, only energies $\Delta_{i,0,j}$ and $\Delta_{i,j,0}$, $1 \le j \le \sigma_i$, are relevant. Therefore, if $\Delta_{i,0,j} > 0$, we can add this energy to $\Delta_{i,j,0}$, i.e. $\Delta'_{i,j,0} := \Delta_{i,0,j} + \Delta_{i,j,0}$ and $\Delta'_{i,0,j} := 0$.

3 SERVERS WITH TWO STATES

We study the variant of DPM in which each server S_i has exactly two states, an active state $s_{i,0}$ and a sleep state $s_{i,1}$, $1 \le i \le m$.

THEOREM 3.1. *Let $\mathcal{I}$ be an instance of DPM in which each server has exactly two states. An optimal schedule for $\mathcal{I}$ can be computed in polynomial time by a combinatorial algorithm that uses a minimum-cost flow computation.*

In the remainder of this section we prove Theorem 3.1. We first show that we may assume w.l.o.g. that the power consumption rates in the sleep states are equal to 0. More specifically, for any problem instance $\mathcal{I}$, an optimal schedule can be derived from an optimal solution to a modified instance $\mathcal{I}'$ in which the power consumption rates in the sleep states are indeed 0. Formally, given $\mathcal{I} = (\mathcal{S}, \mathcal{D})$, define an instance $\mathcal{I}' = (\mathcal{S}', \mathcal{D})$. Set $\mathcal{S}'$ consists of servers $S'_1, \dots, S'_m$, where each server S'_i has again an active state and a sleep state. For any S'_i, let $r'_{i,0} = r_{i,0} - r_{i,1}$ and $r'_{i,1} = 0$, i.e. the rates are reduced by $r_{i,1}$. All other problem parameters of $\mathcal{I}'$, namely the state transition energies and the demand profile, are identical to those of $\mathcal{I}$. The next proposition states that an optimal schedule for $\mathcal{I}$ translates to an optimal schedule for $\mathcal{I}'$ and vice versa. Only the consumed energy differs by $\sum_{i=1}^{m} r_{i,1}(t_n - t_1)$.

PROPOSITION 3.2. *Any schedule Σ for $\mathcal{I}$ that is executed for $\mathcal{I}'$ consumes an energy of $E(\Sigma) - \sum_{i=1}^{m} r_{i,1}(t_n - t_1)$. Any schedule Σ' for $\mathcal{I}'$ that is executed for $\mathcal{I}$ consumes an energy of $E(\Sigma') + \sum_{i=1}^{m} r_{i,1}(t_n - t_1)$.*

In the following let $\mathcal{I} = (\mathcal{S}, \mathcal{D})$ be a problem instance in which the power consumption rates in the servers' sleep states are 0. To simplify notation let $r_i := r_{i,0}$ be the power consumption rate of S_i in the active state, $1 \le i \le m$. Moreover, let $\Delta_i := \Delta_{i,1,0}$ be the energy needed to transition S_i from the sleep state to the active state. We develop an algorithm $\mathcal{A}_1$ that computes an optimal schedule. Based on Proposition 2.2, we focus on schedules that perform state transitions only at the times of T. Given $\mathcal{I} = (\mathcal{S}, \mathcal{D})$, $\mathcal{A}_1$ constructs a network $\mathcal{N}(\mathcal{I})$. Any feasible schedule Σ for $\mathcal{I}$ translates to a feasible flow of cost $E(\Sigma)$ in $\mathcal{N}(\mathcal{I})$. Any feasible flow of cost C in $\mathcal{N}(\mathcal{I})$ can be converted so that it corresponds to a feasible schedule consuming energy C. The conversion requires some work but can be performed in a polynomial number of steps.

3.1 Construction of the Network

Consider any problem instance $\mathcal{I} = (\mathcal{S}, \mathcal{D})$.

Network components. Network $\mathcal{N}(\mathcal{I})$ contains a *component* C_i, for each server S_i, $1 \le i \le m$. Such a component C_i, which is depicted in Figure 1, consists of an *upper path* and a *lower path*. The upper path represents the active state of S_i; the lower path models the server's sleep state. The computing demands change at the times $t_1 < \dots < t_n$ in T. For any t_k, $1 \le k \le n$, there is a vertex $u_{i,k}$ on the upper path. Vertices $u_{i,k}$ and $u_{i,k+1}$ are connected by a directed edge $(u_{i,k}, u_{i,k+1})$ of cost $r_i(t_{k+1} - t_k)$, $1 \le k \le n-1$. This cost is equal to the energy consumed if S_i is in the active state during $[t_k, t_{k+1})$. Similarly, for any t_k, $1 \le k \le n$, there is a vertex $l_{i,k}$ on the lower path. In order to ensure that at least d_k servers are in the active state during $[t_k, t_{k+1})$, if $k < n$, we need two auxiliary vertices $l^a_{i,k}$ and $l^b_{i,k}$. These vertices are again connected by directed edges. There is an edge $(l_{i,k}, l^a_{i,k})$, followed by two edges $(l^a_{i,k}, l^b_{i,k})$ and $(l^b_{i,k}, l_{i,k+1})$, for any k with $1 \le k \le n-1$. The cost of each of these edges is 0 because the energy consumption in the sleep state is 0.

The lower and the upper path are connected by additional edges that model state transitions. Recall that all servers are in the sleep state at times t_1 and t_n. For any k with $1 \le k \le n-1$, there is a

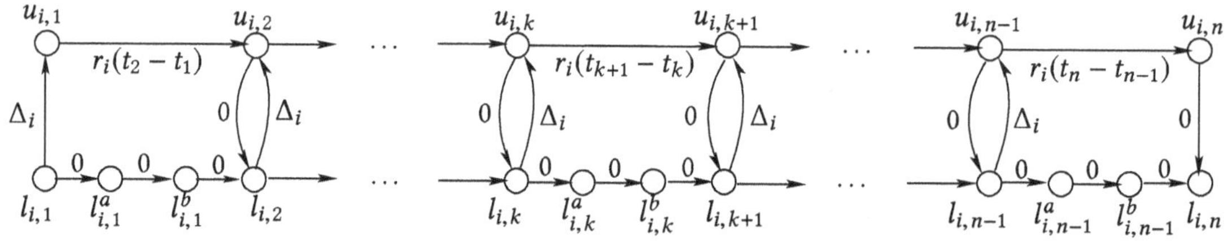

Figure 1: The component C_i for server S_i

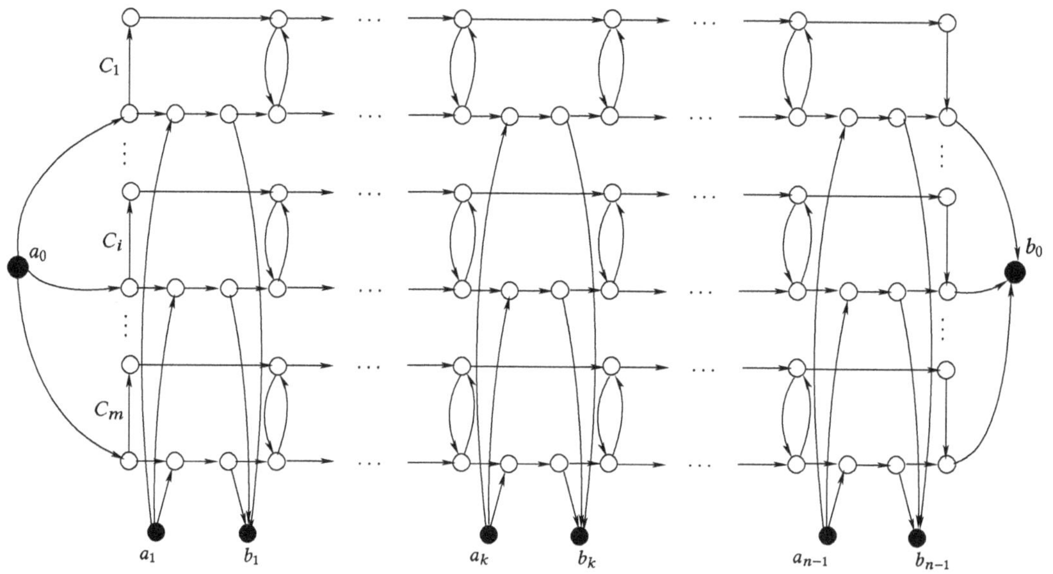

Figure 2: The network $\mathcal{N}(\mathcal{I})$

directed edge $(l_{i,k}, u_{i,k})$ of cost Δ_i, representing a power-up operation of S_i at time t_k. For any k with $1 < k \le n$, there is a directed edge $(u_{i,k}, l_{i,k})$ of cost 0, modeling a power-down operation of S_i at time t_k. The capacity of each edge of C_i is equal to 1.

The entire network. In $\mathcal{N}(\mathcal{I})$ components $C_1, \ldots, C_m$ are aligned in parallel and connected to a source a_0 and a sink b_0. The general structure of $\mathcal{N}(\mathcal{I})$ is depicted in Figure 2. There is a directed edge from a_0 to $l_{i,1}$ in C_i, for any $1 \le i \le m$. Furthermore, there is a directed edge from $l_{i,n}$ to b_0, for any $1 \le i \le m$. Each of these edges has a cost of 0 and a capacity of 1. Vertex a_0 has a supply of m, and b_0 has a demand of m. Hence m units of flow must be shipped through $C_1, \ldots, C_m$. Since all edges have a capacity of 1, one unit of flow must be routed through each C_i, $1 \le i \le m$. Whenever the unit traverses the upper path, S_i is in the active state. Whenever the unit traverses the lower path, S_i is in the sleep state.

In order to ensure that at least d_k servers are in the active state during $[t_k, t_{k+1})$, $1 \le k \le n-1$, we introduce additional sources and sinks. Network $\mathcal{N}(\mathcal{I})$ has a source a_k and a sink b_k with supply/demand d_k, for any $1 \le k \le n-1$. There is a directed edge from a_k to $l^a_{i,k}$ on the lower path of each C_i, $1 \le i \le m$. Furthermore, there is a directed edge from each $l^b_{i,k}$ to b_k, $1 \le i \le m$. The cost and capacity of each of these edges is equal to 0 and 1, respectively. Since d_k flow units have to be shipped from a_k to b_k, there must exist at least d_k components C_i in which the flow unit from a_0 to b_0 traverses the upper path from $u_{i,k}$ to $u_{i,k+1}$. Hence the corresponding servers are in the active state during $[t_k, t_{k+1})$. The encoding length of $\mathcal{N}(\mathcal{I})$ is polynomial in that of $\mathcal{I}$.

Lemma 3.3. *Any feasible schedule Σ in which state transitions are performed only at the times of T corresponds to a feasible flow of cost $E(\Sigma)$ in $\mathcal{N}(\mathcal{I})$.*

3.2 Analysis of Flows

We analyze feasible flows in $\mathcal{N}(\mathcal{I})$. The goal is to show that any feasible flow f can be converted into one that corresponds to a feasible schedule Σ for $\mathcal{I}$; the energy consumed by Σ will be equal to the cost of f. The conversion is not immediate. A feasible flow might not be well-behaved, i.e. flow shipped out of a source a_k is not necessarily routed to b_k, $0 \le k \le n-1$. It may happen that flow leaving a_k is routed to a sink $b_{k'}$, where $k' > k$, or to b_0.

In $\mathcal{N}(\mathcal{I})$ all edge capacities and supplies/demands are integer values. Hence in $\mathcal{N}(\mathcal{I})$ there exists a minimum-cost flow that is integral. A flow f is called integral if the flow $f(e)$ along any edge e takes an integer value. Moreover, there exist polynomial time combinatorial algorithms that compute an integral minimum-cost flow, given a network with integer edge capacities and supplies/demands, see [2].

We will always work with a flow f in $\mathcal{N}(\mathcal{I})$ that is integral. Such a flow translates into a state transition schedule for the servers if,

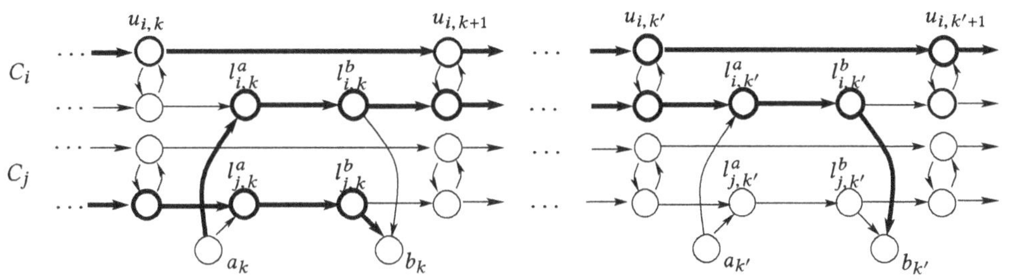

Figure 3: A flow that is not consistent in $[t_{k+1}, t_{k+2})$.

for each C_i and each k, one flow unit traverses either the upper path from $u_{i,k}$ to $u_{i,k+1}$ or the lower path from $l_{i,k}$ to $l_{i,k+1}$. Formally we call an integral flow *consistent in* $[t_k, t_{k+1})$, where $1 \le k \le n-1$, if $f(u_{i,k}, u_{i,k+1}) + f(l_{i,k}, l^a_{i,k}) = 1$ holds for all $i = 1, \ldots, m$. In this definition we only consider flow from $l_{i,k}$ to $l^a_{i,k}$. This will be sufficient for our purposes. An integral flow is called *consistent* if it is consistent in all intervals $[t_k, t_{k+1})$, $1 \le k \le n-1$. In the following we will prove that any feasible integral flow can be converted into one that is consistent. The next lemma identifies properties of feasible flow. Part b) characterizes the shipment of flow that is not consistent and will allow us to generate flow that satisfies consistency.

LEMMA 3.4. *Let f be any feasible integral flow in $\mathcal{N}(\mathcal{I})$.*

a) f is consistent in $[t_1, t_2)$.

b) Suppose that f is consistent in $[t_1, t_2), \ldots, [t_k, t_{k+1})$ but not in $[t_{k+1}, t_{k+2})$. Then there exist components C_i and C_j such that $f(u_{i,k+1}, u_{i,k+2}) + f(l_{i,k+1}, l^a_{i,k+1}) = 2$ and $f(u_{j,k+1}, u_{j,k+2}) + f(l_{j,k+1}, l^a_{j,k+1}) = 0$, cf. Figure 3. In C_i there holds $f(u_{i,k}, u_{i,k+1}) = 1$. One flow unit is shipped from source a_k to $l^a_{i,k}$ and is further routed to $l_{i,k+1}$. In C_j there holds $f(l_{j,k}, l^a_{j,k}) = 1$. This unit is routed via $l^b_{j,k}$ to sink b_k.

3.3 Making a Flow Consistent

Let f be a feasible integral flow in $\mathcal{N}(\mathcal{I})$. We describe how algorithm $\mathcal{A}_1$ modifies f so that the resulting flow is consistent. By Lemma 3.4a), f is consistent in $[t_1, t_2)$. Suppose that f is consistent in $[t_1, t_2), \ldots, [t_k, t_{k+1})$ but not in $[t_{k+1}, t_{k+2})$. $\mathcal{A}_1$ modifies the flow so that it fulfills consistency in $[t_1, t_2), \ldots, [t_{k+1}, t_{k+2})$. The modifications are performed sequentially for all further intervals.

Modifying flow: By assumption, f is consistent in $[t_1, t_2), \ldots, [t_k, t_{k+1})$ but not in $[t_{k+1}, t_{k+2})$. Hence there must exist components C_i and C_j with the properties specified in Lemma 3.4b), see again Figure 3. In C_i a total of two flow units leave $u_{i,k+1}$ and $l_{i,k+1}$ along the upper and lower paths, respectively. On the upper path one flow unit traverses the edge from $u_{i,k}$ and $u_{i,k+1}$. On the lower path one unit is injected from a_k. This unit reaches $l^a_{i,k}$ and continues via $l^b_{i,k}$ to $l_{i,k+1}$. In C_j no flow leaves $u_{j,k+1}$ or $l_{j,k+1}$. A flow unit is shipped from $l_{j,k}$ to $l^a_{j,k}$ and this unit is routed to sink b_k via $l^b_{j,k}$.

While there exist components C_i and C_j as specified above, $\mathcal{A}_1$ works as follows. It determines the smallest integer k', with $k' > k$, such that a flow unit is routed from C_i to sink $b_{k'}$, i.e. $f(l^b_{i,k'}, b_{k'}) = 1$. Such an integer must exist since otherwise a total of two flow units must reach the end of C_i at $u_{i,n}$ and $l_{i,n}$. These two flow units cannot feasibly be routed to b_0 along the unit-capacity edge $(l_{i,n}, b_0)$. Let $P_i(k, k')$ be the path from $l^b_{i,k}$ to $l^b_{i,k'}$ that uses only edges of the lower path of C_i. All edges of $P_i(k, k')$ carry one unit of flow. Similarly, let $P_j(k, k')$ be the path from $l^b_{j,k}$ to $l^b_{j,k'}$ that uses only edges of the lower path of C_j. In the flow modification there are two cases depending on whether or not $P_j(k, k')$ carries flow.

Flow modification, type 1: Suppose that $P_j(k, k')$ does not ship any flow, see Figure 3. Loosely speaking, $\mathcal{A}_1$ replaces flow along $P_i(k, k')$ by flow on $P_j(k, k')$. Formally, the modified flow is as follows. In C_i the flow unit entering $l^b_{i,k}$ is routed to b_k, i.e. $f'(l^b_{i,k}, b_k) = 1$. In C_j algorithm $\mathcal{A}_1$ removes the flow unit leaving $l^b_{j,k}$, i.e. $f'(l^b_{j,k}, b_k) = 0$. For all edges e of $P_i(k, k')$, the algorithm sets $f'(e) = 0$. For all edges e of $P_j(k, k')$, it sets $f'(e) = 1$. Finally it removes the flow unit leaving $l^b_{i,k'}$, i.e. $f'(l^b_{i,k'}, b_{k'}) = 0$, and routes one unit from $l^b_{j,k'}$ to $b_{k'}$, i.e. $f'(l^b_{j,k'}, b_{k'}) = 1$. For all the other edges not considered here, the flow remains unchanged. Obviously, after these modifications, the amount of flow routed into b_k and $b_{k'}$ has not change. The flow conservation law is observed at all vertices of $P_i(k, k')$ and $P_j(k, k')$. Hence the new flow is feasible. Furthermore, the cost of the flow has not changed because the flow update only affects edges of cost 0. Note that $f'(l_{i,k+1}, l^a_{i,k+1}) = 0$ and $f'(l_{j,k+1}, l^a_{j,k+1}) = 1$. Hence restricted to C_i and C_j the new flow is consistent in $[t_{k+1}, t_{k+2})$.

Flow modification, type 2: Assume that some edge of $P_j(k, k')$ carries flow. Then this flow must enter C_j from some source among $a_{k+1}, \ldots, a_{k'}$. $\mathcal{A}_1$ determines the smallest integer k^*, with $k^* > k$, such that $f(a_{k^*}, l^a_{j,k^*}) = 1$. There holds $k^* \le k'$. In component C_i the corresponding edge (a_{k^*}, l^a_{i,k^*}) does not ship flow because all edges of $P_i(k, k')$ carry one unit of flow and no further unit can be injected from a_{k^*}. Let $P_i(k, k^*)$ be the path from $l^b_{i,k}$ to l^a_{i,k^*} that uses only edges of the lower path of C_i. Analogously, let $P_j(k, k^*)$ be the path from $l^b_{j,k}$ to l^a_{j,k^*} that uses only edges of the lower path of C_j. $\mathcal{A}_1$ replaces flow on $P_i(k, k^*)$ by flow on $P_j(k, k^*)$. More specifically, the flow unit routed into $l_{i,k}$ is shipped to b_k, i.e. $f'(l^b_{i,k}, b_k) = 1$. The flow unit on edge $(l^b_{j,k}, b_k)$ is removed. For all edges e of $P_i(k, k^*)$, $\mathcal{A}_1$ sets $f'(e) = 0$. For all edges e of $P_j(k, k^*)$, it sets $f'(e) = 1$. Finally, it sets $f'(a_{k^*}, l^a_{i,k^*}) = 1$ and $f'(a_{k^*}, l^a_{j,k^*}) = 0$. The new flow is feasible, and during the modification the cost has not changed. Restricted to C_i and C_j the new flow is consistent in $[t_{k+1}, t_{k+2})$ because $f'(l_{i,k+1}, l^a_{i,k+1}) = 0$ and $f'(l_{j,k+1}, l^a_{j,k+1}) = 1$.

The above flow modifications do not change flow in components other than C_i and C_j. By repeating the flow update operations for other pairs of network components violating consistency, $\mathcal{A}_1$ obtains a flow that is consistent in $[t_1, t_2), \ldots, [t_{k+1}, t_{k+2})$. The total number of steps to perform the modifications is polynomial in $\mathcal{N}(\mathcal{I})$. The next lemma summarizes the result.

Lemma 3.5. *Let f be a feasible integral flow of cost C in $\mathcal{N}(\mathcal{I})$. Then f can be transformed into a feasible integral flow that is consistent and has cost C. The transformation takes polynomial time.*

3.4 Establishing the Theorem

The next lemma states that a feasible consistent flow properly ships flow from sources to sinks.

Lemma 3.6. *In any feasible integral flow f that is consistent, all flow leaving a_k is routed to b_k, $1 \le k \le n-1$.*

We finish the proof of Theorem 3.1. Given problem instance $\mathcal{I}$, $\mathcal{A}_1$ constructs $\mathcal{N}(\mathcal{I})$ and computes an integral minimum-cost flow f^* using a combinatorial algorithm. Executing the flow modifications described above, the algorithm obtains an integral minimum-cost flow f that is consistent. Lemma 3.6 implies that in f all flow units leaving a_0 are transferred to b_0. By the edge capacity constraints, one unit of flow is transferred through each C_i, $1 \le i \le m$.

$\mathcal{A}_1$ derives a schedule Σ for $\mathcal{I}$ by keeping track of these flow units in $C_1, \ldots, C_m$. Consider component C_i, $1 \le i \le m$. While the flow unit traverses the upper path, server S_i is in the active state. While the flow unit traverses the lower path, S_i is in the sleep state. If the flow traverses an edge $(l_{i,k}, u_{i,k})$, S_i powers up at time t_k. If the flow traverses $(u_{i,k}, l_{i,k})$, the server powers down at time t_k. The energy consumed by S_i is exactly equal to the cost incurred by the flow unit traversing C_i. Hence the energy consumed by Σ is equal to the cost of f, and this is equal to the cost of f^*.

It remains to verify that Σ is feasible. By Lemma 3.6, in f all flow units leaving a_k are shipped to b_k, $1 \le k \le n-1$. Consider any fixed k, $1 \le k \le n-1$. There must exist d_k components C_i such that a flow unit is routed from a_k to $l^a_{i,k}$ and further on to $l^b_{i,k}$ and b_k. Since f is consistent in $[t_k, t_{k+1})$, there holds $f(u_{i,k}, u_{i,k+1}) = 1$. If $f(l_{i,k}, l^a_{i,k}) = 1$, then two units of flow would leave $l^a_{i,k}$, violating the capacity of the outgoing edge. Thus in $[t_k, t_{k+1})$ at least d_k servers are in the active state. Optimality of Σ follows from Proposition 2.2 and Lemma 3.3.

4 SERVERS WITH MULTIPLE STATES

We develop an approximation algorithm for DPM in the general setting that each server may have an arbitrary number of states. Let $\mathcal{I} = (\mathcal{S}, \mathcal{D})$ be an input with τ server types, i.e. each server of $\mathcal{S}$ belongs to one of τ classes, where $\tau \in \mathbb{N}$. Formally, $\mathcal{S}$ is partitioned into $\mathcal{S}_1, \ldots, \mathcal{S}_\tau$. Within each server type/class $\mathcal{S}_i$, $1 \le i \le \tau$, all servers are identical. Every server of $\mathcal{S}_i$ has $\sigma_i + 1$ states $s_{i,0}, \ldots, s_{i,\sigma_i}$ with power consumption rates $r_{i,0} > \ldots > r_{i,\sigma_i}$. Here $s_{i,0}$ is again the active state; the other states are low-power modes. The energy needed to transition from $s_{i,j}$ to $s_{i,0}$ is denoted by $\Delta_{i,j}$, $1 \le j \le \sigma_i$. The state transition energy from the active state to any lower-power state is 0. The servers of $\mathcal{S}_i$ are independent and not synchronized. Over the time horizon each server may reside in individual states and perform state transitions independent of the other servers. Let m_i be the number of servers in $\mathcal{S}_i$. There holds $\sum_{i=1}^{\tau} m_i = m$.

Theorem 4.1. *Let $\mathcal{I}$ be an instance of DPM with τ server types. A schedule whose energy consumption is at most τ times the minimum one for $\mathcal{I}$ can be computed in polynomial time based on a min-cost two-commodity flow computation.*

In the remainder of this section we develop an algorithm $\mathcal{A}_2$ that, given $\mathcal{I} = (\mathcal{S}, \mathcal{D})$, constructs a feasible schedule attaining a τ-approximation on the consumed energy. This establishes Theorem 4.1. By Proposition 2.2 we restrict ourselves to schedules with the following two properties. While a server is in low-power mode, it uses a single state. State transitions are performed only at the times of T.

Algorithm $\mathcal{A}_2$ constructs a network $\mathcal{N}(\mathcal{I})$. Compared to the construction in Section 3, the main differences are as follows. Each network component will represent a class of servers so that the encoding length of $\mathcal{N}(\mathcal{I})$ is polynomial in that of $\mathcal{I}$. A component has a collection of lower paths corresponding to the various low-power modes of the servers. We need a second commodity to ensure that computing demands are met. This will allow us to reduce the number of auxiliary vertices on the lower paths.

Given $\mathcal{N}(\mathcal{I})$, $\mathcal{A}_2$ computes a minimum-cost flow f^*. Since the network has two commodities, f^* is not integral but fractional in general. In a sequence of rounding and packing operations $\mathcal{A}_2$ transforms f^* into an integral one that guides the construction a feasible schedule for $\mathcal{I}$. The cost of the integral flow and the constructed schedule will be at most τ times that of f^*.

4.1 Construction of the Network

We describe $\mathcal{N}(\mathcal{I})$, given $\mathcal{I} = (\mathcal{S}, \mathcal{D})$.

Network components with multiple paths. For every server type i, the network contains a component C_i, $1 \le i \le \tau$. The component represents all the m_i servers of $\mathcal{S}_i$. Exactly m_i flow units will be routed through C_i, modeling the individual states and actions of the servers. Component C_i consists of an *upper path* and σ_i *lower paths*. The general structure is depicted in Figure 4. We search for an optimal schedule in which state transitions are performed only at times $t_1 < \ldots < t_n$ in T, cf. Proposition 2.2. In C_i the upper path corresponds to the active state of the servers of $\mathcal{S}_i$. For any t_k, $1 \le k \le n$, there is a vertex $u_{i,k}$ on the upper path. Vertices $u_{i,k}$ and $u_{i,k+1}$ are connected by a directed edge $(u_{i,k}, u_{i,k+1})$ of cost $r_{i,0}(t_{k+1} - t_k)$, $1 \le k \le n-1$. The cost is equal to energy consumed by one server of $\mathcal{S}_i$ if it resides in the active state during $[t_k, t_{k+1})$. The capacity of $(u_{i,k}, u_{i,k+1})$ and in fact of all edges of C_i is equal to m_i, reflecting that C_i represents m_i servers in $\mathcal{S}_i$.

The σ_i lower paths correspond to the σ_i low-power states. Consider any j with $1 \le j \le \sigma_i$. On lower path j there is a vertex $l_{i,j,k}$ and an auxiliary vertex $l^a_{i,j,k}$, for any $1 \le k \le n-1$. Moreover, there is a final vertex $l_{i,j,n}$. The auxiliary vertices will help to ensure that a total of at least d_k flow units traverse the edges $(u_{i,k}, u_{i,k+1})$ on the upper paths, considering all the components C_i, $1 \le i \le \tau$. We

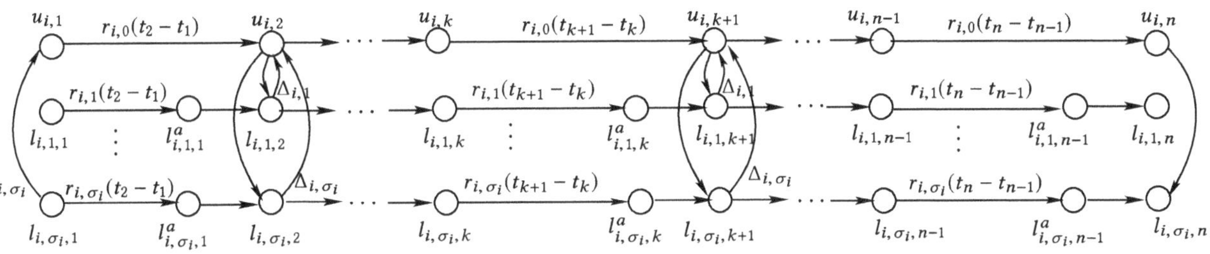

Figure 4: The component C_i for server type i. Unlabeled edges connecting two vertices have cost 0.

do not need a second auxiliary vertex $l^b_{i,j,k}$ because we work with two commodities. On lower path j the vertices are connected as follows. For any k, where $1 \le k \le n-1$, there is a directed edge $(l_{i,j,k}, l^a_{i,j,k})$ of cost $r_{i,j}(t_{k+1}-t_k)$, representing the energy consumed by a server if it is in state $s_{i,j}$ during $[t_k, t_{k+1})$. Furthermore there is an edge $(l^a_{i,j,k}, l_{i,j,k+1})$ of cost 0.

The upper path is connected to the lower paths by additional edges that model state transitions. We assume that at times t_1 and t_n all servers of $\mathcal{S}_i$ are in the deepest low-power state s_{i,σ_i}. Thus there is a directed edge $(l_{i,\sigma_i,1}, u_{i,1})$ of cost Δ_{i,σ_i} modeling possible power-up operations of servers at time t_1. Furthermore there is a directed edge $(u_{i,n}, l_{i,\sigma_i,n})$ of cost 0 representing power-down operations at time t_n. For any $1 < k < n$ and any $1 \le j \le \sigma_i$, there is a directed edge $(u_{i,k}, l_{i,j,k})$ of cost 0 and a directed edge $(l_{i,j,k}, u_{i,k})$ of cost $\Delta_{i,j}$. Since we consider schedules specified in Proposition 2.1, there are no state transitions among low-power states; thus there are no edges between the lower paths. (We remark that on lower path j, $1 \le j < \sigma_i$, we could remove the first and the last vertex but it is not important.) Note again that the capacity of each edge of C_i is m_i.

The network with two commodities. In $\mathcal{N}(\mathcal{I})$ components $C_1, \ldots, C_\tau$ are aligned in parallel and connected to vertices a_0 and b_0. The general composition is similar to that depicted in Figure 2; an accurate figure is given in the full paper. Vertices a_0 and b_0 inject and absorb flow of commodity 1. Specifically, a_0 has a supply of m and b_0 has a demand of m of commodity 1. The connections are as follows. At times t_1 and t_n the servers are in the deepest low-power mode. Hence, for any $1 \le i \le \tau$, there exist directed edges $(a_0, l_{i,\sigma_i,1})$ and $(l_{i,\sigma_i,n}, b_0)$. Each of these edges has a cost of 0 and a capacity of m_i so that m_i flow units can be routed from a_0 to b_0 via C_i.

Network $\mathcal{N}(\mathcal{I})$ contains further sources and sinks that inject and absorb flow of commodity 2. This second commodity will ensure that the computing demands are met. Consider any k with $1 \le k \le n-1$. There is a source a_k and a sink b_k with a supply/demand of $D_k = \sum_{i=1}^{\tau} m_i(\sigma_i - 1) + d_k$ of commodity 2. Vertices a_k and b_k are connected to all lower paths in the components. For any i and j with $1 \le i \le \tau$ and $1 \le j \le \sigma_i$, there is a directed edge $(a_k, l^a_{i,j,k})$ into the auxiliary vertex on lower path j in C_i. Moreover, there is a directed edge $(l_{i,j,k+1}, b_k)$ from the following vertex on the lower path into b_k. Each of these edges has a cost of 0 and a capacity of m_i. Lemma 4.2 below states that in any feasible flow, for any $1 \le k \le n-1$, at least d_k units will be shipped along the edges $(u_{i,k}, u_{i,k+1})$ on the upper paths of the components $C_1, \ldots, C_\tau$.

So far we have specified the total capacity of any edge in $\mathcal{N}(\mathcal{I})$. It remains to specify edge capacity constraints for the two commodities. Consider any $1 \le i \le \tau$. For any edge of C_i, the capacity of commodity 1 is m_i. The same holds true for the edges $(a_0, l_{i,\sigma_i,1})$ and $(l_{i,\sigma_i,n}, b_0)$. On all the edges leaving a_k or entering b_k, $1 \le k \le n-1$, the capacity of commodity 1 is equal to 0. Hence flow of commodity 1 must not traverse these edges. In the network components commodity 2 may only traverse the edges from the auxiliary vertices to the subsequent vertices on the lower paths. Hence commodity 2 has a capacity constraint of m_i on each of the edges $(a_k, l^a_{i,j,k})$, $(l^a_{i,j,k}, l_{i,j,k+1})$ and $(l_{i,j,k+1}, b_k)$, where $1 \le i \le \tau$, $1 \le j \le \sigma_i$ and $1 \le k \le n-1$. For all the other edges in $\mathcal{N}(\mathcal{I})$, commodity 2 has a capacity of 0. Hence all flow from a_k, $1 \le k \le n-1$, must be shipped to b_k via edges $(l^a_{i,j,k}, l_{i,j,k+1})$. The encoding length of $\mathcal{N}(\mathcal{I})$ is polynomial in that of $\mathcal{I}$ because the m_i identical servers of $\mathcal{S}_i$ are modeled by a single component C_i, $1 \le i \le \tau$.

Lemma 4.2, as mentioned above, identifies an important property of feasible flow. Lemma 4.3 states that every optimal schedule with the properties of Proposition 2.2 translates to a feasible flow with the same energy/cost.

LEMMA 4.2. *In $\mathcal{N}(\mathcal{I})$ there exists a feasible flow. Any feasible flow f satisfies $\sum_{i=1}^{\tau} f(u_{i,k}, u_{i,k+1}) \ge d_k$, for $1 \le k \le n-1$.*

LEMMA 4.3. *Let Σ be an optimal schedule as specified in Proposition 2.2. Then Σ corresponds to a feasible flow of cost $E(\Sigma)$ in $\mathcal{N}(\mathcal{I})$.*

4.2 Algorithm Outline & Flow Properties

Given $\mathcal{N}(\mathcal{I})$, algorithm $\mathcal{A}_2$ computes a feasible minimum-cost flow f^*. By Lemma 4.3 the cost of f^*, denoted by *cost*(f^*), is a lower bound on the energy consumed by an optimal schedule for $\mathcal{I}$. Since f^* involves two commodities, it is fractional in general. In particular, it may be fractional on the upper paths of the components. On the corresponding edges the flow has to be raised, for sufficiently many components, so that a feasible schedule for $\mathcal{I}$ can be derived later. $\mathcal{A}_2$ modifies f^* in three main steps. The resulting flow will be integral. (1) First $\mathcal{A}_2$ scales f^* by a factor of τ. (2) Then $\mathcal{A}_2$ modifies the scaled flow so that it becomes integral on the upper paths of the components. Specifically, on edge $(u_{i,k}, u_{i,k+1})$ exactly $d_{i,k} = \min\{m_i, \lfloor \tau f^*(u_{i,k}, u_{i,k+1}) \rfloor\}$ units of flow are routed, where $1 \le i \le \tau$ and $1 \le k \le n-1$. Lemma 4.4 below states that $\sum_{i=1}^{\tau} d_{i,k} \ge d_k$, for any $1 \le k \le n-1$. This property will later admit the construction of a feasible schedule in which the computing demands of $\mathcal{I}$ are met. (3) Given the flow of Step 2, $\mathcal{A}_2$ packs fractional flows on the lower paths of the components $C_1, \ldots, C_\tau$. Using the integral flow obtained in Step 3, $\mathcal{A}_2$ constructs a feasible schedule for $\mathcal{I}$ whose energy consumption is upper bounded by the cost of that flow. Once f^* has been scaled in Step 1, the subsequent flow modifications of Steps 2 and 3 never increase cost. Thus the energy consumed by the schedule is at most $\tau cost(f^*)$.

LEMMA 4.4. *For* $k = 1, \ldots, n-1$, $\sum_{i=1}^{\tau} d_{i,k} \geq d_k$.

Given Lemma 4.4, a natural idea for finding an integral solution is to use a flow computation: Determine a single-commodity minimum-cost flow that ships m_i flow units through component C_i and, importantly, exactly $d_{i,k}$ units along edge $(u_{i,k}, u_{i,k+1})$, where $1 \leq i \leq \tau$ and $1 \leq k \leq n-1$. However, one has to prove that the cost of such a flow is upper bounded by $\tau cost(f^*)$. Such a proof involves arguments and flow modifications contained in Steps 1 and 2 of $\mathcal{A}_2$. Therefore we describe them explicitly as algorithmic steps. Step 3 could indeed be replaced by a min-cost flow computation. However, we instead devise a faster $O(n^2 \sum_{i=1}^{\tau} \sigma_i)$ time routine for constructing an integral flow along the lower paths of the components.

In the following, when describing flow modifications, we will always focus on one particular network component. All flow updates will be performed independently for the components. Hence in the corresponding exposition, we consider an arbitrary but fixed component $C = C_i$, $1 \leq i \leq \tau$. This allows us to simplify notation and omit the index i. On the upper path the vertices are $u_1, \ldots, u_n$. Component C has $\sigma = \sigma_i$ lower paths. On lower path j, $1 \leq j \leq \sigma$, the vertices are $l_{j,k}$ and $l^a_{j,k}$, for $k = 1, \ldots, n-1$, followed by the final vertex $l_{j,n}$. Let $m_c = m_i$ be the number of servers in class S_i represented by $C = C_i$.

Nested structure of flows. We show that in each network component C flow f^* has a crucial property, i.e. it exhibits a nested structure. Let $P_j(k, k')$ be the path from u_k to $u_{k'}$ along lower path j, where $1 \leq j \leq \sigma$ and $1 < k < k' < n$. More specifically, the path consists of $(u_k, l_{j,k})$, followed by the path from $l_{j,k}$ to $l_{j,k'}$ on lower path j, followed by $(l_{j,k'}, u_{k'})$. For $k = 1$ and $1 < k' < n$, we define $P_\sigma(1, k')$ as the path consisting of the edges from $l_{\sigma,1}$ to $l_{\sigma,k'}$ on lower path σ, followed by the edge $(l_{\sigma,k'}, u_{k'})$. For $k' = n$ and $1 < k < n$, path $P_\sigma(k, n)$ consists of edge $(u_k, l_{\sigma,k})$, followed by the edges from $l_{\sigma,k}$ to $l_{\sigma,n}$ on lower path σ. Finally $P(k, k')$ is the path connecting u_k and $u_{k'}$ on the upper path of the component, for any $1 \leq k < k' \leq n$. In the sequel, unless otherwise stated, flow always refers to commodity 1. Consider any path P. We say that P *routes flow* if, for any edge of P, the flow is strictly positive.

The following property of a flow will be important. A flow f in component C is *nested* if it satisfies the following condition. Let $P_i(k_1, k_2)$ and $P_j(k_3, k_4)$ be two paths such that both route flow and $i < j$. Then one of the relations (a–c) holds: (a) $k_2 < k_3$; (b) $k_4 < k_1$; or (c) $k_3 \leq k_1 < k_2 \leq k_4$. Intuitively, the endpoints of the two paths do not alternate. Both endpoints of $P_i(k_1, k_2)$ occur either before, after or in between those of $P_j(k_3, k_4)$.

LEMMA 4.5. *In each component C flow f^* is nested.*

Loop-freeness. Given f^*, $\mathcal{A}_2$ slightly modifies it so that it becomes *loop-free* in each C. A flow is loop-free in C if there exists no vertex u_k such that edges $(l_{i,k}, u_k)$ and $(u_k, l_{j,k})$ both route flow, where $1 \leq i, j \leq \sigma$. Suppose that there exists such a vertex u_k. Since f^* is nested, $i = j$ must hold. Hence $\mathcal{A}_2$ can simply remove $\min\{f^*(l_{i,k}, u_k), f^*(u_k, l_{i,k})\}$ units of flow from both $(l_{i,k}, u_k)$ and $(u_k, l_{i,k})$. By performing these updates one obtains a loop-free flow f^* that is nested.

4.3 Constructing an Integral Flow

We describe the three main flow modification steps.

4.3.1 *Step 1: Flow scaling.* Let f^* be the minimum-cost, loop-free flow. Algorithm $\mathcal{A}_2$ multiplies f^* by a factor of τ on all edges of the network. At the same time it multiplies all edge capacities and supplies/demands by τ. Then it deletes the flow of commodity 2 and the supplies/demands at a_k and b_k, $1 \leq k \leq n-1$. The resulting flow f^1 of commodity 1 is feasible. Additionally, in each component it is nested and loop-free. There holds $cost(f^1) \leq \tau cost(f^*)$.

In Steps 2 and 3 flow f^1 is modified. As indicated above, the modification are executed independently for the components. Therefore, in the description of Steps 2 and 3 we concentrate on one component C that ships τm_c units of flow. The flow modifications never increase the cost. At all times the flow remains nested and loop-free.

4.3.2 *Step 2: Rounding flow on the upper path.* Given f^1, $\mathcal{A}_2$ rounds it so that the flow becomes integral on the upper path of C. Along edge (u_k, u_{k+1}) the amount of flow will be $\min\{m_c, \lfloor \tau f^*(u_k, u_{k+1}) \rfloor\}$. Recall that m_c is the number of servers in the class represented by C. We first describe how to reduce f^1 so that on any edge (u_k, u_{k+1}) the flow is $\lfloor \tau f^*(u_k, u_{k+1}) \rfloor$. $\mathcal{A}_2$ makes four passes over C. First, in Step 2.1, it rounds valleys with low flow. Then, in Steps 2.2 and 2.3, it modifies flow on edge sequences with increasing and decreasing flow, respectively. Finally, in Step 2.4, it takes care of flow peaks. Given this flow, we further reduce it so that the flow on any edge of the upper path does not exceed m_c. At any time, for a current flow f, we say that the flow *increases at u_k* if $k = 1$ and $f(u_1, u_2) > 0$ or if $1 < k < n$ and $f(u_{k-1}, u_k) < f(u_k, u_{k+1})$. Similarly, the flow *decreases at u_k* if $1 < k < n$ and $f(u_{k-1}, u_k) > f(u_k, u_{k+1})$ of if $k = n$ and $f(u_{n-1}, u_n) > 0$. Initially in Step 2, let $f = f^1$.

Step 2.1: Valleys. A *valley* is a path $P(k, k')$, $1 < k < k' < n$, on the upper path of C such that the flow decreases at u_k, increases at $u_{k'}$ and is constant for all the edges of $P(k, k')$. Formally, the last condition indicates that $f(e) = f(u_k, u_{k+1})$, for all edges e of $P(k, k')$. $\mathcal{A}_2$ scans C. Whenever it encounters a valley $P(k, k')$ with a non-integral amount of flow, it invokes the following procedure that reduces the flow to $\lfloor f(u_k, u_{k+1}) \rfloor$.

Flow update procedure: For the given valley $P(k, k')$, the flow decreases at u_k. The procedure determines the smallest j such that flow is routed from u_k to $l_{j,k}$ and shipped on lower path j. In the full paper we prove that $P_j(k, k')$ routes flow. Hence, as $P_j(k, k')$ routes flow, in the unscaled minimum-cost flow f^* path $P_j(k, k')$ also ships flow. Routing the flow on the upper path would have been a feasible option as well. This implies that the total edge cost of $P_j(k, k')$ is upper bounded by that of $P(k, k')$. The procedure updates the flow as follows. It remove $\delta = f(u_k, u_{k+1}) - \lfloor f(u_k, u_{k+1}) \rfloor$ units of flow from $P(k, k')$ and instead routes them along $P_j(k, k')$. This does not increase the cost. The resulting flow in C remains nested. Modifying all valleys takes $O(n\sigma)$ time.

Step 2.2: Flow increases. In a second pass over C algorithm $\mathcal{A}_2$ identifies vertices u_k at which the flow increases. If $f(u_k, u_{k+1})$

is not integral, it is reduced to $\lfloor f(u_k, u_{k+1})\rfloor$. Starting at u_1 or at a vertex representing the end of a valley, $\mathcal{A}_2$ performs a sequence of vertex inspections and possible flow updates. The sequence ends at a vertex at which the flow decreases. The algorithm then searches for the end of the next valley and continues.

Formally, let $u_{k'}$ be a vertex such that $k' = 1$ or $u_{k'}$ is the last vertex of a valley. When located at $u_{k'}$, $\mathcal{A}_2$ determines the smallest k'' with $k'' > k'$ such that the flow decreases at $u_{k''}$. The algorithm inspects the vertices u_k, $k' \le k < k'' - 1$, in order of increasing index. If $f(u_k, u_{k+1})$ is not integral, the procedure described in the next paragraph is invoked, which reduces the flow to $\lfloor f(u_k, u_{k+1})\rfloor$. When the procedure is executed at u_k, there holds $u_k = u_1$ or the flow $f(u_{k-1}, u_k)$ on the preceding edge is integral. The latter condition holds true because if $u_k = u_{k'}$ is the last vertex of a valley, then the flow along the incoming edge has been made integral in Step 2.1. $\mathcal{A}_2$ considers vertices in order of increasing index, starting at $u_{k'}$. When u_k, $k' < k < k'' - 1$, is inspected, the flow on the edges between $u_{k'}$ and u_k is already integral.

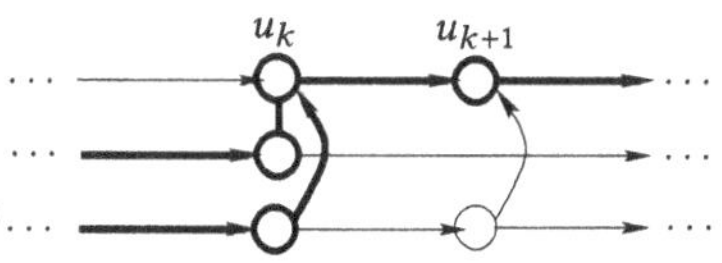

Figure 5: A flow increase at u_k.

Flow update procedure: The procedure updates flow at a vertex u_k where the flow increases and $f(u_k, u_{k+1})$ is not integral. Let again $\delta = f(u_k, u_{k+1}) - \lfloor f(u_k, u_{k+1})\rfloor$. Either $k = 1$ or the flow on (u_{k-1}, u_k) is integral. Hence at least δ units of flow are shipped from lower paths into u_k. While $\delta > 0$, the procedure executes the following steps. Let j be the largest integer such that the flow from $l_{j,k}$ to u_k is positive. Figure 5 depicts the general flow configuration. Let $\delta_j = f(l_{j,k}, u_k)$ and $\delta' = \min\{\delta, \delta_j\}$. The procedure reduces flow on $(l_{j,k}, u_k)$ and (u_k, u_{k+1}) by δ units. Instead it ships δ units of flow from $l_{j,k}$ to u_{k+1} along lower path j, i.e. via $l^a_{j,k}$ and $l_{j,k+1}$. Then δ is reduced by δ'. The flow update decreases the cost of the flow by $(r_0-r_j)(t_{k+1}-t_k) > 0$. Here r_0 and r_j are the cost coefficients along the upper path and lower path j, respectively. More precisely, edge (u_k, u_{k+1}) has a cost of $r_0(t_{k+1}-t_k)$ and $(l_{j,k}, l^a_{j,k})$ has a cost of $r_j(t_{k+1}-t_k)$. The modified flow remains nested; detailed arguments are given in the full paper. The running time of one execution of the procedure is $O(\sigma)$. The running time of the entire pass over C is $O(n\sigma)$.

Step 2.3: Flow decreases. The flow modifications are symmetric to those described in Step 2.2. Algorithm $\mathcal{A}_2$ makes another pass over C, this time from right to left starting at u_n. It searches for vertices u_k at which the flow decreases. If the flow $f(u_{k-1}, u_k)$ on the incoming edge is not integral, then it is reduced to $\lfloor f(u_{k-1}, u_k)\rfloor$. A detailed description is provided in the full version of the paper.

Step 2.4: Peaks. A *peak* is an edge (u_k, u_{k+1}) such that the flow increases at u_k and decreases at u_{k+1}, see also Figure 6. After $\mathcal{A}_2$ has executed Steps 2.1–2.3, the only edges on the upper path with a non-integral amount of flow are peaks. Algorithm $\mathcal{A}_2$ traverses C. For each peak (u_k, u_{k+1}) with a non-integral amount of flow, it invokes the following routine.

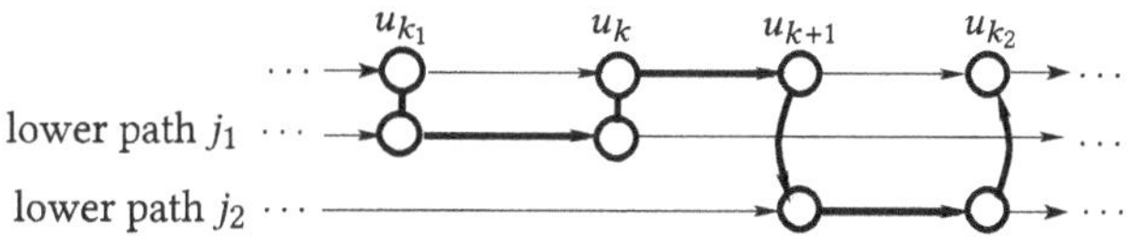

Figure 6: A flow peak on (u_k, u_{k+1}).

Flow update procedure: Again $\delta = f(u_k, u_{k+1}) - \lfloor f(u_k, u_{k+1})\rfloor$. Let j_1 be the largest integer such that $f(l_{j_1,k}, u_k) > 0$, i.e. flow is routed from lower path j_1 to u_k. Let j_2 be the largest integer such that $f(u_{k+1}, l_{j_2,k+1}) > 0$. There are two basic cases.

If $j_1 = j_2$, then let $\delta_1 = f(l_{j_1,k}, u_k)$ and $\delta_2 = f(u_{k+1}, l_{j_2,k+1})$. Furthermore, let $\delta' = \min\{\delta, \delta_1, \delta_2\}$. The procedure removes δ' units of flow from the path connecting $l_{j_1,k}$ and $l_{j_1,k+1}$ along the upper path. Specifically, it removes δ' flow units from the edges $(l_{j_1,k}, u_k)$, (u_k, u_{k+1}) and $(u_{k+1}, l_{j_1,k+1})$. Instead it sends δ' units of flow from $l_{j_1,k}$ to $l_{j_1,k+1}$ via $l^a_{j_1,k}$ on lower path j_1. The reduction in the cost of the flow is $\delta(r_0 - r_{j_1})(t_{k+1} - t_k) + \delta\Delta_{j_1} > 0$. Here Δ_j is the cost of $(l_{j,k}, u_k)$, for any $1 \le j \le \sigma$ and $1 \le k < n-1$.

If $j_1 \ne j_2$, then let k_1 be the largest integer such that $P_{j_1}(k_1, k)$ routes flow. Let δ_1 be the largest value such that every edge of $P_{j_1}(k_1, k)$ routes at least δ_1 units of flow. Similarly, let k_2 be the smallest integer such that $P_{j_2}(k+1, k_2)$ routes flow. Let δ_2 be the largest value such that every edge of $P_{j_2}(k+1, k_2)$ routes at least δ_2 units of flow. Figure 6 shows the case that $j_1 < j_2$. Let $\delta' = \min\{\delta, \delta_1, \delta_2\}$. The procedure removes δ' units of flow from $P_{j_1}(k_1, k)$, edge (u_k, u_{k+1}) and $P_{j_2}(k+1, k_2)$. If $j_1 < j_2$, it instead sends these δ' units on path $P_{j_2}(k_1, k_2)$. If $j_1 > j_2$, it routes the δ' units along $P_{j_1}(k_1, k_2)$. Thus, in any case the deeper low-power state is used. It is not hard to verify that the cost of the flow decreases.

In any case δ is reduced by δ'. In the full paper we prove that the new flow is nested. One call of the procedure takes $O(n^2\sigma)$; the rounding of all peaks can be accomplished in $O(n^3\sigma)$ time.

Step 2.5: Flow reduction to m_c. It remains to reduce the flow to m_c on edges (u_k, u_{k+1}) where the flow after Steps 2.1–2.4 is higher. This can be done using the procedures that handle flow increases and peaks. Details are given in the full paper.

4.3.3 Step 3: Packing flow on the lower paths. Given the flow f^2 constructed in Step 2, $\mathcal{A}_2$ packs flow on the lower paths of the considered component C so that the final flow becomes integral. During the modification the flow on the upper path of C does not change. Moreover, the cost of the flow will not increase.

Auxiliary edges. In order to separate flow that has already been made integral from the original one, we need auxiliary edges. For every edge e in C, except for those in the upper path, we add an auxiliary edge e'. More precisely, for every link $e = (v, w)$ not contained on the upper path, there is the original edge and a new auxiliary edge.

Initially, the flow f^2 is routed on the upper path and the original edges of the lower paths. In a series of rounds $\mathcal{A}_2$ removes flow from the original edges, packs it and adds it to the auxiliary edges. On the auxiliary edges, the flow is always integral. The process ends when there is no flow on the original edges. Then the original edges are removed so that, for each edge, there is only one copy.

We observe that since f^2 is integral on the upper path and loop-free, only integral amounts of flow enter/leave the upper path from/to the lower paths. This invariant will be maintained at all times during the flow transformation. For every edge, the total flow on the original and auxiliary copy will always be at most τm_c.

Matching pairs. The flow packing procedure works with with the notion of a *matching pair*. Such a pair consists of two vertices u_k and $u_{k'}$, $1 < k < k' < n$, with the following properties: (a) Flow is routed from u_k to the lower paths on original edges $(u_k, l_{j,k})$, $1 \le j \le \sigma$; (b) flow is routed into $u_{k'}$ from lower paths on original edges $(l_{j,k'}, u_{k'})$, $1 \le j \le \sigma$; (c) there exists no vertex $u_{k''}$ with $k < k'' < k'$ that satisfies (a) or (b). While there exists a matching pair $\mathcal{A}_2$ executes the following flow packing routine. Unless otherwise stated, $f(e)$ refers to the current flow on the original copy of e.

Packing procedure. Let u_k and $u_{k'}$ be the given matching pair. Let δ_k be the total amount of flow routed from u_k to lower paths on original edges $(u_k, l_{j,k})$, $1 \le j \le \sigma$. Similarly, let $\delta_{k'}$ be the total amount of flow shipped into $u_{k'}$ from lower paths along original edges $(l_{j,k'}, u_{k'})$, $1 \le j \le \sigma$. Both δ_k and $\delta_{k'}$ are integral. If $\delta_k \le \delta_{k'}$, then let J be the set of integers j with $1 \le j \le \sigma$ such that $f(u_k, l_{j,k}) > 0$. Define $\delta_j = f(u_k, l_{j,k})$, for any $j \in J$. There holds $\sum_{j\in J} \delta_j = \delta_k$. If $\delta_k > \delta_{k'}$, then let J be the set of integers j with $1 \le j \le \sigma$ such that $f(l_{j,k'}, u_{k'}) > 0$. Define $\delta_j = f(l_{j,k'}, u_{k'})$, for any $j \in J$. There holds $\sum_{j\in J} \delta_j = \delta_{k'}$. In any case, for $j \in J$, consider the path $P_j(k, k')$. In the full paper we formally prove that $P_j(k, k')$ routes δ_j flow units, for any $j \in J$.

The procedure for packing flow determines the integer $j' \in J$ such that the total edge cost of $P_{j'}(k, k')$ is minimal among $P_j(k, k')$ with $j \in J$. Then, for every $j \in J$, it removes δ_j units of flow from the original edges of $P_j(k, k')$. Finally, it routes $\min\{\delta_k, \delta_{k'}\}$ units of flow on the new edges of $P_{j'}(k, k')$. The new flow remains nested because an already existing routing path with positive flow is selected. The cost does not increase, due to the choice of j'.

Every time the procedure is invoked for a matching pair u_k and $u_{k'}$, the flow leaving u_k or entering $u_{k'}$ on original edges drops to 0. Thus all executions of the procedure take $O(n^2\sigma)$ time. When there exists no matching pair anymore, the remaining flow on original edges along paths $P_\sigma(1, k')$ and $P_\sigma(k, n)$ can be transferred without modification to the auxiliary edges.

4.4 Construction of the Schedule

Let f^3 denote the flow obtained in Step 3.

LEMMA 4.6. *Flow f^3 corresponds to a schedule Σ with τm_i servers of type i, $1 \le i \le \tau$. In $[t_k, t_{k+1})$ exactly $d_{i,k} = \min\{m_i, \lfloor \tau f^*(u_{i,k}, u_{i,k+1}) \rfloor\}$ servers of type i are in the active state, $1 \le i \le \tau$ and $1 \le k \le n-1$. The energy consumed by the servers of type i is equal the cost of f^3 in C_i, $1 \le i \le \tau$.*

LEMMA 4.7. *Let Σ_i be a schedule for τm_i servers of type i in which exactly $d_{i,k}$ servers are in the active state during $[t_k, t_{k+1})$, where $d_{i,k} \le m_i$ and $1 \le k \le n-1$. Then there exists a schedule Σ'_i for m_i servers of type i in which the servers numbered 1 to $d_{i,k}$ are in the active state during $[t_k, t_{k+1})$. The energy consumed by Σ'_i is upper bounded by that of Σ_i.*

Given the integral flow f^3, algorithm $\mathcal{A}_2$ constructs a feasible schedule Σ^* for $\mathcal{I}$. For each server type $\mathcal{S}_i$, $1 \le i \le \tau$, $\mathcal{A}_2$ builds an optimal schedule Σ_i^* such that $d_{i,k}$ of the m_i servers in $\mathcal{S}_i$ are in the active state during $[t_k, t_{k+1})$, $1 \le k \le n-1$. These schedules $\Sigma_1^*, \ldots, \Sigma_\tau^*$ are then combined to form Σ^*. Consider any i with $1 \le i \le \tau$. In a first step, by Lemma 4.7, Σ_i^* just specifies that the servers numbered 1 to $d_{i,k}$ are in the active state during $[t_k, t_{k+1})$, for any $1 \le k \le n-1$. Then, while a server is not required to be active according to the specification, $\mathcal{A}_2$ selects an optimal state. Suppose that at time t_k the number of required servers decreases, i.e. $d_{i,k-1} > d_{i,k}$. Algorithm $\mathcal{A}_2$ determines states for $d_{i,k-1} - d_{i,k}$ servers that may power down. This is done as follows. Initially, $\mu := d_{i,k}$. While $\mu < d_{i,k-1}$, $\mathcal{A}_2$ finds the next time $t_{k'}$ such that $d_{i,k'} \ge \mu + 1$, i.e. at least $\mu + 1$ servers are active. It chooses an optimal state to be assumed by servers numbered $\mu + 1, \ldots, \min\{d_{i,k-1}, d_{i,k'}\}$ at time t_k. This is the state s_{i,j^*} with $j^* = \arg\min_{1\le j\le\sigma_i}\{r_{i,j}(t_{k'} - t_k) + \Delta_{i,j}\}$. Then $\mu := \min\{d_{i,k-1}, d_{i,k'}\}$.

By Lemmas 4.6 and 4.7, the energy consumed by Σ_i^* is upper bounded by the cost incurred by f^3 in component C_i. Thus the energy consumed by the combined schedule Σ^* is at most $cost(f^3) \le \tau cost(f^*)$. Schedule Σ^* is feasible because, by Lemma 4.4, $\sum_{i=1}^{\tau} d_{i,k} \ge d_k$. The proof of Theorem 4.1 is complete.

REFERENCES

[1] The Advanced Configuration and Power Interface. The latest specification 6.1 (January 2016) is available e.g. at UEFI.org.

[2] R.J. Ahuja, T.L. Magnanti and J.B. Orlin. *Network Flows.* Prentice Hall, 1993.

[3] M. Armbrust, A. Fox, R. Griffith, A.D. Joseph, R.H. Katz, A. Konwinski, G. Lee, D.A. Patterson, A. Rabkin, I. Stoica and M. Zaharia. Above the clouds: A Berkeley view of cloud computing. Technical Report No. UCB/EECS-2009-28. EECS Department, University of California, Berkeley, 2009.

[4] J. Augustine, S. Irani and C. Swamy. Optimal power-down strategies. *SIAM J. Comput.*, 37(5):1499–1516, 2008.

[5] Y. Azar, Y. Bartal, E. Feuerstein, A. Fiat, S. Leonardi and A. Rosén. On capital investment. *Algorithmica*, 25(1):22–36, 1999.

[6] L.A. Barroso and U. Hölzle. The case for energy-proportional computing. *IEEE Computer*, 40(12):33–37, 2007.

[7] M. Dayarathna, Y. Wen and R. Fan. Data center energy consumption modeling: A survey. *IEEE Communications Surveys and Tutorials*, 18(1):732–794, 2016.

[8] G. Fettweis and E. Zimmermann. ICT energy consumption – trends and challenges. *Proc. 11th International Symp. on Wireless Personal Multimedia Communications*, 2008.

[9] A. Gandhi and M. Harchol-Balter. How data center size impacts the effectiveness of dynamic power management. *49th Annual Allerton Conference*, 1164–1169, 2011.

[10] A. Gandhi, M. Harchol-Balter and I.J.B.F. Adan. Server farms with setup costs. *Perform. Eval.*, 67(11):1123–1138, 2010.

[11] Z.J. Haas and S. Gu. On power management policies for data centers. *Proc. IEEE Int. Conf. on Data Science and Data Intensive Systems (DSDIS)*, 404–411, 2015.

[12] W. van Heddeghem, S. Lambert, B. Lannoo, D. Colle, M. Pickavet and P. Demeester. Trends in worldwide ICT electricity consumption from 2007 to 2012. *Computer Communications*, 50:64–76, 2014.

[13] Heterogeneous computing. https://en.wikipedia.org/wiki/Heterogeneous_computing

[14] S. Irani, S.K. Shukla and R.K. Gupta. Online strategies for dynamic power management in systems with multiple power-saving states. *ACM Trans. Embedded Comput. Syst.*, 2(3):325–346, 2003.

[15] A.R. Karlin, C. Kenyon and D. Randall. Dynamic TCP acknowledgment and other stories about e/(e-1). *Algorithmica*, 36(3):209–224, 2003.

[16] A.R. Karlin, M.S. Manasse, L. Rudolph and D.D. Sleator. Competitive snoopy caching. *Algorithmica* 3:77–119, 1988.

[17] S. Khuller, J. Li and B. Saha. Energy efficient scheduling via partial shutdown. *Proc. 21st Annual ACM-SIAM Symposium on Discrete Algorithms*, 1360–1372, 2010.

[18] J. Li and S. Khuller. Generalized machine activation problems. *Proc. 22nd Annual ACM-SIAM Symposium on Discrete Algorithms*, 80–94, 2011.

[19] A. Levi and B. Patt-Shamir. Non-additive two-option ski rental. *Theor. Comput. Sci.*, 584:42–52, 2015.

[20] M. Lin, A. Wierman, L.L.H. Andrew and E. Thereska. Dynamic right-sizing for power-proportional data centers. *IEEE/ACM Trans. Netw.*, 21(5):1378–1391, 2013.

[21] Z. Lotker, B. Patt-Shamir and D. Rawitz. Rent, lease, or buy: Randomized algorithms for multislope ski rental. *SIAM J. Discrete Math.* 26(2):718–736, 2012.

[22] K. Wang, M. Lin, F. Ciucu, A. Wierman and C. Lin. Characterizing the impact of the workload on the value of dynamic resizing in data centers. *Proc. IEEE INFOCOM*, 515–519, 2013.

Asymptotically Optimal Approximation Algorithms for Coflow Scheduling

Hamidreza Jahanjou
Northeastern University
Boston, MA 02115
hamid@ccs.neu.edu

Erez Kantor
Northeastern University
Boston, MA 02115
erezk@ccs.neu.edu

Rajmohan Rajaraman
Northeastern University
Boston, MA 02115
rraj@ccs.neu.edu

ABSTRACT

Many modern datacenter applications involve large-scale computations composed of multiple data flows that need to be completed over a shared set of distributed resources. Such a computation completes when all of its flows complete. A useful abstraction for modeling such scenarios is a *coflow*, which is a collection of flows (e.g., tasks, packets, data transmissions) that all share the same performance goal.

In this paper, we present the first approximation algorithms for scheduling coflows over general network topologies with the objective of minimizing total weighted completion time. We consider two different models for coflows based on the nature of individual flows: circuits, and packets. We design constant-factor polynomial-time approximation algorithms for scheduling packet-based coflows with or without given flow paths, and circuit-based coflows with given flow paths. Furthermore, we give an $O(\log n/\log\log n)$-approximation polynomial time algorithm for scheduling circuit-based coflows without given flow paths (here n is the number of network edges).

We obtain our results by developing a general framework for coflow schedules, based on interval-indexed linear programs, which may extend to other coflow models and objective functions and may also yield improved approximation bounds for specific network scenarios. We also present an experimental evaluation of our approach for circuit-based coflows that show a performance improvement of at least %22 on average over competing heuristics.

1 INTRODUCTION

In modern datacenter network applications, a large-scale computation over a big data set is often composed of multiple tasks or multiple data flows that need to be completed over a shared set of distributed resources. Such a computation completes when all the data flows in the computation complete. A useful abstraction for modeling such scenarios is that of a *coflow* [5], which is a collection of flows (e.g., tasks, packets, data transmissions) that all share the same performance goal. Coflows arise frequently in distributed computing and datacenters [2, 5, 6, 13, 23, 28, 29]. A prominent example is parallel data processing; in certain MapReduce computations, the reduce phase at a particular reducer can begin only after all the relevant data from the map phase has arrived at the reducer [10]. Similar examples occur in Dryad [14], and Spark [27].

In this paper, we study the problem of designing coflow schedules that minimize total weighted completion time. We consider two different models for coflows based on the nature of individual flows: circuits and packets.

- **Circuit-based coflows** a flow is a connection request (data transmission) from source to sink on a network.
- **Packet-based coflows** a flow is a packet that needs to be routed from source to sink on a network.

Before going into formal definitions, Figure 1 illustrates a circuit-based coflow scheduling scenario. Three coflows A, B, and C require bandwidth assignment and scheduling on a triangle network with unit edge capacities. Coflow A consists of two flows A_1 of size 2 and A_2 of size 1 whereas the other two have one flow each of size 1. Three solutions are proposed. In (s1), each flow is given a bandwidth of 1/2; all flows are scheduled to run in parallel. The total completion time is $4 + 2 + 4 = 10$. In (s2), coflow A has the highest priority followed by coflow B and C. The total completion time is $2+2+4 = 8$. But, it is possible to do even better by observing that flow C can run at the same time as either flow A_2 or flow B; this gives rise to an optimal solution, shown in (s3), with a total completion time of $4 + 2 + 1 = 7$.

We now present the models and problem formulations, our main results and techniques, and a review of related work.

1.1 Models and Notation

Regardless of the model, the following notation is used. The set of all flows is denoted by $F = \{f_1, ..., f_n\}$. We define a *coflow* F_i to be a subset $\{f_1^i, ..., f_{n_i}^i\}$ of flows such that the set of all coflows, denoted by $\mathcal{F}$, provides a partition of F. Each flow f_i has a source s_i, a destination d_i, and, depending on the model, a size σ_i. Additionally, each flow has a release time r_i at which point it becomes available. Notice that in our formulation each flow has a release time whereas in previous works, release times are at the level of coflows.

We also have a network modeled as a directed graph $G = (V, E)$ which, in the case of circuit-based coflows, also features edge capacities $\{c(e)\}_{e \in E}$.

The completion time of a flow f_i is denoted by c_i. The completion time C_k of a coflow F_k is defined to be the completion time of its

Supported in part by NSF grants Grant CSR-1217981 and CCF-1422715, and a Google Research Award.

SPAA'17, , July 24–26, 2017, Washington, DC, USA.

ACM ISBN 978-1-4503-4593-4/17/07...$15.00
https://doi.org/10.1145/3087556.3087567

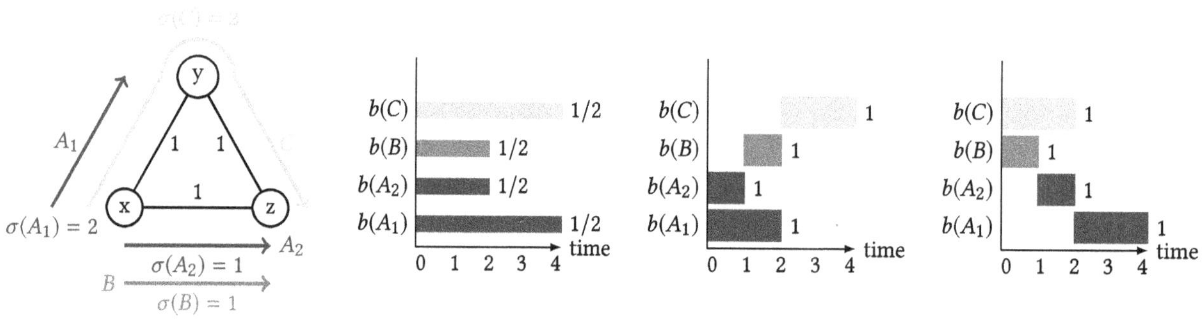

(N) (s1) (s2) (s3)

Figure 1: Three possible bandwidth assignments for the set of coflows $\{A, B, C\}$. Coflow A has two flows (A_1 of size 2 and A_2 of size 1); the other two have each one flow of size 1. The objective is to minimize sum of completion times. (N) The network is a triangle where each edge has unit capacity. Flows are drawn around the edges along with their size. (s1) A bandwidth of 1/2 is assigned to each flow; total completion time is 10. (s2) Priority is given to coflow A then to coflow B and then to coflow C; total completion time is 8. (s3) An optimal solution; total completion time is 7.

last flow; that is,

$$C_k = \max_{f \in F_k} c_f.$$

The goal is to minimize the weighted sum of coflow completion times

$$\overline{C} = \sum_k \omega_k C_k = \sum_k \omega_k \max_{f \in F_k} c_f. \quad (1)$$

Note that if there is only one coflow, the problem reduces to makespan minimization. Similarly, if every coflow has one flow, the problem reduces to minimizing total weighted (flow) completion time. Therefore, in a sense, coflow scheduling bridges two well-studied minimization objectives. In particular, this means that hardness results for either of these problems also hold for coflow scheduling. Below, we consider the particulars of each model.

Circuits. In this model, a flow f_i is a connection request (data transmission) from a source node s_i to a destination node d_i on a network $G = (V, E)$ with edge capacities $\{c(e)\}_{e \in E}$. A coflow is a set of connection requests. To each connection request in F, we need to assign a path p_i (if not given already) and a bandwidth b_i such that $\overline{C}$ is minimized without violating edge capacities. In general, the bandwidth of a connection request is an integrable function of time, $b_i(t)$, and its completion time c_i is defined as the smallest value satisfying

$$\int_0^{c_i} b_i(t)dt = \sigma_i,$$

where σ_i is the size of the connection request.

As we will see, one can assume, without loss of generality, that the bandwidth functions are piece-wise constant. We can further subdivide this problem into two cases: (a) paths are given for each connection request and we only need to assign bandwidths, (b) paths are not given; hence, each connection request requires routing and bandwidth assignment.

Packets. In this case, each flow f_i is a packet residing (at its release time r_i) on its source node s_i waiting to be routed to its destination node $d_i \in V - \{s_i\}$. A coflow is a set of packets. Each link $e \in E$ can serve at most one packet at a time (i.e. edge capacities are set to 1). A coflow F_k completes at time C_k when all of its packets have reached their destination. The goal is to minimize $\overline{C}$.

Model	Paths	Approx.	Hardness
Packet-based	given	$O(1)$	**APX-hard**
	not given		
Circuit-based	given		**NP-hard**
	not given	$O(\frac{\log \lvert E \rvert}{\log\log \lvert E \rvert})$	$\Omega(\frac{\log \lvert E \rvert}{\log\log \lvert E \rvert})$

Table 1: Approximation ratio of our algorithms and corresponding lower bounds for different models.

This model can be seen as a discrete version of circuit-based coflows. As in the previous model, we will consider two subproblems: (a) a path is given for each packet; only scheduling is needed (b) paths are not given; both routing and scheduling are required for each packet.

1.2 Our Results and Techniques

We give asympototically optimal approximation algorithms for minimizing total weighted completion time under the different models defined above.

- We present $O(1)$-approximation algorithms for circuit-based coflows with given paths, packet-based coflows with given paths, and packet-based coflows where paths are not given.
- We present an $O(\log n / \log\log n)$-approximation algorithm for circuit-based coflows where paths are not given.
- We also present an experimental evaluation of our approach for circuit-based coflows which shows %22 or more performance improvement on average over competing heuristics.

Note that, all of the above problems are at least NP-hard. Table 1 summarizes our results.

A noteworthy contribution of our work is a common framework for developing coflow schedules, which applies to all the models we study. The framework consists of three parts. First, we reformulate the coflow scheduling problem as an instance of minimizing total weighted *flow* completion time problem with precedence constraints in form of depth-1 in-trees. Second, we devise an interval-index linear program for each problem instance, and then reduce the problem of finding flow schedules that minimize total weighted completion time (with aforementioned precedences) to multiple instances of the problem of finding flow schedules that minimize makespan. Third, we perform rounding. The specifics of each step varies across models. In particular, the last step is achieved by a careful rounding of the associated linear program solution. Though our approximation bounds are optimal to within constant factors, we have not attempted to optimize these constants. We believe that our framework provides a general approach for solving coflow scheduling problems under diverse models and objectives.

The algorithms given for circuit-based coflows provide the first provable approximation bounds, and apply in the general setting of arbitrary capacitated networks, arbitrary source-sink pairs, arbitrary demands, and arbitrary release times.

To the best of our knowledge, packet-based coflows have not been studied earlier, though related models have been analyzed, as we discuss in previous work.

1.3 Previous Work

Coflows. The notion of coflow was first proposed by Chowdhury and Stoica as *"a networking abstraction to express the communication requirements of prevalent data parallel programming paradigms"* [5, 6]. In [7], Chowdhury et al. present effective heuristics for coflow scheduling without release times on a non-blocking switch network. They also show that coflow scheduling is **NP**-hard for $P \times P$ switches, $P \geq 2$, via a reduction from the concurrent open shop scheduling problem. Approximation algorithms for coflow scheduling on a non-blocking switch with (coflow) release times are given in [15, 23]. Zhao et al. consider coflow scheduling over general network topologies; thereby, routing the flows becomes an additional requirement [29]. They provide heuristics based on the observation that simultaneous routing and scheduling of coflows is required to obtain good performance.

Machine scheduling and task-based coflows. Although coflow scheduling is a relatively recent development, the related problem of scheduling jobs consisting of tasks on parallel machines where a job completes when all of its tasks complete, has been studied before. This model is known in the literature as *order scheduling*; the goal is to minimize the (weighted) sum of job completion times. In their survey, Leung et al., classify order scheduling problems into three categories based on capabilities of the machines [21]. Specifically, in the fully-dedicated case, each machine can process only one type of task. This model, sometimes denoted by $G|| \sum \omega_j C_j$, is also known as the concurrent open shop scheduling since, in contrast to the latter, tasks of a job can be processed at the same time [11]. In the fully-flexible case, all machines can process all types of task. Lastly, in the arbitrary case, unrestricted subsets of machines can process arbitrary subsets of tasks.

Machine scheduling problems are described [12] by three values $\alpha|\beta|\gamma$ where α represents the machine environment, β describes job constraints and γ specifies the objective function to be minimized.

The task-based coflow scheduling model, where a flow is simply a task, corresponds to the fully-flexible case on (unrelated) parallel machines. For this model, Blocher and Chhajed observe that the problem is strongly **NP**-complete even when all machines are identical [4]. Correra, Skutella and Verschae give a 13.5 approximation algorithm for this problem on unrelated machines [9].

Circuit-based coflows. Circuit-based coflow scheduling with fixed paths is a generalization of $1|r_j, pmtn| \sum \omega_j C_j$ which is strongly NP-hard [18]. On the other hand, the version with variable paths is related to congestion minimization. Chuzhoy et al. show that congestion minimization on directed graphs is hard to approximate within $\Omega(\frac{\log |E|}{\log \log |E|})$ unless **NP** has $N^{O(\log \log N)}$-time randomized algorithms [8].

Packet-based coflows. The problem of scheduling packets on store-and-forward networks with given paths is equivalent to the job shop scheduling problem with unit processing times. Leighton, Maggs and Rao [19] show that there exists a schedule achieving a makespan of $O(C+D)$ where C and D denote maximum edge congestion and maximum path dilation respectively. In [20], Leighton et al. give a polynomial-time algorithm for finding such a schedule. Peis et al. [22] show that for all $\epsilon > 0$ there is no $(6/5-\epsilon)$-approximation algorithm for the packet scheduling problem with given paths (minimizing makespan) unless **P** = **NP**. An $O(1)$-approximation algorithm for $J|r_{ij}, p_{ij} = 1| \sum_S C_S$ is given in [24]; the authors consider a generalized minsum objective function.

On the other hand, when paths are not given, Srinvasan and Teo give the first constant-ratio approximation algorithm for packet routing and scheduling to minimize makespan [26]. Koch et al. [16] extend this result to messages which consist of packets having the same source and sink.

The rest of this paper is organized as follows. We study circuit-based coflows in §2 and packet-based coflows in §3. We present experimental results in §4 and conclude in §5.

2 CIRCUIT-BASED COFLOWS

We now consider our main model. In this setting, we have a network $G = (V, E)$ with edge capacities $\{c(e)\}_{e \in E}$. A coflow F_i has a weight $\omega_i \in \mathbb{R}^{\geq 0}$ and consists of a number of connection requests (data transmissions) f_j^i. Each connection request has a source $s_j^i \in V$, a sink $d_j^i \in V$, a release time $r_j^i \in \mathbb{R}^{\geq 0}$ and a size $\sigma_j^i \in \mathbb{R}^{\geq 0}$. A solution must specify a path p_j^i from source to sink (if not given), and a bandwidth function b_j^i for each connection request f_j^i. In general, the bandwidth $b_j^i(t)$ is an integrable function of time such that

$$\int_{r_j^i}^{c_j^i} b_j^i(t)dt = \sigma_j^i, \tag{2}$$

where c_j^i, the completion time of f_j^i, is the smallest value for which the equality holds. In addition, we require that edge capacities are respected. Hence, any solution must satisfy

$$\forall e \in E : \sum_{f_j^i \in P(e)} b_j^i(t) \leq c(e) \tag{3}$$

for all t, where $P(e)$ is the set of paths that use edge e.

There are two natural versions of this problem. In one version, a path p_j^i is given as a part of the input for each connection request f_j^i and we need to assign a bandwidth b_j^i to each request with the goal of minimizing total weighted (coflow) completion time $\overline{C}$ without violating edge capacities. Note that any network topology in which there is a unique path between pairs of vertices, e.g. trees or non-blocking switches, falls into this category. In another version, paths are not given; hence, assigning a (single) path to each connection request becomes an additional requirement.

The rest of this section is organized as follows. First, we present two key lemmas used in deriving our results. Next, in §2.1, we give a 17.6-approximation algorithm for the circuit-based coflow problem with given paths. Finally, in §2.2, an $O(\frac{\log |E|}{\log \log |E|})$-approximation algorithm is presented for the case where paths are not given.

Two lemmas. The following two lemmas are simple but crucial. The first one (Lemma 2.1) states that, without loss of generality, we can assume that bandwidth functions are piece-wise constant.

Lemma 2.1. *Suppose that there exist a capacitated network (G, c) and a set of feasible flows $\{f_1, ..., f_n\}$, where each flow f_i is specified by a triple $(p_i, b_i(t), r_i)$ consisting of its path, bandwidth, and release time. Given two time points $T_1 < T_2$ such that $r_i \le T_1$ for all $i \in [n]$, there exists a set of feasible constant bandwidths $\{b_i'\}_{1\le i\le n}$ with the same delivery amount over the time interval $[T_1, T_2]$.*

Proof. Let σ_i denote the amount of flow delivered on path p_i; that is, $\sigma_i = \int_{T_1}^{T_2} b_i(t)dt$. Define new bandwidths $b_i' = \sigma_i/(T_2 - T_1)$. Clearly, the volume delivered remains the same and release times are respected. Moreover, for any edge e, the sum of flow bandwidths passing through e satisfies $\sum_{i\in P(e)} b_i' \le c(e)$, where $P(e)$ is the set of paths that use e. Indeed, assume that there exists an edge e' for which $\sum_{i\in P(e')} b_i' > c(e')$. Then, it follows that

$$\sum_{i\in P(e')} b_i' = \sum_{i\in P(e')} \sigma_i/(T_2 - T_1) > c(e')$$
$$\Rightarrow \sum_{i\in P(e')} \frac{\int_{T_1}^{T_2} b_i(t)dt}{T_2 - T_1} > c(e')$$
$$\Rightarrow \sum_{i\in P(e')} \int_{T_1}^{T_2} b_i(t)dt > (T_2 - T_1)c(e')$$

which is a contradiction since the total volume delivered can not be more than $(T_2 - T_1)c(e')$. □

The second lemma (Lemma 2.2) shows that it is possible to *discretize* the bandwidth usage.

Lemma 2.2. *Suppose that there exist a capacitated network (G, c), a path p, and a set of feasible flows $\{f_1, ..., f_n\}$ over the path, where each flow f_i has a bandwidth $b_i(t)$ and a release time r_i. Given two time points $T_1 < T_2$ such that $r_i \le T_1$ for all $i \in [n]$, there exists a set of feasible bandwidths $\{b_i''\}_{1\le i\le n}$ such that at any point in time $t \in [T_1, T_2]$, there is at most one active flow (i.e. with non-zero bandwidth). Furthermore, for every flow, the delivery amount over the time interval $[T_1, T_2]$ is as before.*

Proof. Let $c_m = \min_{e\in p} c(e)$ denote the minimum edge capacity of the path. Also, let σ_i denote the volume corresponding to b_i delivered over the time interval; that is, $\sigma_i = \int_{T_1}^{T_2} b_i(t)dt$.

The idea is to assign full bandwidth to flows one at a time. Set $t_0 = 0$ and $t_i = \sum_{k=0}^{i} \frac{\sigma_k}{c_m}$, for $i \in [n]$. Define the new bandwidths as follows. For $i \in [n]$,

$$b_i''(t) = \begin{cases} c_m, & \text{if } t \in (T_1 + t_{i-1}, T_1 + t_i] \\ 0, & \text{otherwise} \end{cases}$$

It is obvious that $b_i''(t)$ is feasible and can be non-zero only in the interval $(T_1 + t_{i-1}, T_1 + t_i]$. Furthermore, this schedule does not require any additional time. Indeed,

$$t_n = \sum_{k=0}^{i} \frac{\sigma_k}{c_m} = \sum_{k=0}^{i} \frac{\int_{T_1}^{T_2} b_i(t)dt}{c_m}$$
$$= \int_{T_1}^{T_2} \sum_{k=0}^{i} \frac{b_i(t)}{c_m} dt \le \int_{T_1}^{T_2} dt = T_2 - T_1.$$

□

2.1 Paths Are Given

In this setting, each connection request comes with a path. We give a 17.6-approximation algorithm for this problem. We begin with an observation.

Observation 2.3. *The circuit-based coflow scheduling with given paths is strongly* **NP***-complete.*

This follows directly from the **NP**-completeness of the scheduling problem $1|pmtn, r_i| \sum \omega_i c_i$ which seeks to minimize total weighted completion time on a single machine with preemption and release times [18]. Indeed, given an instance of the scheduling problem, consider a single edge $e: s \longrightarrow t$ such that every job j with a processing time of p_j corresponds to a coflow consisting of just one flow of size $\sigma_j = p_j$ from s to t and with the corresponding release time. Now, Lemma 2.2 states that we can turn a solution returned by solving the circuit-based coflow problem into a preemptive schedule: simply determine the order of release and completion times on the time line and apply the lemma to each interval.

We follow our general framework for coflow scheduling. In order to get the best approximation ratio, we optimize over some parameters such as interval length.

Reformulation. We transform the problem of minimizing total weighted coflow completion time to an instance of minimizing total weighted flow completion time. To capture completion times at the level of coflows, we (a) introduce a dummy flow f_0^i in each coflow F_i, and (b) assign new weights ω_{ij}' to each flow. In more detail, the dummy flow comes with precedence constraints from $f_j^i, j \ne 0$ to f_0^i, requiring that in each coflow, f_0^i finishes last. In effect, the precedence graph is a forest of n depth-1 in-trees. We set the weight to ω_i for the dummy flow f_0^i (i.e. $\omega_{i0}' = \omega_i$) and to zero for all other flows (i.e. $\omega_{ij}' = 0, j \ne 0$). Finally, note that dummy flows do not have source, destination or size but are required to finish no sooner than other flows in the same coflow. Now, the new objective function to be minimized is $\sum_i \sum_j \omega_{ij}' c_j^i$.

The linear program. In this step, we devise an interval-indexed linear program. The time line is divided into segments $[0, 1], (1, 1+\epsilon]$,

$(1+\epsilon, (1+\epsilon)^2], \dots, (\tau_\ell, \tau_{\ell+1}]$ for $\ell \in \{0, 1, \dots, L\}$, where $\tau_\ell = (1+\epsilon)^{\ell-1}$, $\tau_0 = 0$, $\epsilon > 0$ will be determined later, and L is a sufficiently large integer.

In the linear program below, $x^i_{j\ell}$ is the portion of connection request f^i_j completed in the ℓth interval $(\tau_\ell, \tau_{\ell+1}]$ and $b^i_{j\ell}$ is the bandwidth of p^i_j (i.e. f^i_j's path) during the ℓth interval. Notice that release times are assumed to occur at the start of intervals; we show that this restriction costs us no more than a factor of $1 + \epsilon$. Constraints (6) ensure that the dummy connection request finishes last in each coflow. Constraints (7) calculate the bandwidth of each path p^i_j for every time interval (which is the fraction of flow size delivered, divided by interval length). Constraints (8) ensure that no capacity violation occurs; note that $P(e)$ denotes the set of connection requests whose paths use edge e. Finally, constraints (9) ensure that release times are respected.

$$\text{Minimize } \sum_i \sum_j \omega'_{ij} c^i_j \qquad \textit{subject to}$$

$$\sum_\ell x^i_{j\ell} = 1 \qquad \forall i, j \qquad (4)$$

$$\sum_{\ell \le L} \tau_\ell x^i_{j\ell} \le c^i_j \qquad \forall i, j \qquad (5)$$

$$c^i_j \le c^i_0 \qquad \forall i, j \qquad (6)$$

$$b^i_{j\ell} = \sigma^i_j x^i_{j\ell} / \tau_\ell \qquad \forall i, j, \ell \qquad (7)$$

$$\sum_{f^i_j \in P(e)} b^i_{j\ell} \le c(e) \qquad \forall \ell, e \qquad (8)$$

$$r^i_j > \tau_{\ell+1} \Rightarrow x^i_{j\ell} = 0 \qquad \forall i, \ell \qquad (9)$$

$$x^i_{j\ell} \ge 0 \qquad \forall i, j, \ell, e \qquad (10)$$

Lemma 2.4. *$\frac{1}{1+\epsilon}$ times the optimal value of the above linear program is a lower bound on the weighted sum of completion times for circuit-based coflows with paths and release times.*

Proof. Consider a schedule $\langle p^i_j, b^i_j(t) \rangle$ achieving average coflow completion time $\hat{C}$. We show that it corresponds to a feasible solution to the linear program with an objective value $\le (1+\epsilon)\hat{C}$. Start by setting the variables $x^i_{j\ell}$ for each connection request f^i_j according to the interval in which they finish. Next, note that release times are arbitrary; hence, a connection request may arrive in the middle of an interval. On the other hand, constraints (7) require constant bandwidth in each interval. To remedy this, move all release times to the end of the interval in which they occur and update $x^i_{j\ell}$ if necessary; this clearly increases $\hat{C}$ by no more than a factor of $1 + \epsilon$.

Finally, for each interval $(\tau_\ell, \tau_{\ell+1}]$, apply Lemma 2.1 to get constant bandwidth for each connection request. More precisely, we set

$$b^i_{j\ell} = \frac{\int_{\tau_\ell}^{\tau_{\ell+1}} b^i_j(t)dt}{\tau_\ell}$$

for each f^i_j. Clearly, constraints (7) are satisfied; furthermore, the lemma ensures that constraints (8) stay satisfied as well. This setting of variables satisfies all the remaining constraints as well. □

Rounding. The next step after solving the linear program is to construct a schedule. Let $\{\hat{x}^i_{j\ell}\}_{ij\ell}$ denote an optimal solution to the LP. Set $\hat{b}^i_{j\ell}$ according to equation (7). For some $0 < \alpha \le 1$, define the α-interval h^α_{ij} of a connection request f^i_j to be the interval $(\tau_{h^\alpha_{ij}}, \tau_{h^\alpha_{ij}+1}]$ which contains the earliest point in time that a cumulative α-fraction of the connection request has been completed; that is

$$h^\alpha_{ij} = \min \left\{ \ell : \sum_{t=0}^{\ell} x^i_{jt} \ge \alpha \right\}.$$

The exact value of α will be determined later.

In the schedule, each connection request f^i_j will run entirely in $(\tau_{h^\alpha_{ij}+D}, \tau_{h^\alpha_{ij}+D+1}]$–that is, the Dth interval after its α-interval. The parameter $D \in \mathbb{N}$, the *displacement factor*, will be determined later. Note that the length of this interval is $(1+\epsilon)^{D-1}$ times the cumulative length of intervals from the beginning to the end of the α-interval.

Fix a k. Let $S[k]$ denote the set of connection requests scheduled to run in $(\tau_k, \tau_{k+1}]$. Clearly, the α-interval of all these connection requests is $k - D$. Consider a connection request $f^i_j \in S[k]$. According to the optimal solution obtained by solving the LP, its bandwidth function is

$$\hat{b}^i_j(t) = \begin{cases} \hat{b}^i_{j0}, & \text{if } t \in [0, 1], \\ \hat{b}^i_{j1}, & \text{if } t \in (\tau_1, \tau_2], \\ \vdots & \vdots \\ \hat{b}^i_{jk}, & \text{if } t \in (\tau_{k-D}, \tau_{k-D+1}]. \end{cases}$$

We now define a new constant bandwidth

$$\tilde{b}^i_j = \sum_{\ell=0}^{\ell=k-D} \frac{\alpha^{-1} \hat{b}^i_{j\ell} \tau_\ell}{\tau_k} = \sum_{\ell=0}^{\ell=k-D} \frac{\alpha^{-1} \hat{b}^i_{j\ell}}{(1+\epsilon)^{k-\ell}}. \qquad (11)$$

Observe that we have scaled and added up each bandwidth value depending on how far its interval is from the kth interval. For each connection request in $S[k]$, at least an α fraction of its size σ^i_j was delivered by the end of the α-interval. But now, with the new bandwidth, the entire flow is delivered over the stretched time line. More precisely,

$$\forall f^i_j \in S[k] : \int_0^{\tau_{h^\alpha_{ij}+1}} \hat{b}^i_j(t)dt = \int_0^{\tau_{k-D+1}} \hat{b}^i_j(t)dt = \alpha \tilde{b}^i_j \tau_k.$$

This also means that the new bandwidth and the displacement factor have to satisfy

$$D \ge \left\lceil \log_{1+\epsilon} \frac{1}{\alpha} \right\rceil + 1. \qquad (12)$$

Furthermore, we must ensure that no capacity violation occurs. In the schedule, for every k and for every edge e,

$$\begin{aligned}\sum_{f_j^i \in P(e)} \tilde{b}_j^i &= \sum_{f_j^i \in P(e)} \sum_{\ell=0}^{\ell=k-D} \frac{\alpha^{-1}\hat{b}^i_{j\ell}}{(1+\epsilon)^{k-\ell}} \\ &= \sum_{\ell=0}^{\ell=k-D} \frac{\alpha^{-1}}{(1+\epsilon)^{k-\ell}} \sum_{f_j^i \in P(e)} \hat{b}^i_{j\ell} \\ &\le c(e) \sum_{\ell=0}^{\ell=k-D} \frac{\alpha^{-1}}{(1+\epsilon)^{k-\ell}},\end{aligned}$$

where the inequality follows from constraints (8). Thus, we require that $\sum_{\ell=0}^{\ell=k-D} \frac{\alpha^{-1}}{(1+\epsilon)^{k-\ell}} \le 1$, for all k. Hence,

$$\frac{1}{\epsilon(1+\epsilon)^{D-1}} \le \alpha. \tag{13}$$

Finally, note that the blow up factor in completion time for each connection request in $S[k]$, taking into account the $(1+\epsilon)$-factor loss in the LP, is at most

$$\frac{(1+\epsilon)\tau_{k+1}}{(1-\alpha)\tau_{k-D}} = \frac{(1+\epsilon)^{D+2}}{1-\alpha}. \tag{14}$$

Numerically minimizing (14) subject to (13) and displacement factor constraint (12), we get an approximation factor of 17.5319 for $\alpha = 0.5$, $D = 3$, and $\epsilon \approx 0.5436$.

2.2 Paths Are Not Given

In this section, we consider circuit-based coflow scheduling when paths are not given. Our $O(\frac{\log|E|}{\log\log|E|})$ approximation ratio for this case is asymptotically tight since an $\Omega(\frac{\log|E|}{\log\log|E|})$ hardness follows from hardness of congestion minimization on directed graphs [8]. Recall that, in the congestion minimization problem, given a directed graph and source-sink pairs, the goal is to connect each pair by a path such that congestion, the maximum number of paths crossing an edge, is minimized. But, regarding the source-sink pairs as connection requests of unit size in a single coflow, the congestion is equivalent to makespan, where all edge capacities are set to 1. So, essentially, congestion minimization can be seen as a special case of our problem. We now go over our algorithm.

Algorithm 1: CIRCUIT-BASED COFLOW SCHEDULING

```
input  : Coflows 𝓕, Network (G, c)
Construct the LP 𝓛;
Solve 𝓛; perform rounding and scaling to get flow values x_e^f
    and completion times c_f;
foreach flow f ∈ 𝓕 do
    PathSet[f] = FlowDecomposition(f);
    Path[f] = Rounding(PathSet[f]);
end
return : Flow paths and ordering based on c_f
```

Reformulation. Identical to §2.1.

The linear program. The linear program is similar to §2.1, where we have set $\epsilon = 1$. Notice that constraints (18)-(21) are the usual flow constraints per time interval.

$$\text{Minimize} \sum_i \sum_j \omega'_{ij} c^i_j \qquad \textit{subject to}$$

$$\sum_{\ell} x^i_{j\ell} = 1 \qquad \forall i,j \tag{15}$$

$$\sum_{\ell \le L} \tau_\ell x^i_{j\ell} \le c^i_j \qquad \forall i,j \tag{16}$$

$$c^i_j \le c^i_0 \qquad \forall i,j \tag{17}$$

$$\sum_{\substack{e\in N(v)\\ v\notin\{s^i_j, d^i_j\}}} x^e_{ij\ell} = 0 \qquad \forall i,j,\ell \tag{18}$$

$$\sum_{e\in N(d^i_j)} x^e_{ij\ell} = \sigma^i_j x^i_{j\ell}/\tau_\ell \qquad \forall i,j,\ell \tag{19}$$

$$\sum_{e\in N(s^i_j)} x^e_{ij\ell} = -\sum_{e\in N(d^i_j)} x^e_{ij\ell} \qquad \forall i,j,\ell \tag{20}$$

$$\sum_i \sum_j x^e_{ij\ell} \le c(e) \qquad \forall \ell, e \tag{21}$$

$$r^i_j > \tau_{\ell+1} \Rightarrow x^i_{j\ell} = 0 \qquad \forall i,j,\ell \tag{22}$$

$$x^e_{ij\ell}, x^i_{j\ell} \ge 0 \qquad \forall i,j,\ell,e \tag{23}$$

Next, we show that the optimal value of the linear program gives us a relaxed lower bound.

LEMMA 2.5. *Half the optimal value of the above linear program provides a lower bound on the weighted sum of completion times for circuit-based coflows with release times.*

PROOF. Following the proof of Lemma 2.4, move release times if necessary, set the variables $x^i_{j\ell}$ and calculate bandwidths per interval. Next, set the value of flow variables $x^e_{ij\ell}$ based on the paths p^i_j and the calculated bandwidths. This setting of variables satisfies all constraints. □

Rounding. This step involves scaling followed by flow decomposition and randomized rounding. Let $\langle \hat{x}^e_{ij\ell}, \hat{x}^i_\ell \rangle$ denote an optimal solution to the LP. Analogous to the previous case in §2.1, define the half interval h^i_j of each connection request f^i_j. All connection requests whose half interval is H will be scheduled to run entirely in interval $(\tau_{H+3}, \tau_{H+4}]$. In analogy with §2.1, set $\alpha = \frac{1}{2}$ and $D = 3$. Now, fix a k and let $S[k]$ denote the set of connection requests scheduled to run in $(\tau_k, \tau_{k+1}]$. Perform scaling and adding up of flows for every edge to get updated flow variables

$$\tilde{x}^e_{ij} = \sum_{\ell=0}^{\ell=k-3} \frac{\hat{x}^e_{ij\ell}}{2^{k-\ell-1}}. \tag{24}$$

The calculations in §2.1 apply here as well (where we use inequalities (21) instead of (8)). Hence, the entire size of every connection request is delivered in the new settings and all edge capacities are respected. The next step is to apply the well-known flow decomposition theorem (see e.g. [1]) to the flow variables $\tilde{x}^e_{ij}$ to get a set of flow paths $P_{ij} = \{p_j^i\}$ from s_j^i to d_j^i for each connection request $f_j^i \in S[k]$.

At this point, after computing the flow paths, we have for each k a set of connection requests $S[k]$ expressed in terms of flow paths. Unfortunately, this is not enough since each connection request must have exactly one path from source to sink. What we have, instead, is a *set* of flow paths $P_{ij} = \{p_{j1}^i, ..., p_{jn_{ij}}^i\}$ for each connection request f_j^i. This brings us to the final step.

Let b_j^i denote the total amount of flow in P_{ij};

$$b_j^i = \sum_{k \in [n_{ij}]} |p_{jk}^i|.$$

We apply the randomized rounding technique of Raghavan and Thompson [25] to choose a single path from P_{ij}: we randomly choose a flow path from P_{ij} where the probability of p_{jk}^i being selected is $|p_{jk}^i|/b_j^i$. All of the flow in P_{ij} will go over the chosen path. Let $\bar{b}_e$ denote the total flow passing through e after the rounding. Using a Chernoff-Hoeffding bound, we can show that for every $e \in E$ and every $\delta > 0$:

$$\Pr\left[\bar{b}_e \geq (1+\delta)c(e)\right] \leq \left(\frac{\mathrm{e}^{\delta}}{(1+\delta)^{1+\delta}}\right)^{c(e)/|E|}.$$

Hence,

$$\begin{aligned}\Pr\left[\max_e \frac{\bar{b}_e}{c(e)} \geq (1+\delta)\right] &\leq \sum_e \Pr\left[\frac{\bar{b}_e}{c(e)} \geq (1+\delta)\right] \\ &\leq \sum_e \left(\frac{\mathrm{e}^{\delta}}{(1+\delta)^{1+\delta}}\right)^{c(e)/|E|} \\ &\leq |E|\left(\frac{\mathrm{e}^{\delta}}{(1+\delta)^{1+\delta}}\right)^{(\min_e c(e))/|E|}.\end{aligned}$$

If we set $\delta = O(\frac{\log|E|}{\log\log|E|})$, we obtain that the bandwidth used exceeds the capacity of any edge by at most $O(\frac{\log|E|}{\log\log|E|})$ with probability at most $1/n^c$ for some constant $c > 0$. Consequently, by scaling down the bandwidth allocated by $1+\delta$, and scaling up in time by the same factor, we obtain a feasible set of connection requests with a blowup in completion times at most $O(\frac{\log|E|}{\log\log|E|})$.

3 PACKET-BASED COFLOWS

In this model, a flow corresponds to a *single* packet (flow size is 1) and a coflow is a collection of packets. The schedule is based on discrete time steps. During a step, each packet can either stay at a node (in a queue) or move along an edge with the restriction that at most one packet can use the edge at a time. In §3.1, we observe that when paths are given, we can apply known results for job shop scheduling. Next, in §3.2, we consider the case where paths are not given. We present an $O(1)$-approximation algorithm for this case.

3.1 Paths Are Given

When a path p_j^i is given for each packet f_j^i, the only remaining problem is scheduling. It is well-known that the problem of scheduling packets on a store-and-forward network with fixed paths is an instance of job-shop scheduling. Specifically, each packet f_j^i can be regarded as a job which needs to be executed on a number of machines (edges) in a prescribed order (given by p_j^i) such that a machine can process one job at a time. Consequently, the packet-based coflow problem with given paths, is an instance of shop scheduling $J|r_j, p_{ij} = 1|\sum_S \omega_S C_S$ with unit processing times and a *generalized* min-sum objective; hence, the algorithm of [24] immediately gives an $O(1)$-approximation.

THEOREM 3.1 ([24]). *There exists a polynomial-time $O(1)$ approximation algorithm for the (generalized) min-sum job-shop problem $J(P)|r_j, p_{ij} = 1|\sum_j \omega_j C_j$.*

3.2 Paths Are Not Given

This is the more general case where one needs to both route and schedule packets. We give a polynomial-time $O(1)$-approximation algorithm for this problem.

An ingredient in our solution is the notion of *time-expanded graphs* first introduced by Ford and Fulkerson [17]. In more detail, given a (directed) graph $G = (V, E)$ and n coflows $\{F_i = \{f_1^i, ..., f_{n_i}^i\}\}_{i \in [n]}$, we construct a time-expanded graph G^T as follows. Each node in the time-expanded graph is labeled by a tuple (v, t) where v is a node in G and $0 \leq t \leq T$ is the timestamp. Therefore, the edge set of G^T is

$$\begin{aligned}E(G^T) = &\{((u,t),(v,t+1)) : (u,v) \in E(G),\ 0 \leq t \leq T-1\} \\ &\cup \{((v,t),(v,t+1)) : v \in V(G),\ 0 \leq t \leq T-1\}\end{aligned}$$

where the second group of edges are called queue edges and their role is to simulate packets waiting for one or more rounds at a node. Let us denote by E' the set $E(G^T)$ excluding the queue edges.

The overall idea of the algorithm is as follows. By a net-flow we mean a network flow in the ordinary sense. We express each packet as multiple net-flows to the packet's destination in different times in G^T; this will become clear shortly. The remaining steps involve writing an interval-indexed linear program, assigning packets to intervals, and performing routing and scheduling packets for each interval.

Reformulation. Consider a packet $f_j^i \in F_i$ to be routed from s_j^i to d_j^i in G. Corresponding to this packet, we send a set of net-flows f_{ij}^t in G^T: net-flow f_{ij}^t has node (s_j^i, r_j^i) as source (demand is -1) and node (d_j^i, t) as destination where $t \in \{r_i + 1, ..., T\}$ and sum of demands of these nodes is 1 (the exact values will be determined by solving the linear program below). Also, we set T to a sufficiently large integer (say $|E| \sum_{i \in [n]} n_i$). As before, we introduce dummy flows f_0^i and update weights ω'_{ij} accordingly.

The linear program. Let $T' = \log T$, $\tau_0 = 1$ and $\tau_\ell = 2^{\ell-1}$ for $\ell \in [T']$. Let c_j^i denote the earliest time when a net-flow f_{ij}^t in G^T reaches its destination; that is $c_j^i = \min_t c_{ij}^t$ where c_{ij}^t is the completion time of f_{ij}^t. Variables $x_e^{f_{ij}^t}$ denote the amount of flow corresponding to f_{ij}^t over edge $e \in E(G^T)$. In constraints (25), $f_{ij\ell}$ is the total amount of flow, corresponding to net-flows f_{ij}^t, that enter their destination nodes (d_j^i, t) for $t \in (\tau_\ell, \tau_{\ell+1}]$. By $E((d_{ij}, t))$ we mean the set of incoming edges to (d_{ij}, t) in constraints (25). Moreover, b_{ij}^t is the demand of node (d_j^i, t) and $\mathcal{N}^{f_{ij}^t} x^{f_{ij}^t} = b^{f_{ij}^t}$ specify the obvious requirements of sending a net-flow of size b_{ij}^t

from (s^i_j, r_i) to (d^i_j, t) for $r_i \le t \le T$, as well as flow conservation at nodes other than source and sink.

$$\text{Minimize} \sum_{i\in[n]}\sum_{j=0}^{n_i} \omega'_{ij} c^i_j \qquad \textit{subject to}$$

$$\sum_{\tau_\ell < t \le \tau_{\ell+1}} \sum_{e\in E((d_{ij},t))} x_e^{f^t_{ij}} = f_{ij\ell} \qquad \forall i,j,\ell \qquad (25)$$

$$\sum_{\ell\le T'} \tau_\ell f_{ij\ell} \le c_{ij} \qquad \forall i,j \qquad (26)$$

$$c_{ij} \le c_{i0} \qquad \forall i,j \qquad (27)$$

$$\sum_{i\in[n]}\sum_{j=0}^{n_i}\sum_{t\le\tau_{\ell+1}} x_e^{f^t_{ij}} \le \tau_{\ell+1} \qquad \forall \ell, e \qquad (28)$$

$$\sum_{e\in E'}\sum_{t\le\tau_{\ell+1}} x_e^{f^t_{ij}} \le \tau_{\ell+1} \qquad \forall i,j,\ell \qquad (29)$$

$$\sum_{t\in T} b^t_{ij} = 1 \qquad \forall i,j \qquad (30)$$

$$\mathcal{N}^{f^t_{ij}} x^{f^t_{ij}} = b^{f^t_{ij}} \qquad \forall i,j \qquad (31)$$

$$0 \le x_e^{f^t_{ij}} \le 1 \qquad \forall i,j,t,e \qquad (32)$$

Constraints (28) and (29) restrict respectively the congestion and dilation of packets which reach their destination in interval $[0, \tau_{\ell+1}]$. As can be seen, queue edges don't contribute to path dilation.

LEMMA 3.2. *The optimal value of the linear program (25)-(32) with weights $\omega'_{i0} = \omega_i$ and $\omega'_{ij} = 0, j \ne 0$, is a lower bound on the optimal weighted sum of packet-based coflow completion times.*

PROOF. Given a set $S = \langle \{p^i_j\}, \{q^i_j\} \rangle_{i\in[n], j\in[n_i]}$ of paths $\{p^i_j\}$ and schedules $\{q^i_j\}$, we show that S constitutes a feasible solution to the LP. Without loss of generality, let g denote the maximum amount of time any packet has to wait in the schedule; the existence of $g \in O(1)$ follows from [19] (note that g is the maximum queue size.) Each packet f^i_j is routed, on a path of length $|p^i_j|$, from $s^i_j \in V$ to $d^i_j \in V$ according to the schedule $\{q^i_j\}$ which specifies the amount of time $\in [0, g]$ the packet has to wait before crossing the next edge on its path. Let T^i_j denote the time step when f^i_j reaches its sink. Furthermore, we define $T = \max_{ij} T^i_j$.

For each packet f^i_j, we construct an integral flow $f^{T_{ij}}_{ij}$ in the time-expanded graph G^T. Consider a packet f^i_j with release time r^i_j in G going from s^i_j to d^i_j on a path specified by p^i_j according to the schedule q^i_j and arriving at time T^i_j. The corresponding flow, $f^{T_{ij}}_{ij}$, in G^T from (s^i_j, r^i_j) to (d^i_j, T^i_j) is constructed in steps. We keep a current time step t which is initially set to r^i_j. For each edge $e = (u, v)$ on the path p^i_j, starting from s^i_j, the flow f^i_j follows the edge(s)

$$((u,t),(u,t+1)) \longrightarrow \cdots \longrightarrow ((u,t+h),(v,t+h+1)),$$

in G^T where h is the delay specified by q^i_j before crossing the edge. Next, we update $t \leftarrow t+1$ and repeat until we reach d^i_j. Clearly, T^i_j is the sum of the path length $|p^i_j|$ and total amount of delay prescribed by the schedule q^i_j.

It follows from the construction that constraints (31) are satisfied. Furthermore, since the schedule does not allow more than one packet to cross an edge at the same time, the path followed by a flow is exclusive to that flow except, possibly, the edges $((u,t),(u,t+1))$ which effectively simulate queues. At this point, we can set the value of variables $x_e^{f^t_{ij}}$ according to the flow $f^{T^i_j}_{ij}$. We also set $c^i_j = T^i_j$ and $c^i_0 = \max_{j\in[n_i]} c^i_j$. It is easy to verify that constraints (25)-(27) are satisfied. Regarding congestion constraints (28), observe that, for all ℓ, packets that have reached their destination by time $\tau_{\ell+1}$, can not cause an edge to have a congestion value more than $\tau_{\ell+1}$. The same argument applies to dilation constraints (29). □

Rounding. At a high-level, this step consists of two parts (a) Assign the packets to time intervals; (b) Route and schedule packets in each interval by applying the algorithm of Srinivasan and Teo [26].

Let $\hat{S} = \langle \hat{x}_e^{f^t_{ij}}, \hat{f}_{ij\ell}, \hat{c}^i_j \rangle$ denote an optimal solution to the LP (25)-(32). We start by filtering the solution and assigning packets to intervals. Specifically, define the half-interval of a packet f^i_j to be the interval $(\tau_{h^i_j}, \tau_{h^i_j+1}]$ such that $h^i_j = \min\{\ell : \sum_{t<\ell} \hat{f}_{ijt} \ge \frac{1}{2}\}$; then, set

$$\bar{f}_{ij\ell} = \begin{cases} \hat{f}_{ij\ell}/(1 - \sum_{t\ge\ell} \hat{f}_{ijt}), & \text{if } \tau_{\ell+1} \le h^i_j, \\ 0, & \text{if } \tau_{\ell+1} \ge h^i_j. \end{cases}$$

Also, set the other variables $\bar{x}_e^{f^t_{ij}}$ and $\bar{c}^i_j$ according to (25) and (26) respectively. Clearly, the blowup in each variable and the right hand side of (28)-(29) is at most 2.

Next, we assign each packet f^i_j to its half-interval. Let $P[\ell]$ denote the set of packets that have been assigned to the interval $(\tau_\ell, \tau_{\ell+1}]$. At this stage, we go over all time intervals sequentially and, for each one, route and schedule all packets in it. Fix an ℓ and consider all packets $f^i_j \in P[\ell]$. Collapse the portion of the time-expanded graph G^T, corresponding to the times $t \le \tau_{\ell+1}$, back to G by combining nodes and edges which differ only in time stamp and by removing queue edges altogether.

Observe that the removal of queue edges will not cause any problem since any amount of flow passing through them will have left the queue by the end of the last interval. Now, the filtered solution $\bar{S} = \langle \bar{x}_e^{f^t_{ij}}, \bar{f}_{ij\ell}, \bar{c}^i_j \rangle$ satisfies

$$\sum_{i,j: f^i_j \in F[\ell]} x_e^{f_{ij}} \le \tau_{\ell+2} \qquad \forall e \in E \qquad (33)$$

$$\sum_{e\in E} x_e^{f_{ij}} \le \tau_{\ell+2} \qquad \forall f^i_j \in P[\ell] \qquad (34)$$

$$\bar{\mathcal{N}}^{f_{ij}} x^{f_{ij}} = \bar{b}^{f_{ij}} \qquad \forall f^i_j \in P[\ell] \qquad (35)$$

$$0 \le x_e^{f_{ij}} \le 1 \qquad \forall f^i_j \in P[\ell]\ \forall e \in E \qquad (36)$$

where the constraints $\bar{\mathcal{N}}^{f_{ij}} x^{f_{ij}} = \bar{b}^{f_{ij}}$ express the flow requirements in the collapsed graph. Formally,

Lemma 3.3. *For every $\ell \in [T']$, the set of flows $\bar{x}_e^{f_{ij}}$ corresponding to packets f_j^i in $P[\ell]$ satisfy the LP in (33)-(36) with respect to the (collapsed) graph G.*

This LP is exactly the one considered in [26] and by applying their theorem, we can route and schedule all packets in $P[\ell]$ such that the last packet arrives in time $O(\tau_{\ell+2})$.

Theorem 3.4 ([26]). *There are constants $c', c'' > 0$ such that the following holds. For any packet routing problem on any network, there is a set of paths and a corresponding schedule that can be constructed in polynomial time such that the routing time is at most c' times the optimal, and the maximum queue size at each edge is bounded by c''.*

We do this for $P[1]$, $P[2]$ and so on. Note that the coflow release times are respected. The optimal completion time of a packet $f_j^i \in P[\ell]$ in the LP (25)-(32) is $\hat{c}_j^i = O(\tau_{\ell+1})$. On the other hand, the completion time of the same packet in our algorithm is

$$\tilde{c}_j^i = \sum_{t \leq \ell} O(\tau_{t+1}) = \sum_{t \leq \ell} O(2^t) = O(2^\ell) = O(\tau_{\ell+1}). \quad (37)$$

Consequently, the weighted completion time of our algorithm is within a $O(1)$ factor of the optimal solution.

4 EXPERIMENTS

In this section, we describe some experiments conducted to evaluate the practical performance of our circuit-based algorithm in §2.2.

4.1 Methodology

We use a simulator to assess the performance of our algorithm in practice. Packet-level simulators are not suitable for this setting due to their high level of overhead [3, 29]. Therefore, like previous works [3, 7, 29], we developed a flow-based simulator. At a high level, the simulator is an event queue. Each flow corresponds to an event which happens at its release time. The simulator chooses the next flow based on the ordering prescribed by a scheduling algorithm or scheme. A second event occurs when a flow completes; at which time, its reserved bandwidth is released.

We use a 128-server Fat-Tree with 1Gbs links as the network topology. Due to the complexity of the linear program to be solved, simulations of large instances were prohibitively slow. Each coflow instance is randomly generated with flow release times, flow sizes, and coflow weights based on Poisson distributions. Each result is the average of 10 tries.

4.2 Implementation

We implement Algorithm 1 in §2.2 with some minor tweaks. In particular, to avoid wasting time and bandwidth, each flow starts as soon as it can (in the order prescribed by the linear program), as opposed to starting at the beginning of its half-interval.

The path decomposition algorithm tries to minimize the number of paths per flow by finding the "thickest" paths; this is done using a well-known version of Dijkstra's shortest-path algorithm. We implemented the above algorithm in C++ using Lemon libraries and IBM CPLEX 12.6.3. to solve the linear program.

4.3 Performance

We measure the weighted sum of completion times. As in [29], we compare our algorithm to the following schemes.

- Baseline: flows are routed and ordered randomly.
- Schedule-only: flows are routed randomly; ordering is by minimum completion time which is computed as the ratio of flow size to path bandwidth.
- Route-only: flows are routed for achieving good load balance and edge utilization; ordering is arbitrary.

We investigate the impact of two parameters. First is the number of flows in each coflow, which we refer to as *coflow width*. Second is the number of coflows.

Coflow width. In this case, we fix the number of coflows to 10 and run experiments for coflow widths in $\{4, 8, 16, 32\}$. As illustrated in Figure 2, LP-Based completes *every instance* faster than the baseline, Schedule-only, and Route-only schedules. On average, the improvement over the baseline, Schedule-only and Route-only is by %126, %96, and %22, respectively.

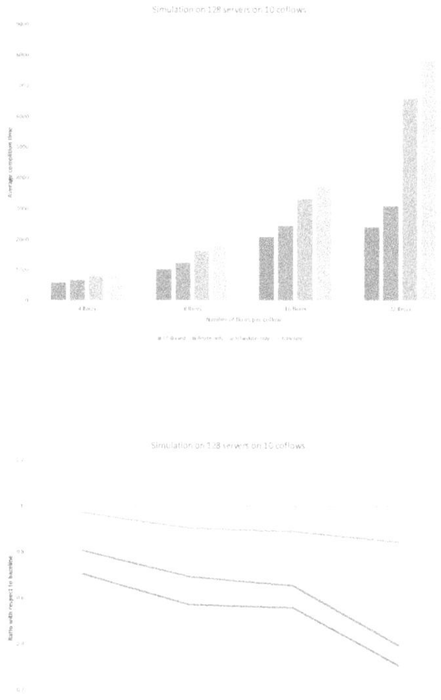

Figure 2: Changing the coflow width; the number of coflows is set to 10.

Number of coflows. Using a fixed coflow width of 16, we vary the number of coflows from 10 to 25, in increments of 5. The results are illustrated in Figure 3. We find that again LP-Based completes *every instance* faster than the baseline as well as the Schedule-only and Route-only schedules. On average, the improvement over the baseline, Schedule-only and Route-only is by factors of %110, %72, and %26, respectively. We note that, as can be seen in the experiments,

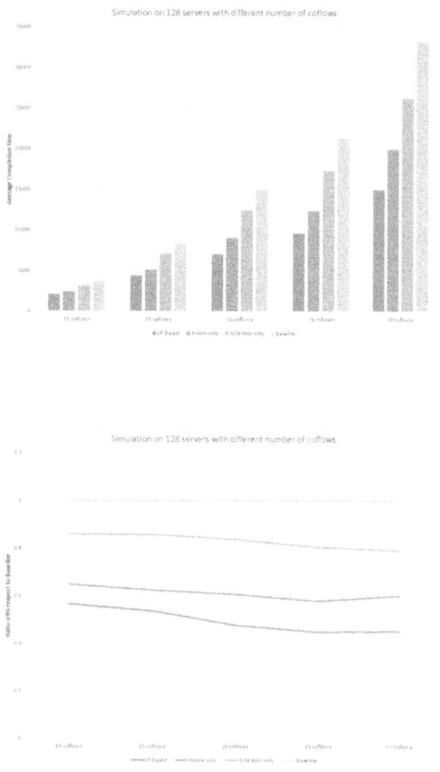

Figure 3: Changing the number of coflows; coflow width is set to 16.

the worst-case approximation ratio of $O(\log|E|/\log\log|E|)$, does not happen in practice. The main reason is that in the fat-tree topology there are a few paths between pairs of servers; furthermore, uniform link bandwidth causes the path decomposition routine to return fewer flow paths. Indeed, in all of our experiments, the path decomposition routine returns one path per flow.

5 CONCLUSION AND OPEN PROBLEMS

We have presented algorithms for scheduling task-based coflows, packet-based coflows, and circuit-based coflows for general networks. All of our algorithms achieve asymptotically-optimal total weighted completion time. An immediate line of further research is to obtain improved constant-factor bounds for general networks and improved algorithms for special network classes that are of particular interest to datacenter applications. More broadly, we would like to pursue algorithms for other important objectives and coflow models. Specifically, we are interested in designing approximation algorithms for the total weighted response time objective, where the response time is the difference between completion time and release time. Another line of research is the design of schedules for coflows in optical networks.

6 ACKNOWLEDGMENTS

We would like to thank the reviewers for their useful comments and pointing out the relevant work done in [9].

REFERENCES

[1] R. K. Ahuja, T. L. Magnanti, and J. B. Orlin. 1993. *Network Flows: Theory, Algorithms, and Applications.*
[2] M. Al-Fares, S. Radhakrishnan, B Raghavan, N. Huang, and A. Vahdat. 2010. Hedera: Dynamic Flow Scheduling for Data Center Networks. In *NSDI.*
[3] Mohammad Al-Fares, Sivasankar Radhakrishnan, Barath Raghavan, Nelson Huang, and Amin Vahdat. 2010. Hedera: Dynamic Flow Scheduling for Data Center Networks. In *USENIX.*
[4] J. D. Blocher and D. Chhajed. 1996. The customer order lead-time problem on parallel machines. *Naval Research Logistics* 43, 5 (1996).
[5] M. Chowdhury and I. Stoica. 2012. Coflow: A Networking Abstraction for Cluster Applications. In *HotNets.*
[6] M. Chowdhury, M. Zaharia, J. Ma, M. I. Jordan, and I. Stoica. 2011. Managing data transfers in computer clusters with orchestra. In *SIGCOMM.*
[7] M. Chowdhury, Y. Zhong, and I. Stoica. 2014. Efficient Coflow Scheduling with Varys. *SIGCOMM, Comput. Commun. Rev.* 44, 4 (2014).
[8] J. Chuzhoy, V. Guruswami, S. Khanna, and K. Talwar. 2007. Hardness of routing with congestion in directed graphs. In *STOC.*
[9] José R. Correa, Martin Skutella, and José Verschae. 2009. *The Power of Preemption on Unrelated Machines and Applications to Scheduling Orders.* Springer Berlin Heidelberg, Berlin, Heidelberg, 84–97. https://doi.org/10.1007/978-3-642-03685-9_7
[10] J. Dean and S. Ghemawat. 2008. MapReduce: simplified data processing on large clusters. *Commun. ACM* 51, 1 (2008).
[11] N. Garg, A. Kumar, and V. Pandit. 2007. Order Scheduling Models: Hardness and Algorithms. In *FSTTCS.*
[12] R.L. Graham, E.L. Lawler, J.K. Lenstra, and A.H.G. Rinnooy Kan. 1979. Optimization and Approximation in Deterministic Sequencing and Scheduling: a Survey. Discrete Mathematics, Vol. 5.
[13] C. Hong, M. Caesar, and B. Godfrey. Finishing flows quickly with preemptive scheduling. In *ACM Conference, SIGCOMM.*
[14] M. Isard, M. Budiu, Y. Yu, A. Birrell, and D. Fetterly. 2007. Dryad: distributed data-parallel programs from sequential building blocks. In *Proc. of the EuroSys Conference.*
[15] S. Khuller and M. Purohit. 2016. Improved Approximation Algorithms for Scheduling Co-Flows. In *SPAA.* Brief Announcement.
[16] R. Koch, B. Peis, M. Skutella, and A.s Wiese. 2009. Real-Time Message Routing and Scheduling. In *Approximation, Randomization, and Combinatorial Optimization. Algorithms and Techniques.* Lecture Notes in Computer Seince, Vol. 5687.
[17] Jr. L. R. Ford and D. R. Fulkerson. 1958. Constructing Maximal Dynamic Flows from Static Flows. *Operations Research* 6, 3 (1958).
[18] J. Labetoulle, E.L. Lawler, J.K. Lenstra, and A.H.G. Rinnooy Kan. 1984. Preemptive Scheduling of Uniform Machines Subject to Release Dates. In *Progress in Combinatorial Optimization*, William R. Pulleyblank (Ed.). Academic Press.
[19] F.T. Leighton, B.M. Maggs, and S.B. Rao. 1994. Packet routing and job-shop scheduling in O(congestion+dilation) steps. *Combinatorica* (1994).
[20] F. T. Leighton, B.M. Maggs, and A.W. Richa. 1999. Fast Algorithms for Finding O(Congestion + Dilation) Packet Routing Schedules. *Combinatorica* 19, 3 (1999).
[21] J. Y-T. Leung, H. Li, and M. Pinedo. 2005. *Order Scheduling Models: An Overview.*
[22] B. Peis, M. Skutella, and A. Wiese. 2009. Packet Routing: Complexity and Algorithms. In *WAOA.*
[23] Z. Qiu, C. Stein, and Y. Zhong. 2015. Minimizing the Total Weighted Completion Time of Coflows in Datacenter Networks. In *SPAA.*
[24] M. Queyranne and M. Sviridenko. 2002. Approximation Algorithms for Shop Scheduling Problems with Minsum Objective. *Journal of Scheduling* (2002).
[25] P. Raghavan and C. Thompson. 1987. Randomized Rounding: A Technique for Provably Good Algorithms and Algorithmic Proofs. *Combinatorica* 7 (1987).
[26] A Srinivasan and C.-P. Teo. 2001. A Constant-Factor Approximation Algorithm for Packet Routing and Balancing Local vs. Global Criteria. *SIAM J. Comput.* 30, 6 (2001).
[27] M. Zaharia, M Chowdhury, M. J. Franklin, S. Shenker, and I. Stoica. 2010. Spark: Cluster Computing with Working Sets. In *HotCloud.*
[28] D. Zats, T. Das, P. Mohan, D. Borthakur, and R. H. Katz. 2012. DeTail: reducing the flow completion time tail in datacenter networks. In *SIGCOMM.*
[29] Y. Zhao, K. Chen, W. Bai, M. Yu, C. Tian, Y. Geng, Y. Zhang, D. Li, and S. Wang. 2015. Rapier: Integrating routing and scheduling for coflow-aware data center networks. In *INFOCOM.*

Online Flexible Job Scheduling for Minimum Span

Runtian Ren
School of Computer Science and Engineering
Nanyang Technological University
Singapore 639798
RENR0002@e.ntu.edu.sg

Xueyan Tang
School of Computer Science and Engineering
Nanyang Technological University
Singapore 639798
asxytang@ntu.edu.sg

ABSTRACT

In this paper, we study an online Flexible Job Scheduling (FJS) problem. The input of the problem is a set of jobs, each having an arrival time, a starting deadline and a processing length. Each job has to be started by the scheduler between its arrival and its starting deadline. Once started, the job runs for a period of the processing length without interruption. The target is to minimize the span of all the jobs – the time duration in which at least one job is running. We study online FJS under both the non-clairvoyant and clairvoyant settings. In the non-clairvoyant setting, the processing length of each job is not known for scheduling purposes. We first establish a lower bound of μ on the competitive ratio of any deterministic online scheduler, where μ is the max/min job processing length ratio. Then, we propose two $O(\mu)$-competitive schedulers: *Batch* and *Batch+*. The Batch+ scheduler is proved to have a tight competitive ratio of $(\mu + 1)$. In the clairvoyant setting, the processing length of each job is known at its arrival and can be used for scheduling purposes. We establish a lower bound of $\frac{\sqrt{5}+1}{2}$ on the competitive ratio of any deterministic online scheduler, and propose two $O(1)$-competitive schedulers: *Classify-by-Duration Batch+* and *Profit*. The Profit scheduler can achieve a competitive ratio of $4+2\sqrt{2}$. Our work lays the foundation for extending several online job scheduling problems in cloud and energy-efficient computing to jobs that have laxity in starting.

KEYWORDS

Job scheduling, span, online algorithm

ACM Reference format:

Runtian Ren and Xueyan Tang. 2017. Online Flexible Job Scheduling for Minimum Span. In *Proceedings of SPAA '17, July 24-26, 2017, Washington DC, USA*, , 12 pages.

DOI: http://dx.doi.org/10.1145/3087556.3087562

1 INTRODUCTION

We study the following scheduling problem: the input is a set of jobs, each having an arrival time, a starting deadline and a processing length. Each job has to be started by the scheduler (algorithm) between its arrival and its starting deadline. Once started, the job runs for a period of the processing length without interruption. The target is to minimize the span of all the jobs, where the span is the time duration in which at least one job is running. We refer to this problem as the *Flexible Job Scheduling* (FJS) problem. In this paper, we consider the online version of FJS, where the scheduler does not have any knowledge of future job arrivals.

In a sense, the objective of FJS is to maximize the parallelism of job execution – a recent trend arising from the prevalence of cloud computing and energy-efficient computing. If the execution of jobs can always be hosted by one server with a sufficient capacity, minimizing the span directly minimizes the running hours of the server. Under the pay-as-you-go billing model of clouds, this minimizes the monetary expense [1]. In energy-efficient computing, this indicates reducing the energy consumption of the server as the power usage of a server normally consists of a component proportional to the time duration when the server is "on" (which represents the power consumed by an idle server) and a component proportional to the total amount of work done (which is fixed for processing a given set of jobs) [4]. If job execution needs to be distributed to multiple servers each with a limited capacity, minimizing the total running hours of the servers can be modeled as the MinUsageTime Dynamic Bin Packing problem [15, 16, 19], for which the competitiveness of scheduling often depends on the span and the time-accumulated resource demand of all the jobs. Thus, minimizing the span also helps enhance the competitiveness of scheduling.

FJS can be seen as a variant of the interval scheduling problem [13, 14]. In interval scheduling, a set of jobs are to be scheduled on machines. After a job arrives, it needs to run for its processing length on a machine non-preemptively and be completed before a deadline. In many cases, each machine can run only one job at a time. A common target of interval scheduling is to schedule a subset of jobs on a given number of machines such that the total weight of the scheduled jobs is maximized [2, 3, 5, 8, 9, 17, 21, 24]. This objective is substantially different from ours in that it attempts to control the parallelism of job execution. Recently, another version of interval scheduling closer to our problem is receiving increasing attention [7, 10, 11, 18, 22]. In this version, each machine can run a fixed number of jobs concurrently. The target is to minimize the total busy time of all the machines used for scheduling all the jobs. Most work along this direction has focused on scheduling jobs in an offline manner, where all the inputs are given in advance. There was only one study on online scheduling for optimizing the busy time [22]. However, it assumed "rigid" jobs that must be started immediately at their arrivals (i.e., each job's deadline is exactly its arrival time plus its processing length). Different from [22], we consider flexible jobs that have laxity in starting. A recent work showed that the offline version of FJS can be solved by dynamic programming [11], but no online scheduler was investigated. Our

SPAA '17, July 24-26, 2017, Washington DC, USA
© 2017 ACM. 978-1-4503-4593-4/17/07...$15.00
DOI: http://dx.doi.org/10.1145/3087556.3087562

work focuses on the online version of FJS and lays the foundation for extending online busy time optimization to flexible jobs.

Contributions of this paper. We study online FJS under both the non-clairvoyant and clairvoyant settings. In the non-clairvoyant setting, the processing length of each job is not known until it completes execution. Thus, the knowledge of processing length cannot be used for scheduling purposes. We establish a lower bound of μ on the competitive ratio of any deterministic online scheduler, where μ is the max/min job processing length ratio. Then, we propose two $O(\mu)$-competitive schedulers: *Batch* and *Batch+*. The Batch scheduler achieves a competitive ratio between 2μ and $(2\mu + 1)$, and the Batch+ scheduler achieves a tight competitive ratio of $(\mu + 1)$. In the clairvoyant setting, the processing length of each job is known at the time of its arrival and this information can be used by the scheduler. We establish a lower bound of $\frac{\sqrt{5}+1}{2}$ on the competitive ratio of any deterministic online scheduler. Then, we propose two $O(1)$-competitive schedulers: *Classify-by-Duration Batch+* and *Profit*. We show that these two schedulers can achieve competitive ratios of $7 + 2\sqrt{6}$ and $4 + 2\sqrt{2}$ respectively.

2 PRELIMINARIES

We first define some key notations for this paper. For any time interval I, we use I^- and I^+ to denote the left and right endpoints of I respectively. For technical reasons, we shall view intervals as half-open, i.e., $I = [I^-, I^+)$. Let $\text{len}(I) = I^+ - I^-$ denote the length of interval I.

For any job J, let $a(J)$, $d(J)$ and $p(J)$ denote J's arrival time, starting deadline (latest possible starting time)[1] and processing length respectively. When a job J arrives at time $a(J)$, its starting deadline $d(J)$ is known and the job can be started at any time between $a(J)$ and $d(J)$. The difference $d(J) - a(J)$ is known as the *laxity* of job J. Once the job is started, it has to run for a processing length $p(J)$ without interruption. A *scheduler* decides the starting times of jobs. If a scheduler Λ starts a job J at time t, we refer to the time interval $\left[t, t + p(J)\right)$ in which J is running as the *active interval* of job J and denote it by $I_\Lambda(J)$. Let $\mathcal{J}$ denote the set of jobs to schedule. The time duration in which at least one job in $\mathcal{J}$ is running is known as the *span* of $\mathcal{J}$. We denote the span of $\mathcal{J}$ induced by a scheduler Λ as $\text{span}_\Lambda(\mathcal{J}) = \text{len}\left(\bigcup_{J\in\mathcal{J}} I_\Lambda(J)\right)$.

Our goal of job scheduling is to minimize the span. We denote the minimum possible span induced by an optimal scheduler as $\text{span}_{min}(\mathcal{J})$. The performance of an online algorithm is often characterized by its *competitive ratio*, i.e., the worst-case ratio between the objective function values of an online solution and an optimal solution [6]. We propose several online schedulers and analyze their competitiveness.

3 NON-CLAIRVOYANT SETTING

We start by considering the non-clairvoyant setting first. In Section 3.1, we show that any deterministic online scheduler has a competitive ratio at least μ, where $\mu = \frac{\max_{J\in\mathcal{J}} p(J)}{\min_{J\in\mathcal{J}} p(J)}$ is the ratio of the maximum job processing length to the minimum job processing length among all the jobs to schedule. In Section 3.2, we introduce a $(2\mu + 1)$-competitive *Batch* scheduler and a $(\mu + 1)$-competitive *Batch+* scheduler.

[1]We assume a starting deadline for each job rather then a completion deadline as one of the settings we study is non-clairvoyant where the processing length of each job is not known.

3.1 Lower Bound on Competitiveness of Online Schedulers

We construct an instance to establish the lower bound μ on the competitive ratio of any deterministic online scheduler. In our instance, each job has one of two processing lengths: 1 or μ, where $\mu > 1$ can be revealed to the scheduler in advance. In the non-clairvoyant setting, an adversary has the freedom of assigning a processing length to a job after it is started. In our instance, each job is assigned the processing length 1 time unit after it is started since the processing lengths of all jobs are at least 1. If a job J is assigned a processing length of 1, it completes execution immediately. If the job is assigned a processing length of μ, it continues to run for another $(\mu - 1)$ time units before completing execution. Let $k \geq 1$ be an integer. We release jobs in up to $(k + 1)$ iterations. For each iteration i, let T_i denote the time to release all the jobs of this iteration. Among all the jobs released in iteration i, the number of concurrently running jobs induced by an online scheduler shall be referred to as the *concurrency* of iteration i. Note that each iteration has its own concurrency and the concurrency normally changes over time.

In the first iteration, we start by releasing $2^{2^{2k}}$ jobs at time $T_1 = 0$. Let the j-th job $(1 \leq j \leq 2^{2^{2k}})$ have a laxity of α^j, where $\alpha > \mu + 1$ is a constant. As long as the concurrency of the first iteration does not exceed $\sqrt{2^{2^{2k}}} = 2^{2^{2k-1}}$ by applying the online scheduler, all the jobs are assigned a processing length of 1 when they are due for the length assignment. If the concurrency never exceeds $2^{2^{2k-1}}$ until all the jobs complete execution, we stop releasing jobs and do not proceed with any further iteration. Otherwise, consider the time t_1 when the concurrency first exceeds $2^{2^{2k-1}}$. Suppose there are m_1 $(m_1 \geq 2^{2^{2k-1}} + 1)$ jobs running at time t_1. Let $J_1, J_2, \ldots, J_{m_1}$ be all these jobs sorted in an increasing order of their laxities. Note that none of these jobs has been assigned the processing length, since all the jobs assigned the processing length so far were assigned a length of 1 and have completed execution. We shall assign a processing length of μ to job J_{m_1} and refer to it as the *earmarked job* of the first iteration. All the other jobs $J_1, J_2, \ldots, J_{m_1-1}$ will be assigned the same processing length of 1. Apart from this, all the jobs started after time t_1 will also be assigned a processing length of 1. Then, we set T_2, the job release time of the second iteration, to the completion time of the earmarked job J_{m_1} of the first iteration.

The above process is repeated iteratively with decreasing number of jobs released in each iteration. In each iteration i $(2 \leq i \leq k)$, we release $2^{2^{2k-i+1}}$ jobs at time T_i. Let the j-th job $(1 \leq j \leq 2^{2^{2k-i+1}})$ have a laxity of α^j. As long as the concurrency of iteration i does not exceed $\sqrt{2^{2^{2k-i+1}}} = 2^{2^{2k-i}}$ by applying the online scheduler, we assign a processing length of 1 to all the jobs. If the concurrency never exceeds $2^{2^{2k-i}}$ until all the jobs released in iteration i complete execution, we do not proceed with any further iteration of job release. Otherwise, let t_i denote the time when the concurrency of iteration i first exceeds $2^{2^{2k-i}}$. Suppose there are m_i $(m_i \geq 2^{2^{2k-i}} + 1)$ jobs running at time t_i, and let $J_1, J_2, \ldots, J_{m_i}$ be all these jobs sorted

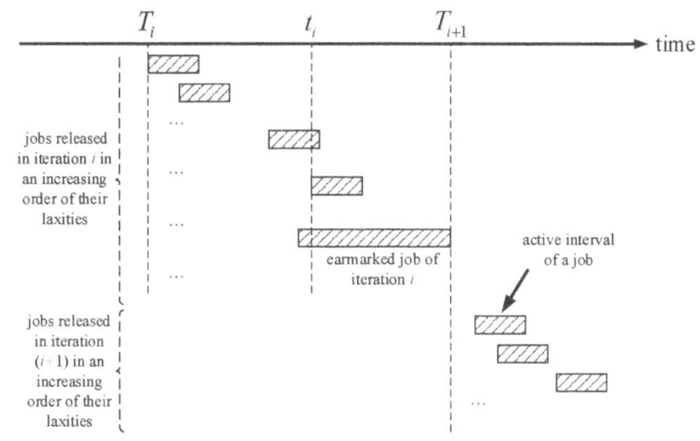

Figure 1: Jobs released in iterations i and $(i + 1)$

in an increasing order of their laxities. We shall assign a processing length of μ to job J_{m_i} and refer to it as the *earmarked job* of iteration i. All the other jobs $J_1, J_2, \ldots, J_{m_i-1}$ will be assigned the same processing length of 1. In addition, we shall assign a processing length of 1 to all the jobs started after time t_i. Then, we set T_{i+1}, the job release time of iteration $(i + 1)$, to the completion time of the earmarked job J_{m_i} of iteration i. Figure 1 illustrates the above process. In the final iteration $(k + 1)$ (if needed), we release 2^{2^k} jobs at time T_{k+1} and directly assign the same processing length of 1 to all these jobs.

We introduce two lemmas for analyzing the online scheduler and the optimal scheduler of the above instance.

LEMMA 3.1. *For each iteration i $(1 \leq i \leq k)$, if there is no earmarked job, the span induced by the online scheduler for all the jobs released in this iteration must be at least $2^{2^{2k-i}}$.*

Proof: An iteration i does not have an earmarked job only if its concurrency never exceeds $2^{2^{2k-i}}$. In this case, all the jobs released in iteration i have the same processing length of 1, so their total length is $2^{2^{2k-i+1}}$. Thus, the span of these jobs is at least $2^{2^{2k-i+1}} / 2^{2^{2k-i}} = 2^{2^{2k-i}}$. □

LEMMA 3.2. *For each iteration i $(2 \leq i \leq k+1)$, all the earmarked jobs of the first $(i-1)$ iterations can be started at the job release time T_i of iteration i.*

Proof: For each iteration j $(1 \leq j < i)$, let t_j denote the time when the concurrency of iteration i first exceeds $2^{2^{2k-j}}$. Among all the m_j $(m_j \geq 2^{2^{2k-j}} + 1)$ jobs active at t_j, let $\widetilde{J_j}$ be the job with the smallest laxity and let $\widehat{J_j}$ be the job with the largest laxity ($\widehat{J_j}$ is the earmarked job of iteration j). Denote the laxity of job $\widehat{J_j}$ by α^{L_j}. Since the jobs released in iteration j have exponentially increasing laxities, it is easy to infer that $L_j \geq m_j \geq 2^{2^{2k-j}} + 1$ and the laxity of job $\widetilde{J_j}$ is at most $\alpha^{L_j - m_j + 1}$. We next show that $T_i \leq T_j + \alpha^{L_j}$ for each $1 \leq j < i$, which suggests that the earmarked job of iteration j can be started at time T_i.

Note that in iteration j, the earmarked job $\widehat{J_j}$ is active at time t_j and has a processing length of μ. Since T_{j+1} is exactly the completion time of job $\widehat{J_j}$, we have $T_{j+1} \leq t_j + \mu$. On the other hand, job $\widetilde{J_j}$ is also active at time t_j and has a processing length of 1. Thus, $\widetilde{J_j}$ must be started no earlier than $t_j - 1$. Since the laxity of $\widetilde{J_j}$ is at most $\alpha^{L_j - m_j + 1}$, $\widetilde{J_j}$'s starting deadline is bounded by $T_j + \alpha^{L_j - m_j + 1}$. As a result, we have $t_j - 1 \leq T_j + \alpha^{L_j - m_j + 1}$. Therefore,

$$T_{j+1} \leq t_j + \mu \leq T_j + (\mu + 1) + \alpha^{L_j - m_j + 1}.$$

Since the above inequality holds for each $1 \leq j < i$. It follows that

$$T_i \leq T_j + (i - j)(\mu + 1) + \sum_{l=j}^{i-1} \alpha^{L_l - m_l + 1}.$$

Now, to prove $T_i \leq T_j + \alpha^{L_j}$, we only need to show $(i - j)(\mu + 1) + \sum_{l=j}^{i-1} \alpha^{L_l - m_l + 1} \leq \alpha^{L_j}$.

For each $j \leq l < i$, we have $L_l \geq m_l \geq 2^{2^{2k-l}} + 1$. Since the total number of jobs released in iteration $(l + 1)$ is $2^{2^{2k-l}}$, we also have $2^{2^{2k-l}} \geq L_{l+1}$. Thus, $L_l \geq L_{l+1} + 1$ for each $j \leq l < i$. Consequently, $L_j \geq L_l + (l - j)$. Note that $m_l \geq 3$. Therefore,

$$\begin{aligned}
\sum_{l=j}^{i-1} \alpha^{L_l - m_l + 1} &= \left(\sum_{l=j+1}^{i-1} \alpha^{L_l - m_l + 1} \right) + \alpha^{L_j - m_j + 1} \\
&< \left(\sum_{l=j+1}^{i-1} \alpha^{L_l - 2} \right) + \frac{\alpha^{L_j}}{\alpha^2} \\
&\leq \left(\frac{\alpha^{L_j}}{\alpha^3} + \frac{\alpha^{L_j}}{\alpha^4} + \cdots + \frac{\alpha^{L_j}}{\alpha^{i-j+1}} \right) + \frac{\alpha^{L_j}}{\alpha^2} \\
&< \left(\sum_{h=2}^{\infty} \frac{1}{\alpha^h} \right) \cdot \alpha^{L_j}
\end{aligned}$$

Since $\alpha > \mu + 1 \geq 2$ and $i - j \leq k$, we have $(i - j)(\mu + 1) < k\alpha$. It is easy to verify that when $\alpha > 2$, $k\alpha < \alpha^{2^k}$ for any $k \geq 1$. Since $L_j \geq m_j \geq 2^{2^{2k-j}} + 1 \geq 2^{2^k} + 1 > 2^k + 1$, we have $\alpha^{2^k} < \frac{1}{\alpha} \cdot \alpha^{L_j}$. As a result, $(i - j)(\mu + 1) < \frac{1}{\alpha} \cdot \alpha^{L_j}$. Thus,

$$(i - j)(\mu + 1) + \sum_{l=j}^{i-1} \alpha^{L_l - m_l + 1} < \left(\sum_{h=1}^{\infty} \frac{1}{\alpha^h} \right) \cdot \alpha^{L_j} = \frac{\alpha^{L_j}}{\alpha - 1} < \alpha^{L_j},$$

where the last inequality holds since $\alpha > 2$. Therefore, $T_i \leq T_j + \alpha^{L_j}$ for each $1 \leq j < i$ and the lemma is proven. □

Now, we derive the ratio between the spans induced by the online scheduler and the optimal scheduler. In the first iteration, if there is no earmarked job, according to Lemma 3.1, the span induced by the online scheduler is at least $2^{2^{2k-1}}$. In this case, the optimal schedule is to start all the jobs immediately once they are released (i.e., at time $T_1 = 0$) so that the induced span is 1. Thus, the ratio between the two spans is at least $2^{2^{2k-1}}$. If there is an earmarked job in the first iteration, the second iteration follows.

If the job releasing process is terminated after i iterations $(2 \leq i \leq k)$, each of the first $(i-1)$ iterations has an earmarked job. Since the jobs of each iteration are released when the earmarked job of the previous iteration completes, the active intervals of these $(i-1)$ earmarked jobs do not overlap. Moreover, by Lemma 3.1, the span induced by the online scheduler for the jobs released in iteration i is at least $2^{2^{2k-i}}$. Thus, the online scheduler must induce a total span at least $(i - 1)\mu + 2^{2^{2k-i}}$. A better schedule is to start all the jobs released in iteration i together with all earmarked jobs of the first $(i-1)$ iterations at time T_i (Lemma 3.2). All the remaining jobs released in the first $(i-1)$ iterations (which have processing lengths of 1) can be started immediately once they are released. In this way, the total span is $\mu + (i-1)$. Therefore, the ratio between the spans induced by the online scheduler and the optimal scheduler is at least $\frac{(i-1)\mu+2^{2^{2k-i}}}{\mu+(i-1)}$.

Finally, if the job releasing process proceeds to iteration $(k+1)$, the span induced by the online scheduler must be at least $k\mu + 1$. A better schedule is to start all the jobs released in iteration $(k+1)$ together with all the earmarked jobs of the previous iterations at time T_{k+1} (Lemma 3.2). All the remaining jobs are started immediately once they are released. This schedule induces a span at most $\mu + k$. So, the ratio between the two spans is at least $\frac{k\mu+1}{\mu+k}$.

In summary, the competitive ratio by applying any deterministic online scheduler is at least

$$\min\left\{2^{2^{2k-1}}, \min_{2\le i\le k}\left\{\frac{(i-1)\mu+2^{2^{2k-i}}}{\mu+(i-1)}\right\}, \frac{k\mu+1}{\mu+k}\right\}.$$

Since $\frac{(i-1)\mu+2^{2^{2k-i}}}{\mu+(i-1)} > \frac{2^{2^k}}{\mu+k}$ and $\frac{k\mu+1}{\mu+k} > \frac{\mu}{\frac{\mu}{k}+1}$, the above competitive ratio can be made arbitrarily close to μ as k goes towards infinity. Thus, we can conclude that:

Theorem 3.3. *For Non-Clairvoyant FJS, no deterministic online scheduler can achieve a competitive ratio less than μ, where μ is the max/min job processing length ratio.*

3.2 Batch Scheduler and Batch+ Scheduler

It is easy to infer that an eager scheduler that starts every job immediately at its arrival cannot achieve any bounded competitive ratio even for any given μ, because it does not make use of any laxity to boost the concurrency of job execution. Similarly, a lazy scheduler that delays the start of each job till its starting deadline cannot achieve any bounded competitive ratio for any given μ either, since it does not take any advantage of the flexibility offered by the laxity. Without any knowledge of job processing length, an intuitive strategy to improve the concurrency of job execution is to start as many jobs as possible simultaneously. In the following, we first propose a *Batch* scheduler and show that it can achieve a competitive ratio of $(2\mu+1)$ for Non-Clairvoyant FJS.

The Batch scheduler determines the starting times of jobs in iterations. In each iteration, the Batch scheduler waits until a job J pending execution hits its starting deadline $d(J)$, i.e., J is the job with the earliest starting deadline among those that have arrived but not yet started execution. We refer to J as the *flag job* of the iteration. If several jobs share the same starting deadline, any one of them can be chosen as the flag job. At time $d(J)$, the Batch scheduler starts all the jobs pending execution and let them run concurrently. Then, the scheduler proceeds to the next iteration to wait for another job to hit its starting deadline and repeats this process.

Theorem 3.4. *For Non-Clairvoyant FJS, the Batch scheduler achieves a competitive ratio between 2μ and $(2\mu+1)$, where μ is the max/min job processing length ratio.*

Proof: Let J_i denote the flag job of iteration i as designated by the Batch scheduler. By definition, the flag jobs $J_1, J_2, J_3, \ldots$

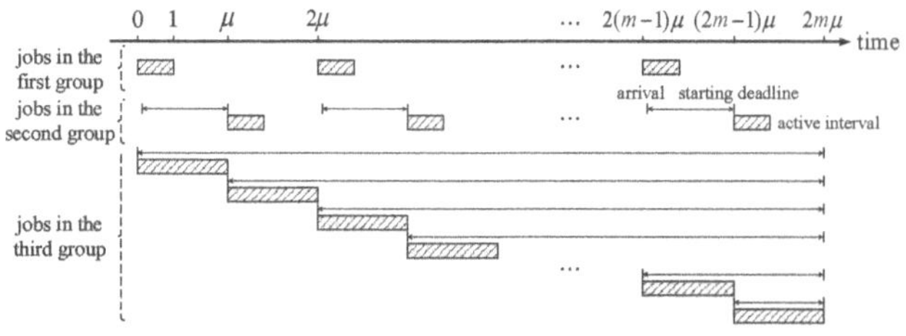

Figure 2: An example schedule induced by Batch

have increasing starting deadlines. To establish a lower bound on the span induced by an optimal scheduler, we choose a subset of the flag jobs, such that their active intervals cannot overlap with each other by any scheduler. First, we choose J_1. Then, we find the lowest-indexed flag job J_h that satisfies $d(J_h) \ge d(J_1) + p(J_1)$ and choose the flag job J_{h+1} if J_{h+1} exists. This selection process is repeated. After a flag job J_i is chosen, we find the lowest-indexed flag job J_j that satisfies $d(J_j) \ge d(J_i) + p(J_i)$ and then choose the flag job J_{j+1} if J_{j+1} exists. By the definition of Batch, J_{j+1} arrives later than $d(J_j)$ and thus, $a(J_{j+1}) > d(J_j) \ge d(J_i) + p(J_i)$. Note that $d(J_i) + p(J_i)$ is the latest possible completion time of job J_i. This implies that the active intervals of J_{j+1} and J_i cannot overlap with each other by any scheduler. Thus, the span induced by an optimal scheduler is at least $\sum_{J\in\mathcal{F}} p(J)$, where $\mathcal{F}$ is the subset of flag jobs chosen.

Next, we derive an upper bound on the span induced by the Batch scheduler. Consider any two flag jobs J_i and J_{i+1} chosen in succession. Since J_j is the lowest-indexed flag job satisfying $d(J_j) \ge d(J_i) + p(J_i)$, for each flag job J_g ($i \le g < j$), it holds that $d(J_g) < d(J_i) + p(J_i)$. This means that all the jobs started in iterations i to $(j-1)$ by the Batch scheduler are started before time $d(J_i) + p(J_i)$. Thus, all these jobs must complete execution by time $d(J_i) + p(J_i) + \mu \cdot p(J_i)$, since the max/min job processing length ratio is μ. Therefore, the span induced by the Batch scheduler for iterations i to $(j-1)$ is bounded by $d(J_i) + p(J_i) + \mu \cdot p(J_i) - d(J_i) = (\mu+1) \cdot p(J_i)$. Similarly, for all the jobs started in iteration j, since they are started simultaneously, their induced span is bounded by the maximum job processing length, which is in turn capped by $\mu \cdot p(J_i)$. Consequently, the span induced by the Batch scheduler for iterations i to j is bounded by $(\mu+1)\cdot p(J_i) + \mu \cdot p(J_i) = (2\mu+1)\cdot p(J_i)$. Putting all the iterations together, the total span induced by the Batch scheduler is bounded by $(2\mu+1) \cdot \sum_{J\in\mathcal{F}} p(J)$, where $\mathcal{F}$ is the subset of flag jobs chosen. Therefore, the competitive ratio of the Batch scheduler is bounded by $(2\mu+1)$.

Now, we construct an instance to show that the competitive ratio of the Batch scheduler is no less than 2μ. Consider three groups of jobs as shown in Figure 2. The first group contains m short jobs, each with a laxity of 0 and a processing length of 1. The i-th short job in the first group arrives at time $2(i-1)\mu$. The second group also contains m short jobs, each with a laxity of $(\mu - \varepsilon)$ and a processing length of 1, where $\varepsilon > 0$ can be arbitrarily small. The i-th short job in the second group arrives at time $2(i-1)\mu + \varepsilon$. The third group contains $2m$ long jobs, all of which have the same starting deadline of $2m\mu$ and a processing length of μ. The i-th long job arrives at time $(i-1)\mu$. By applying the Batch scheduler, the i-th short job in the first group and the $(2i-1)$-th long job in the third group are started together at time $2(i-1)\mu$ in the same iteration. The i-th short job in the second group and the $(2i)$-th long job in the third group are started together at time $(2i-1)\mu$ in the same iteration. Therefore, the total span induced is $2m\mu$. A better schedule is to start all the long jobs in the third group at their (same) starting deadlines and start all the short jobs in the first two groups immediately at their arrivals. This yields a span of $m(1+\varepsilon)+\mu$. Therefore, the ratio between the spans induced by the Batch scheduler and the optimal scheduler is at least $\frac{2m\mu}{m(1+\varepsilon)+\mu}$, which can be made arbitrarily close to 2μ as m goes towards infinity. □

To improve the competitiveness, we can make the Batch scheduler more aggressive. Next, we propose a tight $(\mu+1)$-competitive *Batch+* scheduler. Same as the Batch scheduler, Batch+ also determines the starting times of jobs in iterations. In each iteration, the Batch+ scheduler determines a flag job (the job with the earliest starting deadline) and starts all the pending jobs together with the flag job. What is different from Batch is that, during the active interval of the flag job, the Batch+ scheduler further starts all the newly arriving jobs immediately at their arrivals. Only when the flag job completes execution, the Batch+ scheduler starts the next iteration to buffer incoming jobs and search for a new flag job.

THEOREM 3.5. *For Non-Clairvoyant FJS, the Batch+ scheduler achieves a tight competitive ratio of $(\mu+1)$, where μ is the max/min job processing length ratio.*

Proof: We first show that the Batch+ scheduler is $(\mu+1)$-competitive. Let J_i denote the flag job of iteration i as designated by the Batch+ scheduler. By applying Batch+, all the jobs started in iteration i are started no later than the completion time of J_i, i.e., $d(J_i)+p(J_i)$. Since the max/min job processing length ratio is μ, the span of the jobs started in iteration i is at most $(\mu+1)\cdot p(J_i)$. Therefore, the total span induced by the Batch+ scheduler is at most $(\mu+1)\cdot\sum_{i\geq 1} p(J_i)$. Note that the flag job J_{i+1} of iteration $(i+1)$ must arrive later than $d(J_i)+p(J_i)$. Thus, the active intervals of J_i and J_{i+1} cannot overlap with each other by any scheduler. Therefore, the span induced by an optimal scheduler is at least $\sum_{i\geq 1} p(J_i)$. As a result, the competitive ratio of the Batch+ scheduler is bounded by $(\mu+1)$.

We construct an instance to show that the competitive ratio of $(\mu+1)$ is tight. Consider two groups of jobs as shown in Figure 3. One group contains m short jobs, each with a laxity of 0 and a processing length of 1. The i-th short job arrives at time $(i-1)(\mu+1)$. The other group contains m long jobs, all of which have the same starting deadline of $m(\mu+1)$ and a processing length of μ. The i-th long job arrives at time $(i-1)(\mu+1)+(1-\varepsilon)$, where $\varepsilon>0$ can be arbitrarily small. By applying the Batch+ scheduler, the i-th short job and the i-th long job are started immediately at their

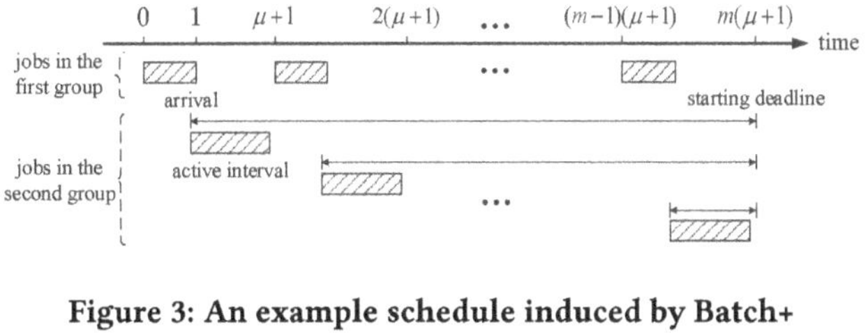

Figure 3: An example schedule induced by Batch+

arrivals in the same iteration, and thus a total span of $m(\mu+1-\varepsilon)$ is induced. An optimal schedule is to start all long jobs at their (same) starting deadlines and start all the short jobs immediately at their arrivals. This yields a span of $m+\mu$. Therefore, the ratio between the spans induced by the Batch+ scheduler and the optimal scheduler is $\frac{m(\mu+1-\varepsilon)}{m+\mu}$, which can be made arbitrarily close to $(\mu+1)$ as m goes towards infinity. □

4 CLAIRVOYANT SETTING

In this section, we study FJS under the clairvoyant setting, where the processing length of each job is known at its arrival. In Section 4.1, we establish a lower bound of $\frac{\sqrt{5}+1}{2}$ on the competitive ratio of any deterministic online scheduler. In Sections 4.2 and 4.3, we propose two $O(1)$-competitive schedulers: a *Classify-by-Duration Batch+* scheduler and a *Profit* scheduler.

4.1 Lower Bound on Competitiveness of Online Schedulers

We first construct an instance to show that any deterministic online scheduler has a competitive ratio of at least $\varphi=\frac{\sqrt{5}+1}{2}$. In our instance, each job has one of two processing lengths: 1 or φ. Let $n\geq 1$ be an integer. We release jobs in up to n iterations. In each iteration, we release two jobs, a short job with a processing length of 1 and a long job with a processing length of φ.

In the first iteration, we release a short job J_1 and a long job J_2 at time 0. Job J_1 has a laxity of 0 and job J_2 has a laxity of $n(\varphi+1)$. Obviously, J_1 must be started immediately at time 0. We check whether the online scheduler starts J_2 during the active interval of J_1, i.e., $[0,1)$. If J_2 is not started within J_1's active interval, we terminate the job releasing process and do not proceed with any further iteration. In this case, the span induced by the online scheduler is $\varphi+1$. The optimal schedule is to start J_1 and J_2 together at time 0, which induces a span of φ. Thus, the ratio between the two spans is $\frac{\varphi+1}{\varphi}=\varphi$. Otherwise, if J_2 is started during the time interval $[0,1)$, the second iteration follows.

The above process is repeated iteratively. As shown in Figure 4, in each iteration i $(2\leq i<n)$, we release a short job J_{2i-1} and a long job J_{2i} at time $(i-1)(\varphi+1)$. Job J_{2i-1} has a laxity of 0 and job J_{2i} has a laxity of $(n-i+1)(\varphi+1)$. We check whether the online scheduler starts J_{2i} during the active interval of J_{2i-1}, i.e., $[(i-1)(\varphi+1),(i-1)(\varphi+1)+1)$. If J_{2i} is not started within J_{2i-1}'s active interval, we terminate the job releasing process and do not proceed with any further iteration. In this case, the span induced by the online scheduler for iteration i is $(\varphi+1)$. Note that in each of the first $(i-1)$ iterations, the long job is started within the active interval of the short job. Since the job release times of two successive iterations are $(\varphi+1)$ apart, the active intervals of all the long jobs do not overlap with each other. Thus, the aggregate span of the first $(i-1)$ iterations is at least $(i-1)\varphi$. Therefore, the total span induced by the online scheduler for all the iterations is at least $(i-1)\varphi+(\varphi+1)$. An optimal schedule is to start all the long jobs together at time $(i-1)(\varphi+1)$ and to start all the short jobs at their respective arrivals. This yields a span of $\varphi+(i-1)$. Thus, the ratio between two spans is at least $\frac{(i-1)\varphi+\varphi+1}{\varphi+(i-1)}=\varphi$. Otherwise,

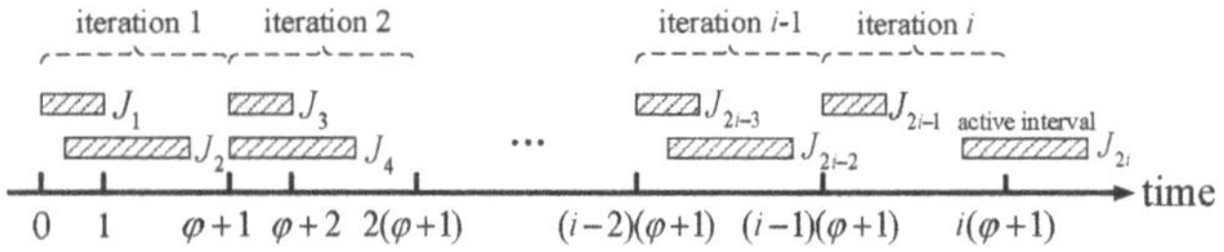

Figure 4: An example of the job release process

if J_{2i} is started during the active interval of J_{2i-1}, iteration $(i+1)$ follows.

In the final iteration n (if needed), we release a short job J_{2n-1} and a long job J_{2n} at time $(n-1)(\varphi+1)$. J_{2n-1} has a laxity of 0 and J_{2n} has a laxity of $(\varphi+1)$. Similar to the earlier argument, the active intervals of all the long jobs in the n iterations do not overlap with each other. Thus, the online scheduler induces a span at least $n\varphi$. An optimal schedule is to start all the long jobs at time $(n-1)(\varphi+1)$ and to start all the short jobs at their respective arrivals. This yields a span of $\varphi+(n-1)$. Thus, the ratio between the spans induced by the online scheduler and the optimal scheduler is at least $\frac{n\varphi}{\varphi+(n-1)}$, which can be made arbitrarily close to φ as n goes towards infinity.

With the above instance, we can conclude that:

THEOREM 4.1. *For Clairvoyant FJS, no deterministic online scheduler can achieve a competitive ratio less than* $\frac{\sqrt{5}+1}{2}$.

4.2 Classify-by-Duration Batch+ Scheduler

As shown in Section 3.1, in the non-clairvoyant setting, the competitiveness of an online scheduler is limited by the max/min job processing length ratio μ. In the clairvoyant setting, with the knowledge of job processing length, a natural strategy to break this limit is to classify jobs into categories according to their lengths and schedule each category separately. In this way, the max/min job processing length ratio of each job category is reduced compared to the whole job set. In this section, we show that applying such a classify-by-duration strategy on the Batch+ scheduler can achieve an $O(1)$ competitive ratio.

We first introduce our *Classify-by-Duration Batch+* (CDB) scheduler. Let α be the max/min job processing length ratio of each job category. Given a base job processing length b, we classify jobs into categories such that each category includes all the jobs with processing length between $b\alpha^{i-1}$ and $b\alpha^{i}$ for an integer i. Whenever a new job arrives, it is put into a category according to its processing length. For each job category, we apply the Batch+ scheduler seperately to decide the starting times of jobs. If the max/min job processing length ratio for the entire set of jobs to schedule is μ, there can be up to $\lceil\log_\alpha \mu\rceil+1$ non-empty job categories produced by the classification. Let $\mathcal{J}_1, \mathcal{J}_2, \dots, \mathcal{J}_{\lceil\log_\alpha \mu\rceil+1}$ denote these job categories. Let $\mathcal{F}_i$ be the set of flag jobs designated by the Batch+ scheduler in the job category $\mathcal{J}_i$. Let $\mathcal{F}=\bigcup_{i=1}^{\lceil\log_\alpha \mu\rceil+1}\mathcal{F}_i$ be all the flag jobs designated by Classify-by-Duration Batch+ in the entire job set.

LEMMA 4.2. *The span induced by the Classify-by-Duration Batch+ scheduler for a set of jobs $\mathcal{J}$ is bounded by $(\alpha+1)$ times the span of all the flag jobs $\mathcal{F}\subseteq\mathcal{J}$ in the schedule.*

Proof: By applying the Batch+ scheduler, the active interval of each flag job J is $\left[d(J), d(J)+p(J)\right)$. Thus, the span of all the flag jobs is $\bigcup_{J\in\mathcal{F}}\left[d(J), d(J)+p(J)\right)$. Such a span may not be a single contiguous time interval. It may be composed of multiple contiguous time intervals that are apart from each other. Let $I_1, I_2, \dots, I_m$ $(m \geq 1)$ be these contiguous intervals. Then, we can divide all the flag jobs $\mathcal{F}$ into m groups, such that the span of each job group $\mathcal{H}_i$ is I_i, i.e., $\bigcup_{J\in\mathcal{H}_i}\left[d(J), d(J)+p(J)\right) = \left[\min_{J\in\mathcal{H}_i} d(J), \max_{J\in\mathcal{H}_i}\left(d(J)+p(J)\right)\right) = I_i$. The span of all the flag jobs can be written as $\sum_{i=1}^{m}\text{len}(I_i)$.

By the argument for the Batch+ scheduler in the proof of Theorem 3.5, the active intervals of all the jobs started in the iteration defined by flag job J must lie inside the time interval $\left[d(J), d(J)+(\alpha+1)\cdot p(J)\right)$. Thus, the span of all the jobs $\mathcal{J}$ is bounded by $\text{len}\left(\bigcup_{J\in\mathcal{F}}\left[d(J), d(J)+(\alpha+1)\cdot p(J)\right)\right)$. For each flag job $J\in\mathcal{H}_i$, we have $d(J)\geq \min_{J\in\mathcal{H}_i} d(J) = I_i^-$ and

$$\begin{aligned} & d(J)+(\alpha+1)\cdot p(J) \\ = \quad & (\alpha+1)\cdot\left(d(J)+p(J)\right)-\alpha\cdot d(J) \\ \leq \quad & (\alpha+1)\cdot\max_{J\in\mathcal{H}_i}\left(d(J)+p(J)\right)-\alpha\cdot\min_{J\in\mathcal{H}_i} d(J) \\ = \quad & \min_{J\in\mathcal{H}_i} d(J)+(\alpha+1)\cdot\left(\max_{J\in\mathcal{H}_i}\left(d(J)+p(J)\right)-\min_{J\in\mathcal{H}_i} d(J)\right) \\ = \quad & I_i^-+(\alpha+1)\cdot\text{len}(I_i). \end{aligned}$$

Hence, $\left[d(J), d(J)+(\alpha+1)\cdot p(J)\right)\subseteq\left[I_i^-, I_i^-+(\alpha+1)\cdot\text{len}(I_i)\right)$. This suggests that the span of all the jobs J is bounded by $\text{len}\left(\bigcup_{i=1}^{m}\left[I_i^-, I_i^-+(\alpha+1)\cdot\text{len}(I_i)\right)\right)$. Since $\bigcup_{i=1}^{m}\left[I_i^-, I_i^-+(\alpha+1)\cdot\text{len}(I_i)\right)$ has a total length capped by $(\alpha+1)\cdot\sum_{i=1}^{m}\text{len}(I_i)$, the lemma is proven. □

With Lemma 4.2, we only need to analyze the span for the flag jobs $\mathcal{F}$. Recall that $\mathcal{F}$ can be classified into the categories $\mathcal{F}_1, \mathcal{F}_2, \dots, \mathcal{F}_m$, As argued in the proof of Theorem 3.5, each flag job designated by the Batch+ scheduler must arrive later than the latest possible completion time of the previous flag job. Thus, the active intervals of any two flag jobs in the same category cannot overlap with each other by any scheduler. In the following, we study the CDB-to-optimal span ratio[2] for any set of jobs with the above property.

LEMMA 4.3. *If a set of jobs $\mathcal{J}$ can be classified into a collection of categories $\mathcal{J}_1, \mathcal{J}_2, \dots, \mathcal{J}_m$ such that*

(a) the max/min job processing length ratio of each category is bounded by α,

(b) the active intervals of any two jobs in the same category cannot overlap by any scheduler,

then the CDB-to-optimal span ratio of $\mathcal{J}$ is bounded by $3+\frac{1}{\alpha-1}$.

Proof: We prove it by an induction on the number of job categories. If $\mathcal{J}$ contains only one job category, then according to property (b), the active intervals of any two jobs in $\mathcal{J}$ cannot overlap by any scheduler. Thus, the span induced by any scheduler is exactly $\sum_{J\in\mathcal{J}} p(J)$. Therefore, the CDB-to-optimal span ratio of $\mathcal{J}$ is 1, which is bounded by $3+\frac{1}{\alpha-1}$.

[2]For simplicity of presentation, we shall refer to the ratio between the spans induced by the Classify-by-Duration Batch+ scheduler and an optimal scheduler as the CDB-to-optimal span ratio.

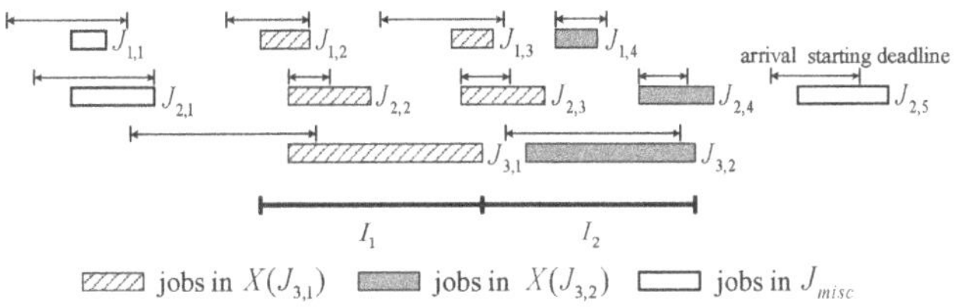

Figure 5: An optimal schedule induced by scheduler A

Suppose that the CDB-to-optimal span ratio is bounded by $3 + \frac{1}{\alpha-1}$ for all job sets containing no more than $(n-1)$ categories. We now show that for any job set $\mathcal{J}$ that contains n categories, its CDB-to-optimal span ratio is also bounded by $3 + \frac{1}{\alpha-1}$. Consider an optimal scheduler A on $\mathcal{J}$, i.e., $\text{span}_A(\mathcal{J}) = \text{span}_{min}(\mathcal{J})$. Let $I_A(J)$ denote the active interval of job $J \in \mathcal{J}$ induced by scheduler A.

We start by deriving a lower bound on the span induced by scheduler A. Assume that $\mathcal{J}$ can be classified into n categories $\mathcal{J}_1, \mathcal{J}_2, \ldots, \mathcal{J}_n$, where $\mathcal{J}_n$ includes jobs with the longest processing lengths. Let $J_{n,1}, J_{n,2}, \ldots, J_{n,q}$ be all the jobs in $\mathcal{J}_n$ sorted in an increasing order of their arrivals. The span induced by scheduler A for all the jobs $\mathcal{J}$ may consist of multiple contiguous time intervals. For each job $J_{n,j}$ $(1 \le j \le q)$, let $I_S(J_{n,j})$ denote the contiguous interval that $J_{n,j}$'s active interval $I_A(J_{n,j})$ falls in. Then, we define an interval I_j for $J_{n,j}$ as

$$I_j = \left[\max\{I_S(J_{n,j})^-, I_A(J_{n,j-1})^+\}, I_A(J_{n,j})^+\right),$$

i.e., I_j is left delimited by the starting point of $I_S(J_{n,j})$ and the ending point of $J_{n,j-1}$'s active interval, and it is right delimited by the ending point of $J_{n,j}$'s active interval. By property (b) of $\mathcal{J}_n$, we can infer that $I_A(J_{n,j}) \subseteq I_j$ and all the I_j's do not overlap with each other. For each I_j, define $X(J_{n,j})$ as the set of all the jobs $J \in \mathcal{J}$ satisfying $I_A(J) \subseteq I_j$ or $I_A(J)^- < I_j^+ < I_A(J)^+$, i.e., these jobs have their active intervals either fully contained in I_j or crossing the ending point of I_j. Obviously, $J_{n,j} \in X(J_{n,j})$. Let $\mathcal{J}_{overlap} = \bigcup_{j=1}^{q} X(J_{n,j})$ and $\mathcal{J}_{misc} = \mathcal{J} \backslash \mathcal{J}_{overlap}$. It is easy to see that the active interval of any job in $\mathcal{J}_{misc}$ does not overlap with any I_j, i.e., $\left(\bigcup_{J \in \mathcal{J}_{misc}} I_A(J)\right) \cap \left(\bigcup_{j=1}^{q} I_j\right) = \emptyset$. Figure 5 illustrates the above definitions with an example of jobs classified into three categories: $\mathcal{J}_1 = \{J_{1,1}, J_{1,2}, J_{1,3}, J_{1,4}\}$, $\mathcal{J}_2 = \{J_{2,1}, J_{2,2}, J_{2,3}, J_{2,4}, J_{2,5}\}$, $\mathcal{J}_3 = \{J_{3,1}, J_{3,2}\}$.

We can thus establish a lower bound on the span induced by the optimal scheduler A as

$$\begin{aligned} \text{span}_{min}(\mathcal{J}) &\ge \text{span}_A(\mathcal{J}_{misc}) + \sum_{j=1}^{q} \text{len}(I_j) \\ &\ge \text{span}_{min}(\mathcal{J}_{misc}) + \sum_{j=1}^{q} \text{len}(I_j), \end{aligned} \quad (1)$$

where $\text{span}_{min}(\mathcal{J}_{misc})$ is the span induced by an optimal scheduler on $\mathcal{J}_{misc}$.

Next, we prove that the span induced by Classify-by-Duration Batch+ for $\mathcal{J}$ has the following upper bound:

$$\text{span}_{CDB}(\mathcal{J}) \le (3 + \frac{1}{\alpha - 1}) \cdot \left(\text{span}_{min}(\mathcal{J}_{misc}) + \sum_{j=1}^{q} \text{len}(I_j)\right). \quad (2)$$

Due to property (b), by applying Classify-by-Duration Batch+ on $\mathcal{J}$, each job in $\mathcal{J}$ is started at its starting deadline. Thus,

$$\begin{aligned} \text{span}_{CDB}(\mathcal{J}) &= \text{len}\left(\bigcup_{J \in \mathcal{J}} \left[d(J), d(J) + p(J)\right)\right) \\ &\le \text{len}\left(\bigcup_{J \in \mathcal{J}_{misc}} \left[d(J), d(J) + p(J)\right)\right) \\ &\quad + \text{len}\left(\bigcup_{J \in \mathcal{J}_{overlap}} \left[d(J), d(J) + p(J)\right)\right) \\ &= \text{span}_{CDB}(\mathcal{J}_{misc}) + \text{span}_{CDB}(\mathcal{J}_{overlap}). \end{aligned}$$

It is obvious that the jobs $\mathcal{J}_{misc}$ come from at most $(n-1)$ categories $\mathcal{J}_1, \mathcal{J}_2, \ldots, \mathcal{J}_{n-1}$. According to the induction hypothesis, the CDB-to-optimal span ratio of $\mathcal{J}_{misc}$ is bounded by $3 + \frac{1}{\alpha-1}$, i.e., $\text{span}_{CDB}(\mathcal{J}_{misc}) \le (3 + \frac{1}{\alpha-1}) \cdot \text{span}_{min}(\mathcal{J}_{misc})$. What remains is to show that $\text{span}_{CDB}(\mathcal{J}_{overlap}) \le (3 + \frac{1}{\alpha-1}) \cdot \sum_{j=1}^{q} \text{len}(I_j)$.

In each job set $X(J_{n,j})$ defined earlier, all the jobs other than $J_{n,j}$ fall in categories $\mathcal{J}_1, \mathcal{J}_2, \ldots, \mathcal{J}_{n-1}$. Recall that the active intervals of all the jobs in each category $\mathcal{J}_i$ cannot overlap by any scheduler. We can thus infer that $X(J_{n,j})$ contains at most one job $\widetilde{J}_i$ from each category $\mathcal{J}_i$ $(1 \le i \le n-1)$ which satisfies $I_A(J_{n,j})^+ < d(\widetilde{J}_i) + p(\widetilde{J}_i)$. Assume on the contrary that there are two jobs $\widetilde{J}_i, \widetilde{J}_i' \in X(J_{n,j}) \cap \mathcal{J}_i$ satisfying this condition. By the argument in the proof of Theorem 3.5, either $d(\widetilde{J}_i) + p(\widetilde{J}_i) \le a(\widetilde{J}_i')$ or $d(\widetilde{J}_i') + p(\widetilde{J}_i') \le a(\widetilde{J}_i)$ holds. This implies that one of these two jobs must arrive after time $I_A(J_{n,j})^+$. On the other hand, by the definition of $X(J_{n,j})$, these two jobs have their active intervals overlapping with I_j by scheduler A. So, they must both arrive before $I_j^+ = I_A(J_{n,j})^+$, which leads to a contradiction. Hence, there is at most one job $\widetilde{J}_i \in X(J_{n,j}) \cap \mathcal{J}_i$ satisfying $I_A(J_{n,j})^+ < d(\widetilde{J}_i) + p(\widetilde{J}_i)$. All the remaining jobs $J \in X(J_{n,j}) \cap \mathcal{J}_i \backslash \{\widetilde{J}_i\}$ must have their completion times $d(J) + p(J) \le I_A(J_{n,j})^+ = I_j^+$. By the definition of $X(J_{n,j})$, J's active interval $I_A(J)$ induced by scheduler A must be fully contained in I_j. Since $I_A(J)^- \le d(J)$, J's starting deadline $d(J)$ must also be in I_j. As a result, J's active interval $\left[d(J), d(J) + p(J)\right)$ induced by Classify-by-Duration Batch+ must be fully contained in I_j. Therefore,

$$\begin{aligned} &\text{len}\left(\bigcup_{J \in X(J_{n,j})} \left[d(J), d(J) + p(J)\right)\right) \\ &= \text{len}\left(\bigcup_{i=1}^{n-1}\left(\bigcup_{J \in X(J_{n,j}) \cap \mathcal{J}_i} \left[d(J), d(J) + p(J)\right)\right)\right) \\ &\quad + \text{len}\left(\left[d(J_{n,j}), d(J_{n,j}) + p(J_{n,j})\right)\right) \\ &\le \text{len}\left(\bigcup_{i=1}^{n-1}\left(\bigcup_{J \in X(J_{n,j}) \cap \mathcal{J}_i \backslash \{\widetilde{J}_i\}} \left[d(J), d(J) + p(J)\right)\right)\right) \\ &\quad + \sum_{i=1}^{n-1} \text{len}\left(\left[d(\widetilde{J}_i), d(\widetilde{J}_i) + p(\widetilde{J}_i)\right)\right) + p(J_{n,j}) \\ &\le \text{len}(I_j) + \left(\sum_{i=1}^{n-1} p(\widetilde{J}_i)\right) + p(J_{n,j}). \end{aligned}$$

Since $\widetilde{J}_i \in \mathcal{J}_i$ and $J_{n,j} \in \mathcal{J}_n$, we have $p(\widetilde{J}_i) \leq \frac{1}{\alpha^{n-1-i}} \cdot p(J_{n,j})$. Note that $I_A(J_{n,j}) \subseteq I_j$, so $p(J_{n,j}) \leq \text{len}(I_j)$. It follows that $p(\widetilde{J}_i) \leq \frac{1}{\alpha^{n-1-i}} \cdot \text{len}(I_j)$. Thus,

$$\begin{aligned}
&\text{len}\Big(\bigcup_{J \in X(J_{n,j})} \big[d(J), d(J)+p(J)\big)\Big) \\
\leq\ & \text{len}(I_j) + \Big(\sum_{i=1}^{n-1} \frac{1}{\alpha^{n-1-i}} \cdot \text{len}(I_j)\Big) + \text{len}(I_j) \\
<\ & \text{len}(I_j) + \frac{1}{1-\frac{1}{\alpha}} \cdot \text{len}(I_j) + \text{len}(I_j) \\
=\ & (3 + \frac{1}{\alpha - 1}) \cdot \text{len}(I_j).
\end{aligned}$$

Therefore,

$$\begin{aligned}
\text{span}_{CDB}(\mathcal{J}_{overlap}) &= \text{len}\Big(\bigcup_{J \in \mathcal{J}_{overlap}} \big[d(J), d(J)+p(J)\big)\Big) \\
&= \text{len}\Big(\bigcup_{j=1}^{q}\Big(\bigcup_{J \in X(J_{n,j})} \big[d(J), d(J)+p(J)\big)\Big)\Big) \\
&\leq \sum_{j=1}^{q} \text{len}\Big(\bigcup_{J \in X(J_{n,j})} \big[d(J), d(J)+p(J)\big)\Big) \\
&< (3 + \frac{1}{\alpha-1}) \cdot \sum_{i=1}^{q} \text{len}(I_j).
\end{aligned}$$

Hence, inequality (2) is proven. Based on (1) and (2), the CDB-to-optimal span ratio of the job set $\mathcal{J}$ with n categories is bounded by $3 + \frac{1}{\alpha-1}$. By induction, the lemma is proven. □

By Lemma 4.3, the CDB-to-optimal span ratio for the set of flag jobs $\mathcal{F}$ is bounded by $3 + \frac{1}{\alpha-1}$, i.e., $\frac{\text{span}_{CDB}(\mathcal{F})}{\text{span}_{min}(\mathcal{F})} \leq 3 + \frac{1}{\alpha-1}$. It is obvious that the minimum possible span of any job set $\mathcal{J}$ is no less than that of its flag jobs $\mathcal{F}$ designated by Classify-by-Duration Batch+, i.e., $\text{span}_{min}(\mathcal{J}) \geq \text{span}_{min}(\mathcal{F})$. Thus, by Lemma 4.2, we have

$$\frac{\text{span}_{CDB}(\mathcal{J})}{\text{span}_{min}(\mathcal{J})} \leq \frac{(\alpha+1) \cdot \text{span}_{CDB}(\mathcal{F})}{\text{span}_{min}(\mathcal{F})} \leq 3\alpha + 4 + \frac{2}{\alpha - 1}.$$

It is easy to derive that $(3\alpha + 4 + \frac{2}{\alpha-1})$ has a minimum value of $7 + 2\sqrt{6} \approx 11.9$ when α is set to $1 + \sqrt{\frac{2}{3}}$.

Theorem 4.4. *The Classify-by-Duration Batch+ scheduler is $(3\alpha + 4 + \frac{2}{\alpha-1})$-competitive for Clairvoyant FJS, where α is the max/min job processing length ratio for each job category. When setting $\alpha = 1+\sqrt{\frac{2}{3}}$, this scheduler is $(7 + 2\sqrt{6})$-competitive.*

4.3 Profit Scheduler

Although the Classify-by-Duration Batch+ scheduler can achieve a constant competitive ratio, it schedules different categories of jobs independently, which may lose some opportunities to optimize the span. Moreover, Classify-by-Duration Batch+ does not make use of any runtime state in scheduling. In fact, with the knowledge of job processing length, we can derive how much the active interval of a new job can overlap with those of currently running jobs. This information would help decide whether starting a new job can make effective use of the existing span. Motivated by this observation, we propose a more competitive *Profit* scheduler that considers all the jobs as a whole.

The Profit scheduler determines the starting times of jobs in iterations. In each iteration, the Profit scheduler waits until a job J_f pending execution hits its starting deadline $d(J_f)$, i.e., J_f is the job with the earliest starting deadline among all pending jobs. Such a job J_f is designated as the *flag job* of this iteration. If several jobs share the same starting deadline, the one with the longest processing length is chosen as the flag job. The Profit scheduler starts the flag job J_f at time $d(J_f)$. For each job J that has arrived before time $d(J_f)$ but not yet started execution, if $p(J) \leq k \cdot p(J_f)$ (where $k > 1$ is an algorithm parameter), the Profit scheduler also starts job J at time $d(J_f)$ in this iteration. This guarantees that at least $\frac{1}{k}$ of J's active interval overlaps with J_f's active interval in the span and such a job J is said to be *profitable* to job J_f. Apart from this, if a job J arrives during the active interval of the flag job J_f and satisfies $p(J) \leq k \cdot \big(d(J_f) + p(J_f) - a(J)\big)$, the Profit scheduler starts job J immediately at its arrival $a(J)$ in this iteration. Since the flag job J_f completes execution at time $d(J_f) + p(J_f)$, the above condition also ensures that at least $\frac{1}{k}$ of J's active interval overlaps with J_f's active interval in the span. Such a job J is also said to be *profitable* to job J_f. Meanwhile, among all the pending jobs not profitable to job J_f, the Profit scheduler watches for any job to hit its starting deadline. Once a job hits its starting deadline, a new iteration is initiated and the above job starting process is repeated. Note that by applying the Profit scheduler, the flag jobs of different iterations may be running concurrently. As a result, it is possible that a new incoming job J is profitable to several running flag jobs when it arrives. In this case, the scheduler starts job J immediately and we attribute J to any iteration of these flag jobs.

In the following text, we analyze the competitive ratio of the Profit scheduler. The analysis framework bears some similarity to that for Classify-by-Duration Batch+, but is more sophisticated than the latter. Let $\mathcal{F}$ be all the flag jobs designated by the Profit scheduler in the entire job set $\mathcal{J}$. The following lemma describes the relation between the spans induced by Profit for $\mathcal{J}$ and $\mathcal{F}$.

Lemma 4.5. *The span induced by the Profit scheduler for a set of jobs $\mathcal{J}$ is bounded by k times the span of all the flag jobs $\mathcal{F} \subseteq \mathcal{J}$ in the schedule.*

Proof: First, we show that each job J started in an iteration with a flag job J_f must have its active interval fall inside the time interval $\big[d(J_f), d(J_f) + k \cdot p(J_f)\big)$. If J arrives before time $d(J_f)$, then $p(J) \leq k \cdot p(J_f)$ and J is started at time $d(J_f)$. Then, the completion time of J satisfies $d(J_f) + p(J) \leq d(J_f) + k \cdot p(J_f)$. If J arrives during the active interval of the flag job J_f, then $p(J) \leq k \cdot \big(d(J_f) + p(J_f) - a(J)\big)$ and J is started at its arrival time $a(J)$. Hence, the completion time of job J satisfies

$$\begin{aligned}
a(J) + p(J) &\leq a(J) + k \cdot \big(d(J_f) + p(J_f) - a(J)\big) \\
&= a(J) + k \cdot p(J_f) - k \cdot (a(J) - d(J_f)) \\
&< a(J) + k \cdot p(J_f) - (a(J) - d(J_f)) \\
&= d(J_f) + k \cdot p(J_f).
\end{aligned}$$

Therefore, all the jobs started in an iteration with a flag job J_f must have their active intervals fall inside $\left[d(J_f), d(J_f)+k\cdot p(J_f)\right)$. As a result, the span of all the jobs $\mathcal{J}$ is bounded by len $\left(\bigcup_{J\in\mathcal{F}}\left[d(J), d(J)+k\cdot p(J)\right)\right)$.

By applying the Profit scheduler, the active interval of each flag job J_f is $\left[d(J_f), d(J_f)+p(J_f)\right)$. Thus, the span of all the flag jobs designated by the Profit scheduler is $\bigcup_{J\in\mathcal{F}}\left[d(J), d(J)+p(J)\right)$. Such a span may consist of multiple contiguous time intervals which are apart from each other. Let $I_1, I_2, \ldots, I_m$ $(m \geq 1)$ be these contiguous intervals. Then, the span of all the flag jobs can be written as $\sum_{i=1}^{m} \text{len}(I_i)$. We can divide all the flag jobs $\mathcal{F}$ into m groups, such that the span of each job group $\mathcal{H}_i$ is I_i, i.e., $\bigcup_{J\in\mathcal{H}_i}\left[d(J), d(J)+p(J)\right) = \left[\min_{J\in\mathcal{H}_i} d(J), \max_{J\in\mathcal{H}_i}\left(d(J)+p(J)\right)\right) = I_i$. For each flag job $J \in \mathcal{H}_i$, we have $d(J) \geq \min_{J\in\mathcal{H}_i} d(J) = I_i^-$ and

$$\begin{aligned}
&d(J) + k\cdot p(J)\\
&\quad= k\cdot\left(d(J)+p(J)\right) - (k-1)\cdot d(J)\\
&\quad\leq k\cdot\max_{J\in\mathcal{H}_i}\left(d(J)+p(J)\right) - (k-1)\cdot\min_{J\in\mathcal{H}_i} d(J)\\
&\quad= \min_{J\in\mathcal{H}_i} d(J) + k\cdot\left(\max_{J\in\mathcal{H}_i}\left(d(J)+p(J)\right) - \min_{J\in\mathcal{H}_i} d(J)\right)\\
&\quad= I_i^- + k\cdot \text{len}(I_i).
\end{aligned}$$

Hence, $\left[d(J), d(J)+k\cdot p(J)\right) \subseteq \left[I_i^-, I_i^- + k\cdot\text{len}(I_i)\right)$. This suggests that the span of all the jobs $\mathcal{J}$ is bounded by len $\left(\bigcup_{i=1}^{m}\left[I_i^-, I_i^- + k\cdot\text{len}(I_i)\right)\right)$. Since $\bigcup_{i=1}^{m}\left[I_i^-, I_i^- + k\cdot\text{len}(I_i)\right)$ has a total length capped by $k\cdot\sum_{i=1}^{m}\text{len}(I_i)$, the lemma is proven. □

With Lemma 4.5, we only need to analyze the span for the flag jobs $\mathcal{F}$. We start by proving a useful lemma for the flag jobs $\mathcal{F}$.

Lemma 4.6. *For any two flag jobs designated by the Profit scheduler, the one with an earlier starting deadline must be completed before the other one.*

Proof: Let J_1 and J_2 be the flag jobs designated by the Profit scheduler in two different iterations. Without loss of generality, suppose J_1 has an earlier starting deadline than J_2, i.e., $d(J_1) < d(J_2)$.[3] If $a(J_2) \geq d(J_1)+p(J_1)$, then $d(J_2)+p(J_2) > a(J_2) \geq d(J_1) + p(J_1)$. If $a(J_2) < d(J_1)+p(J_1)$, since J_2 is also a flag job and is started at its starting deadline $d(J_2) > d(J_1)$, J_2 must not be profitable to J_1. If J_2 arrives before time $d(J_1)$, we have $p(J_2) > k\cdot p(J_1)$ and thus $d(J_2)+p(J_2) > d(J_1)+k\cdot p(J_1) > d(J_1)+p(J_1)$. If J_2 arrives during J_1's active interval $\left[d(J_1), d(J_1)+p(J_1)\right)$, we have $p(J_2) > k\cdot\left(d(J_1)+p(J_1)-a(J_2)\right)$ and it follows that

$$\begin{aligned}
d(J_2)+p(J_2) &> a(J_2) + k\cdot\left(d(J_1)+p(J_1)-a(J_2)\right)\\
&> a(J_2) + \left(d(J_1)+p(J_1)-a(J_2)\right)\\
&= d(J_1)+p(J_1).
\end{aligned}$$

[3]Note that $d(J_1) \neq d(J_2)$. Otherwise, at their (same) starting deadlines, the job with a longer processing length would be chosen as the flag job by the Profit scheduler. Then, the other job is profitable to the flag job and will be started in the same iteration so that it would not become a flag job itself.

Therefore, in any case, J_1 is completed before J_2. □

To study the Profit-to-optimal span ratio,[4] we construct a directed graph $G(\mathcal{F}, E)$ for the set of flag jobs $\mathcal{F}$ as follows. For each flag job $J \in \mathcal{F}$, let $X(J)$ be the set of all the flag jobs $J' \in \mathcal{F}$ satisfying $a(J') < d(J)+p(J)$ and $d(J) < d(J')$, i.e., J' arrives before J completes and J' is started after J. Thus, J' must not be profitable to J. If $X(J) \neq \emptyset$, then among all the jobs in $X(J)$, we choose the job $\widetilde{J}$ with the earliest starting deadline and create a directed edge from $\widetilde{J}$ to J in the graph $G(\mathcal{F}, E)$. Figure 6 shows an example of graph construction. It can be shown that the graph constructed in this way is a collection of rooted trees.

Lemma 4.7. *The directed graph $G(\mathcal{F}, E)$ is a collection of rooted trees.*

Proof: By definition, for each job $J \in \mathcal{F}$ with $X(J) \neq \emptyset$, there is only one job $J' \in X(J)$ which has an edge pointing to J. Moreover, no cycle exists in $G(\mathcal{F}, E)$. Otherwise, suppose a set of edges (J_1, J_2), (J_2, J_3), $\ldots$, (J_{m-1}, J_m), $(J_m, J_1) \in E$ form a cycle. According to the definition of an edge $(J', J) \in E$, we have $d(J) < d(J')$. Consequently, $d(J_1) < d(J_m) < d(J_{m-1}) < \cdots < d(J_3) < d(J_2) < d(J_1)$, which leads to a contradiction. Hence, the lemma is proven. □

Based on Lemma 4.7, for each edge $(J', J) \in E$, we refer to job J' as the *parent* of job J, and refer to J as a *child* of J'. By definition, if job J' is the parent of job J, J' is the job with the earliest starting deadline in $X(J)$. If $X(J) = \emptyset$ for a job J, we refer to J as a *root job*. If a job J does not have any child, we call it a *leaf job*. We next show that to study the Profit-to-optimal span ratio for all the flag jobs $\mathcal{F}$, it is equivalent to study the Profit-to-optimal span ratio for any rooted tree in the graph $G(\mathcal{F}, E)$.

Lemma 4.8. *Given a job $J \in \mathcal{F}$, for each job $J' \in X(J)$, there exists a path from J' to J in the graph $G(\mathcal{F}, E)$.*

Proof: Suppose job J is in a rooted tree T of $G(\mathcal{F}, E)$. Let J_1, J_2, $\ldots$, J_q, J be the sequence of nodes along the path from the root job of tree T to J, i.e., J_1 is the root job of T and is the parent of J_2, J_2 is the parent of J_3, $\ldots$, and J_q is the parent of J. By the definition of edges, we have $d(J) < d(J_q) < d(J_{q-1}) < \cdots < d(J_1)$. We prove that $X(J) \subseteq \{J_1, J_2, \ldots, J_q\}$ by contradiction.

Assume on the contrary that there exists a job $J' \in X(J)$ such that $J' \notin \{J_1, J_2, \ldots, J_q\}$. Since J_q is the parent of J, J_q has the earliest starting deadline among all the jobs in $X(J)$. Thus, $d(J') > d(J_q)$.

We first consider the case that $d(J_i) < d(J') < d(J_{i-1})$ for some i. Since $J' \in X(J)$, we have $a(J') < d(J)+p(J)$. It follows from $d(J) < d(J_i)$ and Lemma 4.6 that $d(J)+p(J) < d(J_i)+p(J_i)$. As a result, $a(J') < d(J_i)+p(J_i)$ and thus $J' \in X(J_i)$. The existence of the edge (J_{i-1}, J_i) suggests that job J_{i-1} has the earliest starting deadline among all the jobs in $X(J_i)$. Therefore, $d(J_{i-1}) < d(J')$, which leads to a contradiction.

Next, we consider the case that $d(J_1) < d(J')$. Similarly, since $a(J') < d(J)+p(J) < d(J_1)+p(J_1)$, we have $J' \in X(J_1)$, but this contradicts the fact that $X(J_1) = \emptyset$ since J_1 is a root job.

[4]For simplicity of presentation, we shall refer to the ratio between the spans induced by the Profit scheduler and an optimal scheduler as the Profit-to-optimal span ratio.

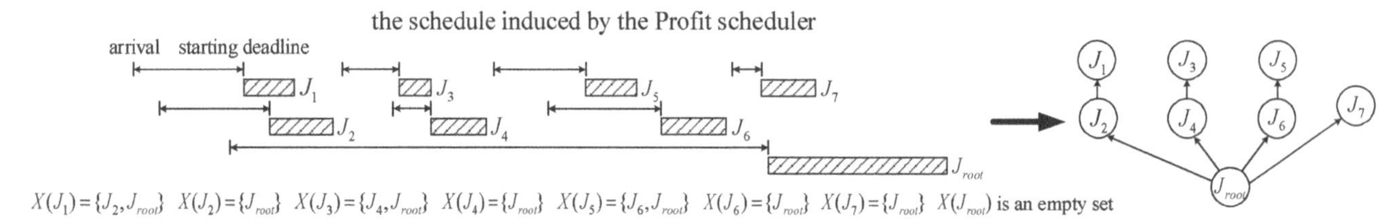

Figure 6: Constructing a graph for flag jobs

Thus, it is proven that $X(J) \subseteq \{J_1, J_2, \ldots, J_q\}$, which implies that there exists a path from each job $J' \in X(J)$ to job J. □

LEMMA 4.9. *If there is no path between two jobs J and J' in the graph $G(\mathcal{F}, E)$, the active intervals of J and J' can never overlap with each other by any scheduler.*

Proof: Without loss of generality, suppose $d(J) < d(J')$. If $a(J') < d(J) + p(J)$, then $J' \in X(J)$. According to Lemma 4.8, there exists a path from J' to J in the graph $G(\mathcal{F}, E)$, which leads to a contradiction. Therefore, we have $a(J') \geq d(J) + p(J)$, i.e., job J' arrives no earlier than the latest possible completion time of job J. Thus, their active intervals cannot overlap with each other by any scheduler. □

LEMMA 4.10. *The Profit-to-optimal span ratio for the flag jobs $\mathcal{F}$ is bounded by a constant C if the Profit-to-optimal span ratio for the flag jobs in any rooted tree of the graph $G(\mathcal{F}, E)$ is bounded by C.*

Proof: According to Lemma 4.7, we can decompose the directed graph $G(\mathcal{F}, E)$ into a collection of rooted trees $T_1(\mathcal{F}_1, E_1)$, $T_2(\mathcal{F}_2, E_2), \ldots, T_m(\mathcal{F}_m, E_m)$, where m is an integer and $\mathcal{F}_i$ is the set of flag jobs in tree T_i. For any two jobs $J \in \mathcal{F}_i$ and $J' \in \mathcal{F}_j$ $(i \neq j)$, there is no path between them in $G(\mathcal{F}, E)$. By Lemma 4.9, the active intervals of J and J' cannot overlap with each other by any scheduler. This suggests that an optimal schedule for the job set $\mathcal{F}_i \cup \mathcal{F}_j$ can be obtained by simply combining the optimal schedules for $\mathcal{F}_i$ and $\mathcal{F}_j$, and thus $\text{span}_{min}(\mathcal{F}_i \cup \mathcal{F}_j) = \text{span}_{min}(\mathcal{F}_i) + \text{span}_{min}(\mathcal{F}_j)$. Consequently, $\text{span}_{min}(\mathcal{F}) = \sum_{i=1}^{m} \text{span}_{min}(\mathcal{F}_i)$.

Note that by applying the Profit scheduler, all the flag jobs are started at their starting deadlines. Thus,

$$\begin{aligned}\text{span}_{Profit}(\mathcal{F}) &= \text{len}\Big(\bigcup_{J\in\mathcal{F}} \big[d(J), d(J)+p(J)\big)\Big) \\ &\leq \sum_{i=1}^{m} \text{len}\Big(\bigcup_{J\in\mathcal{F}_i} \big[d(J), d(J)+p(J)\big)\Big) \\ &= \sum_{i=1}^{m} \text{span}_{Profit}(\mathcal{F}_i).\end{aligned}$$

If the Profit-to-optimal span ratio for any $\mathcal{F}_i$ is bounded by C, i.e., $\text{span}_{Profit}(\mathcal{F}_i) \leq C \cdot \text{span}_{min}(\mathcal{F}_i)$, it follows that $\text{span}_{Profit}(\mathcal{F}) \leq \sum_{i=1}^{m} \big(C \cdot \text{span}_{min}(\mathcal{F}_i)\big) = C \cdot \text{span}_{min}(\mathcal{F})$. □

We now focus on the Profit-to-optimal span ratio for a rooted tree of flag jobs. In the following, we prove an upper bound of $2 + \frac{1}{k} + \frac{1}{k-1}$ on the Profit-to-optimal span ratio for any rooted tree by an induction on the *height* of the rooted tree — the number of edges along the longest path between the root job and the leaf jobs in the rooted tree.

First, consider a rooted tree with a height of 0, i.e., there is only one job J in the tree. Then, the span induced by any scheduler is exactly $p(J)$. Thus, the Profit-to-optimal span ratio for such a tree is 1, which is bounded by $2 + \frac{1}{k} + \frac{1}{k-1}$.

Suppose that the Profit-to-optimal span ratio is bounded by $2 + \frac{1}{k} + \frac{1}{k-1}$ for any rooted tree with a height no more than $(n-1)$. According to Lemma 4.10, this upper bound of the span ratio also holds for a directed graph consisting of a collection of rooted trees, each with a height no more than $(n-1)$. We now show that this upper bound also holds for any rooted tree T with a height of n. Let $\mathcal{J}_T$ be the set of flag jobs in T. Consider an optimal scheduler A on $\mathcal{J}_T$, i.e., $\text{span}_A(\mathcal{J}_T) = \text{span}_{min}(\mathcal{J}_T)$. Let $I_A(J)$ denote the active interval of a job $J \in \mathcal{J}_T$ induced by scheduler A.

We start by determining a lower bound on the span induced by scheduler A. The span induced by scheduler A for the flag jobs $\mathcal{J}_T$ may consist of multiple contiguous time intervals. Let J_{root} be the root job of T and let I_S denote the contiguous interval that J_{root}'s active interval $I_A(J_{root})$ falls in. As illustrated in Figure 7, we define an interval $I_{middle} = \big[I_S^-, I_A(J_{root})^+\big)$, i.e., I_{middle} is left delimited by the starting point of I_S and it is right delimited by the ending point of J_{root}'s active interval. It is obvious that $I_A(J_{root}) \subseteq I_{middle}$ and thus $p(J_{root}) \leq \text{len}(I_{middle})$. Then, we define $\mathcal{J}_{middle}$ as the set of all the jobs $J \in \mathcal{J}_T$ satisfying $I_A(J) \subseteq I_{middle}$ or $I_A(J)^- < I^+_{middle} < I_A(J)^+$, i.e., these jobs have their active intervals either fully contained in I_{middle} or crossing the ending point of I_{middle}. Obviously, $J_{root} \in \mathcal{J}_{middle}$. Let $\mathcal{J}_{left}$ be the set of all the jobs $J \in \mathcal{J}_T$ satisfying $I_A(J)^+ < I^-_{middle}$. Let $\mathcal{J}_{right}$ be the set of all the jobs other than $\mathcal{J}_{left}$ and $\mathcal{J}_{middle}$, i.e., $\mathcal{J}_{right} = \mathcal{J}_T \backslash (\mathcal{J}_{left} \cup \mathcal{J}_{middle})$. Apparently, each job $J \in \mathcal{J}_{right}$ satisfies $I_A(J)^- \geq I^+_{middle} = I_A(J_{root})^+$. We can therefore establish a lower bound on the span induced by the optimal scheduler A as

$$\begin{aligned}&\text{span}_{min}(\mathcal{J}_T) \\ &\quad\geq \text{span}_A(\mathcal{J}_{left}) + \text{len}(I_{middle}) + \text{span}_A(\mathcal{J}_{right}) \\ &\quad\geq \text{span}_{min}(\mathcal{J}_{left}) + \text{len}(I_{middle}) + \text{span}_{min}(\mathcal{J}_{right}), \quad (3)\end{aligned}$$

where $\text{span}_{min}(\mathcal{J}_{left})$ and $\text{span}_{min}(\mathcal{J}_{right})$ are the spans induced by the optimal schedulers on $\mathcal{J}_{left}$ and $\mathcal{J}_{right}$ respectively.

Next, we prove that the span induced by the Profit scheduler for $\mathcal{J}_T$, i.e., $\text{span}_{Profit}(\mathcal{J}_T)$, is bounded by $(2+\frac{1}{k}+\frac{1}{k-1}) \cdot \big(\text{span}_{min}(\mathcal{J}_{left}) + \text{len}(I_{middle}) + \text{span}_{min}(\mathcal{J}_{right})\big)$.

Note that all the jobs in $\mathcal{J}_T$ are flag jobs. Thus, by applying the Profit scheduler, each job in $\mathcal{J}_T$ is started at its starting deadline. It follows that

$$\text{span}_{Profit}(\mathcal{J}_T) = \text{len}\Big(\bigcup_{J\in\mathcal{J}_T} \big[d(J), d(J)+p(J)\big)\Big)$$

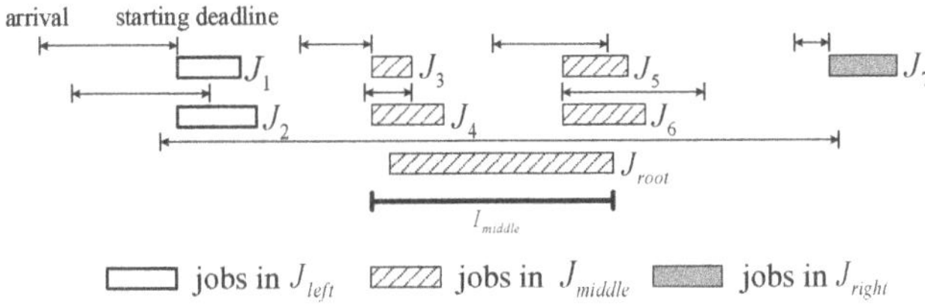

Figure 7: An optimal schedule on a rooted tree

$$\begin{aligned}
&\leq \operatorname{len}\Big(\bigcup_{J\in\mathcal{J}_{left}} \big[d(J), d(J)+p(J)\big)\Big) \\
&\quad + \operatorname{len}\Big(\bigcup_{J\in\mathcal{J}_{middle}} \big[d(J), d(J)+p(J)\big)\Big) \\
&\quad + \operatorname{len}\Big(\bigcup_{J\in\mathcal{J}_{right}} \big[d(J), d(J)+p(J)\big)\Big) \\
&= \operatorname{span}_{Profit}(\mathcal{J}_{left}) + \operatorname{span}_{Profit}(\mathcal{J}_{middle}) \\
&\quad + \operatorname{span}_{Profit}(\mathcal{J}_{right}).
\end{aligned}$$

It can be shown that by applying the graph construction technique for the job set $\mathcal{J}_{left}$, $\mathcal{J}_{left}$ must form a collection of rooted trees, each with a height no more than $(n-1)$. Let $G'(\mathcal{J}_{left}, E_{left})$ be the graph constructed for $\mathcal{J}_{left}$. For each edge $(J, J') \in E_{left}$, by definition, we have $J \in X(J')$. It follows from Lemma 4.8 that there exists a path from J to J' in the rooted tree T of jobs $\mathcal{J}_T$. Thus, every path in G' remains and cannot become shorter in T. Note that $J_{root} \notin \mathcal{J}_{left}$ is a root job that has a path to every node in T. Therefore, the longest path in T must be longer than that in G'. This implies that each rooted tree in G' has height at most $(n-1)$. According to the induction hypothesis and Lemma 4.10, the Profit-to-optimal span ratio of $\mathcal{J}_{left}$ is bounded by $2+\frac{1}{k}+\frac{1}{k-1}$, i.e., $\operatorname{span}_{Profit}(\mathcal{J}_{left}) \leq (2+\frac{1}{k}+\frac{1}{k-1})\cdot \operatorname{span}_{min}(\mathcal{J}_{left})$. Similarly, we have $\operatorname{span}_{Profit}(\mathcal{J}_{right}) \leq (2+\frac{1}{k}+\frac{1}{k-1})\cdot \operatorname{span}_{min}(\mathcal{J}_{right})$. What remains is to show that $\operatorname{span}_{Profit}(\mathcal{J}_{middle}) \leq (2+\frac{1}{k}+\frac{1}{k-1})\cdot \operatorname{len}(I_{middle})$.

Recall that each job in $\mathcal{J}_{middle}$ is started at its starting deadline by the Profit scheduler. This suggests that the starting time of each job $J \in \mathcal{J}_{middle}$ determined by the Profit scheduler must be no earlier than $I_A(J)^-$. Let $J_1, J_2, \ldots, J_m$ be all the jobs in $\mathcal{J}_{middle}\setminus\{J_{root}\}$ sorted in an increasing order of their starting deadlines. Since J_{root} is the root job, by the definition of edges, J_{root} must have a later starting deadline than all the other jobs in $\mathcal{J}_{middle}$. As a result, we have $d(J_1) < d(J_2) < \cdots < d(J_m) < d(J_{root})$. Let J_i be the highest-indexed job satisfying $d(J_i) \leq I_A(J_{root})^+$, if there exists at least one such job. For notational convenience, if such a job does not exist (i.e., $I_A(J_{root})^+ < d(J_1)$), we define $i = 0$.

We first show that the span induced by the Profit scheduler for jobs $\{J_1, J_2, \ldots, J_i\}$ is at most $\operatorname{len}(I_{middle}) + \frac{1}{k}\cdot p(J_{root})$. According to Lemma 4.6, the jobs $J_1, J_2, \ldots, J_i$ must be completed no later than time $d(J_i)+p(J_i)$. If $d(J_i)+p(J_i) \leq I_A(J_{root})^+$, all these jobs must have their active intervals fully contained in I_{middle}. Consequently, the span induced by the Profit scheduler for these jobs is at most $\operatorname{len}(I_{middle})$. If $d(J_i)+p(J_i) > I_A(J_{root})^+$, the span induced by the Profit scheduler for jobs $\{J_1, J_2, \ldots, J_i\}$ is at most

$$\begin{aligned}
&\operatorname{len}\Big(\big[I^-_{middle}, d(J_i)+p(J_i)\big)\Big) \\
&= \operatorname{len}(I_{middle}) + \operatorname{len}\Big(\big[I_A(J_{root})^+, d(J_i)+p(J_i)\big)\Big). \quad (4)
\end{aligned}$$

Since $I_A(J_{root})^+ \in \big[d(J_i), d(J_i)+p(J_i)\big)$, job J_{root} must arrive before job J_i completes in the Profit schedule. This implies that job J_{root} is not profitable to J_i. If J_{root} arrives earlier than time $d(J_i)$, we have $p(J_{root}) > k\cdot p(J_i)$. It follows from $d(J_i) \leq I_A(J_{root})^+$ that $p(J_{root}) > k\cdot\big(d(J_i)+p(J_i)-I_A(J_{root})^+\big) = k\cdot\operatorname{len}\Big(\big[I_A(J_{root})^+, d(J_i)+p(J_i)\big)\Big)$. If J_{root} arrives during J_i's active interval $\big[d(J_i), d(J_i)+p(J_i)\big)$, we have $p(J_{root}) > k\cdot\big(d(J_i)+p(J_i)-a(J_{root})\big)$. Note that $a(J_{root}) \leq I_A(J_{root})^- < I_A(J_{root})^+$. Hence, we have $p(J_{root}) > k\cdot\big(d(J_i)+p(J_i)-I_A(J_{root})^+\big) = k\cdot\operatorname{len}\Big(\big[I_A(J_{root})^+, d(J_i)+p(J_i)\big)\Big)$. Therefore, by inequality (4), the span for the jobs $\{J_1, J_2, \ldots, J_i\}$ is always bounded by $\operatorname{len}(I_{middle}) + \frac{1}{k}\cdot p(J_{root})$.

We next show that if $i < m$, $p(J_{j+1}) > k\cdot p(J_j)$ holds for each $i+1 \leq j \leq m-1$, and $p(J_{root}) > k\cdot p(J_m)$. By the definition of $\mathcal{J}_{middle}$, we have $I_A(J_{j+1})^- < I_A(J_{root})^+$. It follows that $a(J_{j+1}) \leq I_A(J_{j+1})^- < I_A(J_{root})^+ < d(J_{i+1}) \leq d(J_j)$. Thus, when job J_j is started at its starting deadline $d(J_j)$, J_{j+1} must have arrived and is not profitable to J_j, which suggests that $p(J_{j+1}) > k\cdot p(J_j)$. Similarly, since $a(J_{root}) \leq I_A(J_{root})^- < I_A(J_{root})^+ < d(J_{i+1}) \leq d(J_m)$, J_{root} is not profitable to J_m. Hence, $p(J_{root}) > k\cdot p(J_m)$. Together, these relations suggest that $p(J_j) < \frac{1}{k^{m+1-j}}\cdot p(J_{root})$ for each $i+1 \leq j \leq m$.

Therefore, the span induced by the Profit scheduler for $\mathcal{J}_{middle}$ satisfies

$$\begin{aligned}
&\operatorname{span}_{Profit}(\mathcal{J}_{middle}) \\
&\leq \operatorname{len}\Big(\bigcup_{j=1}^{i}\big[d(J_j), d(J_j)+p(J_j)\big)\Big) \\
&\quad + \operatorname{len}\Big(\bigcup_{j=i+1}^{m}\big[d(J_j), d(J_j)+p(J_j)\big)\Big) \\
&\quad + \operatorname{len}\Big(\big[d(J_{root}), d(J_{root})+p(J_{root})\big)\Big) \\
&\leq \operatorname{len}(I_{middle}) + \frac{1}{k}\cdot p(J_{root}) + \sum_{j=i+1}^{m} p(J_j) + p(J_{root}) \\
&< \operatorname{len}(I_{middle}) + (1+\frac{1}{k})\cdot p(J_{root}) + \Big(\sum_{h=1}^{\infty}\frac{1}{k^h}\Big)\cdot p(J_{root}) \\
&= \operatorname{len}(I_{middle}) + (1+\frac{1}{k}+\frac{1}{k-1})\cdot p(J_{root}) \\
&\leq (2+\frac{1}{k}+\frac{1}{k-1})\cdot \operatorname{len}(I_{middle}).
\end{aligned}$$

Now, according to inequality (3), the Profit-to-optimal span ratio for the flag jobs $\mathcal{J}_T$ in a rooted tree T with a height of n is bounded by $2+\frac{1}{k}+\frac{1}{k-1}$. By induction, we can conclude that the Profit-to-optimal span ratio for any rooted tree of flag jobs is bounded by $2+\frac{1}{k}+\frac{1}{k-1}$.

By Lemma 4.10, the Profit-to-optimal span ratio for all the flag jobs $\mathcal{F}$ is bounded by $2+\frac{1}{k}+\frac{1}{k-1}$. It is apparent that the minimum possible span of any job set $\mathcal{J}$ is no less than that of its flag jobs $\mathcal{F}$ designated by the Profit scheduler, i.e., $\operatorname{span}_{min}(\mathcal{J}) \geq$

$\text{span}_{min}(\mathcal{F})$. Thus, by Lemma 4.5, we have

$$\frac{\text{span}_{Profit}(\mathcal{J})}{\text{span}_{min}(\mathcal{J})} \leq \frac{k \cdot \text{span}_{Profit}(\mathcal{F})}{\text{span}_{min}(\mathcal{F})} \leq 2k + 2 + \frac{1}{k-1}.$$

It is easy to derive that $2k + 2 + \frac{1}{k-1}$ has a minimum value of $4 + 2\sqrt{2} \approx 6.9$ when k is set to $1 + \frac{\sqrt{2}}{2}$.

THEOREM 4.11. *The Profit scheduler is* $(2k + 2 + \frac{1}{k-1})$*-competitive for Clairvoyant FJS. When setting* $k = 1 + \frac{\sqrt{2}}{2}$*, this scheduler is* $(2\sqrt{2} + 4)$*-competitive.*

5 CONCLUDING REMARKS

We briefly outline how our results can be used to extend the MinUsageTime Dynamic Bin Packing (DBP) problem. The MinUsageTime DBP problem was defined to model server acquisition and job scheduling in cloud-based systems [15, 16, 19, 23]. In this problem, a set of items (jobs) are to be packed into bins (cloud servers). Each item has an arrival time, a departure time and a size. The item has to be placed in a bin from its arrival to its departure. The size of the item models the resource demand of the job. The total size of the items placed in one bin cannot exceed the bin capacity (server capacity) at any time. The target is to minimize the total usage time of all the bins used for packing. Competitiveness analysis has been carried out for various packing algorithms in the non-clairvoyant and clairvoyant settings [15, 16, 19, 20, 23]. It has been shown that the total bin usage time is bounded by adding the span of all the items and the accumulated time-space demand of all the items. So far, the jobs modeled by MinUsageTime DBP are restricted to "rigid" jobs that must be started immediately at their arrivals. In this case, the span of all the jobs is fixed and independent of the packing algorithm.

To generalize MinUsageTime DBP and model flexible jobs that have laxity in starting, we can apply a scheduling algorithm to determine the starting time of each job and apply a packing algorithm to decide where to place (run) the job when it starts. In this way, the span of all the jobs is affected by the scheduling algorithm. In the non-clairvoyant setting, it is known that a First Fit packing algorithm can achieve a near-optimal $O(\mu)$ competitive ratio for MinUsageTime DBP [20, 23]. Since our Batch+ scheduler is $O(\mu)$-competitive for minimizing the span, integrating Batch+ scheduling with First Fit packing can achieve an $O(\mu)$ competitive ratio for generalized MinUsageTime DBP. In the clairvoyant setting, applying a classify-by-duration strategy to First Fit packing can achieve an $O(\log \mu)$ competitive ratio for MinUsageTime DBP [19]. Since our Profit scheduler is $O(1)$-competitive for minimizing the span, combining Profit scheduling with classify-by-duration First Fit packing can achieve an $O(\log \mu)$ competitive ratio for generalized MinUsageTime DBP.

It was recently brought to our attention a concurrent work by Koehler *et al.* [12] which studied a busy-time scheduling problem on a bounded number of machines. An online case of their problem when the machine capacity is unbounded is equivalent to our Clairvoyant FJS. They independently established the same lower bound of $\frac{\sqrt{5}+1}{2}$ on the competitive ratio of any online scheduler, and proposed a 5-competitive *Doubler* scheduler.

6 ACKNOWLEDGMENTS

This work is supported by Singapore Ministry of Education Academic Research Fund Tier 2 under Grant MOE2013-T2-2-067, and Academic Research Fund Tier 1 under Grant 2013-T1-002-123.

REFERENCES

[1] Amazon EC2 Pricing. http://aws.amazon.com/ec2/pricing/. (2017).
[2] Amotz Bar-Noy, Reuven Bar-Yehuda, Ari Freund, Joseph (Seffi) Naor, and Baruch Schieber. 2001. A unified approach to approximating resource allocation and scheduling. *J. ACM* 48, 5 (2001), 735–744.
[3] Amotz Bar-Noy, Sudipto Guha, Joseph Naor, and Baruch Schieber. 2001. Approximating the throughput of multiple machines in real-time scheduling. *SIAM J. Comput.* 31, 2 (2001), 331–352.
[4] Luiz André Barroso and Urs Hölzle. 2007. The Case for Energy-Proportional Computing. *Computer* 40, 12 (2007), 33–37.
[5] Sanjoy Baruah, Gilad Koren, Decao Mao, Bhubaneswar Mishra, Arvind Raghunathan, Louis Rosier, Dennis Shasha, and Fuxing Wang. 1991. On the competitiveness of on-line real-time task scheduling. In *Proceedings of the 12th IEEE Real-Time Systems Symposium (RTSS)*. 106–115.
[6] Allan Borodin and Ran El-Yaniv. 1998. *Online computation and competitive analysis*. Vol. 53. Cambridge University Press.
[7] Jessica Chang, Samir Khuller, and Koyel Mukherjee. 2014. LP rounding and combinatorial algorithms for minimizing active and busy time. In *Proceedings of the 26th ACM Symposium on Parallelism in Algorithms and Architectures (SPAA)*. 118–127.
[8] Julia Chuzhoy, Rafail Ostrovsky, and Yuval Rabani. 2006. Approximation algorithms for the job interval selection problem and related scheduling problems. *Mathematics of Operations Research* 31, 4 (2006), 730–738.
[9] Ulrich Faigle and Willem M. Nawijn. 1995. Note on scheduling intervals on-line. *Discrete Applied Mathematics* 58, 1 (1995), 13–17.
[10] Michele Flammini, Gianpiero Monaco, Luca Moscardelli, Hadas Shachnai, Mordechai Shalom, Tami Tamir, and Shmuel Zaks. 2010. Minimizing total busy time in parallel scheduling with application to optical networks. *Theoretical Computer Science* 411, 40-42 (2010), 3553–3562.
[11] Rohit Khandekar, Baruch Schieber, Hadas Shachnai, and Tami Tamir. 2015. Real-time scheduling to minimize machine busy times. *Journal of Scheduling* 18, 6 (2015), 561–573.
[12] Frederic Koehler and Samir Khuller. 2017. Busy-Time Scheduling on a Bounded Number of Machines. In *Proceedings of the 15th Algorithms and Data Structures Symposium (WADS)*, to appear.
[13] Antoon W.J. Kolen, Jan Karel Lenstra, Christos H. Papadimitriou, and Frits C.R. Spieksma. 2007. Interval scheduling: A survey. *Naval Research Logistics* 54, 5 (2007), 530–543.
[14] Mikhail Y. Kovalyov, C.T. Ng, and T.C. Edwin Cheng. 2007. Fixed interval scheduling: Models, applications, computational complexity and algorithms. *European Journal of Operational Research* 178, 2 (2007), 331–342.
[15] Yusen Li, Xueyan Tang, and Wentong Cai. 2014. On dynamic bin packing for resource allocation in the cloud. In *Proceedings of the 26th ACM Symposium on Parallelism in Algorithms and Architectures (SPAA)*. 2–11.
[16] Yusen Li, Xueyan Tang, and Wentong Cai. 2016. Dynamic Bin Packing for On-Demand Cloud Resource Allocation. *IEEE Transactions on Parallel and Distributed Systems* 27, 1 (2016), 157–170.
[17] Richard J. Lipton and Andrew Tomkins. 1994. Online Interval Scheduling. In *Proceedings of the 5th ACM-SIAM Symposium on Discrete Algorithms (SODA)*. 302–311.
[18] George B. Mertzios, Mordechai Shalom, Ariella Voloshin, Prudence W.H. Wong, and Shmuel Zaks. 2015. Optimizing busy time on parallel machines. *Theoretical Computer Science* 562 (2015), 524–541.
[19] Runtian Ren and Xueyan Tang. 2016. Clairvoyant Dynamic Bin Packing for Job Scheduling with Minimum Server Usage Time. In *Proceedings of the 28th ACM Symposium on Parallelism in Algorithms and Architectures (SPAA)*. 227–237.
[20] Runtian Ren, Xueyan Tang, Yusen Li, and Wentong Cai. 2016. Competitiveness of Dynamic Bin Packing for Online Cloud Server Allocation. *IEEE/ACM Transactions on Networking* (2016).
[21] Steven S. Seiden. 1998. Randomized online interval scheduling. *Operations Research Letters* 22, 4 (1998), 171–177.
[22] Mordechai Shalom, Ariella Voloshin, Prudence W.H. Wong, Fencol C.C. Yung, and Shmuel Zaks. 2014. Online optimization of busy time on parallel machines. *Theoretical Computer Science* 560 (2014), 190–206.
[23] Xueyan Tang, Yusen Li, Runtian Ren, and Wentong Cai. 2016. On First Fit Bin Packing for Online Cloud Server Allocation. In *Proceedings of the 30th IEEE International Parallel and Distributed Processing Symposium (IPDPS)*. 323–332.
[24] Gerhard J. Woeginger. 1994. On-line scheduling of jobs with fixed start and end times. *Theoretical Computer Science* 130, 1 (1994), 5–16.

Minimizing Total Weighted Flow Time with Calibrations

Vincent Chau
Shenzhen Institutes of Advanced Technology
China
vincentchau@siat.ac.cn

Minming Li
Department of Computer Science
City University of Hong Kong, Hong Kong
minming.li@cityu.edu.hk

Samuel McCauley
IT University of Copenhagen
Denmark
samc@itu.dk

Kai Wang
Department of Computer Science
City University of Hong Kong, Hong Kong
kai.wang@my.cityu.edu.hk

ABSTRACT

In sensitive applications, machines need to be periodically calibrated to ensure that they run to high standards. Creating an efficient schedule on these machines requires attention to two metrics: ensuring good throughput of the jobs, and ensuring that not too much cost is spent on machine calibration.

In this paper we examine flow time as a metric for scheduling with calibrations. While previous papers guaranteed that jobs would meet a certain deadline, we relax that constraint to a tradeoff: we want to balance how long the average job waits with how many costly calibrations we need to perform.

One advantage of this metric is that it allows for online schedules (where an algorithm is unaware of a job until it arrives). Thus we give two types of results. We give an efficient offline algorithm which gives the optimal schedule on a single machine for a set of jobs which are known ahead of time. We also give online algorithms which adapt to jobs as they come. Our online algorithms are constant competitive for unweighted jobs on single or multiple machines, and constant-competitive for weighted jobs on a single machine.

1 INTRODUCTION

Modern industrial products like processors and digital cameras must be manufactured, consistently, to exacting standards. The machines that make these products are high-performance and high-maintenance, and perform very precise tasks. As such, they need to be calibrated before they can be trusted to perform a job. Performing these calibrations can be very expensive, possibly much more than the cost of running the machines. The calibrations are only effective for a set period of time, after which the machine may no longer be accurate, and must be (expensively) recalibrated before running more jobs.

With these costs in mind, recent work has considered scheduling on machines that need to be calibrated [1, 8, 14]. The goal of algorithms in this framework is to minimize the number of calibrations, while ensuring that all jobs complete by their deadlines.

This objective function has an interesting property: in most objective functions (say, minimizing total waiting time, or maximizing number of jobs completed by a deadline), it is generally profitable to schedule a job as early as possible. But to minimize calibrations, the algorithm wants to group jobs together as much as possible, possibly delaying some jobs considerably. The known algorithms in this framework are designed to effectively handle this tradeoff: grouping jobs for more efficient calibrations, while maintaining a reasonable schedule where jobs are not delayed too long.

The original motivation for scheduling with calibrations came directly from the Integrated Stockpile Evaluation (ISE) program to test nuclear weapons periodically. The tests for these weapons require calibrations that are expensive in a monetary (thought not necessarily temporal) sense. This motivation is specified further in [8, 12, 20].

However, this motivation can extend to any context where machines performing jobs must be calibrated periodically. For example, high-precision machines require periodic calibration to ensure precision. Methods for calibrating these machines is itself an area of research; some examples include [23, 25, 27, 28]. Oftentimes, machines are no longer considered to be accurately calibrated after a set period of time. There are many guidelines to determine this *calibration interval*, or period of time between calibrations, both from industry and academia [5, 7, 17, 18, 22, 26].

Calibrations have applications in many areas, including robotics [9, 13, 21], pharmaceuticals [3, 7, 15], and digital cameras [2, 6, 29].

We formally model calibrations as follows. We must ***calibrate*** a machine before it is able to perform tasks. The machine stays ***calibrated*** for $T \geq 2$ time steps, after which it must remain idle until it is recalibrated. We refer to these T time steps following a calibration as an ***interval***. Calibrating a machine is instantaneous, meaning that a machine can be recalibrated between two job executions that run in successive time steps.

We consider the following calibration costs/constraints. In the online setting (Section 3), each calibration has cost G; our objective is to minimize the sum of the calibration cost and the total flow time. In the offline setting (Section 4) we have a budget of K calibrations;

The work described in this paper was supported by a grant from Research Grants Council of the Hong Kong Special Administrative Region, China (Project No. CityU 11268616), by NSFC (No. 61433012, U1435215), by Shenzhen basic research grant JCYJ20160229195940462, by NSF grants CCF 1617618, IIS 1247726, IIS 1251137, CNS 1408695, and CCF 1439084, and by Sandia National Laboratories. Work done in part while Samuel McCauley was visiting the City University of Hong Kong.

SPAA'17, , July 24–26, 2017, Washington, DC, USA.

ACM ISBN 978-1-4503-4593-4/17/07...$15.00
http://dx.doi.org/10.1145/3087556.3087573

the objective is to find the schedule that minimizes total flow time while only calibrating K times.

While minimizing calibrations, we still want to make sure the algorithm provides good throughput for the jobs. In this paper, we want to minimize the average weighted flow time of jobs (the weighted average of the time each job waits, from when it is released to its completion). Because the number of jobs remains constant, minimizing the total flow time is equivalent to minimizing the average; the remainder of the paper only discusses minimizing total flow time for simplicity.

1.1 Results

Our online algorithms include:

- a 3-competitive algorithm for a single machine with unweighted jobs,
- a 12-competitive algorithm for a single machine with weighted jobs, and
- a 12-competitive algorithm for multiple machines with unweighted jobs.

We give a lower bound of 2 for the online case.

For the offline case with one machine and weighted jobs, we give an $O(Kn^3)$ dynamic programming algorithm, where n is the number of jobs and K is the budget for the number of calibrations.

While proving the performance of our algorithms we give several structural lemmas for scheduling with calibrations, which may be useful for future research.

1.2 Related Work

The initial study of scheduling with calibrations was by Bender et al. [8], who considered minimizing the number of calibrations for jobs with release times and deadlines. They gave an optimal solution for a single machine, but were only able to achieve a 2-approximation for multiple machines (except for some special cases).

Later, Fineman and Sheridan extended these results for jobs with non-unit processing times [14]. Their work begins with the observation that minimizing calibrations for jobs with deadlines generalizes the well-known machine minimization problem—as T becomes arbitrarily large, the problem is simply to minimize the number of machines. Somewhat surprisingly, the calibrations for arbitrary T can be minimized nearly as efficiently: an algorithm with a given performance bound for machine minimization leads to an algorithm with similar performance for minimizing calibrations.

More recently, Angel et al. developed dynamic programming algorithms for further generalizations—where for example there are multiple kinds of calibrations, or jobs have nonunit processing times, but are preemptible [1].

Scheduling with calibrations has similarities with some other well-known scheduling problems, such as minimizing idle periods [4], and scheduling on cloud-based machines which must be rented to perform work [19].

2 PRELIMINARIES

Our algorithm must schedule a set of n jobs $\mathcal{J}$ on P machines. Each job j has a release time r_j, a weight w_j, and a processing time $p_j = 1$ (all jobs have identical, unit length). If a job is scheduled to begin at t_j, it ends at $t_j + 1$, and incurs flow $w_j(t_j + 1 - r_j)$.

We assume jobs are indexed in ascending release time order, i.e. $r_1 \leq \ldots \leq r_n$. Furthermore, we assume that there are at most P jobs with any given release time without loss of generality (so if $P = 1$, we assume that all release times are distinct).[1]

We refer to the time period $[t, t + 1)$ as ***time step*** t. We assume all such t, as well as all release times, are integers. We call a time step ***idle*** if no job is being processed during that time step.

A machine can be ***calibrated*** at a time step t for cost G. We refer this time step as the ***calibration time***. This calibration happens instantaneously (the calibration does not prevent the machine from running jobs during both t and $t - 1$, if it is otherwise able). We refer to the T calibrated time steps from t to $t+T-1$ as an ***interval***; we say that the interval ***begins*** at t and ***ends*** at $t + T$. We call an interval ***full*** if the machine is never idle during the interval, and ***non-full*** otherwise.

A schedule $\mathcal{S}$ consists of two parts:

- an assignment of each job j to a time step t and a machine m, and
- a set of calibration times for each machine.

A correct schedule only assigns one job to each time step on any machine, and only assigns jobs to calibrated time steps (i.e. no more than T time steps after the machine was calibrated).

We begin with an observation that if the set of calibration times is given, we can optimally assign the jobs to machines and time steps using an efficient, online algorithm.

Observation 2.1. *Consider a set of calibration times C, a set of jobs $\mathcal{J}$, and a number of machines P, we can optimally assign $\mathcal{J}$ to time steps using the following online algorithm:*
For each time step t:

1. *Add all jobs arriving at t to the set of waiting jobs W.*
2. *For every calibration in C at t, calibrate the next machine in round-robin order.*
3. *For each machine m that is calibrated at t, schedule the highest-weight job $j \in W$ on m at time t. If multiple jobs are tied for heaviest weight, choose the job with earliest release time. Remove j from W.*

Proof. Let $\mathcal{S}$ be the schedule given by this algorithm.

Since the machines are indistinguishable, they can be calibrated in round-robin order without loss of generality. In the case that there are more than P calibrations in less than T time steps, scheduling in round-robin order maximizes the number of calibrated time steps. See [8, Lemma 7] for a thorough discussion.

To show that this is an optimal assignment of jobs to times, we proceed by contradiction. Let t be the first time that $\mathcal{S}$ deviates from every optimal schedule—that is, $\mathcal{S}$ schedules j at t, but there exists an optimal $\mathcal{S}'$ that either schedules j' at t with $w_j \neq w_{j'}$, or chooses not to schedule at all. (Meanwhile, no schedule that matches $\mathcal{S}$ up to $t - 1$ schedules j at t.)

Consider a schedule $\mathcal{S}''$ which is the same as $\mathcal{S}'$, except we swap the times when j and j' are scheduled (if S' does not schedule a job, we let $w_{j'} = 0$ and swap j' with the empty time step at t). Since $w_j \neq w_{j'}$, $w_{j'} < w_j$ by definition of $\mathcal{S}$. Then $\mathcal{S}''$ has smaller weighted flow time than $\mathcal{S}'$, contradicting its optimality.

[1] If more than P jobs have the same release time r, we take the lightest job and increase its release time by 1. Since at most P jobs can be scheduled at r (and it's always cheapest to delay the lightest job), this does not change the optimal cost of the instance.

A similar exchange argument shows that ties can be broken by release time without loss of generality. □

3   ONLINE ALGORITHMS

In this section we consider an online model for scheduling with calibrations. In the online setting, an algorithm first learns about job j at time r_j: before the algorithm makes any decisions at time t, it receives a list of jobs with $r_j = t$, as well as w_j for each such job.

In this section, we limit our calibrations by giving them a (potentially very large) cost that must be balanced with flow. Each calibration costs G; our goal is to minimize

$$G \cdot (\# \text{ calibrations}) + \sum_{j \in \mathcal{J}} w_j(t_j + 1 - r_j)$$

where job j begins at time t_j and ends at time $t_j + 1$.

Our online algorithms do not make any assumptions on G or T. In particular, if $T < G/T$, while our algorithms work as-is, they can be further simplified while achieving equal or better bounds. For example, the "immediate calibrations" in Algorithm 1 can be removed entirely, and the corresponding charging arguments can be considerably simplified. Similarly, if $G/T < 1$, our online algorithms all schedule every incoming job immediately, again greatly simplifying their operation and analysis. We focus on bounds that apply for all G and T, leaving the analysis of online scheduling with calibrations under special cases to future work.

We analyze our algorithms using competitive analysis. An algorithm is said to be α-*competitive* if, for every sufficiently large input I, the algorithm performs at most an α factor worse than the optimal offline algorithm on I [10, 24].

We refer to an optimal schedule for an input $(\mathcal{J}, P)$ as $\text{OPT}(\mathcal{J}, P)$. Our analysis usually considers a fixed input, in which case we refer to an optimal schedule as OPT.

We begin with a lower bound, which shows that no deterministic algorithm is better than 2-competitive.

LEMMA 3.1. *For a single machine and unweighted jobs, any deterministic online algorithm can not be better than $(2-o(1))$-competitive. (The $o(1)$ term depends on T and G.)*

PROOF. The adversary begins by releasing a job at time 0. Our lower bound considers two cases.

(1) If the online algorithm calibrates at time 0, the adversary releases another job at time T. Then the online algorithm incurs calibration cost $2G$ and flow cost 2, with a total cost of $2G + 2$. Meanwhile, the optimal solution can calibrate at $t = 1$, with cost $3 + G$. This gives a competitive ratio of $\frac{2G+2}{G+3} = 2 - \frac{4}{G+3}$.

(2) If the online algorithm waits (does not calibrate immediately) then the adversary releases one more job for each time step from 1 to $T - 1$. Then the online algorithm has cost at least $2T + G$ (since each job has flow at least 2), whereas an optimal algorithm calibrates at time 0 and has cost $T + G$. Thus the competitive ratio is $\frac{2T+G}{T+G} = 2 - \frac{G}{T+G}$.

Thus, the competitive ratio can be arbitrarily close to 2 for large G, and $T \gg G$. □

3.1   Unweighted Single-Machine Algorithm

In this section, we examine a special case where all jobs are unweighted ($w_j = 1$) and must be scheduled on a single machine ($P = 1$). We give a 3-competitive algorithm.

The idea of the algorithm is to delay arriving jobs until their flow is equal to the calibration cost G. However, the algorithm has a maximum number of jobs it can delay, after which it must schedule.

Algorithm 1 Online Unweighted Calibration on One Machine

1: $Q \leftarrow$ empty priority queue of jobs, ordered by release time
2: **for** each time step t **do**
3:     **if** a job j arrives at time t **then**
4:         Insert j in Q
5:     **end if**
6:     **if** t is not calibrated **then**
7:         $f \leftarrow$ flow cost of scheduling all $j \in Q$ starting at $t + 1$
8:         **if** Q contains $\geq G/T$ jobs **or** $f \geq G$ **then**
9:             Calibrate at t
10:         **else**
11:             $p \leftarrow$ total flow of jobs in the most recent calibration
12:             **if** $p < G/2$ **and** a job is released at t **then**
13:                 Calibrate at t
14:             **end if**
15:         **end if**
16:     **end if**
17:     **if** Q is not empty and t is calibrated **then**
18:         Remove the earliest-released job j' from Q
19:         Schedule j' at t
20:     **end if**
21: **end for**

At a high level, Algorithm 1 is similar to known algorithms, like the optimal solution to the ski rental problem. Both delay until a large penalty cost is reached (G total flow in this case).

On the other hand, Algorithm 1 is more aggressive at some points: if there are G/T waiting jobs, or if a job is released after a calibration in which jobs had total flow less than $G/2$, it calibrates regardless of the flow of the current waiting jobs. Interestingly, although the algorithm appears to schedule somewhat early in these cases (especially if G/T is small), it is still 3-competitive.

We bound the algorithm's performance using a charging argument. To begin, we observe that OPT and Algorithm 1 schedule jobs in the same order: release time order (this follows from Observation 2.1). Our proof relies heavily on this structure.

Before proving the competitive ratio, we need a structural lemma to show that we never double-charge to a calibration. Let J_i be the set of jobs scheduled in interval i by Algorithm 1. We partition J_i into two subsets: J_i^E is the set of jobs scheduled earlier in OPT than in Algorithm 1 or at the same time in both, and J_i^L is the set of jobs scheduled strictly later.

LEMMA 3.2. *Consider an interval i scheduled by Algorithm 1 starting at time b_i with nonempty J_i^E. Let i^{OPT} be the earliest interval in OPT containing a job in J_i. Then for all $i' > i$, i^{OPT} contains no jobs in $J_{i'}$.*

Proof. Since J_i^E is nonempty, and both OPT and Algorithm 1 schedule in release time order, the first job in J_i must be in J_i^E. Since the first job in J_i is scheduled in the first time step of i, i^{OPT} must begin no later than i.

Let j' be the first job in J_{i+1}. If j' is released after $b_i + T$, it (and thus all jobs in i') must be scheduled after $b_i + T$ as well, so it cannot be scheduled in i^{OPT}. On the other hand, if j' is released before $b_i + T$, since Algorithm 1 schedules according to Observation 2.1, there must be T jobs in J_i. Then there are $T + 1$ jobs in $J_i \cup \{j'\}$; thus j' cannot be scheduled in i^{OPT}, and neither can any job in $J_{i'}$. □

Theorem 3.3. *Algorithm 1 is 3-competitive.*

Proof. We use a charging argument for each interval i. We charge to both costs in OPT: the cost of calibrating intervals, and the flow of jobs. We argue that each calibration is only charged to once using Lemma 3.2. The flow of each job is only charged to once because we only charge to the flow of jobs in J_i.

We break into two cases: in the first, Algorithm 1 calibrated i due to total flow of G; in the second, the calibration was due to G/T waiting jobs. If Algorithm 1 calibrated $i + 1$ because i had flow at most $G/2$ (but there were less than G/T waiting jobs with total flow less than G), we call $i + 1$ an ***immediate calibration***. If $i + 1$ is an immediate calibration, we consider the cost of i and $i + 1$ simultaneously.

Let b_i be the time when Algorithm 1 schedules interval i. Let f_i be the total flow of all jobs in i released before b_i, and let e_i be the total flow of all jobs in i released on or after b_i. We have $f_i \leq G$ by Algorithm 1, and $e_i \leq G$ since there be at most T incoming jobs, and each is delayed by $|Q| \leq G/T$. As in Lemma 3.2, let i^{OPT} be the earliest interval in OPT containing a job in J_i.

Case 1 (Calibrated due to flow G): We split into two subcases. First, we assume that all jobs in i are scheduled later in OPT than in Algorithm 1 (J_i^E is empty). Then we charge to the flow of the jobs in OPT. Algorithm 1 incurs a cost of $G + f_i + e_i < 2G + e_i$, while OPT incurs a cost of at least $f_i^{OPT} + e_i \geq G + e_i$, leading to a competitive ratio of 2.

Otherwise, (in the second subcase) J_i^E is nonempty. We charge to i^{OPT}; this charging is unique by Lemma 3.2. Algorithm 1 incurs a cost of $G + f_i + e_i < 3G$ while OPT incurs a calibration cost of G; we obtain a competitive ratio of 3.

Case 2 (Calibrated due to G/T waiting jobs): We split into three subcases.

Case 2a (Nonempty J_i^E): First, we assume that J_i^E is nonempty. If there is no immediate calibration following i, we can charge to i^{OPT}. This calibration is only charged to once by Lemma 3.2. Algorithm 1 has cost $G + f_i + e_i < 3G$; we charge to an interval with calibration cost G.

If $f_i + e_i \leq G/2$, and $i + 1$ is an immediate calibration, consider whether interval $i+1$ has a job scheduled earlier in OPT (i.e. whether J_{i+1}^E is empty). If interval $i+1$ has a job scheduled earlier in OPT, we charge to two intervals in OPT: i^{OPT} and $(i + 1)^{OPT}$ (the earliest interval in OPT containing a job in J_{i+1}). Lemma 3.2 shows that these are two different intervals, and that they are not charged to by any other interval. Intervals i and $i + 1$ have total cost $2G + e_i + f_i + e_{i+1} + f_{i+1} < 5G/2$; we charge to a calibration cost of $2G$ in OPT. Otherwise, if all jobs in J_{i+1} are scheduled later in OPT, Algorithm 1 has cost $5G/2 + e_{i+1} + f_{i+1}$, and OPT has cost at least $G + e_{i+1} + f_{i+1}$ (again charging to i^{OPT}). In all cases, we achieve a competitive ratio of 3.

Case 2b (All jobs in J_i delayed at least T): In the second subcase, we assume that J_i^E is empty (all jobs in J_i are scheduled later in OPT), and all jobs in J_i are scheduled at or after $b_i + T$ in OPT. We charge the cost of J_i ($G + e_i + f_i$) to the jobs' flow in OPT, which must be at least $G + e_i + f_i$.

If J_{i+1} is an immediate calibration, all jobs in J_{i+1} have flow cost 1, and must have larger flow cost in OPT. Thus we charge the calibration and flow costs of J_i and J_{i+1} ($2G + e_i + f_i + e_{i+1} + f_{i+1}$) to their flow costs in OPT, which must be at least $G + e_i + f_i + e_{i+1} + f_{i+1}$, giving a competitive ratio of 2.

Case 2c (All jobs delayed; some by a small amount): Finally, we assume that all jobs in J_i are scheduled later in OPT, but at least one is scheduled before $b_i + T$. This means that the interval i^{OPT} must be scheduled before $b_i + T$. This interval contains no jobs in $J_{i'}$ for $i' > i + 1$: if i^{OPT} contains a job from J_{i+1}, this follows from Lemma 3.2; otherwise, all jobs in J_{i+1} (and thus $J_{i'}$) are scheduled after i^{OPT} ends. We charge both i and $i + 1$ to i^{OPT}—even if $i + 1$ is not an immediate calibration.

First, assume that $i+1$ is an immediate calibration. Then i and $i+1$ have total cost at most $2G + e_i + f_i + e_{i+1} + f_{i+1} \leq 5G/2 + |J_{i+1}|$, as each job in J_{i+1} is scheduled immediately. We charge to cost $G + |J_{i+1}|$ in OPT: G from the calibration cost of i^{OPT}, and $|J_{i+1}|$ since each job in J_{i+1} must incur flow cost at least 1 in OPT. This gives a competitive ratio of 5/2.

If $i+1$ is not an immediate calibration (and i has total flow at least $G/2$), these intervals have total cost at most $2G + f_i + e_i + f_{i+1} + e_{i+1}$. Since all jobs in J_i are scheduled later in OPT, we charge to their flow as well as the calibration of i^{OPT}, so OPT has cost at least $G + f_i + e_i$. The ratio between these is minimized when $f_i + e_i$ is minimized, at $f_i + e_i = G/2$. Then Algorithm 1 has cost $5G/2 + f_{i+1} + e_{i+1} < 9G/2$, and OPT has cost at least $3G/2$, giving a competitive ratio of 3. □

3.2 Weighted Single-Machine Algorithm

When jobs have weights (but must be scheduled on a single machine), we follow a similar algorithm to the unweighted case. The main differences are that the algorithm now calibrates if the waiting jobs have total weight G/T, and the algorithm no longer performs immediate calibrations (after an interval with flow $\leq G/2$).

We assume that all algorithms schedule the heaviest possible job first, breaking ties by release time (Observation 2.1). Thus, our algorithm and OPT may schedule jobs in a different order, since which job is scheduled next depends on which time steps are calibrated.

This lack of a common ordering makes charging more difficult. Our solution to this is twofold. First, in Lemma 3.4, we show that we can restrict ourselves to algorithms that schedule in order of release time, losing only a factor 2 in cost. Second, we charge sequences of full intervals (rather than each interval individually). While it is difficult to reason about Algorithm 2's job order within each interval, we show in Lemmas 3.6 and 3.7 that we can make useful statements about its behavior between sequences.

Lemma 3.4. *If an optimal solution of a given instance has cost C_{OPT}, there exists a solution with all jobs scheduled in order of release time with cost at most $2C_{OPT}$.*

Algorithm 2 Online Weighted Calibration on One Machine

```
Q ← empty priority queue of jobs, ordered by release time
for each time step t do
    if a job j arrives at time t then
        Insert j in Q
    end if
    if t is not calibrated then
        f ← flow cost of scheduling all j ∈ Q starting at t + 1
        if Σ_{j∈Q} w_j ≥ G/T or |Q| = T or f ≥ G then
            Calibrate at t
        end if
    end if
    if Q is not empty and t is calibrated then
        Extract the job j′ with smallest weight from Q
        Schedule j′ at t
    end if
end for
```

Proof. We show how to transform an optimal schedule (with C calibrations) into a new schedule where jobs are in release time order. This new schedule will schedule all jobs no later than they were in the original schedule, so the flow cost will be smaller. Furthermore, the new schedule will have no more than $2C$ calibrations. Thus the total cost of the new schedule is at most $2C_{\mathrm{OPT}}$.

Consider each job in the schedule, in order from latest to earliest release time. We maintain the invariant that after considering a job j, it is scheduled at a time t_j such that $t_j \geq r_j$, and all jobs with $r_{j'} > r_j$ have $t_{j'} > t_j$. At intermediate points while constructing this schedule, several jobs may be scheduled at the same time. However, we also maintain that after considering job j, no two jobs with release times at least r_j are scheduled at the same time.

For each job j, move j before all jobs j' with $r_j' > r_j$. In other words, move j to the time step immediately before the job with the next-largest release time is scheduled (even if there is a job already scheduled at this time step).

We now show that these invariants are maintained. Each job j is scheduled before all jobs with later release times by definition. To show $t_j \geq r_j$, we must have all jobs with $r_{j'} > r_j$ scheduled at $t_{j'} \geq r_{j'} \geq r_j + 1$; thus, r_j is a time step before all jobs with later release times are scheduled, so it satisfies the requirement for t_j. Since t_j is the maximum time step satisfying the requirement, $t_j \geq r_j$. Finally, no job with release time larger than r_j can be scheduled at t_j; thus j is not scheduled at the same time as a job with larger release time. Since the invariant was maintained for all jobs with larger release time, the invariant is maintained.

Now we show that there are no more than $2C$ calibrations. Each time we add a job, we add one new time step—this time step is already calibrated, or is adjacent to a sequence of newly-filled time steps, the last of which is adjacent to a calibrated time step.

Consider a sequence of calibrated time steps in the new schedule. All jobs from this sequence must have come from intervals contained in this sequence, as a job j being pushed back never "skips over" an uncalibrated time step. As j is pushed back, it may empty some slots, but we assume that they remain calibrated in the new schedule. Thus, all jobs from this calibrated sequence must come from an interval in this sequence. Let p be the number of previously-uncalibrated slots in this sequence. Then the number of extra calibrations necessary is $\lceil p/T \rceil$. Furthermore, the number of calibrations previously in this interval was at least $\lceil p/T \rceil$. Thus the number of calibrations for each sequence is at most doubled. Thus the total number of calibrations is no more than $2C$. □

In some circumstances we want to charge the online algorithm's flow cost to OPT's calibration cost (like we did for the cases with nonempty J_E in the proof of Theorem 3.3). But if jobs have extremely large weights, our intervals can have correspondingly large flow, even if they are scheduled at release time. Similarly, Algorithm 2 calibrates immediately if the waiting jobs have total weight more than G/T; however, heavy incoming jobs can cause a much larger total queue weight. Lemma 3.5 helps deal with these issues by showing that if we ignore the unavoidable flow cost of w_j for every job, we can bound the total flow of jobs in an interval.

Lemma 3.5. *Let J_i be the set of jobs scheduled in interval i by Algorithm 2, where each $j \in J_i$ is processed at time t_j.*[2] *Then $\sum_{j \in J_i} w_j(t_j - r_j) < 2G$.*

Proof. Let i begin at b_i. The total flow cost of jobs in interval i is the sum of three terms:

(1) the flow incurred by jobs if they had been scheduled at b_i (the value f in Algorithm 2 is this flow at $b_i + 1$),
(2) the flow of incoming jobs scheduled immediately, and
(3) for each time step t, w_j flow for each unfinished $j \in J_i$.

Term 1 is at most G by Algorithm 2, and term 2 does not count towards our cost (since these jobs are scheduled at their release time). Thus, our goal is to show that the total cost of term 3 is at most $G + \sum_{j \in J_i} w_j$.

Let Q_t denote the queue of waiting jobs at time $b_i + t$, not including the job scheduled at $b_i + t$. Then we want to show $\sum_{t=0}^{T-1} \sum_{j \in Q_t} w_j \leq G$.

First we bound the cost of Q_0. At the time step before b_i, Algorithm 2 did not schedule an interval, so the total weight of all waiting jobs was less than G/T. At b_i, any job released at time b_i is added to the queue, and the largest job in Q_0 is removed; thus $\sum_{j \in Q_0} w_j < G/T$.

Now we show that $\sum_{j \in Q_{i-1}} w_j \leq \sum_{j \in Q_i} w_j$. At each time step, a job enters the queue, and a job is popped off the queue to be scheduled. If no job arrives, or if the arriving job does not have the largest weight in the queue, this is a net decrease in weight and we have $Q_i < Q_{i-1}$. If the arriving job has the largest weight in the queue, it is scheduled immediately, and $Q_i = Q_{i-1}$. Thus, $\sum_{t=0}^{T-1} \sum_{j \in Q_t} w_j \leq \sum_{t=0}^{T-1} \sum_{j \in Q_0} w_j < G$. □

As mentioned before, our charging argument considers groups of consecutive intervals. In particular, we partition the schedule of Algorithm 2 into maximal groups of consecutive intervals, called ***sequences***, such that all but the last interval in each sequence is full.[3] This partitioning is unique, since the boundaries between sequences are exactly the non-full intervals. We say a sequence ***ends*** at e_I, the final time step of its last interval, and ***begins*** at b_I, the time step immediately after the previous sequence ends

[2] Thus j finishes at $t_j + 1$ and incurs flow $w_j(t_j + 1 - r_j)$.
[3] The last interval may be full if it is the last interval in the entire schedule.

($b_I = 0$ for the first sequence). Observation 2.1 implies that all jobs scheduled within each sequence I are released on or after b_I.

Let OPT_r be the optimal algorithm that schedules all jobs in order of release time.

The following lemma is the basis of our charging argument. Essentially, we show that for any sequence I, since most of the intervals are full, OPT_r must calibrate all but the last interval earlier than in Algorithm 2.

Lemma 3.6. *For every sequence I, for every $k < |I|$, there are at least k intervals scheduled by OPT_r that:*

- *end after b_I, but*
- *begin no later than the kth interval in I.*

Proof. Assume the contrary: let k^{OPT} be the kth interval scheduled by OPT_r after b_I, and k^I be the kth interval in I, with k^{OPT} scheduled after k^I. Since k^I is full, there were at least kT jobs released between b_I and the time k^I ends. In particular, since OPT_r schedules in release time order, all jobs in k^{OPT} were released by the time k^I ends. This means that k^{OPT} can be scheduled one time step earlier, improving its flow time and contradicting the definition of OPT_r. □

Our final structural lemma shows that we can, in some cases, bound the flow of jobs scheduled later in OPT_r than in Algorithm 2 for a given sequence. The assumptions in the lemma are specific because they closely match our charging scheme.

Lemma 3.7. *Let I be a sequence of intervals scheduled by Algorithm 2 with jobs J_I, and let ℓ be the last interval in I. Let ℓ^{OPT} be the $|I|$th interval in OPT_r containing jobs in J_I. Assume ℓ^{OPT} begins after ℓ ends. Let f_ℓ^q be the total flow of the jobs in ℓ if no new jobs were incoming (corresponding to the value f in Algorithm 2 one time step before ℓ is scheduled), and let f_ℓ be the actual flow incurred by all jobs in ℓ. Then the total flow incurred by OPT_r of all jobs in J_I scheduled in ℓ^{OPT} and later intervals is at least $f_\ell - f_\ell^q$.*

Proof. Deferred to the full version for space. □

Now we are ready to prove the performance of our algorithm. We show that Algorithm 2 is 6-competitive with OPT_r, which implies by Lemma 3.4 that it is 12-competitive with OPT.

Theorem 3.8. *Algorithm 2 is 12-competitive.*

Proof. Consider a sequence of intervals I. We charge the last unit of flow of all jobs scheduled by Algorithm 2 to their last unit of flow in OPT_r.

We charge the remainder of the cost of the kth interval of I to the kth interval of OPT_r ending after b_I, for all $k < I$. In particular, we charge to half its calibration cost, $G/2$. We only charge to half the cost because we will charge to some intervals twice.

For the last interval in I, let ℓ^{OPT} be the $|I|$th interval containing jobs in J_I in OPT_r.

(1) If ℓ^{OPT} begins after e_I and is charged to by two later sequences, we charge to the flow of all jobs in J_I scheduled by OPT_r in ℓ^{OPT} or later.
(2) Otherwise, if $|I| = 1$ and ℓ^{OPT} begins after b_I, we charge to half the calibration cost of ℓ^{OPT}, *and* the flow cost of all jobs in J_I scheduled by OPT_r in ℓ^{OPT} or later.
(3) Otherwise, we charge to one time step of flow for each $j \in J_i$, plus half the calibration cost of ℓ^{OPT}.

First, we show that we charge to any interval i in OPT_r at most twice. By Lemma 3.6, i cannot be charged to by two intervals from the same sequence I. Since all jobs in a sequence I are released after I begins, and all but the last interval charge to earlier intervals by Lemma 3.6, if an interval is charged to by two different sequences, it must be charged to by the $|I|$th interval for some I. Then by the definition of Case 1, it can only be charged to twice.

We now examine the total costs of an interval i with jobs J_i, in a sequence I with jobs J_I. We split into two cases.

Case 1 (i charges to a calibration cost in OPT_r): We charge the flow incurred during the time step in which each job is scheduled to its flow in OPT_r, and the remainder of the cost of i to the kth interval in OPT_r containing jobs from J_I. By Lemma 3.5 we charge a cost of $3G + \sum_{j \in J_i} w_j$ to a cost in OPT of at least $G/2 + \sum_{j \in J_i} w_j$; this leads to a competitive ratio of 6.

Case 2 (i charges to flow): If i charges to flow, by Case 1, there are two intervals i_1, i_2 that charge to the calibration cost of an interval ℓ^{OPT} containing jobs from J_I. If $|I| > 1$, we examine the total cost of i, i_1, and i_2, and lower bound the cost they charge to. Otherwise, if $|I| = 1$, we charge the cost of i directly.

First, for this argument to be correct, we need that for every ℓ^{OPT}, there is only one interval in a sequence of size greater than one that charges to flow in ℓ^{OPT} (since we charge to the calibration cost of ℓ^{OPT} when $|I| > 1$). This follows from Lemma 3.6.

Now, consider the case where $|I| = 1$. The total cost is $G + f_i$, where f_i is the flow in I. Let f_i^{OPT} be the flow of the jobs in J_I incurred in OPT_r. Since all jobs in i (and thus all jobs in J_I) are scheduled after ℓ^{OPT}, and ℓ^{OPT} begins after e_I, they are scheduled beginning at least T time steps later in OPT_r. Immediately, we have $f_i^{OPT} > f_i$. If i was scheduled due to flow G we have $f_i^{OPT} > G$ by definition; if i was scheduled due to G/T weight of waiting jobs, each waits for T additional steps, and again $f_i^{OPT} > G$. Thus $G + f_i$ is at most twice f_i^{OPT}.

Now, consider $|I| > 1$. Let f_i be the flow of all jobs in i, and f_i^q be the flow of all jobs in i incurred if there had been no incoming jobs after i began (see Lemma 3.7). Then by Lemma 3.7, i charges to a flow of at least $f_i - f_i^q$. Either i_1 or i_2 must charge to ℓ^{OPT} using Case 2; without loss of generality we call this i_1. Then i_1 is in a sequence of size 1. In particular, all jobs scheduled in i_1 are scheduled in ℓ^{OPT} or later and must incur at least the same flow.

Then the total cost of i, i_1, and i_2 is $G + f_i + G + f_{i_1} + G + f_{i_2} \leq 5G + f_i + f_{i_1} + \sum_{j \in J_{i_2}} w_j$ by Lemma 3.5. We charge to a cost of $G + (f_i - f_i^q) + f_{i_1} + \sum_{j \in J_{i_2}} w_j$. Since $f_i^q \leq G$, our competitive ratio is

$$\frac{6G + (f_i - f_i^q) + f_{i_1} + \sum_{j \in J_{i_2}} w_j}{G + (f_i - f_i^q) + f_{i_1} + \sum_{j \in J_{i_2}} w_j} \leq 6. \qquad \square$$

3.3 Multiple Machines

We give a competitive online algorithm when jobs can be assigned to multiple machines, and jobs do not have weights.

When there are multiple machines, charging becomes infeasible, as small perturbations in the intervals can lead to significant changes in which jobs belong to which interval (if they are scheduled in order of release time).

Instead, we use another method: the primal-dual approach. This allows us to use linear-programming-based techniques to derive a lower bound on the cost of OPT directly, without charging to intervals containing specific jobs. On the other hand, this seems to come at some loss of efficiency: we only show that our algorithm for multiple machines is 12-competitive.

Our algorithm is an extension of Algorithm 2. We wait until there are G/T waiting jobs or the jobs have total flow G to calibrate. Then, we schedule jobs in order of release time, starting with the machine with smallest index first.

With multiple machines, we need to be careful how we define waiting jobs. In particular, once we calibrate, we want the jobs we will schedule in that interval to no longer count as waiting jobs when deciding if we should calibrate further. Thus, when we calibrate, we assign jobs to the intervals immediately. This means that the guarantee that jobs are scheduled in order of release time does not hold across machines for this algorithm.

In particular, Algorithm 3 schedules jobs explicitly, rather than using the schedule in Observation 2.1. While we are still able to prove a constant approximation ratio, in practice one would almost certainly only use Algorithm 3 to determine calibration times, and use Observation 2.1 for the actual assignments. In particular, Algorithm 3 may schedule jobs late in an interval (in Step 13), incurring extra flow over Observation 2.1's schedule if a largely-empty interval is scheduled concurrently.

Algorithm 3 Online Unweighted Calibration on Multiple Machines

```
1:  Q ← empty priority queue of jobs, ordered by release time
2:  for each time step t do
3:      for all jobs j arriving at time t do
4:          Insert j in Q
5:      end for
6:      for all calibrated machines m idle at t do
7:          Remove the earliest-released job j from Q
8:          Schedule j on m at t
9:      end for
10:     f ← flow cost of scheduling all jobs in Q starting at t + 1
11:     while Q contains ≥ G/T jobs or f ≥ G do
12:         Calibrate at t on the next machine in round robin order
13:         Schedule up to G/T jobs from Q in this interval in re-
            lease time order
14:     end while
15: end for
```

We begin with several simple observations about the flow costs of each interval scheduled by Algorithm 3.

Observation 3.9. *Let i be an interval scheduled on machine m at time step b_i by Algorithm 3. Then*

- *every job in i incurs flow at most $2G/T$ after b_i,*
- *the total flow of all jobs in i is at most $3G$, and*
- *if Algorithm 3 schedules i due to flow ($f \geq G$ in Step 11), the total flow of jobs in i is at least $G - G/T$.*

Proof. Let $j \in J_i$ be in Q at b_i or a later time. Since jobs are scheduled in release time order, and all but the first G/T time steps of i are free, j is scheduled at most $G/T + |Q| \leq 2G/T$ time steps after b_i.

The total flow of all jobs in i is at most G up to time b_i (since all jobs incurring flow before b_i must be released before b_i and thus must be in Q at b_i). There are at most T jobs in i, each of which incurs flow at most $2G/T$ after b_i, giving a total flow of at most $3G$.

Let f be the total flow if the jobs were scheduled at $b_i + 1$ (as defined in Step 10 of Algorithm 3), and f_i be the actual flow of all jobs in I, scheduled beginning at b_i. Since only jobs in Q are waiting at time b_i (by definition), $f \leq f_i + |Q|$. Since $f \geq G$ and $|Q| < G/T$, $f_i \geq G - G/T$. □

In Figure 1 we give the linear program we use to analyze the algorithm. By observation, any schedule $\mathcal{S}$ with total cost C corresponds to a solution to the linear program with cost C. We use the dual of the linear program to lower bound this cost, thus lower bounding the cost of any schedule $\mathcal{S}$.

In particular, the weak duality theorem guarantees that *any* solution to the primal LP has at least the cost of any solution to the dual LP. Our proof shows that at every time step, the cost incurred by Algorithm 3 can be offset by a cost increase in the dual LP, and thus a cost increase in OPT. See [11, 16] for further discussion of this technique.

We have four constraints in the linear program. The first ensures that flow is high until we fully calibrate. The second ensures that the flow being incurred at a given time step can only decrease by 1 from the previous time step (per machine), and only during calibrated time steps. The third ensures that each job j is assigned to at least one machine m. The fourth makes sure that every job incurs flow cost of at least 1. The first and second constraints seem slightly redundant; however, both are necessary for our proof.

These following variable assignments show that any schedule for an online calibrations instance satisfies these constraints (and help explain the intuition behind them). Let $f_{t,j} = 1$ if job j incurs flow at time step t. Let $c_{t,m} = 1$ if an interval begins on machine m at time t. Finally, let $a_{j,m} = 1$ if job j is scheduled on machine m. All variables are 0 in all other cases.

Primal:

$$\begin{aligned}
\text{minimize} \quad & \sum \sum_t f_{t,j} + G \sum c_{t,m} \\
& f_{t,j} + \sum_{t'=r_j-T} c_{t',m} - a_{j,m} \geq 0 \quad \forall j, t \geq r_j, m \\
& \sum_{r_j<t} (f_{t,j} - f_{t-1,j}) + \sum_m \sum_{t'=t-T}^{t} c_{t',m} \geq 0 \quad \forall t \\
& \sum_m a_{j,m} \geq 1 \quad \forall j \\
& f_{r_j,j} = 1 \quad \forall j
\end{aligned}$$

Figure 1: A linear program for scheduling with calibrations.

Taking the dual, we obtain the LP given in Figure 2. All variables are required to be nonnegative in the primal. In the dual, we have $x_{t,j} \geq 0$, $y_t \geq 0$, $v_j \geq 0$, and z_j unbounded.

Theorem 3.10. *Algorithm 3 is 12-competitive.*

Dual:

$$\text{maximize} \sum z_j + \sum v_j$$
$$\sum_p x_{t,j,m} - y_{t+1} + z_j \leq 1 \quad \forall t,j \text{ with } t = r_j$$
$$\sum_p x_{t,j,m} + y_t - y_{t+1} \leq 1 \quad \forall t,j \text{ with } t \neq r_j$$
$$\sum_{j|r_j \leq t+T} \sum_{t'>t} x_{t',j,m} + \sum_{t'=t}^{t+T} y_t \leq G \quad \forall t,m$$
$$\sum_{t>r_j} -x_{t,j,m} + v_j \leq 0 \quad \forall j,m$$

Figure 2: The dual of the linear program given in Figure 1.

Proof. As mentioned earlier, we use the primal dual technique. We set the variables every time Algorithm 3 calibrates (or, in some cases, only after Algorithm 3 calibrates twice. This is similar to when two intervals are charged simultaneously in the proof of Theorem 3.3). In each case, we show that the increase in the dual objective function is at least 1/12 the cost incurred by Algorithm 3. This shows that Algorithm 3 is 12-competitive.

We let $v_j = \max_m \sum_t x_{t,j,m}$. Intuitively, we use $x_{t,j,m}$ to keep track of the flow of job j at time t on machine m. Since Algorithm 3 only assigns flow to one machine, v_j can store the total flow of job j. We set $y_t = G/2T$ for all t, and $z_j = G/2T$ for all j. These variables help contribute to cost when there are a large number of jobs that may not have much flow (i.e. Algorithm 3 calibrates due to G/T waiting jobs).

We examine each interval i one by one and find the increase in the dual LP objective after the interval is scheduled. Let b_i be the time when interval i is scheduled, let m_i be the machine i is scheduled on, and let J_i be the jobs scheduled in i. Our argument is split into cases based on why the algorithm decided to schedule the jobs.

Case 1 (Total flow G): In this case, we calibrate because the waiting jobs have total flow at least G. We split into two subcases. First, assume that there is a job which is released before i ends, and scheduled on m_i, but not scheduled in i. Then there are T total jobs scheduled during i. We keep $x_{t,j,m} = 0$ for all t, m for all $j \in J_i$, but recall that $z_j = G/2T$ for all $j \in J_i$. This gives a total dual cost of $G/2$; since i has total cost at most $4G$ by Observation 3.9, this gives a competitive ratio of 8.

Now we can assume that all jobs scheduled on m_i with $r_j < b_i + T$ are scheduled in i or an earlier interval.

First, we deal with the corner case $T = 1$. Then i has only one job j. We charge to $z_j = G/2$, again giving a competitive ratio of 8.

Otherwise, $T \geq 2$. Note that all jobs on each machine are scheduled in order of release time. For all $t \leq b_i$ and for all jobs $j \in J_i$, let $x_{t,j,m_i} = 1/2$ if job j is waiting at time t, and $x_{t,j,m} = 0$ otherwise. Since the jobs incur at most G flow before b_i, the sum of these $x_{j,t,m}$ is at most $G/2$. Therefore, the third condition is satisfied for all times t, m.

Let f_j be the total flow of job j. By Observation 3.9, $f_j \leq 2G/T + \sum_t 2x_{t,j,m}$. Algorithm 3 incurs cost $G + \sum_{j \in J_i} f_j$.

The dual cost increases by $\sum_{j \in J_i} \left(G/2T + \sum_t x_{t,j,m}\right) \geq \sum_{j \in J_i} f_j/4$. By Observation 3.9, the jobs in J_i have total flow at least $G - G/T \geq G/2$, so $\sum_{j \in J_i} f_j/6 \geq G/12$.

Thus the competitive ratio is

$$\frac{G + \sum_{j \in J_i} f_j}{\sum_{j \in J_i} f_j/4} \leq \frac{G + \sum_{j \in J_i} f_j}{G/12 + \sum_{j \in J_i} f_j/12} \leq 12.$$

Case 2 (G/T waiting jobs): We consider intervals i and $i+1$. These two intervals have cost at most $6G$. We show that the dual increases in cost by at least $G/2$. We set $x_{j,t,m_i} = c$ for all waiting jobs $j \in J_i$,[4] for a constant c defined momentarily. Otherwise, $x_{j,t,m} = 0$ for all t, m for all $j \in J_{i+1}$ and all other $j \in J_i$.

If there are exactly G/T jobs scheduled in i with release time at most b_i, we let $c = 1/2$. If there are more than G/T jobs remaining (e.g. if G/T is not an integer or many jobs are released at b_i), we reduce c until $cT(\#\text{ waiting jobs}) = G/2$.

The third condition is satisfied since only the waiting jobs have $x_{t,j,m_i} > 0$ for $b_i \leq t < b_i + T$; by definition of c the sum of these terms is exactly $G/2$.

By Observation 3.9, Algorithm 3 incurs cost at most $4G + \sum_{j \in J_i} 2G/T + \sum_{j \in J_{i+1}} 2G/T$, while the dual increases by at least $G/2 + \sum_{j \in J_i} G/2T + \sum_{j \in J_{i+1}} G/2T$. This gives a competitive ratio of 8. □

4 OFFLINE SCHEDULING

In this section, rather than a calibration cost, we have a calibration budget K. Our goal is to minimize the flow time while calibrating at most K times on $P = 1$ machine.

This is a generalization of the online model, as we can use a binary search to find the optimal calibration budget (between 1 and n calibrations) for a given calibration cost G.[5]

As before, we consider unit jobs. Our offline solution allows arbitrary weights for each job, and guarantees an optimal solution on one machine.

Lemma 4.1. *Let j be a job scheduled at t_j in interval i starting at b_i. Then in any optimal schedule, either:*

- *j starts at its release time ($t_j = r_j$), or*
- *there is no idle time between b_i and t_j.*

Proof. By contradiction. Let j be the first contradicting job in some optimal schedule; in other words, j is the earliest job scheduled such that $t_j \neq r_j$, and there exists an empty time step t between b_i and t_j.

If r_j does not have a job scheduled, we can schedule j at r_j, strictly improving the flow time of the schedule and achieving a contradiction.

Otherwise, let j' be the job scheduled at r_j. Since all release times are distinct, $r_{j'} < r_j$; since we assumed j is the earliest job violating the lemma, we must have $t > r_j$. Then we can schedule j at t, strictly improving the flow time of the schedule; thus the schedule cannot be optimal. □

[4] By "waiting jobs" we mean the jobs with $r_j \leq t < t_j$.

[5] One may hope for an online result using a calibration budget as well. However, a calibration budget leaves an online algorithm completely helpless: whether it should spend a calibration now, or wait until more jobs have accumulated, depends entirely on the future schedule.

Lemma 4.2. *There exists an optimal schedule such that the last time step of each interval i is a job that is scheduled at its release time.*

Proof. Without loss of generality we assume the last time step of i is not idle (otherwise, we move the calibration back in time until a job is scheduled in the last time step).

First, assume that i is non-full. Then by Lemma 4.1, the last job in j (indeed, all jobs scheduled after an empty time step in i) must be scheduled at its release time.

Otherwise, assume that i is full. For a contradiction, assume that the last job in i is not scheduled at its release time. Let t be the latest release time of any job in i. If $t = b_i + T$, the job released at t must be scheduled at t and we are done. Otherwise, push i back so that it ends immediately after t (in other words, $b_i \leftarrow t + 1 - T$). Since all jobs have distinct release times, all jobs previously in i can still be scheduled in i; if we schedule using Observation 2.1 (without loss of generality), each job is scheduled no later than before. This leads to a schedule with better flow, contradicting the optimality of the original schedule. □

By Lemma 4.1, we have the following corollary.

Corollary 4.3. *In any optimal schedule, for any non-full interval i, any job that is released before the end of interval i must be scheduled in an interval which starts no later than i.*

Proof. Let t be the first idle time step in interval i. No job is released at time t (otherwise time step t will not be idle). For jobs released before t, they can not be scheduled in a time step after t since t is idle and calibrated. For jobs released after t and before the end of interval i, they should be scheduled at its release time according to Lemma 4.1, as time step t is idle. □

With these lemmas in mind, our offline schedule is built around critical jobs.

Definition 4.4. Given a feasible schedule, job j is ***critical*** if it is scheduled at its release time and any job that is released before r_j is scheduled before r_j.

The remainder of the proofs in this section are deferred to the full version for space.

4.1 The Offline Algorithm

By Corollary 4.3, in an optimal schedule, the last job of each non-full interval must be a critical job. We consider two adjacent non-full intervals such that all intervals between them (maybe zero) are full, let jobs j and j', $j < j'$ be the last job of the two non-full intervals respectively, then there must be a group of $\left\lceil \frac{j'-j}{T} \right\rceil$ intervals which only schedule jobs $\{j+1, ..., j'\}$. Moreover, there is at most one non-full interval in the group, and it must be the last interval in the group.[6] Then, we propose a dynamic programming approach to find such groups of intervals and obtain an optimal schedule.

We denote for each job $j \in \mathcal{J}$ a distinct rank $\mu_j \in \{1, 2, ..., n\}$ which corresponds to the ascending order of their weights (break ties by ranking the job of latest release time first). Let $J(u, v, \mu) = \{j \mid r_u \leq r_j \leq r_v, \mu_j > \mu\}$ be the set of jobs that are released during $[r_u, r_v + 1)$ with ranks higher than μ. We define $f(u, v, \mu)$ as the minimum total weighted completion time of jobs in $J(u, v, \mu)$ with a group of exactly $\lceil |J(u, v, \mu)|/T \rceil$ intervals such that the last interval starts at $r_v + 1 - T$ and all intervals in the group are full (except the last one in the case that $|J(u, v, \mu)|$ is not divisible by T). We define $F(k, v)$ as the minimum total weighted completion time of jobs $\{1, ..., v\}$ with at most k calibrations.

Proposition 1.
$$F(k, v) = \min_{u \leq v} \left\{ F\left(k - \left\lceil \frac{v-u+1}{T} \right\rceil, u-1\right) + f(u, v, 0) \right\}$$
We set $F(k, v) \leftarrow +\infty$ if $kT < v$, and $F(k, v) \leftarrow 0$ if $v = 0$.

We maintain the invariant that job v is critical and test for each job u before or equal to job v whether job $u - 1$ is a critical job. Then, we use another dynamic program to calculate the minimum total weighted completion time $f(u, v, 0)$ of jobs $\{u, ..., v\}$.

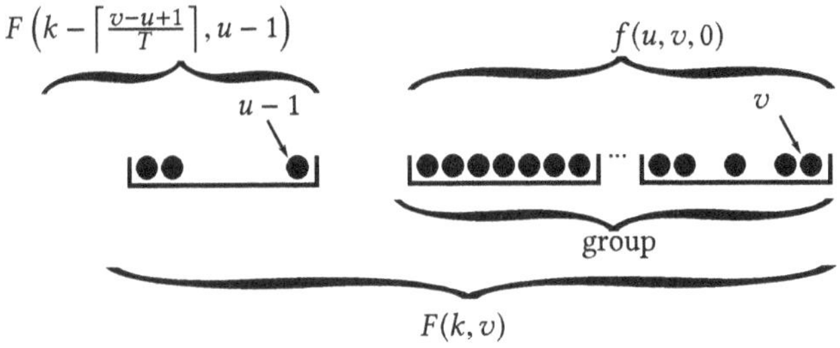

Figure 3: Illustration of Proposition 1

In the following, we show how to compute $f(u, v, \mu)$ for jobs $J(u, v, \mu)$ with a budget of $\lceil |J(u, v, \mu)|/T \rceil$ calibrations.

Let i be the last interval, and $b_i = r_v + 1 - T$ be the time when interval i starts (it ends at $r_v + 1 = b_i + T$). We look for the optimal schedule such that, except for i, all other intervals are full. Without loss of generality, we assume that no two intervals overlap with each other.[7]

Definition 4.5. Given u, v, μ such that $J(u, v, \mu) \neq \emptyset$:

- let $e = \arg\min_{j \in J(u,v,\mu)} \mu_j$ be the job of smallest rank,
- let $\Psi = \{j \mid |J(u, j, \mu)| \mod T \equiv 0,\ j \in J(u, v-1, \mu)\}$ be the set of jobs j such that the number of jobs $J(u, j, \mu)$ is a multiple of T,
- let $j_\ell = \arg\max_{j \in \Psi} r_j$ be the job with latest release time r_ℓ of jobs Ψ if $\Psi \neq \emptyset$, and
- let $s = \min\{h \mid h \equiv |\{j \mid r_j < r_v + 1 - T + h,\ j \in J(u, v, \mu)\}| \mod T\}$.

Lemma 4.6. *As defined above, s is the smallest value such that the machine is completely busy during $[b_i, b_i + s)$, and every job is scheduled at its release time during $[b_i + s, b_i + T)$.*

We focus on where we should schedule the job e of smallest rank. Suppose in the optimal schedule job e is scheduled in interval $i' = [b_{i'}, b_{i'} + T)$ at time step t_e. Firstly, no job except e could be released at t_e, otherwise a schedule with better or equal cost can be

[6] These groups are similar to the sequences defined in Section 3.2, but are used significantly differently.

[7] This can clearly be done by perturbing intervals. We do need to be slightly careful to maintain Lemma 4.2; in particular, if two intervals overlap, we should perturb them by scheduling the first one earlier rather than the second one later.

obtained by swapping the schedule of that job and job e, since job e has the smallest weight. Secondly, jobs that are released before t_e must not be scheduled after t_e. Assume by contradiction that such job i exists. Then a better schedule can be obtained by swapping the schedule of job i and job e. Therefore, any job that is scheduled in interval $[t_e + 1, b_{i'} + T)$ must be scheduled at its release time. Consequently, the last job of i' must be a critical job.

PROPOSITION 2. *We set* $f(u,v,\mu) \leftarrow 0$ *if* $J(u,v,\mu) = \emptyset$; *and* $f(u,v,\mu) \leftarrow \infty$ *if* $\Psi \neq \emptyset$ *and* $b_i \leq r_\ell$.
Otherwise, $f(u,v,\mu) =$

$$\min \begin{cases} f(u,v,\mu_e) + w_e(r_e+1) & \textbf{if } r_e \geq I_{begin} + s \\ f(u,v,\mu_e) + w_e(r_v + 1 - T + s) & \\ & \textbf{if } r_e < I_{begin} + s, s > 0 \\ \min\limits_{j\in\Psi,\ r_j \geq r_e} f(u,j,\mu) + f(j+1,v,\mu) & \textbf{if } \Psi \neq \emptyset \end{cases}$$

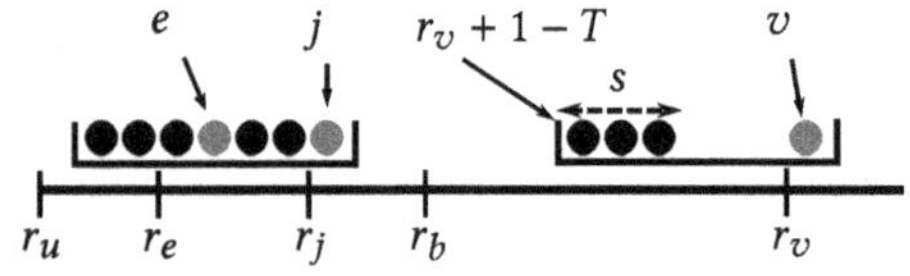

Figure 4: Illustration of Proposition 2

THEOREM 4.7. *This dynamic programming algorithm requires* $O(Kn^3)$ *time.*

5 CONCLUSION

This work is the first to our knowledge to study online scheduling with calibrations, and the first to give algorithms that allow for a tradeoff between throughput and calibrations. However, open problems remain. We would like to tighten the bounds for the single-machine unweighted case: the online algorithm is 3-competitive, while the lower bound is only 2. Can this be tightened?

An interesting open problem is to fully explore the connection with machine minimization. Fineman and Sheridan showed that the problems are essentially equivalent in the offline case with resource augmentation [14]; can a similar statement be made about online scheduling?

REFERENCES

[1] Eric Angel, Evripidis Bampis, Vincent Chau, and Vassilis Zissimopoulos. 2017. On the Complexity of Minimizing the Total Calibration Cost. In *Proceedings of the 11th International Workshop on Frontiers in Algorithmics (FAW '17) (LNCS)*, Vol. 10336. Springer, Heidelberg. To appear.
[2] Richard Baer. 2005. Self-calibrating and/or self-testing camera module. (Sept. 30 2005). US Patent App. 11/239,851.
[3] Surendra K Bansal, Thomas Layloff, Ernest D Bush, Marta Hamilton, Edward A Hankinson, John S Landy, Stephen Lowes, Moheb M Nasr, Paul A St Jean, and Vinod P Shah. 2004. Qualification of analytical instruments for use in the pharmaceutical industry: A scientific approach. *Aaps Pharmscitech* 5, 1 (2004), 151–158.
[4] Philippe Baptiste. 2006. Scheduling unit tasks to minimize the number of idle periods: a polynomial time algorithm for offline dynamic power management. In *Proceedings of the 17th. ACM-SIAM Symposium on Discrete Algorithms (SODA '06)*. SIAM, Philadelphia, 364–367.
[5] HP Barringer. 1995. Cost Effective Calibration Intervals Using Weibull Analysis. In *Proceedings of the 11th. Quality Congress*. American Society For Quality Control, Milwaukee, 1026–1038.
[6] Andrew Barton-Sweeney, Dimitrios Lymberopoulos, and Andreas Savvides. 2006. Sensor localization and camera calibration in distributed camera sensor networks. In *Proceedings of the 3rd. International Conference on Broadband Communications, Networks and Systems (BROADNETS '06)*. IEEE, Piscataway, 1–10.
[7] Beamex. 2007. Traceable and Efficient Calibrations in the Process Industry. (October 2007). https://www.beamex.com/wp-content/uploads/2016/12/CalibrationWorld_2007-03-ENG.pdf.
[8] Michael A. Bender, David P. Bunde, Vitus J. Leung, Samuel McCauley, and Cynthia A. Phillips. 2013. Efficient Scheduling to Minimize Calibrations. In *Proceedings of the 25th. ACM Symposium on Parallelism in Algorithms and Architectures (SPAA '13)*. ACM Press, New York, NY, 280–287.
[9] Rolf Bernhardt and S Albright. 1993. *Robot calibration*. Springer Science & Business Media, Heidelberg.
[10] Allan Borodin and Ran El-Yaniv. 2005. *Online computation and competitive analysis*. Cambridge University Press, Cambridge.
[11] Niv Buchbinder and Joseph Naor. 2009. The design of competitive online algorithms via a primal-dual approach. *Foundations and Trends in Theoretical Computer Science* 3, 2–3 (2009), 93–263.
[12] Chris Burroughs. 2006. New Integrated Stockpile Evaluation program to better ensure weapons stockpile Safety, Security, Reliability. http://www.sandia.gov/LabNews/060331.html. (March 2006). Online; posted March 2006.
[13] Roger C Evans, John E Griffith, David D Grossman, Myron M Kutcher, and Peter M Will. 1982. Method and Apparatus for Calibrating a Robot to Compensate for Inaccuracy of the Robot. (Dec. 7 1982). US Patent 4,362,977.
[14] Jeremy T Fineman and Brendan Sheridan. 2015. Scheduling Non-Unit Jobs to Minimize Calibrations. In *Proceedings of the 27th. ACM Symposium on Parallelism in Algorithms and Architectures (SPAA '15)*. ACM Press, New York, NY, 161–170.
[15] M Forina, MC Casolino, and C De la Pezuela Martínez. 1998. Multivariate calibration: applications to pharmaceutical analysis. *Journal of pharmaceutical and biomedical analysis* 18, 1 (1998), 21–33.
[16] Michel X Goemans and David P Williamson. 1997. *The primal-dual method for approximation algorithms and its application to network design problems*. PWS Publishing Co, Boston. 144–191 pages.
[17] James R. Lakin. 2014. Establishing Calibration Intervals, How Often Should One Calibrate? http://www.inspec-inc.com/home/company/blog/inspec-insights/2014/09/30/establishing-calibration-intervals-how-often-should-one-calibrate. (Sep 2014). Online; posted 30 September 2014.
[18] Kuo-Huang Lin and Bin-Da Liu. 2005. A gray system modeling approach to the prediction of calibration intervals. *IEEE Transactions on Instrumentation and Measurement* 54, 1 (2005), 297–304.
[19] Alexander Mäcker, Manuel Malatyali, Friedhelm Meyer auf der Heide, and Sören Riechers. 2016. Cost-efficient Scheduling on Machines from the Cloud. In *Proceedings of the 10th. International Conference on Combinatorial Optimization and Applications (COCOA '16)*. Springer, Heidelberg, 578–592.
[20] National Nuclear Safety Administration. 2014. Office of Test and Evaluation. http://nnsa.energy.gov/aboutus/ourprograms/defenseprograms/stockpilestewardship/testcapabilitiesand-eval. (September 2014). Online; posted 30 September 2014.
[21] Hoai-Nhan Nguyen, Jian Zhou, and Hee-Jun Kang. 2013. A new full pose measurement method for robot calibration. *Sensors* 13, 7 (2013), 9132–9147.
[22] Emilia Nunzi, Gianna Panfilo, Patrizia Tavella, Paolo Carbone, and Dario Petri. 2005. Stochastic and reactive methods for the determination of optimal calibration intervals. *IEEE Transactions on Instrumentation and Measurement* 54, 4 (2005), 1565–1569.
[23] SR Postlethwaite, DG Ford, and D Morton. 1997. Dynamic calibration of CNC machine tools. *International Journal of Machine Tools and Manufacture* 37, 3 (1997), 287–294.
[24] Daniel D Sleator and Robert E Tarjan. 1985. Amortized efficiency of list update and paging rules. *Commun. ACM* 28, 2 (1985), 202–208.
[25] Tobias Wilken, C Lovis, A Manescau, Tilo Steinmetz, L Pasquini, G Lo Curto, Theodor W Hänsch, Ronald Holzwarth, and Th Udem. 2010. High-precision calibration of spectrographs. *Monthly Notices of the Royal Astronomical Society: Letters* 405, 1 (2010), L16–L20.
[26] Donald W. Wyatt and Howard T. Castrup. 1991. Managing Calibration Intervals. (1991).
[27] G Zhang and R Hocken. 1986. Improving the accuracy of angle measurement in machine calibration. *CIRP Annals-Manufacturing Technology* 35, 1 (1986), 369–372.
[28] Zhengyou Zhang. 2000. A flexible new technique for camera calibration. *IEEE Transactions on Pattern Analysis and Machine Intelligence* 22, 11 (2000), 1330–1334.
[29] Zhengyou Zhang. 2002. Method and system for calibrating digital cameras. (Aug. 20 2002). US Patent 6,437,823.

Tight Bounds for Clairvoyant Dynamic Bin Packing

Yossi Azar
Tel-Aviv University
Tel-Aviv, Israel
azar@tau.ac.il

Danny Vainstein
Tel-Aviv University
Tel-Aviv, Israel
danvainstein@tau.ac.il

ABSTRACT

In this paper we focus on the Clairvoyant Dynamic Bin Packing (DBP) problem, which extends the classical online bin packing problem in that items arrive and depart over time and the departure time of an item is known upon its arrival. The problem naturally arises when handling cloud-based networks. We focus specifically on the MinUsageTime cost function which aims to minimize the overall usage time of all bins that are opened during the packing process. Earlier work has shown a $O(\frac{\log \mu}{\log \log \mu})$ upper bound where μ is defined as the ratio between the maximal and minimal durations of all items. We improve the upper bound by giving an $O(\sqrt{\log \mu})$-competitive algorithm. We then provide a matching lower bound of $\Omega(\sqrt{\log \mu})$ on the competitive ratio of any online algorithm, thus closing the gap with regards to this problem. We then focus on what we call the class of aligned inputs and give a $O(\log \log \mu)$-competitive algorithm for this case, beating the lower bound of the general case by an exponential factor. Surprisingly enough, the analysis of our algorithm that we present, is closely related to various properties of binary strings.

CCS CONCEPTS

•Theory of computation → Scheduling algorithms; Online algorithms;

KEYWORDS

Online Algorithms; Dynamic Bin Packing; Clairvoyant Setting; Competitive Ratio; Analysis of Algorithms

ACM Reference format:
Yossi Azar and Danny Vainstein. 2017. Tight Bounds for Clairvoyant Dynamic Bin Packing. In *Proceedings of SPAA'17, July 24–26, 2017, Washington, DC, USA,* , 10 pages.
DOI: http://dx.doi.org/10.1145/3087556.3087570

1 INTRODUCTION

The classical online bin packing problem has been widely researched [11] [14]. In this problem, items arrive in an online fashion, remain permanently, and must be assigned to bins upon their arrival (without delay). Furthermore, the goal is to minimize the maximum number of bins opened during the packing process. Later, motivated by practical applications (such as cloud computing), the dynamic version of the problem has been introduced and studied [6] [2] [3], namely, the Dynamic Bin Packing (DBP) problem. In this version, items arrive in an online fashion. In addition, items not only arrive but also depart over time. The definition of this variant gives rise to two different settings, i.e., clairvoyant and non-clairvoyant. In the non-clairvoyant setting, the departure time of each item is unknown until its departure, whereas in the clairvoyant setting, the item's departure time is revealed to the online algorithm upon its arrival.

Traditionally one used the goal function of minimizing the maximum number of bins opened throughout the entire process and compare the online algorithm's performance with that of an optimal algorithm. An alternative approach is to use the momentary goal function. In this goal function the online algorithm is compared to the optimal algorithm at every moment with respect to its number of opened bins, i.e., the goal function is defined as the maximal possible (at any moment in time) ratio between the number of bins opened by the online algorithm at that time and the number of bins opened by the optimal algorithm at that same time. In the classical online bin packing problem, since once items arrive they remain permanently, these goal functions collide. Unfortunately, both goal functions fail to distinguish between the case where the online algorithm's cost function is high throughout the entire process and the case where the online algorithm's cost function is only momentarily high and low throughout the rest of the process (in both cases the optimal algorithm's cost function remains low throughout the entire process). Therefore, the MinUsageTime goal function was introduced [7] [9], which better captures the total performance of online algorithms in the dynamic case.

The newly introduced MinUsageTime goal function aims to minimize the total accumulated time of all open bins, throughout the entire packing process [7] [9] (which can also be viewed as the total energy used by the algorithm). This is a problem that typically arises in cloud-based networks. Users apply to use a server bandwidth for a certain period of time, and the aim is to assign users to servers such that the overall time the servers are functioning is minimized, while maintaining the invariant that the overall requested bandwidth applied for by the users does not exceed the server's overall bandwidth. Thus, looking at the users as items and servers as bins, a natural formalization of this problem is the MinUsageTime DBP.

In our paper we focus on the clairvoyant version of this problem. This variant also arises in real-life applications, such as cloud gaming. In such applications, the users' server-time requests can be accurately predicted upon their arrival [8]. This problem was

Supported in part by the Israel Science Foundation (grant No. 1506/16), by the I-CORE program (Center No.4/11) and by the Blavatnik Fund.

SPAA'17, July 24–26, 2017, Washington, DC, USA

978-1-4503-4593-4/17/07...$15.00
DOI: http://dx.doi.org/10.1145/3087556.3087570

defined and researched by Ren *et al.* [10]. In [10], they present a $O(\frac{\log \mu}{\log \log \mu})$-competitive algorithm where μ is defined as the ratio between the maximal and minimal lengths of all items. Furthermore, they show a constant lower bound of $\frac{1+\sqrt{5}}{2}$.

Shalom *et al.* [12] researched a similar problem, namely, the online version of interval scheduling with bounded parallelism. In this problem interval jobs arrive in an online manner and are assigned to machines such that each machine may treat a bounded number of jobs at any given moment. The above problem differs from our MinUsageTime DBP in that all jobs have the same resource demand of $1/g$ for some given g. In [12] a lower bound of g was described. Although they did not explicitly write as much, by choosing appropriate parameters in their analysis one can get a non-constant lower bound for our settings.

A natural question would be to ask whether these upper or lower bounds are tight. We show that in fact, neither is tight. Specifically, we provide an algorithm which combines the First-Fit approach with the Classify-by-Duration approach, to produce a matching upper bound of $O(\sqrt{\log \mu})$ (even when our performance is compared with an optimal algorithm that may repack items at any moment), improving quadratically upon the result given in [10]. As stated above, we also provide a new approach towards establishing a matching lower bound of $\Omega(\sqrt{\log \mu})$ (where the optimal algorithm, to which we compare our performance, may not repack items) which is strictly greater than the bound that can be deduced from [12]. Thus, effectively closing the gap on the competitive ratio of this problem.

To beat the given lower bound, we turn our focus to an interesting class of input, namely, aligned inputs. In this class of input, items of length $\in (2^{i-1}, 2^i]$ may only arrive at multiples of 2^i (i.e. $c \cdot 2^i$ for some $c \in \mathbb{N}$). Note that this may also be viewed as the following: items need to be assigned to a specific bin by the online algorithm at their arrival. However they only start taking up bin space at their appropriate binary times ($c \cdot 2^i$ for some $c \in \mathbb{N}$). We provide an $O(\log \log \mu)$-competitive algorithm, which beats the former lower bound by an exponential factor.

We also note the difference between the Non-Clairvoyant setting and the Clairvoyant one. As opposed to the Clairvoyant case, in the Non-Clairvoyant case, the best competitive ratio for a deterministic algorithm one could hope to achieve is μ which was shown via a lower bound by Li *et al.* [7]. On the other hand, the First-Fit algorithm was shown to perform nearly optimally, achieving a competitive ratio of $\mu + 4$ [13].

Contributions of this paper In this paper, we provide the following results.

- In the Clairvoyant setting, we present a hybrid algorithm that combines the first-fit and classify-by-duration strategies. By reducing the problem to inputs that end at binary times (2^i for some i, depending on the item's duration), we show that the above algorithm achieves a competitive ratio of $O(\sqrt{\log \mu})$. We note that this algorithm does not assume early knowledge of μ, but rather adapts as μ increases.
- We provide a matching lower bound of $\Omega(\sqrt{\log \mu})$ on the competitive ratio of any online algorithm (in the Clairvoyant setting), thus closing the gap for this problem.
- We beat the lower bound by focusing on an interesting family of inputs, namely, aligned input (once again in the Clairvoyant setting). In this type of input, if the item is of duration $\in (2^{i-1}, 2^i]$, it may only arrive at multiples of 2^i (i.e. $c \cdot 2^i$ for some $c \in \mathbb{N}$).
  We provide an $O(\log \log \mu)$-competitive algorithm, which indeed beats the former lower bound by an exponential factor.

Table 1 summarizes the results known in the various settings regarding MinUsageTime DBP.

		Upper Bound	Lower Bound
Clairvoyant	General Inputs	$O(\sqrt{\log \mu})$ [*]	$\Omega(\sqrt{\log \mu})$ [*]
	Aligned Inputs	$O(\log \log \mu)$ [*]	$\Omega(1)$
Non-Clairvoyant	General Inputs	$\mu + 4$ [13]	μ [7]

Table 1: A summary of the asymptotic upper and lower bounds on the competitive ratios of deterministic algorithms in the various settings regarding MinUsageTime DBP. [*] These results are shown in the following chapters.

Related Work The classical online bin packing problem was introduced by Johnson *et al.* [5] and has since been extensively researched. The problem is defined such that items of sizes in [0, 1] are released in an online manner, and these items must be packed into bins while maintaining the invariant that each bin packs at most a load of 1. Our goal under this setting is to minimize the number of bins used. For this problem, the currently best known algorithm is presented by Heydrich *et al.* [4] and has a competitive ratio of roughly 1.58. On the other hand, the current best known lower bound for any deterministic algorithm has been shown to be about 1.54 [1].

Later, the DBP problem was introduced by Coffman *et al.* [6] (which will be later termed as the Non-Clairvoyant DBP problem). This problem generalizes the online bin packing problem such that each item has a departure time as well, which is revealed to the online algorithm only at its departure. Under this setting the goal function remains the same as in the classical online bin packing problem. The current best known algorithm [6] achieves a competitive ratio of 2.788. On the other hand, the current best known lower bound for any deterministic algorithm is 2.666 [15].

Both of the above problems aim to minimize the overall number of bins used. A natural extension would be to look at a different type of goal function, namely, the momentary goal function. In this goal function, the competitive ratio of the online algorithm is defined as the maximum ratio between the number of bins opened by the online algorithm, compared to the number of bins opened by the optimal algorithm, where the maximum is taken over any moment.

Later, a new type of problem was introduced by Li *et al.* [7] [9], namely, the MinUsageTime DBP problem. The goal in this problem is to minimize the overall usage time of all bins being used in the packing process. For this problem, the current best known upper bound is achieved by the First-Fit algorithm and is shown to have a competitive ratio of $\mu + 4$ [13], μ being the max/min item interval length ratio. Furthermore, a lower bound of μ with respect to the competitive ratio of any online algorithm, has been shown in [7].

More recently, Ren *et al.* [10] introduced a variant of this problem where the departure time of an item is revealed to the online algorithm at the time of its arrival. This was termed the Clairvoyant DBP problem, whereas the former problem may sometimes be referred to as the Non-Clairvoyant DBP problem.

For the Clairvoyant DBP problem, the best known upper bound was $O(\log \mu)$ when μ is not known to the online algorithm, and $\min_{n\geq 1} \mu^{\frac{1}{n}} + n + 3 = O(\frac{\log \mu}{\log\log \mu})$, otherwise [10]. On the other hand, as stated earlier, a non constant lower bound exists which appears implicitly in [12]. In this paper, we improve the upper bound to $O(\sqrt{\log \mu})$ even if μ is not known to the online algorithm, and give a matching lower bound of $\Omega(\sqrt{\log \mu})$. Furthermore, we focus on a specific set of aligned inputs (to be formally defined later) which we feel capture the essence of the problem and show a $O(\log\log \mu)$-competitive algorithm for this case.

Techniques We give an overview of the two algorithms presented in our paper, the Hybrid Algorithm (HA) and the Classify-by-Duration-First-Fit (CDFF) algorithm.

- There are two natural strategies one would try using under this setting. The first is to apply the First-Fit strategy, but this is known to be at least $\Omega(\mu)$-competitive. The other is to classify items by their duration, but this is typically as worse as $\Omega(\log \mu)$-competitive (we note that this approach may be tweaked in order to give a $\theta(\frac{\log \mu}{\log\log \mu})$-competitive algorithm). Surprisingly, HA combines the two strategies starting with First-Fit and temporarily switching when needed to the classify-by-duration strategy, to achieve a tight upper bound of $O(\sqrt{\log \mu})$. Specifically, at any moment the algorithm holds two types of bins - general (GN) type bins and classify-by-duration (CD) type bins. Upon arrival of an item, HA looks at the overall load this type of items currently contribute. If the overall load is under a defined threshold, pack this item into any GN-type bin in a First-Fit manner. Otherwise, pack this item into a CD-type bin that holds this specific type. Packing the item into a CD-type bin is also done in a First-Fit manner, however in this case, only CD-type bins that hold this specific type, are considered [1].

  Upon analysing the competitive ratio of our algorithm we defined a reduction on inputs that delays each items' departure time resulting in a moderately small number of different item types such that items of the same type either depart together or do not intersect. We then apply the reduction only to the optimal algorithm (the online algorithm remains oblivious to the reduction) and show the desired competitive ratio.
- CDFF gives a $O(\log\log \mu)$ upper bound for aligned inputs. Given a collection of items, σ, at any moment, t, CDFF classifies all items based on their lengths. Furthermore, CDFF maintains rows of bins for each type of items. However, instead of statically packing types into rows, at any given moment different rows are considered for different types, i.e., items of a specific type are packed into different rows according to their arrival time. This adaptation is what ultimately improves the competitive ratio by an exponential factor. Surprisingly enough, the analysis of CDFF's performance is done by observing various properties of random binary strings which ultimately results in an upper bound of $O(\log\log \mu)$.

  Upon analysing the competitive ratio of CDFF, we first evaluate the algorithm's performance on a very structured input and then relate any other aligned input to it. We then apply the reduction (which was defined earlier) only to the optimal algorithm and show the desired competitive ratio.

[1] We note that using any Any-Fit approach towards packing items into the GN-type bins or the CD-type bins will work just as well.

2 NOTATIONS AND PRELIMINARIES

We first formally define the Clairvoyant MinUsageTime DBP problem.

The input consists of an infinite set of bins, $\{b_1, b_2, \ldots\}$, and a set of items $\sigma = \{r_1, \ldots, r_{|\sigma|}\}$. Each item is associated with an arrival time, t_r, and departure time, f_r. Therefore, each item is associated with a time interval for which it is active, denoted by $I(r) = [t_r, f_r]$. We sometimes denote t_r by $I(r)^-$ and f_r by $I(r)^+$. We also denote the interval length by $l(I(r))$. We further associate each item with a size, denoted by $s(r) \in [0, 1]$. For a given σ, let μ denote the max/min item interval length ratio, meaning, $\mu = \max_{r\in\sigma} l(I(r)) / \min_{r\in\sigma} l(I(r))$. Furthermore, let $d(\sigma)$ denote the total space-time demand of all items in σ, namely, $d(\sigma) = \sum_{r\in\sigma} s(r) \cdot l(I(r))$. Finally, let $span(\sigma) = l(\cup_{r\in\sigma} I(r))$, denote the time during which at least one item in σ is active.

The online algorithm has to pack each item into a single bin at the time of its arrival. Furthermore, the online algorithm has no knowledge of items which have not yet arrived. Nevertheless, at the time of an item's arrival, the online algorithm will also know its departure time (since we are studying the clairvoyant setting). We further assume that the online algorithm cannot repack items, i.e., once it has assigned an item to a bin, it cannot be moved to a different bin. We define the online algorithm's goal function as its MinUsageTime and denote it as ON(σ), i.e., $\text{ON}(\sigma) = \sum_{i=1}^{\infty} span(\{r : r \text{ was assigned to } b_i\})$. We note that we may assume w.l.o.g. that once all items from a given bin depart, that bin is considered closed and never used again.

We define two types of optimal algorithms, repacking and non-repacking, to which we compare our online algorithm's performance. An optimal repacking algorithm is defined as the optimal offline algorithm (in the sense that it sees the entire input together) that may repack items at any moment. An optimal non-repacking algorithm is defined as the optimal offline algorithm that may never repack items. Denote the former as OPT_R and the latter as OPT_{NR}. Given an input, σ, we denote OPT's number of open bins at moment t as $\text{OPT}^t(\sigma)$ and the total load of all active items at moment t as $S_t(\sigma)$.

We characterize an online algorithm's performance by its *competitive ratio*. We say that an online algorithm, ON, is $c - competitive$ for $c \geq 1$, if there exists a constant, $b \geq 0$, such that for any input, σ, $\text{ON}(\sigma) \leq c \cdot \text{OPT}(\sigma) + b$ for a given optimal algorithm.

We define a First-Fit algorithm in the usual way. Given a set of open bins and an incoming item to be packed, we pack the item into the earliest opened bin. If no bins are open, we open a new bin. Furthermore, once all items depart from a given a bin, that bin is closed and never used again.

Lastly, we give the definition on an aligned input.

Definition 2.1. We define an aligned input, σ, as follows: Items of length $\in (2^{i-1}, 2^i]$ may only arrive at multiples of 2^i, i.e., $c \cdot 2^i$ for $c \in \mathbb{N}$. We note that all items that arrive at time t, arrive with some arbitrary order, meaning that our on-line algorithm must handle each item before the next arrives.

3 UPPER BOUND OF $O(\sqrt{\text{LOG}\,\mu})$

Throughout this section we assume that the shortest item's interval is at least 1. Furthermore we assume that the input items form a continuous interval of active items (otherwise we apply our algorithm to each such interval individually).

We first give a few basic observations. Recall that given an input, σ, $\text{OPT}^t_R(\sigma)$ was defined as the number of bins OPT has open at moment t and $S_t(\sigma)$ as the overall load of all active items at moment t. Thus we get the following bound,

- $\text{OPT}_R(\sigma) = \int_{\cup_{r\in\sigma} I(r)} \text{OPT}^t_R(\sigma)\,\text{dt} \geq \int_{\cup_{r\in\sigma} I(r)} \lceil S_t(\sigma)\rceil\,\text{dt}$.

Furthermore, the following two bounds hold,

- the *time − space* bound: $\text{OPT}_R(\sigma) \geq d(\sigma)$.
- the *span* bound: $\text{OPT}_R(\sigma) \geq span(\sigma)$.

The *time − space* bound holds since $d(\sigma) = \int_{\cup_{r\in\sigma} I(r)} S_t(\sigma)\,\text{dt}$. The *span* bound holds since at least one bin must be opened whenever an item is active. Both bounds have been introduced in earlier work [10] [7] [9].

Given the above two bounds a natural question would be to ask whether these bounds are tight. The following lemma shows that this is indeed the case.

Lemma 3.1. *For any sequence of items, σ,*

1. *$OPT_R(\sigma) \leq \int_{t\in span(\sigma)} 2\lceil S_t(\sigma)\rceil dt$.*
2. *$OPT_R(\sigma) \leq 2 \cdot d(\sigma) + 2 \cdot span(\sigma)$.*

Proof. Let $\text{OPT}^t_R(\sigma)$ denote the number of bins OPT has open at time t. In particular,

$$\int_t \text{OPT}^t_R(\sigma)\text{dt} = \text{OPT}_R(\sigma). \tag{1}$$

Since OPT may repack at any moment we can assume that the overall load of any two of OPT's bins is strictly greater than 1 (otherwise OPT may pack the items of both bins into 1 at time t and then repack them as before for time $t' > t$, only improving upon its cost function).

Let $\text{OPT}^t_R(\sigma) = n$ and let $d_1, \ldots, d_n$ denote the loads in OPT's bins at time t and $S_t(\sigma)$ denote the overall load of all active items at time t. Therefore,

$$\text{OPT}^t_R(\sigma) = n < 2\sum_{i=1}^{n} d_i \leq 2\lceil S_t(\sigma)\rceil, \tag{2}$$

where the first inequality follows from the fact that the load of any two bins is strictly greater than 1. By (1) and (2), we get,

$$\text{OPT}_R(\sigma) = \int_t \text{OPT}^t_R(\sigma)\text{dt} \leq \int_t 2\lceil S_t(\sigma)\rceil\text{dt}.$$

Therefore,

$$\begin{aligned}\text{OPT}_R(\sigma) &\leq \int_t 2\lceil S_t(\sigma)\rceil\text{dt} \leq \int_t 2 + S_t(\sigma)\text{dt} \\ &= 2\cdot span(\sigma) + 2\cdot d(\sigma),\end{aligned}$$

which gives us the desired results. □

We now turn to define our online algorithm, HA (Hybrid Algorithm):

HA first classifies the items according to the following types. Define r's type as the tuple $T = (i, c)$ such that $l(I(r)) \in (2^{i-1}, 2^i]$ and $I(r)^- \in ((c-1)\cdot 2^i, c\cdot 2^i]$, such that $1 \leq i \leq \log\mu$ and $c \in \mathbb{N}$. Note that under such definition, given a specific i there may only be two types of items alive at any moment in time (i.e., two different values of c).

We further define two types of bins - GN (general) and CD (classify-by-duration) bins.

Non-formally, HA acts as follows. HA first checks for an open CD-type bin that holds type T items. If such a bin exists, HA will pack r into one of these bins in a First-Fit manner (opening a new CD-type bin if needed). Otherwise, it checks if the overall load of all active items of type T (including the load of the currently handled item) is strictly greater than $\frac{1}{2\sqrt{i}}$. If so, it opens a new CD-type bin and packs r into it, otherwise it packs r into a GN-type bin in a First-Fit manner (opening a new GN-type bin if needed). We note that HA does not need to know μ in advance, but rather adapts as μ grows.

In Algorithm 1 we formally define the algorithm.

```
Upon arrival of request r do
    T = (i, c) ← r's type.
    d ← overall load of all active items of type T, including r.
    if (exists an open CD-type bin that holds type T) then
        Pack r in a first-fit manner over all CD-type bins that
        hold type T. If needed, open a new CD-type bin for r.
    else
        if (d ≤ 1/(2√i)) then
            Pack r in a first-fit manner over all GN-type bins.
            If needed, open a new GN-type bin for r.
        else
            Open a new CD-type bin for r.
        end
    end
Upon departure of request r do
    Remove r from its bin and close bin if needed.
```

Algorithm 1: Description of the Hybrid Algorithm

We first state the main theorem of the section.

Theorem 3.2. *For any sequence of items, σ, $HA(\sigma) = O(\sqrt{\log\mu}) \cdot OPT_R(\sigma)$.*

Before proving Theorem 3.2, we first give the following lemma.

Lemma 3.3. *Given an input, σ, let GN_t denote the number of GN-type bins HA has open at time t. Therefore,*

$$GN_t \leq 2 + 4\sqrt{\log \mu}.$$

Proof. Items of type $T = (i, c)$ add a load of at most $\frac{1}{2\sqrt{i}}$ to the GN-type bins. Since there can be at most 2 types of items active at any given moment, for any given $i \in \{1, \ldots, \log \mu\}$, the overall load in all the GN-type bins is at most,

$$\sum_{i=1}^{\log \mu} \frac{1}{\sqrt{i}}. \tag{1}$$

Since, $\int \frac{1}{\sqrt{x}} = 2\sqrt{x}$ and the fact that $\frac{1}{\sqrt{x}}$ is non-increasing for $x \geq 1$, we get,

$$\sum_{i=1}^{\log \mu} \frac{1}{\sqrt{i}} \leq 1 + \int_{1}^{\log \mu} \frac{1}{\sqrt{x}} \mathrm{dx} = 1 + 2\sqrt{\log \mu}. \tag{2}$$

By (1) and (2), the overall load in all the GN-type bins, at time t, is at most $1 + 2\sqrt{\log \mu}$. Furthermore, this bound holds for all t. Since $i \geq 1$, the load of each item that is packed into the GN-type bins, is at most 1/2. Therefore, if HA would have opened more than $2 + 4\sqrt{\log \mu}$ GN-type bins, at the time of the opening of such a bin, we would have that the overall load of all items in all of the GN-type bins would be strictly greater than $1 + 2\sqrt{\log \mu}$ which would have lead us to a contradiction. Therefore, we know that $GN_t \leq 2 + 4\sqrt{\log \mu}$ as needed. □

Given a type of item, $T = (i, c)$, let k_t^T denote the number of open CD-type bins HA has for type T at time t. Furthermore, let $k_t = \sum_T k_t^T$. We would have liked to have shown that $\mathrm{OPT}_R^t(\sigma) \geq \max\{1, \frac{k_t}{4\sqrt{\log \mu}}\}$ which would have (as we will see) given us the desired competitive ratio. Unfortunately, this is not the case. However, we can make it correct by means of amortization. Specifically, by increasing the cost of OPT, using the following reduction.

Given an input σ, we convert it into an input σ' in the following way:
Let $r \in \sigma$, let $i \in \{1, \ldots, \log \mu\}$ be such that $l(I(r)) \in (2^{i-1}, 2^i]$ and let $c \in \mathbb{N}$ be such that $I(r)^- \in ((c-1) \cdot 2^i, c \cdot 2^i]$.
Given such r, define r' as, $I(r')^- = I(r)^-$ and $I(r')^+ = (c+1) \cdot 2^i$. Thus to convert σ to σ' we simply convert every item in σ as defined above.

Note that every two items of the same type (i.e., $T = (i, c)$) depart together once the reduction is applied. Further note that the reduction simply increases r's length by at most a multiplicative factor of 4. Therefore, we get the following two observations.

Observation 1. $span(\sigma') \leq 4 \cdot span(\sigma)$.

Observation 2. $d(\sigma') = \sum_{r' \in \sigma'} l(I(r')) \cdot s(r') \leq \sum_{r \in \sigma} 4 \cdot l(I(r)) \cdot s(r) = 4 \cdot d(\sigma)$.

The following corollary shows that the optimal algorithm does not lose too much due to the reduction.

Corollary 3.4. *For any sequence of items, σ, let σ' denote the items after the reduction is applied. If the items in σ form a continuous interval of active items, then,*

$$OPT_R(\sigma') \leq 16 \cdot OPT_R(\sigma).$$

Proof.

$$\begin{aligned} \mathrm{OPT}_R(\sigma') &\leq 2 \cdot span(\sigma') + 2 \cdot d(\sigma') \\ &\leq 8 \cdot span(\sigma) + 8 \cdot d(\sigma) \leq 16 \cdot \mathrm{OPT}_R(\sigma), \end{aligned}$$

where the first inequality is due to Lemma 3.1, the second is due to observations 1 and 2 and the last inequality is due to the *time−space* and *span* bounds. □

Recall that k_t is the number of any CD-type bins HA has open at time t.

Lemma 3.5. *Given a sequence of items, σ, let σ' denote the sequence after the above reduction is applied. Furthermore, let k_t be as defined above. Therefore,*

$$OPT_R^t(\sigma') \geq \max\{1, \frac{k_t}{4\sqrt{\log \mu}}\},$$

Proof. We first note that if $k_t = 0$ then the lemma immediately follows (since the items in σ form a continuous interval of active items and by the reduction, so do the items in σ'). Therefore, we shall assume the contrary from now on.

Consider all active items of type $T = (i, c)$ at time t, in σ. Let $\hat{r}_T$ be the first item to arrive out of all considered items. By the above reduction, since all items of a certain type depart together, we have that at the time of $\hat{r}_T$'s arrival, he was the only active item of that type. Furthermore, any items of that type that are released between the time of $\hat{r}_T$'s arrival and t, do not depart. Thus, we can give the following two observations.

Firstly, by the definition of HA, items of this type placed in the GN-type bins, plus the item that opened the first CD bin that accepts only items of this type (there exists such a bin since $k_t^T \geq 1$), contribute an overall load of at least $\frac{1}{2\sqrt{i}} \geq \frac{1}{2\sqrt{\log \mu}}$ (i being such that $T = (i, c)$). This is due to the fact that since HA opened such a bin, we know that exists a moment, $t' \leq t$, such that the overall load of active items of type T, in σ, is at least $\frac{1}{2\sqrt{i}}$ and since σ' is the result of the reduction applied to σ, we know that these items are active at time t as well (this is due to the fact that if items of the same type intersect, they must depart together).

Secondly, we will show that if $k_t^T \geq 2$, the other $k_t^T - 1$ bins of this type contribute an overall load of at least $\frac{k_t^T - 2}{2}$, in σ'. Due to the reduction, it is enough to show that if k CD-type bins for type T were opened until time t, then items packed into these bins, by HA, in σ, contribute a load of at least $\frac{k-1}{2}$ (this is due to that fact by the reduction's definition, all these items will be active at time t). We will prove this using induction on k.

For $k = 2$ the statement follows by the definition of first-fit algorithms. For $k > 2$, consider time t' when bin $k - 1$ was opened. By our induction hypothesis, we know that items of type T that have arrived before time t' contribute a load of $\frac{k-2}{2}$. Again, by the definition of first-fit algorithms, since bin k was opened, all items that have arrived after time t' and before t (including at time t) contribute a load of at least 1/2, giving us the desired result.

Thus, due to the fact that these items depart together, the overall load contributed by type T items, in σ' is at least $\frac{1}{2\sqrt{\log \mu}} + \frac{k_t^T-2}{2} \geq \frac{k_t^T}{4\sqrt{\log \mu}}$, if $k_t^T \geq 2$. Otherwise, $k_t^T = 1$, and the overall load is, once again, at least $\frac{1}{2\sqrt{\log \mu}} \geq \frac{k_t^T}{4\sqrt{\log \mu}}$.

If we sum over all types, by the time-space bound and since there is at least one active item at time t, we get,

$$\mathrm{OPT}_R^t(\sigma') \geq \max\{1, \frac{k_t}{4\sqrt{\log \mu}}\},$$

as needed. □

We now turn to prove our main theorem, i.e., Theorem 3.2.

Proof of Theorem 3.2. Let σ' be σ after we apply the reduction. Therefore,

$$\begin{aligned}\mathrm{HA}_t(\sigma) &= \mathrm{GN}_t + k_t \leq 2 + 4\sqrt{\log \mu} + k_t \\ &\leq 2 + 2 \cdot \max\{4\sqrt{\log \mu}, k_t\} \\ &= 2 + 8\sqrt{\log \mu} \cdot \max\{1, \frac{k_t}{4\sqrt{\log \mu}}\} \\ &\leq O(\sqrt{\log \mu}) \cdot \mathrm{OPT}_R^t(\sigma'),\end{aligned} \tag{1}$$

where the first inequality follows by Lemma 3.3 and the last by Lemma 3.5.
Putting it all together,

$$\begin{aligned}\mathrm{HA}(\sigma) &= \int_t \mathrm{HA}_t(\sigma)\mathrm{dt} \leq O(\sqrt{\log \mu}) \int_t \mathrm{OPT}_R^t(\sigma')\mathrm{dt} \\ &= O(\sqrt{\log \mu}) \cdot \mathrm{OPT}_R(\sigma') \leq O(\sqrt{\log \mu}) \cdot \mathrm{OPT}_R(\sigma) \\ &= O(\sqrt{\log \mu}) \cdot \mathrm{OPT}_R(\sigma),\end{aligned}$$

where the first inequality is due to (1) and the second inequality is due to Corollary 3.4. □

4 LOWER BOUND OF $\Omega(\sqrt{\mathrm{LOG}\, \mu})$

In this section we show a lower bound of $\Omega(\sqrt{\log \mu})$ with respect to the more general adversary, namely, an optimal algorithm that can never repack items. Recall that such an optimal algorithm is denoted as OPT_{NR}.

Definition 4.1. Define σ_t^* as the following sequence of items: At time t, release one item for each length in $\{1, 2, 4, \ldots, 2^{\log \mu}\}$ sequentially, from shortest to longest. Furthermore, let all items be of load $\frac{1}{\sqrt{\log \mu}}$.

Ren *et al.* [10] presented a 4-approximation (off-line) algorithm called the Dual Coloring Algorithm (note that this algorithm is not admitted repacking), that was described and analysed against an optimal algorithm that is admitted repacking. We restate their theorem using our notations.

Theorem 4.2. *For every sequence of items, σ, $DC(\sigma) \leq 4OPT_R(\sigma)$.*

Theorem 4.3. *For every on-line, deterministic and clairvoyant algorithm, ON, exists a sequence of items, σ, such that, $ON(\sigma) \geq \Omega(\sqrt{\log \mu}) \cdot OPT_{NR}(\sigma)$.*

Note that this is the stronger case, in the sense that the lower bound holds even w.r.t. a non-repacking off-line algorithm.

Proof. Let $t_i = i$ for $i = 0, \ldots, \mu - 1$. We now turn to define our adversary.

For all $i = 0, \ldots, \mu - 1$, release a prefix of $\sigma_{t_i}^*$ and stop as soon as ON opens $\sqrt{\log \mu}$ bins. Note that ON is indeed forced to open that many bins since $|\sigma_{t_i}^*| = \log \mu + 1$ and each items' load is $\frac{1}{\sqrt{\log \mu}}$, hence the overall load at that time is at least $\sqrt{\log \mu}$.

We now turn to analyse ON's competitive ratio compared to a repacking optimal off-line algorithm. Since at any moment, $t \leq \mu$, ON is forced to open $\sqrt{\log \mu}$ bins,

$$\mu\sqrt{\log \mu} \leq \mathrm{ON}(\sigma). \tag{1}$$

Let $S_t(\sigma)$ be the overall load of σ at time t. Furthermore, for any given moment t_i, let l_{t_i} denote the length of the last released item in $\sigma_{t_i}^*$ by the adversary (if no items were released, let $l_{t_i} = 0$).
By the definition of our adversary, the last released item in $\sigma_{t_i}^*$, for any t_i, forces ON to open a new bin for it. Therefore, ON must pay for the full duration of each one of these items. Thus, we get,

$$\sum_{i=0}^{\mu-1} l_{t_i} \leq \mathrm{ON}(\sigma). \tag{2}$$

Since the lengths of the items given at any moment, t_i, form a geometric series, the sum of their lengths is at most $2 \cdot l_{t_i}$. Therefore,

$$\int_{t \in [0,2\mu]} S_t(\sigma) = d(\sigma) \leq \frac{1}{\sqrt{\log \mu}} \cdot 2 \cdot \sum_{i=0}^{\mu-1} l_{t_i}. \tag{3}$$

Therefore,

$$\begin{aligned}\mathrm{OPT}_R(\sigma) &\leq 2 \cdot \int_{t \in [0,2\mu]} \lceil S_t(\sigma) \rceil \leq 4\mu + 2 \cdot \int_{t \in [0,2\mu]} S_t(\sigma) \\ &\leq 4\mu + \frac{1}{\sqrt{\log \mu}} \cdot 4 \cdot \sum_{i=0}^{\mu} l_{t_i} \leq \frac{8}{\sqrt{\log \mu}} \mathrm{ON}(\sigma),\end{aligned} \tag{4}$$

where the first inequality follows from Lemma 3.1, the second inequality follows from (3) and the last inequality follows from (1) and (2).

Putting it all together,

$$\begin{aligned}\mathrm{ON}(\sigma) &\geq \Omega(\sqrt{\log \mu}) \cdot \mathrm{OPT}_R(\sigma) \\ &\geq \Omega(\sqrt{\log \mu}) \cdot \mathrm{DC}(\sigma) \geq \Omega(\sqrt{\log \mu}) \cdot \mathrm{OPT}_{NR}(\sigma),\end{aligned}$$

where the first inequality follows from (4), the second inequality follows from Theorem 4.2 and the last inequality follows from the fact that DC is a non-repacking algorithm. □

5 UPPER BOUND OF $O(\mathrm{LOG\,LOG}\, \mu)$ W.R.T ALIGNED INPUTS

Recall the definition of aligned inputs, i.e., that items of length $\in (2^{i-1}, 2^i]$ may only arrive at multiples of 2^i and that items that arrive at the same moment, t, arrive with an arbitrary order (meaning that every item must be handled before the next one arrives). Note that, in particular this means that any items that arrive strictly after $c \cdot 2^i$ and strictly before $(c+1) \cdot 2^i$ must depart by time $(c+1) \cdot 2^i$, for any $c, i \in \mathbb{N}$.

By the definition of binary inputs, we may use the notation t^+ to denote time t after all items arriving at t have arrived and t^- to denote time t after all items that depart at time t have departed and before any other item arrives.

Given such an input, σ, with value μ, we first partition it in the following way. Consider time $t_0 = 0$ and consider all items that arrive at that time. Let μ' denote the length of the longest item that arrived at that time and let $\mu_0 = 2^{\lceil \log \mu' \rceil}$. By the definition of aligned inputs, all items that arrive in the time interval $[t_0, t_0 + \mu_0]$ must also depart in that time interval (this is due to the fact that if an item departs after $t_0 + \mu_0$ then by the definition of aligned inputs, it must have arrived at time t_0. However, in this case that would contradict the definition of μ_0). Therefore, we may remove all items that arrive in this interval (and denote them as σ_0), from σ, and manage them as a separate input. We continue decomposing σ in the same way, resulting in mutually disjoint inputs, $\sigma_0, \sigma_1, \ldots$ (in the sense that no two items from different inputs, intersect). Under such a partition, given any σ_i, changing its starting time, t_i, to 0, results in the input remaining aligned. Therefore, from now on we will assume each σ_i starts at time 0. We note that every σ_i is defined such that an item of length $(\frac{\mu_i}{2}, \mu_i]$ arrives at time 0. In particular, this means that $\mu_i \leq 2\mu$ (where μ is defined by the original input, σ).

This partition can be done in an online manner, therefore we may apply a $f(\mu_i)$-competitive algorithm to each σ_i separately and achieve a $f(2\mu)$-competitive algorithm (where μ is defined with respect to the original input, σ) assuming f is a non-decreasing function. Thus, from now on we shall assume that our input is aligned, an item of length μ arrives at time 0, all items arrive and depart during the time interval, $[0, \mu]$ and μ is a power of 2, i.e., $\mu = 2^n$ for some $n \in \mathbb{N}$.

Before defining our algorithm, CDFF (Classify-by-Duration-First-Fit), we first give a few definitions. We first partition the possible lengths of items, i.e., $\bigcup_{i=0}^{\log \mu}(2^{i-1}, 2^i]$ (note that the interval, $(1/2, 1]$, may only include items of length 1, however we use the entire interval for convenience of notation). By the definition of aligned inputs, at any moment t, the longest item that may arrive is bounded from above (e.g., items of length 1 may arrive any moment, however items of length μ may only arrive at time 0). For any given moment, t, let $(2^{m_t-1}, 2^{m_t}]$ denote the longest interval for which items of length in that interval may arrive. Note that m_t is defined by t and can therefore be computed in an online manner before any items arrive.

We now turn to define CDFF on aligned inputs. At time $t^- = 0^-$, open $\log \mu + 1$ bins, $b_0^1, \ldots, b_{\log \mu}^1$ (some of these bins may remain empty throughout the process). We note that by the definition of aligned inputs, items of any length may arrive. Given an item, r, CDFF first classifies it according to its length, i.e., $l(r) \in (2^{i-1}, 2^i]$, and then packs r into bin $b_{\log \mu - i}^1$. Note that items with larger intervals are packed into bins with smaller lower indexes. For example, an item of length μ is packed into b_0^1 and item of length 1 is packed into $b_{\log \mu}^1$. Once b_i^1 is too full to accept an item, we open b_i^2 and so on and so forth. Meaning, item of length $\in (2^{i-1}, 2^i]$ is put into bin $b_{\log \mu - i}^j$ for minimal j s.t. $b_{\log \mu - i}^j$ can accept said item. Later on, we will address the bins $\{b_i^j\}_j$, for a given i, as the ith row of bins.

We note that although CDFF is defined as having prior knowledge of μ, at time $t^- = 0^-$ it packs items according to type and may therefore adapt as larger items arrive. This means it does not in fact need any prior knowledge of μ. Furthermore, items of length $\in (\frac{\mu}{2}, \mu]$ arrive at time 0, thus, during the following item arrivals CDFF will already know the value of μ.

We turn to define our algorithm for time $t^- > 1$:
Let $(2^{m_t-1}, 2^{m_t}]$ denote the longest interval for which items of length in that interval may arrive. Now, CDFF first classifies items according to their length and then packs items that belong to the ith smallest interval, into row $(m_t - i)$, in a first-fit manner (furthermore, once a bin b_i^j becomes empty, remove it from the ith row and update indexes). Again we note that the bins' numbering is opposite to the interval numbering, i.e., items with interval i are packed into row $m_t - i$. Meaning that given an item r, if $l(r) \in (2^{i-1}, 2^i]$ for $0 \leq i \leq m_t$, then r is packed into $b_{m_t - i}^j$ for a minimal j that can accept it. Figure 1 shows a representation of what CDFF's bins will look like at any moment.

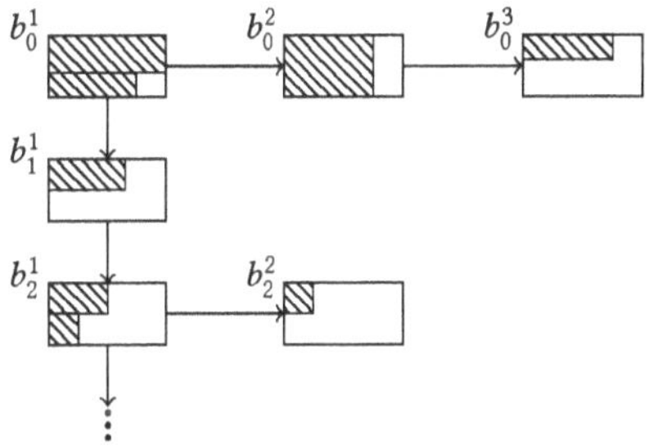

Figure 1: Representation of CDFF's bins at a given moment, t. Each rectangle represents a bin with some load.

In Algorithm 2 we formally define CDFF.

/* Denote b_i^j as bin j in row i of bins. */

Init: Open $log\mu + 1$ bins labelled $b_0^1, \ldots, b_{\log \mu}^1$.

Upon arrival of request r **do**
- $t^- \leftarrow r$'s arrival time.
- $(2^{m_t-1}, 2^{m_t}] \leftarrow$ longest interval for which items of length in that interval may arrive.
- $i \leftarrow r$'s type, i.e., $l(I(r)) \in (2^{i-1}, 2^i]$.
- Pack r into row $m_t - i$ of open bins in a First-Fit manner. If needed open a new bin in that row.

Upon departure of request r **do**
- Remove r from its bin, close the bin and update indexes if necessary.

Algorithm 2: Description of CDFF Algorithm

We first state the main theorem of the section.

THEOREM 5.1. *For any aligned input, σ,*

$$CDFF(\sigma) = O(\log\log\mu)OPT_R(\sigma).$$

Before proving our Theorem 5.1, in the next section we define a specific type of aligned input, namely, binary input, and show that for any binary input, σ_μ such that $\mu = 2^n$, we get $\mathrm{CDFF}(\sigma_\mu) = O(\log\log\mu)\cdot\mathrm{OPT}_R(\sigma_\mu)$. We then argue that in a sense, this is the worst case scenario and that in fact for any aligned input, σ, we have $\mathrm{CDFF}(\sigma) = O(\log\log\mu)\cdot\mathrm{OPT}_R(\sigma)$.

5.1 Upper Bound of $O(\log\log\mu)$ w.r.t Binary Inputs

Definition 5.2. Define a binary input of size $\mu = 2^n$, denoted as σ_μ, as the following collection of items:
For every $i \in \{0, 1, \dots, \log\mu\}$, items of duration 2^i arrive at times, $0\cdot 2^i, 1\cdot 2^i, \dots, (\frac{\mu}{2^i}-1)\cdot 2^i$. Furthermore, all items' loads are $1/\log\mu$.

For example, figures 2 and 3, show what a binary input, σ_8 would look like and how CDFF would handle such an input.

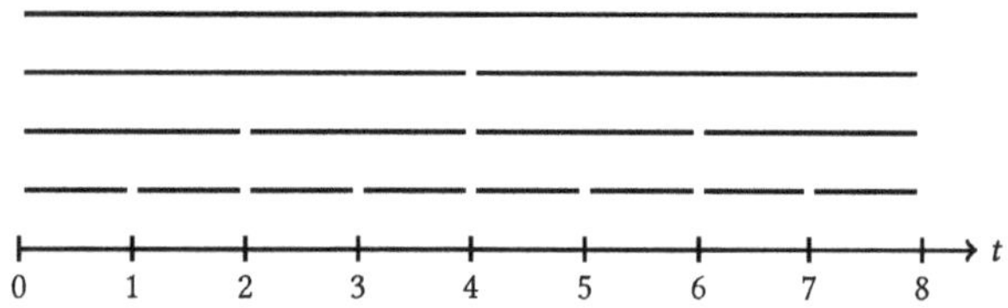

Figure 2: Representation of σ_8. Each segment represents an item.

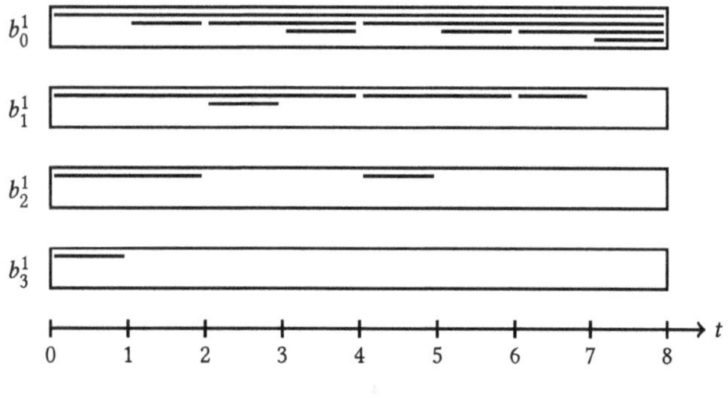

Figure 3: Representation of how CDFF packs σ_8.

PROPOSITION 5.3. *$\forall\mu$: $CDFF(\sigma_\mu) \le (2\log\log\mu + 1)OPT_R(\sigma_\mu)$.*

Surprisingly, our problem is closely related to the binary representation of time t and a few of its properties. In order to prove our proposition, we first give a few definitions and a few lemmas.

Definition 5.4. For $t \in \mathbb{N}$, let $binary(t)$ denote t's binary representation.

Since, by the definition of σ_μ, at time t only items of length 2^i such that $t/2^i \in \mathbb{N}$, may arrive, we get the following observation.

OBSERVATION 3. *Given a binary input, σ_μ, and for any $t \in \{0, 1, \dots, \mu-2, \mu-1\}$, the number of requests that arrive at time t is equal to 1 + the length of the longest sequence of zeros that starts at the least significant bit (LSB) of $binary(t)$.*

For any $t \in \{0, 1, \dots, \mu-1\}$ let $b_t = (1||binary(t)) \in \{0,1\}^{\log\mu+1}$ (where $a||b$ denotes the concatenation of binary strings, a and b). Furthermore, let $b_t = ((b_t)_{\log\mu}, \dots, (b_t)_0)$.
Given σ_μ and time t, we define a mapping, f_t, from items in σ_μ to bits in b_t as follows.

$$\forall r \in \sigma_\mu : f_t(r) = (b_t)_{\log(I(I(r))}. \tag{1}$$

For example, if r is an item of length 1 given at time 0, $f_0(r) = (b_0)_{\log(1)} = (10\cdots0)_0 = 0$.

By the definition of σ_μ, an item of every length is active at every moment, and therefore this mapping is one-to-one and onto the $\log\mu$ least significant bits in b_t. Meaning that every item in σ_μ at any moment has an associated bit and every bit at every moment has an associated item.

LEMMA 5.5. *Let σ_μ be a binary input and let $t \in \{0, 1, \dots, \mu-1\}$. Therefore,*

1. *For any item $r \in \sigma_\mu$, if $f_t(r) = 1$ then r is assigned by CDFF to b_0^1.*
2. *For any item $r \in \sigma_\mu$, if $f_t(r) = 0$ and the maximal sequence of zeros that starts at $(b_t)_{\log(I(I(r))}$ and continues towards the most significant bit (MSB), is of size s (not including $(b_t)_{\log(I(I(r))}$), then r is assigned by CDFF to b_{s+1}^1.*

For example, if $b_t = 1001000$, then item of length 4 will be assigned to bin b_1^1.

PROOF. We will prove this by induction on t.

For $t = 0$, $b_0 = 10\cdots0$ and by the definition of CDFF only the item of length 2^k for $k \in \{0, 1, \dots, \log\mu\}$, is assigned to bin $b^1_{\log\mu-k}$. Furthermore, only one item arrives of each length, meaning that $b^1_{\log\mu-k}$ will indeed have room for the item. Thus 1 and 2 follow.

For $t > 0$, let $b_t = 1||\alpha||\beta$ such that $\beta = 10\cdots0 \in \{0,1\}^k$, $\alpha \in \{0,1\}^{\log\mu+1-k}$ and $k \in \{1, 2, \dots, \log\mu\}$. By Observation 3 we know that the arriving items are of lengths $1, 2, 4, \dots, 2^{k-1}$. By our inductive hypothesis and since items of lengths greater than 2^{k-1} have arrived before time t, we know that these items were assigned to bins correctly. Therefore, it is enough to show that any item of length $l_i = 2^i$ for $i \in \{0, 1, \dots, k-1\}$ is assigned to bin b^1_{k-1-i}.

Every item in σ_μ has a load of $1/\log\mu$ and at any moment there are $\log\mu$ active items, therefore for the entirety of σ_μ, no bin of type b_i^1 will ever be full (and we will never have to open a bin of type b_i^2). By the definition of our algorithm, item of length l_i is assigned to the row of bins, b_{k-1-i}, and will therefore be assigned to bin b^1_{k-1-i} as needed. □

Definition 5.6. For an aligned input, σ, let $\mathrm{CDFF}_{t^+}(\sigma)$ be the amount of open bins in CDFF at time t^+.

Definition 5.7. For $b \in \{0,1\}^n$, let $max_0(b)$ be the length of the longest consecutive sequence of zeros in b.

Corollary 5.8. $\forall t \in \{0, 1, \ldots, \mu - 1\} : CDFF_{t^+}(\sigma_\mu) = \max_0(binary(t)) + 1$.

Proof. If $t = \mu - 1$ then $b_t = \overbrace{(11 \cdots 1)}^{\log \mu + 1 \text{ bits}}$ and by Lemma 5.5 all items are assigned to b_0^1. On the other hand, $\max_0(binary(t)) = \max_0 \overbrace{(11 \cdots 1)}^{\log \mu \text{ bits}} = 0$, implying the correctness of our lemma in this case.

If $t < \mu - 1$, by Lemma 5.5, the item assigned to b_s^1 for maximal s, is the item that has an associated bit 0 with a maximal number of consecutive zeros (counting towards the MSB). This is exactly the bit which is 0 and starts the longest sequence of consecutive 0's in $binary(t)$. Therefore, the length of the longest consecutive sequence of 0's starting at the items' bit (and counting towards MSB) is equal to $\max_0(binary(t)) - 1$ and by Lemma 5.5 this item is assigned to $b^1_{\max_0(binary(t))}$. Since the rows are indexed beginning at 0, $\text{CDFF}_{t^+}(\sigma_\mu) = \max_0(binary(t)) + 1$. □

Lemma 5.9. *Let $b = (b_1, \ldots, b_n) \in \{0,1\}^n$ be n i.i.d. bits such that $Pr[b_i = 1] = 1/2$. Therefore,*

$$E[\max_0(b)] \leq 2 \log n.$$

Proof. By the union bound we have,

$$\Pr[\max_0(b) \geq 2\log n] \leq \sum_{i=1}^{n-2\log n} \Pr[(b_i, \ldots, b_{i+2\log n}) = (0, \ldots, 0)]$$
$$\leq n \cdot \frac{1}{2^{2\log n}} = \frac{1}{n}.$$

Therefore,

$$\text{E}[\max_0(b)] = \sum_{i=1}^{2\log n - 1} i \cdot \Pr[\max_0(b) = i] + \sum_{i=2\log n}^{n} i \cdot \Pr[\max_0(b) = i]$$
$$\leq 2\log n - 1 + n \cdot \Pr[\max_0(b) \geq 2\log n] \leq 2 \log n.$$

□

Corollary 5.10. $\sum_{t=0}^{\mu-1} max_0(binary(t)) \leq 2\mu \cdot \log\log\mu$.

Proof. Let $n = \log \mu$. Therefore,

$$\frac{\sum_{t=0}^{\mu-1} \max_0(binary(t))}{\mu} = \frac{\sum_{b \in \{0,1\}^n} \max_0(b)}{2^n} = \text{E}[\max_0(b)]$$
$$\leq 2\log n = 2\log\log\mu.$$

□

We now turn to prove Proposition 5.3.

Proposition 5.3. $\forall \mu : CDFF(\sigma_\mu) \leq (2\log\log\mu + 1)OPT_R(\sigma_\mu)$.

Proof.

$$\text{CDFF}(\sigma_\mu) = \sum_{t=0}^{\mu-1} \text{CDFF}_t(\sigma_\mu) = \sum_{t=0}^{\mu-1} (\max_0(binary(t)) + 1)$$
$$= \mu + \sum_{t=0}^{\mu-1} \max_0(binary(t)) \leq \mu + 2 \cdot \mu \cdot \log\log\mu$$
$$\leq (2\log\log\mu + 1)\text{OPT}_R(\sigma_\mu),$$

where the first inequality is by Corollary 5.10, the second equality is by Corollary 5.8 and the last inequality is due to the fact that $\text{OPT}_R(\sigma_\mu) \geq \mu$. □

5.2 Upper Bound of $O(\log\log\mu)$ w.r.t Aligned Inputs

In this section we show that CDFF is $O(\log\log\mu)$ - competitive w.r.t. arbitrary aligned inputs. Recall the reduction we used in section 3:

Given an input σ, define σ' as follows:
Let $r \in \sigma$, let $i \in \{1, \ldots, \log\mu\}$ be such that $l(I(r)) \in (2^{i-1}, 2^i]$ and let $c \in \mathbb{N}$ be such that $I(r)^- \in ((c-1) \cdot 2^i, c \cdot 2^i]$.
Given such r, define r' as, $I(r')^- = I(r)^-$ and $I(r')^+ = (c+1) \cdot 2^i$.
Note that in our case, i.e. aligned inputs, $I(r)$ is always equal to $c \cdot 2^i$. Therefore, the reduction simply increases the item's departure time to the next multiple of 2^i.

We now turn to prove that CDFF is $O(\log\log\mu)$ competitive as we did in section 3 - given an input, σ, we compare CDFF(σ) to $\text{OPT}_R(\sigma')$. Then, by Corollary 3.4, we get the desired result.
First we give the following definition.

Definition 5.11. Given σ and σ' such that σ is an arbitrary aligned input and σ' is the input we get by applying the reduction to σ, we define $d_r^{t^+}(\sigma')$ to be the overall load of all items that have ever been packed into row r by CDFF (in σ) and that are active at time t^+ (in σ'). That is, if $e \in \sigma$, then its load is added to $d_r^{t^+}(\sigma')$ only if e was packed by CDFF into row r of bins and $t^+ \in I(e')$ s.t. e' is e after we apply the reduction.

Lemma 5.12. *Given an arbitrary aligned input, σ, if at any moment t^+, CDFF has k open bins in row r, then $d_r^{t^+}(\sigma') \geq \frac{k-1}{2}$.*

Proof. Consider CDFF's r'th row of bins, $b_r^1, \ldots, b_r^k$ at time t^+. We will prove by induction on k that the overall load of all items that have ever been put into one of these bins by CDFF and that are active at time t^+, in σ', is at least $\frac{k-1}{2}$.

The case $k = 1$ is trivial. We now assume we have $k \geq 2$ open bins at time t^+, $b_r^1, \ldots, b_r^k$. By our induction hypothesis we may assume that the overall load of all items that were packed into $b_r^1, \ldots, b_r^{k-1}$ and are active at time t^+ in σ', is at least $\frac{k-2}{2}$. We now show that the overall load of all items that were packed into all k bins and that are active at time t^+ in σ', is at least $\frac{k-1}{2}$. Consider an item that is packed into bin b_r^k and that is active at time t^+ in σ. Denote this item as $\widetilde{r}$, its arrival time as $t_{\widetilde{r}}$ and its load as $s(\widetilde{r})$. If $s(\widetilde{r}) \geq 1/2$ then together with our induction hypothesis, $d_r^{t^+}(\sigma') \geq \frac{k-1}{2}$ as needed.

Otherwise, consider $\widetilde{r}$'s arrival time. Since CDFF packed items into row r, in a First-Fit manner, we know that at time $t_{\widetilde{r}}$ each bin, $b_r^1, \ldots, b_r^{k-1}$, has a load of at least 1/2 and therefore the overall load is at least $\frac{k-1}{2}$. We argue that all items that are active at time $t_{\widetilde{r}}$, in σ, in bins $b_r^1, \ldots, b_r^{k-1}$ are also active at time t^+ in σ', thus concluding our proof. To that end, consider an item in one of the $k-1$ bins, $b_r^1, \ldots, b_r^{k-1}$, that is active at time $t_{\widetilde{r}}$ and denote it as $\hat{r}$ and its arrival time as $t_{\hat{r}}$. By the definition of CDFF we know that if items that arrive at the same time are packed into the same row of bins, then they must depart at the same time (in σ'). Therefore, if $t_{\widetilde{r}} = t_{\hat{r}}$ then, $\hat{r}$ and $\widetilde{r}$ depart together (in σ'). Since $\widetilde{r}$ is active at time t^+ in σ, it is also active at time t^+ in σ', meaning that $t_{\hat{r}}$ is also active at time t^+ in σ', as needed.

Otherwise, $t_{\hat{r}} < t_{\widetilde{r}}$. Since $\hat{r}$ arrived before $\widetilde{r}$ in σ, this is also the case in σ' (since arrival times are not altered). Furthermore, since both items are active at time $t_{\widetilde{r}}$ in σ, this is also the case in σ' (since items' lengths are only increased). Meaning that in σ', $\hat{r}$ arrived strictly before $\widetilde{r}$ and their time intervals intersected. By the definition of σ', $\hat{r}$ must therefore depart after $\widetilde{r}$. In particular this means that $\hat{r}$ is active at time t^+ in σ', as needed. Thus, in any case, we get that $d_r^{t^+}(\sigma') \geq \frac{k-1}{2}$ as needed. □

We now turn to prove our main theorem.

Proof of Theorem 5.1. Let $C_r^{t^+}$ denote CDFF's number of open bins in row r at time t^+. Therefore,

$$\begin{aligned}
\mathrm{CDFF}(\sigma) &= \sum_{t=0}^{\mu-1} \mathrm{CDFF}_{t^+}(\sigma) = \sum_{t=0}^{\mu-1}\sum_{i=1}^{R_{t^+}} C_i^{t^+} \\
&\leq \sum_{t=0}^{\mu-1}\sum_{i=1}^{R_{t^+}} (2 \cdot d_r^{t^+}(\sigma') + 1) \qquad (1) \\
&= \sum_{t=0}^{\mu-1}\sum_{i=1}^{R_{t^+}} 1 + 2 \cdot \sum_{t=0}^{\mu-1}\sum_{i=1}^{R_{t^+}} d_r^{t^+}(\sigma'),
\end{aligned}$$

where the first inequality follows by Lemma 5.12.

The sum $\sum_{t=0}^{\mu-1}\sum_{i=1}^{R_{t^+}}(1)$ represents the number of bins of type b_j^1 open at any given time. We have shown an upper bound for this number in Proposition 5.3, since in σ_μ at any given time items of all lengths available at that time arrive, meaning every bin of such type that could be opened is indeed opened. Therefore,

$$\sum_{t=0}^{\mu-1}\sum_{i=1}^{R_{t^+}} 1 \leq \mu \cdot (2 \log\log \mu + 1). \qquad (2)$$

For any r and t, $d_r^{t^+}(\sigma')$ accounts for loads that are disjoint and therefore no load is counted twice. Thus,

$$\sum_{t=0}^{\mu-1}\sum_{i=1}^{R_{t^+}} d_r^{t^+}(\sigma') \leq d(\sigma'). \qquad (3)$$

Putting it all together,

$$\begin{aligned}
\mathrm{CDFF}(\sigma) &\leq \mu \cdot (2\log\log\mu + 1) + 2 \cdot d(\sigma') \\
&\leq (3 + 2\log\log\mu) \cdot \mathrm{OPT}_R(\sigma') \\
&\leq (8 + 16\log\log\mu) \cdot \mathrm{OPT}_R(\sigma) \\
&= O(\log\log\mu) \cdot \mathrm{OPT}_R(\sigma),
\end{aligned}$$

where the first inequality is due to (1), (2) and (3), the second inequality is due to the *time – space* and *span* bounds (note that the *span* bound follows from our assumption that an item of length μ arrives at time 0) and the last inequality is due to Corollary 3.4. □

6 CONCLUSIONS AND OPEN PROBLEMS

We provide a $O(\sqrt{\log \mu})$-competitive algorithm and show a matching lower bound of $\Omega(\sqrt{\log \mu})$ on the competitiveness of any online algorithm, both bounds are with respect to general inputs. We also provide a $O(\log\log\mu)$-competitive algorithm with respect to aligned inputs. A natural open question would be to either show that with respect to aligned inputs our algorithm is optimal (by improving the lower bound) or improving the upper bound by showing a better performing algorithm. Another natural continuation of the research would be to inspect other interesting families of inputs.

REFERENCES

[1] János Balogh, József Békési, and Gábor Galambos. New lower bounds for certain classes of bin packing algorithms. *Theor. Comput. Sci.*, 440-441:1–13, 2012.
[2] Mihai Burcea. *Online dynamic bin packing.* PhD thesis, University of Liverpool, UK, 2014.
[3] Joseph Wun-Tat Chan, Prudence W. H. Wong, and Fencol C. C. Yung. On dynamic bin packing: An improved lower bound and resource augmentation analysis. *Algorithmica*, 53(2):172–206, 2009.
[4] Sandy Heydrich and Rob van Stee. Beating the harmonic lower bound for online bin packing. In *43rd International Colloquium on Automata, Languages, and Programming, ICALP 2016, July 11-15, 2016, Rome, Italy*, pages 41:1–41:14, 2016.
[5] David S. Johnson, Alan J. Demers, Jeffrey D. Ullman, M. R. Garey, and Ronald L. Graham. Worst-case performance bounds for simple one-dimensional packing algorithms. *SIAM J. Comput.*, 3(4):299–325, 1974.
[6] Edward G. Coffman Jr., M. R. Garey, and David S. Johnson. Dynamic bin packing. *SIAM J. Comput.*, 12(2):227–258, 1983.
[7] Yusen Li, Xueyan Tang, and Wentong Cai. On dynamic bin packing for resource allocation in the cloud. In *26th ACM Symposium on Parallelism in Algorithms and Architectures, SPAA '14, Prague, Czech Republic - June 23 - 25, 2014*, pages 2–11, 2014.
[8] Yusen Li, Xueyan Tang, and Wentong Cai. Play request dispatching for efficient virtual machine usage in cloud gaming. *IEEE Trans. Circuits Syst. Video Techn.*, 25(12):2052–2063, 2015.
[9] Yusen Li, Xueyan Tang, and Wentong Cai. Dynamic bin packing for on-demand cloud resource allocation. *IEEE Trans. Parallel Distrib. Syst.*, 27(1):157–170, 2016.
[10] Runtian Ren and Xueyan Tang. Clairvoyant dynamic bin packing for job scheduling with minimum server usage time. In *Proceedings of the 28th ACM Symposium on Parallelism in Algorithms and Architectures, SPAA 2016, Asilomar State Beach/Pacific Grove, CA, USA, July 11-13, 2016*, pages 227–237, 2016.
[11] Steven S. Seiden. On the online bin packing problem. *J. ACM*, 49(5):640–671, 2002.
[12] Mordechai Shalom, Ariella Voloshin, Prudence W. H. Wong, Fencol C. C. Yung, and Shmuel Zaks. Online optimization of busy time on parallel machines. *Theor. Comput. Sci.*, 560:190–206, 2014.
[13] Xueyan Tang, Yusen Li, Runtian Ren, and Wentong Cai. On first fit bin packing for online cloud server allocation. In *2016 IEEE International Parallel and Distributed Processing Symposium, IPDPS 2016, Chicago, IL, USA, May 23-27, 2016*, pages 323–332, 2016.
[14] André van Vliet. An improved lower bound for on-line bin packing algorithms. *Inf. Process. Lett.*, 43(5):277–284, 1992.
[15] Prudence W. H. Wong, Fencol C. C. Yung, and Mihai Burcea. An 8/3 lower bound for online dynamic bin packing. In *Algorithms and Computation - 23rd International Symposium, ISAAC 2012, Taipei, Taiwan, December 19-21, 2012. Proceedings*, pages 44–53, 2012.

Brief Announcement: Scheduling Parallelizable Jobs Online to Maximize Throughput

Kunal Agrawal, Jing Li, Kefu Lu, Benjamin Moseley
Washington University in St. Louis
1 Brookings Drive, St. Louis, MO 63130
{kunal,li.jing,kefulu,bmoseley}@wustl.edu

ABSTRACT

We consider scheduling parallelizable jobs online to maximize the throughput or profit of the schedule. A set of n jobs arrive online and each job J_i has an associated function $p_i(t)$, the profit obtained for finishing job J_i at time t. Each job has its own arbitrary non-increasing profit function. We consider the case where each job is a parallel job that can be represented as a directed acyclic graph (DAG). We give the first non-trivial results for the profit scheduling problem for DAG jobs showing $O(1)$-competitive algorithms using resource augmentation.

1 INTRODUCTION

Scheduling preemptive jobs online to meet deadlines is a fundamental problem and, consequently, this area has been extensively studied. In a typical setting, there are n jobs that arrive over time. Each job J_i arrives at time r_i, has a deadline d_i, relative deadline $D_i = d_i - r_i$ and a profit or weight p_i that is obtained if the job is completed by its deadline. The ***throughput*** of a schedule is the total profit of the jobs completed by their deadlines, and a popular scheduling objective is to maximize the throughput of the schedule.

In a generalization of the throughput problem, each job J_i is associated with a function $p_i(t)$, which specifies the profit obtained for finishing job J_i at time $r_i + t$. It is assumed that p_i can be different for each job J_i and the functions are arbitrary non-increasing functions. We call this problem the ***general profit*** problem.

In this work, we consider the throughput and general profit scheduling problems in the preemptive online setting for parallel jobs. In this setting, the *online* scheduler is only aware of the job at the time it arrives in the system, and a job is *preemptive* if it can be started, stopped, and resumed from the previous position later. We model each parallel job as a ***directed acyclic graph (DAG)***. Each node in the DAG is a sequence of instructions to be executed; the edges in the DAG represent dependencies. A node can be executed if and only if all of its predecessors have been completed. Therefore, two nodes can potentially run in parallel if neither precedes the other in the DAG. In this setting, each job J_i arrives as a single independent DAG and a profit of p_i is obtained if *all* nodes of the DAG are completed by job J_i's deadline. The DAG model can represent parallel programs written in many widely used parallel languages and libraries, such as OpenMP [25], Cilk Plus [16], Intel TBB [27] and Microsoft Parallel Programming Library [13].

Both the throughput and general profit scheduling problem have been studied extensively for sequential jobs. In the simplest setting, each job J_i has work or processing time W_i to be processed on a single machine. It is known that there exists a deterministic algorithm which is $O(\delta)$-competitive, where δ is the ratio of the maximum to minimum density of a job [10, 11, 20, 32]. The *density* of job J_i is $\frac{p_i}{W_i}$ (the ratio of its profit to its work). In addition, this is the best possible result for any deterministic online algorithm even in the case where all jobs have unit profit and the goal is to complete as many jobs as possible by their deadlines. If the algorithm can be randomized, $\Theta(\min\{\log \delta, \log \Delta\})$ is the optimal competitive ratio [17, 19]. Δ is the ratio of the maximum to minimum job processing time.

These strong lower bounds on the competitive ratio of any online algorithm makes it difficult to differentiate between algorithms and to discover the key algorithmic ideas that work well in practice. To overcome this challenge, the now standard form of analysis in scheduling theory is a *resource augmentation* analysis [18, 30]. In a resource augmentation analysis, the algorithm is given extra resources over the adversary and the competitive ratio is bounded. A s-speed c-competitive algorithm is given a processor that is s times faster than the optimal solution and achieves a competitive ratio of c. The seminal scheduling paper [18] considered the throughput scheduling problem and gave the best possible $(1 + \epsilon)$-speed $O(\frac{1}{\epsilon})$-competitive algorithm for any fixed $\epsilon > 0$.

Since this work, there has been an effort to understand and develop algorithms for more general scheduling environments and objectives. In the identical machine setting where the jobs can be scheduled on m identical parallel machines, a $(1 + \epsilon)$-speed $O(1)$-competitive algorithm is known for fixed $\epsilon > 0$ [4]. This has been extended to the case where the machines have speed scalable processors and the scheduler is energy aware [26]. In the related machines and unrelated machines settings, similar results have been obtained as well [15]. In [23] similar results were obtained in a distributed model.

None of the prior work considers parallel jobs. Parallel DAG jobs have been widely considered in scheduling theory for other objectives [1–3, 14, 22, 24, 28, 29]. There has been an extensive study in the real-time system community on how to schedule parallel DAG jobs by their deadlines [5–9, 12, 21, 22, 29]. These works focus on determining if a set of reoccurring jobs can *all* be completed by their deadlines, in contrast to optimizing throughput or profit.

Results: We give the *first* non-trivial results for scheduling parallelizable DAG jobs online to maximize throughput and then we

SPAA'17, July 24–26, 2017, Washington, DC, USA

ACM ISBN 978-1-4503-4593-4/17/07...$15.00
http://dx.doi.org/10.1145/3087556.3087590

generalize these results to the general profit problem. Two important parameters in the DAG setting are the ***critical-path length*** L_i of job J_i (its execution time on an infinite number of processors) and its total ***work*** W_i (its uninterrupted execution time on a single processor). The value of $\max\{L_i, W_i/m\}$ is a lower bound on the amount of time any 1-speed scheduler takes to complete job J_i on m cores. We will focus on schedulers that are aware of the values of L_i and W_i when the job arrives, but are unaware of the internal structure of the job's DAG. That is, besides L_i and W_i, the only other information a scheduler has on a job's DAG is which nodes are currently available to execute. We call such an algorithm *semi-non-clairvoyant* — for DAG jobs. This is a reasonable model for the real world programs since the DAG generally unfolds dynamically as the program executes. We first state a simple theorem about these schedulers.

Theorem 1.1. *There exists inputs where any semi-non-clairvoyant scheduler requires a speed augmentation of* $2 - 1/m$ *to be* $O(1)$-*competitive for maximizing throughput.*

Scheduling even a single DAG job in time smaller than $\frac{W_i - L_i}{m} + L_i$ is a hard problem even in the offline setting where the entire job structure is known in advance. This is captured by the classic problem of scheduling a precedence constrained jobs to minimize the makespan. For this problem, there is no $2 - \epsilon$ approximation assuming a variant of the unique games conjecture [31]. We can construct a DAG where any semi-non-clairvoyant scheduler will take roughly $\frac{W_i - L_i}{m} + L_i$ time to complete, while a fully clairvoyant scheduler can finish in time W_i/m. By setting the relative deadline to be $D_i = W_i/m = L_i$, every semi-clairvoyant scheduler will require a speed augmentation of $2 - 1/m$ to have bounded competitiveness.

With the previous theorem in place, we cannot hope for a $(1+\epsilon)$-speed $O(1)$-competitive algorithm. To circumvent this hurdle, one could hope to show $O(1)$-competitiveness by either using more resource augmentation or by making an assumption on the input. Intuitively, the hardness comes from having a relative deadline D_i close to $\max\{L_i, W_i/m\}$. In practice, this is unlikely to be the case. We show that so long as $D_i \geq (1+\epsilon)(\frac{W_i - L_i}{m} + L_i)$ then there is a $O(\frac{1}{\epsilon^6})$-competitive algorithm.

Theorem 1.2. *If* $(1+\epsilon)(\frac{W_i - L_i}{m} + L_i) \leq D_i$ *for every job* J_i, *there is a* $O(\frac{1}{\epsilon^6})$-*competitive algorithm for maximizing throughput.*

We note that this immediately implies the following corollaries. One with no assumptions on the input and one for "reasonable jobs."

Corollary 1.3. *There is a* $(2+\epsilon)$-*speed* $O(\frac{1}{\epsilon^6})$-*competitive algorithm for maximizing throughput.*

Corollary 1.4. *There is a* $(1+\epsilon)$-*speed* $O(\frac{1}{\epsilon^6})$-*competitive for maximizing throughput if* $(W_i - L_i)/m + L_i \leq D_i$ *for all jobs* J_i.

The assumption on the job deadline is reasonable as there exists inputs for which even the optimal semi-non-clairvoyant scheduler has unbounded performance if the deadline is any smaller.

For the general profit scheduling problem, we can make the following assumption. For all jobs J_i its general profit function satisfies $p_i(d) = p_i(x_i^*)$, where $0 < d \leq x_i^*$ for some $x_i^* \geq (1+\epsilon)(\frac{W_i - L_i}{m} + L_i)$. This assumption states that there is no additional benefit for completing a job J_i before time x_i^*; this is the natural generalization of the assumption in the throughput case. Using this, we show the following.

Theorem 1.5. *If for every job* J_i *it is the case that* $p_i(d) = p_i(x_i^*)$, *where* $0 < d \leq x_i^*$ *for some value of* $x_i^* \geq (1+\epsilon)(\frac{W_i - L_i}{m} + L_i)$, *there is a* $O(\frac{1}{\epsilon^6})$-*competitive algorithm for the general profit objective.*

Corollary 1.6. *There is a* $(2+\epsilon)$-*speed* $O(\frac{1}{\epsilon^6})$-*competitive algorithm for maximizing general profit.*

2 ALGORITHM FOR JOBS WITH DEADLINES

Here we present an algorithm S for jobs with deadlines and profits for which Theorem 1.2 holds.

On every time step, the algorithm S must decide which jobs to schedule and which ready nodes of each job to schedule. When a job J_i arrives, S calculates a value, n_i — the number of processors "allocated" to J_i. On any time step when S decides to run J_i, it will always allocate n_i processors to J_i. In addition, since S is semi-non-clairvoyant, it is unable to distinguish between ready nodes of J_i; when it decides to allocate n_i nodes to J_i, it arbitrarily picks n_i ready nodes to execute if more than n_i nodes are ready.

In the assumption of Theorem 1.2, each job follows the condition that $(1+\epsilon)(\frac{W_i - L_i}{m} + L_i) \leq D_i$ for some positive constant ϵ.

We define the following **constants**. Let $\delta < \epsilon/2$, $c \geq 1 + \frac{1}{\delta\epsilon}$ and $b = (\frac{1+2\delta}{1+\epsilon})^{1/2} < 1$ be fixed constants. For each job J_i, the algorithm S calculates $n_i = \frac{(W_i - L_i)}{\frac{D_i}{1+2\delta} - L_i}$, where n_i is the number of processors S will give to J_i if it decides to execute J_i on a time step.

Let $x_i = \frac{W_i - L_i}{n_i} + L_i$, which is the number of time steps to complete J_i on n_i dedicated processors (regardless of the order the nodes are executed in). Therefore, job J_i can meet its deadline if it is given n_i dedicated processors for x_i time steps during $[r_i, d_i]$.

We define a ***processor step*** as a unit of time on a single processor and the ***density*** of a job as $v_i = \frac{p_i}{x_i n_i}$. Note that this is a non-standard definition of density. We define the density as $\frac{p_i}{x_i n_i}$ instead of $\frac{p_i}{W_i}$, because we think of J_i requiring $x_i n_i$ processor steps to complete by S. Thus, this definition of density indicates the potential profit per processor step that S can obtain by executing job J_i.

The scheduler S maintains jobs that have arrived but are unfinished in two priority queues. Queue Q stores all the jobs that have been *started* by S. Queue P stores all the jobs that have arrived but have not been started. In both queues, the jobs are sorted according to the density from high to low.

Job Execution: At each time step t, S picks a set of jobs in Q to execute in order from highest to lowest density. If a job J_i has been completed or if its absolute deadline d_i has passed ($d_i > t$), S removes the job from Q. When considering job J_i, if the number of unallocated processors is at least n_i the scheduler assigns n_i processors to J_i for execution. Otherwise, it continues on to the next job. S stops this procedure when either all jobs have been considered or when there are no remaining processors to allocate.

A job J_i is δ-**good** if $D_i \geq (1+2\delta)x_i$. A job is δ-**fresh** at time t if $d_i - t \geq (1+\delta)x_i$. For any set T of jobs, let the set $A(T, v_1, v_2)$ contains all jobs in T with density within the range $[v_1, v_2)$. We define $N(T, v_1, v_2) = \sum_{J_i \in A(T, v_1, v_2)} n_i$. This is the total number of processors that S allocates to jobs in $A(T, v_1, v_2)$. We say that the set of job $A(T, v_1, v_2)$ *requires* $N(T, v_1, v_2)$ processors.

Adding Jobs There are two types of events that may cause S to add a job to Q. Either a job arrives or S completes a job. When a job J_i arrives, S adds it to queue Q if it satisfies the following:

(1) J_i is δ-good;
(2) For all job $J_j \in Q \cup J_i$ it is the case that $N\left(Q \cup J_i, v_j, cv_j\right) \leq bm$. In words, the total number of processors required by jobs in $Q \cup J_i$ with density in the range $[v_j, cv_j)$ is no more than bm.

If these conditions are met, then J_i is inserted into queue Q; otherwise, job J_i is inserted into queue P. When a job is added to Q, we say that the job is ***started*** by S.

When a job completes, S considers the jobs in P from highest to lowest density but first removes all jobs with absolute deadlines that have passed. Then S checks if a job J_i in P can be moved to queue Q by checking if job J_i is δ-fresh and meets condition (2) from above. If both are true, then J_i is moved from queue P to Q.

Remark: Note that the Scheduler S pre-computes a fixed number of processors n_i assigned to each job; this may seem strange. We chose this design because n_i is approximately the minimum number of dedicated cores job J_i requires to complete by $\frac{D_i}{1+2\delta} \to D_i$, without knowing J_i's the DAG structure.

3 ALGORITHM FOR GENERAL PROFIT

The algorithm S' for jobs with general profit functions is similar to S. Due to space, we briefly sketch it and point out the differences.

Assigning cores, deadlines and slots to jobs: When a job J_i arrives, S' calculates a relative deadline D_i and a set of time steps I_i with n_i processors. I_i are the only time steps in which J_i is allowed to run. In each time step t in I_i, we say that J_i is assigned to t.

Note that for the general profit problem, a job J_i has no deadline. Thus, S' computes a D_i by searching all the potential deadlines D to find the minimum valid deadline using a complicated process which we omit due to space. The set of time steps I_i is then determined using the chosen deadline D_i.

From the assumption in Theorem 1.5, for each job J_i the profit function stays the same until $x_i^* \geq (\frac{W_i - L_i}{m} + L_i)(1+\epsilon)$. We set $n_i = \frac{W_i - L_i}{x_i^*/(1+2\delta) - L_i}$, where $\delta < \epsilon/2$. We define its the ***density*** as $v_i = \frac{p_i(D_i)}{x_i n_i} = \frac{p_i(D_i)}{W_i + (n_i - 1)L_i}$, where $x_i := \frac{W_i - L_i}{n_i} + L_i$.

Executing jobs: This procedure is similar to S, with the only difference that S' only picks jobs to execute that have been assigned to time step t.

ACKNOWLEDGMENTS

This work is supported in part by a Google Research Award, a Yahoo Research Award and NSF grants CCF-1617724, CCF-1150036 and CCF-1340571.

REFERENCES

[1] Kunal Agrawal, Yuxiong He, Wen Jing Hsu, and Charles E. Leiserson. 2006. Adaptive Task Scheduling with Parallelism Feedback. In *PPoPP*.
[2] Kunal Agrawal, Yuxiong He, and Charles E. Leiserson. 2007. Adaptive Work Stealing with Parallelism Feedback. In *PPoPP*.
[3] Kunal Agrawal, Jing Li, Kefu Lu, and Benjamin Moseley. 2016. Scheduling Parallel DAG Jobs Online to Minimize Average Flow Time. In *SODA '16*. 176–189.
[4] Nikhil Bansal, Ho-Leung Chan, and Kirk Pruhs. 2011. Competitive Algorithms for Due Date Scheduling. *Algorithmica* 59, 4 (2011), 569–582.
[5] Sanjoy Baruah. 2014. Improved Multiprocessor Global Schedulability Analysis of Sporadic DAG Task Systems. In *ECRTS 2014*. 97–105.
[6] Sanjoy Baruah. 2015. The federated scheduling of constrained-deadline sporadic DAG task systems. In *Proceedings of the 2015 Design, Automation & Test in Europe Conference & Exhibition, DATE 2015*. 1323–1328.
[7] Sanjoy Baruah. 2015. Federated Scheduling of Sporadic DAG Task Systems. In *IPDPS 2015*. 179–186.
[8] Sanjoy Baruah. 2015. The federated scheduling of systems of conditional sporadic DAG tasks. In *EMSOFT 2015*. 1–10.
[9] Sanjoy Baruah, Vincenzo Bonifaci, and Alberto Marchetti-Spaccamela. 2015. The Global EDF Scheduling of Systems of Conditional Sporadic DAG Tasks. In *ECRTS 2015*. 222–231.
[10] Sanjoy K. Baruah, Gilad Koren, Decao Mao, Bhubaneswar Mishra, Arvind Raghunathan, Louis E. Rosier, Dennis Shasha, and Fuxing Wang. 1992. On the Competitiveness of On-Line Real-Time Task Scheduling. *Real-Time Systems* 4, 2 (1992), 125–144.
[11] Sanjoy K. Baruah, Gilad Koren, Bhubaneswar Mishra, Arvind Raghunathan, Louis E. Rosier, and Dennis Shasha. 1991. On-line Scheduling in the Presence of Overload. In *Symposium on Foundations of Computer Science*. 100–110.
[12] Vincenzo Bonifaci, Alberto Marchetti-Spaccamela, Sebastian Stiller, and Andreas Wiese. 2013. Feasibility analysis in the sporadic dag task model. In *ECRTS*.
[13] Colin Campbell and Ade Miller. 2011. *A Parallel Programming with Microsoft Visual C++: Design Patterns for Decomposition and Coordination on Multicore Architectures*. Microsoft Press.
[14] Yuxiong He, Wen-Jing Hsu, and Charles E. Leiserson. 2007. Provably Efficient Online Non-clairvoyant Adaptive Scheduling. In *IPDPS*. http://research.microsoft.com/apps/pubs/default.aspx?id=176942
[15] Sungjin Im and Benjamin Moseley. 2016. General Profit Scheduling and the Power of Migration on Heterogeneous Machines. In *SPAA '16*.
[16] Intel. 2013. Intel CilkPlus. (Sep 2013). https://www.cilkplus.org/.
[17] Bala Kalyanasundaram and Kirk Pruhs. 2000. Fault-Tolerant Real-Time Scheduling. *Algorithmica* 28, 1 (2000), 125–144.
[18] Bala Kalyanasundaram and Kirk Pruhs. 2000. Speed is as powerful as clairvoyance. *J. ACM* 47, 4 (2000), 617–643.
[19] Gilad Koren and Dennis Shasha. 1994. MOCA: A Multiprocessor On-Line Competitive Algorithm for Real-Time System Scheduling. *Theor. Comput. Sci.* 128, 1&2 (1994), 75–97.
[20] Gilad Koren and Dennis Shasha. 1995. Dover: An Optimal On-Line Scheduling Algorithm for Overloaded Uniprocessor Real-Time Systems. *SIAM J. Comput.* 24, 2 (1995), 318–339.
[21] Jing Li, Kunal Agrawal, Chenyang Lu, and Christopher Gill. 2013. Analysis of Global EDF for Parallel Tasks. In *ECRTS '13*.
[22] Jing Li, Jian-Jia Chen, Kunal Agrawal, Chenyang Lu, Christopher D. Gill, and Abusayeed Saifullah. 2014. Analysis of Federated and Global Scheduling for Parallel Real-Time Tasks. In *ECRTS '14*. 85–96.
[23] Brendan Lucier, Ishai Menache, Joseph Naor, and Jonathan Yaniv. 2013. Efficient online scheduling for deadline-sensitive jobs: extended abstract. In *SPAA '13*. 305–314.
[24] Lin Ma, R.D. Chamberlain, and K. Agrawal. 2014. Performance modeling for highly-threaded many-core GPUs. In *Proc. of Int'l Conf. on Application-specific Systems, Architectures and Processors (ASAP)*. 84–91.
[25] OpenMP. 2013. OpenMP Application Program Interface v4.0. (July 2013). http://http://www.openmp.org/mp-documents/OpenMP4.0.0.pdf.
[26] Kirk Pruhs and Clifford Stein. 2010. How to Schedule When You Have to Buy Your Energy. In *APPROX 2010, and RANDOM 2010*. 352–365.
[27] James Reinders. 2010. *Intel threading building blocks: outfitting C++ for multi-core processor parallelism*. O'Reilly Media.
[28] Julien Robert and Nicolas Schabanel. 2008. Non-clairvoyant scheduling with precedence constraints. In *SODA (SODA '08)*. 491–500.
[29] Abusayeed Saifullah, David Ferry, Jing Li, Kunal Agrawal, Chenyang Lu, and Christopher D. Gill. 2014. Parallel Real-Time Scheduling of DAGs. *IEEE Trans. Parallel Distrib. Syst.* 25, 12 (2014), 3242–3252.
[30] Daniel D Sleator and Robert E Tarjan. 1985. Amortized efficiency of list update and paging rules. *Commun. ACM* 28, 2 (1985), 202–208.
[31] Ola Svensson. 2010. Conditional hardness of precedence constrained scheduling on identical machines. In *STOC 2010*. 745–754.
[32] Gerhard J. Woeginger. 1994. On-Line Scheduling of Jobs with Fixed Start and End Times. *Theor. Comput. Sci.* 130, 1 (1994), 5–16.

Brief Announcement: A New Improved Bound for Coflow Scheduling

Mehrnoosh Shafiee and Javad Ghaderi
Department of Electrical Engineering
Columbia University, New York, NY

ABSTRACT

Many data-parallel computing frameworks in today's datacenters consist of multiple computation and communication stages. A stage often cannot start or be completed unless all the required data pieces from the preceding stages are received. *Coflow* is a recently proposed networking abstraction to capture such communication patterns. We consider the problem of efficiently scheduling coflows with release dates in a shared datacenter network so as to minimize the total weighted completion time of coflows. This problem has been shown to be NP-complete, and several polynomial-time approximation algorithms have been recently proposed with provable performance guarantees. Our main result in this paper is a new polynomial-time approximation algorithm that improves the best prior known results. Specifically, we propose a deterministic algorithm with an approximation ratio of 5, which improves the prior best known ratio of 12. For the special case when all the coflows are released at time zero, we obtain an algorithm with an approximation ratio of 4 which improves the prior best known ratio of 8.

KEYWORDS

Scheduling Algorithms, Approximation Algorithms, Coflow, Datacenter Network

1 INTRODUCTION

Many data-parallel computation frameworks, such as MapReduce [3], Dryad [5], Hadoop [13], and Spark [14], alternate between computation and communication stages. Usually, a computation stage produces many pieces of data that need to be processed in remote servers, therefore, it is followed by a communication stage that transfers the intermediate data across the datacenter network. The next computation stage often cannot start unless all the required data pieces from the previous stage are received. Hence, the collective effect of all the flows between the two server groups is more important than that of any of the individual flows.

Recently Chowdhury and Stoica [1] have introduced the *coflow* abstraction to capture these application level communication requirement. *A coflow is defined as a collection of parallel flows whose completion time is determined by the completion time of the last flow in the collection.*

In this paper, we study the coflow scheduling problem with release dates, namely, the algorithmic task of determining when to start serving each flow and at what rate, in order to minimize the weighted sum of completion times of coflows in the system.

1.1 Related Work

The problem of coflow scheduling without release dates was introduced in Varys [2] where the authors proposed a heuristic to minimize the average completion time of coflows. Here, we would like to highlight three papers [6, 7, 10] that are more relevant to our work. The two papers [6, 10] consider the problem of minimizing the total weighted completion time of coflows with release dates. This problem is shown to be NP-complete through its connection with the concurrent open shop problem [2, 10], and then approximation algorithms are proposed which run in polynomial time and return a solution whose value is guaranteed to be within a constant fraction of the optimal. Both papers rely on linear programming relaxation techniques.

In [10], the authors utilize an interval-indexed linear program formulation to partition the coflows into disjoint groups. All coflows that fall into one partition are then viewed as a single coflow, where a polynomial-time algorithm is used to optimize its completion time. The deterministic algorithm proposed in [10] is a 67/3 and 64/3-approximation algorithm for coflow scheduling problem with and without release dates, respectively.

Authors of [6] improved these bounds to 12 and 8, respectively, by constructing an instance of the concurrent open shop problem from the original coflow scheduling problem, and applying the well-known approximation algorithms for the concurrent open shop problem to the constructed instance to obtain an ordering of coflows which is then used in a similar fashion as in [10].

2 MODEL AND PROBLEM STATEMENT

Similar to [2, 10], we abstract out the datacenter network as one giant $N \times N$ non-blocking switch, with N input links connected to N source servers and N output links connected to N destination servers. Thus, the network can be viewed as a bipartite graph with source nodes denoted by set $\mathcal{I}$ on one side and destination nodes denoted by set $\mathcal{J}$ on the other side. Moreover, there are capacity constraints on the input and output links. We assume that all the link capacities are equal and normalized to one.

A coflow is a collection of flows whose completion time is determined by the completion time of the latest flow in the collection. The coflow k can be denoted as an $N \times N$ matrix $D^{(k)}$. Every flow is a triple (i, j, k), where $i \in \mathcal{I}$ is its source node, $j \in \mathcal{J}$ is its destination node, and k is the coflow to which it belongs. The size of

This work is supported by NSF Grants CNS-1652115 and CNS-1565774.

SPAA'17, July 24–26, 2017, Washington, DC, USA
 978-1-4503-4593-4/17/07.
DOI: http://dx.doi.org/10.1145/3087556.3087598

flow (i, j, k) is denoted by d_{ij}^k, which is the (i, j)-th element of the matrix $D^{(k)}$.

There is a set of K coflows denoted by $\mathcal{K}$. Coflow $k \in \mathcal{K}$ is released (arrives) at time r_k which means it can only be scheduled after time r_k. For simplicity, we assume that all flows within a coflow arrive to the system at the same time (as in [10]).

For a source node $i \in \mathcal{I}$ and a coflow $k \in \mathcal{K}$, we define

$$d_i^k = \sum_{j \in \mathcal{J}} d_{ij}^k,$$

which is the aggregate flow that node i needs to transmit for coflow k. d_j^k is defined similarly for destination node $j \in \mathcal{J}$ and coflow $k \in \mathcal{K}$.

We use f_k to denote the finishing (completion) time of coflow k, which, by definition of coflow, is the time when all its flows have finished processing. In other words, for every coflow $k \in \mathcal{K}$, $f_k = \max_{i \in \mathcal{I}, j \in \mathcal{J}} f_{ij}^k$, where f_{ij}^k is the completion time of flow (i, j, k). Then the coflow scheduling problem with release dates is defined as follows. For given positive weights w_k, $k \in \mathcal{K}$, the goal is to minimize the weighted sum of coflow completion times, i.e.,

$$\begin{array}{ll} \text{minimize} & \sum_{k \in \mathcal{K}} w_k f_k \\ \text{subject to} & \text{Capacity and release date constraints.} \end{array}$$

The weights w_k can capture different priority for different coflows.

3 MAIN RESULT

The main contribution of this paper is that we propose a polynomial-time approximation algorithm with the following improved approximation guarantees for the offline coflow scheduling problem.

THEOREM 3.1. *There exists a deterministic 5-approximation algorithm for coflow scheduling with release dates so as to minimize total weighted completion times.*

COROLLARY 3.2. *When all coflows are released at time zero, the approximation ratio of this algorithm is 4.*

The prior best known ratios for this problem is 12 for the case of release dates and 8 for the case of without release dates [6]. Furthermore, our deterministic algorithm has better performance ratios even compared with the randomized algorithms of [6, 10, 12].

4 LINEAR PROGRAMING RELAXATION

In this section, we use *linear ordering variables* (see, e.g., [4, 8, 9]) to present a relaxed linear program of coflow scheduling problem. This formulation is very similar to what has been introduced in [8] for concurrent open shop problem. In the next section, we use the optimal solution to this LP as a subroutine in our deterministic algorithm.

Ordering variables. For each pair of coflows, we define a binary variable which indicates which coflow is completed (finishes all its flows) before the other coflow is completed. Formally, for any two coflows k, k', we introduce a binary variable $\delta_{kk'} \in \{0, 1\}$ such that $\delta_{kk'} = 1$ if coflow k is finished before coflow k', and it is 0 otherwise.

Relaxed Integer Program (IP). We formulate the following Integer Program (IP):

$$\text{(IP)} \ \min \sum_{k \in \mathcal{K}} w_k f_k \tag{1a}$$

$$f_k \geq d_i^k + \sum_{k' \in \mathcal{K}} d_i^{k'} \delta_{k'k} \quad i \in \mathcal{I}, k \in \mathcal{K} \tag{1b}$$

$$f_k \geq d_j^k + \sum_{k' \in \mathcal{K}} d_j^{k'} \delta_{k'k} \quad j \in \mathcal{J}, k \in \mathcal{K} \tag{1c}$$

$$f_k \geq r_k \quad k \in \mathcal{K} \tag{1d}$$

$$\delta_{kk'} + \delta_{k'k} = 1 \quad k, k' \in \mathcal{K} \tag{1e}$$

$$\delta_{kk'} \in \{0, 1\} \quad k, k' \in \mathcal{K}. \tag{1f}$$

The constraint (1b) (similarly (1c)) follows from the definition of ordering variables and the fact that flows incident to a source node i (a destination node j) are processed by a single link of unit capacity. By constraint (1d), each coflow cannot get completed before its release date. This optimization problem is a relaxed integer program for coflow scheduling problem since the set of constraints in (IP) do not capture all the requirements which a feasible schedule should satisfy.

Relaxed Linear Program (LP). In the linear program relaxation, we allow the ordering variables to be fractional. Specifically, we replace the constraint (1f) with the constraints (2b) below. We refer to the obtained linear problem by (LP).

$$\text{(LP)} \ \min \sum_{k=1}^{K} w_k f_k \tag{2a}$$

$$\text{subject to: (1b) – (1e),}$$

$$\delta_{kk'} \in [0, 1] \quad k, k' \in \mathcal{K}. \tag{2b}$$

We denote by $\tilde{f}_k$ the optimal solution to the (LP) for completion time of coflow $k \in \mathcal{K}$. We order coflows based on values of $\tilde{f}_k$ in nondecreasing order. More precisely, we number coflows such that,

$$\tilde{f}_1 \leq \tilde{f}_2 \leq \ldots \leq \tilde{f}_K. \tag{3}$$

Ties are broken arbitrarily. Also, we define $W(k)$ to be the maximum aggregate data that a node should send or receive considering the first k coflows according to the ordering in (3). Specifically,

$$W(k) = \max\{\max_{i \in \mathcal{I}}(\sum_{l=1}^{k} d_i^l), \max_{j \in \mathcal{J}}(\sum_{l=1}^{k} d_j^l)\}. \tag{4}$$

Now we characterize the solution to the linear program (LP).

LEMMA 4.1. $\tilde{f}_k \geq \frac{W(k)}{2}$.

PROOF. Variant versions of this lemma were used in other scheduling problems (see e.g., [4, 8, 9]). We refer to the extended version of this paper [11] for the proof. □

Furthermore, the following lemma establishes a relationship between optimal value of (LP) solution, i.e., $\sum_{k=1}^{K} w_k \tilde{f}_k$ and optimal value of coflow scheduling problem, i.e., $\sum_{k=1}^{K} w_k f_k^{\star}$, where $f_k^{\star}$ is the completion time of coflow k in the optimal schedule.

LEMMA 4.2. $\sum_{k=1}^{K} w_k \tilde{f}_k \leq \sum_{k=1}^{K} w_k f_k^{\star}$.

Proof. Consider an optimal solution to the coflow scheduling problem. We set the ordering variables so as $\delta_{kk'} = 1$ if coflow k precedes coflow k' in this solution, and $\delta_{kk'} = 0$, otherwise. We note that this set of ordering variables and coflow completion times satisfies constraints (1b) and (1c) since the optimal solution should respect capacity constraints on the communication links. It also satisfies constraint (1d). Therefore, the optimal solution can be converted to a feasible solution to (LP). This implies the desired inequality. □

5 APPROXIMATION ALGORITHM

The approximation algorithm is depicted in Algorithm 1 which is a simple list scheduling algorithm based on the ordering in (3). More specifically, the algorithm maintains a list of flows such that for every two flows (i, j, k) and (i', j', k') with $k < k'$, flow (i, j, k) is before flow (i', j', k') in the list. Flows of the same coflow are listed arbitrarily. The algorithm scans the list starting from the first flow and schedules a flow if both its corresponding source and destination links are idle at that time. Upon completion of a flow or arrival of a coflow, the algorithm preempts the schedule, updates the list, and starts scheduling the flows in the updated list.

Algorithm 1 Deterministic Coflow Scheduling Algorithm

Suppose Coflows $\left\{d_{ij}^k\right\}_{i,j=1}^N$ for $k \in \mathcal{K}$ with release dates r_k, $k \in \mathcal{K}$, and weights w_k, $k \in \mathcal{K}$, are given.

1: Solve the linear program (LP) and denote optimal solution by $\{\tilde{f}_k; k \in \mathcal{K}\}$.
2: Order and re-index coflows such that:
$$\tilde{f}_1 \le \tilde{f}_2 \le \ldots \le \tilde{f}_K, \tag{5}$$
where ties are broken arbitrarily.
3: Wait until the first coflow(s) is released.
4: **while** There is some incomplete flow, **do**
5: List the released and incomplete flows respecting the ordering in (5). Let L be the total number of flows in the list.
6: **for** $l = 1$ to L **do**
7: Denote the l-th flow in the list by (i_l, j_l, k_l),
8: **if** Both the links i_l and j_l are unused, **then**
9: Schedule flow (i_l, j_l, k_l).
10: **end if**
11: **end for**
12: **while** No flow is complete and no coflow is released **do**
13: Transmit the flows that get scheduled in line 9 with rate 1.
14: **end while**
15: **end while**

Now we present a sketch of the proof of Theorem 3.1 and Corollary 3.2 regarding performance of Algorithm 1.

Proof of Theorem 3.1. Denote by f_k completion time of coflow k under Algortihm 1. Suppose flow (i, j, k) is the last flow of coflow k that is completed. In general, Algorithm 1 may preempt a flow several times during its execution. For now, suppose flow (i, j, k) is not preempted and use t_k to denote the time when its transmission is started (the arguments can be easily extended to the preemption case as we show at the end of the proof). Therefore
$$f_k = f_{ij}^k = t_k + d_{ij}^k \tag{6}$$
From the algorithm description, t_k is the first time both links i and j are available and there is no flow from i to j before flow (i, j, k) in the list to be scheduled. By definition of $W(k)$ (Equation (4)), node i (similarly node j) has at most $W(k) - d_{ij}^k$ data flow to send by time t_k. Recall that capacity of all links are normalized to 1. Hence,
$$t_k \le r_k + W(k) - d_{ij}^k + W(k) - d_{ij}^k.$$
Combining this inequality with equality (6) yields that: $f_k \le r_k + 2W(k)$. Using Lemma 4.1 and constraint (1d), we can conclude that
$$f_k \le 5\tilde{f}_k,$$
which implies that
$$\sum_{k=1}^K w_k f_k \le 5 \sum_{k=1}^K w_k \tilde{f}_k.$$
This shows approximation ratio of 5 for Algorithm 1 using Lemma 4.2. Finally, if flow (i, j, k) is preempted, the above argument can still be used by letting t_k to be the starting time of its last piece and d_{ij}^k to be the remaining size of its last piece at time t_k. This completes the proof. □

Proof of Corollary 3.2. When all coflows are released at time 0, $t_k \le W(k) - d_{ij}^k + W(k) - d_{ij}^k$. The rest of the argument is similar. Therefore, the algorithm has approximation ratio of 4 when all coflows are release at time 0. □

REFERENCES

[1] M. Chowdhury and I. Stoica. Coflow: A networking abstraction for cluster applications. In *Proceedings of the 11th ACM Workshop on Hot Topics in Networks*, pages 31–36. ACM, 2012.
[2] M. Chowdhury, Y. Zhong, and I. Stoica. Efficient coflow scheduling with varys. In *ACM SIGCOMM Computer Communication Review*, volume 44, pages 443–454. ACM, 2014.
[3] J. Dean and S. Ghemawat. Mapreduce: simplified data processing on large clusters. *Communications of the ACM*, 51(1):107–113, 2008.
[4] L. A. Hall, D. B. Shmoys, and J. Wein. Scheduling to minimize average completion time: Off-line and on-line algorithms. In *SODA*, volume 96, pages 142–151, 1996.
[5] M. Isard, M. Budiu, Y. Yu, A. Birrell, and D. Fetterly. Dryad: distributed data-parallel programs from sequential building blocks. In *ACM SIGOPS Operating Systems Review*, volume 41, pages 59–72. ACM, 2007.
[6] S. Khuller and M. Purohit. Brief announcement: Improved approximation algorithms for scheduling co-flows. In *Proceedings of the 28th ACM Symposium on Parallelism in Algorithms and Architectures*, pages 239–240. ACM, 2016.
[7] S. Luo, H. Yu, Y. Zhao, S. Wang, S. Yu, and L. Li. Towards practical and near-optimal coflow scheduling for data center networks. 2016.
[8] M. Mastrolilli, M. Queyranne, A. S. Schulz, O. Svensson, and N. A. Uhan. Minimizing the sum of weighted completion times in a concurrent open shop. *Operations Research Letters*, 38(5):390–395, 2010.
[9] C. Potts. An algorithm for the single machine sequencing problem with precedence constraints. In *Combinatorial Optimization II*, pages 78–87. Springer, 1980.
[10] Z. Qiu, C. Stein, and Y. Zhong. Minimizing the total weighted completion time of coflows in datacenter networks. In *Proceedings of the 27th ACM symposium on Parallelism in Algorithms and Architectures*, pages 294–303. ACM, 2015.
[11] M. Shafiee and J. Ghaderi. An improved bound for minimizing the total weighted completion time of coflows in datacenters. *arXiv preprint arXiv:1704.08357*, 2017.
[12] M. Shafiee and J. Ghaderi. Scheduling coflows in datacenter networks: Improved bound for total weighted completion time. *ACM SIGMETRICS, Poster Paper*, 2017.
[13] K. Shvachko, H. Kuang, S. Radia, and R. Chansler. The hadoop distributed file system. In *2010 IEEE 26th symposium on mass storage systems and technologies (MSST)*, pages 1–10. IEEE, 2010.
[14] M. Zaharia, M. Chowdhury, M. J. Franklin, S. Shenker, and I. Stoica. Spark: Cluster computing with working sets. *HotCloud*, 10(10-10):95, 2010.

Bounding Laconic Proof Systems by Solving CSPs in Parallel*

Jason Li
Carnegie Mellon University
Pittsburgh, PA 15213
jmli@cs.cmu.edu

Ryan O'Donnell
Carnegie Mellon University
Pittsburgh, PA 15213
odonnell@cs.cmu.edu

ABSTRACT

We show that the basic semidefinite programming relaxation value of any constraint satisfaction problem can be computed in NC; that is, in parallel polylogarithmic time and polynomial work. As a complexity-theoretic consequence we get that $\mathsf{MIP1}[k, c, s] \subseteq \mathsf{PSPACE}$ provided $s/c \leq (.62 - o(1))k/2^k$, resolving a question of Austrin, Håstad, and Pass. Here $\mathsf{MIP1}[k, c, s]$ is the class of languages decidable with completeness c and soundness s by an interactive proof system with k provers, each constrained to communicate just 1 bit.

CCS CONCEPTS

• **Theory of computation → Proof complexity**; **Interactive proof systems**; **Semidefinite programming**;

KEYWORDS

constraint satisfaction problems, semidefinite programming, complexity theory

ACM Reference format:
Jason Li and Ryan O'Donnell. 2017. Bounding Laconic Proof Systems by Solving CSPs in Parallel. In *Proceedings of SPAA '17, Washington DC, USA, July 24-26, 2017*, 5 pages.
https://doi.org/http://dx.doi.org/10.1145/3087556.3087557

1 INTRODUCTION

The famous IP = PSPACE and MIP = NEXP theorems [4, 14, 20] are concerned with the computational power of randomized interactive proof systems. In the multiprover interactive proof (MIP) setup, a randomized (private-coin) polynomial-time verifier is allowed to communicate with k all-powerful, separated provers in an attempt to decide if a given n-bit string x is in a language L. The complexity class $\mathsf{MIP}[k, c, s]$ is the set of languages decidable by such a proof system with completeness c and soundness s; this means that for all $x \in L$, the verifier accepts with probability at least c and for all $x \notin L$, the verifier accepts with probability at most s. It is known that in this definition the precise values of the constants k, c, and s do not really matter: for all $k \geq 2$ and all $0 < s < c \leq 1$ it holds that $\mathsf{MIP}[k, c, s] = \mathsf{NEXP}$ (and also $\mathsf{MIP}[1, c, s] = \mathsf{PSPACE}$).

A significant amount of the original research on interactive proof systems was concerned with the effect of bounding the number of *rounds* of communication. Goldreich and Håstad [6] introduced a refined version of this question in which the number of *bits* communicated by the provers is bounded. Such provers are called *laconic*. This line of research is motivated in part by the fact that several interesting proof systems indeed use laconic provers; for example, in the well-known 1-prover proof systems for Quadratic-Nonresiduosity [9] and Graph-Nonisomorphism [7], the prover communicates just a single bit to the verifier (achieving $c = 1$, $s = 1/2$). An example result in this area, due to Goldreich, Vadhan, and Wigderson [8], is that if $1 > c^2 > s > c/2 > 0$, then the class of languages decided by an interactive proof system with 1 prover communicating 1 bit is precisely SZK.

A recent work of Austrin, Håstad, and Pass [3] focused on the class $\mathsf{MIP1}[k, c, s]$, the restriction of $\mathsf{MIP}[k, c, s]$ in which the provers are restricted to sending just 1 bit. (More precisely, given x, the verifier prepares k questions and an acceptance predicate $\phi : \{0, 1\}^k \to \{0, 1\}$. The questions are sent to the provers simultaneously, and the verifier accepts/rejects according to ϕ's value on the provers' 1-bit responses.) They showed that for any $k \geq 2$ and $c = 1 - \epsilon$ (say), one obtains an intriguing fine-grained hierarchy of complexity classed by varying s. For example, suppose we fix the number of provers to $k = 3$. Austrin et al. show that for any $\epsilon > 0$:

$$\begin{array}{lll} \text{if} & 0 < s < 1/8 - \epsilon, & \mathsf{MIP1}[3, 1 - \epsilon, s] = \mathsf{BPP}; \\ \text{if} & 1/8 + \epsilon < s < 1/4 - \epsilon, & \mathsf{MIP1}[3, 1 - \epsilon, s] = \mathsf{SZK}; \\ \text{if} & 1/4 + \epsilon < s < 1/2 - \epsilon, & \mathsf{AM} \subseteq \mathsf{MIP1}[3, 1 - \epsilon, s] \subseteq \mathsf{EXP}; \\ \text{if} & 1/2 + \epsilon < s < 1 - \epsilon, & \mathsf{MIP1}[3, 1 - \epsilon, s] = \mathsf{NEXP}. \end{array}$$

Narrowing the gap between AM and EXP for $1/4 < s < 1/2$ is quite an interesting open problem. Austrin et al. asked whether, in this range, the upper bound of EXP can be reduced to PSPACE. In this paper we answer the question in the affirmative. More generally, we reduce the upper bound to PSPACE for all parameter ranges k, c, s for which Austrin et al. had an upper bound of EXP:

Theorem 1.1. *Provided* $s/c \leq (.62 - o(1))k/2^k$ *we have* $\mathsf{MIP1}[k, c, s] \subseteq \mathsf{PSPACE}$. *Also, for all* $\epsilon > 0$ *we have* $\mathsf{MIP1}[3, 1 - \epsilon, 1/2 - \epsilon] \subseteq \mathsf{PSPACE}$.

Remark 1.1. *As discussed in Section 2, we can show similar results for MIP systems in which the provers may communicate any fixed number of bits* $c > 1$.

We achieve these new complexity-theoretic upper bounds by showing that the basic semidefinite programming (SDP) value of any constraint satisfaction problem (CSP) can be computed by an

*Computer Science Department, Carnegie Mellon University. Supported in part by NSF grants CCF-0747250, CCF-1116594, CCF-1618679.

ACM ISBN 978-1-4503-4593-4/17/07...$15.00
http://dx.doi.org/10.1145/3087556.3087557

efficient deterministic parallel algorithm — polylogarithmic time and polynomial work.

2 EFFICIENT PARALLEL APPROXIMATION ALGORITHMS FOR CSP SDPS

Here we review the connection between MIP systems and exponential-size CSPs; this connection is standard and appears in Austrin et al.'s work [3, Theorem 5.1]. Suppose $L \in \mathsf{MIP1}[k, c, s]$ and that the associated polynomial-time verifier uses exactly $t(n) = \mathrm{poly}(n)$ random coins on inputs $x \in \{0,1\}^n$. Consider enumerating the actions of the verifier over all its random strings $r \in \{0,1\}^{t(n)}$. For each r, the verifier produces k "questions", along with an acceptance predicate $\phi : \{0,1\}^k \to \{0,1\}$ to be applied to the provers' answers. Thinking of the questions as "CSP variables" to be assigned bits by the provers, we see that on each input $x \in \{0,1\}^n$, the verifier implicitly produces an exponential-size (k-partite) Boolean k-CSP, with a multiset of exactly $2^{t(n)}$ constraints (using various predicates). The optimal value (fraction of constraints satisfied) of this CSP instance is precisely the highest probability with which the provers can cause the verifier to accept. Write $m = 2^{t(n)}$ for the number of constraints in the CSP instance. Now to show that $L \in \mathsf{EXP}$ (say), it suffices to show that for such "implicitly-given" CSPs we can in $\mathrm{poly}(m)$ time distinguish whether the optimal value is at least c or at most s. This is an approximation algorithms problem. In general, the best known polynomial-time approximation algorithms for Boolean k-CSP use semidefinite programming and achieve the approximation ratio $(.62 - o(1))k/2^k$; they are due to Makarychev and Makarychev [15]. This is precisely how Austrin et al. achieve Theorem 1.1 with EXP in place of PSPACE. (The factor-1/2 approximation when $k = 3$ is due to Zwick [24].) Regarding Remark 1.1, it is clear that to handle provers communicating c bits, we just need to investigate the best known [15] approximation algorithms for k-CSPs over a larger alphabet Σ of cardinality 2^c.

As noted by Austrin et al., to achieve the PSPACE upper bound in Theorem 1.1, what we need to do is show that the Makarychev–Makarychev (and Zwick) SDP-based approximation algorithms for m-constraint CSPs can be implemented in $\mathrm{polylog}(m)$ *space*. Let us make this a little more precise. For any arity-k CSP instance $\mathcal{I}$ with arbitrary predicates $\phi : \Sigma^k \to \{0,1\}$ over a constant-size alphabet Σ, there is a certain "basic SDP" relaxation introduced by Raghavendra [18]. It is known [19] to be at least as strong as the ones used by Makarychev–Makarychev and Zwick; i.e., its value, $\mathrm{SDP}(\mathcal{I})$ is known to be as close or closer to $\mathrm{Opt}(\mathcal{I})$. Thus to prove Theorem 1.1, it suffices to prove the following:

THEOREM 2.1. *For any constants*[1] k, q, *and* $\epsilon > 0$, *there is a* $\mathrm{polylog}(m)$*-space Turing Machine that, given as input an* m*-constraint* k*-ary CSP instance* $\mathcal{I}$ *over alphabet* Σ *of size* q*, computes the basic SDP value* $\mathrm{SDP}(\mathcal{I})$ *to within* $\pm\epsilon$.

In fact, we prove the following stronger statement:

THEOREM 2.2. *The algorithm in Theorem 2.1 can be carried out in (log-space uniform)* NC*; equivalently [22], by a (log-space uniform) parallel algorithm using* $\mathrm{poly}(m)$ *deterministic processors and* $\mathrm{polylog}(m)$ *parallel time.*

[1] We could allow k, q, and $1/\epsilon$ to be slightly superconstant; e.g., $\epsilon = \frac{1}{\mathrm{polylog}(m)}$ would be okay. However for simplicity we'll insist they're constant.

This is stronger than Theorem 2.1 because (log-space uniform) $\mathsf{NC} \subseteq \mathsf{polyL}$.

Our proof of Theorem 2.2 is similar to prior works (e.g., [10–12, 23]) that show how to (approximately) solve certain SDPs in NC using the matrix multiplicative weights (MMW) technique of Kale and coauthors [1, 2, 13]. Unfortunately, each specific SDP seems to require its own analysis. Here we use the work of Steurer [21] that shows how the basic $\mathrm{SDP}(\mathcal{I})$ for CSPs can be approximately solved in *serial* quasilinear time, $\widetilde{O}(m)$. We show how to parallelize the algorithm so as to use polylog parallel time, as claimed in Theorem 2.2.

We mention here one important subtlety that arises in translating Steurer's algorithm. Although our complexity-theoretic application Theorem 1.1 is only concerned with space, not time, one may anyway ask whether Steurer's algorithm can be implemented in quasilinear time and polylog space. The subtlety entering into this question has to do with the crucial use of randomness in the algorithm; particularly, the use of the Johnson–Lindenstrauss Lemma while solving the SDP. It seems that it may be possible to perform Steurer's algorithm with $\widetilde{O}(m)$ work and $\mathrm{polylog}(m)$ depth in a standard model of *randomized* parallel computation (for example, this was shown in the special case of approximating Max-Cut by Tangwongsan [23, Chapter 4]). However, in such models, each processor is allowed to store and access any random bits that it uses. When moving to a Turing Machine model, this would seem to necessitate two-way access to a random tape (the "wrong" model of randomized space-bounded computation [16]), as opposed to just a Turing Machine with read-once coin flips. Thus it wouldn't be clear how to get the needed deterministic polylog space algorithm using, say, Nisan's space-derandomization results. Alternatively, one might attempt to directly derandomize the use of the Johnson–Lindenstrauss Lemma using ideas from [5], but it did not seem easy to us to do that in polylog space. See also [17].

Thus in the end, we will only show how to implement Steurer's algorithm in deterministic $\mathrm{polylog}(m)$ parallel time and $\mathrm{poly}(m)$ work, as this is sufficient for Theorem 1.1. (Even $2^{\mathrm{polylog}(m)}$ work would have been sufficient.) By allowing ourselves more than quasilinear work and not insisting on the use of the Johnson–Lindenstrauss Lemma, certain aspects of Steurer's algorithm are simplified. However some effort is still required to prove Theorem 2.1 as parts of Steurer's proof are only sketched, especially the parts concerning arithmetic precision.

3 OUTLINE OF STEURER'S ALGORITHM

Herein we recall Steurer's algorithm from [21] for approximately solving the basic SDP relaxation for CSPs. As is standard, the algorithm actually solves a decision version of the problem: given $\mathcal{I}$ and α, the algorithm outputs YES if $\mathrm{SDP}(\mathcal{I}) \geq \alpha$ and outputs NO if $\mathrm{SDP}(\mathcal{I}) \leq \alpha - \epsilon$. Combining this with a binary search allows the algorithm to approximate $\mathrm{SDP}(\mathcal{I})$ to within $\pm\epsilon$ with only a constant $O(\log(1/\epsilon))$ multiplicative overhead in parallel time and work.

The statement "$\mathrm{SDP}(\mathcal{I}) \geq \alpha$" corresponds to the statement that there exists a PSD matrix X that satisfies certain inequalities. Steurer's algorithm performs MMW iterations in an attempt to find a PSD matrix that is "δ-close" to satisfying all the inequalities.

Steurer's analysis shows two things: that if indeed $\mathrm{SDP}(\mathcal{I}) \geq \alpha$ then a δ-close X will be found after some $T := \mathrm{poly}(k, q, 1/\delta) \cdot \log m$ iterations; and, the existence of a δ-close X implies that $\mathrm{SDP}(\mathcal{I}) \geq \alpha - \mathrm{poly}(k, q) \cdot \delta^{1/4}$. Thus the ϵ-approximate decision problem can be solved with $O(\log m)$ MMW iterations by taking δ to be a constant of the form $\epsilon^4/\mathrm{poly}(k, q)$.

More details. Steurer's algorithm works in a slightly more general setting of CSPs than we need, with a *weighted* list of m *payoffs*, rather than an unweighted list of m predicates. Since we are only concerned approximating $\mathrm{SDP}(\mathcal{I})$ up to a constant $\pm\epsilon$, it is easy to see that we may assume the payoffs and weights are rationals expressible with $\log m + O(1)$ bits. The inputs to Steurer's algorithm are then as follows:

- V, the set of CSP variables, and Σ, the alphabet of cardinality q. We will write $n = |V \times \Sigma|$.
- m, the number of payoffs; their positive weights $w_1, \ldots, w_m$, summing to 1; the scopes $S_1, \ldots, S_m \subset V$ of the payoffs; k, the cardinality of each S_j; and, the payoffs themselves $\phi_1, \ldots, \phi_m : \Sigma^{S_j} \to [-1, 1]$. We may assume m and n are polynomially related.
- α, the target SDP value, and $\delta > 0$, a "closeness" parameter. Both are rational constants.

We also need the following notation:

- $d \in \mathbb{R}^V$ has d_i equal to the normalized degree of variable $i \in V$, i.e., $\frac{1}{k}\sum\{w_j : S_j \ni i\}$.
- $\overline{d} \in \mathbb{R}^n$ is the vector whose (i, a)-entry is d_i for all $a \in \Sigma$.
- $D = \mathrm{diag}(\overline{d})$, i.e., the diagonal matrix with the entries of $\overline{d}$ on the diagonal. We may assume D's entries are rational with common denominator $M = O(m)$.
- Δ_D denotes the set of $n \times n$ PSD matrices X satisfying $D \bullet X = 1$. We define $A \bullet B = \mathrm{tr}(A^T B)$, also equal to the entrywise dot product of A and B.
- ρ is a certain "width" parameter, of the form $\mathrm{poly}(k, q, 1/\delta)$.

We now give the high-level outline of the MMW method as employed by Steurer (with slightly adjusted notation). It constructs certain $n \times n$ matrices Y_t, X_t, and uses the notation $Y_{<t} = \sum_{i<t} Y_i$:

> Main Algorithm:
>
> (1) for $t = 1 \ldots T$ (where, recall, $T = \mathrm{poly}(k, q, 1/\delta) \cdot \log m$)
>
> (2) Compute $X_t = D^{-1/2} E\left(\frac{\delta}{4\rho^2} D^{-1/2} Y_{<t} D^{-1/2}\right) D^{-1/2}$, where $E(Z) := \frac{\exp(Z)}{\mathrm{tr}(\exp(Z))}$.
>
> (3) Call ORACLE(X_t). If this returns "X_t is δ-close" then halt and output YES.
>
> (4) Otherwise it returns matrix A_t and scalar b_t with $A_t \bullet X_t \leq b_t - \delta$.
>
> (5) Set $Y_t = A_t - b_t D$.
>
> (6) Halt and output NO.

Here the subroutine ORACLE(X) will be described later; we mention that it expects $X \in \Delta_D$.

We remark that Steurer's algorithm is actually more complicated than the above because (in an effort to keep the total serial time $\widetilde{O}(m)$) it does not compute X_t explicitly; rather, it uses the (randomized) Johnson–Lindenstrauss Lemma to compute an approximate, low-dimensional Gram representation of X_t. As mentioned earlier, we will omit this step and instead keep the matrices X_t and $Y_{<t}$ explicitly.

Relying on some theorems concerning the "width" and "separation" of the subroutine ORACLE(X), Steurer proves the above Main Algorithm correct. However there is a complication; the algorithm is idealized and cannot be carried out exactly, due to precision issues involved with approximating $D^{-1/2}$ and the matrix exponential. Steurer sketches some details of how to handles this. Because we need to be very careful about our computational model, we provide full details in the next section.

The oracle. We now recall Steurer's ORACLE subroutine, which takes as input a matrix $X \in \Delta_D$. At the heart of this subroutine is a certain family of small linear programs, one for each payoff $j \in [m]$. Given such a j, let X_j denote the $kq \times kq$ PSD submatrix of X formed by the rows and columns associated to $S_j \times \Sigma$. Steurer considers the following dual linear programs:

$$\alpha_j = \max_{\substack{\mu \text{ a distribution} \\ \text{on } \Sigma^{S_j}}} \left\{ \mathop{\mathbf{E}}_{x \sim \mu}[\phi_j(x)] - C \cdot \|X_j - \mathfrak{M}(\mu)\|_\infty \right\} \quad \text{(primal)}$$
$$= \min_{\Upsilon : \|\Upsilon\|_1 \leq C} \{X_j \bullet \Upsilon + P(\Upsilon)\} \quad \text{(dual).}$$

Here $C = 3/\delta$, $\|A\|_\infty$ (respectively $\|A\|_1$) denotes the maximum (respectively, sum) of the absolute values of A's entries, $\mathfrak{M}(\mu)$ is the matrix whose $((i, a), (i', a'))$-entry is $\sum\{\mu(x) : x_i = a, x_{i'} = a'\}$, and

$$P(\Upsilon) = \max_{x \in \Sigma^{S_j}} \Big\{\phi_j(x) - \sum_{i, i' \in S_j} \Upsilon_{(i, x_i), (i', x_{i'})}\Big\}.$$

We may now give the ORACLE algorithm. (The reader may check that the below is equivalent to [21, Figure 2].)

> ORACLE(X):
>
> (1) Solve the dual LP above for α_j and the optimizing Υ_j, for each $j \in [m]$,
>
> (2) If $\sum_j w_j \alpha_j \leq \alpha - \delta$, return $A := \sum_j w_j \Upsilon_j$, $b := \alpha - \sum_j w_t P(\Upsilon_j)$.
>
> (3) Let $s_0 = \overline{d}\,\overline{d}^\top \bullet X - 1$. If $|s_0| \geq \delta$, return $A := -\mathrm{sgn}(s_0)\overline{d}\,\overline{d}^\top$, $b := -\mathrm{sgn}(s_0)$.
>
> (4) Define $s \in \mathbb{R}^n$ by $s_{i,a} = \sum_{(i',a')} d_{i'} X_{(i,a),(i',a')} - X_{(i,a),(i,a)}$.
>
> (5) If $\sum_{(i,a)} |\overline{d}_{i,a} s_{i,a}| \geq \delta$, return $A := -(\overline{d}\,\overline{d}^\top \circ S) - D \cdot \mathrm{diag}(\mathrm{sgn}(s))$, $b := 0$, where $S \in \mathbb{R}^{n \times n}$ is defined by $S_{(i,a),(i',a')} = \frac{1}{2}(\mathrm{sgn}(s_{i,a}) + \mathrm{sgn}(s_{i',a'}))$.

(6) Otherwise, return "X is δ-close".

4 AN EFFICIENT PARALLEL IMPLEMENTATION

In this section we establish Theorem 2.2 by showing that Steurer's algorithm — as described in the previous section — can effectively be carried out by a parallel algorithm using poly(m) processors and polylog(m) parallel time.

Some precision issues. As mentioned, we do not carry out the Main Algorithm literally as written, due to the precision issues arising in Line 2. Instead, in each step of the main loop, our parallel algorithm computes a very good rational approximation $\widehat{X}_t$ to X_t. We will ensure this $\widehat{X}_t$ is always in Δ_D (precisely); thus it always serves as an acceptable argument for ORACLE. If ORACLE($\widehat{X}_t$) returns "$\widehat{X}_t$ is δ-close" then it is correct to output YES (as Steurer's analysis shows). Otherwise, it returns some A_t and b_t with $A_t \bullet \widehat{X}_t \le b_t - \delta$. We will show that this implies $A_t \bullet X_t \le b_t - (2/3)\delta$. It is easy to check that this is sufficient (after slightly adjusting the constant in the definition of T) for the algorithm to still find a δ-close X presuming that SDP($\mathcal{I}$) $\ge \alpha$.

By inspection, we see that the ORACLE subroutine always returns a matrix A satisfying $\|A\|_1 \le \text{poly}(q, 1/\delta)$. (This uses $\|\Upsilon_j\|_1 \le C = O(1/\delta)$, $\sum_j w_j = 1$, and $\sum_{(i,a)} \overline{d}_{i,a} = q$.) Therefore $|A_t \bullet X_t - A_t \bullet \widehat{X}_t| \le \text{poly}(q, 1/\delta) \cdot \|X_t - \widehat{X}_t\|_\infty$, which in turn is at most $\delta/3$ provided $\|X_t - \widehat{X}_t\|_\infty \le 1/p(q, 1/\delta)$, where p denotes some sufficiently large polynomial function. It follows that we can retain correctness by replacing Line 2 of the Main Algorithm by

(2') Compute a matrix $\widehat{X}_t \in \Delta_D$ satisfying $\|X_t - \widehat{X}_t\|_\infty \le 1/p(q, 1/\delta)$.

In fact, we need to address another precision issue here concerning the rational matrix $Y_{<t}$. In order to keep the denominator sizes from increasingly too rapidly, it will be convenient to approximate the A_t and b_t returned by the oracle. We claim that if $\widehat{A}_t$ and $\widehat{b}_t$ agree with A_t and b_t to within $\pm 1/\text{poly}(m)$, entrywise, then the resulting $\widehat{A}_t \bullet X_t - \widehat{b}_t$ will still be accurate to within $\delta/3$. As before, this is sufficient for the overall correctness of the algorithm (after slightly adjusting T). Since δ is a constant, it's clear that rounding b_t to within $\pm 1/\text{poly}(m)$ is harmless. Regarding $|\widehat{A}_t \bullet X_t - A_t \bullet X_t|$, to see that $\pm 1/\text{poly}(m)$ accuracy for A_t is sufficient we use the fact that X_t is PSD with $D \bullet X_t = 1$. Since D's (diagonal) entries are at least $1/O(m)$, we conclude that $\text{tr}(X) \le O(m)$ and hence $\|X_t\|_1 \le \text{poly}(m)$ (using the fact that X_t is PSD). Thus indeed it suffices to have $|\widehat{A}_t - A_t\|_\infty \le 1/\text{poly}(m)$. As a consequence, for some fixed $M' = \text{poly}(m)$ we can replace Line 5 of the Main Algorithm by

(5') Set $Y_t = \widehat{A}_t - \widehat{b}_t D$, where $\widehat{A}_t, \widehat{b}_t$ are rational approximations of A_t, b_t with denominator M'.

In particular, this means that the rational entries of Y_t and $Y_{<t}$ will always have common denominator MM', which has bit-length $O(\log m)$. (Recall that M is the common denominator for entries in D.)

4.1 Parallel Implementation with poly(m) Processors and polylog(m) Parallel Time

Preliminaries. We describe the algorithm in nonuniform fashion; we trust the reader to verify that it can be constructed by an $O(\log m)$-space machine. (This only requires various very simple things; e.g., memory management, simple calculations involving $O(\log m)$-bit integers, etc.) We will also frequently rely on the fact that NC is closed under composition. We remind the reader that the processors are treated as simple RAMs. Since integer multiplication is in NC, we may allow the RAMs to do basic arithmetic on registers containing rational numbers expressible with polylog(m) bits [22].

For storing the matrices Y_t, $Y_{<t}$, and D we will have a processor for each entry, as is standard. As discussed earlier, all of these will have a common denominator of $O(\log m)$ bits. The entries of D need to be computed at the outset of the algorithm; this is easily done with m processors in polylog(m) time using the parallel iterated-addition algorithm.

The Main Algorithm. The loop in Line 1 of the Main Algorithm only gives a multiplicative running time overhead of $O(\log m)$.

We now analyze Line 2'. Recall we have $Y_{<t}$ and D stored with a processor for each entry. We need to compute a $\pm 1/p(q, 1/\delta)$ approximation $\widehat{X}_t$ to $X_t = D^{-1/2} E\left(\frac{\delta}{4\rho^2} D^{-1/2} Y_{<t} D^{-1/2}\right) D^{-1/2}$, and it should also satisfy $\widehat{X}_t \in \Delta_D$. The techniques for this are standard and straightforward. The trace needed for E can be computed efficiently in parallel by iterated-addition. As noted in, e.g., [10], rational approximations square-roots and matrix exponentials (for matrices of constant norm) can be computed even to poly(m) bits in NC, much more than we need. We need to check that the matrix exponential is "sufficiently continuous" that a good approximation in the input leads to a good approximation in the output. This follows from the method used to approximately compute the matrix exponential; namely, truncating the expansion $\exp(Z) = I + Z + Z^2/2 + Z^3/6 + \cdots$ to polylog(m) terms.

There is one more detail to take care of. We can get an initial approximation $\widehat{X}_t$ to X_t that is highly accurate; say, having $\|X_t - \widehat{X}_t\|_\infty \le 1/m^c$ for any large constant c of our choice. This is much more accurate than the constant accuracy for $\widehat{X}_t$ we need. However, whereas $X_t \in \Delta_D$ by construction, we also wish to have $\widehat{X}_t \in \Delta_D$ precisely. This issue is straightforward to fix. We can first replace $\widehat{X}_t$ by $\frac{1}{2}(\widehat{X}_t + \widehat{X}_t^\top)$ to make it symmetric; this doesn't change its entrywise error. The matrix $\widehat{X}_t$ may still fail to be positive semidefinite; however since $\|\widehat{X}_t - X_t\|_\infty \le 1/m^c$, we can fix this by adding some $1/\text{poly}(m)$ multiple of the identity matrix to $\widehat{X}_t$. This $1/\text{poly}(m)$ can be as small as we like, by taking c large. Thus again we only lose $\pm 1/\text{poly}(m)$ in entrywise accuracy. Finally, we can ensure $D \bullet \widehat{X}_t = 1$ exactly by dividing $\widehat{X}_t$ by $D \bullet \widehat{X}_t$; again, since D's entries are in $[1/O(m), 1]$, this will again only cost us $\pm 1/\text{poly}(m)$ in accuracy, taking the initial c large enough.

In Line 3–4 of the Main Algorithm, the call to subroutine ORACLE, will be analyzed below. As we will see, the A_t and b_t it returns will involve rationals with $m \cdot \text{polylog}(m)$ bits; this is okay, however, by closure of FNC under composition.

Finally, the rounding in Line $5'$ can certainly be done in NC, as can the updating of $Y_{<t}$.

The Oracle. We now show that ORACLE is in NC. The input is a matrix $\widehat{X}$, stored by n^2 processors, each entry being a rational number expressible with $O(\log m)$ bits. Thus each linear program that the oracle needs to solve has bit-complexity $O(\log m)$. Therefore we can devote m processors to these LPs, one for each constraint, and each processor can use a standard serial algorithm to solve its LP in polylog(m) time. Actually, we need to allow each processor polylog(m) registers for this, but that is not a problem. The resulting solutions $\alpha_j, \Upsilon_j, P(\Upsilon_j)$ will be rationals with polylog(m) bit-complexity.

In Line 2 of ORACLE($\widehat{X}$) we first need to compute $\sum_j w_j \alpha_j$. This can be done in NC using iterated-addition and integer multiplication algorithms. Due to a potential lack of common denominators for the α_j's, the resulting quantity may require as many as $m \cdot \text{polylog}(m)$ bits; as mentioned before, however, this is not a problem. If we need to return A, b at this stage, note that again they can be computed via iterated-addition in polylog(m) time. Finally, lines 3, 4, 5 are similar; it's easy to see that $\overline{d}\,\overline{d}^{\top}$, s_0, s, and S can be computed in NC.

REFERENCES

[1] Sanjeev Arora, Elad Hazan, and Satyen Kale. 2005. Fast algorithms for approximate semidefinite programming using the multiplicative weights update method. In *Proceedings of the 46th Annual IEEE Symposium on Foundations of Computer Science.* 339–348.

[2] Sanjeev Arora and Satyen Kale. 2007. A combinatorial, primal-dual approach to semidefinite programs. In *Proceedings of the 39th Annual ACM Symposium on Theory of Computing.* 227–236.

[3] Per Austrin, Johan Håstad, and Rafael Pass. 2013. On the power of many one-bit provers. ACM, 215–220.

[4] László Babai, Lance Fortnow, and Carsten Lund. 1991. Non-Deterministic Exponential Time has Two-Prover Interactive Protocols. *Computational Complexity* 1 (1991), 3–40.

[5] Lars Engebretsen, Piotr Indyk, and Ryan O'Donnell. 2002. Derandomized dimensionality reduction with applications. In *Proc. 13th ACM-SIAM Symposium on Discrete Algorithms.* 705–712.

[6] Oded Goldreich and Johan Håstad. 1998. On the complexity of interactive proofs with bounded communication. *Inform. Process. Lett.* 67 (1998), 205–214.

[7] Oded Goldreich, Silvio Micali, and Avi Wigderson. 1991. Proofs that Yield Nothing but Their Validity or all languages in NP have zero-knowledge proof systems. *J. ACM* 38, 3 (1991), 691–729.

[8] Oded Goldreich, Salil Vadhan, and Avi Wigderson. 2002. On interactive proofs with a laconic prover. *Computational Complexity* 11, 1–2 (2002), 1–53.

[9] Shafi Goldwasser, Silvio Micali, and Charles Rackoff. 1989. The knowledge complexity of interactive proofs. *SIAM Journal of Computing* 18, 1 (1989), 186–208.

[10] Rahul Jain, Zhengfeng Ji, Sarvagya Upadhyay, and John Watrous. 2010. QIP = PSPACE. *Commun. ACM* 53, 12 (2010), 102–109.

[11] Rahul Jain, Sarvagya Upadhyay, and John Watrous. 2009. Two-Message Quantum Interactive Proofs Are in PSPACE. In *Proceedings of the 50th Annual IEEE Symposium on Foundations of Computer Science.* 534–543.

[12] Rahul Jain and John Watrous. 2009. Parallel approximation of non-interactive zero-sum quantum games. In *Proceedings of the 24th Annual Computational Complexity Conference.* 243–253.

[13] Satyen Kale. 2007. *Efficient algorithms using the multiplicative weights update method.* Ph.D. Dissertation. Princeton University.

[14] Carsten Lund, Lance Fortnow, Howard Karloff, and Noam Nisan. 1992. Algebraic Methods for Interactive Proof Systems. *J. ACM* 39, 4 (1992), 859–868.

[15] Konstantin Makarychev and Yury Makarychev. 2014. Approximation algorithm for non-Boolean Max-k-CSP. *Theory of Computing* 10, 13 (2014), 341–358.

[16] Noam Nisan. 1990. On read-once vs. multiple access to randomness in logspace. 179–184.

[17] Periklis Papakonstantinou. 2013. Is uniform RNC contained in polylog space? Theoretical Computer Science Stack Exchange. (2013). http://cstheory.stackexchange.com/q/18538.

[18] Prasad Raghavendra. 2009. *Approximating NP-hard problems: efficient algorithms and their limits.* Ph.D. Dissertation. University of Washington.

[19] Prasad Raghavendra and David Steurer. 2009. How to round any CSP. In *Proceedings of the 50th Annual IEEE Symposium on Foundations of Computer Science.* IEEE, 586–594.

[20] Adi Shamir. 1992. IP = PSPACE. *J. ACM* 39, 4 (1992), 869–877.

[21] David Steurer. 2010. Fast SDP algorithms for constraint satisfaction problems. In *Proceedings of the 21st Annual ACM-SIAM Symposium on Discrete Algorithms.* 684–697.

[22] Larry Stockmeyer and Uzi Vishkin. 1984. Simulation of parallel random access machines by circuits. *SIAM J. Comput.* 13, 2 (1984), 409–422.

[23] Kanat Tangwongsan. 2011. *Efficient Parallel Approximation Algorithms.* Ph.D. Dissertation. Carnegie Mellon University.

[24] Uri Zwick. 1998. Approximation Algorithms for Constraint Satisfaction Problems Involving at Most Three Variables per Constraint. In *Proceedings of the 9th Annual ACM-SIAM Symposium on Discrete Algorithms.* 201–210.

Matrix Multiplication, a Little Faster

Elaye Karstadt
The Hebrew University of Jerusalem
elayeek@cs.huji.ac.il

Oded Schwartz
The Hebrew University of Jerusalem
odedsc@cs.huji.ac.il

ABSTRACT

Strassen's algorithm (1969) was the first sub-cubic matrix multiplication algorithm. Winograd (1971) improved its complexity by a constant factor. Many asymptotic improvements followed. Unfortunately, most of them have done so at the cost of very large, often gigantic, hidden constants. Consequently, Strassen-Winograd's $O\left(n^{\log_2 7}\right)$ algorithm often outperforms other matrix multiplication algorithms for all feasible matrix dimensions. The leading coefficient of Strassen-Winograd's algorithm was believed to be optimal for matrix multiplication algorithms with 2×2 base case, due to a lower bound of Probert (1976).

Surprisingly, we obtain a faster matrix multiplication algorithm, with the same base case size and asymptotic complexity as Strassen-Winograd's algorithm, but with the coefficient reduced from 6 to 5. To this end, we extend Bodrato's (2010) method for matrix squaring, and transform matrices to an alternative basis. We prove a generalization of Probert's lower bound that holds under change of basis, showing that for matrix multiplication algorithms with a 2×2 base case, the leading coefficient of our algorithm cannot be further reduced, hence optimal. We apply our technique to other Strassen-like algorithms, improving their arithmetic and communication costs by significant constant factors.

CCS CONCEPTS

•**Mathematics of computing → Computations on matrices;** •**Computing methodologies → Linear algebra algorithms;**

KEYWORDS

Fast Matrix Multiplication, Bilinear Algorithms

1 INTRODUCTION

Strassen's algorithm [37] was the first sub-cubic matrix multiplication algorithm, with complexity $O\left(n^{\log_2 7}\right)$. Winograd [40] reduced the leading coefficient from 7 to 6 by decreasing the number of additions and subtractions from 18 to 15. In practice, Strassen-Winograd's algorithm often performs better than some asymptotically faster algorithms [3] due to these smaller hidden constants. The leading coefficient of Strassen-Winograd's algorithm was believed to be optimal, due to a lower bound on the number of additions[1] for matrix multiplication algorithms with 2×2 base case, obtained by Probert [31].

We obtain a method for improving the practical performance of Strassen and Strassen-like fast matrix multiplication algorithms by improving the hidden constants inside the O-notation. To this end, we extend Bodrato's (2010) method for matrix squaring, and transform matrices to an alternative basis.

1.1 Strassen-like Algorithms

Strassen-like algorithms are a class of divide-and-conquer algorithms which utilize a base $\langle n_0, m_0, k_0; t\rangle$-algorithm: multiplying an $n_0 \times m_0$ matrix by an $m_0 \times k_0$ matrix using t scalar multiplications, where n_0, m_0, k_0 and t are positive integers. When multiplying an $n \times m$ matrix by an $m \times k$ matrix, the algorithm splits them into blocks (each of size $\frac{n}{n_0} \times \frac{m}{m_0}$ and $\frac{m}{m_0} \times \frac{k}{k_0}$, respectively), and works block-wise, according to the base algorithm. Additions and multiplication by scalar in the base algorithm are interpreted as block-wise additions. Multiplications in the base algorithm are interpreted as block-wise multiplication via recursion. We refer to a Strassen-like algorithm by its base case. Hence, an $\langle n, m, k; t\rangle$-algorithm may refer to either the algorithm's base case or the corresponding block recursive algorithm, as obvious from context.

1.2 Known Strassen-like algorithms

Since Strassen's original discovery, many fast matrix multiplication algorithms followed and improved the asymptotic complexity [6, 12, 13, 26, 29, 32, 33, 36, 38, 39]. Some of these improvements have come at the cost of very large, often gigantic, hidden constants. Le Gall [26] estimated that even if matrix multiplication could be done in $O\left(n^2\right)$ arithmetic operations, it is unlikely to be applicable as the base case sizes would have to be astronomical.

Recursive fast matrix multiplication algorithms with reasonable base case size for both square and rectangular matrices have been discovered [3, 20, 24, 25, 29, 30, 35]. Thus, they have manageable hidden constants, some of which are asymptotically faster than Strassen's algorithm. While many fast matrix multiplication algorithms fail to compete with Strassen's in practice due to their hidden constants. However, some have achieved competitive performance (e.g., Kaporin's [21] implementation of Laderman et al.'s algorithm [24]).

Recently, Smirnov presented several fast matrix multiplication algorithms derived by computer aided optimization tools [35], including an $\langle 6, 3, 3; 40\rangle$-algorithm with asymptotic complexity of $O\left(n^{\log_{54} 40^3}\right)$, faster than Strassen's algorithm. Ballard and Benson [3] later presented several additional fast Strassen-like algorithms,

[1] From here on, when referring to addition and subtraction count we say additions.

SPAA'17, July 24-26, 2017, Washington, DC, USA

978-1-4503-4593-4/17/07...$15.00
DOI: 10.1145/3087556.3087579

found using computer aided optimization tools as well. They implemented several Strassen-like algorithms, including Smirnov's $\langle 6,3,3;40\rangle$-algorithm, on shared-memory architecture in order to demonstrate that Strassen and Strassen-like algorithms can outperform classical matrix multiplication in practice (such as, Intel's MKL), on modestly sized problems (at least up to n=13000), in a shared-memory environment. Their experiments also showed Strassen's algorithm outperforming Smirnov's algorithm in some of the cases.

1.3 Previous work

Bodrato [7] introduced the intermediate representation method, for repeated squaring and for chain matrix multiplication computations. This enables decreasing the number of additions between consecutive multiplications. Thus, he obtained an algorithm with a 2×2 base case, which uses 7 multiplications, and has a leading coefficient of 5 for chain multiplication and for repeated squaring, for every multiplication outside the first one. Bodrato also presented an invertible linear function which recursively transforms a $2^k \times 2^k$ matrix to and from the intermediate transformation. While this is not the first time that linear transformations are applied to matrix multiplication, the main focus of previous research on the subject was on improving asymptotic performance rather than reducing the number of additions [10, 17].

Very recently, Cenk and Hasan [8] showed a clever way to apply Strassen-Winograd's algorithm directly to $n \times n$ matrices by forsaking the uniform divide-and-conquer pattern of Strassen-like algorithms. Instead, their algorithm splits Strassen-Winograd's algorithm into two linear divide-and-conquer algorithms which recursively perform all pre-computations, followed by vector multiplication of their results, and finally performs linear post-computations to calculate the output. Their method enables reuse of sums, resulting in a matrix multiplication algorithm with arithmetic complexity of $5n^{\log_2 7} + 0.5 \cdot n^{\log_2 6} + 2n^{\log_2 5} - 6.5n^2$. However, this comes at the cost of increased communication costs and memory footprint.

1.4 Our contribution

We present the Alternative Basis Matrix Multiplication method, and show how to apply it to existing Strassen-like algorithms (see Sections 3). While basis transformation is, in general, as expensive as matrix multiplications, some can be performed very fast (e.g., Hadamard in $O\left(n^2 \log n\right)$ using FFT [11]). Fortunately, so is the case for our basis transformation (see Section 3.1). Thus, it is a worthwhile trade-off of reducing the leading coefficient in exchange of an asymptotically insignificant overhead (see Section 3.2). We provide analysis as to how these constants are affected and the impact on both arithmetic and IO-complexity.

We discuss the problem of finding alternative bases to improve Strassen-like algorithms (see Section 5), and present several improved variants of existing algorithms, most notable of which are the alternative basis variant of Strassen's $\langle 2,2,2;7\rangle$-algorithm which reduces the number of additions from 15 to 12 (see Section 3.3), and the variant of Smirnov's $\langle 6,3,3;40\rangle$-algorithm with leading coefficient reduced by about 83.2%.[2]

[2]Files containing the encoding/decoding matrices and the corresponding basis transformations can be found at https://github.com/elayeek/matmultfaster.

Theorem 1.1 (Probert's lower bound). *[31] 15 additions are necessary for any $\langle 2,2,2;7\rangle$-algorithm.*

Our result seemingly contradicts Probert's lower bound. However, his bound implicitly assumes that the input and output are represented in the standard basis, thus there is not contradiction. We extend Probert's lower bound to account for alternative bases (see Section 4):

Theorem 1.2 (Basis invariant lower bound). *12 additions are necessary for any matrix multiplication algorithm that uses a recursive-bilinear algorithm with a 2×2 base case with 7 multiplications, regardless of basis.*

Our alternative basis variant of Strassen's algorithm performs 12 additions in the base case, matching the lower bound in Theorem 1.2. Hence, it is optimal.

2 PERLIMINARIES

2.1 The communication bottleneck

Fast matrix multiplication algorithms have lower IO-complexity than the classical algorithm. That is, they communicate asymptotically less data within the memory hierarchy and between processors. The IO-compleixty is measured as a function of the number of processors P, the local memory size M, and the matrix dimension n. Namely, the communication costs of a parallel $\langle n_0, n_0, n_0; t\rangle$-algorithm are $\Theta\left(\left(\frac{n}{\sqrt{M}}\right)^{\log_{n_0} t} \frac{M}{P}\right)$ [1, 2, 4, 34]. Thus, parallel versions of Strassen's algorithm which minimize communication cost outperform the well tuned classical matrix multiplication in practice, both in shared-memory [3, 14, 23] and distributed-memory architectures [1, 16, 27].

Our $\langle 2,2,2;7\rangle$-algorithm not only reduces the arithmetic complexity by 16.66%, but also the IO-complexity by 20%, compared to Strassen-Winograd's algorithm. Hence, performance gain should be in range of 16-20% on a shared-memory machine.

2.2 Encoding and Decoding matrices

Fact 2.1. Let R be a ring, and let $f : R^n \times R^m \to R^k$ be a bilinear function which performs t multiplications. There exist $U \in R^{t\times n}$, $V \in R^{t\times m}$, $W \in R^{t\times k}$ such that

$$\forall x \in R^n,\ y \in R^m\ f(x,y) = W^T\left((U\cdot x) \odot (V \cdot y)\right)$$

where $\odot$ is element-wise vector product (Hadamard product).

Definition 2.2. (Encoding/Decoding matrices). We refer to the $\langle U, V, W\rangle$ of a recursive-bilinear algorithm as its encoding/decoding matrices (where U, V are the encoding matrices and W is the decoding matrix).

Definition 2.3. Let R be a ring, and let $A \in R^{n\times m}$ a matrix. We denote the vectorization of A by $\vec{A}$. We use the notation $U_{\ell,(i,j)}$ when referring to the element in the $\ell'th$ row on the column corresponding with the index (i,j) in the vectorization of A. For ease of notation, we sometimes write $A_{i,j}$ rather than $\vec{A}_{(i,j)}$.[3]

[3]All basis transformations and encoding/decoding matrices assume row-ordered vectorization of matrices.

Table 1: $\langle 2, 2, 2; 7\rangle$-algorithms

Algorithm	Additions	Arithmetic Computations	I/O-Complexity
Strassen [37]	18	$7n^{\log_2 7} - 6n^2$	$6 \cdot \left(\frac{\sqrt{3} \cdot n}{\sqrt{M}}\right)^{\log_2 7} \cdot M - 18n^2 + 3M$
Strassen-Winograd [40]	15	$6n^{\log_2 7} - 5n^2$	$5 \cdot \left(\frac{\sqrt{3} \cdot n}{\sqrt{M}}\right)^{\log_2 7} \cdot M - 15n^2 + 3M$
Ours	12	$5n^{\log_2 7} - 4n^2 + 3n^2 \log_2 n$	$4 \cdot \left(\frac{\sqrt{3} \cdot n}{\sqrt{M}}\right)^{\log_2 7} \cdot M - 12n^2 + 3n^2 \cdot \log_2 \left(\sqrt{2} \cdot \frac{n}{\sqrt{M}}\right) + 5M$

Table 2: Alternative Basis Algorithms

Algorithm	Linear Operations	Improved Linear Operations	Arithmetic Leading Coefficient	Improved Leading Coefficient	Computations Saved
$\langle 2, 2, 2; 7\rangle$ [40]	15	12	6	5	16.6%
$\langle 3, 2, 3; 15\rangle$[3]	64	52	15.06	7.94	47.3%
$\langle 2, 3, 4; 20\rangle$[3]	78	58	9.96	7.46	25.6%
$\langle 3, 3, 3; 23\rangle$[3]	87	75	8.91	6.57	26.3%
$\langle 6, 3, 3; 40\rangle$[35]	1246	202	55.63	9.39	83.2%

Fact 2.4. (Triple product condition). [22] Let R be a ring, and let $U \in R^{t \times n \cdot m}$, $V \in R^{t \times m \cdot k}$, $W \in R^{t \times n \cdot k}$. $\langle U, V, W\rangle$ are encoding/decoding matrices of an $\langle n, m, k; t\rangle$-algorithm if and only if:

$$\forall i_1, i_2 \in [n], k_1, k_2 \in [m], j_1, j_2 \in [k]$$

$$\sum_{r=1}^{t} U_{r,(i_1,k_1)} V_{r,(k_2,j_1)} W_{r,(i_2,j_2)} = \delta_{i_1,i_2} \delta_{k_1,k_2} \delta_{j_1,j_2}$$

where $\delta_{i,j} = 1$ if $i = j$ and 0 otherwise.

Notation 2.5. Denote the number of nonzero entries in a matrix by $nnz(A)$, and the number of rows/columns by $rows(A)$, $cols(A)$.

Remark 2.6. The number of linear operations used by a bilinear algorithm is determined by its encoding/decoding matrices. The number of additions performed by each of the encoding is:

$$\texttt{AdditionsU} = nnz(U) - rows(U)$$

$$\texttt{AdditionsV} = nnz(V) - rows(V)$$

The number of additions performed by the decoding is:

$$\texttt{AdditionsW} = nnz(W) - cols(W)$$

The number of scalar multiplication performed by each of the encoding/decoding is equal to the total number of matrix entries which are not 1, −1, and 0.

3 ALTERNATIVE BASIS MATRIX MULTIPLICATION

Fast matrix multiplication algorithms are bilinear computations. The number of operations performed in the linear phases of such algorithms (the application of their encoding/decoding matrices $\langle U, V, W\rangle$ in the case of matrix multiplication, see Definition 2.2) depends on basis of representation. In this section, we detail how alternative basis algorithms work and address the effects of using alternative bases on arithmetic complexity and IO-complexity.

Definition 3.1. Let R be a ring and let ϕ, ψ, υ be automorphisms of $R^{n \cdot m}$, $R^{m \cdot k}$, $R^{n \cdot k}$ (respectively). We denote a Strassen-like algorithm which takes $\phi(A)$, $\psi(B)$ as inputs and outputs $\upsilon(A \cdot B)$ using t multiplications by $\langle n, m, k; t\rangle_{\phi,\psi,\upsilon}$-algorithm. If $n = m = k$ and $\phi = \psi = \upsilon$, we use the notation $\langle n, n, n; t\rangle_{\phi}$-algorithm. This notation extends the $\langle n, m, k; t\rangle$-algorithm notation as latter applies when the three basis transformations are the identity map.

Given a recursive-bilinear, $\langle n, m, k; t\rangle_{\phi,\psi,\upsilon}$-algorithm, *ALG*, alternative basis matrix multiplication works as follows:

Algorithm 1 Alternative Basis Matrix Multiplication Algorithm

Input: $A \in R^{n \times m}$, $B^{m \times k}$
Output: $n \times k$ matrix $C = A \cdot B$
1: **function** $ABS(A, B)$
2: $\tilde{A} = \phi(A)$ ▷ $R^{n \times m}$ basis transformation
3: $\tilde{B} = \psi(B)$ ▷ $R^{m \times k}$ basis transformation
4: $\tilde{C} = ALG(\tilde{A}, \tilde{B})$ ▷ $\langle n, m, k; t\rangle_{\phi,\psi,\upsilon}$-algorithm
5: $C = \upsilon^{-1}(\tilde{C})$ ▷ $R^{n \times k}$ basis transformation
6: **return** C

Lemma 3.2. *Let R be a ring, let $\langle U, V, W\rangle$ be the encoding/decoding matrices of an $\langle n, m, k; t\rangle$-algorithm, and let ϕ, ψ, υ be automorphisms of $R^{n \cdot m}$, $R^{m \cdot k}$, $R^{n \cdot k}$ (respectively). $\left\langle U\phi^{-1}, V\psi^{-1}, W\upsilon^{T}\right\rangle$ are encoding/decoding matrices of an $\langle n, m, k; t\rangle_{\phi,\psi,\upsilon}$-algorithm.*

Proof. $\langle U, V, W\rangle$ are encoding/decoding matrices of an $\langle n, m, k; t\rangle$-algorithm. Hence, for any $A \in R^{n \times m}$, $B \in R^{m \times k}$

$$W^T \left(\left(U \cdot \vec{A}\right) \odot \left(V \cdot \vec{B}\right) \right) = \overrightarrow{A \cdot B}$$

Hence,

$$\upsilon\left(\overrightarrow{A \cdot B}\right) = \upsilon\left(W^T\left(U \cdot \vec{A} \odot V \cdot \vec{B}\right)\right)$$
$$= \left(W\upsilon^T\right)^T \left(U\phi^{-1} \cdot \phi\left(\vec{A}\right) \odot V\psi^{-1} \cdot \psi\left(\vec{B}\right)\right)$$

□

Corollary 3.3. *Let R be a ring, and let ϕ, ψ, υ be automorphisms of $R^{n \cdot m}$, $R^{m \cdot k}$, $R^{n \cdot k}$ (respectively). $\langle U, V, W \rangle$ are encoding/decoding matrices of an $\langle n, m, k; t \rangle_{\phi, \psi, \upsilon}$-algorithm if and only if $\left\langle U\phi, V\psi, W\upsilon^{-T} \right\rangle$ are encoding/decoding matrices of an $\langle n, m, k; t \rangle$-algorithm.*

3.1 Fast basis transformation

Definition 3.4. Let R be a ring and let $\psi_1 : R^{n_0 \times m_0} \to R^{n_0 \times m_0}$ be a linear map. We recursively define a linear map $\psi_{k+1} : R^{n \times m} \to R^{n \times m}$ (where $n = n_0^{\ell_1}$, $m = m_0^{\ell_2}$ for some $\ell_1, \ell_2 \leq k+1$) by $(\psi_{k+1}(A))_{i,j} = \psi_k(\psi_1(A))_{i,j}$, where $A_{i,j}$ are $\frac{n}{n_0} \times \frac{m}{m_0}$ sub-matrices.

Note that ψ_{k+1} is a linear map. For convenience, we omit the subscript of ψ when obvious from context.

Claim 3.5. *Let R be a ring, let $\psi_1 : R^{n_0 \times m_0} \to R^{n_0 \times m_0}$ be a linear map, and let $A \in R^{n \times m}$ (where $n = n_0^{k+1}$, $m = m_0^{k+1}$). Define $\tilde{A}$ by $\left(\tilde{A}\right)_{i,j} = \psi_k\left(A_{i,j}\right)$. Then $\psi_1\left(\tilde{A}\right) = \psi_{k+1}(A)$.*

Proof. ψ_1 is a linear map. Hence, for any $i \in [n_0]$, $j \in [m_0]$, $(\psi_1(A))_{i,j}$ is a linear sum of elements of A. Therefore, there exist scalars $\left\{x_{r,\ell}^{(i,j)}\right\}_{r \in [n_0],\, \ell \in [m_0]}$ such that

$$(\psi_{k+1}(A))_{i,j} = \psi_k(\psi_1(A))_{i,j} = \psi_k\left(\sum_{r,\ell} x_{r,\ell}^{(i,j)} \cdot A_{r,\ell}\right)$$

By linearity of ψ_k

$$= \sum_{r,\ell} x_{r,\ell}^{(i,j)} \psi_k\left(A_{r,\ell}\right) = \left(\psi_1\left(\tilde{A}\right)\right)_{i,j}$$

□

Claim 3.6. *Let R be a ring, let $\psi_1 : R^{n_0 \times m_0} \to R^{n_0 \times m_0}$ be an invertible linear map, and let ψ_{k+1} as defined above. ψ_{k+1} is invertible and its inverse is $\left(\psi_{k+1}^{-1}(A)\right)_{i,j} = \psi_k^{-1}\left(\psi_1^{-1}(A)\right)_{i,j}$.*

Proof. Define $\tilde{A}$ by $\left(\tilde{A}\right)_{i,j} = \psi_k\left(A_{i,j}\right)$ and define ψ_{k+1}^{-1} by $\left(\psi_{k+1}^{-1}(A)\right)_{i,j} = \psi_k^{-1}\left(\psi_1^{-1}(A)\right)_{i,j}$. Then:

$$\left(\psi_{k+1}^{-1}(\psi_{k+1}(A))\right)_{i,j} = \psi_k^{-1}\left(\psi_1^{-1}(\psi_{k+1}(A))\right)_{i,j}$$

By Claim 3.5

$$= \psi_k^{-1}\left(\psi_1^{-1}\left(\psi_1\left(\tilde{A}\right)\right)\right)_{i,j} = \psi_k^{-1}\left(\tilde{A}\right)_{i,j}$$

By definition of $\tilde{A}$

$$= \psi_k^{-1}\left(\psi_k(A)_{i,j}\right) = A_{i,j}$$

□

We next analyze the arithmetic complexity and IO-complexity of fast basis transformations. For convenience and readability, we presented here the square case only. The analysis for rectangular matrices is similar.

Claim 3.7. *Let R be a ring, let $\psi_1 : R^{n_0 \times n_0} \to R^{n_0 \times n_0}$ be a linear map, and let $A \in R^{n \times n}$ where $n = n_0^k$. The arithmetic complexity of computing $\psi(A)$ is*

$$F_\psi(n) = \frac{q}{n_0^2} n^2 \log_{n_0} n$$

where q is the number of linear operations performed by ψ_1.

Proof. Let $F_\psi(n)$ be the number of additions required by ψ. Each step of the recursion consists of computing n_0^2 sub-problems and performs q additions of sub-matrices. Therefore, $F_\psi(n) = n_0^2 F_\psi\left(\frac{n}{n_0}\right) + q\left(\frac{n^2}{n_0}\right)$ and $F_\psi(1) = 0$. Thus,

$$F_\psi(n) = n_0^2 F_\psi\left(\frac{n}{n_0}\right) + q\left(\frac{n}{n_0}\right)^2$$
$$= \sum_{k=0}^{\log_{n_0}(n)-1} \left(n_0^2\right)^k \left(q\left(\frac{n}{n_0^{k+1}}\right)^2\right)$$
$$= \frac{q}{n_0^2} n^2 \cdot \sum_{k=0}^{\log_{n_0}(n)-1} \left(\frac{n_0^2}{n_0^2}\right)^k = \frac{q}{n_0^2} n^2 \cdot \log_{n_0}(n)$$

□

Claim 3.8. *Let R be a ring and let $\psi_1 : R^{n_0 \times n_0} \to R^{n_0 \times n_0}$ be a linear map, and let $A \in R^{n \times n}$ where $n = n_0^k$. The IO-complexity of computing $\psi(A)$ is*

$$IO_\psi(n, M) \leq \frac{3q}{n_0^2} n^2 \log_{n_0}\left(\sqrt{2}\frac{n}{\sqrt{M}}\right) + 2M$$

where q is the number of linear operations performed by ψ_1.

Proof. Each step of the recursion consists of computing n_0^2 sub-problems and performs q linear operations. The base case occurs when the problem fits entirely in the fast memory (or local memory in parallel setting), namely $2n^2 \leq M$. Each addition requires at most 3 data transfers (one of each input and one for writing the output). Hence, a basis transformation which performs q linear operations at each recursive steps has the recurrence:

$$IO_\psi(n, M) \leq \begin{cases} n_0^2 IO_\psi\left(\frac{n}{n_0}, M\right) + 3q \cdot \left(\frac{n}{n_0}\right)^2 & 2n^2 > M \\ 2M & otherwise \end{cases}$$

Therefore

$$IO_\psi(n, M) \leq n_0^2 IO_\psi\left(\frac{n}{n_0}, M\right) + 3q\left(\frac{n}{n_0}\right)^2$$
$$= \sum_{k=0}^{\log_{n_0}\left(\frac{n}{\sqrt{\frac{M}{2}}}\right)-1} \left(n_0^2\right)^k \left(3q\left(\frac{n}{n_0^{k+1}}\right)^2\right) + 2M$$
$$= \frac{3q}{n_0^2} n^2 \cdot \sum_{k=0}^{\log_{n_0}\left(\sqrt{2}\cdot\frac{n}{\sqrt{M}}\right)-1} \left(\frac{n_0^2}{n_0^2}\right)^k + 2M$$
$$= \frac{3q}{n_0^2} n^2 \cdot \log_{n_0}\left(\sqrt{2} \cdot \frac{n}{\sqrt{M}}\right) + 2M$$

□

3.2 Computing matrix multiplication in alternative basis

Claim 3.9. *Let $\phi_1, \psi_1, \upsilon_1$ be automorphisms of $R^{n_0 \times m_0}, R^{m_0 \times k_0}, R^{n_0 \times k_0}$ (respectively), and let ALG be an $\langle n_0, m_0, k_0; t \rangle_{\phi_1, \psi_1, \upsilon_1}$ algorithm. For any $A \in R^{n \times m}$, $B \in R^{m \times k}$:*

$$ALG\left(\phi_\ell\left(A\right), \psi_\ell\left(B\right)\right) = \upsilon_\ell\left(A \cdot B\right)$$

where $n = n_0^\ell$, $m = m_0^\ell$, $k = k_0^\ell$.

Proof. Denote $\tilde{C} = ALG\left(\phi_{\ell+1}\left(A\right), \psi_{\ell+1}\left(B\right)\right)$ and the encoding/decoding matrices of ALG by $\langle U, V, W \rangle$. We prove by induction on ℓ that $\tilde{C} = \upsilon_\ell\left(A \cdot B\right)$. For $r \in [t]$, denote

$$S_r = \sum_{i \in [n_0], j \in [m_0]} U_{r,(i,j)} \left(\phi_1\left(A\right)\right)_{i,j}$$

$$T_r = \sum_{i \in [m_0], j \in [k_0]} V_{r,(i,j)} \left(\psi_1\left(B\right)\right)_{i,j}$$

The base case, $\ell = 1$, holds by Lemma 3.2 since ALG is an $\langle n_0, m_0, k_0; t \rangle_{\phi_1, \psi_1, \upsilon_1}$-algorithm. Note that this means that for any $i \in [n_0]$, $j \in [k_0]$

$$\left(\upsilon_1\left(AB\right)\right)_{i,j} = \left(W^T\left(\left(U \cdot \phi_1\left(A\right)\right) \odot \left(V \cdot \psi_1\left(B\right)\right)\right)\right)_{i,j}$$

$$= \sum_{r \in [t]} W_{r,(i,j)} \left(S_r \cdot T_r\right)$$

Next, we assume the claim holds for $\ell \in \mathbb{N}$ and show for $\ell + 1$. Given input $\tilde{A} = \phi_{\ell+1}\left(A\right)$, $\tilde{B} = \psi_{\ell+1}\left(B\right)$, ALG performs t multiplications $P_1, \ldots, P_t$. For each multiplication P_r, its left hand side multiplicand is of the form

$$L_r = \sum_{i \in [n_0], j \in [m_0]} U_{r,(i,j)} \tilde{A}_{i,j}$$

By Definition 3.4, $\left(\phi_{\ell+1}\left(A\right)\right)_{i,j} = \phi_\ell\left(\phi_1\left(A\right)\right)_{i,j}$. Hence,

$$= \sum_{i \in [n_0], j \in [m_0]} U_{r,(i,j)} \left(\phi_\ell\left(\phi_1\left(A\right)\right)_{i,j}\right)$$

From linearity of ϕ_ℓ

$$= \phi_\ell\left(\sum_{i \in [n_0], j \in [m_0]} U_{r,(i,j)} \left(\phi_1\left(A\right)\right)_{i,j}\right)$$

$$= \phi_\ell\left(S_r\right)$$

And similarly, the right hand multiplication R_r is of the form

$$R_r = \psi_\ell\left(T_r\right)$$

Note that for any $r \in [t]$, S_r, T_r are $n_0^\ell \times m_0^\ell$ and $m_0^\ell \times k_0^\ell$ matrices, respectively. Hence, by the induction hypothesis,

$$P_r = ALG\left(\phi_\ell\left(S_r\right), \psi_\ell\left(T_r\right)\right) = \upsilon_\ell\left(S_r \cdot T_r\right)$$

Each entry in the output $\tilde{C}$ is of the form:

$$\tilde{C}_{i,j} = \sum_{r \in [t]} W_{r,(i,j)} P_r$$

$$= \sum_{r \in [t]} W_{r,(i,j)} \upsilon_\ell\left(S_r \cdot T_r\right)$$

By linearity of υ_ℓ

$$= \upsilon_\ell\left(\sum_{r \in [t]} W_{r,(i,j)} \left(S_r \cdot T_r\right)\right)$$

And, as noted in the base case:

$$\left(\upsilon_1\left(A \cdot B\right)\right)_{i,j} = \left(\sum_{r \in [t]} W_{r,(i,j)} \left(S_r \cdot T_r\right)\right)_{(i,j)}$$

Hence,

$$\tilde{C}_{i,j} = \upsilon_\ell\left(\upsilon_1\left(A \cdot B\right)\right)_{i,j}$$

Therefore, by Definition 3.4, $\tilde{C} = \upsilon_{\ell+1}\left(A \cdot B\right)$ □

Notation 3.10. When discussing an $\langle n_0, n_0, n_0; t \rangle_{\phi, \psi, \upsilon}$-algorithm, we denote $\omega_0 = \log_{n_0} t$.

Claim 3.11. *Let ALG be an $\langle n_0, n_0, n_0; t \rangle_{\phi, \psi, \upsilon}$-algorithm which performs q linear operations at its base case. The arithmetic complexity of ALG is*

$$F_{ALG}\left(n\right) = \left(1 + \frac{q}{t - n_0^2}\right) n^{\omega_0} - \left(\frac{q}{t - n_0^2}\right) n^2$$

Proof. Each step of the recursion consists of computing t subproblems and performs q linear operations (additions/multiplication by scalar) of sub-matrices. Therefore $F_{ALG}\left(n\right) = tF_\psi\left(\frac{n}{n_0}\right) + q\left(\frac{n}{n^0}\right)^2$ and $F_{ALG}\left(1\right) = 1$. Thus,

$$F_{ALG}\left(n\right) = \sum_{k=0}^{\log_{n_0} n - 1} t^k \cdot q \cdot \left(\frac{n}{n_0^{k+1}}\right)^2 + t^{\log_{n_0} n} \cdot F_{ALG}\left(1\right)$$

$$= \frac{q}{n_0^2} n^2 \cdot \sum_{k=0}^{\log_{n_0} n - 1} \left(\frac{t}{n_0^2}\right)^k + n^{\omega_0}$$

$$= \frac{q}{n_0^2} n^2 \left(\frac{\left(\frac{t}{n_0^2}\right)^{\log_{n_0} n} - 1}{\frac{t}{n_0^2} - 1}\right) + n^{\omega_0} q \left(\frac{n^{\omega_0} - n^2}{t - n_0^2}\right) + n^{\omega_0}$$

□

Claim 3.12. *Let ALG be an $\langle n_0, n_0, n_0; t \rangle_{\phi, \psi, \upsilon}$-algorithm which performs q linear operations at its base case. The IO-complexity of ALG is*

$$IO_{ALG}\left(n, M\right) \leq \left(\frac{q}{t - n_0^2}\right)\left(M\left(\sqrt{3} \cdot \frac{n}{\sqrt{M}}\right)^{\omega_0} - 3n^2\right) + 3M$$

Proof. Each step of the recursion consists of computing n_0^2 subproblems and performs q linear operations. The base case occurs when the problem fits entirely in the fast memory (or local memory in parallel setting), namely $3n^2 \leq M$. Each addition requires at most 3 data transfers (one of each input and one for writing the output). Hence, a basis transformation which performs q linear operations at each recursive steps has the recurrence:

$$IO_{ALG}(n,M) \le \begin{cases} t \cdot IO_{\psi}\left(\frac{n}{n_0}, M\right) + 3q \cdot \left(\frac{n}{n_0}\right)^2 & 3n^2 > M \\ 3M & otherwise \end{cases}$$

Therefore

$$\begin{aligned} IO_{ALG}(n,M) &\le \sum_{k=0}^{\log_{n_0} \frac{n}{\sqrt{\frac{M}{3}}}-1} t^k \cdot 3q \left(\frac{n}{n_0^{k+1}}\right)^2 + 3M \\ &= \frac{3q}{n_0^2} n^2 \sum_{k=0}^{\log_{n_0} \frac{n}{\sqrt{\frac{M}{3}}}-1} \left(\frac{t}{n_0^2}\right)^k + 3M \\ &= \frac{3q}{n_0^2} n^2 \left(\frac{\left(\frac{t}{n_0^2}\right)^{\log_{n_0} \frac{n}{\sqrt{\frac{M}{3}}}} - 1}{\frac{t}{n_0^2} - 1} \right) + 3M \\ &= q \left(\frac{M\left(\sqrt{3} \cdot \frac{n}{\sqrt{M}}\right)^{\omega_0} - 3n^2}{t - n_0^2} \right) + 3M \end{aligned}$$

□

Corollary 3.13. *If ABS (Algorithm 1) performs q linear operations at the base case, then its arithmetic complexity is*

$$F_{ABS}(n) = \left(1 + \frac{q}{t - n_0^2}\right) n^{\omega_0} - \left(\frac{q}{t - n_0^2}\right) n^2 + O\left(n^2 \log n\right)$$

Proof. The number of flops performed by the algorithm is the sum of: (1) the number of flops performed by the basis transformations (denoted ϕ, ψ, υ) and (2) the number of flops performed by the recursive bilinear algorithms ALG.

$$F_{ABS}(n) = F_{ALG}(n) + F_{\phi}(n) + F_{\psi}(n) + F_{\upsilon}(n)$$

The result immediately follows from Claim 3.7 and Claim 3.11 □

Corollary 3.14. *If ABS (Algorithm 1) performs q linear operations at the base case, then its IO-complexity is*

$$\begin{aligned} IO_{ALG}(n,M) \le& \left(\frac{3q}{t - n_0^2}\right)\left(M\left(\frac{\sqrt{3} \cdot n}{\sqrt{M}}\right)^{\omega_0} - n^2\right) \\ &+ 3M + O\left(n^2 \log \frac{n}{\sqrt{M}}\right) \end{aligned}$$

Proof. The IO-complexity is the sum of: (1) the IO-complexity of the recursive bilinear algorithms ALG and (2) the IO-complexity of the basis transformations (denoted ϕ, ψ, υ).

$$\begin{aligned} IO_{ABS}(n,M) =& IO_{ALG}(n,M) + IO_{\phi}(n,M) \\ &+ IO_{\psi}(n,M) + IO_{\upsilon}(n,M) \end{aligned}$$

The result immediately follows from Claim 3.8 and Claim 3.12. □

3.3 Optimal $\langle 2,2,2;7\rangle$-algorithm

We now present a basis transformation $\psi_{opt} : R^4 \to R^4$ and an $\langle 2,2,2;7\rangle_{\psi}$-algorithm which performs only 12 linear operations.

Notation 3.15. Let, ψ_{opt} refer to the following transformation:

$$\psi_{opt} = \begin{pmatrix} 1 & 0 & 0 & 0 \\ 0 & 1 & -1 & 1 \\ 0 & 0 & -1 & 1 \\ 0 & 1 & 0 & 1 \end{pmatrix} \quad \psi_{opt}^{-1} = \begin{pmatrix} 1 & 0 & 0 & 0 \\ 0 & 1 & -1 & 0 \\ 0 & -1 & 0 & 1 \\ 0 & -1 & 1 & 1 \end{pmatrix}$$

For convenience, when applying ψ to matrices, we omit the vectorization and refer to it as $\psi : R^{2\times 2} \to R^{2\times 2}$:

$$\psi_{opt}(A) = \psi_1 \begin{pmatrix} A_{1,1} & A_{1,2} \\ A_{2,1} & A_{2,2} \end{pmatrix} = \begin{pmatrix} A_{1,1} & A_{1,2} - A_{2,1} + A_{2,2} \\ A_{21} - A_{2,2} & A_{1,2} + A_{2,2} \end{pmatrix}$$

Where $A_{i,j}$ can be ring elements or sub-matrices. ψ_{opt}^{-1} is defined analogously. Both ψ_{opt} and ψ_{opt}^{-1} extend recursively as in Definition 3.4.

$$\left\langle U_{opt}, V_{opt}, W_{opt} \right\rangle =$$

$$\left\langle \begin{pmatrix} 0 & 0 & 0 & 1 \\ 0 & 0 & 1 & 0 \\ 0 & 1 & 0 & 0 \\ 1 & 0 & 0 & 0 \\ 0 & 1 & -1 & 0 \\ -1 & 1 & 0 & 0 \\ 0 & -1 & 0 & 1 \end{pmatrix}, \begin{pmatrix} 0 & 0 & 0 & 1 \\ 0 & 0 & 1 & 0 \\ 0 & 1 & 0 & 0 \\ 1 & 0 & 0 & 0 \\ 0 & -1 & 0 & 1 \\ 0 & 1 & -1 & 0 \\ -1 & 1 & 0 & 0 \end{pmatrix}, \begin{pmatrix} 0 & 0 & 0 & 1 \\ 0 & 0 & 1 & 0 \\ 0 & 1 & 0 & 0 \\ 1 & 0 & 0 & 0 \\ 1 & 1 & 0 & 0 \\ 0 & -1 & 0 & -1 \\ 0 & 1 & 1 & 0 \end{pmatrix} \right\rangle$$

Figure 1: $\langle U, V, W\rangle$ are the encoding/decoding matrices of our $\langle 2,2,2;7\rangle_{\psi_{opt}}$-algorithm which performs 12 linear operations

Claim 3.16. *$\left\langle U_{opt}, V_{opt}, W_{opt} \right\rangle$ are encoding/decoding matrices of an $\langle 2,2,2;7\rangle_{\psi_{opt}}$-algorithm.*

Proof. Observe that

$$\left\langle U_{opt} \cdot \psi_{opt}, V_{opt} \cdot \psi_{opt}, W_{opt} \cdot \psi_{opt}^{-T} \right\rangle =$$

$$\left\langle \begin{pmatrix} 0 & 1 & 0 & 1 \\ 0 & 0 & -1 & 1 \\ 0 & 1 & -1 & 1 \\ 1 & 0 & 0 & 0 \\ 0 & 1 & 0 & 0 \\ -1 & 1 & -1 & 1 \\ 0 & 0 & 1 & 0 \end{pmatrix}, \begin{pmatrix} 0 & 1 & 0 & 1 \\ 0 & 0 & -1 & 1 \\ 0 & 1 & -1 & 1 \\ 1 & 0 & 0 & 0 \\ 0 & 0 & 1 & 0 \\ 0 & 1 & 0 & 0 \\ -1 & 1 & -1 & 1 \end{pmatrix}, \begin{pmatrix} 0 & 0 & 1 & 1 \\ 0 & -1 & 0 & 1 \\ 0 & 1 & -1 & -1 \\ 1 & 0 & 0 & 0 \\ 1 & 1 & -1 & -1 \\ 0 & -1 & 0 & 0 \\ 0 & 0 & -1 & 0 \end{pmatrix} \right\rangle$$

It is easy to verify that $\left\langle U_{opt} \cdot \psi_{opt}, V_{opt} \cdot \psi_{opt}, W_{opt} \cdot \psi_{opt}^{-T} \right\rangle$ satisfy the triple product condition in Fact 2.4. Hence, they are encoding/decoding algorithm of an $\langle 2,2,2;7\rangle$-algorithm. By Corollary 3.3, the claim follows. □

Claim 3.17. *Let R be a ring, and let $A \in R^{n\times n}$ where $n = 2^k$. The arithmetic complexity of computing $\psi_{opt}(A)$ is*

$$F_{\psi_{opt}}(n) = n^2 \log_2 n$$

The same holds for computing $\psi_{opt}^{-1}(A)$.

Proof. Both ψ_{opt}, ψ_{opt}^{-1} perform $q = 4$ linear operations at each recursive step and has base case size of $n_0 = 2$. The lemma follows immediately from Claim 3.7. □

Claim 3.18. *Let R be a ring, and let $A \in R^{n\times n}$ where $n = 2^k$. The I/O-complexity of computing $\psi_{opt}(A)$ is*

$$IO_{\psi_{opt}}(n, M) \le 2n^2 \log_2\left(\sqrt{2}\frac{n}{\sqrt{M}}\right) + 2M$$

Proof. Both ψ_{opt}, ψ_{opt}^{-1} perform $q = 4$ linear operations at each recursive step. The lemma follows immediately from Claim 3.8 with base case $n_0 = 2$. □

Corollary 3.19. *Our $\langle 2, 2, 2; 7\rangle_{\psi_{opt}}$-algorithm's arithmetic complexity is $F_{opt}(n) = 5n^{\log_2 7} - 4n^2$.*

Proof. Our $\langle 2, 2, 2; 7\rangle_{\psi_{opt}}$-algorithm has a 2×2 base case and performs 7 multiplications. Applying Fact 2.6 to its encoding/decoding matrices $\langle U_{opt}, V_{opt}, W_{opt}\rangle$, we see that it performs 12 linear operations. The result follows immediately from Claim 3.11 □

Corollary 3.20. *Our $\langle 2, 2, 2; 7\rangle_{\psi_{opt}}$-algorithm's IO-complexity is*

$$IO_{opt}(n, M) \le 12 \cdot \left(\sqrt{3} \cdot M\left(\frac{n}{\sqrt{M}}\right)^{\log_2 7} - 3n^2\right) + 3M$$

Proof. Our algorithm has a 2×2 base case and performs 7 multiplications. By applying Fact 2.6 to its encoding/decoding matrices (as shown in Figure 1), we see that it performs 12 linear operations. The result follows immediately from Claim 3.12. □

Corollary 3.21. *The arithmetic complexity of* ABS *(Algorithm 1) with our $\langle 2, 2, 2; 7\rangle_{\psi_{opt}}$-algorithm is*

$$F_{ABS}(n) = 5n^{\log_2 7} - 4n^2 + 3n^2 \log_2 n$$

Proof. The proof is similar to that of Corollary 3.13 □

Corollary 3.22. *The IO-complexity of* ABS *(Algorithm 1) with our $\langle 2, 2, 2; 7\rangle_{\psi_{opt}}$-algorithm is*

$$IO_{ALG}(n, M) \le 4 \cdot \left(\frac{\sqrt{3}\cdot n}{\sqrt{M}}\right)^{\log_2 7} \cdot M - 12n^2 + 3n^2 \cdot \log_2\left(\sqrt{2} \cdot \frac{n}{\sqrt{M}}\right) + 5M$$

Proof. The proof is similar to that of Corollary 3.14 □

Theorem 3.23. *Our $\langle 2, 2, 2; 7\rangle_{\psi_{opt}}$-algorithm's sequential and parallel IO-complexity is bound by $\Omega\left(\left(\frac{n}{\sqrt{M}}\right)^{\omega_0} \frac{M}{P}\right)$ (where P is the number of processors, 1 in the sequential case, and $\omega_0 = \log_2 7$).*

Proof. We refer to the undirected bipartite graph defined by the decoding matrix of our a Strassen-like algorithm as its decoding graph (i.e., the edge (i, j) exists if $W_{i,j} \neq 0$). In [2], Ballard et al. proved that for any square recursive-bilinear Strassen-like algorithm with $n_0 \times n_0$ base case which performs t multiplications, if the decoding graph is connected then these bounds apply with $\omega_0 = \log_{n_0} t$. The decoding graph of our algorithm is connected. Hence, the claim is true. □

4 BASIS-INVARIANT LOWER BOUND ON ADDITIONS FOR 2 × 2 MATRIX MULTIPLICATION

In this section we prove Theorem 1.2 which says that 12 additions are necessary to compute 2×2 matrix multiplication recursively with base case of 2×2 and 7 multiplications, irrespective of basis. Theorem 1.2 completes Probert's lower bound which says that for standard basis, 15 additions are required.

Definition 4.1. Denote the permutation matrix which swaps row-order for column-order of vectorization of an $I \times J$ matrix by $P_{I\times J}$.

Lemma 4.2. *[19] Let $\langle U, V, W\rangle$ be the encoding/decoding matrices of an $\langle m, k, n; t\rangle$-algorithm. Then $\langle WP_{n\times m}, U, VP_{n\times k}\rangle$ are encoding/decoding matrices of an $\langle n, m, k; t\rangle$-algorithm.*

We use the following results, shown by Hopcroft and Kerr [20]:

Lemma 4.3. *[20] If an algorithm for 2×2 matrix multiplication has k left (right) hand side multiplicands from the set $S = \{A_{1,1}, (A_{1,2} + A_{2,1}), (A_{1,1} + A_{1,2} + A_{2,1})\}$, where additions are done modulo 2, then it requires at least $6 + k$ multiplications.*

Corollary 4.4. *[20] Lemma 4.3 also applies for the following definitions of S:*

(1) $(A_{1,1} + A_{2,1}), (A_{1,2} + A_{2,1} + A_{2,2}), (A_{1,1} + A_{1,2} + A_{2,2})$
(2) $(A_{1,1} + A_{1,2}), (A_{1,2} + A_{2,1} + A_{2,2}), (A_{1,1} + A_{2,1} + A_{2,2})$
(3) $(A_{1,1} + A_{1,2} + A_{2,1} + A_{2,2}), (A_{1,2} + A_{2,1}), (A_{1,1} + A_{2,2})$
(4) $A_{2,1}, (A_{1,1} + A_{2,2}), (A_{1,1} + A_{2,1} + A_{2,2})$
(5) $(A_{2,1} + A_{2,2}), (A_{1,1} + A_{1,2} + A_{2,2}), (A_{1,1} + A_{1,2} + A_{2,1})$
(6) $A_{1,2}, (A_{1,1} + A_{2,2}), (A_{1,1} + A_{1,2} + A_{2,2})$
(7) $(A_{1,2} + A_{2,2}), (A_{1,1} + A_{2,1} + A_{2,2}), (A_{1,1} + A_{1,2} + A_{2,1})$
(8) $A_{2,2}, (A_{1,2} + A_{2,1}), (A_{1,2} + A_{2,1} + A_{2,2})$

Corollary 4.5. *Any 2×2 matrix multiplication algorithm where a left hand (or right hand) multiplicand appears at least twice (modulo 2) requires 8 or more multiplications.*

Proof. Immediate from Lemma 4.3 and Corollary 4.4 since it covers all possible linear sums of matrix elements, modulo 2. □

Fact 4.6. A simple counting argument shows that any 7×4 binary matrix with less than 10 non-zero entries has a duplicate row (modulo 2) or an all zero row.

Lemma 4.7. *Irrespective of basis transformations ϕ, ψ, υ, the encoding matrices U, V, of an $\langle 2, 2, 2; 7\rangle_{\phi,\psi,\upsilon}$-algorithm contain no duplicate rows.*

Proof. Let $\langle U, V, W\rangle$ be encoding/decoding matrices of an $\langle 2, 2, 2; 7\rangle_{\phi,\psi,\upsilon}$-algorithm. By Corollary 3.3, $\langle U\phi, V\psi, W\upsilon^{-T}\rangle$ are encoding/decoding matrices of a $\langle 2, 2, 2; 7\rangle$-algorithm. Assume, w.l.o.g, that U contains a duplicate row, which means that $U\phi$ contains a duplicate row as well. In that case, $\langle U\psi, V\psi, W\upsilon^{-T}\rangle$ is a $\langle 2, 2, 2; 7\rangle$-algorithm in which one of the encoding matrices contains a duplicate row, in contradiction to Corollary 4.5. □

Lemma 4.8. *Irrespective of basis transformations ϕ, ψ, υ, the encoding matrices U, V, of a $\langle 2, 2, 2; 7\rangle_{\phi,\psi,\upsilon}$-algorithm have at least 10 non-zero entries.*

Proof. No row in U, V can be zeroed out since otherwise the algorithm would require less than 7 multiplications. The result then follows from Fact 4.6 and Lemma 4.7. □

Lemma 4.9. *Irrespective of basis transformations ϕ, ψ, υ, the decoding matrix W of an $\langle 2,2,2;7\rangle_{\phi,\psi,\upsilon}$-algorithm has at least 10 non-zero entries.*

Proof. Let $\langle U, V, W\rangle$ be encoding/decoding matrices of an $\langle 2,2,2;7\rangle_{\phi,\psi,\upsilon}$-algorithm and suppose by contradiction that W has less than 10 non-zero entries. W is a 7×4 matrix. By Fact 4.6, it either has a duplicate row (modulo 2) or an all zero row. Corollary 3.3 states that $\left\langle U\phi, V\psi, W\upsilon^{-T}\right\rangle$ are encoding/decoding matrices of a $\langle 2,2,2;7\rangle$-algorithm. By Lemma 4.2, because $\left\langle U\phi, V\psi, W\upsilon^{-T}\right\rangle$ define a $\langle 2,2,2;7\rangle$-algorithm, so does $\left\langle W\upsilon^{-T}P_{2\times 2}, U\phi, V\psi P_{2\times 2}\right\rangle$. Hence $W\upsilon^{-T}P_{2\times 2}$ is an encoding matrix of a $\langle 2,2,2;7\rangle$-algorithm which has duplicate or all zero rows, contradicting Corollary 4.5. □

Proof (of Theorem 1.2). Lemma 4.8 and 4.9 then show that each encoding/decoding matrix must contain at least 10 non-zero entries. By Remark 2.6, the number of additions used by each of the encoding matrix is $nnz(U) - rows(U)$ (and analogously for V) and the number of additions used by the decoding is $nnz(W) - cols(W)$. Hence, 12 additions are necessary for an $\langle 2,2,2;7\rangle_{\phi,\psi,\upsilon}$-algorithm irrespective of basis transformations ϕ, ψ, υ. □

5 OPTIMAL ALTERNATIVE BASES

To apply our alternative basis method to other Strassen-like matrix multiplication algorithms, we find bases which reduce the number of linear operations performed by the algorithm. As we mentioned in Fact 2.6, the non-zero entries of the encoding/decoding matrices determine the number of linear operations performed by an algorithm. Hence, we want our encoding/decoding matrices to be as sparse as possible, and ideally to have only entries of the form -1, 0 and 1. From Lemma 3.2 and Corollary 3.3 we see that any $\langle n,m,k;t\rangle$-algorithm and dimension compatible basis transformations ϕ, ψ, υ can be composed into an $\langle n,m,k;t\rangle_{\phi,\psi,\upsilon}$-algorithm. Therefore, the problem of finding a basis in which a Strassen-like algorithm performs the least amount of linear operations is closely tied to the Matrix Sparsification problem:

Problem 5.1. Matrix Sparsification Problem (MS): Let U be an $m\times n$ matrix of full rank, find an invertible matrix A such that

$$A = \underset{A\in GL_n}{\texttt{argmin}}\left(nnz(UA)\right)$$

That is, finding basis transformations for a Strassen-like algorithm consists of three independent MS problems. Unfortunately, MS is not only NP-Hard [28] to solve, but also NP-Hard to approximate to within a factor of $2^{\log^{.5-o(1)} n}$ [15] (Over $\mathbb{Q}$, assuming NP does not admit quasi-polynomial time deterministic algorithms). There seem to be very few heuristics for matrix sparsification (e.g., [9]), or algorithms under very limiting assumptions (e.g., [18]). Nevertheless, for existing Strassen-like algorithms with small base cases, the use of search heuristics to find bases which significantly sparsify the encoding/decoding matrices of several Strassen-like algorithms proved useful. Our resulting alternative basis Strassen-like algorithms are summarized in Table 2. Note, particularly, our alternative basis version of Smirnov's $\langle 6,3,3;40\rangle$-algorithm, which is asymptotically faster than Strassen's, where we have reduced the number of linear operations in the bilinear-recursive algorithm from 1246 to 202, thus reducing the leading coefficient by 83.2%.

6 IMPLEMENTATION AND PRACTICAL CONSIDERATIONS

6.1 Recursion cutoff point

Implementations of fast matrix multiplication algorithms often take several recursive steps then call the classical algorithm from a vendor-tuned library. This gives better performance in practice due to two main reasons: (1) the asymptotic improvement of Strassen-like algorithms makes them faster than classical algorithms by margins which increase with matrix size, and (2) vendor-tuned libraries have extensive built-in optimization, which makes them perform better than existing implementations of fast matrix multiplication algorithms on small matrices.

We next present theoretical analysis for finding the optimal number of recursive steps without tuning.

Claim 6.1. *Let* ALG *be an $\langle n,n,n;t\rangle$-algorithm with q linear operations at the base case. The arithmetic complexity of running ALG for ℓ steps, then switching to classical matrix multiplication is:*

$$F_{ALG}(n,\ell) = \frac{q}{t-n_0^2}\left(\left(\frac{t}{n_0^2}\right)^{\ell} - 1\right)\cdot n^2 + \\ + t^{\ell}\left(2\left(\frac{n}{n_0^{\ell}}\right)^3 - \left(\frac{n}{n_0^{\ell}}\right)^2\right)$$

Proof. Each step of the recursion consists of computing t sub-problems and performs q linear operations. Therefore, $F_{ALG}(n,\ell) = t\cdot F_{ALG}\left(\frac{n}{n_0},\ell-1\right) + q\left(\frac{n}{n^0}\right)^2$ and $F_{ALG}(n,0) = 2n^3 - n^2$. Thus

$$\begin{aligned} F_{ALG}(n,\ell) &= \sum_{k=0}^{\ell-1} t^k\cdot q\cdot\left(\frac{n}{n_0^{k+1}}\right)^2 + t^{\ell}\cdot F_{ALG}\left(\frac{n}{n_0^{\ell}}\right) \\ &= \frac{q}{n_0^2}n^2\left(\frac{\left(\frac{t}{n_0^2}\right)^{\ell}-1}{\frac{t}{n_0^2}-1}\right) + t^{\ell}\left(2\left(\frac{n}{n_0^{\ell}}\right)^3 - \left(\frac{n}{n_0^{\ell}}\right)^2\right) \\ &= \frac{q}{t-n_0^2}\left(\left(\frac{t}{n_0^2}\right)^{\ell}-1\right)\cdot n^2 + t^{\ell}\left(2\left(\frac{n}{n_0^{\ell}}\right)^3 - \left(\frac{n}{n_0^{\ell}}\right)^2\right) \end{aligned}$$

□

When running an alternative basis algorithm for a limited number of recursive steps, the basis transformation needs to be computed only for the same number of recursive steps. If the basis transformation is computed for more steps than the alternative basis multiplication, the classical algorithm will compute incorrect results as it does not account for the input being represented in an alternative basis. This introduces a small saving in the runtime of basis transformation.

Claim 6.2. *Let R be a ring and let $\psi_1 : R^{n_0 \times n_0} \to R^{n_0 \times n_0}$ be an invertible linear map, let $A \in R^{n \times n}$ where $n = n_0^k$, and let $\ell \leq k$. The arithmetic complexity of computing $\psi_\ell(A)$ is*

$$F_\psi(n, \ell) = \frac{q}{n_0^2} n^2 \cdot \ell$$

Proof. Let $F_{\psi_\ell}(n)$ be the number of additions required by ψ_ℓ. Each recursive consists of computing n_0^2 sub-problems and performing q linear operations. Therefore, $F_\psi(n, \ell) = n_0^2 \cdot F_\psi\left(\frac{n}{n_0}, \ell - 1\right) + q \cdot \left(\frac{n}{n_0}\right)^2$ and $F_\psi(n, 0) = 0$

$$F_{\psi_\ell}(n) = \sum_{k=0}^{\ell-1} \left(n_0^2\right)^k \cdot q \left(\frac{n}{n_0^{k+1}}\right)^2$$
$$= \frac{q}{n_0^2} n^2 \cdot \sum_{k=0}^{\ell-1} \left(\frac{n_0^2}{n_0^2}\right)^k = \frac{q}{n_0^2} n^2 \cdot \ell$$

□

6.2 Performance experiments

We next present performance results for our $\langle 2, 2, 2; 7\rangle_{\psi_{opt}}$-algorithm. All experiments were conducted on a single compute node of HLRS's Hazel Hen, with two 12-core (24 threads) Intel Xeon CPU E5-2680 v3 and 128GB of memory.

We used a straightforward implementation of both our algorithm and Strassen-Winograd's [40] algorithm using OpenMP. Each algorithm runs for a pre-selected number of recursive steps before switching to Intel's MKL DGEMM routine. Each DGEMM call uses all threads, matrix additions are always fully parallelized. All results are the median over 6 experiments.

In Figure 2 we see that our algorithm outperforms Strassen-Winograd's, with the margin of improvement increasing with each recursive step and nearing the theoretical improvement.

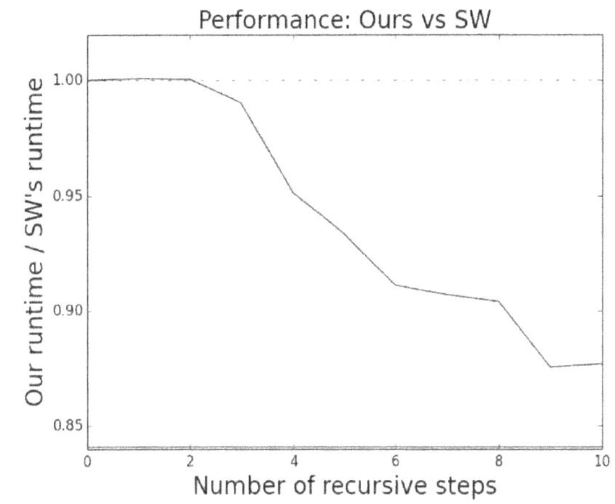

Figure 2: Comparing the performance of our $\langle 2, 2, 2; 7\rangle_{\psi_{opt}}$-algorithm to Strassen-Winograd's on square matrices of fixed dimension $N = 32768$. The graph shows our algorithm's runtime, normalized by Strassen-Winograd's algorithm's runtime, as a function of the number of recursive steps taken before switching to Intel's MKL DGEMM. The top horizontal (at 1) line represents Strassen-Winograd's performance and the bottom horizontal line (at 0.83) represents the theoretical ratio when taking the maximal number of recursive steps.

7 DISCUSSION

Our method obtained novel variants of existing Strassen-like algorithms, reducing the number of linear operations required. Our algorithm also outperforms Strassen-Winograd's algorithm for any matrix dimension $n \geq 32$. Furthermore, we've obtained an alternative basis algorithm of Smirnov's $\langle 6, 3, 3; 40\rangle$-algorithm, reducing the number of additions by 83.8%. While the problem of finding bases which optimally sparsify an algorithm's encoding/decoding matrices is NP-Hard (see Section 5), it is still solvable for many fast matrix multiplication algorithms with small base cases. Hence, finding basis transformations could be done in practice using search heuristics, leading to further improvements.

We leave large scale implementations for future research but note that both kernels of our alternative basis algorithms (basis transformation and recursive-bilinear algorithms) are known to be highly parallelizable recursive divide-and-conquer algorithms, and admit various communication minimizing parallelization techniques (e.g., [1, 5]).

ACKNOWLEDGMENTS

Research is supported by grants 1878/14, and 1901/14 from the Israel Science Foundation (founded by the Israel Academy of Sciences and Humanities) and grant 3-10891 from the Ministry of Science and Technology, Israel. Research is also supported by the Einstein Foundation and the Minerva Foundation. This work was supported by the PetaCloud industry-academia consortium. This research was supported by a grant from the United States-Israel Bi-national Science Foundation (BSF), Jerusalem, Israel. This work was supported by the HUJI Cyber Security Research Center in conjunction with the Israel National Cyber Bureau in the Prime Minister's Office. We acknowledge PRACE for awarding us access to Hazel Hen at GCS@HLRS, Germany.

REFERENCES

[1] Grey Ballard, James Demmel, Olga Holtz, Benjamin Lipshitz, and Oded Schwartz. 2012. Communication-optimal parallel algorithm for strassen's matrix multiplication. In *Proceedings of the twenty-fourth annual ACM symposium on Parallelism in algorithms and architectures*. ACM, 193–204.

[2] Grey Ballard, James Demmel, Olga Holtz, and Oded Schwartz. 2012. Graph expansion and communication costs of fast matrix multiplication. *Journal of the ACM (JACM)* 59, 6 (2012), 32.

[3] Austin R Benson and Grey Ballard. 2015. A framework for practical parallel fast matrix multiplication. *ACM SIGPLAN Notices* 50, 8 (2015), 42–53.

[4] Gianfranco Bilardi and Lorenzo De Stefani. 2016. The I/O complexity of Strassen's matrix multiplication with recomputation. *arXiv preprint arXiv:1605.02224* (2016).

[5] Gianfranco Bilardi, Michele Scquizzato, and Francesco Silvestri. 2012. A Lower Bound Technique for Communication on BSP with Application to the FFT. In *European Conference on Parallel Processing*. Springer, 676–687.

[6] Dario Bini, Milvio Capovani, Francesco Romani, and Grazia Lotti. 1979. O ($n^{2.7799}$) complexity for n× n approximate matrix multiplication. *Information processing letters* 8, 5 (1979), 234–235.

[7] Marco Bodrato. 2010. A Strassen-like matrix multiplication suited for squaring and higher power computation. In *Proceedings of the 2010 International Symposium on Symbolic and Algebraic Computation*. ACM, 273–280.

[8] Murat Cenk and M Anwar Hasan. 2017. On the arithmetic complexity of strassen-like matrix multiplications. *Journal of Symbolic Computation* 80 (2017), 484–501.

[9] S Frank Chang and S Thomas McCormick. 1992. A hierarchical algorithm for making sparse matrices sparser. *Mathematical Programming* 56, 1 (1992), 1–30.

[10] Henry Cohn and Christopher Umans. 2003. A group-theoretic approach to fast matrix multiplication. In *Foundations of Computer Science, 2003. Proceedings. 44th Annual IEEE Symposium on.* IEEE, 438–449.

[11] James W Cooley and John W Tukey. 1965. An algorithm for the machine calculation of complex Fourier series. *Mathematics of computation* 19, 90 (1965), 297–301.

[12] Don Coppersmith and Shmuel Winograd. 1982. On the asymptotic complexity of matrix multiplication. *SIAM J. Comput.* 11, 3 (1982), 472–492.

[13] Don Coppersmith and Shmuel Winograd. 1990. Matrix multiplication via arithmetic progressions. *Journal of symbolic computation* 9, 3 (1990), 251–280.

[14] Paolo D'alberto, Marco Bodrato, and Alexandru Nicolau. 2011. Exploiting parallelism in matrix-computation kernels for symmetric multiprocessor systems: Matrix-multiplication and matrix-addition algorithm optimizations by software pipelining and threads allocation. *ACM Transactions on Mathematical Software (TOMS)* 38, 1 (2011), 2.

[15] Lee-Ad Gottlieb and Tyler Neylon. 2010. Matrix sparsification and the sparse null space problem. In *Approximation, Randomization, and Combinatorial Optimization. Algorithms and Techniques.* Springer, 205–218.

[16] Brian Grayson and Robert Van De Geijn. 1996. A high performance parallel Strassen implementation. *Parallel Processing Letters* 6, 01 (1996), 3–12.

[17] Vince Grolmusz. 2008. Modular representations of polynomials: Hyperdense coding and fast matrix multiplication. *IEEE Transactions on Information Theory* 54, 8 (2008), 3687–3692.

[18] Alan J Hoffman and ST McCormick. 1984. A fast algorithm that makes matrices optimally sparse. *Progress in Combinatorial Optimization* (1984), 185–196.

[19] John Hopcroft and Jean Musinski. 1973. Duality applied to the complexity of matrix multiplications and other bilinear forms. In *Proceedings of the fifth annual ACM symposium on Theory of computing.* ACM, 73–87.

[20] John E Hopcroft and Leslie R Kerr. 1971. On minimizing the number of multiplications necessary for matrix multiplication. *SIAM J. Appl. Math.* 20, 1 (1971), 30–36.

[21] Igor Kaporin. 2004. The aggregation and cancellation techniques as a practical tool for faster matrix multiplication. *Theoretical Computer Science* 315, 2-3 (2004), 469–510.

[22] Donald E Knuth. 1981. The Art of Computer Programming, Volume 2: Seminumerical Algorithms, Addison-Wesley. *Reading, MA* (1981).

[23] Bharat Kumar, C-H Huang, P Sadayappan, and Rodney W Johnson. 1995. A tensor product formulation of Strassen's matrix multiplication algorithm with memory reduction. *Scientific Programming* 4, 4 (1995), 275–289.

[24] Julian Laderman, Victor Pan, and Xuan-He Sha. 1992. On practical algorithms for accelerated matrix multiplication. *Linear Algebra and Its Applications* 162 (1992), 557–588.

[25] Julian D Laderman. 1976. A noncommutative algorithm for multiplying 3× 3 matrices using 23 multiplications. In *Am. Math. Soc*, Vol. 82. 126–128.

[26] François Le Gall. 2014. Powers of tensors and fast matrix multiplication. In *Proceedings of the 39th international symposium on symbolic and algebraic computation.* ACM, 296–303.

[27] Benjamin Lipshitz, Grey Ballard, James Demmel, and Oded Schwartz. 2012. Communication-avoiding parallel strassen: Implementation and performance. In *Proceedings of the International Conference on High Performance Computing, Networking, Storage and Analysis.* IEEE Computer Society Press, 101.

[28] S Thomas McCormick. 1983. *A Combinatorial Approach to Some Sparse Matrix Problems.* Technical Report. DTIC Document.

[29] V Ya Pan. 1978. Strassen's algorithm is not optimal trilinear technique of aggregating, uniting and canceling for constructing fast algorithms for matrix operations. In *Foundations of Computer Science, 1978., 19th Annual Symposium on.* IEEE, 166–176.

[30] V Ya Pan. 1982. Trilinear aggregating with implicit canceling for a new acceleration of matrix multiplication. *Computers & Mathematics with Applications* 8, 1 (1982), 23–34.

[31] Robert L Probert. 1976. On the additive complexity of matrix multiplication. *SIAM J. Comput.* 5, 2 (1976), 187–203.

[32] Francesco Romani. 1982. Some properties of disjoint sums of tensors related to matrix multiplication. *SIAM J. Comput.* 11, 2 (1982), 263–267.

[33] Arnold Schönhage. 1981. Partial and total matrix multiplication. *SIAM J. Comput.* 10, 3 (1981), 434–455.

[34] Jacob Scott, Olga Holtz, and Oded Schwartz. 2015. Matrix multiplication I/O-complexity by path routing. In *Proceedings of the 27th ACM symposium on Parallelism in Algorithms and Architectures.* ACM, 35–45.

[35] AV Smirnov. 2013. The bilinear complexity and practical algorithms for matrix multiplication. *Computational Mathematics and Mathematical Physics* 53, 12 (2013), 1781–1795.

[36] Andrew James Stothers. 2010. On the complexity of matrix multiplication. (2010).

[37] Volker Strassen. 1969. Gaussian elimination is not optimal. *Numerische mathematik* 13, 4 (1969), 354–356.

[38] Volker Strassen. 1986. The asymptotic spectrum of tensors and the exponent of matrix multiplication. In *Foundations of Computer Science, 1986., 27th Annual Symposium on.* IEEE, 49–54.

[39] Virginia Vassilevska Williams. 2012. Multiplying matrices faster than Coppersmith-Winograd. In *Proceedings of the forty-fourth annual ACM symposium on Theory of computing.* ACM, 887–898.

[40] Shmuel Winograd. 1971. On multiplication of 2× 2 matrices. *Linear algebra and its applications* 4, 4 (1971), 381–388.

A Communication-Avoiding Parallel Algorithm for the Symmetric Eigenvalue Problem

Edgar Solomonik
University of Illinois at Urbana-Champaign
Department of Computer Science

Grey Ballard
Wake Forest University
Department of Computer Science

James Demmel
University of California, Berkeley
Department of Mathematics & Department of Electrical Engineering and Computer Science

Torsten Hoefler
ETH Zurich
Computer Science Department

ABSTRACT

Many large-scale scientific computations require eigenvalue solvers in a scaling regime where efficiency is limited by data movement. We introduce a parallel algorithm for computing the eigenvalues of a dense symmetric matrix, which performs asymptotically less communication than previously known approaches. We provide analysis in the Bulk Synchronous Parallel (BSP) model with additional consideration for communication between a local memory and cache. Given sufficient memory to store c copies of the symmetric matrix, our algorithm requires $\Theta(\sqrt{c})$ less interprocessor communication than previously known algorithms, for any $c \leq p^{1/3}$ when using p processors. The algorithm first reduces the dense symmetric matrix to a banded matrix with the same eigenvalues. Subsequently, the algorithm employs successive reduction to $O(\log p)$ thinner banded matrices. We employ two new parallel algorithms that achieve lower communication costs for the full-to-band and band-to-band reductions. Both of these algorithms leverage a novel QR factorization algorithm for rectangular matrices.

1 INTRODUCTION

The eigenvalue decomposition of a symmetric matrix A is $A = UDU^T$ where D is a diagonal matrix of eigenvalues and the columns of the orthogonal matrix U are the eigenvectors of A. Dense symmetric eigensolvers typically reduce the matrix to a tridiagonal matrix with the same eigenvalues, compute the eigenvalues D of this tridiagonal matrix [17], and, if desired, apply the orthogonal transformation backwards to compute the eigenvectors U. Although algorithms for tridiagonalizing a symmetric matrix require the same asymptotic amount of work as one-sided decompositions such as LU and QR factorization, they have a more complex dependency structure, which makes communication-efficient parallelization challenging. Efficient execution of scientific applications such as electronic structure methods, which compute eigenvalue decompositions of a sequence of symmetric matrices (see, e.g. Hartree-Fock method [21, 26]), requires scalable symmetric eigensolvers.

We analyze the scalability of parallel algorithms in a Bulk Synchronous Parallel (BSP) cost model [39]. In addition to quantifying horizontal communication (data movement between processors) and synchronization, we augment the BSP model with an additional bandwidth cost parameter for vertical communication (data movement between memory and cache). There are known algorithms for Cholesky, LU, and QR factorization [3, 35, 38], which for $n \times n$ input matrices on a p-processor system, have horizontal communication complexity $W = O(n^2/\sqrt{cp})$, require $S = O(\sqrt{cp})$ synchronizations, and use $M = O(cn^2/p)$ memory per processor. Most commonly, 2D processor grids are used by algorithms that achieve this communication complexity for $c = 1$, but 3D processor grids and more complicated schemes are needed to achieve the complexity with any $c \in [1, p^{1/3}]$ and obtain practical performance improvements [35]. For Cholesky factorization, which is simpler than LU and QR, these algorithms attain communication lower bounds $W = O\left(\frac{n^3}{pM^{1/2}}\right)$ [7] and $W \cdot S = \Omega(n^2)$ [34], for a range of W parameterized by c.

The best previously known algorithms for solving the symmetric eigenvalue problem directly, use 2D parallelizations and achieve the cost $W = O(n^2/\sqrt{p})$. We introduce algorithms that reduce the horizontal communication cost asymptotically by a factor of $\sqrt{c}$, while using a factor of c more memory and $\sqrt{c}$ more synchronizations, in the same fashion as previously done for one-sided factorizations. The new algorithms generalize of previous approaches, and the flexibility offered by the parameter c increases the dimensionality of the tuning space for symmetric eigensolver implementations. In particular, employing a large c is attractive for bandwidth-constrained problems on massively-parallel architectures.

Our algorithms focus on reducing the symmetric matrix to thinner and thinner banded matrices with the same eigenvalues. This "successive band reduction" approach [10, 11], i.e. reducing to an

Grey Ballard was supported by an appointment to the Sandia National Laboratories Truman Fellowship in National Security Science and Engineering, sponsored by Sandia Corporation (a wholly owned subsidiary of Lockheed Martin Corporation) as Operator of Sandia National Laboratories under its U.S. Department of Energy Contract No. DE-AC04-94AL85000. James Demmel was supported by US Dept. of Energy, Office of Science, Office of Advanced Scientific Computing Research, Grant DOE DE-SC0010200, and ASPIRE Lab industrial sponsors and affiliationliates Intel, Google, Hewlett-Packard, Huawei, LGE, NVIDIA, Oracle, and Samsung. Edgar Solomonik was supported by a US. Dept. of Energy Computational Science Graduate Fellowship and an ETH Zurich Postdoctoral Fellowship.

SPAA '17, July 24-26, 2017, Washington DC, USA

ACM ISBN 978-1-4503-4593-4/17/07...$15.00
https://doi.org/10.1145/3087556.3087561

intermediate banded matrix rather than directly to tridiagonal, has been used to reduce vertical communication and synchronization costs [8]. Further, in practice, algorithms using a two-stage (full-to-banded and banded-to-tridiagonal) approach [5, 25] have been shown to outperform libraries that reduce directly to tridiagonal (like ScaLAPACK [12]). However, a disadvantage of successive band reduction is an increase in cost of the back transformations done to compute eigenvectors. Unlike the forward application of transformations whose computation cost scales linearly with the matrix band-width, known algorithms for back transformations require $O(n^3)$ operations for each intermediate band-width used.

The BSP model allows us to formulate and analyze algorithms as compositions of a set of common building-blocks. We leverage algorithms for matrix multiplication and QR factorization within our symmetric eigensolvers. For QR factorization, we extends known algorithms for tall-and-skinny matrices [16] and square matrices [38] to be efficient for arbitrary rectangular matrices.

We use these building blocks to define algorithms for reducing a dense matrix to a banded matrix, and a banded matrix to a thinner band-width, while preserving eigenvalues. Our main algorithm combines these, using $O(\log p)$ intermediate band-widths. The algorithm is work-efficient for computing eigenvalues, requires $O(n^2/\sqrt{cp})$ horizontal communication, $O(n^2 \log p/\sqrt{cp})$ vertical communication, and $O(\sqrt{cp}\log^2 p)$ synchronizations (BSP supersteps). Known approaches for back-transformations to compute eigenvectors require the same asymptotic amount of computation for matrices of any band-width, meaning our approach may require a computation cost of $O(n^2 k \log p/p)$ if k eigenvectors are needed. We leave the analysis of back-transformation computation for future work, but propose a potential approach to reduce the number of intermediate band-widths needed by our symmetric eigensolver.

2 THEORETICAL COST MODEL

We use the Bulk Synchronous Parallel (BSP) model [39] with an additional parameter to measure the cost of traffic between memory and cache. We derive asymptotic bounds on the parallel running-time of our algorithms for this two-level architectural model, with consideration for both communication between processors and in the memory hierarchy of each processor. The BSP model permits an all-to-all communication to be done with unit synchronization cost, which will allow us to construct BSP algorithms for general matrix distributions and compose them without significant overhead.

We employ cost notation typically used for the α–β communication model. As all stored and communicated datasets in this paper consist exclusively of floating-point numbers, we quantify sizes in terms of 'words' (floating-point numbers of a given precision). We model the memory hierarchy of each processor by a main 'slow' memory (i.e. DRAM) and a 'fast' memory (i.e. cache). We permit interprocessor (horizontal) communication to move data between main memories of different processors, and intraprocessor (vertical) communication to move data between main memory and cache of a single processor. Our architectural model is characterized by the following parameters:

- p – processors on a fully-connected network,
- M – words of memory owned by each processor,
- H – words of cache owned by each processor,
- γ – time to compute a floating point operation,
- β – time to send or receive a word,
- ν – time to move a word between cache and memory,
- α – time to perform a (global) synchronization.

We bound the cost of each algorithm by measuring four quantities:

- F – number of local floating point operations performed (computation cost),
- W – number of words of data moved between processors (horizontal communication cost),
- Q – number of words of data moved between main memory and cache (vertical communication cost),
- S – number of BSP supersteps (synchronization cost).

If at each superstep $i \in [1, S]$, processor j performs F_i^j local operations, sends and receives W_i^j total words, and performs Q_i^j reads and writes to memory, then the costs of the BSP algorithm are

$$F = \sum_{i=1}^{S} \max_{j\in[1,p]} F_i^j, \quad W = \sum_{i=1}^{S} \max_{j\in[1,p]} W_i^j, \quad Q = \sum_{i=1}^{S} \max_{j\in[1,p]} Q_i^j,$$

and the BSP execution time of this algorithm is

$$T = \Theta(\gamma \cdot F + \beta \cdot W + \nu \cdot Q + \alpha \cdot S).$$

This model does not consider overlap between communication and computation (or between other costs), as such overlap does not affect the overall asymptotic time.

We simplify asymptotic cost expressions by assuming $\gamma \leq \beta$. Further, we write only vertical communication terms which are not associated with horizontal communication or with computations that achieve a factor of $\sqrt{H}$ cache reuse (optimal for matrix multiplication [27]). These simplifications correspond to the assumptions on the relative communication times, $\nu \leq \beta$ and the floating point rate $\nu \leq \gamma \cdot \sqrt{H}$. However, general vertical communication cost upper-bounds may be obtained from our stated results for arbitrary ν by reinserting the term $O(\nu \cdot (F/\sqrt{H} + W))$.

We will provide asymptotic bounds for the BSP cost of all algorithms in the paper. Sometimes, we will employ algorithms as building blocks whose cost has been analyzed in the standard $\alpha - \beta$ model, which is restricted to point-to-point messaging (pairwise synchronization). These algorithms are trivially translated to the BSP model used in this paper, which is less restrictive (allows bulk synchronizations).

Throughout the paper, we will assume that matrix dimensions are greater than and divisible by the number of processors. When it is clear that the asymptotic costs would not be affected, we will also omit floors and ceilings when subdividing the number of processors and matrix dimensions.

3 BUILDING BLOCKS

We first state known results and provide minor extensions to quantify the complexity of matrix multiplication and of QR factorization in our cost model. These results will be critical in the cost analysis of the new symmetric eigensolvers, which use matrix multiplication and QR factorization as subroutines.

3.1 Matrix Multiplication

Our symmetric eigensolvers will perform matrix multiplications, often of nonsquare matrices. We consider the BSP cost of multiplication of arbitrary rectangular matrices with any starting distribution. Additionally, we specially consider the BSP cost of a matrix multiplication of a pre-replicated matrix with another matrix in an arbitrary distribution. We start with the vertical communication cost of a matrix multiplication done by a single processor.

Lemma 3.1. *The multiplication of matrices of dimensions $m \times n$ and $n \times k$ can be done by a single processor in time,*

$$O(\gamma \cdot mnk + \nu \cdot [mn + mk + nk]).$$

The Rec-Mult algorithm [22, Theorem 1] obtains the vertical communication cost given in Lemma 3.1. We omit the usual term $O(\nu \cdot mnk/\sqrt{H})$, since we have $\nu \leq \gamma \cdot \sqrt{H}$.

We now consider the full BSP cost of parallel rectangular matrix multiplication. The communication cost of square matrix multiplication is well known [1, 3, 9, 14, 29, 31]. The horizontal costs of rectangular matrix multiplication have also been analyzed within the α–β communication model, where a recursive algorithm was proposed [15] that attains the communication lower bound. We show that the algorithm in [15] can be executed within the time specified in the subsequent Lemma, for any initial load balanced distribution of the matrices. It is possible to also design different matrix multiplication algorithms in the BSP model with a $\Theta(\log p)$ factor less in synchronization cost, but the overall synchronization costs of our QR and symmetric eigensolve algorithms would not improve. We parameterize the memory used by the algorithm by a parameter v, which controls how many block matrix multiplications are performed.

Lemma 3.2. *For any $v \geq 1$, the multiplication of matrices of dimensions $m \times n$ and $n \times k$ in any load-balanced starting layout can be done in BSP time,*

$$O\left(\gamma \cdot \frac{mnk}{p} + \beta \cdot \left[\frac{mn + nk + mk}{p} + v^{1/3}\left(\frac{mnk}{p}\right)^{2/3}\right] + \alpha \cdot v \log p\right),$$

using $M = O\left(\frac{mn+nk+mk}{p} + \left(\frac{mnk}{vp}\right)^{2/3}\right)$ memory.

Proof. We consider the cost of the recursive 'CARMA' algorithm [15]. The algorithm assumes specific initial matrix layouts, but does not assume any initial data is replicated. Therefore, starting from load balanced layouts, the BSP time to move to the layouts specified by CARMA is $O(\beta \cdot \frac{mn+nk+mk}{p} + \alpha)$. Because the computation is load balanced, the computation cost is $O(\gamma \cdot mnk/p)$. The latency cost of the CARMA algorithm is an upper-bound on the number of BSP supersteps necessary to execute it. In [15], the latency cost is shown to be $O\left(\frac{mnk}{pM^{3/2}} \log p\right) = O(v \log p)$. The communication cost of CARMA is presented in cases for 1D, 2D, and 3D processor grids. We show that the postulated BSP time upper-bound holds for all cases.

We first argue that the vertical communication cost of the local matrix multiplications (given by Lemma 3.1) is dominated by horizontal communication due to the assumption $\beta \geq \nu$. In the 3D case, the operand matrix blocks are nearly square, and either one of the operands or the output is always communicated, so horizontal communication cost dominates vertical communication cost. In the 1D and 2D cases, each processor performs a single local matrix multiplication, where the largest operand has size $O(\frac{mn+nk+mk}{p})$, since it is the local block of the largest matrix.

We leverage previous analysis [15] to derive the horizontal communication cost. Let $d_1 = \min(m, n, k)$, $d_2 = \text{median}(m, n, k)$, and $d_3 = \max(m, n, k)$. If $p < d_3/d_2$ (1D case), then $d_1 d_2 < d_1 d_3/p$, so the provided cost $O(\beta \cdot d_1 d_2) = O(\beta \cdot (mn + nk + mk)/p)$. If $d_3/d_2 \leq p \leq d_2 d_3/d_1^2$ (2D case), then the provided cost $O(\beta \cdot \sqrt{d_1^2 d_2 d_3/p}) = O(\beta \cdot (mn + nk + mk)/p)$. Finally, if $p > d_2 d_3/d_1^2$ (3D case), the provided cost $O(\beta \cdot [mnk/(p\sqrt{M}) + (mnk/p)^{2/3}]) = O(\beta \cdot v^{1/3}(mnk/p)^{2/3})$. □

The algorithm analyzed in Lemma 3.2 allows any initial load balanced matrix distributions. We now consider Algorithm 3.1, which assumes an initial distribution with replicated data and subsequently can multiply certain matrices in less time than given by Lemma 3.2. In Algorithm 3.1, one of the input matrices is stored redundantly on $c = p^{2\delta-1}$ 2D processor grids for any $c \in [1, p^{1/3}]$ ($\delta \in [1/2, 2/3]$). The parameterization by δ is the same as α in [38], while c is the same replication factor as in [35]. The parameter w controls the number of supersteps in Algorithm 3.1.

The algorithm permits the distribution to be defined as a blocking of the matrices after permutation by $P^{(1)}, P^{(2)}$. Our analysis assumes the blocking is roughly, but not necessarily exactly load balanced, permitting both cyclic and block-cylic matrix factorization algorithms where different processors perform updates (matrix multiplications) with a slightly different amount of local data at each step. We will employ Algorithm 3.1 with cyclic distributions, for which $P^{(1)}_{ij} = 1$ for $i = (j \bmod q)(m/q) + \lfloor j/q \rfloor$ and $P^{(2)}_{jk} = 1$ for $k = (j \bmod q)(n/q) + \lfloor j/q \rfloor$. On each processor grid layer, the algorithm executes a variant of the SUMMA algorithm [40], which communicates the operand B and reduces the output C. This variant is chosen, since we will use the algorithm with the operand A being larger in dimensions than B and C.

Lemma 3.3. *Consider Algorithm 3.1 for multiplication of matrices A and B of dimensions $m \times n$ and $n \times k$, where the initial distributions of A and B satisfy the stated requirements for permutations $P^{(1)}$ and $P^{(2)}$ where each block A_{ij} of $P^{(1)}AP^{(2)}$ has dimensions $O(m/p^{1-\delta}) \times O(n/p^{1-\delta})$. Then, using $M = O(mn/p^{2(1-\delta)} + (mk + nk)/(wp^{\delta}))$ memory for any $w \in [1, p^{1-\delta}]$, the algorithm can be executed in BSP time,*

$$O\left(\gamma \cdot \frac{mnk}{p} + \beta \cdot \frac{mk + nk}{p^{\delta}} + \alpha \cdot w\right),$$

when $H \geq mn/p^{2(1-\delta)}$ and the copies of A start inside cache, and otherwise with an extra cost of $O(\nu \cdot \frac{wmn}{p^{2(1-\delta)}})$.

Proof. As required by Algorithm 3.1, B starts in any load-balanced distribution over the p processors. As the initial layout is load-balanced the redistribution done on line 4 costs $O(\beta \cdot nk/p + \alpha)$. The gather on line 9 and reduce-scatter on line 11 are dual communication patterns that together have cost $O(\beta \cdot (mk + nk)/(qcw) + \alpha)$.

Algorithm 3.1 $[C] \leftarrow$ Streaming-MM$(A, B, P^{(1)}, P^{(2)}, \Pi)$

Require: Given positive integers p, m, n, k, w and $\delta \in [1/2, 2/3]$: Π is a grid of $q \times q \times c$ processors with $q = p^{1-\delta}$ and $c = p^{2\delta-1}$, A is $m \times n$, B is $n \times k$. For each $l \in [1, c]$, $\Pi[i, j, l]$ owns all elements in A_{ij}, defined by square permutation matrices $P^{(1)}$, $P^{(2)}$, as $P^{(1)}AP^{(2)} = \begin{bmatrix} A_{11} & \cdots & A_{1q} \\ \vdots & \ddots & \vdots \\ A_{q1} & \cdots & A_{qq} \end{bmatrix}$.

B is in any load balanced layout over all p processors.
Let $z = wc$
Partition B into blocks: $P^{(2)T}B = \begin{bmatrix} B_{11} & \cdots & B_{1z} \\ \vdots & & \vdots \\ B_{q1} & \cdots & B_{qz} \end{bmatrix}$.
Redistribute B so that each $\Pi[i, j, l]$ owns $k/(zq)$ columns of B_{jh} for each $h \in \{l, l+c, \ldots, l+(w-1)c\}$.
% *Execute loop iterations in parallel*
for $i \in [1, q], j \in [1, q], l \in [1, c]$ **do**
  % *Execute loop iterations in sequence*
  for $h \in \{l, l+c, \ldots, l+(w-1)c\}$ **do**
    Gather B_{jh} on $\Pi[i, j, l]$
    Compute $\bar{C}_{ijh} = A_{ij} \cdot B_{jh}$ on $\Pi[i, j, l]$
    Reduce-scatter $C_{ih} = \sum_{j=1}^{c} \bar{C}_{ijh}$ so that each $\Pi[i, j, l]$ owns $k/(zq)$ columns of C_{ih}

Require: $C = A \cdot B$ is distributed so that each processor in Π owns mk/p elements of C.

Over all w iterations of index h, we get $O(\beta \cdot (mk+nk)/(qc) + \alpha \cdot w) = O(\beta \cdot (mk+nk)/p^{\delta} + \alpha \cdot w)$.

The w local matrix multiplications take time,

$$O\left(\gamma \cdot \frac{mnk}{p} + \nu \cdot \left(\frac{wmn}{p^{2(1-\delta)}} + \frac{mk+nk}{p^{\delta}}\right)\right),$$

by Lemma 3.1. However, if the entire matrix A starts in cache, which is possible if $H \geq mn/p^{2(1-\delta)}$, it suffices to read only the entries of B_{jh} from memory into cache and write the entries of $\bar{C}_{ijh}$ out to memory. In this case, the vertical communication cost is $O(\nu \cdot \frac{mk+nk}{qc}) = O(\nu \cdot \frac{mk+nk}{p^{\delta}})$. This term is dominated by the interprocessor communication term since $\beta \geq \nu$. The memory usage corresponds to the storage necessary for each block: A_{ij}, B_{jh}, and $\bar{C}_{ijh}$, $M = O\left(\frac{mn}{p^{2(1-\delta)}} + \frac{mk+nk}{wp^{\delta}}\right)$. □

3.2 QR Factorization

We will use QR factorization within our symmetric eigensolver algorithms to obtain orthogonal transformations that introduce zeros when applied to the symmetric matrix. The vertical communication cost of executing a sequential QR factorization is proportional to that of matrix multiplication.

LEMMA 3.4. *The QR factorization of an $m \times n$ matrix A with $m \geq n$ can be done sequentially in time, $O(\gamma \cdot mn^2 + \nu \cdot mn)$.*

The sequential Communication-Avoiding QR (CAQR) algorithm achieves the vertical communication cost given above [16]. The Householder representation, lower trapezoidal $m \times n$ matrix U and upper-triangular $n \times n$ matrix T so that $Q = I - UTU^T$, may be obtained with the cost of Lemma 3.4 using Householder reconstruction [6].

We first consider parallel QR factorization of square matrices.

LEMMA 3.5. *The QR factorization of an $n \times n$ matrix A distributed in any load-balanced layout can be computed using $M = O\left(\frac{n^2}{p^{2(1-\delta)}}\right)$ memory for any $\delta \in [1/2, 2/3]$ in BSP time,*

$$O\left(\gamma \cdot \frac{n^3}{p} + \beta \cdot \frac{n^2}{p^{\delta}} + \alpha \cdot p^{\delta}\right).$$

The QR algorithm given by [38] in the BSP model achieves the costs given in Lemma 3.5. The vertical communication cost was not analyzed in [38]. However, the algorithm consists purely of distributed matrix multiplications or QR factorizations, which by Lemma 3.1 and Lemma 3.4 have a vertical communication cost proportional to the matrix sizes. As the analysis in [38] assumes all matrices that participate in multiplication or QR factorization are communicated, due to $\nu < \beta$, the horizontal communication cost dominates the vertical communication costs associated with these operations.

We now adapt the QR algorithm from [38] to handle rectangular matrices with a desirable asymptotic cost (the embedding used in [38] is inefficient for tall-and-skinny matrices). Our adaptation is based on a binary QR reduction tree, with QR factorizations of nearly square matrices done at every node in the tree performed using the algorithm from [38]. An approach employing a QR reduction tree using Givens rotations goes back to [23], a blocked flat tree approach (optimal sequentially) was presented in [24], and a parallel block reduction tree approach was given earlier in [13]. Our approach is closest to the TSQR algorithm [16], except a set of up to $q_{\max}$ processors works on each tree node.

Algorithm 3.2 computes the QR factorization of an $m \times n$ matrix, outputting the first n columns of the orthogonal Q factor, as well as the $n \times n$ upper-triangular matrix R. The algorithm assumes the existence of a sequential routine 'QR' and a parallel routine for (nearly) square matrices 'square-QR'.

THEOREM 3.6. *Algorithm 3.2 can compute the QR factorization of any $m \times n$ matrix A with $m \geq n$ in a load-balanced layout, using $M = O\left(\left(\frac{n^{\delta}m^{1-\delta}}{p^{1-\delta}}\right)^2\right)$ memory for any $\delta \in [1/2, 2/3]$, in BSP time,*

$$O\left(\gamma \cdot \frac{mn^2}{p} + \beta \cdot \left(\frac{m^{\delta}n^{2-\delta}}{p^{\delta}} + \frac{mn}{p}\right) + \alpha \cdot \left(\frac{np}{m}\right)^{\delta} \log^2 p\right).$$

PROOF. We assume without loss of generality that m/n and p are powers of two. Let $T(\bar{m})$ be the cost of Algorithm 3.2 for an $\bar{m} \times n$ matrix using p processors. Note that m corresponds to the number of rows in the original input matrix, while $\bar{m}$ will be used to refer to the number of rows at a given recursive step. We select the maximum number of processors to be used in base-case square QR factorizations to be $q_{\max} = \frac{pn}{m} \log(p)^{1/\delta}$, in order to minimize synchronization cost while achieving an optimal horizontal communication cost.

The cost of the sequential base case of Algorithm 3.2 is, by Lemma 3.4, $T_{\text{bs1}}(\bar{m}) = O(\gamma \cdot \bar{m}n^2 + \nu \cdot \bar{m}n)$. When reaching the square base case (dimension $2n \times n$, since m/n is a power of two), we employ the square QR algorithm [38] with up to $q_{\max} = \frac{pn}{m} \log(p)^{1/\delta}$

Algorithm 3.2 $[Q, R] \leftarrow$ rect-QR(A, Π)

Require: Given positive integers $p, m, n, q_{\max}$ and $\delta \in [1/2, 2/3]$: Π is a set of p processors, A is $m \times n$, m/n and p are powers of two, and each $\Pi[i]$ owns mn/p elements of A.

1: **if** $p = 1$ **then** Compute $[Q, R] = \text{QR}(A)$ sequentially and exit.

2: **if** $m \leq 2n$ **then** Compute $[Q, R] =$ square-QR$(A, \Pi[1 : \min(p, q_{\max})])$ and exit.

3: Let $r = \min(p, \lceil \frac{m}{2n} \rceil)$ and partition $A = \begin{bmatrix} A_1^T & \cdots & A_r^T \end{bmatrix}^T$ so that each A_i is $m/r \times n$

4: *% Execute loop iterations in parallel*

5: **for** $i \in [1, r]$ **do**

6: $\quad [W_i, R_i] =$ rect-QR$(A_i, \Pi[(i-1)(p/r)+1 : i(p/r)])$

7: $[Z, R] =$ rect-QR$\left(\begin{bmatrix} R_1^T & \cdots & R_r^T \end{bmatrix}^T, \Pi\right)$

8: Partition $Z = \begin{bmatrix} Z_1^T & \cdots & Z_r^T \end{bmatrix}^T$ so that each Z_i is $n \times n$

9: *% Execute loop iterations in parallel*

10: **for** $i \in [1, r]$ **do**

11: $\quad$ Compute $Q_i = W_i Z_i$ using $\Pi[(i-1)(p/r) + 1 : i(p/r)]$

Require: $A = Q \cdot R$ where $Q = \begin{bmatrix} Q_1^T & \cdots & Q_r^T \end{bmatrix}^T$ is $m \times n$ with orthogonal columns, R is $n \times n$ and upper-triangular, both are distributed in load balanced layouts across Π.

processors. We can bound the cost of this QR by Lemma 3.5. We break the cost into two cases: $T_{\text{bp}}(\bar{p}) = T_{\text{bp1}}(\bar{p})$ when $\bar{p} < q_{\max}$ and $T_{\text{bp}}(\bar{p}) = T_{\text{bp2}}$ when $\bar{p} \geq q_{\max}$, where

$$T_{\text{bp1}}(\bar{p}) = O(\gamma \cdot n^3/\bar{p} + \beta \cdot n^2/\bar{p}^{\delta} + \alpha \cdot \bar{p}^{\delta}),$$

$$T_{\text{bp2}} = O\left(\gamma \cdot \frac{mn^2}{p \log(p)^{1/\delta}} + \beta \cdot \frac{m^{\delta} n^{2-\delta}}{p^{\delta} \log p} + \alpha \cdot \left(\frac{np}{m}\right)^{\delta} \log p\right).$$

The square QR algorithm requires that the matrix be embedded into a slanted panel [38]. This can be done generally by using a somewhat larger matrix, but in all except the first recursive call, the $2b \times b$ matrix will have the structure of two stacked upper-triangular matrices. The rows of these upper-triangular matrices can be interleaved to produce a slanted panel without embedding into a larger matrix.

The recursive calls on line 6 always immediately encounter one of the base-cases. The only time base cases can have a matrix with dimension other than $2n \times n$ is during the invocations on line 6 at the first recursive step of the algorithm, and only when $m > 2np$. Therefore, we consider this first recursive step of Algorithm 3.2 separately. The cost of the first recursive step, when $m > 2np$, includes

- the cost of a potential redistribution, $O(\beta \cdot mn/p + \alpha)$,
- the cost of the invocations on line 6 (which lead to base cases), $T_{\text{bs1}}(m/p)$, since $r = \min(p, \lceil m/2n \rceil) = p$,
- the cost of the matrix multiplications on line 11, which are done concurrently, each by a single processor, is $O(\gamma \cdot mn^2/p + \nu \cdot mn/p)$.

Therefore, the total BSP time of the algorithm for $m > 2np$ is

$$\begin{aligned} T(m) &= T(np) + T_{\text{bs1}}\left(\frac{m}{p}\right) + O\left(\gamma \cdot \frac{mn^2}{p} + \beta \cdot \frac{mn}{p}\right) \\ &= T(np) + O(\gamma \cdot mn^2/p + \beta \cdot mn/p + \alpha). \end{aligned}$$

The cost of this initiale step for $m > 2np$ is no greater than the cost in the theorem. Subsequent recursive calls into line 11 or the case when $m \leq 2np$, the matrix multiplications done on line 11 involve matrices of size at most $2n \times n$, each executed using $pn/\bar{m}$ processors. By Lemma 3.2 with $v = (pn/\bar{m})^{2-3\delta}$, these matrix multiplications (done concurrently) take time, $T_{\text{MM}}(\bar{m}) =$

$$O\left(\gamma \cdot \frac{\bar{m}n^2}{p} + \beta \cdot \left(\frac{\bar{m}n}{p} + \frac{\bar{m}^{\delta} n^{2-\delta}}{p^{\delta}}\right) + \alpha \cdot \left(\frac{pn}{\bar{m}}\right)^{2-3\delta} \log p\right)$$

and use $M = O\left(\left(\frac{n^{\delta} \bar{m}^{1-\delta}}{p^{1-\delta}} \log p\right)^2\right)$ memory. When combined with the concurrent recursive calls on line 11 on matrices of size $2n \times n$ with $pn/\bar{m}$ processors and the recursive call on line 7 on a matrix of size $\bar{m}/2 \times n$ with all p processors, we obtain the following BSP time recurrence for $\bar{m} \leq 2np$,

$$T(\bar{m}) = T(\bar{m}/2) + T_{\text{bp}}(pn/\bar{m}) + T_{\text{MM}}(\bar{m}),$$

where $T_b(pn/\bar{m})$ is a base case where up to $q_{\max}$ processors perform the QR. We consider the two cases (for $\bar{m} \leq 2np$),

$$T(\bar{m}) = T(\bar{m}/2) + T_{\text{MM}}(\bar{m}) + \begin{cases} T_{\text{bp1}}(pn/\bar{m}) & : pn/\bar{m} < q_{\max} \\ T_{\text{bp2}} & : pn/\bar{m} \geq q_{\max} \end{cases}$$

Since $q_{\max} = \frac{pn}{m} \log(p)^{1/\delta}$, and $\bar{m}$ decreases by a factor of two at each step, up to the first $(1/\delta) \log \log p$ recursive steps make the call on line 6 with more than $q_{\max}$ processors. The computation and communication cost of these calls are no greater than that of matrix multiplication (part of $T_{\text{MM}}(\bar{m})$), while the synchronization cost increases geometrically, up to the latency cost in T_{bp2}. Therefore, the recurrence is asymptotically equivalent to (for $\bar{m} \leq 2np$),

$$\begin{aligned} T(\bar{m}) &= T(\bar{m}/2) + T_{\text{MM}}(\bar{m}) + T_{\text{bp2}} \\ &= T(\bar{m}/2) + O\left(\gamma \cdot \left(\frac{\bar{m}n^2}{p} + \frac{mn^2}{p \log(p)^{1/\delta}}\right)\right. \\ &\quad \left. + \beta \cdot \left(\frac{\bar{m}n}{p} + \frac{\bar{m}^{\delta} n^{2-\delta}}{p^{\delta}} + \frac{m^{\delta} n^{2-\delta}}{p^{\delta} \log p}\right) + \alpha \cdot \left(\frac{pn}{m}\right)^{\delta} \log p\right). \end{aligned}$$

Since, $\bar{m} \leq 2np$, one of the base-cases is reached after $\log p$ steps, and so the above time is the one postulated in the theorem. □

Alternate communication-efficient formulations of a rectangular QR algorithm are also possible (for instance by combining column-recursion [20] with communication-efficient matrix multiplication, see [32]). We would like to work with the Householder representation to apply orthogonal transformations efficiently in our symmetric eigensolver algorithms, so we give the following corollary.

Corollary 3.7. *The Householder representation of the $m \times n$ orthogonal matrix Q computed by Algorithm 3.2, $Q = (I - UTU_1^T)$, where U_1 is the lower triangular top $n \times n$ block of U, while T is upper-triangular and $U^T U = T^{-1} + T^{-T}$, can be obtained with the same cost and memory usage as in Theorem 3.6.*

Proof. The Householder representation U, T can be obtained stably by executing $[U_1, W_1] = \text{LU}(Q_1 - S)$ where Q_1 is the top $n \times n$ block of Q and S is a diagonal sign matrix, then computing $U = QW_1^{-1}$ and $T = W_1 U_1^{-T}$ [6]. The matrices U_1, W_1, U_1^{-1}, and W_1^{-1} can be obtained by a parallel non-pivoted LU factorization algorithm augmented to subtract S as in [6], which makes the matrix diagonally dominant. The LU algorithms in [37] and [35] both obtain the desired costs. We use the former in our analysis.

When executed using pn/m processors, the algorithm in [37] takes BSP time, $O(\gamma \cdot mn^2/p + \beta \cdot m^\delta n^{2-\delta}/p^\delta + \alpha \cdot (np/m)^\delta)$. This cost was presented in [37], modulo analysis of vertical communication cost, but as the algorithm is based purely on parallel multiplication of square matrices, the vertical communication cost is dominated by the horizontal communication cost. The algorithm also outputs the inverses of the triangular factors [37], so matrix multiplications suffice to compute $U = QW_1^{-1}$ and $T = W_1 U_1^{-T}$. These can be done using all the processors in time, $O(\gamma \cdot mn^2/p + \beta \cdot m^\delta n^{2-\delta}/p^\delta + \alpha)$ with $M = O\left(\left(\frac{n^\delta m^{1-\delta}}{p^{1-\delta}}\right)^2\right)$ memory. As these costs and memory usage are no greater than in Theorem 3.6, we arrive at the postulated conclusion. □

4 SYMMETRIC EIGENSOLVERS

Algorithms for blocked computation of the eigenvalue decomposition of a symmetric matrix via a tridiagonal matrix were studied by [18, 19, 28]. These algorithms reduce an $n \times n$ symmetric matrix A to a matrix B with band-width b and the same eigenvalues as A via a series of $k = (n-b)/b$ orthogonal transformations,

$$B = Q_1^T \cdots Q_k^T A Q_k \cdots Q_1,$$

where each Q_i is representable in terms of b Householder vectors, aggregated in a trapezoidal matrix U_i, as $Q_i = (I - U_i T_i U_i^T)$.

A key property employed by these algorithms is that each two-sided trailing matrix update of blocked Householder transformations may be done as a rank-$2b$ symmetric update. To compute the two-sided transformation $Q^T X Q$ where $X = X^T$ and $Q = (I - UTU^T)$, we can write

$$\begin{aligned} Q^T X Q &= (I - UT^T U^T) X (I - UTU^T) \\ &= X + UV^T + VU^T, \end{aligned} \quad (4.1)$$

where $V = \frac{1}{2} UT^T U^T XUT - XUT$. This form of the update is cheaper to compute than the explicit two-sided update and is easy to aggregate by appending additional vectors to U (to aggregate the Householder form itself requires computing a larger T matrix). Since the trailing matrix update does not have to be applied immediately, but only to the columns which are factorized, this two-sided update can also be aggregated and used in a left-looking algorithm. For instance, to multiply $Q^T X Q$ by a matrix Y, we can compute

$$Q^T X Q Y = XY + UV^T Y + VU^T Y. \quad (4.2)$$

Returning to algorithms that compute a series of k two-sided transformations, we note that when computing V_2 from U_2 (to apply Q_2), we need to multiply U_2 by a submatrix of $Q_1^T A Q_1$, which can be done without applying Q_1, using the above form. Left-looking algorithms which generalize this idea and employ a delayed trailing matrix update have been used to reduce directly to tridiagonal form ($b = 1$) [18].

However, there are disadvantages to reducing the symmetric matrix directly to tridiagonal form, since it requires that a vector be multiplied by the trailing matrix for each computation of V_i of which there are $n-2$. These matrix-vector multiplications require $O(n)$ synchronizations and $O(n)$ transfers of the trailing matrix between memory and cache (so long as it does not fit into cache).

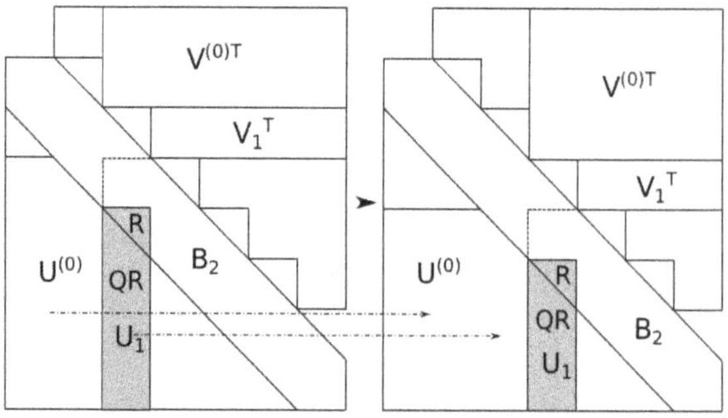

Figure 1: A depiction of matrices used in Algorithm 4.1 for two subsequent recursive steps.

These disadvantages motivated approaches where the matrix is not reduced directly to tridiagonal form, but rather to banded form, which allows for $b > 1$ Householder vectors to be computed via QR at each step without needing to touch the trailing matrix from within the QR. After such a reduction to banded form, it is then necessary to reduce the banded matrix to tridiagonal form. However, this can be significantly less expensive because the trailing matrix is banded and requires less work and vertical communication to update than during the full-to-banded reduction step.

Such a multi-stage reduction approach was introduced by [10, 11] with the aim of achieving BLAS 3 reuse. These algorithms can reduce the banded matrix to tridiagonal or perform more stages of reduction, employing multiple intermediate band-widths. Performing more stages of successive band reduction can improve the synchronization cost of the overall approach, from $O(n)$ as needed if reducing to tridiagonal form directly, to $O(\sqrt{p})$ as shown by [8]. ELPA [5] is a distributed-memory library implementing a two-step reduction approach, motivated by reducing vertical communication cost. ELPA employs the parallel banded-to-tridiagonal algorithm introduced by [30]. Performance studies by [5] have demonstrated that this approach is particularly beneficial for large matrices.

We first introduce an algorithm for reducing a full dense matrix to banded form, with up to $O(p^{1/6})$ less horizontal communication than previously known schemes. We subsequently introduce an algorithm for reducing a banded matrix to a smaller band-width, again with less communication than known approaches. Both of these reduction algorithms use a parallel routine 'QR', which performs QR factorization and outputs the Householder representation (U, T) of the Q factor. We then give a combined, 2.5D symmetric eigensolver algorithm, that uses the first algorithm to reduce the dense symmetric matrix to band-width $\frac{n}{\max(p^{2-3\delta}, \log p)}$, then uses $O(\log p)$ calls to our band-to-band reduction, to arrive at a band-width of n/p, which is small enough to allow for efficient sequential computation of eigenvalues. The resulting symmetric eigensolver has the same BSP complexity as QR factorization (Lemma 3.5), modulo logarithmic factors in the number of processors for the vertical communication and synchronization costs.

Algorithm 4.1 $[B] \leftarrow$ 2.5D-Full-to-Band$(A, U^{(0)}, V^{(0)}, \Pi, b)$

Require: Given nonnegative integers p, n, m, b and $\delta \in [1/2, 2/3]$, $z = (bp^\delta/n)^{(1-\delta)/\delta}$: Π is a grid of $q \times q \times c$ processors where $q = p^{1-\delta}$ and $c = p^{2\delta-1}$ and $b \bmod q = 1$, A is an n-by-n symmetric matrix, $U^{(0)}$ and $V^{(0)}$ are n-by-m matrices where $U^{(0)}$ is trapezoidal (zero in top right upper b-by-b triangle) and $V^{(0)}$ is dense, A (stored as a nonsymmetric matrix), $U^{(0)}$, and $V^{(0)}$ are distributed cyclically over $\Pi[:,:,k]$ for each $k \in [1, c]$.

1: **if** $n \leq b$ **then**

2: Compute $B = A + U^{(0)}V^{(0)T} + V^{(0)}U^{(0)T}$ and exit.

3: Subdivide $A = \begin{bmatrix} A_{11} & A_{21}^T \\ A_{21} & A_{22} \end{bmatrix}$ where A_{11} is b-by-b

4: Subdivide $U^{(0)} = \begin{bmatrix} U_1^{(0)} \\ U_2^{(0)} \end{bmatrix}$ and $V^{(0)} = \begin{bmatrix} V_1^{(0)} \\ V_2^{(0)} \end{bmatrix}$ where $U_1^{(0)}$ and $V_1^{(0)}$ are b-by-m

5: Compute $\begin{bmatrix} \bar{A}_{11} \\ \bar{A}_{21} \end{bmatrix} = \begin{bmatrix} A_{11} \\ A_{21} \end{bmatrix} + U^{(0)}V_1^{(0)T} + V^{(0)}U_1^{(0)T}$

6: *% Compute QR of matrix panel*

7: $[U_1, T, R] \leftarrow \text{QR}(\bar{A}_{21}, \Pi[:, 1:z, :])$

8: Compute $W = A_{22}U_1 + U_2^{(0)}(V_2^{(0)T}U_1) + V_2^{(0)}(U_2^{(0)T}U_1)$

9: Compute $V_1 = \frac{1}{2}U_1(T^T(U^T(WT))) - WT$

10: Replicate U_1 and V_1 so that they are distributed cyclically over $\Pi[:,:,k]$ for each $k \in [1, c]$

11: *% Recursively reduce the trailing matrix to banded form*

12: $B_2 = $ 2.5D-Full-to-Band$(A_{22}, [U_2^{(0)}, U_1], [V_2^{(0)}, V_1], \Pi, b)$

13: $B = \left[\begin{array}{c|c} \bar{A}_{11} & R^T \quad 0 \\ \hline R & \\ 0 & B_2 \end{array}\right]$

Ensure: B is a symmetric n-by-n matrix with band-width b and the same eigenvalues as $A + U^{(0)}V^{(0)T} + V^{(0)}U^{(0)T}$.

4.1 Full-to-Band Reduction

Algorithm 4.1 reduces a symmetric n-by-n matrix A to band-width b using replication of data and aggregation. It achieves a horizontal communication cost of $W = O(n^2/p^\delta)$, when the amount of available memory on each processor is $M = O(n^2/p^{2(1-\delta)})$. The algorithm is left looking, meaning it updates the next matrix panel (line 5) immediately prior to performing the QR of the panel. Figure 1 displays the key matrices employed in Algorithm 4.1, specifically the third and fourth steps of recursion.

The algorithm replicates the matrix A and aggregates as well as replicates the updates $U^{(0)}$ and $V^{(0)}$ (these update matrices should have $m = 0$ columns for the initial invocation of Algorithm 4.1) over $c = p^{2\delta-1}$ layers of $q^2 = p^{2(1-\delta)}$ processors. In the definition of the algorithm and the analysis we assume that c and q are integers for any given p. Each of these replicated matrices is stored in a 2D cyclic distribution on each processor grid layer, adhering to the layout assumptions of Algorithm 3.1. A cyclic layout yields local blocks which can be used within sequential routines the same way as done in a blocked layout. The assumption $b \bmod q = 1$ ensures that whenever each new panel of U and V is replicated (U_1 and V_1 on line 10), they can be concatenated to previously replicated panels while maintaining a perfectly load balanced cyclic distribution.

Algorithm 4.1 performs the update correctly since, first, the computation of $W = \bar{A}U$ where $\bar{A} = Q^TAQ$ (line 8) follows the identity Eqn. (4.2). Further, as computed on line 9, V takes the desired form,

$$V = \left(\frac{1}{2}UT^TU^T - I\right)WT = \frac{1}{2}UT^TU^T\bar{A}UT - \bar{A}UT,$$

the same one as the aggregated update matrix derived in Eqn. (4.1). Consequently, the eigenvalues of the original matrix are preserved in the resulting banded matrix due to the ensured condition on the result of the tail recursion, which performs the update and factorization of the trailing matrix. In the base case, the matrix dimension is less than or equal to the desired matrix band-width, which means it suffices to perform the aggregated update and return the result, which would appear in the lower right block of the full banded matrix. We now analyze the execution time of Algorithm 4.1.

Lemma 4.1. *Algorithm 4.1 can reduce any symmetric n-by-n matrix (input in any evenly-distributed layout and with $n \geq p$) to a banded matrix with the same eigenvalues and any band-width $n/p^\delta \leq b \leq n/\log p$, using $M = O(n^2/p^{2(1-\delta)})$ memory for any $\delta \in [1/2, 2/3]$, when $H > 3n^2/p^{2(1-\delta)}$, in BSP time,*

$$O\left(\gamma \cdot \frac{n^3}{p} + \beta \cdot \frac{n^2}{p^\delta} + \alpha \cdot p^\delta \log^2 p\right).$$

If $H \leq 3n^2/p^{2(1-\delta)}$, then there is an additional vertical communication cost of $O(\nu \cdot (n/b)n^2/p^{2(1-\delta)})$.

Proof. Since $b \geq n/p^\delta$, we assume without loss of generality that $b \bmod p^{1-\delta} = 0$. We also note that since $b \geq n/p^\delta$, $z = (bp^\delta/n)^{(1-\delta)/\delta} \geq 1$. We note that the dimensions of A, $U^{(0)}$, and $V^{(0)}$ at any recursive step will always be less than the dimension of the original matrix, n. Algorithm 4.1 assumes A, $U^{(0)}$, and $V^{(0)}$ are initially replicated. Since each $b \times b$ block of these matrices is distributed cyclically and since $b \bmod q = 0$ ($q = p^{1-\delta}$), the submatrix extraction and concatenation done between recursive steps, can preserve perfect load balance without communication. To satisfy initial assumptions of the first invocation of Algorithm 4.1, we need to replicate the A matrix. Since, by assumption, it is distributed over all processors initially, the replication can be done with $O(n^2/q^2) = O(n^2/p^{2(1-\delta)})$ horizontal communication cost.

At each recursive step, Algorithm 4.1 performs a QR factorization, several matrix multiplications, and replicates U_1 and V_1. Each $O(n) \times b$ QR factorization is done using a processor subgrid of dimensions $p^{1-\delta} \times z \times p^{2\delta-1}$ with a total of $zp^\delta = p(b/n)^{(1-\delta)/\delta}$ processors (picked to minimize both communication and synchronization) using Algorithm 3.2. By Theorem 3.6 and the fact that $z \geq 1$, it takes BSP time,

$$O\left(\gamma \cdot \frac{n^{1/\delta}b^{3-1/\delta}}{p} + \beta \cdot \frac{nb}{p^\delta} + \alpha \cdot \frac{b}{n}p^\delta \log^2 p\right),$$

using $M = O\left(\left(\frac{b^\delta n^{1-\delta}}{(zp^\delta)^{1-\delta}}\right)^2\right) = O\left(\left(\frac{n(b/n)^{(2\delta-1)/\delta}}{p^{1-\delta}}\right)^2\right)$ memory.

The two matrix multiplications on line 5 and the five matrix multiplications on line 8 (done right to left), all correspond to an $O(n) \times O(n)$ replicated matrix multiplied by an $O(n) \times b$ rectangular matrix. By Lemma 3.3, with $w = \max(1, bp^{2-3\delta}/n)$, using $M = O(n^2/p^{2(1-\delta)} + nb/(wp^{\delta})) = O(n^2/p^{2(1-\delta)})$ memory, the time to compute these matrix multiplications is, if $U^{(0)}$ and $V^{(0)}$ start in cache,

$$O\left(\gamma \cdot \frac{n^2 b}{p} + \beta \cdot \frac{nb}{p^{\delta}} + \alpha \cdot w\right).$$

In general (for any cache size), there is an additional cost of $O(\nu \cdot \frac{(n/b)n^2}{p^{2(1-\delta)}})$. The memory usage needed for these matrix multiplications is greater than that needed for the QR factorizations done by each set of processors. Since $n^{1/\delta}b^{3-1/\delta} < n^2 b$ the computation cost of these matrix multiplications also dominates that of the QR factorizations.

The matrix multiplications needed to compute line 9 from right to left either operate on an $O(n) \times b$ matrix and a $b \times b$ matrix, like $W \cdot T$, or result in a $b \times b$ matrix, like $U^T \cdot (WT)$. By Lemma 3.2 any matrix multiplication where two of the matrix dimensions are b and one is $O(n)$, with $v = p^{2-3\delta}$, takes BSP time,

$$O\left(\gamma \cdot \frac{nb^2}{p} + \beta \cdot \left[\frac{nb}{p} + \frac{n^{2/3}b^{4/3}}{p^{\delta}}\right] + \alpha \cdot p^{2-3\delta} \log p\right).$$

Since $b \leq n/\log p$, the above communication cost is never greater than that of the larger matrix multiplications, i.e. $n^{2/3}b^{4/3}/p^{\delta} \leq nb/p^{\delta}$. The synchronization cost of the QR factorizations dominates that of of the matrix multiplications.

Replicating U_1 and V_1 over c subsets of q^2 processors (line 10) can be done in time, $O\left(\beta \cdot nb/p^{2(1-\delta)} + \alpha\right)$.

Therefore, the cost over all $n/b - 1$ recursive steps when all replicated matrices fit into cache (when $H > 3n^2/p^{2(1-\delta)}$) is the total cost postulated in the theorem. In the second scenario (when $H < 3n^2/p^{2(1-\delta)}$), the algorithm incurs an extra additive factor of $O\left((n/b)\frac{wn^2}{p^{2(1-\delta)}}\right)$ in vertical communication cost. The memory usage is dominated by the replicated matrix multiplication (invocation of Lemma 3.3 above), which is also as stated in the theorem. □

4.2 Band-to-Band Reduction

We now consider algorithms for reducing a banded matrix to a smaller band-width, while preserving eigenvalues. We start by recalling a parallel algorithm designed for small band-widths [8], then present Algorithm 4.2, which is designed to exploit additional parallelism given larger starting band-widths. Algorithm 4.2 describes the QR factorizations and applications necessary to reduce a symmetric banded matrix A from band-width b to band-width $h = b/k$ via bulge chasing. The algorithm eliminates n/h trapezoidal panels via QR factorization, each of which generate bulges of nonzeros in the trailing matrix. Each bulge is subsequently chased down the band by $O(n/b)$ eliminations again done by QR factorizations. Every new panel elimination is done immediately after the previously generated bulge is chased twice (including its initial panel elimination). Figure 2 depicts the QR factorizations necessary to eliminate a trapezoidal panel and chase two bulges generated from eliminating the first two panels, which are done concurrently in the algorithm. This type of pipelined successive band reduction approach was first considered by [10, 11]. The CA-SBR algorithm in [8] is similar, but assigns each processor a set of bulge chases at

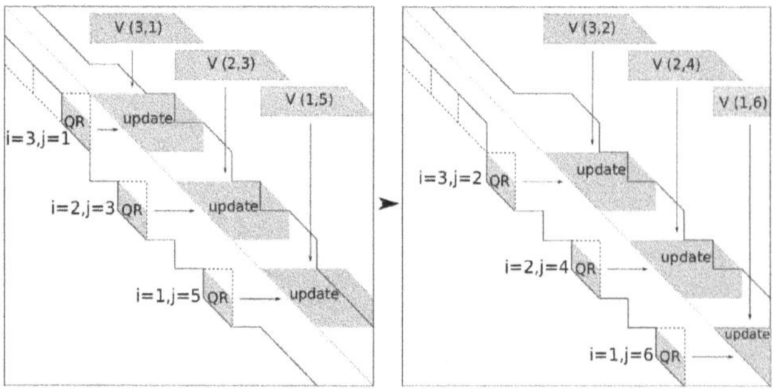

Figure 2: QR factorizations and updates in iterations $(i,j) \in \{(3,1),(2,3),(1,5)\}$ (left) and $(i,j) \in \{(3,2),(2,4),(1,6)\}$ (right) of Algorithm 4.1 with $k = 2$. These two sets of iterations are executed concurrently by processor groups $\hat{\Pi}_1$, $\hat{\Pi}_3$, and $\hat{\Pi}_5$ (left) and $\hat{\Pi}_2$, $\hat{\Pi}_4$, and $\hat{\Pi}_6$ (right), respectively. Only the unique part of the trailing matrix update is shown, while the pseudocode performs both symmetric reflections of it. Each matrix V is labeled with the iteration in which it is computed.

each pipeline step, rather than performing each bulge chase with a set of processors as done in Algorithm 4.2.

Lemma 4.2. *An $n \times n$ symmetric matrix (input in any load-balanced layout) of band-width $b \leq n/p$ can be reduced to one with the same eigenvalues and band-width $b/2$, using $M = O(nb/p)$ memory, in BSP time,*

$$O\left(\gamma \cdot \frac{n^2 b}{p} + \beta \cdot nb + \nu \cdot \frac{n^2}{p} + \alpha \cdot p\right).$$

Proof. We consider the cost of one step of the CA-SBR algorithm [8]. A redistribution from any initial layout costs $O(\beta \cdot nb + \alpha)$. The analysis in [8] shows that the cost of reducing from bandwidth b to $b/2$ has the computation, horizontal communication, and synchronization costs, as well as the memory usage postulated in the lemma. The algorithm consits of a bulge chase pipeline, executed in $O(p)$ parallel steps, in which each processor works on $O(n/p)$ columns, chasing $O(n/(pb))$ bulges $O(n/(pb))$ times, for a total of $O(n^2/(p^2b^2))$ bulge chases. Since each bulge chase consists of a QR factorization and a matrix multiplication, with matrices of size $O(b) \times O(b)$, by Lemma 3.1 and Lemma 3.4, the vertical communication cost is $O(\nu \cdot b^2)$ for each bulge chase. Summing the costs of the bulge chases over all parallel steps yields the postulated total cost. □

We now consider the cost of Algorithm 4.2. Its primary innovation is to perform each QR factorization and update in parallel using a subset of processors, leveraging both pipelined parallelism across different bulge chases as well as parallelism within a bulge chase. When the band-width becomes smaller, fewer processors are used to execute each bulge chase.

Lemma 4.3. *Algorithm 4.2 can reduce an $n \times n$ symmetric matrix (input in any evenly-distributed layout) of band-width $b \geq n/p$ to one with the same eigenvalues and band-width b/k, using $M = O((n^{1-\delta}b^{\delta}/p^{1-\delta})^2)$ memory for any $\delta \in [1/2, 2/3]$ and any*

Algorithm 4.2 $[B] \leftarrow$ 2.5D-Band-to-Band(A, Π, b, k)

Require: Given positive integers b, p, n, k and $h = b/k$ with $n \bmod b \equiv 0$ and $b \bmod k \equiv 0$: A is a banded symmetric matrix of dimension n with band-width $b \leq n$, $\hat{\Pi}_j \subset \Pi$ is the jth group of $\hat{p} \equiv pb/n$ processors for $j \in [1, n/b]$.

1: Set $B = A$
2: Let $B[(j-1)b+1 : jb\, , (j-1)b+1 : jb]$ be replicated in $\hat{\Pi}_j$ over $(bp/n)^{2\delta-1}$ subsets of $(bp/n)^{2(1-\delta)}$ processors.
3: *% Iterate over panels of B*
4: **for** $i \in [1, n/h - 1]$ **do**
5: *% $\hat{\Pi}_j$ applies chase j of bulge i as soon as $\hat{\Pi}_{j-1}$ executes chase $(j-1)$*
6: **for** $j = 1 : \lfloor (n - ih - 1)/b \rfloor$ **do**
7: *% Define row and column offsets*
8: Let $o_{\rm blg} = (i-1)h + (j-1)b$, $o_{\rm qr.r} = o_{\rm blg} + h$
9: **if** $j = 1$ **then** $o_{\rm qr.c} = o_{\rm qr.r} - h$, $o_{\rm v} = 0$
10: **else** $o_{\rm qr.c} = o_{\rm qr.r} - b$, $o_{\rm v} = b - h$, $o_{\rm up.c} = o_{\rm qr.c} + h$
11: *% Define index ranges needed for bulge chase*
12: $n_{\rm r} = \min(n - o_{\rm qr.r}, b)$, $n_{\rm c} = \min(n - o_{\rm up.c}, h + 3b)$
13: $I_{\rm qr.rs} = o_{\rm qr.r} + (1 : n_{\rm r})$, $I_{\rm qr.cs} = o_{\rm qr.c} + (1 : h)$
14: $I_{\rm v.rs} = o_{\rm v} + (1 : n_{\rm r})$, $I_{\rm up.cs} = o_{\rm up.c} + (1 : n_{\rm c})$
15: *% Perform a rectangular parallel QR factorization*
16: $[U, T, R] \leftarrow \mathrm{QR}(B[I_{\rm qr.rs}, I_{\rm qr.cs}], \hat{\Pi}_j[1 : ph/n])$
17: $B[I_{\rm qr.rs}, I_{\rm qr.cs}] = \begin{bmatrix} R \\ 0 \end{bmatrix}$, $B[I_{\rm qr.cs}, I_{\rm qr.rs}] = \begin{bmatrix} R \\ 0 \end{bmatrix}^T$
18: *% Perform trailing matrix updates*
19: $W = B[I_{\rm up.cs}, I_{\rm qr.rs}]UT$, $V = -W$
20: $V[I_{\rm v.rs}, :] = V[I_{\rm v.rs}, :] + \frac{1}{2}U(T^T(U^T W[I_{\rm v.rs}, :]))$
21: $B[I_{\rm qr.rs}, I_{\rm up.cs}] = B[I_{\rm qr.rs}, I_{\rm up.cs}] + UV^T$
22: $B[I_{\rm up.cs}, I_{\rm qr.rs}] = B[I_{\rm up.cs}, I_{\rm qr.rs}] + VU^T$

Ensure: B is a banded matrix with band-width h and the same eigenvalues as A

$k \leq 1 + p^{2-3\delta}$, *in BSP time,*

$$O\left(\gamma \cdot \frac{n^2 b}{p} + \beta \cdot \frac{n^{1+\delta} b^{1-\delta}}{p^\delta} + \alpha \cdot \frac{k^\delta n^{1-\delta} p^\delta}{b^{1-\delta}} \log p\right).$$

Proof. The cost of each inner loop iteration (loop on line 6) can be derived from the costs of the matrix multiplications and QR done inside it. Let the pair (i, j) correspond to the the ith iteration of the outer loop and jth iteration of the inner loop. Figure 2 displays the QR factorizations and updates computed during a few such iterations. Each iteration computes a QR factorization of a matrix with dimensions at most $(b-h) \times h$, $B[I_{\rm qr.rs}, I_{\rm qr.cs}]$ on line 16 with $\bar{p} = pb/(nk^{(1-\delta)/\delta})$ processors. The BSP time to compute such a QR factorization is by Theorem 3.6 for $\delta \in [1/2, 2/3]$,

$$O\left(\gamma \cdot \frac{bh^2}{\bar{p}} + \beta \cdot \frac{b^\delta h^{2-\delta}}{\bar{p}^\delta} + \alpha \cdot \bar{p}^\delta \log(\bar{p})\right)$$
$$= O\left(\gamma \cdot \frac{nb^2}{k^{3-1/\delta} p} + \beta \cdot \frac{n^\delta b^{2-\delta}}{kp^\delta} + \alpha \cdot k^{\delta-1}(pb/n)^\delta \log p\right)$$

The amount of memory needed for this QR factorization is given in Lemma 3.6 as

$$M = O\big((h^\delta b^{1-\delta}/\bar{p}^{1-\delta})^2\big) = O((n^{1-\delta} b^\delta/(p^{1-\delta} k^{(2\delta-1)/\delta}))^2).$$

The matrix multiplications to form the V matrix are on lines 19 and 20, while those to perform the updates are on lines 21 and 22. The matrix multiplications on line 20 should be done from right to left. We can then observe that the most costly matrix multiplications in Algorithm 4.2 are $B[I_{\rm up.cs}, I_{\rm qr.rs}]U$ on line 19 and the updates UV^T and VU^T on lines 21 and 22. In the first case, a $(3b-h)\times(b-h)$ is multiplied by a $(b-h) \times h$ matrix, while the update UV^T involve $(3b-h) \times h$ matrix multiplied by an $h \times (b-h)$ matrix (VU^T is just the transpose of the former). In both cases, by Lemma 3.2 with $v = \hat{p}^{2-3\delta}/(k-1)$ (we subtract one from k to make sure $v \geq 1$), the BSP time to compute the matrix multiplications using $\hat{p}$ processors is

$$O\left(\gamma \cdot \frac{b^2 h}{\hat{p}} + \beta \cdot \frac{b^2}{k\hat{p}^\delta} + \alpha \cdot \frac{\hat{p}^{2-3\delta}}{k} \log p\right)$$
$$= O\left(\gamma \cdot \frac{nb^2}{kp} + \beta \cdot \frac{n^\delta b^{2-\delta}}{kp^\delta} + \alpha \cdot \frac{(pb/n)^{2-3\delta}}{k} \log p\right),$$

with a memory footprint of $M = O(b^2/\hat{p} + (b^2 h/(v\hat{p}))^{2/3}) = O((b/\hat{p}^{1-\delta})^2) = O((n^{1-\delta} b^\delta/p^{1-\delta})^2)$, which is greater than the memory needed to perform the QR factorizations. The other matrix multiplications have strictly lower cost and the cost of redistributions necessary for all of these matrix multiplications is included in the horizontal communication cost of Lemma 3.2. As A and B are stored in load balanced layouts, each processor subset can obtain the submatrix which it factorizes and the submatrix which it updates at every iteration with $O(b^2/\hat{p})$ horizontal communication.

Thus, the overall cost for each iteration of Algorithm 4.2 is the sum of the two different costs above,

$$O\left(\gamma \cdot \frac{nb^2}{kp} + \beta \cdot \frac{n^\delta b^{2-\delta}}{kp} + \alpha \cdot k^{\delta-1}(pb/n)^\delta \log p\right).$$

For a given outer loop (line 4) iteration i, each j loop iteration (line 6) is done by a different processor group. The total number of inner loop iterations is roughly $(n/h)(n/b)/2$ and they are pipelined among n/b groups of processors, up to $n/(2b)$ of them working concurrently on different bulge chases at any given time. Consequently, the algorithm can be executed in $O(n/h)$ phases, where at the ith phase, $\min(i-1, (n-ih)/(2b))$ processor groups chase bulges concurrently and the ith panel is eliminated. At each phase, a synchronization and data exchange is required between the QR factorization and trailing matrix updates computed by adjacent active processor groups. Therefore, the BSP cost of each recursive step of the algorithm corresponds to the cost of computing $O(n/h) = O(kn/b)$ inner loop iterations using one processor group, which corresponds to the cost postulated in the lemma. □

4.3 Complete Symmetric Eigensolver

Algorithm 4.3 combines our algorithms for full-to-band reduction (Algorithm 4.1) with multiple subsequent stages of band-to-band reduction (Algorithm 4.2) and band-halving steps of the CA-SBR algorithm from [8], which we refer to as CA-BR. Algorithm 4.1 reduces the symmetric matrix to one with band-width at most

Algorithm 4.3 $[D] \leftarrow$ 2.5D-Symmetric-Eigensolver(A, Π)

Require: Given positive integers p, n, and $\delta \in [1/2, 2/3]$ with $n \bmod b \equiv 0$, A is a symmetric matrix of dimension n.

Let $b = \frac{n}{\max(p^{2-3\delta}, \log p)}$, $k = 2$, and $\zeta = (1-\delta)/\delta$
Execute B = 2.5D-Full-to-Band$(A, \{\}, \{\}, \Pi, b)$
for $i = 0 : \log_2(bp^\delta/n) - 1$ **do**
  Let $\bar{\Pi} = \Pi[1 : p/k^{i\zeta}]$
  Gather B onto $\bar{\Pi}$
  Execute B = 2.5D-Band-to-Band$(B, b/k^i, \bar{\Pi}, k)$
Let $\bar{\Pi} = \Pi[1 : p^\delta]$
for $i = 0 : \log_2(p^{1-\delta}) - 1$ **do**
  Execute B = CA-BR$(B, n/(p^\delta k^i), \bar{\Pi}, k)$
Gather B onto a processor and compute its eigenvalues D

Ensure: D is a vector containing the eigenvalues of A

$n/\log p$. Algorithm 4.2 is then used to successively half the band-width to n/p^δ. Subsequently, the CA-BR algorithm (same function signature as 2.5D-Band-to-Band) is used to reduce the band-width to n/p. At that point, the matrix is small enough for one processor to compute the eigenvalues efficiently.

For every 2.5D-Band-to-Band step that reduces the band-width by a factor of k, Algorithm 4.2 reduces the number of processors used by k^ζ where $\zeta = (1-\delta)/\delta$. The parameter ζ is chosen to be $(1-\delta)/\delta$ so that the per-stage horizontal cost term $O(nb/p^\delta)$ does not increase at each recursive step, since $n(b/k)/(p/k^\zeta)^\delta = nb/p^\delta$. Decreasing the number of active processors in this way also keeps the synchronization cost equal at every stage. Overall, we now obtain a parallel algorithm that has horizontal communication of $O(n^2/p^\delta)$, vertical communication of $O(n^2 \log p/p^\delta)$, and $O(p^\delta \log^2 p)$ synchronizations. Modulo logarithmic cost factors in vertical communication and synchronization, this amounts to the same communication cost as the best known algorithms for LU and QR factorization [3, 35, 38].

Theorem 4.4. *Algorithm 4.3 computes the eigenvalues of a symmetric n-by-n matrix (input in any evenly-distributed layout), using* $M = O(n^2/p^{2(1-\delta)})$ *memory for any* $\delta \in [1/2, 2/3]$*, in BSP time,*

$$O\left(\gamma \cdot \frac{n^3}{p} + \beta \cdot \frac{n^2}{p^\delta} + \nu \cdot \frac{n^2 \log p}{p^\delta} + \alpha \cdot p^\delta \log^2 p\right).$$

Proof. The cost of the gather/redistribution of B onto $\bar{\Pi}$ is dominated by the subsequent 2.5D-Band-to-Band invocation. The cost of computing the eigenvalues of B sequentially at the end is $O(\gamma \cdot n^3/p + \beta \cdot n^2/p + \alpha)$, since the band-width is n/p [8]. We employ Lemma 4.1 with $b = \frac{n}{\max(p^{2-3\delta}, \log p)}$ to obtain the cost of 2.5D-Full-to-Band. The computation, horizontal communication, and synchronization costs are the same for 2.5D-Full-to-Band as the ones postulated in Theorem 4.4. The vertical communication cost term incurred for small cache sizes, $O(\nu \cdot (n/b)n^2/p^{2(1-\delta)})$ is bounded by $O(\nu \cdot [n^2/p^\delta + n^2 \log p/p^{2/3}]) = O(\nu \cdot n^2 \log p/p^\delta)$.

We now consider the memory footprint and cost of the invocations of 2.5D-Band-to-Band. By Lemma 4.3 with $k = 2$, the memory usage is $M = O((n^{1-\delta}\bar{b}^\delta/\bar{p}^{1-\delta})^2)$, where $\bar{b} = b/k^i$ where $\bar{p} = p/k^{i\zeta}$ at iteration i. We observe that $(n^{1-\delta}\bar{b}^\delta/\bar{p}^{1-\delta})^2 = O(n^2/p^{2(1-\delta)})$ for all iterations i, because at each subsequent iteration $\bar{b}$ decreases by k while $\bar{p}$ decreases by k^ζ, and so $\bar{b}^\delta/\bar{p}^{1-\delta} \leq b^\delta/p^{1-\delta} \leq n^\delta/p^{1-\delta}$ for all i, since $k^{(1-\delta)\zeta}/k^\delta = k^{(1-\delta)^2/\delta}/k^\delta \leq k^{1-\delta}/k^\delta \leq 1$. The cost of each band reduction with starting band-width $\bar{b}$ and $\bar{p}$ processors is by Lemma 4.3 with $k = 2$,

$$O\left(\gamma \cdot \frac{n^2\bar{b}}{\bar{p}} + \beta \cdot \frac{n^{1+\delta}\bar{b}^{1-\delta}}{\bar{p}^\delta} + \alpha \cdot \frac{n^{1-\delta}\bar{p}^\delta}{\bar{b}^{1-\delta}} \log p\right).$$

The computation cost clearly decreases with each iteration i. The horizontal communication cost is $O(nb/p^\delta) = O(n^2/(p^\delta \log p))$ (since $b \leq n/\log p$) at each iteration, since

$$\frac{\bar{b}^{1-\delta}}{\bar{p}^\delta} = \frac{(b/k^i)^{1-\delta}}{(p/k^{i\zeta})^\delta} = \frac{b^{1-\delta}}{p^\delta}.$$

Therefore, over all $O(\log p)$ iterations, the bandwidth cost of the SBR invocations is $O(n^2/p^\delta)$. Finally, the synchronization cost is $\frac{n^{1-\delta}\bar{p}^\delta}{\bar{b}^{1-\delta}} \log p = O(p^\delta \log p)$ at each iteration, since $\bar{p}^\delta/\bar{b}^{1-\delta} = p^\delta/b^{1-\delta}$. Thus, the overall synchronization cost is as postulated.

The time for CA-BR using p^δ processors starting from band-width n/p^δ and reducing it to n/p is via Lemma 4.2, $O(\gamma \cdot \frac{n^3}{p^{2\delta}} + \beta \cdot \frac{n^2}{p^\delta} + \nu \cdot \frac{n^2 \log p}{p^\delta} + \alpha \cdot p^\delta \log p)$. Computing the eigenvalues of a matrix with band-width n/p sequentially costs $O(\gamma \cdot \frac{n^3}{p})$ [8]. □

Algorithm	W (β)	Q (ν)	S (α)
ScaLAPACK [12]	$n^2/\sqrt{p}$	n^3/p	$n \log p$
ELPA [4]	$n^2/\sqrt{p}$	-	$n \log p$
CA-SBR [8]	$n^2/\sqrt{p}$	$n^2 \log n/\sqrt{p}$	$\sqrt{p}(\log^2 p + \log n)$
Theorem 4.4	n^2/p^δ	$n^2 \log p/p^\delta$	$p^\delta \log^2 p$

Table 1: Asymptotic costs for computing eigenvalues, with $\delta \in [1/2, 2/3]$. All variants have $O(n^3/p)$ computation cost.

A disadvantage of this multi-stage approach arises when eigenvectors are required in addition to eigenvalues. The cost of the back-transformations scales linearly with the number of band-reduction stages (each stage requires $O(n^2)$ memory and $O(n^3)$ computation). We leave the consideration of eigenvector construction for future work. To reduce the number of band-reduction stages when $\delta < 2/3$, one can use $k = p^{2-3\delta}$ with each invocation of 2.5D-Band-to-Band, but this results in a greater synchronization cost. It may also be possible to improve the 2.5D-Band-to-Band algorithm by using aggregation as in the 2.5D-Full-to-Band algorithm.

5 CONCLUSION

Table 1 provides a comparison of communication and synchronization costs to previous work. Our new direct method for computing the eigenvalues of a symmetric matrix, performs up to $p^{1/6}$ less horizontal communication than alternatives. The vertical communication cost (Q) for ScaLAPACK assumes $H < n^2/p$ and arises from the matrix-vector multiplications computing V for each column. For CA-SBR, Q is inferred from Lemma 4.2. For ELPA, we assume the full-to-band step reduces to band-width $b = \sqrt{H}$, in which case either (when $\sqrt{H} > n/p$) the banded matrix fits in cache, or $\nu \cdot Q = O(\nu \cdot [n^3/(pb) + nb^2]) = O(\gamma \cdot F/\sqrt{H})$ [4].

The new 2.5D-Symmetric-Eigensolver algorithm trades off a variable amount of extra work, synchronization, and memory usage for a lower communication cost. Implementations of the algorithms in this paper permit optimizations such as

- alternating between left-looking partial updates and complete trailing matrix updates in Algorithm 4.1,
- smaller bulge width in Algorithm 4.2 to increase parallelism in the bulge chase pipeline,
- lookahead [2, 36] (overlapping QR with updates).

Our analysis shows that a carefully parameterized collage of parallel algorithms and optimizations yields asymptotic cost improvements with minimal overhead. We combine approaches (2.5D algorithms, aggregation, successive band reduction) that have been successful on modern architectures [5, 6, 33], so our innovations should pave the path for practical improvements in scalability of applications computing singular values or eigenvalues of matrices.

REFERENCES

[1] R. C. Agarwal, S. M. Balle, F. G. Gustavson, M. Joshi, and P. Palkar. 1995. A three-dimensional approach to parallel matrix multiplication. *IBM Journal of Research and Development* 39 (September 1995), 575–582. Issue 5.
[2] Ramesh C Agarwal and Fred G Gustavson. 1988. A parallel implementation of matrix multiplication and LU factorization on the IBM 3090. In *Proceedings of the IFIP WG*, Vol. 2. 217–221.
[3] Alok Aggarwal, Ashok K. Chandra, and Marc Snir. 1990. Communication complexity of PRAMs. *Theoretical Computer Science* 71, 1 (1990), 3 – 28.
[4] Thomas Auckenthaler. 2012. *Highly scalable eigensolvers for petaflop applications.* Ph.D. Dissertation. Universität München.
[5] T. Auckenthaler, H.-J. Bungartz, T. Huckle, L. Krämer, B. Lang, and P. Willems. 2011. Developing algorithms and software for the parallel solution of the symmetric eigenvalue problem. *Journal of Computational Science* 2, 3 (2011), 272 – 278. https://doi.org/10.1016/j.jocs.2011.05.002 Social Computational Systems.
[6] G. Ballard, J. Demmel, L. Grigori, M. Jacquelin, H. D. Nguyen, and E. Solomonik. 2014. Reconstructing Householder Vectors from Tall-Skinny QR. In *Proceedings of the 28th IEEE International Symposium on Parallel and Distributed Processing (IPDPS '14).* 1159–1170. https://doi.org/10.1109/IPDPS.2014.120
[7] Grey Ballard, James Demmel, Olga Holtz, and Oded Schwartz. 2011. Minimizing Communication in Numerical Linear Algebra. *SIAM J. Matrix Anal. Appl.* 32, 3 (2011), 866–901. https://doi.org/10.1137/090769156
[8] Grey Ballard, James Demmel, and Nicholas Knight. 2015. Avoiding Communication in Successive Band Reduction. *ACM Transactions on Parallel Computing* 1, 2, Article 11 (Feb. 2015), 37 pages. https://doi.org/10.1145/2686877
[9] Jarle Berntsen. 1989. Communication efficient matrix multiplication on hypercubes. *Parallel Comput.* 12, 3 (1989), 335–342.
[10] C. Bischof, B. Lang, and X. Sun. 2000. Algorithm 807: The SBR Toolbox – Software Successive Band Reduction. *ACM Trans. Math. Software* 26, 4 (Dec 2000), 602–616.
[11] C. Bischof, B. Lang, and X. Sun. 2000. A Framework for Symmetric Band Reduction. *ACM Trans. Math. Software* 26, 4 (Dec 2000), 581–601.
[12] L. S. Blackford, J. Choi, A. Cleary, E. D'Azevedo, J. Demmel, I. Dhillon, J. Dongarra, S. Hammarling, G. Henry, A. Petitet, K. Stanley, D. Walker, and R. C. Whaley. 1997. *ScaLAPACK Users' Guide.* SIAM, Philadelphia, PA, USA. Also available from http://www.netlib.org/scalapack/.
[13] Rudnei Dias da Cunha, Dulcenéia Becker, and James Carlton Patterson. 2002. New parallel (rank-revealing) QR factorization algorithms. In *Euro-Par 2002 Parallel Processing.* Springer, 677–686.
[14] Eliezer Dekel, David Nassimi, and Sartaj Sahni. 1981. Parallel Matrix and Graph Algorithms. *SIAM J. Comput.* 10, 4 (1981), 657–675.
[15] J. Demmel, D. Eliahu, A. Fox, S. Kamil, B. Lipshitz, O. Schwartz, and O. Spillinger. 2013. Communication-Optimal Parallel Recursive Rectangular Matrix Multiplication. In *Proceedings of the 27th IEEE International Symposium on Parallel and Distributed Processing (IPDPS '13).* 261–272. https://doi.org/10.1109/IPDPS.2013.80
[16] James Demmel, Laura Grigori, Mark Hoemmen, and Julien Langou. 2012. Communication-optimal Parallel and Sequential QR and LU Factorizations. *SIAM Journal on Scientific Computing* 34, 1 (2012), A206–A239. https://doi.org/10.1137/080731992
[17] Inderjit S. Dhillon, Beresford N. Parlett, and Christof Vömel. 2006. The Design and Implementation of the MRRR Algorithm. *ACM Trans. Math. Software* 32, 4 (Dec. 2006), 533–560. https://doi.org/10.1145/1186785.1186788
[18] Jack J Dongarra, Danny C Sorensen, and Sven J Hammarling. 1989. Block reduction of matrices to condensed forms for eigenvalue computations. *J. Comput. Appl. Math.* 27, 1 (1989), 215–227.
[19] Jack J Dongarra and Robert A van de Geijn. 1992. Reduction to condensed form for the Eigenvalue problem on distributed memory architectures. *Parallel Comput.* 18, 9 (1992), 973 – 982. https://doi.org/10.1016/0167-8191(92)90011-U
[20] E. Elmroth and F. Gustavson. 1998. New serial and parallel recursive QR factorization algorithms for SMP systems. In *Applied Parallel Computing. Large Scale Scientific and Industrial Problems.*, B. Kågström et al. (Ed.). Lecture Notes in Computer Science, Vol. 1541. Springer, 120–128.
[21] V. Fock. 1930. Näherungsmethode zur Lösung des quantenmechanischen Mehrkörperproblems. *Zeitschrift für Physik* 61, 1-2 (1930), 126–148. https://doi.org/10.1007/BF01340294
[22] M. Frigo, C. E. Leiserson, H. Prokop, and S. Ramachandran. 1999. Cache-Oblivious Algorithms. In *Proceedings of the 40th Annual Symposium on Foundations of Computer Science (FOCS '99).* IEEE Computer Society, Washington, DC, USA, 285.
[23] Gene H Golub, Robert J Plemmons, and Ahmed Sameh. 1986. *Parallel block schemes for large-scale least-squares computations.* University of Illinois Press. 171–179 pages.
[24] Brian C. Gunter and Robert A. Van De Geijn. 2005. Parallel Out-of-core Computation and Updating of the QR Factorization. *ACM Trans. Math. Software* 31, 1 (March 2005), 60–78. https://doi.org/10.1145/1055531.1055534
[25] Azzam Haidar, Hatem Ltaief, and Jack Dongarra. 2011. Parallel Reduction to Condensed Forms for Symmetric Eigenvalue Problems Using Aggregated Fine-grained and Memory-aware Kernels. In *Proceedings of 2011 International Conference for High Performance Computing, Networking, Storage and Analysis (SC '11).* ACM, New York, NY, USA, Article 8, 11 pages. https://doi.org/10.1145/2063384.2063394
[26] D. R. Hartree. 1928. The Wave Mechanics of an Atom with a Non-Coulomb Central Field. Part I. Theory and Methods. *Mathematical Proceedings of the Cambridge Philosophical Society* 24 (1 1928), 89–110. Issue 01. https://doi.org/10.1017/S0305004100011919
[27] Hong Jia-Wei and H. T. Kung. 1981. I/O complexity: The red-blue pebble game. In *Proceedings of the thirteenth annual ACM symposium on Theory of computing (STOC '81).* ACM, New York, NY, USA, 326–333.
[28] Thierry Joffrain, Tze Meng Low, Enrique S. Quintana-Ortí, Robert van de Geijn, and Field G. Van Zee. 2006. Accumulating Householder Transformations, Revisited. *ACM Trans. Math. Software* 32, 2 (June 2006), 169–179. https://doi.org/10.1145/1141885.1141886
[29] S. Lennart Johnsson. 1993. Minimizing the communication time for matrix multiplication on multiprocessors. *Parallel Comput.* 19 (November 1993), 1235–1257. Issue 11.
[30] B. Lang. 1993. A Parallel Algorithm for Reducing Symmetric Banded Matrices to Tridiagonal Form. *SIAM Journal on Scientific Computing* 14, 6 (1993), 1320–1338. https://doi.org/10.1137/0914078
[31] W. F. McColl and A. Tiskin. 1999. Memory-Efficient Matrix Multiplication in the BSP Model. *Algorithmica* 24 (1999), 287–297. Issue 3.
[32] Edgar Solomonik. 2014. *Provably Efficient Algorithms for Numerical Tensor Algebra.* Ph.D. Dissertation. University of California, Berkeley.
[33] Edgar Solomonik, Abhinav Bhatele, and James Demmel. 2011. Improving Communication Performance in Dense Linear Algebra via Topology Aware Collectives. In *Proceedings of 2011 International Conference for High Performance Computing, Networking, Storage and Analysis (SC '11).* ACM, New York, NY, USA, Article 77, 11 pages. https://doi.org/10.1145/2063384.2063487
[34] Edgar Solomonik, Erin Carson, Nicholas Knight, and James Demmel. 2014. Tradeoffs Between Synchronization, Communication, and Computation in Parallel Linear Algebra Computations. In *Proceedings of the 26th ACM Symposium on Parallelism in Algorithms and Architectures.* ACM, 307–318. https://doi.org/10.1145/2612669.2612671
[35] Edgar Solomonik and James Demmel. 2011. Communication-Optimal Parallel 2.5D Matrix Multiplication and LU Factorization Algorithms. In *Euro-Par 2011 Parallel Processing.* Lecture Notes in Computer Science, Vol. 6853. Springer Berlin Heidelberg, 90–109. https://doi.org/10.1007/978-3-642-23397-5_10
[36] Peter Strazdins. 2001. A comparison of lookahead and algorithmic blocking techniques for parallel matrix factorization. *International Journal Parallel and Distributed Systems and Networks* 4, 1 (2001), 26–35.
[37] A. Tiskin. 2002. Bulk-Synchronous Parallel Gaussian Elimination. *Journal of Mathematical Sciences* 108 (2002), 977–991. Issue 6. https://doi.org/10.1023/A:1013588221172
[38] A. Tiskin. 2007. Communication-efficient parallel generic pairwise elimination. *Future Generation Computer Systems* 23, 2 (2007), 179 – 188.
[39] Leslie G Valiant. 1990. A bridging model for parallel computation. *Commun. ACM* 33, 8 (1990), 103–111.
[40] R. A. Van De Geijn and J. Watts. 1997. SUMMA: Scalable Universal Matrix Multiplication Algorithm. *Concurrency: Practice and Experience* 9, 4 (1997), 255–274.

Sharing is Caring: Multiprocessor Scheduling with a Sharable Resource

Peter Kling
University of Hamburg
Vogt-Kölln-Str. 30
Hamburg, Germany
peter.kling@uni-hamburg.de

Alexander Mäcker
Paderborn University
Heinz Nixdorf Institute
Fürstenallee 11
Paderborn, Germany
alexander.maecker@upb.de

Sören Riechers
Paderborn University
Heinz Nixdorf Institute
Fürstenallee 11
Paderborn, Germany
soeren.riechers@upb.de

Alexander Skopalik
Paderborn University
Heinz Nixdorf Institute
Fürstenallee 11
Paderborn, Germany
alexander.skopalik@upb.de

ABSTRACT

We consider a scheduling problem on m identical processors sharing an arbitrarily divisible resource. In addition to assigning jobs to processors, the scheduler must distribute the resource among the processors (e.g., for three processors in shares of 20%, 15%, and 65%) and adjust this distribution over time. Each job j comes with a size $p_j \in \mathbb{R}$ and a resource requirement $r_j > 0$. Jobs do not benefit when receiving a share larger than r_j of the resource. But providing them with a fraction of the resource requirement causes a linear decrease in the processing efficiency. We seek a (non-preemptive) job and resource assignment minimizing the makespan.

Our main result is an efficient approximation algorithm which achieves an approximation ratio of $2+1/(m-2)$. It can be improved to an (asymptotic) ratio of $1+1/(m-1)$ if all jobs have unit size. Our algorithms also imply new results for a well-known bin packing problem with splittable items and a restricted number of allowed item parts per bin.

Based upon the above solution, we also derive an approximation algorithm with similar guarantees for a setting in which we introduce so-called tasks each containing several jobs and where we are interested in the average completion time of tasks (a task is completed when all its jobs are completed).

CCS CONCEPTS

• **Theory of computation → Scheduling algorithms**;

This work is partially supported by the German Research Foundation (DFG) within the Collaborative Research Center "On-The-Fly Computing" (SFB 901) and the German Academic Exchange Service (DAAD).

SPAA '17, July 24–26, 2017, Washington, DC, USA

ACM ISBN 978-1-4503-4593-4/17/07...$15.00
https://doi.org/10.1145/3087556.3087578

KEYWORDS

multiprocessor scheduling; approximation algorithm; resource constraints; shared resources; bin packing with cardinality constraints and splittable items

1 INTRODUCTION

Multiprocessor scheduling is a classical resource allocation problem. In its simplest version, a computing system consisting of m identical processors has to execute n independent jobs of possibly different workloads. The objective is to find an assignment of jobs to processors that minimizes some quality of service measure like the makespan (latest completion time of any job) or average completion time (average time a job has to wait for its completion). Specific results differ widely depending on additional model parameters: Is preemption (pausing and resuming jobs) allowed? Can jobs be migrated from one to another processor? Is there any additional knowledge about the jobs (like size, priority, or dependencies)? Leung [14] gives a good overview of these and many more.

This work considers the following multiprocessor model: In addition to the processors and (non-preemptive) jobs, there is a *common finite resource* (think of bandwidth or power supply) that is to be shared by the processors. The scheduler controls the resource assignment, which can be adjusted over time. We assume that the resource can be divided arbitrarily between the processors. For example, the scheduler might distribute the total available bandwidth for a few processor cycles in portions of 20%, 35%, and 45% among three available processors and change it later to 10%, 85%, and 5%, depending on how communication intensive the currently processed jobs are.

The dependence of different jobs on the resource might vary a lot. In the bandwidth example, some jobs might be very data-intensive and require a lot of communication while others do not communicate at all. We model this aspect via a job's *resource requirement*. This is a positive value that indicates what portion of the resource is needed to finish one unit of the job's workload. Providing the job with a higher share of the resource does not speed it up (it cannot use the excess bandwidth). But assigning it a significantly smaller share might slow the job down drastically. As a first step towards such a *scalable resource* model in job scheduling, we consider a performance decrease that depends linearly on the resource: for example, if a job of unit size receives $1/k$-th ($k > 1$) of its resource requirement during each time step it is executed, its processing takes $\lceil k \rceil$ steps. Note that this model gives insights on scenarios where resource requirement is the bottleneck of the system, which is often the case in today's big data applications. In contrast, the aspect of processing power is disregarded by assuming that sufficient processing power is available at any time.

The first part of this article studies the above model for the objective of minimizing the makespan. We refer to this problem as ***Shared Resource Job-Scheduling*** (SoS) (see Section 1.1 for the full, formal specification). In the second part, we extend this model to the setting of *composed services*, where the processors have to finish a set of *tasks* and each task consists itself of a set of jobs (each of which has its own resource requirement). A task is finished when all its jobs are finished. We aim at minimizing the average completion time of all tasks. This is a typical setting in cloud computing, where users submit applications (tasks) composed of many smaller parts (jobs) and require the output of all these parts. We refer to this setting as ***Shared Resource Task-Scheduling*** (SaS).

1.1 Model & Notation

Consider a system of $m \in \mathbb{N}$ processors from the set $M := [m] = \{1,2,\ldots,m\}$ and $n \in \mathbb{N}$ *jobs* from the set $J := [n]$. There is a *resource* that is to be shared by the processors. In each time step $t \in \mathbb{N}$, each processor i is assigned a share $R_i(t) \in [0,1]$ of the resource. The resource may not be overused, such that we require $\sum_{i \in [m]} R_i(t) \leq 1$. Each processor can process at most one job per time step and each job can be processed by at most one processor. A job j has a *processing volume (size)* $p_j \in \mathbb{R}_{>0}$ and a *resource requirement* $r_j \in \mathbb{R}_{>0}$. Note that we will assume $p_j \in \mathbb{N}$ for convenience throughout this paper, but all our results carry over to $p_j \in \mathbb{R}_{>0}$ (also see explanation below Equation (1)). Without loss of generality, we assume $r_1 \leq r_2 \leq \cdots \leq r_n$. The resource requirement specifies what portion of the resource is needed to finish one unit of a job's processing volume. More exactly, assume job j is processed by processor i during time step t. Then exactly $\min(R_i(t)/r_j, 1)$ units of j's processing volume are finished during that time step. A job is *finished* once all p_j units of its processing volume have been finished. Preemption and migration of jobs is not allowed. The objective is to find a *schedule* S (i.e., a resource and job assignment) having minimal *makespan* $|S|$ (the number of time steps until all jobs are finished). We refer to this problem as ***Shared Resource Job-Scheduling*** (SoS). As a special case, we sometimes consider $p_j = 1$ for all $j \in J$. We refer to this as the setting of jobs with unit size.

During our analysis, it will be convenient to adopt the following perspective on SoS: Given a schedule S, consider job j processed on processor i during time step t. Without loss of generality, we assume $R_i(t) \leq r_j$ (setting $R_i(t)$ to $\min\{R_i(t), r_j\}$ yields a valid schedule with the same makespan). Let t_1 and t_2 denote the time steps when j was started and finished, respectively. Since j is finished, we have $\sum_{t=t_1}^{t_2} R_i(t)/r_j \geq p_j$. Rearranging yields $\sum_{t=t_1}^{t_2} R_i(t) \geq r_j \cdot p_j$. Thus, if we define $s_j := r_j \cdot p_j$ as the *total resource requirement* of job j, we can think of j as being finished once the total resource shares it received over time equal (at least) s_j. We define $s_j(t) := s_j - \sum_{t'=t_1}^{t} R_i(t')$ as the total resource requirement remaining after time step t. Note that job j is finished in the first time step t for which $s_j(t) = 0$. We use $J(t) := \{j \in J \mid s_j(t) > 0\}$ to denote the set of jobs that are not finished after time step t. Throughout the paper, for any set S, we write $\max S := \max_{s \in S} s$.

A polynomial time algorithm A is called to have an *(absolute) approximation ratio* of α if, on any instance I, the schedule S produced by A satisfies $|S|/|\text{OPT}| \leq \alpha$, where OPT denotes an optimal solution for I. A has an *asymptotic ratio* of α if, on any instance, $|S| = \alpha \cdot |\text{OPT}| + o(|\text{OPT}|)$.

Lower Bounds. Let OPT denote an optimal schedule. Two simple lower bounds for any schedule, including OPT, are $\lceil s_0(J) \rceil$ and $\frac{1}{m} \cdot \sum_{j \in J} \lceil s_j/r_j \rceil$. The former holds since each job needs to receive a total of s_j resource shares over time. The latter holds since each job must be split in at least $\lceil s_j/r_j \rceil$ parts, and each such part needs a dedicated machine in one time step to be processed. Thus, we have

$$|\text{OPT}| \geq \max\left\{\lceil s_0(J) \rceil, \frac{1}{m} \cdot \sum_{j \in J} \left\lceil \frac{s_j}{r_j} \right\rceil\right\}. \quad (1)$$

Note that these lower bounds on OPT remain valid if allowing $p_j \in \mathbb{R}$ and rescaling $p'_j := \lceil p_j \rceil$ and $r'_j := s_j/p'_j$, as this modification maintains the s_j and by $\lceil p'_j \rceil = \lceil p_j \rceil$ the bound in Equation (1) remains the same. Also, the lower bounds remain valid for the preemptive setting as they are only based on observations of the overall workload.

1.2 Related Work

In the following we survey related problems, focusing on *resource constrained scheduling* and *bin packing with cardinality constraints*. As it turns out, the latter is among the most relevant related work, as it can be seen as a special case of our problem (except for the difference that preemption is allowed).

Bin Packing. The problem supposedly closest related to SoS is *bin packing with cardinality constraints and splittable items* as introduced in [4]. In this problem, a set of n items needs to be packed into as few bins of capacity one as possible. In contrast to standard bin packing, items can have an arbitrary size in $(0,\infty)$ and may be split and distributed among different bins. However, there is a constraint on the maximum number of (parts of) different items that may be packed into a single bin given by some predefined value k. Chung et al. [4] proved this problem to be strongly NP-hard for $k = 2$ and provided a simple approximation algorithm with asymptotic approximation ratio of $3/2$ (also for $k = 2$). Epstein and van Stee [7] extended the NP-hardness to any fixed $k \geq 2$. They also gave efficient algorithms with asymptotic approximation ratio $7/5$ for $k = 2$ and an absolute approximation ratio of $2 - 1/k$ for $k \geq 2$, respectively. Finally, Epstein et al. [5] presented an efficient polynomial-time approximation scheme (EPTAS) for the case $k = o(n)$. They also proved that for $k = \Theta(n)$ a polynomial-time approximation algorithm with a ratio smaller than $3/2$ cannot exist unless P = NP.

Note that bin packing with cardinality constraints and splittable items is, except for the lack of the notion "preemption", equivalent to SoS with unit size jobs: If items correspond to jobs of size one and each bin is identified with one time step, the packing of a bin describes the jobs executed in this time step and the part size of an item corresponds to the share of the resource the respective job gets. The cardinality constraint k corresponds to having k processors.

A variant of bin packing with cardinality constraints and splittable items, which is motivated by a scheduling problem similar to SoS, was studied by König et al. [12]. This work assumes the items to be edges of a tree and the goal is to find a packing into as few bins as possible such that no bin contains (parts of) items incident to more than k nodes. They proved this problem to be NP-hard in the strong sense for any constant value k and constant degree of the underlying tree. Concerning approximations, two algorithms are presented: For paths NextFit achieves an asymptotic approximation ratio of $2-1/(2(k-1))$ and for general trees an algorithm with approximation ratio $5/2$ was given.

Scheduling. Another strain of closely related works is resource constrained scheduling. Garey and Graham [8] considered a model in which a set of jobs needs to be processed on m parallel processors. Additionally, they assume ℓ resources to be part of the system and, in addition to a workload, each job also has a requirement on each of the resources. In contrast to our model, however, each job needs to be assigned its full resource requirement at each step during its execution. They studied list-scheduling algorithms for this problem and proved an approximation ratio of at most $\min\left\{\frac{m+1}{2}, \ell+2-\frac{2\ell+1}{m}\right\}$.

For the restriction to a single resource, the results discussed above directly imply that their list scheduling algorithm achieves an approximation factor of $3-\frac{3}{m}$. Niemeier and Wiese [15] improved these results by presenting a $(2+\varepsilon)$-approximation algorithm for this problem using techniques such as grouping and linear programming. They also proved that this problem cannot be approximated within an (absolute) approximation ratio less than $\frac{3}{2}$ by a straightforward reduction from the Partition problem. Finally, Jansen et al. [10] very recently presented an asymptotic fully polynomial-time approximation scheme (AFPTAS) for this problem.

A simplified variant of our scheduling problem was studied by Brinkmann et al. [3]. They focused solely on the resource assignment aspect of the problem: Each job was already assigned to one of the m processors, and even the order in which the jobs on each processor had to be processed was fixed. Further restricting the problem to jobs of the same computational size, they proved NP-completeness for variable m and proposed a natural combinatorial approximation algorithm that achieved an approximation ratio of $2-1/m$. They also provided an optimal algorithm for two processors based on dynamical programming. The case for non-unit size jobs as well as incorporating the job assignment (instead of assuming it given) were left as the central open issues. In [2], an exact algorithm was given that runs in polynomial time for any fixed $m \geq 2$. Another related, older scheduling problem that allows an arbitrary (continuous) assignment of a given resource to multiple processors was considered under the name *discrete-continuous* scheduling, but provided mostly heuristic results (cf. [11, 16]).

With respect to Section 4, where we consider a model generalization for tasks that are composed of multiple jobs, [13] should be mentioned. Here, a production model is considered, where tasks represent orders and each job of an order must be processed on a subset of specific machines. In particular they consider a similar objective function for this setting (see Section 4). However, note that these *order scheduling models* do not consider resource sharing in our sense, but instead only the allocation to the (non-identical) machines.

Apart from these resource constrained scheduling results, one should at least briefly mention the related classical multiprocessor makespan scheduling problem. Here, a set of jobs needs to be scheduled on m identical machines so as to minimize the makespan. Note that in the special case of SoS in which all jobs have negligible resource requirements, both problems become equivalent. For scheduling identical machines, a PTAS is known [1] if m is part of the input and for fixed m even an FPTAS is possible [9].

1.3 Our Contribution

We study a new scheduling model for a setting of parallel processors sharing a common scarce resource in terms of its complexity and approximations. Our model is an extension of a simpler variant studied in [3] and is closely related to a well-known bin packing problem [4]. Precisely, our results are as follows:

- We prove SoS and SaS to be strongly NP-hard (Section 2).
- For SoS, we design and analyze a polynomial time algorithm with an approximation ratio of $2+1/(m-2)$ for jobs of arbitrary size and (asymptotically) $1+1/(m-1)$ for unit size jobs (Section 3). Our algorithm is based on the idea of a *maximal sliding window*: We order jobs by non-decreasing resource requirement and (for each time step) create a sliding window trying to find a subset of consecutive jobs such that $m-1$ of these jobs can be finished and the full resource can be used.
- Our algorithm implies the same (asymptotic) guarantee of $1+1/(k-1)$ for bin packing with splittable items and cardinality constraint k. Besides a known PTAS, which has a quite high running time, the best known fast algorithm for this problem has an approximation ratio of $2-1/(k-1)$. For computing centers typically containing a huge amount of processors, this ratio approaches 2 whereas our algorithm is almost optimal.
- We generalize our algorithm to obtain an asymptotic approximation ratio of $2+4/(m-3)$ for SaS where jobs are grouped into tasks and where we aim at minimizing the average completion time of all tasks (Section 4).

2 COMPLEXITY

In the following, we explore the complexity of the SoS problem.

Theorem 2.1. *The SoS problem with jobs of unit size is strongly NP-hard for $m=2$.*

Proof. Bin packing with cardinality constraints and splittable items is equal to our setting with preemption. The NP-hardness of SoS, even for unit size jobs, can hence be shown similarly to the reduction found in [4]. For completeness sake and to show its adaptivity to our setting, it can be found in the full version of this paper. □

Note that the hardness of the general SoS problem directly follows. This also holds for the SaS problem, as it contains the SoS problem as a special case.

As stated before, there is a PTAS [6] for bin packing with cardinality constraints and splittable items if the cardinality constraint (corresponding to the number of processors in our model) is in $o(n)$. This bin packing variant is similar to the unit size version of our problem, but with preemption. However, this PTAS can be adapted easily to the setting without preemption by restricting the set of solutions to non-preemptive schedules. For unit size jobs, this implies a better approximation ratio than our algorithm in Section 3, but at the cost of very high running time.

3 APPROXIMATION ALGORITHM

We provide some additional notation for this section: Let $j \in J, U \subseteq J$ and $t \in \mathbb{N}_0$. We define $r(U) := \sum_{j \in U} r_j$ and $s_t(U) := \sum_{j \in U} s_j(t)$. We say job j is *fractured* at time t if $s_j(t) = k \cdot r_j + q_j(t)$ for some $k \in \mathbb{N}_0$ and $q_j(t) \in (0, r_j)$ (i.e., $s_j(t)$ is not an integer multiple of r_j). Note that, since $s_j(0) = s_j = p_j \cdot r_j$ and $p_j \in \mathbb{N}$, initially no job is fractured. We also define $L_t(U) := \{j \in J(t-1) \mid j < \min U\}$ as the set of jobs remaining at the beginning of time step t that have a resource requirement smaller than any job in U ("left of U"). Similarly, $R_t(U) := \{j \in J(t-1) \mid j > \max U\}$. For convenience, we define $L_t(\emptyset) := \emptyset$ and $R_t(\emptyset) := J(t-1)$.

We continue with the central definition of *maximal (job) windows*, a subset of remaining jobs that can be processed efficiently (see algorithmic intuition below). Our algorithm will ensure that it always processes jobs from such a window. The bulk of the analysis goes towards proving that we can always find a maximal window.

Definition 3.1 (Job Window). A subset of unfinished jobs $W \subseteq J(t-1)$ is called a *job window* for time step t if

(a) $j_1, j_2 \in W \Rightarrow J(t-1) \cap \{j_1, j_1+1, \ldots, j_2\} \subseteq W$,
(b) $r(W \setminus \{\max W\}) < 1$,
(c) $|\{j \in W \mid q_j(t-1) > 0\}| \leq 1$, and
(d) $j \in J(t-1) \setminus W \Rightarrow s_j(t-1) = s_j$.

We say W is *k-maximal* if, additionally, it has size $|W| \leq k$ and the following properties hold:

(e) $|W| < k \Rightarrow L_t(W) = \emptyset$ and
(f) $r(W) < 1 \Rightarrow R_t(W) = \emptyset$.

In other words a window W (of size $\leq m$) is a set of consecutive jobs (Property (a)) such that we can assign all but the rightmost job their full resource requirements (Property (b)). Moreover, W contains all started jobs and at most one of these is fractured (Properties (c) and (d)). To be k-maximal, a window of size at most k must contain either exactly k jobs or lie at the left border, and either utilize the full resource or lie at the right border (Properties (e) and (f)).

Algorithmic Intuition. We design our algorithm such that it has three key properties:

- During any time step t, it processes jobs from an $(m-1)$-maximal window $W_t \subseteq J(t-1)$ (Lemma 3.7).
- If the window W_t is at the left border of the remaining jobs (i.e., $L_t(W_t) = \emptyset$), then this remains true for all $W_{t'}$ with $t' > t$ (Lemma 3.8(a)).
- If the window W_t is at the right border of the remaining jobs (i.e., $R_t(W_t = \emptyset)$), then this remains true for all $t' > t$ (Lemma 3.8(b)).

Note that if W_t is *not* at the left border of the remaining jobs, Properties (b) and (e) of Definition 3.1 imply that we can assign the resource such that at least $m-2$ jobs (all of W except for $\max W_t$) receive their full resource requirement r_j during time step t. Similarly, if W_t is not at the right border of the remaining jobs, Property (f) implies that we can utilize the full resource during time step t.

```
1   for (t, W) ← (1, ∅); J(t−1) ≠ ∅; t ← t+1:
2       W ← W ∩ J(t−1)
3       W ← GrowWindowLeft(W, t, m−1, 1)
4       W ← GrowWindowRight(W, t, m−1, 1)
5       W ← MoveWindowRight(W, t, 1)
6
7       if ∃ fractured job ι ∈ W: F ← {ι}
8       else:                    F ← ∅
9       if r(W \ F) ≥ 1:
10          process each job j ∈ W \ (F ∪ {max W}) with resource rⱼ
11          if F = {ι}:
12              process job ι with resource qι(t)
13          process job max W with the remaining resource
14      else:
15          process each job j ∈ W \ F with resource rⱼ
16          if F = {ι}:
17              process job ι with resource min {1−r(W \ F), sι(t−1)}
18          if resource left and Rₜ(W) ≠ ∅:
19              assign remaining resource to job min Rₜ(W)
20              W ← W ∪ min Rₜ(W)
```

Listing 1: Approximation algorithm for SoS.

```
1   GrowWindowLeft(W, t, size, R)
2       while (|W| < size and Lₜ(W) ≠ ∅) and r(W) < R:
3           W ← W ∪ {max Lₜ(W)}
4       return W
5
6   GrowWindowRight(W, t, size, R)
7       while (r(W) < R and Rₜ(W) ≠ ∅) and |W| < size:
8           W ← W ∪ {min Rₜ(W)}
9       return W
10
11  MoveWindowRight(W, t, R)
12      while (r(W) < R and Rₜ(W) ≠ ∅) and s_min W = s_min W(t−1):
13          W ← (W \ {min W}) ∪ {min Rₜ(W)}
14      return W
```

Listing 2: Auxiliary procedures. The parameters *size* and *R* are only to facilitate the algorithm from Section 4. In this section, we call these only with *size* = $m-1$ and *R* = 1.

Consider the first time step T such that $L_T(W_T) \cup R_T(W_T) = \emptyset$. In particular, W_T contains all remaining jobs. It is not hard to see that these can be finished by our algorithm in $|\text{OPT}|$ time steps. On the other hand, up to time step T the three key properties and the above observations imply that in each time step either at least $m-2$ jobs receive their full resource requirement or the full resource is utilized. In the former case, the lower bound from Equation (1) implies $T \leq \frac{m}{m-2} \cdot |\text{OPT}|$. In the latter case, the same bound implies $T \leq |\text{OPT}|$. Together, this yields an approximation ratio of at most $\frac{m}{m-2} + 1 = 2 + \frac{m-2}{m}$.

A slightly more careful but similar analysis yields Theorem 3.3. We proceed to describe our algorithm. Afterward we show that the three key properties hold and formalize the above argument.

3.1 Algorithm Description

In the following we describe our algorithm. The corresponding pseudocode can be found in Listing 1 (with some auxiliary procedures outsourced to Listing 2). If not explicitly stated otherwise, references to lines refer to Listing 1. Note that the implementation as shown in Listing 1 has only pseudo-polynomial running time. It is not hard to adapt it such that it yields polynomial running time; we describe how to do that in the proof of Theorem 3.3.

Lines 2 to 5 compute an $(m-1)$-maximal window W for this time step. Lines 7 to 20 compute the resource assignment of this time step. The computation of the maximal window W starts by removing any jobs that were finished in the last time step (Line 2). Lines 3 to 5 take the resulting window and greedily grow it first left, then right, and finally move it as far to the right as possible. This way, W becomes $(m-1)$-maximal for this time step.

To compute the resource assignment, let $F := \{\iota\}$ be the set containing the only fractured job of W (or $F := \emptyset$ if there is no fractured job). We distinguish two cases:

Case 1: $r(W \setminus F) \geq 1$

Note that $\iota \neq \max W$, as otherwise Property (b) of Definition 3.1 violates the case assumption. Each job $j \in W$ except for ι and $\max W$ receives its full resource requirement r_j. Job ι receives resource $q_\iota(t-1)$. Any remaining resource is assigned to $\max W$.

Case 2: $r(W \setminus F) < 1$

In this case, each job $j \in W$ except for ι receives its full resource requirement r_j. Job ι receives resource $\min\{1-r(W \setminus F), s_\iota(t-1), r_\iota\}$. If there is resource left, we use it to process $\min R_t(W)$ (this is the only case where we use all m instead of only $m-1$ processors). In that case, we add $\min R_t(W)$ to W.

Our analysis requires that there is always at most one fractured job[1]. The case distinction above is chosen with this goal in mind: If there is no fractured job, all $j \in W \setminus \{\max W\}$ receive their full resource requirement. The remaining resource goes to $\max W$, possibly fracturing it. If there is already a fractured job ι, doing the same might fracture a second job ($\max W$). Instead, we distinguish whether $r(W \setminus \{\iota\}) \geq 1$ or not. If so, we "unfracture" ι and instead fracture $\max W$; $r(W \setminus \{\iota\}) \geq 1$ guarantees that we can still use the full resource, even if $s_\iota(t-1) = \varepsilon \ll r_\iota$. Otherwise, $r(W \setminus \{\iota\}) < 1$ allows us to assign all $j \in W \setminus \{\iota\}$ their full resource requirement and keep only ι fractured (it gets the remaining resource). This case might leave us with some unecessarily wasted resource (if $s_\iota(t-1) = \varepsilon \ll r_\iota$ and $R_t(W) \neq \emptyset$). If so, we finish ι and use the (so far unused) m-th processor to start a new job. We gather this discussion in the following observation.

Observation 3.2. Given an $(m-1)$-maximal window W for the current time step, Lines 7 to 20 compute a resource assignment for jobs in W such that at least $|W|-1$ jobs $j \in W$ receive their full resource requirement r_j, at most one job is fractured after this time step, and at most $|W|$ jobs are started (and not finished) after this time step.

3.2 Analysis

The goal of this section is to prove the following theorem.

THEOREM 3.3. *The algorithm from Listing 1 generates a schedule S with approximation ratio $2 + \frac{1}{m-2}$. If jobs have unit size, we get the stronger guarantee $|S| \leq (1 + \frac{2}{m-2}) \cdot |\text{OPT}| + 1$. The algorithm can be implemented with a running time of $O((m+n) \cdot n)$.*

It is not hard to see that for jobs of unit size, a minor algorithm modification avoids to reserve the m-th processor: If jobs have unit size, we have $s_j = r_j$ for all $j \in J$. Note that there will be always at most one started (and, thus, at most one fractured) job: Indeed, by the while loops of the auxiliary procedures, the window can contain at most one job with $s_j = r_j > 1$ (this will be $\max W$). Since for all jobs $j \in W \setminus \{\max W\}$ we have $s_j = r_j \leq 1$ and $r(W \setminus \{\max W\}) < 1$ (Property (b) of Definition 3.1), such j will be finished in the current time step. We can treat the only started job ι in step t as a job with resource requirement $s_\iota(t-1)$ and reorder the jobs accordingly. The next time step will either finish ι or it will once more be the only started job. This modification does not need the reserved processor, so we can use m-maximal instead of $(m-1)$-maximal windows, improving the approximation factor for unit size jobs from $\frac{m}{m-2} = 1 + \frac{2}{m-2}$ to $\frac{m}{m-1} = 1 + \frac{1}{m-1}$. The analysis is analogous to the one given below for the unmodified algorithm.

We now start to provide tools for the proof of Theorem 3.3. We start with some auxiliary claims and then prove the above mentioned key properties in Lemmas 3.7 and 3.8

Claim 3.4. *If Properties (a) to (d) from Definition 3.1 hold for W right before we call the auxiliary procedures, then they also hold at any later point in this time step.*

PROOF. Property (a) holds since jobs are added one by one at the left/right borders (Lines 3 and 8 in Listing 2) or one job is removed at the left border and another added at the right border (Line 13). Property (b) is enforced by the while loops' conditions. Property (c) holds since only unstarted (and, thus, unfractured) jobs are added to W. Finally, Property (d) holds since the while loop in Line 12 of Listing 2 ensures that no started jobs are removed. □

Claim 3.5. *If $W = \emptyset$ after Line 2 of Listing 1 in time step t and no job in $J(t-1)$ is started, then W is an $(m-1)$-maximal window when* `MoveWindowRight` *exits.*

PROOF. We have $W = \emptyset$ right before the auxiliary procedures are called. In particular, W is a (trivial) window for time step t. We apply Claim 3.4 to get that Properties (a) to (d) of Definition 3.1 hold when `MoveWindowRight` exits. Since the while loops ensure that the window size is at most $m-1$, it remains to show that Properties (e) and (f) hold after the auxiliary procedures.

For Property (e), note that $L_t(W) = L_t(\emptyset) = \emptyset$. Thus, procedure `GrowWindowLeft` exits immediately, leaving $W = \emptyset$. Now, if `GrowWindowRight` exits because of $|W| = m-1$, Property (e) holds (and remains true since `MoveWindowRight` does not change the size of W). Otherwise, if `GrowWindowRight` exits because the condition "$r(W) < 1 \wedge R_t(W) \neq \emptyset$" is violated, `MoveWindowRight` exits immediately for the same reason. But then, we still have $\min J(t-1) \in W$ (impplying $L_t(W) = \emptyset$) and Property (e) holds.

For Property (f), note that `MoveWindowRight` cannot exit because of the condition "$s_{\min W} = s_{\min W}(t-1)$" (there are no started jobs). Thus, it can only exit because one of the other two conditions is violated, which immediately implies Property (f). □

Claim 3.6. *If $W \neq \emptyset$ after Line 2 of Listing 1 in time step t and the window $\tilde{W}$ computed in the previous time step was $(m-1)$-maximal, then W is a $(m-1)$-maximal window when* `MoveWindowRight` *exits.*

PROOF. We have $W = \tilde{W} \cap J(t-1)$ right before the auxiliary procedures are called. $\tilde{W}$ was a maximal window, and removing finished jobs cannot violate Properties (a) to (d) of Definition 3.1. We apply Claim 3.4 to get that Properties (a) to (d) hold when procedure `MoveWindowRight` exits. It remains to show that Properties (e) and (f) hold after the auxiliary procedures.

For Property (e), we first show that it holds after `GrowWindowLeft`. When we call `GrowWindowLeft` for window W, note that $L_t(W) = L_{t-1}(\tilde{W})$. Thus, if $L_{t-1}(\tilde{W}) = \emptyset$, Property (e) holds trivially after

[1] Otherwise, we could end up with $m-1$ fractured jobs $j \in W$, each with $s_j(t-1) = \varepsilon \ll r_j$. This may cause almost the full resource to be wasted during that step.

GrowWindowLeft (the while loop exits immediately because of the condition "$L_t(W) \neq \emptyset$"). If $L_{t-1}(\tilde{W}) \neq \emptyset$, since Property (e) holds for window $\tilde{W}$, we have $|\tilde{W}| = m-1$. Note that for all $j \in L_t(W) = L_{t-1}(\tilde{W})$ and $j' \in \tilde{W}$ we have $r_j \leq r_{j'}$ (by the job ordering). This implies that we cannot violate condition "$r(W) < 1$" of the while loop of GrowWindowLeft before adding $|\tilde{W}| - |W|$ jobs. Moreover, we cannot violate "$|W| \leq m-1$" before adding $|\tilde{W}| - |W|$ jobs (since $|W| + (|\tilde{W}| - |W|) = |\tilde{W}| \leq m-1$). Thus, GrowWindowLeft adds at least min $\{|L_t(W)|, |\tilde{W}| - |W|\}$ jobs to W. If the minimum equals $|L_t(W)|$ we added all jobs left of W and Property (e) holds. If the minimum equals $|\tilde{W}| - |W|$, Property (e) holds since the resulting window has size at least $|W| + (|\tilde{W}| - |W|) = |\tilde{W}| = m-1$.

So Property (e) holds for W right before GrowWindowRight. We show that it still holds after procedure MoveWindowRight. The statement is trivial if $|W| = m-1$ (both procedures do not decrease W). Otherwise, we use that W has Property (e) to get $L_t(W) = \emptyset$. If GrowWindowRight exits because the condition "$r(W) < 1 \wedge R_t(W) \neq \emptyset$" got violated, MoveWindowRight exits immediately for the same reason, leaving $L_t(W) = \emptyset$. Otherwise, if GrowWindowRight exits because of $|W| = m-1$, this is maintained by MoveWindowRight and, thus, Property (e) holds after MoveWindowRight.

All that remains is to prove that Property (f) holds after procedure MoveWindowRight. Consider the conditions of the while loop in Line 12 of Listing 2. Property (f) holds if the while loop exits because the condition "$r(W) < 1 \wedge R_t(W) \neq \emptyset$" got violated. So assume it exits only because of the condition "$s_{\min W} = s_{\min W}(t-1)$". At that moment, we have a window W with $r(W) < 1$, $R_t(W) \neq \emptyset$, and $s_{\min W} > s_{\min W}(t-1)$. The first two imply that $|W| = m-1$, since otherwise GrowWindowRight would not have exited. The inequality $s_{\min W} > s_{\min W}(t-1)$ implies that job min W is already started, so it must have been in the last time step's window $\tilde{W}$. Now, since W has maximal size $m-1$ and its leftmost job was also in $\tilde{W}$, we get $r(\tilde{W}) \leq r(W) < 1$ as well as $R_t(W) \subseteq R_{t-1}(\tilde{W})$. But since $\tilde{W}$ had Property (f), we know $R_{t-1}(\tilde{W}) = \emptyset$. Together, $R_t(W) = \emptyset$, a contradiction. □

Lemma 3.7. *Fix $t \in \mathbb{N}_0$ and consider the job window W processed during time step t. Then W is an $(m-1)$-maximal window for time step t.*

Proof. We prove the statement inductively. In the first time step $t = 1$, we start with $W = \emptyset$ (initialization by the for loop) and no job has been started. We apply Claim 3.5 to get that W is an $(m-1)$-maximal window after the auxiliary procedures. For $t > 1$ we either have $W = \emptyset$ or $W \neq \emptyset$ after Line 2 of Listing 1. In the former case, we once more apply Claim 3.5. In the latter case, we apply Claim 3.6. In both cases, we get that W is an $(m-1)$-maximal window after the auxiliary procedures, proving the desired statement. □

Lemma 3.8. *Let $\tilde{W} \subseteq J(t-2)$ and $W \subseteq J(t-1)$ be the $(m-1)$-maximal windows processed during time step $t-1$ and t, respectively. Then*

(a) $L_{t-1}(\tilde{W}) = \emptyset \Rightarrow L_t(W) = \emptyset$ and
(b) $R_{t-1}(\tilde{W}) = \emptyset \Rightarrow R_t(W) = \emptyset \wedge r(W) \leq r(\tilde{W})$.

Proof. For (a), note that W starts out as $\tilde{W} \cap J(n-1)$ in time step t. Since $L_t(W) = L_{t-1}(\tilde{W}) = \emptyset$, we only add jobs from $R_t(W) = R_{t-1}(\tilde{W})$. All these jobs have a larger resource requirement than any job in $\tilde{W}$. As a consequence, after GrowWindowRight we have $|W| \leq |\tilde{W}|$. If $|W| < |\tilde{W}| \leq m-1$, MoveWindowRight exits immediately and we have $L_t(W) = \emptyset$. Otherwise, if $|W| = |\tilde{W}|$ after GrowWindowRight, we must have $r(W) \geq r(\tilde{W})$ and $R_t(W) \subseteq R_{t-1}(\tilde{W})$. Since $\tilde{W}$ is $(m-1)$-maximal in time step $t-1$, this implies either $r(W) \geq 1$ or $R_t(W) = \emptyset$, such that MoveWindowRight exits immediately and leaves $L_t(W) = \emptyset$. This proves (a). The first part of Statement (b) follows analogously. The second part holds either since $|W| = |\tilde{W}| = m-1$ and jobs that were finished in $\tilde{W}$ are exchanged for jobs with at most the same resource requirement, or since $W \subseteq \tilde{W}$ (if $L_{t-1}(\tilde{W}) = \emptyset$). □

With these lemmas, we are ready to prove Theorem 3.3.

Proof of Theorem 3.3. We consider the schedule S produced by our algorithm from Listing 1. By Lemma 3.7, the jobs processed during each time step $t \in \mathbb{N}$ are contained in a maximal window W_t for time step t. We define $T_L := \min\{t \in \mathbb{N} \mid |W_t| < m-1\}$ and, similarly, $T_R := \min\{t \in \mathbb{N} \mid r(W_t) < 1\}$. By Properties (e) and (f) of Definition 3.1 and Lemma 3.8 we have $L_t(W_t) = R_t(W_t) = \emptyset$ and $r_t(W_t) < 1$ for all $t \geq \max\{T_L, T_R\} =: T$. In particular, the former implies $W_t = J(t-1)$ for all $t \geq T$. Combining these insights we get that for each $t \geq T$, each of the at most $|W_t| \leq |W_T| < m-1$ remaining jobs gets its full resource requirement. Thus, each $j \in W_T$ is finished after exactly $\lceil s_j(T-1)/r_j \rceil$ additional time steps. Let $p := \max\{s_j(T-1)/r_j \mid j \in W_T\}$. Note that $|S| = T-1+\lceil p \rceil$. We distinguish two cases:

Case 1: $T = T_L$

For each $t < T$ we have $|W_t| = m-1$. Thus, by Observation 3.2, at least $|W_t| - 1 = m-2$ jobs $j \in W_t$ receive their full resource requirement r_j. Remember that $p_j = s_j / r_j$. An average argument gives

$$T-1 \leq \frac{\sum_{j \in J} p_j - \lceil p \rceil}{m-2} \leq |\text{Opt}| \cdot \frac{m}{m-2} - \frac{\lceil p \rceil}{m-2}.$$

Combining everything with the lower bound $|\text{Opt}| \geq \lceil p \rceil$ we compute

$$|S| = T-1+\lceil p \rceil \leq |\text{Opt}| \cdot \frac{m}{m-2} - \frac{\lceil p \rceil}{m-2} + \lceil p \rceil$$
$$\leq |\text{Opt}| \cdot \left(\frac{m}{m-2} + 1 - \frac{1}{m-2}\right) = |\text{Opt}| \cdot \left(2 + \frac{1}{m-2}\right).$$

Case 2: $T = T_R$

For each $t < T$ we have $r(W_t) \geq 1$. Using that Opt cannot overuse the resource, we see $T-1 \leq r(J) \leq |\text{Opt}|$. Similar to the first case, we compute $|S| = T-1+\lceil p \rceil \leq 2 \cdot |\text{Opt}|$.

The result for jobs of unit size follows by realizing that $|S| = T-1+1 = T$. Thus, the bounds above give $|S| \leq |\text{Opt}| \cdot \left(1 + \frac{2}{m-2}\right) + 1$ (Case 1) and $|\text{Opt}| + 1$ (Case 2).

For the the running time, first note that the implementation given in Listing 1 has actually pseudo-polynomial running time (it depends on the sum $\sum_{j \in J} p_j$, since each job j needs a dedicated processor for at least p_j time steps). However, note that if no job is finished in the current time step, the maximal window in the next step will be identical to the current maximal window. With this observation, we can calculate via a simple linear equation after how many step with the current maximal window the first job in the window will be finished. This allows us to "skip" time steps where no job is finished. Thus, given the maximal window in a time step t, we go over the O(m) jobs in the window and find the first one(s) that will be finished under the current resource assignment. To compute the next maximal window, we remove the finished jobs and grow the window left/right. This can be computed in time $O(|W|) = O(m)$ (each adding/removal can be implemented trivially in constant time using doubly linked lists). Then we move the window up to n steps to the right, which can be done in time $O(n)$. Since this always eliminates at least one job from the old maximal window, this repeats at most $O(n)$ times, yielding a total running time of $O(n\cdot(m+n))$. □

As the lower bounds on Opt are still valid for the preemptive setting (see description below Equation (1)), and the upper bounds of the algorithm obviously do not increase by allowing preemption, our results for unit size jobs carry over to bin packing with cardinality constraints and splittable items. Our algorithm scales well with the number of processors in contrast to existing simple (i.e. fast) algorithms, but (obviously) does not reach the approximation ratio of the existing EPTAS [5]. Note that in the following corollary, k denotes the cardinality constraint as this is common notion in the related literature.

Corollary 3.9. *Our results give an algorithm for bin packing with cardinality constraints and splittable items [4] with asymptotic approximation ratio* $1+1/(k-1)$ *and running time* $O((k+n)n)$.

Proof. The lower bounds on the optimum remain valid for the preemptive setting as they only use a notion of overall workload. Also, our algorithm still computes a valid solution, as the preemptive setting removes a constraint. The claim follows. □

4 THE SHARED RESOURCE TASK-SCHEDULING PROBLEM

Computational tasks often consist of multiple parts that may be executed in parallel and independently of each other. Such situations often arise in the context of composed cloud services that consist of several smaller services that can be executed in parallel in a computing center.

We now consider the model where a set of tasks needs to be executed and where each task consists of multiple unit size jobs, i.e. given a task set $\mathcal{T} = \{T_1,\dots,T_k\}$ each containing a set of jobs $T_i = \{j_{i1},\dots,j_{in_i}\}$ with $p_{ik} = 1$ for all i,k. The objective is to minimize the average completion time, where the completion time f_i of a task T_i denotes the time the last job of this task is finished, i.e. $f_i := \max\{t : s_j(t-1) > 0 \text{ for some } j \in T_i\}$. This is equivalent to minimizing the sum of completion times, which we consider throughout this section. Note that this model uses a composed objective: for a single task we aim to minimize the latest completion time of the involved jobs, while over all tasks we aim to minimize the average completion time. Similar measures were considered, for example, in [13] (for *order scheduling models*, where a task consists of jobs and each job needs to be processed on a subset of specific machines).

We denote the set of unfinished tasks after time t by $T(t)$, the set of unfinished jobs of task i after time t by $J_i(t)$, and the remaining resource requirement for set U by $\tilde{r}(U)$.

4.1 Prerequisites

Our algorithm for this setting partitions the set of tasks into two sets $\mathcal{T}_1$ and $\mathcal{T}_2$. For each task, we consider the average resource requirement of its jobs. The tasks with jobs that have a high resource requirement belong to $\mathcal{T}_1$, those with jobs that have a low resource

```
1  for (t,S,W,i) ← (1,∅,∅,1); T(t−1) ≠ ∅; t ← t+1:
2      m' ← m
3      while (r̃(S)+r̃(J_i(t−1)) ≤ 1):
4          S ← S∪T_i; i ← i+1; m' ← m' − |J_i(t−1)|
5          process all jobs in T_i with their full resource requirement
6      W ← W ∩ J_i(t−1)
7      W ← GrowWindowLeft(W, t, m', 1−r̃(S))
8      W ← GrowWindowRight(W, t, m', 1−r̃(S))
9      W ← MoveWindowRight(W, t, 1−r̃(S))
10     if ∃ fractured job ι ∈ W: F ← {ι}
11     else: F ← ∅
12     process each job j ∈ W\(F∪{max W}) with resource r_j
13     if F = {ι}:
14         process job ι with resource q_ι(t)
15     process job max W with the remaining resource
```

Listing 3: Algorithm for task set $\mathcal{T}_1$.

requirement belong to $\mathcal{T}_2$. The algorithm schedules both sets of tasks independently in parallel, each on (roughly) half the processors with half the resource.

We begin with the tasks that have high resource requirements. Here, the available resource is R instead of 1 as in the previous section. Note that the auxiliary procedures called in the algorithms in Listing 3 (Lines 7 to 9) and Listing 4 (Lines 8 to 10) are applied only to the currently considered task instead of the whole set of jobs.

Lemma 4.1. *For a set of tasks* $\mathcal{T} = \{T_1,\dots,T_k\}$ *with* $\frac{r(T)}{|T|} > \frac{R}{(m-1)}$ *for all* $T \in \mathcal{T}$*, the algorithm in Listing 3 computes a schedule such that the completion time* f_i *of task* T_i *is bounded by* $f_i \le \left\lceil \frac{\sum_{l=1}^{i} r(T_l)}{R} \right\rceil$.

Proof. The algorithm in Listing 3 processes tasks by increasing index and proceeds according to the algorithm in Listing 1 and Section 3 separately for each task.

Note that for a task $T_i = \{J_{i1},\dots,J_{in_i}\}$ the average size of the jobs is more than $R/(m-1)$. We inductively prove that $\frac{\tilde{r}(J_i(t))}{|J_i(t)\setminus F|} \ge \frac{R}{m-1}$ remains true for each unfinished task T_i after any time step t. This would imply that after time step t there is a sliding window using the full resource R in that time step (except in the last time step of the schedule) and hence the lemma would follow. We distinguish two cases.

Case 1: First consider the case in which there is no transition between tasks in the current time step $t+1$. As we have $\frac{\tilde{r}(J_i(t))}{|J_i(t)\setminus F|} \ge \frac{R}{m-1}$ and $|F| \le 1$, the algorithm always finds an m-maximal window using the full resource R in time step $t+1$. By Property (e) from Section 3, we have that (i) the windows has size m or (ii) $L_t(W) = \emptyset$. In case (i), $\tilde{r}(J_i(t))$ is reduced by R and $|J_i(t)\setminus F|$ by at least $m-1$, thus $\frac{\tilde{r}(J_i(t+1))}{R} = \frac{\tilde{r}(J_i(t))-R}{R} \ge \frac{|J_i(t)\setminus F|-(m-1)}{m-1} \ge \frac{|J_i(t+1)\setminus F|}{m-1}$. In case (ii), the jobs from $J_i(t)$ with the smallest resource requirement are finished, thus the ratio $\frac{\tilde{r}(J_i(t))}{|J_i(t)\setminus F|} \ge \frac{R}{m-1}$ can only increase. The claim follows.

Case 2: Now consider the case that there is a transition between tasks. That is, there is an arbitrary number of tasks that is finished in Line 3 of Listing 3. Those tasks used $m-m'$ processors, hence at least $m-m'-1$ processors were occupied with full jobs. By induction hypothesis and by the average size of jobs in task set $\mathcal{T}$, at least a resource of $\frac{m-m'-1}{m-1}\cdot R$ was used. Hence, the resource available to the sliding window determined in Lines 7 to 9 is at most $\frac{m'}{m-1}\cdot R$. By Lemma 3.7, we

```
1   for (t,S,W,i) ← (1,∅,∅,1); T(t−1) ≠ ∅; t ← t+1:
2       m′ ← m
3       while (r̃(S)+r̃(J_i(t−1)) ≤ 1) and (|S|+|J_i(t−1)| ≤ m):
4           S ← S ∪ T_i; i ← i+1; m′ ← m′ − |J_i(t−1)|
5           process all jobs in T_i with their full resource requirement
6       m′ ← min{m′, ⌊(1−r̃(S)) · (m−1)/R⌋ + 1}; R ← (m′−1) · R/(m−1)
7       W ← W ∩ J_i(t−1)
8       W ← GrowWindowLeft(W, t, m′, 1−r̃(S))
9       W ← GrowWindowRight(W, t, m′, 1−r̃(S))
10      W ← MoveWindowRight(W, t, 1−r̃(S))
11      if ∃ fractured job ι ∈ W: F ← {ι}
12      else: F ← ∅
13      process each job j ∈ W \ (F ∪ {max W}) with resource r_j
14      if F = {ι}:
15          process job ι with resource q_ι(t)
16      process job max W with the remaining resource
```

Listing 4: Algorithm for task set $\mathcal{T}_2$.

conclude that we computed an m'-maximal window. Now, we either have (a) $|W| = m'$ or (b) $|W| < m'$. In case (a), $\tilde{r}(W)$ was reduced by at most $\frac{m'}{m-1} \cdot R$, whereas $|T_i \setminus F|$ was reduced by exactly $|W| = m'$. Hence $\frac{\tilde{r}(J_i(t+1))}{R} \geq \frac{\tilde{r}(J_i(t)) - m'R/(m-1)}{R} \geq \frac{|J_i(t) \setminus F| - m'}{m-1} = \frac{|J_i(t+1) \setminus F|}{m-1}$ in case (b) with $|W| < m'$, we know $L_t(W) = \emptyset$ by Property (e) from Section 3, implying that the smallest jobs of the new task were executed. The claim follows, as the average size of jobs in each task is at least $R/m-1$.

□

We now consider tasks with jobs that have low resource requirements on average.

Lemma 4.2. *For a set of tasks $\mathcal{T} = \{T_1, \ldots, T_k\}$ with $\frac{r(T)}{|T|} \leq \frac{R}{(m-1)}$ for all $T \in \mathcal{T}$, the algorithm in Listing 4 computes a schedule such that the completion time f_i of task T_i is bounded by $f_i \leq \left\lceil \frac{\sum_{l=1}^{i} |T_l|}{m-1} \right\rceil$.*

Proof. Let $t_i := \frac{\sum_{l=1}^{i} |T_l|}{m-1}$. We show that the following properties hold for every task T_i

(i) T_i is finished at $f_i \leq \lceil t_i \rceil$.
(ii) The number of processors occupied by tasks $T_1 \ldots, T_i$ in time step $\lceil t_i \rceil$ is at most $m_i := (t_i - (\lceil t_i \rceil - 1))(m-1)$.
(iii) Tasks $T_1 \ldots, T_i$ occupy at most a resource of $m_i \cdot \frac{R}{m-1}$ in time step $\lceil t_i \rceil$.

These properties obviously hold for T_1. For the sake of induction, assume they are true for the tasks $T_1, \ldots, T_i$. We distinguish the case two cases whether task T_{i+1} is finished in step f_i or not.

Case 1: If T_{i+1} is finished in time step f_i, it is among those tasks added during the loop in Line 3. Then $f_{i+1} = f_i \leq \lceil t_i \rceil \leq \lceil t_{i+1} \rceil$ and Statement (i) directly follows. For (ii), T_{i+1} uses $|T_{i+1}|$ processors, hence the number of processors used by tasks $T_1, \ldots, T_{i+1}$ in time step f_i is at most $m_i + |T_{i+1}| = (t_{i+1} - (\lceil t_i \rceil - 1))(m-1) = m_{i+1}$. Finally, by $\frac{r(T_{i+1})}{|T_{i+1}|} \leq \frac{R}{(m-1)}$, the resource occupied by tasks $T_1, \ldots, T_{i+1}$ in time step f_i is at most $m_i \cdot \frac{R}{m-1} + r(T_{i+1}) \leq m_i \cdot \frac{R}{m-1} + |T_{i+1}| \cdot \frac{R}{m-1} = m_{i+1} \cdot \frac{R}{m-1}$, which shows (iii).

Case 2: In the case that T_{i+1} is not finished in time step f_i, we will start task T_{i+1} with $m' \geq m - m_i$ processors and allow a resource of at most $(m'-1) \cdot \frac{R}{m-1}$ in this time step (and the full resource in any following non-transitional time step). Since the average resource per full non-fractured job in our sliding window (Lines 8 to 10) is $\frac{R}{m-1}$, we get an analogue statement to Lemma 3.8 from Section 3. That is, we will (a) finish $m'-1$ jobs in f_i and $m-1$ jobs in any time step $t \in (f_i, f_{i+1})$ or (b) use the full resource in any time step $t \in (f_i, f_{i+1})$.

In case (a), we have

$$\begin{aligned} f_{i+1} &\leq f_i + \left\lceil \frac{|T_{i+1}| - (m'-1)}{m-1} \right\rceil \\ &\leq t_i + \frac{m'-1}{m-1} + \left\lceil \frac{|T_{i+1}| - (m'-1)}{m-1} \right\rceil \\ &= \left\lceil \frac{\sum_{k=1}^{i} |T_k| + |T_{i+1}|}{m-1} \right\rceil = \lceil t_{i+1} \rceil, \end{aligned}$$

which yields (i). For (ii), the number of occupied processors in time step $\lceil t_{i+1} \rceil$ is at most $\sum_{k=1}^{i+1} |T_k| - (\lceil t_{i+1} \rceil - 1) \cdot (m-1) = m_{i+1}$. For (iii), observe that the average resource of the window is non-increasing by Lemma 3.8 (b). In particular, the resource used at time $\lceil t_{i+1} \rceil$ is at most $m_{i+1} \cdot \frac{R}{m-1}$.

For case (b), by using $\frac{r(T)}{|T|} \leq \frac{R}{(m-1)}$ in the first inequality, we will finish the task at time

$$\begin{aligned} f_{i+1} &\leq \lceil t_i \rceil + \left\lceil \frac{r(T_{i+1}) - (m'-1) \cdot R/(m-1)}{R} \right\rceil \\ &\leq t_i + \frac{m'-1}{m-1} + \left\lceil \frac{|T_{i+1}| - (m'-1)}{m-1} \right\rceil = \lceil t_{i+1} \rceil, \end{aligned}$$

which yields (i). By using the same reasoning without rounding, the resource used in time step $\lceil t_{i+1} \rceil$ by tasks $T_1, \ldots, T_{i+1}$ can be upper bounded by

$$\left(t_i + \frac{r(T_{i+1}) - (m'-1) \cdot \frac{R}{(m-1)}}{R} - (\lceil t_{i+1} \rceil - 1) \right) \cdot R$$

$$\leq (t_{i+1} - (\lceil t_{i+1} \rceil - 1)) \cdot R = m_{i+1} \cdot \frac{R}{m-1},$$

which yields (iii). For (ii), it remains to be shown that the number of processors occupied at time $\lceil t_{i+1} \rceil$ by jobs from tasks $T_1 \ldots, T_{i+1}$ is at most m_{i+1}. Since (a) did not hold, less than m processors were occupied at some time step prior to t_{i+1}. This implies that the remaining full jobs must have an average size of more than $\frac{R}{m-1}$. The claim follows.

□

We now give bounds for the optimal algorithm.

Lemma 4.3. *The sum of completion times of the optimal solution can be bounded as follows.*

(a) Given a set of tasks $\mathcal{T} = \{T_1, \ldots, T_k\}$ with $R_l \leq R_{l+1}$ for all l, we have $\text{Opt}_{\mathcal{T}} \geq \sum_{i=1}^{k} \left\lceil \sum_{l=1}^{i} R_l \right\rceil$.
(b) Given a set of tasks $\mathcal{T} = \{T_1, \ldots, T_k\}$ with $|T_l| \leq |T_{l+1}|$ for all l, we have $\text{Opt}_{\mathcal{T}} \geq \sum_{i=1}^{k} \left\lceil \sum_{l=1}^{i} \frac{|T_k|}{m} \right\rceil$.

Proof. We first prove (a). As the optimal solution cannot overuse the resource, there is obviously an order $\mathcal{T} = \{T_{\sigma_1}, \ldots, T_{\sigma_l}\}$ such that $\text{Opt}_{\mathcal{T}} \geq \sum_{i=1}^{k} \left\lceil \sum_{l=1}^{i} R_{\sigma_l} \right\rceil$. We denote the bounds on the completion times as $f_i := \left\lceil \sum_{l=1}^{i} R_l \right\rceil$ and $f_i' := \left\lceil \sum_{l=1}^{i} R_{\sigma_l} \right\rceil$. We prove $f_i \leq f_i'$ for all i which directly implies (a). Let i be arbitrary. Assume $f_i > f'_i$. Then $\left\lceil \sum_{l=1}^{i} R_l \right\rceil > \left\lceil \sum_{l=1}^{i} R_{\sigma_l} \right\rceil$, hence $\sum_{l=1}^{i} R_l > \sum_{l=1}^{i} R_{\sigma_l}$. This is a contradiction to $R_l \leq R_{l+1}$ for all l.

For (b), as the optimal solution cannot finish more than m jobs per time step, there is an order $\mathcal{T} = \{T_{\sigma_1},\dots,T_{\sigma_l}\}$ such that $\text{OPT}_{\mathcal{T}} \geq \left\lceil \sum_{l=1}^{i} \frac{|T_{\sigma_l}|}{m} \right\rceil$. Now, denote $f_i := \left\lceil \sum_{l=1}^{i} \frac{|T_l|}{m} \right\rceil$, $f'_i := \left\lceil \sum_{l=1}^{i} \frac{|T_{\sigma_l}|}{m} \right\rceil$. Assume $f_i > f'_i$ for some i. Hence $\sum_{l=1}^{i} |T_l| > \sum_{l=1}^{i} |T_{\sigma_l}|$. A contradiction. □

To upper bound rounding errors later, the following lemma proves to be useful.

Lemma 4.4. *Given $z \in \mathbb{N}_{\geq 3}$ and $\{x_1,\dots,x_k\} \in \mathbb{R}_{\geq 1/z}$ such that $x_i + 1/z \leq x_{i+1}$ for all $i \in \{1,\dots,k-1\}$, there is a $q \in \mathbb{N}_0$ such that*

$$\sum_{i=1}^{k}\left(\left\lceil \frac{z}{\lfloor (z-1)/2 \rfloor}\cdot x_i \right\rceil - \frac{z}{\lfloor (z-1)/2 \rfloor}\cdot \lceil x_i \rceil\right) \leq q, \text{ and} \tag{2}$$

$$\sum_{i=1}^{k} \lceil x_i \rceil \geq \frac{2}{3}(\sqrt{q}-2)^3 + (k-q). \tag{3}$$

Proof. First, denote $err_i := \left\lceil \frac{z}{\lfloor (z-1)/2 \rfloor}\cdot x_i \right\rceil - \frac{z}{\lfloor (z-1)/2 \rfloor}\cdot \lceil x_i \rceil$. Also, let $E_{>0} := \{i \in \{1,\dots,k\} : err_i > 0\}$ and $E_{\leq 0}$ analogously. Clearly, we have

$$err_i \leq \left(\frac{z}{\lfloor (z-1)/2 \rfloor}\cdot x_i + 1\right) - \frac{z}{\lfloor (z-1)/2 \rfloor}\cdot x_i = 1$$

for all $i \in \{1,\dots,k\}$. We choose $q = |E_{>0}|$, so (2) follows. We further show that

$$x_i \in \left[l, \frac{\lfloor (z-1)/2 \rfloor}{z}\cdot\left(\left\lceil \frac{(l+1)\cdot z}{\lfloor (z-1)/2 \rfloor}\right\rceil - 1\right)\right] \text{ for } l \in \mathbb{N}_0 \tag{4}$$

implies $err_i \leq 0$. Note that (4) implies $\lceil x_i \rceil \leq l+1$. We upper bound

$$\left\lceil \frac{z}{\lfloor (z-1)/2 \rfloor}\cdot x_i \right\rceil \leq \left\lceil \frac{(l+1)\cdot z}{\lfloor (z-1)/2 \rfloor}\right\rceil - 1 \leq \frac{(l+1)\cdot z}{\lfloor (z-1)/2 \rfloor} = \frac{z}{\lfloor (z-1)/2 \rfloor}\cdot \lceil x_i \rceil. \tag{5}$$

Now, each x_i, $i \in E_{>0}$ has to be in an open interval of the form

$$\left(\frac{\lfloor (z-1)/2 \rfloor}{z}\cdot\left(\left\lceil \frac{l\cdot z}{\lfloor (z-1)/2 \rfloor}\right\rceil - 1\right), l\right) \tag{6}$$

for some $l \in \mathbb{N}$ since otherwise $err_i \leq 0$ by Inequality (5). The length of each such interval can be upper bounded by

$$\begin{aligned}
& l - \frac{\lfloor (z-1)/2 \rfloor}{z}\cdot\left(\left\lceil \frac{l\cdot z}{\lfloor (z-1)/2 \rfloor}\right\rceil - 1\right) \\
&= \frac{\lfloor \frac{z-1}{2} \rfloor}{z}\cdot\left(\frac{l\left(z-2\left(\lfloor \frac{z-1}{2} \rfloor\right)\right)}{\lfloor (z-1)/2 \rfloor} - \left\lceil \frac{l\left(z-2\left(\lfloor \frac{z-1}{2} \rfloor\right)\right)}{\lfloor (z-1)/2 \rfloor}\right\rceil + 1\right) \\
&\leq \frac{\lfloor (z-1)/2 \rfloor}{z}\cdot\left(\frac{l(z-2\cdot(z-2)/2)}{\lfloor (z-1)/2 \rfloor} - \left\lceil \frac{l(z-2\cdot(z-1)/2)}{\lfloor (z-1)/2 \rfloor}\right\rceil + 1\right) \\
&\leq \frac{\lfloor (z-1)/2 \rfloor}{z}\cdot\left(\frac{2l}{\lfloor (z-1)/2 \rfloor} - 1 + 1\right) = \frac{2l}{z},
\end{aligned}$$

where the first equality is just a transformation, the second inequality bounds the floor and ceiling functions and the last inequality follows from $\frac{l(z-2\cdot(z-1)/2)}{\lfloor (z-1)/2 \rfloor} = \frac{l}{\lfloor (z-1)/2 \rfloor} > 0$. Hence, at most $2l$ different x_i can be in the lth such interval. Considering the first p such intervals, they can contain at most $\sum_{l=1}^{p} 2l = p(p+1)$ different x_i. This leads to $x_i > p$ for all $i > p(p+1)$. We conclude

$$\begin{aligned}
\sum_{i=1}^{k} \lceil x_i \rceil &= \sum_{i \in E_{>0}} \lceil x_i \rceil + \sum_{i \in E_{\leq 0}} \lceil x_i \rceil \\
&\geq \left(\sum_{p=1}^{\lfloor \sqrt{q} \rfloor - 1} \sum_{i=(p-1)p+1}^{p(p+1)} p\right) + (k-q) \\
&\geq \sum_{p=1}^{\lfloor \sqrt{q} \rfloor - 1} 2p^2 + (k-q) \\
&= \frac{2\cdot(\lfloor \sqrt{q} \rfloor - 1)\cdot(\lfloor \sqrt{q} \rfloor - 1/2)\cdot\lfloor \sqrt{q} \rfloor}{3} + (k-q) \\
&\geq \frac{2}{3}(\sqrt{q}-2)^3 + (k-q),
\end{aligned}$$

where the first inequality is by rearranging the sum and omitting some summands as well as $\lceil x_i \rceil \geq 1$ for all i and the last equality is by a well-known formula for summing up squares. □

4.2 Approximation Algorithm

We are now ready to describe our algorithm. The algorithm divides the tasks into task sets

$$\mathcal{T}_1 = \left\{T \in \mathcal{T} \,\middle|\, \frac{|T|}{\sum_{J_i \in T} r_i} < m-1\right\} \text{ and } \mathcal{T}_2 = \left\{T \in \mathcal{T} \,\middle|\, \frac{|T|}{\sum_{J_i \in T} r_i} \geq m-1\right\}.$$

We assign $\lfloor m/2 \rfloor$ processors to task set $\mathcal{T}_1$ and $\lceil m/2 \rceil$ processors to task set $\mathcal{T}_2$. Denote the sum of completion times of the task using our algorithm by S and the optimal sum of completion times by OPT. The partial sum of completion times of tasks from $\mathcal{T}_1$ and $\mathcal{T}_2$ are called $\text{OPT}_{\mathcal{T}_1}$ and $\text{OPT}_{\mathcal{T}_2}$, respectively. Also, let $k_1 = |\mathcal{T}_1|$, $k_2 = |\mathcal{T}_2|$ (implying $k = k_1 + k_2$). We prove the following lemmata.

Lemma 4.5. *Scheduling $\mathcal{T}_1$ using the algorithm in Listing 3 with $\lfloor \frac{m}{2} \rfloor$ processors and a resource of $R = \frac{\lfloor m/2 \rfloor - 1}{m-1} < \frac{1}{2}$, there is a $q_1 \in \mathbb{N}_0$ such that the sum of completion times is at most $\left(2 + \frac{4}{m-3}\right)\text{OPT}_{\mathcal{T}_1} + q_1$ as well as*

$$\text{OPT}_{\mathcal{T}_1} \geq \frac{2}{3}(\sqrt{q_1}-2)^3 + (k_1 - q_1). \tag{7}$$

Proof. For all $T \in \mathcal{T}_1$, we have

$$\frac{r(T)}{|T|} > \frac{1}{m-1} = \frac{(\lfloor m/2 \rfloor - 1)/(m-1)}{\lfloor m/2 \rfloor - 1}$$

by construction of $\mathcal{T}_1$. Assume the tasks $\mathcal{T}_1 = \{T_1,\dots,T_{k_1}\}$ are ordered by non-decreasing overall resource requirement (i.e., $r(T_1) \leq r(T_2) \leq \dots \leq r(T_{k_1})$). Applying Lemma 4.1, we know that the full resource of $\frac{\lfloor m/2 \rfloor - 1}{m-1}$ is used in every time step. Hence, the tasks are scheduled such that the sum of their completion times is

$$S_{\mathcal{T}_1} = \sum_{i=1}^{k_1}\left\lceil \frac{\sum_{l=1}^{i} r(T_l)}{(\lfloor m/2 \rfloor - 1)/(m-1)}\right\rceil = \sum_{i=1}^{k_1}\left\lceil \frac{m-1}{(\lfloor m/2 \rfloor - 1)}\sum_{l=1}^{i} r(T_j)\right\rceil.$$

From Lemma 4.3 (a), we have $\text{OPT}_{\mathcal{T}_1} \geq \sum_{i=1}^{k_1}\left\lceil \sum_{l=1}^{i} r(T_j)\right\rceil$. Now, using Lemma 4.4 with $x_i := \sum_{l=1}^{i} r(T_j)$ and $z := m-1$, we conclude that there is a $q_1 \in \mathbb{N}_0$ such that

$$S_{\mathcal{T}_1} \leq \frac{m-1}{(\lfloor m/2 \rfloor - 1)}\text{OPT}_{\mathcal{T}_1} + q_1 \leq \left(2 + \frac{4}{m-3}\right)\text{OPT}_{\mathcal{T}_1} + q_1$$

together with Property (7), which proves the claim. □

Lemma 4.6. *Scheduling $\mathcal{T}_2$ using the algorithm in Listing 4 with $\lceil \frac{m}{2} \rceil$ processors and a resource of $R=\frac{1}{2}$, there is a $q_2 \in \mathbb{N}_0$ such that the sum of completion times is at most $\left(2+\frac{4}{m-2}\right)\mathrm{Opt}_{\mathcal{T}_2}+q_2$ and*

$$\mathrm{Opt}_{\mathcal{T}_2} \geq \frac{2}{3}(\sqrt{q_2}-2)^3+(k_2-q_2). \quad (8)$$

Proof. For all $T \in \mathcal{T}_2$, we have

$$\frac{r(T)}{|T|} \leq \frac{1}{m-1} = \frac{1/2}{(m+1)/2-1} \leq \frac{1/2}{\lceil m/2 \rceil -1}$$

by construction of $\mathcal{T}_2$. Assume the tasks $\mathcal{T}_2=\{T_1,\ldots,T_{k_2}\}$ are ordered by non-decreasing number of jobs (i.e., $|T_1| \leq |T_2| \leq \cdots \leq |T_{k_2}|$). By Lemma 4.2, we have $S_{\mathcal{T}_2}=\sum_{i=1}^{k_2}\left\lceil \frac{|T_i|}{\lceil m/2 \rceil -1}\right\rceil$, and from Lemma 4.3 (b) we have $\mathrm{Opt}_{\mathcal{T}_2} \geq \sum_{i=1}^{k_2}\left\lceil \frac{|T_i|}{m}\right\rceil$. Now, observing $\lceil m/2 \rceil = \lfloor (m+1)/2 \rfloor$ and using Lemma 4.4 with $x_i := \frac{|T_i|}{m}$ and $z := m$, we conclude that there is a $q_2 \in \mathbb{N}_0$ with

$$S_{\mathcal{T}_1} \leq \frac{m}{\lfloor \frac{(m+1)}{2} \rfloor -1}\cdot \mathrm{Opt}_{\mathcal{T}_2}+q_2 \leq \left(2+\frac{4}{m-2}\right)\mathrm{Opt}_{\mathcal{T}_2}+q_2$$

together with Property (8). □

For our final result, we need the following technical lemma.

Lemma 4.7. *Given $q_1,q_2,k_1,k_2 \in \mathbb{N}_0$ and $k \in \mathbb{N}$ such that $q_1+q_2 \leq k$. Then*

$$\frac{q_1+q_2}{\frac{2}{3}(\sqrt{q_1}-2)^3+\frac{2}{3}(\sqrt{q_2}-2)^3+k-(q_1+q_2)} = \mathrm{O}\left(k^{-1/5}\right)$$

with respect to k.

Proof. If $q_1+q_2 \leq k^{4/5}$,

$$\begin{aligned}&\frac{q_1+q_2}{\frac{2}{3}(\sqrt{q_1}-2)^3+\frac{2}{3}(\sqrt{q_2}-2)^3+k-(q_1+q_2)}\\ &\leq \frac{q_1+q_2}{-2\cdot\frac{16}{3}+k-(q_1+q_2)} < \frac{k^{4/5}}{k-k^{4/5}-11} \leq \frac{1}{k^{1/5}-12}.\end{aligned}$$

On the other hand, if $k^{4/5} < q_1+q_2 \leq k$, then $q_1 > 1/2k^{4/5} > 1/4k^{4/5}$ or $q_2 > 1/4k^{4/5}$. Hence

$$\begin{aligned}&\frac{q_1+q_2}{\frac{2}{3}(\sqrt{q_1}-2)^3+\frac{2}{3}(\sqrt{q_2}-2)^3+k-(q_1+q_2)}\\ &\leq \frac{q_1+q_2}{\frac{2}{3}(\sqrt{q_1}-2)^3+\frac{2}{3}(\sqrt{q_2}-2)^3} \leq \frac{k}{\frac{2}{3}(\frac{1}{2}k^{2/5}-2)^3}.\end{aligned}$$

The claim follows. □

We are now ready to state the main results of this section. Note that we use $\mathrm{o}(1)$ with respect to the number of tasks.

Theorem 4.8. *Splitting up $\mathcal{T}$ into task sets $\mathcal{T}_1$ and $\mathcal{T}_2$ and scheduling them separately with the algorithms from Listing 3 and Listing 4 results in a sum of completion times of*

$$\left(\left(2+\frac{4}{(m-3)}\right)+\mathrm{o}(1)\right)\cdot \mathrm{Opt}.$$

Proof. By $S = S_{\mathcal{T}_1} + S_{\mathcal{T}_2}$ and $\mathrm{Opt} = \mathrm{Opt}_{\mathcal{T}_1} + \mathrm{Opt}_{\mathcal{T}_2}$ as well as Lemma 4.5 and Lemma 4.6, there are $q_1,q_2 \in \mathbb{N}_0$ such that

$$\begin{aligned}S &\leq \left(2+\frac{4}{m-3}\right)\mathrm{Opt}_{\mathcal{T}_1}+q_1+\left(2+\frac{4}{m-2}\right)\mathrm{Opt}_{\mathcal{T}_2}+q_2\\ &\leq \left(2+\frac{4}{m-3}\right)(\mathrm{Opt}_{\mathcal{T}_1}+\mathrm{Opt}_{\mathcal{T}_2})+q_1+q_2\end{aligned}$$

and

$$\mathrm{Opt} \geq \frac{2}{3}(\sqrt{q_1}-2)^3+(k_1-q_1)+\frac{2}{3}(\sqrt{q_2}-2)^3+(k_2-q_2).$$

Dividing S by Opt, using these inequalities, and applying Lemma 4.7 completes the proof. □

If we denote the total number of jobs by $n=\sum_{i=1}^{k} n_i$ and by applying the same arguments as in the proof of Theorem 3.3, we get a bound on the running time.

Corollary 4.9. *The algorithms can be implemented with a running time of $\mathrm{O}((m+n)\cdot n)$.*

REFERENCES

[1] Noga Alon, Yossi Azar, Gerhard J Woeginger, and Tal Yadid. 1998. Approximation schemes for scheduling on parallel machines. *Journal of Scheduling* 1, 1 (1998), 55–66.

[2] Ernst Althaus, André Brinkmann, Peter Kling, Friedhelm Meyer auf der Heide, Lars Nagel, Sören Riechers, Jiří Sgall, and Tim Süß. 2017. Scheduling shared continuous resources on many-cores. *Journal of Scheduling* (2017).

[3] André Brinkmann, Peter Kling, Friedhelm Meyer auf der Heide, Lars Nagel, Sören Riechers, and Tim Süß. 2014. Scheduling Shared Continuous Resources on Many-Cores. In *Proceedings of the 26th ACM Symposium on Parallelism in Algorithms and Architectures (SPAA '14)*. ACM, 128–137.

[4] Fan Chung, Ronald Graham, Jia Mao, and George Varghese. 2006. Parallelism versus Memory Allocation in Pipelined Router Forwarding Engines. *Theory of Computing Systems* 39, 6 (2006), 829–849.

[5] Leah Epstein, Asaf Levin, and Rob van Stee. 2012. Approximation Schemes for Packing Splittable Items with Cardinality Constraints. In *Algorithmica*. Vol. 62. Springer, 102–129.

[6] Leah Epstein and Rob van Stee. 2007. Approximation schemes for packing splittable items with cardinality constraints. In *Proceedings of the 5th International Workshop on Approximation and Online Algorithms (WAOA '07)*. Springer, 232–245.

[7] Leah Epstein and Rob van Stee. 2011. Improved results for a memory allocation problem. *Theory of Computing Systems* 48, 1 (2011), 79–92.

[8] Michael R Garey and Ronald L. Graham. 1975. Bounds for multiprocessor scheduling with resource constraints. *SIAM J. Comput.* 4, 2 (1975), 187–200.

[9] Ellis Horowitz and Sartaj Sahni. 1976. Exact and approximate algorithms for scheduling nonidentical processors. *Journal of the ACM (JACM)* 23, 2 (1976), 317–327.

[10] Klaus Jansen, Marten Maack, and Malin Rau. 2016. Approximation schemes for machine scheduling with resource (in-) dependent processing times. In *Proceedings of the Twenty-Seventh Annual ACM-SIAM Symposium on Discrete Algorithms*. Society for Industrial and Applied Mathematics, 1526–1542.

[11] Joanna Józefowska and Jan Weglarz. 1998. On a Methodology for Discrete-continuous Scheduling. *European Journal of Operational Research* 107, 2 (1998), 338–353.

[12] Jürgen König, Alexander Mäcker, Friedhelm Meyer auf der Heide, and Sören Riechers. 2016. Scheduling with Interjob Communication on Parallel Processors. In *Proceedings of the 10th Annual International Conference on Combinatorial Optimization and Applications (COCOA '16)*. Springer, 563–577.

[13] Joseph YT Leung, Haibing Li, and Michael Pinedo. 2005. Order Scheduling Models: An Overview. In *Multidisciplinary Scheduling: Theory and Applications*. Springer, 37–53.

[14] Joseph Y-T. Leung. 2004. *Handbook of Scheduling: Algorithms, Models, and Performance Analysis*. Chapman & Hall/CRC.

[15] Martin Niemeier and Andreas Wiese. 2015. Scheduling with an Orthogonal Resource Constraint. *Algorithmica* 71, 4 (2015), 837–858.

[16] Jan Weglarz, Joanna Józefowska, Marek Mika, and Grzegorz Waligóra. 2011. Project Scheduling with Finite or Infinite Number of Activity Processing Modes – A Survey. *European Journal of Operational Research* 208, 3 (2011), 177–205.

Brief Announcement: Graph Matching in Massive Datasets

Soheil Behnezhad* University of Maryland
Mahsa Derakhshan* University of Maryland
Hossein Esfandiari† University of Maryland
Elif Tan‡ Ankara University
Hadi Yami* University of Maryland

ABSTRACT

In this paper we consider the maximum matching problem in large bipartite graphs. We present a new algorithm that finds the maximum matching in a few iterations of a novel edge sampling technique. This algorithm can be implemented in big data settings such as *streaming setting* and *MapReduce setting*, where each iteration of the algorithm maps to one pass over the stream, or one MapReduce round of computation, respectively. We prove that our algorithm provides a $1-\varepsilon$ approximate solution to the maximum matching in $1/\varepsilon$ rounds which improves the prior work in terms of the number of passes/rounds. Our algorithm works even better when we run it on real datasets and finds the exact maximum matching in 4 to 8 rounds while sampling only about %1 of the edges.

1 INTRODUCTION

The best offline algorithm known for the maximum matching problem runs in $O(m\sqrt{n})$ time and $O(m)$ space [13] for a graph G with n vertices and m edges. For massive graphs, this is quite inefficient, especially when the input graph is dense (i.e., $m \gg n$). To overcome this problem, there are several recent attempts to design efficient algorithms in *streaming* and/or *distributed* settings (e.g. MapReduce)[2–4, 7, 9, 11, 12]. All of these algorithms give approximate solutions to the maximum matching, i.e., for some $0 < \alpha \leq 1$ they report a solution which is at least α fraction of the maximum matching.

In streaming setting, a graphs is given as a sequence of edges. The algorithm is allowed to take a few passes over the input (usually constant or logarithmic), and has access to a local memory significantly smaller than the input graph (i.e. $o(n^2)$).

McGregor [12] provided a $1-\varepsilon$ approximation algorithm for unweighted general graphs and a $0.5-\varepsilon$ approximation algorithm for weighted graphs in constant (exponential in $1/\varepsilon$) passes over the input, using $\tilde{O}(n)$ space. For bipartite unweighted graphs, Ahn and Guha [1] improved the number of passes to $O(1/\varepsilon^2 \log\log 1/\varepsilon)$. On a related note, Ahn and Guha [2] later presented a MapReduce algorithm that achieves a $1-\varepsilon$ approximation in $O(p/\varepsilon)$ rounds, using $O(n^{1+1/p})$ local space.

There are also some recent attempts towards estimating the size of the maximum matching in these settings [3, 4, 7, 9] and some attempts to find the maximum matching when its size is small [4–6].

In this paper, we present an algorithm that finds the maximum matching in a few iterations of a novel edge sampling technique. Our algorithm iteratively samples the edges of the input graph based on the minimum vertex cover of the currently sampled edges. In fact, each iteration of the algorithm maps to one pass over the stream in the streaming setting, or one Map-Reduce round of computation. We prove that after $1/\varepsilon$ iterations our algorithm gives a $1-\varepsilon$ approximation, improving the result of Ahn and Guha [1] in terms of the number of passes.

The simplicity of our algorithm makes it implementable in common big data settings such as streaming and Map-Reduce models. Our experiments indicate that on real world datasets, it works much better than our theoretical guarantees. More precisely, it finds the exact maximum matching in 4 to 8 of rounds, while sampling only about %1 of edges in total.

2 NOTATIONS

The input, denoted by $\mathcal{G}$, is an undirected bipartite graph with n vertices. Throughout this paper, $\mathcal{V}(\mathcal{G})$ denotes the vertex set of $\mathcal{G}$ and $\mathcal{E}(\mathcal{G})$ denotes the edge set of $\mathcal{G}$. For any arbitrary subgraph H of $\mathcal{G}$, $\mathcal{G} \setminus H$ is a subgraph of $\mathcal{G}$ where $\mathcal{V}(\mathcal{G} \setminus H) = \mathcal{V}(\mathcal{G}) - \mathcal{V}(H)$ and an edge $\{u, v\} \in \mathcal{E}(\mathcal{G})$ is in $\mathcal{E}(\mathcal{G} \setminus H)$ if and only if u and v are not in $\mathcal{V}(H)$. We may also abuse this notation and use $\mathcal{G} \setminus V$ when V is a subset of $\mathcal{V}(\mathcal{G})$ and not a sub-graph of $\mathcal{G}$. Moreover, we denote the set of edges in the maximum matching of a graph G by $\mathcal{M}_G$.

3 ALGORITHM

In this section we explain our algorithm to find a maximum matching in bipartite graphs (Figure 1). The input graph $\mathcal{G}$ and a real number α are given. Our algorithm consists of

*Supported in part by NSF CAREER award CCF-1053605, NSF BIGDATA grant IIS-1546108, NSF AF:Medium grant CCF-1161365, DARPA GRAPHS/AFOSR grant FA9550-12-1-0423, and another DARPA SIMPLEX grant. Emails: {soheil,mahsaa,hadiyami}@cs.umd.edu.
†Supported in part by Google PhD Fellowship in Market Algorithms. Email: hossein@cs.umd.edu.
‡Supported by TUBITAK-2219 International Postdoctoral Research Scholarship Programme. Email: etan@ankara.edu.tr.

SPAA '17, July 24-26, 2017, Washington DC, USA

ACM ISBN 978-1-4503-4593-4/17/07.
https://doi.org/10.1145/3087556.3087601

```
 1: procedure MAXIMUMMATCHINGBYSAMPLING(𝒢, α)
 2:     𝒮₀, 𝒞₀ ← ∅
 3:     i ← 1
 4:     while |ℰ(𝒢 \ 𝒞ᵢ₋₁)| > 0 do
 5:         U ← nα edges sampled u.a.r from 𝒢 \ 𝒞ᵢ₋₁
 6:         𝒮ᵢ ← 𝒮ᵢ₋₁ ∪ U
 7:         𝒞ᵢ ← vertices in minimum vertex cover of 𝒮ᵢ
 8:         i ← i + 1
 9:     end while
10:     return maximum matching of 𝒮ᵢ₋₁
11: end procedure
```

Figure 1: Maximum Matching via Sampling

several rounds, and in each round, we add some edges to our sample until there are no more valid edges to add. More precisely, $\mathcal{S}_i$ denotes our sample at round i and $\mathcal{C}_i$ denotes a minimum vertex cover of $\mathcal{S}_i$. Initially $\mathcal{S}_0$ and $\mathcal{C}_0$ are empty sets. For any $i > 0$, $\mathcal{S}_i$ is the union of $\mathcal{S}_{i-1}$ and a sample of at most $n\alpha$ edges chosen uniformly at random from the candidate set $\mathcal{E}(\mathcal{G} \setminus \mathcal{C}_{i-1})$. This means in the first round the candidate edges that we sample from is the edge set of $\mathcal{G}$, and $\mathcal{S}_1$ is a set of $n\alpha$ edges that are chosen uniformly at random from $\mathcal{E}(\mathcal{G})$. We continue this until round r where there are no edges in the candidate set $\mathcal{E}(\mathcal{G} \setminus \mathcal{C}_r)$. This implies that all the edges in $\mathcal{G}$ are covered by $\mathcal{C}_r$. Note that in a bipartite graph the size of the minimum vertex cover is equal to the size of the maximum matching by König's theorem [10]. Hence we have $|\mathcal{M}_{\mathcal{S}_r}| = |\mathcal{C}_r|$. On the other hand $\mathcal{C}_r$ is also a vertex cover of $\mathcal{G}$ since it covers every edge in $\mathcal{G}$, therefore the size of the maximum matching of $\mathcal{G}$ is at most $|\mathcal{C}_r|$. This means $|\mathcal{M}_{\mathcal{G}}| = |\mathcal{M}_{\mathcal{S}_r}|$ and it suffices to return the maximum matching of our last sample when there are no edges in the candidate set.

4 ANALYSIS

In this section we analyze Algorithm 1 and show that by setting $\alpha = \sqrt{n}$, our algorithm gives a $(1-\varepsilon)$-approximation for the maximum matching problem in streaming setting, using $O(\frac{n^{1.5}}{\varepsilon})$ space and $O(\frac{1}{\varepsilon})$ passes.

We first prove that every edge that is not covered by the vertex cover in the i-th round is added to the sample in the next round, with high probability. We define the notion of *critical induced subgraphs* as follows:

Definition 4.1 (Critical Induced Subgraph). An induced subgraph $\mathcal{K}$ of $\mathcal{G}$ is *critical*, if $|\mathcal{E}(\mathcal{K})| \geq n^{1.5}$.

We show that the probability that Algorithm 1 does not sample any edge from an arbitrary critical induced subgraph in the first round is too small that even the union bound over all critical induced subgraphs is still very low. This means that with high probability any critical induced subgraph has at least one edge in $\mathcal{S}_1$.

LEMMA 4.2. *With probability at least $1 - (\frac{2}{e})^n$, any critical induced subgraph of $\mathcal{G}$ has at least one edge in $\mathcal{S}_1$, if $\alpha = \sqrt{n}$.*

PROOF. Let $\mathcal{K}$ be an arbitrary critical induced subgraph of $\mathcal{G}$. For any arbitrary edge w of $\mathcal{G}$, let $\bar{P}(w, \mathcal{S}_1)$ denote the probability that w is not in $\mathcal{S}_1$. We also use $\bar{P}(\mathcal{K}, \mathcal{S}_1)$ to denote the probability that none of the edges of $\mathcal{K}$ are in $\mathcal{S}_1$. By fixing a random edge x of $\mathcal{K}$ we first give an upper bound for $\bar{P}(x, \mathcal{S}_1)$ to further show $\bar{P}(\mathcal{K}, \mathcal{S}_1)$ is very small.

Note that we sample $n\sqrt{n}$ edges of $\mathcal{E}(\mathcal{G})$ uniformly at random in the first step, thus $\bar{P}(x, \mathcal{S}_1) = 1 - \frac{n\sqrt{n}}{|\mathcal{E}(\mathcal{G})|}$. This means $\bar{P}(x, \mathcal{S}_1)$ has the highest value when $|\mathcal{E}(\mathcal{G})|$ is large, but the number of the edges in a graph with n vertices could not be more than n^2. Therefore

$$\bar{P}(x, \mathcal{S}_1) < 1 - \frac{n\sqrt{n}}{n^2} = 1 - \frac{1}{\sqrt{n}}. \tag{1}$$

We take advantage of the fact that all the edges in $\mathcal{S}_1$ are chosen uniformly at random to give an upper bound for $\bar{P}(\mathcal{K}, \mathcal{S}_1)$ using $\bar{P}(x, \mathcal{S}_1)$. Boolean random variables in $\{X_1, \ldots, X_n\}$ are *negatively correlated* if:

$$\Pr[\bigwedge_{i \in S} X_i = 1] \leq \prod_{i \in S} \Pr[X_i] \qquad \forall S \subseteq \{1, \ldots, n\} \tag{2}$$

For any edge w of $\mathcal{G}$, we define the boolean random variable $\bar{X}(w, \mathcal{S}_1)$ to be 1 if w is not in $\mathcal{S}_1$ and 0 otherwise (note that $\bar{P}(w, \mathcal{S}_1) = \Pr[\bar{X}(w, \mathcal{S}_1)]$). Since the edges in $\mathcal{S}_1$ are chosen uniformly at random, the boolean random variables in $\mathcal{X}_{\mathcal{G}} = \{\bar{X}(y, \mathcal{S}_1) \mid y \in \mathcal{E}(\mathcal{G})\}$ are negatively correlated [8], therefore the probability that none of the edges of $\mathcal{K}$ are in $\mathcal{S}_1$, is not more than $(1 - n^{-0.5})^{|\mathcal{E}(\mathcal{K})|}$, more formally let $\mathcal{X}_{\mathcal{K}} = \{\bar{X}(y, \mathcal{S}_1) \mid y \in \mathcal{E}(\mathcal{K})\}$, since $\mathcal{X}_{\mathcal{K}} \subseteq \mathcal{X}_{\mathcal{G}}$ by (2):

$$\Pr[\bigwedge_{r \in \mathcal{X}_{\mathcal{K}}} r = 1] \leq \prod_{r \in \mathcal{X}_{\mathcal{K}}} \Pr[r] = \bar{P}(x, \mathcal{S}_1)^{|\mathcal{E}(\mathcal{K})|}$$

and by (1):

$$\bar{P}(x, \mathcal{S}_1)^{|\mathcal{E}(\mathcal{K})|} \leq (1 - \frac{1}{\sqrt{n}})^{|\mathcal{E}(\mathcal{K})|}$$

therefore:

$$\Pr[\bigwedge_{r \in \mathcal{X}_{\mathcal{K}}} r = 1] = \bar{P}(\mathcal{K}, \mathcal{S}_1) \leq (1 - \frac{1}{\sqrt{n}})^{|\mathcal{E}(\mathcal{K})|}. \tag{3}$$

Note that $\mathcal{K}$ is a critical induced subgarph of $\mathcal{G}$ and by definition $|\mathcal{E}(\mathcal{K})| \geq n\sqrt{n}$, thus $\bar{P}(\mathcal{K}, \mathcal{S}_1) \leq (1 - n^{-0.5})^{n\sqrt{n}}$ and by using the fact that $(1 - \frac{1}{x})^x < \frac{1}{e}$ for any real number $x \geq 1$, we get:

$$\bar{P}(\mathcal{K}, \mathcal{S}_1) \leq (1 - \frac{1}{\sqrt{n}})^{n\sqrt{n}} = ((1 - \frac{1}{\sqrt{n}})^{\sqrt{n}})^n < (\frac{1}{e})^n.$$

On the other hand every subset of $\mathcal{V}(\mathcal{G})$ is equivalent to an induced subgraph of $\mathcal{G}$. Therefore the total number of critical induced subgraphs of $\mathcal{G}$ does not exceed 2^n. This means the probability that there is at least one critical induced subgraph of $\mathcal{G}$ that has no edge in $\mathcal{S}_1$, which is equal to the union bound of $\bar{P}(\mathcal{K}, \mathcal{S}_1)$ for all possible critical induced subgraphs, is not more than $2^n \times (\frac{1}{e})^n = (\frac{2}{e})^n$. □

Using Lemma 4.2, we give an $n^{1.5}$ upper bound for the size of $\mathcal{E}(\mathcal{G}/\mathcal{C}_i)$ with high probability. This means every edge in $\mathcal{G}/\mathcal{C}_i$ could be added to the sample in the next round.

LEMMA 4.3. *With probability at least $1-(\frac{2}{e})^n$ every edge in $\mathcal{G}/\mathcal{C}_{i-1}$ is in $\mathcal{S}_i$, for any $i>1$, If $\alpha=\sqrt{n}$.*

PROOF. Note that since $\alpha=\sqrt{n}$, in Line 6 of Algorithm 1, $n\sqrt{n}$ edges of $\mathcal{G}/\mathcal{C}_{i-1}$ are added to the sample. Therefore if the number of edges in $\mathcal{G}/\mathcal{C}_{i-1}$ is less than $n\sqrt{n}$ (which we prove with high probability is the case), $\mathcal{S}_i$ will contain them all as desired.

To prove $|\mathcal{E}(\mathcal{G}/\mathcal{C}_{i-1})|\le n\sqrt{n}$ with high probability, recall that by Lemma 4.2, all critical induced subgraphs of $\mathcal{G}$ have at least one edge in $\mathcal{S}_1$ with probability $1-(\frac{2}{e})^n$. We show if $|\mathcal{E}(\mathcal{G}/\mathcal{C}_{i-1})|>n\sqrt{n}$ there exists a critical induced subgraph of $\mathcal{G}$ that does not have any edge in $\mathcal{S}_1$, and therefore it happens only with probability $(\frac{2}{e})^n$. To do so, we first prove if an edge e is in $\mathcal{S}_1$, then it cannot be in $\mathcal{G}/\mathcal{C}_{i-1}$. To see this, note that e has to be in $\mathcal{S}_{i-1}$ since the sample set at each round is a super set of the sample set at the previous round (Line 6 of Algorithm 1). This means the vertex cover $\mathcal{C}_{i-1}$ of $\mathcal{S}_{i-1}$, contains at least one of the vertices of e to cover it, which implies at least one of the vertices of e is not in $\mathcal{G}/\mathcal{C}_{i-1}$, and therefore $e\notin\mathcal{E}(\mathcal{G}/\mathcal{C}_{i-1})$. Note that if the number of edges in $\mathcal{G}/\mathcal{C}_{i-1}$ is more than $n\sqrt{n}$, then $\mathcal{G}/\mathcal{C}_{i-1}$ is a critical induced subgraph of $\mathcal{G}$ by Definition 4.1 which does not have any edge in $\mathcal{S}_1$ (or otherwise that edge could not have appeared in $\mathcal{G}/\mathcal{C}_{i-1}$). By Lemma 4.2 this happens only with probability $(\frac{2}{e})^n$.

We proved with probability at least $1-(\frac{2}{e})^n$, the number of edges in candidate set $\mathcal{G}/\mathcal{C}_{i-1}$ is too small that we can sample them all. □

Theorem 4.5 states that after $\frac{1}{\varepsilon}$ rounds, the maximum matching of the sample is a $(1-\varepsilon)$-approximation for the maximum matching of $\mathcal{G}$ with high probability. To prove this, we first show in Lemma 4.4, that at least $|\mathcal{M}_\mathcal{G}|-|\mathcal{M}_{\mathcal{S}_i}|$ edges of $\mathcal{M}_\mathcal{G}$ are in $\mathcal{S}_{i+1}-\mathcal{S}_i$ with high probability. Then using this lemma we show that before reaching the (1-ε)-approximation, at each round, the size of the maximum matching of the sample increases by at least $\varepsilon|\mathcal{M}_\mathcal{G}|$. Using this observation we give an upper bound for the number of rounds before reaching the approximation.

LEMMA 4.4. *If $|\mathcal{M}_{\mathcal{S}_i}|<|\mathcal{M}_\mathcal{G}|$, and we set $\alpha=\sqrt{n}$, with probability at least $1-(\frac{2}{e})^n$, at least $|\mathcal{M}_\mathcal{G}|-|\mathcal{M}_{\mathcal{S}_i}|$ edges of $\mathcal{M}_\mathcal{G}$ are in $\mathcal{S}_{i+1}-\mathcal{S}_i$.*

PROOF. Let k_i denote $|\mathcal{M}_\mathcal{G}|-|\mathcal{M}_{\mathcal{S}_i}|$. Note that $|\mathcal{C}_i|=|\mathcal{M}_{\mathcal{S}_i}|$ since any subgraph of a bipartite graph is also a bipartite graph and the size of the minimum vertex cover of any bipartite graph is equal to the size of its maximum matching. Therefore $|\mathcal{M}_\mathcal{G}|-|\mathcal{C}_i|=k_i$. This means $\mathcal{C}_i$ does not cover at least k_i edges of $\mathcal{M}_\mathcal{G}$, since no two edges of $\mathcal{M}_\mathcal{G}$ could be covered with the same vertex. By Lemma 4.3 every edge in $\mathcal{G}/\mathcal{C}_i$ is in $\mathcal{S}_{i+1}$ with probability at least $1-(\frac{2}{e})^n$, therefore at least k_i edges of $\mathcal{M}_\mathcal{G}$ are added to $\mathcal{S}_{i+1}$ with probability at least $1-(\frac{2}{e})^n$. □

THEOREM 4.5. *$\mathcal{M}_{\mathcal{S}_r}$ is a (1-ε)-approximation for $\mathcal{M}_\mathcal{G}$ with probability at least $1-(\frac{2}{e})^{\frac{n}{\varepsilon}}$, if $r\ge\frac{1}{\varepsilon}$ and $\alpha=\sqrt{n}$.*

Dataset	Nodes	Edges	Maximum Matching
`Wiki-Vote`	14230	13595753	7115
`Facebook`	8078	5608736	4039
`Enron-Email`	73384	60599542	36692
`Twitter`	58316	195413186	60810
`Slashdot`	154720	189796532	77360

Table 1: Properties of the datasets

PROOF. Let k_i denote $|\mathcal{M}_\mathcal{G}|-|\mathcal{M}_{\mathcal{S}_i}|$. Note that in Line 6 of Algorithm 1 every edge in $\mathcal{S}_i$ is in $\mathcal{S}_{i+1}$, thus $|\mathcal{M}_{\mathcal{S}_i}|\le|\mathcal{M}_{\mathcal{S}_{i+1}}|$. This implies that the size of the matching of the sample is increasing at each round. Therefore for any $m'\le|\mathcal{M}_\mathcal{G}|$ there exists a round i such that $m'\le\mathcal{M}_{\mathcal{S}_t}$.

Using Lemma 4.4 we find a lower bound for the size of the maximum matching in round r based on k_r. Lemma 4.4 states that in round i of this algorithm with probability at least $1-(\frac{2}{e})^n$, $\mathcal{S}_{i+1}$ includes at least k_i new edges from $\mathcal{M}_\mathcal{G}$. Since for each round j where $j\le i$ we have $k_j\ge k_i$, in each round before r with probability at least $1-(\frac{2}{e})^n$, at least k_r new edges from $\mathcal{M}_\mathcal{G}$ are added to the sampled graph. Therefore the total number of edges form $\mathcal{M}_\mathcal{G}$ that are guaranteed to be in the $\mathcal{S}_r$ with probability at least $1-(\frac{2}{e})^{\frac{n}{\varepsilon}}$ is greater than $(r-1)\times\varepsilon|\mathcal{M}_\mathcal{G}|$. Considering these, we have the equation below which shows after round r the minimum number of $\mathcal{M}_\mathcal{G}$ edges the sampled graph has, is smaller than the number of its maximum matching size.

$$(r-1)\times\varepsilon|\mathcal{M}_\mathcal{G}|<(1-\varepsilon)|\mathcal{M}_\mathcal{G}|$$

This equation states that the number of maximum rounds for having a $(1-\varepsilon)$-approximation with probability at least $1-(\frac{2}{e})^{\frac{n}{\varepsilon}}$ is $\frac{1}{\varepsilon}$. Therefore we have a (1-ε)-approximation for $\mathcal{M}_\mathcal{G}$ with probability at least $1-(\frac{2}{e})^{\frac{n}{\varepsilon}}$. □

5 EMPIRICAL RESULTS

In this section we describe our experiments on several datasets.

5.1 Datasets

We present our empirical results on the 2-hop neighborhood graph of `Twitter`, `Facebook`, `Slashdot`, `Wiki-Vote`, and `Enron-Email` datasets from *SNAP*[1], a publicly available dataset collection. Note that these networks are not necessarily bipartite. To make them bipartite, we create two partitions by duplicating the original graph's vertex set and adding an edge from a vertex v in a partition to vertex u in the other partition if there is an edge from v to u in the original graph.

Table 1 shows some of the relevant properties of our datasets.

5.2 Experiments

In order to practically evaluate Algorithm 1, we run it on our datasets for different values of α in the range 1-10 to find a maximum matching. We also run it on different induced

[1] http://snap.stanford.edu/data/

α	1	2	5	10	20
Wiki-Vote	8	6	5	4	3
Facebook	4	3	2	3	2
Enron-Email	7	6	4	4	3
Twitter	8	7	5	4	4
Slashdot	8	6	4	4	4

Table 2: The number of rounds until we find the maximum matching for different values of α.

α	1	2	5	10	20
Wiki-Vote	0.7%	0.8%	1.6%	2.5%	2.7%
Facebook	0.6%	0.7%	1.4%	1.6%	2.9%
Enron-Email	0.6%	0.8%	1.3%	2.2%	2.7%
Twitter	0.3%	0.5%	0.7%	1.3%	1.7%
Slashdot	0.6%	0.7%	1.1%	1.7%	2.2%

Table 3: The ratio of sampled edges until we find the maximum matching for different values of α.

subgraphs of the datasets to compare the results for different number of vertices. To find an induced subgraph of our datasets, we first randomly choose a subset of vertices in the original network and construct the bipartite graph for those users (this means for any selected user we have two vertices).

Some of the important implications of our empirical results are as follows:

Different number of vertices. as the number of vertices of the induced subgraph increases, the ratio of edges sampled by the algorithm to find a maximum matching decreases accordingly. This property of our algorithm is specially very important for solving large input graphs, which is indeed the main focus of our approach. This property could be observed in Figure 2 (a).

Different values of α. For very large values of α, Algorithm 1 clearly samples all the edges in the first round. However, by decreasing α, although the expected number of rounds needed to find the maximum matching increases, the ratio of edges that we sample decreases. This could be observed in Table 2 and Table 3. Note that even in the worst case (where $\alpha = 1$) the number of rounds does not exceed 8 on any dataset. The above-mentioned property means one can pick a desirable α to balance the number of rounds versus the ratio of sampled edges.

Approximation factor in different rounds. Note that after each round, the approximation factor gets better and better until when we find the maximum matching. According to Figure 2 (b), even when $\alpha = 1$, we can get a 0.8-approximation for all datasets by at most 4 rounds and it takes at most 7 rounds to find the optimal maximum matching.

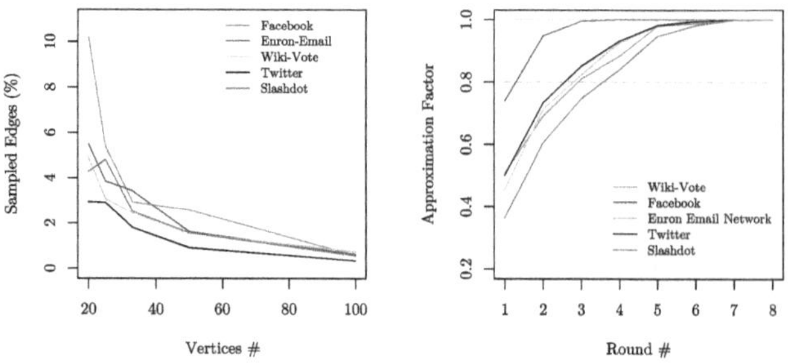

(a) (b)

Figure 2

REFERENCES

[1] K. J. Ahn and S. Guha. Linear programming in the semi-streaming model with application to the maximum matching problem. *Inf. Comput.*, 222:59–79, 2013.

[2] K. J. Ahn and S. Guha. Access to data and number of iterations: Dual primal algorithms for maximum matching under resource constraints. In *Proceedings of the 27th ACM on Symposium on Parallelism in Algorithms and Architectures*, pages 202–211. ACM, 2015.

[3] M. Bury and C. Schwiegelshohn. Sublinear estimation of weighted matchings in dynamic data streams. *arXiv preprint arXiv:1505.02019*, 2015.

[4] R. Chitnis, G. Cormode, H. Esfandiari, M. Hajiaghayi, A. McGregor, M. Monemizadeh, and S. Vorotnikova. Kernelization via sampling with applications to dynamic graph streams. *arXiv preprint arXiv:1505.01731*, 2015.

[5] R. Chitnis, G. Cormode, H. Esfandiari, M. Hajiaghayi, and M. Monemizadeh. Brief announcement: New streaming algorithms for parameterized maximal matching & beyond. In *Proceedings of the 27th ACM on Symposium on Parallelism in Algorithms and Architectures*, pages 56–58. ACM, 2015.

[6] R. Chitnis, G. Cormode, M. Hajiaghayi, and M. Monemizadeh. Parameterized streaming: maximal matching and vertex cover. In *Proceedings of the Twenty-Sixth Annual ACM-SIAM Symposium on Discrete Algorithms*, pages 1234–1251. SIAM, 2015.

[7] H. Esfandiari, M. T. Hajiaghayi, V. Liaghat, M. Monemizadeh, and K. Onak. Streaming algorithms for estimating the matching size in planar graphs and beyond. In *Proceedings of the Twenty-Sixth Annual ACM-SIAM Symposium on Discrete Algorithms*, pages 1217–1233. SIAM, 2015.

[8] K. Joag-Dev and F. Proschan. Negative association of random variables with applications. *The Annals of Statistics*, pages 286–295, 1983.

[9] M. Kapralov, S. Khanna, and M. Sudan. Approximating matching size from random streams. In *Proceedings of the Twenty-Fifth Annual ACM-SIAM Symposium on Discrete Algorithms*, pages 734–751. SIAM, 2014.

[10] D. Konig. Gráfok és mátrixok. matematikai és fizikai lapok, 38: 116–119, 1931.

[11] S. Lattanzi, B. Moseley, S. Suri, and S. Vassilvitskii. Filtering: a method for solving graph problems in mapreduce. In *Proceedings of the twenty-third annual ACM symposium on Parallelism in algorithms and architectures*, pages 85–94. ACM, 2011.

[12] A. McGregor. Finding graph matchings in data streams. In *Approximation, Randomization and Combinatorial Optimization. Algorithms and Techniques*, pages 170–181. Springer, 2005.

[13] S. Micali and V. V. Vazirani. An $o(\sqrt{|v|}|e|)$ algoithm for finding maximum matching in general graphs. In *Foundations of Computer Science, 1980., 21st Annual Symposium on*, pages 17–27. IEEE, 1980.

Brief Announcement: Using Multi-Level Parallelism and 2-3 Cuckoo Filters for Set Intersection Queries and Sparse Boolean Matrix Multiplication

David Eppstein
Univ. of California, Irvine
eppstein@uci.edu

Michael T. Goodrich
Univ. of California, Irvine
goodrich@uci.edu

ABSTRACT

We use multi-level parallelism and a new type of data structures, known as ***2-3 cuckoo*** filters, to answer set intersection queries faster than previous methods, with applications to improved sparse Boolean matrix multiplication.

KEYWORDS

set intersection, 2-3 cuckoo filters, Boolean matrix multiplication

1 INTRODUCTION

Assume we have a collection, $S_1, S_2, \ldots$, of sets, of variable sizes, which can be preprocessed and represented in some canonical data structures stored in main memory. In a ***set-intersection query***, we are then given the names of two sets, S_i and S_j, and are asked to produce a listing of the members in the common intersection, $S_i \cap S_j$. As discussed by Amossen and Pagh [2], such queries have applications in sparse Boolean matrix multiplication.

In this paper, we provide asymptotic improvements to such set-intersection queries, for pairs of sets of different sizes, by taking advantage of bit-level parallelism, i.e., an ability to compute AC^0 functions on pairs of binary words in constant time, including such operations as AND, OR, XOR, and MSB (most-significant set bit). This computational model is known as the ***practical RAM*** model [11], and we refer to a parallel shared-memory extension of this model as the ***practical PRAM*** model.

Related Work. In 1996, Miltersen [11] introduced the ***practical RAM*** model, which has inspired futher research for algorithms in this model (e.g., see [3, 12]). Bille *et al.* [4] present a data structure that can compute the intersection of t sets of total size n in expected time $O(n(\log^2 w)/w + kt + \log w)$. Kopelowitz *et al.* [9] introduce a data structure for computing set intersections for pairs of sets of roughly the same size and use it to list the triangles in a graph G in $O(m\lceil(\alpha(G)\log^2 w)/w + \log w\rceil + k)$ expected time, where $\alpha(G)$ denotes the arboricity of G. Eppstein *et al.* [6] improve this bound to $O(m\lceil(\alpha(G)\log w)/w\rceil + k)$ expected time, using a data structure they call "2-3 cuckoo hash-filters," but their construction is likewise limited to pairwise intersections of sets of roughly the same size.

SPAA '17, July 2017, Washington, DC USA

ACM ISBN 978-1-4503-4593-4/17/07.
https://doi.org/10.1145/3087556.3087599

Lingas [10] shows how to multiply two $n \times n$ Boolean matrices in time $O(n^2 s^{0.188})$, where s is the number of non-zero entries in the output matrix. Amossen and Pagh [1, 2] also study the sparse Boolean matrix multiplication problem, and approach it, as we do, as an application of set-intersection data structures. They show how to perform Boolean matrix multiplication in time $O(m^{0.86}s^{0.41} + (ms)^{2/3})$, where m is the number of non-zero entries in the input matrices [1].

Our Results. We show how to use 2-3 cuckoo hash tables and filters to quickly compute the common intersection of pairs of sets of varying sizes, with applications to sparse Boolean matrix multiplication. We show that these two simple ideas allow us to compute set-intersection queries for pairs of sets of total size n in expected time $O(n(\log w)/w + k)$. This, in turn, leads to new algorithms for sparse Boolean matrix multiplication running in expected time $O(n^2 + nm(\log w)/w)$. Finally, we show how to implement our solutions to compute set-intersection queries in $O(\log n)$ time in the practical PRAM model.

2 2-3 CUCKOO HASH-FILTERS

We begin by reviewing the 2-3 cuckoo hash-filter data structure of Eppstein *et al.* [6], Suppose, then, we wish to maintain a set, S, of n elements taken from a universe such that each element can be stored in a single memory word, where $w \geq \log n$. We maintain S using the following three components, T, C, and F:

- A hash table T of size $O(n)$, using three pseudo-random hash functions h_1, h_2, and h_3, which map elements of S to triples of distinct integers in the range $[0, n-1]$. Each element x in S is stored, if possible, in two of the three possible locations for x based on these hash functions.
- We also store a stash cache [8], C, of size λ, where λ is bounded by a constant. C stores elements for which it was not possible to store properly in two distinct locations in T.
- A table, F, having $O(n)$ cells, that parallels T, so that $F[j]$ stores a non-zero fingerprint digest, $f(x)$, for an element x, if and only if $T[j]$ stores a copy of x. The digest $f(x)$ is a non-zero random hash function comprising δ bits, where $\delta = \Theta(\log w)$. The table F is called a 2-3 ***cuckoo filter***, and it is stored in a packed format, so that we store $O(w/\log w)$ cells of F per memory word. In addition to the vector F, we store a bit-mask, M, that is the same size as F and has all 1 bits in the corresponding cell of F that is occupied.

We assume we can read and write individual cells of F and M in $O(1)$ time. These cells amount to subfields of words of $O(\log w)$ size, which can be read from or written to using standard bit-level operations, such as AND, OR, XOR, etc.

Parallel Construction Algorithm. Since the method for constructing a 2-3 cuckoo filter, F, is the same as that for a 2-3 hash table, T, that is parallel to it, without loss of generality, let us describe how to construct T. We assume we have n elements that need to be added to T and that T has size that is at least $6(1+\epsilon)n$, for a constant $\epsilon > 0$. We also assume that we have a stash cache, C, of constant size, λ. Eppstein *et al.* [6] describe a sequential algorithm for constructing a 2-3 cuckoo hash-filter.

We describe here a parallel algorithm, which can easily be simulated sequentially if one desires a sequential algorithm (which would only use bit-level parallelism). Different than Eppstein *et al.*, we proceed in a sequence of rounds. In each round, we have some set, S, of elements that have yet to be added to T. Initially, S is the entire set of n elements, where we create two copies of each element, where each copy functions somewhat independently. In a given round, each element in S has 3 locations in T where it can be placed, with at most one of these places being a location where it was previously displaced (initially there are no such previous locations). For each such element, x, we read each of the 2 (or initially 3) locations, $T[h_i(x)]$, where it was not previously displaced, and consider the following possible cases: (1) If one of these locations, $T[h_i(x)]$ is empty, then we choose one of these empty locations at random and try to inject x at that location. (2) Otherwise, we choose a location, $T[h_i(x)]$, at random, that does not already hold x and we try to inject x into that location.

Since we are implementing this computation in parallel in the practical PRAM model, we need to deal with the likely possibility that the injection step performed for multiple elements simultaneously might involve concurrent writes; hence, we assume we are operating in the practical CRCW PRAM model where write conflicts are resolved arbitrarily. After we perform this injection step in $O(1)$ time, we collect all the elements that failed to be injected, and let this set be the set S for the next round. This collection step can easily be done in $O(\log n)$ time using $O(n)$ work (e.g., see [7]). We repeat this process for $D \log n$ rounds, where D is a constant. If the size of the set S at the end of this process is at most λ, then we set the stash cache equal to S (which could even be empty) and we consider the construction of T a success. Otherwise, we consider the construction of T to be a failure.

If the construction of T succeeds, then we create a parallel (i.e., mirrored) copy of T as a hash filter, F, by replacing each element with its fingerprint of size $O(\log w)$ and compressing every block of size $O(w/\log w)$ words in T into a single work for F. If the construction of T fails, however, then we instead sort the elements of the original set, S, of n elements and just use this sorted copy of S to represent S. Following the analysis of Eppstein *et al.* [6], we can show:

THEOREM 2.1. *For any constant integer $s \geq 1$, the (constant) size, s, S of the stash in a 2-3 cuckoo hash table after all items have been inserted satisfies* $\Pr(S \geq s) = \tilde{O}(n^{-s})$, *where $\tilde{O}$ ignores polylogarithmic factors.*

3 LISTS OF 2-3 CUCKOO HASH-FILTERS

We construct our data structure for S as follows.

1. Sort the elements of S according to a global total order for all sets, and divide this sorted listing of S into intervals, $I_1, I_2, \ldots,$, such that each interval I_j contains a subset, S_j, of S of $O(w/\log w)$ elements.

2. For each subset S_j in parallel, use the algorithm given above to construct a 2-3 cuckoo hash-filter for S_j with a stash of constant size, λ. If the construction for some S_j fails, then simply fallback to representing this subset as a sorted listing of its elements.

3. For each subset, S_j, that had a failed cuckoo construction, subdivide S_j into smaller intervals, $I_{j,1}, I_{j,2}, \ldots$, such that each interval contains exactly one element of S_j, and construct a single-element 2-3 cuckoo hash-filter for each.

4. For each subset, S_j, that had a successful cuckoo construction, subdivide S_j into $O(\lambda)$ smaller intervals, $I_{j,1}, I_{j,2}, \ldots$, so that each interval contains at most one stash element. Then copy the 2-3 cuckoo filter for S_j into $O(\lambda)$ copies, one for each $I_{j,k}$ interval, removing the elements of S_j that do not belong to $I_{j,k}$, so that no 2-3 cuckoo filter in this group has a non-empty stash.

Given our construction methods, and known results for parallel sorting (e.g., see [7]), it is straightforward to show that we can construct the above representation for each set in a collection of total size n in $O(\log n)$ time using expected work $O(n \log n)$ in the practical (CRCW) PRAM model.

Intersecting 2-3 Cuckoo Hash-Filters. Let us review the method of Eppstein *et al.* [6] for intersecting a pair of 2-3 cuckoo hash-filters that are the same size. Suppose then that we have two subsets, S_i, and S_j, for which we wish to compute a representation of the intersection of these two sets. We begin our set-intersection algorithm by computing a vector of $O(1)$ words that identifies the matching non-empty cells in F_i and F_j. For example, we could compute the vector defined by the following bit-wise vector expression:

$$A = (M_i \text{ AND NOT } (F_i \text{ XOR } F_j)). \quad (1)$$

We view A as being a parallel vector to F_i and F_j. Note that a cell, $A[r]$, consists of δ bits and this cell is all 1s if and only if $F_i[r]$ stores a fingerprint digest for some element and $F_i[r] = F_j[r]$, since fingerprint digests are non-zero. Thus, we can create the list, L, of members of the common intersection of S_i and S_j, by visiting each word of A and storing to L the element in $T_i[r]$ corresponding to each cell, $A[r]$, that is all 1s, but doing so only after confirming that $T_i[r] = T_j[r]$. Doing the listing can be done in time $O(1+k+t)$, where k is the number of elements in the intersection and t is the number of false positives, by using bit-level operations in the practical RAM model (e.g., see [5]).

Answering Set-Intersection Queries. Let us next describe our algorithm for answering a query asking for the intersection of two sets, S_1 and S_2, of possibly different sizes. Let n_1 (n_2)denote the size of S_1 (S_2), and let $n = n_1 + n_2$.

Let us assume that S_1 and S_2 are each represented using the lists of 2-3 cuckoo hash-filters. Furthermore, as explained above, there are no stashes and every subset has a hash-filter. The goal of our algorithm is to compute a cuckoo hash-filter representation that contains all the elements in $S_1 \cap S_2$, plus possibly some false positives that our algorithm identifies as high-probability elements belonging to this common intersection. After we have performed the core part of algorithm, then, we can simply go through the list of cuckoo-filters and confirm which elements actually belong to the common intersection.

Because of the way our algorithm works, it produces a cuckoo-filter representation for the common intersection, where $S_1 \cap S_2$ is represented as a sorted list of intervals (no two consecutive of which are empty), such that for each interval, I, we have a cuckoo filter, F_I, and a backing 2-3 cuckoo table, T_I, where, for each non-zero fingerprint, $F_I[j]$, there is a corresponding element, $x = T_I[j]$, with x being a confirmed element in S_1. The cuckoo filter, F_I, might not be a 2-3 cuckoo filter, however. Nevertheless, after our core algorithm completes, our representation allows us to examine each non-zero cuckoo filter fingerprint in a filter F_I, lookup its corresponding element, x, in a backing 2-3 cuckoo table, T_I, and then perform a search for x in the global hash table, H_2 for S_2. Thus, after one additional lookup for each such element, x, we can confirm or discard x depending on whether it is or isn't in the common intersection.

Our algorithm for constructing this representation of $S_1 \cap S_2$, and then culling out false positives, is as follows.

1. Merge the list of interval boundaries for S_1 and S_2 according to the global total order for sets. This step can be done in parallel in $O(\log n)$ time and $O(n(\log w)/w)$ work.

2. For each overlapping interval, $I_{1,j}$ and $I_{2,k}$, where $I_{1,j}$ is from S_1 and $I_{2,k}$ is from S_2, intersect these two subsets using the bit-parallel intersection algorithm for 2-3 cuckoo filters derived using Equation 1 above (but skipping the lookups in the corresponding 2-3 cuckoo table and any lookups for elements in stashes). Let $F_{j,k}$ denote the resulting (now partial) 2-3 cuckoo filter. This step can be implemented in parallel in $O(1)$ time and $O(n(\log w)/w)$ work, since the total number of overlapping pairs of intervals is $O(n(\log w)/w)$.

3. For each interval, $I_{1,j}$, collect all the partial 2-3 cuckoo hash-filters, $F_{j,k}$, computed in the previous step for $I_{1,j}$. Compute the bit-wise OR of these filters. Let F_j denote the resulting partial 2-3 cuckoo filter for $I_{1,j}$, and let **F** denote the collection of all such filters (note that there is potentially a non-empty partial cuckoo filter, F_j, for each interval in S_1). This step can be implemented in parallel in $O(1)$ time and $O(n(\log w)/w)$ work, since the total number of overlapping pairs of intervals is $O(n(\log w)/w)$.

4. For each interval $I_{1,j}$, and each element, x, in the 2-3 cuckoo hash table for $I_{1,j}$ that has a corresponding fingerprint belonging to F_j in **F**, do a lookup in each of the global hash tables H_1 and H_2 to determine if x is indeed a common element in the sets S_1 and S_2. Let Z denote the set of all such elements so determined to belong to this common intersection. This step can be implemented in $O(\log n)$ time and $O(n(\log w)/w + k + p)$ work, where k is the size of the output and p is the number of false positives, that is, elements that have a non-zero fingerprint in some F_j but nevertheless are not in the common intersection, $S_1 \cap S_2$.

Theorem 3.1. *Given two sets, S_1 and S_2, represented using ultra-compact 2-3 cuckoo hash-filters, one can compute a listing of the k elements in $S_1 \cap S_2$ in $O(\log n)$ time using $O(n(\log w)/w + k)$ expected work in the practical CRCW PRAM model (or sequentially in this expected time).*

Sparse Boolean Matrix Multiplication. Suppose we are given two Boolean $n \times n$ matrices, A and B, and asked to compute $C = A \times B$, where the scalar plus (+) operation is Boolean OR and the scalar times operation is Boolean AND. Our method for producing C involves using the above data structure to represent the indices of the non-zero elements in each row of A and each column of B. Producing these representations using ultra-compact 2-3 cuckoo hash-filters can be done in $O(\log n)$ time and $O(n)$ expected work in the practical CRCW PRAM model, for each such row and column, because we don't need to perform a separate sorting step. The set of indices for each row of A and each column of B are already sorted. Furthermore, note that the number of non-zero entries in any row or column of A or B can vary dramatically, which is why we need a set representation that can vary as well, while still providing an efficient way to answer set-intersection queries.

To compute the Boolean product, we use perform a set-intersection query for each row i of A and each column j of B, cutting the computation short as soon as we have determined if the intersection is empty or not. Then $C[i,j] = 1$ if and only if this intersection is non-empty. By the results given above, the performance of this algorithm can be characterized as in the following theorem.

Theorem 3.2. *The product of two $n \times n$ Boolean matrices can be computed in $O(\log n)$ time and expected $O(n^2 + nm(\log w)/w)$ work in the practical CRCW PRAM model, or sequentially in $O(n^2 + nm(\log w)/w)$ expected time in the practical RAM model, where m is the number of non-zero entries in the input matrices.*

Acknowledgments. This article reports on work supported by the DARPA under agreement no. AFRL FA8750-15-2-0092. The views expressed are those of the authors and do not reflect the official policy or position of the Department of Defense or the U.S. Government. This work was also supported in part from NSF grants 1228639, 1526631, 1217322, 1618301, and 1616248.

REFERENCES

[1] Rasmus Resen Amossen and Rasmus Pagh. 2009. Faster Join-projects and Sparse Matrix Multiplications. In *ICDT*. 121–126. https://doi.org/10.1145/1514894.1514909

[2] R. R. Amossen and R. Pagh. 2011. A new data layout for set intersection on GPUs. In *IPDPS*. 698–708. https://doi.org/10.1109/IPDPS.2011.71

[3] Arne Andersson, Peter Bro Miltersen, and Mikkel Thorup. 1999. Fusion trees can be implemented with AC^0 instructions only. *Theor. Comput. Sci.* 215, 1-2 (1999), 337–344. https://doi.org/10.1016/S0304-3975(98)00172-8

[4] Philip Bille, Anna Pagh, and Rasmus Pagh. 2007. Fast evaluation of union-intersection expressions. In *ISAAC (LNCS)*, Vol. 4835. 739–750. https://doi.org/10.1007/978-3-540-77120-3_64

[5] David Eppstein. 2016. Cuckoo Filter: Simplification and Analysis. In *SWAT (LIPIcs)*, Vol. 53. 8:1–8:12. https://doi.org/10.4230/LIPIcs.SWAT.2016.8

[6] David Eppstein, Michael T. Goodrich, Michael Mitzenmacher, and Manuel Torres. 2017. 2-3 Cuckoo Filters for Faster Triangle Listing and Set Intersection. In *PODS*.

[7] Joseph JáJá. 1992. *An Introduction to Parallel Algorithms*. Vol. 17. Addison-Wesley.

[8] Adam Kirsch, Michael Mitzenmacher, and Udi Wieder. 2010. More robust hashing: Cuckoo hashing with a stash. *SIAM J. Comput.* 39, 4 (2010), 1543–1561. https://doi.org/10.1137/080728743

[9] Tsvi Kopelowitz, Seth Pettie, and Ely Porat. 2015. Dynamic Set Intersection. In *SODA*. 470–481. https://doi.org/10.1007/978-3-319-21840-3_39

[10] Andrzej Lingas. 2011. A Fast Output-Sensitive Algorithm for Boolean Matrix Multiplication. *Algorithmica* 61, 1 (2011), 36–50. https://doi.org/10.1007/s00453-010-9441-x

[11] Peter Bro Miltersen. 1996. Lower bounds for static dictionaries on RAMs with bit operations but no multiplication. In *ICALP (LNCS)*, Vol. 1099. 442–453. https://doi.org/10.1007/3-540-61440-0_149

[12] Mikkel Thorup. 2003. On AC^0 implementations of fusion trees and atomic heaps. In *SODA*. 699–707. http://dl.acm.org/citation.cfm?id=644108.644221

Invited Talk: Some Sequential Algorithms are Almost Always Parallel

Guy E. Blelloch
Carnegie Mellon University
Pittsburgh, PA, USA
guyb@cs.cmu.edu

ABSTRACT

Over the years many interesting and efficient parallel algorithms have been developed to solve a wide variety of problems, but not much attention has been paid to studying the inherent parallelism in sequential algorithms—i.e., understanding the depth of their dependence structure, and how shallow dependence structures might be used to develop efficient parallel implementations.

In this talk I will describe recent work on analyzing the dependence depth of iterative sequential algorithms—ones that loop over a collection of elements. Many of these algorithms have deep dependence chains in the worst case, but shallow chains (polylog w.h.p.) if the elements are randomly ordered. Examples include many fundamental algorithms: the Knuth shuffle for random permutations, sorting by insertion into a binary search tree, greedy maximal independent set (MIS), greedy maximal matching, greedy graph-coloring, counting cycles in a permutation, incremental k-dimensional linear programming, and incremental 2d Delaunay triangulation. An advantage of the approach is that it can lead to very simple and efficient parallel algorithms. Our MIS algorithm, for example can be coded in a dozen or so lines, and is significantly faster than Luby's algorithm on modern multicore machines. Also the approach encourages snapping the view that sequential and parallel algorithms are distinct, and instead thinking of algorithms, in general, as collections of instructions with dependences among them

BIOGRAPHY

Guy Blelloch is a Professor of Computer Science at Carnegie Mellon University. He received a BA in Physics and BS in Engineering from Swarthmore College in 1983, and a PhD in Computer Science from MIT in 1988. His research interests are in algorithms and programming languages and how they interact, with an emphasis on parallel computation. He has worked on programming-language based cost models along with provable implementation bounds, on bounding costs in runtime scheduling and parallel garbage collection, and designed the Nesl programming language. He has developed a variety of parallel algorithms, including algorithms for graph connectivity, set cover, semi sorting, suffix trees, balanced trees, hashing, shortest paths, and Delaunay triangulation. His work has both been in models that are communication conscious, e.g. accounting for caching, and not. He is most proud of developing a sophomore level algorithms and data structures course at Carnegie Mellon in which parallelism is taught from the start. He is an ACM Fellow for his contributions in parallel computation, and was general chair of the ACM Symposium on Parallelism in Algorithms and Architecture (SPAA) from 2011–2015.

PODC'17 & SPAA'17, July 24-27, 2017, Washington, DC, USA.
© 2017 Copyright is held by the author/owner(s).
ACM ISBN 978-1-4503-4992-5/17/07 & 978-1-4503-4593-4/17/07.
DOI: http://dx.doi.org/10.1145/3087801.3087871

Distributed Partial Clustering

Sudipto Guha
University of Pennsylvania
Philadelphia, PA 19104, United States
sudipto@cis.upenn.edu

Yi Li
Nanyang Technological University
Singapore
yili@ntu.edu.sg

Qin Zhang
Indiana University Bloomington
Bloomington, IN 47401, United States
qzhangcs@indiana.edu

ABSTRACT

Recent years have witnessed an increasing popularity of algorithm design for distributed data, largely due to the fact that massive datasets are often collected and stored in different locations. In the distributed setting communication typically dominates the query processing time. Thus it becomes crucial to design communication efficient algorithms for queries on distributed data. Simultaneously, it has been widely recognized that partial optimizations, where we are allowed to disregard a small part of the data, provide us significantly better solutions. The motivation for disregarded points often arise from noise and other phenomena that are pervasive in large data scenarios.

In this paper we focus on partial clustering problems, k-center, k-median and k-means, in the distributed model, and provide algorithms with communication sublinear of the input size. As a consequence we develop the first algorithms for the partial k-median and means objectives that run in subquadratic running time. We also initiate the study of distributed algorithms for clustering uncertain data, where each data point can possibly fall into multiple locations under certain probability distribution.

1 INTRODUCTION

The challenge of optimization over large quantities of data has brought communication efficient *distributed* algorithms to the fore. From the perspective of optimization, it has also become clear that *partial optimizations*, where we are allowed to disregard a small part of the input, enable us to provide significantly better optimization solutions compared with those which are forced to account for the whole input. While several algorithms for distributed clustering have been proposed, partial optimizations for clustering problems, introduced by Charikar et al. [4], have not received as much attention. While the results of Chen [6] improve the approximation ratios, the running time of the k-median and k-means versions have not been improved and the (at least) quadratic running times have remained as a barrier.

In this paper we study partial clustering under the standard (k, t)-median/means/center objective functions, where k is the number of centers we can use and t is the maximum number of points we can ignore. In the distributed setting, let s denote the number of sites. The (k, t)-center problem has recently been studied by Malkomes et al. [19], who gave a 2-round $O(1)$-approximation algorithm with $\tilde{O}(sk + st)$ bits of communication[1], assuming that each point can be encoded in $O(1)$ bits. In fact, we observe that results from streaming algorithms [14] can in fact provide us 1-round $O(1)$-approximation algorithms with $\tilde{O}(sk + st)$ bits of communication for (k, t)-center, (k, t)-median, and (k, t)-means. However, in many scenarios of interest, we have $n > t \gg k$ and $t \gg s$. Thus the st term generates a significant communication burden. In this paper we reduce $\tilde{O}(st)$ to $\tilde{O}(t)$ for the (k, t)-center problem, as well as for (k, t)-median and (k, t)-means problems and unify their treatment. We also provide the first subquadratic algorithms for median and means version of this problem.

Large data sets often have erroneous values. Stochastic optimization has recently attracted a lot of attention in the field of databases, and has substantiated as a subfield called 'uncertain/probabilistic databases' (see, e.g., [20]). For the clustering problem, a method of choice is to first model the underlying uncertainty and then cluster the uncertain data. Clustering under uncertainty has been studied in centralized models [8, 15], but the algorithms proposed therein do not consider communication costs. Note that it typically requires significantly more communication to communicate a distribution (for an uncertain point) than a deterministic point, and thus black box adaptations of centralized algorithms do not work well in the distributed setting. In this paper we propose communication-efficient distributed algorithms for handling *both* data uncertainty and partial clustering. To the best of our knowledge neither distributed clustering of uncertain data nor partial clustering of uncertain data has been studied. We note that both problems are fairly natural, and likely to be increasingly useful as distributed cloud computing becomes commonplace.

Models and Problems. We study the clustering problems in the *coordinator* model, in which there are s sites and one central coordinator, who are connected by a star communication network with the coordinator at the center. However, direct communication between sites can be simulated by routing via the coordinator, which at most doubles the communication. The computation is in terms of rounds. At each round, the coordinator sends a message (could be an empty message) to each site and every site sends a message (could be an empty message) back to the coordinator. The coordinator outputs the answer at the end. The input $\mathbb{A}$ is partitioned into $(\mathbb{A}_1, \dots, \mathbb{A}_s)$ among the s sites. Let $n_i = |\mathbb{A}_i|$, and $n = |\mathbb{A}| = \sum_{i \in [s]} n_i$ be the total input size.

We will consider clustering over a graph with n nodes and an oracle distance function $d(\cdot, \cdot)$. An easy example of such is points

Sudipto Guha was supported in part by NSF award 1546151. Qin Zhang was supported in part by NSF CCF-1525024 and IIS-1633215.

SPAA '17, July 24-26, 2017, Washington DC, USA

ACM ISBN 978-1-4503-4593-4/17/07...$15.00
https://doi.org/10.1145/3087556.3087568

[1] We hide poly log n factors in the $\tilde{O}$ notation.

in Euclidean space. More complicated examples correspond to documents and images represented in a feature space and the distance function is computed via a kernel. We now give the definitions of (k,t)-center/median/means.

Definition 1.1 ((k, t)-center,median,means). Let $\mathbb{A}$ be a set of n points and k, t are integer parameters $(1 \le k \le n, 0 \le t \le n)$. In the (k,t)-median problem we want to compute

$$\min_{K,\mathbb{O}\subseteq\mathbb{A}} \sum_{p\in\mathbb{A}\setminus\mathbb{O}} d(p,K) \quad \text{subject to} \quad |K| \le k \text{ and } |\mathbb{O}| \le t,$$

where $d(p,K) = \min_{x\in K} d(p,x)$. We typically call K the *centers* and $\mathbb{O}$ the *outliers*. In the (k,t)-means and the (k,t)-center problem we replace the objective function $\sum_{p\in\mathbb{A}\setminus\mathbb{O}} d(p,K)$ with $\sum_{p\in\mathbb{A}\setminus\mathbb{O}} d^2(p,K)$ and $\max_{p\in\mathbb{A}\setminus\mathbb{O}} d(p,K)$ respectively.

In the definition above, we assume that centers are chosen from the input points. In the Eucldiean space, such restriction will only affect the approximation by a factor of 2.

For the uncertain data, we follow the assigned clustering introduced in [8]. Let $\mathcal{P}$ be a finite set of points in a metric space. There are n input nodes $\mathbb{A}$, where node j follows an independent distribution $\mathcal{D}_j$ over $\mathcal{P}$. Each site i knows the distributions $\mathcal{D}_j$ associated with the nodes $j \in \mathbb{A}_i$.

Definition 1.2 (Clustering Uncertain Data). In clustering with uncertainty, the output is a subset $K \subseteq \mathcal{P}$ of size k (centers), a subset $\mathbb{O} \subseteq \mathcal{P}$ of size at most t (ignored points), as well as a mapping $\pi : \mathbb{A} \to K$. In every realization $\sigma : \mathbb{A} \to \mathcal{P}$ of the values of the input nodes, node $j \in \mathbb{A}$ (now realized as $\sigma(j) \in \mathcal{P}$) is assigned to the same center $\pi(j) \in K$. In uncertain (k,t)-median, the goal is to minimize the expected cost

$$\mathop{\mathbb{E}}_{\sigma\sim\prod_{j\in\mathbb{A}}\mathcal{D}_j}\left[\sum_{j\in\mathbb{A}\setminus\mathbb{O}} d(\sigma(j),\pi(j))\right] = \sum_{j\in\mathbb{A}\setminus\mathbb{O}} \mathop{\mathbb{E}}_{\sigma\sim\mathcal{D}_j}[d(\sigma(j),\pi(j))]. \tag{1}$$

The definition of uncertain (k,t)-means is basically the same as uncertain (k,t)-median, except that we replace the objective function (1) with $\sum_{j\in\mathbb{A}\setminus\mathbb{O}} \mathbb{E}_{\sigma\sim\mathcal{D}_j}\left[d^2(\sigma(j),\pi(j))\right]$. For uncertain (k,t)-center, we have two objectives:

$$\max_{j\in\mathbb{A}\setminus\mathbb{O}}\left(\mathop{\mathbb{E}}_{\sigma\sim\mathcal{D}_j}[d(\sigma(j),\pi(j))]\right) \tag{2}$$

$$\mathop{\mathbb{E}}_{\sigma\sim\prod_j\mathcal{D}_j}\left[\max_{j\in\mathbb{A}\setminus\mathbb{O}} d(\sigma(j),\pi(j))\right] \tag{3}$$

Note that these two objectives are *not* equivalent, since $\mathbb{E}$ and max do not commute in Equation (3) and we cannot equate it to (2). Equation (2) is in the same spirit as Equation (1), and corresponds to a *per point* measurement. We term this problem as uncertain (k,t)-center-pp. Equation (3) corresponds to a more *global* measurement and we term this problem as uncertain (k,t)-center-g. This version was considered in [8, 15].

Our Results. We present our main results in Table 1 and only present the results based on 2 rounds. The full set of our results can be found in Appendix A. We use T to denote the runtime to compute 1-median/means of a node distribution, B to denote the information needed to encode a point, and I to denote the information needed to encode a node in the uncertain data case. In the column of *Local Time*, the first is the local computation time of all sites, and the second is the local computation time at the coordinator. Observe that the total running time is $\tilde{O}(\sum_i n_i^2)$, which becomes $\tilde{O}(n^2/s)$ if the partitions are balanced. This shows that we can reduce the running time by distributing the clustering across many sites.

In particular we have obtained the following. All algorithms finish in 2 rounds in the coordinator model. We say a solution is an (α,β)-approximation if it is a solution of cost αC while excluding βt points, where C is the optimum cost for excluding t points.

(1) We give $(O(1),1)$-approximation algorithms with $\tilde{O}((sk+t)B)$ communication for the (k,t)-median (Section 3) and the (k,t)-center (Theorem 4.3) problems. The lower bounds in [5] for the $t=0$ case indicate that these communication costs are tight, if we want to output all the outliers (which our algorithms do), up to logarithmic factors. We also give an $(O(1+1/\epsilon), 1+\epsilon)$-approximation algorithm with $\tilde{O}((sk+t)B)$ communication for the (k,t)-median (with better running time) and the (k,t)-means (Theorem 3.6) problems.
(2) We show that for (k,t)-median/means and (k,t)-center-pp the above results are achievable even on uncertain data (Theorem 5.6). For uncertain (k,t)-center-g we obtain an $(O(1+1/\epsilon), 1+\epsilon)$-approximation algorithm with $\tilde{O}(skB+tI+s\log\Delta)$ communication, where I is the information to encode the distribution of an uncertain point, and Δ is the ratio between the maximum pairwise distance and the minimum pairwise distance in the dataset (Theorem 5.14).

Our results for the (k,t)-center problem improves that in [19]. And as far as we are concerned, our results on distributed (k,t)-median/means and of uncertain input are the first of their kinds. Our results for distributed (k,t)-median or means also lead to *subquadratic* time constant factor approximation centralized algorithms, which have been left open for many years.

Technical Overview. The high level idea of our algorithms is fairly natural: Each site first performs a *preclustering*, i.e., it computes some local solution on its own dataset. Then each site sends the centers of the local solution, number of attached points to each center and the ignored points to the coordinator, who will then solve the induced *weighted* clustering problem.

A major difficulty is to determine how many points to ignore in the local solution at each site. Certainly for the sake of safety each site can ignore t points and send all ignored t points to the coordinator for a final decision. This would however incur $\Theta(st)$ bits of communication. To reduce the communication of this part to $O(t)$, we hope to find $\{t_1,\ldots,t_s\}$ such that $\sum_i t_i = t$ and each site i sends a solution with just t_i ignored points. At the cost of an extra round of communication, we solve the minimization problem $\sum_i f_i(t_i)$ subject to $\sum_i t_i = t$ for convex functions $\{f_i\}$. It is tempting to take $f_i(t_i)$ to be the cost of local solution with t_i ignored points on site i, however, such f_i is not necessarily convex. The remedy is to take a lower convex hull of f_i instead, which can be shown to have only a mild effect on the solution cost. The convex hull of t points can be found in $O(t\log t)$ time, and we can further reduce the runtime without compromising approximation ratio by computing local solutions on each site for only $\log t$ geometrically increasing values of t_i.

Objective	Approx.	Centers	Ignored	Rounds	Total Comm.	Local Time
median	$O(1)$	k	t	2	$\tilde{O}((sk+t)B)$	$\tilde{O}(n_i^2)$, $\tilde{O}(k^2t^2(sk+t)^3)$
	$O(1+1/\epsilon)$		$(1+\epsilon)t$		$\tilde{O}((sk+t)B)$	$\tilde{O}(n_i^2)$, $\tilde{O}((sk+t)^2)$
means	$O(1+1/\epsilon)$	k	$(1+\epsilon)t$	2	$\tilde{O}((sk+t)B)$	$\tilde{O}(n_i^2)$, $\tilde{O}((sk+t)^2)$
center	$O(1)$	k	t	2	$\tilde{O}((sk+t)B)$	$\tilde{O}((k+t)n_i)$, $\tilde{O}((sk+t)^2)$
uncertain median/ means/ center-pp	as in the regular case above					$+O(n_i T)$, unchanged
center-g	$O(1+1/\epsilon)$	k	$(1+\epsilon)t$	2	$\tilde{O}(skB+tI+s\log\Delta)$	$\tilde{O}(n_i^2\log\Delta)$, $\tilde{O}((sk+t)^2)$

Table 1: Results based on a 2 round algorithms. T denotes the runtime to compute 1-median/mean of a node distribution[2], B the information encoding a point and I the information encoding a node in the uncertain data case. Δ is the ratio between the maximum pairwise distance and the minimum pairwise distance in the dataset.

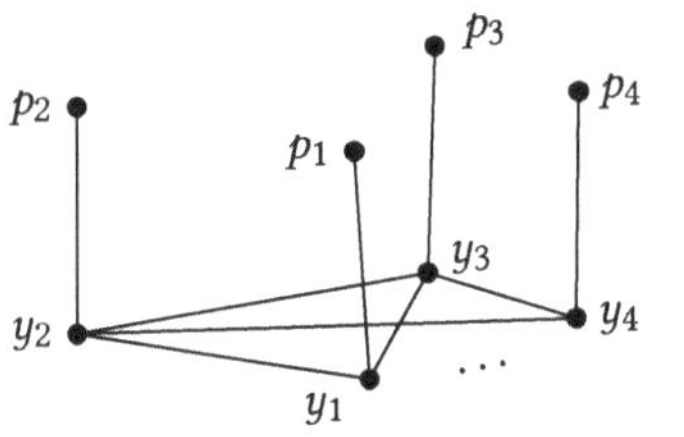

Figure 1: An example of a compressed graph produced

For uncertain data, it is natural to reduce the clustering problems to the deterministic case. To this end, we 'collapse' each node j to its optimal center in $\mathcal{P}$. For instance, for the (k,t)-median problem, each node j is 'collapsed' to $y_j = \arg\min_{y \in \mathcal{P}} \mathbb{E}_\sigma[d(\sigma(j), y)]$, called the 1-median of node j. It may be tempting to consider the clustering problem on the set of 1-medians, but the 'collapse' cost is lost, hence we construct a *compressed graph* G that allows us to keep track of the collapse costs. The graph looks like a clique with tentacles, see Figure 1. The 1-medians form a clique in G with edge weight being the distance in the underlying metric space; for each 1-median y_j, we add a tentacle (an edge) from y_j to a new vertex p_j with edge weight being the collapse cost $\mathbb{E}_\sigma[d(\sigma(j), y_j)]$. We manage to show that the original clustering problem is equivalent, up to a constant factor in cost, to the clustering problem on the compressed graph where the facility vertices are 1-medians $\{y_j\}$ and the demand vertices are $\{p_j\}$. Our previous framework for deterministic data is then applied to the compressed graph.

Lastly, for the global center problem with uncertain data, we build upon the approach developed in [15], which uses a truncated distance function $\mathcal{L}_\tau(x,y) = \max\{d(x,y) - \tau, 0\}$ instead of the usual metric distance $d(\cdot,\cdot)$. Our algorithm performs a parametric search on τ, and applies our previous framework to solve the global problem using local solutions. Now in the analysis of the approximation ratio we need to relate the optimum solution to the solution with truncated distance function, which is a fairly nontrivial task.

Related Work. In the centralized model, Charikar et al. gives a 3-approximation algorithm for (k,t)-center, and an $(O(1), O(1))$ bicriteria algorithm for (k,t)-median [4]. This bicriteria was later removed by Chen [6], who designed an $O(1)$-approximation algorithm using $\tilde{O}(k^2(k+t)^2n^3)$ time. Feldman and Schulman studied the (k,t)-median problem with different loss functions using the *coreset* technique [12].

On uncertain data, Cormode and McGregor considered k-center/median/means where each $\mathcal{D}_i$ is a discrete distribution [8]. Guha and Munagala provided a technique to reduce the uncertain k-center to the deterministic k-median problem [15]. Wang and Zhang studied the special case of k-center on the line [21]. We refer the readers to the survey by Aggarwal [1].

Clustering on distributed data has been studied only recently. In the coordinator model, in the d-dimensional Euclidean space, Balcan et al. obtained $O(1)$-approximation algorithms with $\tilde{O}((kd+sk)B)$ bits of communication for both k-median and k-means [2]. Their results on k-means were further improved by Liang et al. [18] and Cohen et al. [7]. Chen et al. provided a set lower bounds for these problems [5]. In the MapReduce model, Ene et al. designed several $O(1)$-approximation $O(1)$-round algorithms for the k-center and the k-median problems [11]. Im and Moseley further studied the partial clustering variant [16], however their algorithms require communication polynomial in n. Cormode et al. studied the k-center maintenance problem in the distributed data stream model where the coordinator can keep track of the cluster centers at any time step [9].

2 PRELIMINARIES

Notation. We use the following notations in this paper.

- $\mathrm{sol}(Z,k,t,d)$: A solution (computed by an algorithm) to the median/means/center problem on point set Z with at most k centers and at most t outliers, under the distance function d;
- $\mathrm{opt}(Z,k,t,d)$: An optimal solution to the median/means or center problem on point set Z with at most k centers and at most t outliers, under d;
- $C_{\mathrm{sol}}(Z,k,t,d)$: The cost of the solution $\mathrm{sol}(Z,k,t,d)$;
- $C_{\mathrm{opt}}(Z,k,t,d)$: The cost of the solution $\mathrm{opt}(Z,k,t,d)$;
- $\pi(j)$: The center to which point j is attached.

When Z lies in a metric space and d agrees with the distance function on the metric space, we omit the parameter d in the notations above.

Combining Preclustering Solutions. We review a theorem from [14], which concerns 'combining' local solutions into a global solution. The problems considered in the theorem have *no* outliers

[2]For a general discrete distribution on m points in Euclidean space with $\mathcal{P}$ be the whole space, $T = O(m)$ [10]; for special distributions such as normal distribution, $T = O(1)$.

($t = 0$) and lie in a metric space, so we abbreviate the notation $\mathsf{sol}(Z, k, t, d)$ to $\mathsf{sol}(Z, k)$, etc.

Theorem 2.1 ([14]). *Suppose that $\mathbb{A} = \mathbb{A}_1 \uplus \cdots \uplus \mathbb{A}_s$ (disjoint union) and $\{\mathsf{sol}(\mathbb{A}_i, k)\}$ are the preclustering solutions at sites. Let $\mathbb{M} = \{\pi(j) : j \in \mathbb{A}\}$ and $L = \sum_{j \in \mathbb{A}} d(j, \pi(j))$, where $\pi(j)$ denotes the preclustering assignment. Consider the weighted k-median problem on $\mathbb{M}$ where the weight of $m \in \mathbb{M}$ is defined to be the number of points that are assigned to m in the preclustering, that is, $|\{j \mid j \in \mathbb{A}, \pi(j) = m\}|$. Then*

- *(i) There exists a weighted k-median solution $\mathsf{sol}(\mathbb{M}, k)$ such that $C_{\mathsf{sol}}(\mathbb{M}, k) \le 2(L + C_{\mathsf{opt}}(\mathbb{A}, k))$.*
- *(ii) Given any weighted k-median solution $\mathsf{sol}(\mathbb{M}, k)$, there exists a k-median solution $\mathsf{sol}(\mathbb{A}, k)$ such that $C_{\mathsf{sol}}(\mathbb{A}, k) \le \mathsf{sol}(\mathbb{M}, k) + L$.*

Consequently, there exists a k-median solution $\mathsf{sol}(\mathbb{A}, k)$ such that $C_{\mathsf{sol}}(\mathbb{A}, k) \le 2\gamma(L + C_{\mathsf{opt}}(\mathbb{A}, k)) + L$ and centers are restricted to $\mathbb{M}$, where γ is the best approximation ratio for the k-median problem.

Corollary 2.2. *The result in Theorem 2.1 extends to*

- *(i) the k-center problem;*
- *(ii) the k-means problem with weaker constants, using a relaxed triangle inequality;*
- *(iii) the (k, t)-median/means/center approximation on the weighted point set $\mathbb{M}$ (with γ being the corresponding bicriteria approximation ratio),* provided *the preclustering does not ignore any points. Otherwise the total number of ignored points is the sum of the ignored points in the clustering and preclustering phases.*

3 (k, t)-MEDIAN AND (k, t)-MEANS

Our algorithm for distributed (k, t)-median clustering is provided in Algorithm 1. For integer pairs (i, q), we consider the lexicographical order as partial order, that is,

$$(i_1, q_1) \prec (i_2, q_2) \quad \text{if} \quad \begin{cases} i_1 < i_2; \text{ or} \\ i_1 = i_2 \text{ and } q_1 < q_2. \end{cases} \tag{4}$$

Remark 1. *In Line 17 of Algorithm 1, (i) no input point is ignored in the preclustering; (ii) if the preclustering aggregated q points but the coordinator's algorithm chooses less than q copies (to exclude exactly t) then the proofs are not affected in any way.*

We begin with a theorem about approximating (k, t)-median or means with a different trade-off from that in [4].

Theorem 3.1 (Proof Omitted). *Let $\epsilon > 0$. We can compute $\mathsf{sol}(Z, k, (1+\epsilon)t)$ and $\mathsf{sol}(Z, (1+\epsilon)k, t)$ for the (k, t)-median problem in $\tilde{O}(|Z|^2)$ time such that*

$$C_{\mathsf{sol}}(Z, k, (1+\epsilon)t) \le \max\{6, 6/\epsilon\} \cdot C_{\mathsf{opt}}(Z, k, t), \text{ and}$$
$$C_{\mathsf{sol}}(Z, (1+\epsilon)k, t) \le \max\{6, 6/\epsilon\} \cdot C_{\mathsf{opt}}(Z, k, t).$$

The result extends to the (k, t)-means problem with a slightly larger constant.

Throughout the rest of the section, we denote by t_i^* the number of ignored points from $\mathbb{A}_i$ in the global optimum solution $\mathsf{opt}(\mathbb{A}, k, t)$. We need the following lemmas.

[4] *Stably* means that when $\ell(i_1, q_1) = \ell(i_2, q_2)$, the sorting algorithm puts $\ell(i_1, q_1)$ before $\ell(i_2, q_2)$ if $(i_1, q_1) \prec (i_2, q_2)$ as defined in (4).

[4] Element of *rank* r means the r-th element in a sorted list

---

Algorithm 1 Distributed $(k, (1+\epsilon)t)$-median clustering

Input: $\mathbb{A} = \mathbb{A}_1 \uplus \cdots \uplus \mathbb{A}_s$, $k \ge 1$, $t \ge 0$ and $\rho > 1$

Output: $\mathsf{sol}(\mathbb{A}, k, (1+\epsilon)t)$ such that $C_{\mathsf{sol}}(\mathbb{A}, k, (1+\epsilon)t) = O(1 + 1/\epsilon) \cdot C_{\mathsf{opt}}(\mathbb{A}, k, t)$

1: **for** each site i **do**

2: $\quad \mathbb{I} \leftarrow \{\lfloor \rho^r \rfloor : 1 \le r \le \lfloor \log_\rho t \rfloor, r \in \mathbb{Z}\} \cup \{0, t\}$

3: $\quad$ Compute $\mathsf{sol}(\mathbb{A}_i, 2k, q)$ for each $q \in \mathbb{I}$

4: $\quad$ Compute the (lower) convex hull of the point set $\{(q, C_{\mathsf{sol}}(\mathbb{A}_i, 2k, q))\}_{q \in \mathbb{I}}$, which induces a function $f_i(\cdot)$ defined on $\{0, \ldots, t\}$

5: $\quad$ Send the function $f_i(\cdot)$ to the coordinator

6: **end for**

7: Coordinator computes $\ell(i, q) = f_i(q-1) - f_i(q)$ for each $1 \le i \le s$ and each $1 \le q \le t$

8: Coordinator *stably* sorts all $\{\ell(i, q)\}$ in decreasing order[3]

9: Coordinator finds $\ell(i_0, q_0)$ of rank[4] ρt and sends $\ell(i_0, q_0)$, i_0 and q_0 to all sites

10: **for** each site i **do**

11: $\quad t_i \leftarrow \max\{q : \ell(i, q) \ge \ell(i_0, q_0)\}$ $\quad \triangleright$ define $\max \emptyset = 0$

12: $\quad$ **if** $i = i_0$ **then**

13: $\quad\quad t_i \leftarrow \min\{q \in \mathbb{I} : q \ge q_0 \text{ and } C_{\mathsf{sol}}(\mathbb{A}_i, 2k, q_0) = f_{i_0}(q_0)\}$

14: $\quad$ **end if**

15: $\quad$ Send the coordinator the $2k$ centers built in $\mathsf{sol}(\mathbb{A}_i, 2k, t_i)$, the number of points attached to each center, and the t_i unassigned points

16: **end for**

17: Coordinator considers the union of the centers obtained from each site and the unassigned points, and applies Theorem 3.1 and outputs $\mathsf{sol}(\mathbb{A}, k, (1+\epsilon)t)$.

Lemma 3.2. *It holds that $\sum_i C_{\mathsf{opt}}(\mathbb{A}_i, k, t_i^*) \le 2C_{\mathsf{opt}}(\mathbb{A}, k, t)$. For (k, t)-means the constant changes from 2 to 4.*

Proof. We shall use an argument used in [14]. Let π_{opt} be the center projection function and K be the set of optimum centers in the optimal solution $\mathsf{opt}(\mathbb{A}, k, t)$. For each $\mathbb{A}_i$, we construct a solution $\mathsf{sol}(\mathbb{A}_i, k, t_i^*)$ by excluding the points excluded in $\mathsf{opt}(\mathbb{A}, k, t)$ and choosing $\{\arg\min_{u \in \mathbb{A}_i} d(u, k) : k \in K\}$ to be the centers. Then

$$C_{\mathsf{sol}}(\mathbb{A}_i, k, t_i^*) \le 2 \sum_{x \in \mathbb{A}_i} d(x, \pi_{\mathsf{opt}}(x)).$$

Summing over i yields $\sum C_{\mathsf{sol}}(\mathbb{A}_i, k, t_i^*) \le 2C_{\mathsf{opt}}(\mathbb{A}, k, t)$. The result for k-means follows from applying triangle inequality with $(a+b)^2 \le 2(a^2 + b^2)$. □

Lemma 3.3. *The $t_1, \ldots, t_s$ computed in Step 11 of Algorithm 1 minimizes $\sum_i f_i(t_i)$ subject to $\sum_i t_i \le \rho t$ and $0 \le t_i \le t$.*

Proof. Suppose that $t_1', \ldots, t_s'$ is a minimizer. Since $f_i(\cdot)$ is non-increasing for all i, it must hold that $\sum_i t_i' = \rho t$. By the definition of t_i, it also holds that $\sum_i t_i = \rho t$. If $(t_1', \ldots, t_s') \ne (t_1, \ldots, t_s)$, there must exist i, j such that $t_i' > t_i$ and $t_j' < t_j$. By the definition of t_i and the sorting of $\{\ell(i, q)\}$, we know that

$$\ell(i, t_i + 1) \le \ell(i_0, q_0), \quad \ell(j, t_j) \ge \ell(i_0, q_0).$$

From convexity of f_i and that $t_i' \geq t_i + 1$ and $t_j' + 1 \leq t_j$, it follows that

$$f_i(t_i' - 1) - f_i(t_i') \leq \ell(i_0, q_0) \leq f_j(t_j') - f_j(t_j' + 1)$$

which means that increasing t_j' by 1 and decreasing t_i' by 1 will not decrease the sum

$$G(q_1', \ldots, q_s') := \sum_i (f_i(0) - f_i(t_i')).$$

Therefore $\sum_i f_i(t_i') = \sum_i f_i(0) - G(t_1', \ldots, t_s')$ will not increase. We can continue this procedure until $(t_1', \ldots, t_s') = (t_1, \ldots, t_s)$. □

Lemma 3.4. *It holds for all $i \neq i_0$ that $t_i \in \mathbb{I}$ and $C_{\mathrm{sol}}(\mathbb{A}_i, 2k, t_i) = f_i(t_i)$, where i_0 is computed in Step 9 and t_i's in Step 11 of Algorithm 1.*

Proof. Since $0 \in \mathbb{I}$, we need only to consider the i's with $t_i \neq 0$. By the selection of i_0 and q_0, it must hold that

$$\ell(i, t_i) \geq \ell(i_0, q_0) > \ell(i, t_i + 1) \quad \text{for} \quad i < i_0$$
$$\ell(i, t_i) > \ell(i_0, q_0) \geq \ell(i, t_i + 1) \quad \text{for} \quad i > i_0,$$

which implies that $\ell(i, t_i) > \ell(i, t_i + 1)$ whenever $i \neq i_0$, i.e.,

$$f_i(t_i - 1) - f_i(t_i) > f_i(t_i) - f_i(t_i + 1), \quad i \neq i_0.$$

Hence $(i, f_i(t_i))$ is a vertex of the convex hull for all $i \neq i_0$, that is, $t_i \in \mathbb{I}$ and $f_i(t_i) = C_{\mathrm{sol}}(\mathbb{A}_i, 2k, t_i)$. □

Now we are ready to bound the 'goodness' of local solutions.

Lemma 3.5. *Let $\rho = 2$. It holds that $\sum_i C_{\mathrm{sol}}(\mathbb{A}_i, 2k, t_i) \leq 12 \cdot C_{\mathrm{opt}}(\mathbb{A}, 2k, t)$ and $\sum_i t_i \leq 3t$, where $t_1, \ldots, t_s$ are computed in Step 11 and may be updated in Step 15 of Algorithm 1.*

Proof. Let $\hat{t}_i = \min\{q \in \mathbb{I} : q \geq t_i^*\}$. It follows from Lemma 3.2 with $\sum_i t_i^* \leq t$ that

$$2C_{\mathrm{opt}}(\mathbb{A}, k, t) \geq \sum_i C_{\mathrm{opt}}(\mathbb{A}_i, k, t_i^*) \geq \sum_i C_{\mathrm{opt}}(\mathbb{A}_i, k, \hat{t}_i) \geq \frac{1}{6} \sum_i C_{\mathrm{sol}}(\mathbb{A}_i, 2k, \hat{t}_i),$$

where the last inequality follows from Theorem 3.1 (applied with $\epsilon = \rho - 1 = 1$). Observe that $\hat{t}_i \leq 2t_i^*$ and thus $\sum_i \hat{t}_i \leq 2 \sum_i t_i^* \leq 2t$, and

$$\sum_i C_{\mathrm{sol}}(\mathbb{A}_i, 2k, \hat{t}_i) \geq \sum_i f_i(\hat{t}_i) \geq \sum_i f_i(t_i),$$

where the last equality follows from Lemma 3.3, and t_i's are computed in Step 11.

Now, by Lemma 3.4, $f_i(t_i) = C_{\mathrm{sol}}(\mathbb{A}_i, 2k, t_i)$ for all except one i. The exceptional t_i will be replaced by a bigger value, which will not increase $f_i(t_i)$ by the monotonicity of f_i, and the first part follows. This update will increase $\sum_i t_i$ by at most t and thus $\sum_i t_i \leq 3t$. □

Lemma 3.5 and Theorem 3.1 together give the following. Note that $|\mathbb{I}| = O(\log t)$.

Theorem 3.6. *For the distributed (k, t)-median problem, Algorithm 1 with $\rho = 2$ outputs $\mathrm{sol}(\mathbb{A}, k, (1+\epsilon)t)$ satisfying $C_{\mathrm{sol}}(\mathbb{A}, k, (1+\epsilon)t)) \leq O(1 + 1/\epsilon) \cdot C_{\mathrm{opt}}(\mathbb{A}, k, t)$. The sites communicate a total of $\tilde{O}(sk + t)$ bits of information with the coordinator over 2 rounds. The runtime at each site is $\tilde{O}(n_i^2)$ and the runtime at the coordinator is $\tilde{O}((sk + t)^2)$. The same result holds for (k, t)-means with larger constants in the approximation ratio and the runtime.*

Proof. The communication cost is straightforward. By Lemma 3.5, the coordinator will solve the problem of at most $2sk + 3t$ points. The claims on approximation ratio and the runtime then follow from Theorem 3.1, noting that it takes time $O(\mathbb{I} \log \mathbb{I}) = \tilde{O}(1)$ to find the convex hull. □

If we were only interested in the clustering and not the list of ignored points, we could set $\rho = 1 + \delta$ and change line 12 to line 15 of Algorithm 1 to the following. The sites do not send the ignored nodes but just the number of them, and the exceptional site runs a slightly more convoluted algorithm.

12: **if** $i \neq i_0$ **then**
13: Send the coordinator t_i, the $2k$ centers built in $\mathrm{sol}(\mathbb{A}_i, 2k, t_i)$ and the number of points attached to each center
14: **else**
15: $t_{i,1} = \max\{q \in \mathbb{I} : q \leq t_i \text{ and } C_{\mathrm{sol}}(\mathbb{A}_i, 2k, q) = f_i(q)\}$
16: $t_{i,2} = \min\{q \in \mathbb{I} : q \geq t_i \text{ and } C_{\mathrm{sol}}(\mathbb{A}_i, 2k, q) = f_i(q)\}$
17: Combine $\mathrm{sol}(\mathbb{A}_i, 2k, t_{i,1})$ and $\mathrm{sol}(\mathbb{A}_i, 2k, t_{i,2})$ to form a solution $\mathrm{sol}(\mathbb{A}_i, 4k, t_i)$ by taking the union of the medians, attaching each point to the closest center among the combined centers, and ignoring the points with largest t_i distances.
18: Send to the coordinator t_i, the combined centers and the number of points attached to each center.
19: **end if**

Observe that Lemma 3.5 still holds with $\sum_i t_i \leq (1 + \delta)t$, since we are not changing the exceptional t_i. For the exceptional site i, suppose that $t_i = (1 - \theta)t_{i,1} + \theta t_{i,2}$ for some $\theta \in (0, 1)$, we have $(1 - \theta)f_i(t_{i,1}) + \theta f_i(t_{i,2}) \leq f_i(t_i)$. We now argue the next critical lemma.

Lemma 3.7. $C_{\mathrm{sol}}(\mathbb{A}_i, 4k, t_i) \leq (1 - \theta)f_i(t_{i,1}) + \theta f_i(t_{i,2})$.

Proof. We will prove the lemma by carefully designing an assignment of $n - t_i$ points to the $4k$ centers which is bounded above by the right hand side. Since choosing the minimum $n - t_i$ distances will only result in a smaller value, the lemma would follow.

For $j = 1, 2$, let π_j be the center projection function in $\mathrm{sol}(\mathbb{A}_i, 2k, t_{i,j})$ and P_i the set of clustered points in $\mathrm{sol}(\mathbb{A}_i, 2k, t_{i,j})$. For $x \in P_1 \cap P_2$, we attach x to the nearer one between the two centers $\pi_1(x)$ and $\pi_2(x)$, and the incurred cost is

$$\min\{d(x, \pi_1(x)), d(x, \pi_2(x))\} \leq (1 - \theta)d(x, \pi_1(x)) + \theta d(x, \pi_2(x)). \tag{5}$$

For $x \in P_1 \Delta P_2$, since only one of $\pi_1(x)$ and $\pi_2(x)$ exist, we abbreviate it as $\pi(x)$ for simplicity. Define $h(x)$ for each $x \in P_1 \Delta P_2$ as

$$h(x) = \begin{cases} (1 - \theta) \cdot d(x, \pi(x)), & x \in P_1 \setminus P_2; \\ \theta \cdot d(x, \pi(x)), & x \in P_2 \setminus P_1. \end{cases}$$

Let $r = |P_1 \cap P_2|$, $r_1 = |P_1 \setminus P_2|$ and $r_2 = |P_2 \setminus P_1|$. It holds that $r + r_1 = n - t_{i,1}$ and $r + r_2 = n - t_{i,2}$, thus $r_1 > r_2$ and

$$(1 - \theta)r_1 + \theta r_2 = n - t_i - r.$$

Define $Q_1 = P_1 \setminus P_2$ and $Q_2 = P_2 \setminus P_1$. Pick $x = \arg\min_{z \in Q_1 \cup Q_2} h(z)$. If $x \in Q_1$, pick an arbitrary $u \in Q_2$, otherwise pick $u \in Q_1$. Attach x to $\pi(x)$ in the $4k$-center solution we are constructing and mark u

as outlier. Note that this incurs a cost of

$$d(x,\pi(x)) \le \begin{cases} (1-\theta)d(x,\pi(x)) + \theta d(u,\pi(u)), & x \in Q_1; \\ (1-\theta)d(u,\pi(u)) + \theta d(x,\pi(x)), & x \in Q_2, \end{cases} \tag{6}$$

by our choice of x, because one of the combination terms is exactly $h(x)$ and it is smaller than $h(u)$, which is exactly the other term. Then we remove x and u from Q_1 or Q_2 depending on the case. Now, $|Q_1| = r_1 - 1$ and $|Q_2| = r_2 - 1$, and note that

$$(1-\theta)(r_1 - 1) + \theta(r_2 - 1) = n - t_i - r - 1.$$

Since $r_1 > r_2$, we can continue this process until $Q_2 = \emptyset$. At this point we have run the procedure above r_2 times, and it holds that

$$(1-\theta)r_1 = n - t_i - r - r_2.$$

Note that $r_1 \ge n - t_i - r - r_2$, so we can choose $E \subseteq Q_1$ to be the points with smallest $n - t_i - r - r_2$ values of h. Attach points in E to their respective centers and mark the remaining points in Q_1 as outliers. This incurs a cost of

$$\sum_{x\in E} d(x,\pi(x)) \le \frac{n - t_i - r - r_2}{r_1} \sum_{x\in Q_1} d(x,\pi(x)) = (1-\theta)\sum_{x\in Q_1} d(x,\pi(x)) \tag{7}$$

In total we have assigned $r + r_2 + (n - t_i - r - r_2) = n - t_i$ points as desired. The desired upper bound on cost follows from (i) summing both sides of (5) over $P_1 \cap P_2$; (ii) summing both sides of (6) over x and the corresponding u during the pairing procedure; and (iii) Equation (7). Note that (ii) covers $(P_1 \triangle P_2) \setminus Q_1$, where Q_1 is the post-pairing set. □

As a consequence of Lemma 3.7, $C_{\mathrm{sol}}(\mathbb{A}_i, 4k, t_i) \le f_i(t_i)$. Thus the upper bound on the approximation ratio still holds. Finally, note that $|\mathbb{I}| = \tilde{O}(1/\delta)$ and we conclude that

THEOREM 3.8. *For the distributed (k,t)-median problem, the modified Algorithm 1 with $\rho = 1 + \delta$ outputs $\mathrm{sol}(\mathbb{A}, k, (2+\epsilon+\delta)t)$ satisfying $C_{\mathrm{sol}}(\mathbb{A}, k, (2+\epsilon+\delta)t) \le O(1+1/\epsilon)\cdot C_{\mathrm{opt}}(\mathbb{A},k,t)$. The sites communicate a total of $\tilde{O}(s\delta^{-1} + skB)$ bits of information with the coordinator over 2 rounds. The runtime on site i is $\tilde{O}(n_i^2/\delta)$ and the runtime on the coordinator is $\tilde{O}((sk)^2)$. The same result holds for (k,t)-means with a larger constant in the approximation ratio.*

3.1 Subquadratic-time Centralized Algorithm

We now show an unusual application of Theorem 3.6 in speeding up existing constant-factor approximation algorithms for (k,t)-median (or means). Note that the centralized bicriteria approximation algorithms in Charikar [4] are $\tilde{O}(n^3)$ from n points, and while the modifications in Theorem 3.1 improve the running time to $\tilde{O}(n^2)$, this leaves open the important question: *Are there algorithms with provable constant factor approximation guarantees which are subquadratic?* Observe that the question is even more pertinent in the context of unicriterion approximation, for which the only known result is a $\tilde{O}(n^3k^2t^2)$-time constant-factor approximation of (k,t)-median [6]. In the sequel we show that the running time can be brought to almost linear time. The improvement arises from the fact that we can simulate a distributed algorithm sequentially.

LEMMA 3.9. *Suppose that we are given a $\tilde{O}(n^{1+\alpha_0}k^2)$ time algorithm for bicriteria approximation which produces 2k centers or 2t outliers with approximation factor γ, where $\alpha_0 \le 1$. Then we can produce a similar algorithm with running time $\tilde{O}(t^2) + \tilde{O}\left(n^{\frac{2+2\alpha_0}{2+\alpha_0}}k^2\right)$ and approximation $c_0\gamma$ for some absolute constant $c_0 > 0$.*

PROOF. We will apply Theorem 3.6 after dividing the data arbitrarily in s pieces of size n/s. The sequential simulation of the s sites will take time $\tilde{O}(s\,(n/s)^{1+\alpha_0}k^2)$ based on the statement of the lemma. The coordinator will require time $\tilde{O}((sk+t)^2) = \tilde{O}(s^2k^2) + \tilde{O}(t^2)$. Observe that we can now balance $n^{1+\alpha_0} = s^{2+\alpha_0}$, which provides us the optimum s to use and achieve a running time of

$$\tilde{O}(t^2) + \tilde{O}(s^2k^2) = \tilde{O}(t^2) + \tilde{O}\left(n^{\frac{2+2\alpha_0}{2+\alpha_0}}k^2\right).$$ □

THEOREM 3.10. *Let $\alpha > 0$ and suppose that $t \le \sqrt{n}$. There exists a centralized algorithm for the (k,t)-median problem that runs in $\tilde{O}(n^{1+\alpha}k^2)$ time and outputs a solution $\mathrm{sol}(\mathbb{A},k,2t)$ satisfying $C_{\mathrm{sol}}(\mathbb{A},k,2t) \le (1+1/\alpha)^{O(1)}C_{\mathrm{opt}}(\mathbb{A},k,t)$.*

PROOF. Note that the algorithm in Theorem 3.1 has runtime $\tilde{O}(n^2)$, so we can take $\alpha_0 = 1$ in Lemma 3.9 to obtain an algorithm of approximation ratio $\gamma = 6$ and runtime $\tilde{O}(t^2 + n^{4/3}k^2)$, which is $\tilde{O}(n^{4/3}k^2)$ by our assumption that $t \le \sqrt{n}$. Repeatedly applying Lemma 3.9 for j times gives an algorithm of runtime $\tilde{O}(n^{1+1/(2^j-1)}k^2)$ and approximation ratio $(c_0\gamma)^j$. Let $j = \log(1+1/\alpha)$, the runtime becomes $O(n^{1+\alpha}k^2)$ and the approximation ratio $(1+1/\alpha)^{\log(c_0\gamma)} = (1+1/\alpha)^{O(1)}$. □

REMARK 2. *We remark that*

(i) *the theorem above also holds for $\mathrm{sol}(\mathbb{A},2k,t)$, where the number of centers, instead of the outliers, is relaxed.*
(ii) *for the unicriterion approximation, if we use the algorithm of runtime $\tilde{O}(n^3t^2k^2)$ from [6] instead of the result of Theorem 3.1, we need to balance s^3 and $s(n/s)^{1+\alpha_0}$ for an analogy of Lemma 3.9, which will eventually lead to an algorithm of runtime $O(n^{1+\alpha}t^2k^2)$, provided that $t \le n^{1/5}$.*

4 (k,t)-CENTER CLUSTERING

Our algorithm for (k,t)-center clustering is presented in Algorithm 2. It is similar to Algorithm 1 but only simpler, because the preclustering stage admits a simpler algorithm due to Gonzalez [13]. For the k-center problem on a point set Z of n points, Gonzalez's algorithm outputs a re-ordering of points in Z, say, $p_1,\ldots,p_n$, such that for each $1 \le r \le n$, the solution $\mathrm{sol}(Z,r)$ of choosing $\{p_1,\ldots,p_r\}$ as the r centers is a 2-approximation for the r-center problem on Z, i.e., $C_{\mathrm{sol}}(Z,r) \le 2C_{\mathrm{opt}}(Z,r)$.

The core argument is that the k-center algorithm of Gonzalez can be used to simultaneously (a) precluster the local data into local solutions and (b) provide a witness that can be compared globally.

REMARK 3. *In Algorithm 2, (i) none of the original points is ignored in the preclustering, and (ii) it is possible that the preclustering aggregated q points but the coordinator's algorithm chooses less than q copies to exclude exactly t points. This does not affect the proofs of (k,t)-center clustering.*

Algorithm 2 Distributed (k, t)-center clustering

1: **for** each site i **do**
2: Run Gonzalez's algorithm and obtain a re-ordering $\{a_1, \dots, a_{n_i}\}$ of the points in $\mathbb{A}_i$
3: **for** each $1 \le q \le t$ **do**
4: Compute $\ell(i, q) \leftarrow \min\{d(a_j, a_{k+q}) : j < k + q\}$
5: **end for**
6: **end for**
7: Sites and coordinator sort $\{\ell(i, q)\}$, and follow the subsequent steps as in Algorithm 1, where the coordinator in the last step runs the algorithm in [4] for the k-center problem with exactly t outliers.

We now analyze the performance of Algorithm 2. Denote by t_i^* the number of points ignored from $\mathbb{A}_i$ in the global optimum solution $\text{opt}(\mathbb{A}, k, t)$. First we show two structural lemmas.

Lemma 4.1. $2C_{\text{opt}}(\mathbb{A}_i, k, t) \ge \max_i C_{\text{opt}}(\mathbb{A}_i, k, t_i^*)$.

Proof. Use the same argument in the proof of Lemma 3.2. □

Lemma 4.2. $\max_i C_{\text{opt}}(\mathbb{A}_i, k, t_i^*) \ge \min_{\sum_i t_i \ge t} \left(\max_i C_{\text{opt}}(\mathbb{A}_i, k, t_i) \right)$.

Proof. It follows from the fact that $\sum_i t_i^* = t$. □

Theorem 4.3. *For the distributed (k, t)-center problem, Algorithm 2 outputs $\text{sol}(\mathbb{A}, k, t)$ satisfying $C_{\text{sol}}(\mathbb{A}, k, t) \le O(1) \cdot C_{\text{opt}}(\mathbb{A}, k, t)$. The sites communicate a total of $\tilde{O}((sk + t)B)$ bits of information to the coordinator over 2 rounds. The runtime on site i is $\tilde{O}((k + t)n_i)$ and the runtime on the coordinator is $\tilde{O}((sk + t)^2)$.*

Proof. The approximation ratio follows from a similar argument to that of Theorem 3.6, using Lemma 4.1 and 4.2. The coordinator runtime follows from [4, Theorem 3.1] and the site runtime from [13], noting that we need only the first $k + t$ points of the reordering of each $\mathbb{A}_i$. The communication cost is clear from Algorithm 2. □

5 CLUSTERING UNCERTAIN INPUT

Recall that in the setting of clustering with uncertainty there is an underlying metric space $(\mathcal{P}, d)$. We are given a set of input nodes $j \in \mathbb{A}$ which correspond to distributions $\mathcal{D}_j$ on $\mathcal{P}$. In this section we shall use nodes to indicate the input and points to indicate deterministic objects in the metric space $\mathcal{P}$. We shall denote by $\sigma(j)$ a realization of node j and by $\pi(j)$ the center node to which j is attached. Our goal in the (k, t)-median problem in this context is to compute

$$\min_{\substack{K \subseteq \mathcal{P}, \mathbb{O} \subseteq \mathbb{A} \\ |K| \le k, |\mathbb{O}| \le t}} \left[\sum_{j \in \mathbb{A} \setminus \mathbb{O}} \left(\min_{\pi(j)} \mathbb{E}_{\sigma} \left[d(\sigma(j), \pi(j)) \right] \right) \right]. \quad (8)$$

For (k, t)-means we use $d^2(\cdot, \cdot)$ and for (k, t)-center-pp we use $\max_j$ instead of $\sum_j$.

Define $\hat{d} : \mathbb{A} \times \mathcal{P} \to \mathbb{R}$ as $\hat{d}(j, p) = \mathbb{E}_{\sigma}[d(\sigma(j), p)]$, the objective function (8) is then reduced to the usual (k, t)-median problem with the new distance function $\hat{d}$. However, this definition only allows the computation of distance between an input node and a point in $\mathcal{P}$. To extend $\hat{d}$ to a pair of input nodes, the site holding $\mathbb{A}_i$ will need to know the point set $\bigcup_{j \in \mathbb{A}_{i'}} \text{supp}(\mathcal{D}_j)$ from some other site i'. This will blow up the communication cost, and thus naively using this distance function in combination with the algorithms developed previously will not work well. To circumvent this issue we combine the notion of 1-median introduced in [8] along with the framework in Theorem 2.1, and introduce a compression scheme to evaluate distances.

Definition 5.1. For each node j, define its 1-median and 1-mean to be

$$y_j = \arg\min_{y \in \mathcal{P}} \mathbb{E}_{\sigma}[d(\sigma(j), y)], \quad y_j' = \arg\min_{y \in \mathcal{P}} \mathbb{E}_{\sigma}[d^2(\sigma(j), y)],$$

respectively.

Definition 5.2 (Compressed graph). The compressed graph $G(\mathbb{A})$ is a weighted graph on vertices $\mathcal{P} \cup \{p_j\}_{j \in \mathbb{A}}$, where the edges are as follows: (1) each pair $(u, v) \in \mathcal{P}$ is an edge with weight $d(u, v)$, and (2) for each $j \in \mathbb{A}$, the vertex p_j is connected only to y_j with weight $\ell_j = \mathbb{E}_{\sigma}[d(\sigma(j), y_j)]$. Define the distance $d_G(u, v)$ between two vertices u, v in G to be the length of the shortest path between u and v in G.

For the compressed graph G, we can also consider the following (k, t)-median problem, where we restrict the demand points to $\{p_j\}$ and the possible centers to $\{y_j\}$, and the distance function is the length of shortest path on G. We continue to use the notations $\text{sol}(G, k, t)$, $C_{\text{sol}}(G, k, t)$, etc., to denote the solution and the corresponding cost of (k, t)-median problem on G. The following two lemmas show that (k, t)-median problem in Eqn (8) is, up to some constant factor in the approximation ratio, equivalent to the (k, t)-median problem on the compressed graph.

Lemma 5.3. *If there exists a solution $\text{sol}(\mathbb{A}, k, t)$ of cost $C_{\text{sol}}(\mathbb{A}, k, t)$ to the objective in Equation (8), then there exists a solution $\text{sol}(G(\mathbb{A}), k, t)$ on the compressed graph such that $C_{\text{sol}}(G(\mathbb{A}), k, t) \le 5C_{\text{sol}}(\mathbb{A}, k, t)$.*

Proof. Let $\mathbb{A}'$ be the set of clustered nodes in the feasible (k, t)-median solution of the original problem with the objective in (8). Define the set of center points $M = \{y_j : j \in \mathbb{A}'\}$. For each $j \in \mathbb{A}'$, let $y_{\pi(j)} = \arg\min_{y \in M} d(\pi(j), y)$. Let $\text{sol}(G(\mathbb{A}), k, t)$ be the solution of connecting each point p_j ($j \in \mathbb{A}'$) to $y_{\pi(j)}$ in the compressed graph G. We try to upper bound the cost $C_{\text{sol}}(G(\mathbb{A}), k, t)$:

$$\begin{aligned} C_{\text{sol}}(G(\mathbb{A}), k, t) &= \sum_{j \in \mathbb{A}'} d_G(y_{\pi(j)}, p_j) && \text{(definition of } C_{\text{sol}}) \\ &= \sum_{j \in \mathbb{A}'} \left(d(y_{\pi(j)}, y_j) + d_G(y_j, p_j) \right) && \text{(definition of } d_G) \\ &\le \sum_{j \in \mathbb{A}'} d(y_{\pi(j)}, \pi(j)) + \sum_{j \in \mathbb{A}'} d(\pi(j), y_j) + \sum_{j \in \mathbb{A}'} d_G(y_j, p_j) \\ & && \text{(triangle inequality)} \\ &\le 2 \sum_{j \in \mathbb{A}'} d(\pi(j), y_j) + \sum_{j \in \mathbb{A}'} \ell_j, \end{aligned}$$

where the last line follows from $d(y_{\pi(j)}, \pi(j)) \le d(\pi(j), y_j)$ by the definition (optimality) of $y_{\pi(j)}$.

Observe that for any realization $\sigma(j)$, it holds that

$$d(y_j, \pi(j)) \le d(y_j, \sigma(j)) + d(\sigma(j), \pi(j)).$$

Taking expectation over σ,

$$d(y_j,\pi(j)) \le \mathop{\mathbb{E}}_{\sigma} d(y_j,\sigma(j)) + \mathop{\mathbb{E}}_{\sigma} d(\sigma(j),\pi(j)) = \ell_j + \mathop{\mathbb{E}}_{\sigma} d(\sigma(j),\pi(j)).$$

Summing over $j \in \mathbb{A}'$,

$$\sum_{j\in\mathbb{A}'} d(y_j,\pi(j)) \le \sum_{j\in\mathbb{A}'} \ell_j + \sum_{j\in\mathbb{A}'} \mathop{\mathbb{E}}_{\sigma} d(\sigma(j),\pi(j)) \le \sum_{j\in\mathbb{A}'} \ell_j + C_{\text{opt}}(\mathbb{A},k,t). \tag{9}$$

We next bound $\sum_{j\in\mathbb{A}'}\ell_j$. This is exactly the cost of connecting each $j \in \mathbb{A}'$ to its 1-median, which is the optimal solution of at most $n-t$ centers for $\mathbb{A}'$. The optimal cost for $n-t$ centers is clearly less than that for k centers and hence $\sum_{j\in\mathbb{A}'}\ell_j \le C_{\text{opt}}(\mathbb{A},k,t)$.

Therefore $C_{\text{sol}}(G(\mathbb{A}),k,t) \le 2\cdot 2C_{\text{opt}}(\mathbb{A},k,t) + C_{\text{opt}}(\mathbb{A},k,t) = 5C_{\text{opt}}(\mathbb{A},k,t)$ as claimed. □

Lemma 5.4. *If there exists a solution* $\text{sol}(G(\mathbb{A}),k,t)$ *of cost* $C_{\text{sol}}(G(\mathbb{A}),k,t)$ *on the compressed graph, then there exists a solution* $\text{sol}(\mathbb{A},k,t)$ *for the problem formulated in* (8) *such that* $C_{\text{sol}}(\mathbb{A},k,t) \le 2C_{\text{sol}}(G(\mathbb{A}),k,t)$.

Proof. Let $\mathbb{A}''$ be the set of clustered nodes in $\text{sol}(G(\mathbb{A}),k,t)$. A similar argument of increasing the number of centers as in Lemma 5.3 yields that $\sum_{j\in\mathbb{A}''}\ell_j \le C_{\text{sol}}(G(\mathbb{A}),k,t)$. Suppose that p_j is assigned to $\pi(j)$ in $\text{sol}(G(\mathbb{A}),k,t)$ in the compressed graph. Note that $\pi(j) \in \mathcal{P}$. Let $\text{sol}(\mathbb{A},k,t)$ be the solution of attaching j to $\pi(j)$ in $\mathcal{P}$, and the cost can be bounded as

$$\begin{aligned}
C_{\text{sol}}(\mathbb{A},k,t) &= \sum_{j\in\mathbb{A}''} \mathop{\mathbb{E}}_{\sigma}(d(\sigma(j),\pi(j))) && \text{(definition of } C_{\text{sol}})\\
&\le \sum_{j\in\mathbb{A}''} \mathop{\mathbb{E}}_{\sigma}\left(d(\sigma(j),y_j)\right) + \sum_{j\in\mathbb{A}''} d(y_j,\pi(j)) && \text{(triangle inequality)}\\
&\le \sum_{j\in\mathbb{A}''} \ell_j + \sum_{j\in\mathbb{A}''} d_G(p_j,\pi(j)) && \text{(definition of } d_G\text{, see below)}\\
&\le 2C_{\text{sol}}(G(\mathbb{A}),k,t), && \text{(definition of } C_{\text{sol}})
\end{aligned}$$

where the third line follows from $d_G(p_j,\pi(j)) = d(p_j,y_j)+d(y_j,\pi(j)) \ge d(y_j,\pi(j))$. □

The equivalence between the original problem and the one on the compressed graph also holds for the (k,t)-center-pp and the (k,t)-means problems.

Lemma 5.5. *Lemma 5.3 and Lemma 5.4 both hold*

(a) for (k,t)-center-pp with the same constants; and
(b) for (k,t)-means with slightly larger constants.

Proof. (a) Observe that $\sum_j$ is replaced with $\max_j$ and Equation (9) rewrites to

$$\max_{j\in\mathbb{A}'} d(y_j,\pi(j)) \le \max_{j\in\mathbb{A}'} \ell_j + C_{\text{opt}}(\mathbb{A},k,t).$$

The remainder of the equations hold with this transformation.

(b) Note that we used triangle inequality in the proof above. Although the square of the distance does not obey the triangle inequality, we can nevertheless apply $(a+b)^2 \le 2a^2+2b^2$ after the triangle inequality. The derivations above will go through and the results hold with slightly larger constants. □

Algorithm 3 A Compression Scheme for Distributed Partial Clustering of Uncertain Data

1: **for** each site i **do**
2: Compute $\ell_j = \mathbb{E}_\sigma[d(\sigma(j),y_j)]$ for all $j \in \mathbb{A}_i$
3: Construct the compressed graph of $\mathbb{A}_i$ as described in Definition 5.2
4: Run any algorithm corresponding to Section 3 and Section 4 on the compressed graph, with the following change: whenever the site has to communicate p_j, it also sends y_j (or y_j') and the values of $\mathbb{E}_\sigma[d(\sigma(j),y_j)]$ (or $\mathbb{E}_\sigma[d^2(\sigma(j),y_j')]$).
5: **end for**

The overall algorithm is summarized in Algorithm 3. Note that we cannot just cluster the $\{y_j\}$; the graph is necessary. To implement the algorithm, we need to show that each site is able to compute the distance function individually. Indeed, note that any site that contains p_j will also contain the corresponding y_j or y_j' and the value $\mathbb{E}_\sigma[d(\sigma(j),y_j)]$ or $\mathbb{E}_\sigma[d^2(\sigma(j),y_j')]$ respectively. Therefore the distance oracle on the graph can be implemented by the site in constant time.

Theorem 5.6. *For the distributed (k,t)-median problem, Algorithm 3 outputs* $\text{sol}(\mathbb{A},k,(1+\epsilon)t)$ *such that* $C_{\text{sol}}(\mathbb{A},k,(1+\epsilon)t) = O(1+1/\epsilon)\cdot C_{\text{opt}}(\mathbb{A},k,t)$. *The sites communicate a total of* $\tilde{O}((sk+t)B)$ *bits of information to the coordinator over 2 rounds. The runtime on site i is* $\tilde{O}(n_i^2+n_iT)$, *where T is the runtime to compute 1-median, and the runtime on the coordinator is* $\tilde{O}((sk+t)^2)$. *The same result holds for the (k,t)-median and center-pp problems with larger constants.*

Proof. By Lemma 5.4 for the median problem and Lemma 5.5 for the means and center-pp problems, it suffices to show that we can solve the (k,t)-median problem on the compressed graph. The result then follows from Theorem 3.6 and Theorem 3.8 with the following amendments: When a site sends the t or t_i potential outliers, it needs to send the y_j and the corresponding values $\mathbb{E}_\sigma[d(\sigma(j),y_j)]$ or $\mathbb{E}_\sigma[d^2(\sigma(j),y_j')]$, which at most doubles the communication cost. The runtime is increased by $O(n_iT)$ due to Step 2 since computing ℓ_j on the compressed graph takes $O(T)$ time. □

Other results claimed in Table 2 follow from analogous amendments to Theorem 3.8.

The global k-Center case. We now focus on (k,t)-center-g. In this setting $\mathcal{D}_j$'s are independent and we optimize

$$\min_{\substack{K\subseteq\mathcal{P},\,\mathbb{O}\subseteq\mathbb{A}\\|K|\le k,\,|\mathbb{O}|\le t}} \left(\mathop{\mathbb{E}}_{\sigma\sim\prod_j\mathcal{D}_j}\left[\max_{j\in\mathbb{A}\setminus\mathbb{O}} d(\sigma(j),\pi(j))\right]\right).$$

Definition 5.7 (Truncated distance [15]). For $\tau \ge 0$, define $\mathcal{L}_\tau : \mathcal{P}\times\mathcal{P} \to \mathbb{R}$ as $\mathcal{L}_\tau(u,v) = \max\{d(u,v)-\tau, 0\}$ and $\rho_\tau : \mathbb{A}\times\mathcal{P} \to \mathbb{R}$ as $\rho_\tau(j,u) = \mathbb{E}_\sigma[\mathcal{L}_\tau(\sigma(j),u)]$. Note that $\mathcal{L}_\tau(\cdot,\cdot)$ is not a metric for $\tau > 0$.

Definition 5.8. Given a node set $Z \subseteq \mathbb{A}$, let $\mathcal{P}(Z) \subseteq \mathcal{P}$ be the associated point set corresponding to possible realizations of nodes in Z. Let $\text{sol}(Z,k,t,\rho_\tau)$ and $\text{opt}(Z,k,t,\rho_\tau)$ be a solution by algorithm and the global optimum solution respectively to the (k,t)-median problem on node set Z where the centers are restricted to $\mathcal{P}(Z)$

and the weighted assignment cost of assigning node $j \in Z$ to center $m \in \mathcal{P}(Z)$ is $\rho_\tau(j, m)$. The costs $C_{\text{sol}}(Z, k, t, \rho_\tau)$ and $C_{\text{opt}}(Z, k, t, \rho_\tau)$ are defined analogously.

Let $d_{\min}$ and $d_{\max}$ denote the minimum and the maximum distance, respectively, between two distinct points in $\mathcal{P}$ and let $\Delta = d_{\max}/d_{\min}$. The algorithm is presented in Algorithm 4.

Algorithm 4 Algorithm for (k, t)-center-g

1: All parties compute $d_{\min}$ and $d_{\max}$
2: Each party creates $\mathbb{T} = \{2^i d_{\min}/18 : 0 \le i \le \lceil \log_2 \Delta \rceil + 2\}$
3: **for** each $\tau \in \mathbb{T}$ **do**
4: All parties run Algorithm 2 with the following changes: when it calls Algorithm 1 as a subroutine, $\text{sol}(\mathbb{A}_i, 2k, q)$ in Algorithm 1 is replaced with $\text{sol}(\mathbb{A}_i, 2k, q, \rho_{6\tau})$ and the sites obtain the numbers of local outliers $\{t_i(\tau)\}$
5: **end for**
6: Coordinator finds $\hat{\tau} = \min\{\tau \in \mathbb{T} : \sum_i C_{\text{sol}}(\mathbb{A}_i, 2k, t_i(\tau), \rho_{6\tau}) \le 12\tau\}$
7: Coordinator solves (k, t)-center-g on the preclustering solutions $\text{sol}(\mathbb{A}_i, 2k, t_i(\hat{\tau}), \rho_{6\tau})$ and outputs $\text{sol}(\mathbb{A}, k, (1+\epsilon)t)$.

Now we try to analyze the performance of Algorithm 4. We first show an analogy of Theorem 3.1 that we can compute a constant approximation to $C_{\text{opt}}(Z, k, t, \rho_\tau)$. The proof is omitted.

Lemma 5.9. *Let $\tau \ge 0$. For the (k, t)-center problem on Z, we can compute in $\tilde{O}((k + t)|Z|)$ time* $\text{sol}(Z, k, (1+\epsilon)t, \rho_{9\tau})$ *or* $\text{sol}(Z, (1+\epsilon)k, t, \rho_{3\tau})$ *such that*

$$C_{\text{sol}}(Z, k, (1+\epsilon)t, \rho_{9\tau}) \le \max\{6, 6/\epsilon\} \cdot C_{\text{opt}}(Z, k, t, \rho_\tau)$$
$$C_{\text{sol}}(Z, (1+\epsilon)k, t, \rho_{3\tau}) \le \max\{6, 6/\epsilon\} \cdot C_{\text{opt}}(Z, k, t, \rho_\tau)$$

We next show that the $\hat{\tau}$ computed in Step 6 is a good choice of τ and will ensure that the preclustering solutions $\text{sol}(\mathbb{A}_i, 2k, t_i(\hat{\tau}), \rho_{2\hat{\tau}})$ can be combined to yield a good global solution. Specifically we have the following two lemmas.

Lemma 5.10. *The $\hat{\tau}$ computed in Step 6 satisfies the following two conditions.*

(i) $\sum_i C_{\text{sol}}(\mathbb{A}_i, 2k, t_i(\hat{\tau}), \rho_{6\hat{\tau}}) \le 12\hat{\tau}$;
(ii) $\sum_i C_{\text{opt}}(\mathbb{A}_i, k, t_i', \rho_{2\hat{\tau}}) \ge 2\hat{\tau}$ *for all* $\{t_i'\}$ s.t. $\sum_i t_i' \le t$,

Proof. Note that $\tau_{\max} = \max \mathbb{T} > d_{\max}/6$, it always holds that $\rho_{6\tau_{\max}} = 0$. Thus the condition $\sum_i C_{\text{sol}}(\mathbb{A}_i, 2k, t_i(\tau_{\max}), \rho_{6\tau_{\max}}) \le 12\tau_{\max}$ holds, and $\hat{\tau}$ exists and satisfies condition (i).

Next we show that condition (ii) holds. Let $\{t_i'\}$ be an arbitrary sequence satisfying that $\sum_i t_i' \le t$. Similarly to the proof of Lemma 3.3, one can show that $\sum_i C_{\text{sol}}(\mathbb{A}_i, 2k, t_i', \rho_{6\hat{\tau}}) \ge \sum_i C_{\text{sol}}(\mathbb{A}_i, 2k, t_i(\hat{\tau}), \rho_{6\hat{\tau}})$, using the fact that $\sum_i t_i' \le t < \rho t = \sum_i t_i$. Combining with Lemma 5.9 with $\epsilon = 1$, we have that

$$6\sum_i C_{\text{opt}}(\mathbb{A}_i, k, t_i', \rho_{2\hat{\tau}}) \ge \sum_i C_{\text{sol}}(\mathbb{A}_i, 2k, t_i', \rho_{6\hat{\tau}}) \ge \sum_i C_{\text{sol}}(\mathbb{A}_i, 2k, t_i(\hat{\tau}), \rho_{6\hat{\tau}}) \ge 12\hat{\tau},$$

whence condition (ii) follows. □

Lemma 5.11. *Suppose that $\hat{\tau}$ satisfies the condition (i) and (ii) of Lemma 5.10, a γ-approximation of the weighted center-g problem induced by preclustering* $\text{sol}(\mathbb{A}_i, 2k, t_i(\hat{\tau}), \rho_{6\hat{\tau}})$ *is an $O(\gamma)$ approximation of $C_{\text{opt}}(\mathbb{A}, k, t)$.*

To prove this lemma, we need the following two auxiliary lemmas.

Lemma 5.12. $2C_{\text{opt}}(\mathbb{A}, k, t, \rho_\tau) \ge \sum_i C_{\text{opt}}(\mathbb{A}_i, k, t_i^*, \rho_{2\tau})$, *where t_i^* is the number of ignored nodes from $\mathbb{A}_i$ in the global optimum solution* $\text{opt}(\mathbb{A}, k, t, \rho_\tau)$.

Proof. Fix a realization of the nodes. The proof mimics Lemma 3.2 for each realization. It then uses the observation that $\mathcal{L}_\tau(u_1, u_2) + \mathcal{L}_\tau(u_2, u_3) \ge \mathcal{L}_{2\tau}(u_1, u_3)$ and takes the expectation. □

Lemma 5.13. *If $C_{\text{opt}}(Z, k, t, \rho_\tau) \ge \tau$ then $C_{\text{opt}}(Z, k, t) \ge \tau/3$.*

Proof. The case of $t = 0$ (no outliers) is proved in [15, Lemma 4.4]. For a general $t > 0$, let $Z' \subseteq Z$ be the set of clustered point in $\text{opt}(Z, k, t)$, then $C_{\text{opt}}(Z', k, 0, \rho_\tau) = C_{\text{opt}}(Z, k, t, \rho_\tau) \ge \tau$, thus $C_{\text{opt}}(Z, k, t) = C_{\text{opt}}(Z', k, 0) \ge \tau/3$. □

Proof of Lemma 5.11. It follows from Lemma 5.12 and condition (ii) of Lemma 5.10 that

$$2C_{\text{opt}}(\mathbb{A}, k, t, \rho_{\hat{\tau}}) \ge \sum_i C_{\text{opt}}(\mathbb{A}_i, k, t_i^*, \rho_{2\hat{\tau}}) \ge 2\hat{\tau},$$

where t_i^* is the number of ignored nodes from $\mathbb{A}_i$ in the global optimum solution $\text{opt}(\mathbb{A}, k, t, \rho_{\hat{\tau}})$. It then follows from Lemma 5.13 that $C_{\text{opt}}(\mathbb{A}, k, t) \ge \hat{\tau}/3$,

To simplify the notation, in the rest of the proof we shorthand $t_i(\hat{\tau})$ as t_i. Let $\mathbb{A}_i^* \subseteq \mathbb{A}_i$ be the set of nodes clustered in the global optimum solution $\text{opt}(\mathbb{A}, k, t)$. Consider "collapsing" the nodes in $\mathbb{A}_i^*$ to their corresponding centers in $\text{sol}(\mathbb{A}_i, 2k, t_i, \rho_{6\hat{\tau}})$ while keeping the same centers in $\text{sol}(\mathbb{A}, k, t)$. If a node in $\mathbb{A}_i^*$ is marked as an outlier in $\text{sol}(\mathbb{A}_i, 2k, t_i, \rho_{2\hat{\tau}})$ then it is not moved, and it continues to be excluded from the calculation. This movement increases the expectation of the maximum assignment by $6\hat{\tau} + C_{\text{sol}}(\mathbb{A}_i, 2k, t_i, \rho_{2\hat{\tau}})$. Now consider the same process where we collapse $\mathbb{A}_i^*$ for all i. The total increase across the different i is $6\hat{\tau} + \sum_i C_{\text{sol}}(\mathbb{A}_i, 2k, t_i, \rho_{6\hat{\tau}})$ because the increase in $6\hat{\tau}$ arises from distance truncation and is common. Thus we achieve a solution of cost at most

$$\gamma\left(C_{\text{opt}}(\mathbb{A}, k, t) + 6\hat{\tau} + \sum_i C_{\text{sol}}(\mathbb{A}_i, 2k, t_i, \rho_{6\hat{\tau}})\right).$$

Now consider "expanding" the nodes of $\mathbb{A}_i$ from the preclustering to the distribution $\mathcal{D}_j$. By that logic the expected maximum can increase by at most $2\hat{\tau} + \sum_i C_{\text{sol}}(\mathbb{A}_i, 2k, t_i, \rho_{2\hat{\tau}})$, which by condition (i) of Lemma 5.10 totals to $O(\gamma\hat{\tau}) = O(\gamma)C_{\text{opt}}(\mathbb{A}, k, t)$. The lemma follows. □

We state the main theorem for the (k, t)-center-g problem to conclude this section.

Theorem 5.14. *For the distributed (k, t)-center-g problem, Algorithm 4 outputs* $\text{sol}(\mathbb{A}, k, (1+\epsilon)t)$ *satisfying* $C_{\text{sol}}(\mathbb{A}, k, (1+\epsilon)t) = O(1 + 1/\epsilon) \cdot C_{\text{opt}}(\mathbb{A}, k, t)$. *The sites communicate a total of $\tilde{O}(skB + s\log\Delta + tI)$ bits of information to the coordinator over 2 rounds, where I is the bit complexity to encode a node. The runtime at site i is $\tilde{O}((k + t)n_i \log\Delta)$ and the runtime at the coordinator is $\tilde{O}((sk + t)^2)$.*

Objective	Approx.	Centers	Ignored	Rounds	Total Comm.	Local Time
median	$O(1)$	k	t	1 2	$\tilde{O}((sk+st)B)$ $\tilde{O}((sk+t)B)$	$\tilde{O}(n_i^2)$, $\tilde{O}(k^2 s^3 t^5)$ $\tilde{O}(n_i^2)$, $\tilde{O}(k^2 t^2 (sk+t)^3)$
			$(2+\delta)t$	2	$\tilde{O}(s/\delta + skB)$	$\tilde{O}(n_i^2)$, $\tilde{O}(s^2 k^7)$
means/ median	$O(1+1/\epsilon)$	k, $(1+\epsilon)t$ or $(1+\epsilon)k$, t		1 2	$\tilde{O}((sk+st)B)$ $\tilde{O}((sk+t)B)$	$\tilde{O}(n_i^2)$, $\tilde{O}((sk+st)^2)$ $\tilde{O}(n_i^2)$, $\tilde{O}((sk+t)^2)$
		k $(1+\epsilon)k$	$(2+\epsilon+\delta)t$ $(2+\delta)t$	2	$\tilde{O}(s/\delta + skB)$	$\tilde{O}(n_i^2)$, $\tilde{O}((sk)^2)$
center	$O(1)$	k	t	1 2	$\tilde{O}((sk+st)B)$ $\tilde{O}((sk+t)B)$	$\tilde{O}((k+t)n_i)$, $\tilde{O}((sk+st)^2)$ $\tilde{O}((k+t)n_i)$, $\tilde{O}((sk+t)^2)$
			$(2+\delta)t$	2	$\tilde{O}(s/\delta + skB)$	$\tilde{O}(n_i^2)$, $\tilde{O}((sk)^2)$
uncertain median/ means/ center-pp	as in the regular case above					$+O(n_i T)$, unchanged
center-g	$O(1+1/\epsilon)$ $O(1)$	k	$(1+\epsilon)t$ t	2 1	$\tilde{O}(skB + tI + s\log\Delta)$ $\tilde{O}(s(kB+tI)\log\Delta)$	$\tilde{O}(n_i^2 \log\Delta)$, $\tilde{O}((sk+t)^2)$ $\tilde{O}((k+t)n_i \log\Delta)$, $\tilde{O}(s^2(k+t)^2)$

Table 2: Our results. T denotes the runtime to compute 1-median/mean of a node distribution, I is the information encoding a node in the uncertain data case, B the information encoding a point and Δ the ratio between the maximum pairwise distance and the minimum pairwise distance in the dataset.

Proof. The claim on approximation ratio follows from Lemma 5.11. To determine $\hat{\tau}$, the communication cost increases by a factor of $\log\Delta$; to send the preclustering solutions, the communication cost for sending the outliers increases by a factor of I. The runtime follows from Lemma 5.9 with an increase of a factor of $\log\Delta$. □

We remark that the dependence on $\log\Delta$ can be removed with another pass where each site computes a τ_i using binary search. The discussion is omitted in the interest of simplicity.

Other results claimed in Table 2 follow from analogous amendments to Theorem 3.8.

REFERENCES

[1] Charu C. Aggarwal. A survey of uncertain data clustering algorithms. In *Data Clustering: Algorithms and Applications*, pages 457–482. 2013.

[2] Maria-Florina Balcan, Steven Ehrlich, and Yingyu Liang. Distributed k-means and k-median clustering on general communication topologies. In *Proceedings of NIPS*, pages 1995–2003, 2013.

[3] Moses Charikar and Sudipto Guha. Improved combinatorial algorithms for the facility location and k-median problems. In *Proceedings of FOCS*, pages 378–388, 1999.

[4] Moses Charikar, Samir Khuller, David M. Mount, and Giri Narasimhan. Algorithms for facility location problems with outliers. In *Proceedings of SODA*, pages 642–651, 2001.

[5] Jiecao Chen, He Sun, D. Woodruff, and Qin Zhang. Communication-optimal distributed clustering. In *Proceedings of NIPS*, 2016.

[6] Ke Chen. A constant factor approximation algorithm for k-median clustering with outliers. In *Proceedings of SODA*, pages 826–835, 2008.

[7] Michael B. Cohen, Sam Elder, Cameron Musco, Christopher Musco, and Madalina Persu. Dimensionality reduction for k-means clustering and low rank approximation. In *Proceedings of STOC*, pages 163–172, 2015.

[8] Graham Cormode and Andrew McGregor. Approximation algorithms for clustering uncertain data. In *Proceedings of PODS*, pages 191–200, 2008.

[9] Graham Cormode, S Muthukrishnan, and Wei Zhuang. Conquering the divide: Continuous clustering of distributed data streams. In *Proceedings of ICDE*, pages 1036–1045. IEEE, 2007.

[10] M. E. Dyer. On a multidimensional search technique and its application to the euclidean one centre problem. *SIAM J. Comput.*, 15(3):725–738, 1986.

[11] Alina Ene, Sungjin Im, and Benjamin Moseley. Fast clustering using mapreduce. In *Proceedings of SIGKDD*, pages 681–689, 2011.

[12] Dan Feldman and Leonard J. Schulman. Data reduction for weighted and outlier-resistant clustering. In *Proceedings of SODA*, pages 1343–1354, 2012.

[13] Teofilo F. Gonzalez. Clustering to minimize the maximum intercluster distance. *Theor. Comput. Sci.*, 38:293–306, 1985.

[14] Sudipto Guha, Adam Meyerson, Nina Mishra, Rajeev Motwani, and Liadan O'Callaghan. Clustering data streams: Theory and practice. *IEEE Trans. on Knowl. and Data Eng.*, 15(3):515–528, 2003.

[15] Sudipto Guha and Kamesh Munagala. Exceeding expectations and clustering uncertain data. In *Proceedings of PODS*, pages 269–278, 2009.

[16] Sungjin Im and Benjamin Moseley. Brief announcement: Fast and better distributed mapreduce algorithms for k-center clustering. In *Proceedings of SPAA*, pages 65–67, 2015.

[17] Kamal Jain and Vijay V. Vazirani. Approximation algorithms for metric facility location and k-median problems using the primal-dual schema and lagrangian relaxation. *J. ACM*, 48(2):274–296, 2001.

[18] Yingyu Liang, Maria-Florina Balcan, Vandana Kanchanapally, and David P. Woodruff. Improved distributed principal component analysis. In *Proceedings of NIPS*, pages 3113–3121, 2014.

[19] Gustavo Malkomes, Matt J. Kusner, Wenlin Chen, Kilian Q. Weinberger, and Benjamin Moseley. Fast distributed k-center clustering with outliers on massive data. In *Proceedings of NIPS*, pages 1063–1071, 2015.

[20] Dan Suciu, Dan Olteanu, R. Christopher, and Christoph Koch. *Probabilistic Databases*. Morgan & Claypool Publishers, 1st edition, 2011.

[21] Haitao Wang and Jingru Zhang. One-dimensional k-center on uncertain data. *Theoretical Computer Science*, 602:114 – 124, 2015.

A THE FULL SET OF OUR RESULTS

We summarize the full set of our results in Table 2. Besides the main results that already appear in Table 1, all the 1-round results in Table 2 basically follow from setting $t_i = t$ for all sites i. The results for (k,t)-median/means that ignore $(2+\delta)t$ or $(2+\epsilon+\delta)t$ points basically follow from Theorem 3.8, where for (k,t)-median with k centers (unicriterion) we need to apply again the 1-round result, and for (k,t)-median/means with $(1+\epsilon)k$ centers we simply use the second inequality of Theorem 3.1 instead of the first one at the final clustering step at the coordinator. The result for (k,t)-center that ignore $(2+\delta)t$ points is due to the following modifications on Algorithm 4: sites do not send the total $(1+\delta)t$ local outliers to the coordinator, and thereafter the coordinator performs the second level clustering with (another) t outliers, we have $(2+\delta)t$ outliers in total.

Distributed Detection of Cycles

Pierre Fraigniaud*
Institut de Recherche en Informatique Fondamentale
CNRS and University Paris Diderot
France
pierre.fraigniaud@irif.fr

Dennis Olivetti†
Gran Sasso Science Institute
L'Aquila, Italy
dennis.olivetti@gssi.infn.it

ABSTRACT

Distributed property testing in networks has been introduced by Brakerski and Patt-Shamir (2011), with the objective of detecting the presence of large dense sub-networks in a distributed manner. Recently, Censor-Hillel et al. (2016) have shown how to detect 3-cycles in a constant number of rounds by a distributed algorithm. In a follow up work, Fraigniaud et al. (2016) have shown how to detect 4-cycles in a constant number of rounds as well. However, the techniques in these latter works were shown not to generalize to larger cycles C_k with $k \geq 5$. In this paper, we completely settle the problem of cycle detection, by establishing the following result. For every $k \geq 3$, there exists a distributed property testing algorithm for C_k-freeness, performing in a constant number of rounds. All these results hold in the classical CONGEST model for distributed network computing. Our algorithm is 1-sided error. Its round-complexity is $O(1/\epsilon)$ where $\epsilon \in (0,1)$ is the property testing parameter measuring the gap between legal and illegal instances.

1 INTRODUCTION

1.1 Context

1.1.1 Property Testing. The objective of (sequential) *property testing* [21] is the design of efficient mechanisms for detecting whether data-structures satisfy a given property. In the context of networks, a vast literature has been dedicated to testing the presence or absence of specific patterns like triangles, cycles, cliques, etc. (see, e.g., [2, 3, 11, 22]). A property testing mechanism, a.k.a. *tester*, is a centralized algorithm $\mathcal{A}$ which is given the ability to probe nodes with queries of the form $\text{deg}(i)$ returning the degree of the ith node, and $\text{adj}(i,j)$ returning the identity of the jth neighbor of the ith node. Beside its running time, the quality of a tester is typically measured by the number of queries that it must perform before deciding whether or not the network satisfies the considered property.

Property testing finds its main interest when the problem is relaxed by simply requiring the tester to distinguish between instances satisfying the property, and instances that are *far* from satisfying that property. In the context of networks, several notions of farness have been considered. We consider here the so-called *sparse* model: Given any $\epsilon \in (0,1)$, an n-node m-edge network G is said to be ϵ-far from satisfying a graph property $\mathcal{P}$ if adding and/or removing at most ϵm edges to/from G cannot result in a network satisfying $\mathcal{P}$.

A tester for a graph property $\mathcal{P}$ is a randomized algorithm $\mathcal{A}$ that is required to accept or reject any given network instance, under the following two constraints:

- G satisfies $\mathcal{P} \Longrightarrow \Pr[\mathcal{A} \text{ accepts } G] \geq 2/3$;
- G is ϵ-far from satisfying $\mathcal{P} \Longrightarrow \Pr[\mathcal{A} \text{ rejects } G] \geq 2/3$.

The success guarantee 2/3 is arbitrary, as one can boost any success guarantee by repetition.

In the case of instances which are nearly satisfying $\mathcal{P}$ but not quite, the algorithm can output either ways. Hence, a tester for $\mathcal{P}$ is a mechanism enabling to detect degraded instances (i.e., instances that are far from satisfying a desired property $\mathcal{P}$) with arbitrarily large probability, while correct instances are accepted also with arbitrarily large probability.

A tester is 1-sided error if

- G satisfies $\mathcal{P} \Longrightarrow \Pr[\mathcal{A} \text{ accepts } G] = 1$.

1.1.2 Distributed Property Testing. Distributed property testing has been introduced in [6], and recently revisited in [7, 20]. In networks, a *distributed* tester is a distributed algorithm running at every node in parallel (every node executes the same code). After having inspected its surrounding, i.e., the nodes in its vicinity, every node outputs accept or reject. One says that $\mathcal{A}$ accepts a network G if and only if all nodes output accept. That is, $\mathcal{A}$ rejects if at least one of the nodes outputs reject.

In this paper, we are focussing on the detection of cycles, one of the most basic and central structures in graph theory, with impact on Ramsey theory and block design. Let $k \geq 3$. A k-node cycle, or k-cycle for short, is denoted by C_k. A network G is C_k-free if and only if G does not contain a k-node cycle as a subgraph. A case of particular interest is $k = 3$, and a C_3 is often called triangle.

*Additional support from ANR Project DESCARTES and Inria Project GANG.
†Additional support from ANR Project DESCARTES.

SPAA '17, July 24-26, 2017, Washington DC, USA

ACM ISBN 978-1-4503-4593-4/17/07...$15.00
https://doi.org/10.1145/3087556.3087571

It has been shown in [7] that, in the classical CONGEST model[1] for distributed computing [29], there exists a distributed property testing algorithm for triangle-freeness performing in $O(1/\epsilon^2)$ rounds. This result has been extended in [20] where it is proved that there exists a distributed property testing algorithm for C_4-freeness performing in $O(1/\epsilon^2)$ rounds as well.

Perhaps surprisingly, the techniques in [7, 20] do not extend to larger cycles. Indeed, using explicit constructions of so-called Behrend graphs, it was proved in [20] that these techniques fail for most values of $k \geq 5$. That is, these techniques cannot result in a tester performing in a constant number of rounds in all graphs, even if the constant is allowed to be a function of $1/\epsilon$. The existence of distributed property testing algorithms for C_k-freeness performing in a constant number of rounds was left open for k larger than 4.

1.2 Our results

We completely settle the problem of cycle detection, for every possible length $k \geq 3$. Specifically, we prove that, for every $k \geq 3$, there exists a 1-sided error distributed property testing algorithm for C_k-freeness, performing in $O(1/\epsilon)$ rounds in the CONGEST model.

Essentially, we reduce the problem of detecting k-cycles to the problem of detecting whether a given edge e belongs to some C_k. At first glance, the latter problem may seem to be much more simple. Indeed, it does not require to deal with the link congestion caused by the simultaneous testing of several edges. However, the problem remains actually quite challenging as, in the CONGEST model, even collecting the identities of the nodes at distance 2 from a given node u might be impossible to achieve in $o(n)$ rounds in n-node network. Indeed, u may have constant degree, with $\Omega(n)$ neighbors at distance 2. To overcome this difficulty, we proceed by pruning the set of information transmitted between nodes, namely by pruning the set of candidate cycles passing through the given edge e. This pruning is at the risk of discarding candidate cycles that would have turned out to be actual cycles. Nevertheless, our pruning mechanism guarantees that at least one actual cycle remains in the current set of candidate cycles throughout the execution of the algorithm.

Interestingly, the use of randomization is limited to the reduction of the general problem of testing C_k-freeness to the problem of detecting whether there exists a k-cycle passing through a given edge e. Indeed, our algorithm solving the latter problem is *deterministic*. In particular, the aforementioned pruning mechanism is deterministic. That is, the existence of an actual cycle passing through e among the restricted set of candidate cycles kept at each round is not a property that holds under some statistical guarantee, but it holds systematically.

Moreover, our algorithm for testing the existence of a k-cycle passing through a given edge e does not rely on the ϵ-farness assumption. That is, even if there is just a single k-cycle passing through e, that cycle will be detected by our algorithm.

After the acceptance of the paper, we became aware of the existence of a combinatorial lemma due to Erdős et al. [14], stating the following. Let V be a set of size n, and let us fix two integers p and q with $p + q \leq n$. Then, for any set $F \subseteq \mathcal{P}(V)$ of subsets of size at most p of V, there exists a subset $\widehat{F}$ of F of cardinality at most $\binom{p+q}{p}$ such that, for every set $C \subseteq V$ of size at most q, if there is a set $L \in F$ such that $L \cap C = \emptyset$, then there also exists $\widehat{L} \in \widehat{F}$ such that $\widehat{L} \cap C = \emptyset$. This combinatorial result has been used in different contexts, including the design of sequential parametrized algorithms for the longest path problem [26]. Our technique for detecting cycles can also be viewed as a distributed implementation of this combinatorial lemma.

1.3 Related Work

1.3.1 Property Testing. The property of H-freeness has been the subject of a lot of investigation in classical (i.e., sequential) property testing.

In the so-called *dense* model, most solutions exploit the *graph removal lemma*, which essentially states that, for every k-node graph H, and every $\epsilon > 0$, there exists $\delta > 0$ such that every n-node graph containing at most δn^k (induced) copies of H can be transformed into an (induced) H-free graph by deleting at most ϵn^2 edges. This lemma was first proved for the case $k = 3$, and later generalized to subgraphs H of any size [13], and further to induced subgraphs [1]. It is possible to exploit this lemma for testing the presence of any (induced or not) subgraph of constant size, in constant time. Notice that δ is a fast growing function of ϵ and k. The growth of the function was later improved in [3] under some assumptions. For more details on the graph removal lemma, see [10].

Cycle-detection has also been considered in the so-called sparse model. On bounded degree graphs, cycle-freeness can be tested with $O(\frac{1}{\epsilon^3} + \frac{d}{\epsilon^2})$ queries [22] by a 2-sided error algorithm, where d is the maximum degree of the graph. However, if we restrict ourselves to 1-sided error algorithms, then the problem becomes harder. A lower bound of $\Omega(\sqrt{n})$ queries was established in [11]. The same paper presents a tester requiring $\widetilde{O}(poly(1/\epsilon)\sqrt{n})$ queries in arbitrary graphs, and another tester requiring $\widetilde{O}(poly(d^k/\epsilon)\sqrt{n})$ queries in graphs with maximum degree d for detecting cycles of length at least k. Detecting triangles requires at least $\Omega(n^{1/3})$ queries, and at most $O(n^{6/7})$ queries (see [2]). The same lower bound holds for detecting any non bipartite subgraph H, and for 2-sided error algorithms as well. For some specific subgraphs H, the lower bound can even be as high as $\Omega(n^{1/2})$.

1.3.2 Distributed Property Testing. Distributed property testing has been introduced in [6], and fully formalized in [7].

The authors of that latter paper show that, in the dense model, any tester for a *non-disjointed* property can be emulated in the distributed setting with just a quadratic slowdown, i.e., if a sequential tester makes q queries, then it can be converted

[1] *The CONGEST model states that all nodes perform synchronously in a sequence of rounds; At each rounds, messages of $O(\log n)$ bits can be exchanged along the edges of the network.*

into a distributed tester that performs in $O(q^2)$ rounds. This simulation exploits the fact that any dense tester can be converted to a tester that first chooses some nodes uniformly at random, gathers their edges, and then performs centralized analysis of the obtained data (see [23]).

The authors of [7] also provide distributed testers for the sparse model, showing that it is possible to test triangle-freeness in $O(1/\epsilon^2)$ rounds, cycle-freeness in $O(1/\epsilon \log n)$ rounds, and, in bounded degree graphs, bipartiteness in

$$O(poly(1/\epsilon \log(n/\epsilon)))$$

rounds. Their work was inspired by [6], where a constant-time distributed algorithm for finding a linear-size ϵ-near clique is proposed, under the assumption that the graph contains a linear-size ϵ^3-near clique. (An ϵ-near clique is a set of nodes where all but an ϵ fraction of pairs of nodes have edges between them).

The result in [7] regarding testing triangle-freeness was extended in [20], where it is shown that, for every 4-node connected graph H, there exists a distributed tester for H-freeness performing in $O(1/\epsilon^2)$ rounds. Also, [20] provides a proof that the approach in [7, 20] fails to test C_k-freeness in a constant number of rounds, whenever $k \geq 5$.

1.3.3 Distributed Decision. Distributed property testing fits into the larger framework of *distributed decision*. The seminal paper [27] was perhaps the first to identify the connection between the ability to locally check the correctness of a solution in a distributed manner, and the ability to design an efficient deterministic distributed algorithm for constructing a correct solution. Since then, there have been a huge amount of contributions aiming at studying variant of distributed decision, in the deterministic setting (see, e.g., [19]), the anonymous setting (see, e.g., [12]), the probabilistic setting (see, e.g., [15, 18]), the non-deterministic setting (see, e.g., [24, 25]), and even beyond (see, e.g., [4, 17]). We refer to [16] for a survey on distributed decision.

1.3.4 Distributed Cycle Detection. Cycle detection has been investigated in various parallel and distributed computing frameworks, in particular for its connection to deadlock detection in routing or databases. We refer to, e.g., [5, 8, 9, 28] for cycle detection in message passing, bulk-synchronization, self-stabilizing, and other models of parallel and distributed computing.

2 MODEL AND DEFINITIONS

2.1 The CONGEST Model

We are considering the classical CONGEST model for distributed network computing [29]. The network is modeled as a connected simple graph (no self-loops, and no parallel edges). The nodes of the graph are computing entities exchanging messages along the edges of the graph. Nodes are given arbitrary distinct identities (IDs) in a range polynomial in n, in n-node networks. Hence, every ID can be stored on $O(\log n)$ bits.

In the CONGEST model, all nodes start simultaneously, and execute the same algorithm in parallel. Computation proceeds synchronously, in a sequence of *rounds*. At each round, every node

- performs some individual computation,
- sends messages to neighbors in the network, and
- receives messages sent by neighbors.

The main constraint imposed by the CONGEST model is a restriction of the amount of data that can be transferred between neighboring nodes during a round: messages are bounded to be of $O(\log n)$ bits.

The $O(\log n)$-bit bound on the message size enables the transmission of a constant number of IDs between nodes at each round. The CONGEST model is well suited for analyzing the impact of limiting the throughput of a network on its capacity to solve tasks efficiently. The complexity of a distributed algorithm in the CONGEST model is expressed in number of rounds.

In this paper, we are mostly interested in solving tasks locally. Hence, we are mainly focussing on the design of algorithms performing in a constant number of rounds in the CONGEST model.

2.2 Distributed Property Testing

2.2.1 Definition. Let $\mathcal{P}$ be a graph property like, e.g., planarity, cycle-freeness, bipartiteness, C_k-freeness, etc. Let $\epsilon \in (0, 1)$. Recall that a graph G is said to be ϵ-far from satisfying $\mathcal{P}$ if removing and/or adding at most ϵm edges to/from G cannot result in a graph satisfying $\mathcal{P}$.

A distributed property testing algorithm for $\mathcal{P}$ is a randomized algorithm which performs as follows. Initially, every node is only given its ID as input. After a certain number of rounds, every node must output a value in $\{\text{accept}, \text{reject}\}$. The algorithm is correct if and only if the following two conditions are satisfied.

- if G satisfies $\mathcal{P}$, then

$$\Pr[\text{every node outputs accept}] \geq 2/3;$$

- if G is ϵ-far from satisfying $\mathcal{P}$, then

$$\Pr[\text{at least one node outputs reject}] \geq 2/3.$$

The algorithm is 1-sided error if, whenever G satisfies $\mathcal{P}$, the probability that every node outputs accept equals 1, i.e., if G satisfies $\mathcal{P}$, then

$$\Pr[\text{every node outputs accept}] = 1.$$

2.2.2 C_k-Freeness. Let $k \geq 3$. A k-node cycle, or simply k-cycle for short, consists of k nodes x_i, and k edges $\{x_i, x_{i+1 \bmod k}\}$, $i = 0, \ldots, k-1$. Such a graph is denoted by C_k.

Given a graph G, its set of nodes (resp., edges) is denoted by $V(G)$ (resp., $E(G)$). Throughout the paper, $n = |V(G)|$, and $m = |E(G)|$.

Recall that a graph H is a *subgraph* of a graph G if and only if

$$V(H) \subseteq V(G) \text{ and } E(H) \subseteq E(G).$$

Definition 2.1. A network G is C_k-free if and only if G does not contain a k-node cycle as a subgraph.

Our objective is the design of efficient distributed property testing algorithms for C_k-freeness, for all $k \geq 3$.

3 DETECTING CYCLES

In this section, we establish our main result.

THEOREM 3.1. *For every $k \geq 3$, there exists a 1-sided error distributed property testing algorithm for C_k-freeness performing in $O(\frac{1}{\epsilon})$ rounds in the* CONGEST *model.*

The rest of the section is dedicated to the proof of the theorem. Let us fix $k \geq 3$. We need to show that there exists a distributed tester for C_k-freeness performing in $O(\frac{1}{\epsilon})$ rounds, satisfying

- if G is C_k-free, then

$$\Pr[\text{every node outputs accept}] = 1.$$

- if G contains a cycle C_k then

$$\Pr[\text{at least one node outputs reject}] \geq 2/3.$$

Our tester algorithm for detecting C_k proceeds in two phases:

(1) determining a candidate edge e susceptible to belong to some cycle C_k, if any;
(2) checking the existence of a cycle C_k passing through e.

Only the first phase is randomized, the second phase is fully deterministic.

3.1 Description of Phase 1

Every edge is assigned to its extremity with smallest identity. Every node picks a random integer $r(e) \in [1, m^2]$ for each edge e that is assigned to it, called the rank of e. (By construction, $O(\log n)$ random bits per edge are sufficient). For each edge e, the extremity of e which computed its rank sends $r(e)$ to the other extremity. Then, every node u selects the edge e_u of lowest rank among all its incident edges, where ties are broken arbitrarily (e.g., based on the ID of extremities), and starts performing the second phase, which consists in checking whether there exists a cycle C_k passing through e_u.

To avoid congestion, every node performs only instructions of Phase 2 related to the edge with smallest rank it ever become aware of during the execution of the algorithm (again, ties are broken arbitrarily), in a way similar to the prioritized search in [7]. Specifically, if a node u currently involved in checking the existence of a cycle C_k passing through e receives a message related to checking the existence of a cycle C_k passing through $e' \neq e$, then u discards this message if

$$r(e') > r(e),$$

and otherwise switches to checking the existence of cycles passing through e'. This guarantees that no two messages corresponding to checking the existence of a cycle C_k passing through two different edges ever traverse an edge in the same direction at the same round. Moreover, if there is a unique edge e with minimum rank, then no nodes discard messages related to checking the existence of a cycle C_k passing through e, and thus the checking phase for e will not be interrupted.

Before analyzing Phase 1, we now describe Phase 2, which is the core of the property testing algorithm for C_k-freeness. For simplifying the presentation, let us fix some edge

$$e = \{u, v\},$$

and let us describe Phase 2 for edge e only, assuming that no other checks for other edges are running concurrently. Likewise, the reader can assume that e is the unique edge with minimum rank in G, which guarantees that the Phase 2 for e will not be slowed down by messages corresponding to Phase 2 applied to other edges.

3.2 Description of Phase 2

We describe the algorithm used to check whether there exists a cycle C_k passing through a given edge e. The algorithm proceeds in $\lfloor \frac{k}{2} \rfloor$ rounds. At each round $t = 1, \ldots, \lfloor \frac{k}{2} \rfloor$ of the algorithm, sequences of t IDs are exchanged between nodes participating to the search for C_k. Every node which receives some sequences at round t concatenates its own ID to each received sequence, and sends the resulting collection of sequences to all its neighbors.

For instance, to detect a C_5 passing through $e = \{u, v\}$, nodes u and v send their IDs to their neighbors at Round 1 (see Fig. 1). A node may thus receive 0, 1, or 2 IDs depending on whether it is adjacent to none, one, or both nodes u and v. Each node x which received at least one of these IDs has now a set $\mathcal{R}$ of sequences of the form $(\mathrm{ID}(w))$ where $w \in \{u, v\}$. Such node appends its own ID to each sequence, and sends the resulting set of sequences to all its neighbors at Round 2. A node z that, at Round 2, receives a sequence $(\mathrm{ID}(u), \mathrm{ID}(x))$, and a sequence $(\mathrm{ID}(v), \mathrm{ID}(y))$ from distinct neighbors x and y, respectively, detects the presence of the cycle (u, x, z, y, v).

This "append-and-forward" technique can be trivially extended to detect C_k, for arbitrary $k \geq 5$. However, a node of high degree may have to forward very many sequences during a round (this is typically the case of a node connected to u and/or v via many vertex-disjoint paths of same length), violating the bandwidth restriction of the CONGEST model.

The main concern of our algorithm is to limit the maximum number of different sequences of IDs to be sent by each node during the execution. Yet, it is crucial that nodes forward sufficiently many sequences of IDs to guarantee detection. For instance, in the graph depicted on Fig. 1, nodes x and y both receive $\mathrm{ID}(u)$ and $\mathrm{ID}(v)$ at the first round. If x forwards only the sequence $(\mathrm{ID}(u), \mathrm{ID}(x))$, and y forwards only the sequence $(\mathrm{ID}(u), \mathrm{ID}(y))$, the 5-cycle will not be detected by z.

In other words, discarding too many sequences may prevent the algorithm from detecting the cycle, while forwarding too many sequences overloads the communication links. We show that sending a constant number of sequences is sufficient to guarantee cycle detection whenever these sequences are carefully chosen.

The pseudocode of our algorithm is depicted as Algorithm 1.

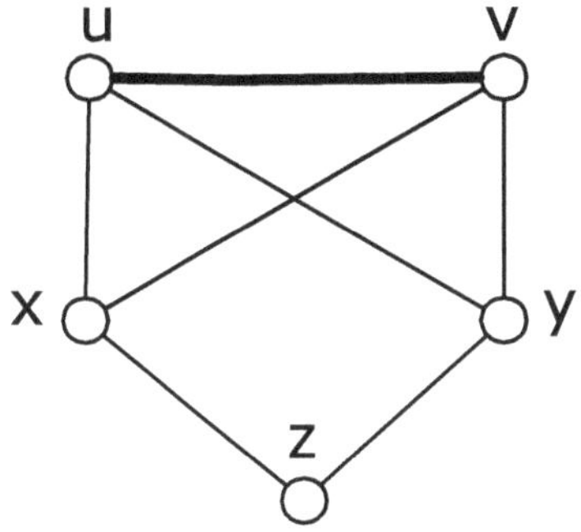

Figure 1: *Detecting C_5 passing through $\{u,v\}$*

3.3 Description of Algorithm 1

Algorithm 1 is essentially of the form "append-and-forward" (cf. Instruction 24), but selects only a few lists to be sent at each round. The "seed" lists are just formed by $\text{ID}(u)$ and $\text{ID}(v)$ (cf. Instruction 3). The algorithm proceeds in $\lfloor \frac{k}{2} \rfloor$ rounds (cf. the for-loop of Instruction 9). At each round, every node that received non-empty messages collects all IDs that were contained in these messages, distinct from its own ID, in a set $\mathcal{I}$ (cf. Instructions 11-13). Then, at round t, a set of $k-t$ "fake" IDs are added in $\mathcal{I}$ (cf. Instruction 14). Intuitively, these fake IDs represent the yet unknown IDs of nodes which could potentially form a C_k together with the nodes of some list received by the current node at this round. In order to form the collection $\mathcal{S}$ of lists that will be sent to neighbors at the next round (cf. Instruction 28), the collection $\mathcal{X}$ of all possible sets X of $k-t$ IDs are constructed, including fake IDs (cf. Instruction 15).

The core of the algorithm is the construction of $\mathcal{S}$ by the Instructions from 16 to 24. Before describing this crucial part of Algorithm 1 in detail, let us complete the description of the final part of the algorithm.

At Round $\lfloor \frac{k}{2} \rfloor$, all lists of IDs sent and received at this round, or received during the previous round, are considered, and stored in a set of lists $\mathcal{R}$ (cf. Instructions 32-36). If a node w has two lists L_1 and L_2 in $\mathcal{R}$ such that

$$|L_1 \cup L_2 \cup \{\text{ID}(w)\}| = k,$$

then Node w outputs "yes". Before showing that a cycle C_k formed by all nodes with IDs in $L_1 \cup L_2 \cup \{\text{ID}(w)\}$ exists if and only if $|L_1 \cup L_2 \cup \{\text{ID}(w)\}| = k$, we first return to the core of Algorithm 1, that is the set up of the set of lists $\mathcal{R}$.

Construction of the set of lists to be sent at each round. For comfort and ease of reading, we repeat below the instructions performed by Algorithm 1 for computing the set $\mathcal{S}$ of ordered sequences to be sent to all neighboring nodes.

$\mathcal{S} \leftarrow \emptyset$
for all $L \in \mathcal{R}$ **do**
  $\mathcal{C} \leftarrow \{X \in \mathcal{X} : X \cap L = \emptyset\}$
  if $\mathcal{C} \neq \emptyset$ **then**
    $\mathcal{S} \leftarrow \mathcal{S} \cup \{L\}$
    $\mathcal{X} \leftarrow \mathcal{X} \setminus \mathcal{C}$
  end if
end for
append *myid* at the tail of each $L \in \mathcal{S}$

Recall that $\mathcal{R}$ denotes the set of all ordered sequences L of IDs received at this round, and $\mathcal{X}$ denotes the collection of all sets of $k-t$ elements in $\mathcal{I}$, where $\mathcal{I}$ is the set of all collected IDs at this round, including the fake IDs in $\{-1, -2, \ldots, -k+t\}$.

For each sequence $L \in \mathcal{R}$ the algorithm takes the decision whether to include L in $\mathcal{S}$ or not. For this purpose, the algorithm checks whether there is a set $X \subseteq \mathcal{I}$ with $k-t$ elements which does not intersect L. If this is the case, such a list L is added to $\mathcal{S}$. The intuition is that L (of length $t-1$ at round t) may potentially be extended by adding the current node, plus $k-t$ other nodes, so that to form a cycle C_k.

For instance, Fig. 2 displays the case where

$$L = (y_1, y_2, \ldots, y_{t-1})$$

and

$$X = \{x_1, x_2, \ldots, x_{k-t}\}$$

are considered by some node z, depicted as a star $\star$ on the figure. The nodes in L are depicted in light grey, while the nodes in X are depicted in black. Note that X is a set, and the ordering of the x_i's on the figure is arbitrary. The list L is placed in $\mathcal{S}$ because there are $k-t$ nodes, i.e., those in X, which can potentially form a k-cycle with z and all the nodes in L.

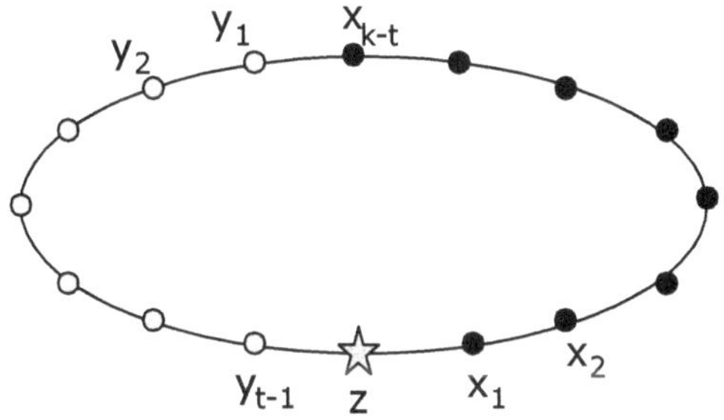

Figure 2: *Construction of $\mathcal{R}$*

Importantly, the sets $X \in \mathcal{C}$ are then removed from $\mathcal{X}$. The intuition is that if there is a k-cycle formed by the nodes in $L' \cup \{z\} \cup X$ for some list $L' \in \mathcal{R}$ where z is the actual node, then the nodes in $L \cup \{z\} \cup X$ also form a k-cycle, and therefore there is no need to keep both L and L'. Therefore, as soon as L has been identified, all witnesses sets $X \in \mathcal{C}$ can safely be removed from $\mathcal{X}$.

Algorithm 1 C_k detection for edge $e = \{u,v\}$ executed by node with ID $myid$.

1: **function** DETECTCK(u,v)
2:    **if** $myid = u$ **or** $myid = v$ **then**   ▷ initial computation at round 1
3:       $\mathcal{S} \leftarrow \{(myid)\}$ ▷ $\mathcal{S}$ is a set of sequences of IDs
4:    **else**
5:       $\mathcal{S} \leftarrow \varnothing$
6:    **end if**
7:    **send** $\mathcal{S}$ **to** all neighbors   ▷ send operation at round 1
8:    **receive** messages **from** all neighbors   ▷ receive operation at round 1
9:    **for** $t = 2$ **to** $\lfloor\frac{k}{2}\rfloor$ **do**   ▷ rounds 2 to $\lfloor\frac{k}{2}\rfloor$
10:       **if** non-empty messages have been received at round $t-1$ **then**
11:          $\mathcal{R} \leftarrow$ set of all ordered sequences of IDs received at round $t-1$ ▷ $\mathcal{R}$ contains sequences of $t-1$ IDs
12:          remove from $\mathcal{R}$ all sequences containing $myid$
13:          $\mathcal{I} \leftarrow$ set of IDs included in at least one sequence in $\mathcal{R}$
14:          $\mathcal{I} \leftarrow \mathcal{I} \cup \{-1,\ldots,-k+t\}$ ▷ add $k-t$ distinct "fake" IDs to $\mathcal{I}$
15:          $\mathcal{X} \leftarrow$ collection of all sets X of $k-t$ IDs in $\mathcal{I}$
16:          $\mathcal{S} \leftarrow \varnothing$ ▷ initializes the set of sequences to be sent
17:          **for all** $L \in \mathcal{R}$ **do**
18:             $\mathcal{C} \leftarrow \{X \in \mathcal{X} : X \cap L = \varnothing\}$ ▷ $\mathcal{C}$ is a sub-collection of sets X of $k-t$ IDs
19:             **if** $\mathcal{C} \neq \varnothing$ **then**
20:                $\mathcal{S} \leftarrow \mathcal{S} \cup \{L\}$ ▷ $\mathcal{S}$ contains ordered sequences of existing IDs
21:                $\mathcal{X} \leftarrow \mathcal{X} \setminus \mathcal{C}$
22:             **end if**
23:          **end for**
24:          append $myid$ at the tail of each $L \in \mathcal{S}$ ▷ $\mathcal{S}$ contains sequences of t IDs
25:       **else**
26:          $\mathcal{S} \leftarrow \varnothing$
27:       **end if**
28:       **send** $\mathcal{S}$ **to** all neighbors   ▷ send operation at round t
29:       **receive** messages **from** all neighbors   ▷ receive operation at round t
30:    **end for**
31:    **if** non-empty messages have been received at any round $1,\ldots,\lfloor\frac{k}{2}\rfloor$ **then**
32:       **if** k is odd **then**
33:          $\mathcal{R} \leftarrow \{$sequences received at round $\lfloor\frac{k}{2}\rfloor\}$ ▷ $\mathcal{R}$ contains sequences of equal length
34:       **else**
35:          $\mathcal{R} \leftarrow \mathcal{S} \cup \{$sequences received at round $\lfloor\frac{k}{2}\rfloor - 1\}$ ▷ $\mathcal{R}$ contains sequences of lengths differing by at most 1
36:       **end if**
37:       **if** $\exists L_1, L_2 \in \mathcal{R} : |L_1 \cup L_2 \cup \{myid\}| = k$ **then**
38:          output reject   ▷ a C_k has been detected
39:       **else** output accept
40:       **end if**
41:    **else** output accept
42:    **end if**
43: **end function**

For instance, considering again the example of Fig. 2, as long as L has been placed in $\mathcal{S}$, the set X can be removed from $\mathcal{X}$ since it could only be used to identify another sequence

$$L' = (y'_1, y'_2, \ldots, y'_{t-1})$$

potentially forming a k-cycle with X, while we are not interested in enumerating all cycles C_k but just in determining whether there is one.

Note here the role of the fake IDs that were added to $\mathcal{I}$. First, observe that the first sequence $L \in \mathcal{R}$ that is considered in the for-loop (the order in which these sequence are taken is arbitrary) is necessarily placed in $\mathcal{S}$. Indeed,

$$X = \{-1, -2, \ldots, -k+t\}$$

is in $\mathcal{X}$, and for sure does not intersect L. Second, notice that the fact that all sets $X \in \mathcal{C}$ can be safely removed from $\mathcal{X}$ is not obvious if X contains fake IDs because X then does not fully specify the cycle. Nevertheless, we shall show that those sets can still be removed, without preventing the algorithm to detect a cycle, if there is one.

To give a more precise intuition of the use of fake IDs in our algorithm, let us consider a cycle of length 9, where node IDs are from 1 to 9, consecutively around the cycle (hence, the edges are $\{1,2\},\ldots,\{8,9\}$ and $\{1,9\}$. Let us assume that one wants to detect C_9, starting from the edge {1,9}. Then, in particular, when node 3 receives the sequence $(1,2)$ from node 2, we want that node to send the sequence $(1,2,3)$ to node 4. This is the role of Lines 16-24 in Algorithm 1, where $\mathcal{R}$ contains just the sequence $(1,2)$. In Algorithm 1, if one would not add fake IDs to $\mathcal{I}$, then $\mathcal{I} = 1,2$, and $\mathcal{X}$ would become empty as one cannot construct sequences of length $k-t = 9-3 = 6$ using IDs from $\mathcal{I}$. As a consequence, $\mathcal{C}$ would also be empty as it results from an intersection with the empty set, and we would not add $(1,2)$ to $\mathcal{S}$. It would follow that node 3 does not send any sequence. Instead, if we add the fake IDs $-1,,-6$ to $\mathcal{I}$, then the sequence $(-1,\ldots,-6)$ is in $\mathcal{X}$, and since $(1,2)$ is disjoint with $\{-1,\ldots,-6\}$, the sequence $(1,2)$ is added to $\mathcal{S}$, and the sequence $(1,2,3)$ will be sent, as desired.

3.4 Analysis of Algorithm 1

We start by proving the correctness of the algorithm, before analyzing its performances.

LEMMA 3.2. *For every $t = 1,\ldots,\lfloor\frac{k}{2}\rfloor$, every sequence L contained in a non-empty set $\mathcal{S}$ sent at round t is composed of t distinct IDs, and forms a simple path in the graph with one extremity equal to the sender, and the other equal to u or v.*

PROOF. By induction on t. The lemma trivially holds for $t = 1$ (cf. Instruction 3). All messages set to be sent at round $t+1$ are constructed by appending the ID of the current node to sequences L received at round t (cf. Instruction 24), and these sequences L do not contain the ID of the current node (cf. Instruction 12). Therefore, every sequence sent at round $t+1$ are composed of $t+1$ distinct IDs. Moreover, by induction, a sequence L received at round t by a node x from a neighboring node y forms a simple path in the graph with one extremity equal to y. Therefore, as long as $\mathrm{ID}(x) \notin L$ (which is guarantied by Instruction 12), the sequence $L \cup \{\mathrm{ID}(x)\}$ forms a simple path in the graph with one extremity equal to x. The other extremity remains unchanged, and thus equal to u or v. □

LEMMA 3.3. *For any graph G, and every edge $e = \{u,v\}$ of G, Algorithm 1 running on G satisfies that all nodes output* accept *if and only if there are no C_k passing through the edge e.*

PROOF. Let us assume that some node w outputs reject, and let us show that there is indeed a k-cycle passing through e. From Instruction 37, this node w satisfies that there exist two sequences $L_1, L_2 \in \mathcal{R}$ such that

$$|L_1 \cup L_2 \cup \{\mathrm{ID}(w)\}| = k.$$

By Lemma 3.2, both sequences are simple paths of length at most $\lfloor\frac{k}{2}\rfloor$ from u or v to a neighbor of w. Let

$$L_1 = (x_1, x_2, \ldots, x_\ell),$$

and

$$L_2 = (y_1, y_2, \ldots, y_m),$$

where $\ell \le \lfloor k/2 \rfloor$ and $m \le \lfloor k/2 \rfloor$.

- If k is odd, $|L_1 \cup L_2 \cup \{\mathrm{ID}(w)\}| = k$ implies that $\ell = m = \lfloor k/2 \rfloor$, w is distinct from every x_i and every y_j, and every x_i is distinct from every y_j, $i = 1,\ldots,\ell$, $j = 1,\ldots,m$. In particular, since $x_1 \neq y_1$, we have $\{x_1, y_1\} = \{u,v\}$. It follows that
$$(x_1, x_2, \ldots, x_\ell, w, y_m, y_{m-1}, \ldots, y_1)$$
is a k-cycle passing through e.
- If k is even, then we claim that
$$L_1 \in \mathcal{S} \text{ and } L_2 \notin \mathcal{S}$$
or
$$L_1 \notin \mathcal{S} \text{ and } L_2 \in \mathcal{S}.$$
Indeed, let us consider two distinct sequences L and L' in $\mathcal{S}$. Since they are both of length $k/2$, and since they both contain $\mathrm{ID}(w)$, we have $|L \cup L' \cup \{\mathrm{ID}(w)\}| \le k-1$. Thus, at least a sequence must not be contained in $\mathcal{S}$. Moreover, if $|L \cup L' \cup \{myid\}| = k$, then at least one of the two sequences must belong to $\mathcal{S}$ because the sequences received at round $k/2-1$ are of length $k/2-1$. Hence the claim holds.
So, let us now assume, w.l.o.g., that $L_1 \in \mathcal{S}$ and $L_2 \notin \mathcal{S}$. It follows that L_1 is of length $k/2$ and contains $\mathrm{ID}(w)$, and that L_2 is of length $k/2$ without containing $\mathrm{ID}(w)$. The equality $|L_1 \cup L_2 \cup \{\mathrm{ID}(w)\}| = k$ then implies that w is distinct from every x_i and every y_j, and every x_i is distinct from every y_j, $i = 1,\ldots,\ell$, $j = 1,\ldots,m$. In particular, since $x_1 \neq y_1$, we have $\{x_1, y_1\} = \{u,v\}$. It follows that
$$(x_1, x_2, \ldots, x_\ell, w, y_m, y_{m-1}, \ldots, y_1)$$
is a k-cycle passing through e.

Therefore, for both cases, k even or odd, the existence of a node which outputs reject implies the existence of a cycle passing through e.

Conversely, let us assume that there is a k-cycle passing through e, and let us show that at least one node detects that cycle (i.e., outputs reject). Observe that a modified version of the algorithm where the construction of $\mathcal{S}$ in the for-loop of Instruction 17 is replaced by

$$\mathcal{S} \leftarrow \mathcal{R}$$

clearly detects the cycle. Indeed, at each round t, all the possible paths of length t from the edge to the actual node are transmitted. However, there can be too many such paths, and transmitting all of them would not fit with the constraints of the CONGEST model. Hence, some paths are discarded by Algorithm 1. Yet, we show that Algorithm 1 keeps sufficiently many options for detecting the cycle. Let us fix some round $t \in \{2,\ldots,\lfloor\frac{k}{2}\rfloor\}$, and a node w. Let us consider a discarded sequence

$$L = (x_1, x_2, \ldots, x_{t-1})$$

at w. Let us assume that the cycle includes that sequence of nodes, that is the cycle is of the form

$$x_1, x_2, \ldots, x_{t-1}, w, y_1, \ldots, y_{k-t}$$

where $\{x_1, y_{k-t}\} = \{u, v\}$. Since the sequence has been discarded, we have

$$\{X \in \mathcal{X} : X \cap L = \emptyset\} = \emptyset$$

where $\mathcal{X}$ is the collection of all sets X of $k-t$ IDs in $\mathcal{I}$, and $\mathcal{I}$ is the collection of all IDs included in at least one sequence in $\mathcal{R}$, complemented with the $k-t$ "fake" IDs

$$\{-1, \ldots, -k+t\}.$$

This implies that all sets $X \in \mathcal{X}$ that intersect L have been removed from $\mathcal{X}$ when considering other sequences in the for-loop. In particular the set

$$X = \{y_1, \ldots, y_{k-t}\}$$

has been removed when considering another sequence

$$L' = (z_1, z_2, \ldots, z_{t-1}).$$

Since $L' \cap \{y_1, \ldots, y_{k-t}\} = \emptyset$, we get that there is actually another cycle,

$$z_1, z_2, \ldots, z_{t-1}, w, y_1, \ldots, y_{k-t}$$

where $\{z_1, y_{k-t}\} = \{u, v\}$. Therefore, Algorithm 1 satisfies that, at every round $t \in \{2, \ldots, \lfloor \frac{k}{2} \rfloor\}$, if w belongs to a cycle

$$x_1, x_2, \ldots, x_{t-1}, w, y_1, \ldots, y_{k-t}$$

passing through $e = \{x_1, y_{k-t}\}$, and w receives the sequence $x_1, x_2, \ldots, x_{t-1}$, then Algorithm 1 guarantees that if w does not send the sequence $x_1, x_2, \ldots, x_{t-1}, w$ to y_1, then w necessarily sends another sequence $z_1, z_2, \ldots, z_{t-1}, w$ to y_1 where

$$z_1, z_2, \ldots, z_{t-1}, w, y_1, \ldots, y_{k-t}$$

is a cycle passing through $e = \{z_1, y_{k-t}\}$. Therefore, the nodes antipodal to e (that is, the nodes at distance $\lceil \frac{k}{2} \rceil - 1$ from e in the cycle) will detect a cycle at round $\lfloor \frac{k}{2} \rfloor$, and will output reject, as desired. □

In the next lemma, we show that, for a fixed k, the messages exchanged during the execution of Algorithm 1 are of constant size.

LEMMA 3.4. *For every $t = 1, \ldots, \lfloor \frac{k}{2} \rfloor$, every message sent by nodes at round t is composed of at most $(k-t+1)^{t-1}$ ordered sequences of t IDs.*

PROOF. For the ease of notation, we rephrase the statement of the lemma as: For every $t = 0, \ldots, \lfloor \frac{k}{2} \rfloor - 1$, every message sent by nodes at round $t+1$ is composed of at most $(k-t)^t$ ordered sequences of $t+1$ IDs.

Let us fix $t \in \{0, \ldots, \lfloor \frac{k}{2} \rfloor - 1\}$, and a node w, and let us focus on round $t+1$. For $i = 0, \ldots, t$, let us then define property P_i stating:

for every set of $t-i$ IDs, w sends at most $(k-t)^i$ sequences that contain that set.

Note that Property P_t establishes the lemma.

Property P_0 stating that, for every set of t IDs, w sends at most one sequence that contains that set, follows from the fact that, in the construction of $\mathcal{S}$ in the for-loop of Instruction 17, this set will be sent only once, in one of all its possible orderings.

Let us assume that P_{i-1} holds, and let us establish P_i. Consider the case where, during the execution of the for-loop of Instruction 17, we already added $(k-t)^i$ sequences to $\mathcal{S}$ containing the same $t-i$ elements $x_1, x_2, \ldots, x_{t-i}$. That is, $\mathcal{S}$ contains

$$\{x_1, x_2, \ldots, x_{t-i}, y_{1,1}, y_{1,2}, \ldots, y_{1,i}\}$$
$$\{x_1, x_2, \ldots, x_{t-i}, y_{2,1}, y_{2,2}, \ldots, y_{2,i}\}$$
$$\vdots$$
$$\{x_1, x_2, \ldots, x_{t-i}, y_{(k-t)^i,1}, y_{(k-t)^i,2}, \ldots, y_{(k-t)^i,i}\}$$

After these sequences have been added to $\mathcal{S}$, the remaining sequences in $\mathcal{X}$ must contain at least one element of each such sequences. That is, for every $X \in \mathcal{X}$,

$$(x_1 \in X) \vee (x_2 \in X) \vee \ldots \vee (x_{t-i} \in X)$$

or

$$\bigwedge_{j=1}^{(k-t)^i} \Big((y_{j,1} \in X) \vee (y_{j,2} \in X) \vee \ldots \vee (y_{j,i} \in X) \Big) \quad (1)$$

Indeed, if a sequence does not contain $x_1, x_2, \ldots, x_{t-i}$, then it should contain an element $y_{a,b}$ for each sequence. We can now apply the induction hypothesis to show that the same element $y_{a,b}$ cannot appear more than $(k-t)^{i-1}$ times. Indeed, the sequence $x_1, x_2, \ldots, x_{t-i}, y_{a,b}$ is of length $t-(i-1)$, and therefore, by induction, it cannot appear more than $(k-t)^{i-1}$ times.

Therefore, since there are $(k-t)^i = (k-t)^{i-1} \cdot (k-t)$ sequences in $\mathcal{S}$ containing the same $t-i$ elements $x_1, x_2, \ldots, x_{t-i}$, Eq. (1) implies that a sequence $X \in \mathcal{X}$ must contain $k-t$ different elements. However, sequences in X are of size $k-t-1$. Therefore, the formula in Eq. (1) cannot be satisfied. It follows that, for every $X \in \mathcal{X}$,

$$(x_1 \in X) \vee (x_2 \in X) \vee \ldots \vee (x_{t-i} \in X).$$

Let us now consider another sequence

$$L = (x_1, x_2, \ldots, x_{t-i}, z_1, \ldots, z_i)$$

taken from $\mathcal{R}$. This sequence will not be added to $\mathcal{S}$ because every sequence $X \in \mathcal{X}$ contains at least one element from $\{x_1, x_2, \ldots, x_{t-i}\}$, which implies that $L \cap X \neq \emptyset$. □

3.5 Proof of Theorem 3.1

Let us first compute the probability of detecting a cycle in a network which is ϵ-far from being C_k-free. We exploit the fact that, in such a network, there must be many edge-disjoint copies of C_k, as stated below:

LEMMA 3.5 ([20]). *Let H be any graph. Let G be an m-edge graph that is ϵ-far from being H-free. Then G contains at least $\epsilon m / |E(H)|$ edge-disjoint copies of H.*

Hence, a graph G that is ϵ-far from being C_k-free contains at least $\epsilon m/k$ edge-disjoint copies of C_k, i.e., ϵm edges belong to edge-disjoint cycles.

LEMMA 3.6. *The probability that there is a unique edge with minimum rank after the execution of Phase 1 is at least $1/e^2$.*

PROOF. The probability that there are no collisions while choosing for each edge a random number from $[1, m^2]$ is

$$\begin{aligned} \frac{m^2-1}{m^2} \times \ldots \times \frac{m^2-m}{m^2} &\geq \left(\frac{m^2-m}{m^2}\right)^m \\ &= \left(1-\frac{1}{m}\right)^m \\ &\geq \left(e^{\frac{-2}{m}}\right)^m \\ &= \frac{1}{e^2} \end{aligned}$$

where the last inequality holds whenever $m \geq 2$. □

Let G be a graph that is ϵ-far from being C_k-free. Let $\mathcal{E}$ be the event:

there is a unique edge with minimum rank after the execution of Phase 1, and this edge belongs to a k-cycle.

Combining the previous two lemmas, we get that

$$\Pr[\mathcal{E}] \geq \epsilon/e^2.$$

Now, if event $\mathcal{E}$ holds, then, by Lemma 3.3, at least one node will output reject, as desired. To boost the probability of detecting a cycle in a graph that is ϵ-far from being C_k-free, we repeat the whole process $\frac{e^2}{\epsilon}\ln 3$ times. In this way, the probability that $\mathcal{E}$ holds in at least one of these repetitions is at least 2/3 as desired.

By Lemma 3.4, each repetition of the whole process of executing Phases 1 and 2 requires a constant number of rounds. This completes the proof of Theorem 3.1. □

4 CONCLUSION

In this paper, we have proved that, for every $k \geq 3$, there exists a 1-sided error distributed property testing algorithm for C_k-freeness, performing in $O(1/\epsilon)$ rounds. We mention hereafter some possible directions for further work.

It was proved in [20] that, for every graph pattern H with at most 4 nodes, there exists a distributed property testing algorithm for H-freeness, performing in constant number of rounds, and the question of whether a distributed property testing algorithm for H-freeness exists for every arbitrarily large pattern H was left open in [20]. The techniques in this paper does not seem to extend to arbitrary patterns. To see why, consider H as a k-cycle with a chord between two nodes. The pruning technique in Algorithm 1 discarding some sequences of nodes is oblivious to the neighborhood of the nodes in these sequences. Hence, while Algorithm 1 makes sure to keep at least one sequence corresponding to a cycle, if such cycle exists, it may well discard the sequence corresponding to the cycle in H, and keep a sequence without a chord. It was also pointed out in [20] that their techniques do not seem to extend to *induced* subgraphs[2]. The same apparently holds for the techniques in this paper. The reasons are the same as for detecting a given graph pattern H. Indeed, our pruning mechanism is not adapted to detect an induced cycle. It may well discard a sequence corresponding to the induced cycle, and keep a sequence with chords.

We believe that proving or disproving the existence of distributed property testing algorithms for H-freeness, as a subgraph or as an induced subgraph, are potentially challenging but definitely rewarding issues whose study is susceptible to shed new light on the CONGEST model, and, more generally, to improve our understanding of local distributed computing in presence of bandwidth limitation.

REFERENCES

[1] Noga Alon, Eldar Fischer, Michael Krivelevich, and Mario Szegedy. 2000. Efficient Testing of Large Graphs. *Combinatorica* 20, 4 (2000), 451–476.
[2] Noga Alon, Tali Kaufman, Michael Krivelevich, and Dana Ron. 2008. Testing Triangle-Freeness in General Graphs. *SIAM J. Discrete Math.* 22, 2 (2008), 786–819.
[3] Noga Alon and Asaf Shapira. 2006. A Characterization of Easily Testable Induced Subgraphs. *Combinatorics, Probability & Computing* 15, 6 (2006), 791–805.
[4] Alkida Balliu, Gianlorenzo D'Angelo, Pierre Fraigniaud, and Dennis Olivetti. 2017. What Can Be Verified Locally?. In *34th Symposium on Theoretical Aspects of Computer Science (STACS)*.
[5] Azzedine Boukerche and Carl Tropper. 1998. A Distributed Graph Algorithm for the Detection of Local Cycles and Knots. *IEEE Trans. Parallel Distrib. Syst.* 9, 8 (1998), 748–757.
[6] Zvika Brakerski and Boaz Patt-Shamir. 2011. Distributed discovery of large near-cliques. *Distributed Computing* 24, 2 (2011), 79–89.
[7] Keren Censor-Hillel, Eldar Fischer, Gregory Schwartzman, and Yadu Vasudev. 2016. Fast Distributed Algorithms for Testing Graph Properties. In *30th Int. Symposium on Distributed Computing (DISC) (LNCS)*, Vol. 9888. Springer, 43–56.
[8] Pranay Chaudhuri. 1999. A Self-Stabilizing Algorithm for Detecting Fundamental Cycles in a Graph. *J. Comput. Syst. Sci.* 59, 1 (1999), 84–93.
[9] Pranay Chaudhuri. 2002. An optimal distributed algorithm for finding a set of fundamental cycles in a graph. *Comput. Syst. Sci. Eng.* 17, 1 (2002), 41–47.
[10] David Conlon and Jacob Fox. 2012. Graph removal lemmas. *CoRR* abs/1211.3487 (2012).
[11] Artur Czumaj, Oded Goldreich, Dana Ron, C. Seshadhri, Asaf Shapira, and Christian Sohler. 2014. Finding cycles and trees in sublinear time. *Random Struct. Algorithms* 45, 2 (2014), 139–184.
[12] Yuval Emek, Christoph Pfister, Jochen Seidel, and Roger Wattenhofer. 2014. Anonymous networks: randomization = 2-hop coloring. In *33rd ACM Symposium on Principles of Distributed Computing*. 96–105.
[13] Paul Erdös, Peter Frankl, and Vojtech Rödl. 1986. The asymptotic number of graphs not containing a fixed subgraph and a problem for hypergraphs having no exponent. *Graphs and Combinatorics* 2, 1 (1986), 113–121.
[14] Paul Erdős, András Hajnal, and J. W. Moon. 1964. A Problem in Graph Theory. *The American Mathematical Monthly* 71, 10 (1964), 1107–1110.
[15] Laurent Feuilloley and Pierre Fraigniaud. 2015. Randomized Local Network Computing. In *27th ACM Symposium on Parallelism in Algorithms and Architectures (SPAA)*. 340–349.
[16] Laurent Feuilloley and Pierre Fraigniaud. 2016. Survey of Distributed Decision. *Bulletin of the EATCS* 119 (2016), 41–65.
[17] Laurent Feuilloley, Pierre Fraigniaud, and Juho Hirvonen. 2016. A Hierarchy of Local Decision. In *43rd Int. Colloquium on Automata, Languages, and Programming (ICALP)*. 118:1–118:15.
[18] Pierre Fraigniaud, Mika Göös, Amos Korman, Merav Parter, and David Peleg. 2014. Randomized distributed decision. *Distributed Computing* 27, 6 (2014), 419–434.

[2] *A graph H is an induced subgraph of a graph G iff $V(H) \subseteq V(G)$ and $E(H) = E(G[V(H)])$, i.e., for every $(u,v) \in V(H) \times V(H)$, we have $\{u,v\} \in E(H) \iff \{u,v\} \in E(G)$. (In other words, H is isomorphic to the subgraph of G induced by the nodes in H).*

[19] Pierre Fraigniaud, Amos Korman, and David Peleg. 2013. Towards a complexity theory for local distributed computing. *J. ACM* 60, 5 (2013), 35:1–35:26.
[20] Pierre Fraigniaud, Ivan Rapaport, Ville Salo, and Ioan Todinca. 2016. Distributed Testing of Excluded Subgraphs. In *30th Int. Symposium on Distributed Computing (DISC) (LNCS)*, Vol. 9888. Springer, 342–356.
[21] Oded Goldreich (Ed.). 2010. *Property Testing — Current Research and Surveys*. Vol. LNCS 6390. Springer.
[22] Oded Goldreich and Dana Ron. 2002. Property Testing in Bounded Degree Graphs. *Algorithmica* 32, 2 (2002), 302–343.
[23] Oded Goldreich and Luca Trevisan. 2003. Three theorems regarding testing graph properties. *Random Struct. Algorithms* 23, 1 (2003), 23–57.
[24] Mika Göös and Jukka Suomela. 2016. Locally Checkable Proofs in Distributed Computing. *Theory of Computing* 12, 1 (2016), 1–33.
[25] Amos Korman, Shay Kutten, and David Peleg. 2010. Proof labeling schemes. *Distributed Computing* 22, 4 (2010), 215–233.
[26] Burkhard Monien. 1985. How to find long paths efficiently. In *Analysis and design of algorithms for combinatorial problems*. North-Holland Math. Stud., Vol. 109. North-Holland, Amsterdam, 239–254.
[27] Moni Naor and Larry J. Stockmeyer. 1995. What Can be Computed Locally? *SIAM J. Comput.* 24, 6 (1995), 1259–1277.
[28] Gabriele Oliva, Roberto Setola, Luigi Glielmo, and Christoforos N. Hadjicostis. 2016. Distributed Cycle Detection and Removal. *IEEE Transactions on Control of Network Systems* PP, 99 (2016).
[29] David Peleg. 2000. *Distributed Computing: A Locality-Sensitive Approach*. SIAM, Philadelphia.

Distributed Graph Clustering by Load Balancing

He Sun
University of Bristol
Bristol, UK
h.sun@bristol.ac.uk

Luca Zanetti
University of Bristol
Bristol, UK
luca.zanetti@bristol.ac.uk

ABSTRACT

Graph clustering is a fundamental computational problem with a number of applications in algorithm design, machine learning, data mining, and analysis of social networks. Over the past decades, researchers have proposed a number of algorithmic design methods for graph clustering. However, most of these methods are based on complicated spectral techniques or convex optimisation, and cannot be applied directly for clustering many networks that occur in practice, whose information is often collected on different sites. Designing a simple and distributed clustering algorithm is of great interest, and has wide applications for processing big datasets.

In this paper we present a simple and distributed algorithm for graph clustering: for a wide class of graphs that are characterised by a strong cluster-structure, our algorithm finishes in a poly-logarithmic number of rounds, and recovers a partition of the graph close to an optimal partition. The main component of our algorithm is an application of the *random matching model* of load balancing, which is a fundamental protocol in distributed computing and has been extensively studied in the past 20 years. Hence, our result highlights an intrinsic and interesting connection between graph clustering and load balancing.

At a technical level, we present a purely algebraic result characterising the *early behaviours* of load balancing processes for graphs exhibiting a cluster-structure. We believe that this result can be further applied to analyse other gossip processes, such as rumour spreading and averaging processes.

CCS CONCEPTS

• **Theory of computation → Graph algorithms analysis; Distributed algorithms; Random walks and Markov chains;**

KEYWORDS

graph clustering; load balancing; spectral graph theory

1 Introduction

Analysis of large-scale networks has brought significant advances to our understanding of complex systems. One of the most relevant features possessed by networks occurring in practice is a strong cluster-structure, i.e., an organisation of nodes into clusters such that nodes within the same cluster are highly connected in contrast to nodes from different clusters. Recovering this cluster-structure is the aim of graph clustering, which is an important research topic in many disciplines, including computer science, physics, biology, and sociology. For instance, graph clustering is widely used in finding communities in social networks, webpages dealing with similar topics, and proteins having the same specific function within the cell in protein-protein interaction networks [13]. Most algorithms for graph clustering, however, require advanced algorithm design techniques such as spectral methods, or convex optimisation, which may make the algorithms difficult to be implemented in the setting of big data, where graphs may be allocated in sites that are physically remote. For this reason, designing a simple and distributed algorithm is of great interest in practice, and has received considerable attention in recent years [6, 20, 31].

In this work we propose a simple and distributed graph clustering algorithm that is mainly based on the following classical load balancing process (random matching model): assume that there is an application running on a parallel network with n processors. Every processor has initially a certain amount of loads (jobs) and the processors are connected by an arbitrary graph G. A load balancing process in the random matching model consists of synchronous rounds: in each round a random matching of G is generated in a distributed way, and every two matched nodes average their loads evenly. This process continues until every node has almost the same amount of load. Despite its low communication cost (at most $\lfloor n/2 \rfloor$ edges are involved in each round for load distribution) and highly distributed properties (every node only contacts its neighbors in the entire process), load balancing has been proven to be very efficient [27], and has been widely used in various domains, including scheduling [30], hashing [23], routing [10], and numerical computation such as solving partial differential equations [32].

1.1 Structure of Clusters

Let $G = (V, E)$ be an undirected graph with n nodes. For any set S, let the conductance of S be

$$\phi_G(S) \triangleq \frac{|E(S, V \setminus S)|}{\mathrm{vol}(S)},$$

where $E(S, V \setminus S)$ is the set of edges between S and $V \setminus S$, and $\mathrm{vol}(S)$ is the number of edges with at least one endpoint in S. Intuitively, nodes in S form a cluster if $\phi_G(S)$ is small, i.e., there are few edges connecting the nodes of S to the nodes in $V \setminus S$. We call subsets of nodes (i.e. *clusters*) $A_1, \ldots, A_k$ a *k-way partition* of G if $A_i \cap A_j = \emptyset$ for different i and j, and $\bigcup_{i=1}^{k} A_i = V$. Moreover, we define the *k-way expansion constant* by

$$\rho(k) \triangleq \min_{\text{partition } A_1,\ldots,A_k} \max_{1 \leqslant i \leqslant k} \phi_G(A_i).$$

SPAA '17, July 24-26, 2017, Washington DC, USA

ACM ISBN 978-1-4503-4593-4/17/07...$15.00
https://doi.org/10.1145/3087556.3087569

Computing the exact value of $\rho(k)$ is coNP-hard, and a sequence of results show that $\rho(k)$ can be approximated by algebraic quantities relating to the matrices of G. For instance, Lee et al. [22] proved the following high-order Cheeger inequality:

$$\frac{1-\lambda_k}{2} \leqslant \rho(k) \leqslant O\left(k^2\right)\sqrt{1-\lambda_k}, \tag{1}$$

where $1 = \lambda_1 \geqslant \cdots \geqslant \lambda_n \geqslant -1$ are the eigenvalues of the random walk matrix of G. Based on (1), we know that a large gap between $(1-\lambda_{k+1})$ and $\rho(k)$ guarantees (i) existence of a k-way partition $S_1, \ldots S_k$ with bounded $\phi_G(S_i) \leqslant \rho(k)$, and (ii) any $(k+1)$-way partition $A_1, \ldots, A_{k+1}$ of G contains a subset A_i with significantly higher conductance $\rho(k+1) \geqslant (1-\lambda_{k+1})/2$ compared with $\rho(k)$. Peng et al. [25] formalise these observations by defining the parameter

$$\Upsilon \triangleq \frac{1-\lambda_{k+1}}{\rho(k)},$$

and shows that a suitable lower bound on the value of Υ implies that G has k well-defined clusters.

Throughout the rest of the paper, we assume that $S_1, \ldots, S_k$ is a k-way partition that achieves $\rho(k)$, and there is a known threshold $\beta > 0$ such that $|S_i| \geqslant \beta n$ for any $1 \leqslant i \leqslant k$, i.e., the clusters have balanced size. We say G is *well-clustered* if

$$\Upsilon = \omega\left(k^5 \frac{1}{\beta^3} \log^4 \frac{1}{\beta} \log n\right). \tag{2}$$

Notice that (2) can be written as $\Upsilon = \omega(\log n)$ when the number of clusters k is a constant, and the sizes of all the clusters are almost balanced. For simplicity, we assume that G is a d-regular graph, and we will discuss in Section 4.5 how to generalise our result to almost-regular graphs, as long as the ratio between the maximum and minimum degree is upper bounded by a constant.

1.2 Our Results

We investigate the power of random matching model of load balancing, a widely studied process in distributed computing [4, 11, 15, 17, 26, 27]. We propose a high-dimensional version of this random matching model, and show that the proposed algorithm can be used for graph clustering. Our algorithm is decentralised, and very easy to implement. Moreover, our approach corresponds to a natural centralised algorithm for graph clustering, which is also new to the best of our knowledge. Our main result is summarised as follows:

THEOREM 1.1. *There exists a distributed algorithm such that, for any well-clustered graph $G = (V, E)$ with n nodes and k clusters $S_1, \ldots, S_k$ that satisfies (2), finishes in $T \triangleq \Theta\left(\frac{\log n}{1-\lambda_{k+1}}\right)$ rounds and, with constant probability, at the end of the algorithm the following statements hold:*

(1) Each node v receives a label ℓ_v such that the total number of misclassified nodes is $o(n)$, i.e., there exists a permutation of the labels σ such that

$$\left|\bigcup_{i=1}^{k} \{v | v \in S_i \text{ and } \ell_v \neq \sigma(i)\}\right| = o(n);$$

(2) The total information exchanged among these n nodes, i.e., the message complexity, is $O(T \cdot n \cdot k \log k)$ words.

An important scenario for graph clustering is the case where G consists of $k = \Theta(1)$ clusters $S_1, \ldots, S_k$, where $|S_i| = \Theta(n/k)$, every $G[S_i]$ is a spectral expander, and has conductance $\phi_G(S_i) = O(1/\text{poly}\log n)$ for $i = 1, \ldots, k$. It is easy to verify that for such graph G our gap assumption (2) on Υ holds, and our algorithm finishes in $O(\log n)$ rounds with message complexity $O(n \log n)$. Moreover, the non-distributed version of our algorithm runs in $O(n \log n)$ time once we have an oracle which outputs a random neighbour of any node. That is, when the input graph is d-regular with $d = \omega(\log n)$, our algorithm runs in *sub-linear time*. This example shows a clear distinction between our algorithm and most other graph clustering algorithms, which usually require at least linear-time. Hence, the techniques presented in our paper might be of interest for designing algorithms for other models of computation as well, e.g., local algorithms, and algorithms for property testing.

1.3 Related Work

There is a large amount of literature on graph clustering, and our work is most closely related to efficient algorithms for graph clustering under different formulations of clusters. Oveis Gharan and Trevisan [24] formulate the notion of clusters with respect to the *inner* and *outer* conductance: a cluster S should have low outer conductance, and the conductance of the induced subgraph by S should be high. Under a assumption between λ_{k+1} and λ_k, they present a polynomial-time algorithm which finds a k-way partition $\{A_i\}_{i=1}^k$ that satisfies the inner- and outer-conductance condition. To ensure that every A_i has high inner conductance, they assume that $\lambda_{k+1} \geqslant \text{poly}(k)\lambda_k^{1/4}$, which has a stronger polynomial dependency on λ_k.

Another line of research closely related to our result is the design of local algorithms for finding a subset of nodes of low conductance, e.g., [16, 29]. In particular, Allen-Zhu et al. [1] studies a cluster structure with a gap assumption similar to ours, and presents a local algorithm with better approximation guarantee than previously known algorithms under that gap assumption. However, there is substantial difference between our algorithm and most local algorithms [1, 16, 29] for the following reasons: (1) We need to run a local algorithm k times in order to find k clusters. However, as the output of each execution of a local algorithm only returns an *approximate* cluster, the approximation ratio of the final output cluster might not be guaranteed when the value of k is large. (2) For many instances, our algorithm requires only a poly-logarithmic number of rounds, while local algorithms run in time proportional to the volume of the output set. It is unclear how these algorithms could finish in a poly-logarithmic number of rounds, even if we were able to implement them in the distributed setting.

Recently, Becchetti et al. [3] studies a distributed process to partition an almost-regular graph into clusters, and their analysis focuses mostly on graphs generated randomly from stochastic block models. In contrast to ours, their algorithm requires each node to exchange information with all of its neighbours in each round, and has significantly higher communication cost for a dense graph.

We also notice that the distributed algorithm presented in Kempe et al. [21] for computing the top k eigenvectors of the adjacency matrix of a graph can be applied for graph clustering. Their algorithm is, however, much more involved than ours. Moreover, for an input graph G of n nodes, the number of rounds required in their algorithm is proportional to the mixing time of a random walk in G. For a graph consisting of multiple expanders connected by a few edges, their algorithm requires a polynomial number of rounds, while ours only requires a poly-logarithmic number of rounds.

Finally, we point out that our work is closely related to multiple random walks [2, 9, 12], other variants of load balancing processes [14], and runtime analysis of gossip algorithms [7, 8, 18, 19].

1.4 Organisation

The remaining part of the paper is organised as follows: Section 2 lists the notations used in the paper, and discusses necessary knowledge of load balancing. Section 3 presents our algorithm, and Section 4 gives a detailed analysis of our algorithm.

2 Preliminaries

2.1 Notations

Let $G = (V, E)$ be an undirected graph with n nodes and m edges. For any set $S, T \subseteq V$, we define $E(S,T)$ to be the set of edges between S and T, i.e., $E(S,T) \triangleq \{\{u,v\} | u \in S \text{ and } v \in T\}$. For two sets X and Y, the symmetric difference of X and Y is defined as $X \Delta Y \triangleq (X \setminus Y) \cup (Y \setminus X)$.

For any d-regular graph G, the random walk matrix of G is defined by $\mathbf{P} = (1/d) \cdot \mathbf{A}$, where $\mathbf{A}$ is the adjacency matrix of G defined by $\mathbf{A}_{u,v} = 1$ if $\{u,v\} \in E(G)$, and $\mathbf{A}_{u,v} = 0$ otherwise. For this matrix, we will denote its n eigenvalues with $\lambda_1 \geqslant \cdots \geqslant \lambda_n$, with their corresponding orthonormal eigenvectors $f_1, \ldots, f_n$.

For any set S of nodes, let $\chi_S \in \mathbb{R}^n$ be the normalised indicator vector of S, where $\chi_S(v) = 1/|S|$ if $v \in S$, and $\chi_S(v) = 0$ otherwise. In particular, we simply write χ_v instead of $\chi_{\{v\}}$ when the set $S = \{v\}$. The Euclidean norm of any vector $x \in \mathbb{R}^n$ is defined by $\|x\| \triangleq \sqrt{\sum_{i=1}^n x_i^2}$, and the spectral norm of any matrix $\mathbf{M} \in \mathbb{R}^{n \times n}$ is defined as

$$\|\mathbf{M}\| \triangleq \max_{x \in \mathbb{R}^n \setminus \{0\}} \frac{\|\mathbf{M}x\|}{\|x\|}.$$

Given two symmetric $n \times n$ matrices A, B, we write $A \preceq B$ if $x^\intercal A x \leqslant x^\intercal B x$ holds for any $x \in \mathbb{R}^n$.

2.2 The Matching Model for Load Balancing

One of the key components used in our algorithm is the random matching model for load balancing [5, 26, 27], in which one generates a random matching in each round and every two matched nodes balance their loads evenly. There are several simple and distributed randomised protocols to generate such matching, and in the present paper we use the following protocol [5]: (1) every node is either *active* or *non-active* with probability 1/2; (2) every *active* node chooses one of its neighbours v uniformly at random; (3) every non-active node v chosen by exactly one of its neighbours is included in the matching together with its neighbour u.

We use a matching matrix $\mathbf{M}^{(t)} \in \mathbb{R}^{n \times n}$ to express the matching used in round t: for every matched nodes u and v, we have $\mathbf{M}^{(t)}_{u,u} \triangleq 1/2$, $\mathbf{M}^{(t)}_{v,v} \triangleq 1/2$, and $\mathbf{M}^{(t)}_{u,v} \triangleq 1/2$, $\mathbf{M}^{(t)}_{v,u} \triangleq 1/2$; if u is not matched, then $\mathbf{M}^{(t)}_{u,u} \triangleq 1$ and $\mathbf{M}^{(t)}_{u,v} \triangleq 0$ if $u \neq v$. With slight abuse of notation, we also use $\mathbf{M}^{(t)}$ to express the set of edges included in the matching in round t.

The following lemma describes the properties of matrix $\mathbf{M}^{(t)}$, and is originally proven in [5].

Lemma 2.1 ([5]). *Let $\bar{d} = \left(1 - \frac{1}{2d}\right)^{d-1}$. Then, the following statements hold for any $t \geqslant 1$:*

(1) $\mathbb{E}\left[\mathbf{M}^{(t)}\right] = \left(1 - \frac{\bar{d}}{4}\right)\mathbf{I} + \frac{\bar{d}}{4} \cdot \mathbf{P}$;

(2) $\mathbf{M}^{(t)}$ is a projection matrix, i.e., $\left(\mathbf{M}^{(t)}\right)^2 = \mathbf{M}^{(t)}$;

Proof. We start with the first statement. By definition, it holds for any edge $\{u,v\}, u \neq v$, that

$$\begin{aligned}
&\mathbb{P}[\{u,v\} \text{ is included in a matching in round } t] \\
&= 2 \cdot \mathbb{P}[u \text{ is active}] \cdot \mathbb{P}[v \text{ is non-active}] \\
&\quad \cdot \mathbb{P}[\{u,v\} \text{ is chosen as a matching}] \\
&= 2 \cdot \frac{1}{4} \cdot \frac{1}{d}\left(1 - \frac{1}{2d}\right)^{d-1} \\
&= \frac{1}{2} \cdot \frac{\bar{d}}{d}.
\end{aligned}$$

Hence, we have for any edge $\{u,v\}, u \neq v$, that

$$\begin{aligned}
\mathbb{E}\left[\mathbf{M}^{(t)}_{u,v}\right] &= \frac{1}{2} \cdot \mathbb{P}[\{u,v\} \text{ is included in a matching in round } t] \\
&= \frac{1}{2} \cdot \frac{1}{2} \cdot \frac{\bar{d}}{d} = \frac{\bar{d}}{4} \cdot \mathbf{P}_{u,v}.
\end{aligned}$$

Similarly, we have for any vertex u that

$$\begin{aligned}
\mathbb{E}\left[\mathbf{M}^{(t)}_{u,u}\right] &= \frac{1}{2} \cdot \mathbb{P}[u \text{ is included in a matching in round } t] \\
&\quad + \mathbb{P}[u \text{ is not included in a matching}] \\
&= \frac{1}{2} \cdot \frac{\bar{d}}{2} + \left(1 - \frac{\bar{d}}{2}\right) = 1 - \frac{\bar{d}}{4}.
\end{aligned}$$

Combining these two equations gives us the first statement.

The second statement follows from the fact that, for any $x \in \mathbb{R}^n$, $\mathbf{M}^{(t)}x$ is the projection of x on the subspace

$$\left\{y \in \mathbb{R}^n \mid y(u) = y(v) \text{ for any } \{u,v\} \in \mathbf{M}^{(t)}\right\}.$$

∎

3 Algorithm

Now we present the distributed algorithm for graph clustering. For completeness, in Section 3.1 we will first present the detailed implementation of our algorithm in the distributed setting. In Section 3.2 we will discuss our algorithm in a more abstract way, and show its connection to load balancing processes.

3.1 Formal Description

At the initialisation step, every node v picks a random number from 1 to n^3, which is used as the identification of node v. It is easy to show that, with high probability, all the nodes pick different numbers. We assume that this holds in the remaining part of the paper, and use $\mathsf{ID}(v)$ to represent the ID of node v. Our algorithm consists of three procedures:

The Seeding Procedure: Every node v repeats the following experiment for

$$\bar{s} \triangleq \frac{3}{\beta}\ln\frac{1}{\beta}$$

trials, where in each trial node v becomes *active* with probability $1/n$. For every node v that has been active at least once, node v sets its initial state as $\mathsf{State}_v(0) = \{(\mathsf{ID}(v), 0)\}$. Every non-active node v sets $\mathsf{State}_v(0) = \emptyset$. For simplicity, we call $\mathsf{ID}(v)$ and x the *prefix* and *suffix* of vector $(\mathsf{ID}(v), x)$.

The Averaging Procedure: The averaging procedure proceeds for T rounds, where in each round t each node v computes its state $\mathsf{State}_v(t)$ through the following operations: (1) nodes apply the distributed algorithm described in Section 2.2 to generate a matching; (2) each node v computes the vector $\mathsf{State}_v(t)$ in round t as follows: If node v is not involved in any matching, then node v sets its state in round t as $\mathsf{State}_v(t) = \mathsf{State}_v(t-1)$. Otherwise node v is matched to node u in round t, and their states are computed based on the following rule, where both $\mathsf{State}_u(t)$ and $\mathsf{State}_v(t)$ are set to be empty initially:

- If there is $(\mathsf{ID}(w), x) \in \mathsf{State}_u(t-1)$ and $(\mathsf{ID}(w), y) \in \mathsf{State}_v(t-1)$ with the same prefix, then both of u and v adds the vector $(\mathsf{ID}(w), (x+y)/2)$ to $\mathsf{State}_u(t)$ and $\mathsf{State}_v(t)$.
- For any vector $(\mathsf{ID}(w), x) \in \mathsf{State}_u(t-1)$ that does not share a common prefix with any vector in $\mathsf{State}_v(t-1)$, both of u and v adds the vector $(\mathsf{ID}(w), x/2)$ to $\mathsf{State}_u(t)$ and $\mathsf{State}_v(t)$ respectively.
- For any vector $(\mathsf{ID}(w), y) \in \mathsf{State}_v(t-1)$ that does not share a common prefix with any vector in $\mathsf{State}_u(t-1)$, both of u and v adds the vector $(\mathsf{ID}(w), y/2)$ to $\mathsf{State}_u(t)$ and $\mathsf{State}_v(t)$ respectively.

The Query Procedure: The query procedure assigns every node v to a label ℓ_v, and any two nodes u, v belong to the same cluster if and only if $\ell_u = \ell_v$. Formally, based on $\mathsf{State}_v(T)$ node v uses

$$\ell_v = \min\left\{\mathsf{ID}(w) \mid (\mathsf{ID}(w), x) \in \mathsf{State}_v(T) \bigwedge x \geqslant \frac{1}{\sqrt{2\beta}n}\right\}$$

as the label of the cluster it belongs to, and ℓ_v is set to be an arbitrary ID if there is no vector $(\mathsf{ID}(w), x) \in \mathsf{State}_v(T)$ satisfying $x \geqslant 1/\left(\sqrt{2\beta}n\right)$.

3.2 Connection to Multi-Dimensional Load Balancing

From the formal description above, it is easy to see that the prefix of any vector is only used to identify from which node the corresponding unit load is generated, and loads from the vectors with different prefix will not be balanced during the execution of the algorithm. Therefore, we can view our algorithm as a multi-dimensional load balancing process, which is described as follows.

The seeding procedure consists of $\bar{s} \triangleq (3/\beta)\ln(1/\beta)$ trials, where in each trial every node becomes *active* with probability $1/n$. For simplicity, we use s to denote the number of active nodes at the end of these $\bar{s}$ trials, and use $v_1, \cdots, v_s$ to denote these active nodes. Moreover, we introduce s vectors $x^{(0,1)}, \ldots, x^{(0,s)} \in \mathbb{R}^n$, where $x^{(0,i)} = \chi_{v_i}$ for any $1 \leqslant i \leqslant s$.

After that, the averaging procedure proceeds for T rounds, where in each round t the nodes apply the distributed algorithm described in Section 2.2 to generate a matching $\mathbf{M}^{(t)}$, and update the vectors $x^{(t,i)}$ as follows: if nodes u and v are matched in round t, then they simply average their load evenly, i.e.,

$$x^{(t,i)}(u) = x^{(t,i)}(v) = \frac{x^{(t-1,i)}(u) + x^{(t-1,i)}(v)}{2}, \qquad i = 1, \ldots, s;$$

otherwise, for every unmatched node u, node u simply sets

$$x^{(t,i)}(u) = x^{(t-1,i)}(u), \qquad i = 1, \ldots, s.$$

Notice that the evolution of these s load vectors can be described by $x^{(t,i)} = \mathbf{M}^{(t)} x^{(t-1,i)}$ for any $i = 1, \ldots, s$.

Finally, at the query procedure every node v checks its coordinates $x^{(T,1)}(v), \ldots, x^{(T,s)}(v)$, and uses

$$\ell_v = \min\left\{i \mid x^{(T,i)}(v) \geqslant \frac{1}{\sqrt{2\beta}n}\right\}$$

as the label of the cluster it belongs to. If no such index i exists, the algorithm assigns node v an arbitrary label $\ell_v \in \{1, \ldots, s\}$.

As a side remark, notice that, compared with the standard load balancing process in which the configuration for any round is expressed by an n-dimensional vector, in our algorithm there are s vectors of dimension n in each round. However, in each round the *same* matching matrix is applied to update these s vectors. Notice that, since $\mathbb{E}[s] = \bar{s}$, the expected communication cost is low, i.e., $O(T \cdot \bar{s} \cdot n)$. Secondly, as an interesting feature, our algorithm does not need to know the exact number of clusters k, and a lower bound of β suffices for our algorithm. Thirdly, the number of rounds T required by our algorithm relates to an upper bound of the *local mixing time* of a cluster, i.e., the time required for a random walk to become mixed inside a cluster. In particular, a value of $T = \Theta\left(\frac{\log n}{1-\lambda_{k+1}}\right)$ suffices and this value is typically a poly-logarithmic function of n for most graphs exhibiting a strong cluster-structure.

4 Analysis

In this section we analyse the algorithm, and prove Theorem 1.1. Remember that the configuration of our algorithm is expressed by s vectors $x^{(t,1)}, \ldots, x^{(t,s)}$, and these vectors are updated with respect to the *same* matching matrix in each round. To elaborate the intuitions behind our analysis, we first look at the standard load balancing process (the 1-dimensional case), and use the symbols $y^{(t)} \in \mathbb{R}^n$ to express the load distribution in round t for the 1-dimensional load balancing process, where $y^{(0)} \triangleq \chi_u$ for some node u, and the load distribution in round $t+1$ is defined by

$$y^{(t+1)} \triangleq \mathbf{M}^{(t)} y^{(t)}. \tag{3}$$

It is well-known that the sequence $\left\{y^{(t)}\right\}_{t=1}^{\infty}$ converges to the stationary distribution of a random walk in G, i.e., the first eigenvector f_1 of $\mathbf{P}$ [5, 28], and $y^{(t)}$ is close to f_1 when t is the mixing time of a random walk in G [27]. Studying the early behaviour of load balancing processes, however, is more complicated, and we will show that the early behaviour of this process depends on the cluster-structure of G.

Our starting point is to study the load distribution $y^{(T)}$. Informally, our choice of T corresponds to the time when a random walk gets well mixed and the resulting distribution becomes stable in S_i, as long as the random walk always stays in S_i. This happens if a random walk starts from a *good node* in S_i so that it won't leave S_i quickly. We will prove that there are enough good nodes so that, if the load balancing process above starts with χ_u for a good node u, then $y^{(T)}$ is close to a linear combination of $\chi_{S_1}, \cdots, \chi_{S_k}$. This implies that $y^{(T)}(u)$ and $y^{(T)}(v)$ are approximately the same if u and v belong to the same cluster.

Generalising this argument, we study the multi-dimensional load balancing process and prove the following fact: if the load balancing process starts with s vectors $x^{(0,1)}, \dots, x^{(0,s)}$, then two nodes u, v belong to the same cluster if the values node u maintains, i.e., $\left(x^{(T,1)}(u), \dots, x^{(T,s)}(u)\right)$, are similar with the values node v maintains.

4.1 Proof Sketch

We first focus on the load balancing process for the 1-dimensional case, and study the changes in vectors $\left\{y^{(t)}\right\}_{t=1}^{\infty}$. We will prove that $y^{(T)}$ is close to the projection of the initial vector $y^{(0)}$ on the subspace spanned by $f_1, \dots, f_k$. Formally, we denote by $\mathbf{Q}$ the projection matrix onto the subspace spanned by $f_1, \dots, f_k$ of $\mathbf{P}$, and show the following result:

LEMMA 4.1. *It holds for any $t \geqslant T$ and any constant $c > 0$ that*

$$\mathbb{E}\left[\left\|\mathbf{Q}y^{(0)} - y^{(t)}\right\|\right] \leqslant 2\sqrt{t \cdot (1-\lambda_k)}\left\|\mathbf{Q}y^{(0)}\right\| + o\left(n^{-c}\right),$$

where the expectation is over all possible random matchings chosen during the first t rounds.

To explain the statement above, notice that every sampled random matching matrix $\mathbf{M}^{(j)}$ in any round j satisfies

$$\mathbb{E}\left[\mathbf{M}^{(j)}\right] = \left(1 - \frac{\bar{d}}{4}\right)\mathbf{I} + \frac{\bar{d}}{4} \cdot \mathbf{P}$$

by Lemma 2.1, i.e., the expected behaviour of a single round load balancing is the same as a 1-step lazy random walk. Therefore, we can imagine that $y^{(T)}$ will be close to $\mathbf{Q}y^{(0)}$ in T rounds, as there is a gap between λ_k and λ_{k+1}, and the contributions of $f_1, \dots, f_k$ towards $y^{(T)}$ will become dominant. Each sampled matrix $\mathbf{M}^{(j)}$ in each round j, however, can differ from $\mathbb{E}\left[\mathbf{M}^{(j)}\right]$ significantly, affecting the distribution of the load vectors in all subsequent rounds. Lemma 4.1 states that, although the above event could occur, in expectation $\left\|\mathbf{Q}y^{(0)} - y^{(t)}\right\|$ is small.

REMARK 1. *Notice that the bound in Lemma 4.1 is* increasing *in t. This is due to the fact that, although the distribution of a random walk becomes stable inside a cluster in T rounds, after $t \gg T$ steps the distribution of such random walk will converge to the uniform distribution of the whole graph, and the error term will increase with respect to t.*

Next, we will show that when the underlying graph G is well-clustered, there is an orthonormal set $\{\widehat{\chi}_i\}_{i=1}^k$, each $\widehat{\chi}_i$ being in the span of $\{\chi_{S_1}, \dots, \chi_{S_k}\}$, such that $\widehat{\chi}_i$ is close to f_i. Combining this with Lemma 4.1, we will prove that $\mathbf{Q}y^{(0)}$ is almost constant on each cluster.

LEMMA 4.2. *For any $1 \leqslant i \leqslant k$ there exists $\widehat{\chi}_i$ in the span of $\{\chi_{S_1}, \dots, \chi_{S_k}\}$, such that*

$$\|\widehat{\chi}_i - f_i\| \leqslant \mathcal{E} \triangleq \Theta\left(k\sqrt{\frac{k}{\Upsilon}}\right).$$

Moreover, $\{\widehat{\chi}_i\}_{i=1}^k$ form an orthonormal set.

Lemma 4.2 bounds the ℓ_2-distance between $\widehat{\chi}_i$ and f_i for $i = 1, \dots, k$. We will next show that there are enough "good" nodes that have "small" contribution to $\sum_{i=1}^k \|\widehat{\chi}_i - f_i\|^2$. If we start the load balancing process at one of these good nodes, then the load distribution $y^{(T)}$ will be close to a vector that is constant on the coordinates corresponding to nodes in some cluster S_j, and 0 otherwise. Formally, for every node v, let

$$\alpha_v \triangleq \sqrt{\sum_{i=1}^k (f_i(v) - \widehat{\chi}_i(v))^2} \tag{4}$$

be the contribution of node v to the total error $\sum_{i=1}^k \|\widehat{\chi}_i - f_i\|^2$ from Lemma 4.2. We call a node v *good* if

$$\alpha_v \leqslant k\mathcal{E}\sqrt{\frac{C \log n \log(1/\beta)}{\beta n}}$$

for some constant C and call v a *bad* node otherwise. The following lemma shows that, when staring the 1-dimensional load balancing process from a good node v in a cluster S_j, the expected distance between $y^{(T)}$ and χ_{S_j} can be bounded.

LEMMA 4.3. *Let S_j be any cluster, and $v \in S_j$ be a good node. Starting the load balancing process for T rounds with the initial load vector $y^{(0)} = \chi_v$, we have that*

$$\mathbb{E}\left[\left\|y^{(T)} - \chi_{S_j}\right\|\right] = O\left(k \cdot \mathcal{E} \cdot \sqrt{\frac{\log n \cdot \log(1/\beta)}{\beta \cdot n}}\right).$$

Based on these lemmas, we are ready to prove Theorem 1.1.

PROOF OF THEOREM 1.1. The seeding procedure consists of $\bar{s}$ trials, where in each trial a node is active with probability $1/n$. Hence, the total number of active nodes s satisfies $\mathbb{E}[s] = \bar{s}$ and, by Markov inequality, $s = O(\bar{s})$ with probability at least $1 - c$ for an arbitrary small constant $c > 0$. We assume this holds in the remaining part of the proof.

For any fixed cluster S_j, the probability that no node in S_j is active in any one of the $\bar{s}$ trials is at most

$$\prod_{v \in S_j}\left(1 - \frac{1}{n}\right)^{\bar{s}} \leqslant \prod_{v \in S_j} e^{-\bar{s}/n} = e^{-\bar{s}\sum_{v \in S_j} 1/n} \leqslant e^{-\bar{s}\beta} \leqslant e^{-3\ln\beta^{-1}} \leqslant e^{-3}/k$$

where we use the fact $1 - x \leqslant e^{-x}$ for $x \leqslant 1$ in the first inequality, and the assumption that $|S_j| \geqslant \beta n, \beta \leqslant 1/k$. Applying a union bound, with probability at least $1 - e^{-3}$ there is at least one active node in each cluster.

Let $\mathcal{I} = \{v_1, \dots, v_s\}$ be the set of active nodes, and denote by $\mathcal{S}(v)$ the cluster to which node v belongs to. By the definition of

α_v and the fact $\sum_v \alpha_v^2 = k\mathcal{E}^2$, the number of bad nodes is at most

$$k\mathcal{E}^2 \cdot \left(k\mathcal{E}\sqrt{\frac{C\log n \log(1/\beta)}{\beta n}}\right)^{-2} = \frac{\beta n}{C \cdot k \log n \log(1/\beta)}$$

by the averaging argument. Hence, the probability that in any given trial a bad node is active is at most

$$\frac{1}{n} \cdot \frac{\beta n}{C \cdot k \log n \log(1/\beta)} = \frac{\beta}{C \cdot k \log n \log(1/\beta)},$$

and with constant probability all the active nodes are good. From now on we assume that this event occurs.

Now we apply Lemma 4.3 on each coordinate of the multi-dimensional load vector, and obtain

$$\mathbb{E}\left[\left\|x^{(T,i)} - \chi_{S(v_i)}\right\|\right] = O\left(k \cdot \mathcal{E} \cdot \sqrt{\frac{\log n \cdot \log(1/\beta)}{\beta \cdot n}}\right)$$

for $i = 1, 2, \ldots, s$. By Markov inequality and the union bound, with constant probability it holds for all $i = 1, \ldots, s$ that

$$\left\|x^{(T,i)} - \chi_{S(v_i)}\right\|^2 = O\left(\bar{s} \cdot k \cdot \mathcal{E} \cdot \sqrt{\frac{\log n \cdot \log(1/\beta)}{\beta \cdot n}}\right)^2. \quad (5)$$

To analyse the performance of the query procedure, notice that node v can be misclassified only if there is $i \in \{1, \ldots, s\}$ such that

$$\left|x^{(T,i)}(v) - \chi_{S(v_i)}(v)\right|^2 \geqslant \frac{1}{2\beta n^2}.$$

By a simple averaging argument and assuming (5) holds, the number of misclassified nodes is at most

$$\begin{aligned}
&\sum_{i=1}^{s}\sum_{v\in V} \mathbb{1}\left\{\left|x^{(T,i)} - \chi_{S(v_i)}(v)\right|^2 \geqslant \frac{1}{2\beta n^2}\right\} \\
&\leqslant \sum_{i=1}^{s} O\left(\bar{s} \cdot k \cdot \mathcal{E} \cdot \sqrt{\frac{\log n \cdot \log(1/\beta)}{\beta \cdot n}}\right)^2 \cdot 2\beta n^2 \\
&= O\left(\bar{s}^3 \cdot k^2 \cdot \mathcal{E}^2 \log\frac{1}{\beta} \log n\right) n \\
&= O\left(k^2 \cdot \mathcal{E}^2 \cdot \frac{1}{\beta^3} \log^4\frac{1}{\beta} \cdot \log n\right) n.
\end{aligned}$$

Combining this with the definition of $\mathcal{E}$ gives us that

$$\begin{aligned}
&\sum_{i=1}^{s}\sum_{v\in V} \mathbb{1}\left\{\left|x^{(T,i)} - \chi_{S(v_i)}(v)\right|^2 \geqslant \frac{1}{2\beta n^2}\right\} \\
&= O\left(k^2 \cdot \mathcal{E}^2 \cdot \frac{n}{\beta^3} \log^4\frac{1}{\beta} \cdot \log n\right) \\
&= O\left(\frac{k^5}{\Upsilon} \cdot \frac{n}{\beta^3} \log^4\frac{1}{\beta} \cdot \log n\right) \\
&= o(n),
\end{aligned}$$

where the last equality holds by the assumption on Υ.

The total information exchanged follows from the fact that the algorithm finishes in T rounds, and in each round only matched nodes exchange the information of $O(k \log k)$ words. ■

4.2 Proof of Lemma 4.1

Proof of Lemma 4.1. Without loss of generality, we denote by $\mathbf{Q}^{\perp} \triangleq \mathbf{I} - \mathbf{Q}$ the projection on the subspace spanned by the eigenvectors $f_{k+1}, \ldots, f_n$. Since $\mathbf{Q}y^{(t)}$ and $\mathbf{Q}^{\perp}y^{(t)}$ are orthogonal to each other, it holds that

$$\begin{aligned}
&\mathbb{E}\left[\left\|\mathbf{Q}y^{(0)} - y^{(t)}\right\|^2\right] \\
&= \mathbb{E}\left[\left\|\mathbf{Q}y^{(0)} - \left(\mathbf{Q} + \mathbf{Q}^{\perp}\right)y^{(t)}\right\|^2\right] \\
&= \mathbb{E}\left[\left\|\mathbf{Q}y^{(0)} - \mathbf{Q}y^{(t)}\right\|^2\right] + \mathbb{E}\left[\left\|\mathbf{Q}^{\perp}y^{(t)}\right\|^2\right]. \quad (6)
\end{aligned}$$

Proving that the first term in (6) is small corresponds to show that after $t \approx T$ rounds the contribution of the top k eigenvectors $f_1, \ldots, f_k$ to $y^{(t)}$ is dominant, while proving that the second term is small means that the contribution of the bottom k eigenvectors $f_{k+1}, \ldots, f_n$ to $y^{(t)}$ becomes negligible. This is what we would expect if at each round we were able to apply directly the expected matrix $\mathbb{E}\left[\mathbf{M}^{(t)}\right]$. We prove that in expectation these facts hold, although different matching matrices $\mathbf{M}^{(t)}$ are applied in different rounds.

Formally, we analyse the first term in (6) and have that

$$\begin{aligned}
&\mathbb{E}\left[\left\|\mathbf{Q}\left(y^{(0)} - y^{(t)}\right)\right\|^2\right] \\
&= \mathbb{E}\left[\sum_{i=1}^{k}\left\langle y^{(0)} - y^{(t)}, f_i\right\rangle^2\right] \\
&= \sum_{i=1}^{k}\mathbb{E}\left[\left(\left\langle y^{(0)}, f_i\right\rangle - \left\langle y^{(t)}, f_i\right\rangle\right)^2\right] \\
&= \sum_{i=1}^{k}\left(\left\langle y^{(0)}, f_i\right\rangle^2 + \mathbb{E}\left[\left\langle y^{(t)}, f_i\right\rangle^2\right] - 2\left\langle y^{(0)}, f_i\right\rangle\mathbb{E}\left[\left\langle y^{(t)}, f_i\right\rangle\right]\right) \\
&\leqslant \sum_{i=1}^{k}\left(2\left\langle y^{(0)}, f_i\right\rangle^2 - 2\left\langle y^{(0)}, f_i\right\rangle\mathbb{E}\left[\left\langle y^{(t)}, f_i\right\rangle\right]\right), \quad (7)
\end{aligned}$$

where the last inequality uses the fact that, for every t, $\mathbf{M}^{(t)}$ is a projection matrix with norm at most one, and therefore

$$\mathbb{E}\left[\left\langle y^{(t)}, f_i\right\rangle^2\right] \leqslant \left\langle y^{(0)}, f_i\right\rangle^2.$$

Also, since at every round t the picked matrix $\mathbf{M}^{(t)}$ is independent from previous matchings, it holds that

$$\begin{aligned}
\mathbb{E}\left[\left\langle y^{(t)}, f_i\right\rangle\right] &= y^{(0)\intercal}\mathbb{E}\left[\mathbf{M}^{(t)} \cdots \mathbf{M}^{(1)}\right] f_i \\
&= y^{(0)\intercal}\mathbb{E}\left[\mathbf{M}^{(0)}\right]^t f_i \\
&= \left(1 - \frac{\bar{d} - \bar{d} \cdot \lambda_i}{4}\right)^t \left\langle y^{(0)}, f_i\right\rangle, \quad (8)
\end{aligned}$$

Therefore, it holds that

$$\begin{aligned}
&\mathbb{E}\left[\left\|\mathbf{Q}y^{(0)} - \mathbf{Q}y^{(t)}\right\|^2\right] \\
&\leqslant \sum_{i=1}^{k}\left(2\left\langle y^{(0)}, f_i\right\rangle^2 - 2\left(1 - \frac{\bar{d} - \bar{d} \cdot \lambda_i}{4}\right)^t \left\langle y^{(0)}, f_i\right\rangle^2\right) \\
&\leqslant 2t \cdot (1 - \lambda_k)\left\|\mathbf{Q}y^{(0)}\right\|^2. \quad (9)
\end{aligned}$$

To bound the second term in (6), we study the total expected norm of $y^{(t)}$, and prove that, for any $\ell, t \geqslant 1$, it holds that

$$\mathbb{E}\left[\mathbf{M}^{(t)}\mathbf{P}^{\ell}\mathbf{M}^{(t)}\right] \preceq \left(1-\frac{\bar{d}}{8}\right)\mathbf{P}^{\ell} + \frac{\bar{d}}{8}\mathbf{P}^{\ell+1}. \qquad (10)$$

To see this, we fix two nodes u, v. Then, the value of ${\mathbf{M}^{(t)}\mathbf{P}^{\ell}\mathbf{M}^{(t)}}_{u,v}$ depends on how nodes u and v are matched in round t:

Case 1: If both of u and v are not involved in the matching in round t, then ${\mathbf{M}^{(t)}\mathbf{P}^{\ell}\mathbf{M}^{(t)}}_{u,v} = \mathbf{P}^{\ell}_{u,v}$.

Case 2: If u is not involved in the matching but v is matched to a node $\sigma(v) \neq v$, then ${\mathbf{M}^{(t)}\mathbf{P}^{\ell}\mathbf{M}^{(t)}}_{u,v} = (1/2)\cdot\mathbf{P}^{\ell}_{u,v} + (1/2)\cdot\mathbf{P}^{\ell}_{u,\sigma(v)}$.

Case 3: Similarly, if u is matched to $\sigma(u) \neq u$ but v is not involved in the matching in round t, then ${\mathbf{M}^{(t)}\mathbf{P}^{\ell}\mathbf{M}^{(t)}}_{u,v} = (1/2)\cdot\mathbf{P}^{\ell}_{u,v} + (1/2)\cdot\mathbf{P}^{\ell}_{\sigma(u),v}$.

Case 4: If u is matched to $\sigma(u) \neq u$ and v to $\sigma(v) \neq v$, then ${\mathbf{M}^{(t)}\mathbf{P}^{\ell}\mathbf{M}^{(t)}}_{u,v} = (1/4)\cdot\left(\mathbf{P}^{\ell}_{u,v} + \mathbf{P}^{\ell}_{\sigma(u),v} + \mathbf{P}^{\ell}_{u,\sigma(v)} + \mathbf{P}^{\ell}_{\sigma(u),\sigma(v)}\right)$.

Notice that the exact value of $\mathbb{E}\left[{\mathbf{M}^{(t)}\mathbf{P}^{\ell}\mathbf{M}^{(t)}}_{u,v}\right]$ depends on how node v can be reached from node u from one or two matching edges in round t, as well as a walk of length ℓ. Hence, we can write

$$\mathbb{E}\left[{\mathbf{M}^{(t)}\mathbf{P}^{\ell}\mathbf{M}^{(t)}}_{u,v}\right] = \alpha_1\mathbf{P}^{\ell}_{u,v} + \alpha_2{\mathbf{P}^{\ell+1}}_{u,v} + \alpha_3{\mathbf{P}^{\ell+2}}_{u,v},$$

where $\alpha_1+\alpha_2+\alpha_3 = 1$. In particular, since the first case occurs with probability at most $(1-\bar{d}/4)$, it holds that $\alpha_1 \leqslant 1-\bar{d}/8$. Then, (10) follows from the fact that $\mathbf{P}^{\ell+2} \preceq \mathbf{P}^{\ell+1} \preceq \mathbf{P}^{\ell}$, and we have that

$$\begin{aligned}
&\mathbb{E}\left[\left\|y^{(t)}\right\|^2\right] \\
&= {y^{(0)}}^{\intercal}\,\mathbb{E}\left[\mathbf{M}^{(t)}\mathbf{M}^{(t-1)}\cdots\mathbf{M}^{(1)}\mathbf{M}^{(1)}\cdots\mathbf{M}^{(t-1)}\mathbf{M}^{(t)}\right]y^{(0)} \\
&\leqslant {y^{(0)}}^{\intercal}\left(\left(1-\frac{\bar{d}}{8}\right)\mathbf{I} + \frac{\bar{d}}{8}\cdot\mathbf{P}\right)^{t} y^{(0)}. \qquad (11)
\end{aligned}$$

To bound $\mathbb{E}\left[\left\|\mathbf{Q}y^{(t)}\right\|^2\right]$, we use (8) and obtain that

$$\begin{aligned}
\mathbb{E}\left[\left\|\mathbf{Q}y^{(t)}\right\|^2\right] &= \sum_{i=1}^{k}\mathbb{E}\left[\left\langle y^{(t)}, f_i\right\rangle^2\right] \\
&\geqslant (1-2t(1-\lambda_k))\sum_{i=1}^{k}\left\langle y^{(0)}, f_i\right\rangle^2 \\
&= (1-2t(1-\lambda_k))\left\|\mathbf{Q}y^{(0)}\right\|^2, \qquad (12)
\end{aligned}$$

where the first inequality follows from the Jensen's inequality. Combining (11), (12) and the fact that $\left\langle \mathbf{Q}y^{(t)}, \mathbf{Q}^{\perp}y^{(t)}\right\rangle = 0$, we obtain that

$$\begin{aligned}
&\mathbb{E}\left[\left\|\mathbf{Q}^{\perp}y^{(t)}\right\|^2\right] \\
&= \mathbb{E}\left[\left\|y^{(t)}\right\|^2\right] - \mathbb{E}\left[\left\|\mathbf{Q}y^{(t)}\right\|^2\right] \\
&\leqslant {y^{(0)}}^{\intercal}\left(\left(1-\frac{\bar{d}}{8}\right)\mathbf{I} + \frac{\bar{d}}{8}\cdot\mathbf{P}\right)^{t} y^{(0)} - (1-2t(1-\lambda_k))\left\|\mathbf{Q}y^{(0)}\right\|^2 \\
&\leqslant 2t(1-\lambda_k)\left\|\mathbf{Q}y^{(0)}\right\|^2 + \left(1-\frac{\bar{d}}{8}+\frac{\bar{d}}{8}\lambda_{k+1}\right)^{t} \\
&\leqslant 2t(1-\lambda_k)\left\|\mathbf{Q}y^{(0)}\right\|^2 + o(n^{-c}), \qquad (13)
\end{aligned}$$

where (13) holds for a large constant $c > 0$ due to our choice of $t \geqslant T$.

Finally, combining (9) with (13) gives us that

$$\mathbb{E}\left[\left\|\mathbf{Q}y^{(0)} - y^{(t)}\right\|^2\right] \leqslant t\cdot(1-\lambda_k)\left\|\mathbf{Q}y^{(0)}\right\|^2 + o\left(n^{-c}\right),$$

and Lemma 4.1 holds by applying the Jensen's inequality. ∎

4.3 Proof of Lemma 4.2

To prove Lemma 4.2, we need the following lemma:

Lemma 4.4 ([25]). *Let $\{S_i\}_{i=1}^{k}$ be a k-way partition of G achieving $\rho(k)$, and let $\Upsilon = \Omega\left(k^2\right)$. Assume that $\widetilde{\chi}_i$ is the projection of f_i in the span of $\{\chi_{S_1}, \ldots, \chi_{S_k}\}$. Then, it holds for any $1 \leqslant i \leqslant k$ that*

$$\|\widetilde{\chi}_i - f_i\| = O\left(\sqrt{\frac{k}{\Upsilon}}\right).$$

Proof of Lemma 4.2. Since $\{f_i\}_{i=1}^{k}$ is an orthonormal set, it holds by Lemma 4.4 that $\{\widetilde{\chi}_i\}_{i=1}^{k}$ are *almost* orthonormal. Hence, our task is to construct an orthonormal set $\{\widehat{\chi}_i\}_{i=1}^{k}$ based on $\{\widetilde{\chi}_i\}_{i=1}^{k}$, which can be achieved by applying the Gram-Schmidt orthonormalisation procedure. The error bound follows from the fact that

$$\left\langle \widetilde{\chi}_i, \widetilde{\chi}_j\right\rangle = O\left(\sqrt{\frac{k}{\Upsilon}}\right)$$

holds for $i \neq j$. ∎

4.4 Proof of Lemma 4.3

Proof. We first show that χ_{S_i} is the projection of the initial load vector $y^{(0)} = \chi_v$ in the span of $\{\chi_{S_1}, \ldots, \chi_{S_k}\}$. Since every $\widehat{\chi}_i$ $(1 \leqslant i \leqslant k)$ is a linear combination of vectors in $\{\chi_{S_i}\}_{i=1}^{k}$, and $\widehat{\chi}_1, \ldots, \widehat{\chi}_k$ are orthonormal by Lemma 4.2, we have that $\mathrm{span}\{\widehat{\chi}_1, \ldots, \widehat{\chi}_k\} = \mathrm{span}\{\chi_{S_1}, \ldots, \chi_{S_k}\}$. Hence,

$$\begin{aligned}
\sum_{i=1}^{k}\langle\chi_v, \widehat{\chi}_i\rangle\,\widehat{\chi}_i &= \sum_{i=1}^{k}\left\langle\chi_v, \frac{\chi_{S_i}}{\|\chi_{S_i}\|}\right\rangle\frac{\chi_{S_i}}{\|\chi_{S_i}\|} \\
&= \left\langle\chi_v, \chi_{S_j}\right\rangle\frac{\chi_{S_j}}{\|\chi_{S_j}\|^2} = \chi_{S_j}, \qquad (14)
\end{aligned}$$

where the first equality holds by the fact that $\mathrm{span}\{\widehat{\chi}_1, \ldots, \widehat{\chi}_k\} = \mathrm{span}\{\chi_{S_1}, \ldots, \chi_{S_k}\}$, the second equality holds since χ_v is orthogonal to every χ_{S_ℓ} with $\ell \neq j$, and the third equality holds by the fact that $\langle\chi_v, \chi_{S_j}\rangle = 1/|S_j| = \|\chi_{S_j}\|^2$.

Based on this, we bound the expected distance between $y^{(T)}$ and χ_{S_j}. By the triangle inequality, it holds that

$$\mathbb{E}\left[\left\|y^{(T)} - \chi_{S_j}\right\|\right] \leqslant \mathbb{E}\left[\left\|\mathbf{Q}\chi_v - y^{(T)}\right\|\right] + \left\|\mathbf{Q}\chi_v - \chi_{S_j}\right\|, \qquad (15)$$

where the expectation is over all possible random matchings generated within the first T rounds. By Lemma 4.1, we have that

$$\mathbb{E}\left[\left\|\mathbf{Q}\chi_v - y^{(T)}\right\|\right] \leqslant 2\sqrt{T\cdot(1-\lambda_k)}\,\|\mathbf{Q}\chi_v\| + o\left(n^{-c}\right). \qquad (16)$$

For the second term in the right hand side of (15), by the triangle inequality we have that

$$\begin{aligned}
&\left\|Q\chi_v - \chi_{S_j}\right\| \\
&= \left\|\sum_{i=1}^{k}\langle\chi_v, f_i\rangle f_i - \sum_{i=1}^{k}\langle\chi_v, f_i\rangle\widehat{\chi}_i + \sum_{i=1}^{k}\langle\chi_v, f_i\rangle\widehat{\chi}_i - \sum_{i=1}^{k}\langle\chi_v, \widehat{\chi}_i\rangle\widehat{\chi}_i\right\| \\
&\leqslant \left\|\sum_{i=1}^{k}\langle\chi_v, f_i\rangle f_i - \sum_{i=1}^{k}\langle\chi_v, f_i\rangle\widehat{\chi}_i\right\| \\
&\quad + \left\|\sum_{i=1}^{k}\langle\chi_v, f_i\rangle\widehat{\chi}_i - \sum_{i=1}^{k}\langle\chi_v, \widehat{\chi}_i\rangle\widehat{\chi}_i\right\| \qquad (17)
\end{aligned}$$

To bound the first term in (17), we have that

$$\begin{aligned}
\left\|\sum_{i=1}^{k}\langle\chi_v, f_i\rangle f_i - \sum_{i=1}^{k}\langle\chi_v, f_i\rangle\widehat{\chi}_i\right\| &\leqslant \sum_{i=1}^{k}|\langle\chi_v, f_i\rangle|\,\|f_i - \widehat{\chi}_i\| \\
&\leqslant \mathcal{E}\sum_{i=1}^{k}|\langle\chi_v, f_i\rangle| \leqslant k\mathcal{E}\,\|Q\chi_v\| \qquad (18)
\end{aligned}$$

where the first line follows from the triangle inequality, the second follows by Lemma 4.2, and the last follows by the Cauchy-Schwarz inequality. To bound the second term in (17), we have that

$$\begin{aligned}
\left\|\sum_{i=1}^{k}\left(\langle\chi_v, f_i\rangle - \langle\chi_v, \widehat{\chi}_i\rangle\right)\widehat{\chi}_i\right\| &= \left\|\sum_{i=1}^{k}\left(f_i(v) - \widehat{\chi}_i(v)\right)\widehat{\chi}_i\right\| \\
&= \sqrt{\sum_{i=1}^{k}\left(f_i(v) - \widehat{\chi}_i(v)\right)^2\|\widehat{\chi}_i\|^2} \\
&= \alpha_v
\end{aligned}$$

where the second inequality follows from the orthonormality of $\{\widehat{\chi}_i\}_i$, and the third equality from the definition of α_v and, again, the orthonormality of $\{\widehat{\chi}_i\}_i$. Thus, we rewrite (17) as

$$\left\|Q\chi_v - \chi_{S_j}\right\| \leqslant k\cdot\mathcal{E}\cdot\|Q\chi_v\| + \alpha_v. \qquad (19)$$

Combining (15), (16) with (19), we have that

$$\begin{aligned}
\mathbb{E}\left[\left\|y^{(T)} - \chi_{S_j}\right\|\right] &\leqslant \left(\sqrt{T\cdot(1-\lambda_k)} + k\cdot\mathcal{E}\right)\|Q\chi_v\| + \alpha_v \\
&= O\left(k\cdot\mathcal{E}\sqrt{\log n}\right)\|Q\chi_v\| + \alpha_v, \qquad (20)
\end{aligned}$$

where the last equality follows by (1) and the fact that

$$\sqrt{T\cdot(1-\lambda_k)} = O\left(\sqrt{\frac{(1-\lambda_k)\log n}{1-\lambda_{k+1}}}\right) = O\left(k\cdot\mathcal{E}\sqrt{\log n}\right).$$

Hence, it suffices to bound $\|Q\chi_v\|^2$. Direct calculation shows that

$$\begin{aligned}
\|Q\chi_v\|^2 &= \sum_{i=1}^{k}\langle\chi_v, f_i\rangle^2 \\
&= \sum_{i=1}^{k}\langle\chi_v, \widetilde{\chi}_i - (\widetilde{\chi}_i - f_i)\rangle^2 \\
&= \sum_{i=1}^{k}\left(\langle\chi_v, \widetilde{\chi}_i\rangle - \langle\chi_v, \widetilde{\chi}_i - f_i\rangle\right)^2 \\
&\leqslant \sum_{i=1}^{k}2\left(\langle\chi_v, \widetilde{\chi}_i\rangle^2 + \langle\chi_v, \widetilde{\chi}_i - f_i\rangle^2\right) \qquad (21) \\
&= 2\left\|\chi_{S_j}\right\|^2 + 2\langle\chi_v, \widetilde{\chi}_i - f_i\rangle^2 \qquad (22) \\
&\leqslant 2\left\|\chi_{S_j}\right\|^2 + 2\alpha_v^2 \qquad (23)
\end{aligned}$$

where (21) follows from the inequality

$$(a-b)^2 \leqslant 2(a^2+b^2),$$

(22) follows from (14), and (23) follows from the definition of α_v. Hence, it holds that $\|Q\chi_v\| = O\left(\left\|\chi_{S_j}\right\| + \alpha_v\right)$, and we can rewrite (20) as

$$\begin{aligned}
\mathbb{E}\left[\left\|y^{(T)} - \chi_{S_j}\right\|\right] &= O\left(k\cdot\mathcal{E}\sqrt{\log n}\cdot\left(\left\|\chi_{S_j}\right\| + \alpha_v\right)\right) + \alpha_v \\
&= O\left(k\cdot\mathcal{E}\sqrt{\log n}\cdot\left\|\chi_{S_j}\right\| + \alpha_v\right),
\end{aligned}$$

where the last equality follows from the assumption on Υ. Then the lemma follows from by the definition of α_v and the fact that

$$\left\|\chi_{S_j}\right\| = \frac{1}{\sqrt{|S_j|}} \leqslant \frac{1}{\sqrt{\beta n}}.$$

■

4.5 Analysis for Almost-Regular Graphs

Finally, we show that our algorithm and analysis can be easily modified to work for *almost-regular graphs*, i.e., the graphs for which the ratio between maximum degree $\Delta = \max_{v\in V}\{d_v\}$ and the minimum degree $\delta = \min_{v\in V}\{d_v\}$ is upper bounded by some constant. We also assume each node knows an upper bound $D \geqslant \Delta$ of the maximum degree such that $D/\delta = \Theta(\Delta/\delta)$. With these assumptions, we only need to slightly modify the seeding procedure, in which every node v sets to be active with probability $\frac{1}{2} + \frac{D-d_v}{2D}$, instead of $1/2$ for the case of regular graphs. The Averaging and Query procedures remain the same.

To show our algorithm and analysis holds for almost-regular graphs, we view the underlying almost-regular graph G as a D-regular graph $G^\star$, which is obtained from G by adding $D - d_v$ self-loops to each node v. Then, the conductance of any set S is almost the same in G and $G^\star$, since

$$\phi_{G^\star}(S) = \frac{|E_G(S, V\setminus S)|}{D\cdot|S|} = \Theta\left(\frac{|E_G(S, V\setminus S)|}{\mathrm{vol}(S)}\right) = \Theta\left(\phi_G(S)\right).$$

It is also easy to see that the $(k+1)$th eigenvalues of the random walk matrix of G and $G^\star$ differ by at most a constant factor, and therefore $G^\star$ is well-clustered. Hence, Theorem 1.1 holds for almost-regular graphs as well.

REFERENCES

[1] Zeyuan Allen-Zhu, Silvio Lattanzi, and Vahab S. Mirrokni. 2013. A local algorithm for finding well-connected clusters. In *30th International Conference on Machine Learning (ICML'13)*. 396–404.

[2] Noga Alon, Chen Avin, Michal Koucký, Gady Kozma, Zvi Lotker, and Mark R. Tuttle. 2008. Many random walks are faster than one. In *20th Annual ACM Symposium on Parallel Algorithms and Architectures (SPAA'08)*. 119–128.

[3] Luca Becchetti, Andrea Clementi, Emanuele Natale, Francesco Pasquale, and Luca Trevisan. 2017. Find your place: Simple distributed algorithms for community detection. In *28th Annual ACM-SIAM Symposium on Discrete Algorithms (SODA'17)*. 940–959.

[4] Petra Berenbrink, Colin Cooper, Tom Friedetzky, Tobias Friedrich, and Thomas Sauerwald. 2015. Randomized diffusion for indivisible loads. *J. Comput. Syst. Sci.* 81, 1 (2015), 159–185.

[5] Stephen Boyd, Arpita Ghosh, Balaji Prabhakar, and Devavrat Shah. 2006. Randomized gossip algorithms. *IEEE Transactions on Information Theory* 52, 6 (2006).

[6] Jiecao Chen, He Sun, David P. Woodruff, and Qin Zhang. 2016. Communication-optimal distributed clustering. In *29th Advances in Neural Information Processing Systems (NIPS'16)*. 3720–3728.

[7] Flavio Chierichetti, Silvio Lattanzi, and Alessandro Panconesi. 2010. Almost tight bounds for rumour spreading with conductance. In *42nd Annual ACM Symposium on Theory of Computing (STOC'10)*. 399–408.

[8] Flavio Chierichetti, Silvio Lattanzi, and Alessandro Panconesi. 2010. Rumour spreading and graph conductance. In *21st Annual ACM-SIAM Symposium on Discrete Algorithms (SODA'10)*. 1657–1663.

[9] Colin Cooper, Alan M. Frieze, and Tomasz Radzik. 2009. Multiple random walks in random regular graphs. *SIAM Journal on Discrete Mathematics* 23, 4 (2009), 1738–1761.

[10] George Cybenko. 1989. Dynamic load balancing for distributed memory multiprocessors. *J. Parallel and Distrib. Comput.* 7 (1989), 279–301.

[11] Robert Elsasser and Thomas Sauerwald. 2010. Discrete load balancing is (almost) as easy as continuous load balancing. In *29th Annual ACM-SIGOPT Principles of Distributed Computing (PODS'10)*. 346–354.

[12] Robert Elsasser and Thomas Sauerwald. 2011. Tight bounds for the cover time of multiple random walks. *Theoretical Computer Science* 412, 24 (2011), 2623–2641.

[13] Santo Fortunato. 2010. Community detection in graphs. *Physics Reports* 486, 3 (2010), 75–174.

[14] Tobias Friedrich, Martin Gairing, and Thomas Sauerwald. 2012. Quasirandom load balancing. *SIAM J. Comput.* 41, 4 (2012), 747–771.

[15] Tobias Friedrich and Thomas Sauerwald. 2009. Near-perfect load balancing by randomized rounding. In *41st Annual ACM Symposium on Theory of Computing (STOC'09)*. 121–130.

[16] Shayan Oveis Gharan and Luca Trevisan. 2012. Approximating the expansion profile and almost optimal local graph clustering. In *53rd Annual IEEE Symposium on Foundations of Computer Science (FOCS'12)*. 187–196.

[17] Bhaskar Ghosh, S. Muthukrishnan, and Martin H. Schultz. 1996. First and second order diffusive methods for rapid, coarse, distributed load balancing. In *8th Annual ACM Symposium on Parallel Algorithms and Architectures (SPAA'96)*. 72–81.

[18] George Giakkoupis. 2011. Tight bounds for rumor spreading in graphs of a given conductance. In *28th International Symposium on Theoretical Aspects of Computer Science (STACS'11)*. 57–68.

[19] George Giakkoupis and Thomas Sauerwald. 2012. Rumor spreading and vertex expansion. In *23rd Annual ACM-SIAM Symposium on Discrete Algorithms (SODA'12)*. 1623–1641.

[20] Pan Hui, Eiko Yoneki, Shu Yan Chan, and Jon Crowcroft. 2007. Distributed community detection in delay tolerant networks. In *Proceedings of 2nd ACM/IEEE International Workshop on Mobility in the Evolving Internet Architecture*.

[21] David Kempe and Frank McSherry. 2004. A decentralized algorithm for spectral analysis. In *36th Annual ACM Symposium on Theory of Computing (STOC'04)*. 561–568.

[22] James R. Lee, Shayan Oveis Gharan, and Luca Trevisan. 2014. Multiway spectral partitioning and higher-order Cheeger inequalities. *Journal of the ACM* 61, 6 (2014), 37:1–37:30.

[23] Gurmeet Singh Manku. 2004. Balanced binary trees for ID management and load balance in distributed hash tables. In *23rd Annual ACM-SIGOPT Principles of Distributed Computing (PODS'04)*. 197–205.

[24] Shayan Oveis Gharan and Luca Trevisan. 2014. Partitioning into expanders. In *25th Annual ACM-SIAM Symposium on Discrete Algorithms (SODA'14)*. 1256–1266.

[25] Richard Peng, He Sun, and Luca Zanetti. 2017. Partitioning well-clustered graphs: spectral clustering works! *SIAM J. Comput.* 46, 2 (2017), 710–743.

[26] Yuval Rabani, Alistair Sinclair, and Rolf Wanka. 1998. Local divergence of markov chains and the analysis of iterative load balancing schemes. In *39th Annual IEEE Symposium on Foundations of Computer Science (FOCS'98)*. 694–705.

[27] Thomas Sauerwald and He Sun. 2012. Tight bounds for randomized load balancing on arbitrary network topologies. In *53rd Annual IEEE Symposium on Foundations of Computer Science (FOCS'12)*. 341–350.

[28] Devavrat Shah. 2009. Gossip Algorithms. *Foundations and Trends in Networking* 3, 1 (2009), 1–125.

[29] Daniel A. Spielman and Shang-Hua Teng. 2013. A local clustering algorithm for massive graphs and its application to nearly linear time graph partitioning. *SIAM J. Comput.* 42, 1 (2013), 1–26.

[30] Sonesh Surana, Brighten Godfrey, Karthik Lakshminarayanan, Richard M. Karp, and Ion Stoica. 2006. Load balancing in dynamic structured peer-to-peer systems. *Performance Evaluation* 63, 3 (2006), 217–240.

[31] Wenzhuo Yang and Huan Xu. 2015. A divide and conquer framework for distributed graph clustering. In *32nd International Conference on Machine Learning (ICML'15)*. 504–513.

[32] Dongliang Zhang, Changjun Jiang, and Shu Li. 2009. A fast adaptive load balancing method for parallel particle-based simulations. *Simulation Modelling Practice and Theory* 17, 6 (2009).

Fast Scheduling in Distributed Transactional Memory

Costas Busch
Louisiana State University
Baton Rouge, LA
busch@csc.lsu.edu

Maurice Herlihy
Brown University
Providence, RI
herlihy@cs.brown.edu

Miroslav Popovic
University of Novi Sad
Novi Sad, Serbia
miroslav.popovic@rt-rk.uns.ac.rs

Gokarna Sharma
Kent State University
Kent, OH
sharma@cs.kent.edu

ABSTRACT

We investigate scheduling algorithms for distributed transactional memory systems where transactions residing at nodes of a communication graph operate on shared, mobile objects. A transaction requests the objects it needs, executes once those objects have been assembled, and then possibly forwards those objects to other waiting transactions. Minimizing execution time in this model is known to be NP-hard for arbitrary communication graphs, and also hard to approximate within any factor smaller than the size of the graph. Nevertheless, networks on chips, multi-core systems, and clusters are not arbitrary. Here, we explore efficient execution schedules in specialized graphs likely to arise in practice: Clique, Line, Grid, Cluster, Hypercube, Butterfly, and Star. In most cases, when individual transactions request k objects, we obtain solutions close to a factor $O(k)$ from optimal, yielding near-optimal solutions for constant k. These execution times approximate the TSP tour lengths of the objects in the graph. We show that for general networks, even for two objects ($k = 2$), it is impossible to obtain execution time close to the objects' optimal TSP tour lengths, which is why it is useful to consider more realistic network models. To our knowledge, this is the first attempt to obtain provably fast schedules for distributed transactional memory.

CCS CONCEPTS

•Theory of computation → Design and analysis of algorithms; Distributed algorithms; •Computer communication networks → Network architecture and design; Distributed networks;

KEYWORDS

Transactional memory; distributed systems; execution time; approximation; data-flow model; scheduling; contention

SPAA '17, July 24-26, 2017, Washington DC, USA

DOI: 10.1145/3087556.3087565

1 INTRODUCTION

Concurrent processes (threads) need to synchronize to avoid introducing inconsistencies in shared data objects. Traditional synchronization mechanisms such as locks and barriers have well-known limitations and pitfalls, including deadlock, priority inversion, reliance on programmer conventions, and vulnerability to failure or delay. *Transactional memory* [15, 34] (TM) has emerged as an alternative. Using TM, code is split into *transactions*, blocks of code that appear to execute atomically with respect to one another. Transactions are executed *speculatively*: synchronization conflicts or failures may cause an executing transaction to *abort*: its effects are rolled back and the transaction is restarted. In the absence of conflicts or failures, a transaction typically *commits*, causing its effects to become visible.

Several commercial processors provide direct hardware support for TM, including Intel's Haswell [18] and IBM's Blue Gene/Q [13], zEnterprise EC12 [25], and Power8 [4]. There are proposals for adapting TM to clusters of GPUs [2, 11, 23]. Here, we consider *distributed* TM systems appropriate for rack-scale or cluster-scale networks of nodes linked by a modern communication network [2, 16, 23, 33, 36].

We consider a *data-flow* of transaction execution [16, 33], in which each transaction executes at a single node, but data objects are mobile. A transaction initially requests the objects it needs, and executes only after it has assembled them. When the transaction commits, it releases its objects, possibly forwarding them to other waiting transactions.

In a distributed TM, execution time is dominated by the costs of moving objects from one transaction to another. The goal of a *transaction scheduling algorithm* (sometimes called *contention management*) is to minimize delays caused by data conflicts and data movement.

Here, we consider scheduling algorithms in a synchronous data-flow model where time is divided into discrete steps [3]. The network is modeled as a weighted graph G, where transactions reside at nodes, edges are communication links, and edge weights are communication delays. At any time step, a node may perform three actions: (1) it may receive objects from adjacent nodes, (2) it executes any transaction that has assembled its required objects, and (3) it may forward objects to adjacent nodes. A transaction's execution step models when it commits. That transaction may have started earlier, but may have been blocked while assembling the objects it needed.

We provide offline algorithms to compute conflict-free schedules. We consider batch problem instances where transactions and objects initially reside at different nodes of G. Each node has a single transaction and each object has a single copy. The objective is to minimize the total execution time (makespan) until all transactions complete. The schedule determines the time step when each transaction executes and commits. After a transaction commits, it forwards its objects to any next requesting transactions in the execution order. Typically, an object is sent along a shortest path, implying that the transfer time depends on the distance in G between the sender and receiver nodes. Execution time depends on both the objects' traversal times and on inter-transaction data dependencies.

It is known [3] through a reduction from vertex coloring that determining the shortest execution time in arbitrary graphs is NP-hard, and even hard to approximate within a sub-linear factor of n, the number of nodes in G. Fortunately, however, networks for rack-scale and cluster-scale computing centers are not likely to be arbitrary [7]. Here, we focus on the kinds of specialized networks likely to arise in practice, such as Clique, Line, Grid, Cluster, Hypercube, Butterfly, and Star [5, 10, 22, 24, 27]. For example, the clique graph has implications on the hypercube and butterfly which are typical supercomputer topologies. The line graph represents bus system architectures, for example connecting boards in a rack. The grid graph represents systems on chips or multi-cores (e.g. XMOS architecture, Intel Xeon Phi). The cluster graph is an abstraction of clusters of computers found in data centers. Star graphs correspond to hubs, multiplexer, concentrators, and switches, which are normally used on supercomputers, clusters, and data centers.

1.1 Contributions

Suppose we have a set of w shared objects $O = \{o_1, \ldots, o_w\}$. We consider scheduling problems where each node holds a single transaction, and each transaction requests k objects (out of w). In most of the problems that we study, a transaction's set of k objects is chosen arbitrarily. We make two kinds of contributions.

Lower Bounds. A trivial lower bound for the execution time of the transactions is the longest shortest path that any object has to follow. This path length is within a constant factor from the optimal TSP tour length of the object. Using the probabilistic method, we demonstrate the existence of a scheduling problem on the grid, with 2 objects per transaction, where every schedule must have execution time $\Omega(n^{1/40}/\log n)$ factor away from the optimal TSP tour length of any object. The same lower bound holds also for trees. Therefore, we cannot expect in general to compute schedules that respect the optimal TSP length of any object. Nevertheless, the specialized graphs and scheduling problems considered here admit approximations that beat this lower bound.

Upper Bounds. We give polynomial time algorithms that compute execution schedules for a variety of graphs: Clique, Line, Grid, Cluster, Hypercube, Butterfly, and Star. These are the kinds of graphs one would expect to find in multiprocessor systems, Networks-on-chip (NoCs), or rack-scale or cluster-scale distributed systems [5, 7, 10, 22, 24, 27]. For one transaction per node requesting k objects out of w, we obtain the following results:

Clique: In any clique (complete graph) of n nodes there is a schedule which is within a factor $O(k)$ from optimal.

Line: In any line graph of n nodes there is a schedule which is within a factor $O(1)$ from optimal (asymptotically optimal).

Grid: In a $n \times n$ grid where each transaction requests a random set of k objects, we show that with high probability there is a schedule which is within a factor $O(k \log m)$ from optimal, where $m = \max(n, w)$.

Cluster: We consider a cluster graph which consists of cliques with β nodes connected to each other through bridge edges of weight $\gamma \geq \beta$. We show that there is a schedule which is a factor $O(\min(k\beta, \log_c^k m))$, for some constant c.

In the Hypercube and Butterfly graphs the results are extensions of the results in cliques scaled by a $\log n$ factor, since a shortest path connecting two nodes has length $O(\log n)$, instead of 1 in cliques. We also consider the Star graph topology where there is a central node that connects rays each consisting of β nodes. We observe that the analysis of the Star graph has many similarities with the Cluster and Line graphs and we show that there is a schedule which is a factor $O(\log \beta \cdot \min(k\beta, \log_c^k m))$ from optimal, for a constant c.

When k is a constant, in all graph cases we either obtain asymptotically optimal schedules or we obtain schedules within a poly-log factor from optimal. In most cases, with the only exception of the Grid, for the input problem we assume that each transaction holds an arbitrary set of k objects. In the Grid, a transaction holds a randomly-chosen set of k objects, and the reason for doing this is that the TSP lower bound on the Grid prohibits good schedules for arbitrary input problems, even when $k = 2$.

The main approach for computing the schedules is to appropriately apply a greedy schedule which colors the dependency graph of the transactions, where each color represents a different time step. The result in the Clique is a direct application of the greedy schedule. The result in the Grid is a repeated application of the greedy schedule in subgrid graphs carefully chosen such that the greedy schedule within each of them is efficient. The result in the Cluster graph is an application of the greedy schedule within the constituent cliques and also carefully synchronizing the object movements between the cliques. In all cases the resulting approximation factor compares the execution time to the TSP object tour lengths.

Our results for the data-flow model also apply to restricted versions of other models where objects may be replicated or versioned (Section 1.2).

1.2 Related Work

Transaction scheduling problems are widely studied in (tightly-coupled) multi-core systems. Several scheduling algorithms with provable upper and lower bounds, and impossibility results are given [1, 12, 31, 32], besides several other scheduling algorithms that are evaluated only experimentally [17, 35]. Dragojevic *et al.* [9], provide some theoretical evaluation of conflict prediction for online schedulers and also an experimental algorithm. These scheduling algorithms, however, are not suitable for scheduling in distributed TMs as they do not typically deal with communication cost in accessing shared resources.

Several researchers [2, 8, 23] present techniques to implement distributed TMs. However, they either use global lock, serialization lease, or commit-time broadcasting technique which may not scale well with the size of the network. Moreover, they do not provide formal analysis of either the execution time or the communication cost.

Most of the previous work [16, 19, 33, 36] on the data-flow model of distributed TMs focused on minimizing only the *communication cost* – the total distance traversed by all the objects in G. However, these works studied communication cost for scheduling problem instances with only a single shared object. Kim and Ravindran [19] provided communication cost bounds for special workloads and problem instances with multiple shared objects. The execution time minimization is considered by Zhang *et al.* [36]. However, the graph topology G they considered is arbitrary, except for the assumption of the known diameter D. Therefore, their result is not suitable for the specialized networks we study in this paper. Moreover, they do not study lower bound on execution time whereas we provide for the first time an execution time lower bound, improving significantly on the known TSP lower bound, even for the instances with only two shared objects. Busch *et al.* [3] considered minimizing both the execution time and communication cost. They showed that it is impossible to simultaneously minimize execution time and communication cost, that is, minimizing execution time implies high communication cost (and vice-versa).

There are distributed TM proposals that employ replication and multi-versioning [23, 28]. In replicated TMs, multiple copies are available for each shared object, whereas multiple versions of each object are available in multi-versioning TMs [23]. Kim and Ravindran [20] studied transaction scheduling in replicated distributed TMs. In the *control-flow* model [30], objects are immobile and transactions either move to the network nodes where the required objects reside, or invoke remote procedure calls. Hendler *et al.* [14] studied a lease based hybrid (combining data-flow with control-flow) distributed TM which dynamically determines whether to migrate transactions to the nodes that own the leases, or to demand the acquisition of these leases by the node that originated the transaction. Palmieri *et al.* [26] present a comparative study of data-flow versus control-flow models for distributed TMs in partially-replicated environments. Others have studied the speculative transaction execution [29] in replicated environments, and transaction scheduling using consistent snapshots [20, 23, 28, 29] for replicated and multiversioning environments. These works provide no theoretical analysis of execution time or communication cost.

1.3 Roadmap

In Section 2 we give the model and preliminaries, including the basic greedy schedule. We present result for Cliques in Section 3, where we also explain the implications for the Hypercube, Butterfly, and other related graphs. In Section 4 we give the scheduling algorithm for the Line graph, and in Section 5 we give the scheduling algorithm for the Grid graph. We present the result for the Cluster graph in Section 6, and the related result for the Star graph in Section 7. We prove our lower bound on execution time based on the TSP object tours in Section 8. Finally, we give our conclusions in Section 9.

2 MODEL AND PRELIMINARIES

2.1 Distributed TM Model

We assume a synchronous communication model: at each time step a node receives messages, performs a local computation, and then transmits messages to adjacent nodes. The message size is sufficient to convey the information about an object over the network, and there is no limit on the number of messages that may concurrently traverse an edge.

Let $O = \{o_1, \ldots, o_w\}$ denote w shared memory objects. Each object has a value which can be read or modified (written). The shared objects reside at nodes and are mobile, that is, an object can move from node to node in a message. There is a single copy of each object. A transaction T_i is an atomic code sequence executed at a node v_i which requires a set of objects $O(T_i) \subseteq O$. Transaction T_i can finish execution and commit at a specific time step once all the objects it needs have been gathered at v_i. A transaction T_i may modify some of its objects while others may remain unchanged. Initially, an object is at an arbitrary node of G.

Consider a set of m transactions $\mathcal{T} = \{T_1, T_2, \ldots, T_m\}$, where $m \leq n$, with at most one transaction per node. This batch problem setting is similar to the one usually considered for scheduling in multi-core systems [1, 31]. The transactions are distributed across network nodes and at most n transactions execute concurrently. Conflicts among transactions in accessing shared objects are defined in the usual way, where an aborting transaction restarts immediately.

A *scheduling algorithm* $\mathcal{A}$ determines the time step $t(T_i)$ when a transaction executes. The schedule is feasible if the objects that each transaction requests have moved to the transaction's node at time $t(T_i)$. Let $\mathcal{E}$ be an execution schedule based on $\mathcal{A}$.

Definition 2.1 (Execution Time). For a set of transactions $\mathcal{T}$ in graph G, the time of an execution $\mathcal{E}$ is the time elapsed until the last transaction finishes its execution in $\mathcal{E}$. The execution time of scheduling algorithm $\mathcal{A}$ is the maximum time over all possible executions for $\mathcal{T}$.

2.2 Chernoff Bounds

In our analysis, we use the following Chernoff bounds:

Lemma 2.2 (Chernoff Bounds). *Let $X_1, \ldots, X_n$ be independent random variables such that $X_i \in \{0, 1\}$, for $1 \leq i \leq n$. Let $X = \sum_{i=1}^{n} X_i$ and let $\mu = E[X]$. Then,*

$$\Pr(X \geq (1+\delta)\mu) \leq e^{-\frac{\delta^2\mu}{3}}, \quad 0 < \delta < 1, \tag{1}$$

$$\Pr(X \leq (1-\delta)\mu) \leq e^{-\frac{\delta^2\mu}{2}}, \quad 0 < \delta < 1. \tag{2}$$

2.3 Greedy Schedule

Consider a set of transactions in a graph G. In the *dependency graph* H each node corresponds to a transaction, and an edge between two nodes corresponds a dependency (conflict) that arises when the respective transactions share one or more objects. The weight of an edge in H represents the distance between the respective transactions. We can schedule the transactions in G using a *greedy schedule* which assigns execution times to transactions based on a coloring of H. A valid coloring of H assigns a unique positive integer to each transaction such that two adjacent transactions receive colors which differ by at least the weight of the incident edge that connects them. The colors correspond to the distinct time steps where respective transactions execute.

A lower bound for the execution time schedule is the maximum weight of any edge in H, since some object will require so much time to be transferred from one node to another in G. The weighted degree of a transaction in H is the sum of the weights of the edges adjacent to the transaction. Let Γ denote the maximum weighted degree of all transactions in H. A greedy coloring scheme assigns colors to the transactions of H one after the other, giving the smallest available color. It can be shown that H can be colored with $\Gamma + 1$ colors in polynomial time [3]. Let Δ be the maximum (non weighted) degree of H. Then a $\Gamma + 1$ coloring gives a $\Delta + 1$ factor approximation to the optimal schedule in G, since the maximum edge weight is a lower bound. The $O(\Delta)$ approximation assumes that the objects are initially positioned in the first transaction in the greedy schedule.

3 COMPLETE GRAPH

Scheduling Problem. Consider a unweighted complete graph (clique) G with n nodes where every node is connected to every other node with an edge of weight 1. Every node holds one transaction. There are w objects $O = \{o_1, \ldots, o_w\}$. Each transaction uses an arbitrary subset of k objects, where $1 \le k \le w$.

Algorithm and Analysis. For the algorithm, we use the greedy schedule of Section 2.3. The analysis if as follows.

THEOREM 3.1 (COMPLETE GRAPH). *In the complete graph the greedy schedule gives a $O(k)$ approximation to the optimal schedule.*

PROOF. Let A_i denote the set of transactions that use object o_i. Denote $\ell_i = |A_i|$ and $\ell = \max_i \ell_i$. Every transaction uses k objects, and every object is used by at most ℓ transactions. Therefore, the maximum weighted degree in the dependency graph is $k\ell$, and hence the dependency graph can be colored with at most $k\ell + 1$ colors. At the same time, the length of the schedule is at least ℓ, since an object has to visit every transaction that requests it. Consequently, the schedule is an $O(k)$ factor approximation of the optimal. □

3.1 Hypercube and Other Graphs

The result on complete graphs has implications to other graphs as well. In a hypercube graph [21] with n nodes there is a path of length $\log n$ connecting any pair of nodes. Therefore, the hypercube graph can be represented as a complete graph with n nodes where the weight of any edge is between 1 and $\log n$. Thus, similar to the proof of Theorem 3.1, the maximum weighted degree in the dependency graph is $k\ell \log n$, and hence it can be colored with with $O(k\ell \log n)$ colors. Since $\Omega(\ell)$ is a lower bound, this gives a $O(k \log n)$ approximation.

Generalizing, in any graph where the maximum distance between any pair of nodes is d (diameter), the greedy algorithm gives a $O(k\ell d)$ schedule. For each object o_i let χ_i denote the shortest path length that connects all transactions in A_i. Let $\chi = \max_i \chi_i$. Clearly, χ is a lower bound on execution time. Since $\chi \ge \ell$, we get a $O(kd)$ approximation for execution time. In Butterfly networks [21] and $\log n$-dimensional grids [6], $d = O(\log n)$ which gives a similar bound to the hypercube, $O(k \log n)$. If for a specific scheduling problem χ is asymptotically larger than ℓ then we can get a tighter approximation.

4 LINE GRAPH

Scheduling Problem. Consider a line graph $L = (V, E)$ which is a sequence of n nodes, $V = \{v_1, \ldots, v_n\}$, where there is an edge (v_i, v_{i+1}) of weight 1 for any $1 \le i < n - 1$. Assume an orientation of the nodes in L from left to right, so that v_1 is the leftmost while v_n is the rightmost. Let O be a set of shared objects and suppose that each node executes a transaction which uses an arbitrary subset of O. Assume that each object is initially in a node with a transaction that requests it.

Algorithm. Let ℓ be the longest shortest walk of any object in O. Let $L_{i,z} = (V_{i,z}, E_{i,z})$ denote the subgraph with up to z nodes $V_{i,z} = \{v_i, v_{i+1}, \ldots, v_{i+z-1}\}$, where $E_{i,z} \subseteq E$ consists only of the edges connecting nodes in $V_{i,z}$. If $i+z-1 > n$, then we ignore all the nodes with subscript higher than n. Let $S = \{L_{x,\ell} : x = y\ell + 1,\ y \ge 0\}$, denote a decomposition of L into consecutive line subgraphs each of size ℓ. Let S_1 (S_2) denote the subset of S consisting of the $L_{x,\ell}$ with even (odd) index y in the definition of S. Namely, S_1 consists of the even subsequence of the line subgraphs of length ℓ, while S_2 consists of the odd subsequence of the line subgraphs. We schedule the transactions in two phases. (If $\ell = n$ then we only have Phase 1.) In the first phase we execute the transactions in S_1 while in the second phase we execute the transactions in S_2.

Phase 1: The first phase consists of two periods:
- *Period 1:* In the first period, each object is positioned to the leftmost node of a node in S_1 that needs it. This period has duration $\ell - 1$.
- *Period 2:* In the second period we execute the transactions in S_1. Within each subgraph $L' \in S_1$, the transactions execute from left to right. This period has duration ℓ. Suppose that $L' = (V', E') \in S_1$ where $V' = \{v_{i_1}, v_{i_2}, \ldots, v_{i_\ell}\}$. In the first time step of the period we execute the transaction (if any) in the first node v_{i_1} of L' and then immediately all the objects in v_{i_1} which are needed by transactions on the right move to the second node v_{i_2}. In the second time step we execute the transaction in v_{i_2} (if any) and then the objects in v_{i_2} move to v_{i_3} (if needed by transactions on the right). This repeats until the transaction (if any) in v_{i_ℓ} executes.

Phase 2: The second phase consists of two periods:
- *Period 1:* In the first period, each remaining object (still needed by an non-executed transaction) is positioned to the leftmost node that needs it. This period has duration $\ell - 1$.
- *Period 2:* In the second period we execute the transactions in S_2. Within each subgraph $L' \in S_2$, the transactions execute from left to right, similar to phase 1, period 2. This period has duration ℓ.

Analysis. The reason for having two phases (when $\ell < n$) is to allow a gap of ℓ nodes between subgraphs of length ℓ. The gap allows to execute in parallel the transactions in the subgraphs of each phase, since there is no object that will be needed concurrently by two subgraphs of a phase, since ℓ is a bound on the shortest walk of any object. Phase 1, period 1, finishes within $\ell - 1$ steps since each object moves to a node in S_1 at distance at most $\ell - 1$ from its original position. In phase 1, period 2, no object can be requested simultaneously by different subgraphs of S_1, since the maximum walk length is ℓ. Therefore, transactions in different subgraphs of S_1 can execute in parallel. Since each subgraph has ℓ nodes, ℓ steps suffice to execute all transactions in S_1. A similar analysis holds for the second phase. This execution has total duration $4\ell - 2$ steps which is asymptotically optimal (within a factor 4).

Theorem 4.1 (Line Graph). *For the line graph, for any arbitrary input instance there is an execution schedule with asymptotically optimal time.*

5 GRID GRAPH

Scheduling Problem. Consider a $n \times n$ grid graph $G = (V, E)$ where $|V| = n^2$. Every node has a coordinate (x, y), $1 \le x, y \le n$, and connects with its four neighbors (up, down, left, right) with an edge of weight 1. Assume an orientation of the grid on the plane such that node $(1, 1)$ appears at the top left. Nodes at the border of the grid connect with three neighbors and the corner nodes connect to two neighbors. There are w objects $O = \{o_1, \ldots, o_w\}$. Each node holds a transaction that uses a random subset of k objects, where $1 \le k \le w$. Initially, each object is at one of the nodes (if any) that needs it.

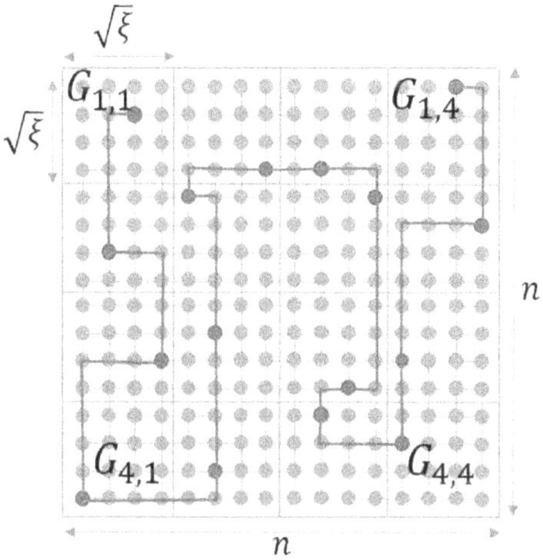

Figure 1: A grid of size 16×16 with subgrids of size 4×4. It depicts the path of an object.

Algorithm. Let $m = \max(n, w)$ and $\xi = (27w \ln m)/k$. Assume for simplicity that ξ and $\sqrt{\xi}$ are integers (otherwise, we may simply use ceilings which do not affect the proven asymptotic bounds). If $\sqrt{\xi} < n$, decompose the grid into subgrids $G_{i,j}$ of size $\sqrt{\xi} \times \sqrt{\xi}$. Assume also for simplicity that $\sqrt{\xi}$ divides n, since otherwise we obtain partial subgrids at the borders of G that have size smaller than $\xi \times \xi$, but those can be treated similarly to complete subgrids without affecting the analysis. The top-left corner of subgrid $G_{i,j}$ is positioned at node $((i-1)\sqrt{\xi}+1, (j-1)\sqrt{\xi}+1)$, where $1 \le i, j \le n/\sqrt{\xi}$. Note that G can be divided into $n/\sqrt{\xi}$ columns of subgrids, where each column consists of $n/\sqrt{\xi}$ subgrids. If $\sqrt{\xi} \ge n$, then there is only one subgrid, which is the whole of G.

The schedule executes the transactions in each subgrid separately, one subgrid at a time. The schedule follows a column major order of subgrids, starting from the leftmost column and ending at the rightmost column of subgrids (see Figure 1). In the jth column of subgrids the order of subgrids is top to bottom if j is odd, while the order is bottom to top if j is even. The first subgrid is $G_{1,1}$ at the top of the leftmost column. All transactions within $G_{1,1}$ execute and once they finish then execution continues with the transactions in subgrid $G_{2,1}$ immediately below. When all transactions within $G_{2,1}$ finish execution, then the execution continues in subgrid $G_{3,1}$ immediately below, and so on, until the last subgrid $G_{n/\sqrt{\xi},1}$ (at the bottom) of the first column. Then the execution continues in the second column starting with the bottom subgrid $G_{n/\sqrt{\xi},2}$ at the bottom, and then it executes the subgrids above in the second column in a similar way until the topmost subgrid. The third column of subgrids is processed top to bottom. The execution continues in a similar way, alternating the direction in each column of subgrids, and it ends when all transactions complete at the last subgrid of the rightmost column.

Within a subgrid $G_{i,j}$ an object may be requested by multiple nodes. We use the greedy schedule described in Section 2.3 to execute the transactions within each subgrid. We will refer to this as the *internal schedule* of each subgrid. Between the internal schedule of two consecutive subgrids there is a *transition period* where objects move from one subgrid to the next. Initially, before execution in $G_{1,1}$ starts, all required objects move to $G_{1,1}$ and position themselves to the respective first node that needs them in the internal schedule of $G_{1,1}$. Once execution in a subgrid finishes then the objects move from the current subgrid to the next subgrid in the order. Once the next subgrid has all the objects positioned in the first node of its internal schedule, then execution begins according to the internal schedule. Whenever objects move from one node to another they follow a shortest path in G.

Note that there may be the case that some object may not be requested by the current subgrid in the column order. In this case, the object moves directly to the immediately next subgrid in the order that contains a transaction that requests it. The object waits there until the respective subgrid becomes the current one to execute.

Analysis. Suppose for now that $\xi \le n^2$. Consider a subgrid $G_{i,j} = (V', E')$, with ξ nodes $v_{i_1}, \ldots, v_{i_\xi}$. Consider an object $o_z \in O$. Let $X_y \in \{0, 1\}$ denote an event such that $X_y = 1$ if object o_z is used by a transaction in node n_y in $G_{i,j}$, and otherwise $X_y = 0$. Let $X = \sum_{v_y \in V'} X_y$. Denote $L = 9 \ln m$ and $U = 45 \ln m$.

Lemma 5.1. *For $\xi \le n^2$, $\Pr(L < X < U) \ge 1 - 2/m^4$.*

Proof. There are $\binom{w}{k}$ subsets of k objects. The number of these subsets containing object o_z is $\binom{w-1}{k-1}$. Therefore, the probability that node n_y picks object o_z is $\binom{w-1}{k-1}/\binom{w}{k} = k/w$, or equivalently,

$\Pr(X_y = 1) = k/w$. We have that $E[X_y] = k/w$, which implies that

$$\mu = E[X] = E\left[\sum_{v_y \in V'} X_y\right] = \sum_{v_y \in V'} E[X_y] = \frac{\xi k}{w} = 27 \ln m.$$

Let $\delta = 2/3$. Using the Chernoff bound in Equation 1 we get $\Pr(X \geq U) = \Pr(X \geq 45 \ln m) \leq e^{-4 \ln m} = 1/m^4$. Similarly, using the Chernoff bound in Equation 2 we get $\Pr(X \leq L) = \Pr(X \leq 9 \ln m) < e^{-4 \ln m} = 1/m^4$. By combining the two bounds, we get the desired result. □

Lemma 5.2. *For $\xi \leq n^2$, with probability at least $1 - 2/m$, each of the w objects is used by more than L and less than U transactions in each subgrid of G.*

Proof. From Lemma 5.1, any specific object o_z within a specific subgrid is used by more than L and less than U transactions with probability at least $1 - 2/m^4$. Considering now all subgrids, which do not exceed $n^2 \leq m^2$, we get that object o_z is used by more than L and less than U transactions with probability at least $1 - 2m^2/m^4 = 1 - 2/m^2$. Considering now all w objects, where $w \leq m$, we get that each of the w objects is used by more than L and less than U transactions in each subgrid of G, with probability at least $1 - 2m/m^2 = 1 - 2/m$. □

Lemma 5.3. *For $\xi \leq n^2/9$, any schedule requires at least $\Omega(n^2/\sqrt{\xi})$ time steps to execute all the transactions in G, with probability at least $1 - 2/m$.*

Proof. From Lemma 5.2, each object is requested by more than $L \geq 1$ transactions within each grid. Thus the object has to visit at least one node in all n^2/ξ subgrids. Consider now the *odd* subgrids $G_{i,j}$, where i and j are odd numbers. Note that there are at least $n^2/(4\xi)$ odd subgrids, since $\xi \leq n^2/9$. The shortest walk to connect the respective nodes within the odd subgrids is at least $(n^2/(4\xi) - 1)\sqrt{\xi} = \Omega(n^2/\sqrt{\xi})$ since the shortest walk has to cross *even* subgrids between any two odd subgrids with a path of length at least $\sqrt{\xi}$, and no odd subgrid is repeated in the best case. □

Lemma 5.4. *For $\xi \leq n^2$, our algorithm requires $O(kn^2 \log m/\sqrt{\xi})$ time steps to execute all the transactions in G, with probability at least $1 - 2/m$.*

Proof. The execution time is divided into phases of internal grid execution and phases of transferring the objects from one subgrid to the next.

From Lemma 5.2, each object is requested by less than U transactions within each grid with probability at least $1 - 2/m$ (and by more than L transactions). The diameter of a subgrid is less than $2\sqrt{\xi}$, and each transaction uses exactly k objects. Therefore, the weighted degree of the dependency graph is bounded by $2\sqrt{\xi}Uk = O(k\sqrt{\xi}\log m)$ which is also the time spent in each subgrid for the internal schedule. Since there are n^2/ξ subgrids, the total time spent in internal executions is $O((n^2/\xi) \cdot k\sqrt{\xi}\log m) = O(kn^2 \log m/\sqrt{\xi})$.

At most $2n = O(n)$ steps are needed to move the objects from their original positions to the transactions that request them in the first subgrid $G_{1,1}$. Once execution in the column order starts, the time to move the objects from one subgrid to the immediately next in the same column, is no more than $3\sqrt{\xi}$. This is also the same time to move the objects from the last subgrid of the current column to the first subgrid of the next column (since these subgrids are adjacent). Since there are in total n^2/ξ subgrids, it takes total time $3\sqrt{\xi}(n^2/\xi - 1) = O(n^2/\sqrt{\xi})$ time steps to transfer the objects between subgrids. Since $\xi \leq n^2$, this bound remains the same even if we consider the additional $O(n)$ time to initially position the objects in the first subgrid.

Combining the above bounds, we obtain that the total time spent is $O(kn^2 \log m/\sqrt{\xi})$. □

Theorem 5.5. *The grid scheduling algorithm provides an $O(k \log m)$ approximation to the optimal schedule with probability at least $1 - \Theta(1/m)$.*

Proof. For $\xi \leq n^2/9$, the result follows from Lemma 5.3 and Lemma 5.4.

Consider now the case $\xi > n^2/9$. Then, there are no more that 9 subgrids. The bounds with respect to U in Lemma 5.1 and Lemma 5.2 still hold. Therefore, each object is used by less than U transactions in each subgrid with probability at least $1 - 2/m$. Consequently, an object is used by less than $9U$ transactions in total in G. Thus, the maximum number of other transactions that a transaction conflicts with is less than $9Uk$ (with high probability).

We apply the greedy schedule in the whole G. If each object is requested by at most one transaction, then the execution takes trivially 1 time step, which is optimal. Suppose now that some object is requested by at least two transactions. Let τ be the maximum distance between any pair of transactions that request the same object. Since objects are originally positioned at some transaction that needs them, it takes at most τ time steps to position the objects in the first transaction according to the greedy schedule. In the dependency graph the maximum weighted degree is bounded by $9Uk\tau$. Therefore, the total time to execute the transactions is bounded by $\tau + 9Uk\tau + 1 = O(Uk\tau) = O(\tau k \log m)$. Since τ is a lower bound for the execution time, we obtain an $O(k \log m)$ approximation. □

6 CLUSTER GRAPH

Scheduling Problem. The communication graph $G = (V, E)$ consists of α sub-graphs (clusters) $C_1, \ldots, C_\alpha$ such that each C_i is a complete graph with β nodes and edge weights 1 (see left part of Figure 2). In each cluster C_i there is a designated bridge node such that between any pair of clusters there is a bridge edge connecting the respective bridge nodes. Each bridge edge has weight γ. We assume that $\gamma \geq \beta$, namely, the clusters are far apart from each other. Each node of G holds one transaction with k arbitrary objects from the set of transactions $O = \{o_1, \ldots, o_w\}$.

Algorithm. If each object is used only within one cluster, then we apply the greedy schedule within each cluster in parallel. Otherwise, if there are objects used by more than one cluster, the algorithm uses one of the two following approaches, whichever gives smaller execution time. Let $m = \max(n, w)$. Let σ denote the maximum number of clusters that any object is requested to.

Approach 1: We execute the transactions in G using the greedy schedule of Section 2.3.

Approach 2: The details of this approach appear in Algorithm 1. The algorithm consists of $\psi = \lceil \sigma/(24 \ln m) \rceil$ phases. We

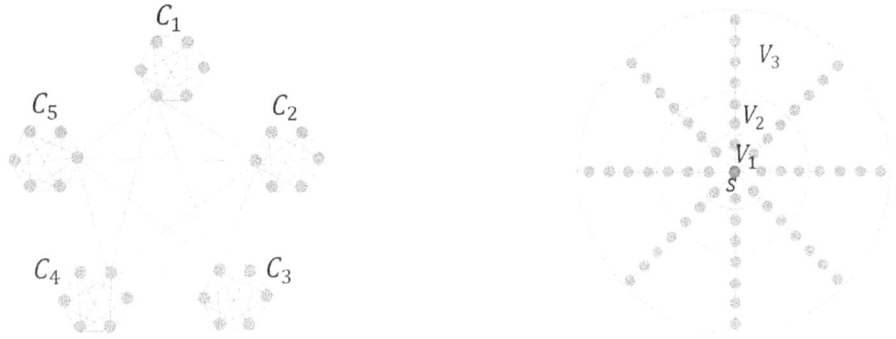

Figure 2: Left: A graph with 5 clusters where each cluster C_i is a complete graph with 6 nodes; links within clusters have weight 1, while links between clusters have weight γ. Right: A star graph with 8 rays, each ray consisting of 7 nodes; the rings depict the set of segments V_1, V_2, V_3.

assign each cluster to a uniform randomly chosen phase, and execute all the transactions of the cluster in that phase. A phase consists of $\zeta = 2 \cdot 40^k \lceil \ln^{k+1} m \rceil$ rounds, where each round has duration $\beta + \gamma + 2$ time steps. Within each round an object *gets active in some cluster*, namely, the object picks uniformly at random one of the clusters (if any) that has a transaction that needs it at that phase and the object moves to that cluster. A transaction is enabled when all its objects are activated (in the analysis we show that a transaction is enabled with certain probability). In a round, within each cluster, the enabled transactions execute using the greedy schedule of Section 2.3. The duration of a round guarantees that there is enough time to execute the enabled transactions within each cluster.

Analysis. If we use Approach 1, then in the transaction dependency graph the weighted degree of a transaction is bounded by $k\sigma\beta(\gamma + 2)$, since any pair of transactions in different clusters are at distance $\gamma + 2$ from each other (through the respective bridges), and a transaction requests k objects and each object visits at most $\sigma\beta$ transactions.

Lemma 6.1. *Using Approach 1, the algorithm executes all transaction within time $O(k\sigma\beta\gamma)$ time steps.*

Now, consider Approach 2. For any object $o_i \in O$, let Z_i denote the set of clusters that have at least one transaction that uses o_i. We have that $\sigma = \max_i |Z_i|$, and hence, $|Z_i| \leq \sigma$. Let Φ_p be the set of clusters which are randomly assigned in phase p. Let $S_{i,p} = Z_i \cap \Phi_p$ denote the clusters which use object o_i and are assigned in phase p. Let $\xi = \max_{i,p} |S_{i,p}|$ denote the maximum number of clusters assigned in any phase for any object.

Lemma 6.2. $\Pr(\xi > 40 \ln m) < 1/m$.

Proof. Since there are $\psi = \lceil \sigma/(24 \ln m) \rceil$ phases, each cluster in Z_i picks phase ρ with probability $1/\psi$. Therefore, the expected number of clusters in Z_i that pick phase j is $|Z_i|/\psi \leq \sigma/\psi \leq 24 \ln m$. From the Chernoff bound in Equation 1, by setting $\delta = 2/3$ we obtain $\Pr(|S_{i,p}| > 40 \ln m) < 1/m^3$. Since the number of phases is bounded by $\sigma \leq \alpha \leq n \leq m$, and the number of objects is bounded by $w \leq m$, the result follows by taking the union bound over all phases and objects. □

Algorithm 1: Cluster Schedule (Approach 2)

```
Input: Graph G with n nodes and clusters C_1, ..., C_α, where
       each transaction in G uses k objects in set
       O = {o_1, ..., o_w}
Output: An execution schedule for the transactions
Let Z_i be the set of clusters that have transactions that use o_i;
m ← max(n, w); σ ← max_i |Z_i|; ψ ← ⌈σ/(24 ln m)⌉;
  ζ ← 2 · 40^k ⌈ln^{k+1} m⌉;
//Assign each cluster to a phase
for j ← 1 to α do
    x ← random(1, ψ);
    Φ_x ← Φ_x ∪ C_j; //Φ_x are the clusters of phase x
//Execute the transactions in each phase
for phase p ← 1 to ψ do
    for round r ← 1 to ζ do
        foreach object o_i ∈ O do
            //A_i is the cluster in which object o_i activates
            A_i ← nil;
            if Z_i ∩ Φ_p ≠ ∅ then
                A_i ← a random uniformly chosen cluster from
                  set Z_i ∩ Φ_p;
                Move o_i to the bridge node of cluster A_i (if
                  A_i ≠ nil);
        E ← ∅; //set of enabled transactions
        foreach cluster C_y ∈ Φ_p do
            foreach transaction T ∈ C_y do
                if all objects of T have been activated in C_y
                  (A_i = C_y for each o_i ∈ T) then
                    E ← E ∪ {T};
        Execute all enabled transactions in E using the greedy
          schedule of Section 2.3;
```

Consider now some phase p, where $1 \leq p \leq \psi$. Let T_x denote a transaction that has not executed yet (in a previous phase) and is in one of the clusters, say C_y, assigned to phase p (namely, $C_y \in \Phi_p$).

Lemma 6.3. *If $\xi \leq 40 \ln m$, then with probability at least $1 - 1/m^2$, transaction T_x will execute in phase p.*

Proof. Within phase p, transaction T_x will execute in a round that it gets enabled. Let $o_{z_1}, \ldots, o_{z_k}$ denote the objects of transaction T_x. Each object o_{z_j} may be needed by up to ξ clusters within phase ϕ (recall that $|S_{z_j,p}| \leq \xi$). In a round, object o_{z_j} becomes active in cluster C_y with probability at least $1/\xi$, since the object picks randomly one of the at most ξ available clusters for it (in $S_{z_j,p}$). Thus, transaction T_x becomes enabled with probability at least $1/\xi^k$. For the number of rounds ζ, it holds that $\zeta \geq 2\xi^k \ln m$. Thus, T_x does not get enabled in phase ϕ with probability at most

$$\left(1 - \frac{1}{\xi^k}\right)^{\zeta} \leq \left(1 - \frac{1}{\xi^k}\right)^{2\xi^k \ln m} \leq \left(\frac{1}{e}\right)^{2 \ln m} = \frac{1}{m^2}.$$

□

Lemma 6.4. *Using Approach 2, with probability at least $1 - 2/m$, all transactions execute within time $O(\sigma\gamma 40^k \ln^k m)$.*

Proof. Each transaction belongs to some assigned cluster of some phase. Assuming that $\xi \leq 40 \ln m$, from Lemma 6.3 each transaction will execute at the phase its cluster gets assigned with probability at least $1 - 1/m^2$. Therefore, all $n \leq m$ transactions will finish by the end of the last phase, with probability at least $1 - m/m^2 = 1 - 1/m$. Combining this with Lemma 6.2, we get that with probability at least $1-2/m$ all transactions complete execution by the end of the last (ψth) phase.

It only remains to establish that a round has enough time steps to execute the transactions. Clearly, in a round there can be no more than β enabled transactions within a cluster. It takes $\gamma + 2$ steps to transfer objects from one cluster to another through the respective bridge nodes. Therefore, the duration of a round, $\beta + \gamma + 2$, suffices to execute all enabled transactions and then transfer them to the respective cluster that will be used in the next round. There are ζ rounds, and $\lceil \sigma/(24 \ln m) \rceil$ phases. Consequently, since $\beta \leq \gamma$, the total number of time steps is:

$$\lceil \sigma/(24 \ln m) \rceil \cdot \zeta \cdot (\beta + \gamma + 2) = O(\sigma\gamma 40^k \ln^k m).$$

□

Theorem 6.5 (cluster graph). *With probability at least $1 - \Theta(1/m)$, the cluster graph algorithm will execute all the transactions in time within $O(\min(k\beta, 40^k \ln^k m))$ factor from optimal.*

Proof. If each transaction is used in only one cluster, then with the same analysis as in Theorem 3.1, we obtain an $O(k)$ approximation to the optimal solution. In any other case, $\Omega(\sigma\gamma)$ is a lower bound, since each object will have to move to at least $\sigma - 1$ different clusters after the initial one, and it takes $\gamma + 2$ steps to reach a node from one cluster to another through the respective bridge nodes.

If Approach 1 is used, then from Lemma 6.1 the algorithm executes all transaction within time $O(k\sigma\beta\gamma)$ time steps, which is a $O(k\beta)$ factor from optimal.

If Approach 2 is used, then from Lemma 6.4 with probability at least $1 - 2/m$, all transactions execute in time $O(\sigma\gamma 40^k \ln^k m)$, which is a $O(40^k \ln^k m)$ factor from optimal.

Combining all the approximation factors from the three different cases we obtain the desired result, as needed. □

Note that the time bound of Theorem 6.5 may also be written as $O(\min(k\beta, \log_c^k m))$, where c is a constant such that $40 = 1/\ln c$. For constant k, Theorem 6.5 gives a poly-log approximation for the optimal execution time.

Corollary 6.6. *For constant k, with high probability the cluster graph algorithm will execute the transactions in time within a poly-log factor of m from optimal.*

7 STAR GRAPH

A star graph G consists of α rays where each ray is a line graph with β nodes (see right part of Figure 2). There is a *center node* s which is adjacent to the tip of each ray. Every edge in the star graph G has weight 1. We consider scheduling problems where each node holds a transaction that uses k arbitrary objects out of the object set $O = \{o_1, \ldots, o_w\}$.

A star graph can be analyzed similarly to the cluster graph (Section 6) in combination with the analysis of the line graph (Section 4). We divide each ray into $\eta = \lceil \log \beta \rceil$ segments (log is base 2) of exponentially increasing lengths. In particular, consider a ray r and assume that it contains nodes $v_1, \ldots, v_\beta$, such that v_1 is adjacent to the center s, while v_β is the furthest from s. The ith segment of r, where $1 \leq i \leq \eta$, consists of the nodes $v_{2^{i-1}}, \ldots, v_{2^i-1}$. Note that the last segment may be truncated. The ith segment, $i < \eta$, has 2^{i-1} nodes, while the last segment has no more than $\beta/2 + 1$ nodes. Every node of the ith segment is at distance at least 2^{i-1} from the center s.

We start the schedule by executing the transaction in the center node s. We then continue execution with the transactions in the rays. The execution in the rays is performed in different time periods, one period dedicated for each segment length. Let V_i denote the set of nodes of G which are in the ith segment in each ray (see the rings in the right part of Figure 2). There are η periods where the ith period is dedicated to execute the transactions in V_i.

Consider now the ith period. Each ray segment of V_i can be treated as if it is a cluster. The clusters (segments) communicate through s, with paths of length $2 \cdot 2^{i-1} = 2^i$ (from one tip of the segment to the next). This is similar to directly connecting two nodes of the clusters with a link (bridge edge) of weight $\gamma = 2^i$. Since each segment is a line graph, the transactions in it can execute sequentially in time no more that the length of each segment (see also Section 4). Let σ_i denote the maximum number of segments in V_i that an object has to visit due to transactions requesting it. If $\sigma_i = 1$ (i.e. an object visits one segment only), then we can execute the transactions in the segments in parallel in $O(2^i)$ time. So assume that $\sigma_i > 1$.

Using a greedy schedule similar to Approach 1 of the Cluster graph, we can prove (similar to Lemma 6.1) that the transactions in V_i can execute in time $O(k\sigma_i 2^{2i})$ (for size of cluster we have $O(2^i)$). When using the schedule similar to Approach 2 of the Cluster graph, we can prove (similar to Lemma 6.4) that with high probability, the transactions in V_i can execute in time $O(\sigma_i 2^i c^k \ln^k m)$, for some constant c, where $m = \max\{n, w\}$. Noting that $\Omega(\sigma_i 2^i)$ is a lower bound for the execution, we obtain that the transactions in V_i can execute in time which is within factor $O(\min(k2^i, c^k \ln^k m))$ from optimal. Since we have η periods, we get that the approximation factor is $O(\eta \max_i \min(k2^i, c^k \ln^k m)) = O(\log \beta \cdot \min(k\beta, c^k \ln^k m))$.

Theorem 7.1 (Star graph). *There is an execution schedule in the star graph, which with high probability all transactions execute within time $O(\log \beta \cdot \min(k\beta, c^k \ln^k m))$ factor from the optimal schedule, for some constant c.*

For constant k, Theorem 7.1 gives a schedule which is within a poly-log factor from optimal.

Corollary 7.2. *For constant k, there is a schedule in the star graph which with high probability the transactions execute within time a poly-log factor of β and m from optimal.*

8 A LOWER BOUND FOR EXECUTION TIME

The *shortest walk* of an object minimizes the total distance to visit all the transactions that require the object. The maximum shortest walk of any object is a lower bound for the execution time. Note that an optimal TSP tour length of an object is no more than twice its shortest walk length. In other words, half of the maximum optimal TSP tour length of any object is a lower bound on the execution time as well.

We use the probabilistic method to prove the existence of scheduling problem instances on graphs with n nodes, such that the optimal TSP tour length of any object is $O(n^{4/5})$ and yet, any possible schedule has execution time $\Omega(n^{4/5+1/40}/\log n)$. The problem instances use two objects per transaction. We consider two kinds of graphs, grid graphs and tree graphs. We first give the grid description and then provide the tree description which is a straightforward modification based on the grid.

8.1 Lower Bound on Grids

Consider a graph G which is a $s \times s\sqrt{s}$ grid of nodes, for a total of $n = s^{5/2}$ nodes (see left part of Figure 3). Divide the grid into s subgraphs (blocks) $H_1, \ldots, H_s$, each having s rows and $\sqrt{s}$ columns. (For simplicity assume that $\sqrt{s}$ is an integer.) Within each block, a node is connected to four neighbor nodes (up, down, left, right) by an edge of weight 1, except for the corner nodes or side nodes of the block which are connected to two or three neighbors within the same block, respectively. Adjacent blocks H_i and H_{i+1}, where $1 \le i < s$, are connected to each other through horizontal edges of weight s between two neighbor nodes.

Each node in H_i holds a transaction, for all $1 \le i \le s$. The set of objects is $O = A \cup B$, such that $A = \{a_1, \ldots, a_s\}$ and $B = \{b_1, \ldots, b_s\}$. Object $a_i \in A$ is used by all the transactions in block H_i, for any $1 \le i \le s$. Initially, each object a_i resides in the top left corner node in H_1. In each block H_i, each transaction picks randomly and uniformly one of the objects in B, for any $1 \le i \le s$. Initially, each object $b_i \in B$ resides in some node of H_1 that uses it (if any, otherwise in an arbitrary node of H_1).

We first bound the shortest walks (and hence, TSP tours) for the objects. Let ℓ_i denote the shortest path length (number of edges) for object $b_i \in B$. Let $\ell = \max_i \ell_i$. We can prove the following results:

Lemma 8.1. $\Pr(\ell \le 5s^2) > 1 - s^2 e^{-\sqrt{s}/12}$.

Lemma 8.2. *Any set of λ transactions, where $s^{3/8} \le \lambda \le s$ and $s \ge e^{7 \cdot 80}$, that execute in any block H_i during a period of s time steps, requires at least $\lambda^{3/5}$ unique objects of B, with probability at least $1 - s^{-s^{3/8}/161}$.*

The union probability of Lemmas 8.1 and 8.2 is fast reaching 1. Therefore, these two lemmas imply that for any large enough s there is a problem instance I_s such that the maximum path length of any object in B is bounded by $5s^2$. Since objects in A have shortest path length in their blocks of length at most $s\sqrt{s}$, the bound of $5s^2$ applies for all objects in O. Moreover, in any period of s time steps, sets of λ executed transactions use at least $\lambda^{3/5}$ different objects of B. Therefore, we have the following result:

Corollary 8.3. *For any $s \ge e^{7 \cdot 80}$, there is a problem instance I_s on the grid graph such that:*

- *the shortest path length of any object is at most $5s^2$, and*
- *any set of λ transactions within any block H_i, where $s^{3/8} \le \lambda \le s$, which execute during a period of s time steps, use at least $\lambda^{3/5}$ distinct objects of B.*

The following theorem applies to problem instances I_s as given by Corollary 8.3.

Theorem 8.4 (Execution Time Lower Bound). *There are problem instances on the grid graph with two objects per transaction, such that every execution schedule has duration $\Omega(s^{33/16}/\log s) = \Omega(n^{4/5+1/40}/\log n)$, and every object has TSP tour length at most $O(s^2) = O(n^{4/5})$.*

8.2 Lower Bound on Trees

The lower bound construction of graph G for trees is very similar to the lower bound construction on grids. The main difference is in the structure of the blocks $H_1, \ldots, H_s$ (see right part of Figure 3). Each block is a tree such that the leftmost column is connected, and each row is connected and attached to the leftmost column. The weights of the edges within the block are equal to 1. The trees of the adjacent blocks are connected through the topmost row, where the edge weight between two blocks is s.

All the results for the grid graph hold also verbatim for the tree graph. Therefore, similar to Theorem 8.4, we obtain that there are problem instances on the tree graph with two objects per transaction such that every execution schedule has duration $\Omega(n^{4/5+1/40}/\log n)$ and every object has TSP tour length $O(n^{4/5})$.

9 CONCLUSION

We presented a comprehensive set of bounds for various specialized network topologies. If the system is not completely synchronous, then our bounds are affected by the synchronicity factor (maximum delay divided by minimum delay). There are some open questions. It would be interesting to extend the results to the online setting, where the set of transactions to be executed are not known ahead of time. It would also be interesting to examine the impact of congestion, where network links have bounded capacity.

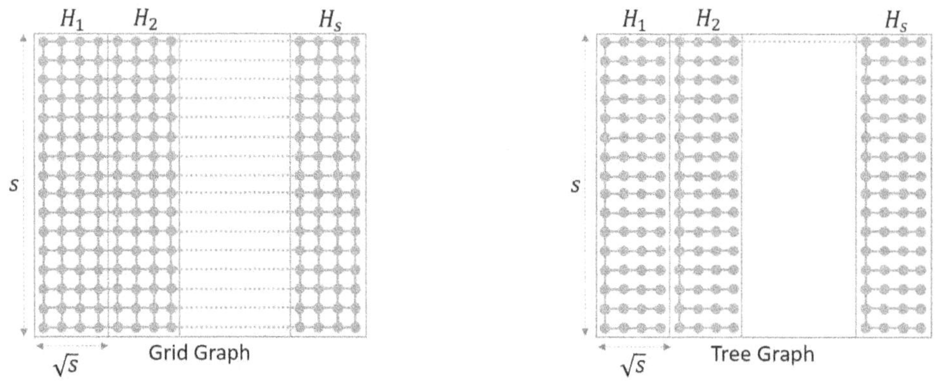

Figure 3: Left: grid graph; Right: tree graph.

ACKNOWLEDGMENTS

This work is supported by the National Science Foundation grants 1320835 and 1420673, and partly supported by the Serbian Ministry of Education & Science, through grants No. III 44009, and TR 32031.

REFERENCES

[1] Hagit Attiya, Leah Epstein, Hadas Shachnai, and Tami Tamir. 2010. Transactional Contention Management as a Non-Clairvoyant Scheduling Problem. *Algorithmica* 57, 1 (2010), 44–61.
[2] Robert L. Bocchino, Vikram S. Adve, and Bradford L. Chamberlain. 2008. Software transactional memory for large scale clusters. In *PPoPP.* 247–258.
[3] Costas Busch, Maurice Herlihy, Miroslav Popovic, and Gokarna Sharma. 2015. Impossibility Results for Distributed Transactional Memory. In *PODC.* 207–215. DOI:http://dx.doi.org/10.1145/2767386.2767433
[4] Harold W. Cain, Maged M. Michael, Brad Frey, Cathy May, Derek Williams, and Hung Q. Le. 2013. Robust architectural support for transactional memory in the power architecture. In *ISCA.* 225–236. DOI:http://dx.doi.org/10.1145/2485922.2485942
[5] Henri Casanova, Arnaud Legrand, and Yves Robert. 2008. *Parallel Algorithms* (1st ed.). Chapman & Hall/CRC.
[6] M. Y. Chan. 1989. Embedding of D-dimensional Grids into Optimal Hypercubes. In *SPAA.* 52–57. DOI:http://dx.doi.org/10.1145/72935.72941
[7] Paolo Costa, Hitesh Ballani, Kaveh Razavi, and Ian Kash. 2015. R2C2: A Network Stack for Rack-scale Computers. In *SIGCOMM.* 551–564. DOI:http://dx.doi.org/10.1145/2785956.2787492
[8] Maria Couceiro, Paolo Romano, Nuno Carvalho, and Luís Rodrigues. 2009. D2STM: Dependable Distributed Software Transactional Memory. In *PRDC.* 307–313.
[9] Aleksandar Dragojević, Rachid Guerraoui, Anmol V. Singh, and Vasu Singh. 2009. Preventing Versus Curing: Avoiding Conflicts in Transactional Memories. In *PODC.* 7–16. DOI:http://dx.doi.org/10.1145/1582716.1582725
[10] Michel Dubois, Murali Annavaram, and Per Stenstrm. 2012. *Parallel Computer Organization and Design.* Cambridge University Press, New York, NY, USA.
[11] Wilson W. L. Fung, Inderpreet Singh, Andrew Brownsword, and Tor M. Aamodt. 2011. Hardware transactional memory for GPU architectures. In *MICRO.* 296–307.
[12] Rachid Guerraoui, Maurice Herlihy, and Bastian Pochon. 2005. Toward a Theory of Transactional Contention Managers. In *PODC.* 258–264.
[13] Ruud Haring, Martin Ohmacht, Thomas Fox, Michael Gschwind, David Satterfield, Krishnan Sugavanam, Paul Coteus, Philip Heidelberger, Matthias Blumrich, Robert Wisniewski, Alan Gara, George Chiu, Peter Boyle, Norman Chist, and Changhoan Kim. 2012. The IBM Blue Gene/Q Compute Chip. *IEEE Micro* 32, 2 (2012), 48–60.
[14] Danny Hendler, Alex Naiman, Sebastiano Peluso, Francesco Quaglia, Paolo Romano, and Adi Suissa. 2013. Exploiting Locality in Lease-Based Replicated Transactional Memory via Task Migration. In *DISC.* 121–133.
[15] Maurice Herlihy and J. Eliot B. Moss. 1993. Transactional Memory: Architectural Support for Lock-free Data Structures. In *ISCA.* 289–300.
[16] Maurice Herlihy and Ye Sun. 2007. Distributed transactional memory for metric-space networks. *Distributed Computing* 20, 3 (2007), 195–208.
[17] William N. Scherer III and Michael L. Scott. 2005. Advanced contention management for dynamic software transactional memory. In *PODC.* 240–248.
[18] Intel. 2012. http://software.intel.com/en-us/blogs/2012/02/07/transactional-synchronization-in-haswell. (2012).
[19] Junwhan Kim and Binoy Ravindran. 2010. On Transactional Scheduling in Distributed Transactional Memory Systems. In *SSS.* 347–361.
[20] Junwhan Kim and B. Ravindran. 2013. Scheduling Transactions in Replicated Distributed Software Transactional Memory. In *CCGrid.* 227–234.
[21] F. Thomson Leighton. 1992. *Introduction to Parallel Algorithms and Architectures: Array, Trees, Hypercubes.* Morgan Kaufmann Publishers Inc., San Francisco, CA, USA.
[22] Dawei Li, Jie Wu, Zhiyong Liu, and Fa Zhang. 2017. Towards the Tradeoffs in Designing Data Center Network Architectures. *IEEE Transactions on Parallel and Distributed Systems* 28, 1 (Jan. 2017), 260–273. DOI:http://dx.doi.org/10.1109/TPDS.2016.2610970
[23] Kaloian Manassiev, Madalin Mihailescu, and Cristiana Amza. 2006. Exploiting Distributed Version Concurrency in a Transactional Memory Cluster. In *PPoPP.* 198–208.
[24] Marek Michalewicz, Lukasz Orlowski, and Yuefan Deng. 2015. Creating Interconnect Topologies by Algorithmic Edge Removal: MOD and SMOD Graphs. *Supercomput. Front. Innov.: Int. J.* 2, 4 (March 2015), 16–47.
[25] Takuya Nakaike, Rei Odaira, Matthew Gaudet, Maged M. Michael, and Hisanobu Tomari. 2015. Quantitative comparison of hardware transactional memory for Blue Gene/Q, zEnterprise EC12, Intel Core, and POWER8. In *ISCA.* 144–157. DOI:http://dx.doi.org/10.1145/2749469.2750403
[26] Roberto Palmieri, Sebastiano Peluso, and Binoy Ravindran. 2015. Transaction Execution Models in Partially Replicated Transactional Memory: The Case for Data-Flow and Control-Flow. In *Transactional Memory.* 341–366. DOI:http://dx.doi.org/10.1007/978-3-319-14720-8_16
[27] Sudeep Pasricha and Nikil Dutt. 2008. *On-Chip Communication Architectures: System on Chip Interconnect.* Morgan Kaufmann Publishers Inc., San Francisco, CA, USA.
[28] Sebastiano Peluso, Pedro Ruivo, Paolo Romano, Francesco Quaglia, and Luís Rodrigues. 2012. When Scalability Meets Consistency: Genuine Multiversion Update-Serializable Partial Data Replication. In *ICDCS.* 455–465. DOI:http://dx.doi.org/10.1109/ICDCS.2012.55
[29] Paolo Romano, Roberto Palmieri, Francesco Quaglia, Nuno Carvalho, and Luís Rodrigues. 2014. On speculative replication of transactional systems. *J. Comput. Syst. Sci.* 80, 1 (2014), 257–276. DOI:http://dx.doi.org/10.1016/j.jcss.2013.07.006
[30] Mohamed M. Saad and Binoy Ravindran. 2011. Snake: Control Flow Distributed Software Transactional Memory. In *SSS.* 238–252. DOI:http://dx.doi.org/10.1007/978-3-642-24550-3_19
[31] Gokarna Sharma and Costas Busch. 2012. A Competitive Analysis for Balanced Transactional Memory Workloads. *Algorithmica* 63, 1-2 (2012), 296–322.
[32] Gokarna Sharma and Costas Busch. 2012. Window-Based Greedy Contention Management for Transactional Memory: Theory and Practice. *Distrib. Comput.* 25, 3 (2012), 225–248.
[33] Gokarna Sharma and Costas Busch. 2014. Distributed Transactional Memory for General Networks. *Distrib. Comput.* 27, 5 (2014), 329–362.
[34] Nir Shavit and Dan Touitou. 1997. Software Transactional Memory. *Distrib. Comput.* 10, 2 (1997), 99–116.
[35] Richard M. Yoo and Hsien-Hsin S. Lee. 2008. Adaptive transaction scheduling for transactional memory systems. In *SPAA.* 169–178.
[36] Bo Zhang, Binoy Ravindran, and Roberto Palmieri. 2014. Distributed Transactional Contention Management as the Traveling Salesman Problem. In *SIROCCO.* 54–67. DOI:http://dx.doi.org/10.1007/978-3-319-09620-9_6

Is Our Model for Contention Resolution Wrong?

Confronting the Cost of Collisions*

William C. Anderton
Department of Computer Science and Engineering
Mississippi State University
MS, USA, 39762
wca36@msstate.edu

Maxwell Young
Department of Computer Science and Engineering
Mississippi State University
MS, USA, 39762
myoung@cse.msstate.edu

ABSTRACT

Randomized binary exponential backoff (BEB) is a popular algorithm for coordinating access to a shared channel. With an operational history exceeding four decades, BEB is currently an important component of several wireless standards.

Despite this track record, prior theoretical results indicate that under bursty traffic (1) BEB yields poor makespan and (2) superior algorithms are possible. To date, the degree to which these findings manifest in practice has not been resolved.

To address this issue, we examine one of the strongest cases against BEB: n packets that simultaneously begin contending for the wireless channel. Using Network Simulator 3, we compare against more recent algorithms that are inspired by BEB, but whose makespan guarantees are superior. Surprisingly, we discover that these newer algorithms significantly underperform.

Through further investigation, we identify as the culprit a flawed but common abstraction regarding the cost of collisions. Our experimental results are complemented by analytical arguments that the number of collisions – and not solely makespan – is an important metric to optimize. We argue that these findings have implications for the design of contention-resolution algorithms.

CCS CONCEPTS

• **Networks → Network algorithms**; • **Theory of computation → Distributed algorithms**;

KEYWORDS

Contention resolution; backoff; wireless; collisions

*This work is supported by the National Science Foundation grant CCF 1613772 and by a research gift from C Spire. William Cooper Anderton was an undergraduate student in the Computer Science and Engineering Department at Mississippi State University when this research was performed and this paper was accepted.

SPAA'17, July 24–26, 2017, Washington, DC, USA.

ACM ISBN 978-1-4503-4593-4/17/07...$15.00
https://doi.org/10.1145/3087556.3087584

1 INTRODUCTION

Randomized binary exponential backoff (***BEB***) plays a critical role in coordinating access by multiple devices to a shared communication medium. Given its importance, BEB has been studied at length and is known to yield good throughput under well-behaved traffic [3, 4, 15, 36, 37, 39, 44, 58, 66].

In contrast, when traffic is "bursty", BEB is suspected to perform sub-optimally. Under a ***single batch*** of n ***packets*** that simultaneously begin contending for the channel, Bender et al. [10] prove that BEB has $\Theta(n \log n)$ ***makespan*** (the amount of time until all packets are successfully transmitted). More recent algorithms have been proposed [10–13, 31, 32, 40] with improved makespan regardless of the traffic type.

Together, these results beg the question: *How do newer algorithms compare to BEB in practice?* Here, we make progress towards an answer by restricting ourselves to bursty traffic – in particular, the simplest instance of such traffic: a single burst (***batch***) of packets. This is a prominent case where BEB is anticipated to do poorly, and it should be a straightforward (if laborious) exercise to discover which of the following situations is true:

(1) A newer contention-resolution algorithm outperforms BEB.
(2) BEB outperforms newer contention-resolution algorithms.

Interestingly, neither of these outcomes is very palatable. In one form or another, BEB has operated in networks for over four decades and it remains an essential ingredient in several wireless standards. Bursty traffic can arise in practice [70, 74] and its impact has been examined [14, 19, 35, 64]. If (1) holds, then BEB is potentially in need of revision and the ramifications of this are hard to overstate.

Conversely, if (2) holds, then theoretical results are not translating into improved performance. At best, this is a matter of asymptotics. At worst, this indicates a problem with the abstract model upon which newer results are based. In this latter case, it is important to understand what assumptions are faulty so that the abstract model can be revised.

1.1 A Common Model

Given n stations, the problem of ***contention resolution*** addresses the amount of time until any one of the stations transmits alone. A natural consideration is the time until a subset of k stations each transmits alone; this often falls under the same label, but is also referred to as k-selection (see [6]).

We focus on the case of $k = n$. Here, much of the algorithmic work shares an abstract model. Three common assumptions are:

- *A0.* Time is discretized into ***slots***, each of which may accommodate a packet.
- *A1.* If a single packet is transmitted in a slot, the packet ***succeeds***, but ***failure*** occurs if two or more packets transmit simultaneously due to a ***collision***.
- *A2.* The failure of a transmission is known to the sender with negligible delay beyond the single slot in which the failure occurred.

Assumption A0 is near universal, but technically inaccurate for reasons discussed in Section 1.2. To summarize, slots in a contention window are used to obtain ownership of the channel. However, transmission of the full packet may occur past this contention-window slot while all other stations pause their execution. Therefore, this assumption is sufficiently close to reality that we should not expect performance to deviate greatly as a result.

Examples of assumption A1 abound (for example [6, 11–13, 20, 32, 48]), although variations exist. A compelling alternative is the signal-to-noise-plus-interference (SINR) model [7, 55] which is less strict about failure in the event of simultaneous transmissions. Another model that has received attention is the affectance model [43]. Nevertheless, these all share the reasonable assumption that simultaneous transmissions may negatively impact performance.

Assumption A2 is also widely adopted (see the same examples for A1) and implicitly addresses two quantities that affect performance: the time to transmit a packet, and the time to receive any feedback on success or failure. Assigning a delay of 1 slot to these quantities admits a model where the problem of contention resolution is treated separately from the functionality for collision detection. Such functionality is provided by a medium access control (MAC) protocol – of which the contention-resolution algorithm is only one component – and is not captured by A2.

1.1.1 Demonstrating a Flawed Assumption. Our main thesis is that A2 is flawed in the wireless setting; that is, the cost of failure is far more significant than the abstract model acknowledges. This is not a matter of minor adjustments to the assumption, or an artifact of hidden constants in the algorithms examined. Rather, the way in which failures – in particular, collisions – are detected cannot be isolated from the problem of contention resolution.

Several corollaries follow from this thesis, all indicating that accounting for such failures should be incorporated into algorithm design. For a range of wireless settings, contention-resolution algorithms that ignore this will likely not perform as advertised when deployed within a MAC protocol (see Section 5.2). We demonstrate this for the popular IEEE 802.11g standard.

1.2 Overview of BEB in IEEE 802.11g

To understand our findings, it is helpful to summarize IEEE 802.11g and how BEB operates within it. However, outside of this section and the description of our experimental setup, discussion of such aspects and terminology is kept to a minimum. Throughout, we will often use interchangeably the terms *packets* and *stations* depending on the context; the two uses are equivalent given that each station seeks to transmit a single packet in the single-batch case.

Exponential backoff [53] is a widely deployed algorithm for distributed multiple access. Informally, a backoff algorithm operates over a ***contention window (CW)*** wherein each ***station*** makes a single randomly-timed access attempt. In the event of two or more simultaneous attempts, the result is a collision and none of the stations succeed. Backoff seeks to avoid collisions by dynamically increasing the contention-window size such that stations succeed.

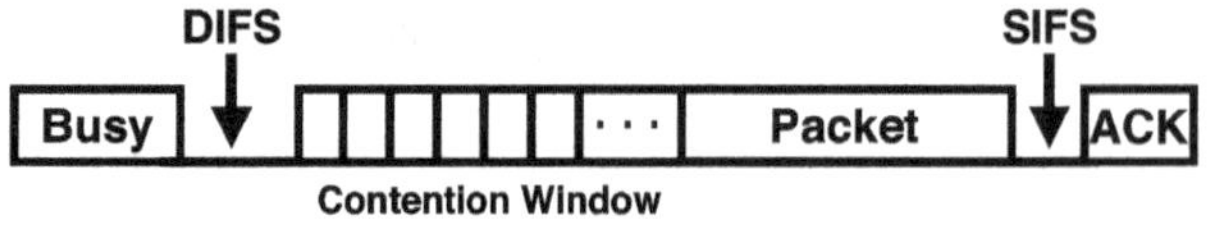

Figure 1: Illustration of DCF.

IEEE 802.11 handles contention resolution via the ***distributed coordination function (DCF)*** which employs BEB; as the name suggests, successive CWs double in size under BEB. The operation of DCF is summarized as follows. Prior to transmitting data, a station first senses the channel for a period of time known as a ***distributed inter-frame space (DIFS)***. If the channel is not in use over the DIFS, the station transmits its data; otherwise, it waits until the current transmission finishes and then initiates BEB.

For a contention window of size CW, a timer value is selected uniformly at random from $[0, CW - 1]$. So long as the channel is sensed to be idle, the timer counts down and, when it expires, the station transmits. However, if at any prior time the channel is sensed busy, BEB is *paused for the duration of the current transmission*, and then resumed (not restarted) after another DIFS.

After a station transmits, it awaits an **acknowledgement (ACK)** from the receiver. If the transmission was successful, then the receiver waits for a short amount of time known as a ***short inter-frame space (SIFS)*** – of shorter duration than a DIFS – before sending the ACK. Upon receiving an ACK, the station learns that its transmission was successful. Otherwise, the station waits for an ACK-timeout duration before *concluding that a collision occurred.*

This series of actions is referred to as ***collision detection***; the cost of which lies at the heart of our argument. If a collision is detected, then the station must attempt a retransmission via the same process with its CW doubled.

Figure 1 illustrates the operation of DCF. Note that both the transmission of data and the acknowledgement process occur "outside" of the backoff component of DCF. Yet, the focus of many algorithmic results is solely on the slots of this backoff component.

Finally, RTS/CTS (request-to-send and clear-to-send) is an optional mechanism. Informally, a station will send an RTS message and await an CTS message from the receiver prior to transmitting its data. Due to increased overhead, RTS/CTS is often only enabled for large packets. Therefore, we focus on the case where RTS/CTS is disabled, although our experiments show that our findings continue to hold when this mechanism is used (see Section 3.2).

2 EXPERIMENTAL SETUP

We employ Network Simulator 3 (NS3) [28] which is a widely used network simulation tool in the research community [72]. Our experimental setup is described here for the purposes of reproducibility.[1]

Our reasons for using NS3 are twofold. First, wireless communication is difficult to model and employing NS3 helps allay concerns that our findings are an artifact of poorly-modeled wireless effects.

[1]Our simulation code and data will be made available at www.maxwellyoung.net.

Parameter	Value
Data rate	54 Mbits/sec
Wireless specification	802.11g
Slot duration	9μs
SIFS	16μs
DIFS	34μs
ACK timeout	75μs
Preamble	20μs
Transport layer protocol	UDP
Packet overhead	64 bytes
Contention-window size min.	1
Contention-window size max.	1024
RTS/CTS	Off

Table 1: Parameter values used in our experiments.

Second, given the assumptions upon which contention-resolution algorithms are based, NS3 can reveal whether we are being led astray by an assumption that appears reasonable, but results in a *significant* discrepancy between theory and practice.

Table 1 provides our experimental parameters. Path-loss models with default parameters are known to be faithful [67] and, therefore, our experiments employ the log-distance propagation loss model in NS3. For transmission and reception of packets (frames), we use the YANS [50] module which provides an additive-interference model.

At the MAC layer, we make use of IEEE 802.11g and we implement changes to the growth of the contention window based on the algorithms we investigate. All experiments use IPv4 and UDP.

The amount of overhead for each packet is 64-bytes: 8 bytes for UDP, 20 bytes for IP, 8 bytes for an LLC/Snap header, and 28 bytes of additional overhead at the MAC layer.

The duration of an acknowledgement (ACK) timeout is specified by the most recent IEEE 802.11 standard[2] to be roughly the sum of a SIFS (16μs), standard slot time (9μs), and preamble (20μs); a total of 45μs. However, in practice, this is subject to tuning. In our experiments, an ACK-timeout below 55μs gave markedly poor performance; there is insufficient time for the ACK before the sender decides to retransmit. We use the default value of 75μs in NS3 since this is the same order of magnitude and performs well.

In our experiments, n stations are placed in a $40m \times 40m$ grid, and they are laid out starting at the south-west corner of the grid moving left to right by 1 meter increments, and then up when the current row is filled. A wireless access point (AP) is located (roughly) at the center of the grid. We do not simulate additional terrain or environmental phenomena; our goal is to test the performance under ideal conditions without complicating factors.

Our experiments are computationally intensive. Computing resources are provided by the High Performance Computing Collaboratory (HPC^2) at Mississippi State University. We employ four identical Linux (CentOS) systems, each with 16 processors (Intel Xeon CPU E5-2690, 2.90GHz) and 396 GB of memory.

[2]This is a large document; please see Section 10.3.2.9, page 1317 of [2].

When a station wishes to transmit a packet:

- Set the window size $W = 1$.
- Repeat until the packet is successfully transmitted:
  - Choose a slot t in the window uniformly at random. Try to transmit in slot t.
  - If the transmission failed, then: (i) wait until the end of the window, and (ii) set $W \leftarrow (1+r)W$.

Figure 2: Generic algorithm for LLB, LB, and BEB where $r = 1/\lg\lg W$, $r = 1/\lg W$, and $r = 1$, respectively.

3 A SINGLE BATCH

We examine a single batch of n packets that simultaneously begin their contention for the channel. As algorithmic competitors for BEB, we take Log-Backoff (LB), LogLog-Backoff (LLB) from [10] and Sawtooth-Backoff (STB) from [33, 41]. Both LLB and LB are closely related to BEB in that they execute using a CW that increases in size monotonically. The typical pseudocode for algorithms LLB, LB, and BEB is provided in Figure 2.

In contrast, STB is non-monotonic and executes over a doubly-nested loop. The outer loop sets the current window size W to be double that used in the preceding outer loop; this is like BEB. Additionally, for each such W, the inner loop executes over $\lg W$ windows of size $W, W/2, W/4, \ldots, 2$ and, for each window, a slot is chosen uniformly at random for the packet to transmit; this is the "backon" component of STB.

Algorithm	Contention-Window Slots
BEB	$\Theta(n \log n)$
Log-Backoff	$\Theta\left(\frac{n \log n}{\log\log n}\right)$
LogLog-Backoff	$\Theta\left(\frac{n \log\log n}{\log\log\log n}\right)$
Sawtooth-Backoff	$\Theta(n)$

Table 2: Known guarantees on the number of CW slots for a batch of n packets for BEB, LB, LLB [10] and STB [33, 41].

Our Metrics. For a single batch of n packets, algorithmic results address the number of slots required to complete all n packets. These slots correspond only to those belonging to contention windows, even though many results refer to this as makespan. To avoid confusion, we will refer to this metric more explicitly by ***contention-window slots (CW slots)***.

Table 2 summarizes the known with-high-probability[3] guarantees on CW slots. Note that LB, LLB, and STB each have superior guarantees over BEB, with STB achieving $\Theta(n)$ CW slots which is asymptotically optimal.

We also make use of a second metric. As described in Section 1.2, events occur outside of contention windows (such as SIFS, DIFS, full packet transmission, ACK timeouts). To denote the duration – including the time spent in contention windows – between when the single batch of packets arrives and when the last packet successfully transmits, we refer to ***total time***.[4]

[3]With probability at least $1 - 1/n^c$ for a tunable constant $c > 1$.

[4]We exclude the time required for a station to associate with the access point and ARP requests/replies. This would only (unfairly) strengthen the effects we observe.

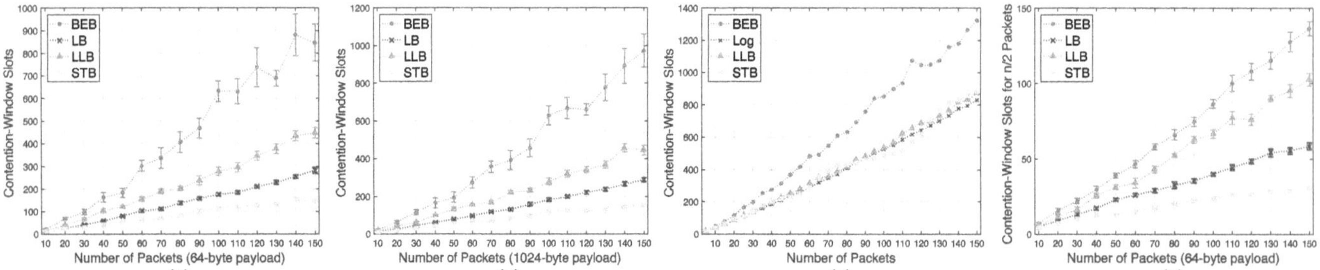

(3) (4) (5) (6)

Figures 3-6. Median values are reported: (3) and (4) CW slots from NS3 experiments with 30 trials for each value of n with 64B and 1024B payloads, respectively, (5) CW slots via Java simulation with 50 trials for each value of n, (6) number of CW slots required to finish $n/2$ packets from NS3 experiments with 20 trials for each value of n. Bars represent 95% confidence intervals.

3.1 Theory and Experiment

We begin by comparing the number of CW slots. The algorithms we investigate are designed to reduce this quantity since all slots in the abstract model occur within some contention window. Under this metric, LLB, LB, and STB are expected to outperform BEB.

Throughout, when we report on performance, we are referring to median values for $n = 150$. Percentage increases or decreases are calculated as $100 \times (A - B)/B$ where B is always the value for BEB (the "old" algorithm) and A corresponds to a value for one of LLB, LB, or STB (the "new" algorithms).

3.1.1 Contention-Window Slots. We provide results from our NS3 experiments using both small packets, with a 64-byte (B) payload, and large packets, with a 1024B payload.

Figures 3 and 4 illustrate our experimental findings with respect to CW slots.[5] The behavior generally agrees with theoretical predictions that each of LLB, LB, and STB should outperform BEB.

Interestingly, LLB incurs a greater number of CW slots than LB despite despite the former's better asymptotic guarantees. We suspect this is an artifact of hidden constants/scaling and evidence of this is presented later in Section 5.1.

Nevertheless, LLB, LB, and STB demonstrate improvements over BEB, giving a respective decrease of 49.4%, 68.2%, and 83.0%, respectively, with a 64B payload. Similarly, LLB, LB, STB demonstrate a respective decrease of 54.2%, 69.9%, 84.2% with a 1024B payload.

For comparison, Figure 5 depicts CW slots derived from a simple Java simulation that implements only the assumptions of the abstract model (it ignores wireless effects, details in the protocol stack, etc.). Our NS3 results also roughly agree with this data in terms of magnitude of values and the separation of BEB from the other algorithms; albeit, the performances of LLB, LB, and STB do not separate cleanly in this data.

Finally, Figure 6 presents the number of CW slots (for 64B) required to complete half the packets, and we make two observations. First, the remaining $n/2$ packets are responsible for the bulk of the CW slots. Second, the improvement over BEB decreases to 25.0%, 56.4%, and 77.7% for LLB, LB, and STB, respectively (and similarly for 1024B). This difference is due to "straggling" packets which survive until relatively large windows are reached. This impacts BEB more than other algorithms given its rapidly increasing window size (and, unlike STB, it does not have a "backon" component).

Result 1. *Experiment confirms theoretical predictions that LLB, LB, and STB outperform BEB with respect to CW slots.*

3.1.2 Total Time. It is tempting to consider the single-batch scenario settled. However, if we focus on the total time for both the 64B and 1024B payload sizes, then a different picture emerges.

The degree to which these newer algorithms outperform BEB is erased as seen from Figures 7 and 8. In fact, the order of performance is reversed with total time ordered from least to greatest as BEB, LLB, LB, STB. For 64B payloads, LLB, LB, and STB suffer an increase of 5.6%, 19.3%, and 26.5%, respectively, over BEB. For 1024B payloads, the increase is 9.1%, 25.4%, and 35.4%, respectively. Notably, the larger packet size seems to favor BEB.

What about the time until $n/2$ packets are successfully transmitted? Perhaps newer algorithms do better for the bulk of packets, but suffer from a few stragglers? Interestingly, Figures 9 and 10 suggest that this is not the case. Indeed, for a 64B payload, BEB performs even better over LLB, LB, and STB with the latter exhibiting an increase of 13.1%, 17.3%, 25.4%, respectively. Similarly, for 1024B, the percent increase is 10.1%, 16.6%, 26.6%, respectively.

Result 2. *In comparison to BEB, the total time for each of LLB, LB, and STB is significantly worse.*

These findings are troubling since, arguably, total time is a more important performance metric in practice than CW slots. Critically, we note that this behavior is detected only through the use of NS3; it is not apparent from the simpler Java simulation. What is the cause of this phenomenon?

3.2 The Cost of Collisions

The number of ACK timeouts per station provides an important hint. As Figure 8 shows, the newer algorithms are incurring substantially more ACK timeouts which, in turn, corresponds to more (re)transmissions.

This evidence points to collisions as the main culprit. In particular, the way in which collision detection is performed means that each collision is costly in terms of time. In support of our claim, we decompose this delay into three portions using BEB (for $n = 150$) as an example throughout:

[5] The following common approach is used to identify outliers in our data. Let Δ be the distance between the first and third quartiles. Any data point that falls outside a distance of 1.5Δ from the median is declared an outlier. We emphasize this results in very few points being discarded; for example, only a *single* n value for our 64B experiments had 5 outliers (out of 30 trials), and the vast a majority had none.

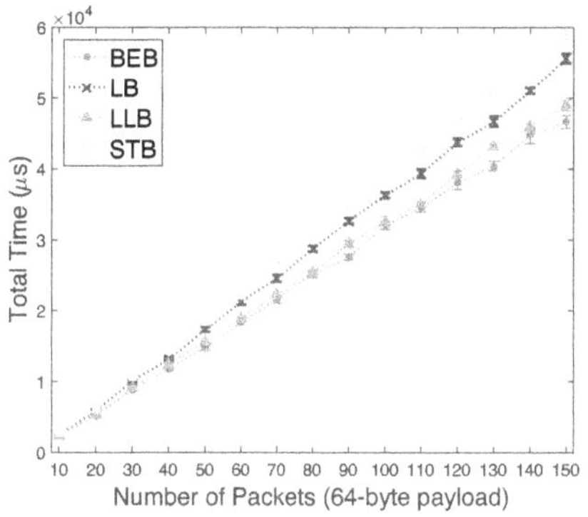

(7)

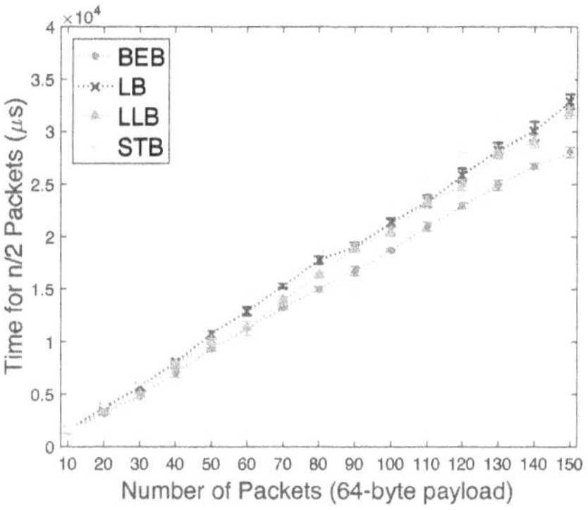

(9)

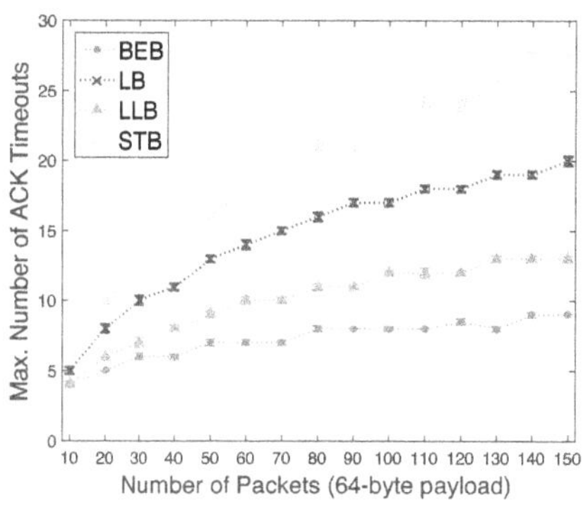

(11)

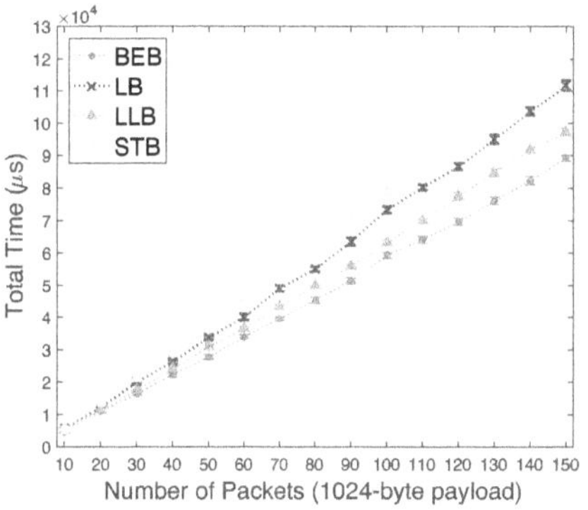

(8)

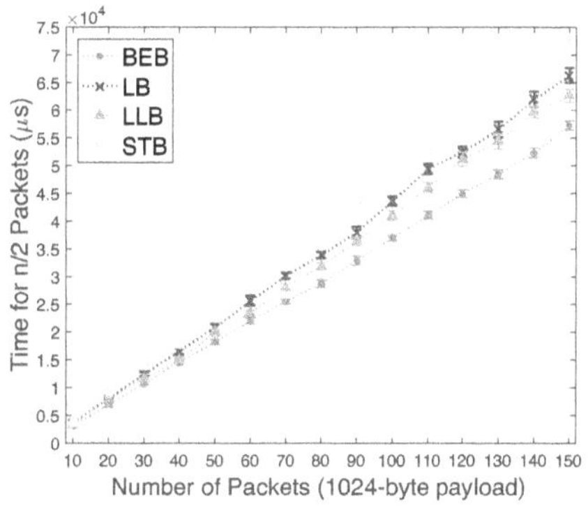

(10)

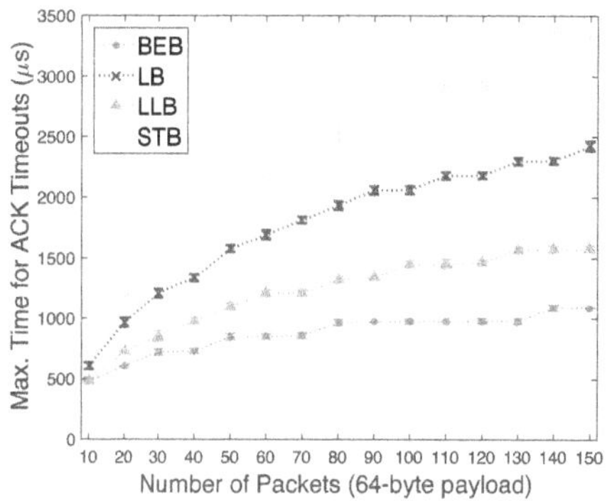

(12)

Figures 7-12. NS3 results with the median reported from 30 trials for each value of n: (7) and (8) total time for 64B and 1024B payloads, (9) and (10) time required to complete $n/2$ packets with a 64B payload and 1024B payloads, (11) the maximum number of ACK timeouts per station over all stations with a 64B payload, (12) corresponding time spent waiting for ACK timeouts by the station with maximum ACK timeouts. Data plotted with 95% confidence intervals.

(I) Transmission Time. (Re)transmissions are expensive. A packet of size 128B (64B payload plus 64B overhead) requires roughly $19\mu s$ plus the associated $20\mu s$ preamble. The maximum number of ACK timeouts for BEB – and, thus, the number of collisions – experienced by an unlucky station is 9.

Most collisions should involve only a handful of stations given the growth of CWs. (Why? Recall from Figure 6 that $n/2$ packets require the vast majority of CW slots to finish. These $n/2$ packets succeed only in larger windows – of size roughly equal to or greater than n for BEB – and do not finish immediately due to collisions, each of which should involve only a few stations given such window sizes). If two stations are involved in each collision, this results in $75(9/2)$ non-overlapping (or ***disjoint***) collisions, for an aggregate duration of roughly $75(9/2)(19\mu s + 20\mu s) = 13,163\mu s$.[6]

(II) ACK Timeouts. Given a collision, the AP fails to obtain the transmission and the corresponding stations incur an ACK timeout before concluding that a collision occurred. This delay is significant – roughly $1,100\mu s$ for BEB with $n = 150$ (see Figure 12) – but an order-of-magnitude less than the transmission time.

(III) Contention-Window Slots. BEB incurs 886 CW slots for $n = 150$, each of duration $9\mu s$, spent in CWs which yields $7,974\mu s$.

[6]We do not add the time for the final/successful transmissions (this would only increase the value); our focus is on the transmissions associated with collisions.

For BEB at $n = 150$, these three values yield a very conservative lower bound on the total time of $22,237\mu s$; for instance, we have not accounted for the SIFS and DIFS. This back-of-the-envelope calculation conforms to the magnitude of values observed in Figure 7, and it highlights two important facts. First, both transmission time and CW slots contribute significantly to total time, with ACK timeouts being a distant third. Second, collisions greatly impact total time – far more than CW slots – by forcing retransmissions.

Underlining this second point, we note that the transmission time for the 1024B payload is larger at roughly $75(9/2)(161\mu s + 20\mu s) = 61,088\mu s$.[7] By comparison, the CW slots contribute roughly $973 \times 9\mu s = 8,757\mu s$.

ACK Timeout ≈ Collision. It is true that not all ACK timeouts necessarily imply that the corresponding packet suffered a collision. For example, an ACK might be lost due to wireless effects even if the packet was transmitted without any collision. Note that, in such a case, the sending station still diagnoses that a collision has occurred and so the same costs described in (I)-(III) hold.

For our simple NS3 setup, virtually all ACK failures result from a collision. This is evident from Figure 13 which illustrates a trial with $n = 20$ under BEB using a 64B payload. Collisions occur only when

[7]The number of ACK timeouts for 1024B is roughly the same, even though packet size has increased. This aligns with our findings in Section 4.

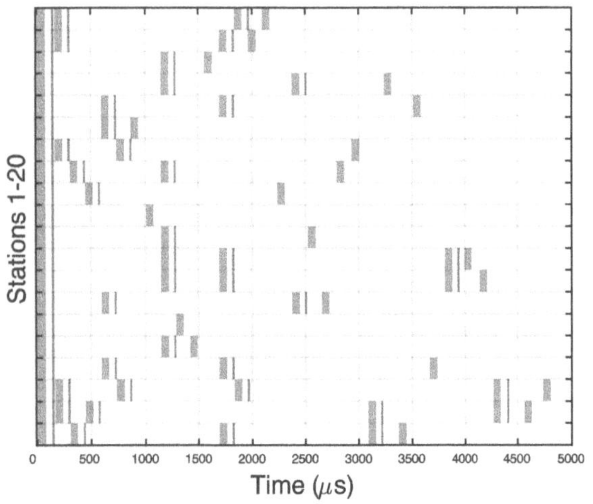

Figure 13. Execution of BEB with 20 stations.

two or more stations transmit (duration of transmission denoted by a thick blue line) at the same time and the result is an ACK timeout event (indicated by a thin red line); in all other cases, the transmission is successful and the corresponding ACK is received.

Disjoint Collisions. We observe that the total time does not grow linearly with the maximum number of ACK timeouts – equivalently, collisions – experienced by a station. Under LB, an unlucky station suffers roughly twice the number of ACK timeouts, but the total time of LB is not twice that of BEB.

Why? Consider n stations where each collision involves only two stations. Then, there are $n/2$ disjoint collisions and each is added to the total time. In contrast, consider the opposite extreme where all n stations transmit at the same time and collide. Then, there is one collision which adds only a single failed transmission time to the total time.

The number of stations involved in a single collision is larger for algorithms whose CWs grow more slowly, such as LB and LLB. For STB, a similar phenomenon is at work; the backon component yields collisions involving many stations. That is, LB, LLB, and STB are closer to the second case, while BEB is closer to the first.

From our experimental results, we see assumption A2 is not accurate with regards to the cost of failure:

Result 3. *The impact from collision detection is not properly accounted for by A2. This impact is primarily a function of:*

- *transmission time, and*
- *time spent in contention windows,*

with the former dominating.

RTS/CTS. Although it is not examined in detail in our work, we briefly remark on the use of RTS/CTS. When enabled, stations can experience collisions among the RTS frames (instead of the packets). These are smaller in size (20B), but the remainder of the total-time calculation remains the same, and additional time is incurred due to additional inter-frame spaces and the transmission of CTS frames.

For very large packets, we may expect RTS/CTS to mitigate the transmission-time cost, but not for small to medium-sized packets where the overhead from this mechanism might even cause worse performance. Ultimately, we observe the same qualitative behavior when RTS/CTS is enabled. For example, without RTS/CTS, recall from Section 3.1.2 that the total time for LLB (BEB's closest competitor) increases by 5.6% and 9.1% for the 64B and 1024B, respectively, over BEB. With RTS/CTS, the increases are 10.7% and 7.5%.

3.2.1 Backing Off Slowly is Bad. The reason for the discrepancy between theory and experiment is now apparent. LLB increases each successive contention window by a smaller amount than BEB; in other words, LLB is *backing off more slowly*; the same is true of LB. Informally, this slower-backoff behavior is the reason behind the superior number of CW slots for LB and LLB since they linger in CWs where the contention is "just right" for a significant fraction of the packets to succeed. However, backing off slowly also inflicts a greater number of collisions.

Note that BEB backs off faster, jumping away from such favorable contention windows and thus incurring many empty slots. This is undesirable from the perspective of optimizing the number of CW slots. However, the result is fewer collisions. Given the empirical results, this appears to be a favorable tradeoff.

We explicitly note that LLB backs off faster than LB. In this way, LLB is "closer" to BEB and, therefore, is not outperformed as badly as illustrated in Figures 7 and 8.

Result 4. *For algorithm design, optimizing CW slots at the expense of increased collisions is a poor design choice.*

Can we quantify the tradeoff between CW slots and collisions? From our discussion in Section 3.2, the total time for an algorithm A, denoted by $\mathcal{T}_A$, is approximated as:

$$\mathcal{T}_A = C_A \cdot (P + \rho) + \mathcal{W}_A \cdot s$$

where C_A is the number of disjoint collisions, P is the transmission time for a packet, ρ is the preamble duration, $\mathcal{W}_A$ is the corresponding number of CW slots, and s is the duration of a slot.

Abstracting further, we may treat ρ and s as constants to get:

$$\mathcal{T}_A = \Theta\left(C_A \cdot P + \mathcal{W}_A\right)$$

In other words, total time depends on the number of disjoint collisions (which depends on n) — each of which has a severity that depends on P — and the number of CW slots (which depends on n).

How does P behave? We assume it is proportional to packet size. For small values of n, it seems reasonable to consider $P = \Theta(1)$. However, if we are interested in the asymptotic behavior of $\mathcal{T}_A$, then P should not be treated as a constant. Arguably, as n scales, the number of bits required to address devices must also increase, and it is not uncommon to assume P scales as the logarithm of n.

Previous results have already established $\mathcal{W}_A$, so the parameter of interest is C_A, which we investigate next.

4 BOUNDS ON COLLISIONS

In order to provide additional support for our empirical findings, we derive asymptotic bounds on C_A. In comparison to BEB, we demonstrate that STB is asymptotically equal while both LLB and LB suffer from asymptotically more disjoint collisions.

Our arguments are couched in terms of packets and slots, but what follows is a balls-into-bins analysis. To bound C_A, we are interested in the number of bins (where bins make up the slots in a CW) that contain two or more balls; this is a disjoint collision (or just a *collision*). The second column of Table 3 presents our results.

4.1 Upper Bounding Collisions in BEB

CLAIM 1. *For a single batch of n packets, with high probability the number of collisions for BEB is $O(n)$.*

PROOF. In the execution of BEB, consider a contention window of size $n2^i$ for an integer $i \geq 0$; let the windows be indexed by i. Note that up to window $i = 0$, we have $O(n)$ collisions since there are $O(n)$ slots by the sum of a geometric series.

Let the indicator random variable $X_j = 1$ if slot j in window i is a collision; $X_j = 0$ otherwise. We map this to a balls-and-bins problem, where a ball corresponds to a packet and a bin corresponds to a slot in a contention window.

$$Pr[X_j = 1] = O\left(\binom{n}{2}\left(\frac{1}{n2^i}\right)^2\left(1 - \frac{1}{n2^i}\right)^{n-2}\right) = O\left(\frac{1}{2^{2i}}\right)$$

Pessimistically, assume n balls are dropped in each consecutive window i; in actuality, packets finish over these windows and reduce the probability of collisions. Let $L_i = \sum_{j=1}^{n2^i} X_j$ be the number of collisions in window i. By linearity of expectation:

$$E[L_i] = \sum_{j=1}^{n2^i} E\left[X_j\right] = O\left(\frac{n}{2^i}\right)$$

Using the method of bounded differences [29], w.h.p. L_i is tightly bounded to its expectation. By [10], w.h.p. BEB finishes within $m = O(\lg\lg n)$ windows and so $C_{BEB} = \sum_{i=0}^{m} L_i = O(n/2^i) = O(n)$. □

4.2 Lower Bounding Collisions in LLB and LB

The specification of LLB analyzed here is slightly different from the description in Section 3; the contention window size doubles, but each such window of size w is repeated for $\lg\lg w$ iterations. With respect to CW slots and disjoint collisions, this is asymptotically equivalent to the strictly monotonic version described earlier [10].

The window size of interest is $\Theta(n/\lg\lg\lg n)$, since LLB finishes within a window of this magnitude [10]. We first prove an upper bound of $o(n)$ successes in a single execution of this window. This allows us to claim $\Omega(\lg\lg n)$ iterations exist where $\Theta(n)$ packets remain unfinished. Next, we prove that for each such iteration, $\Omega(n/\lg\lg\lg n)$ collisions occur yielding a total of $\Omega(n\lg\lg n/\lg\lg\lg n)$ collisions.

LEMMA 4.1. *Assume ϵn packets and a CW of size $cn/\lg\lg\lg n$ for a sufficiently large constant $\epsilon \leq 1$ and sufficiently small constant $c > 0$. With high probability, at most $O(n/(\lg\lg n)^d)$ packets succeed in the CW for a constant $d > 1$ depending on ϵ and c.*

PROOF. Let $Y_j = 1$ if a packet succeeds in slot j, otherwise $Y_j = 0$. We have:

$$\begin{aligned} Pr[Y_j = 1] &= \binom{\epsilon n}{1}\left(\frac{\lg\lg\lg n}{cn}\right)\left(1 - \frac{\lg\lg\lg n}{cn}\right)^{\epsilon n-1} \\ &\leq \frac{\epsilon\lg\lg\lg n}{c(\lg\lg n)^{\epsilon\lg(e)/c}} \leq O\left(\frac{1}{c(\lg\lg n)^d}\right) \end{aligned}$$

for a constant $d > 1$ where the last line follows from noting that $\epsilon\lg(e)/c > 1$ for a sufficiently large constant ϵ and a sufficiently small constant $c > 0$. Let $Y = \sum_j Y_j$, then:

$$E[Y] = O\left(\frac{n}{(\lg\lg n)^d}\right)$$

By the method of bounded differences, w.h.p. this is tight. □

CLAIM 2. *For a single batch of n packets, with high probability LOGLOG-BACKOFF experiences $\Omega\left(\frac{n\lg\lg n}{\lg\lg\lg n}\right)$ collisions.*

PROOF. We focus on a contention window w of size $cn/\lg\lg\lg n$ for a sufficiently small constant $c > 0$. Conservatively, we do not count collisions prior to this window (counting these can only improve our result).

Prior to this window, w.h.p. $o(n)$ packets have succeeded. To see this, note that w.h.p. no packet finishes prior to a window of size $\Theta(n/\lg n)$. The number of intervening windows before reaching size $cn/\lg\lg\lg n$ is less than $\lg\lg n$. Pessimistically assume each intervening window has size $cn/\lg\lg\lg n$, then each results in $O(n/(\lg\lg n)^d)$ successful packets w.h.p. by Lemma 4.1 for $d > 1$. Each such intervening window executes $O(\lg\lg n)$ times. Therefore, the total number of packets finished is still $O(n/(\lg\lg n)^{d'})$ for a constant d' depending only d, and so $\Omega(n)$ packets remain.

In this window, assume that ϵn packets exist for some constant $\epsilon > 0$. Let $X_j = 1$ if slot j contains a collision; otherwise, $X_j = 0$. Then we have $Pr[X_j = 1]$:

$$\begin{aligned} &= 1 - \sum_{k=0}^{1}\binom{\epsilon n}{k}\left(\frac{\lg\lg\lg n}{cn}\right)^k\left(1 - \frac{\lg\lg\lg n}{cn}\right)^{\epsilon n-k} \\ &\geq 1 - \left(1 - \frac{\lg\lg\lg n}{cn}\right)^{\epsilon n} - \frac{\epsilon\lg\lg\lg n}{c}\left(1 - \frac{\lg\lg\lg n}{cn}\right)^{\epsilon n-1} \\ &\geq 1 - O\left(\frac{\epsilon\lg\lg\lg n}{c\,(\lg\lg n)^{2\epsilon\lg(e)/c}}\right) \text{by Taylor series} \\ &= \Omega(1) \end{aligned}$$

Let $X = \sum_j X_j$. The expected number of collisions over the contention window w is:

$$E[X] = \sum_j E[X_j] = \Omega\left(\frac{cn}{\lg\lg\lg n}\right)$$

By the method of bounded differences, w.h.p. this is tight.

The window w is executed $\lg\lg(cn/\lg\lg\lg n) = \Omega(\lg\lg n)$ times. By Lemma 4.1, $O(n/(\log\log n)^d)$ packets are succeeding in each such execution for some constant $d > 1$ given c is sufficiently small. Thus, there will be at least ϵn packets remaining in each execution for some sufficiently small constant $\epsilon > 0$. By the above lower bound on the number of collisions, w.h.p. this results in $C_{LLB} = \Omega(cn\lg\lg n/\lg\lg\lg n)$ collisions. □

An argument similar to that used to support Claim 2 yields:

CLAIM 3. *For a single batch of n packets, with high probability LOG-BACKOFF experiences $\Omega\left(\frac{n\lg n}{\lg\lg n}\right)$ collisions.*

4.3 Upper Bounding Collisions in STB

For a single batch of n packets, it is known that w.h.p. STB has $\mathcal{W}_{STB} = O(n)$ and this is a trivial upper bound on the number of collisions. A straightforward argument allows us to derive a lower bound of $\Omega(n)$.

CLAIM 4. *For a single batch of n packets, with high probability SAWTOOTH-BACKOFF experiences $\Omega(n)$ collisions.*

PROOF. Consider a window of size $n/8$. The total number of slots up to the end of this window (including all the backon windows) is less than $n/2$; therefore, more than $n/2$ packets have not finished by

Algorithm A	Num. of Collisions C_A	Total Time $\mathcal{T}_A$
BEB	$O(n)$	$O(n \cdot P + n \log n)$
LB	$\Theta\left(\frac{n \log n}{\log \log n}\right)$	$\Omega\left(\frac{n \log n}{\log \log n} \cdot P\right)$
LLB	$\Theta\left(\frac{n \log \log n}{\log \log \log n}\right)$	$\Omega\left(\frac{n \log \log n}{\log \log \log n} \cdot P\right)$
STB	$\Theta(n)$	$\Theta(n \cdot P)$

Table 3: Asymptotic bounds on collisions and total time.

this point. In the next window, which has size $n/4$, the probability of a collision is constant. Therefore, the expected number of collisions is $C_{STB} = \Omega(n)$ and this is tight by the method of bounded differences. □

Although BEB and STB are asymptotically equal in the number of collisions suffered, we expect the hidden constant in the big-O notation for STB to be larger due to the backon component. We consider this question, amongst others involving asymptotic performance, later in Section 5.1.

4.4 Asymptotic Behavior of Total Time

Plugging in the results from Section 4, our formula for $\mathcal{T}_A = \Theta(C_A \cdot P + \mathcal{W}_A)$ yields the third column Table 3.

Recall that for small n, treating P as a constant is reasonable. However, for large values of n, one may argue that P ought to be treated as a slowly growing function of n, such as $\Omega(\log n)$. In this case, we note that both $\mathcal{T}_{LB}$ and $\mathcal{T}_{LLB}$ exceed $\mathcal{T}_{BEB}$ asymptotically. In fact, even a smaller bound $P = \omega(\lg n \lg\lg\lg n / \lg\lg n)$ is sufficient to yield this asymptotic behavior.

> **Result 5.** *Theoretical bounds on total time imply that LLB and LB should underperform both BEB and STB for sufficiently large n and P.*

This analysis offers support for our conjecture that the number of collisions is an important metric – perhaps more so than the number of CW slots – when it comes to the design of contention-resolution algorithms.

With respect to total time, recall that in Section 3.1.2 an increase in packet size was seen to favor BEB over LLB, the latter being the closest competitor to BEB in our experiments (although, STB is asymptotically superior and we address this issue in Section 5.1). This aligns with the above discussion. Furthermore, as empirical support for our claim, we use NS3 to examine the relative performance of these two algorithms as packet size increases in Figure 14.

As the packet size grows, LLB performs increasingly worse than BEB. We fit a linear regression model of LLB - BEB on the number of packets. This fitting model implies that when the payload size increases by 100B, the average increase in total time for LLB is roughly 700μs more than the increase experienced by BEB. The increase rate is statistically significant (p-value less than 0.001).

5 DISCUSSION

We have presented our evidence for why assumption A2 is flawed. In this section, we conclude our argument by considering a few unresolved observations, and discussing the legitimacy of our findings in the context of other protocols/networks.

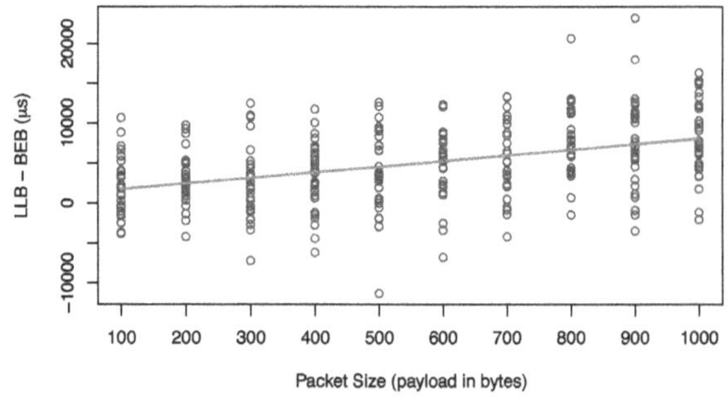

Figure 14. The difference in total time between LLB and BEB for $n = 150$ as packet size increases (30 trials per size).

5.1 Oddities at Small Scale

A few issues remain unaddressed:

(i) In terms of asymptotic bounds on CW slots, the newer algorithms are ordered "best" to "worst" as STB, LLB, and LB. Yet, Figure 3 shows LB outperforming LLB.
(ii) In terms of asymptotic bounds on the number of collisions, the newer algorithms are ordered "best" to "worst" as STB, LLB, and LB. Yet, Figure 11 shows STB suffering a larger number of ACK timeouts than both LLB and LB.
(iii) BEB and STB have an asymptotically equal number of collisions, but STB is expected to suffer more and this is supported by Figures 7 and 8. What is the long-term behavior?

As we discussed previously in Section 2, NS3 is valuable in revealing flawed assumptions via the extraordinary level of detail it provides; however, this also prevents experimentation with NS3 at larger scales. We attempt to shed light on (i) - (iii) by examining larger values of n in order to see if our predictions are met, and we employ our simpler Java simulation for this task.

To address (i), we look at $n \leq 10^5$ as plotted in Figure 15. Now we see that STB performs best in terms of CW slots, and that LLB is indeed outperforming LB. This supports prior theoretical results for CW slots given sufficiently large n.

In regard to (ii), we again take $n \leq 10^5$ and plot the ratio of collisions: LB vs STB and LLB vs STB. Figure 16 demonstrates that the number of collisions for LB quickly exceeds STB. The tougher case is LLB which only begins to evidence a greater number of collisions at approximately $n = 30,000$. Nevertheless, we observe a trend towards exceeding parity, as expected. Moreover, the sluggish trajectory is not surprising given our analysis in Section 4.

Finally, for (iii), we observe that the number of collisions for STB is larger than BEB by roughly a factor of 2 over this large range of n. Note that the plot of BEB/STB is (roughly) flat, as expected from our asymptotic analysis of collisions.

5.2 Scope of Our Findings

In this section, we consider to what extent our findings are an artifact of IEEE 802.11g, and whether LB, LLB, STB might do better inside other protocols.

IEEE 802.11g uses a truncated BEB, is this significant? In our experiments, the maximum congestion-window size is 1024 which differs from the abstract model where no such upper bound exists. However, even for $n = 150$, this maximum is rarely reached during

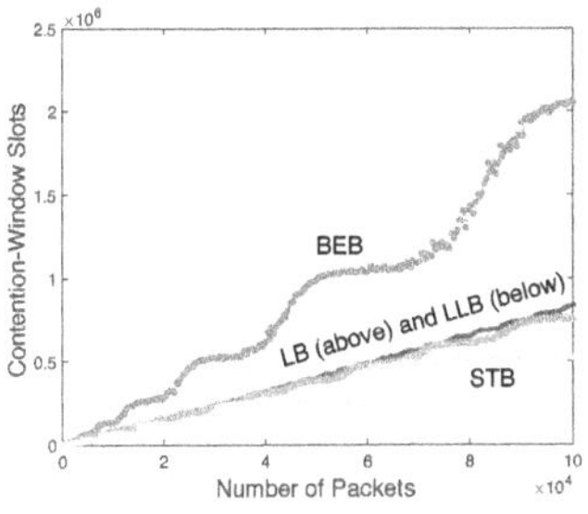

(15)

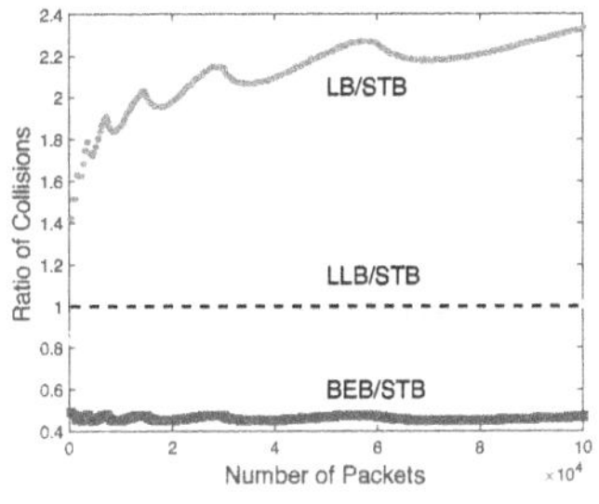

(16)

Figures 15-16. Results from Java simulation results with 200 **trials per** $n \leq 10^6$ **in increments of** 400**: (15) CW slots with median values plotted, (16) ratio of median number of collisions for BEB, LLB, and LB versus STB.**

an execution of BEB and this does not seem to have any noticeable impact on the trend observed in Figures 3 and 4.

What if smaller packets are used? During a collision, the time lost to transmitting would be reduced. In an extreme case, if the transmission of a packet fit within a slot, this would align more closely with A2.

Due to overhead, packet size has a lower bound in IEEE 802.11. Additionally, in NS3, there is a 12-byte payload minimum which translates into a minimum packet size of 76 bytes for our experiments.[8] The same qualitative behavior is observed in terms of CW slots and total time. For total time, the increase by LLB, LB, and STB is 6.6%, 17.8%, and 20.6%.

Alternatives to 802.11 might see more significant decreases. However, there is a tradeoff for *any* protocol. A smaller packet implies a reduced payload given the need for control information (for routing, error-detection, etc.) and this means that throughput is degraded.

What if the ACK-timeout duration is reduced or acknowledgements are removed altogether? This would also bring us closer to A2, although less so than having smaller packets – the delay from ACK timeouts does not dominate as discussed in Section 3.2. In our experiments, the ACK-timeout is $75\mu s$ (recall Section 2) and values below this threshold will lead a station to consider its packet lost before the ACK can be received. This results in unnecessary retransmissions and, ultimately, poor throughput.

Totally removing acknowledgements (or some form of feedback) is difficult in many settings since, arguably, they are critical to *any* protocol that provides reliability; more so when transmissions are subject to disruption by other stations over a shared channel.

To what extent do these findings generalize to other protocols? We do *not* claim that our findings hold for all protocols. If (a) sufficiently small packets are feasible *and* (b) reliability is not paramount, performance should align better with theoretical guarantees derived from using assumption A2.

We *do* claim that the performance of how collision detection is performed – and which is ignored under A2 – seems common to several other protocols. Examples include members of the IEEE 802.11 family, IEEE 802.15.4 (for low-rate wireless networks), and IEEE 802.16 (WiMax). These employ some form of backoff and, regarding (a) and (b), each incurs header bloat and uses feedback via acknowledgements or a timeout to determine success or failure. This is a significant slice of current wireless standards that, given our findings, could *potentially* experience performance degradation if BEB is replaced by LB, LLB, and STB.

Result 6. *Designing contention-resolution algorithms using assumption A2 seems likely to translate into poor performance in practice for a range of protocols.*

A setting where the abstract model may be valid is networks of multi-antenna devices. If a collision can be detected more efficiently, perhaps by a separate antenna, the delay due to transmission time can be reduced. Canceling the signal at the sending device so that other transmissions (that would cause the collision) can be detected is challenging. However, this is possible (for an interesting application, see [38]) and such schemes have been proposed using multiple-input multiple-output (MIMO) antenna technology [46, 54].

Finally, we note that future standards may satisfy (a) and (b). A possible setting is the Internet-of-Things (IoT); for example, [9] characterizes IoT transmissions as "small" and "intermittent, delay-sensitive, and short-lived". To reduce delay, the authors argue for removing much of the control messaging used by traditional MAC protocols. Therefore, this setting seems more closely aligned with A2. However, using this same logic, [9] also argues for the removal of any backoff-like contention-resolution mechanism. Nevertheless, these standards are in flux and we may see protocols that avoid the issues we identify here.

6 A SIZE-ESTIMATION APPROACH

Given our findings, we consider an alternative approach to the design of contention-resolution algorithms. Feedback is a useful ingredient as it allows stations to tune their sending probabilities. For windowed algorithms, this feedback is obtained via collisions which, as we have seen, is costly.

To avoid this problem, we examine a different approach. Stations first estimate n and then execute ***fixed backoff*** where the size of each contention window is set to this one-time estimate. So long as the algorithm avoids an underestimate, the large number of collisions incurred by BEB, LB, LLB and STB should be avoided.

Prior work in [13, 16–18, 40] examines size estimation as a means for improving performance, although the methods and traffic assumptions differ (see Section 7). Our goal is to experiment with an algorithm for a single batch of arrivals, whose specification lends itself to implementation, and whose improved performance manifests for practical values of n.

To this end, the size-estimation component of our algorithm, Best-of-k, specified in Figure 17 is a variant of a well-known "folklore" result (see [45]). For $k = \Theta(1)$, a significant overestimate may occur, but the amount by which it can underestimate is bounded; w.h.p. the estimate will be $\Omega(n/\log n)$.

Dummy packets of 28 bytes are used in the size-estimation phase; this small size is possible because the packets contain none of the upper-layer headers (these are not used in our IEEE 802.11 experiments since routing requires the upper-layer headers). Execution

[8]This is set within the UdpClient class of NS3.

Best-of-k
- For $i = 0$ to 10, do:
  - For each of k consecutive slots, do:
    - With probability $\frac{1}{2^i}$, send dummy packet; otherwise, sense the channel.
  - If channel is clear for more than $k/2$ slots, then:
    - $W \leftarrow 2^i$
    - Terminate and start executing fixed backoff using a contention window of size W

Figure 17. The Best-of-k contention-resolution algorithm.

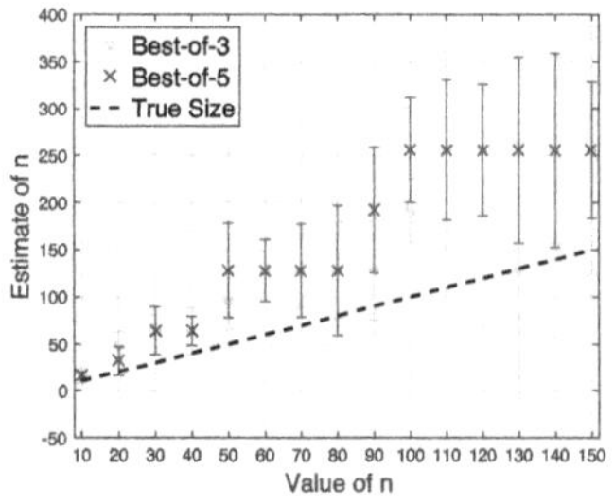

(18)

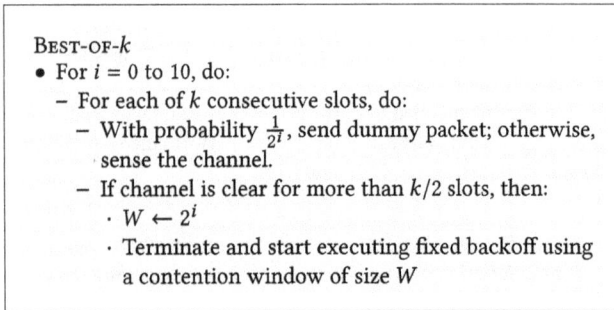

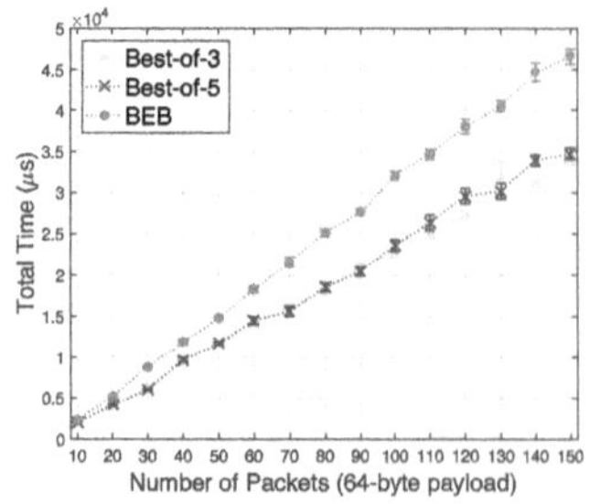

(19)

Figures 18-19. Median values are reported for NS3 results with 20 trials for each value of n: (18) estimation values, (19) total time (μs) for BEB, Best-of-3, and Best-of-5. Bars represent 95% confidence intervals.

proceeds in $35\mu s$ rounds during which a dummy packet is transmitted. Channel sensing is used to distinguish "busy" from "clear"; therefore, we avoid any collision detection and the use of any acknowledgements for these dummy packets.

As expected, for $k = 3$, the estimates are somewhat noisy, but this improves with $k = 5$; see Figure 18. Notably, increasing k does not significantly impact performance since the time required to run the size-estimation component is negligible (less than 5%) of the total time; instead, running fixed backoff is the main source of delay. We also observe that only overestimates occur, as predicted. This has the benefit of yielding good performance due to the lack of collisions. As demonstrated by Figure 19, both versions of the size-estimation approach outperform BEB, with $k = 3$ and $k = 5$ yielding a decrease in total time of 26.0% and 24.7% respectively.

Result 7. *A size-estimation approach to designing contention-resolution algorithms appears promising.*

Finally, we note our assumption of synchronization might not hold in a dynamic setting. Furthermore, a real-world deployment would likely be "messier" with respect to interference from other devices/networks running different applications, impact of terrain and weather on transmissions, etc. and our simple setup does not account for such phenomena. Additional methods would be needed to address these issues. However, as an initial proof of concept, our results suggest an approach to contention resolution that *may* compete with BEB in the single-batch case.

7 RELATED WORK

Exponential backoff has been studied under Poisson-distributed traffic (see [36, 37, 44, 58]). Guarantees on stability are known [3, 4, 39], and under saturated conditions [15].

There is a vast body of literature addressing the performance of IEEE 802.11 (for examples, see [1, 26, 30, 51, 56, 71, 75]). There are several results that focus on the performance of BEB within IEEE 802.11; however, they do not address issues of the abstract model, bursty traffic, or the newer algorithms examined here. Nonetheless, we summarize those works that are most closely related.

Under continuous traffic, windowed backoff schemes are examined in [68] with a focus on the tradeoff between throughput and fairness. The authors focus on polynomial backoff and demonstrate via analysis and NS2 (the predecessor to NS3) simulations that quadratic backoff is a good candidate with respect to both metrics.

Work in [49] addresses saturated throughput (each station always has a packet ready to be transmitted) of exponential backoff; roughly, this is the maximum throughput under stable packet arrival rates. Custom simulations are used to confirm these findings.

In [65], the authors propose backoff algorithms where the size of the contention window is modified by a small constant factor based on the number of successful transmissions observed. NS2 simulations are used to demonstrate improvements over BEB within 802.11 for a steady stream of packets (i.e. non-bursty traffic).

Lastly, in [52], the authors examine a variation on backoff where the contention window increases multiplicatively by the logarithm of the current window size (confusingly, also referred to as "logarithmic backoff"). NS2 simulations imply an advantage to their variant over BEB within IEEE 802.11, again for non-bursty traffic.

In regard to size-estimation approaches, there is prior work on tuning the probability of a transmission under Poisson-distributed traffic [34, 42, 47]. Subsequent work in [17, 18] offers (custom) simulation and analytical results on performance improvements assuming that the transmission interval for which a station backs off is sampled from the geometric distribution. In [16], the authors propose a method for estimating the number of contending stations under saturation conditions, and custom simulations demonstrate the accuracy of this approach. More recent work in [13] proposes a size-estimation scheme with small (asymptotic) sending and listening costs; however, no experimental results are provided and implementing this scheme may be challenging.

Regarding the time required for a single successful transmission, [73] demonstrates a lower-bound of $\Omega(\log \log n)$. In different communication models, other bounds are known [31, 32].

A class of tree-based algorithms for contention resolution is proposed in [20]. Work in [11] addresses the case of heterogeneous packet sizes. The case where packets can arrive dynamically is examined in [22, 23, 27].

Energy efficiency is important to multiple access in many low-power wireless networks [13, 21, 45]. When the communication channel is subject to adversarial disruption, several results address the challenge of multiple access [8, 12, 57, 59–63, 69]. Finally, deterministic broadcast protocols have also received significant attention [5, 24, 25].

8 CONCLUDING REMARKS

We have presented evidence that a model commonly used for designing contention-resolution algorithms is not adequately accounting for the cost of collisions. A number of interesting questions remain.

In terms of analytical work, we have argued for why collisions matter at small scale and asymptotically, but what is the optimal tradeoff between collisions and CW slots? Does this change when we consider multi-hop networks or long-lived bursty traffic? Assuming that this tradeoff is known, can we design algorithms that leverage this information?

Regarding future experimental work, it may be of interest to perform a similar evaluation on other protocols. For example, much of what is examined in this work seems to apply to contention resolution under IEEE 802.15.4, and we expect collisions to be similarly expensive. However, are there subtle differences in the protocol that allow IEEE 802.15.4 to avoid collisions? What about newer wireless standards? Understanding any such behavior may aid in the design of future contention-resolution algorithms.

Acknowledgements. We are grateful to David Dampier for providing us with access to the computing resources at HPC^2.

REFERENCES

[1] 2014. How Penalty Leads to Improvement: A Measurement Study of Wireless Backoff in IEEE 802.11 Networks. *Computer Networks* 75, Part A (2014), 37 – 57.

[2] 2016. IEEE Standard for Information Technology–Telecommunications and Information Exchange Between Systems Local and Metropolitan Area Networks – Specific Requirements - Part 11: Wireless LAN Medium Access Control (MAC) and Physical Layer (PHY) Specifications. *IEEE Std 802.11-2016 (Revision of IEEE Std 802.11-2012)* (2016), 1–3534.

[3] H. Al-Ammal, A. L. Goldberg, and P. MacKenzie. 2001. An Improved Stability Bound for Binary Exponential Backoff. *Theory of Computing Systems* 34, 3 (2001), 229–244.

[4] Hesham Al-Ammal, Leslie Ann Goldberg, and Phil MacKenzie. 2000. *Binary Exponential Backoff Is Stable for High Arrival Rates.* Springer Berlin Heidelberg, Berlin, Heidelberg, 169–180.

[5] Lakshmi Anantharamu, Bogdan S. Chlebus, and Mariusz A. Rokicki. 2009. Adversarial Multiple Access Channel with Individual Injection Rates. In *Proceedings of the 13th International Conference on Principles of Distributed Systems (OPODIS).* 174–188.

[6] Antonio Fernández Anta and Miguel A. Mosteiro. 2010. *Contention Resolution in Multiple-Access Channels: k-Selection in Radio Networks.* 378–388.

[7] Chen Avin, Yuval Emek, Erez Kantor, Zvi Lotker, David Peleg, and Liam Roditty. 2009. SINR Diagrams: Towards Algorithmically Usable SINR Models of Wireless Networks. In *Proceedings of the 28th ACM Symposium on Principles of Distributed Computing (PODC).*

[8] Baruch Awerbuch, Andrea Richa, and Christian Scheideler. 2008. A Jamming-Resistant MAC Protocol for Single-Hop Wireless Networks. In *Proceedings of the 27th ACM Symposium on Principles of Distributed Computing (PODC).* 45–54.

[9] A. Bakshi, L. Chen, K. Srinivasan, C. E. Koksal, and A. Eryilmaz. 2016. EMIT: An Efficient MAC Paradigm for the Internet of Things. In *IEEE INFOCOM 2016 - The 35th Annual IEEE International Conference on Computer Communications.* 1–9.

[10] Michael A. Bender, Martin Farach-Colton, Simai He, Bradley C. Kuszmaul, and Charles E. Leiserson. 2005. Adversarial Contention Resolution for Simple Channels. In *Proc. 17th Annual ACM Symposium on Parallelism in Algorithms and Architectures (SPAA).* 325–332.

[11] Michael A. Bender, Jeremy T. Fineman, and Seth Gilbert. 2006. Contention Resolution with Heterogeneous Job Sizes. In *Proceedings of the 14th Conference on Annual European Symposium (ESA).* 112–123.

[12] Michael A. Bender, Jeremy T. Fineman, Seth Gilbert, and Maxwell Young. 2016. How to Scale Exponential Backoff: Constant Throughput, Polylog Access Attempts, and Robustness. In *Proceedings of the Twenty-Seventh Annual ACM-SIAM Symposium on Discrete Algorithms (SODA '16).* 636–654.

[13] Michael A. Bender, Tsvi Kopelowitz, Seth Pettie, and Maxwell Young. 2016. Contention Resolution with Log-logstar Channel Accesses. In *Proceedings of the 48th Annual ACM SIGACT Symposium on Theory of Computing (STOC 2016).* 499–508.

[14] B. N. Bhandari, R. V. Raja Kumar, and S. L. Maskara. 2008. Performance of IEEE 802.16 MAC Layer Protocol Under Conditions of Self-Similar Traffic. In *TENCON 2008 - 2008 IEEE Region 10 Conference.* 1–4.

[15] Giuseppe Bianchi. 2006. Performance Analysis of the IEEE 802.11 Distributed Coordination Function. *IEEE Journal on Selected Areas in Communications* 18, 3 (Sept. 2006), 535–547.

[16] Giuseppe Bianchi and Ilenia Tinnirello. 2003. Kalman Filter Estimation of the Number of Competing Terminals in an IEEE 802.11 Network. In *Proceedings of the 22nd Annual Joint Conference of the IEEE Computer and Communications Societies (INFOCOM)*, Vol. 2. 844–852.

[17] Frederico Cali, Marco Conti, and Enrico Gregori. 2000. Dynamic Tuning of the IEEE 802.11 Protocol to Achieve a Theoretical Throughput Limit. *IEEE/ACM Transactions on Networking* 8, 6 (2000), 785–799.

[18] Frederico Cali, Marco Conti, and Enrico Gregori. 2000. IEEE 802.11 Protocol: Design and Performance Evaluation of an Adaptive Backoff Mechanism. *IEEE Journal on Selected Areas in Communications* 18, 9 (2000), 1774–1786.

[19] B. Canberk and S. Oktug. 2009. Self Similarity Analysis and Modeling of VoIP Traffic under Wireless Heterogeneous Network Environment. In *Telecommunications, 2009. AICT '09. Fifth Advanced International Conference on.* 76–82.

[20] J. Capetanakis. 2006. Tree Algorithms for Packet Broadcast Channels. *IEEE Trans. Inf. Theor.* 25, 5 (Sept. 2006), 505–515.

[21] Yi-Jun Chang, Tsvi Kopelowitz, Seth Pettie, Ruosong Wang, and Wei Zhan. 2017. Exponential Separations in the Energy Complexity of Leader Election . In *Proceedings of the Annual ACM SIGACT Symposium on Theory of Computing (STOC).*

[22] Bogdan S. Chlebus, Leszek Gasieniec, Dariusz R. Kowalski, and Tomasz Radzik. 2005. On the Wake-up Problem in Radio Networks. In *Proceedings of the 32nd International Colloquium on Automata, Languages and Programming (ICALP).* 347–359.

[23] Bogdan S. Chlebus and Dariusz R. Kowalski. 2004. A Better Wake-up in Radio Networks. In *Proceedings of 23rd ACM Symposium on Principles of Distributed Computing (PODC).* 266–274.

[24] Bogdan S. Chlebus, Dariusz R. Kowalski, and Mariusz A. Rokicki. 2006. Adversarial queuing on the multiple-access channel. In *Proc. Twenty-Fifth Annual ACM Symposium on Principles of Distributed Computing (PODC.* 92–101.

[25] Bogdan S. Chlebus, Dariusz R. Kowalski, and Mariusz A. Rokicki. 2012. Adversarial Queuing on the Multiple Access Channel. *ACM Transactions on Algorithms* 8, 1 (2012), 5.

[26] Nakjung Choi, Yongho Seok, Yanghee Choi, Sungmann Kim, and Hanwook Jung. 2005. P-DCF: Enhanced Backoff Scheme for the IEEE 802.11 DCF. In *2005 IEEE 61st Vehicular Technology Conference*, Vol. 3.

[27] Marek Chrobak, Leszek Gasieniec, and Dariusz R. Kowalski. 2007. The Wake-Up Problem in Multihop Radio Networks. *SIAM J. Comput.* 36, 5 (2007), 1453–1471.

[28] NS-3 Consortium. 2017. NS-3. (2017). www.nsnam.org.

[29] Devdatt Dubhashi and Alessandro Panconesi. 2009. *Concentration of Measure for the Analysis of Randomized Algorithms* (1st ed.). Cambridge University Press.

[30] Andrezj Duda. 2008. Understanding the Performance of 802.11 Networks. In *2008 IEEE 19th International Symposium on Personal, Indoor and Mobile Radio Communications.* 1–6.

[31] Jeremy T. Fineman, Seth Gilbert, Fabian Kuhn, and Calvin Newport. 2016. Contention Resolution on a Fading Channel. In *Proceedings of the 2016 ACM Symposium on Principles of Distributed Computing (PODC '16).* 155–164.

[32] Jeremy T. Fineman, Calvin Newport, and Tonghe Wang. 2016. Contention Resolution on Multiple Channels with Collision Detection. In *Proceedings of the 2016 ACM Symposium on Principles of Distributed Computing (PODC '16).* 175–184.

[33] Mihály Geréb-Graus and Thanasis Tsantilas. 1992. Efficient Optical Communication in Parallel Computers. In *Proceedings 4th Annual ACM Symposium on Parallel Algorithms and Architectures (SPAA).* 41–48.

[34] Mario Gerla and Leonard Kleinrock. 1977. Closed Loop Stability Controls for S-aloha Satellite Communications. In *Proceedings of the Fifth Symposium on Data Communications (SIGCOMM '77).* 2.10–2.19.

[35] Sayeed Ghani. 2010. The Impact of Self Similar Traffic on Wireless LAN. In *Proceedings of the 6th International Wireless Communications and Mobile Computing Conference (IWCMC '10).* 52–56.

[36] L.A. Goldberg and P.D. MacKenzie. 1996. *Analysis of Practical Backoff Protocols for Contention Resolution with Multiple Servers.* ALCOM-IT Technical Report TR-074-96. Warwick. http://www.dcs.warwick.ac.uk/~leslie/alcompapers/contention.ps.

[37] Leslie Ann Goldberg, Philip D. MacKenzie, Mike Paterson, and Aravind Srinivasan. 2000. Contention Resolution with Constant Expected Delay. 47, 6 (Nov. 2000), 1048–1096.

[38] Shyamnath Gollakota, Haitham Hassanieh, Benjamin Ransford, Dina Katabi, and Kevin Fu. 2011. They Can Hear Your Heartbeats: Non-invasive Security for Implantable Medical Devices. In *Proceedings of the ACM SIGCOMM 2011 Conference (SIGCOMM '11).* 2–13.

[39] Jonathan Goodman, Albert G. Greenberg, Neal Madras, and Peter March. 1988. Stability of Binary Exponential Backoff. *J. ACM* 35, 3 (June 1988), 579–602.

[40] Albert G. Greenberg, Philippe Flajolet, and Richard E. Ladner. 1987. Estimating the Multiplicities of Conflicts to Speed Their Resolution in Multiple Access Channels. *JACM* 34, 2 (April 1987), 289–325.

[41] Ronald I. Greenberg and Charles E. Leiserson. 1985. Randomized Routing on Fat-Trees. In *Proc. of the Symp. on Foundations of Computer Science (FOCS).* 241–249.

[42] Bruce Hajek and Timothy van Loon. 1982. Decentralized Dynamic Control of a Multiaccess Broadcast Channel. *IEEE Trans. Automat. Control* 27, 3 (1982), 559–569.

[43] Magnús M. Halldórsson and Roger Wattenhofer. 2009. *Wireless Communication Is in APX.* Springer Berlin Heidelberg, Berlin, Heidelberg, 525–536.

[44] Johan Hastad, Tom Leighton, and Brian Rogoff. 1987. Analysis of Backoff Protocols for Multiple Access Channels. In *STOC'87*. New York, New York, 241–253.

[45] Tomasz Jurdziński, Mirosław Kutyłowski, and Jan Zatopiański. 2002. Energy-Efficient Size Approximation of Radio Networks with No Collision Detection. In *Proceedings of the 8th Annual International Conference (COCOON)*. 279–289.

[46] M. Kawahara, K. Nishimori, T. Hiraguri, and H. Makino. 2014. A New Propagation Model for Collision Detection using MIMO Transmission in Wireless LAN Systems. In *2014 IEEE International Workshop on Electromagnetics (iWEM)*. 34–35.

[47] Frank P. Kelly. 1985. Stochastic Models of Computer Communication Systems. *Journal of the Royal Statistical Society, Series B (Methodological)* 47, 3 (1985), 379–395.

[48] J. Komlos and A. Greenberg. 2006. An Asymptotically Fast Nonadaptive Algorithm for Conflict Resolution in Multiple-access Channels. *IEEE Trans. Inf. Theor.* 31, 2 (Sept. 2006), 302–306.

[49] Byung-Jae Kwak, Nah-Oak Song, and L. E. Miller. 2005. Performance Analysis of Exponential Backoff. *IEEE/ACM Transactions on Networking* 13, 2 (2005), 343–355.

[50] Mathieu Lacage and Thomas R. Henderson. 2006. Yet Another Network Simulator. In *Proceeding from the 2006 Workshop on NS-2: The IP Network Simulator (WNS2 '06)*.

[51] Jiandong Li, Zygmunt J. Haas, Min Sheng, and Yanhui Chen. 2003. Performance Evaluation of Modified IEEE 802.11 MAC for Multi-Channel Multi-Hop Ad Hoc Networks. *Journal of Interconnection Networks* 4, 3 (2003), 345–359.

[52] Saher S. Manaseer, Mohamed Ould-Khaoua, and Lewis M. Mackenzie. 2009. On the Logarithmic Backoff Algorithm for MAC Protocol in MANETs. In *Integrated Approaches in Information Technology and Web Engineering: Advancing Organizational Knowledge Sharing*. IGI Global, Chapter 12, 174–184.

[53] Robert M. Metcalfe and David R. Boggs. 1976. Ethernet: Distributed Packet Switching for Local Computer Networks. *CACM* 19, 7 (July 1976), 395–404.

[54] Y. Morino, T. Hiraguri, T. Ogawa, H. Yoshino, and K. Nishimori. 2014. Analysis Evaluation of Collision Detection Scheme Utilizing MIMO Transmission. In *2014 IEEE 10th International Conference on Wireless and Mobile Computing, Networking and Communications (WiMob)*. 28–32.

[55] T. Moscibroda. 2007. The Worst-Case Capacity of Wireless Sensor Networks. In *2007 6th International Symposium on Information Processing in Sensor Networks*. 1–10.

[56] Qiang Ni, Lamia Romdhani, and Thierry Turletti. 2004. A Survey of QoS Enhancements for IEEE 802.11 Wireless LAN: Research Articles. *Wireless Communications and Mobile Computing* 4, 5 (Aug. 2004), 547–566.

[57] Adrian Ogierman, Andrea Richa, Christian Scheideler, Stefan Schmid, and Jin Zhang. 2014. Competitive MAC under adversarial SINR. In *IEEE Conference on Computer Communications (INFOCOM)*. 2751–2759.

[58] Prabhakar Raghavan and Eli Upfal. 1995. Stochastic Contention Resolution With Short Delays. In *Proceedings of the Twenty-Seventh Annual ACM Symposium on the Theory of Computing (STOC)*. 229–237.

[59] Andrea Richa, Christian Scheideler, Stefan Schmid, and Jin Zhang. 2010. A Jamming-Resistant MAC Protocol for Multi-Hop Wireless Networks. In *Proceedings of the International Symposium on Distributed Computing (DISC)*. 179–193.

[60] Andrea Richa, Christian Scheideler, Stefan Schmid, and Jin Zhang. 2011. Competitive and Fair Medium Access Despite Reactive Jamming. In *Proceedings of the 31st International Conference on Distributed Computing Systems (ICDCS)*. 507–516.

[61] Andrea Richa, Christian Scheideler, Stefan Schmid, and Jin Zhang. 2012. Competitive and Fair Throughput for Co-Existing Networks Under Adversarial Interference. In *Proceedings of the 31st ACM Symposium on Principles of Distributed Computing (PODC)*.

[62] Andrea Richa, Christian Scheideler, Stefan Schmid, and Jin Zhang. 2013. An Efficient and Fair MAC Protocol Robust to Reactive Interference. *IEEE/ACM Transactions on Networking* 21, 1 (2013), 760–771.

[63] Andrea Richa, Christian Scheideler, Stefan Schmid, and Jin Zhang. 2013. Competitive Throughput in Multi-Hop Wireless Networks Despite Adaptive Jamming. *Distributed Computing* 26, 3 (2013), 159–171.

[64] N. I. Sarkar and K. W. Sowerby. 2009. The Effect of Traffic Distribution and Transport Protocol on WLAN Performance. In *Telecommunication Networks and Applications Conference (ATNAC), 2009 Australasian*. 1–6.

[65] M. Shurman, B. Al-Shua'b, M. Alsaedeen, M. F. Al-Mistarihi, and K. A. Darabkh. 2014. N-BEB: New Backoff Algorithm for IEEE 802.11 MAC Protocol. In *2014 37th International Convention on Information and Communication Technology, Electronics and Microelectronics (MIPRO)*. 540–544.

[66] Nah-Oak Song, Byung-Jae Kwak, and Leonard E. Miller. 2003. On the Stability of Exponential Backoff. *Journal of Research of the National Institute of Standards and Technology* 108, 4 (2003).

[67] M. Stoffers and G. Riley. 2012. Comparing the NS-3 Propagation Models. In *Proceedings of the IEEE 20th International Symposium on Modeling, Analysis and Simulation of Computer and Telecommunication Systems*. 61–67.

[68] X. Sun and L. Dai. 2015. Backoff Design for IEEE 802.11 DCF Networks: Fundamental Tradeoff and Design Criterion. *IEEE/ACM Transactions on Networking* 23, 1 (2015), 300–316.

[69] Henry Tan, Chris Wacek, Calvin Newport, and Micah Sherr. 2014. *A Disruption-Resistant MAC Layer for Multichannel Wireless Networks.* 202–216.

[70] Shahram Teymori and Weihua Zhuang. 2005. *Queue Analysis for Wireless Packet Data Traffic.* Springer Berlin Heidelberg, Berlin, Heidelberg, 217–227.

[71] I. Tinnirello, G. Bianchi, and Y. Xiao. 2010. Refinements on IEEE 802.11 Distributed Coordination Function Modeling Approaches. *IEEE Transactions on Vehicular Technology* 59, 3 (2010), 1055–1067.

[72] Elias Weingärtner, Hendrik Vom Lehn, and Klaus Wehrle. 2009. A Performance Comparison of Recent Network Simulators. In *Proceedings of the 2009 IEEE International Conference on Communications (ICC'09)*. 1287–1291.

[73] Dan E. Willard. 1986. Log-logarithmic Selection Resolution Protocols in a Multiple Access Channel. *SIAM J. Comput.* 15, 2 (May 1986), 468–477.

[74] J. Yu and A. P. Petropulu. 2006. Study of the Effect of the Wireless Gateway on Incoming Self-Similar Traffic. *IEEE Transactions on Signal Processing* 54, 10 (2006), 3741–3758.

[75] Y. H. Zhu, X. Z. Tian, and J. Zheng. 2011. Performance Analysis of the Binary Exponential Backoff Algorithm for IEEE 802.11 Based Mobile Ad Hoc Networks. In *2011 IEEE International Conference on Communications (ICC)*. 1–6.

Optimal Reissue Policies for Reducing Tail Latency

Tim Kaler
MIT CSAIL
tfk@mit.edu

Yuxiong He
Microsoft Research
yuxhe@microsoft.com

Sameh Elnikety
Microsoft Research
samehe@microsoft.com

ABSTRACT

Interactive services send redundant requests to multiple different replicas to meet stringent tail latency requirements. These additional (reissue) requests mitigate the impact of non-deterministic delays within the system and thus increase the probability of receiving an on-time response.

There are two existing approaches of using reissue requests to reduce tail latency. (1) Reissue requests immediately to one or more replicas, which multiplies the load and runs the risk of overloading the system. (2) Reissue requests if not completed after a fixed delay. The delay helps to bound the number of extra reissue requests, but it also reduces the chance for those requests to respond before a tail latency target.

We introduce a new family of reissue policies, **Single-Time / Random** (SingleR), that reissue requests after a delay d with probability q. SingleR employs randomness to bound the reissue rate, while allowing requests to be reissued early enough so they have sufficient time to respond, exploiting the benefits of both immediate and delayed reissue of prior work. We formally prove, within a simplified analytical model, that SingleR is optimal even when compared to more complex policies that reissue multiple times.

To use SingleR for interactive services, we provide efficient algorithms for calculating optimal reissue delay and probability from response time logs through data-driven approach. We apply iterative adaptation for systems with load-dependent queuing delays. The key advantage of this data-driven approach is its wide applicability and effectiveness to systems with various design choices and workload properties.

We evaluated SingleR policies thoroughly. We use simulation to illustrate its internals and demonstrate its robustness to a wide range of workloads. We conduct system experiments on the Redis key-value store and Lucene search server. The results show that for utilizations ranging from 40-60%, SingleR reduces the 99th-percentile latency of Redis by 30-70% by reissuing only 2% of requests, and the 99th-percentile latency of Lucene by 15-25% by reissuing 1% only.

1 INTRODUCTION

Interactive online services, such as web search, financial trading, and games require consistently low response times to attract and retain users [13, 24]. The service providers therefore define strict targets for *tail latencies* — 95th percentile, 99th percentile or higher response times [6, 7, 14, 31] to deliver consistently fast responses to user requests. For many distributed and layered services, a request could span several servers and the responses are aggregated, in which case the slower servers typically dominate the response time [18]. As a result, tail latencies are more suitable performance metrics than averages in latency-sensitive applications that employ concurrency.

Variability in a service's response-time can lead to tail-latencies that are several orders of magnitude larger than the average or median. Rare work-intensive requests can have a disproportionate impact on tail-latency by causing other requests to be delayed. Other, often nondeterministic, factors also play a significant role: random load-balancing can lead to short-term skew between machines; background tasks on servers can lead to temporary shortages in CPU cycles, memory, and disk bandwidth; network congestion can increase latency and reduce throughput of communication channels. Reducing tail latency, influenced by all of these contributing factors, is challenging.

The judicious use of redundant computation is often a highly effective technique for reducing tail-latency in interactive services. The basic idea is to exploit inter-machine parallelism by sending multiple copies of a request to replicated servers in order to boost the probability of receiving at least one timely response. This technique is widely used by interactive services, yet despite its prevalence there has been little guidance on optimizing its usage.

We develop a methodology for designing reissue policies that is composed of 3 steps. First, we define several families of reissue policies of varied complexity. These reissue policies are parametrized by variables such as: a) if to reissue a request, b) when to reissue a request, and c) how many times to reissue a request. We choose an optimal family of policies among the candidates guided by a theoretical analysis under a simplified model where the system's response-time distributions are static. Second, we provide an algorithm to find the optimal values for the policy's parameters using response-time logs, solving the constrained optimization problem efficiently. Third, we provide iterative algorithms for refining a policy's parameters in response to changes in system load, and for adjusting the total fraction of requests that are reissued to minimize tail-latency.

Related work and challenges. This technique of reissuing latency-sensitive requests is not new. It has been employed by a wide variety of systems such as key-value stores [4, 19, 26, 29], distributed request-response workflows [15], DNS lookup [2, 27], TCP flows [8, 30], and web-search [6]. Existing systems that reissue requests to reduce tail-latency predominantly employ one of two strategies.

For systems that run at low utilization, the common approach is to perform *immediate reissue* of requests — i.e. dispatch multiple copies of all requests. The effectiveness of immediate reissue has been investigated in previous studies [8, 26, 27, 30]. The primary advantage of the immediate reissue approach is that all copies of a request have an equal chance to respond before a tail-latency deadline since they are dispatched at the same time. This advantage is a motivation within RepFlow [30] for employing immediate reissue for the replication of short TCP flows (under 100KB). The disadvantage of immediate reissue, however, is that its impact on overall load renders it ineffective for systems with moderate and high utilization. A recent study in [27] on memcached, for example, shows that immediate reissue can degrade performance at utilizations as low as 10%.

For systems that run at higher utilization, an alternative approach is to perform *delayed reissue* of requests [5, 6, 15, 29] — i.e. dispatch a second copy of a request after a delay d, which we refer to as **Single-Time / Deterministic** policy or SingleD. The SingleD

SPAA '17, July 24-26, 2017, Washington DC, USA

ACM ISBN 978-1-4503-4593-4/17/07...$15.00
https://doi.org/10.1145/3087556.3087566

policy family corresponds to the scheme proposed in "The Tail at Scale" by Dean and Barroso [6], where, for example, the delay d could be decided using 95th-percentile latency of the workload. The advantage of delayed reissue is that we save the cost of reissuing the requests that would respond fast anyway. However, if the delay d is picked to be too large, then there may not be sufficient time for a reissue request to respond before the latency target.

Along the line of analytical work, prior work only studied immediate reissues for average latency under very specific arrival/service time distributions. Joshi, et.al. [16, 17] study the impact of immediate reissuing on log-concave and log-convex service-time distributions. Gardner, et.al. [10] present an exact analysis of immediate reissue for poisson arrivals and exponential service-times. Lee et.al. [20] consider minimizing average latency by reissuing requests with a known cancellation overhead. Shah et.al. [25] analyze the effectiveness of immediate reissuing in the MDS queue model.

When it comes to developing effective reissue policies for reducing tail-latency on a wide range of workloads and systems, many questions remain largely unanswered. The problem is challenging for multiple reasons: (1) The impact of reissuing is complex: one must weigh the odds of reducing tail latency by sending a duplicate request against the increase in system utilization caused by adding load. (2) There is a large search space with many different choices of which requests to reissue and when. (3) The complex and different workload properties of various interactive services, such as service-time distributions, arrival patterns, request correlations, and system settings make it difficult to derive general strategies for reducing tail latency. (4) Analytical work using queueing theory is challenging even when making strong assumptions about response-time distributions (e.g. drawn from exponential family), and conclusions draw from such simple models are hard to generalize to more complex systems.

Methodology and Key Results. The goal of our work is to find a reissue policy that minimizes a workload's kth percentile tail latency by issuing a fixed percentage (or budget) of redundant requests. We explore the space and devise reissue policies in a principled manner — directed by theoretical analysis to identify the key insights of effective reissue policies, and driven by empirical data from actual systems for wide applicability.

We introduce a new family of reissue policies, **Single-Time / Random** (SingleR), that reissue requests after a delay d with probability q. The use of randomness in SingleR provides an important degree of freedom that allows to bound the reissue budget while also ensuring that reissue requests have sufficient time to respond, exploiting the benefits of both immediate and delayed reissue of prior work.

Using a simplified analytical model, we formally prove that SingleR is the optimal trade-off between the immediate and delayed reissue strategies. More precisely, we define the ***Multiple-Time / Random*** (MultipleR) policies which reissue requests multiple times with different delays and reissue probabilities. We prove that, surprisingly, the optimal policies in MultipleR and SingleR are equivalent. It is a powerful result, restraining the complexity of reissue policies to one time reissue only while guaranteeing the effectiveness of SingleR.

Next, we present how to apply SingleR for interactive services through a data-driven approach to efficiently find the appropriate parameters, reissue time and probability, given sampled response times of the workloads. Our approach takes into account correlations between primary and reissue request response times. It is computationally efficient, finding optimal values of the parameters in close to linear time, with respect to the data size.

Moreover, we show how to devise reissue policies for systems which are sensitive to added load by adaptively refining a reissue policy in response to feedback from the system. This method remains oblivious to many system design details, relies on iterative adaptation to discover a system's response-time distributions and its response to added load. This data-driven approach is performed in a principled manner: every refined policy is the solution to a well defined optimization problem based on updated response-time distributions, applicable to a wide range of workloads with varying properties.

Empirical evaluation. We illustrate the properties of SingleR using both simulation and system experiments. Through careful simulation, we illustrate two key points: 1) the use of randomization in SingleR is especially important for workloads with correlated service times and queueing delays, 2) the effectiveness of SingleR is robust to varied workload properties and design choices including: utilization, service-time distribution, target latency percentiles, service-time correlations, and load-balancing/request-prioritization strategies.

We also evaluate SingleR using two distributed systems based on Redis [32] and Lucene enterprise search [21]. We demonstrate that, on a wide range of utilizations from 20-60%, SingleR is able to reduce tail-latency significantly while reissuing only a small number of requests. Even at 40-60% utilization, which is high for interactive services, SingleR reduces the 99th-percentile latency of Redis by 30-70% while reissuing only 2% of requests, and the 99th-percentile latency of Lucene by 15-25% while reissuing just 1% of requests.

Summary of contributions.

(1) We introduce the SingleR reissue policy family that reissues requests after a delay d with probability q. It exploits randomness to permit the timely reissue of requests with bounded budget, achieving the benefits of both immediate and delayed reissue (Section 2).
(2) We prove within a simplified analytical model that the optimal policies in MultipleR and SingleR are equivalent. Reissuing more than once does not offer additional benefit — SingleR is simple and effective. (Section 3).
(3) We show how to apply SingleR for interactive services by providing efficient algorithms for obtaining reissue delay and probability parameters from response time logs. (Section 4).
(4) We evaluate SingleR using both simulation and system experiments on Redis key value store and Lucene search server (Section 5 and Section 6).

Note that our methodology for developing reissue policies utilizes multiple performance models of increasing complexity. This is a strategic choice that allows us to make definitive design choices that are guided by theoretical insights. The proof that SingleR is optimal relative to SingleD and MultipleR operates in a simplified model in which policies reissue only a fixed fraction of requests, and where the service's response-time distributions are static and uncorrelated. This simplified model allows us to address questions about the general structure of reissue policies that are otherwise intractable. Our algorithms for finding the optimal SingleR policy for a specific interactive service operates in a less constrained model where response-times may be correlated. Our techniques for adaptively refining SingleR policies are in a more general model in which a system may have load-dependent queueing delays — i.e. reissue requests perturb the response-time distribution. The sequence of decisions made with respect to performance model are not arbitrary. As shown in the empirical analysis of SingleR on simulated workloads in Section 5 and in real-world systems in Section 6 these steps lead to effective reissue policies and the insights made in simpler models are readily recognizable in our empirical results.

2 DETERMINISTIC VS RANDOM REISSUE

In this section, we introduce the ***Single-Time / Random*** (SingleR) policies, which reissues a request with probability q after a delay

d. We show how the incorporation of randomness within SingleR policies enables requests to be reissued earlier while still meeting a specified reissue budget. This allows for SingleR to reduce tail-latency significantly even when constrained by a small reissue budget.

This section is organized as follows. Section 2.1 presents the model and terminology. Section 2.2 defines the ***Single-Time / Deterministic*** (SingleD) policies which formalize the "delayed reissue" strategy of prior work. We present SingleR policies in Section 2.3 and discuss their benefits over SingleD in Section 2.4.

2.1 Model and Terminology

We shall, for the moment, operate within a simplified performance model in which there are no queueing delays and query response-times are independent and identically distributed. Later, in Section 4.2 we describe how these limitations can be overcome to adapt our techniques to workloads with correlated response-times and queueing delays.

Formally, we consider an interactive workload to be a collection of queries where each query is composed of exactly one ***primary request*** that is dispatched at time $t=0$ and zero or more ***reissue requests*** dispatched at times $d \geq t$.

The response-time of a query is based on the length of time between the dispatch of the primary request and the arrival of any reply from either a primary or reissue request.

The ***reissue rate*** of a workload consisting of N queries and M reissue requests is defined as the ratio M/N.

We look for a reissue policy that minimizes a workload's kth percentile tail-latency with the reissue rate equal to a given ***reissue budget*** B.

2.2 The SingleD Policies

The ***Single-Time / Deterministic*** (SingleD) policy family is a 1-parameter family of policies that is parametrized by a ***reissue delay*** d. A SingleD policy reissues a request if a response has not been received after d seconds.

Let the random variable X denote the response time of the primary request and Y denote the response time of the reissue request. A query Q completes before time t if its primary response-time X is less than t, or if the reissue request response-time Y is less than $t-d$. The probability that the query Q responds before time t is given by Equation (1).

$$\Pr(Q \leq t) = \Pr(X \leq t) + \Pr(X > t)\Pr(Y \leq t-d) \quad (1)$$

The expected number of reissue requests created by a SingleD policy is equal to the number of primary requests that respond after time d, i.e., the reissue budget is

$$B = \Pr(X > d) . \quad (2)$$

Therefore, if a system can tolerate 10% additional requests, then the delay d is chosen for the SingleD policy such that $\Pr(X > d) = 1/10$. The smaller the delay d, more requests are reissued, and the higher the budget B.

2.3 The SingleR Policies

The ***Single-Time / Random*** (SingleR) policy family is a 2-parameter family of policies that is parametrized by a ***reissue delay*** d and a ***reissue probability*** q. A SingleR policy reissues a request with probability q if a response has not been received after d seconds.

A query Q responds before time t if the primary request responds before time t, or if a reissue request was created and its response time is less than $t-d$. The probability that Q completes before time t while employing SingleR is given by Equation (3).

$$\Pr(Q \leq t) = \Pr(X \leq t) + q \cdot \Pr(X > t)\Pr(Y \leq t-d) \quad (3)$$

The reissue budget is

$$B = q \cdot \Pr(X > d) \quad (4)$$

Given Equation (3) and (4), we write the constrained optimization problem which identifies the reissue delay and probability parameters of the optimal SingleR policy given the primary and reissue response time distributions X and Y.

Optimal Policy For SingleR.
Given tail-latency percentile k, a reissue budget B, and policy family SingleR

$$\begin{aligned} \underset{d,\, q}{\text{minimize}} \quad & t \\ \text{subject to} \quad & \Pr(X \leq t) + q \cdot \Pr(X > t)\Pr(Y \leq t-d) \geq k, \\ & q \cdot \Pr(X \geq d) \leq B \end{aligned}$$

2.4 Randomization Is Essential

The use of randomization in SingleR allows the reissue budget, and thus the added resource and system load, to be bounded while also ensuring that requests can be reissued early enough so they have sufficient time to respond. This may not be allowed under SingleD, which we illustrate in the following example.

Suppose, for example, that we want to minimize a workload's 95th percentile tail-latency by reissuing no more than 5% of all queries. Clearly, this cannot be achieved using a SingleD policy — its limited reissue budget forces it to reissue requests later than the original 95th percentile tail-latency.

In general, a SingleD policy cannot reduce *any* workload's kth percentile latency with budget $B < 1-k$. Randomization is an essential part of an effective reissue policy.

3 SINGLE VS MULTIPLE REISSUE

As we saw in Section 2, randomness provides SingleR policies an important degree of freedom that enables a continuous trade-off between the advantages of immediate and delayed reissuing. A natural question arises: can we obtain an even better policy family by introducing additional degrees of freedom?

In this section, we address this question by introducing MultipleR policies that can reissue requests more than once, at multiple different times, and with different probabilities. We prove a surprising fact: for a given reissue budget B and tail-latency percentile k, the optimal MultipleR and SingleR policies achieve the same tail-latency reduction.

Note that we continue to operate in the simplified model described in Section 2.1 in which there are no queueing delays and query response-times are independent and identically distributed. These limitations will be lifted in Section 4.2 as we show how to adapt SingleR policies to handle correlated response-times and queueing delays.

3.1 Multiple Time Policies

The ***Multiple-Time / Random*** (MultipleR) policy family contains policies that can reissue requests multiple times. A policy that reissues a request at-most n times consists of a sequence of n delays $d_1, d_2, \ldots, d_n$ and n probabilities $q_1, q_2, \ldots, q_n$. Like SingleR, the MultipleR family explores the space between two extremes — the "immediate reissue" and "delayed reissue" strategies. Specifically, the reissue times d_i of a MultipleR policy lie between 0, the time of immediate reissue, and d', the time selected by a "delayed reissue" SingleD policy, where $\Pr(X > d') = B$. For any d_i, since $d_i \leq d'$, the following condition holds

$$\Pr(X > d') \geq B . \quad (5)$$

For the purpose of our later arguments, we also define the ***Double-Time / Random*** (DoubleR) policy family. The DoubleR family is a subset of MultipleR and contains policies that reissue requests at most twice.

3.2 Single Is Optimal

We prove the optimality of SingleR in two steps: (1) We show in Theorem 3.1 that the optimal policies in the SingleR and DoubleR families achieve identical tail-latency reduction; (2) Finally, we prove a generalization in Theorem 3.2 for MultipleR policies that have $n > 2$ reissue times.

Theorem 3.1. *The optimal SingleR and DoubleR reissue policies achieve the same kth percentile tail-latency when given the same reissue budget B.*

Proof. Consider the optimal SingleR policy with budget B that minimizes t, the kth percentile tail-latency. Suppose that this policy reissues requests at time d^*. Then, the probability that a query using the optimal SingleR policy responds before time t is given by Equation (6) below.

$$\Pr(Q \le t) = \Pr(X \le t) + G^*_{SR} \tag{6}$$

where,

$$G^*_{SR} = \frac{B}{\Pr(X > d^*)} \Pr(X > t) \Pr(Y \le t - d^*) \,. \tag{7}$$

The first term $\Pr(X \le t)$ is the probabilitity that the primary request returns before the tail-latency deadline. The term G^*_{SR} corresponds to the case for which the primary request misses the deadline, but the reissue request responds on-time.

Now consider a DoubleR policy with reissue times d_1, d_2 and reissue probabilities q_1, q_2. The probability that a query using this policy reponds before time t is given by Equation (8) below.

$$\Pr(Q \le t) = \Pr(X \le t) + G_1 + G_2 \tag{8}$$

where,

$$G_1 = q_1 \Pr(X > t) \Pr(Y_1 \le t - d_1) \tag{9}$$

$$G_2 = q_2 (1 - q_1 \Pr(Y_1 \le t - d_1)) \Pr(X > t) \Pr(Y_2 \le t - d_2) \tag{10}$$

The term G_1 corresponds to the case for which the primary request misses the deadline, but the first reissue request responds on-time. Lastly, the third term G_2 corresponds to the case where both the primary and first reissue request miss the deadline, but the second reissue request responds on-time.

We shall show that $G_1 + G_2 \le G^*_{SR}$. After this has been shown, it follows that no DoubleR policy can achieve a lower tail-latency than a SingleR policy with the same budget.

First, we provide a bound on G_1.

Consider a SingleR policy that reissues requests at time d_1 with probability $B \cdot \Pr(X > d_1)^{-1}$. Using this policy, the probability that a query returns before time t is given by

$$\Pr(Q \le t) = \Pr(X \le t) + G_{SR,1} \tag{11}$$

where,

$$G_{SR,1} = \frac{B}{\Pr(X > d_1)} \Pr(X > t) \Pr(Y \le t - d_1) \,. \tag{12}$$

Since G^*_{SR} is the optimal policy for a budget B, we have that

$$G_{SR,1} \le G^*_{SR} \,. \tag{13}$$

Multiplying both sides of Inequality (13) by $q_1 \Pr(X > d_1) B^{-1}$ gives us the upper bound on G_1 shown in Inequality (14).

$$G_1 \le \frac{q_1 \Pr(X > d_1)}{B} G^*_{SR} \tag{14}$$

Second, we provide an upper bound on G_2.

We begin by formulating an upper bound on G_2 that is a function of q_1. This requires a sequence of observations. We note that the budget constraint for the DoubleR policy implies the following inequality:

$$q_1 \Pr(X > d_1) + q_2 \Pr(X > d_2)(1 - q_1 \Pr(Y_1 \le d_2 - d_1)) \le B \tag{15}$$

Then, given q_1 Inequality (15) implies the following upper bound on q_2:

$$q_2 \le \frac{B - q_1 \Pr(X > d_1)}{\Pr(X > d_2)(1 - q_1 \Pr(Y_1 \le d_2 - d_1))} \,. \tag{16}$$

Finally, we incorporate this bound on q_2 into the expression for G_2 given in Equation (10) to obtain an upper bound on G_2 as a function of q_1.

$$G_2 \le \frac{B - q_1 \Pr(X > d_1)}{\Pr(X > d_2)} \gamma \Pr(X > t) \Pr(Y_2 \le t - d_2) \tag{17}$$

where, $\gamma = (1 - q_1 \Pr(Y_1 \le t - d_1))/(1 - q_1 \Pr(Y_1 \le d_2 - d_1))$. Note that γ is at most 1 since d_2 is less than t which allows us to omit γ in Inequality (17) to obtain a simpler (albeit weaker) upper bound on G_2.

Now consider a SingleR policy that reissues at time d_2 with probability $B \Pr(X > d_2)^{-1}$. The probability that a query using this policy responds before time t is given by:

$$\Pr(Q \le t) = \Pr(X \le t) + G_{SR,2} \tag{18}$$

where,

$$G_{SR,2} = \frac{B}{\Pr(X > d_2)} \Pr(X > t) \Pr(Y_2 \le t - d_2) \,. \tag{19}$$

We have that for all positive a that $a G_{SR,2} \le a G^*_{SR}$. Let $a = 1 - q_1 \Pr(X > d_1) B^{-1}$, which is strictly positive since the budget constraint on the DoubleR policy implies the inequality $q_1 \Pr(X > d_1) < B$.

Then, combining Equation (19) and Inequality (17) we have that

$$\begin{aligned} G_2 &\le \left(1 - \frac{q_1 \Pr(X > d_1)}{B}\right) G_{SR,2} \\ &\le \left(1 - \frac{q_1 \Pr(X > d_1)}{B}\right) G^*_{SR} \,. \end{aligned} \tag{20}$$

Together the upper bounds on G_1 and G_2 imply that $G_1 + G_2 \le G^*_{SR}$, completing the proof. □

Theorem 3.2. *The optimal SingleR and MultipleR reissue policies achieve the same kth percentile tail-latency when given the same reissue budget B.*

Proof. Assume as an inductive hypothesis that the theorem holds for n- and $(n+1)$-time MultipleR policies. The base cases for 1-time and 2-time MultipleR policies follows from Theorem 3.1.

Consider an optimal $(n+2)$-time MultipleR policy P_{n+2} with reissue times $d_1, \ldots, d_{n+2}$. To complete the inductive argument, we will show that there exists an $(n+1)$-time MultipleR policy with reissue times $d_1, \ldots, d_n, d'$ that achieves the same kth percentile tail-latency.

Let P_n be the n-time MultipleR policy obtained by taking the first n reissue times and reissue probabilities in P_{n+2}. The policy P_n consumes budget $\alpha B (\le B)$, where $\alpha \le 1$.

Let $Q[P_n]$ be a random variable representing the response-time distribution of a query reissued using policy P_n.

Let's now transform the original problem to a new but equivalent problem of minimizing the kth percentile tail-latency of a workload W' with primary response-time distribution $Q[P_n]$ and reissue response-time distribution Y.

We want to show that, for the workload W', a reissue policy with budget $(1 - \alpha)B$ that reissues at times d_{n+1} and d_{n+2} is a DoubleR policy. In particular, we want to show that its budget and reissue times satisfy the condition of Inequality (5) under MultipleR definition, i.e., the following two inequalities hold:

$$\Pr(Q[P_n] \geq d_{n+1}) \geq (1-\alpha)B \quad (21)$$

$$\Pr(Q[P_n] \geq d_{n+2}) \geq (1-\alpha)B \quad (22)$$

In order to show that Inequality (21) and Inequality (22) hold, we use the induction hypothesis for n-time MultipleR policies to obtain a lower-bound on $\Pr(Q[P_n] \geq d_{n+1})$ and $\Pr(Q[P_n] \geq d_{n+2})$.

Let $k' = (1-\Pr(Q[P_n] > d_{n+1}))$ so that d_{n+1} is the k'th percentile tail-latency of $Q[P_n]$. Consider the original workload W with primary response-time X and reissue response-time Y. By the induction hypothesis for n-time MultipleR policies, there exists a SingleR policy P_{SR} with budget αB that achieves a k'th percentile tail-latency that is at most d_{n+1}. Suppose that P_{SR} reissues requests at time d^*. Then, we have that

$$\Pr(Q[P_n] > d_{n+1}) \geq \Pr(Q[P_{SR}] > d_{n+1}) \quad (23)$$

and that

$$\frac{\Pr(Q[P_{SR}] > d_{n+1})}{\Pr(X > d_{n+1})} = 1 - \frac{\alpha B \Pr(Y \leq d_{n+1} - d^*)}{\Pr(X > d^*)} \quad (24)$$

By the definition of MultipleR we have that $\Pr(X > d_{n+1}) \geq B$ and by the definition of SingleR that $\Pr(X > d^*) \geq B$. Together with Inequality (23) this implies that

$$\Pr(Q[P_n] > d_{n+1}) \geq \Pr(Q[P_{SR}] > d_{n+1}) \geq (1-\alpha)B \quad (25)$$

Which proves that Inequality (21) holds. The proof that Inequality (22) holds follows an identical argument.

Therefore, we have shown that for the workload W' the policy which reissues requests at times d_{n+1} and d_{n+2} is a DoubleR policy. By Theorem 3.1 it follows that there exists a SingleR policy that reissues at some time d' which achieves the same kth percentile tail-latency as this DoubleR policy. We can, therefore, replace the $(n+2)$-time MultipleR policy with an $(n+1)$-time MultipleR policy that reissues at times $d_1,...,d_n,d'$ that achieves the same kth percentile tail-latency — completing the proof. □

Analysis with Correlation. The analysis in Theorem 3.1 may be extended (with additional assumptions) to the case in which primary and reissue response times are correlated. Consider a DoubleR policy that reissues requests at times d_1,d_2, and let Q_1 represent the probability that either the primary or first reissue request (issued at time d_1) responds before time t. Then the analysis in Theorem 3.1 holds if a) $\Pr(Y_2 \leq t-d_2 | Q_1 > t) \leq \Pr(Y_2 \leq t-d_2 | X > t)$, and b) $\Pr(Y_1 \leq d_2-d_1) | X > d_2) \leq \Pr(Y_1 \leq t-d_1 | X > t)$. The first assumption (a) is fairly modest and is employed to simplify Inequality (15). Intuitively, assumption (a) states that the likelihood of a second reissue request responding before time $t-d_2$ decreases (or is unchanged) if the first reissued request fails. The second assumption (b) is a technical requirement that allows our proof to use the budget constraint in Inequality (15) in the correlated case. Specifically, assumption (b) ensures that γ in Inequality (17) is at most 1. Informally, assumption (b) states that the positive correlation between primary and reissue response-times is weaker in the tail of the distribution (i.e. near time t) than it is near the reissue times d_1,d_2. We note that in the case where assumption (b) fails to hold, derived bounds on γ can still be used to obtain competitive ratios.

The optimality of SingleR is a powerful result, restraining the complexity of reissue policies to one time reissue only while guaranteeing its effectiveness.

4 SINGLER FOR INTERACTIVE SERVICES

This section presents how to use SingleR for interactive services: We use a data-driven approach to efficiently find the appropriate parameters, reissue time and probability, given sampled response times of the workloads. We develop the parameter search algorithm in 3 steps. (1) We start from a simple model in Section 4.1, assuming the response times of primary and reissue requests are independent.

```
ComputeOptimalSingleR(R_X, R_Y, k, B):
1  Q ← R_X
2  d* ← min{Q}
3  t ← max{Q}
4  while Q ≠ ∅
5      d ← min{Q}
6      Q ← Q − {d}
7      α ← SingleRSuccessRate(R_X, R_Y, B, t, d)
8      while α > k and t > d
9          Q ← Q − {t}
10         t ← max{Q}
11         d* ← d
12         α ← SingleRSuccessRate(R_X, R_Y, B, t, d)
13 q ← 1 − DiscreteCDF(R_X, d*)
14 return (d*, q)

SingleRSuccessRate(R_X, R_Y, B, t, d):
15 Pr(X ≤ t) ← DiscreteCDF(R_X, t)
16 Pr(X > d) ← 1 − DiscreteCDF(R_X, d)
17 Pr(Y ≤ t − d) ← DiscreteCDF(R_Y, t − d)
18 q ← B / Pr(X > d)
19 α ← Pr(X ≤ t) + q · (1 − Pr(X ≤ t)) · Pr(Y ≤ t − d)
20 return α

DiscreteCDF(R, t):
21 s ← |{x ∈ R; x < t}|
22 return s / |R|
```

Figure 1: Pseudocode for the data-driven algorithm for finding the optimal SingleR policy.

We present an algorithm ComputeOptimalSingleR that computes optimal reissue time and probability, minimizing tail latency. Our algorithm is computationally efficient, taking $O(N \log N)$ time where N is the number of response time samples. (2) We extend the algorithm in Section 4.2 to incorporate correlation between reissue and primary requests, guaranteeing optimality on parameter selection while offering the same computational efficiency of $O(N \log N)$. (3) We show how to adaptively refine a SingleR policy to take into account additional queueing delays introduced to the system by the reissue requests in Section 4.3.

4.1 Parameter Search

The ComputeOptimalSingleR(R_X,R_Y,k,B) procedure (in Figure 1) computes the optimal SingleR policy to minimize the kth percentile tail-latency of an interactive service with reissue budget B. The response-time distributions for the service are represented using two sets of samples: a set R_X of response times for primary requests; and, a set R_Y of response times for reissued requests, accommodating the cases in which these distributions differ, e.g., when reissue requests are executed using dedicated or specialized resources. The output of the procedure is the reissue time d^* and the reissue probability q for the SingleR policy.

ComputeOptimalSingleR searches for the optimal reissue time. We preserve the following invariant throughout the procedure — the SingleR policy that reissues requests at time d^* achieves a kth percentile tail-latency of at most t. The procedure begins on lines 2–3 by selecting a trivial policy that reissues all requests at time $d^* \leftarrow \min\{R_X\}$ and achieves a kth percentile tail-latency of $t \leftarrow \max\{R_X\}$. A search is then performed on lines 4–12 for each reissue time $d \in R_X$ to determine if the SingleR policy reissuing at time d achieves a kth percentile tail-latency smaller than t. For each time d, the success-rate α of the SingleR policy that reissues at time d is computed on line 7, which is the probability that a query is serviced before time t. If this success rate is greater than the tail-latency percentile target k, we replace d^* with $d^* \leftarrow d$ and decrease t to $\max\{R_X - \{t\}\}$ while preserving the invariant. This iterative refinement of the policy is repeated on lines 8–12 until the success rate α of the SingleR policy reissuing at time d is less than k. By then, we find the optimal d^* value, and its corresponding q value is computed at line 13.

Complexity. ComputeOptimalSingleR is computationally efficient with complexity of $\Theta(N + Sort(N))$ where N is the number of samples, and $Sort(N)$ is the time required to sort N response times. In particular, the list of potential reissue times Q is initialized with N response times. Each time SingleRSuccessRate is invoked one element is removed from Q. Therefore, SingleRSuccessRate can be invoked at most N times. SingleRSuccessRate evaluates three cumulative distribution functions DiscreteCDF on lines 15–17. Although the success rate α computed on line 19 is not necessarily monotonic as a function of (t,d), its composite CDFs are monotonic in t, d, and $t-d$ respectively. As a result, the amortised cost of DiscreteCDF is $O(1)$ with a careful analysis considering order statistics and using finger search tree [3, 12]. DiscreteCDF takes pre-sorted response time samples as inputs, where the sorting takes $\Theta(Sort(N))$ time. Summing them together, the complexity of ComputeOptimalSingleR is $\Theta(N + Sort(N))$.

4.2 Incorporating Response-Time Correlations

The response-time of a request can be divided into two components: the amount of time a request waits in a server's queue before being processed (the ***queueing time***), and the time required execute the request (the ***service time***). The response-times of primary and reissue requests, however, will often be correlated. For example, queries within a workload can have different service times: a query with high service time (e.g., many instructions) is likely to take long for both primary and reissue requests. The system's instantaneous load may be similar upon the arrival of the primary and reissue requests.

Correlations between primary and reissue requests influence the probability that a reissue request will respond before a tail-latency deadline. This influence can be taken into account in ComputeOptimalSingleR by modifying line 19 of SingleRSuccessRate in Figure 1 to use the conditional distribution $\Pr(Y \leq t-d | X > t)$ in place of $\Pr(Y \leq t-d)$.

The conditional distribution $\Pr(Y \leq t-d | X > t)$ may be estimated efficiently by using a 2D orthogonal range query data structure [1, 22] over pairs (t_x, t_y) where t_x and t_y are the primary and reissue response times.

Each range query performed within SingleRSuccessRate takes $O(\log N)$ time, and SingleRSuccessRate is invoked at most $2N$ times by ComputeOptimalSingleR. Therefore, the procedure ComputeOptimalSingleR which takes into account correlation computes the optimal SingleR policy in $\Theta(N \lg N)$ time.

4.3 Iterative Adaptation for Queue Delays

The queueing delay of requests in a workload depends on the arrival process to a service. The use of a reissue policy can perturb this arrival process and change the response-time distributions used by ComputeOptimalSingleR to find a SingleR policy.

The impact of added load on a workload's response-time distributions can be significant. Consider the inverse CDFs illustrated in Figure 2a for *Original* and *Primary* requests[1]. The *Original* curve illustrates the inverse CDF of the original primary response-time distribution of the system when no requests are reissued. The *Primary* curve illustrates the new inverse CDF of the primary response-time distribution when using a SingleR policy with a 30% reissue budget. The impact of these reissue requests on the primary response-time distribution is dramatic: the 85th percentile grows from 50 to 350.

[1] The corresponding simulation setup for Figure 2a is discussed in Section 5.

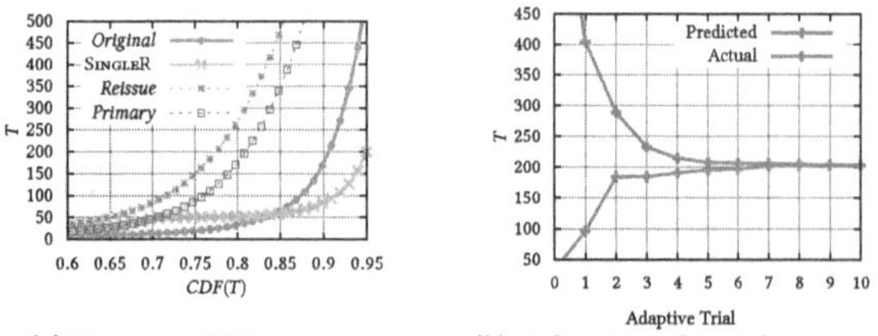

(a) Inverse CDF. (b) Adaptive algorithm.

Figure 2: Convergence of the adaptive SingleR policy on a workload with correlated service-times and queueing delays.

We employ an adaptive approach to iteratively refine a SingleR policy in-response to changes in the response-time distribution. First, we begin with a reissue policy P that reissues requests at time $d = 0$ with probability B. We then execute the system with the reissue policy and sample the response-time distributions of primary and reissue requests. The sampled response-time distributions are used within ComputeOptimalSingleR to compute the optimal SingleR policy P_{local} for these response-time distributions. Next, we obtain a new policy P' that has reissue delay $d' = d + \lambda(d_{local} - d)$ where λ is a learning rate. Finally, this process is repeated until the empirical kth percentile tail-latency converges to the value predicted by ComputeOptimalSingleR and the empirical reissue rate converges to B.

This adaptive approach is based upon two observations: a) using the same budget, reissuing later tend to impact load more as it is more likely to reissue requests with more work and higher resource demands; and, b) small changes to the reissue delay result in only small changes to the response-time distributions. Observation (a) implies that the predicted kth percentile tail-latency at each step of ComputeOptimalSingleR increases after each step of the algorithm. Observation (b) implies that for sufficiently small λ that the true optimal reissue time d_{opt} lies between d' and d_{local} at each step of the algorithm.

Figure 2b shows the 95th percentile tail-latency achieved on each step of the adaptive algorithm using a learning rate of 0.2 for a SingleR policy with a reissue budget of 30%. Convergence can be detected by comparing the policy optimizer's predicted tail-latency with the observed latency when using the policy. For this workload, convergence is achieved after ≈ 6 iterations.

4.4 Extended Scenarios

The tools and algorithms presented in the preceding sections can be applied to handle common scenarios that occur in practice. Since space limitations prohibit an exhaustive examination of each of these scenarios, we shall instead sketch a few strategies for addressing common use cases.

Varying load / response-time distributions. In practice a system's response-time distribution can vary over time on both short (hourly, daily), and long (monthly, yearly) time scales. The iterative algorithm for adaptively refining a SingleR policy can be applied in an on-line fashion to address these temporal variation, but requires modifications which depend on specific application needs and the time-scale of interest to properly balance exploration and exploitation in its search.

Selecting optimal reissue budget. The adaptive algorithm described in this section assumes the use of a fixed reissue budget. As we learned in Section 2, SingleR policies are able to reduce tail-latency in a "smooth" fashion even with very small reissue budgets. As a consequence, the tail-latency reduction of SingleR as a function of the reissue budget tends to be a parabola whose extrema can be readily found through simple binary search techniques.

To evaluate the practicality of this simple approach, we implemented a simple budget selection procedure that performs the following steps: 1) set $\delta = 1\%$ and set *best-budget* = 0; 2) for budget *best-budget*+δ run the adaptive SINGLER policy optimizer for 5 adaptive trials to produce reissue policy P; 3) collect response-time data from the system when using reissue policy P; 4) if the budget *best-budget*+δ has smaller 99th percentile tail-latency than *best-budget*, then set $\delta = 3\delta/2$. Otherwise, set $\delta = -\delta/2$. An example of this binary search procedure is presented later in Figure 8 as part of our system experiments in Section 6.

Meeting tail-latency with minimal resources. Interactive services often formulate service-level agreements (SLA) that guarantee a fixed latency for $k\%$ of all requests. In such a scenario, a system designer may be interested in minimizing the resources required to satisfy the SLA. Given a particular tail-latency target T, the budget can be minimized using either a brute force search, starting at small reissue rates, or by using a variation of the binary search procedure for finding the optimal budget that transforms tail-latency values L using the function $f(L) = \min\{T, L\}$.

5 SIMULATIONS

In this section we use a discrete-time event simulator to carefully evaluate the behavior and tail-latency impact of SINGLER policies. Simulation allows us to vary workload and system properties covering a wide range of scenarios.

First, we provide simulation results on three types of workloads: *Independent, Correlated,* and *Queueing*, corresponding to the three workload models in Section 4. This experiment demonstrates two points: a) Randomness in SINGLER is, in fact, especially important for workloads with correlated service-times and queueing delays; and, b) The optimal SINGLER policy takes workload characteristics into account in order to maximize the value of each reissued request.

Next, we conduct a sensitivity study that varies the *Queueing* workload along many dimensions: utilization, service time distribution, percentile targets, strength of service-time correlations, load balancing strategies, and request prioritization strategies. The results demonstrate SINGLER is effective and robust over varying workloads and system design properties.

5.1 Simulated Workload

Figure 3 provides simulation results on a set of three workloads: *Independent, Correlated,* and *Queueing*. The service-times in each workload are drawn from a PARETO distribution with shape parameter 1.1 and mode 2.0.

In the *Independent* workload, the service-times of primary and reissue requests are independent and have no queueing delays (i.e. there are an infinite number of servers). In the *Correlated* workload, the primary and reissue request service-times are correlated via the relationship $Y = rx + Z$ where x is the sampled primary request service-time, Z is an independently drawn service-time, and $r = 0.5$ is a linear correlation ratio. In the *Queueing* workload, requests have correlated service-times and arrive according to a Poisson process. The request is dispatched to the FIFO queue of one of 10 servers selected uniformly at random. The arrival rate is chosen to achieve a system utilization of 30%.

Figure 3a compares the 95th percentile tail-latency reduction achieved by the optimal SINGLER and SINGLED policies for varied reissue budgets. For the *Queueing* workload, both the SINGLER and SINGLED policies are selected using adaptive policy refinement (for the SINGLED policy this adaptive refinement is needed to ensure the reissue budget is satisfied). Figure 3b illustrates the "remediation rate" of SINGLER and SINGLED policies. The ***remediation rate*** measures the average value of added (i.e. actually issued) reissue requests and is defined to be the probability that a primary request X exceeds a tail-latency target t, but the reissued request Y responds before time $t-d$, i.e. $\Pr(X > t \cap Y < t-d)$. Figure 3c plots the reissue times and probabilities used by the optimal SINGLER policy for each budget.

5.2 Benefits of Randomization

The results of Figure 3a illustrates the benefits of randomization in reissue policies. For all three workloads, there exists a range of reissue budgets for which the SINGLED policy is ineffective at reducing the 95th percentile tail-latency. On the *Independent* workload a SINGLED policy is unable to achieve any tail-latency reduction when the reissue budget is less than 5%. On the *Correlated* workload, SINGLED policies are ineffective for reissue budgets less than 10%. Worst of all, SINGLED policies actually *increases* the 95th percentile latency of the *Queueing* workload with reissue budgets less than 10% — since these reissued requests increase system load.

In contrast, SINGLER is able to reduce the 95th percentile tail-latency for all reissue budgets on the *Independent* and *Correlated* workloads. On the *Queueing* workload, SINGLER begins to reduce tail-latency once the reissue budget is greater than 3%. For all three workloads, randomization allows for SINGLER to achieve better tail-latency reduction than SINGLED for budgets less than 15%.

5.3 Impact of Correlation and Queueing

The procedure outlined in Section 4 for finding an optimal SINGLER policy takes into account the properties of the primary and reissue response-time distributions, and adapts to queueing delays. By inspecting the three workloads in Figure 3, we can gain insight into how SINGLER reissue policies are able to outperform SINGLED.

The goal of COMPUTEOPTIMALSINGLER is to find a SINGLER policy that minimizes the workload's kth percentile tail-latency with a reissue budget of B. One can think of COMPUTEOPTIMALSINGLER as searching over all policies that use budget B in order to find the policy which maximizes the value of each added request. A convenient measure of the "value" of each reissue request is its remediation rate — i.e. the probability that the redundancy provided by the reissue request was necessary for the query to meet its tail-latency target.

Figure 3c illustrates the way in which SINGLER changes its choice of reissue delay and probability based upon the reissue budget and workload characteristics. We shall discuss the behavior of SINGLER policies for each of our three workloads in the case where the reissue budget is 10%.

On the *Independent* workload, the optimal SINGLER policy reissues requests with probability 0.7 at a time d where approximately 15% primary requests remain outstanding — resulting in approximately 10% of all requests being reissued in total. On the *Correlated* workload, the optimal SINGLER policy chooses to reissue requests with probability 0.4 at a time d where 25% of requests are outstanding.

On the *Correlated* workload, the optimal SINGLER policy must reissue requests earlier due to service-time correlations. When optimizing its success rate it takes into account the fact that if a query's primary request exceeds a tail latency target, there is a higher chance of its reissue request responding slowly. By reissuing requests earlier in time, the probability that the reissued request will help tail latency (i.e. the remediation rate) increases. Therefore, on this workload the optimal policy reissues requests earlier at a time d when 40% of requests are outstanding, and reissues with a smaller probability of 25%.

On the *Queueing* workload, the optimal SINGLER policy reissues requests with probability 0.8 at a time d where approximately 13% of requests are outstanding. Although this workload's service-times are correlated, the latency of requests in the tail of the response-time distribution is dominated by queueing delays which depends on the service process as well as on request arrival process and load balancing. Indeed, we can observe in Figure 4b that the addition of queueing delays dampens the strength of correlation between

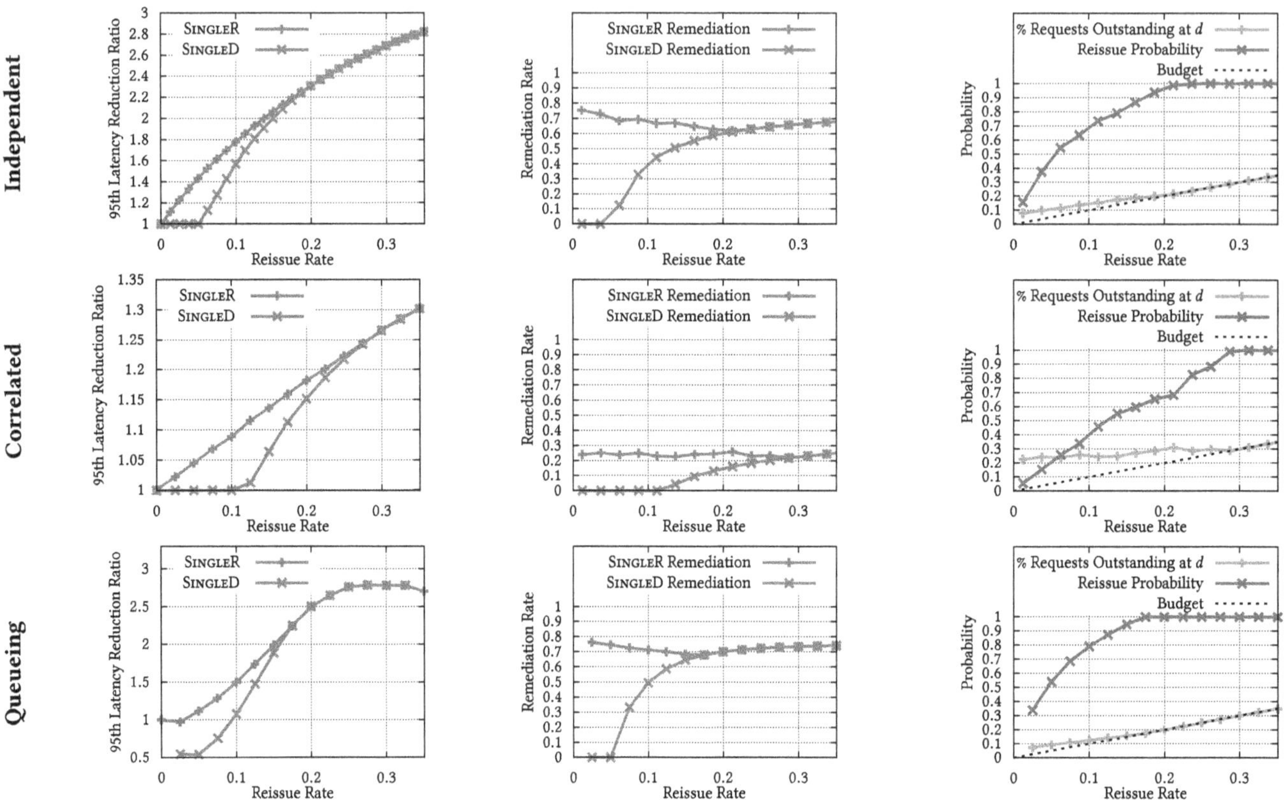

(a) Tail-latency reduction ratio.

(b) Reissue remediation rate.

(c) Reissue time and probability.

Figure 3: Simulation results for SINGLER and SINGLED policies with varied reissue budgets on three simulated workloads: *Independent, Correlated,* and *Queueing.*

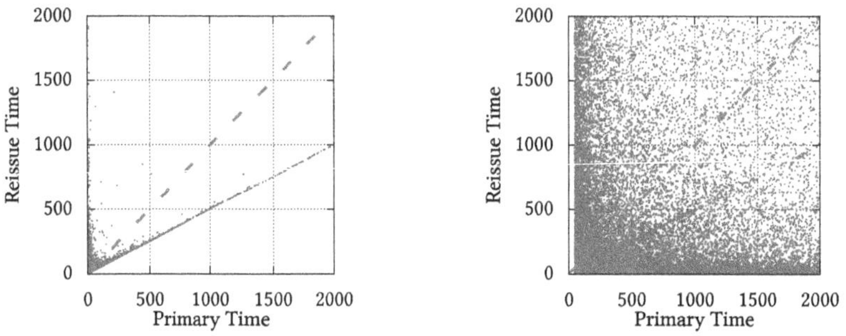

(a) *Correlated*

(b) *Queueing*

Figure 4: Response-time correlations between primary and reissue requests on the *Correlated* and *Queueing* workloads. The service-time X of the primary request is drawn from a Pareto distribution with shape 1.1 and mode 2. The service-time Y of a reissued request is drawn from $Y = rx + Z$, where x is the observed service-time of the primary request, Z is drawn from a Pareto distribution with shape 1.1 and mode 2, and $r = 0.5$.

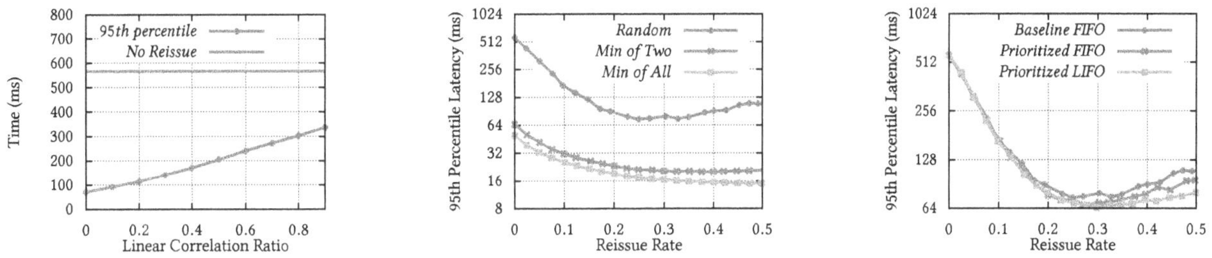

(a) Correlation (b) Load-balancing (c) Queuing

Figure 5: Illustrates impact of correlation ratio (Figure 5a), load-balancing strategies (Figure 5b), and server's queue-management policies (Figure 5c) on the 95th percentile tail-latency of the *Queueing* workload.

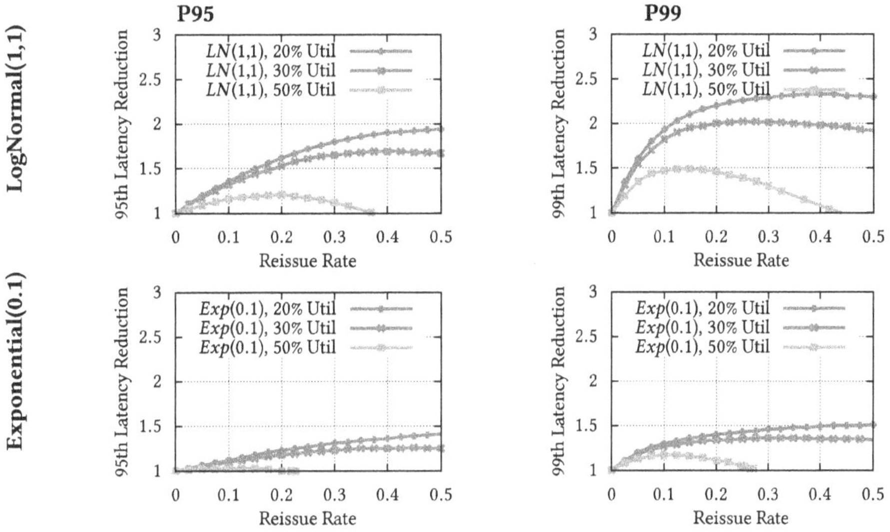

Figure 6: The 95th percentile tail-latency *P*95 and the 99th percentile tail-latency *P*99 for Exp(0.1) and LogNormal(1,1) distributions with varied reissue rates and system utilization.

primary and reissue requests. Although the preexisting correlation can still be observed, the structure of the joint-distribution exhibits more randomness due to request queueing time. This provides an explanation for why SingleR, and reissuing in general, can achieve more latency reduction on the Queueing workload than the Correlated workload, as shown in Figure 3a.

This experiment shows that SingleR optimizes the choice of reissue time and probability based upon workload characteristics, maximizing the benefit of reissued requests for tail-latency reduction.

5.4 Sensitivity Study

We study the sensitivity of SingleR to workload properties and design choices, including: utilization, service-time distribution, target latency percentiles, correlation among requests, load-balancing among servers, and changing the priority processing reissued requests. As a baseline, we use a variant of the Queueing workload from Section 5.1 without service-time correlations unless otherwise specified.

Utilization, Service Time Distribution and Percentiles. We use LogNormal(1,1) and Exponential(0.1) as service time distributions and measure P95 and P99 tail latency reduction for three utilization levels: 20%, 30%, and 50%.

Figure 6 illustrates the *P*95 and *P*99 tail-latency reduction (Y-axis) achieved by SingleR policies over a range of reissue budgets (X-axis) compared to the original tail-latencies when no requests are reissued. The results demonstrate: (1) Reissue obtains higher benefit under less loaded systems, but even at rather high load of 50% utilization, SingleR achieves latency reduction of up to 1.5 times. (2) The benefit of reissue tends to increase for higher target percentiles.

Correlation. We use the same default Pareto distribution to model service time, and progressively increase the service time correlation ratio r between the primary request and its corresponding reissued request (defined in Section 5.1). The *P*95 latency without reissue is 567, and is independent of the correlation ratio r. Figure 5a reports *P*95 latency of SingleR using a fixed reissue rate of 25% as a function of the correlation ratio. As expected, the less service-times are correlated the larger benefit reissuing has on tail-latency. Even when primary and reissue requests are strongly correlated (e.g. $r = 1$) SingleR is still able to reduce the response-times of queries delayed due to queueing delays.

Load-balancing. Figure 5b shows the impact of different load-balancing strategies on tail latency. We make two observations: (1) Using more sophisticated load-balancing strategies such as *Min-of-2* (select the server with shorter queue among two randomly selected servers to dispatch a request) or *Min-of-All* (select the server with the shortest queue among all servers to dispatch a request) helps reduce the *P*95 tail-latency relative to the simpler *Random* strategy that picks a server uniformly at random. (2) In all cases, SingleR reduces the *P*95th latency by a factor of 2 or more.

Changing priority of reissued requests. We study three priority settings: (1) *Baseline FIFO* corresponds to a server maintaining a FIFO single queue, and does not differentiate between primary and reissue requests. (2) *Prioritized FIFO* corresponds to a server that maintains two separate FIFO queues for primary and reissue requests, and only processes reissue requests when the primary queue is empty: preventing multiple reissued requests from delaying a primary request. (3) *Prioritized LIFO* is the same as *Prioritized FIFO* but processes the reissue queue in LIFO order. Figure 5c compares the three systems and shows that changing the priority scheme has a modest impact on the tail latency improvements of SingleR.

The overall results in this section show that SingleR and its adaptive policy optimizer is robust and reduces the tail latency for these different system design choices and workload characteristics.

6 EXPERIMENTAL EVALUATION

We evaluate SingleR policies in two distributed systems based on Redis [32] which is a key-value store that supports stored procedures, and Lucene [21] which is an enterprise search engine. Our main target is reducing the *P*99 tail latency.

6.1 Experimental Setup and Workloads

We use a cluster of 10 servers to execute the workload. Each server has a dual-core 2.4 GHz Intel E5-2676 processor and 32GB of RAM. The data sets and its associated indices both for Redis and for Lucene fit in the main memory. To execute each query workload, we employ several machines emulating clients that send requests in an open loop with exponential inter-arrival times.

To enable request reissuing, we assign each primary request a timestamp, and add it to a FIFO queue so that the request can be reissued later. A *reissue thread* consumes the entries from the FIFO queue, and dispatches the request to a server after a policy-specified delay. Prior to sending a reissue request, the completion status of its associated query is checked using a client-local boolean array.

All reported system utilizations refer to CPU utilization on a single core as measured by the Linux *sysstat* [11] utility. We use 10 adaptive iterations (with learning rate $\lambda = 0.5$) to compute the SingleD and SingleR policies satisfying the reissue budget. The measured reissue rate and the target reissue budget tend to closely agree with the predictions of the reissue policy optimizer and thus we report only the empirical rate in all figures.

6.2 Redis Set-Intersection Workload

The Redis workload consists of set-intersection queries performed over a synthetic collection of 1000 sets. Each set stores a random subset of integers in the range 1 and 10^6, and set cardinalities are distributed according to a lognormal distribution. Query traces consist of 40,000 intersections between randomly selected pairs of sets.

The service-time distribution for the Redis set-intersection workload is illustrated in Figure 9 discretized into 20 msec bins. Over 98% of set-intersection queries in this workload have a service-time less than 10 msec. Indeed, the workload's mean service time $\mu_R = 2.366$ milliseconds and standard deviation $\sigma_R = 8.64$ may lead us to expect request latencies to be well-behaved, even in the tail.

A handful of queries (≈ 20), however, have service times greater than 150 msec. These queries correspond to the rare case in which an intersection is performed between two abnormally large sets. These rare queries do little to skew the aggregate statistics of the workload's service-time distribution, but have a substantial impact on tail-latency. As shown in Figure 7b, the 99th percentile tail-latency for the set-intersection workload is 900 msec when one does not reissue requests.

These "queries of death" are a common problem in database applications, and their impact on tail-latency can be difficult to predict apriori. In particular, the influence of these requests depends to a large extent on the queueing mechanisms used in the system. In Redis, requests are serviced in a round-robin fashion from each active client connection in a batch. If even a single client issues a long-running request, then the requests of all other clients will be delayed until completion. Furthermore, in an open-loop system such delays lead to a backlog of requests that further extends the impact of the slow request for multiple rounds.

Tail Latency Reduction under SingleR and SingleD. On the *Redis* workload, the SingleR and SingleD policies are able to reduce the *P*99 latency at 40% utilization from 900 milliseconds to 400 milliseconds. SingleR is able to meet this target *P*99 latency with a budget of just $\approx 3.5\%$, whereas SingleD requires a budget of at least 5%. For reissue budgets between 3 and 5%, the reissue probability of SingleR increases from 0.8 to 1.0 so that for budgets greater than 5% SingleR and SingleD are equivalent.

Figure 7a shows the *P*99 latency in msec (Y-axis) against the reissue rates between 0 and 6% (X-axis) for SingleR and SingleD. Both Redis (top figure) and Lucene (bottom figure) running at 40% baseline utilization without any reissue.

We make two observations: First, both the SingleR and SingleD curves illustrate reduced tail latency relative to the baseline system without reissuing. Second, we note that the SingleR policy achieves strictly better tail-latencies than SingleD for small reissue rates. For example at 2% reissue rate in Redis, SingleR reduces the *P*99 latency to 405 msec, compared to 900 msec for the baseline system and 820 msec for SingleD.

Varied System Utilization. Next, we illustrate the performance of SingleR under three system utilization levels: 20%, 40%, and 60% in Figure 7b, which depicts the *P*99 latency against fixed reissue rate. For all utilizations between 20–60%, SingleR is able to reduce the 99th percentile tail latency.

In particular, at 60% utilization (which is very high for interactive services) SingleR with a 3% reissue rate reduces the Redis *P*99 latency from 1750 msec to 1000 msec, and the Lucene *P*99 latency from 1603 msec to 1157 msec.

The best latency reduction occurs when choosing the optimal reissue rate, which depends on the system utilization. For 20% utilization, we illustrate the process of finding the optimal reissue rate via binary search in Figure 8. At 20% utilization the best reissue budget is approximately 8%. At both 40% and 60% utilization, the best reissue rate is approximately 5%.

Figure 7c illustrates the best tail-latency achieved by a SingleR policy for the Redis workload for utilizations between 20% and 60%. The *Best Reissue Rate* curve illustrates the *P*99 latency achieved by the best SingleR policy (with reissue rate determined via a binary search procedure), and the *No Reissue* curve illustrates the *P*99 latency of the baseline system without reissuing.

6.3 Lucene Search Workload

The Lucene search workload consists of search queries over a corpus of 33 million articles from the English Wikipedia dataset [9]. Queries are drawn randomly from a set of 10,000 queries from the Lucene nightly regression tests [23].

The service-time distribution for queries in the search workload contrasts with set-intersection in that it is not as highly skewed towards very-low latencies. The distribution for search service-times is illustrated in Figure 9 discretized into 20 msec bins. Approximately 90% of all requests have service times between 1 and 70 msec, and the overall distribution has mean service-time $\mu_L = 39.73$ msec with standard deviation $\sigma_L = 21.88$.

Similar to the set-intersection workload, the search workload also has rare slow queries. Approximately 1% of search queries have service-times greater than 100 msec. The impact of these slow queries on tail-latency, however, is different in Lucene than in Redis. At 40% utilization, the search workload's 99th percentile

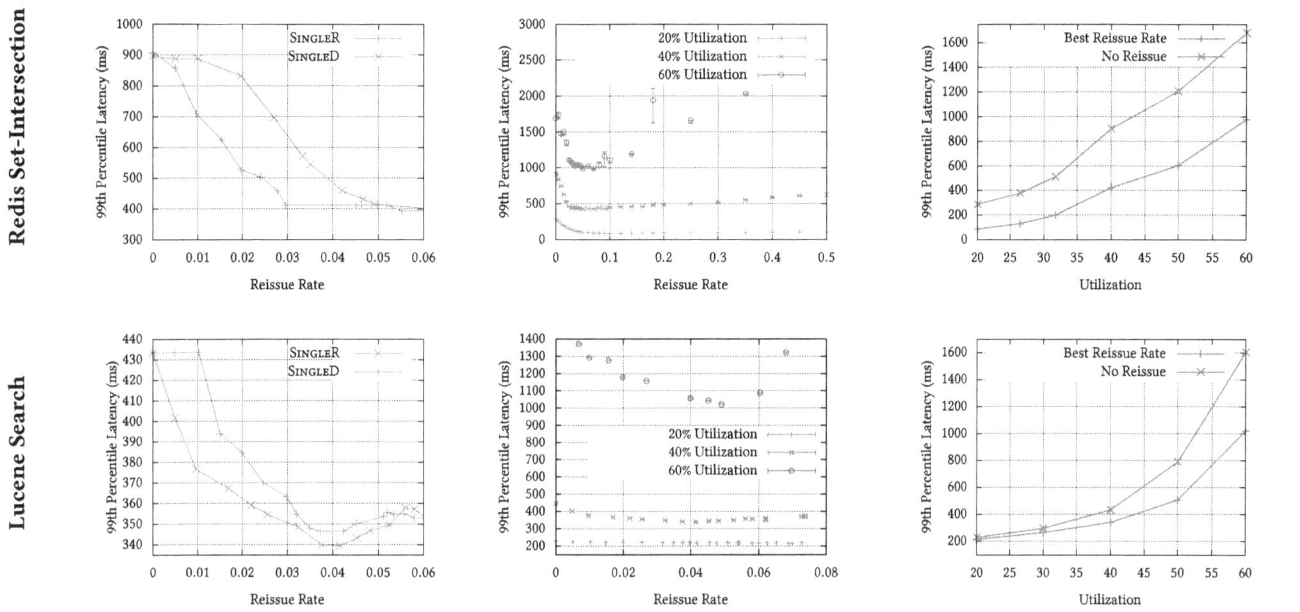

(a) SINGLER vs SINGLED (b) Latency vs Reissue Rate (c) Best Latency vs Utilization

Figure 7: System experiment results for the Redis and Lucene workloads. Figure 7a compares the *P*99 latency of SINGLER and SINGLED for reissue budgets between 0 and 6% at 40% utilization. Figure 7b shows the *P*99 latency for SINGLER with varied reissue rates for 20%, 40%, and 60% utilization. Figure 7c shows the *P*99 latency achieved when using the best reissue budget and a SINGLER policy for utilizations ranging from 20% to 60%.

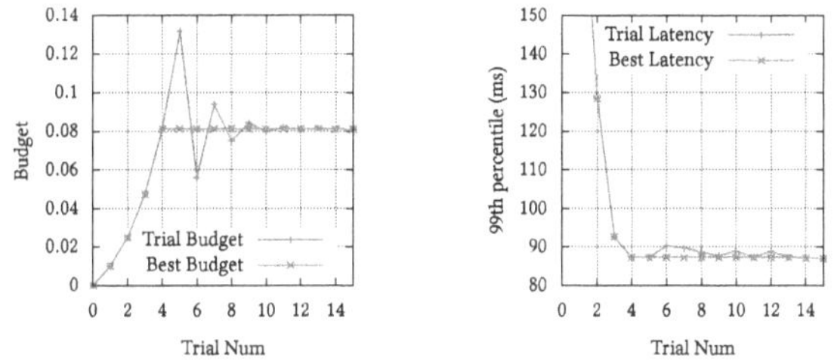

Figure 8: Illustration of binary search for optimal budget for the *Intersection Counting* query to minimize 99th percentile tail-latency. 20% utilization.

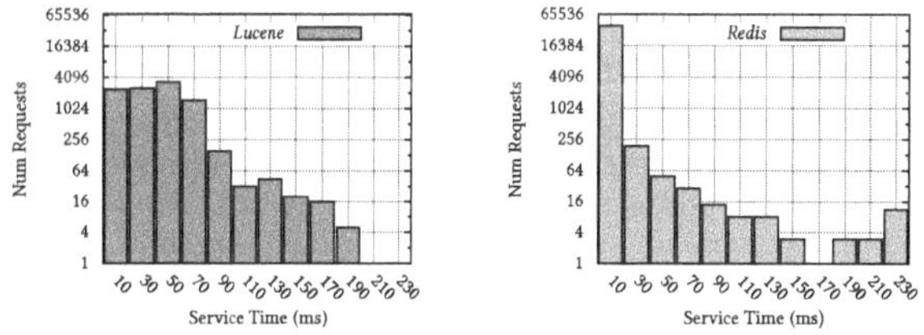

Figure 9: Service time distributions for the Redis set-intersection and Lucene search workloads.

latency is ≈435 msec when there are no reissued requests. This is not entirely due to the differences in service-time distribution, although it certainly is an important influence. The Lucene search server also differs in how it manages concurrent requests. Requests from all open connections are placed into a single FIFO queue which results in relatively good tail-latency behavior — FIFO is, in fact, optimal for light-tailed service-time distributions [28].

Tail Latency Reduction under SingleR and SingleD. On the *Lucene* workload, we observe in Figure 7a that SINGLER reduces Lucene's $P99$ latency at 40% utilization from 433 milliseconds to 339 milliseconds, and the SINGLED policy reduces $P99$ to 346 milliseconds. This gap, while small, is not merely measurement noise — all reported values reflect the median of multiple runs.

The improved performance of the SINGLER policy is due to its use of randomization that allows it to reissue queries earlier than SINGLED. At 40% utilization, the optimal reissue rate for SINGLER is 4%, and the optimal policy reissues requests with probability approximately 0.75. As the reissue rate grows the achieved latency gap between SINGLER and SINGLED closes, and the reissue probability of the optimal SINGLER policy converges to 1.0. Randomization is more valuable on the Lucene search workload than it was for Redis because of the much higher mean service time of requests.

Varied System Utilization. Next, we illustrate the performance of SINGLER under three system utilization levels: 20%, 40%, and 60% in Figure 7b, which depicts the $P99$ latency against fixed reissue rate.

SINGLER reduces the tail-latency of Lucene search workload for all utilizations between 20–60%. At 60% utilization (high load), SINGLER reduces the $P99$ latency from 1603 to 1157 msec. Figure 7c illustrates the best tail-latency achieved by a SINGLER policy for the Lucene workload for utilizations between 20% and 60%. The *Best Reissue Rate* curve illustrates the $P99$ latency achieved by the best SINGLER policy (with reissue rate determined via a binary search procedure), and the *No Reissue* curve illustrates the $P99$ latency of the baseline system without reissuing. We observe significant tail latency reduction due to SINGLER over the baseline.

7 CONCLUSION

We have illustrated principled methods of generating reissue policies for interactive services. By operating within a simplified model, we were able to prove that SINGLER is an optimal compromise between the commonly used immediate and delayed reissue strategies. There are a few general lessons that we think are useful to impart: a) there is little reason to choose a reissue policy more complex than SINGLER if that additional complexity does not leverage application-specific insight; and, b) reissue policies that reduce tail-latency as a "smooth" function of their budget admit relatively simple strategies for adapting to load-dependent queueing delays and searching for optimal reissue budgets. As we have shown, we were able to adapt SINGLER policies to systems and workloads with a wide range of properties through iterative adaptation. As we have seen, this leads to a simple process for finding effective reissue policies in real systems: SINGLER is able to reduce tail-latency in simulated and real-world workloads even when reissuing a small fraction of requests.

REFERENCES

[1] Pankaj K Agarwal. 1996. *Range Searching.* Technical Report. DTIC Document.
[2] David G Andersen, Hari Balakrishnan, M Frans Kaashoek, and Rohit N Rao. 2005. Improving web availability for clients with MONET. In *Proceedings of the 2nd conference on Symposium on Networked Systems Design & Implementation-Volume 2.* USENIX Association, 115–128.
[3] Mark R Brown and Robert E Tarjan. 1980. Design and analysis of a data structure for representing sorted lists. *SIAM journal on computing* 9, 3 (1980), 594–614.
[4] Fay Chang, Jeffrey Dean, Sanjay Ghemawat, Wilson C. Hsieh, Deborah A. Wallach, Mike Burrows, Tushar Chandra, Andrew Fikes, and Robert E. Gruber. 2008. Bigtable: A Distributed Storage System for Structured Data. *ACM Trans. Comput. Syst.* 26, 2, Article 4 (June 2008), 26 pages. https://doi.org/10.1145/1365815.1365816
[5] Inc. DataStax. 2016. DataStax Distribution of Apache Cassandra 3.x. (2016). http://docs.datastax.com/en/cassandra/3.x/pdf/cassandra3x.pdf
[6] Jeffrey Dean and Luiz André Barroso. 2013. The Tail at Scale. *Commun. ACM* 56, 2 (2013), 74–80.
[7] Giuseppe DeCandia, Deniz Hastorun, Madan Jampani, Gunavardhan Kakulapati, Avinash Lakshman, Alex Pilchin, Swaminathan Sivasubramanian, Peter Vosshall, and Werner Vogels. 2007. Dynamo: amazon's highly available key-value store. In *SOSP.*
[8] Tobias Flach, Nandita Dukkipati, Andreas Terzis, Barath Raghavan, Neal Cardwell, Yuchung Cheng, Ankur Jain, Shuai Hao, Ethan Katz-Bassett, and Ramesh Govindan. 2013. Reducing web latency: the virtue of gentle aggression. In *ACM SIGCOMM Computer Communication Review,* Vol. 43. ACM, 159–170.
[9] Wikimedia Foundation. 2016. Wikipedia: Database. (2016). https://en.wikipedia.org/wiki/Wikipedia:Database_download
[10] Kristen Gardner, Samuel Zbarsky, Sherwin Doroudi, Mor Harchol-Balter, and Esa Hyytia. 2015. Reducing latency via redundant requests: Exact analysis. In *Proceedings of the 2015 ACM SIGMETRICS International Conference on Measurement and Modeling of Computer Systems.* ACM, 347–360.
[11] Sébastien Godard. 2004. Sysstat: System performance tools for the Linux OS. (2004).
[12] Leo J Guibas, Edward M McCreight, Michael F Plass, and Janet R Roberts. 1977. A new representation for linear lists. In *Proceedings of the ninth annual ACM symposium on Theory of computing.* ACM, 49–60.
[13] James Hamilton. 2009. The Cost of Latency. (2009). http://per-spect-ives-.mvdirona.com-/2009/10/31/TheCostOfLatency.aspx
[14] Y. He, S. Elnikety, J. Larus, and C. Yan. 2012. Zeta: Scheduling Interactive Services with Partial Execution. In *ACM Symposium on Cloud Computing (SOCC).* 12.
[15] Virajith Jalaparti, Peter Bodik, Srikanth Kandula, Ishai Menache, Mikhail Rybalkin, and Chenyu Yan. 2013. Speeding up distributed request-response workflows. *ACM SIGCOMM Computer Communication Review* 43, 4 (2013), 219–230.
[16] Gauri Joshi, Emina Soljanin, and Gregory Wornell. 2015. Efficient Redundancy Techniques for Latency Reduction in Cloud Systems. *arXiv preprint arXiv:1508.03599* (2015).
[17] Gauri Joshi, Emina Soljanin, and Gregory Wornell. 2015. Queues with redundancy: Latency-cost analysis. *ACM SIGMETRICS Performance Evaluation Review* 43, 2 (2015), 54–56.
[18] Saehoon Kim, Yuxiong He, Seung-won Hwang, Sameh Elnikety, and Seungjin Choi. 2015. Delayed-Dynamic-Selective (DDS) Prediction for Reducing Extreme Tail Latency in Web Search. In *Proceedings of the Eighth ACM International Conference on Web Search and Data Mining (WSDM '15).* ACM, New York, NY, USA, 7–16. https://doi.org/10.1145/2684822.2685289
[19] Avinash Lakshman and Prashant Malik. 2010. Cassandra: A Decentralized Structured Storage System. *SIGOPS Oper. Syst. Rev.* 44, 2 (April 2010), 35–40. https://doi.org/10.1145/1773912.1773922
[20] Kangwook Lee, Ramtin Pedarsani, and Kannan Ramchandran. 2015. On Scheduling Redundant Requests with Cancellation Overheads. In *Proc. of the 53rd Annual Allerton conference on Communication, Control, and Computing.*
[21] Apache Lucene. 2010. Apache lucene. (2010).
[22] George S Lueker. 1978. A data structure for orthogonal range queries. In *Foundations of Computer Science, 1978., 19th Annual Symposium on.* IEEE, 28–34.
[23] Mike McCandless. 2010. Lucene Nightly Benchmarks. (2010). http://people.apache.org/~mikemccand/lucenebench
[24] Eric Schurman and Jake Brutlag. 2009. The user and business impact of server delays, additional bytes, and HTTP chunking in web search. In *Velocity Conference.*
[25] Nihar B Shah, Kangwook Lee, and Kannan Ramchandran. 2014. The MDS queue: Analysing the latency performance of erasure codes. In *Information Theory (ISIT), 2014 IEEE International Symposium on.* IEEE, 861–865.
[26] Christopher Stewart, Aniket Chakrabarti, and Rean Griffith. 2013. Zoolander: Efficiently Meeting Very Strict, Low-Latency SLOs.. In *ICAC,* Vol. 13. 265–277.
[27] Ashish Vulimiri, Oliver Michel, P Godfrey, and Scott Shenker. 2012. More is less: reducing latency via redundancy. In *Proceedings of the 11th ACM Workshop on Hot Topics in Networks.* ACM, 13–18.
[28] Adam Wierman and Bert Zwart. 2012. Is tail-optimal scheduling possible? *Operations research* 60, 5 (2012), 1249–1257.
[29] Zhe Wu, Curtis Yu, and Harsha V. Madhyastha. 2015. CosTLO: Cost-Effective Redundancy for Lower Latency Variance on Cloud Storage Services. In *12th USENIX Symposium on Networked Systems Design and Implementation (NSDI 15).* USENIX Association, Oakland, CA, 543–557. https://www.usenix.org/conference/nsdi15/technical-sessions/presentation/wu
[30] Hong Xu and Baochun Li. 2014. RepFlow: Minimizing flow completion times with replicated flows in data centers. In *INFOCOM, 2014 Proceedings IEEE.* IEEE, 1581–1589.
[31] Jeonghee Yi, Farzin Maghoul, and Jan Pedersen. 2008. Deciphering mobile search patterns: A study of Yahoo! mobile search queries. In *ACM International Conference on World Wide Web (WWW).* 257–266.
[32] Jeremy Zawodny. 2009. Redis: Lightweight key/value store that goes the extra mile. *Linux Magazine* 79 (2009).

Impact of Knowledge on Election Time in Anonymous Networks

Yoann Dieudonné*
Laboratoire MIS, Université de Picardie Jules Verne
33 rue Saint-Leu
Amiens 80000, France
yoann.dieudonne@u-picardie.fr

Andrzej Pelc†
Département d'informatique, Université du Québec en Outaouais
C.P. 1250, succ. Hull
Gatineau, Québec J8X 3X7, Canada
pelc@uqo.ca

ABSTRACT

Leader election is one of the basic problems in distributed computing. This is a symmetry breaking problem: all nodes of a network must agree on a single node, called the leader. If the nodes of the network have distinct labels, then such an agreement means that all nodes have to output the label of the elected leader. For anonymous networks, the task of leader election is formulated as follows: every node v of the network must output a simple path, which is coded as a sequence of port numbers, such that all these paths end at a common node, the leader. In this paper, we study deterministic leader election in arbitrary anonymous networks.

It is well known that deterministic leader election is impossible in some networks, regardless of the allocated amount of time, even if nodes know the map of the network. This is due to possible symmetries in it. However, even in networks in which it is possible to elect a leader knowing the map, the task may be still impossible without any knowledge, regardless of the allocated time. On the other hand, for any network in which leader election is possible knowing the map, there is a minimum time, called the *election index*, in which this can be done. Informally, the election index of a network is the minimum depth at which views of all nodes are distinct. Our aim is to establish tradeoffs between the allocated time τ and the amount of information that has to be given *a priori* to the nodes to enable leader election in time τ in all networks for which leader election in this time is at all possible. Following the framework of *algorithms with advice*, this information (a single binary string) is provided to all nodes at the start by an oracle knowing the entire network. The length of this string is called the *size of advice*. For a given time τ allocated to leader election, we give upper and lower bounds on the minimum size of advice sufficient to perform leader election in time τ.

We focus on the two sides of the time spectrum. For the smallest possible time, which is the election index of the network, we show that the minimum size of advice is linear in the size n of the network, up to polylogarithmic factors. On the other hand, we consider large values of time: larger than the diameter D by a summand, respectively, linear, polynomial, and exponential in the election index; for these values, we prove tight bounds on the minimum size of advice, up to multiplicative constants. We also show that constant advice is not sufficient for leader election in all graphs, regardless of the allocated time.

CCS CONCEPTS

• **Theory of computation → Distributed algorithms**; • **Mathematics of computing →** *Discrete mathematics*;

KEYWORDS

Leader election; anonymous network; advice; deterministic distributed algorithm; time

*Partially supported by the European Regional Development Fund (ERDF) and the Hauts-de-France region under Project TOREDY.
†Partially supported by NSERC discovery grant 8136 – 2013, and by the Research Chair in Distributed Computing at the Université du Québec en Outaouais.

SPAA '17, July 24-26, 2017, Washington DC, USA

ACM ISBN 978-1-4503-4593-4/17/07...$15.00
https://doi.org/http://dx.doi.org/10.1145/3087556.3087563

1 INTRODUCTION

Background. Leader election is one of the basic problems in distributed computing [35]. This is a symmetry breaking problem: all nodes of a network must agree on a single node, called the leader. It was first formulated in [34] in the study of local area token ring networks, where, at all times, exactly one node (the owner of a circulating token) is allowed to initiate communication. When the token is accidentally lost, a leader must be elected as the initial owner of the token.

If the nodes of the network have distinct labels, then agreeing on a single node means that all nodes output the label of the elected leader. However, in many applications, even if nodes have distinct identities, they may decide to refrain from revealing them, e.g., for privacy or security reasons. Hence it is important to design leader election algorithms that do not rely on knowing distinct labels of nodes, and that can work in anonymous networks as well. Under this scenario, agreeing on a single leader means that every node has to output a simple path (coded as a sequence of port numbers) to a common node.

Model and Problem Description. The network is modeled as a simple undirected connected n-node graph with diameter D, for $n \geq 3$. Nodes do not have any identifiers. On the other hand, we assume that, at each node v, each edge incident to v has a distinct *port number* from $\{0, \dots, d-1\}$, where d is the degree of v. Hence, each edge has two corresponding port numbers, one at each of its endpoints. Port numbering is *local* to each node, i.e., there is no relation between port numbers at the two endpoints of an edge. Initially, each node knows only its own degree. The task of leader election is formulated as follows. Every node v must output a sequence $P(v) = (p_1, q_1, \ldots, p_k, q_k)$ of nonnegative integers. For each node v, let $P^*(v)$ be the path starting at v, such that port numbers p_i and q_i correspond to the i-th edge of $P^*(v)$, in the order from v to the other end of this path. All paths $P^*(v)$ must be simple paths in the graph (i.e., paths without repeated nodes) that end at a common node, called the leader. In this paper, we consider deterministic leader election algorithms.

In the absence of port numbers, there would be no way to identify the elected leader by non-leaders, as all ports, and hence all neighbors, would be indistinguishable to a node. Security and privacy reasons for not revealing node identifiers do not apply in the case of port numbers.

The central notion in the study of anonymous networks is that of the view of a node [44]. Let G be a graph and let v be a node of G. We first define, for any $l \geq 0$, the *truncated view* $\mathcal{V}^l(v)$ at depth l, by induction on l. $\mathcal{V}^0(v)$ is a tree consisting of a single node x_0. If $\mathcal{V}^l(u)$ is defined for any node u in the graph, then $\mathcal{V}^{l+1}(v)$ is the port-labeled tree rooted at x_0 and defined as follows. For every node v_i, $i = 1, \ldots, k$, adjacent to v, there is a child x_i of x_0 in $\mathcal{V}^{l+1}(v)$ such that the port number at v corresponding to edge $\{v, v_i\}$ is the same as the port number at x_0 corresponding to edge $\{x_0, x_i\}$, and the port number at v_i corresponding to edge $\{v, v_i\}$ is the same as the port number at x_i corresponding to edge $\{x_0, x_i\}$. Now node x_i, for $i = 1, \ldots, k$, becomes the root of the truncated view $\mathcal{V}^l(v_i)$.

The *view* from v is the infinite rooted tree $\mathcal{V}(v)$ with labeled ports, such that $\mathcal{V}^l(v)$ is its truncation to level l, for each l.

We use the extensively studied $\mathcal{LOCAL}$ communication model [39]. In this model, communication proceeds in synchronous rounds and all nodes start simultaneously. In each round, each node can exchange arbitrary messages with all of its neighbors and perform arbitrary local computations. The information that v gets about the graph in r rounds is precisely the truncated view $\mathcal{V}^r(v)$, together with degrees of leaves of this tree. Denote by $\mathcal{B}^r(v)$ the truncated view $\mathcal{V}^r(v)$ whose leaves are labeled by their degrees in the graph, and call it the *augmented truncated view* at depth r. If no additional knowledge is provided *a priori* to the nodes, the decisions of a node v in round r in any deterministic algorithm are a function of $\mathcal{B}^r(v)$. Note that all augmented truncated views can be canonically coded as binary strings, and hence the set of all augmented truncated views can be ordered lexicographically. The *time* of leader election is the minimum number of rounds sufficient to complete it by all nodes. It is well known that the synchronous process of the $\mathcal{LOCAL}$ model can be simulated in an asynchronous network using time-stamps.

Unlike in labeled networks, if the network is anonymous then leader election is sometimes impossible, regardless of the allocated time, even if the network is a tree and its topology is known. This is due to symmetries, and the simplest example is the two-node graph. It follows from [44] that if nodes know the map of the graph (i.e., its isomorphic copy with all port numbers indicated) then leader election is possible if and only if views of all nodes are distinct. We will call such networks *feasible* and restrict attention to them. However, even in the class of feasible networks, leader election is impossible without any *a priori* knowledge about the network. This simple observation follows from a slightly stronger result proved in Proposition 4.4. On the other hand, for any fixed feasible network G, whose map is given to the nodes, there is a minimum time, called the *election index* and denoted by $\phi(G)$, in which leader election can be performed. The election index of a network is equal to the smallest integer ℓ, such that the augmented truncated views at depth ℓ of all nodes are distinct. This will be proved formally in Section 2. The election index is always a strictly positive integer because there is no graph all of whose nodes have different degrees (indeed, the degrees of the n nodes of a simple connected graph are integers between 1 and $n-1$ included).

Our aim is to establish tradeoffs between the allocated time and the amount of information that has to be given *a priori* to the nodes to enable them to perform leader election. Following the framework of *algorithms with advice*, see, e.g., [10, 13, 18, 38], this information (a single binary string) is provided to all nodes at the start by an oracle knowing the entire network. The length of this string is called the *size of advice*. It should be noted that, since the advice given to all nodes is the same, this information does not increase the asymmetries of the network (unlike in the case when different pieces of information could be given to different nodes) but only helps to harvest the existing asymmetries and use them to elect the leader. Hence the high-level formulation of our problem is the following. What is the minimum amount of identical information that can be given to nodes to enable them to use asymmetries present in the graph to elect a leader in a given time?

Of course, since the faithful map of the network is the total information about it, asking about the minimum size of advice to solve leader election in time τ is meaningful only in the class of networks G for which $\phi(G) \leq \tau$, because otherwise, no advice can help. The central problem of this paper can be now precisely formulated as follows.

> For a given time τ, what is the minimum size of advice that permits leader election in time τ, for all networks G for which $\phi(G) \leq \tau$?

The paradigm of algorithms with advice has been proven very important in the domain of network algorithms. Establishing a strong lower bound on the minimum size of advice sufficient to accomplish a given task in a given time permits to rule out entire classes of algorithms and thus focus only on possible candidates. For example, if we prove that $\Omega(n/\log n)$ bits of advice are needed to perform a certain task in n-node networks (as we do in this paper for leader election in minimum possible time), this rules out all potential algorithms that can work using only the size n of the network, as n can be given to the nodes using $O(\log n)$ bits. Lower bounds on the size of advice give us impossibility results based strictly on the *amount* of initial knowledge allowed in a model. This is much more general than the traditional approach based on specific categories of information given to nodes, such as the size, diameter, or maximum node degree.

Our results. For a given time τ allocated to leader election, we give upper and lower bounds on the minimum size of advice sufficient to perform leader election in time τ for networks with election index at most α. An upper bound U for a class of networks C means that, for all networks in C, leader election in time τ is possible given advice of size $O(U)$. We prove such a bound by constructing advice of size $O(U)$ together with a leader election algorithm for all networks in the class C, that uses this advice and works in time τ. A lower bound L for a class of networks C means that there exist networks in C for which leader election in time τ requires advice of size $\Omega(L)$. We prove such a bound by constructing a subclass C' of C such that no leader election algorithm running in time τ with advice of size $o(L)$ can succeed for all networks in C'.

We focus on the two sides of the time spectrum. For the smallest possible time, which is the election index of the network, we show that the minimum size of advice is linear in the size n of the network, up to polylogarithmic factors. More precisely, we establish a general upper bound $O(n \log n)$ and lower bounds $\Omega(n \log \log n)$ and $\Omega(n(\log \log n)^2 / \log n)$, for election index equal to 1 and larger than 1, respectively.

On the other hand, we consider large values of time: those exceeding the diameter D by a summand, respectively, linear, polynomial, and exponential in the election index; for these values, we prove tight bounds on the minimum size of advice, up to multiplicative constants. More precisely, for any positive integer α, consider the class of networks with election index at most α. Let $c > 1$ be an integer constant. For any graph of election index $\phi \leq \alpha$ in this class, consider leader election algorithms working in time, respectively, at most $D + \phi + c$, at most $D + c\phi$, at most $D + \phi^c$, and at most $D + c^{\phi}$. Hence the additive offset above D in the time of leader election is asymptotically equal to ϕ in the first case, it is linear in ϕ but with a multiplicative constant larger than 1 in the second case, it is polynomial in ϕ but super-linear in the third case, and it is exponential in ϕ in the fourth case. In the considered class we show that the minimum size of advice is $\Theta(\log \alpha)$ in the first case, it is $\Theta(\log \log \alpha)$ in the second case, it is $\Theta(\log \log \log \alpha)$ in the third case, and it is $\Theta(\log(\log^* \alpha))$ in the fourth case. Hence, perhaps surprisingly, the jumps in the minimum size of advice, when the time of leader election varies between the above milestones, are all exponential. We also show that constant advice is not sufficient for leader election in all graphs, regardless of the allocated time.

Related work. The first papers on leader election focused on the scenario where all nodes have distinct labels. Initially, it was investigated for rings in the message passing model. A synchronous algorithm based on label comparisons was given in [28]. It used $O(n \log n)$ messages. An asynchronous algorithm using $O(n \log n)$ messages was given, e.g., in [40]. Leader election was also investigated in the radio communication model, both in the deterministic [30, 33, 37] and in the randomized [42] scenarios.

Many authors [3–6, 43, 44] studied leader election in anonymous networks. In particular, [6, 44] characterize message-passing networks in which leader election is feasible. In [43], the authors study the problem of leader election in general networks, under the assumption that node labels exist but are not unique. They characterize networks in which leader election can be performed and give an algorithm which achieves election when it is feasible. In [12, 14], the authors study message complexity of leader election in rings with possibly nonunique labels. In [11], the authors investigate the feasibility of leader election among anonymous agents that navigate in a network in an asynchronous way.

Providing nodes or agents with arbitrary types of knowledge that can be used to increase efficiency of solutions to network problems has previously been proposed in [1, 10, 13, 16–18, 31, 32, 36, 38, 41]. This approach was referred to as *algorithms with advice*. The advice is given either to the nodes of the network or to mobile agents performing some task in a network. In the first case, instead of advice, the term *informative labeling schemes* is sometimes used if (unlike in our scenario) different nodes can get different information.

Several authors studied the minimum size of advice required to solve network problems in an efficient way. In [32], given a distributed representation of a solution for a problem, the authors investigated the number of bits of communication needed to verify the legality of the represented solution. In [16], the authors compared the minimum size of advice required to solve two information dissemination problems using a linear number of messages. In [18], it was shown that advice of constant size given to the nodes enables the distributed construction of a minimum spanning tree in logarithmic time. In [13], the advice paradigm was used for online problems. In the case of [38], the issue was not efficiency but feasibility: it was shown that $\Theta(n \log n)$ is the minimum size of advice required to perform monotone connected graph clearing. In [10], the task of drawing an isomorphic map by an agent in a graph was considered, and the problem was to determine the minimum advice that has to be given to the agent for the task to be feasible.

Among papers studying the impact of information on the time of leader election, the papers [21, 25, 36] are closest to the present work. In [36], the authors investigated the minimum size of advice sufficient to find the largest-labelled node in a graph, all of whose nodes have distinct labels. The main difference between [36] and the present paper is that we consider networks without node labels. This is a fundamental difference: breaking symmetry in anonymous networks relies heavily on the structure of the graph, rather than on labels, and, as far as results are concerned, much more advice is needed for a given allocated time. In [21], the authors investigated the time of leader election in anonymous networks by characterizing this time in terms of the network size, the diameter of the network, and an additional parameter called the level of symmetry, similar to our election index. This paper used the traditional approach of providing nodes with some parameters of the network, rather than any type of advice, as in our setting. Finally, the paper [25] studied leader election under the advice paradigm for anonymous networks, but restricted attention to trees. It should be stressed that leader election in anonymous trees and in arbitrary anonymous networks present completely different difficulties. The most striking difference is that, in the case of trees, for the relatively modest time equal to the diameter D, leader election can be done in feasible trees without any advice, as all nodes can reconstruct the map of the tree. This should be contrasted with the class of arbitrary networks, in which leader election with no advice is impossible. Our results for large election time values (exceeding the diameter D) give a hierarchy of sharply differing tight bounds on the size of advice in situations in which leader election in trees can be performed with no advice at all.

2 PRELIMINARIES

We use the word "graph" to mean a simple undirected connected graph with unlabeled nodes and all port numbers fixed. In the sequel we use the word "graph" instead of "network".

We will use the following characterization of the election index.

Proposition 2.1. *The election index of a feasible graph is equal to the smallest integer ℓ, such that the augmented truncated views at depth ℓ of all nodes are distinct.*

The value of the election index is estimated in the following proposition, which is an immediate consequence of the main result of [27].

Proposition 2.2. *For any n-node feasible graph of diameter D, its election index is in $O(D \log(n/D))$.*

3 ELECTION IN MINIMUM TIME

We start this section by designing a leader election algorithm working in time ϕ, for any graph of size n and election index ϕ, and using advice of size $O(n \log n)$. The high-level idea of the algorithm is the following. The oracle knowing the graph G produces the advice consisting of three items: the integer ϕ, A_1 and A_2. This is done using Algorithm ComputeAdvice(G). The integer ϕ serves the nodes to determine for how long they have to exchange information with their neighbors. The item A_1 is the most difficult to construct. Its aim is to allow every node that knows its augmented truncated view at depth ϕ (which is acquired in the allocated time ϕ) to construct a unique integer label from the set $\{1, 2, \ldots, n\}$. Recall that the advice is the same for all nodes, and hence each node has to produce a distinct label using this common advice, relying only on its (unique) augmented truncated view at depth ϕ. The third item in the advice, that we call A_2, is a labeled BFS tree of the graph G. (To avoid ambiguity, we take the *canonical* BFS tree, in which the parent of each node u at level $i + 1$ is the node at level i corresponding to the smallest port number at u.) The labels of nodes are equal to those that nodes will construct using item A_1, the root is the node labeled 1, and all port numbers in the BFS tree (that come from the graph G) are faithfully given. More precisely, A_2 is the *code* of this tree, i.e., a binary string of length $O(n \log n)$ which permits the nodes to reconstruct unambiguously this labeled tree (the details are given below). After receiving the entire advice, Algorithm Elect works as follows. Each node acquires its augmented truncated view at depth ϕ, then positions itself in the obtained BFS tree, thanks to the unique constructed label, and outputs the sequence of port numbers corresponding to the unique path from itself to the root of this BFS tree.

The main difficulty is to produce item A_1 of the advice succinctly, i.e., using only $O(n \log n)$ bits, and in such a way that allows nodes to construct unique *short* labels. Note that a naive way in which nodes could attribute themselves distinct labels would require no advice at all and could be done as follows. Nodes could list all possible augmented truncated views at depth ϕ, order them lexicographically in a canonical way, and then each node could adopt as its label the rank in this list. However, already for $\phi = 1$, there are $\Omega(n)^{\Omega(n)}$ different possible augmented truncated views at depth 1, and hence these labels would be of size $\Omega(n \log n)$. Now item A_2 of the advice would have to give the tree with all these labels, thus potentially requiring at least $\Omega(n^2 \log n)$ bits, which significantly exceeds the size of advice that we want to achieve. This is why item A_1 of the advice is needed, and must be constructed in a subtle way. On the one hand, it must be sufficiently short (use only $O(n \log n)$ bits) and on the other hand it must allow nodes to construct distinct labels of size $O(\log n)$. Then item A_2 of the advice can be given using also only $O(n \log n)$ bits.

We now give some intuitions concerning the construction of item A_1 of the advice. This item can be viewed as a carefully constructed *trie*, cf. [2], which is a rooted binary tree whose leaves correspond to objects, and whose internal nodes correspond to yes/no queries concerning these objects. The left child of each internal node corresponds to port 0 and to the answer "no" to the query, and the right child corresponds to port 1 and to the answer "yes" to the query. The object in a given leaf corresponds to all answers on the branch from the root to the leaf, and must be unique. In our case, objects in leaves of the trie are nodes of the graph, and queries serve to discriminate all views $\mathcal{B}^{\phi}(v)$, for all nodes v of the graph G. Since each node v knows its augmented truncated view $\mathcal{B}^{\phi}(v)$, after learning the trie it can position itself as a leaf of it and adopt a unique label from the set $\{1, 2 \ldots, n\}$.

As an example, consider the case $\phi = 1$. All augmented truncated views at depth 1 can be coded by binary sequences of length $O(n \log n)$. In this case the queries at internal nodes of the trie are of two types: "Is the binary representation of your augmented truncated view at depth one of length smaller than t?" (this query is coded as $(0, t)$), and "Is the jth bit of the binary representation of your augmented truncated view at depth one equal to 1?" (this query is coded as $(1, j)$). Since both the possible lengths t and the possible indices j are of size $O(\log n)$, the entire trie can be coded as a binary sequence of length $O(n \log n)$, because there are n leaves of the trie.

For $\phi > 1$ the construction is more complicated. Applying the same method as for $\phi = 1$ (by building a large trie discriminating between all augmented truncated views at depth ϕ, using similar questions as above, only concerning depth ϕ instead of depth 1) is impossible, because the sizes of the queries would exceed $\Theta(\log n)$. Actually, queries would be of size $\Omega(\phi \log n)$, resulting in advice of size $\Omega(\phi n \log n)$, and not $O(n \log n)$. Hence we apply a more subtle strategy. The upper part of the trie is as for the case $\phi = 1$. However, this is not sufficient, as in this case there exist nodes u and v in the graph such that $\mathcal{B}^1(u) = \mathcal{B}^1(v)$ but $\mathcal{B}^{\phi}(u) \neq \mathcal{B}^{\phi}(v)$, and hence such a small trie would not discriminate between all augmented truncated views at depth ϕ. Hence leaves of this partial trie, corresponding to sets of nodes in the graph that have the same augmented truncated view at depth 1, have to be further developed, by adding sub-tries rooted at these leaves, to further discriminate between all augmented truncated views at depth ϕ. This is done recursively in such a way that these further queries are still of size $O(\log n)$, and constitutes the main difficulty of the advice construction.

The details of Algorithm ComputeAdvice and of Algorithm Elect using it are in the Appendix.

The next theorem shows that Algorithm Elect, executed on any n-node graph, performs leader election in time equal to the election index of this graph, using advice of size $O(n \log n)$.

Theorem 3.1. *For any n-node graph G with election index ϕ, the following properties hold:*

(1) *Algorithm* ComputeAdvice(G) *terminates and returns a binary string of length $O(n \log n)$.*

(2) *Using the advice returned by Algorithm* `ComputeAdvice(G)`, *Algorithm* `Elect` *performs leader election in time* ϕ.

We now prove two lower bounds on the size of advice for election in the minimum time, i.e., in time equal to the election index ϕ. For $\phi = 1$ we establish the lower bound $\Omega(n \log\log n)$, and for $\phi > 1$ we establish the lower bound $\Omega(n(\log\log n)^2/\log n)$. Both these bounds differ from our upper bound $O(n \log n)$ only by a polylogarithmic factor.

The high-level idea of the proofs of these bounds is the following. Given a positive integer ϕ we construct, for arbitrarily large integers n, families of n-node graphs with election index ϕ and with the property that each graph of such a family must receive different advice for any election algorithm working in time ϕ for all graphs of this family. This property is established by showing that, if two graphs G_1 and G_2 from the family received the same advice, some nodes v_1 in G_1 and v_2 in G_2 would have to output identical sequences of port numbers because they have identical augmented truncated views at depth ϕ, which would result in failure of leader election in one of these graphs. Since the constructed families are large enough, the above property implies the desired lower bound on the size of advice for at least one graph in the family.

We start with the construction of a family $\mathcal{F}(x) = \{C_1, \dots, C_y\}$ of labeled $(x+1)$-node cliques, for $x \geq 2$. All these cliques will have node labels $r, v_0, v_1, \dots, v_{x-1}$. We first define a clique C by assigning its port numbers. Assign port number i, for $0 \leq i \leq x-1$, to the port at r corresponding to the edge $\{r, v_i\}$. The rest of the port numbers are assigned arbitrarily. We now show how to produce the cliques of the family $\mathcal{F}(x)$ from the clique C. Consider all sequences of x integers from the set $\{1, \dots, x-1\}$. There are $y = (x-1)^x$ such sequences. Let $(s_1, \dots, s_y)$ be any enumeration of them. Let $s_t = (h_0, h_1, \dots, h_{x-1})$, for a fixed $t = 1, \dots, y$. The clique C_t is defined from clique C by assigning port $(p + h_j) \mod x$ instead of port p at node v_j, for all pairs $0 \leq j, p \leq x-1$.

We first consider the election index $\phi = 1$.

Theorem 3.2. *For arbitrarily large integers n, there exist n-node graphs with election index 1, such that leader election in time 1 in these graphs requires advice of size* $\Omega(n \log\log n)$.

Proof. (Sketch) Fix an integer $k \geq 2^{16}$, and let $x = \lceil 2\log k / \log\log k \rceil$. We have $k \leq y = (x-1)^x$. We first define a graph H_k using the family $\mathcal{F}(x)$, cf. Fig. 1.

Consider a ring of size k with nodes $w_1, \dots, w_k$. Attach an isomorphic copy of the clique C_t to node w_t, by identifying w_t with node r of this copy and taking all other nodes different from the nodes of the ring. (The term "isomorphic" means that all port numbers are preserved.) All attached cliques are pairwise node-disjoint. Assign ports x and $x+1$ corresponding to edges of the ring at each of its nodes, in the clockwise order. This concludes the construction of graph H_k.

Finally we produce a family $\mathcal{G}_k$ consisting of $(k-1)!$ graphs as follows. Keep the clique at node w_1 of the ring in H_k fixed, and permute arbitrarily cliques attached to all other nodes of the ring. Then delete all node labels.

The proof relies on the following two claims, proved in the Appendix. The first claim establishes the election index of graphs in $\mathcal{G}_k$.

Claim 3.1. *All graphs in the family* $\mathcal{G}_k$ *have election index 1.*

The next claim will imply a lower bound on the number of different pieces of advice needed to perform election in the family $\mathcal{G}_k$ in time 1.

Claim 3.2. *Consider any election algorithm working for the family* $\mathcal{G}_k$ *in time 1. The advice given to distinct graphs in this family must be different.*

Our lower bound will be shown on the family $\mathcal{G} = \bigcup_{k=2^{16}}^{\infty} \mathcal{G}_k$. Consider an election algorithm working in all graphs of this family in time 1. For any $k \geq 2^{16}$, let $n_k = k(\lceil 2\log k / \log\log k \rceil + 1)$. Graphs in the family $\mathcal{G}_k$ have size n_k. By Claim 3.1, all these graphs have election index 1. By Claim 3.2, all of them must get different advice. Since, for any $k \geq 2^{16}$, there are $(k-1)!$ graphs in $\mathcal{G}_k$, at least one of them must get advice of size $\Omega(\log((k-1)!)) = \Omega(k \log k)$. We have $k \log k \in \Theta(n_k \log\log n_k)$. Hence there exists an infinite sequence of integers n_k such that there are n_k-node graphs with election index 1 that require advice of size $\Omega(n_k \log\log n_k)$ for election in time 1. □

We next consider the election index $\phi > 1$. The lower bound in this case uses a construction slightly more complicated than for $\phi = 1$. Note that a straightforward generalization of the previous construction would lead to a lower bound $\Omega(n \log\log n/\phi)$ which would be too weak for our purpose, as ϕ can be much larger than polylogarithmic in n.

Theorem 3.3. *Let* ϕ *be an integer larger than 1. For arbitrarily large integers n, there exist n-node graphs with election index* ϕ*, such that leader election in time* ϕ *in these graphs requires advice of size* $\Omega(n(\log\log n)^2/\log n)$.

4 ELECTION IN LARGE TIME

In this section we study the minimum size of advice sufficient to perform leader election when the allocated time is large, i.e., when it exceeds the diameter of the graph by an additive offset which is some function of the election index ϕ of the graph. We consider four values of this offset, for an integer constant $c > 1$: $\phi + c$, $c\phi$, ϕ^c, and c^ϕ. In the first case the offset is asymptotically equal to ϕ, in the second case it is linear in ϕ but the multiplicative constant is larger than 1, in the third case it is polynomial in ϕ but super-linear, and in the fourth case it is exponential in ϕ. Note that, even in the first case, that calls for the fastest election among these four cases (in time $D + \phi + c$), the allocated time is large enough for all nodes to see all the differences in truncated views of other nodes, which makes a huge difference between leader election in such a time and in the minimum possible time ϕ. For all these four election times, we establish tight bounds on the minimum size of advice that enables election in this time, up to multiplicative constants.

We start by designing an algorithm that performs leader election in time at most $D + x + 1$, for any graph of diameter D and election index ϕ, provided that nodes receive as input an integer $x \geq \phi$. Note that nodes of the graph know neither D nor ϕ. We will then show how to derive from this generic algorithm four leader election algorithms using larger and larger time and smaller and smaller advice.

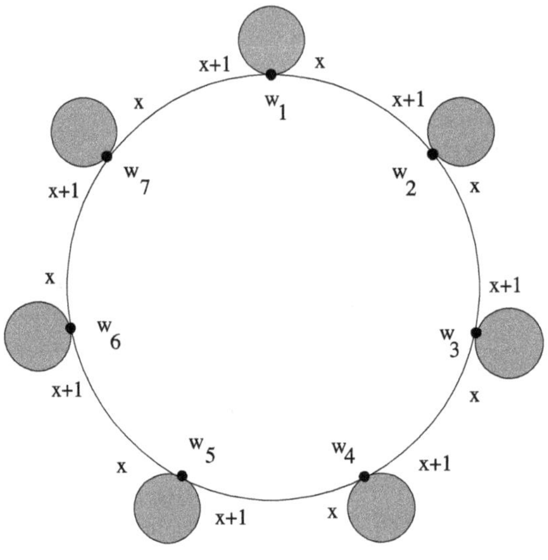

Figure 1: A representation of the graph H_7. The grey discs represent cliques from $\mathcal{F}(x)$.

The high-level idea of Algorithm `Generic`(x) is the following. Nodes of the graph communicate between them and acquire augmented truncated views at increasing depths. Starting from round x, they discover augmented truncated views at depth x of an increasing set of nodes. They stop in the round when no new augmented truncated views at depth x are discovered. At this time, we have the guarantee that all nodes learned all augmented truncated views at depth x. Hence, to solve leader election, it suffices that every node outputs a sequence of port numbers leading to a node with the lexicographically smallest augmented truncated view at depth x. Since $x \geq \phi$, the augmented truncated view at depth x of every node is unique in the graph, in view of Proposition 2.1. Hence all nodes output sequences of port numbers leading to the same node.

The detailed description of Algorithm `Generic` is in the Appendix. The following lemma establishes the correctness of Algorithm `Generic` and estimates its execution time.

Lemma 4.1. *For any graph G of diameter D and election index ϕ, Algorithm* `Generic`(x)*, with any parameter $x \geq \phi$, is a correct leader election algorithm and works in time at most $D + x + 1$.*

We now describe four algorithms, called `Election`$_i$, for $i = 1, 2, 3, 4$, working for graphs of diameter D and election index ϕ. Recall the notation ${}^i c$ defined by induction as follows: ${}^0 c = 1$ and ${}^{i+1}c = c^{{}^i c}$. Intuitively it denotes a tower of powers. For an integer constant $c > 1$, let $T_1 = D+\phi+c$, $T_2 = D+c\phi$, $T_3 = D+\phi^c$, and $T_4 = D+c^{\phi}$. Let A_1 be the binary representation of ϕ, let A_2 be the binary representation of $\lfloor \log \phi \rfloor$, let A_3 be the binary representation of $\lfloor \log \log \phi \rfloor$, and let A_4 be the binary representation of $\log^* \phi$. Hence the size of A_1 is $O(\log \phi)$, the size of A_2 is $O(\log \log \phi)$, the size of A_3 is $O(\log \log \log \phi)$, and the size of A_4 is $O(\log(\log^* \phi))$. Define the following integers. $P_1 = \phi$, $P_2 = 2^{\lfloor \log \phi \rfloor + 1} - 1$, $P_3 = 2^{2^{\lfloor \log \log \phi \rfloor + 1}} - 1$, and $P_4 = {}^{(\log^* \phi)+1}2 - 1$.

Algorithm `Election`$_i$ uses advice A_i and will be shown to work in time T_i:

Algorithm 1 `Election`$_i$

`Generic`(P_i)

Theorem 4.2. *Let G be a graph of diameter D and election index ϕ. Let $c > 1$ be any integer constant.*

(1) *Algorithm* `Election`$_1$ *solves leader election in G in time at most $D + \phi + c$ and using $O(\log \phi)$ bits of advice.*
(2) *Algorithm* `Election`$_2$ *solves leader election in G in time at most $D + c\phi$ and using $O(\log \log \phi)$ bits of advice.*
(3) *Algorithm* `Election`$_3$ *solves leader election in G in time at most $D + \phi^c$ and using $O(\log \log \log \phi)$ bits of advice.*
(4) *Algorithm* `Election`$_4$ *solves leader election in G in time at most $D + c^{\phi}$ and using $O(\log(\log^* \phi))$ bits of advice.*

Proof. 1. Algorithm `Election`$_1$ uses advice A_1 which is the binary representation of ϕ of size $O(\log \phi)$. It first computes ϕ using A_1, and then calls Algorithm `Generic`(ϕ). In view of Lemma 4.1, Algorithm `Generic`(ϕ) solves leader election in G in time at most $D + \phi + 1 \leq D + \phi + c$. This proves part 1 of the theorem.

2. Algorithm `Election`$_2$ uses advice A_2 which is the binary representation of $\lfloor \log \phi \rfloor$ of size $O(\log \log \phi)$. It first computes $\lfloor \log \phi \rfloor$ using A_2, then computes $P_2 = 2^{\lfloor \log \phi \rfloor + 1} - 1$ and calls Algorithm `Generic`(P_2). Notice that $P_2 \geq \phi$. In view of Lemma 4.1, Algorithm `Generic`(P_2) solves leader election in G in time at most $D + P_2 + 1 = D + 2^{\lfloor \log \phi \rfloor + 1}$. This is at most $D + 2\phi$ and hence at most $D + c\phi$, since c is an integer larger than 1.

3. Algorithm `Election`$_3$ uses advice A_3 which is the binary representation of $\lfloor \log \log \phi \rfloor$ of size $O(\log \log \log \phi)$. It first computes $\lfloor \log \log \phi \rfloor$ using A_3, then computes $P_3 = 2^{2^{\lfloor \log \log \phi \rfloor + 1}} - 1$ and calls Algorithm `Generic`(P_3). Notice that $P_3 \geq \phi$. In view of Lemma 4.1, Algorithm `Generic`(P_3) solves leader election in G in time at most $D + P_3 + 1 = D + 2^{2^{\lfloor \log \log \phi \rfloor + 1}}$. This is at most $D + \phi^2$ and hence at most $D + \phi^c$, since c is an integer larger than 1.

4. Algorithm $\texttt{Election}_4$ uses advice A_4 which is the binary representation of $\log^* \phi$ of size $O(\log(\log^* \phi))$. It first computes $\log^* \phi$ using A_4, then computes $P_4 = {}^{(\log^* \phi)+1}2 - 1$ and calls Algorithm $\texttt{Generic}(P_4)$. Notice that $P_4 \geq \phi$. In view of Lemma 4.1, Algorithm $\texttt{Generic}(P_4)$ solves leader election in G in time at most $D + P_4 + 1 = D + {}^{(\log^* \phi)+1}2$. This is at most $D + 2^\phi$ and hence at most $D + c^\phi$, since c is an integer larger than 1. □

Remark. Notice that the first part of the theorem remains valid for $c = 1$, and the proof remains the same. Hence, it is possible to perform leader election in time $D+\phi+1$ using $O(\log \phi)$ bits of advice. We do not know if the same is true for the time $D+\phi$, but in this time it is possible to elect a leader using $O(\log D + \log \phi)$ bits of advice. Indeed, it suffices to provide the nodes with values of the diameter D and of the election index ϕ. Equipped with this information, each node u learns $\mathcal{B}^{D+\phi}(u)$ in time $D + \phi$. Then, knowing D, it knows that nodes that it sees in this augmented truncated view at distance at most D from the root of this view represent all nodes of the graph. Knowing the value of ϕ, node u can reconstruct $\mathcal{B}^\phi(v)$, for each such node v, and hence find in $\mathcal{B}^{D+\phi}(u)$ a representation of the node w in the graph, whose augmented truncated view $\mathcal{B}^\phi(v)$ is lexicographically smallest. Finally, the node u can output a sequence of port numbers corresponding to one of the shortest paths from u to w in $\mathcal{B}^{D+\phi}(u)$.

The following theorem provides matching lower bounds (up to multiplicative constants) on the minimum size of advice sufficient to perform leader election in time corresponding to our four milestones.

Theorem 4.3. *Let α be a positive integer, and let $c > 1$ be any integer constant.*

(1) *Consider any leader election algorithm such that for all positive integers D and ϕ, this algorithm works in time at most $D + \phi + c$, for all graphs of diameter D and election index ϕ. There exist graphs with election index at most α such that this algorithm in these graphs requires advice of size $\Omega(\log \alpha)$.*
(2) *Consider any leader election algorithm such that for all positive integers D and ϕ, this algorithm works in time at most $D + c\phi$, for all graphs of diameter D and election index ϕ. There exist graphs with election index at most α such that this algorithm in these graphs requires advice of size $\Omega(\log \log \alpha)$.*
(3) *Consider any leader election algorithm such that for all positive integers D and ϕ, this algorithm works in time at most $D + \phi^c$, for all graphs of diameter D and election index ϕ. There exist graphs with election index at most α such that this algorithm in these graphs requires advice of size $\Omega(\log \log \log \alpha)$.*
(4) *Consider any leader election algorithm such that for all positive integers D and ϕ, this algorithm works in time at most $D + c^\phi$, for all graphs of diameter D and election index ϕ. There exist graphs with election index at most α such that this algorithm in these graphs requires advice of size $\Omega(\log(\log^* \alpha))$.*

Proof. (Sketch) The high-level idea of the proof relies on the construction of (ordered) families of graphs with controlled growth of election indices, and with the property that, for any election algorithm working in the prescribed time, graphs from different families must receive different advice. Since the growth of election indices in the constructed sequence of families is controlled (it is linear in part 1), this implies the desired lower bound on the size of advice. In order to prove that advice in different families must be different, we have to show that otherwise the algorithm would fail in one of these families. The difficulty lies in constructing the families of graphs in such a way as to confuse the hypothetical algorithm in spite of the fact that, as opposed to the situation in Theorems 3.2 and 3.3, the algorithm has now a lot of time: nodes can see all the differences in augmented truncated views of other nodes. In this situation, the way to confuse the algorithm is to make believe two nodes that they are in a graph with a smaller diameter and thus have to stop early, outputting a path to the leader, while in reality they are in a graph of large diameter, and each of them has seen less than "half" of the graph, which results in outputting by each of them a path to a different leader. These nodes are fooled because their augmented truncated views in the large graph at the depth requiring them to stop in the smaller graph are the same as in this smaller graph. In order to assure this, parts of the smaller graph must be carefully reproduced in the large graph, which significantly complicates the construction and the analysis. □

We close this section by showing that constant advice is not enough for leader election in all feasible graphs, regardless of the allocated time.

Proposition 4.4. *There is no algorithm using advice of constant size and performing leader election in all feasible graphs.*

Proof. We define a family $\mathcal{H}$ of graphs, called *hairy rings*, for which we will prove that no algorithm with advice of constant size performs correct leader election for all graphs in $\mathcal{H}$. Let R_n be the ring of size $n \geq 3$, with port numbers 0,1 at each node, in clockwise order. Let S_k, for any integer $k \geq 2$, be the $(k + 1)$-node tree with k leaves, called the k-star.

The only node of degree larger than 1 of the k-star is called its *central node*. For $k = 1$, S_k is defined as the two-node graph with the central node designated arbitrarily, and for $k = 0$, S_k is defined as the one-node graph, with the unique node being its central node. The class $\mathcal{H}$ is the set of all graphs that can be obtained in the following way. For all $n \geq 3$, attach to every node v of every ring R_n some graph S_k, for $k \geq 0$, by identifying its central node with the node v, in such a way that, for every ring, the star of maximum size attached to it is unique. Assign missing port numbers in any legal way, i.e., so that port numbers at a node of degree d are from 0 to $d - 1$. Every graph obtained in this way is feasible because it has a unique node of maximum degree. An example of a hairy ring is depicted in Fig. 2a.

For any graph H in $\mathcal{H}$ we define a *cut* of H as follows, see Fig. 2b. Let H be a graph resulting from a ring R_n by attaching stars. Fix any node $w = w_1$ of this ring. Let $w_1, \ldots, w_n$ be nodes of this ring listed in clockwise order. The cut of H at node w is the graph resulting from H by removing the edge $\{w_1, w_n\}$. Node $w = w_1$ is called the first node of the cut and node w_n is called the last node of the cut. For any integer $\gamma \geq 2$, the γ-*stretch* of H starting at node w is the graph defined as follows, see Fig. 2c. Take γ pairwise disjoint

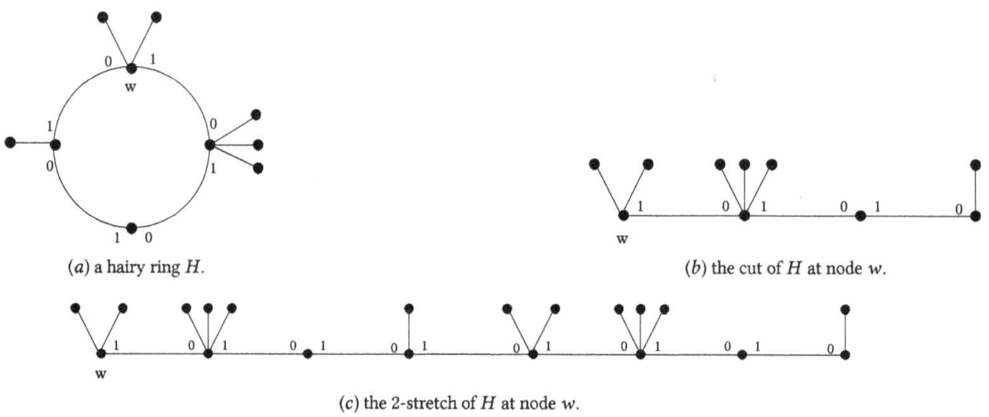

Figure 2: Illustration of a hairy ring and its different transformations used in the proof of Proposition 4.4.

isomorphic copies of the cut of H at w. For $1 < i \leq \gamma$, attach the ith copy to the $(i-1)$th copy joining the first node a_i of the ith copy with the last node b_{i-1} of the $(i-1)$th copy by an edge with port 0 at a_i and port 1 at b_{i-1} . The first node of the first copy is called the first node of the γ-stretch, and the last node of the last copy is called the last node of the γ-stretch.

Suppose that there exists a leader election algorithm $\mathcal{A}$ which uses advice of constant size to perform leader election in all hairy rings from the family $\mathcal{H}$. Let c be the smallest integer such that a total of c pieces of advice are sufficient to elect a leader in every graph from $\mathcal{H}$ by algorithm $\mathcal{A}$. Let $H_1, \ldots, H_c$ be graphs from $\mathcal{H}$ for which algorithm $\mathcal{A}$ uses different pieces of advice. Let N be the maximum of sizes of all graphs $H_1, \ldots, H_c$, and let T be the maximum execution time of $\mathcal{A}$, for all graphs $H_1, \ldots, H_c$.

Let $\gamma = 4(N+T)$ and let G_j be the γ-stretch of H_j starting at some node u_j of H_j, for $j \leq c$. We define the graph G as follows. Take pairwise disjoint isomorphic copies of graphs G_j, for $j \leq c$. For every $1 < j \leq c$, attach G_j to G_{j-1} joining the first node c_i of the ith copy with the last node d_{i-1} of the $(i-1)$th copy by an edge with port 0 at c_i and port 1 at d_{i-1}. Finally, take a γ-star and join its central node by edges to the first node of G_1 and to the last node of G_γ, assigning missing port numbers in any legal way. The graph G obtained in this way is in $\mathcal{H}$ because it has a unique node of maximum degree which is $\gamma + 2$. Let n_{H_j} be the size of the ring that was used in the construction of H_j. Let a_j be the (unique) node of G_j at distance $n_{H_j}(N+T)$ from u_j, at the end of a simple path all of whose ports are 0's and 1's. Let b_j be the (unique) node of G_j at distance $3n_{H_j}(N+T)$ from u_j, at the end of a simple path all of whose ports are 0's and 1's. Call these nodes the *foci* of G_j. Each of them corresponds to the first node of the cut serving to define G_j. Let z_j be the node in H_j at which this cut was done.

By definition of graphs $H_1, \ldots, H_c$, the advice received by graph G when algorithm $\mathcal{A}$ is performed, is the same as that received by some graph H_{j_0}. In H_{j_0} the node z_{j_0} executing algorithm $\mathcal{A}$ must stop after time at most T. By construction, the augmented truncated view $\mathcal{B}^T(z_{j_0})$ in H_{j_0} is the same as the augmented truncated views $\mathcal{B}^T(a_{j_0})$ and $\mathcal{B}^T(b_{j_0})$ in G. Hence nodes a_{j_0} and b_{j_0} executing algorithm $\mathcal{A}$ in G must also stop after time at most T. Node z_{j_0} in H_{j_0} must output a sequence of port numbers of length smaller than $2N$ because the size of H_{j_0} is at most N. Hence nodes a_{j_0} and b_{j_0} executing algorithm $\mathcal{A}$ in G must also output a sequence of port numbers of length smaller than $2N$, corresponding to simple paths in G of length smaller than N, starting, respectively at nodes a_{j_0} and b_{j_0}. However, the distance between a_{j_0} and b_{j_0} in G is at least $2N$, hence the other extremities of these simple paths must be different. It follows that the leaders elected by nodes a_{j_0} and b_{j_0} executing algorithm $\mathcal{A}$ in G are different, and hence this algorithm is not correct for the class $\mathcal{H}$. □

5 CONCLUSION

We established almost tight bounds on the minimum size of advice sufficient for election in minimum possible time (i.e., in time equal to the election index ϕ) and tight bounds on this size for several large values of time. The first big jump occurs between time ϕ and time $D+\phi$, where D is the diameter of the graph. In the first case, the size of advice is (roughly) linear in the size n of the graph, and in the second case it is at most logarithmic in n, in view of Proposition 2.2 and of the remark after Theorem 4.2. The intriguing open question left by our results is how the minimum size of advice behaves in the range of election time strictly between ϕ and $D+\phi$, i.e., for time sufficiently large to elect if the map were known, but possibly too small for all nodes to see the augmented truncated views at depth ϕ of all other nodes, and hence to realize all the differences in views. Note that, for time exactly $D+\phi$, all nodes see all these differences, although, without any advice, they cannot realize that they see all of them: this is why some advice is needed for time $D+\phi$.

In this paper we defined leader election in anonymous networks similarly as in [25]: a node has to output a simple path to the leader. There is, however, another natural definition of leader election in this context: it can be argued that it is enough for every node to learn a port corresponding to a shortest path towards the leader, as then, e.g., in the case when all nodes have to send some messages to the leader, packets could be routed to the leader from node to node, using only this local information. This is indeed true, if nodes want to cooperate with others by revealing the local port towards the leader when retransmitting packets. In some applications, however, such a cooperation may be uncertain, and even when it happens, it may slow down transmissions, as the local port has to be retrieved from the memory of the relaying node. Hence, both definitions may be suitable in different applications. It would be interesting to compare the size of advice needed for fast leader election in both these variations.

REFERENCES

[1] S. Abiteboul, H. Kaplan, T. Milo, Compact labeling schemes for ancestor queries, Proc. 12th Annual ACM-SIAM Symposium on Discrete Algorithms (SODA 2001), 547–556.
[2] A.V. Aho, J.E. Hopcroft, J.D. Ullman, Data Structures and Algorithms, Addison-Wesley 1983.
[3] D. Angluin, Local and global properties in networks of processors. Proc. 12th Annual ACM Symposium on Theory of Computing (STOC 1980), 82–93.
[4] H. Attiya and M. Snir, Better computing on the anonymous Ring, Journal of Algorithms 12, (1991), 204-238.
[5] H. Attiya, M. Snir, and M. Warmuth, Computing on an anonymous ring, Journal of the ACM 35, (1988), 845-875.
[6] P. Boldi, S. Shammah, S. Vigna, B. Codenotti, P. Gemmell, and J. Simon, Symmetry breaking in anonymous networks: Characterizations. Proc. 4th Israel Symposium on Theory of Computing and Systems, (ISTCS 1996), 16-26.
[7] P. Boldi and S. Vigna, Computing anonymously with arbitrary knowledge, Proc. 18th ACM Symp. on Principles of Distributed Computing (PODC 1999), 181-188.
[8] J.E. Burns, A formal model for message passing systems, Tech. Report TR-91, Computer Science Department, Indiana University, Bloomington, September 1980.
[9] F. Chierichetti, personal communication.
[10] D. Dereniowski, A. Pelc, Drawing maps with advice, Journal of Parallel and Distributed Computing 72 (2012), 132–143.
[11] D. Dereniowski, A. Pelc, Leader election for anonymous asynchronous agents in arbitrary networks, Distributed Computing 27 (2014), 21-38.
[12] S. Dobrev and A. Pelc, Leader election in rings with nonunique labels, Fundamenta Informaticae 59 (2004), 333-347.
[13] Y. Emek, P. Fraigniaud, A. Korman, A. Rosen, Online computation with advice, Theoretical Computer Science 412 (2011), 2642–2656.
[14] P. Flocchini, E. Kranakis, D. Krizanc, F.L. Luccio and N. Santoro, Sorting and election in anonymous asynchronous rings, Journal of Parallel and Distributed Computing 64 (2004), 254-265.
[15] P. Fraigniaud, C. Gavoille, D. Ilcinkas, A. Pelc, Distributed computing with advice: Information sensitivity of graph coloring, Distributed Computing 21 (2009), 395–403.
[16] P. Fraigniaud, D. Ilcinkas, A. Pelc, Communication algorithms with advice, Journal of Computer and System Sciences 76 (2010), 222–232.
[17] P. Fraigniaud, D. Ilcinkas, A. Pelc, Tree exploration with advice, Information and Computation 206 (2008), 1276–1287.
[18] P. Fraigniaud, A. Korman, E. Lebhar, Local MST computation with short advice, Theory of Computing Systems 47 (2010), 920–933.
[19] G.N. Fredrickson and N.A. Lynch, Electing a leader in a synchronous ring, Journal of the ACM 34 (1987), 98-115.
[20] E. Fusco, A. Pelc, How much memory is needed for leader election, Distributed Computing 24 (2011), 65-78.
[21] E. Fusco, A. Pelc, Knowledge, level of symmetry, and time of leader election, Distributed Computing 28 (2015), 221-232.
[22] E. Fusco, A. Pelc, Trade-offs between the size of advice and broadcasting time in trees, Algorithmica 60 (2011), 719–734.
[23] E. Fusco, A. Pelc, R. Petreschi, Use knowledge to learn faster: Topology recognition with advice, Information and Computation 247 (2016), 254-265.
[24] C. Gavoille, D. Peleg, S. Pérennes, R. Raz. Distance labeling in graphs, Journal of Algorithms 53 (2004), 85-112.
[25] C. Glacet, A. Miller, A. Pelc, Time vs. information tradeoffs for leader election in anonymous trees, Proc. 27th Annual ACM-SIAM Symposium on Discrete Algorithms (SODA 2016), 600-609.
[26] M.A. Haddar, A.H. Kacem, Y. Métivier, M. Mosbah, and M. Jmaiel, Electing a leader in the local computation model using mobile agents. Proc. 6th ACS/IEEE International Conference on Computer Systems and Applications (AICCSA 2008), 473-480.
[27] J. Hendrickx, Views in a graph: To which depth must equality be checked?, *IEEE Transactions on Parallel and Distributed Systems* 25 (2014) 1907-1912.
[28] D.S. Hirschberg, and J.B. Sinclair, Decentralized extrema-finding in circular configurations of processes, Communications of the ACM 23 (1980), 627-628.
[29] D. Ilcinkas, D. Kowalski, A. Pelc, Fast radio broadcasting with advice, Theoretical Computer Science, 411 (2012), 1544-1557.
[30] T. Jurdzinski, M. Kutylowski, and J. Zatopianski, Efficient algorithms for leader election in radio networks. Proc., 21st ACM Symp. on Principles of Distributed Computing (PODC 2002), 51-57.
[31] M. Katz, N. Katz, A. Korman, D. Peleg, Labeling schemes for flow and connectivity, SIAM Journal of Computing 34 (2004), 23–40.
[32] A. Korman, S. Kutten, D. Peleg, Proof labeling schemes, Distributed Computing 22 (2010), 215–233.
[33] D. Kowalski, and A. Pelc, Leader election in ad hoc radio networks: A keen ear helps, Journal of Computer and System Sciences 79 (2013), 1164-1180.
[34] G. Le Lann, Distributed systems - Towards a formal approach, Proc. IFIP Congress, 1977, 155–160, North Holland.
[35] N.L. Lynch, Distributed Algorithms, Morgan Kaufmann Publ. Inc., San Francisco, USA, 1996.
[36] A. Miller, A. Pelc: Election vs. selection: Two ways of finding the largest node in a graph, Proc. 28th ACM Symposium on Parallelism in Algorithms and Architectures (SPAA 2016), 377-386.
[37] K. Nakano and S. Olariu, Uniform leader election protocols for radio networks, IEEE Transactions on Parallel and Distributed Systems 13 (2002), 516-526.
[38] N. Nisse, D. Soguet, Graph searching with advice, Theoretical Computer Science 410 (2009), 1307-1318.
[39] D. Peleg, Distributed Computing, A Locality-Sensitive Approach, SIAM Monographs on Discrete Mathematics and Applications, Philadelphia 2000.
[40] G.L. Peterson, An $O(n \log n)$ unidirectional distributed algorithm for the circular extrema problem, ACM Transactions on Programming Languages and Systems 4 (1982), 758-762.
[41] M. Thorup, U. Zwick, Approximate distance oracles, Journal of the ACM, 52 (2005), 1–24.
[42] D.E. Willard, Log-logarithmic selection resolution protocols in a multiple access channel, SIAM J. on Computing 15 (1986), 468-477.
[43] M. Yamashita and T. Kameda, Electing a leader when procesor identity numbers are not distinct, Proc. 3rd Workshop on Distributed Algorithms (WDAG 1989), LNCS 392, 303-314.
[44] M. Yamashita and T. Kameda, Computing on anonymous networks: Part I - Characterizing the solvable cases, IEEE Trans. Parallel and Distributed Systems 7 (1996), 69-89.

Swarm-based Incast Congestion Control in Datacenters Serving Web Applications

Haoyu Wang
University of Virginia
Department of Computer Science
Charlottesville, Virginia 22904, USA
hw8c@virginia.edu

Haiying Shen
University of Virginia
Department of Computer Science
Charlottesville, Virginia 22904, USA
hs6ms@virginia.edu

Guoxin Liu
Clemson University
Department of ECE
Clemson, South Carolina 29604, USA
guoxinl@clemson.edu

ABSTRACT

In Web applications served by datacenter nowadays, the incast congestion at the front-end server seriously degrades the data request latency performance due to the vast data transmissions from a large number data servers for a data request in a short time. Previous incast congestion control methods usually consider the direct data transmissions from data servers to the front-end server, which makes it difficult to control the sending speed or adjust workloads due to the transient transmission of only a few data objects from each data server. In this paper, we propose a Swarm-based Incast Congestion Control (*SICC*) system. *SICC* forms all target data servers of one request in the same rack into a swarm. In each swarm, a data server (called hub) is selected to forward all data objects to the front-end server, so that the number of data servers concurrently connected to the front-end server is reduced, which avoids the incast congestion. Also, the continuous data transmission from hubs to the front-end server facilitates the development of other strategies to further control the incast congestion. To fully utilize the bandwidth, *SICC* uses a two-level data transmissior
control method to adjust the data transmission speeds of l
query redirection method further reduces the request late
balancing the transmission remaining times between hubs.
periments in simulation and on a real cluster demonstrate th
outperforms other incast control methods in improving thro
and reducing the data request latency.

KEYWORDS

Incast Congestion; Congestion Control; Data Center

ACM Reference format:
Haoyu Wang, Haiying Shen, and Guoxin Liu. 2017. Swarm-base
Congestion Control in Datacenters Serving Web Applications. In *Prc
of SPAA'17, July 24-26, 2017, Washington DC, USA*, , 10 pages.
DOI: http://dx.doi.org/10.1145/3087556.3087559

SPAA'17, July 24-26, 2017, Washington DC, USA
© 2017 ACM. 978-1-4503-4593-4/17/07...$15.00
DOI: http://dx.doi.org/10.1145/3087556.3087559

1 INTRODUCTION

Web applications, such as online social networks (e.g., Facebook), Web search systems (e.g., Google) and online content publishers (e.g., Youtube), become the top sources of Internet traffic today [1]. The datacenter serving these applications usually support tremendous workloads. For example, Facebook serves a billion reads per second [2]. It is important to guarantee that the data requests from users are served successfully with low latency because it affects the quality of experience of users and also is negatively proportional to the incomes of the Web application providers. Take Amazon for example, its sale degrades by one percent if the latency of its Web presentation increases as small as 100ms [3]. The typical data request latency inside a storage system of Yahoo is on larger than 100ms [4] to meet the user satisfaction. However, the packet loss always occurs during data requesting due to traffic congestion and the bandwidth usually becomes the bottleneck of the performance [5–7]. The traffic congestion also greatly increase the data request latency due to the retransmissions of dropped packets. Therefore,

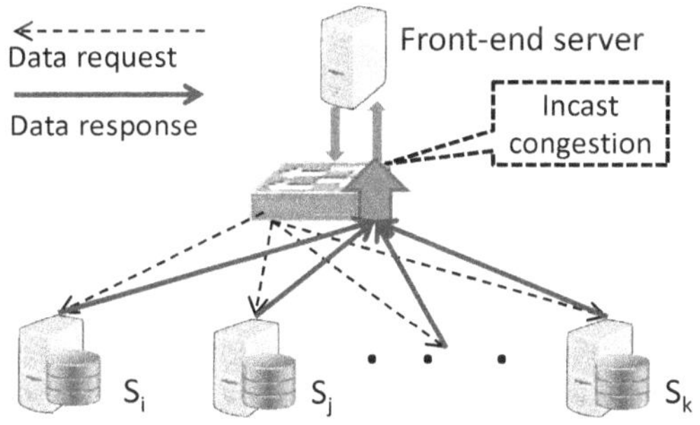

Figure 1: An example of incast congestion.

In Web applications, a data request for a Web page presentation needs to retrieve thousands of data objects currently [2, 8]. As shown in the Figure 1, for a data request, the front-end server sends out data queries concurrently to all targeted data servers, and receives hundreds or thousands of data responses simultaneously. The heavy network traffic in a short time may not reach the front-end server in time due to the bandwidth limitation. The traffic then overflows the switch buffer capacity and causes packet loss, which introduces an extra delay due to retransmissions. This kind of congestion is named as *incast congestion*, which is a major cause of the delay of data requests in datacenter [2, 9].

The root cause of incast congestion is the many-to-one communication pattern between a front-end server and many data servers. Therefore, many previous methods have been proposed to handle the incast congestion problem by reducing the number of data servers concurrently connected to the front-end server. We classify these methods to three groups. The first group [10–17] improves the sliding window protocol. This approach measures the actual packet throughput variation to decide the size of the sliding window at the front-end server. When the sliding window has an available slot of download link bandwidth, the front-end server sends a query to a data server. However, there is a delay between the new query sending and the response receiving so that the download link bandwidth cannot be fully utilized. Therefore, this approach cannot meet the stringent low service latency requirement of the current Web applications. The second group [18–20] uses data reallocation that tries to reallocate or replicate the data objects of a request to a small number of servers. However, the data reallocation method requires that many requests share concurrently requested data objects (e.g., user data in online social networks) and the data replication method generates a high overhead due to data replication and consistency maintenance [21, 27]. The third group [22–24] pre-determines a certain time interval between any two consecutive responses in order to limit the number of responses during a short time arriving at the front-end server. However, the network status varies over time and between different data servers, so it is difficult to pre-determine the interresponse interval to fully utilize the bandwidth while avoiding congestion. If we improve this approach to dynamically determine the interresponse interval based on current network status of individual data servers, it is not applicable to the current Web applications which needs hundreds or thousands of responses for one data request because of the high overhead for the front-end server to keep track of the network status of such a large number of data servers.

More importantly, all of these previous approaches usually consider the direct data transmissions from data servers to the front-end server for a request, which leads to very fast ($178\mu s$ seconds) transmission of only a few (1 or 2) data objects from each data server [2, 25, 26] for current Web applications. The transient transmission makes it difficult to timely control the sending speed or to adjust the workloads on different data servers without knowing their current transmission speeds to reduce latency. A very large number of data servers for one data request make these tasks even more formidable.

To handle the aforementioned problems, in this paper, we propose a Swarm-based Incast Congestion Control method (*SICC*). It also makes data transmission long-lasting to effectively control data transmission speeds and adjust workloads on different data servers to fully utilize bandwidth to reduce service latency. SICC forms all target data servers of one request in the same rack into a swarm. In each swarm, a data server (called hub) is selected to forward all data objects to the front-end server, so that the number of data servers concurrently connected to the front-end server is reduced. Also, instead of sending out data object queries sequentially, the front-end server sends out data queries simultaneously, so that it can receive the responses continuously without the delay on the data servers for waiting for the data queries. The long-lasting data transmission from hubs to the front-end server allows it to adjust the hubs' transmission speeds and redirect the requests to balance the workloads among them according to their current data transmission speeds. Also, each hub can receive many packets for compression in order to save bandwidth consumption for transmitting many packets.

SICC consists of the following methods.

Proximity-aware swarm based data transmission. The front-end server dynamically clusters all target data servers of a request in the same rack into a swarm. The hub in each swarm is responsible for collecting all data responses from its swarm and sends the responses continually to the front-end server. Hubs can form a multi-level tree to further reduce the number of concurrently connected servers to avoid incast congestion.

Two-level data transmission speed control. Each front-end server adjusts the data transmission speed of each hub based on its network status in order to fully utilize its bandwidth while avoiding congestion. It also adjusts its received data response traffic to its edge switch to avoid congestion at the aggregation router to avoid packet loss.

Packet compression and object query redirection. Each hub combines several data objects together to one packet to reduce the number of packets in transmission to reduce traffic. Also, the front-end server redirects data queries from an overloaded hub to an underloaded hub to reduce the longest data transmission latency in all hubs for a request.

The rest of this paper is organized as follows. Section 2 presents the related work. Section 3 presents the design of *SICC* in detail. Sections 4 and 5 present the performance evaluation of *SICC* in comparison with other methods a model on a simulator and a prototype on a real cluster, respectively. Section 6 concludes this paper with remarks on our future work.

2 RELATED WORK

There are many works focusing on the incast congestion control problem. We classify the previously proposed methods to three groups: improved sliding window protocols, data server reduction and transmission delay control.

Many works improve the sliding window protocol [28] to solve the incast congestion problem by limiting the number of concurrently connected data servers in order to reduce the number of concurrent responses. ICTCP [10] adjusts the receive window according to the ratio of the actual throughput over the expected throughput. When the ratio decreases, the window size is increased to use more available bandwidth and vice verse. It divides the slot into two sub-slots and then uses all the traffic received in the first sub-slot to calculate the available bandwidth as quota for window increase on the second sub-slot. Zhang *et al.* [14] modeled the TCP incast congestion problem based on their observation that the TCP throughput is affected by two kinds of timeouts, which are for waiting all other senders to finish and for the retransmission caused by incast congestion. To improve the downlink bandwidth utilization, DCTCP [12, 13] reduces the window size by a flexible ratio according to current network status, such as the round trip delay (RTD) and package loss rate.

Although all of the above methods can control the incast congestion by adjusting the size of the sliding window, they introduce extra round trip delay when the front-end server waits for response of new requests while the window is moving.

The methods in [18–20] use data reallocation or data replication to increase the number of data objects queried from each server, so that the number of concurrently requested servers is reduced. However, it needs data reallocation to store simultaneously requested data together in the same server. In [18, 20], concurrently requested data objects are replicated to several servers close to each other, so that a request can target a small number of servers nearby. In [19], all servers are divided into several RAID groups, and all concurrently requested data objects are put into one of the groups, so that each data request only communicates with data servers in one RAID group. The above methods can avoid the incast congestion to a certain extent by reducing the number of concurrently connected servers. However, they need data reallocation or replication, which introduce extra network loads.

In [22–24], a short delay is introduced between two consecutive requests by manually scheduling the second response in short delay. Therefore, the concurrent number of connec servers is reduced to avoid incast congestion. In [22], the insert one unit time delay between two consecutive requ methods in [23, 24] asks the target server to wait for a time before transmitting the requested data, so that the of concurrently connected data servers is reduced. Howe pre-determined delay for all data queries in a data reques adapt to the network status varying over time and between data servers. This delay adaptation is a non-trivial task for Web applications because they have thousands of data ob a request and it is difficult to profile the network status thousands of data servers and decide the delay individual

Previous methods use the direct connection between dat to the front-end server. The transient data transmission fr data server to the front-end server for a request makes it to control the sending speed or adjust workloads betw servers. To overcome this problem, we solve the incast co problem using a completely different approach. We set o local servers as a hub to collect all the requested data object so that the number of concurrently connected data serve front-end server is reduced to avoid the incast congest long-lasting data transmission between hubs and the fr server enables data response speed control, package compression, and query redirection among data replicas to further reduce the request latency.

3 SWARM BASED INCAST CONGESTION CONTROL

In this section, we present the details of Swarm based Incast Congestion Control (*SICC*). A swarm is formed by all data servers of a request in the same rack. In *SICC*, the front-end server dynamically forms a proximity-aware swarm structure with all data servers for a request, and selects one data server from each swarm as the hub to connect to it in order to reduce the number of concurrently connected data servers to avoid the incast congestion. By monitoring the actual packet transmission speed of each hub and the traffic in the uplink of edge switch, each front-end server controls the data transmission speed of hub servers to fully utilize its bandwidth without causing congestion in its edge switch and aggregation router. *SICC* has two enhancements, a packet compression method and object query redirection method, to further reduce the network overhead and data request latency.

3.1 Proximity-aware Swarm based Data Transmission

To avoid incast congestion, *SICC* also reduces the number of concurrently connected data servers to the front-end server. For this purpose, rather than relying on sliding window protocol (that causes an extra delay) or data reallocation (that generates extra overhead), *SICC* introduces another layer between the requester (front-end server) and the responsers (data servers) of a request (Figure 2), which consists of several data servers called hubs. Hubs are responsible for data transmission between the front-end server and the data servers. We use h_i to denote the hub of the ith swarm, and H

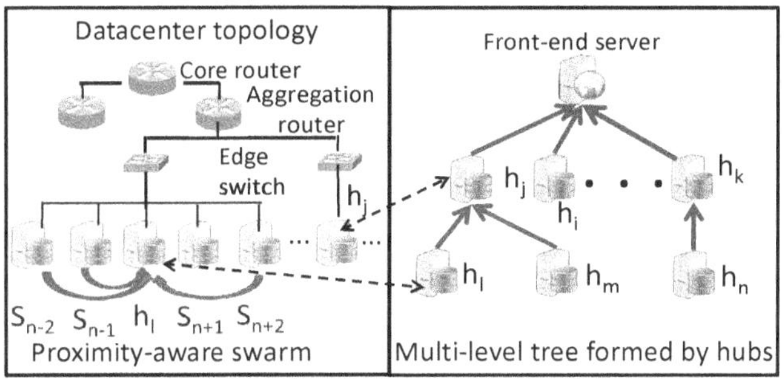

Figure 2: The multilevel tree with proximity-aware swarms.

For a data request, *SICC* forms the target data servers to swarms with each swarm consisting of data servers in the same rack. The server with the largest spare capacity to handle I/O among each rack is selected as the hub of each rack. In order to maintain the multi-level structure, we also select another server in the rack with larger spare capacity as the backup for the hub. When the current hub fails, the backup server will serve as the hub. A hub forwards data object queries from the front-end server to the target data servers, and then forwards the data responses from the data servers to the front-end server. Each hub continuously sends all queried data objects to the front-end server, starting from the data objects stored inside it and then the received data objects from other data servers inside its swarm sequentially. Since the number of data servers in a swarm is limited and also the number of hub servers, this one-to-many communication pattern is unlikely to cause incast congestion. Also, because data servers and the hub are in the same rack, the data transmission efficiency will be enough.

Note this structure is dynamically created for each request rather than fixed and it does not need to be maintained. The front-end server sends its data object queries to each hub along with its swarm information. Then, each hub knows the data servers to forward the queries. After receiving queries from a hub, the data servers know the hub to send their data responses. Finally, the hub forwards the data responses to the front-end server. If the hub layer has too many hubs that will generate incast congestion, we transform the hub layer to a tree structure. We will explain the tree creation later on.

We create the transient swarm structure from the data servers of a request to be used specifically for the request rather than creating a global tree from all data servers in the datacenter for all requests because of three reasons. First, the transient structure does not need to be maintained by periodical probing between connected servers, which avoids generating more network load. Second, transmitting data through a much smaller structure greatly reduces the latency. Third, the data servers without the requested data objects do not need to involve in the data transmission for the request, which saves data transmission time since the establishment of the data transmission connection takes a certain time. Though the front-end server needs to create a swarm structure for each request, this computing latency is negligible as is shown in Section 4.6.

Next, we discuss how to determine a suitable number of hubs. If there are too many hubs in the system, the number of concurrently received packets in a short time can still cause incast congestion. Generally, Assume the bandwidth of downlink is B_d Gbps, the bandwidth of uplink is B_u Gbps, the average size of a packet as $\bar{s}$, and the buffer size of the edge switch is S_e MB. In the case that all hubs' packets arrive at the edge switch of the front-end server in a short time, the largest number of hubs (denoted by M) connecting front-end server at a time without causing the increment of the queue size in the edge switch is

$$M = \frac{\frac{S_e}{B_d} * B_u}{\bar{s}}. \tag{1}$$

Assume that there are m requests sent from the front-end server at a time on average, then the number of hubs for one request is $N = M/m$.

In a large-scale datacenter with a lot of racks, we also need to constrain the number of hubs directly connecting to the front-end server to be less than N. To achieve this, as shown in Figure 2, all hubs need to form a multi-level tree structure with the front-end server as the root. Each child hub transmits all its requested data objects to its parent hub continuously, which transmits the data further to its parent. In order to reduce the network load, we try to reduce the transmission switches and data size in data transmission. Then, we follow two rules when building the tree.

Rule 1: We form the tree with proximity-awareness to reduce the number of transmission switches. That is, two hubs (including their children) under the same aggregation router are linked together in the tree.

Rule 2: We ensure that a hub's child always has a smaller number of requested data objects (including the data objects inside its child hub) than its parent in the tree structure.

Algorithm 1 shows the procedure to build the multi-level tree from the target data servers of a request. Based on Rule 1, *SICC* clusters target data servers inside the same rack into a proximity-aware swarm (Line 1). Inside a swarm, based on Rule 2, the data server storing the largest number of queried data objects is selected to be the hub by the front-end server, and the hub enqueues into queue Q_h (Lines 2-4). Thus, the hub can communicate with its proximity close data servers directly through the edge switch with minimized path length as 1. Due to the clustering of data servers, the number of hubs is much smaller than the number of target data servers, so that the total number of concurrently connected data servers to the front-end server is reduced to avoid the incast congestion.

Algorithm 1: Building a multi-level tree from hubs.

```
1  Cluster target data servers in each rack into a swarm;
2  /*Selecting a hub from each swarm*/
3  for each swarm do
4      Select the data server with the largest number of requested
         data objects as the hub; Enqueue the hub in to queue Q_h;
5  Sort the hubs in Q_h in an ascending order of the number of
     stored requested data objects;
6  /*Creating multi-level tree from the hubs*/
7  while |Q_h| > N do
8      Dequeue a hub h_i from Q_h;
9      Select a hub h_j
         with the smallest number of data objects and under the
         same aggregation router as h_i; Link h_i as a child to h_j;
10     while h_j has less than N children and h_i has children do
11         Transmit the last child from h_i to be a child of h_j;
12     Update h_j's number of requested data objects by add h_i's;
13     Update h_j's position at Q_h accordingly;
```

When the number of hubs connecting the front-end servers is larger than N, which tends to generate incast congestion, a multi-level tree is formed from the hubs to limit the number of concurrent connections to the front-end server no larger than N. By following Rule 1, we first sort all hubs in an ascending order of the number of their stored requested data objects Q_h (Line 5). Q_h contains hubs in an ascending order of the number of requested data objects contained in the subtree with the root of each hub. While the number of hubs connecting the front-end servers is larger than N (Line 7), starting from the first hub h_i (Line 8), we try to form a subtree to connect it (as the child) and a hub nearby (as the parent) (Lines 9-13). According to Rule 1 and Rule 2, we try to link a hub to the hub with the smallest number of data objects among the hubs under the same aggregate router (Lines 9-10). Also, in order to balance the workloads among hubs and reduce the number of levels of the tree to reduce the network load of data transmission, if h_i is a parent hub of other hubs, it transfers each of its child from the one with the largest number of requested data objects to be a child of h_j until all h_i's children are transferred or h_j has N children (Lines 10-11). After that, the number of requested data objects reported by h_j is updated by adding the number of data objects reported by h_i (Line 12), and h_j's position in the queue should be updated accordingly based on the number of requested data objects contained in its subtree (Line 13).

3.2 Two-Level Data Transmission Speed Control

3.2.1 Congestion Avoidance at the Front-End Server. For a data request, the front-end server sends out the data queries concurrently to all hubs in the swarm structure. While collecting all data responses from target data servers inside the same swarm, a hub continuously sends out all data responses to the front-end server. The sum of the bandwidths of the hubs' upload links may still be larger than the bandwidth of the download link of the front-end server, which may cause incast congestion.

To avoid the incast congestion caused by the hubs, we control the data transmission speed of each hub in each short time period (denoted by t_i ($i \in N^+$)) in order to fully utilize the bandwidth of the front-end server while avoiding overflows. Fortunately, the long-lasting data transmissions from hubs to the front-end servers enable to learn the transmission speeds of hubs in time t_{i-1} to adjust their assigned bandwidth in time t_i. We use $b^a_{h_i}$ to denote the assigned data transmission speed of hub h_i, and use $b^r_{h_i}$ to denote the real data transmission speed from hub h_i to the front-end server measured during the last short time period. We use B_p to denote the downlink bandwidth that the front-end server plans or is assigned to use for the next time period. At initial, B_p is set to $(B_d - B_a)$, where B_d denotes its bandwidth capacity, and B_a denotes its actual received total size of packets during time t_{i-1}. We will explain how to update B_p later on.

At the initial time of each short time period, without considering the different network status of each hub, the front-end server can allocate its bandwidth evenly to each hub as:

$$b^a_{h_i} = \frac{B_p}{|H|}. \tag{2}$$

However, the network status of each hub varies over time and the loads on different hubs are different, so some hubs may not fully utilize their assigned transmission speed $b^a_{h_i}$ while others need a transmission speed higher than $b^a_{h_i}$. In order to fully utilize the bandwidth of the front-end server without causing congestion, we reassign the over-assigned bandwidth to other hubs that need more bandwidth. We use H^o and H^u to denote the set of hubs with $b^a_{h_i} < b^r_{h_i}$ (over-utilized hubs) and the set of hubs with $b^a_{h_i} > b^r_{h_i}$ (under-utilized hubs), respectively. Therefore, we reassign the data transmission speed of hubs in H^o to:

$$b^a_{h_i} = b^a_{h_i} + \frac{\sum_{h_j \in H^u}(b^a_{h_j} - b^r_{h_j})}{|H^o|}, \tag{3}$$

and the data transmission speed of hubs in H^u to:

$$b^a_{h_i} = b^r_{h_i}. \tag{4}$$

The front-end server periodically adjusts the assigned bandwidth to each hub after each short time period. Since the expected and upper bound of data transmission speed is always $\sum_{h_i \in H} b^a_{h_i}$ which equals B_p, the front-end server overflow of the download link is avoided and the bandwidth is fully utilized.

3.2.2 Congestion Avoidance at the Aggregation Router. Considering a number of front-end servers in the same rack, due to their sharing of the uplink of the edge-switch (Figure 2), the incast congestion may occur at the uplink of the edge-switch (i.e., downlink of the aggregation router) if all front-end servers in the same rack receive many data responses at the same time. To avoid the overflow at the uplink of edge-switches, the front-end servers need to cooperatively adjust the data transmission speeds for data responses in their downlinks on the edge-switch. That is, B_p used in Equation (2) for the next time period is proactively adjusted.

At the beginning of each period t_i, each front-end server asks the total size of all queueing packets (denoted by q_{t_i}) in the aggregation router's port, which is connected to the uplink of its edge switch. We use S_a to denote the size of the buffer in the aggregation router for package queueing and use T to denote a threshold to judge a possible incoming congestion at the uplink of the edge switch. If $\frac{q_{t_i}}{S_a} \geq T$, each front-end server cuts down its B_p to avoid the congestion:

$$B_p = B_p * (1 - \beta * \frac{q_{t_i}}{S_a}), \tag{5}$$

where β is the upper bound of the decrement of the bandwidth. We used a sliding window [28] like congestion control strategy by reducing the planned bandwidth by a certain percentage. Largely reducing the planned bandwidth leads to low bandwidth utilization. Therefore, *SICC* adjusts the planned bandwidth according to the congestion conditions measured by $\frac{q_{t_i}}{S_a}$. A larger q_{t_i} compared to the buffer size S_a indicates a more serious congestion in the edge bandwidth uplink, which needs a larger decrement on B_p. After updating B_p, all the data transmission speeds of hubs are updated by keeping the same portion of their sharing of the B_p in last period based on Equation (2).

To fully utilize the bandwidth of the uplink, we need to enlarge B_p when there is no predicted congestion. Then, we set

$$B_p = \min\{B_d, B_p * (1 + \alpha * \frac{B_a}{B_p})\}, \tag{6}$$

where α is the upper bound of the increment of the bandwidth. Instead of using a slow increase as in the sliding window protocol, *SICC* increases the planned bandwidth by a certain percentage according to the network status. A larger B_a means that the hub fully utilized its planed bandwidth in current period, which indicates a better network status during packet routing. Thus, we increased B_p faster with a larger $\frac{B_a}{B_p}$. On the other hand, a smaller B_a indicates a busy network during data transmission. Therefore, B_p is increased more slowly with a smaller $\frac{B_a}{B_p}$.

3.3 Packet Compression and Object Query Redirection

3.3.1 Packet Compression. The data object is usually very small and no larger than 1KB [2], such as the text content of one friend post and status in online social networks. To put each data object in one packet, a large amount of the bandwidth along the path from a hub to the front-end server is consumed by transferring the packet headers compared to its small payload. Thus, the network resource utilization is reduced.

Actually, the maximum payload of a packet can be much larger than the size of a data object. For example, the packet in Ethernet is 1,500 bytes. Therefore, a hub can combine several data objects into the same packet until the maximum allowed payload is reached. It reduces the total number of packets needed to be sent to the front-end server through inter-rack communication and saves the bandwidth otherwise needed to transmit a large number of packet heads. As a result, the network resource utilization is increased.

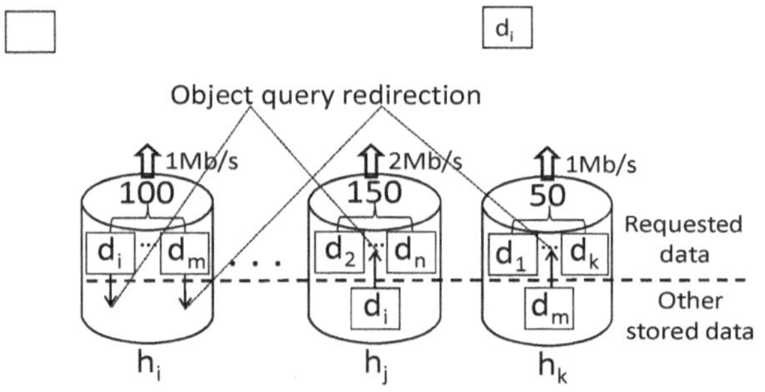

Figure 3: An example of query redirection.

3.3.2 Query Redirection. The data request response latency depends on the hub that is the last one finishing the data transmission to the front-end server regardless of the transmission speeds of the other hubs. Therefore, an incast congestion control method needs to reduce the longest data transmission latency in all hubs. To achieve this, *SICC* needs to balance the number of data objects transmitted from different hubs according to their data transmission speeds to minimize the data response latency. We define the data transmission progress rate of hub h_i (denoted by p_{h_i}) as:

$$p_{h_i} = \frac{|D_{h_i}| * \bar{s}}{b^r_{h_i}}, \quad (7)$$

where D_{h_i} denotes the set of all data objects stored in the data servers in the subtree of h_i that have not been transmitted yet. The data transmission progress rate p_{h_i} actually denotes the expected remaining time to finish the data transmission. In order to reduce the longest data request latency among all hubs, we need to balance the data transmission progress rate among them.

For each data object, there are usually several data replicas stored by different data servers over the datacenter in order to achieve high data availability [29, 30]. Therefore, if a hub has a long data remaining transmission time, the front-end server can redirect some of the hub's queries to another hub whose subtree has data servers hosting replicas of the data objects of the queries. As shown in Figure 3, h_i has a higher remaining time than h_j and h_k. The request of d_i and d_j are redirected from h_i to h_j and h_k, respectively. To do this, we define the average transmission remaining time as

$$\bar{p} = \frac{\sum_{h_i \in H} p_{h_i}}{|H|}. \quad (8)$$

For any hub with $p_{h_i} > \bar{p}$, we define it as a low-progress hub, and use D_l to denote the set of all low-progress hubs; for any hub with $p_{h_i} < \bar{p}$, we define it as a high-progress hub, and use D_h to denote the set of all high-progress hubs.

We aim to redirect some queries from each hub h_i in D_l to the hubs in D_h to make h_i a non-less-progress hub. We loop all data objects $d_k \in D_{h_i}$ until h_i is not a low-progress hub. Specifically, for each data object $d_k \in D_{h_i}$, if there exists a data replica inside the swarm of a high-progress hub h_j in D_h, we redirect the data query of d_k from h_i to h_j. We then update D_{h_i} and D_{h_j}, and recalculate p_{h_i} and p_{h_j} accordingly. By comparing with $\bar{p}$, if the hub h_i (h_j) is no longer a low (high) progress hub, it is removed from D_l (D_h). In this way, all hubs for a request are expected to have a similar data transmission progress rate, and the longest data request latency among all the hubs is reduced.

4 PERFORMANCE EVALUATION

We simulated 3000 data servers [31] in a datacenter, which forms a typical three-layer fat-tree [5] with 60 data servers inside a rack [32]. Front-end servers were randomly selected from servers. The capacity of downlink, uplink and buffer size of each edge-switch were set to 1Gbps, 1Gbps [33] and 100KB, respectively. We assume a 1:4 over-subscription ratio at the ToR tier.We set the default number of requested data objects of a data request to 1000 [2]. Each data object has three replicas [30] randomly distributed among all data servers [34]. We set the size of each packet to a value randomly chosen from [20, 1000]B [2]. The timeout of TCP packet retransmission was set to 10 ms [35]. As [10, 36, 37], we first simulated the incast congestion scenario with one front-end server requesting data objects from multiple data servers. For each experiment, the front-end server continuously initiates 10,000 data requests one after each other, and we measure the average performance per request after the front-end server receives all queried data objects. Later on, we test the scenario of multiple front-end servers. We assume that there is no any physical failure in the simulation.

We compared *SICC* with previous incast congestion control methods: *One-all*, the sliding window protocol (*SW*) [2], and *ICTCP* [10].

One-all We use *One-all* as a baseline. In this method, the front-end server simultaneously sends out queries to all target data servers, which start the data transmission to the front-end server right after receiving the queries.

SW The sliding window protocol (SW) [2] reduces the concurrently connected data servers to the front-end server using the typical sliding window protocol, which increases the window size till the occurrence of incast congestion and then decreases the size.

ICTCP [10] improves the sliding window protocol by adjusting the receiving window according to the ratio of the actual throughput over the expected throughput. It divides the slot into two sub-slots and then uses all the traffic received in the first sub-slot to calculate the available bandwidth as quota for window increase on the second sub-slot. In the following sections, we first measure the performance of *SICC* without enhancements, and then measure the effectiveness of each enhancement method.

4.1 Performance of Data Request Latency

A data request consists of many data queries for different data objects. The latency of a query is defined as the time elapsed from the time when the front-end server initiates the query to the time when it receives the data object. The longest query latency among the queries of a request is the request's latency. Figure 4(a) shows the data request latency of different methods versus the number of data queries. Figure 4(b) shows the CDF of data queries over time

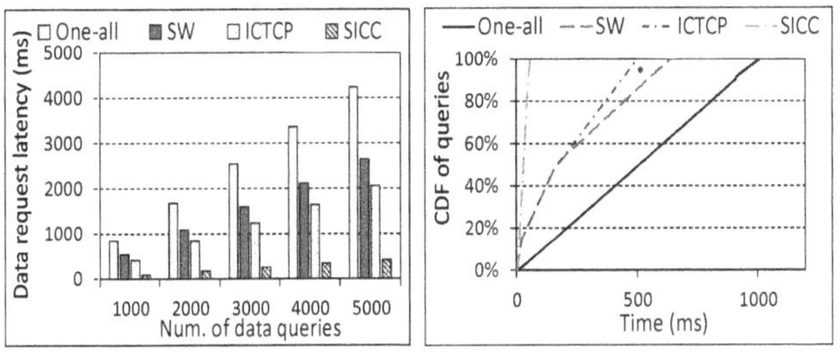

(a) Data request latency (b) CDF of queries

Figure 4: Performance of response latency.

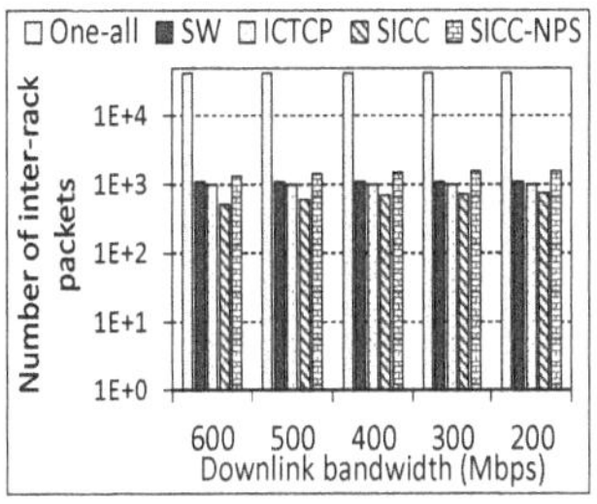

Figure 5: Inter-rack traffic cost reduction

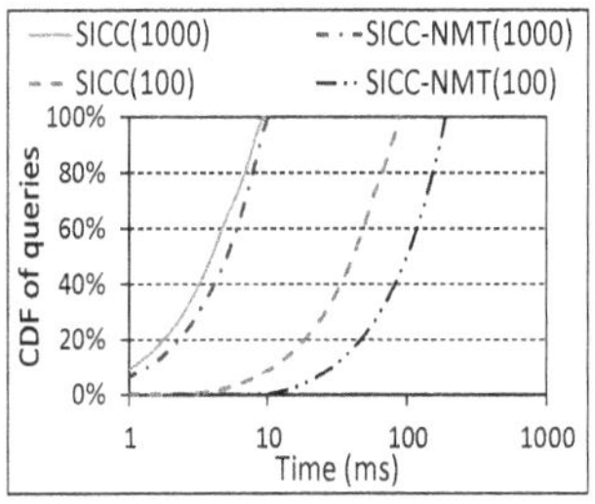

Figure 6: Effectiveness of swarm-based multi-level tree.

of one data request. From both figures, we see that the data request latency follows *SICC<ICTCP<SW<One-all*. In *One-all*, all target data servers send data packets to the front-end server during a short time, which causes incast congestion and retransmissions for dropped packets, thus leading to the highest latency. *SW* reduces the concurrently connected data servers through the sliding window protocol. Thus, it generates a shorter data request latency than *One-all* due to lighter incast congestion. *SW* generates a longer service latency than *ICTCP*, which improves the sliding window protocol to avoid increasing the window size beyond the bandwidth of the uplink. However, the sliding window cannot fully utilize the bandwidth while moving the window forwards, and a delay is generated between querying sending and response receiving for a new available slot. *SICC* generates a shorter latency than *ICTCP* since *SICC* receives all data responses continuously by fully utilizing the bandwidth of the downlink. Figure 4(a) also shows that the data request latency of all methods increases proportional to the number of data queries of a request. More queries mean that more data objects need to be transmitted to each hub, leading to a longer data transmission time. The figures indicate that *SICC* generates the shortest data request latency among all methods by avoiding congestion and fully utilizing the downlink bandwidth.

4.2 Performance in Reducing Inter-Rack Traffic

Inter-rack communication usually has a higher latency than intra-rack communication. Also, the network resources of inter-rack communication are highly required since the resources are shared by many servers under different racks. The bandwidth of links of an aggregation router is much smaller than the total downlink bandwidth of all data servers connecting to this router. Therefore, it is necessary to reduce the number of inter-rack packets. Figure 5 shows the number of inter-rack packets (including retransmitted packets) on a logarithmic scale generated by different methods while the downlink bandwidth decreases from 600Mbps to 200Mbps. We use *SICC-NPS* to denote *SICC* without the Proximity-aware Swarm method (PS), in which each hub randomly selects the same amount of target data servers as in *SICC-NPS* among all data servers as its swarm children. From the figure, we see that the result follows *One-all>SICC-NPS>SW>ICTCP>SICC*. *One-all* generates the largest number of inter-rack packets since the packet retransmissions caused by the incast congestion generate extra inter-rack packets. *SICC-NPS* can mitigate incast congestion so that it generates a smaller number of inter-rack packets than *One-all*. *SICC-NPS* generates a larger number of inter-rack packets than *SW*. This is because, in *SICC-NPS*, most packets between hubs and data servers in their swarms are transmitted between racks due to the proximity-unaware clustering. In *SW*, all data servers transmit the packets directly to the front-end server without another forwarding layer between hubs and the front-end server as in *SICC-NPS*. *ICTCP* also has direct transmission without an additional forwarding layer. Since *ICTCP* avoids more incast congestion and hence reduces more packet retransmissions than *SW*, it generates a smaller number of inter-rack packets than *SW*. *SICC* generates the smallest number of inter-rack packets due to its proximity-aware swarm creation, packet compression method to send several data packets together, and the incast congestion control that avoids packet retransmission. This figure indicates that *SICC* is the most effective in reducing the number of inter-rack packets to reduce request latency and save the inter-rack network resources.

4.3 Performance of Swarm based Multi-Level Tree

We then measure the effectiveness of the swarm based multi-level tree to reduce the data request latency by avoiding the incast congestion. We use *SICC-NMT* to denote *SICC* without the Multi-level Tree (MT), so that all hubs directly connect to the front-end server. Figure 6 shows the CDF of the queries over time of different methods versus downlink bandwidth capacity and (x) in the figure means that the downlink is xMbps. It shows that *SICC-NMT* generates a longer data request latency than *SICC* due to the incast congestion caused by packets concurrently sent from all hubs. The figure also shows that a larger downlink bandwidth leads to a smaller response latency. By fully utilizing the bandwidth, *SICC(1000)* generates approximate one-tenth of the data request latency of *SICC(100)* even though it has a higher depth of multi-level tree. Since each hub starts transmitting data objects continuously from currently stored and received requested data objects, it does not need to wait for receiving all data objects from its children. Therefore, by sending and receiving data objects continuously, the hub can fully utilize its assigned bandwidth. Therefore, a tree with a large depth does not increase the data request latency. The figure further shows that with a smaller downlink bandwidth, *SICC-NMT* generates much longer latency than *SICC*. This is because, with a smaller downlink

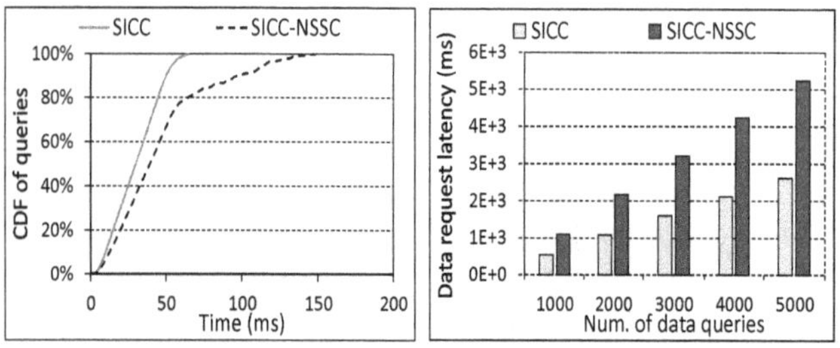

(a) CDF of queries of a single front-end server (b) Data request latency with multi-front-end servers

Figure 7: Effectiveness of two-level speed control.

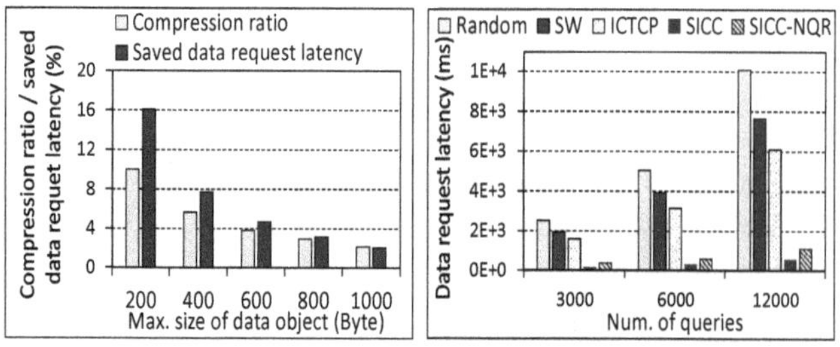

(a) Packet compression. (b) Query redirection

Figure 8: Effectiveness of the enhancement methods

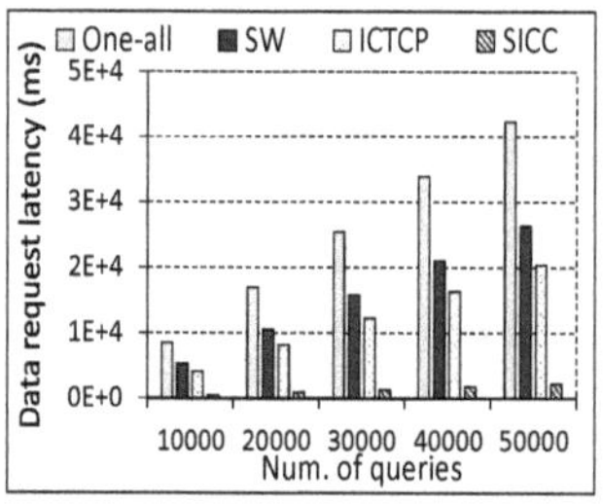

Figure 9: Performance of scalability.

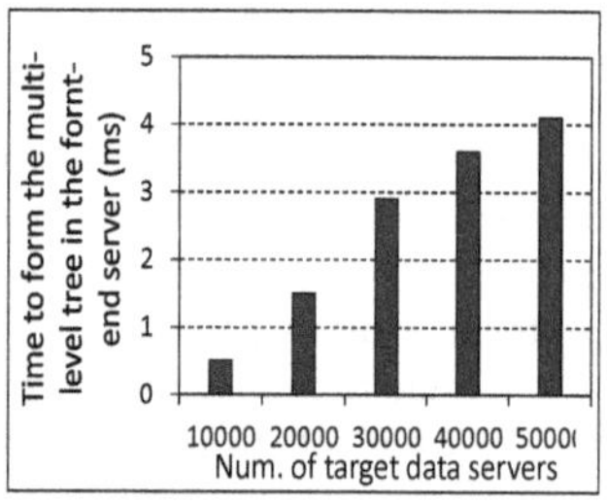

Figure 10: Computing time for tree creation.

bandwidth, there should be fewer hubs directly connect to the front-end server. Therefore, *SICC-NMT* generates more serious incast congestion because it has more hubs connecting to the front-end server. In summary, the figure indicates that the multi-level tree can avoid incast congestion caused by many hubs directly connecting the front-end server, and its depth hardly affects the data request latency.

4.4 Two-level Data Transmission Speed Control

In this section, we measure the performance of our two-level data transmission Speed Control method (SSC). We use *SICC-NSSC* to denote *SICC* without this method. We adjust the assigned downlink bandwidth to each hub in every 10ms. We first present the performance of congestion control at the front-end server side and then at the aggregation router. For each experiment, we set the probability of each hub becoming overloaded to 50%, and the overloaded hub has an actual data transmission speed as 10% of its initially assigned data transmission speed. Figure 7(a) shows the CDF of queries over time of *SICC* and *SICC-NSSC*. It shows that *SICC* has a much smaller data request latency than *SICC-NSSC*. This is because *SICC* reassigns the data transmission speeds of hubs according to their actual data transmission speeds. Together with the query redirection method, *SICC* can fully utilize the bandwidth of downlink to reduce the query latency. *SICC-NSSC* also leverages query redirection to balance the progress, but without speed control, it cannot fully utilize the bandwidth, leading to a longer data request latency. The figure indicates that the data transmission speed control can effectively reduce the data query latency when the hubs are overloaded by fully utilizing the bandwidth of the edge switch downlink.

We then present the performance of congestion avoidance at the aggregation router. We set all data servers inside a rack as front-end servers, each of which conducts a request concurrently. We set $\alpha = \beta = 20\%$, $T = 10\%$ and $B_a = 200KB$. Figure 7(b) shows the average data request latency of *SICC* and *SICC-NSSC* versus the number of queries per request. It shows that *SICC-NSSC* generates a much longer data request latency than *SICC*. This is because, without the speed control method, all front-end servers aim to receive the packets at the speed of their downlink bandwidth. It causes incast congestion at the aggregation router. Then, a timeout delay is introduced to all front-end servers due to packet loss. The figure indicates that the speed control can effectively reduce the data request latency by avoiding the incast congestion at the aggregation router side.

4.5 Performance of Enhancement Methods

We first measure the effectiveness of the packet compression method in reducing the number of inter-rack packets and data request latency. In order not to count the inter-rack packets between hubs in the multi-level tree to show packet compression's sole effectiveness in reducing the number of inter-rack packets, we connected all hubs directly to the front-end server. We measure the compression ratio by n/n', where n and n' represent the number of inter-rack packets generated by *SICC* without and with packet compression, respectively. Recall that the size of a data object was randomly chosen from [20, 1000]B. In this test, the size of a data object was randomly chosen from [20, x]B, where the maximum size of a data object x was varied from 200B to 1000B with a step size as 200B. Figure 8(a) shows the compression ratio, which is always much larger than 1. It implies that the packet compression effectively reduces the number of packets transmitted from hubs. figure, we can

We also see that the compression ratio decreases as the size of the data objects increases. This is because a large maximum size of a data object leads to a lower probability to fit two packets into the same Ethernet packet with the maximum payload limitation. Besides, the figure shows the saved data request latency calculated by $(l' - l)/l'$, where l and l' are the data request latency of *SICC* with and without packet compression, respectively. It shows that the packet compression can reduce the data request latency. This is because a larger payload in packets leads to higher bandwidth utilization and then a shorter data request latency while transmitting

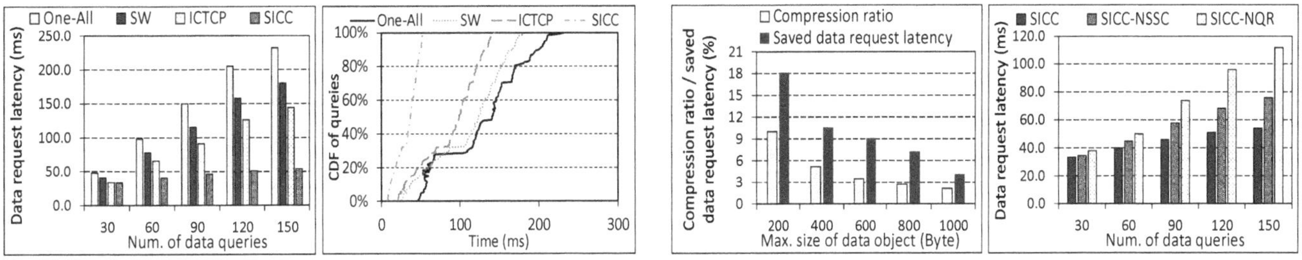

(a) Data request latency (b) CDF of queries (c) Effectiveness of packet compression (d) Effectiveness of speed control and query redirection

Figure 11: Performance on a real cluster.

the same amount of data. It indicates that the packet compression method is effective in reducing the data request latency of *SICC*.

We then measure the effectiveness of the query redirection in reducing the data request latency. We use the same scenario as in Section 4.4. We use *SICC-NQR* to denote *SICC* without the Query Redirection method (QR). Figure 8(b) shows the data request latency of different methods with different number of queries. It shows the same order among all methods as shown in Figure 4(a) due to the same reasons. *SICC-NQR* generates a longer data request latency than *SICC* because of the longer latency to transmit requested data from overloaded hubs while *SICC* can redirect the requests to balance the data transmission progress rate. The figure indicates that the query redirection method effectively reduces data request latency by balancing the data transmission progress rates among hubs.

4.6 Performance of Scalability

In this section, we measure the data request latency of different methods in a large-scale datacenter. We enlarge the number of data servers by 50 times. We varied the number of queries of a request from 10,000 to 50,000 with a step size as 10,000 to measure the performance. Figure 9 shows the data request latency of all different methods. We see that *SICC* always generates the shortest data request latency among all methods. Also, as the number of queries increases, its data request latency slowly increases proportionally while those of other methods increase rapidly. This is because *SICC* effectively controls all hubs data transmission progress rate and speed and the number of hubs connecting to it to avoid the incast congestion and fully utilize the bandwidth. The figure also shows the same order among all other methods as shown in Figure 4(a) due to the same reasons. The figure indicates that *SICC* generates the shortest request latency, and its performance is more scalable than other methods in a large-scale datacenter.

We also measure the time to create the multi-level tree with proximity-aware swarms in a front-end server. We measured the computing time in a laptop with 4GB memory and Dual-core 2.5GHz CPU. The computing time in a powerful front-end server in practice will be much smaller. Figure 10 shows the computing time to create the multi-level tree versus the number of target data servers. We set the number of requested data objects in each target data server to a value randomly chosen from [1, .., 10]. It shows that more target data servers lead to a higher computing time. This is because more data servers from more swarms, and there are more hubs to form the multi-level tree, increasing the computing workload. However, the computing time is around 4ms to computing a multi-level tree with 50,000 data servers, and less than 1ms for 10,000 data servers. Therefore, the latency to form the tree introduces a small delay, which is much smaller than 100ms as the typical budget for a data request in a datacenter serving Web applications [4].

5 EVALUATION ON A REAL TESTBED

We implemented *SICC* and other comparison methods on the Palmetto cluster [38], a high-performance supercomputer in Clemson University. The servers are with 2.4G Intel Xeon CPUs E5-2665 (16 cores), 64GB RAM, 240GB hard disk and 10G NICs. The OS of each server is Linux 64-bit version. The switchs are Brocade MLXeâĂŘ32 switchsWe which can provide 40Gbps. The CPU, Memory and hard disk are never a bottleneck in any of our experiments. We randomly selected 150 servers from all servers and one front-end server in them, each of which has the downlink and uplink as 10Gbps. We randomly distributed 150 data objects into the data servers, the size and the number of replicas of each data object follow the same distribution as in Section 4. We use a batch-processing application, the Apache Hadoop mapreduce framework [34] to simulate the web application workload. The workload consists of WordCount (counting unique words in text) and PageRank (Implementation of PageRank algorithm) [39]. All other settings are the same as in Section 4.

Figure 11(a) shows the data request latency of all methods versus the number of queries. Figure 11(b) shows the CDF of queries over time of all incast control methods. They exhibit the same order and trends as in Figure 4(a) and Figure 4(b) due to the same reasons. The figure indicates that *SICC* generates the shortest data request latency of all methods on the testbed.

Figure 11(c) shows the compression ratio and the saved data request latency of the packet compression method. It shows the same trends as in Figure 8(a) due to the same reasons. It indicates that the packet compression method is effective in reducing data request latency by reducing the number of packets.

Figure 11(d) shows the data request latency of *SICC* without data transmission speed control or query redirection. It shows that *SICC-NSSC* and *SICC-NQR* generate longer data request latency than *SICC* due to the same reasons as in Figures 7(a) and 8(b), respectively. The figure shows that the data transmission speed control and query redirection reduce the data request latency of *SICC* without each of them by 40.3% and 107%, respectively when there are 1500 requested data objects. The figure indicates that the two methods can effectively improve the request latency of *SICC*.

6 CONCLUSION

Previous incast congestion control methods are not applicable to datacenter serving current Web applications because of their stringent low delay requirements and typical data access features (i.e., a very large number of responses and very fast transmission for each response). To solve this problem, we proposed a Swarm-based Incast Congestion Control method (*SICC*). *SICC* clusters the proximity-close data servers in the same rack into swarms, selects a data server as a hub to collect all transmitted data inside its swarm and continuously forwards it to the front-end server, so that the number of concurrently connected data servers to the front-end server is reduced, which avoids the incast congestion. Also, the long-lasting transmission by transmitting data together from a hub enables *SICC* to sophisticatedly control the data transmission speed to avoid congestion while fully utilizing the bandwidth. This feature also enables *SICC* to have two enhancement methods: packet compression and query redirection. The packet compression method combines different packets to one packet to increase the payload of a packet to improve the bandwidth utilization. The query redirection method transmits the data queries from swarms with long remaining data transmission latency to swarms with short remaining data transmission latency in order to reduce the data request latency. The experiments in simulation and on a real cluster show that *SICC* achieves the shortest data request latency compared with other incast control methods.

In the future, we will further consider how to make data transmission bypass congestion during the routing in order to further reduce the data request latency.

7 ACKNOWLEDGEMENTS

This research was supported in part by U.S. NSF grants ACI-1719397, CNS-1733596 and Microsoft Research Faculty Fellowship 8300751.

REFERENCES

[1] Facebook Passes Google In Time Spent On Site For First Time Ever. http://www.businessinsider.com/chart-of-the-day-time-facebook-google-yahoo-2010-9, [accessed in July 2015].

[2] R. Nishtala, H. Fugal, S. Grimm, M. Kwiatkowski, H. Lee, H. C. Li, R. McElroy, M. Paleczny, D. Peek, P. Saab, D. Stafford, T. Tung, and V. Venkataramani. Scaling Memcache at Facebook. In *Proc. of NSDI*, 2013.

[3] R. Kohavl and R. Longbotham. Online Experiments: Lessons Learned, 2007. http://exp-platform.com/Documents/IEEEComputer2007Online Experiments.pdf, [accessed in July 2015].

[4] B. F. Cooper, R. Ramakrishnan, U. Srivastava, A. Silberstein, P. Bohannona, H.-A. Jacobsen, N. Puz, D. Weaver, and R. Yerneni. PNUTS: Yahoo!s Hosted Data Serving Platform. In *Proc. of VLDB*, 2008.

[5] M. Al-Fares, A. Loukissas, and A. Vahdat. A Scalable, Commodity Data Center Network Architecture. In *Proc. of SIGCOMM*, 2008.

[6] L. Yan, K. Chen, H. Shen, and G. Liu. Mobilecopy: Resisting correlated node failures to enhance data availability in dtns. In *Proc. of SECON*, 2015.

[7] R. Mittal, N. Dukkipati, E. Blem, H. Wassel, M. Ghobadi, A. Vahdat, Y. Wang, D. Wetherall, and D. Zats. Timely: Rtt-based congestion control for the datacenter. In *Proc. of SIGCOMM*, 2015.

[8] Z. Li, H. Shen, J. Denton, and W. Ligon. Comparing application performance on hpc-based hadoop platforms with local storage and dedicated storage. In *Proc. of Big Data*, 2016.

[9] G. Liu, H. Shen, and H. Wang. Computing load aware and long-view load balancing for cluster storage systems. In *Proc. of Big Data*, 2015.

[10] H. Wu, Z. Feng, C. Guo, and Y. Zhang. ICTCP: Incast Congestion Control for TCP in Data-Center Networks. *TON*, 2013.

[11] D. Wischik, C. Raiciu, A. Greenhalgh, and M. Handley. Design, Implementation and Evaluation of Congestion Control for Multipath TCP. In *Proc. of NSDI*, 2011.

[12] M. Alizadeh, A. G. Greenberg, D. A. Maltz, J. Padhye, P. Patel, B. Prabhakar, S. Sengupta, and M. Sridharan. Data center TCP (DCTCP). In *Proc. of SIGCOMM*, 2010.

[13] B. Vamanan, J. Hasan, and T. N. Vijaykumar. Deadline-Aware Datacenter TCP (D2TCP). In *Proc. of SIGCOMM*, 2012.

[14] J. Zhang, F. Ren, and C. Lin. Modeling and Understanding TCP Incast in Data Center Networks. In *Proc. of INFOCOM*, 2011.

[15] C. Raiciu, S. Barre, C. Pluntke, A. Greenhalgh, D. Wischik, and M. Handley. Improving Datacenter Performance and Robustness with Multipath TCP. *ACM SIGCOMM Comput. Commun. Rev.*, 2011.

[16] J. Mudigonda, P. Yalagandula, M. Al-Fares, and J. C. Mogul. SPAIN: COTS Data-Center Ethernet for Multipathing over Arbitrary Topologies. In *Proc. of NSDI*, 2010.

[17] V. Vasudevan, A. Phanishayee, H. Shah, E. Krevat, D. G Andersen, G. R Ganger, G. A Gibson, and B. Mueller. Safe and effective fine-grained tcp retransmissions for datacenter communication. In *Proc. of SIGCOM*, 2009.

[18] A. Phanishayee, E. Krevat, V. Vasudevan, D. G. Andersen, G. R. Ganger, G. A Gibson, and S. Seshan. Measurement and Analysis of TCP Throughput Collapse in Cluster-based Storage Systems. In *Proc. of FAST*, 2008.

[19] E. Krevat, V. Vasudevan, A. Phanishayee, D. G. Andersen, G. R. Ganger, G. A. Gibson, and S. Seshan. On Application-Level Approaches to Avoiding TCP Throughput Collapse in Cluster-based Storage Systems. In *Proc. of PDSW*, 2007.

[20] J. M. Pujol, V. Erramilli, G. Siganos, X. Yang, N. Laoutaris, P. Chhabra, and P. Rodriguez. The Little Engine(s) that Could: Scaling Online Social Networks. In *Proc. of SIGCOMM*, 2010.

[21] G. Liu, H. Shen, and H. Chandler. Selective Data replication for Online Social Networks with Distributed Datacenters. In *Proc. of ICNP*, 2013.

[22] Y. Yang, H. Abe, K. Baba, and S. Shimojo. A Scalable Approach to Avoid Incast Problem from Application Layer. In *Proc. of COMPSACW*, 2013.

[23] M. Podlesny and C. Williamson. An Application-Level Solution for the TCP-Incast Problem in Data Center Networks. In *Proc. of IWQoS*, 2011.

[24] M. Podlesny and C. Williamson. Solving the TCP-Incast Problem with Application-Level Scheduling. In *Proc. of MASCOTS*, 2012.

[25] H. Shen, A. Sarker, L. Yu, and F. Deng. Probabilistic network-aware task placement for mapreduce scheduling. In *Proc. of Cluster*, 2016.

[26] G. Liu, H. Shen, and H. Wang. Deadline guaranteed service for multi-tenant cloud storage. *Trans. on Parallel and Distributed Systems, TPDS*, 2016.

[27] Z. Li, H. Shen, W. B. Ligon III, and J. Denton. An exploration of designing a hybrid scale-up/out hadoop architecture based on performance measurements. *Trans. on Parallel and Distributed Systems, TPDS*, 2016.

[28] L. L. Peterson and B. S. Davie. *Computer Networks: A Systems Approach*. Elsevier, 2007.

[29] K. Shvachko, H. Kuang, S. Radia, and R. Chansler. The Hadoop Distributed File System. In *Proc. of MSST*, 2010.

[30] Amazon DynnamoDB. http://aws.amazon.com/dynamodb/, [accessed in July 2015].

[31] Y. Chen, A. Ganapathi, R. Griffith, and R. Katz. The Case for Evaluating MapReduce Performance Using Workload Suites. In *Proc. of MASCOTS*, 2011.

[32] T. Benson, A. Akella, and D. A. Maltz. Network Traffic Characteristics of Data Centers in the Wild. In *Proc. of IMC*, 2010.

[33] Cisco Nexus 3064 Switch. http://www.cisco.com/c/en/us/products/switches/nexus-3064-switch/, [accessed in July 2015].

[34] K. Shvachko, H. Kuang, S. Radia, and R. Chansler. The Hadoop Distributed File System. In *Proc. of MSST*, 2010.

[35] V. Paxson, M. Allman, J. Chu, and M. Sargent. Computing TCP's Retransmission Timer. Technical report, 2011.

[36] J. Zhang, F. Ren, L. Tang, and C. Lin. Taming TCP Incast Throughput Collapse in Data Center Networks. In *Proc. of ICNP*, 2013.

[37] G. Liu, H. Shen, and H. Wang. Towards long-view computing load balancing in cluster storage systems. *Trans. on Parallel and Distributed Systems, TPDS*, 2016.

[38] Palmetto Cluster. http://citi.clemson.edu/palmetto/.

[39] S. Huang, J. Huang, J. Dai, T. Xie, and B. Huang. The hibench benchmark suite: Characterization of the mapreduce-based data analysis. In *ICDE Workshops*. 2011.

Brief Announcement: Approximation Algorithms for Unsplittable Resource Allocation Problems with Diseconomies of Scale

Antje Bjelde*
School of Business and Economics
Humboldt University Berlin
Spandauer Straße 1
Berlin 10789, Germany
antje.bjelde@hu-berlin.de

Max Klimm†
School of Business and Economics
Humboldt University Berlin
Spandauer Straße 1
Berlin 10789, Germany
max.klimm@hu-berlin.de

Daniel Schmand
School of Business and Economics
RWTH Aachen University
Kackertstraße 7
Aachen 52072, Germany
schmand@oms.rwth-aachen.de

ABSTRACT

We study general resource allocation problems with a diseconomy of scale. Given a finite set of commodities that request certain resources, the cost of each resource grows superlinearly with the demand for it, and our goal is to minimize the total cost of the resources. In large systems with limited coordination, it is natural to consider local dynamics where in each step a single commodity switches its allocated resources whenever the new solution after the switch has smaller total cost over all commodities. This yields a deterministic and polynomial time algorithm with approximation factor arbitrarily close to the *locality gap*, i.e., the worst case ratio of the cost of a local optimal and a global optimal solution. For costs that are polynomials with non-negative coefficients and maximal degree d, we provide a locality gap for weighted problems that is tight for all values of d. For unweighted problems, the locality gap asymptotically matches the approximation guarantee of the currently best known centralized algorithm [Makarychev, Srividenko FOCS14] but only requires local knowledge of the commodities.

CCS CONCEPTS

• **Theory of computation → Routing and network design problems; Distributed algorithms; Network games;**

KEYWORDS

Approximation Algorithm; Distributed Algorithm; Locality Gap; Energy Efficiency; Congestion Games

ACM Reference format:

Antje Bjelde, Max Klimm, and Daniel Schmand. 2017. Brief Announcement: Approximation Algorithms for Unsplittable Resource Allocation Problems with Diseconomies of Scale. In *Proceedings of SPAA '17, Washington DC, USA, July 24-26, 2017,* 3 pages.
https://doi.org/http://dx.doi.org/10.1145/3087556.3087597

*Work of this author is supported by Einstein Center for Mathematics Berlin and Caroline von Humboldt Completion Grant.
†Work of this author is supported by Einstein Center for Mathematics Berlin.

ACM ISBN 978-1-4503-4593-4/17/07...$15.00
https://doi.org/http://dx.doi.org/10.1145/3087556.3087597

1 INTRODUCTION AND RELATED WORK

We consider a finite set of resources R and a finite set of commodities $N = \{1, \dots, n\}$. For each commodity $i \in N$, we are given (explicitly or implicitly) a set $S_i \subseteq 2^R$ of feasible solutions and a weight $w_i \in \mathbb{R}_{\geq 0}$. The cost of each resource r is determined by a non-negative convex function $c_r : \mathbb{R}_{\geq 0} \to \mathbb{R}_{\geq 0}$. Given a solution $\mathbf{s} = (s_1, \dots, s_n)$ with $s_i \in S_i$, the cost for commodity i is defined as $C_i(\mathbf{s}) := w_i \sum_{r \in s_i} c_r(w_r(\mathbf{s}))$, where $w_r(\mathbf{s}) := \sum_{j \in N: r \in s_j} w_j$ is the total weight put on resource r under solution $\mathbf{s}$. We are interested in finding solutions $\mathbf{s}$ that minimize the total cost of the commodities, i.e., that minimize $C(\mathbf{s}) := \sum_{i=1}^{n} C_i(\mathbf{s}) = \sum_{r \in R} w_r(\mathbf{s}) c_r(w_r(\mathbf{s}))$. We denote the space of all feasible solutions by $\mathbf{S} = S_1 \times S_2 \times \dots \times S_n$ and an instance of a resource allocation problem by $I = (\mathbf{S}, (w_i)_{i \in N}, (c_r)_{r \in R})$. A resource allocation problem is called *unweighted* if $w_i = 1$ for all $i \in N$ and *weighted*, otherwise. For a solution $\mathbf{s} \in \mathbf{S}$ and a commodity $i \in N$, we write $\mathbf{s} = (s_i, \mathbf{s}_{-i})$ implying that $s_i \in S_i$ and $\mathbf{s}_{-i} \in S_1 \times \dots \times S_{i-1} \times S_{i+1} \times \dots \times S_n$.

We call a solution *local optimal*, if its cost cannot be decreased by reallocating a single commodity, that is, $C(\mathbf{s}) \leq C(s_i', \mathbf{s}_{-i})$ for all $i \in N$ and $s_i' \in S_i$. We are interested in the cost guarantees achieved by local optimal solutions. These guarantees are captured by the notion of a locality gap. For an instance I of a resource allocation problem, the *locality gap* is defined as $\max\{C(\mathbf{s})/C(\mathbf{s}') : \mathbf{s}, \mathbf{s}' \in \mathbf{S} \text{ and } \mathbf{s} \text{ is a local optimum}\}$.

Minimization problems of this kind appear in different contexts. In the area of energy efficient algorithms, resources model computing devices that can run at different speeds. As the speed is increased, the energy consumption increases superlinearly. Frequently, it is assumed that energy consumption can be modeled by a function $C_r(x) = k_r x^{q_r} = x k_r x^{q_r - 1}$ of the speed x where $k_r > 0$ and $q_r \in (1, 3]$ are device-specific parameters, see, e.g., Albers [3] for a reference. In the area of traffic networks, resources correspond to roads in a street network. The time needed to traverse a road increases with the total traffic on the road. Popular models are the travel time functions put forward by the US Bureau of Public Roads (BPR) which are of the form $c_r(x) = k_r(1 + 0.15(x/z_r)^4)$ where $k_r > 0$ and $z_r > 0$ are road-specific parameters and x is the load of the resource, see [13]. When minimizing the total congestion cost, we are interested in minimizing the average travel time of a unit of demand which is given by $C_r(x) = x c_r(x)$.

As a running example, it is useful to consider the most natural case where the set of resources R corresponds to the set of edges E

of a graph $G = (V, E)$. Each commodity is specified by a source node u_i and a target v_i. The set S_i of feasible solutions of commodity i corresponds to the set of simple (u_i, v_i)-paths in G. We note, however, that all our results continue to hold in a more general setting where the set of feasible solutions $S_i \subset 2^R$ is arbitrary. We only need to make the minimal assumption that each commodity can efficiently optimize over its set S_i as long as the vector of feasible solution $\mathbf{s}_{-i}$ of the other commodities is fixed. In fact, we only need to require that this optimization over S_i can be done efficiently within arbitrary precision. We assume:

(1) *For every constant $\alpha \geq 1$, every commodity $i \in N$, there is a polynomial algorithm (oracle) $\mathfrak{O}_{i,\alpha} : \mathbf{S}_{-i} \to S_i$ that, given a partial solution $\mathbf{s}_{-i} \in \mathbf{S}_{-i}$ as input, computes a feasible solution $s_i' \in S_i$ with $C(s_i', \mathbf{s}_{-i}) \leq \alpha \min_{s_i \in S_i} C(s_i, \mathbf{s}_{-i})$.*
(2) *A feasible solution $\mathbf{s} \in \mathbf{S}$ can be computed in polynomial time.*

Clearly, when the sets S_i corresponds to the set of paths in a network, this assumption is satisfied as shortest paths can be computed efficiently.

Currently, the approximation algorithm with the best performance guarantee for this problem is due to Makarychev and Sviridenko [9]. They propose a convex programming relaxation of the problem and show that for monomials with degree d, the integrality gap is equal to the $(d + 1)$-st Bell number B_{d+1}. Using a randomized rounding technique, this yields a randomized algorithm with approximation guarantee $B_{d+1} + \epsilon$ for any $\epsilon > 0$ which can be shown to be of order $[O(d/\log d))]^{d+1}$, see [5]. However, the linear programming approach of Makarychev and Sviridenko has the disadvantage that it requires a large amount of central coordination as the convex program has to be solved by a single central authority and the routing decisions of the commodities are based on the solution of the linear programming relaxation. This may be infeasible to implement in large systems without a central authority that is able to collect the data and solve the program. In fact, when optimizing large decentralized networks such as the Internet with respect to the energy consumption or the total delay, such a central authority is usually absent.

For the optimization of such decentralized systems, it is natural to consider improvement dynamics where the system starts in an arbitrary state $\mathbf{s}$ and at each step one commodity chooses another path if it decreases their share of the cost, i.e., commodity i switches from path P to path Q if

$$\sum_{r \in P \setminus Q} c_r(w_r(\mathbf{s})) > \sum_{r \in Q \setminus P} c_r(w_r(\mathbf{s}) + w_i),$$

where $w_r(\mathbf{s})$ denotes the load of resource r in state $\mathbf{s}$. The stable points of these dynamics are the Nash equilibria of the underlying congestion game. There is a vast amount of literature quantifying the price of anarchy of congestion games, i.e., determining the worst case ratio of the total cost in a Nash equilibrium and the total cost of an optimal solution. Most relevant to our work, Aland et al. [2] showed that the price of anarchy for both weighted and unweighted congestion games with polynomial travel time functions c_r with maximal degree d (that correspond to polynomial total cost functions C_r with maximum degree $d + 1$) is of order $[O(d/\log d)]^{d+1}$. Unfortunately, this result does not yield an efficient distributed approximation algorithm since for weighted commodities, the improvement dynamics may cycle (cf. Harks et al. [8]) and Nash equilibria may even be fully absent (cf. Harks and Klimm [7]). For unweighted commodities the improvement dynamics are guaranteed to converge by a potential function argument due to Rosenthal [11], but the convergence may take a number of steps that is exponential in the size of the underlying network, see Ackermann et al. [1]. These issues make these dynamics unfavorable in practice.

In order to obtain polynomial convergence for the unweighted case, Awerbuch et al. [4] studied an approximate version of the improvement dynamics where each commodity only switches if the potential function drops by a factor of $1 + \delta$. They showed that after a polynomial sequence of δ-best replies, a solution is reached which is an $(5/2 + O(\delta))$-approximation to the minimal congestion cost in the case of linear cost functions. For polynomial cost functions with maximum degree d and positive coefficients, their approach yields a $(d^{d-o(1)} + O(\delta))$-approximation. The technique of Awerbuch et al. however, relies on the existence of a potential function and thus, cannot be applied to resource allocation problems with weighted commodities and non-linear cost functions.

To overcome this issue, we study a different improvement dynamics where the system again starts in an arbitrary state $\mathbf{s}$, but all commodities take the impact of their path choices on the other commodities into account. More formally, we require that commodity i switches from path P to path Q if this switch decreases the overall cost of the solution, i.e.,

$$\sum_{r \in P \setminus Q} \Big(w_r(\mathbf{s}) c_r\big(w_r(\mathbf{s})\big) - \big(w_r(\mathbf{s}) - w_i\big) c_r\big(w_r(\mathbf{s}) - w_i\big) \Big)$$
$$> \sum_{r \in Q \setminus P} \Big(\big(w_r(\mathbf{s}) + w_i\big) c_r\big(w_r(\mathbf{s}) + w_i\big) - w_r(\mathbf{s}) c_r\big(w_r(\mathbf{s})\big) \Big).$$

This approach has the advantage that the total cost of the current solution is monotonically decreasing in each step, which implies that the dynamics reach a local optimum after a finite number of steps. In contrast to the long history of papers quantifying the efficiency of Nash equilibria, much less is known regarding the efficiency of local optimal solutions. This is the main issue addressed in this paper.

By analyzing the locality gap of the local optimal solutions, we provide the first non-trivial analysis of a local search algorithm that is guaranteed to converge both for the weighted and unweighted case of the problem.

2 OUR RESULTS AND TECHNIQUES

We study local improvement dynamics for general resource allocation problems with convex costs. In particular, we are interested in quantifying the locality gap. We assume that the cost functions $c_r(x)$ are polynomials with non-negative coefficients and maximal degree d, i.e. $c_r(x) = \sum_{j \in J} \alpha_j^r x^j$ with $J \subset [0, d]$, $\alpha_j^r \geq 0$ for all $j \in J$ and all $r \in R$. This imposes a total cost of $x c_r(x)$ on resource r under load x.[1]

[1]This is the standard form for the total cost in the congestion game literature. The speed scaling literature usually writes the total cost of a resource as x^q for some $q > 1$. Clearly, both forms are equivalent up to a shift in the exponent.

Our general algorithm is based on local search. The local search starts in an arbitrary solution $s \in S$. In each iteration, the oracles $\mathfrak{O}_{i,\alpha}$ are called to find a commodity that has an alternative solution $s_i' \in S_i$ such that $(1+\delta)C(s_i', s_{-i}) \leq C(s)$ for some sufficiently small $\delta > 0$. When no such commodity is found, the algorithm stops and returns the solution.

Orlin et al. [10] showed that every local search problem admits a PTAS in the sense that an $(1+\delta)$-approximate local optimal solution can be computed in polynomial time via approximate local improvements steps. In order to determine how well local optimal solutions approximate the global minimum, we use the notion of smoothness used by Chen et al. [6] to analyze the price of anarchy of altruistic versions of unweighted congestion games with linear costs. It builds upon a similar notion of (λ, μ)-smoothness due to Roughgarden [12].

For unweighted resource allocation problems, we show that the locality gap is of order $[O(d/\log d)]^{d+1}$.

Theorem 2.1. *For every unweighted resource allocation problem with polynomial cost functions with non-negative coefficients and maximal degree d the following hold for some $\alpha \in O((2d/\log d)^{d+1})$:*

1. *The locality gap is α.*
2. *For any $\epsilon > 0$ there is a polynomial time $\alpha+\epsilon$-approximation algorithm for the minimization of the total costs.*

For concrete values of d, we can evaluate the locality gap explicitly.

Theorem 2.2. *For any $\epsilon > 0$ there is a polynomial time $\alpha_d + \epsilon$-approximation for every unweighted resource allocation problem with polynomial cost functions with maximal degree d and non-negative coefficients, where $\alpha_1 = 3$, $\alpha_2 = 13$, $\alpha_3 = 61$, $\alpha_4 = 391$, and $\alpha_5 = 2,157$.*

For the case of linear cost functions, it has been shown by Chen et al. [6] that the bound on the locality gap of 3 is tight. We provide a lower bound on the locality gap for general polynomials with maximum degree d.

Theorem 2.3. *There is an unweighted resource allocation problem with monomial costs with degree d and locality gap $\lfloor \frac{d}{\log(d+2)} - 1 \rfloor^{d+1}$.*

For weighted resource allocation problems, we obtain a locality gap for all values of d.

Theorem 2.4. *For every weighted resource allocation problem with polynomial costs with non-negative coefficients and maximal degree d, the following hold for $\alpha = 1/(\sqrt[d+1]{2}-1)^{d+1} \in O\big(((d+1)/\log 2)^{d+1}\big)$:*

1. *The locality gap is at most α.*
2. *For any $\epsilon > 0$, there is a polynomial time $\alpha+\epsilon$-approximation algorithm for the minimization of the total costs.*

Specifically, the locality gap is $3 + 2\sqrt{2} \approx 5.829$ for $d = 1$ and the locality gap is $15\sqrt[3]{2} + 12\sqrt[3]{4} + 19 \approx 56.948$ for $d = 2$.

This locality gap is tight.

Theorem 2.5. *There is a resource allocation problem with monomial costs with degree d and locality gap arbitrarily close to $\big(\sqrt[d+1]{2} - 1\big)^{-(d+1)} \in O\big((\frac{d+1}{\log 2})^{d+1}\big)$.*

Further, the problem is APX-hard.

Theorem 2.6. *For all $\alpha < 1.02$, there is no polynomial time α-approximation algorithm for unweighted resource allocation problems with linear cost functions, unless* P = NP.

We can thus conclude: by considering approximate improvement dynamics where commodities switch to another path only when the total cost is decreased by at least a factor of $1 + \delta$, where $\delta > 0$ is arbitrary, the dynamics are guaranteed to converge to an approximate local optimal solution in a polynomial number of steps. We show that by sacrificing an additional factor of $1 + \delta$, all locality gaps above yield a *deterministic*, *combinatorial* and *distributed* algorithm for the minimization of the total cost with the corresponding approximation guarantee. For weighted resource allocation problems, this yields the first deterministic algorithm, the first combinatorial algorithm, and the first distributed algorithm with non-trivial approximation guarantee as the algorithm of Makarychev and Srividenko relies on the centralized solution of a linear program and the randomized rounding of its solution.

For unweighted problems with linear cost, our asymptotic approximation guarantee of $[O(d/\log d)]^{d+1}$ is a slight improvement over the asymptotic behavior of the algorithm by Awerbuch et al. whose asymptotic behavior is of order $d^{d-o(1)}$. Our calculation of the concrete approximation guarantees for maximum degree up to ten suggests that our approximation is in fact better than the one by Awerbuch et al. for all $d \geq 9$. The approximation guarantee of $[O(d/\log d)]^{d+1}$ asymptotically matches the currently best known guarantee of Makarychev and Srividenko, but in contrast to the their algorithm, our algorithm is deterministic, can be implemented in a distributed fashion, and does not rely on the approximate solution of a convex program.

REFERENCES

[1] H. Ackermann, H. Röglin, and B. Vöcking. On the impact of combinatorial structure on congestion games. *J. ACM*, 55(6):1–22, 2008.

[2] S. Aland, D. Dumrauf, M. Gairing, B. Monien, and F. Schoppmann. Exact price of anarchy for polynomial congestion games. *SIAM J. Comput.*, 40(5):1211–1233, 2011.

[3] S. Albers. Energy-efficient algorithms. *Commun. ACM*, 53:86–96, 2010.

[4] B. Awerbuch, Y. Azar, A. Epstein, V. S. Mirrokni, and A. Skopalik. Fast convergence to nearly optimal solutions in potential games. In *Proc. 9th ACM Conf. Electron. Commerce*, pages 264–273, 2008.

[5] D. Berend and T. Tassa. Improved bounds on bell numbers and on moments of sums of random variables. *Probability and Mathematical Statistics*, 30:185–205, 2010.

[6] P.-A. Chen, B. De Keijzer, D. Kempe, and G. Schäfer. The robust price of anarchy of altruistic games. In N. Chen, E. Elkind, and E. Koutsoupias, editors, *Proc. 7th Int. Workshop Internet and Network Econ.*, volume 7090 of *LNCS*, pages 383–390, 2011.

[7] T. Harks and M. Klimm. On the existence of pure Nash equilibria in weighted congestion games. *Math. Oper. Res.*, 37(3):419–436, 2012.

[8] T. Harks, M. Klimm, and R. H. Möhring. Characterizing the existence of potential functions in weighted congestion games. *Theory Comput. Syst.*, 49(1):46–70, 2011.

[9] K. Makarychev and M. Sviridenko. Solving optimization problems with diseconomies of scale via decoupling. In *Proc. 55th Annu. IEEE Symp. Found. Comput. Sci.*, pages 571–580, 2014.

[10] J. B. Orlin, A. P. Punnen, and A. S. Schulz. Approximate local search in combinatorial optimization. *SIAM J. Comput.*, 33(5):1201–1214, 2004.

[11] R. W. Rosenthal. A class of games possessing pure-strategy Nash equilibria. *Internat. J. Game Theory*, 2(1):65–67, 1973.

[12] T. Roughgarden. Intrinsic robustness of the price of anarchy. In *Proc. 41st Annu. ACM Symp. Theory Computing*, pages 513–522, 2009.

[13] U.S. Bureau of Public Roads. *Traffic assignment manual.* U.S. Department of Commerce, Urban Planning Division, Washington, DC, 1964.

Brief Announcement: Towards Fault-Tolerant Bin Packing for Online Cloud Resource Allocation

Chuanyou Li
School of Computer Science and Engineering
Nanyang Technological University, Singapore
chuanyou.li@gmail.com

Xueyan Tang
School of Computer Science and Engineering
Nanyang Technological University, Singapore
asxytang@ntu.edu.sg

ABSTRACT

We consider an online fault-tolerant bin packing problem that models the reliable resource allocation in cloud-based systems. In this problem, any feasible packing algorithm must satisfy an exclusion constraint and a space constraint. The exclusion constraint is generalized from the fault-tolerance requirement and the space constraint comes from the capacity planning. The target of bin packing is to minimize the number of bins used. We first derive a lower bound on the number of bins needed by any feasible packing algorithm. Then we study two heuristic algorithms mirroring and shifting. The mirroring algorithm has a low utilization of the bin capacity. Compared with the mirroring algorithm, the shifting algorithm requires fewer numbers of bins. However, in online packing, the process of opening bins by the shifting algorithm is not smooth. It turns out that even for packing a few items, the shifting algorithm needs to quickly open a large number of bins. We therefore propose a new heuristic algorithm named mixing which can gradually open new bins for incoming items. We prove that the mixing algorithm is feasible and show that it balances the number of bins used and the process of opening bins.

KEYWORDS

Fault-tolerance, Bin packing, Online algorithm

1 INTRODUCTION

Cloud is a type of Internet-based computing paradigm which provides shared computing resources on demand. Cloud-based applications and services are growing explosively. Enormous application requirements promote the cloud to upgrade and equip increasing number of servers. The fast progress of cloud computing needs to face two fundamental issues. First, resource utilization, which aims at meeting the computational demands with minimum amount of cloud resources. Second, fault tolerance, whose target is to enhance the reliability, as failures are more prone to happen when the scale of the cloud grows.

Cloud resource allocation can be modeled as a bin packing problem [3]: given a set of items, the target is to pack the items into a minimum number of bins while guaranteeing that the aggregate size of the items in each bin does not exceed the bin capacity. For its online version, each item must be placed into a bin without the knowledge of subsequent items. In this paper, we consider a new version of the bin packing problem, which is called the fault-tolerant bin packing problem. This problem follows the online setting and needs to tolerate up to f faulty bins which stop serving any items.

To ensure fault tolerance, the primary-standby replication scheme is involved: each item is replicated and has $f + 1$ replicas which are composed of one primary and f standbys. For the primary-standby replication scheme, a primary replica is indispensable. The primary replica takes more responsibilities and has a higher workload than a standby replica [14]. Accordingly, for each item, a value $l \in (0, 1)$ is used to denote the workload of its primary replica and the workload of each standby replica is assumed to be l/η where $\eta > 1$ is the workload ratio between the primary and a standby. In the case of failures, when a standby replica becomes the new primary, its workload increases to l.

For the fault-tolerant bin packing problem, any feasible algorithm should satisfy an exclusion constraint and a space constraint. The exclusion constraint is generalized from the fault-tolerance requirement. For each item, its $f + 1$ replicas need to be dispersed to $f + 1$ different bins, such that no matter which f bins turn to be faulty, one correct replica is still available.

Definition 1.1. A fault-tolerant bin packing algorithm $\mathfrak{A}$ satisfies the exclusion constraint if and only if it never places two (or more than two) replicas of the same item in the same bin.

The space constraint arises from the resource limitation of a bin. We consider two scenarios. First, there is no faulty bin in the system. Second, no more than f faulty bins arise in the system. For the first case, during the placement, a fault-tolerant bin packing algorithm $\mathfrak{A}$ should ensure that the total workloads of the replicas placed in a bin does not exceed the bin capacity W. The second case is a little more complex. When a faulty primary arises, a process of switching standby to primary will be involved. Note that when $f > 1$, a service has more than 1 standby replicas. It could be the case that there exist several different switching strategies for which one standby is selected to become the new primary. Furthermore, as the switching process leads to workload expansion on the standby, it could happen that some bad switching strategies will lead to overloaded bins. Before giving a formal definition of the space constraint, we first define the concept of a valid switching strategy.

Definition 1.2. Given a set of faulty bins, a switching strategy (standby to primary) is valid if and only if it satisfies the following two properties: (1) for each faulty primary replica, one of its correct standby replica is selected to become the new primary; (2) there are no overloaded bins after workload expansion.

SPAA'17, July 24–26, 2017, Washington, DC, USA

DOI: http://dx.doi.org/10.1145/3087556.3087596

Definition 1.3. A fault-tolerant bin packing algorithm $\mathfrak{A}$ satisfies the space constraint if and only if it satisfies the following two properties: (1) there are no overloaded bins before any failure happens; (2) a valid switching strategy always exists as long as there are no more than f faulty bins.

Definition 1.4. A fault-tolerant bin packing algorithm $\mathfrak{A}$ is named feasible if and only if it satisfies both the exclusion constraint and the space constraint.

2 TECHNICAL CONTRIBUTIONS

To pack a set of items, we first derive a lower bound on the number of bins required by any feasible algorithm.

THEOREM 2.1. *To place a set of items with a total workload L of all primary replicas, any feasible fault-tolerant bin packing algorithm $\mathfrak{A}$ requires at least* $\frac{(\eta f+\eta L+fL)+\sqrt{(\eta L+fL+\eta f)^2-4\eta(f^2L+fL)}}{2\eta}$ *bins.*

We then propose three feasible heuristic algorithms named mirroring $\mathfrak{A}_{mr}$, shifting $\mathfrak{A}_{st}$ and mixing $\mathfrak{A}_{mx}$. The mirroring algorithm $\mathfrak{A}_{mr}$ places primary replicas and standby replicas separately. Any bin that is used to place primary replicas has f "mirror images", which are f bins that are used to place the corresponding standby replicas. The original idea of mirroring algorithm is from [11].

THEOREM 2.2. *The mirroring algorithm $\mathfrak{A}_{mr}$ is feasible.*

THEOREM 2.3. *To place a set of items with a total workload L of all primary replicas, the mirroring algorithm $\mathfrak{A}_{mr}$ requires at most* $(\lfloor \frac{L}{l\lfloor 1/l \rfloor} \rfloor + 1)(f + 1)$ *bins.*

In the mirroring algorithm $\mathfrak{A}_{mr}$, any bin that is used to place the primary replicas has another f bins dedicated to placing the corresponding standby replicas. The utilization of the bin capacity by the mirroring algorithm is inefficient. Because of failures, all the standby replicas located in the same bin might switch to primary and expand their workloads together. To meet the space constraint, a large amount of the reserved space should be maintained in each bin hosting standby replicas. To reduce the number of bins used, we design the shifting algorithm $\mathfrak{A}_{st}$ to decrease the amount of reserved space. The idea of $\mathfrak{A}_{st}$ is derived from [4]. We generalize the basic idea by replication and make it adapt to any f faulty bins in our model. Similar to the mirroring algorithm, the shifting algorithm $\mathfrak{A}_{st}$ also places primary replicas and standby replicas separately. The difference is that for primary replicas hosted in the same bin, $\mathfrak{A}_{st}$ disperses their standby replicas into f different bins.

THEOREM 2.4. *The shifting algorithm $\mathfrak{A}_{st}$ is feasible.*

THEOREM 2.5. *To place a set of items with a total workload L of all primary replicas, the shifting algorithm $\mathfrak{A}_{st}$ requires at most* $(\lfloor \frac{L}{\lfloor \frac{l+\eta-l\eta}{l} \rfloor \lfloor \frac{1}{l} \rfloor l} \rfloor + 1)(\lfloor \frac{l+\eta-l\eta}{l} \rfloor + f\lfloor \frac{1}{l} \rfloor)$ *bins.*

The shifting algorithm $\mathfrak{A}_{st}$ saves the amount of reserved space by ensuring that at most one standby in each bin might switch to primary in the case of failures. Compared with $\mathfrak{A}_{mr}$, $\mathfrak{A}_{st}$ reduces the number of bins used. However, in online packing, the process of opening bins by $\mathfrak{A}_{st}$ is not smooth. Even for packing a few items, $\mathfrak{A}_{st}$ needs to quickly open a large number of bins. In order to smooth the process of opening bins, we propose the new mixing

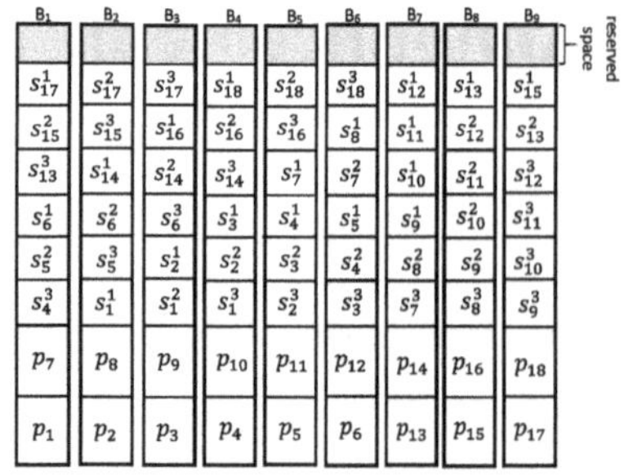

Figure 1: Example of the algorithm $\mathfrak{A}_{mx}$ (f = 3)

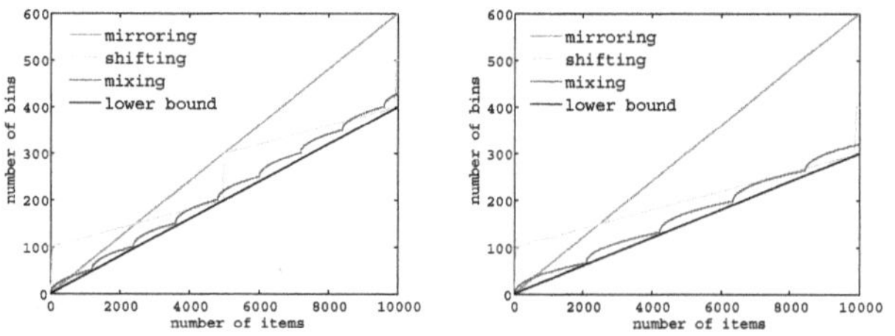

(a) $l = 0.02, \eta = 2$ (b) $l = 0.02, \eta = 4$

Figure 2: Numerical examples

algorithm $\mathfrak{A}_{mx}$. $\mathfrak{A}_{mx}$ opens new bins gradually and organizes them into a sequence of bin groups. Each bin hosts at most $x = \lfloor \frac{\eta-\eta l+l}{\eta l+fl} \rfloor$ primary replicas. When a new item arrives, if there exists one bin in the current bin group hosting less than x primary replicas but not enough bins to host f more standby replicas, $\mathfrak{A}_{mx}$ opens f new bins and adds them into the current group. If no bin in the current group can host one more primary replica, $\mathfrak{A}_{mx}$ opens $2f$ new bins and organizes them as a new group. Suppose p_i represents the ith arriving item's primary replica and suppose each s^k_i ($1 \leq k \leq f$) represents one of the ith item's standby replicas. Figure 1 shows an example of the placement by assuming $x = 2$ and $f = 3$.

THEOREM 2.6. *The mixing algorithm $\mathfrak{A}_{mx}$ is feasible.*

THEOREM 2.7. *To place a set of items with a total workload L of all primary replicas, the mixing algorithm $\mathfrak{A}_{mx}$ requires at most* $\frac{L}{l\lfloor \frac{\eta-\eta l+l}{\eta l+fl} \rfloor} + f(\lfloor \frac{\eta-\eta l+l}{\eta l+fl} \rfloor + 1)$ *bins.*

We conclude that when $l < 1/2$, the mixing algorithm $\mathfrak{A}_{mx}$ outperforms the mirroring algorithm $\mathfrak{A}_{mr}$. The number of bins required by the mixing algorithm may be slightly more than that by the shifting algorithm, but the process of opening bins for $\mathfrak{A}_{mx}$ is much more smooth than $\mathfrak{A}_{st}$. Figure 2 shows two numerical examples. For both examples, we set $f = 2$ and $l = 0.02$. In Figure 2(a), η is set to 2 and in Figure 2(b), η is set to 4. In both examples, we can see that the number of bins required by the mixing algorithm increases smoothly. Even for packing 10000 items, the mixing algorithm is still the best among the three heuristic algorithms. Besides, when η increases, both $\mathfrak{A}_{mx}$ and $\mathfrak{A}_{st}$ require fewer number of bins. However, $\mathfrak{A}_{mr}$ cannot benefit from the growth of η.

3 RELATED WORK

The classical bin packing problem has been extensively studied [3][5]. It is well known that even in the offline setting, the classical bin packing problem is NP-hard [6]. Numerous heuristic algorithms have been proposed. So far, for classical online bin packing, the best upper bound on the competitive ratio is 1.58889 which is achieved by the HARMONIC++ algorithm [12]. The best known lower bound for any online packing algorithm is 1.54037 [1].

Fault tolerance is a key issue in parallel and distributed computing and has been studied for many years. To achieve fault tolerance, replication is a fundamental mechanism. Based on various replication schemes, there are a large number of fault-tolerance protocols (*e.g.*, a family of protocols based on Paxos [8]) which focus on the consistency problem among different replicas. Recently with the rapid growth of cloud computing, replication is receiving increasing attention to enhance the reliability of resource allocation in the cloud. Shen *et al.* [13] proposed an Availability-on-Demand mechanism. The mechanism consists of a scheduler that manages computing resources. To enhance the availability, each virtual machine (VM) is replicated. When placing VMs to the physical servers, the scheduler ensures the primary and the backups are located in different servers. Yanagisawa *et al.* [14] studied dependable VM allocation in a bank private cloud. Similar to our work, they also considered the resource demands might fluctuate in the case of failures. A mixed integer programming approach was proposed to solve the resource allocation problem. The above two papers focused on empirical performance and did not provide any theoretical analysis. O. Beaumont *et al.* [2] studied the impact of the reliability constraint on the complexity of resource allocation problems. They proved several fundamental complexity results and proposed a basic randomized allocation algorithm. M. Korupolu *et al.* [7] studied failure-aware placement problems under adversarial and probabilistic failure models. Both [2] and [7] targeted to minimize the number of disrupted items in the case of failures or the probability for more than a given number of items to fail together. Different from these studies, we aim to ensure that each item always has at least one survival replica as long as the number of faulty bins are no more than f.

Our problem is closely related to a fault-tolerant server consolidation problem studied recently [11][4]. In the latter problem, to achieve fault tolerance, each task is divided into several replicas which are dispersed in different servers. Every replica inherits part of the original task workload. In the case of failures, the faulty replica's workload can be directed to other replicas hosted by correct servers. One typical application area of server consolidation is in multi-tenant database systems. Schaffner *et al.* [11] studied robust tenant placement for in-memory database clusters. Daudje *et al.* [4] conducted a follow-up study and proposed a heuristic algorithm called the shifting algorithm. Compared with the mirroring algorithm proposed in [11], the shifting algorithm achieves a better competitive ratio. A major difference of our fault-tolerant bin packing problem from the above problem is that each standby replica created has a base workload that is independent of whether the standby switches to the primary or not. This is a reasonable model for many practical scenarios. For example, in the case of database replication, read requests are normally executed by the primary only, whereas write requests must be executed by all the replicas for maintaining the consistency [11][14]. The study of [4], however, does not consider such a constraint. If standby replicas do not involve any base workload, one can in fact simply create idle servers to host standby replicas and let these servers take over the faulty servers when failures occur. In our fault-tolerant bin packing problem, both the mirroring and the shifting algorithms are also studied. The shifting algorithm has better performance. However, the process of opening bins by the shifting algorithm is not smooth in the online setting. We propose a new algorithm named mixing which can balance the number of bins used and the process of opening bins. Furthermore, our work addresses a generalized requirement to tolerate up to f failures.

Another variant of the bin packing problem for modeling cloud resource allocation has been defined and studied in recent years [9][10]. The objective of this variant is to minimize the accumulated bin usage time, which is different from our target to minimize the number of bins used in this paper. Besides, no fault-tolerance constraint was considered in the above variant.

ACKNOWLEDGMENTS

This work is supported by Singapore Ministry of Education Academic Research Fund Tier 1 under Grant 2013-T1-002-123.

REFERENCES

[1] J. Balogh, J. Békési, and G. Galambos. 2012. New lower bounds for certain classes of bin packing algorithms. *Theor. Comput. Sci.* 440-441 (2012), 1–13.

[2] O. Beaumont, L. Eyraud-Dubois, and H. Larchevêque. 2013. An Availability-on-Demand Mechanism for Datacenters. In *Proc. of the 27th IEEE International Symposium on Parallel and Distributed Processing (IPDPS)*. 55–66.

[3] E. G. Coffman, J. Csirik, G. Galambos, S. Martello, and D. Vigo. 2013. Bin packing approximation algorithms: Survey and classification. *Handbook of Combinatorial Optimization (second edition)* (2013), 455–531.

[4] K. Daudjee, S. Kamali, and A. Lopez-Ortiz. 2014. On the online fault-tolerant server consolidation problem. In *Proc. of the 26th ACM Symposium on Parallelism in Algorithms and Architectures (SPAA)*. 12–21.

[5] G. Galambos and G. J. Woeginger. 1995. On-line bin packing - A restricted survey. *Math. Meth. of OR* 42, 1 (1995), 25–45.

[6] M. R. Garey and D. S. Johnson. 1979. *Computers and Intractability: A Guide to the Theory of NP-Completeness.* W. H. Freeman.

[7] M. R. Korupolu and R. Rajaraman. 2016. Robust and Probabilistic Failure-Aware Placement. In *Proc. of the 28th ACM Symposium on Parallelism in Algorithms and Architectures (SPAA)*. 213–224.

[8] L. Lamport. 1998. The Part-Time Parliament. *ACM Trans. Comput. Syst.* 16, 2 (1998), 133–169.

[9] Y. Li, X. Tang, and W. Cai. 2014. On dynamic bin packing for resource allocation in the cloud. In *Proc. of the 26th ACM Symposium on Parallelism in Algorithms and Architectures (SPAA)*. 2–11.

[10] R. Ren and X. Tang. 2016. Clairvoyant Dynamic Bin Packing for Job Scheduling with Minimum Server Usage Time. In *Proc. of the 28th ACM Symposium on Parallelism in Algorithms and Architectures (SPAA)*. 227–237.

[11] J. Schaffner, T. Januschowski, M. Kercher, T. Kraska, H. Plattner, M. J. Franklin, and D. Jacobs. 2013. RTP: Robust tenant placement for elastic in-momory database clusters. In *Proc. of the ACM International Conference on Management of Data (SIGMOD)*. 773–784.

[12] S. S. Seiden. 2002. On the online bin packing problem. *Journal of the ACM* 49, 5 (2002), 640–671.

[13] S. Shen, A. Iosup, A. Israel, W. Cirne, D. Raz, and D. H. J. Epema. 2015. An Availability-on-Demand Mechanism for Datacenters. In *Proc. of the 15th IEEE/ACM International Symposium on Cluster, Cloud and Grid Computing (CCGrid)*. 495–504.

[14] H. Yanagisawa, T. Osogami, and R. Raymond. 2013. Dependable virtual machine allocation. In *Proc. of the 32nd Annual IEEE International Conference on Computer Communications (INFOCOM)*. 629–637.

Concurrent Data Structures for Near-Memory Computing

Zhiyu Liu
Computer Science Department
Brown University
zhiyu_liu@brown.edu

Irina Calciu
VMware Research Group
icalciu@vmware.com

Maurice Herlihy
Computer Science Department
Brown University
mph@cs.brown.edu

Onur Mutlu
Computer Science Department
ETH Zürich
onur.mutlu@inf.ethz.ch

ABSTRACT

The performance gap between memory and CPU has grown exponentially. To bridge this gap, hardware architects have proposed near-memory computing (also called processing-in-memory, or PIM), where a lightweight processor (called a PIM core) is located close to memory. Due to its proximity to memory, a memory access from a PIM core is much faster than that from a CPU core. New advances in 3D integration and die-stacked memory make PIM viable in the near future. Prior work has shown significant performance improvements by using PIM for embarrassingly parallel and data-intensive applications, as well as for pointer-chasing traversals in *sequential* data structures. However, current server machines have hundreds of cores, and algorithms for concurrent data structures exploit these cores to achieve high throughput and scalability, with significant benefits over sequential data structures. Thus, it is important to examine how PIM performs with respect to modern *concurrent* data structures and understand how concurrent data structures can be developed to take advantage of PIM.

This paper is the first to examine the design of *concurrent* data structures for PIM. We show two main results: (1) naive PIM data structures *cannot* outperform state-of-the-art concurrent data structures, such as pointer-chasing data structures and FIFO queues, (2) novel designs for PIM data structures, using techniques such as combining, partitioning and pipelining, can outperform traditional concurrent data structures, with a significantly simpler design.

KEYWORDS

concurrent data structures; parallel programs; processing-in-memory; near-memory computing

1 NEAR-MEMORY COMPUTING

The performance gap between memory and CPU has grown exponentially. Memory vendors have focused mainly on improving memory capacity and bandwidth, sometimes even at the cost of higher memory access latencies [11, 12, 14, 35, 37–39, 42, 43]. To provide higher bandwidth with lower access latencies, hardware architects have proposed near-memory computing (also called *processing-in-memory*, or PIM), where a lightweight processor (called a PIM core) is located close to memory. A memory access from a PIM core is much faster than that from a CPU core. Near-memory computing is an old idea that has been intensively studied in the past (e.g., [17, 20, 21, 32, 34, 44, 45, 51]), but so far has not yet materialized. However, new advances in 3D integration and die-stacked memory likely make near-memory computing viable in the near future. For example, one PIM design [1, 2, 9, 53] assumes that memory is organized in multiple vaults, each having an in-order PIM core to manage it. These PIM cores can communicate through message passing, but do not share memory, and cannot access each other's vaults.

This new technology promises to revolutionize the interaction between computation and data, as it enables memory to become an active component in managing the data. Therefore, it invites a fundamental rethinking of basic data structures and promotes a tighter dependency between algorithmic design and hardware characteristics.

Prior work has already shown significant performance improvements by using PIM for embarrassingly parallel and data-intensive applications [1, 3, 29, 53, 54], as well as for pointer-chasing traversals [23, 30] in *sequential* data structures. However, current server machines have hundreds of cores, and algorithms for concurrent data structures exploit these cores to achieve high throughput and scalability, with significant benefits over sequential data structures (e.g., [19, 27, 46, 52]). Unlike prior work, we focus on *concurrent* data structures for PIM and we show that naive PIM data structures *cannot* outperform state-of-the-art concurrent data structures. In particular, the lower-latency access to memory provided by PIM cannot compensate for the loss of parallelism in data structure manipulation. For example, we show that even if a PIM memory access is two times faster than a CPU memory access, a sequential PIM linked-list is still slower than a traditional concurrent linked-list accessed in parallel by only three CPU cores.

Therefore, to be competitive with traditional concurrent data structures, PIM data structures need new algorithms and new approaches to leverage parallelism. As the PIM technology approaches fruition, it is crucial to investigate how to best utilize it to exploit the lower latencies, while still leveraging the vast amount of previous research related to concurrent data structures.

In this paper, we provide answers to the following key questions: 1) How do we design and optimize data structures for PIM? 2) How

SPAA '17, July 24-26, 2017, Washington DC, USA

DOI: http://dx.doi.org/10.1145/3087556.3087582

do these optimized PIM data structures compare to traditional CPU-managed concurrent data structures? To answer these questions, even before the hardware becomes available, we develop a simplified model of the expected performance of PIM. Using this model, we investigate two classes of data structures.

First, we analyze *pointer chasing data structures* (Section 4), which have a high degree of inherent parallelism and low contention, but which incur significant overhead due to hard-to-predict memory access patterns. We propose using techniques such as combining and partitioning the data across vaults to reintroduce parallelism for these data structures.

Second, we explore *contended data structures* (Section 5), such as FIFO queues, which can leverage CPU caches to exploit their inherent high locality. As they exploit the fast on-chip caches well, FIFO queues might not seem to be a good fit for leveraging PIM's faster memory accesses. Nevertheless, these data structures exhibit a high degree of contention, which makes it difficult, even for the most advanced data structures, to obtain good performance when many threads access the data concurrently. We use pipelining of requests, which can be done very efficiently in PIM, to design a new FIFO queue suitable for PIM that can outperform state-of-the-art concurrent FIFO queues [25, 41].

The contributions of this paper are as follows:

- We propose a simple and intuitive model to analyze the performance of PIM data structures and of concurrent data structures. This model considers the number of atomic operations, the number of memory accesses and the number of accesses that can be served from the CPU cache.
- Using this model, we show that the lower-latency memory accesses provided by PIM are *not* sufficient for sequential PIM data structures to outperform efficient traditional concurrent data structures.
- We propose new designs for PIM data structures using techniques such as combining, partitioning and pipelining. Our evaluations show that these new PIM data structures can outperform traditional concurrent data structures, with a significantly simpler design.

The paper is organized as follows. In Section 2, we briefly describe our assumptions about the hardware architecture. In Section 3, we introduce a simplified performance model that we use throughout this paper to estimate the performance of our data structures using the hardware architecture described in Section 2. In Sections 4 and 5, we describe and analyze our PIM data structures and use our model to compare them to prior work. We also use current DRAM architectures to simulate the behavior of our data structures and evaluate them compared to state-of-the-art concurrent data structures. Finally, we present related work in Section 6 and conclude in Section 7.

2 HARDWARE ARCHITECTURE

In an example architecture utilizing PIM memory [1, 2, 9, 53], multiple CPUs are connected to the main memory, via a shared crossbar network, as illustrated in Figure 1. The main memory consists of two parts—one is a standard DRAM accessible by CPUs, and the other, called the *PIM memory*, is divided into multiple partitions, called *PIM vaults* or simply *vaults*. According to the *Hybrid Memory Cube (HMC)* specification 1.0 [15], each HMC consists of 16 or 32 vaults and has a total size of 2GB or 4GB (so each vault's size is roughly 100MB).[1] We assume the same specifications in our PIM model, although the size of the PIM memory and the number of its vaults can be bigger. Each CPU core also has access to a hierarchy of L1 and L2 caches backed by DRAM, and a last level cache shared among multiple cores.

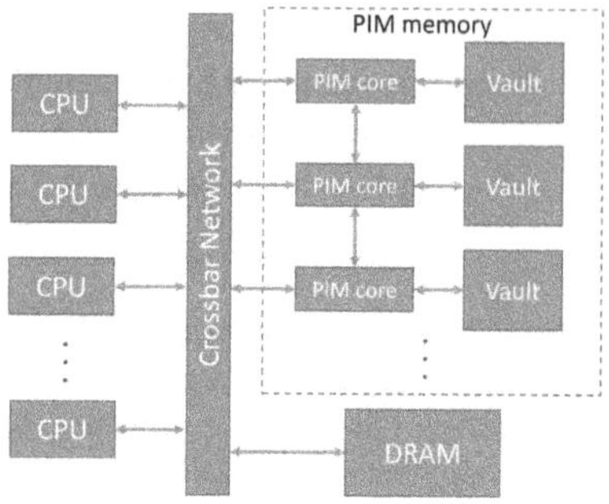

Figure 1: An example PIM architecture

Each vault has a *PIM core* directly attached to it. We say a vault is *local* to the PIM core attached to it, and vice versa. A PIM core is a lightweight CPU that may be slower than a full-fledged CPU with respect to computation speed [1]. A PIM core can be thought of as an in-order CPU with a small private L1 cache. A vault can be accessed only by its local PIM core.[2] Recent work proposes efficient cache coherence mechanisms between PIM cores and CPUs (e.g., [2, 9]), but this introduces additional complexity. We show that we can design efficient concurrent PIM data structures even if there is no coherence. Although a PIM core has lower performance than a state-of-the-art CPU core, it has fast access to its local vault.

A PIM core communicates with other PIM cores and CPUs via messages. Each PIM core, as well as each CPU, has buffers for storing incoming messages. A message is guaranteed to eventually arrive at the buffer of its receiver. Messages from the same sender to the same receiver are delivered in FIFO order: the message sent first arrives at the receiver first. However, messages from different senders or to different receivers can arrive in an arbitrary order.

We assume that a PIM core can only perform read and write operations to its local vault, while a CPU also supports more powerful atomic operations, such as *Compare-And-Swap (CAS)* and *Fetch-And-Add (F&A)*. Virtual memory can be realized efficiently if each PIM core maintains its own page table for the local vault [30].

3 PERFORMANCE MODEL

We propose the following simple performance model to compare our PIM-managed data structures with existing concurrent data structures. For read and write operations, we assume

$$\mathcal{L}_{cpu} = r_1 \mathcal{L}_{pim} = r_2 \mathcal{L}_{llc}$$

where $\mathcal{L}_{cpu}$ is the latency of a memory access by a CPU, $\mathcal{L}_{pim}$ is the latency of a local memory access by a PIM core, and $\mathcal{L}_{llc}$

[1] These small sizes are preliminary, and it is expected that each vault will become larger when PIM memory is commercialized.

[2] Alternatively, we could assume that a PIM core has direct access to the remote vaults, but such accesses are slower than those to the local vault.

is the latency of a last-level cache access by a CPU. Based on the latency numbers in prior work on PIM memory, in particular on the Hybrid Memory Cube [6, 15], and on the evaluation of operations in multiprocessor architectures [16], we may further assume

$$r_1 = r_2 = 3.$$

The latencies of operations may vary significantly on different machines. Our assumption that $r_1 = r_2 = 3$ is mainly to make the performance analysis later in the paper more concrete with actual latency numbers. In our performance model, we ignore the costs of accesses to other cache levels, such as L1 or L2, as they are negligible in the concurrent data structures we consider.

We assume that the latency of a CPU performing an atomic operation, such as a CAS or a F&A, to a cache line is

$$\mathcal{L}_{atomic} = r_3 \mathcal{L}_{cpu}$$

where $r_3 = 1$, even if the cache line is currently in the cache. This is because an atomic operation hitting in the cache is usually as costly as a memory access by a CPU [16]. When there are k atomic operations competing for a cache line concurrently, we assume that they are executed sequentially, that is, they complete in times $\mathcal{L}_{atomic}, 2\mathcal{L}_{atomic}, ..., k \cdot \mathcal{L}_{atomic}$, respectively.

We also assume that the size of a message sent by a PIM core or a CPU core is at most the size of a cache line. Given that a message transferred between a CPU and a PIM core goes through the crossbar network, we assume that the latency for a message to arrive at its receiver is

$$\mathcal{L}_{message} = \mathcal{L}_{cpu}$$

We make the conservative assumption that the latency of a message transferred between two PIM cores is also $\mathcal{L}_{message}$. Note that the message latency we consider here is the transfer time of a message through a message passing channel, that is, the elapsed time between the moment when a PIM or a CPU core finishes sending off the message and the moment when the message arrives at the buffer of its receiver. We ignore the time spent in other parts of a message passing procedure, such as in *preprocessing and constructing the message*, and in *actually sending the message*, as it is negligible compared to the time spent in the message transfer [6].

4 LOW-CONTENTION DATA STRUCTURES

In this section, we consider data structures with low contention. Pointer chasing data structures, such as linked-lists and skip-lists, fall in this category. These are data structures whose operations need to de-reference a non-constant sequence of pointers before completing. We assume these data structures support operations such as add(x), delete(x) and contains(x), which follow "next node" pointers until reaching the position of node x. When these data structures are too large to fit in the CPU caches and access uniformly random keys, they incur expensive memory accesses, which cannot be easily predicted, making the *pointer chasing* operations the dominating overhead of these data structures. Naturally, these data structures have provided early examples of the benefits of near-memory computing [23, 30], as the entire pointer chasing operation could be performed by a PIM core with fast memory access, and only the final result returned to the application.

However, these data structures have inherently low contention. Lock-free algorithms [19, 27, 46, 52] have shown that these data structures can scale to hundreds of cores under low contention [10]. Unfortunately, each vault in PIM memory has a single core. As a consequence, prior work has compared PIM data structures only with sequential data structures, *not* with carefully crafted concurrent data structures.

We analyze linked-lists and skip-lists, and show that the naive PIM data structure in each case cannot outperform the equivalent CPU-managed concurrent data structure even for a small number of cores. Next, we show how to use state-of-the art techniques from concurrent computing to optimize data structures for near-memory computing such that they outperform well-known concurrent data structures designed for multi-core CPUs.

4.1 Linked-lists

We first describe a naive PIM linked-list. The linked-list is stored in a vault, maintained by the local PIM core. Whenever a CPU[3] wants to perform an operation on the linked-list, it sends a request to the PIM core. The PIM core then retrieves the message, executes the operation, and sends the result back to the CPU. The PIM linked-list is sequential, as it can only be accessed by one PIM core.

Performing pointer chasing on sequential data structures using PIM cores is not a new idea. Prior work ([1, 23, 30]) has shown that pointer chasing can be done more efficiently by a PIM core for a sequential data structure. However, we are not aware of any prior comparison between the performance of PIM-managed data structures and *concurrent* data structures, for which CPUs can perform operations in parallel. In fact, our analytical and experimental results show that the naive PIM-managed linked-list is not competitive with a concurrent linked-list that uses fine-grained locks [24].

We use the *combining optimization* proposed by flat combining [25] to improve this data structure: a PIM core can execute all concurrent requests by CPU cores using *a single* traversal over the linked-list.

The role of the PIM core in our PIM-managed linked-list is very similar to that of the combiner in a concurrent linked-list implemented using *flat combining* [25], where, roughly speaking, threads compete for a "combiner lock" to become the combiner, and the combiner takes over all operation requests from other threads and executes them. Therefore, we consider the performance of the flat-combining linked-list as an indicator of the performance of our proposed PIM-managed linked-list.

Based on our performance model, we can calculate the approximate expected throughput (in operations per second) of each of the linked-lists mentioned above, when there are p CPUs making operation requests concurrently. We assume that a linked-list consists of nodes with integer keys in the range of $[1, N]$. Initially a linked-list has n nodes with keys generated independently and uniformly at random from $[1, N]$. The keys of the operation requests are generated the same way. To simplify the analysis, we assume that the size of the linked-list does not fluctuate much. This is achieved when the number of add() requests is similar to the number of delete() requests. We assume that a CPU makes a new operation request

[3] We use the term CPU to refer to a CPU core, as opposed to a PIM core.

immediately after its previous one completes. Assuming that $n \gg p$ and $N \gg p$, the approximate expected throughput (per second) of each of the concurrent linked-lists is presented in Table 1, where $\mathcal{S}_p = \sum_{i=1}^{n} (\frac{i}{n+1})^p$.

Algorithm	Throughput
Linked-list with fine-grained locks	$\frac{2p}{(n+1)\mathcal{L}_{cpu}}$
Flat-combining linked-list without combining	$\frac{2}{(n+1)\mathcal{L}_{cpu}}$
PIM-managed linked-list without combining	$\frac{2}{(n+1)\mathcal{L}_{pim}}$
Flat-combining linked-list with combining	$\frac{p}{(n-\mathcal{S}_p)\mathcal{L}_{cpu}}$
PIM-managed linked-list with combining	$\frac{p}{(n-\mathcal{S}_p)\mathcal{L}_{pim}}$

Table 1: Throughput of linked-lists

We calculate the throughput values in Table 1 in the following manner. In the linked-list with fine-grained locks, which has $(n+1)$ nodes including a dummy head node, each thread (CPU) executes its own operations to the linked-list. The key of a request is generated uniformly at random, so the average number of memory accesses by one thread for one operation is $(n+1)/2$ and hence the throughput of one thread is $2/((n+1)\mathcal{L}_{cpu})$. There are p threads running in parallel, so the total throughput is $2p/((n+1)\mathcal{L}_{cpu})$. The throughput of the flat-combining and the PIM-managed linked-lists without the combining optimization is calculated in a similar manner. For the flat-combining and the PIM-managed linked-lists with combining, it suffices to prove that the average number of memory accesses by a PIM core (or a combiner) batching and executing p random operation requests in one traversal is $n - \mathcal{S}_p$, which is essentially the expected number of pointers a PIM core (or a combiner) needs to go through to reach the position for the request with the largest key among the p requests. Note that we have ignored certain communication costs incurred in some linked-lists, such as the latency of a PIM core sending a result back to a waiting thread, and the latency of a combiner maintaining the combiner lock and the publication list in the flat-combining linked-list (we will discuss the publication list in more detail in Section 5), as they are negligible compared to the dominant costs of traversals over linked-lists.

It is easy to see that the PIM-managed linked-list with combining outperforms the linked-list with fine-grained locks, which is the best one among other linked-lists, if $\frac{\mathcal{L}_{cpu}}{\mathcal{L}_{pim}} = r_1 > \frac{2(n-\mathcal{S}_p)}{n+1}$. Given that $0 < \mathcal{S}_p \leq \frac{n}{2}$, the PIM-managed linked-list can outperform the linked-list with fine-grained locks as long as $r_1 \geq 2$. If we assume $r_1 = 3$, as estimated by prior work, the throughput of the PIM-managed linked-list with combining should be at least 1.5 times the throughput of the linked-list with fine-grained locks. Without combining, however, the PIM-managed linked-list *cannot* outperform the linked-list with fine-grained locks accessed by $p \geq r_1$ concurrent threads. On the other hand, the PIM-managed linked-list is expected to be r_1 times better than the flat-combining linked-list, with or without the combining optimization applied to both.

We implemented the linked-list with fine-grained locks and the flat-combining linked-list with and without the combining optimization. We tested them on a Dell server with 512 GB RAM and 56 cores on four Intel Xeon E7-4850v3 processors running at 2.2 GHz. To eliminate NUMA access effects, we ran experiments with only one processor, which is a NUMA node with 14 cores, a 35 MB shared L3 cache, and a private L2/L1 cache of size 256 KB/64 KB per core. Each core has 2 hyperthreads, for a total of 28 hyperthreads.

The throughput of each of the linked-lists, measured in operations per second, is presented in Figure 2. The results confirm the validity of our analysis in Table 1. The throughput of the flat-combining linked-list without the combining optimization is worse than the linked-list with fine-grained locks. Since the throughput of the flat-combining linked-list is a good indicator of the performance of the PIM-managed linked-list, we triple the throughput of the flat-combining linked-list to obtain the expected throughput of the PIM-managed linked-list, based on the assumption that $r_1 = 3$. As we can see, it is still below the throughput of the one with fined-grained locks. However, with the combining optimization, the performance of the flat-combining linked-list improves significantly and our PIM-managed linked-list with the combining optimization now outperforms all other data structures. We conclude that our PIM-managed linked-list is effective.

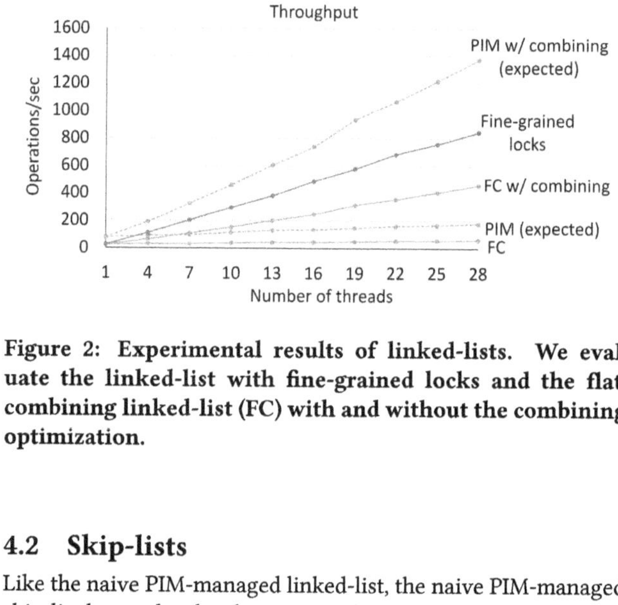

Figure 2: Experimental results of linked-lists. We evaluate the linked-list with fine-grained locks and the flat-combining linked-list (FC) with and without the combining optimization.

4.2 Skip-lists

Like the naive PIM-managed linked-list, the naive PIM-managed skip-list keeps the skip-list in a single vault and CPU cores send operation requests to the local PIM core that executes those operations. As we will see, this skip-list is less efficient than some existing skip-list algorithms.

Unfortunately, the combining optimization *cannot* be applied to skip-lists effectively. The reason is that for any two distant nodes in the skip-list, the paths threads must traverse to reach such nodes do *not* have large overlapping sub-paths. FloDB [7] uses a multi-insert operation for skip-lists, similar to the combining optimization we use for linked-lists. However, FloDB can ensure that the operations performed in a single traversal are close together because the operations are first grouped using a hash-table.

On the other hand, PIM memory usually consists of many vaults and PIM cores. For instance, the first generation of Hybrid Memory Cube [15] has up to 32 vaults. Hence, a PIM-managed skip-list can achieve much better performance if we can exploit the parallelism of multiple vaults. Here we present our PIM-managed skip-list with a *partitioning optimization*: A skip-list is divided into partitions of disjoint ranges of keys, stored in different vaults, so that a CPU sends its operation request to the PIM core of the vault to which the key of the operation belongs.

Figure 3 illustrates the structure of a PIM-managed skip-list. Each partition of a skip-list starts with a *sentinel node* which is a node with maximum height. For simplicity, assume that the max height H_{max} is predefined. A partition covers a key range between the key of its sentinel node and the key of the sentinel node of the next partition. CPUs also store a copy of each sentinel node in regular DRAM (see Figure 1) and this copy has an extra variable indicating the vault containing the sentinel node. The number of nodes with max height is very small with high probability, so the sentinel nodes can likely be found in the CPU caches because CPUs access them frequently.

When a CPU performs an operation for a key on the skip-list, it first compares the key with those of the sentinels, discovers which vault the key belongs to, and then sends its operation request to that vault's PIM core. After the PIM core retrieves the request, it executes the operation in the local vault and sends the result back to the CPU.

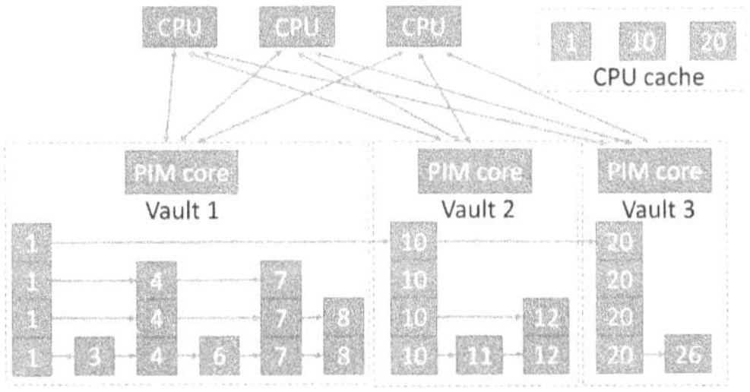

Figure 3: A PIM-managed skip-list with three partitions

We now discuss how we implement the PIM-managed skip-list when the key of each operation is an integer generated uniformly at random from range $[0, n]$ and the PIM memory has k vaults available. Initially we can create k partitions starting with fake sentinel nodes with keys 0, $1/k$, $2/k$,..., $(n-1)/k$, respectively, and allocate each partition in a different vault. The sentinel nodes are never deleted. If a new node to be added has the same key as a sentinel node, we insert it immediately after the sentinel node.

We compare the performance of our PIM-managed skip-list with k partitions to the performance of a flat-combining skip-list [25] and a lock-free skip-list [27], accessed concurrently by p CPUs. We also apply the partitioning optimization to the flat-combining skip-list, so that k combiners are in charge of k partitions of the skip-list. To simplify the comparison, we assume that all skip-lists have the same initial structure, i.e. skip-lists with partitions have extra sentinel nodes. We execute an equal number of add() and remove() requests, so that the size of the skip-list does not change dramatically. The keys of requests are generated uniformly at random.

The approximate throughput of each of these skip-lists is presented in Table 2, where β is the average number of nodes an operation has to access in order to find the location of its key in a skip-list ($\beta = \Theta(\log N)$, where N is the size of the skip-list). In the lock-free skip-list, p threads execute their own operations in parallel, so the throughput is roughly $p/(\beta\mathcal{L}_{cpu})$. Without the partitioning optimization, a combiner in the flat-combining skip-list and a PIM core in the PIM-managed skip-list both have to execute operations one by one sequentially, leading to throughput of roughly $\frac{1}{(\beta\mathcal{L}_{cpu})}$ and $\frac{1}{(\beta\mathcal{L}_{pim}+\mathcal{L}_{message})}$ respectively, where $\mathcal{L}_{message}$ is incurred by the PIM core sending a message with a result back to a CPU. After dividing these two skip-lists into k partitions, we can achieve a speedup of k for both of them, as k PIM cores and k combiners can serve requests in parallel now. Note that we have ignored certain costs in the lock-free skip-list and the two flat-combining skip-lists, such as the cost of a combiner's operations on the publication list in a flat-combining skip-list and the cost of CAS operations in the lock-free skip-list, so their actual performance could be even worse than what we show in Table 2.

Algorithm	Throughput
Lock-free skip-list	$\frac{p}{\beta\mathcal{L}_{cpu}}$
Flat-combining skip-list	$\frac{1}{\beta\mathcal{L}_{cpu}}$
PIM-managed skip-list	$\frac{1}{(\beta\mathcal{L}_{pim}+\mathcal{L}_{message})}$
Flat-combining skip-list with k partitions	$\frac{k}{\beta\mathcal{L}_{cpu}}$
PIM-managed skip-list with k partitions	$\frac{k}{(\beta\mathcal{L}_{pim}+\mathcal{L}_{message})}$

Table 2: Throughput of skip-lists

The results in Table 2 imply that the PIM-managed skip-list with k partitions is expected to outperform the second best skip-list, the lock-free skip-list, when $k > \frac{(\beta\mathcal{L}_{pim}+\mathcal{L}_{message})p}{\beta\mathcal{L}_{cpu}}$. Given that $\mathcal{L}_{message} = \mathcal{L}_{cpu} = r_1\mathcal{L}_{pim}$ and $\beta = \Theta(\log N)$, $k > p/r_1$ should suffice. It is also easy to see that the performance of the PIM-managed skip-list is $\frac{\beta r_1}{\beta + r_1} \approx r_1$ times better than the flat-combining skip-list, when they have the same number of partitions.

Our experimental evaluation reveals similar results, as presented in Figure 4. We have implemented and run the flat-combining skip-list with different numbers of partitions and compared them with the lock-free skip-list. As the number of partitions increases, the performance of the flat-combining skip-list improves, attesting to the effectiveness of the partitioning optimization. Again, we believe the performance of the flat-combining skip-list is a good indicator of the performance of our PIM-managed skip-list. Therefore, according to the analytical results in Table 2, we can triple the throughput of a flat-combining skip-list to estimate the expected performance of a PIM-managed skip-list. As Figure 4 illustrates, when our PIM-managed skip-list has 8 or 16 partitions, it is expected to outperform the lock-free skip-list with up to 28 hardware threads.

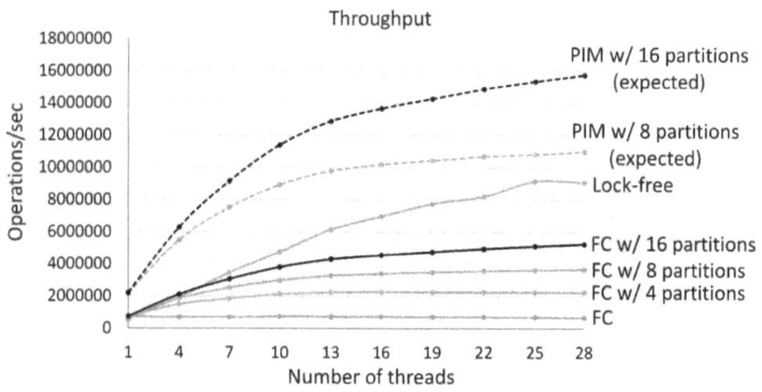

Figure 4: Experimental results of skip-lists. We evaluated the lock-free skip-list and the flat-combining skip-list (FC) with different numbers (1, 4, 8, 16) of partitions.

4.2.1 Skip-list Rebalancing. The PIM-managed skip-list performs well with a uniform distribution of requests. However, if the distribution of requests is *not* uniform, a static partitioning scheme will result in unbalanced partitions, with some PIM cores potentially being idle, while others having to serve a majority of the requests. To address this problem, we introduce a non-blocking protocol for migrating consecutive nodes from one vault to another.

The protocol works as follows. A PIM core p that manages a vault v' can send a message to another PIM core q, managing vault v, to request some nodes to be moved from v' to v. First, p sends a message notifying q of the start of the migration. Then p sends messages to q for adding those nodes into v one by one in ascending order according to the keys of the nodes. After all the nodes have been migrated, p sends notification messages to CPUs so that they can update their copies of sentinel nodes accordingly. After p receives acknowledgement messages from all CPUs, it notifies q of the end of migration. To keep the node migration protocol simple, we don't allow q to move those nodes to another vault again until p finishes its node migration.

During the node migration, p can still serve requests from CPUs. Assume that a request with key k_1 is sent to p when p is migrating nodes in a key range containing k_1. If p is about to migrate a node with key k_2 at the moment and $k_1 \geq k_2$, p serves the request itself. Otherwise, p must have migrated all nodes in the subset containing key k_1, and therefore p forwards the request to q which will serve the request and respond directly to the requesting CPU.

This skip-list is correct, because a request will eventually reach the vault that currently contains nodes in the key range that the request belongs to. If a request arrives to p which no longer holds the partition the request belongs to, p simply replies with a rejection to the CPU and the CPU will resend its request to the correct PIM core, because it has already updated its sentinels and knows which PIM core it should contact now.

Using this node migration protocol, the PIM-managed FIFO queue can support two rebalancing schemes: 1) If a partition has too many nodes, the local PIM core can move nodes in a key range to a vault that has fewer nodes; 2) If two consecutive partitions are both small, we can merge then by moving one to the vault containing the other.

In practice, we expect that rebalancing will not happen very frequently, so its overhead can be ameliorated by the improved efficiency resulting from the rebalanced partitions.

5 CONTENDED DATA STRUCTURES

In this section, we consider data structures that are often contended when accessed by many threads concurrently. In these data structures, operations compete for accessing one or more locations, creating a contention spot, which can become a performance bottleneck. Examples include head and tail pointers in queues and the top pointer of a stack.

These data structures have good locality; therefore, the contention spots are often found in shared CPU caches, such as the last-level cache in a multi-socket machine when shared by threads running on a single socket. Therefore, these data structures might seem to be a poor fit for near-memory computing: the advantage of faster memory access provided by PIM cannot be exercised because the frequently accessed data might stay in the CPU cache. However, such a perspective does not consider the overhead introduced by contention in a concurrent data structure where *many* threads access the *same* locations.

As a representative example of this class of data structures, we consider a FIFO queue, where concurrent enqueue and dequeue operations compete for the head and the tail of the queue, respectively. Although a naive PIM FIFO queue is not a good replacement for a well crafted concurrent FIFO queue, we show that, counterintuitively, PIM can still have benefits over a traditional concurrent FIFO queue. In particular, we exploit the *pipelining* of requests from CPUs, which can be done very efficiently in PIM, to design a PIM FIFO queue that can outperform state-of-the-art concurrent FIFO queues, such as the flat-combining FIFO queue [25] and the F&A FIFO queue [41].

5.1 FIFO queues

The structure of our PIM-managed FIFO queue is shown in Figure 5. A queue consists of a sequence of *segments*, each containing consecutive nodes of the queue. A segment is allocated in a PIM vault, with a head node and a tail node pointing to the first and the last nodes of the segment, respectively. A vault can contain multiple (likely non-consecutive) segments. There are two special segments—the *enqueue segment* and the *dequeue segment*. To enqueue a node, a CPU sends an enqueue request to the PIM core of the vault containing the enqueue segment. The PIM core then inserts the node to the head of the segment. Similarly, to dequeue a node, a CPU sends a dequeue request to the PIM core of the vault holding the dequeue segment. The PIM core then removes the node at the tail of the dequeue segment and sends the node back to the CPU.

Initially, the queue consists of an empty segment that acts as both the enqueue segment and the dequeue segment. When the length of the enqueue segment exceeds some threshold, the PIM core maintaining it notifies another PIM core to create a new segment as the new enqueue segment.[4] When the dequeue segment becomes empty and the queue has other segments, the dequeue segment

[4] Alternative designs where a CPU decides when to create new segments based on more complex criteria are also possible. We leave such designs as future work.

Algorithm 1 PIM-managed FIFO queue

```
1: procedure enq(cid, u)
2:     if enqSeg == null then
3:         send message(cid, false);
4:     else
5:         if enqSeg.head ≠ null then
6:             enqSeg.head.next = u;
7:             enqSeg.head = u;
8:         else
9:             enqSeg.head = u;
10:            enqSeg.tail = u;
11:        enqSeg.count = enqSeg.count + 1;
12:        send message(cid, true);
13:        if enqSeg.count > threshold then
14:            cid′ = the CID of the PIM core chosen to maintain the new segment;
15:            send message(cid′, newEnqSeg());
16:            enqSeg.nextSegCid = cid′;
17:            enqSeg = null;

18: procedure newEnqSeg()
19:     enqSeg = new Segment();
20:     segQueue.enq(engSeg) ;
21:     notify the CPUs of the new enqueue segment;

22: procedure deq(cid)
23:     if deqSeg == null then
24:         send message(cid, false);
25:     else
26:         if deqSeg.tail ≠ null then
27:             send message(cid, deqSeg.tail);
28:             deqSeg.tail = deqSeg.tail.next;
29:         else
30:             if deqSeg == enqSeg then
31:                 send message(cid, null);
32:             else
33:                 send message(deqSeg.nextSegCid, newDeqSeg());
34:                 deqSeg = null;
35:                 send message(cid, false);

36: procedure newDeqSeg()
37:     deqSeg = segQueue.deq();
38:     notify the CPUs of the new dequeue segment;
```

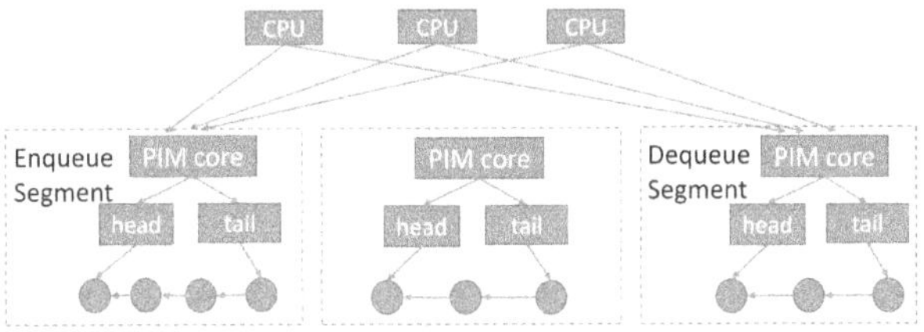

Figure 5: A PIM-managed FIFO queue with three segments

is deleted and the segment that was created first among all the remaining segments is designated as the new dequeue segment. This segment was created when the old dequeue segment acted as the enqueue segment and exceeded the length threshold. If the enqueue segment is different from the dequeue segment, enqueue and dequeue operations can be executed by two different PIM cores in parallel, improving the throughput. The F&A queue [41] also allows parallel enqueue and dequeue.

The pseudo-code of the PIM-managed FIFO queue is presented in Algorithm 1. Each PIM core has local variables *enqSeg* and *deqSeg* that are references to local enqueue and dequeue segments. When *enqSeg* (or *deqSeg*) is not null, it indicates that the PIM core is currently holding the enqueue (or dequeue) segment. Each PIM core also maintains a local queue *segQueue* for storing local segments. CPUs and PIM cores communicate via message(*cid, content*) calls, where *cid* is the unique core ID (CID) of the receiver and *content* is either a request or a response to a request.

Once a PIM core receives an *enqueue* request enq(*cid, u*) of node *u* from a CPU whose CID is *cid*, it first checks if it is holding the enqueue segment (line 2). If so, the PIM core enqueues *u* (lines 5-12), and otherwise sends back a message informing the CPU that the request is rejected (line 3) so that the CPU can resend its request to the right PIM core holding the enqueue segment (we will explain later how the CPU can find the right PIM core). After enqueuing *u*, the PIM core may find that the enqueue segment is longer than the threshold (line 13). If so, it sends a message with a newEnqSeg() request to the PIM core of another vault that is chosen to create a new enqueue segment. The PIM core then sets its *enqSeg* to null, indicating that it no longer deals with enqueue operations. Note that the CID *cid* of the PIM core chosen for creating the new segment is recorded in *enqSeg.nextSegCid* for future use in dequeue requests. As Procedure newEnqSeg() in Algorithm 1 shows, The PIM core receiving this newEnqSeg() request creates a new enqueue segment and enqueues the segment into its *segQueue* (lines 19-20). Finally, it notifies the CPUs of the new enqueue segment (we will discuss this notification in more detail later in this section).

Similarly, when a PIM core receives a *dequeue* request deq(*cid*) from a CPU with CID *cid*, it first checks whether it is holding the dequeue segment (line 23). If so, the PIM core dequeues a node and sends it back to the CPU (lines 26-28). Otherwise, it informs the CPU that this request has failed (line 24) and the CPU will have to resend its request to the right PIM core. If the dequeue segment is empty (line 29) and the dequeue segment is not the same as the enqueue segment (line 32), which implies that the FIFO queue is not empty, the PIM core sends a message with a newDeqSeg() request to the PIM core with CID *deqSeg.nextSegCid*. We know that this PIM core must hold the next segment, according to how we create new segments in enqueue operations, as shown in lines 14-16. Upon receiving the newDeqSeg() request, the PIM core retrieves from its *segQueue* the oldest segment it has created and makes it the new dequeue segment (line 37). Finally the PIM core notifies the CPUs that it is holding the new dequeue segment now.

We now explain how CPUs and PIM cores coordinate to make sure that the CPUs can find the right enqueue and dequeue segments, when their attempts fail due to enqueue/dequeue segment changes. We only discuss how to deal with enqueue segments, because the same methods can be applied to dequeue segments. A straightforward way to inform the CPUs is to have the owner PIM core of the new enqueue segment send notification messages to them (line 21) and wait until all the CPUs send back acknowledgment messages. However, if there is a slow CPU core that doesn't reply in time, the PIM core has to wait for it and therefore other CPUs cannot have their requests executed. A more efficient, non-blocking method is to have the PIM core start serving new requests immediately after it has sent off the notifications to all CPUs. A CPU does not have to reply to those notifications in this case, but if its request later fails, it needs to send messages to all PIM cores to ask which PIM core is currently in charge of the enqueue segment. In either case, the correctness of the queue is guaranteed: at any time, there is only one enqueue segment and only one dequeue segment; only requests sent to them will be executed.

The PIM-managed FIFO queue can be further optimized. For example, the PIM core holding the enqueue segment can combine multiple pending enqueue requests and store the nodes to be enqueued in an array as a "fat" node of the queue, in order to reduce memory accesses. This optimization is also used in the flat-combining FIFO queue [25]. Even without this optimization, the PIM-managed FIFO queue still performs well, as we will show next.

5.2 Pipelining and Performance Analysis

We compare the performance of three concurrent FIFO queues—our PIM-managed FIFO queue, the flat-combining FIFO queue and the F&A-based FIFO queue [41]. The F&A-based FIFO queue is the most efficient concurrent FIFO queue we are aware of, where threads perform F&A operations on two shared variables, one for enqueues and the other for dequeues, to compete for slots in the FIFO queue to enqueue and dequeue nodes (see [41] for more details). The flat-combining FIFO queue we consider is based on the one proposed by [25], with a modification that threads compete for two "combiner locks", one for enqueues and the other for dequeues. We further simplify it based on the assumption that the queue is always non-empty, so that it doesn't have to deal with synchronization issues between enqueues and dequeues when the queue is empty. These assumptions give an advantage to the flat combining queue, to make it competitive with the two other queues, which can perform parallel enqueue and dequeue.

Let us first assume that a queue is long enough such that the PIM-managed FIFO queue has more than one segment, and enqueue and dequeue requests can be executed separately. Since enqueue/dequeue segment changes are infrequent, the overhead of such changes is negligible and therefore not included in our analysis. For example, if the threshold of segment length in line 13 of enq(*cid*, *u*) is a large integer *n*, then, in the worst case, changing an enqueue or dequeue segment happens only once every *n* requests. Moreover, a segment change only entails sending one message and a few steps of local computation. In our analysis, we focus on dequeue operations, because enqueues and dequeues are isolated from each other in all three FIFO queues when queues are long enough. The analysis of enqueues is similar.

Assume there are p concurrent dequeue requests by p threads. In the F&A queue, each thread needs to perform a F&A operation on a shared variable, serializing access to this shared variable. Therefore, the execution time of p requests is at least $p\mathcal{L}_{atomic}$. If we assume that each CPU makes a request immediately after its previous request completes, the throughput (per second) of the F&A queue is at most $\frac{1}{\mathcal{L}_{atomic}}$.

The flat-combining FIFO queue maintains a sequential FIFO queue and threads submit their requests into a *publication list*. The publication list consists of slots, one for each thread, to store their requests. After writing a request into the list, a thread competes with others for acquiring a lock to become the "*combiner*", which incurs one last-level cache access. The combiner then goes through the publication list to retrieve requests, executes operations for those requests, and writes results back to the list, while other threads with pending requests spin on their own slots, waiting for the results. The combiner therefore makes two last-level cache accesses[5] to each slot other than its own, one for reading the request and one for writing the result back. Thus, the execution time of p requests in this FIFO queue is at least $(2p-1)\mathcal{L}_{llc}$ and the throughput (per second) of this FIFO queue is at most $\frac{1}{2\mathcal{L}_{llc}}$ for large enough p.

Note that our analysis of the F&A-based and the flat-combining queues is performed in favor of them, as we consider only partial costs of their executions. We have ignored the latency of accessing and modifying queue nodes in the two FIFO queue algorithms. For dequeues, this latency can be high: nodes to be dequeued in a long queue are unlikely to be cached, so the combiner has to perform a sequence of memory accesses to dequeue them one by one. Moreover, the F&A-based queue may also suffer performance degradation under heavy contention, because contended F&A operations may perform worse in practice [16].

The performance of our PIM-managed FIFO queue seems poor at first sight: although a PIM core can update the queue efficiently, it takes a lot of time for the PIM core to send results back to CPUs one by one. To improve its performance, the PIM core can *pipeline* the execution of requests, as illustrated in Figure 6(a). Suppose p CPUs send p dequeue requests concurrently to the PIM core. The PIM core then retrieves a request from its message buffer (step 1 in the figure), dequeues a node (step 2) for the request, and sends the node back to the CPU (step 3). We can hide the message latency in step 3 as follows. After sending the message containing the node in step 3, the PIM core *immediately* retrieves the next request to execute, without blocking to wait for the previous message to arrive at its receiver. This way, the PIM core *pipelines* requests by overlapping the latency of message transfer in step 3 and the latency of memory accesses and local computations in steps 1 and 2 across multiple requests (see Figure 6(b)). Note that the PIM core still executes everything sequentially: it first sends the message for the current request before serving the next one.

The throughput of a PIM core is given by the costs of its memory accesses and local computations, as long as it has enough bandwidth to keep sending messages back to CPUs. In this FIFO queue algorithm, the PIM core sends a single small message per request, so bandwidth is unlikely to become a bottleneck.

Figure 6(b) illustrates that the execution time of p requests is the sum of the execution times of the first two steps for the p requests, plus the message transfer time of step 3 for the last request. During steps 1-2 of a dequeue, the PIM core only makes one memory access to read the node to be dequeued, and two L1 cache accesses to read and modify the tail node of the dequeue segment. Therefore, the total execution time of p requests, including the time $\mathcal{L}_{message}$ that

[5] We assume the combiner finds the slots in the last-level cache, to the benefit of the flat combining algorithm. If the slots are not found in cache, the cost will be higher, as the combiner will incur memory accesses instead.

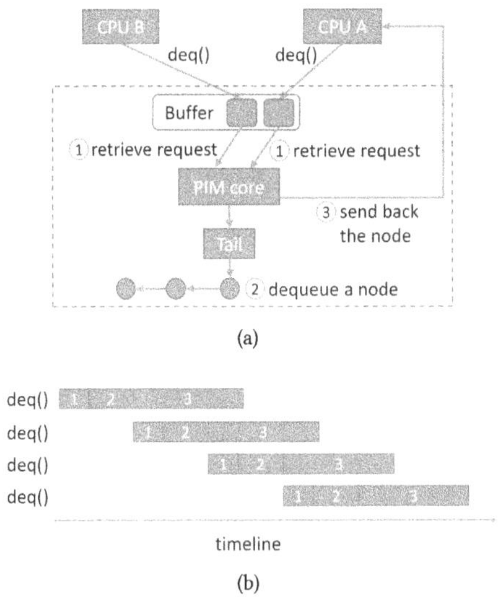

Figure 6: (a) The pipelining optimization, where a PIM core can start executing a new deq() (step 1 of deq() for CPU B), without waiting for the dequeued node of the previous deq() to return to CPU A (step 3). (b) The timeline of pipelining four deq() requests.

the CPUs spend in sending their requests to a PIM core concurrently at the beginning this execution, is $\mathcal{L}_{message} + p(\mathcal{L}_{pim} + \epsilon) + \mathcal{L}_{message}$, where $p(\mathcal{L}_{pim} + \epsilon)$ is the sum of the execution times of the first two steps for the p requests, and the second $\mathcal{L}_{message}$ is message transfer time of step 3 for the last request. ϵ is the total latency of the PIM core making two L1 cache accesses and sending one message. ϵ is negligible in our performance model.

Assume that each CPU makes another request immediately after it receives the result of its previous request and that there are enough (at least $2\mathcal{L}_{message}/\mathcal{L}_{pim}$) CPUs sending requests. We can prove that the PIM core can always find another request in its buffer after it executes one. Let x be the throughput of the PIM core in one second. By the same analysis as above, we have $\mathcal{L}_{message} + x(\mathcal{L}_{pim} + \epsilon) + \mathcal{L}_{message} = 1$, where 1 represents one second. Therefore, the throughput (per second) of the PIM-managed FIFO queue is approximately

$$x = \frac{1 - 2\mathcal{L}_{message}}{\mathcal{L}_{pim} + \epsilon} \approx \frac{1 - 2\mathcal{L}_{message}}{\mathcal{L}_{pim}} \approx \frac{1}{\mathcal{L}_{pim}},$$

since $\mathcal{L}_{message}$ is usually only hundreds of nanoseconds and much smaller than 1 (second).

Comparing the throughput values of the three FIFO queue algorithms, we can conclude that the PIM-managed FIFO queue with pipelining outperforms the other two FIFO queues when $2r_1/r_2 > 1$ and $r_1 r_3 > 1$. If we assume $r_1 = r_2 = 3$ and $r_3 = 1$, then the throughput of our PIM-managed FIFO queue is expected to be twice the throughput of the flat-combining queue and three times that of the F&A queue.[6]

[6] This does not imply that the F&A queue is faster than the flat combining queue, since we only consider part of the costs of these queues in our analysis.

When the PIM-managed FIFO queue is short, it may contain only one segment which deals with both enqueue and dequeue requests. In this case, its throughput is only half of the throughput shown above, but it is still at least as good as the throughput of the other two FIFO queues.

6 RELATED WORK

The PIM model is undergoing a renaissance. Studied for decades (e.g., [17, 20, 21, 32, 34, 44, 45, 51]), this model has recently re-emerged due to advances in 3D-stacked technology that can stack memory dies on top of a logic layer [8, 31, 33, 36, 40]. For example, a 3D-stacked memory prototype called the Hybrid Memory Cube [15] was recently released by industry, and the model has again become the focus of architectural research. Different PIM-based architectures have been proposed, either for general purpose workloads or for specific applications [1–6, 9, 13, 22, 23, 29, 30, 47–50, 53–55].

The PIM model has several advantages, including low energy consumption and high bandwidth (e.g., [1, 4, 53, 54]). Here, we focus on one more: low memory access latency [6, 23, 30, 40]. To our knowledge, we are the first to utilize PIM memory for designing efficient *concurrent data structures.* Although some researchers have studied how PIM memory can help speed up concurrent operations to data structures, such as parallel graph processing [1] and parallel pointer chasing on linked data structures [30], the applications they consider require very simple, if any, synchronization between operations. In contrast, operations to concurrent data structures can interleave in arbitrary orders, and therefore have to correctly synchronize with one another in all possible execution scenarios. This makes designing concurrent data structures with correctness guarantees, like linearizability [28], very challenging.

No prior work compares the performance of data structures in the PIM model with that of state-of-the-art concurrent data structures in the classical shared memory model. We analyze and evaluate concurrent linked-lists and skip-lists, as representatives of pointer-chasing data structures, and concurrent FIFO queues, as representatives of contended data structures. For linked-lists, we compare our PIM-managed implementation with well-known approaches such as fine-grained locking [24] and flat combining [18, 25, 26]. For skip-lists, we compare our implementation with a lock-free skip-list [27] and a skip-list with flat combining and the partitioning optimization. For FIFO queues, we compare our implementation with the flat-combining FIFO queue [25] and the F&A-based FIFO queue [41].

7 CONCLUSION

In this paper, we study how to design efficient data structures that can take advantage of the promising benefits offered by the Processing in Memory (PIM) paradigm. We analyze and compare the performance of our new PIM-managed data structures with traditional concurrent data structures that were proposed in the literature to take advantage of multiple processors. To this end, we develop a simplified performance model for PIM. Using this model, along with empirical performance measurements from a modern system, we show that naive PIM-managed data structures *cannot* outperform traditional concurrent data structures, due to the lack of parallelism and the high communication cost between the CPUs and the PIM cores. To improve the performance of PIM data structures, we propose novel designs for low-contention pointer-chasing data structures, such as linked-lists and skip-lists, and for contended data structures, such as FIFO queues. We show that our new PIM-managed data structures can outperform state-of-the-art concurrent data structures, making PIM memory a promising platform for managing data structures. We conclude that it is very promising to examine novel data structure designs for the PIM paradigm, and hope future work builds upon our analyses to develop other types of PIM-managed data structures.

REFERENCES

[1] Junwhan Ahn, Sungpack Hong, Sungjoo Yoo, Onur Mutlu, and Kiyoung Choi. A scalable processing-in-memory accelerator for parallel graph processing. In *Proceedings of the 42nd Annual International Symposium on Computer Architecture*, ISCA '15, pages 105–117, New York, NY, USA, 2015. ACM.

[2] Junwhan Ahn, Sungjoo Yoo, Onur Mutlu, and Kiyoung Choi. PIM-enabled instructions: A low-overhead, locality-aware processing-in-memory architecture. In *Proceedings of the 42nd Annual International Symposium on Computer Architecture*, ISCA '15, pages 336–348, New York, NY, USA, 2015. ACM.

[3] Berkin Akin, Franz Franchetti, and James C. Hoe. Data reorganization in memory using 3D-stacked DRAM. In *Proceedings of the 42nd Annual International Symposium on Computer Architecture*, ISCA '15, pages 131–143, New York, NY, USA, 2015. ACM.

[4] Erfan Azarkhish, Christoph Pfister, Davide Rossi, Igor Loi, and Luca Benini. Logic-base interconnect design for near memory computing in the Smart Memory Cube. *IEEE Trans. VLSI Syst.*, 25(1):210–223, 2017.

[5] Erfan Azarkhish, Davide Rossi, Igor Loi, and Luca Benini. High performance AXI-4.0 based interconnect for extensible Smart Memory Cubes. In *Proceedings of the 2015 Design, Automation & Test in Europe Conference & Exhibition*, DATE '15, pages 1317–1322, San Jose, CA, USA, 2015. EDA Consortium.

[6] Erfan Azarkhish, Davide Rossi, Igor Loi, and Luca Benini. Design and evaluation of a processing-in-memory architecture for the Smart Memory Cube. In *Proceedings of the 29th International Conference on Architecture of Computing Systems – ARCS 2016 - Volume 9637*, pages 19–31, New York, NY, USA, 2016. Springer-Verlag New York, Inc.

[7] Oana Balmau, Rachid Guerraoui, Vasileios Trigonakis, and Igor Zablotchi. FloDB: Unlocking memory in persistent key-value stores. In *Proceedings of the Twelfth European Conference on Computer Systems*, EuroSys '17, pages 80–94, New York, NY, USA, 2017. ACM.

[8] Bryan Black, Murali Annavaram, Ned Brekelbaum, John DeVale, Lei Jiang, Gabriel H. Loh, Don McCaule, Pat Morrow, Donald W. Nelson, Daniel Pantuso, Paul Reed, Jeff Rupley, Sadasivan Shankar, John Shen, and Clair Webb. Die stacking (3D) microarchitecture. In *Proceedings of the 39th Annual IEEE/ACM International Symposium on Microarchitecture*, MICRO 39, pages 469–479, Washington, DC, USA, 2006. IEEE Computer Society.

[9] Amirali Boroumand, Saugata Ghose, Brandon Lucia, Kevin Hsieh, Krishna Malladi, Hongzhong Zheng, and Onur Mutlu. LazyPIM: An efficient cache coherence mechanism for processing-in-memory. *IEEE Computer Architecture Letters*, 2016.

[10] Irina Calciu, Siddhartha Sen, Mahesh Balakrishnan, and Marcos K. Aguilera. Black-box concurrent data structures for NUMA architectures. In *Proceedings of the Twenty-Second International Conference on Architectural Support for Programming Languages and Operating Systems*, ASPLOS '17, pages 207–221, New York, NY, USA, 2017. ACM.

[11] Kevin K. Chang. *Understanding and Improving Latency of DRAM-Based Memory Systems.* PhD thesis, Carnegie Mellon University, Pittsburgh, PA, USA, 2017.

[12] Kevin K. Chang, Abhijith Kashyap, Hasan Hassan, Saugata Ghose, Kevin Hsieh, Donghyuk Lee, Tianshi Li, Gennady Pekhimenko, Samira Khan, and Onur Mutlu. Understanding latency variation in modern DRAM chips: Experimental characterization, analysis, and optimization. In *Proceedings of the 2016 ACM SIGMETRICS International Conference on Measurement and Modeling of Computer Science*, SIGMETRICS '16, pages 323–336, New York, NY, USA, 2016. ACM.

[13] Kevin K. Chang, Prashant J. Nair, Donghyuk Lee, Saugata Ghose, Moinuddin K. Qureshi, and Onur Mutlu. Low-cost inter-linked subarrays (LISA): enabling fast inter-subarray data movement in DRAM. In *IEEE International Symposium on High Performance Computer Architecture, HPCA 2016, Barcelona, Spain, March 12-16, 2016*, pages 568–580, 2016.

[14] Kevin K. Chang, A. Giray Yaglikci, Saugata Ghose, Aditya Agrawal, Niladrish Chatterjee, Abhijith Kashyap, Donghyuk Lee, Mike O'Connor, Hasan Hassan, and Onur Mutlu. Understanding reduced-voltage operation in modern dram devices: Experimental characterization, analysis, and mechanisms. In *to appear in Proceedings of the 2017 ACM SIGMETRICS International Conference on Measurement and Modeling of Computer Science*, SIGMETRICS '17.

[15] Hybrid Memory Cube Consortium. Hybrid Memory Cube specification 1.0, 2013.

[16] Tudor David, Rachid Guerraoui, and Vasileios Trigonakis. Everything you always wanted to know about synchronization but were afraid to ask. In *Proceedings of the Twenty-Fourth ACM Symposium on Operating Systems Principles*, SOSP '13, pages 33–48, New York, NY, USA, 2013. ACM.

[17] Duncan G. Elliott, W. Martin Snelgrove, and Michael Stumm. Computational RAM: A memory-SIMD hybrid and its application to DSP. In *Proceedings of the IEEE 1992 Custom Integrated Circuits Conference*, CICC '92, pages 30.6.1–30.6.4, Piscataway, NJ, USA, 1992. IEEE Press.

[18] Panagiota Fatourou and Nikolaos D. Kallimanis. Revisiting the combining synchronization technique. In *Proceedings of the 17th ACM SIGPLAN Symposium on Principles and Practice of Parallel Programming*, PPoPP '12, pages 257–266, New York, NY, USA, 2012. ACM.

[19] Keir Fraser. Practical lock-freedom. Technical Report UCAM-CL-TR-579, University of Cambridge, Computer Laboratory, February 2004.

[20] Maya Gokhale, Bill Holmes, and Ken Iobst. Processing in memory: The Terasys massively parallel PIM array. *Computer*, 28(4):23–31, April 1995.

[21] Mary Hall, Peter Kogge, Jeff Koller, Pedro Diniz, Jacqueline Chame, Jeff Draper, Jeff LaCoss, John Granacki, Jay Brockman, Apoorv Srivastava, William Athas, Vincent Freeh, Jaewook Shin, and Joonseok Park. Mapping irregular applications to DIVA, a PIM-based data-intensive architecture. In *Proceedings of the 1999 ACM/IEEE Conference on Supercomputing*, SC '99, New York, NY, USA, 1999. ACM.

[22] M. Hashemi, O. Mutlu, and Y. N. Patt. Continuous Runahead: Transparent hardware acceleration for memory intensive workloads. In *Proceedings of the 49th Annual IEEE/ACM International Symposium on Microarchitecture*, MICRO '16, Oct 2016.

[23] Milad Hashemi, Khubaib, Eiman Ebrahimi, Onur Mutlu, and Yale N. Patt. Accelerating dependent cache misses with an enhanced memory controller. In *Proceedings of the 43rd International Symposium on Computer Architecture*, ISCA '16, pages 444–455, Piscataway, NJ, USA, 2016. IEEE Press.

[24] Steve Heller, Maurice Herlihy, Victor Luchangco, Mark Moir, William N. Scherer, and Nir Shavit. A lazy concurrent list-based set algorithm. In *Proceedings of the 9th International Conference on Principles of Distributed Systems*, OPODIS'05, pages 3–16, Berlin, Heidelberg, 2006. Springer-Verlag.

[25] Danny Hendler, Itai Incze, Nir Shavit, and Moran Tzafrir. Flat combining and the synchronization-parallelism tradeoff. In *Proceedings of the Twenty-second Annual ACM Symposium on Parallelism in Algorithms and Architectures*, SPAA '10, pages 355–364, New York, NY, USA, 2010. ACM.

[26] Danny Hendler, Itai Incze, Nir Shavit, and Moran Tzafrir. Scalable flat-combining based synchronous queues. In *Proceedings of the 24th International Conference on Distributed Computing*, DISC'10, pages 79–93, Berlin, Heidelberg, 2010. Springer-Verlag.

[27] Maurice Herlihy and Nir Shavit. *The Art of Multiprocessor Programming.* Morgan Kaufmann Publishers Inc., San Francisco, CA, USA, 2008.

[28] Maurice P. Herlihy and Jeannette M. Wing. Linearizability: A correctness condition for concurrent objects. *ACM Trans. Program. Lang. Syst.*, 12(3):463–492, July 1990.

[29] Kevin Hsieh, Eiman Ebrahimi, Gwangsun Kim, Niladrish Chatterjee, Mike O'Connor, Nandita Vijaykumar, Onur Mutlu, and Stephen W. Keckler. Transparent offloading and mapping (TOM): Enabling programmer-transparent near-data processing in GPU systems. In *Proceedings of the 43rd International Symposium on Computer Architecture*, ISCA '16, pages 204–216, Piscataway, NJ, USA, 2016. IEEE Press.

[30] Kevin Hsieh, Samira Khan, Nandita Vijaykumar, Kevin K Chang, Amirali Boroumand, Saugata Ghose, and Onur Mutlu. Accelerating pointer chasing in 3D-stacked memory: Challenges, mechanisms, evaluation. In *IEEE 34th International Conference on Computer Design, ICCD 2016*, pages 25–32. IEEE, 2016.

[31] Joe Jeddeloh and Brent Keeth. Hybrid memory cube new DRAM architecture increases density and performance. In *Symposium on VLSI Technology, VLSIT 2012*, pages 87–88. IEEE, 2012.

[32] Yi Kang, Wei Huang, Seung-Moon Yoo, Diana Keen, Zhenzhou Ge, Vinh Vi Lam, Josep Torrellas, and Pratap Pattnaik. FlexRAM: Toward an advanced intelligent memory system. In *Proceedings of the IEEE International Conference On Computer Design*, ICCD '99.

[33] Joonyoung Kim and Younsu Kim. HBM: Memory solution for bandwidth-hungry processors. *2014 IEEE Hot Chips 26 Symposium (HCS)*, 00:1–24, 2014.

[34] Peter M. Kogge. EXECUBE-a new architecture for scaleable MPPs. In *Proceedings of the 1994 International Conference on Parallel Processing - Volume 01*, ICPP '94, pages 77–84, Washington, DC, USA, 1994. IEEE Computer Society.

[35] Donghyuk Lee. *Reducing DRAM Latency at Low Cost by Exploiting Heterogeneity.* PhD thesis, Carnegie Mellon University, Pittsburgh, PA, USA, 2017.

[36] Donghyuk Lee, Saugata Ghose, Gennady Pekhimenko, Samira Khan, and Onur Mutlu. Simultaneous multi-layer access: Improving 3D-stacked memory bandwidth at low cost. *ACM Trans. Archit. Code Optim.*, 12(4):63:1–63:29, January 2016.

[37] Donghyuk Lee, Samira Khan, Lavanya Subramanian, Saugata Ghose, Rachata Ausavarungnirun, Gennady Pekhimenko, Vivek Seshadri, and Onur Mutlu.

Design-induced latency variation in modern dram chips: Characterization, analysis, and latency reduction mechanisms. In *to appear in Proceedings of the 2017 ACM SIGMETRICS International Conference on Measurement and Modeling of Computer Science*, SIGMETRICS '17.

[38] Donghyuk Lee, Yoongu Kim, Gennady Pekhimenko, Samira Manabi Khan, Vivek Seshadri, Kevin Kai-Wei Chang, and Onur Mutlu. Adaptive-latency DRAM: optimizing DRAM timing for the common-case. In *21st IEEE International Symposium on High Performance Computer Architecture, HPCA 2015, Burlingame, CA, USA, February 7-11, 2015*, pages 489–501, 2015.

[39] Donghyuk Lee, Yoongu Kim, Vivek Seshadri, Jamie Liu, Lavanya Subramanian, and Onur Mutlu. Tiered-latency DRAM: A low latency and low cost DRAM architecture. In *19th IEEE International Symposium on High Performance Computer Architecture, HPCA 2013, Shenzhen, China, February 23-27, 2013*, pages 615–626, 2013.

[40] Gabriel H. Loh. 3D-stacked memory architectures for multi-core processors. In *Proceedings of the 35th Annual International Symposium on Computer Architecture*, ISCA '08, pages 453–464, Washington, DC, USA, 2008. IEEE Computer Society.

[41] Adam Morrison and Yehuda Afek. Fast concurrent queues for x86 processors. In *Proceedings of the 18th ACM SIGPLAN Symposium on Principles and Practice of Parallel Programming*, PPoPP '13, pages 103–112, New York, NY, USA, 2013. ACM.

[42] Onur Mutlu. Memory scaling: a systems architecture perspective. In *Proceedings of the 5th International Memory Workshop*, IMW '13, 2013.

[43] Onur Mutlu and Lavanya Subramanian. Research problems and opportunities in memory systems. *Supercomputing Frontiers and Innovations*, 1, 2014.

[44] Mark Oskin, Frederic T. Chong, and Timothy Sherwood. Active pages: A computation model for intelligent memory. In *Proceedings of the 25th Annual International Symposium on Computer Architecture*, ISCA '98, pages 192–203, Washington, DC, USA, 1998. IEEE Computer Society.

[45] David Patterson, Thomas Anderson, Neal Cardwell, Richard Fromm, Kimberly Keeton, Christoforos Kozyrakis, Randi Thomas, and Katherine Yelick. A case for intelligent RAM. *IEEE Micro*, 17(2):34–44, March 1997.

[46] W. Pugh. Concurrent maintenance of skip lists. Technical report, University of Maryland at College Park, 1990.

[47] Vivek Seshadri, Kevin Hsieh, Amirali Boroumand, Donghyuk Lee, Michael A. Kozuch, Onur Mutlu, Phillip B. Gibbons, and Todd C. Mowry. Fast bulk bitwise AND and OR in DRAM. *IEEE Comput. Archit. Lett.*, 14(2):127–131, July 2015.

[48] Vivek Seshadri, Yoongu Kim, Chris Fallin, Donghyuk Lee, Rachata Ausavarungnirun, Gennady Pekhimenko, Yixin Luo, Onur Mutlu, Phillip B. Gibbons, Michael A. Kozuch, and Todd C. Mowry. RowClone: Fast and energy-efficient in-DRAM bulk data copy and initialization. In *Proceedings of the 46th Annual IEEE/ACM International Symposium on Microarchitecture*, MICRO-46, pages 185–197, New York, NY, USA, 2013. ACM.

[49] Vivek Seshadri, Donghyuk Lee, Thomas Mullins, Hasan Hassan, Amirali Boroumand, Jeremie Kim, Michael A. Kozuch, Onur Mutlu, Phillip B. Gibbons, and Todd C. Mowry. Buddy-ram: Improving the performance and efficiency of bulk bitwise operations using DRAM. *CoRR*, abs/1611.09988, 2016.

[50] Vivek Seshadri and Onur Mutlu. The processing using memory paradigm: In-DRAM bulk copy, initialization, bitwise AND and OR. *CoRR*, abs/1610.09603, 2016.

[51] Harold S. Stone. A logic-in-memory computer. *IEEE Trans. Comput.*, 19(1):73–78, January 1970.

[52] J. Valois. *Lock-free Data Structures*. PhD thesis, Rensselaer Polytechnic Institute, Troy, NY, USA, 1996.

[53] Dongping Zhang, Nuwan Jayasena, Alexander Lyashevsky, Joseph L. Greathouse, Lifan Xu, and Michael Ignatowski. TOP-PIM: Throughput-oriented programmable processing in memory. In *Proceedings of the 23rd International Symposium on High-performance Parallel and Distributed Computing*, HPDC '14, pages 85–98, New York, NY, USA, 2014. ACM.

[54] Qiuling Zhu, Berkin Akin, H. Ekin Sumbul, Fazle Sadi, James C. Hoe, Larry T. Pileggi, and Franz Franchetti. A 3D-stacked logic-in-memory accelerator for application-specific data intensive computing. In *IEEE International 3D Systems Integration Conference, 3DIC 2013, San Francisco, CA, USA, October 2-4, 2013*, pages 1–7, 2013.

[55] Qiuling Zhu, Tobias Graf, H. Ekin Sumbul, Larry T. Pileggi, and Franz Franchetti. Accelerating sparse matrix-matrix multiplication with 3D-stacked logic-in-memory hardware. In *IEEE High Performance Extreme Computing Conference, HPEC 2013, Waltham, MA, USA, September 10-12, 2013*, pages 1–6, 2013.

Lower Bounds in the Asymmetric External Memory Model

Riko Jacob
IT University of Copenhagen
Rued Langgaards Vej 7
DK-2300 København S, Denmark
rikj@itu.dk

Nodari Sitchinava*
University of Hawaii at Mānoa
Information and Computer Sciences
1680 East West Road, POST 317
Honolulu, HI 96822, USA
nodari@hawaii.edu

ABSTRACT

Motivated by the asymmetric read and write costs of emerging non-volatile memory technologies, we study lower bounds for the problems of sorting, permuting and multiplying a sparse matrix by a dense vector in the asymmetric external memory model (AEM). Given an AEM with internal (symmetric) memory of size M, transfers between symmetric and asymmetric memory in blocks of size B and the ratio ω between write and read costs, we show $\Omega(\min\{N, \frac{\omega N}{B} \log_{\frac{\omega M}{B}} \frac{N}{B}\})$ lower bound for the cost of permuting N input elements. This lower bound also applies to the problem of sorting N elements. This proves that the existing sorting algorithms in the AEM model are optimal to within a constant factor for reasonable ranges of parameters N, M, B, and ω. We also show a lower bound of $\Omega\left(\min\left\{H, \frac{\omega H}{B} \log_{\frac{\omega M}{B}} \frac{N}{\max\{\delta, M\}}\right\}\right)$ for the cost of multiplying an $N \times N$ matrix with at most $H = \delta N$ non-empty entries by a vector with N elements.

KEYWORDS

Asymmetric external memory; AEM; asymmetric read-write; NVMs; sorting; permuting; lower bounds; sparse matrix vector multiplication; SpMxV

1 INTRODUCTION

Recent advances in Phase-Change Memory, Memristor-based Resistive RAM, and Spin-Torque Transfer Magnetic RAM technologies place non-volatile memory (NVM) technology on the path to become dominant memory technology in the near future. Relative to current DRAM, NVM provides better energy usage and higher density. However, the most significant difference between NVM and DRAM is the asymmetry in the cost of reading and writing data, sometimes by orders of magnitude [8, 9, 12, 15]. Such drastic difference in read and write costs motivated recent studies on the effects of read-write asymmetry on algorithm design.

*This material is based upon work supported by the National Science Foundation under Grant No. 1533823.

SPAA '17, July 24-26, 2017, Washington DC, USA

978-1-4503-4593-4/17/07...$15.00
DOI: 10.1145/3087556.3087583

Most of the studies in the past focused largely on the effects of read-write asymmetry in the NAND flash memories [2, 3, 10, 13, 14, 17]. But recently, several papers focused on models designed specifically for the NVM [4, 6, 7].

Blelloch et al. [6] define (M, ω)*-Asymmetric RAM (ARAM)* model to analyze algorithms in the setting with asymmetric read and write costs. The model consists of a small symmetric memory of size M and unbounded asymmetric memory, which contains the input. To perform any computation on the data, it must be first brought into the symmetric memory. Write accesses to the asymmetric memory cost ω times more than read accesses. If an algorithm performs Q_r read accesses and Q_w write accesses to the asymmetric memory, the *cost* Q of an algorithm is defined as $Q = Q_r + \omega Q_w$. The model also defines *time* T of an algorithm to be equal to the total number of read and write accesses to the symmetric memory, which represents the time it takes to perform computations to within a constant factor, similar to how time complexity is defined in the standard (symmetric) RAM model.

A related (symmetric) *external memory (EM)* model was introduce by Aggarwal and Vitter [1]. The EM model consists of two-level memory hierarchy, with the faster *internal memory* of size M and the slower *external memory* of unbounded size, but symmetric unit cost, *I/O cost*, of accessing the external memory. To perform computation on data, it has to be first brought into the internal memory, and the transfer is performed in contiguous blocks of size $B \geq 1$ elements. The cost Q of an algorithm in the EM model is defined to be the total number of read and write accesses to the external memory. It is assumed that the cost of accessing the external memory is significantly larger than accessing internal memory, therefore, the EM model focuses only on the I/O cost and does not count the number of accesses to the internal memory.

The natural generalization of the EM model to the asymmetric setting [7] defines the (M, B, ω)*-Asymmetric External Memory (AEM)* model as an EM model with each write access to the external memory costing ω times more than a read access. The cost Q of an algorithm, which performs Q_r read and Q_w write accesses (I/Os) to the external memory of the (M, B, ω)-AEM model, is defined as $Q = Q_r + \omega Q_w$. Similarly to the (symmetric) EM model, this definition of the AEM model does not consider accesses (and, equivalently, computation) in the internal memory to be part of the cost. Also, notice that the (M, ω)-ARAM model is equivalent to the $(M, 1, \omega)$-AEM model.

Blelloch et al. study a number of algorithms in the (M, B, ω)-AEM [7] and (M, ω)-ARAM [6] models. In addition they prove lower bounds to a number of problems in the (M, ω)-ARAM model [6].

1.1 Our contributions

In this paper we focus on the problems of sorting, permuting and multiplying a sparse matrix by a dense vector in the (M, B, ω)-AEM model.

Of the three previously published [7] sorting algorithms in the (M, B, ω)-AEM model, sample sort and heapsort achieve the cost $O(\omega n \log_{\omega m} n)$ unconditionally. However, to achieve the same bound, the mergesort relies on the assumption that $\omega < B$. In Section 3, we show that we can implement mergesort in the (M, B, ω)-AEM model with the same cost without relying on any assumptions.

In Section 4 we show an $\Omega(\min\{N, \omega n \log_{\omega m} n\})$ lower bound for the problem of permuting N elements. Since every sorting algorithm must be able to perform an arbitrary permutation, this lower bound also applies to the problem of sorting N elements and matches the sorting upper bound to within a constant factor for reasonable ranges of the parameters ω, B, M and N. In addition to proving the permutation lower bound via the standard counting method, we also prove it via reduction to the unit-cost flash memory model of Ajwani et al. [2]. This result shows a close relationship between the (M, B, ω)-AEM and the unit-cost flash model, which might make this reduction of independent interest.

Finally, in Section 5 we present a lower bound on the cost of multiplying a sparse matrix with a dense vector in the (M, B, ω)-AEM model.

2 PRELIMINARIES

To simplify notation throughout this paper, we define the following variables, which are standard in the literature on the EM model:

- N : size of the input vector/array or a dimension of a matrix
- $H = \delta N$: number of non-zero entries in a sparse matrix
- M : internal (symmetric) memory size
- B : block size
- $m = \lceil M/B \rceil$
- $n = \lceil N/B \rceil$
- $h = \lceil H/B \rceil = \Theta(\delta n)$
- ω : ratio in cost between a write and a read access to the external (asymmetric) memory

Similar to [5], to prove our lower bounds, we distinguish between an *algorithm* and a *program* in the following way. An algorithm is one description of how the (M, B, ω)-AEM model handles an arbitrary input. In particular the size of the input, the permutation, or the structure of the sparse matrix is not fixed, and there are loops and branches. In contrast, a program is a fixed sequence of I/O operations and internal memory move operations (and additions/multiplication in the semi-ring). Accordingly, a program implements one particular permutation or one particular conformation (structure of the non-zero entries, together with a layout) of a sparse matrix. Each such program is a straight line program that performs the same set of operations no matter what values are given as input. We can view the inputs and outputs to such programs as an ordered list of numbers and their meaning is given solely by their position in the ordering, rather than their values.

Clearly, an algorithm gives rise to a family of programs – one for each permutation or sparse matrix conformation. Hence, a lower bound on the cost of any program for some permutation or sparse matrix of a certain size induces the corresponding lower bound on the cost of any algorithm. For all considered problems we give upper bounds on the cost by means of describing an algorithm and lower bounds by arguments about programs.

3 MERGE SORT

In this section we present a multi-way mergesort which achieves $O(\omega n \log_{\omega m} n)$ read and $O(n \log_{\omega m} n)$ write I/Os for any value of ω.

Our AEM mergesort follows the standard framework for multi-way mergesort algorithms: We divide the array into $d = \omega m$ subarrays, each of size $O(N/d)$, recursively sort each one and merge d newly sorted subarrays into a single sorted array. At the base case, using the algorithm for sorting small arrays by Blelloch et al [7, Lemma 4.2], we can sort each subarray of size $N' \leq \omega M$ elements in $O(\omega n')$ read I/Os and $O(n')$ write I/Os (for a total cost of $O(\omega n')$ each), where $n' = N'/B$. If the cost of performing d-way merging of the subarrays is $O(\omega n)$, then the cost of the overall algorithm is defined by the following recurrence:

$$Q(N, M, B, \omega) = \begin{cases} d \cdot Q(N/d, M, B, \omega) + O(\omega n) & \text{if } N > \omega M \\ O(\omega n) & \text{if } N \leq \omega M \end{cases}$$

which solves to $Q(N, M, B, \omega) = O(\omega n \log_d n) = O(\omega n \log_{\omega m} n)$.

Thus, it remains to show how to perform ωm-way merging of sorted subarrays, which collectively contain N elements, within the desired $O(\omega n)$ cost.

3.1 Merging ωm sorted arrays

For ease of exposition, let M be a constant fraction of the available internal memory. This does not affect the asymptotic bounds above and provides us with sufficient space to store a constant number of additional words of auxiliary data with each element in the internal memory.

To merge ωm sorted arrays, we proceed in $R = \lceil N/M \rceil$ rounds. At the end of each round we write a batch of the next M smallest elements across all ωm arrays in sorted order in contiguous addresses of external memory. Next, we show how to perform each round in $O(\omega m)$ read and $O(m)$ write I/Os, for a total of $O(N/M \cdot \omega m) = O(\omega n)$ read and $O(N/M \cdot m) = O(n)$ write I/Os.

Let A_i, $0 \leq i < \omega m$, be the i-th sorted array to be merged. If $\omega > B$, then we do not even have enough space in the internal memory to maintain the pointers to the next element of A_i in external memory. Therefore, we must maintain these pointers in external memory. To reduce the number of times we have to perform a write I/O to update these pointers, rather than maintaining a pointer $ptr[i]$ to the next element e of A_i that is not in internal memory, we maintain the pointer $b[i]$ to the *block* of A_i that contains e. This way, we have to update each $b[i]$ in external memory only after B elements are merged from A_i, i.e., at most once for each of n blocks. Therefore, the total write I/Os required to update the pointers $b[i]$ for merging N elements of ωm arrays is at most $O(n)$. Let π denote the largest element stored in internal memory at the time. The next element to be considered from an array A_i is the smallest element that is larger than π. Note that it is always in the block pointed to by $b[i]$. Thus, we can always determine the correct element within the $b[i]$-th block to be processed next. Initially, all $b[i]$s are set to point to the first block of each array A_i. This initialization takes $O(\lceil \omega m/B \rceil) = O(\omega m)$ write I/Os.

In each round we scan the current elements of the arrays A_i (as detailed later) and maintain M smallest elements in internal memory. Since internal computations are not counted in the cost of an AEM algorithm, we can, for example, maintain them in a sorted array $\mathcal{M}$. The round ends when the next unprocessed element of **every** A_i is larger than the largest element of $\mathcal{M}$, at which point we write $\mathcal{M}$ to external memory using $O(m)$ write I/Os.

Initializing $\mathcal{M}$: Starting with an empty array $\mathcal{M}$, we read two blocks from each array A_i, $0 < i < \omega m$, starting with the $b[i]$-th block. Every time a block is read, its elements that are larger than π are merged into $\mathcal{M}$. If $\mathcal{M}$ grows beyond the size M, it is truncated down to exactly M elements.

Identifying active arrays: We call an array A_i *active*, if more blocks from that array might need to be loaded, i.e., the largest element of the last block read from A_i (a) is not the last element of A_i and (b) is among the M smallest in the internal memory so far. Otherwise, we call A_i *inactive*. Observe that once $\mathcal{M}$ contains M elements the values of the elements of $\mathcal{M}$ can only decrease during that round. Therefore, once an array becomes inactive, it does not need to be considered again until the next round. Observe, that it is easy to identify active arrays by re-reading the blocks from the initialization phase and comparing the last element read from each array with the largest element in $\mathcal{M}$. For every inactive array we can also update $b[i]$, if it has changed.

The efficiency of our merging algorithm relies on the following observation.

Lemma 3.1. *After $\mathcal{M}$ has been initialized, there are at most $m = M/B$ active arrays for the rest of the round of the algorithm.*

Proof. Since more than B elements are read from each array, and $\mathcal{M}$ contains at most M elements, there can be at most M/B blocks from each array with the last element in $\mathcal{M}$, i.e., satisfying the condition (b) in the definition of active arrays. □

Merging from active arrays: According to Lemma 3.1, there is enough space in internal memory to maintain one block from each active array. Observe that the initialization step ensures that one block from each active array is already present in the internal memory. Let μ be the largest value that the algorithm should write out during the round. If μ were known to the algorithm, it could simply read from each A_i all the elements smaller than μ and merge them. As it is not known, the algorithm uses a classical M/B-way merge on the active arrays to load the right elements.

More precisely, for any active A_i let s_i be the maximal element already loaded into the internal memory. Recall that if $s_i > \pi$, the array A_i is no longer active. Let j be be the index of the array with the smallest element among all s_i. In each step the algorithm loads the next block from A_j, merges it into $\mathcal{M}$, updates s_j and repeats until there are no more active arrays, which means $\mu = \pi$. At this point, $\mathcal{M}$ contains M smallest elements, which are written out into external memory in sorted order.

Theorem 3.2. *Merging ωm sorted arrays, containing in total N elements, takes $O(\omega(n + m))$ read and $O(n + m)$ write I/Os.*

Proof. As has been argued earlier, since the $b[i]$ pointers are updated in external memory only once per block, the cost to maintain $b[i]$s is at most $O(n)$ write I/Os. Additional writes are only to output M next smallest elements in each of $R = \lceil N/M \rceil$ rounds for a total of $R \cdot m = O\left(\left(\frac{N}{M} + 1\right) \cdot m\right) = O(n + m)$ write I/Os.

To compute the number of reads, observe that the use of π by the algorithm implies that if in some round, array A_i contains an element that is greater than π, then at most one block from A_i (the one containing the smallest element larger than π) is read from external memory. Thus, the number of reads in each round is at most $\sum_{i=1}^{\omega m} \left(\frac{N_i}{B} + 1\right)$, where N_i is the number of elements from A_i that should be written out in that round. Since in each round $\sum_i N_i = M$ (only M elements are to be written out per round), $\sum_i^{\omega m}(N_i/B+1) \leq m + \omega m$, and over $R = \lceil N/M \rceil$ rounds the number of reads adds up to $R \cdot (m+\omega m) = O\left(\left(1 + \frac{N}{M}\right) \cdot (m + \omega m)\right) = O(\omega(n+m))$ I/Os. □

4 PERMUTATION LOWER BOUNDS

As explained in the introduction, we formulate this lower bounds for programs and this implies the corresponding lower bound for algorithms. Our approach to proving permutation lower bound in the AEM model follows the framework of Hong and Kung [11]: We defined an ωm-round to be a sequence of operations of an (M, B, ω)-AEM program of cost at most ωm. Thus, a round may consist of any combination of r read and w write I/Os, as long as $r + \omega w \leq \omega m$. Additionally, all but the last round must have the cost of at least $\omega(m - 1)$.

We say a program is *round-based*, if it performs computation in ωm-rounds and at the beginning and the end of each round the internal memory is empty. We upper bound the progress that any round-based program can make in any particular round, which gives us a lower bound on the number of rounds that any program must perform for the whole computation, resulting in the lower bound for the whole program (and hence algorithm). We also show that every program $\mathcal{P}$ in the (M, B, ω)-AEM model can be converted into a round-based program $\mathcal{P}'$, without increasing the cost by more than a constant factor (Lemma 4.1). Thus, a lower bound for $\mathcal{P}'$ implies a lower bound for $\mathcal{P}$ (Corollary 4.2).

Lemma 4.1. *Any program $\mathcal{P}$ in the (M, B, ω)-AEM with the overall cost of $Q(N, M, B, \omega)$ can be implemented as a round-based program $\mathcal{P}'$ in the $(2M, B, \omega)$-AEM with cost*

$$Q'(N, 2M, B, \omega) = O(Q(N, M, B, \omega))$$

Proof. Split $\mathcal{P}$ into rounds of cost at least $\omega(m - 1)$ and at most ωm. To simulate each round of $\mathcal{P}$ on the $(2M, B, \omega)$-AEM, $\mathcal{P}'$ logically partition the internal memory of size $2M$ into two halves: $\mathcal{M}'$ and $\mathcal{M}''$. $\mathcal{M}'$ will maintain the contents of the internal memory of $\mathcal{P}$, while $\mathcal{M}''$ will buffer the data being written by $\mathcal{P}$ to the external memory in each round. At the start of each round, $\mathcal{P}'$ initializes $\mathcal{M}'$ by reading the contents of the internal memory of $\mathcal{P}$ from the end of the previous round (this step is skipped during the first round.) For every write operation of $\mathcal{P}$, $\mathcal{P}'$ copies the block into $\mathcal{M}''$, instead of writing it to the external memory. For every read operation of $\mathcal{P}$, $\mathcal{P}'$ loads the block from the external memory if and only if it is not present in $\mathcal{M}''$ already; otherwise $\mathcal{P}'$ copies the block from $\mathcal{M}''$ to $\mathcal{M}'$. When the cost limit of a round is reached, $\mathcal{P}'$ writes the contents of $\mathcal{M}''$ to the external memory and deletes the contents of both $\mathcal{M}'$ and $\mathcal{M}''$. This completes the simulation of a round.

Observe that $\mathcal{P}'$ fulfills the requirements of a round-based program. Since the cost of each round of $\mathcal{P}$ is at most ωm, all elements to be written during the round of $\mathcal{P}$ fit in $\mathcal{M}''$. Excluding the reads required to initialize the contents of $\mathcal{M}'$ at the beginning of each round, the number of read and write accesses of $\mathcal{P}'$ is at most the same as those of $\mathcal{P}$. Additional reads required for initializing $\mathcal{M}'$ cost at most ωm in each round, starting with the second one. If $\mathcal{P}$ consists of at least two rounds, this additional cost in each round can be charged to the cost of the previous one, thus, increasing the overall cost only by a constant factor. If $\mathcal{P}$ consists of only one round, there is no additional cost, because the first round of $\mathcal{P}'$ does not perform the initialization. □

Corollary 4.2. *Any problem which requires cost Q on (M, B, ω)-AEM using a round-based program, requires cost $\Omega(Q)$ to be solved on the $(M/2, B, \omega)$-AEM.*

Similar to the (symmetric) EM model, to prove non-trivial lower bound for permutation, we must assume that each element is indivisible and new elements cannot be generated. To emphasize this point from now on we will refer to such indivisible elements as *atoms*.

With this, we are ready to prove the lower bound for the cost of permuting an array of N elements, stored in $n = N/B$ consecutive blocks in the external memory. We take two approaches to prove the lower bound. In the first approach, we perform a simulation of the (M, B, ω)-AEM permutation program in the unit-cost flash model [2]. Thus, the existing lower bounds in the unit-cost model will imply a lower bound in the (M, B, ω)-AEM model. In the second approach, we prove the lower bound directly via the counting argument. The second approach provides a slightly stronger lower bound for some parameter ranges, due to some inefficiencies in the simulation. However, the simulation result might be of independent interest because it implies a close relationship between the (M, B, ω)-AEM and the unit-cost flash model.

4.1 Lower bound via reduction to the unit-cost flash model

In the symmetric external memory model we could assume (by a simulation that has only a constant slowdown) that reading a block erases it on disc (and that there is no copying or deleting of elements). In the asymmetric model, this is not true because a simulation, which writes the contents of every block that is read back to the external memory, might increase the cost of the program by a factor of ω. Hence the following arguments are based on a more refined trace of the program where we follow which copy of an atom is actually used in the output. This leads to the notion of a read operation 'using' some of the atoms of a block, meaning that the copies read are the ones eventually leading to the output.

In the following, we use a simulation of AEM in the unit-cost flash memory model of [2]. That model is an external memory model where the size of the blocks that are written is bigger than the size of the blocks that are read. This means that when one big block is written, it consists of several small blocks that can be read independently. Moreover, the cost of reading and writing is proportional to the number of elements in the block. Hence, similar to the AEM model, a single write operation is more expensive than a single read operation. Not too surprisingly, we choose a situation where the factor between the two is ω, more precisely, the write blocks are of size B as the AEM blocks, and the read blocks are of size B/ω. For this to make sense, B should be a multiple of ω (or somewhat bigger such that rounding is irrelevant). Still, the symmetry in the cost per element for reading and writing simplifies matters and we have (see [2]) upper and lower bounds for sorting and permuting as if all blocks were small. Interestingly, for the task of permuting, which is about moving around indivisible elements/atoms, there is a close connection between the two models. Observe that in a round-based program for permuting in the AEM model, only a $1/\omega$ fraction of the atoms read during a round can be written. Hence, the average number of *useful* atoms brought into the internal memory during a read operation is B/ω, which is precisely the size of the read block of the associated flash model. The only challenge with simulating an AEM program in the flash model is that in a single read I/O the AEM program can choose an arbitrary subset of the B/ω atoms of the block, whereas in the flash model a read of B/ω elements must happen from the contiguous memory. It is easy to address this challenge if we know how a big block is going to be read in the future. However, this is well defined and easy to determine, because we are considering *programs* and not *algorithms*.

With this, we are ready to describe the simulation.

Lemma 4.3. *Assume there is a round-based program $\mathcal{P}_A$ for (M, B, ω)-AEM that computes the permutation π over N elements with cost Q. Assume $B > \omega$ and B is a multiple of ω. Then there is a program $\mathcal{P}_F$ in the unit-cost flash memory model with read block of size B/ω and write block of size B that performs I/Os of total volume of $2N + 2QB/\omega$. (i.e., an I/O volume corresponding to Q small (read-) blocks).*

Proof. Observe that a read operation is an implicit copy operation: The atom is both in internal memory and in the block. Clearly, only one of the two copies will be moved further to become part of the output. If this is the copy that is in internal memory, we can think of the atom being deleted from the block. Because $\mathcal{P}_A$ is a program, at the time when the block is written, we can determine for all atoms the time when they will be removed from the block. We normalize $\mathcal{P}_A$ to write the block such that the atoms inside the block are ordered by the time they will be removed. We create $\mathcal{P}'_A$ from $\mathcal{P}_A$ by first doing one read and write scan over the input and then executing $\mathcal{P}_A$. This scan has I/O volume $2N$, can easily be round-based and has the effect that all read operation happen on normalized blocks, i.e., on blocks that are internally ordered by removal time. In particular, all read operations use only a contiguous interval of the atoms inside the block. To simulate $\mathcal{P}_A$ with $\mathcal{P}_F$ we keep the indices (names) of blocks. Every write operation of $\mathcal{P}_A$ is replicated directly in $\mathcal{P}_F$. A read operation of $\mathcal{P}_A$ leads to several read operations of small blocks, just enough to cover the interval of atoms that are actually removed from the block by this read operation. Observe that in this way every read operation of $\mathcal{P}_A$ induces at most 2 read operations in $\mathcal{P}_F$ that are not using (removing from the block) all of the read atoms. What remains is to determine the I/O volume of $\mathcal{P}_F$, which is simplified by $\mathcal{P}_F$ being round-based. Clearly, for any round the number k of effectively read atoms is equal to the number of atoms written. Let w be the number of block writes in the round, leading to a cost of ωw, and the bound $k \leq Bw$. The I/O volume for writing in $\mathcal{P}_F$ is Bw. Let r be the number of block read operations of $\mathcal{P}_A$, with cost r. All non-full read operations in $\mathcal{P}_F$ will have a volume of $2rB/\omega$. The full read operations have a total volume of at most $k \leq Bw$. Hence the overall volume of a round in $\mathcal{P}_F$ is $Bw + 2rB/\omega + k \leq 2Bw + 2rB/\omega \leq 2(\omega w + r)B/\omega$. Summing over all rounds and accounting for the initial read and write scan leads to the theorem. □

Using the classical lower bound on permuting [1] we get:

COROLLARY 4.4.

$$Q(N, M, B, \omega) = \Omega\left(\min\left\{N, \omega n \log_{\omega m} n\right\}\right) - 2\omega n$$

Note that the parameter range for which this lower bound is non-trivial depends on the constant factor of the Ω.

4.2 Lower bound via counting

In this section we prove the lower bound for permutation directly. It is a combination of the counting argument of [1] and the rounds introduced in the previous section.

Observe that when performing a permutation, any atom that is read from external memory but is not written back to the external memory does not contribute to generating a permutation. Therefore, we require that atoms are moved between the external memory and internal memory as follows. When reading a block B_i from external memory, a program must decide which subset S of atoms of B_i will be kept in internal memory to be written later. Exact copies of the atoms in S are created in internal memory, while destroying their copies in the external memory. The rest of the atoms of B_i are left unchanged in the external memory. When writing an internal memory block B_i' to the external memory, some atoms of B_i' can be set to be empty. However, writing B_i' to external memory replaces everything in the destination block B_i with the contents of B_i', i.e., any non-empty atom in B_i is destroyed. Since an atom can exist either in the internal memory or in the external memory, but not both, and since there is no way to generate destroyed atoms, writing to external memory can only be performed into empty blocks (either a new block location or all atoms of the destination block had been destroyed via moving them into internal memory in prior reads).

We upper bound the number $P(R)$ of permutations a round-based algorithm can generate after R rounds using the above rules. Since every correct algorithm must be able to generate every possible permutation, the inequality $P(R) \geq N!$ will provide us with the lower bound on the number of rounds R required to generate these permutations. Finally, since every round (except possibly for the last one) costs $\Theta(\omega m) = \Theta(\omega M/B)$, every algorithm's cost to permute N atoms is $\Omega(\omega m R)$. More precisely, we count the number of different normalized programs with ℓ I/Os, where we make sure that every permutation requires a different program.

Typically, we are interested in algorithms which at the end of computation, place the output within the first $\lceil N/B \rceil = \lceil n \rceil$ contiguous blocks of external memory. However, for our lower bound we only require the final output to reside in $\lceil n \rceil$ blocks of external memory, without the requirement for these blocks to be adjacent. Clearly, any lower bound with this relaxation holds in the more stringent setting of requiring the output to be in the fully contiguous space in external memory.

In the original permutation lower bound proof in the (symmetric) EM model, Aggarwal and Vitter [1] argued that the $B!$ permutation within each of $\lceil N/B \rceil$ blocks should be counted only once (see [1] for detailed argument). They count them only when a block B_i is read for the first time. However, in the AEM model, a read of a block might not necessarily use all the atoms of a block, so we cannot argue that we can count those $B!$ permutations when we read the block for the first time. Instead, we can count them the last time a block is written. And since the final output is written into $\lceil N/B \rceil$ blocks and each final block (except the last one) contains exactly B atoms, counting the $B!$ permutations within each final block B_i during the final writing of B_i to the external memory adds up to a total of $B!^{N/B}$ permutations. Thus, when counting the upper bound $P(R)$ on the number of generated permutations, we simply ignore the permutations within each block and require that $P(R) \geq \frac{N!}{B!^{N/B}}$. One can think of this as a normalization (selecting one out of many programs that create the same permutation), where until the block is finally written, the relative order of the atoms within that block is the same as in the input. This effectively reduces the content of a block to be an (unordered) subset of the input atoms.

Let us compute the multiplicative factor of permutations that the r-th round can generate. Let $\mathcal{N}_r$ be the set of non-empty blocks in the external memory at the beginning of the r-th round. Note, $|\mathcal{N}_r| \leq N$ because every atom can only be moved and no new atoms are generated.

Let us compute the number of ways to pick up to M atoms in external memory to bring into the internal memory. There are $\binom{|\mathcal{N}_r|}{\omega M/B} \leq \binom{N}{\omega M/B}$ ways to pick $\omega M/B$ blocks from the input residing in the external memory. Out of the chosen ωM atoms in the $\omega M/B$ blocks, there are $\leq \binom{\omega M}{M} 2^M$ ways to pick up to M atoms to keep in internal memory: $\binom{\omega M}{M}$ ways to pick exactly M atoms out of ωM possible ones and 2 ways for each of these M atoms to decide whether to keep it in the internal memory or not.

Since we empty the internal memory between the rounds, at the end of the r-th round we have to write all the atoms that we chose to bring into the internal memory back to the external memory. Even if we chose to bring all M atoms into internal memory, there are $\frac{M!}{B!^{M/B}}$ ways to permute M elements, without counting the permutations within each block, since we are ignoring those. Finally, each block in the internal memory can be written to $\leq 2|\mathcal{N}_r| + 1$ distinct locations in the external memory: one of $|\mathcal{N}_r|$ blocks of $\mathcal{N}_r$ which might have become empty due to reading at the beginning of r-th round, or one of the $|\mathcal{N}_r| + 1$ locations between the blocks of $\mathcal{N}_r$. So the choice of writing $\leq M/B$ blocks from the internal memory to the external memory provides a multiplicative factor of at most $(2|\mathcal{N}_r| + 1)^{M/B} \leq (3N)^{M/B}$.

Thus, the total number of permutations that can be generated after R rounds is at most

$$P(R) \leq \left[\binom{N}{\frac{\omega M}{B}}\binom{\omega M}{M} 2^M \frac{M!}{B!^{M/B}} (3N)^{M/B}\right]^R \tag{1}$$

Using the inequalities $\binom{n}{k} \leq \left(\frac{n \cdot e}{k}\right)^k$ and $\left(\frac{k}{3}\right)^k \leq k! \leq \left(\frac{k}{2}\right)^k$, the above expression simplifies to

$$
\begin{aligned}
P(R) &\le \left[\left(\frac{Ne}{\omega M/B}\right)^{\omega M/B}(e\omega)^M 2^M\left(\frac{3M}{2B}\right)^M (3N)^{M/B}\right]^R\\
&\le \left[\left(\frac{N^{1+\frac{1}{\omega}}\cdot 3^{\frac{1}{\omega}}e}{\omega M/B}\right)^{\omega M/B}(3e\omega m)^M\right]^R\\
&\le \left[\left(\frac{N^{1+\frac{1}{\omega}}\cdot 3^{\frac{1}{\omega}}e}{\omega m}\right)(3e\omega m)^{B/\omega}\right]^{\omega mR}
\end{aligned}
$$

Since we must have $\frac{N!}{B!^{N/B}} \le P(R)$,

$$
\begin{aligned}
\omega mR &\ge \frac{\log\frac{N!}{B!^{N/B}}}{\log\left(\left(\frac{N^{1+\frac{1}{\omega}}\cdot 3^{\frac{1}{\omega}}e}{\omega m}\right)(3e\omega m)^{B/\omega}\right)}\\
&\ge \frac{N\log(2N/3B)}{\log\left(\frac{N^{1+\frac{1}{\omega}}\cdot 3^{\frac{1}{\omega}}e}{\omega m}\right)+(B/\omega)\log(3e\omega m)}\\
&\ge \frac{N\log(N/2B)}{2\cdot\max\left\{\log\left(\frac{N^{1+\frac{1}{\omega}}\cdot 3^{\frac{1}{\omega}}e}{\omega m}\right),\frac{B}{\omega}\log(3e\omega m)\right\}}
\end{aligned}
$$

Observe that $\log\left(\frac{N^{1+\frac{1}{\omega}}\cdot 3^{\frac{1}{\omega}}e}{\omega m}\right) = O\left(\frac{\omega+1}{\omega}\log N\right) \le c\log N$, for some constant $c > 0$ and sufficiently large N (the last inequality following from the fact that $\omega \ge 1$, i.e., $\frac{\omega+1}{\omega} \le 2$).

Assuming $\omega \le N/B$ or, equivalently, $\omega B \le N$, we distinguish two cases, depending on which term in the denominator dominates:

(1) If $B \ge \frac{c\omega\log N}{\log(3e\omega m)}$ then $\omega mR = \Omega(n\log_{\omega m} n)$

(2) If $B < \frac{c\omega\log N}{\log(3e\omega m)}$ then
$\log\frac{N}{2B} = \log\frac{N}{2\sqrt{B}\cdot B} \ge \log\frac{N}{2\sqrt{Bc\omega\log N}}$
$\ge \log\frac{N}{2\sqrt{cN\log N}} = \Omega(\log N)$
and, therefore, $\omega mR = \Omega(N)$.

Thus, we obtain the following lower bound on the cost of any round-based algorithm:

$$Q(N,\omega,M,B) = \Omega(\omega mR) = \Omega\left(\min\left\{N,\omega n\log_{\omega m} n\right\}\right)$$

Combining with Corollary 4.2, we obtain the following theorem:

THEOREM 4.5. *Assuming that $\omega \le N/B$, the cost of permuting N elements of an array in the (M,B,ω)-AEM model is at least*

$$\Omega\left(\min\left\{N,\omega n\log_{\omega m} n\right\}\right)$$

5 COMPLEXITY OF SPMXV, COLUMN MAJOR LAYOUT

In this section we will mainly prove a lower bound for computing the product $\mathbf{A}\cdot x$ between a sparse matrix $\mathbf{A}$ by a dense vector x in the (M,B,ω)-AEM model. This proof extends the ideas of [5] to the (M,B,ω)-AEM model. In an attempt to be somewhat self contained, we present a complete but concise whole proof.

We consider an $N\times N$ matrix $\mathbf{A}$ stored in the column-major order in the external memory. This means that the non-zero entries of $\mathbf{A}$ are stored in the following way: Start with the first column, list the non-zero elements for increasing row index, then take the second column, and so on. The stored list consists of triples (i,j,a_{ij}). $\mathbf{A}$ consists of a total of $H = \delta\cdot N$ non-zero entries, for some integer $\delta \ge 1$, i.e., on average every column or row has δ non-zero entries.

We start by stating the upper bounds in the (M,B,ω)-AEM model. They follow the well-known algorithms in the (symmetric) EM model. Similar to permuting, for each conformation of the matrix, there is a direct or naive algorithm that produces the output vector in its natural order. For each output element y_i, the program considers all entries a_{ij} in the i-th row of $\mathbf{A}$, multiplying it by x_i and adding the result to y_i. The cost of this program in the (M,B,ω)-AEM model is $O(H+\omega n)$.

Alternatively, there is a sorting based algorithm. It performs a simultaneous scan of $\mathbf{A}$ (in column-major order) and x and replaces the matrix entry a_{ij} with the elementary product $a_{ij}x_j$. Next, it divides the matrix into δ meta columns, and sorts the N entries of the meta column by the row indices of the entries, virtually reordering the meta columns into row-major layout. This essentially results in δ dense vectors, which need to be added up to yield the overall result.

The cost of this algorithm in the (M,B,ω)-AEM model is dominated by sorting the input and writing the output for a total of $O\left(\omega h\log_{\omega m}\frac{N}{\max\{\delta,B\}}+\omega n\right)$. The $\max\{\delta,B\}$ term in the logarithm arises from the fact that each column is already sorted by the row indices and the base case of the mergesort is a sorted sequence of δ elements.

Hence, the upper bound for SpMxV problem in the (M,B,ω)-AEM model is (note, the last term ωn is the cost of writing the output):

$$Q(N,H,\omega,M,B) = O\left(\min\left\{H,\omega h\log_{\omega m}\frac{N}{\max\{\delta,B\}}\right\}+\omega n\right)$$

When proving the permutation lower bounds in Section 4, we had to assume indivisibility of individual elements, i.e., that no new elements can be created by combining several elements or combining subset of bits from several elements. To that end, the only operation that was allowed was moving individual elements as atomic/indivisible entities between the external and internal memories. Since matrix multiplication inherently generates new elements via multiplications and additions, we must relax these constraints.

Following the approach of [5], we work with the semi-ring model, i.e., we consider only algorithms or programs that work over an arbitrary semi-ring. This means in particular that we restrict our attention to algorithms that do not rely on the existence of inverse elements and cancellation. This would disallow an algorithm like Strassen's matrix-matrix multiplication algorithm [16], but it is less of a restriction here because there are no known algorithms for SpMxV that use this. As for the other lower bounds, we consider programs that work only for one particular conformation of matrices, i.e., the structure of $\mathbf{A}$ is fixed, and the semi-ring atoms signifying the a_{ij} are stored in the input in column major layout. This task is actually already difficult for the input vector being the all ones vector, meaning that we only have to compute the sum of the elements of each row.

The proof of the following theorem is an adaptation of the proof of Theorem 6.2 in [5] to our situation. Note that the assumption

$\omega \cdot \delta \cdot M \cdot B \leq N^{1-\varepsilon}$ is presumably stronger than necessary. We use it here to simplify the calculations significantly in comparison to the original proof in [5].

Theorem 5.1. *Consider any semi-ring program in the (M,B,ω)-AEM model, where $B > 2$, $M > 4B$ and $\omega \cdot \delta \cdot M \cdot B \leq N^{1-\varepsilon}$, for a constant $\varepsilon > 0$. There is a sparse $N \times N$ matrix $\mathbf{A}$ with precisely $\delta \geq 1$ non-zero entries per column such that for $\mathbf{A}$ stored in column major layout, multiplying $\mathbf{A}$ with the all ones vector incurs a cost of at least*

$$Q(N,H,\omega,M,B) = \Omega\left(\min\left\{H, \omega h \log_{\omega m} \frac{N}{\max\{\delta,B\}}\right\}\right)$$

Proof. Assume the program is round-based, which by Corollary 4.2 is irrelevant for the statement of the theorem. A configuration of a program describes which atoms are stored in which memory cell at a certain time. We trace the computation backward, i.e., there is a unique final configuration, and we count how many different initial configurations are possible if R many rounds are available. Since we are working with programs, rather than algorithms, we can assume that all atoms are actually used for the output. Because we consider multiplying with the all ones vector, all atoms used by the program are (partial) sums $\sum_{j \in S} a_{ij}$ for some S, including the input elements for $|S| = 1$ and the output elements for S consisting of all (non empty) columns of that row. It is sufficient to trace the program by marking for each atom the row it belongs to. In this abstract trace, the final configuration is fixed. Additionally, the initial configuration of this trace identifies the conformation of the input matrix (because it is stored in column major layout and has precisely δ entries per column). Further we insist on the atoms stored in one block being sorted by the row they belong to. This effectively means that a block stores a subset of rows. To account for the additional choice of the program to change this order in the input blocks, we introduce the function τ below. So far we follow precisely the approach of [5]. Since the program is round-based, it suffices to focus on configurations with empty internal memory between the rounds. Also, note that the configurations can be described by the choices of atoms (initial or intermediate) within the blocks with the order within each block being irrelevant.

For permuting, in both the simulation in the flash model and in the counting lower bound it is important that the amount of data usefully read equals the amount (usefully) written. This is no longer true for the task of SpMxV because here the data read might be partial sums of the same row that are added together to form an atom that is written out. Fortunately, this reduction in volume is fairly limited: Every correct program for the task performs exactly $(\delta - 1)N$ additions. If a round of the computation does not perform any additions, the number of effectively read elements and written elements is identical. The number of additions performed during one round is precisely the difference between the number of elements read and written. Let $s_r, r = 1, \ldots, R$ be the number of additions in round r. We have $\sum_{r=1}^{R} s_r = (\delta - 1)N$. Because round r writes at most M atoms, it can usefully read at most $M + s_r$ atoms.

For a fixed configuration after executing the round, we are interested in the number of different possible configurations before the round. First, we fix the blocks this round uses for reading and writing; this gives a certain multiplicity we will see in the formulas. If an atom is written out and read in again within one round, we don't record this individual movement, but only the net effect of the round. Having fixed this, there is a well defined set of rows for which intermediate results are written in this round; its size is at most M.

In each round r, we have at most $\omega \frac{M}{B}$ read operations, each reading $c_k \leq B$ atoms, and in total reading $\sum_k c_k \leq M + s_r$ atoms. For a fixed choice of where the output is written to, the memory content (as a subset of size at most M of rows) is fixed. We calculate the number of different configurations that are possible before the round, not (yet) accounting for the choice of block where input is read from (i.e. only considering content).

$$\begin{aligned}\prod_{k=1}^{\omega \frac{M}{B}} \binom{M}{c_k} &\leq \binom{\sum_{k=1}^{\omega \frac{M}{B}} M}{\sum_{k=1}^{\omega \frac{M}{B}} c_k} \leq \binom{\omega \frac{M}{B} M}{M + s_r} \\ &\leq \left(\frac{e\omega \frac{M}{B} M}{M + s_r}\right)^{M+s_r} \leq \left(\frac{e\omega M}{B}\right)^{M+s_r}\end{aligned}$$

Here, the first inequality follows from a combinatorial argument: To describe all choices, we can create a marked/disjoint union of the individual universes. The individual subsets lead to a subset of size 'sum of the sizes'.

By choosing the addresses of the involved blocks, which is at most H, the total number of different preceding configurations for round r is at most

$$H^{(\omega+1)\frac{M}{B}} \cdot \left(\frac{e\omega M}{B}\right)^{M+s_r} .$$

Multiplying this over R rounds bounds the number of different set-wise starting configurations, which must be enough to handle all different conformations of sparse matrices:

$$\prod_{r=1}^{R} H^{(\omega+1)\frac{M}{B}} \cdot \left(\frac{e\omega M}{B}\right)^{M+s_r} = H^{R(\omega+1)\frac{M}{B}} \cdot \left(\frac{e\omega M}{B}\right)^{Mr+(\delta-1)N}$$

Additionally, the algorithm is free to choose the s_r and the order of atoms within the input block, and we get the following inequality that bounds R:

$$H^{R(\omega+1)\frac{M}{B}} \cdot \left(\frac{e\omega M}{B}\right)^{Mr+(\delta-1)N} \cdot H^R \geq \binom{N}{\delta}^N / \tau(N,\delta,B),$$

using the definition of [5] for τ:

$$\tau(N,\delta,B) = \begin{cases} 3^{\delta N} & \text{if } B < \delta, \\ 1 & \text{if } B = \delta, \\ (2eB/\delta)^{\delta N} & \text{if } B > \delta. \end{cases}$$

Solving for R we get

$$\begin{aligned}R(\omega+1)\frac{M}{B}\log H + (Mr + (\delta-1)N)\log\left(\frac{e\omega M}{B}\right) + R\log H \geq \\ \geq \delta N \log\frac{N}{\delta} - \log\tau(N,\delta,B),\end{aligned}$$

$$R\left(2\omega\frac{M}{B}\log H + M\log\frac{e\omega M}{B} + \log H\right)$$
$$\geq \delta N\left(\log\left(\frac{N}{\delta}\frac{B}{e\omega M}\right)\right) - \log\tau(N,\delta,B)$$

implying that the cost is

$$Q(\cdot) = R\omega\frac{M}{B} \geq \frac{\delta N\log\frac{N}{\delta} - \log\tau(N,\delta,B) - \log\frac{B}{e\omega M}}{2\log H + \frac{B}{\omega}\log\frac{e\omega M}{B} + \frac{B}{\omega M}\log H}$$

Simplifying the enumerator using the definition of τ, this is:

$$Q(\cdot) = R\omega\frac{M}{B} \geq \frac{\delta N\log\left(\frac{N}{\max\{3\delta,2eB\}}\frac{B}{e\omega M}\right)}{2\log H + \frac{B}{\omega}\log\frac{e\omega M}{B} + \frac{B}{\omega M}\log H}$$

We distinguish cases by the leading term of the denominator. The last term is always dominated by the first, so we can ignore it for asymptotic considerations. If the first term in the denominator dominates the second one, we use the assumption $\omega\cdot\delta\cdot M\cdot B \leq N^{1-\varepsilon}$ to conclude $Q(\cdot) = \Omega(H)$. If, on the other hand, the second term in the denominator dominates the first one, then

$$\begin{aligned} Q(\cdot) &\geq \frac{\omega\delta N}{3B}\left(\frac{\log\frac{N}{\max\{3\delta,2eB\}}}{\log\frac{e\omega M}{B}} - 1\right) \\ &= \Omega\left(\omega h\log_{\omega m}\frac{N}{\max\{\delta,B\}}\right) \end{aligned}$$

matching the bound of the sorting-based algorithm. □

REFERENCES

[1] Alok Aggarwal and S. Vitter, Jeffrey. 1988. The Input/Output Complexity of Sorting and Related Problems. *Commun. ACM* 31, 9 (Sept. 1988), 1116–1127. DOI: http://dx.doi.org/10.1145/48529.48535

[2] Deepak Ajwani, Andreas Beckmann, Riko Jacob, Ulrich Meyer, and Gabriel Moruz. 2009. *On Computational Models for Flash Memory Devices.* Springer Berlin Heidelberg, Berlin, Heidelberg, 16–27. DOI: http://dx.doi.org/10.1007/978-3-642-02011-7_4

[3] Avraham Ben-Aroya and Sivan Toledo. 2011. Competitive Analysis of Flash Memory Algorithms. *ACM Trans. Algorithms* 7, 2, Article 23 (March 2011), 37 pages. DOI: http://dx.doi.org/10.1145/1921659.1921669

[4] Naama Ben-David, Guy E. Blelloch, Jeremy T. Fineman, Phillip B. Gibbons, Yan Gu, Charles McGuffey, and Julian Shun. 2016. Parallel Algorithms for Asymmetric Read-Write Costs. In *Proceedings of the 28th ACM Symposium on Parallelism in Algorithms and Architectures (SPAA '16).* ACM, New York, NY, USA, 145–156. DOI: http://dx.doi.org/10.1145/2935764.2935767

[5] Michael A. Bender, Gerth Stølting Brodal, Rolf Fagerberg, Riko Jacob, and Elias Vicari. 2010. Optimal Sparse Matrix Dense Vector Multiplication inthe I/O-Model. *Theory of Computing Systems* 47, 4 (2010), 934–962. DOI: http://dx.doi.org/10.1007/s00224-010-9285-4

[6] Guy E. Blelloch, Jeremy T. Fineman, Phillip B. Gibbons, Yan Gu, and Julian Shun. 2015. Efficient Algorithms with Asymmetric Read and Write Costs. In *Proceedings of the 24th Annual European Symposium on Algorithms (ESA '16).* 14:1–14:18.

[7] Guy E. Blelloch, Jeremy T. Fineman, Phillip B. Gibbons, Yan Gu, and Julian Shun. 2015. Sorting with Asymmetric Read and Write Costs. In *Proceedings of the 27th ACM Symposium on Parallelism in Algorithms and Architectures (SPAA '15).* ACM, New York, NY, USA, 1–12. DOI: http://dx.doi.org/10.1145/2755573.2755604

[8] Xiangyu Dong, Norman P. Jouppi, and Yuan Xie. 2009. PCRAMsim: System-level Performance, Energy, and Area Modeling for Phase-change Ram. In *Proceedings of the 2009 International Conference on Computer-Aided Design (ICCAD '09).* ACM, New York, NY, USA, 269–275. DOI: http://dx.doi.org/10.1145/1687399.1687449

[9] Xiangyu Dong, Xiaoxia Wu, Guangyu Sun, Yuan Xie, H. Li, and Yiran Chen. 2008. Circuit and microarchitecture evaluation of 3D stacking magnetic RAM (MRAM) as a universal memory replacement. In *2008 45th ACM/IEEE Design Automation Conference.* 554–559.

[10] Eran Gal and Sivan Toledo. 2005. Algorithms and Data Structures for Flash Memories. *ACM Comput. Surv.* 37, 2 (June 2005), 138–163. DOI: http://dx.doi.org/10.1145/1089733.1089735

[11] Jia-Wei Hong and H. T. Kung. 1981. I/O Complexity: The Red-blue Pebble Game. In *Proceedings of the Thirteenth Annual ACM Symposium on Theory of Computing (STOC '81).* ACM, New York, NY, USA, 326–333. DOI: http://dx.doi.org/10.1145/800076.802486

[12] Hyojun Kim, Sangeetha Seshadri, Clement L. Dickey, and Lawrence Chiu. 2014. Evaluating Phase Change Memory for Enterprise Storage Systems: A Study of Caching and Tiering Approaches. *Trans. Storage* 10, 4, Article 15 (Oct. 2014), 21 pages. DOI: http://dx.doi.org/10.1145/2668128

[13] Suman Nath and Phillip B. Gibbons. 2008. Online Maintenance of Very Large Random Samples on Flash Storage. *Proc. VLDB Endow.* 1, 1 (Aug. 2008), 970–983. DOI: http://dx.doi.org/10.14778/1453856.1453961

[14] Hyoungmin Park and Kyuseok Shim. 2009. FAST: Flash-aware External Sorting for Mobile Database Systems. *J. Syst. Softw.* 82, 8 (Aug. 2009), 1298–1312. DOI: http://dx.doi.org/10.1016/j.jss.2009.02.028

[15] Moinuddin K. Qureshi, Sudhanva Gurumurthi, and Bipin Rajendran. 2011. *Phase Change Memory: From Devices to Systems.* Morgan & Claypool Publishers.

[16] Volker Strassen. 1969. Gaussian Elimination is Not Optimal. *Numer. Math.* 13, 4 (Aug. 1969), 354–356. DOI: http://dx.doi.org/10.1007/BF02165411

[17] Stratis D. Viglas. 2014. Write-limited Sorts and Joins for Persistent Memory. *Proc. VLDB Endow.* 7, 5 (Jan. 2014), 413–424. DOI: http://dx.doi.org/10.14778/2732269.2732277

Hand-Over-Hand Transactions with Precise Memory Reclamation

Tingzhe Zhou
Lehigh University
tiz214@lehigh.edu

Victor Luchangco
Oracle Labs
victor.luchangco@oracle.com

Michael Spear
Lehigh University
spear@lehigh.edu

ABSTRACT

In this paper, we introduce *revocable reservations*, a transactional memory mechanism to reserve locations in one transaction and check whether they are unchanged in a subsequent transaction without preventing reserved locations from being reclaimed in the interim. We describe several implementations of revocable reservations, and show how to use revocable reservations to implement lists and trees with a transactional analog to hand-over-hand locking. Our evaluation of these data structures shows that revocable reservations allow precise and immediate reclamation within transactional data structures, without sacrificing scalability or introducing excessive latency.

CCS CONCEPTS

• **Computing methodologies → Parallel computing methodologies; Concurrent computing methodologies;**

KEYWORDS

Transactional Memory, Concurrency, Synchronization, Data Structures, Memory Management

ACM Reference format:

Tingzhe Zhou, Victor Luchangco, and Michael Spear. 2017. Hand-Over-Hand Transactions with Precise Memory Reclamation. In *Proceedings of SPAA '17, Washington DC, USA, July 24-26, 2017,* 10 pages.
https://doi.org/10.1145/3087556.3087587

1 INTRODUCTION

Transactional memory (TM) [18] facilitates the implementation of concurrent data structures: instead of using locks, a programmer can simply designate a block of code to be executed as a transaction, and the system is responsible for executing the transaction atomically. Transactional memory implementations typically use speculation to execute multiple transactions concurrently. If concurrent transactions conflict, one or more of them is aborted and re-executed. To detect conflicts, a transaction typically maintains a "read set" of locations; the transaction is aborted if any of these locations are changed before the transaction commits.

Like critical sections in lock-based implementations, it is desirable to keep transactions as small as possible, in both time and space (i.e., duration and number of locations accessed): smaller transactions are less likely to conflict and abort. Furthermore, existing hardware support for transactional memory (HTM) [24] typically has capacity limits, forcing large transactions to fall back to slower software implementations (STM) [26].

Many operations on pointer-based data structures can be partitioned into a read-only *traversal phase* followed by an *update phase.* In the traversal phase, the operation follows a chain of nodes until it finds a node satisfying some condition. The found node is updated in the update phase. (The update phase is empty if the operation does not modify the data structure.) Some lock-based implementations reduce the size of critical sections of such operations by using *hand-over-hand locking*: An operation traverses the data structure by acquiring the lock for each node it traverses and then releasing each lock after the lock to the next node is acquired. The locks for all nodes accessed in the update phase must also be acquired, and they are not released until the end of the operation. Thus, during the traversal phase, each lock is held only while the next lock in the chain is acquired. This series of overlapping critical sections gives rise to the term hand-over-hand locking, and guarantees the atomicity of the entire operation.

Early release [17] and *elastic transactions* [13] achieve a similar effect for transactions by removing locations from a transaction's read set so that subsequent updates to the "released" locations do not cause the transaction to abort. Although they do not make transactions smaller, these techniques make transactions less likely to abort by reducing the size of their read sets. However, they cannot be applied to transactions executed by HTM, which provides no support for releasing locations.

We propose to hew more closely to hand-over-hand locking by dividing an operation's traversal phase into several read-only transactions, and executing the update phase as a single transaction. However, we cannot ensure atomicity by overlapping transactions as hand-over-hand locking overlaps critical sections. Instead, we introduce a mechanism to link consecutive transactions by "reserving" a location at the end of a transaction and checking the reservation at the beginning of the next transaction, aborting if the location has changed since the previous transaction committed. The composition of these linked transactions appears atomic because no updates are done until the final transaction.

One problem with reservations as described thus far: What happens if a reserved location is reclaimed? In that case, even reading the location in the next transaction may not be safe (e.g., it may result in a segmentation fault). We can avoid this problem by treating a reservation as a kind of hazard pointer [23], deferring the reclamation of reserved locations. Such deferral is not a significant concern for garbage-collected languages. However, in languages like C and C++, custom allocators are required, which must delay reclamation

SPAA '17, July 24-26, 2017, Washington DC, USA

ACM ISBN 978-1-4503-4593-4/17/07...$15.00
https://doi.org/10.1145/3087556.3087587

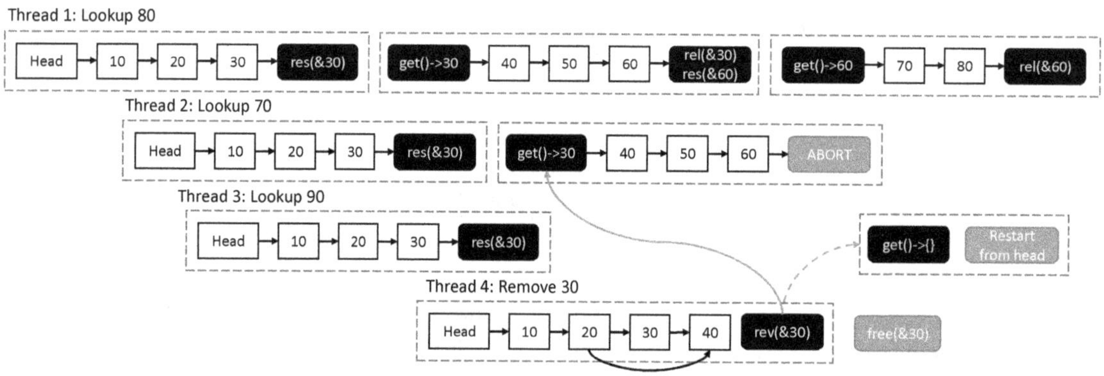

Figure 1: Concurrent operations on a linked list, with hand-over-hand transactions and revocable reservations. Time advances to the right. Dashed boxes indicate transactions, and filled black rectangles represent operations on the revocable reservation shared object ("res", "get", "rel", and "rev" correspond to reserving a value, getting a previously reserved value, releasing a reservation, and revoking all reservations for a specific value).

of some locations until all possible concurrent reads complete. It is difficult to bound the time between logical removal and physical reclamation [11], and many scalable techniques accept unbounded worst-case delay for a bounded [23] or unbounded [9] number of items. To avoid these delays, a system might fall back to complex or expensive measures when the amount of unreclaimed memory becomes too great [3, 6–8]. However, there will always remain programs whose correctness depends on memory being reclaimed immediately, hence the need for *precise* memory reclamation.

To avoid this problem, we introduce *revocable reservations*, which allow threads to revoke all reservations to a specified location. A subsequent transaction that checks a reservation will see that it has been revoked and therefore not attempt to access the formerly reserved location. By leveraging features of HTM, particularly the immediacy of aborts, concurrent operations are able to revoke these reservations and immediately reclaim memory, without compromising correctness.

To see how hand-over-hand transactions work with revocable reservations, consider the execution shown in Figure 1, in which four threads perform operations on a linked-list based set using hand-over-hand transactions. Threads T_1, T_2 and T_3 invoke *Lookup* with values 80, 70 and 90 respectively. Each of these threads executes an initial transaction that traverses the first four nodes in the list (including the head), and then commits that transaction, reserving the node N with value 30. Then T_1 and T_2 start new transactions to continue traversing the list starting from the reserved node N, and T_1 commits its transaction, releasing N and reserving a new node (with value 60). Concurrently, thread T_4 invokes *Remove*(30), finding the relevant node (N) with its first transaction. Because it wants to remove and free N, it calls *Revoke*(N) before committing, which revokes the reservations of T_2 and T_3. (By this time, T_1 has already released N and reserved a different node, so it is not affected and can complete its operation.) This revocation conflicts with T_2's use of its reservation at the beginning of its second transaction, so this transaction must be aborted. T_3 begins its second traversal transaction after T_4 commits, so when T_3 checks its reservation, it finds that its reservation has been revoked, and so retries its operation from the beginning (i.e., begins traversing from the head). Note that had T_4 removed 20 or 40 rather than 30, for example, the reservations of T_2 and T_3 would not have been revoked, so they could have continued with their operations unaffected.

We present several approaches to implementing revocable reservations, which differ in both asymptotic overhead and likelihood of conflict. We implemented and evaluated these variants in the context of singly and doubly linked lists, and unbalanced binary search trees. We found performance to be competitive with the state of the art in both transactional and nonblocking data structures, without sacrificing immediate memory reclamation.

2 SPECIFICATION

A *revocable reservation* is a shared object that provides four methods, *Reserve*, *Get*, *Release*, and *Revoke*. Each of these operations takes a "reference" as a parameter. The object maintains a set of references for each thread. A thread adds and removes references from its set using *Reserve* and *Release* respectively. *Revoke* removes a reference from every thread's set. *Get* checks whether a reference is in the caller's set, returning **nil** if it is not. These methods must be called from within transactions, so they always appear atomic, and we can define their behavior precisely with a sequential specification, which appears in Listing 1.

Note that conflicts among operations on a revocable reservation always involve operations with same reference, one of which must be a call to *Revoke*. In particular, concurrent calls to *Reserve*, *Get*, and *Release* never conflict with each other.

The revocable reservation implementations we describe in the next section also provide a *Register* method, which is invoked by a thread before it invokes any other operation on the revocable reservation. Although not formally part of the specification, this operation is useful for maintaining the set of threads that may use the object, and thus for whom a set of references must be maintained.

Listing 1: Sequential specification for the revocable reservation shared object

```
𝒯 = set of all threads
ℛ = set of all references
states
  refs : 𝒯 → Set(ℛ); initially refs(t) = {} for all t ∈ 𝒯
procedure Reserve(r : ℛ) for thread t
  requires r ∉ refs(t)
  refs(t) ← refs(t) ∪ r
procedure Release(r : ℛ) for thread t
  requires r ∈ refs(t)
  refs(t) ← refs(t) \ r
function Get(r : ℛ) for thread t
  return { r    if r ∈ refs(t),
         { nil  if r ∉ refs(t).
procedure Revoke(r : ℛ) for thread t
  ∀ t'∈𝒯 : refs(t') ← refs(t') \ r
```

Listing 2: Basic revocable reservation algorithm (RR-FA): a linked list simulates a fully associative cache of reservations. All functions are called from an active transaction.

```
Variables ("t" subscript indicates per-thread):
  LL   : List⟨Node⟨ℛ⟩⟩
  N_t  : Node⟨ℛ⟩
function Register()
  if N_t = nil then
    N_t ← new Node(nil)
    LL.appendNode(N_t)
function Reserve(r : ℛ)
  N_t.value ← r
function Release()
  N_t.value ← nil
function Get()
  return N_t.value
function Revoke(r : ℛ)
  for n ∈ LL do
    if n.value = r then
      n.value ← nil
```

3 IMPLEMENTATIONS

In this section, we present two families of revocable reservation implementations. The first adheres strictly to the specification in Section 2. The second provides a relaxed guarantee, inspired by STM: a *Get* may return **nil** even when the previously reserved reference was not revoked. To simplify the presentation, the algorithms in this section only support one reservation per thread. Extending the algorithms to support per-thread sets of reserved references is straightforward.

System Model. We assume a shared memory multiprocessor with coherent caches, and a TM implementation that provides a total order on transactions. The consequence of these requirements is that all writes to any single location must be ordered, and all operations performed within a transaction must appear to execute without any interleaving of transactional operations by other threads. We do not require Strong Isolation [1, 5, 27], and thus both HTM and opaque [15] STM are compatible with our algorithms. When STM is used, it must support privatization safety [21]. This is not a requirement of our algorithms, but rather a consequence of the desire for memory to be immediately reclaimed.

3.1 Strict Implementations

Our first three implementations of revocable reservations resemble fully associative, direct-mapped, and set-associative caches. These implementations strictly adhere to the specification in Section 2. There is significant overlap among the three implementations; to save space, we only present pseudocode for the first in Listing 2.

Fully Associative Reservations. RR-FA resembles a fully associative cache: through the *Register* method, threads "own" nodes in a linked list, and each thread t leaves its node N_t in the list from the time it first performs an operation on an RR-FA-protected list until the point where t terminates. To reserve reference r, t stores r in N_t; to release, t stores **nil** in N_t. To get its reservation, t reads from N_t. To revoke reservations on reference r, a thread traverses the list, and whenever it finds that a node stores r, it writes **nil** to that node.

To support multiple reservations per thread, we would replace the *value* field with a set. Then *Reserve* would append to the set, *Release* would remove an element from the set, and *Get* would test the set for membership. *Revoke* would remove from each thread's set, potentially increasing asymptotic complexity. All methods of the revocable reservation are performed within a transaction, which simplifies coordination of threads' accesses to these sets.

The complexity of *Revoke* is linear in the thread count. *Revoke* is also prone to low-level conflicts: From the time a revoking thread t accesses some node N_i until t's revoking transaction commits, any release or reserve by t_i will cause t's transaction to abort. On the other hand, *Reserve*, *Release*, and *Get* have $O(1)$ complexity with low constant overhead. As long as each thread's node is in a separate cache line, these methods should not experience false transaction conflicts.

Direct Mapped Reservations. RR-DM (direct mapped) replaces *LL* with an array of unsorted, doubly linked lists, and uses a hash function to assign references to these lists. Each thread is still assigned a single node, which can be present in at most one list at any time. To revoke reservations on a reference r, a thread traverses through the list in the array position to which that reference hashes, and in any node where it observes r, it writes **nil**. To reserve a node, a thread sets the value in its node, and then inserts its node into the appropriate list. To release a reservation, the thread must set its node's value to **nil**, and should remove its node from the list. As a contention-avoiding optimization, in RR-DM, a thread can delay removing the node from its list until a subsequent transaction. The *Get* method is unchanged from RR-FA.

RR-DM reduces the common-case overhead of *Revoke*, but the worst case is unchanged. The asymptotic complexity of *Reserve* and *Release* is unchanged, but the constants are higher: each now inserts or removes from a doubly linked list. More significantly, simultaneous calls to *Reserve* and *Release* from different threads can now result in transaction conflicts on one of the reservation object's lists. To reduce contention, each list begins with a sentinel node.

Set Associative Reservations. RR-SA (set associative) replaces the single array of doubly linked lists in RR-DM with A arrays. Each thread is assigned to an array via a mapping function. In *Reserve*

and *Release*, the calling thread chooses the appropriate array, and then operates as in RR-DM. *Get* is unchanged from RR-DM and RR-FA. However, *Revoke* must now traverse a list in each of the A arrays, resulting in $O(A + T)$ complexity, where T is the number of threads.

RR-SA does not change the complexity of *Reserve* or *Release*, nor does it reduce the constants in these methods relative to RR-DM. However, it does reduce the likelihood that concurrent invocations of *Reserve* and *Release* will result in transaction conflicts, since these methods are unlikely to access the same lists. The cost of this improvement is additional overhead in *Revoke*, which now must traverse A lists (though the total number of entries in those lists cannot exceed the number of threads).

Correctness. In the absence of concurrent calls to *Revoke*, the correctness of the cache-inspired implementations is straightforward: a thread writes a reference into a thread-specific location to reserve it, reads from that location to get it, and clears that location to release it. Thus the overall correctness of the algorithm reduces to ensuring that revoking r prevents subsequent calls to *Get* from returning r. In each algorithm, revocation traverses every possible location where a node might store r, and whenever that value is found, it is replaced with **nil**. Since every method is called from a transaction, there are no concurrent interleavings to complicate the argument.

3.2 Relaxed Implementations

In our relaxed implementations, after t_i reserves reference r_i, its subsequent calls to *Get* may return **nil** on account of another thread calling *Revoke*(r_j) or *Reserve*(r_j), for $r_j \neq r_i$. In exchange for this relaxation, these algorithms have smaller constant and asymptotic overhead, and less likelihood of transaction contention.

Exclusive Ownership. RR-XO is inspired by the idea of ownership in STM, and is presented in Listing 3. Again, all functions are called from a transactional context, but now a hash function provides a many-to-one mapping from memory locations to positions in an array (OWN) of thread identifiers. Every thread is assigned a unique identifier through *Register*, starting with the value 0. The value -1 has special meaning. To reserve a reference r, a thread writes r to its thread-local variable R_t, and writes its unique identifier ID_t into the array at the position determined by *hash*(p). *Release* is a local operation, which sets R_t to **nil** but does not update the shared array of identifiers. To revoke reference r, a thread writes -1 in the shared array in the position determined by *hash*(p). To perform a *Get* of reference r, thread t must check that ID_t is still in the table at the expected position. If so, the value in R_t is returned; otherwise **nil** is returned. To support multiple reservations per thread, R_t can be replaced with a set. Since R_t is only accessed by thread t, this does not introduce new concurrency challenges.

In RR-XO, all methods run in constant time. *Release* only accesses thread-local data, and can never cause transactions to conflict. Unlike the strict algorithms, *Reserve* must write to shared memory, and two threads cannot reserve the same reference simultaneously. *Get* retains its constant-time complexity, but it must read from shared memory to determine if R_t remains valid. In exchange for these

Listing 3: Exclusive Owner Revocable Reservation algorithm (RR-XO): an array of thread IDs is used to indicate which thread currently holds a reservation for all references that hash to any given array entry.

```
Variables ("_t" subscript indicates per-thread):
  OWN   : N[]
  ID    : N      // initially 0
  ID_t  : N      // initially -1
  R_t   : R      // initially nil

function Register()
    if ID_t = −1 then
        ID_t ← ID
        ID ← ID + 1

function Reserve(r : R)
    R_t ← r
    OWN[hash(r)] ← ID_t

function Release()
    R_t ← nil

function Get()
    if OWN[hash(R_t)] = ID_t then
        return R_t
    else
        return nil

function Revoke(r : R)
    OWN[hash(r)] ← −1
```

increases in overhead, *Revoke* reduces to a single constant-time write.

Shared Ownership. RR-SO extends RR-XO similarly to how RR-SA extends RR-DM: it introduces multiple arrays of thread identifiers. Each thread is assigned to a specific array, and operates identically to RR-XO for the *Get*, *Reserve*, and *Release* methods. To revoke, a thread must write -1 to the appropriate position in each of the arrays of thread identifiers. We refer to this "shared (read) ownership" variant as RR-SO.

With A ownership arrays, RR-SO increases the complexity of *Revoke* to $O(A)$. It does not change the complexity of the other operations. The main benefit is that threads will rarely cause transaction conflicts when they reserve the same reference, since they are likely to be assigned to different ownership arrays.

Versioned Reservations. RR-V (Listing 4) uses versioning to share reservations without increasing the overhead of *Revoke*. The OWN array is replaced with a version array (V), which stores counters. These counters function like ownership records [10] in STM. To reserve reference r, t writes r to a thread-local field R_t, and then records the counter associated with that reference in thread-local V_t. The *Get* method checks that the value in the counter array is still V_t. To release, the thread writes **nil** to R_t, and to revoke reference r, the counter associated with r is incremented.

In RR-V, all operations have constant overhead. *Reserve* no longer writes to shared memory, and thus should not cause transaction conflicts. The use of version numbers allows any number of threads to simultaneously reserve the same reference, unlike the limits of 1 and A in RR-XO and RR-SO, respectively. *Revoke* is still $O(1)$, but must read and write to shared memory, instead of writing a constant.

Correctness. Due to the use of hash functions, a revoke of r_1 could invalidate a reservation of r_2 if r_1 and r_2 hash to the same

Listing 4: Version-based Revocable Reservation algorithm (RR-V): an array of integers is used to coordinate revocation and reservation operations.

```
Variables ("t" subscript indicates per-thread):
    V     : N[]
    ID    : N          // initially 0
    ID_t  : N          // initially -1
    R_t   : R          // initially nil
    V_t   : N

function Register()
1    if ID_t = -1 then
2        ID_t ← ID
3        ID ← ID + 1

function Reserve(r : R)
4    R_t ← r
5    V_t ← V[hash(r)]

function Release()
6    R_t ← nil

function Get()
7    if V[hash(R_t)] = V_t then
8        return R_t
9    else
10       return nil

function Revoke(r : R)
11   V[hash(r)] ← V[hash(r)] + 1
```

Listing 5: Singly linked list with revocable reservations. Nodes consist of a value and a next pointer, and the head initially points to a sentinel node.

```
Variables:
    RR    : RevocableReservation
    head  : Node⟨T⟩              // Head of the list
    W     : N                    // Nodes to visit per transaction

function Apply(key : T, λ_found, λ_notfound)
1    while true do
2        transaction
             // Initialize
3            (prev, i) ← (RR.Get(), 0)
4            if prev = nil then
5                (prev, i) ← (head, scatter(W))
             // Traverse
6            curr ← prev.next
7            while curr ≠ nil ∧ curr.val < key ∧ i < W do
8                (prev, curr, i) ← (curr, curr.next, i + 1)
             // Match
9            if curr ≠ nil ∧ curr.val = key then
10               res ← λ_found(prev, curr)
11               RR.Release()
12               return res
             // No Match
13           if curr = nil ∨ curr.val > key then
14               res ← λ_notfound(prev, curr)
15               RR.Release()
16               return res
             // Next Window
17           RR.Release()
18           RR.Reserve(curr)

function Lookup(key : T)
19   λ_found ← function (prev : Node, curr : Node)
20       return true
21   λ_notfound ← function (prev : Node, curr : Node)
22       return false
23   return Apply(key, λ_found, λ_notfound)

function Insert(key : T)
24   λ_found ← function (prev : Node, curr : Node)
25       return false
26   λ_notfound ← function (prev : Node, curr : Node)
27       n ← new Node(key)
28       n.next ← curr
29       prev.next ← n
30       return true
31   return Apply(key, λ_found, λ_notfound)

function Remove(key : T)
32   λ_found ← function (prev : Node, curr : Node)
33       prev.next ← curr.next
34       RR.Revoke(curr)
35       delete(curr)
36       return true
37   λ_notfound ← function (prev : Node, curr : Node)
38       return false
39   return Apply(key, λ_found, λ_notfound)
```

position in *OWN* or *V*. Still, we can reason about correctness in the absence of hash conflicts. In the absence of concurrency, the correctness of the three implementations follows immediately from the implementation. As in the previous subsection, the correctness of a call to *Get* in the face of a concurrent call to *Revoke* requires discussion. Calls to *Revoke* do not overwrite t's reference in R_t. However, since every call to *Get* that returns reference r accesses the metadata (in *OWN* or *V*) associated with r, and revoking r writes that metadata, the TM implementation will ensure that a conflict manifests, and a revoked r will not be used. Furthermore, RR-XO and RR-SO limit the ability of threads to concurrently hold a reservation on a reference. This limitation affects progress, but not correctness: if t_i has reserves reference r, and then thread t_j also reserves r, such that ID_i is no longer in *OWN*, t_i will mistake t_j's call to *Reserve* for a call to *Revoke*, but will not return an incorrect value.

4 USING REVOCABLE RESERVATIONS

In this section, we briefly sketch three concurrent data structures that use revocable reservations: a singly linked list, a doubly linked list, and an unbalanced binary search tree.

4.1 Singly Linked List

Listing 5 presents a concurrent singly linked list implementation that uses revocable reservations. The behavior of this code corresponds to the illustration in Figure 1. We represent the common functionality of the *Insert*, *Lookup*, and *Remove* functions as the *Apply* function (lines 1–18). *Apply* takes a search key and two functions, which are run when the key is found, or is not found, respectively. Lines 19–39 provide implementations of the two functions suitable for *Lookup*, *Insert*, and *Remove* operations.

Initially, the thread does not have a reservation, and the *Get* on line 3 returns **nil**. In this case, the thread will start from the head of the list, and will begin traversing forward. Typically, a thread will access a maximum of W nodes per iteration of the while loop. To reduce contention on revocable reservation metadata, it may be desirable to have threads shorten their initial traversal; this is achieved by the scatter function, which ensures that each thread's first traversal in *Apply* will be of some number between 1 and W nodes (subsequent transactions will traverse up to W nodes). During traversal, the counter i tracks the remaining nodes before a transaction must commit and start a new window. This provides the hand-over-hand behavior we desire, ensuring that traversals that progress far into the list do not conflict with modifications to nodes at the beginning of the list.

When there are no concurrent *Remove* operations, a thread will reserve its current position on line 18, commit its transaction, and then immediately get that position on line 3. If a concurrent *Remove* invalidates the traversing thread's start position (via *Revoke*), then the traversal either (a) aborts, and then discovers that its reservation is now **nil**, or (b) is between transactions, and will discover that its reservation has become **nil**. In either case, the thread will restart its search from the head of the list (line 5).

4.2 Doubly Linked List

Due to space constraints, we do not present full pseudocode for the doubly linked list algorithm; it is not significantly different from the singly linked list. We add a "previous" pointer to each node in the list, and during insertions and removals, we must set both the next and previous pointers; since updates are performed transactionally, the code to achieve this behavior is identical to a sequential doubly linked list. The only substantiative change relates to the removal code. In the singly linked list, the previous and current nodes are needed when unlinking a node, but in the doubly linked list, the current node suffices: its predecessor and successor are both reachable from it. This affords an optimization: rather than perform the unlinking and revoking operations from within `Apply`, a *Remove* that finds a node with matching key can reserve the node, commit the transaction, and then use a new transaction to perform both the unlinking step and the *Revoke*. If this transaction discovers that its reservation has been invalided, then it must mean that a concurrent transaction removed the same node, in which case the operation can return **false**: it can appear to happen immediately after the concurrent *Remove* operation.

The appeal of this optimization is that it avoids costly calls to *Revoke* from within traversing transactions. However, in our relaxed implementations, it is not correct: If *Get* returns **nil**, it may mean that an unrelated *Revoke* (RR-V) or even a concurrent *Reserve* (RR-XO and RR-SO) has incorrectly invalided the reservation. For these algorithms, if the final call to *Get* in a *Remove* operation returns **nil**, we must retry the entire operation.

4.3 Unbalanced Binary Search Tree

Lastly, we discuss an unbalanced binary search tree that uses revocable reservations. We focus on an internal tree, and again employ a sentinel node at the root, to simplify the case where the first element reached in a traversal is the target of a removal operation. Our implementation does not save parent pointers in tree nodes, but each node does store whether it is the left or right child of its parent.

Since the tree is not balanced, the *Lookup* and *Insert* operations are nearly identical to corresponding singly linked list code: a *Lookup* traverses until it finds its target node, and an *Insert* traverses until it either finds the value it is trying to insert, or it reaches a **nil** node, at which point it adds its value. Neither of these operations needs to revoke reservations, and both need only one reservation during their hand-over-hand traversals.

The complexity of the algorithm is in the *Remove* operation. If the value to be removed is in a leaf node, or if it is in a node that only has one child, then it can be removed in the same manner as in a singly linked list. With regard to the reservation mechanism, these code paths need only revoke reservations on one node: the node to be removed. Revoking the node to remove is necessary, since another thread's search may have reserved the node that is being deleted. However, we need not revoke the node's parent or its child (if any): If a concurrent *Apply* reserved the parent, then the removal of the node cannot invalidate the *Apply*'s most recent traversal, and the removal will be detected when the operation starts its next transaction. Similarly, if the concurrent *Apply* reserved the child, then it must not be searching for the removed value, and the removal cannot have affected the success of the next transaction issued by the operation, because the subtree rooted at the child has not changed.

When the value to be removed is in a node with two children, we must find a node to swap into its place. We choose the leftmost descendant of the node's right child for the swap. If that node is a leaf, it is removed from the tree by writing **nil** to its parent's left child. Otherwise, it is removed from the tree by promoting its right child to its parent's left child.

When we remove a value stored in a node with two children, we do not extract the node holding the value from the tree. Instead, we overwrite its value and then extract the leftmost descendant node of the right child from the tree. Clearly, the node that is extracted must be revoked. However, the fact that its value moves upward in the tree means that concurrent operations that have performed a *Reserve* anywhere on the path from *curr* to $leftmost$ may be invalid. Let v be the value to delete, and l be the value of the leftmost descendant of the right child. l will be written into v's node using a transaction, so there is never a time where it could appear that l is not in the tree. However, suppose a concurrent thread t_C is performing an operation with a value of l. If t_C has traversed to a point between the node holding v and the node holding l, and has reserved that node, then when it begins its next transaction, it will continue searching from a point below the point where l has been moved, and thus it will incorrectly return that l is not in the tree.

A sufficient condition to remedy this situation is for the thread removing v to perform a *Revoke* on every node in the path from v to l. The revocation causes concurrent threads on that path to restart their traversal from the root of the tree, thereby ensuring that they do not resume from a point that has become invalid.

5 EVALUATION

To evaluate the performance of revocable reservations, we conducted a series of stress-test microbenchmarks. Our evaluation platform is a 4-core/8-thread Intel Core i7-4770 CPU running at 3.40GHz. This CPU supports Intel's TSX extensions for HTM [19]. It has 8 GB of RAM and runs a Linux 4.3 kernel. We used the TM support in the GCC 5.3.1 compiler. Results are the average of 5 trials. Across all experiments, variance was below 3%.

We evaluate four data structures: singly and doubly linked lists and internal and external unbalanced binary search trees. We consider the six revocable reservation implementations, and an implementation in which every data structure operation is performed within a single hardware transaction. GCC's language-level support for HTM falls back to a serial mode after hardware transactions fail twice. For the lists, this policy is adequate, but for the trees, we changed the number to 8, as it improved the performance of all implementations.

In the singly linked list experiments, we compare against a lock-free list based on the work of Harris [16] and Michael [22]. We provide two versions of the list: one that never reclaims memory, and one that uses hazard pointers [23]. The former approximates the best-case performance of an epoch-based allocator or garbage collector, but has no bounds on memory overheads. The latter is significantly more expensive, but can bound memory consumption more tightly. Our implementations adhere to the C++11 standard. With hazard pointers, performance is best when threads only reclaim after 64 deletions, so we report that result.

Our list experiments also include a transactional hazard pointer implementation. Algorithmically, operations are identical to those in Listing 5, except that memory reclamation is deferred via hazard pointers, instead of being performed immediately. We also provide a reference-counted version of this implementation. These algorithms most closely resemble work by Liu et al. [20], and benefit from only accessing hazard pointers once per internal transaction.

We consider both internal and external trees. This affords an opportunity to compare against an existing lock-free unbalanced search tree [25], taken from SynchroBench [14]. Note that this algorithm leaks memory.

We discovered two sources of sensitivity when running the experiments. First, there is a relationship between the number of threads and the optimal transaction window size (variable W in Listing 5). We determined the best window size for each thread count and data structure, and used these values. Second, the choice of memory allocator had a significant impact on scalability. This is a known issue with TM [2]. We performed each experiment with three allocators: the Linux system allocator, Hoard [4] and jemalloc [12]. In our charts, we report performance for whatever allocator was most stable: Hoard for the lists, jemalloc for the trees. We also observed significant improvements for all implementations when memory allocation and reclamation was performed outside of transactions. This suggests TM-aware allocators as a future research topic.

5.1 Linked Lists

Figure 2 presents a singly linked list benchmark. In each experiment, we pre-populate the list to a 50% filled state, and then perform 1M operations per thread. We vary the key range (6-bit or 10-bit) and operation mix (0, 33, or 80% lookups, with the remaining operations split evenly among inserts and removes). In the 6-bit experiments, we omit results for the lock-free implementations: hazard pointers (LFHP) perform the worst, and the lock-free list without any memory reclamation (LFLeak) performs best, but neither scales.

With small key ranges, transactions cannot scale: any list modification operation is likely to access a location that has recently been read by a concurrent transaction. However, hand-over-hand transactions exceed the baseline single-transaction implementation (HTM) in most cases, especially when lookups do not dominate. The experiments also show that when transactions are small, the cost of *Revoke* is important: the implementations with $O(1)$ *Revoke* (RR-XO, RR-SO, and RR-V) perform significantly better than those with $O(T)$ overhead (RR-FA, RR-DM, RR-SA).

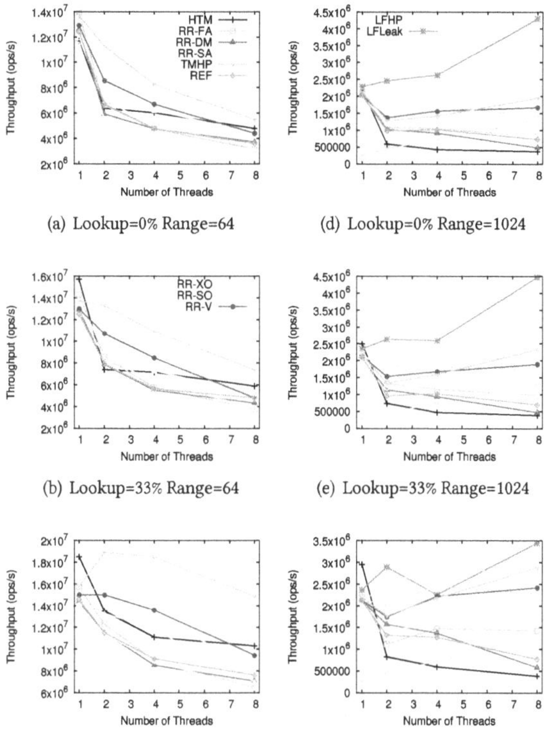

(a) Lookup=0% Range=64
(d) Lookup=0% Range=1024
(b) Lookup=33% Range=64
(e) Lookup=33% Range=1024
(c) Lookup=80% Range=64
(f) Lookup=80% Range=1024

Figure 2: Singly linked list microbenchmark

Even with `scatter` optimizations, transactional reference counting (REF) performs poorly. This is despite optimizations that put reference counts in separate cache lines, read only for the first and last node of each transaction. Additionally, for small lists we can quantify the cost of precise reclamation by contrasting performance with transactional hazard pointers (TMHP). By deferring reclamation and performing reclamation in batches, reclamation exhibits more locality with allocator metadata, and hence has lower latency. Furthermore, since TMHP does not write to shared reservation metadata, it scales better for small key ranges.

With 10-bit key ranges, the bottlenecks in many of our reservation-based algorithms decrease. *Revoke* represents a smaller fraction of total execution time, and the overall performance of each reservation implementation becomes a function of the propensity for *Reserve* and *Release* to cause conflicts: RR-DM performs worst, since threads must insert and remove their nodes from doubly linked lists, and RR-SA performance varies between RR-DM and RR-FA, depending on the value of A (in the charts, $A = 8$).

For high lookup ratios, the relaxed implementations perform best. They avoid the per-access overheads of the leaky list, and their costs relative to transactional hazard pointers are amortized over a longer transaction execution. Interestingly, this workload experiences the longest reclamation delays for the hazard pointer and epoch-based reclamation strategies. Revocable reservations eliminate all reclamation delay while delivering good performance.

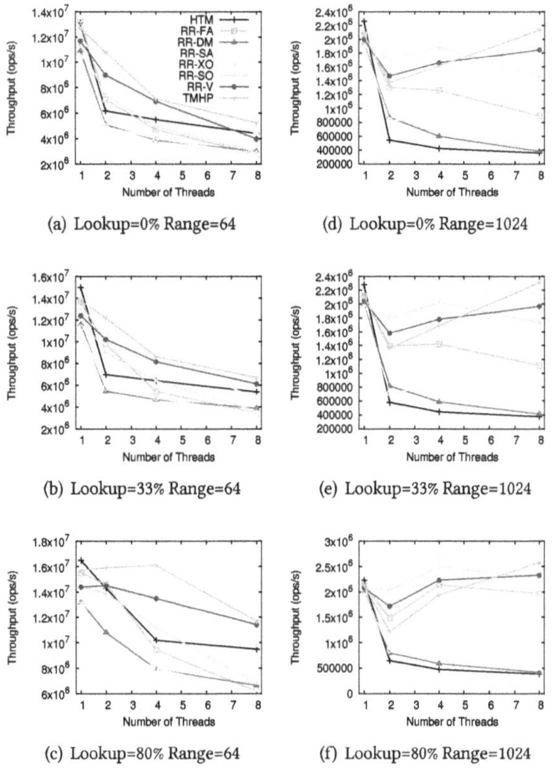

(a) Lookup=0% Range=64 (d) Lookup=0% Range=1024

(b) Lookup=33% Range=64 (e) Lookup=33% Range=1024

(c) Lookup=80% Range=64 (f) Lookup=80% Range=1024

Figure 3: Doubly linked list microbenchmark

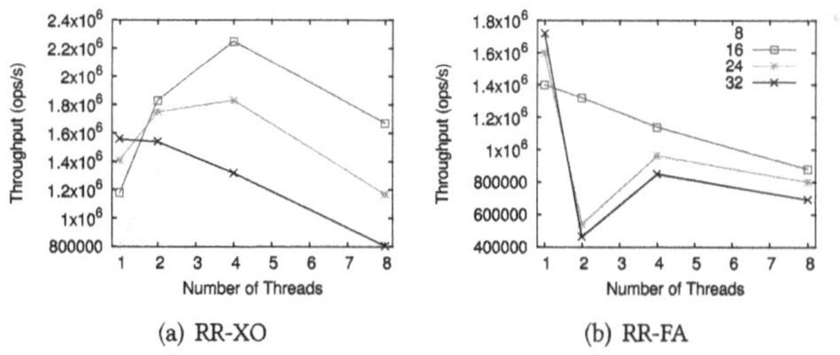

(a) RR-XO (b) RR-FA

Figure 4: Impact of window size

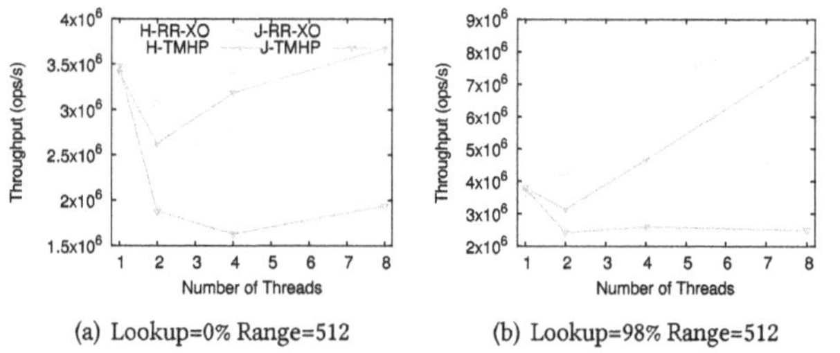

(a) Lookup=0% Range=512 (b) Lookup=98% Range=512

Figure 5: Impact of allocator

Figure 3 presents results for the doubly linked list. We no longer report reference counting, since it performs poorly, and we do not report lock-free doubly linked list performance: the only known algorithms make use of simulated multi-word compare-and-swap, and perform significantly worse than the lock-free singly linked list. The main difference between the two list algorithms is that *Remove* operations can unlink in a separate transaction from the one that finds the target node. This is beneficial for scaling, since the writing transaction is smaller. It also reduces conflicts in the reservation mechanism: if a call to *Revoke* aborts due to conflicts with a concurrent *Reserve*, the enclosing transaction retries immediately, without performing a traversal.

Overall, the doubly linked list trends are similar to the singly linked list. We observe a slightly smaller gap between the reservation mechanisms and TMHP, suggesting that the separate unlink-and-revoke transaction reduces conflicts and contention within the reservation mechanism. The remaining differences stem from TMHP's ability to batch its deferred reclamation.

5.2 Window Size

Figure 4 shows the impact of window size on our algorithms. We highlight RR-FA and RR-XO, which are representative of the strict and relaxed techniques. The experiments use 10-bit keys and a 33% lookup ratio. On the one hand, smaller windows are less likely to result in transactional conflicts. On the other, smaller windows increase latency, since there are overheads at each transaction boundary. In addition, for RR-XO, scattering the initial window size is an important optimization, since threads will otherwise conflict when reserving nodes.

At one thread, there are no conflicts, and all transactions fit within the hardware capacity, even with a window size of 32. The advantage of a large window diminishes rapidly, especially in RR-FA, where revocation is more likely to cause false conflicts with calls to *Reserve* and *Release*. Since the likelihood of conflicts increases with the thread count, higher counts favor smaller windows. In addition, at 8 threads, each hardware transaction's capacity is effectively halved, since our CPU has four two-way threaded cores. Up to 4 threads, a window size of 16 is best. At 8 threads, the balance tips in favor of a window size of 8.

This experiment suggests future work in dynamic tuning of the window size. Doing so will entail hand-crafting the transactions, instead of using GCC TM support: GCC TM does not expose the fact of an abort, or its cause, to the programmer. Without that information, it is not possible to implement a data structure-specific tuning mechanism.

5.3 The Impact of Allocator Algorithm

To illustrate the impact of the memory allocator on performance, Figure 5 contrasts the performance of transactional hazard pointers (TMHP) with the RR-XO algorithm for a doubly linked list. We conduct two experiments, with 0% and 98% lookup ratios, on a list holding 9-bit keys. Curves prefixed with "J-" use jemalloc, and curves prefixed with "H-" use Hoard.

This case is the most extreme that we observed in all of our experiments: TMHP exposes a pathological behavior in jemalloc,

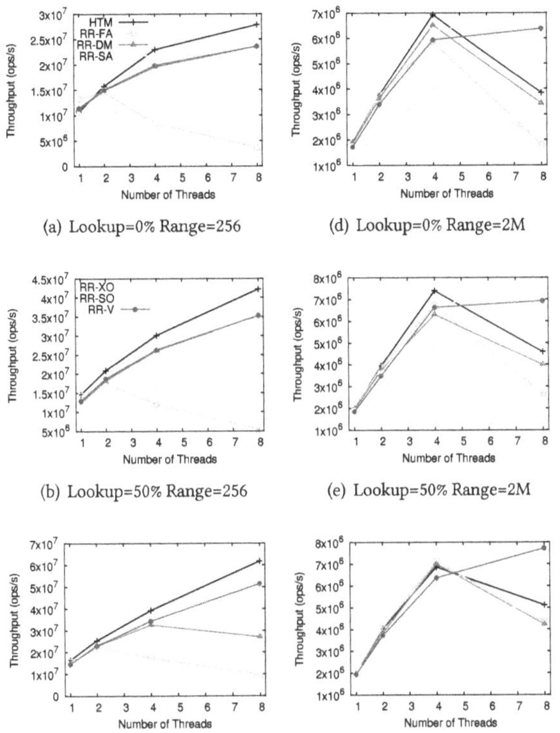

(a) Lookup=0% Range=256 (d) Lookup=0% Range=2M

(b) Lookup=50% Range=256 (e) Lookup=50% Range=2M

(c) Lookup=80% Range=256 (f) Lookup=80% Range=2M

Figure 6: Internal binary search tree microbenchmark

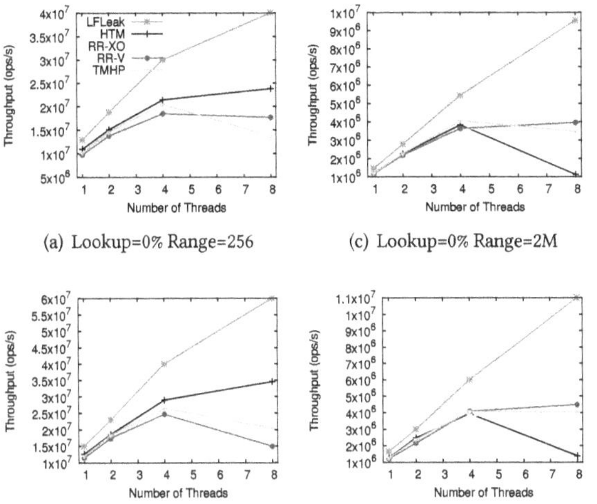

(a) Lookup=0% Range=256 (c) Lookup=0% Range=2M

(b) Lookup=50% Range=256 (d) Lookup=50% Range=2M

Figure 7: External binary search tree microbenchmark

resulting in poor scalability. This is especially peculiar at the 98% lookup ratio, where memory allocation and deallocation are rare. The impact of the allocator was roughly the same for our six implementations of revocable reservations on the doubly linked list.

5.4 Unbalanced Search Trees

We now turn our attention to binary search trees. When a tree has logarithmic depth, performing operations within a single transaction should deliver good performance: even with 2M entries in the tree, the average traversal should only touch about 22 nodes, and should fit in the hardware cache. Thus the potential for reservations to improve performance is diminished. However, since the trees are not balanced, occasional large traversals are possible. Without hand-over-hand transactions, these traversals are likely to exceed cache size, and cause program-wide serialization of transactions.

Figure 6 presents an internal tree microbenchmark, which has mixed (0, 50, or 80%) lookups. We now consider 8-bit and 21-bit keys. In each experiment, the data structure is pre-populated with random keys to reach a 50% fill rate. We are not aware of internal trees that use hazard pointers, and the lock-free tree in SynchroBench is an external tree, so we can only compare our six algorithms against an algorithm where each data structure operation is a single transaction (HTM).

In the small (8-bit) key range experiment, our best implementations use a large window at low thread counts, and the entire operation fits in a single transaction. Thus differences relative to the HTM curve at one thread indicate the cost of reservations, and differences at higher thread counts reveal bottlenecks or contention due to the reservation mechanism. As in the list curves, we see that the relaxed implementations RR-XO and RR-V offer the best performance: all overheads are constant, and threads are unlikely to reserve the same nodes.

For the large key range experiment, there is an inflection point after 4 threads, due to hardware multithreading. The HTM algorithm exceeds the cache, and serializes. In contrast, reservation-based algorithms can use a smaller window size and complete. However, only RR-XO and RR-V scale well. The cause of poor performance in the other algorithms is the overhead of calling *Revoke* for multiple references. Recall that in the tree, a removal must revoke reservations on the path between the found node and the node whose value will be swapped. In RR-SA and RR-SO, each call to *Revoke* visits A locations ($A = 8$). In RR-DM, k *Revoke* operations result in $O(k)$ unique accesses.

Lastly, Figure 7 presents the performance of an external binary search tree that uses revocable reservations. We also include results for a nonblocking external tree [25] that leaks memory (LFLeak), and a tree that uses hand-over-hand transactions and hazard pointers (TMHP).

With no memory reclamation overheads, no overheads on transaction boundaries, and a highly optimized lock-free implementation, LFLeak performs significantly better at all thread levels, and scales linearly. The difference between LFLeak and the other algorithms makes it difficult to observe their performance, so we omitted the weaker-performing reservation algorithms. The best reservation algorithms, RR-XO and RR-V, exhibit the same relationship to HTM as in the internal tree experiments. In addition, we see that the performance of TMHP is almost indistinguishable from these algorithms. In the absence of multiple calls to *Revoke*, the other reservation algorithms performed better than in the internal tree, though still below RR-XO and RR-V.

6 CONCLUSIONS AND FUTURE WORK

This paper introduces revocable reservations, which allow concurrent data structure designers to make use of hand-over-hand transactions and still immediately reclaim memory. We presented six implementations of revocable reservations, three of which allow for spurious revocation of reserved references. We also presented concurrent list and tree data structures that employ revocable reservations and hand-over-hand transactions. We found that the relaxed algorithms performed best, often enabling hand-over-hand transactions to provide better scalability and resilience than coarse-grained transactions, with minimal cost relative to hazard pointer implementations that sacrifice immediate reclamation. However, our revocable reservations did not outperform hand-crafted lock-free data structures that do not bound memory overheads.

Our experiments showed the value of adjusting the number of locations accessed per transaction. We used the thread count as a heuristic, but contention would be a better metric. We plan to explore techniques wherein language-level transactions can reliably and safely expose abort counts and abort causes to the programmer, to enable such optimization in a standards-compliant way. We also found that our concurrent data structures were sensitive to the choice of allocator, with unpredictable and occasionally pathological behaviors. These findings suggest that there is still opportunity to improve on the state of the art in memory allocation, possibly by considering TM-aware allocation strategies and algorithms.

Overall, we found the use of revocable reservations to be straightforward, and their application to lists and unbalanced trees did not require much data structure redesign. Based on this experience, we believe they will be a valuable technique for other concurrent data structures, such as balanced trees and hash tables, for which existing scalable algorithms rely on deferred memory reclamation.

Acknowledgments

We thank Dave Dice and Tim Harris for their advice and guidance during the conduct of this research. At Lehigh University, this work was supported in part by the National Science Foundation under Grant CAREER-1253362, and through financial support from Oracle. Any opinions, findings, and conclusions or recommendations expressed in this material are those of the authors and do not necessarily reflect the views of the National Science Foundation.

REFERENCES

[1] Martín Abadi, Tim Harris, and Mojtaba Mehrara. 2009. Transactional Memory with Strong Atomicity Using Off-the-Shelf Memory Protection Hardware. In *Proceedings of the 14th ACM Symposium on Principles and Practice of Parallel Programming*. Raleigh, NC.

[2] Alexandro Baldassin, Edson Borin, and Guido Araujo. 2015. Performance Implications of Dynamic Memory Allocators on Transactional Memory Systems. In *Proceedings of the 20th ACM Symposium on Principles and Practice of Parallel Programming*. San Francisco, CA.

[3] Oana Balmau, Rachid Guerraoui, Maurice Herlihy, and Igor Zablotchi. 2016. Fast and Robust Memory Reclamation for Concurrent Data Structures. In *Proceedings of the 28th ACM Symposium on Parallelism in Algorithms and Architectures*. Asilomar State Beach, CA.

[4] Emery Berger, Kathryn McKinley, Robert Blumofe, and Paul Wilson. 2000. Hoard: A Scalable Memory Allocator for Multithreaded Applications. In *Proceedings of the 9th International Conference on Architectural Support for Programming Languages and Operating Systems*. Cambridge, MA.

[5] Colin Blundell, E Christopher Lewis, and Milo M. K. Martin. 2006. Subtleties of Transactional Memory Atomicity Semantics. *Computer Architecture Letters* 5, 2 (Nov. 2006).

[6] Anastasia Braginsky, Alex Kogan, and Erez Petrank. 2013. Drop the Anchor: Lightweight Memory Management for Non-Blocking Data Structures. In *Proceedings of the 25th ACM Symposium on Parallelism in Algorithms and Architectures*. Montreal, Quebec, Canada.

[7] Trevor Brown. 2015. Reclaiming Memory for Lock-Free Data Structures: There has to be a Better Way. In *Proceedings of the 34th ACM Symposium on Principles of Distributed Computing*. Portland, OR.

[8] Nachshon Cohen and Erez Petrank. 2015. Efficient Memory Management for Lock-Free Data Structures with Optimistic Access. In *Proceedings of the 27th ACM Symposium on Parallelism in Algorithms and Architectures*. Portland, OR.

[9] Mathieu Desnoyers, Paul McKenney, Alan Stern, Michel Dagenais, and Jonathan Walpole. 2012. User-Level Implementations of Read-Copy Update. *IEEE Transactions on Parallel and Distributed Systems* 23, 2 (2012), 375–382.

[10] Dave Dice, Ori Shalev, and Nir Shavit. 2006. Transactional Locking II. In *Proceedings of the 20th International Symposium on Distributed Computing*. Stockholm, Sweden.

[11] Aleksandar Dragojevic, Maurice Herlihy, Yossi Lev, and Mark Moir. 2011. On The Power of Hardware Transactional Memory to Simplify Memory Management. In *Proceedings of the 30th ACM Symposium on Principles of Distributed Computing*. San Jose, CA.

[12] Jason Evans. 2017. jemalloc memory allocator. (2017). http://http://jemalloc.net/.

[13] Pascal Felber, Vincent Gramoli, and Rachid Guerraoui. 2017. Elastic Transactions. *J. Parallel and Distrib. Comput.* 100 (Feb. 2017), 103–127.

[14] Vincent Gramoli. 2015. More Than You Ever Wanted to Know about Synchronization. In *Proceedings of the 20th ACM Symposium on Principles and Practice of Parallel Programming*. San Francisco, CA.

[15] Rachid Guerraoui and Michal Kapalka. 2008. On the Correctness of Transactional Memory. In *Proceedings of the 13th ACM Symposium on Principles and Practice of Parallel Programming*. Salt Lake City, UT.

[16] Tim Harris. 2001. A Pragmatic Implementation of Non-Blocking Linked Lists. In *Proceedings of the 15th International Symposium on Distributed Computing*. Lisbon, Portugal.

[17] Maurice P. Herlihy, Victor Luchangco, Mark Moir, and William N. Scherer III. 2003. Software Transactional Memory for Dynamic-sized Data Structures. In *Proceedings of the 22nd ACM Symposium on Principles of Distributed Computing*. Boston, MA.

[18] Maurice P. Herlihy and J. Eliot B. Moss. 1993. Transactional Memory: Architectural Support for Lock-Free Data Structures. In *Proceedings of the 20th International Symposium on Computer Architecture*. San Diego, CA.

[19] Intel Corporation. 2012. Intel Architecture Instruction Set Extensions Programming (Chapter 8: Transactional Synchronization Extensions). (Feb. 2012).

[20] Yujie Liu, Tingzhe Zhou, and Michael Spear. 2015. Transactional Acceleration of Concurrent Data Structures. In *Proceedings of the 27th ACM Symposium on Parallelism in Algorithms and Architectures*. Portland, OR.

[21] Vijay Menon, Steven Balensiefer, Tatiana Shpeisman, Ali-Reza Adl-Tabatabai, Richard Hudson, Bratin Saha, and Adam Welc. 2008. Practical Weak-Atomicity Semantics for Java STM. In *Proceedings of the 20th ACM Symposium on Parallelism in Algorithms and Architectures*. Munich, Germany.

[22] Maged Michael. 2002. High Performance Dynamic Lock-Free Hash Tables and List-Based Sets. In *Proceedings of the 14th ACM Symposium on Parallel Algorithms and Architectures*. Winnipeg, Manitoba, Canada.

[23] Maged Michael. 2004. Hazard Pointers: Safe Memory Reclamation for Lock-Free Objects. *IEEE Transactions on Parallel and Distributed Systems* 15, 6 (June 2004), 491–504.

[24] Takuya Nakaike, Rei Odaira, Matthew Gaudet, Maged M. Michael, and Hisanobu Tomari. 2015. Quantitative Comparison of Hardware Transactional Memory for Blue Gene/Q, zEnterprise EC12, Intel Core, and POWER8. In *Proceedings of the 42nd Annual International Symposium on Computer Architecture*. Portland, OR.

[25] Aravind Natarajan and Neeraj Mittal. 2014. Fast concurrent lock-free binary search. In *Proceedings of the 19th ACM SIGPLAN symposium on Principles and practice of parallel programming*. Orlando, FL.

[26] Nir Shavit and Dan Touitou. 1995. Software Transactional Memory. In *Proceedings of the 14th ACM Symposium on Principles of Distributed Computing*. Ottawa, ON, Canada.

[27] Tatiana Shpeisman, Vijay Menon, Ali-Reza Adl-Tabatabai, Steven Balensiefer, Dan Grossman, Richard L. Hudson, Kate Moore, and Bratin Saha. 2007. Enforcing Isolation and Ordering in STM. In *Proceedings of the 2007 ACM Conference on Programming Language Design and Implementation*. San Diego, CA.

Optimal Local Buffer Management for Information Gathering with Adversarial Traffic*

Stefan Dobrev†
Inst. of Mathematics
Slovak Academy of Sciences
Bratislava, Slovakia
Stefan.Dobrev@savba.sk

Manuel Lafond‡
School of Eng. and Comp, Sci.
Université d'Ottawa
Ottawa, Canada
lafonman@iro.umontreal.ca

Lata Narayanan§
Dept. Comp. Sci. & Soft.Eng.
Concordia University
Montréal, Canada
lata@cs.concordia.ca

Jaroslav Opatrny
Dept. Comp. Sci. & Soft.Eng.
Concordia University
Montréal, Canada
opatrny@cs.concordia.ca

ABSTRACT

We consider a problem of routing on directed paths and trees to a single destination, with rate-limited, adversarial traffic. In particular, we focus on local buffer management algorithms that ensure no packet loss, while minimizing the size of the required buffers.

While a centralized algorithm for the problem that uses constant-sized buffers has been recently shown [21], there is no known *local* algorithm that achieves a sub-linear buffer size. In this paper we show tight bounds for the maximum buffer size needed by ℓ-local algorithms for information gathering on directed paths and trees, where an algorithm is called ℓ-local if the decision made by each node v depends only on the sizes of the buffers at most ℓ hops away from v.

We show three main results:

- a lower bound of $\Omega(c \log n/\ell)$ for all ℓ-local algorithms on both directed and undirected paths, where c is an upper bound on the link capacity and injection rate.
- a surprisingly simple 1-local algorithm for directed paths that uses buffers of size $O(\log n)$, when $c = 1$.
- a natural 2-local extension of this algorithm to directed trees, for $c = 1$, with the same asymptotic bound.

Our $\Omega(\log n)$ lower bound is significantly lower than the $\Omega(n)$ lower bound for greedy algorithms, and perhaps surprisingly, there is a matching upper bound. The algorithm that achieves it can be summarized in two lines: If the size of your buffer is odd, forward a message if your successor's buffer size is equal or lower. If your buffer size is even, forward a message only if your successor's buffer size is strictly lower. For trees, a simple arbitration between siblings is added.

*

†Supported by VEGA grant

‡Supported in part by NSERC grant.

§Supported in part by NSERC grant.

SPAA '17, July 24-26, 2017, Washington, DC, USA

ACM ISBN 978-1-4503-4593-4/17/07...$15.00
https://doi.org/10.1145/3087556.3087577

CCS CONCEPTS

- **Theory of computation** → *Network flows*;

KEYWORDS

Buffers, Buffer size, Routing, Trees, Directed paths, Information gathering, Local algorithms, Adversarial traffic

1 INTRODUCTION

Buffer or queue management in packet-switched networks has been an extensive subject of study for decades. Early theoretical work in the area studied *static* routing problems; the source-destination pairs corresponding to a finite set of packets is given as input to the network, and the goal is to route packets from their sources to their respective destinations, while minimizing the worst-case arrival time as well as the maximum size of buffer needed. In the case when multiple routes use the same link, a node may need to store incoming packets in a buffer, and to use a *buffer management* or *scheduling* policy that dictates which packet, if any, should be forwarded along each output port in each step. Well-known examples of scheduling policies include First-In-First-Out (FIFO), Last-in-First-Out (LIFO), Furthest-to-Go (FTG), Nearest-to-Go (NTG), etc. The policy used for buffer management has an impact on many crucial quality-of-service parameters for networks.

More recently, buffer management has been studied in the context of *dynamic* routing, where packets are continuously injected into the network. In a seminal paper, Borodin *et al* [11] introduced an *adversarial* model for traffic to analyze the *worst-case performance* of a scheduling strategy for dynamic routing. In this model, time proceeds in discrete steps. Given a network, in every step, an adversary injects packets at a certain set of nodes, and specifies, for each packet, a path to a destination, where it is *consumed.* The scheduling policy now chooses at most one packet to forward over each link of the network. Clearly, the network would be overwhelmed if the adversary generates more packets than can be sustained by the bandwidth in the network. Therefore, the adversary is assumed to be *rate-constrained.*

A key question is whether a given scheduling policy is *stable* for a given network, i.e., whether the sizes of the buffers remain bounded. One class of scheduling strategies that has been extensively studied is the so-called *greedy* or *work-conserving* policies, wherein a packet is always forwarded along an edge e if there are packets waiting to use e. It has been shown that there are work-conserving policies that are stable; however, the worst case buffer size can be polynomial in the size of the network. Even for a path, the worst-case buffer size for the greedy algorithm is $\Omega(n)$ [23].

In this paper, we study a class of routing problems called *information gathering* or *convergecast*, where the network has a special node called the *sink node*, and all packets generated in the network are destined for the sink. Such a communication pattern has been widely studied, particularly in the case of sensor networks, where sensor nodes collect data and forward it to a sink node for processing. We are interested in *ℓ-local* scheduling policies: every node must make its decision based on the contents of its own buffer, and knowledge of the buffer sizes of nodes in its ℓ-neighborhood. The goal of our work is to find upper and lower bounds on the buffer size required to achieve convergecast on trees with *no packet loss*, while using a *local* scheduling policy.

1.1 Related work

Adversarial queuing theory was introduced in [11] as a new approach to the study of queueing networks in general, and in particular, to the performance of scheduling algorithms in the context of dynamic packet routing in a network. The authors proposed a fixed-rate adversary to generate the input consisting of the nodes where new packets are injected into the network, together with specific paths to their respective destinations. The main question considered in [11] was the *stability* of a queuing discipline for a particular network, *viz.* given a network G and a scheduling policy S, is there a constant M (which can depend on the size of the network but is independent of the length of the input stream) so that for any input stream, the size of all buffers in the network remain bounded by M? Related questions of interest that were posed were the existence of universally stable policies, i.e. stable for all networks, and universally stable networks, i.e. stable for all policies of a given class. It was shown in [11] that every greedy queueing discipline is stable for rate 1 adversaries on any DAG, and that Furthest-to-Go is stable for rate 1 adversaries in a uni-directional ring. Andrews et al [5] extended the result by showing that every greedy queueing discipline is stable for rate 1 adversaries in a unidirectional ring. They also showed that certain scheduling policies, such as Farthest-to-Go (FTG), Nearest-to-Source (NTS), Longest-in-System (LIS), and Shortest-in-System (SIS) are *universally stable,* while common policies such as FIFO, LIFO, and NTG, and Farthest-from-source (FTS) are not. However, the aforementioned policies were shown to require queues and delays of size exponential in the size of the network in the worst case. Finally, they give a local distributed and randomized scheduling policy that uses polynomial size buffers in the worst case. For further studies of this problem see for example, [3, 4, 6, 8, 10, 12, 19, 20].

Aeillo et al [2] proposed the related *Competitive Network Throughput* model in which the buffer size at every node is fixed to a constant B in advance, and the goal is to minimize the number of dropped packets. They show that all greedy protocols have bounded competitive ratio on DAGs. NTG, FTS, and LIS have competitive ratios that are bounded for all networks, while FTG, NTS, SIS have an unbounded competitive ratio on cycles. For the line network, it has been shown that if $B = 1$, any online deterministic algorithm is $\Omega(n)$-competitive while for $B > 1$, a competitive ratio of $O(\sqrt{n})$ can be achieved. For further research using this framework, see for example [1, 7, 9, 13, 14, 16, 23].

For information gathering on a line, all greedy protocols are identical from the point of view of throughput or packet loss. A lower bound of $\Omega(\sqrt{n})$ on the competitive ratio of the greedy protocol was given in [2]. Rosen and Scalosub [23] give tight bounds on the competitive ratio of the greedy algorithm as a function of the injection rate of the adversary and the buffer size B. Their results imply that the greedy policy requires $\Theta(n)$-sized buffers to assure no packet loss. Further studies in lines, rings, and trees, were done by Azar and Zachut [9] and for directed grids in [14, 15].

The papers closest to our work are [21] and [17]. Patt-Shamir and Miller [21] study the same problem as this paper. They consider a more general injection model with injection rate ρ (equal to link capacities) and burstiness bounded by σ. In this model they give a centralized algorithm that achieves information gathering without packet loss using buffers of size $\sigma + 2\rho$ [1] and provide a matching lower bound. The algorithm, called *Forward-If-Empty (FIE)*, is unavoidably centralized, relying on simultaneously forwarding long *trains* of packets. They also analyze several local algorithms and for each of them show that in the worst case the buffer sizes are either unbounded, or at least $\Omega(n)$.

Kothapalli and Scheideler [17] study the competitive ratio of the buffer size achieved by algorithms for the problem of information gathering on an *undirected* path. Their adversarial model is significantly different and much stronger than ours: their adversary can not only choose the site of packet injection, but can also decide which edges are active. They show a lower bound of $\Omega(\log n)$ on buffer sizes, as well as an algorithm which asymptotically matches this bound. Their algorithm forward packets in both directions, and therefore does not work on the directed path. In a follow-up paper [18], the authors show that any deterministic algorithm requires $\Omega(n)$-sized buffers in spider-graphs in the worst case.

[1] Actually, it can be shown that the algorithm as it is formulated in [21] uses for $\rho > 1$ buffers of size $\Omega(\log \rho)$. However, it can be easily corrected by not activating a single path and taking ρ packets along it, but by having ρ activating steps, each applying to a single packet.

1.2 Our results

We start by pointing out that a slight variation of the *Local-Downhill* algorithm, shown in [21] to require buffers of size $\Omega(n)$ in paths, can in fact work with buffers of size $O(\sqrt{n})$, improving upon the other local algorithms presented there.

We then show a tight bound of $\Theta(\log n)$ on the buffer size needed by any local algorithm for information gathering on directed paths and trees. On one hand, we prove a lower bound of $\Omega(c \log n/\ell)$ (more precisely $c(1 + (\log n - 2\log \ell - 1)/2\ell)$) for the buffer sizes required by ℓ-local algorithms on directed paths of length n, where the injection rate of the adversary and the link capacity are both c. The lower bound also holds for bidirectional paths, albeit with a constant factor that is worse by a factor of 4. This is significantly tighter than the result of [17], and it applies to arbitrary constant locality ℓ.

On the other hand, for $c = 1$, we give local algorithms for directed paths and trees that require buffers of size $O(\log n)$. For the directed path, we give a very simple 1-local algorithm that achieves an upper bound of $\log n+3$, i.e. within a factor of 2 of the lower bound. In comparison with the algorithm from [17], our algorithm is simpler, achieves a better bound and works on a directed line, while the algorithm of [17] balances queues by sending packets away from the sink. However, the adversary considered in [17] is stronger, and thus the results are not comparable. For the directed tree, we give a very simple 2-local algorithm that achieves an upper bound of $O(\log n)$. This is in contrast with the lower bound of $\Omega(n)$ shown in [18] for spider graphs, emphasizing the difference between our adversary models.

To the best of our knowledge, the previous best local algorithm for convergecast in trees required buffer size $\Omega(n)$ in the worst case. While our algorithms are very simple to specify and implement, the analysis of both algorithms is based on a sophisticated book-keeping scheme.

After this paper was accepted, we were notified that the same algorithm for paths and trees was independently and concurrently proposed by Patt-Shamir and Rosenbaum [22].

2 NOTATION AND PRELIMINARIES

We consider tree networks of n nodes. The root of the tree, denoted s, is the sink node, which *consumes* packets. The nodes model hosts or routers in a communication network, and the edges represent communication links between them. Each edge can forward at most c packets along every outgoing link in every step. We consider an adversary of rate c; in every time step, the adversary injects a total of at most c packets at some nodes in the network. Our lower bounds work for any c, while our algorithms assume that $c = 1$. Since every packet is to be routed to the sink, the path taken by a packet is assumed to be the unique shortest path to the sink and does not need to be specified. As is common in the literature, we assume that time is divided into steps, each of which can be divided into 2 mini-steps. In the first mini-step, the adversary injects $\leq c$ packets into the network, and can choose the locations for the injections arbitrarily. In the second mini-step, each node uses its scheduling policy to forward at most c packets on each of its outgoing links.

For every node v, we denote by $s(v)$ its *successor* along the path to the sink. The *height* of a node v is the number of packets in its buffer, and is denoted by $h(v)$. A *configuration* C specifies the state of the network at the beginning of a given step. For our purposes, a configuration is specified by the heights of all nodes in the network. We denote the height of a node x in configuration C by $h_C(x)$. We assume that $h_C(s)$ is always 0. Let C be a configuration at the start of a step, and C' be the configuration at the start of the following step. We use shorthands $h(x)$ and $h'(x)$ for $h_C(x)$ and $h_{C'}(x)$, respectively. Throughout the paper, we denote by t the node into which the adversary injected a packet.

3 LOWER BOUNDS

In this section, we show lower bounds on the buffer size of ℓ-local algorithms for information gathering on paths; i.e. a node sees the buffer states of all other nodes up to hop distance ℓ, but not more.

THEOREM 3.1. *Any ℓ-local algorithm for information gathering on a directed path with link capacities c requires buffers of size $\Omega(c \log n/\ell)$.*

PROOF. Let n_0 be the largest number of form $\ell 2^i$ that is smaller than n. The adversary works in stages. At the beginning of stage i, at time t_i, it assumes that there is a contiguous block B_i of nodes of size $K_i = n_0/2^i$ such that the average message density in B_i is at least $H_i = c(1+i/2\ell)$, i.e. the total number of messages M_i in the block B_i is at least $K_i H_i$. We show that as long as $K_i \geq 2\ell$, in $x_i = K_i/2\ell$ steps, the adversary is able to construct a block B_{i+1} of size K_{i+1} and average density H_{i+1}. This implies a lower bound of $\lceil H_{i'} \rceil$, where $i' = \log(n_0/2\ell)$ is the number of stages.

We start by showing that the assumption holds for stage $i = 0$. In each of the first n_0 steps, the adversary injects c messages at the leftmost node of the path. Set the initial block B_0 to be the leftmost n_0 nodes; i.e. $K_0 = n_0$ and $t_0 = n_0$. This yields $H_0 = c$, as none of the messages had time to travel outside block B_0.

Consider now the inductive step i.e. assume the inductive hypothesis holds for stage i. First, consider a scenario in which the adversary injects c messages at the rightmost node of B_i for $x_i = K_i/2\ell$ steps starting at time step $t_i + 1$. As the number of injected messages equals the available outflow from B_i, the number of messages in B_i cannot decrease.

Let M_r and M_l be the number of messages in the right and left half of B_i, respectively, at time $t_{i+1} = t_i + x_i$. By the inductive assumption it holds $M_l + M_r \geq K_i H_i$. If $M_r \geq H_{i+1}K_{i+1} = (H_i + c/2\ell)K_i/2 = H_i K_i/2 + cK_i/4\ell = H_i K_i + cx_i/2$, then the right half of K_i satisfies the condition for stage $i+1$ at time t_{i+1} and we are done. Otherwise, we have $M_l = H_i K_i - M_r \geq H_i K_i/2 - cx_i/2$.

Consider now an alternative scenario, in which the adversary instead injects messages into the leftmost node of B_i. As x_i is chosen in such a way that the information from the

boundary of B_i is not able to reach the middle of B_i in time t_{i+1}, the flow of messages through the middle link is the same in both scenarios. Hence, the number of messages in the left half of B_i is now $M_l + cx_i \geq H_iK_i/2 - cx_i/2 + cx_i = H_{i+1}K_{i+1} + cx_i/2 = H_{i+1}K_{i+1}$.
Therefore, the adversary can always select a scenario in which the assumption for level $i+1$ are satisfied. This argument holds as long as $x_i \geq 1$, i.e. $K_i \geq 2l$. The number of stages is $\log(n_0/2\ell) = \lfloor \log(n/2\ell^2) \rfloor$, resulting in maximal buffer size of at least $c(1 + (\log n - 2\log \ell - 1)/2\ell) \in \Omega(c \log n/\ell)$ □

COROLLARY 3.2. *If the insertion model allows for insertion of c messages with additional burstiness of δ [21], then then the adversary can force buffers of size* $c(1 + (\log n - 2\log \ell - 1)/2\ell) + \delta \in \Omega(c\log n/\ell + \delta)$.

PROOF. The adversary follows the same approach, and in the final stage adds an insertion burst of additional δ messages. □

A natural question is whether giving the algorithm the power to forward messages in both directions might help it to overcome the $\Omega(\log n)$ barrier. We answer this question in the negative and show below that using bidirectional links only reduces the constant factor in the lower bound:

THEOREM 3.3. *Any ℓ-local algorithm for information gathering on an undirected path with link capacities c requires buffers of size $\Omega(c\log n/\ell)$.*

PROOF. Omitted due to lack of space. □

4 1-LOCAL ALGORITHM FOR PATHS

In this section, we give an optimal 1-local algorithm for buffer management that achieves information gathering on a directed path using $\Theta(\log n)$ buffer size, for injection rate and link capacity $c = 1$. Recall that the local algorithms discussed in [21] have either unbounded buffer size (e.g., *FIE*) or use buffers of size $\Omega(n)$ (*Downhill*, *Greedy*). In fact, a simple modification of *Downhill* can be shown to achieve significant improvement to $O(\sqrt{n})$:

THEOREM 4.1. *Consider the local algorithm* Downhill-or-Flat *which forwards a packet whenever the buffer of its successor contains equal or smaller number of packets than its own buffer. Algorithm* Downhill-or-Flat *uses buffers of size* $\Theta(\sqrt{n})$.

PROOF. Omitted. □

Looking at the lower-bound examples given by Miller and Pat-Shamir for various local algorithms, we notice that:

- when the adversary injects at the left, the algorithm should efficiently (at throughput 1) forward messages to the right, otherwise the messages pile up on the left (*FIE* and *Downhill* fail in this). In particular, this suggests forwarding messages to the right if the buffer heights are equal.
- when the adversary injects at the right, the messages should not keep arriving from the left, otherwise they pile up on the right (*Greedy* fails in this, but also *Downhill-or-Flat*).

These two requirements seem contradictory, with no apparent way to satisfy them both. The main idea of our algorithm is to satisfy the first requirement for messages on odd heights, and the second one on even heights. If the adversary starts injecting at the right, the packets start to pile up to the next height, switching to the "stopped" behaviour and spreading the piling up leftwards instead of up. If the adversary starts injecting on the left into stopped even-height nodes, the height raises to even and the packets start efficiently flowing to the right. In this way, the algorithm automatically adapts to the adversary's behaviour. Before having a closer look at

Algorithm 1: Algorithm Odd-Even executed by node v

```
1 if If h(v) is odd then
2 |  forward a packet to your successor s(v) iff
  |  h(s(v)) ≤ h(v)
3 else
4 |  forward a packet to your successor s(v) iff
  |  h(s(v)) < h(v)
5 end
```

the behaviour of Algorithm Odd-Even, let us introduce some notation. Let us call a node an *up* node if its height went up, and a *down* node if its height went down, i.e. $h(x) < h'(x)$ for *up* node x and $h(x) > h'(x)$ when x is a *down* node; the nodes of unchanged height are *steady*. Note that as the link capacity is 1, the height of a *down* node is always reduced by 1, while an *up* node can have its height raised by 1 or by 2 (if it received from its predecessor and from the adversary, but did not send – at any round there can be at most one such node, called 2*up*). There is a special type of *up* node: the node that went up from 0 to 1, while all the nodes in front of it are of height 0. We will call it a *leading-zero* node. Note that there might not be an *leading-zero* node in the network.

Consider first a round in which the adversary did not inject any message. In such case, *up* and *down* nodes must alternate in the sense that the first node in any chain of sending nodes is always *down*, and the first node following this chain is always The injection of a message by an adversary merely raises the height of the injected node by one, e.g. making an *up* node out of a *steady* one, or a 2*up* node out of an *up* one.

4.1 Balanced Matchings

In order to show that the heights of nodes do not go up too much, if the height of a node x goes up, we would like to "charge" that increase to another node y whose height went down in the same round. Intuitively speaking, this is as if y *gave* one if its packets to x.

We say that a non-steady node x is a *neighbour* of a non-steady node y iff there are only *steady* nodes between them.

Definition 4.2. A set P of node pairs is a *balanced matching* for a configuration C' iff

- every *up* node is paired with a neighbouring *down* node, except possibly for the *leading-zero* node
- every *down* node is paired with a neighbouring *up* or $2up$ node, except possibly the rightmost *down* node
- the $2up$ node, if any, is paired with its two neighbouring *down* nodes
- no *steady* node is paired with another node

These possible pairs (and one triple) will be called *down-up*, *up-down* and *down-2up-down* intervals, based on the type of nodes when traversing from the left. In what follows, the *down-2up-down* interval will implicitly be treated as a *down-up* interval followed by an *up-down* interval.

Algorithm 2: Creating a Balanced Matching

```
Set X to be the set of non-steady nodes of C', with the
  2up node (if any) treated as two consecutive up nodes.
while X contains at least two nodes do
  | processing from the left, let x and y be the first two
  | non-steady nodes in X.
  | pair x with y and remove them from X
end
```

CLAIM 1. *At most one non-steady node remains unmatched after executing Algorithm 2, and it is either the rightmost* down *node, or the* leading-zero.

PROOF. First, note that Algorithm 2 fails to make *up-down* or *down-up* pairs only if there are three consecutive *down* or *up* nodes. However, this never happens: If there is no injection, the *down* and *up* nodes alternate. If there is an injection at node t, it can either make a *steady* node out of a *down* node, make an *up* node out of a *steady* node or make a $2up$ node out of an *up* node. In any case, as before the injection the *up* and *down* nodes alternated, at most two consecutive *up* nodes are created and there are no two consecutive *down* nodes.

As each iteration of the while loop removes two non-steady nodes, only the rightmost non-steady node remains unmatched, and only in case the number of non-steady nodes was even (counting the $2up$ node as 2 and the *down*-and-injected node as 0). Hence, it remains to be shown that if the remaining node is an *up* node, it must be a *leading-zero*. If there is *leading-zero*, by its definition it is the rightmost *up* node and we are done. Consider the chain of sending nodes ending in the sink. If there is no *leading-zero* node, the neighbour of the sink must be of non-zero height and hence this chain is non-empty. If there is no injection into this chain, the first node of this chain must go down and being the rightmost non-steady node, the lemma holds.

Finally, if there is injection into this chain, as the *down* and *up* nodes alternate for non-injection case, before the injection the number of non-steady nodes was odd (starting with *down* and finishing with *down*). The injection either creates a rightmost *up* node (if inserted inside the chain), which will pair with the *down* node at the beginning of the chain, or it transforms the rightmost *down* node into a *steady* one. In either case, no unpaired non-steady node remains. □

LEMMA 4.3. *Algorithm 2 creates a balanced matching.*

PROOF. Consider the processing of X in the while loop. As the *up* and *down* nodes alternate, starting with a *down* node, *down-up* intervals are created before encountering the injected node. If an injection creates two neighboring *up* nodes, switching to *up-down* intervals starting at the injected node takes care of all the remaining non-steady nodes, with Claim 1 taking care of the last non-steady node, if there is any. Note that by construction no steady node is paired. □

The pairs of the balanced matching will be called *matching pairs.*

The adversary could conceivably create a high-height node v by first cheaply creating a lot of low-height nodes and then charging those while increasing the height of v; we prevent that be requiring $h_C(y) \geq h_C(x)$. The next lemma shows that this requirement, as well as monotonicity of the intervals between the nodes of the matching pairs, is indeed satisfied:

LEMMA 4.4. *Let (x_d, x_u) be a matching pair with x_u being the* up *node of this pair. Then $h(x_u) \leq h(x_d)$.*

Moreover, if (x_d, x_u) is a down-up *interval, then $h(z) \geq h(s(z))$ for all nodes $z \neq x_u$ between x_d and x_u, and if (x_u, x_d) is an* up-down *interval, then $h(z) \leq h(s(z))$ for all nodes $z \neq x_d$ between x_u and x_d.*

PROOF. Let us first consider the case of (x_d, x_u) being a *down-up* interval, i.e. x_d is behind x_u. As x_d went down, $x_d \neq t$ and it sent a message to $s(x_d)$), i.e. $h(x_d) \geq h(s(x_d))$. As none of the nodes between x_d and x_u changed their height, each one of them must have received and sent a message[2]. Combining with the fact that in any chain of sending nodes, the node heights are non-increasing yields the lemma.

If (x_u, x_d) is an *up-down* interval, then x_d has sent to $s(x_d)$, but received nothing from its predecessor $pr(x_d)$. If none of the nodes from x_u to $pr(x_d)$ has sent a message, then their heights form a non-decreasing sequence and the lemma holds. However, there cannot be a node x' between x_u and x_d that has sent a message – the first non-steady successor of such a node would be an *up* node, violating the definition of *up-down* interval. □

4.2 Attachment Scheme

If $h(x_d) > h(x_u)$, the adversary pays for raising the height of x_u by lowering the height of a costlier, higher height node, a net loss. However, the case of $h(x_d) = h(x_u)$ allows the adversary to raise a node height without losing the effort invested into another node of higher height. The core of the proof is to show that in Algorithm Odd-Even such a situation cannot occur too often. To accomplish this, when x_u charges to x_d and $h(x_d) = h(x_u)$, we take note that x_d "gave" x_u a

[2]Observe that if a node sends a message and receives injection, it is not included in the balanced matching

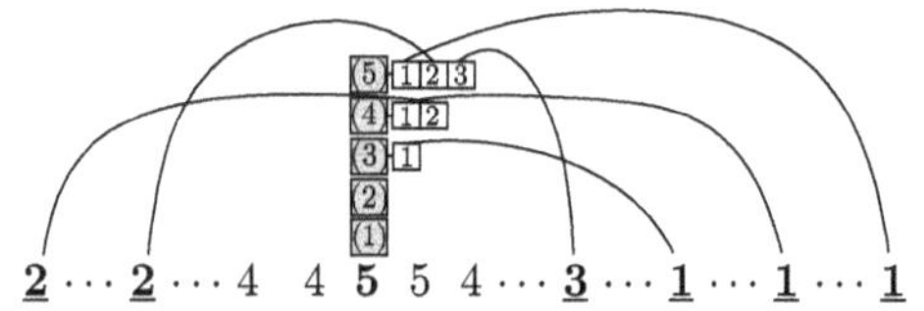

Figure 1: An illustration of a node x of height 5 and all the nodes attached to its packet slots. Only the node heights are shown, and the nodes are depicted from left to right in decreasing order of distance from the sink.The gray boxes correspond to the packets of x, each accompanied with its available slots and attachments. Residues attached to a packet of x appear in boldface and underlined.

packet by *attaching* x_d with the new $h'(x_u)$-th packet of x_u. This attachment will remain until either x_d changes height or until x_u loses its $h'(x_u)$-th packet. In this way, creating a node x of height $h+1$ uses up two nodes of height h: both x itself (as it is no more of height h), but also a node y that attached to x. Taken to its conclusion, this means that creating a node of height h incurs cost exponential in h – provided the attached node is not reused for another *up* node. The key observation (and design goal) is that once a node y gives away a packet and becomes attached, it cannot be charged again by another *up* node as long as this attachment persists. Such a y then becomes useless to the adversary, and we will thus call y a *residue* - it is a leftover that resulted from the creation of a node of higher height.

In order to maintain proper bookkeeping, some attachments may need to be "passed" to other nodes. To keep track of the fact that y virtually gives a packet to x, we create a pointer from x to y. However, when y virtually received this packet from some other node z in a previous step, it would have had a pointer to z; we retain this history by directly creating a pointer from x to z. Intuitively, the greater the height of a node, the more pointers it will have. We formalize all this in the notion of an *attachment scheme* defined below. For $i \geq 3$, a packet $x[i]$ has $i-2$ available *slots* denoted $x[i,1], x[i,2], \ldots, x[i,i-2]$. Note that every slot $x[i,j]$ satisfies $1 \leq j \leq h(x)-2$.

Definition 4.5. An *attachment scheme* A for a configuration C is a set of ordered pairs of the form $(x[i,j], y)$, where $x[i,j]$ is a packet slot and y is a node distinct from x, such that

(1) $j = h(y)$;
(2) each packet slot or node is attached to exactly one element, i.e. for any $(x'[i',j'],y') \in A$ distinct from $(x[i,j],y)$, we have $x[i,j] \neq x'[i',j']$ and $y \neq y'$;

If $(x[i,j],y) \in A$, we say that slot $x[i,j]$ is attached to node y, and similarly that node y is attached to slot $x[i,j]$ (we may also say $x[i,j]$ is the *guardian* of a *residue* y, as will be explained later). We may sometimes write (x,y) instead of $(x[i,j],y)$ when the values of i,j are irrelevant. The node y attached to $x[i,j]$ is denoted $att_A(x[i,j])$.

Figure 1 illustrates a node x with all its available packet slots attached to a node of appropriate height.

LEMMA 4.6. *Let A be an attachment scheme for a configuration C. Let $m := \max_{x\in V} h_C(x)$, and assume $m \geq 3$. Then there are at least $2^{m-2}-1$ distinct nodes that are a residue of A.*

PROOF. For a node $x \in V$, denote by $R'(x)$ the set of residues of A that are attached to a packet slot of x, i.e. $R'(x) = \bigcup_{3\leq i\leq h(x)} \bigcup_{1\leq j\leq i-2} \{att_A(x[i,j])\}$. Define $R(x)$ inductively as follows: if $h(x) \leq 3$, then $R(x) = R'(x)$, and if $h(x) \geq 4$, then $R(x) = R'(x) \cup \bigcup_{x'\in R'(x)} R(x')$. That is, $R(x)$ is the set of residue nodes that are attached to x directly or indirectly. Observe that for any two x and x' with $h(x) = h(x')$, we have $|R(x)| = |R(x')|$.

For an integer p, denote by $r(p)$ the cardinality of $R(x)$ for a node x such that $h(x) = p$. We show that $r(p) = 2^{p-2}-1$. We have $r(1) = r(2) = 0$, since nodes of height 1 or 2 have no available slots for residues. For $p \geq 3$, a node x with $h(x) = p$ has a packet $x[p]$ with each slot $x[p,1], \ldots, x[p,p-2]$ attached to a residue, and there are $p-2$ of those. Also, for each $1 \leq i \leq p-2$, the residue $att_A(x[p,i])$ implies the existence of $r(i)$ other residue nodes. Moreover, the packet $x[p-1]$ implies the existence of $r(p-1)$ residue nodes. Note that by Rule 2 of attachment schemes, no residue is double-counted. Thus, we get $r(p) = p-2+\sum_{i=1}^{p-1} r(i) = p-2+r(p-1)+\sum_{i=1}^{p-2} r(i) = p-2+r(p-1)+r(p-1)-(p-3) = 1+2r(p-1) = 2^{p-2}-1$, when $r(2) = 0$ (the third equality is due to $r(p-1) = p-3+\sum_{i=1}^{p-2} r(i)$). The Lemma follows by setting $p = m$. □

LEMMA 4.7. *Let A be an attachment scheme for a configuration C. Then $\max_{x\in V} h_C(x) \leq \log n + 3$.*

PROOF. By Lemma 4.6, if $m := \max_{x\in V} h_C(x)$, then there are at least $2^{m-2}-1$ nodes that are a residue. Since all these nodes are distinct, we have $2^{m-2}-1 \leq n$, which yields $m \leq \log n + 3$. □

4.3 Maintaining an Attachment Scheme

Due to lack of space, proofs of lemmas are omitted in this subsection.

If for every configuration C, there exists an attachment scheme, it follows from Lemma 4.7 that the height of every node in the path is always upper bounded by $\log n + 3$. We now proceed to show by induction that every configuration indeed admits an attachment scheme. The initial configuration consists of height 0 (i.e. slot-free) nodes, hence it vacuously admits an attachment scheme. If a configuration C admits an attachment scheme, then we will show that the next configuration C' also admits one. The transition from C to C' is done by handling separately and independently the matching pairs of C': We present an algorithm which processes a matching pair $\{x_u, x_d\}$ by changing the heights of its nodes to their new values in C' and rearranging some attachments coincident with x_u or x_d so that an attachment scheme is maintained.

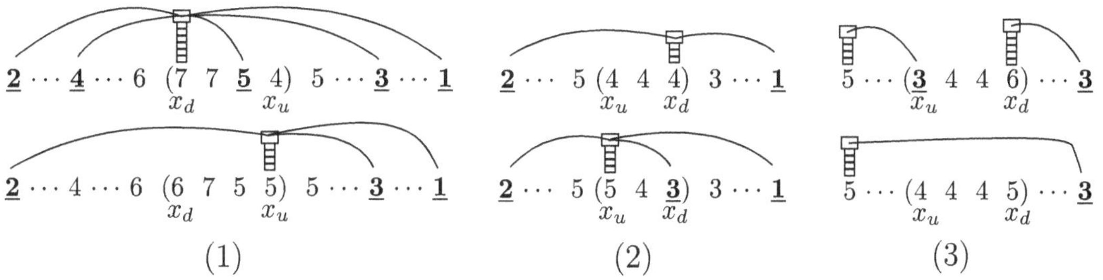

Figure 2: Three examples of applying Algorithm 4. Top: the state before, bottom: the state after. The parentheses surround the processed matching pair. We only represent the packets, attachments and residues of interest. (1) A down-up interval illustrating how x_d passes all possible attachments to x_u (line 7 of Algorithm 4). Note that the residues of value 4 and 5 gets detached in $C_{P'}$. (2) An up-down interval in which $h_d = h_u = 4$. Here x_d passes all its attachments, in addition to becoming a residue attached to x_u (line 9). (3) An up-down interval in which x_u was a residue attached to some slot $z[i, h_u]$ (here z is the node of value 5), and $x_d[h_d, h_u]$ is attached to a node y (y is the node of value 3). After processing, y is attached to $z[i, h_u]$ (line 18).

In order to carry out the inductive step, we need to strengthen the definition of an attachment scheme:

Definition 4.8. An attachment scheme A is *valid*, if in addition to Rules 1 and 2, the following rules are satisfied for each residue y and its guardian x of A:

(3) if $h(y)$ is even, then x is in front of y;
(4) if $h(y)$ is odd, then x is behind y;
(5) for every node z on the path between x and y, $h(z) \geq h(y)$.

Let P be a subset of matching pairs of a balanced matching of C'. We say that C_P is an *intermediate configuration* for P iff $\forall x, x \in P : h_{C_P}(x) = h(x)$, while $\forall x, x \notin P : h_{C_P}(X) = h'(x)$.

We will need the following three technical lemmas:

LEMMA 4.9. *If (x_u, x_d) is a matching pair with $h(x_u) = h(x_d) = h$ then x_u is not a residue.*

The following lemma is crucial in proving that the residues are not shared:

LEMMA 4.10. *Let y be a residue of A. Then y is not a* down *node.*

LEMMA 4.11. *The following facts hold when Algorithm 4 processes a matching pair (x_d, x_u):*

(1) *after being processed, no* up *node remains a residue of another node*
(2) *no existing slot has become empty*
(3) *no new empty slot has been created*
(4) *whenever an attachment to residue y is transferred*
   a) *from x_d to x_u on line 7*
   b) *from z to x_d on line 15*
   c) *from x_d to z on line 18*
   $h'(w) \geq h'(y)$ holds for all nodes between the nodes transferring the attachment (endpoints included)
(5) *the relative order (in front of, or behind) between residues and their guardians never changes*

Algorithm 3: Processing a balanced matching.

Input : Configurations C and C' and an attachment scheme A for C
Output: An attachment scheme A' for C'', where C'' differs from C' (and equals C) only for the possible *down-2up-down* triple, the *leading-zero* and the unmatched rightmost *down* node

```
Let M be a balanced matching for C'
Set P := M and A' := A
while P ≠ ∅ do
    Let (x_d, x_u) be a matching pair from P
    Set A' := processPair(C_P, A', x_d, x_u);
    Set P := P \ {x_d, x_u};
end
Return (A')
```

This allows us to prove that all the rules of the attachment scheme are satisfied:

LEMMA 4.12. *Processing one pair by Algorithm 4 maintains all the rules of the attachment scheme.*

We can now prove the upper bound on buffer sizes.

THEOREM 4.13. *Algorithm Odd-Even uses buffers of size at most* $\log n + 3$.

PROOF. It follows from Lemma 4.12 that processing all pairs of a balanced matching by Algorithm 4 (including the two pairs concerning *down-2up-down* interval) maintains a valid attachment scheme. What remains to be dealt with is the right-most *down* node and the *leading-zero* node. The last one is not a problem, as it was of height 0 and hence not a residue, nor does it have a packet slot, as it is of height 1. The right-most *down* node could have only released some attachments, and did not gain any, so it does not need any sophisticated (creation/passing) attachment processing (by Lemma 4.10 it was not a residue, so no empty slots were created either).

Algorithm 4: Handling a matching pair.

function *processPair* (C_P, A_P, x_d, x_u);
Input : An intermediate configuration C_P, an attachment scheme A_P for C_P, and a matching pair $(x_d, x_u) \in P$ with x_d and x_u being the *up* and *down* nodes, respectively.
Output : An attachment scheme $A_{P'}$ for $C_{P'}$, where P' is obtained from P by removing (x_d, x_u).
Let $h_d := h(x_d)$ and $h_u := h(x_u)$
Let $A' := A_P$.
if *there is a slot* $x_d[i, h_u]$ *such that* $(x[i, h_u], x_u) \in A'$ *and* $i \neq h_d$ **then**
  Swap the $x_d[i, h_u]$ and $x_d[h_d, h_u]$ attachments: in A', replace $(x_d[i, h_u], x_u)$ by $(x_d[i, h_u], att_{A_P}(x_d[h_d, h_u]))$ and replace $(x_d[h_d, h_u], att_{A_P}(x_d[h_d, h_u]))$ by $(x_d[h_d, h_u], x_u)$. ; `// Here we ensure that when` x_u `gets detached, it does not leave slot` $x_d[i, h_u]$ `empty`
end
Pass all possible attachments from the $x_d[h_d]$ packet to the $x_u[h_u + 1]$ packet and remove the others, i.e. remove from A' all the attachments $\{(x_d[h_d, i], att_{A_P}(x_d[h_d, i])) : 1 \leq i \leq h_d - 2\}$ and add to A': $\{(x_u[h_u + 1, j], att_{A_P}(x_d[h_d, j])) : 1 \leq j \leq \min(h_d - 2, h_u - 1)\}$
if $h_d = h_u$ *and* $h_d \geq 2$ **then**
  Add $(x_u[h_u + 1, h_u - 1], x_d)$ to A'
end
if x_u *is a residue of* A_P **then**
  Let $z[i, h_u]$ be the packet slot attached to x_u in A'
  Remove the $(z[i, h_u], x_u)$ attachment from A'
  if $h_d = h_u + 1$ **then**
    Add to A' the attachment $(z[i, h_u], x_d)$
  else if $h_d \geq h_u + 2$ *and* $z \neq x_d$ **then**
    Let $y = att_{A'}(x_d[h_d, h_u])$
    Add to A' the attachment $(z[i, h_u], y)$
end
Return A' as $A_{P'}$

Note that handling the *down-2up-down* interval as a sequence of two intervals sharing an *up* node is perfectly fine: from the point of the right pair this looks the same as if t was of height $h(t) + 1$ and received a message from the left. Lemma 4.7 now completes the proof of the theorem. ☐

5 2-LOCAL ALGORITHM FOR TREES

Notice that in this section, due to lack of space, all proofs are omitted.

The first observation is that lookahead of 1 is not sufficient: Consider node u having $\sqrt{n}$ neighbours and the same schedule as discussed in its caption. When the packets arrive simultaneously to v's, each v_i will send a packet to u, forcing u to need buffer of size $\sqrt{n}$.

Hence, we consider a 2-local algorithm. The algorithm is a straightforward generalization of Algorithm Odd-Even:

Algorithm 5: Algorithm Tree

if *the height h of the node is odd* **then**
  forward a packet to your successor iff its height is at most h and you have the highest priority among your siblings
else
  forward a packet to your successor iff its height is less than h and you have the highest priority among your siblings`// even height` h
end

The algorithm is completed by specifying the priority scheme: A sibling with a higher height has higher priority. Among the siblings of the same maximal height, choose arbitrarily.

Let us now introduce more nomenclature. An internal node v of in-degree at least 2 will be called an *intersection*. For a fixed round, in each intersection there will be at most one incoming packet; the branch where it comes from will be called a *priority line*[3]. A non-priority line ends in a *blocked* node. Hence, the tree can be viewed as a set of lines, starting in leaves and ending in blocked nodes, with one branch, called *drain* making it all the way to the sink. One of the lines might contain the injected node – we will call it the *injected* line. All other lines are *normal*. Note that the *up* and *down* nodes on non-injected lines alternate, starting with a *down* node (exactly like in paths) and ending with a *leading-zero* or *down* node if the line is a *drain*, otherwise ending with an *up* node.

Algorithm 6: Balanced Matching on a Tree

For each line, apply the balanced matching algorithm for paths:
if *the injection was on the priority line to the sink* **then**
  we are done, nothing left to do
else
  while *there is an unmatched* up *node* x_u **do**
    Let v be first intersection in front of x_u, and let p_v be the priority line containing v.
    Let x_d be the first *down* node behind v on p_v.
    Remove the pairs (including the one containing x_d) in front of x_d on the line of x_d
    Add (x_d, x_u) to the set of matching pairs
    Process the remainder of the x_d's line using the algorithm for paths (i.e. add up-down pairs while possible)
  end
end

[3]It can happen that the intersection has no incoming packet. In such a case, we choose as the priority line, the line into which there was an injection; if no such line is behind, select arbitrarily.

The first step is a generalization of balanced matchings to trees: The matchings for each normal line translate directly (they are each just a collection of *down-up* intervals from left to right). If the injected line is also the *drain* one, this is handled as in the single line case with injection. But if the injected and *drain* lines are different, let v be the intersection on which the injected line blocks. As each normal blocked line has an equal number of *up* and *down* nodes, the injected line has an excess of one *up* node: Applying Algorithm 2 leaves it with the rightmost *up* node x unpaired. At this moment, it is impossible to carry on constructing balanced matching as a union of balanced matchings of the lines: We need to introduce *crossover pairs* containing nodes from different lines. This is what is done in the while loop: As the last non-steady node y of the priority line is *down*, we pair x with y to form a *crossover pair*. Since we have removed y from its line, we need to re-do its pairings that were in front of y, switching to *up-down* intervals. This possibly leaves another unmatched *up* node at the end, which needs to be handled in the same manner. We make these crossover pairs until we eventually reach the drain, where the *up-down* matchings do not leave an unmatched *up* node at the end. An example of applying Algorithm 6 is shown in Figure 3. Hence, a tree-version of Lemma 4.3 holds:

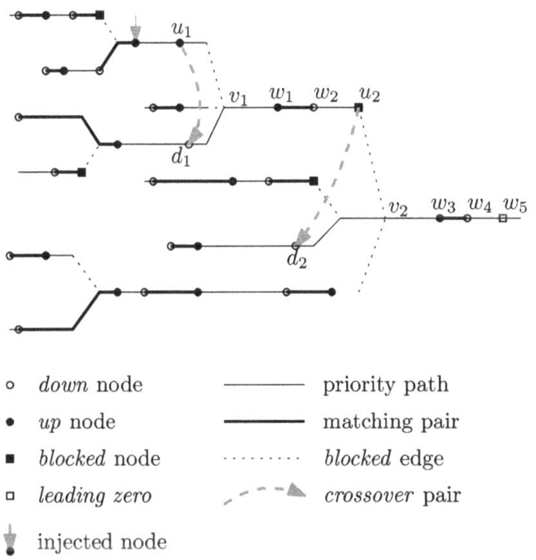

Figure 3: Constructing balanced matching on a tree. Due to adding the (u_1, d_1) matching, the matchings $(d1, w1)$ and $(w2, u2)$ were removed and replaced by $(w1, w2)$, leaving u_2 unpaired. This forced the (d_2, u_2) matching, then switching the (d_2, w_3) and (w_4, w_5) into (w_3, w_4) and leaving w_5 unpaired.

LEMMA 5.1. *Algorithm 6 creates a balanced matching.*

We will often make use of the following simple property of matching pairs.

LEMMA 5.2. *Let x_u be an* up *node lying on a priority path p that is not the drain, and let v be intersection node on which p does not have priority. Then x_u is matched with a node x_d behind v.*

In paths, the notion of *between* two nodes is straightforward. In trees, we will generalize it to fit our purpose: *between* x and y is satisfied by all nodes on the path from x to y, *except* for the node v (if any) in which this path changes direction from forward to backward. This node will be called the *tip* of the crossover pair.

Before introducing the tree-version of Lemma 4.4 we need a bit more notation: Let (x, y) be a crossover pair with tip v. $p_v(z)$ will denote the predecessor of v on the path from z to v. If clear from the context, we will omit the subscript v.

We now show a tree-version of Lemma 4.4:

LEMMA 5.3. *Let (x_d, x_u) be a matching pair with x_u being the* up *node of this pair. Then $h(x_u) \leq h(x_d)$ and $h(z) \geq h(x_u)$ for all nodes z between x_u and x_d.*

Moreover, the nodes on the path from x_d to x_u appear in non-increasing order of height, with the possible exception of the tip v between x_d and x_u.

The attachment scheme is defined analogously as for the path case. However, in order to limit technicalities, we limit Rule 2 to residues of even value. This implies that Lemmas 4.6 and 4.7 yield a $2 \log n + O(1)$ bound.

The Rules 3, 4 and 5 are replaced as follows:

Definition 5.4. For each pair (x, y) of an attachment scheme, where y is a residue and x is its guardian, the following rules must be satisfied:

(6) if $h(y)$ is even, x is not behind y;
(7) if (x, y) is not a crossover pair, then $h(z) \geq h(y)$ holds for every node z on the path between y and $p(y)$; otherwise if (x, y) is a crossover pair, $h(z) \geq h(y)$ holds for every node z on the path between y and $p(y)$, and $h(z) > h(y)$ holds for every node z on the path between x and $p(x)$.

This allows us to prove (using the same arguments; note that the proof is not valid for odd-height residues) the tree-version of Claim 4.10:

CLAIM 2. *Let x be an even-height residue of A. Then x does not go down.*

In the rest of the proof, when we discuss residues and attachments, we limit ourselves to even height residues and corresponding attachment pairs.

First, we show that Lemma 4.9 holds also for trees. As this was the only necessary ingredient for Fact 2, this implies that after running Algorithm 4 on every matching pair, the resulting attachment scheme is still full.

LEMMA 5.5. *If (x_u, x_d) is a matching pair with $h_u = h_d = h$, then x_u is not a residue.*

The proofs of Facts 1, 2 and 3 of Lemma 4.11, as well as the proofs from Lemma 4.12 that Rules 1 and 2 are satisfied are based on the behaviour of Algorithm 4, using in addition only Claim 4.10 and Lemma 4.9; using Claim 2 and Lemma 5.5 instead, the same proofs apply to trees without need for any modifications.

We prove that, after running Algorithm 4 on a single matching pair, crossover or not, Rules 6 and 7 are satisfied directly (here we do not refer to Facts 4 and 5). As before, $h(x)$ is the height of a node at the start of the round, and $h'(x)$ its height after the round.

We first establish that unmodified attachments are still valid, then proceed with the new attachments created by the algorithm.

LEMMA 5.6. *Let (x, y) be an attachment of A that has not changed after running Algorithm 4 on a matching pair. Then (x, y) still satisfies Rules 6 and 7.*

LEMMA 5.7. *Let (x_u, x_d) be a new attachment created on line 9. Then (x_u, x_d) satisfies Rules 6 and 7.*

LEMMA 5.8. *Let (x_u, y) be an attachment formed by passing y from x_d to x_u on line 7 of Algorithm 4. Then (x_u, y) satisfies Rules 6 and 7.*

LEMMA 5.9. *Let (z, x_d) be an attachment formed by swapping the residue of z from x_u to x_d on line 15 of Algorithm 4. Then (z, x_d) satisfies Rules 6 and 7.*

LEMMA 5.10. *Let (z, y) be an attachment formed on line 18 of Algorithm 4. Then (z, y) satisfies Rules 6 and 7.*

We have shown that after running Algorithm 4 on a given matching pair (x_d, x_u), all the unmodified attachments are still valid, and the newly created ones also satisfy the required rules. As before, after processing every single matching pair, we reach the final configuration along with a full attachment scheme. As the handling of the possible *leading-zero*, *down-2up-down* intervals, and unpaired rightmost *down* node is the same as for paths, this completes the proof that a full attachment scheme is maintained in trees. Combining with Lemmas 4.6 and 4.7 yields:

THEOREM 5.11. *Algorithm Tree uses buffers of size at most $O(\log n)$.*

6 CONCLUSIONS

We studied the information gathering problem in paths and trees under the assumption of adversarial traffic. Given an adversary that can inject at most c packets into the network in every step, we showed an $\Omega(\log n)$ lower bound on the buffer space needed to ensure no packet loss. For $c = 1$, we gave deterministic local algorithms that match this bound for directed paths and trees. The existence of local algorithms with $O(\log n)$ buffers for higher rate adversaries remains open. A natural question to ask is if our algorithms generalize to arbitrary routing patterns, or to DAGs. Another intriguing direction for further research is the delay characteristics of our algorithm as well as those of other algorithms proposed in the literature (for example [17]).

REFERENCES

[1] W. Aiello, Y. Mansour, S. Rajagopolan, and A. Rosén. 2005. Competitive Queue Policies for Differentiated Services. *Journal of Algorithms* 55, 2 (2005), 113–141.

[2] W. Aiello, R. Ostrovsky, E. Kushilevitz, and A. Rosén. 2003. Dynamic routing with fixed size buffers. In *Proceedings of SODA*. 771–780.

[3] C. Alvarez, M. Blesa, and M. Serna. 2004. A characterization of universal stability in the adversarial queueing model. *SIAM J. Comput.* 34, 1 (2004), 41–66.

[4] M. Andrews. 2004. Instability of FIFO in session-oriented networks. *Journal of Algorithms* 50, 2 (2004), 232–245.

[5] M. Andrews, B. Awerbuch, A. Fernández, T. Leighton, Z. Liu, and J. Kleinberg. 2001. Universal-stability Results and Performance Bounds for Greedy Contention-resolution Protocols. *J. ACM* 48, 1 (Jan. 2001), 39–69.

[6] M. Andrews, A. Fernandez, A. Goel, and L. Zhang. 2005. Source routing and scheduling in packet networks. *J. ACM* 52, 4 (2005), 582–601.

[7] S. Angelov, S. Khanna, and K. Kunal. 2009. The network as a storage device: dynamic routing with bounded buffers. *Algorithmica* 55 (2009), 71–94.

[8] E. Anshelevich, D. Kempe, and Kleinberg. J. 2008. Stability of load balancing algorithms in dynamic adversarial systems. *SIAM Journal of Computing* 37, 5 (2008), 1656–1673.

[9] Y. Azar and R. Zachut. 2005. Packet routing and information gathering in lines, rings, and trees. In *Proceedings of ESA*. 484–495.

[10] R. Bhattacharjee, A. Goel, and Z. Lotker. 2005. Instability of FIFO at arbitrarily low rates in the adversarial queueing model. *SIAM J. Comput.* 34, 2 (2005), 318–332.

[11] A. Borodin, J. Kleinberg, P. Raghavan, M. Sudan, and D. P. Williamson. 2001. Adversarial Queuing Theory. *J. ACM* 48, 1 (2001), 13–38.

[12] J. Diaz, D. Koukopoulos, S. Nikoletseas, M. Serna, P. Spirakis, and D. Thilikos. 2001. Stability and non-stability of the FIFO protocol. In *Proceedings of SPAA*. 48–52.

[13] G. Even and M. Medina. 2010. An $O(\log n)$-Competitive Online Centralized Randomized Packet-Routing Algorithm for Lines. In *Proceedings of ICALP, Part II*. 139–150.

[14] G. Even and M. Medina. 2011. Online packet routing in grids with bounded buffers. In *Proceedings of SPAA*. 215–224.

[15] G. Even and M. Medina. 2016. Online packet routing in grids with bounded buffers. *Algorithmica* (2016). https://doi.org/10.1007/s00453-016-0177-0

[16] E. Gordon and A. Rosén. 2005. Competitive Weighted Throughput Analysis of Greedy Protocols on DAGs. In *Proceedings of PODC*. 227–236.

[17] K. Kothapalli and C. Scheideler. 2003. Information gathering in adversarial systems: lines and cycles. In *Proceedings of SPAA*. 333–342.

[18] K. Kothapalli and C. Scheideler. 2006. Lower bounds for information gathering in adversarial systems. In *Proceedings of International Conference on Distributed Computing in Sensor Systems*.

[19] D. Koukopoulos, M. Mavronicolas, S. Nikoletseas, and P. Spirakis. 2002. On the stability of compositions of universally stable, greedy contention-resolution protocols. In *Proceedings of DISC*. 88–102.

[20] Z. Lotker, B. Patt-Shamir, and A. Rosén. 2004. New stability results for adversarial queueing. *SIAM J. Comput.* 33, 3 (2004), 286–303.

[21] A. Miller and B. Patt-Shamir. 2016. Buffer Size for Routing Limited-Rate Adversarial Traffic. In *Proceedings of Distributed Computing: 30th International Symposium, DISC 2016*. 328–341.

[22] B. Patt-Shamir and W. Rosenbaum. 2017. The Space Requirement of Local Forwarding on Acyclic Networks. In *Proceedings of PODC, to appear*.

[23] A. Rosén and G. Scalosub. 2007. Rate vs. Buffer Size: Greedy Information Gathering on the Line. In *Proceedings of the Nineteenth Annual ACM Symposium on Parallel Algorithms and Architectures ((SPAA))*. 305–314.

Brief Announcement: Parallel Dynamic Tree Contraction via Self-Adjusting Computation

Umut A. Acar
Carnegie Mellon University, USA
Inria, France
umut@cs.cmu.edu

Vitaly Aksenov
Inria, France
ITMO University, Russia
aksenov@rain.ifmo.ru

Sam Westrick
Carnegie Mellon University, USA
swestric@cs.cmu.edu

ABSTRACT

Dynamic algorithms are used to compute a property of some data while the data undergoes changes over time. Many dynamic algorithms have been proposed but nearly all are sequential. In this paper, we present our ongoing work on designing a parallel algorithm for the dynamic trees problem, which requires computing a property of a forest as the forest undergoes changes. Our algorithm allows insertion and/or deletion of both vertices and edges anywhere in the input and performs updates in parallel. We obtain our algorithm by applying a dynamization technique called self-adjusting computation to the classic algorithm of Miller and Reif for tree contraction.

1 INTRODUCTION

In many applications, algorithms operate on data that changes dynamically over time. For example, an algorithm may compute the heaviest subtree in an edge-weighted tree and may be required to update the result as the tree undergoes changes, e.g., as vertices or edges are inserted and/or deleted. Dynamic algorithms have been studied extensively; several papers review prior work [16, 17, 33]. Nearly all of the prior work on dynamic algorithms considers *sequential dynamic algorithms.* There is relatively little work on *parallel dynamic algorithms,* which would take advantage of parallelism when performing updates.

As an example dynamic problem, consider the classic problem of *dynamic trees.* This problem requires computing various properties of a forest of trees as edges and vertices are inserted and deleted [37]. Algorithms and data structures for dynamic trees have been studied extensively since the early '80s, including Link-Cut Trees [37, 38], Euler-Tour Trees [24, 41], Topology Trees [20], RC-Trees [3, 4], and, more recently, Top Trees [10, 40, 42]. These algorithms are work efficient: they allow the insertion/deletion of a single edge in logarithmic time (some in expectation, some amortized). Some of these algorithms have also been implemented [4, 42] and have been shown to perform well in practice. The algorithms and implementations, however, are all sequential. In prior work, Reif and Tate [35] give a parallel algorithm for dynamic trees but their algorithm is not fully dynamic: it allows changes only at the leaves of a tree and does not support deletions, leaving it to future work.

SPAA '17, July 24-26, 2017, Washington DC, USA

ACM ISBN 978-1-4503-4593-4/17/07.
https://doi.org/10.1145/3087556.3087595

We are interested in designing a parallel algorithm for the dynamic trees problem. There are at least two challenges here.

- Dynamic algorithms are traditionally designed to handle small changes to the input. Small changes, however, do not generate sufficient parallelism. Larger *batches of changes* can generate parallelism but this requires generalizing the algorithms.
- Dynamic algorithms and parallel algorithms on their own are usually quite complex to design, analyze, and implement. Since parallel dynamic algorithms combine the features of both, their implementation can become a significant hurdle.

We believe that it is possible to overcome these challenges by using a technique called *dynamization.* The basic idea is to "dynamize" a static (non-dynamic) algorithm by recording carefully chosen intermediate results computed by the static algorithm and re-using these results when the data changes as a result of dynamic updates. In sequential algoritms, dynamization has been used for a variety of problems, e.g., by Bentley and Saxe [11], Overmars [31], Mulmuley [30], and many others. We believe that parallel algorithms are particularly amenable to dynamization, because they minimize dependencies between subcomputations. In this paper, we outline a parallel algorithm for dynamic trees by dynamizing Miller and Reif's tree contraction algorithm [28, 29] by using self-adjusting computation [1, 2, 27], which, for the purposes of this paper, can be viewed a dynamization technique. The resulting dynamic parallel algorithm allows insertion and deletion of any number of vertices or edges anywhere in the input forest (as long as no cycles are created) and supports parallel updates.

2 THE ALGORITHM

Our approach is based on the technique of *self-adjusting computation* for dynamizing static algorithms. The idea behind this technique is to use a *construction* algorithm to build a *computation graph,* which captures important data and control dependencies in the execution of the static algorithm. When the input data is changed, a *change-propagation* algorithm is used to update the computation by identifying the pieces of the computation affected by the change and re-building them. Change-propagation can be viewed as selectively re-executing the static algorithm while re-using results unaffected by the changes made.

Construction algorithm. The construction algorithm performs randomized tree contraction on an input forest F and produces a computation graph C_F. At a high level, it follows Miller and Reif's algorithm [28] by proceeding in rounds of contraction. Each round takes a forest as input and produces a smaller forest for the next round by applying the rake and compress operations. The rake operation deletes all leaves; the compress operation deletes certain vertices that have one child. Using tree contraction to compute a property of a tree requires specifying application-specific data and how such data is handled during rake and compress [4, 28, 29]. Because this can be done orthogonally, we don't consider application-specific data in this paper.

The construction algorithm produces the computation graph C_F by storing a snapshot of the contraction of F at each round. Each snapshot consists of the configurations of vertices in the forest at that round. We define the *configuration* of a vertex v at round i in forest F, written $\kappa_F^i(v)$, as the set

$$\kappa_F^i(v) = \left\{(u, \ell_F^i(u)) \,\middle|\, u \text{ is a neighbor of } v \text{ at round } i \text{ in } F\right\}$$

where $\ell_F^i(u)$ is a boolean indicating whether or not u is a leaf at round i in forest F. The configuration of a vertex captures all of the information necessary to specify the treatment of that vertex by Miller and Reif's algorithm. This information allows us to perform change-propagation efficiently by identifying the parts of the computation that are affected by an input change.

Change-propagation algorithm. Consider some input forest F. Executing the construction algorithm on F yields a computation graph C_F. Suppose we now wish to modify the input forest F by applying a set $\mathcal{M}$ of deletions and insertions of edges and vertices. Let G be the forest given by applying the changes $\mathcal{M}$ to F. Instead of redoing the computation on G (which would require linear work), we provide a change-propagation algorithm that uses the computation graph C_F to perform the update more efficiently and quickly.

Given a change set $\mathcal{M}$, our change-propagation algorithm edits C_F and returns the updated computation graph C_G. An important property of change-propagation is that the updated computation graph C_G is identical to one that would be obtained by running the construction algorithm on forest G. Change-propagation can thus be iterated as many times as desired.

Change-propagation mimics the execution of the construction algorithm, but does so efficiently by only editing the parts of C_F which are affected by the input change $\mathcal{M}$. As in the construction algorithm, change-propagation proceeds in rounds but distinguishes between two classes of vertices at each round:

- *Unaffected vertices* are those that would be contracted in G in the same manner as in the contraction of forest F. A vertex v is unaffected at round i iff $\kappa_F^i(v) = \kappa_G^i(v)$.
- *Affected vertices* are those that would be contracted differently in G than in F. A vertex v is affected at round i iff $\kappa_F^i(v) \neq \kappa_G^i(v)$.

Each round of change-propagation takes a set of affected vertices as input and produces a new set of affected vertices for the next round. It updates the computation graph by deleting all edges which touch an affected vertex before re-running contraction (in parallel) for the affected vertices only. To produce the set of affected vertices for the next round, change-propagation only needs to keep track of what changes it makes to the computation graph.

Analysis. In the full version of the paper, we plan to establish the following two results. For a forest of size n and a batch of m insertions and/or deletions,

- change-propagation performs $O(m \log \frac{n+m}{m})$ work in expectation, and
- change-propagation exposes plenty of parallelism, i.e., its span (parallel time) is poly-logarithmic in n and m.

Size	Runtime		Self Speedup	Work Improvement	Speedup
m	$T_1^{C(m)}$	$T_{39}^{C(m)}$	$\frac{T_1^{C(m)}}{T_{39}^{C(m)}}$	$\frac{T_1^*}{T_1^{C(m)}}$	$\frac{T_1^*}{T_{39}^{C(m)}}$
10^2	0.004	0.004	1	260	260
10^3	0.04	0.04	1	26	26
10^4	0.28	0.14	2	3.71	7.43
$3 \cdot 10^4$	1.03	0.19	5.42	1.01	5.47

Figure 1: Execution times (in seconds) and speedups of change-propagation for m edges inserted into a forest of size $n = 10^6$, where $T_1^* = 1.04$.

Notice that the work bound gives us $O(\log n)$ work for a single change, and it gracefully approaches $O(n)$ work as m approaches n.

Implementation. We completed a relatively unoptimized implementation of our algorithm by using a fork-join parallelism library in C++ [5] which is similar to Cilk [21]. We also implemented Miller and Reif's tree contraction algorithm for comparison.

We generated a random forest of size $n = 10^6$ where at least 60% of the vertices lie on a chain (i.e., have exactly 2 neighbors). On this forest, using one processor, Miller and Reif's algorithm took 1.04 seconds, while our construction algorithm took 2.25 seconds. Since our construction algorithm constructs a computation graph by recording the configuration of vertices, the 2-factor overhead over Miller and Reif's algorithm seems reasonable. With the same input, our construction algorithm runs in 0.28 seconds on 39 processors, leading to a self-speedup of 8.04.

Figure 1 shows the results for our change-propagation algorithm for inserting m randomly chosen edges ($10^2 \leq m \leq 3 \cdot 10^4$). We write T_1^* for the time of Miller and Reif's algorithm on 1 processor, and $T_p^{C(m)}$ for the time of change-propagation inserting m edges on p processors. The work improvement column measures the decrease in work achieved by our algorithm. For small m, the work improvement is significant. As m increases, the work improvement decreases, converging to the work of the static algorithm at ~3% of the input size. The speedup captures the cumulative effect of both work improvement and benefits of parallelism. On a small number of changes ($m = 100$), there is little parallelism but our change-propagation still achieves significant speedup over the static algorithm due to work improvement. As m increases, work improvement decreases but the amount of parallelism increases, leading to reasonable speedups even with moderately large changes.

3 RELATED WORK

Tree contraction and dynamic trees. Tree contraction, originally introduced by Miller and Reif, [28, 29] has become a crucial technique for computing properties of trees in parallel. It has been studied extensively since its introduction and been used in many applications, e.g., expression evaluation, finding least-common ancestors, common subexpression evaluation, and computing various properties of graphs (e.g., [18, 19, 25, 26, 28, 29, 34, 36]). Prior work has established a connection between the tree contraction and dynamic trees problem of Sleator and Tarjan [37] by showing that tree contraction can be dynamized to solve the dynamic trees problem [3, 4]. That work considers sequential updates only. In this paper, we outline how this connection can be generalized to take advantage of parallelism.

Parallel dynamic algorithms. Historically, parallel and dynamic algorithms have been studied mostly separately, with a few exceptions. Pawagi and Kaser propose a parallel (fully) dynamic algorithm that allows insertion and deletion of arbitrary number of vertices and edges as a batch [32]. Acar et al present a parallel dynamic algorithm for well-spaced points sets that allow insertion and deletion of arbitrary number of points simultaneously as a batch [6].

Self-Adjusting Computation. Our approach is based on the technique of self-adjusting computation for dynamizing static algorithms [1, 2, 23, 27]. Prior work applied self-adjusting computation to problems in several areas including in dynamic data structures [3, 4], computational geometry [7, 8], large data sets [13, 15], and machine learning algorithms [9, 39]. All of this prior work assumes a sequential model of computation. There has been some progress in generalizing self-adjusting computation to support parallelism [6, 12–14, 22].

ACKNOWLEDGMENTS

This research is supported by the National Science Foundation (CCF-1629444, CCF-1320563, and CCF-1408940), European Research Council (ERC-2012-StG-308246), and by Microsoft Research.

REFERENCES

[1] Umut A. Acar, Guy E. Blelloch, Matthias Blume, Robert Harper, and Kanat Tangwongsan. An experimental analysis of self-adjusting computation. *ACM Trans. Prog. Lang. Sys.*, 32(1):3:1–53, 2009.

[2] Umut A. Acar, Guy E. Blelloch, and Robert Harper. Adaptive functional programming. *ACM Trans. Prog. Lang. Sys.*, 28(6):990–1034, 2006.

[3] Umut A. Acar, Guy E. Blelloch, Robert Harper, Jorge L. Vittes, and Maverick Woo. Dynamizing static algorithms with applications to dynamic trees and history independence. In *ACM-SIAM Symposium on Discrete Algorithms*, pages 531–540, 2004.

[4] Umut A. Acar, Guy E. Blelloch, and Jorge L. Vittes. An experimental analysis of change propagation in dynamic trees. In *Workshop on Algorithm Engineering and Experimentation*, 2005.

[5] Umut A. Acar, Arthur Charguéraud, and Mike Rainey. Scheduling parallel programs by work stealing with private deques. In *PPoPP '13*, 2013.

[6] Umut A. Acar, Andrew Cotter, Benoît Hudson, and Duru Türkoğlu. Parallelism in dynamic well-spaced point sets. In *Proceedings of the 23rd ACM Symposium on Parallelism in Algorithms and Architectures*, 2011.

[7] Umut A. Acar, Andrew Cotter, Benoît Hudson, and Duru Türkoğlu. Dynamic well-spaced point sets. *Journal of Computational Geometry: Theory and Applications*, 2013.

[8] Umut A. Acar, Benoît Hudson, and Duru Türkoğlu. Kinetic mesh-refinement in 2D. In *SCG '11: Proceedings of the 27th Annual Symposium on Computational Geometry*, 2011.

[9] Umut A. Acar, Alexander Ihler, Ramgopal Mettu, and Özgür Sümer. Adaptive Bayesian inference. In *Neural Information Processing Systems (NIPS)*, 2007.

[10] Stephen Alstrup, Jacob Holm, Kristian de Lichtenberg, and Mikkel Thorup. Maintaining information in fully-dynamic trees with top trees, 2003. The Computing Research Repository (CoRR)[cs.DS/0310065].

[11] Jon Louis Bentley and James B. Saxe. Decomposable searching problems I: Static-to-dynamic transformation. *Journal of Algorithms*, 1(4):301–358, 1980.

[12] Pramod Bhatotia, Pedro Fonseca, Umut A. Acar, Björn B. Brandenburg, and Rodrigo Rodrigues. iThreads: A threading library for parallel incremental computation. In *Proceedings of the Twentieth International Conference on Architectural Support for Programming Languages and Operating Systems, ASPLOS '15*, pages 645–659, 2015.

[13] Pramod Bhatotia, Alexander Wieder, Rodrigo Rodrigues, Umut A. Acar, and Rafael Pasquini. Incoop: MapReduce for incremental computations. In *ACM Symposium on Cloud Computing*, 2011.

[14] Sebastian Burckhardt, Daan Leijen, Caitlin Sadowski, Jaeheon Yi, and Thomas Ball. Two for the price of one: A model for parallel and incremental computation. In *ACM SIGPLAN Conference on Object-Oriented Programming, Systems, Languages, and Applications*, 2011.

[15] Yan Chen, Umut A. Acar, and Kanat Tangwongsan. Functional programming for dynamic and large data with self-adjusting computation. In *International Conference on Functional Programming (ICFP '14)*, pages 227–240, Sep 2014.

[16] Y.-J. Chiang and R. Tamassia. Dynamic algorithms in computational geometry. *Proceedings of the IEEE*, 80(9):1412–1434, 1992.

[17] Camil Demetrescu, Irene Finocchi, and Giuseppe F. Italiano. *Handbook on Data Structures and Applications*, chapter 36: Dynamic Graphs. CRC Press, 2005.

[18] Krzysztof Diks and Torben Hagerup. More general parallel tree contraction: Register allocation and broadcasting in a tree. *Theoretical Computer Science*, 203(1):3 – 29, 1998.

[19] David Eppstein and Zvi Galil. Parallel algorithmic techniques for combinational computation. *Annual review of computer science*, 3(1):233–283, 1988.

[20] Greg N. Frederickson. A data structure for dynamically maintaining rooted trees. *Journal Algorithms*, 24(1):37–65, 1997.

[21] Matteo Frigo, Charles E. Leiserson, and Keith H. Randall. The implementation of the Cilk-5 multithreaded language. In *PLDI*, pages 212–223, 1998.

[22] Matthew Hammer, Umut A. Acar, Mohan Rajagopalan, and Anwar Ghuloum. A proposal for parallel self-adjusting computation. In *DAMP '07: Declarative Aspects of Multicore Programming*, 2007.

[23] Matthew A. Hammer, Umut A. Acar, and Yan Chen. CEAL: a C-based language for self-adjusting computation. In *ACM SIGPLAN Conference on Programming Language Design and Implementation*, 2009.

[24] Monika R. Henzinger and Valerie King. Randomized fully dynamic graph algorithms with polylogarithmic time per operation. *Journal of the ACM*, 46(4):502–516, 1999.

[25] Joseph Jaja. *An introduction to parallel algorithms.* Addison Wesley Longman Publishing Company, 1992.

[26] Richard M. Karp and Vijaya Ramachandran. Parallel algorithms for shared-memory machines. In *Handbook of Theoretical Computer Science, Volume A: Algorithms and Complexity (A)*, pages 869–942. 1990.

[27] Ruy Ley-Wild, Umut A. Acar, and Matthew Fluet. A cost semantics for self-adjusting computation. In *Proceedings of the 26th Annual ACM Symposium on Principles of Programming Languages*, 2009.

[28] Gary L. Miller and John H. Reif. Parallel tree contraction, part I: Fundamentals. *Advances in Computing Research*, 5:47–72, 1989.

[29] Gary L. Miller and John H. Reif. Parallel tree contraction, part 2: Further applications. *SIAM Journal on Computing*, 20(6):1128–1147, 1991.

[30] Ketan Mulmuley. Randomized multidimensional search trees: Lazy balancing and dynamic shuffling (extended abstract). In *Proceedings of the 32nd Annual IEEE Symposium on Foundations of Computer Science*, pages 180–196, 1991.

[31] Mark H. Overmars. *The Design of Dynamic Data Structures.* Springer, 1983.

[32] Shaunak Pawagi and Owen Kaser. Optimal parallel algorithms for multiple updates of minimum spanning trees. *Algorithmica*, 9:357–381, 1993.

[33] G. Ramalingam and T. Reps. A categorized bibliography on incremental computation. In *Principles of Programming Languages*, pages 502–510, 1993.

[34] S. Rao Kosaraju and Arthur L. Delcher. *Optimal parallel evaluation of tree-structured computations by raking (extended abstract)*, pages 101–110. 1988.

[35] John H. Reif and Stephen R. Tate. Dynamic parallel tree contraction (extended abstract). In *SPAA*, pages 114–121, 1994.

[36] Julian Shun, Yan Gu, Guy E. Blelloch, Jeremy T. Fineman, and Phillip B. Gibbons. Sequential random permutation, list contraction and tree contraction are highly parallel. In *Proceedings of the Twenty-sixth Annual ACM-SIAM Symposium on Discrete Algorithms*, SODA '15, pages 431–448, 2015.

[37] Daniel D. Sleator and Robert Endre Tarjan. A data structure for dynamic trees. *Journal of Computer and System Sciences*, 26(3):362–391, 1983.

[38] Daniel Dominic Sleator and Robert Endre Tarjan. Self-adjusting binary search trees. *Journal of the ACM*, 32(3):652–686, 1985.

[39] Özgür Sümer, Umut A. Acar, Alexander Ihler, and Ramgopal Mettu. Adaptive exact inference in graphical models. *Journal of Machine Learning*, 8:180–186, 2011.

[40] Robert Tarjan and Renato Werneck. Self-adjusting top trees. In *Proceedings of the Sixteenth Annual ACM-SIAM Symposium on Discrete Algorithms (SODA)*, 2005.

[41] Robert E. Tarjan. Dynamic trees as search trees via euler tours, applied to the network simplex algorithm. *Mathematical Programming*, 78:167–177, 1997.

[42] Robert E. Tarjan and Renato F. Werneck. Dynamic trees in practice. *J. Exp. Algorithmics*, 14:5:4.5–5:4.23, January 2010.

Brief Announcement: STAR (Space-Time Adaptive and Reductive) Algorithms for Dynamic Programming Recurrences with more than O(1) Dependency

Yuan Tang, Shiyi Wang*
School of Software, Fudan University
Shanghai, China
yuantang@fudan.edu.cn

ABSTRACT

It's important to hit a space-time balance for a real-world algorithm to achieve high performance on modern shared-memory multi-core and many-core systems. However, a large class of dynamic programs with more than $O(1)$ dependency achieved optimality either in space or time, but not both. In the literature, the problem is known as the fundamental space-time tradeoff. We propose the notion of "Processor-Adaptiveness". In contrast to the prior "Processor-Awareness", our approach does not partition statically the problem space to the processor grid, but uses the processor count P to just upper bound the space and cache requirement in a cache-oblivious fashion. In the meantime, our processor-adaptive algorithms enjoy the full benefits of "dynamic load-balance", which is a key to achieve satisfactory speedup on a shared-memory system, especially when the problem dimension n is reasonably larger than P. By utilizing the "busy-leaves" property of runtime scheduler and a program managed memory pool that combines the advantages of stack and heap, we show that our STAR (Space-Time Adaptive and Reductive) technique can help these dynamic programs to achieving sublinear time bounds while keeping to be asymptotically work-, space-, and cache-optimal. The ***key achievement*** of this paper is to obtain the first sublinear $O(n^{3/4} \log n)$ time and optimal $O(n^3)$ work GAP algorithm; If we further bound the space and cache requirement of the algorithm to be asymptotically optimal, there will be a factor of P increase in time bound without sacrificing the work bound. If $P = o(n^{1/4}/\log n)$, the time bound stays sublinear and may be a better tradeoff between time and space requirements in practice.

CCS CONCEPTS

•Theory of computation →Divide and conquer; Dynamic programming; •Computing methodologies →Shared memory algorithms;

KEYWORDS

space-time balance, cache-oblivious algorithm, matrix multiplication, dynamic program with more than $O(1)$ dependency, work-time model, the shared-memory multicore system

1 INTRODUCTION

It's important to hit a space-time balance for a real-world algorithm to achieve high performance on modern shared-memory multi-core and many-core systems. However, a large class of DP (Dynamic Programming) recurrences with more than $O(1)$ dependency, including the general MM (matrix multiplication), Strassen-like fast MM, LWS, GAP, and Parenthesis, have algorithms with either sublinear (parallel) time bound (time bound for short) [1] but sub-optimal space and cache bound [10], or optimal space and cache but superlinear time bound [4, 6, 8]. To the best of our knowledge, there are no prior approach that can simultaneously achieve a sublinear time as well as optimal work, space and cache bound in one algorithm for DP recurrences with more than $O(1)$ dependency, especially in a cache-oblivious fashion.

Let's take the general MM $C = A \otimes B$ on a closed semiring $SR = (S, \oplus, \otimes, 0, 1)$ as an example, where S is a set of elements, $\oplus$ and $\otimes$ are binary operations on S, and 0, 1 are additive and multiplicative identities, respectively. The general MM not only is a DP problem with $O(n)$ dependency [2], but also serves as a basic building block for more complicated DP algorithms such as LWS, GAP, and Parenthesis to achieve sublinear time bounds [10]. The general MM can be computed in a recursive divide-and-conquer fashion as follows. At each level of recursion, the computation of an MM of dimension n (i.e. n-by-n) is divided into four equally sized quadrants, which require updates from eight

Figure 1: Acronyms and notations

MM	Matrix Multiplication
DP	Dynamic Programming
COP	Cache-Oblivious Parallel
RWS	Randomized Work-Stealing
CAS	Compare-And-Swap
n	Problem dimension
P	Number of processing cores
ϵ_i	small constant
M	Cache size
B	cache line size
T_1	Work
T_∞	Time (span, depth, critical path length)
T_p	Parallel running time on p cores
T_1/T_∞	Parallelism
Q_1	Serial cache complexity
Q_p	Parallel cache complexity on P threads
ND	Nested Dataflow
$a \parallel b$	task b has *no* dependency on a
$a ; b$	task b has *full* dependency on a
$a \rightsquigarrow b$	task b has *partial* dependency on a

---

*Yuan Tang is the corresponding author and also affiliated with Shanghai Key Lab. of Intelligent Information Processing and the State Key Lab. of Comp. Arch. ICT, CAS

SPAA'17, July 24-26, 2017, Washington DC, USA
© 2017 Copyright held by the owner/author(s). 978-1-4503-4593-4/17/07...$15.00
DOI: http://dx.doi.org/10.1145/3087556.3087593

---

[1]If we view a parallel computation as a DAG, the time bound T_∞ denotes the critical path length.
[2]The update of each cell of the output matrix requires $O(n)$ reads and computation from the two input matrices

sub-MMs of dimension $n/2$ as shown in Equation (1).

$$\begin{bmatrix} C_{00} & C_{01} \\ C_{10} & C_{11} \end{bmatrix} = \begin{bmatrix} A_{00} & A_{01} \\ A_{10} & A_{11} \end{bmatrix} \otimes \begin{bmatrix} B_{00} & B_{01} \\ B_{10} & B_{11} \end{bmatrix}$$
$$= \begin{bmatrix} A_{00} \otimes B_{00} & A_{00} \otimes B_{01} \\ A_{10} \otimes B_{00} & A_{10} \otimes B_{01} \end{bmatrix} \oplus \begin{bmatrix} A_{01} \otimes B_{10} & A_{01} \otimes B_{11} \\ A_{11} \otimes B_{10} & A_{11} \otimes B_{11} \end{bmatrix} \quad (1)$$

Depending on the availability of extra space, the computation of the eight sub-MMs can be scheduled to run either completely in parallel (Figure 2a) or in two parallel steps (Figure 2b). The Figures 2a and 2b show the two algorithms. More sophisticated approaches are feasible in the literature and will be discussed in Section 2.

We can calculate the time and space bounds of the two algorithms by the recurrences of Equations (2), (3), and (4). The MM-n^2-SPACE algorithm (Figure 2b) uses no extra space than the input and output matrices so there is no recurrece for its space requirement. We can see that the MM-n^3-SPACE algorithm (Figure 2a) has an optimal $O(\log n)$ time bound if counting only the data dependency but a poor $O(n^3)$ space bound; By contrast, the MM-n^2-SPACE algorithm has an optimal $O(n^2)$ space bound, but a sub-optimal $O(n)$ time bound. We care about an algorithm's space bound not only because operating system will disable a computation from executing if it exceeds the space quota, but also because it's a good indicator of cache bound. The cache bound characterizes the amount of data movement (communication) between levels of cache hierarchy throughout the computation. On modern computing system with a hierarchy of caches, data movement usually has a heavier unit weight than arithmetic operations, thus has more impact on the overall performance. By a similar recurrence calculation, we can see that the MM-n^3-SPACE algorithm has a sub-optimal $O(n^3/B)$ serial cache bound [3], in contrast to the optimal $O(n^3/(B\sqrt{M}))$ bound of the MM-n^2-SPACE algorithm. In the literature, it is known as the fundamental space-time tradeoff.

$$T_{\infty,\text{MM-}n^3\text{-SPACE}}(n) = T_{\infty,\text{MM-}n^3\text{-SPACE}}(n/2) + T_{\infty,\text{MADD}}(n) \quad (2)$$
$$S_{\text{MM-}n^3\text{-SPACE}}(n) = 8S_{\text{MM-}n^3\text{-SPACE}}(n/2) + n^2 \quad (3)$$
$$T_{\infty,\text{MM-}n^2\text{-SPACE}}(n) = 2T_{\infty,\text{MM-}n^2\text{-SPACE}}(n/2) \quad (4)$$

A real-world MM algorithm may employ some tuning technique (e.g. 2.5D MM algorithm [16]) to go somewhere in the middle ground of the two extremes. However, an interesting research question is if it is possible to achieve a sublinear time bound, while in the meantime keeping to be asymptotically work-, space-, and cache-optimal.

Our Contributions

- ***Key Achievement:*** We solve an open problem raised in Galil and Park's paper [10] more than 20 years ago. That is, we have the first sublinear $O(n^{3/4} \log n)$ time and optimal $O(n^3)$ work GAP algorithm. If we further bound the space and cache requirement of the algorithm to be asymptotically optimal, i.e. $O(n^2)$ and $O(n^3/(B\sqrt{M}))$ respectively, there will be a factor of P increase in time bound without sacrificing the work bound. If $P = o(n^{1/4}/\log n)$, the time bound stays sublinear and may be a better tradeoff between time and space in practice.

[3] The parallel cache complexity is determined in large by the runtime scheduler and is proportional to the serial cache bound.

- We propose the notion of "***Processor-Adaptiveness***". In contrast to the prior "Processor-Awareness", our approach does not partition statically the problem space to the processor grid, but uses the processor count P to just upper bound the space and cache requirement in a cache-oblivious fashion. Moreover, our processor-adaptive approach enjoys the full benefits of "*dynamic load-balance*", which is a key to achieving satisfactory speedup on a shared-memory multi-core and many-core system, especially when the problem dimension n is reasonably larger than P. We argue that taking the processor count P as a parameter to algorithm design and implementation is easy and straightforward in most state-of-the-art multi-threaded programming languages such as Cilk and OpenMP. Moreover, the parameter P does not require any tuning during the computation in contrast to the cache parameters.
- By utilizing the "busy-leaves" property of the runtime scheduler, we can bound the space requirement of our STAR (Space-Time Adaptive and Reductive) algorithms to be asymptotically optimal; By a program-managed memory pool that combines the advantages of stack and heap, our STAR technique can further bound the serial cache misses to be asymptotically optimal in a cache-oblivious fashion.
- We show by experiments that our STAR algorithms do improve the parallel cache misses due to a better time bound and can outperform the classic cache-oblivious parallel algorithms when the problem dimension is reasonably large, especially when the application is more "memory-intensive" than "computation-intensive", provided that the same kernel function is employed to compute the same-sized base cases.

2 RELATED WORKS

Galil and Park [9, 10] proposed to solve the dynamic programming recurrences by the methods of matrix closure, matrix product, and indirection. Their work is a great motivation for this paper. By their methods, they achieved sublinear parallel time bounds algorithms for a large class of dynamic programming recurrences with more than $O(1)$ dependency. Their work, however, doesn't consider the space or cache requirements. Moreover, their GAP algorithm is not work-optimal.

Hybrid r-way divide-and-conquer algorithms with different values of r at different levels of recursion have been considered in by Chowdhury et al [5]. These algorithms can reach parallel cache complexity matching the best serial cache bounds. Their approach are processor-aware.

Tang et al. [17] proposed Eager and Lazy cache-oblivious wavefront (COW) technique to strike the best of cache complexity and parallelism for a large class of dynamic programming problems. Dinh et al. [7] extended the research to the ND (Nested Dataflow) parallel programming model.

The optimizations, as well as various tradeoffs among work, space, time, communication bounds, on the general matrix multiplication on a semiring or Strassen-like fast algorithm has been

```
MM-n^3-SPACE(C, A, B)
// C ← A × B
if (sizeof(C) ≤ BASE_SIZE)
    BASE-KERNEL(C, A, B)
    return
D ← alloc(sizeof(C))
// Run all 8 sub-MMs concurrently
MM-n^3-SPACE(C00, A00, B00) || MM-n^3-SPACE(C01, A00, B01)
|| MM-n^3-SPACE(C10, A10, B00) || MM-n^3-SPACE(C11, A10, B01)
|| MM-n^3-SPACE(D00, A01, B10) || MM-n^3-SPACE(D01, A01, B11)
|| MM-n^3-SPACE(D10, A11, B10) || MM-n^3-SPACE(D11, A11, B11)
; // sync
// Merge matrix D into C by addition
madd(C, D)
free (D)
return
```

(a) The $O(n^3)$ space recursive MM algorithm

```
MM-n^2-SPACE(C, A, B)
// C ← A × B
if (sizeof(C) ≤ BASE_SIZE)
    BASE-KERNEL(C, A, B)
    return
// Run the first 4 sub-MMs concurrently
MM-n^2-SPACE(C00, A00, B00) || MM-n^2-SPACE(C01, A00, B01)
|| MM-n^2-SPACE(C10, A10, B00) || MM-n^2-SPACE(C11, A10, B01)
; // sync
// Run the next 4 sub-MMs concurrently
MM-n^2-SPACE(C00, A01, B10) || MM-n^2-SPACE(C01, A01, B11)
|| MM-n^2-SPACE(C10, A11, B10) || MM-n^2-SPACE(C11, A11, B11)
; // sync
return
```

(b) The $O(n^2)$ space recursive MM algorithm

Figure 2: Recursive Divide-And-Conquer MM algorithms. "||" and ";" are symbols of linguistic constructs of the ND (Nested Dataflow) parallel programming model [7] (Figure 1).

studied for decades, including at least [1–3, 11–13, 15, 16]. The basic idea of these prior works on the tradeoffs between work, space, time and / or communication overheads for general matrix multiplication or Strassen-like fast algorithms is to switch manually back and forth between the serial algorithm to save and reuse space and the parallel algorithm to increase the parallelism. There are some differences between these prior works and the STAR techniques. First, our work focus on the shared-memory multicore architecture, on which the dynamic load-balance is a key to achieve satisfactory speedup, especially when the problem dimension n is reasonably large compared to the processor count P; By utilizing the "busy-leaves" property of the runtime scheduler, our STAR technique can upper bound the space requirement to be optimal without tuning; By a program managed memory pool, we combine the advantages of stack and heap, thus bound the serial cache-optimality; By having a sublinear critical path length, we reduce asymptotically the parallel cache misses.

Shun et al. [14] alleviates the problem of "concurrent writes" to the same memory location by prioritizing the operations, thus reduce the number of writes. However, not all operations can be prioritized and reduced such as those for the general matrix multiplication.

ACKNOWLEDGMENTS

We gratefully thank the PACMAN group at Tsinghua University for providing some equipment for experiments. This research is supported in part by the Open Funding of State Key Laboratory of Computer Architecture, ICT, CAS (No. CARCH201606).

REFERENCES

[1] G. Ballard, J. Demmel, O. Holtz, B. Lipshitz, and O. Schwartz. Communication-optimal parallel algorithm for strassen's matrix multiplication. In *Proceedings of the Twenty-fourth Annual ACM Symposium on Parallelism in Algorithms and Architectures*, SPAA '12, pages 193–204, New York, NY, USA, 2012. ACM.

[2] A. R. Benson and G. Ballard. A framework for practical parallel fast matrix multiplication. In *Proceedings of the 20th ACM SIGPLAN Symposium on Principles and Practice of Parallel Programming*, PPoPP 2015, pages 42–53, New York, NY, USA, 2015. ACM.

[3] B. Boyer, J.-G. Dumas, C. Pernet, and W. Zhou. Memory efficient scheduling of strassen-winograd's matrix multiplication algorithm. In *Proceedings of the 2009 International Symposium on Symbolic and Algebraic Computation*, ISSAC '09, pages 55–62, New York, NY, USA, 2009. ACM.

[4] R. Chowdhury. *Cache-efficient Algorithms and Data Structures: Theory and Experimental Evaluation.* PhD thesis, Department of Computer Sciences, The University of Texas at Austin, Austin, Texas, 2007.

[5] R. Chowdhury and V. Ramachandran. Cache-efficient Dynamic Programming Algorithms for Multicores. In *Proceedings of ACM Symposium on Parallelism in Algorithms and Architectures (SPAA)*, pages 207–216, 2008.

[6] R. Chowdhury and V. Ramachandran. The cache-oblivious Gaussian elimination paradigm: Theoretical framework, parallelization and experimental evaluation. *Theory of Computing Systems*, 47(4):878–919, 2010.

[7] D. Dinh, H. V. Simhadri, and Y. Tang. Extending the nested parallel model to the nested dataflow model with provably efficient schedulers. In *SPAA'16*, Pacific Grove, CA, USA, 11 - 13 2016.

[8] M. Frigo, C. E. Leiserson, H. Prokop, and S. Ramachandran. Cache-oblivious algorithms. *ACM Trans. Algorithms*, 8(1):4:1–4:22, Jan. 2012.

[9] Z. Galil and R. Giancarlo. Speeding up dynamic programming with applications to molecular biology. *Theoretical Computer Science*, 64:107–118, 1989.

[10] Z. Galil and K. Park. Parallel algorithms for dynamic programming recurrences with more than $O(1)$ dependency. *Journal of Parallel and Distributed Computing*, 21:213–222, 1994.

[11] J. Huang, T. M. Smith, G. M. Henry, and R. A. van de Geijn. Implementing strassen's algorithm with blis. *CoRR*, 2016.

[12] B. Kumar, C. Huang, P. Sadayappan, and R. W. Johnson. A tensor product formulation of strassen's matrix multiplication algorithm with memory reduction. *Scientific Programming*, 4(4):275–289, 1995.

[13] F. W. McColl and A. Tiskin. Memory-efficient matrix multiplication in the bsp model. *Algorithmica*, 24(3):287–297, 1999.

[14] J. Shun, G. E. Blelloch, J. T. Fineman, and P. B. Gibbons. Reducing contention through priority updates. In *SPAA*, pages 152–163, 2013.

[15] T. M. Smith, R. v. d. Geijn, M. Smelyanskiy, J. R. Hammond, and F. G. V. Zee. Anatomy of high-performance many-threaded matrix multiplication. In *Proceedings of the 2014 IEEE 28th International Parallel and Distributed Processing Symposium*, IPDPS '14, pages 1049–1059, Washington, DC, USA, 2014. IEEE Computer Society.

[16] E. Solomonik and J. Demmel. Communication-optimal parallel 2.5d matrix multiplication and lu factorization algorithms. In *Proceedings of the 17th International Conference on Parallel Processing - Volume Part II*, Euro-Par'11, pages 90–109, Berlin, Heidelberg, 2011. Springer-Verlag.

[17] Y. Tang, R. You, H. Kan, J. J. Tithi, P. Ganapathi, and R. A. Chowdhury. Cache-oblivious wavefront: Improving parallelism of recursive dynamic programming algorithms without losing cache-efficiency. In *PPoPP'15*, San Francisco, CA, USA, Feb.7 - 11 2015.

Near Optimal Parallel Algorithms for Dynamic DFS in Undirected Graphs*

Shahbaz Khan
Department of CSE, IIT Kanpur
Kanpur, UP, India 208016
shahbazk@cse.iitk.ac.in

ABSTRACT

Depth first search (DFS) tree is a fundamental data structure for solving various graph problems. The classical algorithm [37] for building a DFS tree requires $O(m + n)$ time for a given undirected graph G having n vertices and m edges. Recently, Baswana et al. [5] presented a simple algorithm for updating the DFS tree of an undirected graph after an edge/vertex update in $\tilde{O}(n)$ [1] time. However, their algorithm is strictly sequential. We present an algorithm achieving similar bounds that can be easily adopted to the parallel environment.

In the parallel environment, a DFS tree can be computed from scratch using $O(m)$ processors in expected $\tilde{O}(1)$ time [2] on an EREW PRAM, whereas the best deterministic algorithm takes $\tilde{O}(\sqrt{n})$ time [2, 17] on a CRCW PRAM. Our algorithm can be used to develop optimal time (upto *poly* $\log n$ factors) deterministic parallel algorithms for maintaining fully dynamic DFS and fault tolerant DFS of an undirected graph.

(1) *Parallel Fully Dynamic DFS*:
Given any arbitrary online sequence of vertex or edge updates, we can maintain a DFS tree of an undirected graph in $\tilde{O}(1)$ time per update using m processors on an EREW PRAM.

(2) *Parallel Fault tolerant DFS*:
An undirected graph can be preprocessed to build a data structure of size $O(m)$, such that for any set of k updates (where k is constant) in the graph, a DFS tree of the updated graph can be computed in $\tilde{O}(1)$ time using n processors on an EREW PRAM. For constant k, this is also work optimal (upto *poly* $\log n$ factors).

Moreover, our fully dynamic DFS algorithm provides, in a seamless manner, nearly optimal (upto *poly* $\log n$ factors) algorithms for maintaining a DFS tree in the semi-streaming environment and a restricted distributed model. These are the first parallel, semi-streaming and distributed algorithms for maintaining a DFS tree in the dynamic setting.

*The full version of the paper is available in [23]
[1] $\tilde{O}()$ hides the poly-logarithmic factors.

SPAA '17, July 24-26, 2017, Washington DC, USA

ACM ISBN 978-1-4503-4593-4/17/07...$15.00
http://dx.doi.org/10.1145/3087556.3087576

CCS CONCEPTS

• **Theory of computation → Dynamic graph algorithms**; **Parallel algorithms**; Streaming, sublinear and near linear time algorithms; Distributed algorithms; • **Mathematics of computing →** *Graph algorithms*;

KEYWORDS

parallel, dynamic, DFS, graph, algorithm, streaming, distributed

1 INTRODUCTION

Depth First Search (DFS) is a well known graph traversal technique. Right from the seminal work of Tarjan [37], DFS traversal has played a central role in the design of efficient algorithms for many fundamental graph problems, namely, strongly connected components, topological sorting [39], dominators in directed graph [38], edge and vertex connectivity [11] etc.

Let $G = (V, E)$ be an undirected connected graph having n vertices and m edges. The DFS traversal of G starting from any vertex $r \in V$ produces a spanning tree called a DFS tree rooted at r in $O(m + n)$ time. For any rooted spanning tree of G, a non-tree edge of the graph is called a *back edge* if one of its endpoints is an ancestor of the other in the tree. Otherwise, it is called a *cross edge*. A necessary and sufficient condition for any rooted spanning tree to be a DFS tree is that every non-tree edge is a back edge. Thus, many DFS trees are possible for any given graph from a given root r. However, if the traversal is performed strictly according to the order of edges in the adjacency lists of the graph, the resulting DFS tree will be unique. Ordered DFS tree problem is to compute the order in which the vertices are visited by this unique DFS traversal.

An algorithmic graph problem is modeled in a dynamic environment as follows. There is an online sequence of updates on the graph, and the objective is to update the solution of the problem efficiently after each update. In particular, the time taken to update the solution has to be much smaller than that of the best static algorithm for the problem. A dynamic graph algorithm is said to be *fully dynamic* if it handles both insertion and deletion updates, otherwise it is called *partially dynamic*. Another, and more restricted, variant of a dynamic environment is the fault tolerant environment. Here the aim is to build a compact data structure, for a given problem, that is resilient to failures of vertices/edges and can efficiently report the solution after a given set of failures.

Recently, Baswana et al. [5, 6] presented a fully dynamic algorithm for maintaining a DFS tree of an undirected graph in $\tilde{O}(\sqrt{mn})$ time per update. They also presented an algorithm for updating the DFS tree after a single update in $\tilde{O}(n)$ time. Prior to this work, only partially dynamic algorithms were known for DFS trees [7, 8, 14].

Now, major applications of dynamic graphs in the real world involve a huge amount of data, which makes recomputing the solution after every update infeasible. Due to this large size of data, it also becomes impractical for solving such problems on a single sequential machine because of both memory and computation costs involved. Thus, it becomes more significant to explore these dynamic graph problems on a computation model that efficiently handles large storage and computations. In the past three decades a lot of work has been done to address dynamic graph problems in parallel [9, 13, 33, 35], semi-streaming [3, 18, 21, 28], and distributed (also called dynamic networks) [4, 22, 24, 36] environments.

In this paper, we address the problem of maintaining dynamic DFS tree efficiently in the parallel environment and demonstrate its applications in semi-streaming and distributed environments.

1.1 Existing results

In spite of the simplicity of a DFS tree, designing efficient parallel, distributed or streaming algorithms for a DFS tree has turned out to be quite challenging. Reif [31] showed that the ordered DFS tree problem is *P*-Complete. For many years, this result seemed to imply that general DFS tree problem, i.e., computing any DFS tree of the graph, is also inherently sequential. However, Aggarwal et al. [1, 2] proved that the general DFS tree problem is in *RNC*[2] by designing a randomized EREW PRAM[3] algorithm that takes $\tilde{O}(1)$ time. But the fastest deterministic algorithm for computing general DFS tree in parallel still takes $\tilde{O}(\sqrt{n})$ time [2, 17] in CRCW PRAM[4], even for undirected graphs. Moreover, general DFS tree problem has been shown to be in *NC* for some special graphs including DAGs [16] and planar graphs [19] (see [15] for a survey). Whether general DFS tree problem is in *NC* is still a long standing open problem.

In the semi-streaming environment, the input graph is accessed in form of a stream of graph edges, where an algorithm can perform multiple passes on this stream but is allowed to use only $O(n)$ local space. The DFS tree can be trivially computed using $O(n)$ passes, where each pass adds one vertex to the DFS tree. However, computing the DFS tree in $\tilde{O}(1)$ passes is considered hard [12]. To the best of our knowledge, it is an open problem to compute a DFS tree using even $o(n)$ passes in any relaxed streaming environment [29, 32].

Computing a DFS tree in a distributed setting was widely studied in 1980's and 1990's. A DFS tree can be computed in $O(n)$ rounds, with different trade offs between number of messages passed, and size of each message. A DFS tree can be built using $O(n)$ messages if we allow messages of size $O(n)$ [25, 27, 34], and using $O(m)$ messages if we limit the message size to be $\tilde{O}(1)$ [10, 26, 40].

Thus, to maintain a DFS tree in the dynamic setting, each update requires $\tilde{O}(\sqrt{n})$ time on a CRCW PRAM in deterministic parallel setting, $O(n)$ passes in semi-streaming setting and $O(n)$ rounds in distributed setting, which is very inefficient. Hence, exploring the dynamic DFS in parallel, semi-streaming and distributed models seems to be a long neglected problem of practical significance.

[2] *NC* is the class of problems solvable using $O(n^{c_1})$ processors in parallel $O(\log^{c_2} n)$ time, for any constants c_1, c_2. The class *RNC* extends *NC* to allow access to randomness.
[3] Exclusive Read Exclusive Write (EREW) restricts any two processors to simultaneously read or write the same memory cell. Concurrent Read Concurrent Write (CRCW) does not have this restriction.
[4] It essentially shows DFS to be NC equivalent of minimum-weight perfect matching, which is in RNC whereas its best deterministic algorithm requires $\tilde{O}(\sqrt{n})$ time.

We present optimal algorithms (up to *poly* log *n* factors) for maintaining a fully dynamic DFS tree for an undirected graph under both edge and vertex updates on these models.

1.2 Our Results

We consider an extended notion of updates wherein an update could be either insertion/deletion of a vertex or insertion/deletion of an edge. Furthermore, an inserted vertex can be added with any set of incident edges to the graph. In the parallel setting, our main result can be succinctly described as follows.

Theorem 1.1. *Given an undirected graph and its DFS tree, it can be preprocessed to build a data structure of size* $O(m)$ *in* $O(\log n)$ *time using m processors on an EREW PRAM, such that for any update in the graph, a DFS tree of the updated graph can be computed in* $O(\log^3 n)$ *time using n processors on an EREW PRAM.*

With this result at the core, we easily obtain the following results.

(1) *Parallel Fully Dynamic DFS*:
Given an arbitrary online sequence of updates, we can maintain a DFS tree of an undirected graph in $O(\log^3 n)$ time per update using m processors on an EREW PRAM.
(2) *Parallel Fault tolerant DFS*:
An undirected graph can be preprocessed to build a data structure of size $O(m)$, such that for any set of $k(\leq \log n)$ updates in the graph, a DFS tree of the updated graph can be computed in $O(k \log^{2k+1} n)$ time using n processors on an EREW PRAM.

Our fully dynamic algorithm and fault tolerant algorithm (for constant k), clearly take optimal time (up to *poly* log *n* factors) for maintaining a DFS tree. Our fault tolerant algorithm (for constant k) is also work optimal (upto *poly* log *n* factors) since a single update can lead to $\Theta(n)$ changes in the DFS tree. Moreover, our result also establishes that maintaining fully dynamic DFS for an undirected graph is in *NC* (which is still an open problem for static DFS).

1.3 Applications of Parallel Fully Dynamic DFS

Our parallel fully dynamic DFS algorithm can be seamlessly adapted to the semi-streaming and distributed environments as follows.

(1) *Semi-streaming Fully Dynamic DFS*:
Given any arbitrary online sequence of vertex or edge updates, we can maintain a DFS tree of an undirected graph using $O(\log^2 n)$ passes over the input graph per update by a semi-streaming algorithm using $O(n)$ space.
(2) *Distributed Fully Dynamic DFS*:
Given any arbitrary online sequence of vertex or edge updates, we can maintain a DFS tree of an undirected graph in $O(D \log^2 n)$ rounds per update in the synchronous $\mathcal{CONGEST}(n/D)$ model using $O(nD \log^2 n + m)$ messages of size $O(n/D)$ requiring $O(n)$ space on each processor, where D is diameter of the graph.

Our semi-streaming algorithm clearly takes optimal number of passes (up to *poly* log *n* factors) for maintaining a DFS tree. Our distributed algorithm that works in a restricted $CONGEST(B)$ [5]

[5] $CONGEST(B)$ model is the standard $\mathcal{CONGEST}$ model [30] where message size is relaxed to B words.

model, also arguably requires optimal rounds (up to *poly* log *n* factors) because it requires $\Omega(D)$ rounds to propagate the information of the update throughout the graph. Since almost the whole DFS tree may need to be updated due to a single update in the graph, every algorithm for maintaining a DFS tree in the distributed setting will require $\Omega(D)$ rounds [6]. This essentially improves the state of the art for the classes of graphs with $o(n)$ diameter.

1.4 Overview

We now describe a brief overview of our result. Baswana et al. [5] proved that updating a DFS tree after any update in the graph is equivalent to *rerooting* disjoint subtrees of the DFS tree. They also presented an algorithm to reroot a DFS tree T (or its subtree), originally rooted at r to a new root r', in $\tilde{O}(n)$ time. It starts the traversal from r' traversing the path connecting r' to r in T. Now, the subtrees hanging from this path are essentially the components of the *unvisited graph* (the subgraph induced by the unvisited vertices of the graph) due to the absence of *cross edges*. In the updated DFS tree, every such subtree, say τ, shall hang from an edge emanating from τ to the path from r' to r. Let this edge be (x, y), where $x \in \tau$. Thus, we need to recursively reroot τ to the new root x and hang it from (x, y) in the updated DFS tree. Note that this rerooting can be independently performed for different subtrees hanging from tree path from r' to r.

At the core of their result, they use a property of the DFS tree, that they called *components* property, to find the edge (x, y) efficiently, using a data structure $\mathcal{D}_0$. However, as evident from the discussion above, their rerooting procedure can be strictly sequential in the worst case. This is because the size of a subtree τ to be rerooted can be almost equal to that of the original tree T. As a result, $O(n)$ sequential reroots may be required in the worst case. Our main contribution is an algorithm that performs this rerooting efficiently in parallel.

Our algorithm ensures that rerooting is completed in $\tilde{O}(1)$ steps as follows. At any point of time, we ensure that every component c of the *unvisited graph* is either of type $C1$, having a single subtree of T, or of type $C2$, having a path p_c and a set of subtrees of T having edges to p_c. Note that in [5] every component of the unvisited graph is of type $C1$. We define three types of traversals, namely, *path halving* (also used by [5]), *disintegrating traversal* and *disconnecting traversal*. We prove that using a combination of $O(1)$ such traversals, for every component c of the unvisited graph, either the length of p_c is halved or the size of largest subtree in c is halved. Moreover, these traversals can be performed in $O(\log n)$ time on $|c|$ processors using the *components* property and a data structure $\mathcal{D}$ (answering similar queries as $\mathcal{D}_0$). However, since our algorithm ensures that each vertex is queried by $\mathcal{D}$ only $\tilde{O}(1)$ times (unlike [5]), our data structure $\mathcal{D}$ is much simpler than $\mathcal{D}_0$.

Furthermore, both our algorithm and the algorithm by [5] use the non-tree edges of the graph only to answer queries on data structure $\mathcal{D}$ (or $\mathcal{D}_0$). The remaining operations (except for queries on $\mathcal{D}$) required by our algorithm can be performed using only edges of T in $O(n)$ space. As a result, our algorithm being efficient in parallel setting (unlike [5]), can also be adapted to the semi-streaming and distributed model as follows. In the semi-streaming model, the passes over the input graph are used only to answer the queries on $\mathcal{D}$, where the parallel queries on $\mathcal{D}$ made by our algorithm can be answered simultaneously using a single pass. Our distributed algorithm only needs to store the current DFS tree at each node and the adjacency list of the corresponding vertex abiding the restriction of $O(n)$ space at each node. Again, the distributed computation is only used to answer queries on $\mathcal{D}$.

[6] For an algorithm maintaining the whole DFS tree at each node, even our message size is optimal. In the worst case, an update of size $O(n)$ (vertex insertion with arbitrary set of edges) have to be propagated throughout the network. In $O(D)$ rounds, it can only be propagated using messages of size $\Omega(n/D)$ (see full paper [23] for details).

2 PRELIMINARIES

Let $G = (V, E)$ be any given undirected graph on n vertices and m edges. The following notations will be used throughout the paper.

- $par(w)$: Parent of w in T.
- $T(x)$: The subtree of T rooted at vertex x.
- $path(x, y)$: Path from vertex x to vertex y in T.
- $LCA(x, y)$: Lowest common ancestor of x and y in T.
- $root(T')$: Root of a subtree T' of T, i.e., $root(T(x)) = x$.
- T^* : The updated DFS tree computed by our algorithm.

A subtree T' is said to be *hanging* from a path p if the $root(T')$ is a child of some vertex on the path p and does not belong to the path p. Unless stated otherwise, a component refers to a connected component of the unvisited graph. We refer to a path p in a DFS tree T as an *ancestor-descendant* path if one of its endpoints is an ancestor of the other in T.

For our distributed algorithm, we use synchronous $CONGEST(B)$ model [30]. For the dynamic setting, Henzinger et al. [20] presented a model that has a *preprocessing* stage followed by an alternating sequence of non-overlapping stages for *update* and *recovery*. We use this model with an additional space restriction of $O(n)$ size at each node. Without this restriction, the whole graph can be stored at each node, where an algorithm can trivially propagate the update to each node and the updated solution can be computed locally. Also, we allow the deletion updates to be *abrupt*, i.e., the deleted link/node becomes unavailable for use instantly after the update.

In order to handle disconnected graphs, we add a dummy vertex r with edges to all the vertices. Our algorithm maintains a DFS tree rooted at r in this augmented graph, where each child subtree of r is a DFS tree of a connected component of the original graph.

We shall now define some queries that are performed by our algorithm on the data structure $\mathcal{D}$ (similar queries on $\mathcal{D}_0$ also used in [5]). Let $v, w, x, y \in V$, where $path(x, y)$ and $path(v, w)$ (if required) are ancestor-descendant paths in T. Also, no vertex in $path(v, w)$ is a descendant of any vertex in $path(x, y)$. We define the following queries.

(1) $Query(w, path(x, y))$: among all the edges from w that are incident on $path(x, y)$ in G, return an edge that is incident nearest to x on $path(x, y)$.
(2) $Query(T(w), path(x, y))$: among all the edges from $T(w)$ that are incident on $path(x, y)$ in G, return an edge that is incident nearest to x on $path(x, y)$.
(3) $Query(path(v, w), path(x, y))$: among all the edges from $path(v, w)$ that are incident on $path(x, y)$ in G, return an edge that is incident nearest to x on $path(x, y)$.

Let the *descendant* vertices of the three queries described above be w, $T(w)$ and $path(v, w)$ respectively. A set of queries on the data structure $\mathcal{D}$ are called *independent* if the *descendant* vertices of these queries are disjoint.

Baswana et al. [5] described the *components* property as follows.

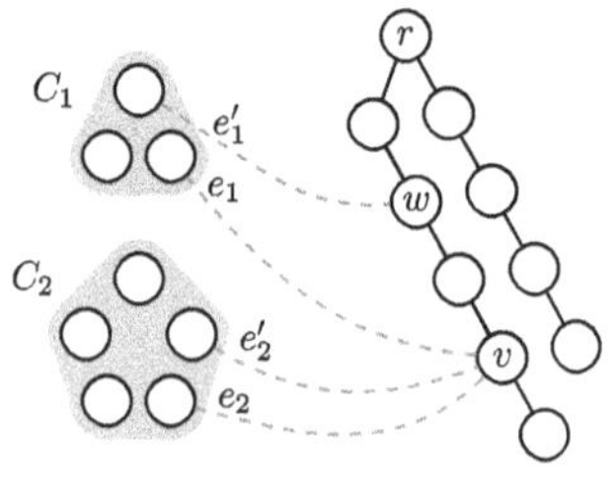

Figure 1: Edges e_1' and e_2' can be ignored during the DFS traversal (reproduced from [6]).

Lemma 2.1 (Components Property [5]). *Let T^* be the partially built DFS tree and v be the vertex currently being visited. Let $C_1, .., C_k$ be the connected components of the subgraph induced by the unvisited vertices. For any two edges e_i and e_i' from C_i that are incident respectively on v and some ancestor (not necessarily proper) w of v in T^*, it is sufficient to consider only e_i during the DFS traversal, i.e., the edge e_i' can be safely ignored.*

Ignoring e_i' during the DFS traversal, as stated in the components property, is justified because e_i' will appear as a back edge in the resulting DFS tree (refer to Figure 1). The edge e_i can be found by querying the data structure $\mathcal{D}$ (or $\mathcal{D}_0$ in [5]). The DFS tree is then updated after any update in the graph by reducing it to *rerooting* disjoint subtrees of the DFS tree using the components property. Rerooting a subtree $T(v)$ at a new root $r' \in T(v)$ involves restructuring the tree $T(v)$ to be now rooted at r', such that the new tree is also a DFS tree of the subgraph induced by $T(v)$. This reduction will henceforth be referred as the *reduction* algorithm and can be succinctly described as follow (see Appendix A for details).

Theorem 2.2. *Given an undirected graph G and its DFS tree T, any graph update can be reduced to independently rerooting disjoint subtrees of T by performing $O(1)$ sets of independent queries on the data structure $\mathcal{D}$ and $O(1)$ sets of LCA queries on T, where each set has at most n queries.*

3 REROOTING A DFS TREE

We now describe the algorithm to reroot a subtree $T(r_0)$ of the DFS tree T, from its original root r_0 to the new root r^*. Also, let the data structure $\mathcal{D}$ be built on T (see Section 2). We maintain the following invariant: at any moment of the algorithm, every component c of the unvisited graph can be of the following two types:

- C1: Consists of a single subtree τ_c of the DFS tree T.
- C2: Consists of a single *ancestor-descendant* path p_c and a set $\mathcal{T}_c$ of subtrees of the DFS tree T having at least one edge to p_c. Note that for any $\tau_1, \tau_2 \in \mathcal{T}_c$, there is no edge between τ_1 and τ_2 since T is a DFS tree.

Moreover, for every component c we also have a vertex $r_c \in c$ from which the DFS tree of the component c would be rooted in the final DFS tree T^*.

The algorithm is divided into $\log n$ *phases*, where each phase is further divided into $\log n$ *stages*. At the end of phase $\mathcal{P}_i$, every subtree of any component c (τ_c or subtrees in $\mathcal{T}_c$) has at most $n/2^i$ vertices. During phase $\mathcal{P}_i$, every component has at least one *heavy* subtree (having $> n/2^i$ vertices). If no such tree exists, we move the component to the next phase. We denote the set of these heavy subtrees by $\mathbb{T}_c$. For notational convenience, we refer to the heaviest subtree of every component c as τ_c, even for components of type $C2$. Hence, for any component of type $C1$ or $C2$, we have $\tau_c \in \mathbb{T}_c$. Clearly the algorithm ends after $\log n$ phases as every component of the unvisited graph would be empty.

At the end of stage $\mathcal{S}_j$ of a phase, the length of p_c in each component c is at most $n/2^j$. If $|p_c| \leq n/2^j$, we move the component c to the next stage. Further, for any component c of type $C1$, the value of $|p_c|$ is zero, so we move such components to the last stage of the phase, i.e., $\mathcal{S}_{\log n}$. Clearly at the end of $\log n$ stages, each component would be of type $C1$.

In the beginning of the algorithm, we have the component induced by $T(r_0)$ of type $C1$ where $r_c = r^*$. Note that during each stage, different connected components of the unvisited graph can be processed independent of each other in parallel.

Algorithm

We now describe how a component c in phase $\mathcal{P}_i$ and stage $\mathcal{S}_j$ is traversed by our algorithm. The aim is to build a partial DFS tree for the component c rooted at r_c, that can be attached to the partially built DFS tree T^* of the updated graph. Note that this has to be performed in such a manner that every component of the unvisited part of c is of type $C1$ or $C2$ only.

Now, in order to move to the next phase, we need to ensure that for every component c' of the unvisited part of c, $|\tau_{c'}| \leq n/2^i$. As described above, after $\log n$ stages every component c' is of type $C1$. Thus, we perform a *disintegrating traversal* of τ_c which ensures that every component of the unvisited part of c can be moved to the next phase.

During $\mathcal{S}_j$, in order to move to the next stage, we need to ensure that for every component c' of the unvisited part of c, either $|p_{c'}| \leq n/2^j$ (moving it to next stage) or $|\tau_{c'}| \leq n/2^i$ (moving it to next phase). The component is processed based on the location of r_c in c as follows. If $r_c \in p_c$, we perform *path halving* which ensures the components move to the next stage. If $r_c \in \tau \notin \mathbb{T}_c$, we perform a *disconnecting traversal* of τ followed by *path halving* of p_c, such that the unvisited components of τ are no longer connected to residual part of p_c, moving them to the next phase. The remaining components of c moves to the next stage due to path halving.

We shall refer to disintegrating traversal, path halving and disconnecting traversal as the *simpler* traversals. The difficult case is when $r_c \in \tau \in \mathbb{T}_c$. Here, some trivial cases can be directly processed by the *simpler* traversals mentioned above. For the remaining cases we perform *heavy subtree traversal* of τ which shall ensure that the unvisited part of c reduces to those requiring *simpler* traversals. Refer to the full paper [23] for pseudocodes of the algorithm.

We now describe the different types of traversals in detail. For any component c, we refer to the smallest subtree of $\tau \in \mathbb{T}_c$ that has more than $n/2^i$ vertices as $T(v_H)$. Since $n/2^{i-1} \geq |\tau| > n/2^i$, v_H is unique. Also, let $r' = root(\tau)$ (if $r_c \in \tau$) and $v_l = LCA(r_c, v_H)$.

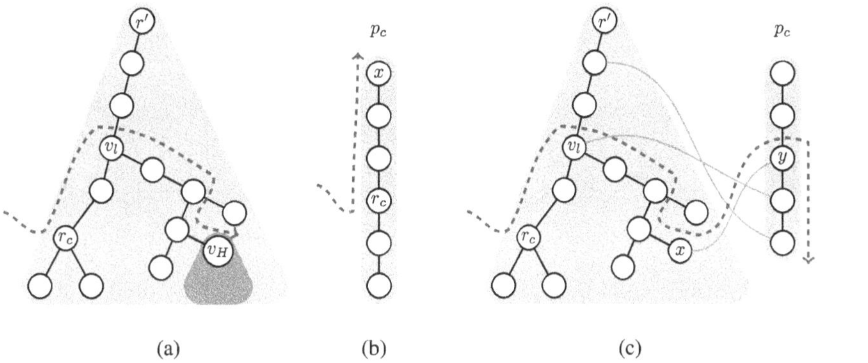

Figure 2: The three *simpler* traversals (shown using blue dotted lines), (a) Disintegrating traversal, (b) Path Halving, and (c) Disconnecting traversal.

3.1 Disintegrating Traversal

Consider a component c of type $C1$ with new root $r_c \in \tau_c$ in phase $\mathcal{P}_i$ $(n/2^i < |\tau_c| \leq n/2^{i-1})$. We first find the vertex v_H. We then traverse along the tree path $path(r_c, v_H)$, adding it to T^* (see Figure 2 (a)). Now, the unvisited part of c consists of $path(par(v_l), r')$ (say p) and the subtrees hanging from $path(r_c, r')$ and $path(v_l, v_H)$. Notice that p is an ancestor-descendant path of T and each subtree has at most $n/2^i$ vertices. Each subtree not having an edge to p corresponds to a separate component of type $C1$. The path p and the remaining subtrees (having an edge to p) form a component of type $C2$. For each component c^*, we also need to find the new root r_{c^*} for the updated DFS tree of the component. Using the components property, we know r_{c^*} has the lowest edge from c^* on the path p^*, where p^* is the newly attached path to T^* described above. Both these queries (finding an edge to p and the lowest edge on p^*) can be answered by our data structure $\mathcal{D}$ (see Section 2). Thus, every component c^* can be identified and moved to next phase.

Remark. *If $r_c = r'$, this traversal can also be performed on a subtree from a component c of type $C2$ achieving similar result. This is possible because no new path p would be formed and we still get components of type $C1$ and $C2$ (being connected to a single path p_c).*

3.2 Path Halving

Consider a component of type $C2$ with $r_c \in p_c = path(x, y)$. We first find the farther end of p_c, say x, where $|path(r_c, x)| \geq |path(r_c, y)|$. We then traverse from r_c to x adding $path(r_c, x)$ to the tree T^* (see Figure 2 (b)). The component c' of type $C2$ thus formed will have $p_{c'}$ of length at most half of p_c. Now, the subtrees in c having an edge to $p_{c'}$ would be a part of c'. The remaining subtrees would form individual components of type $C1$. Again, the new root of each component can be found using $\mathcal{D}$ by querying for the lowest edge on the $path(r_c, x)$ added to T^*.

3.3 Disconnecting Traversal

Consider a component of type $C2$ with $r_c \in \tau$, where $\tau \notin \mathbb{T}_c$. We traverse τ from r_c to reach p_c, which is then followed by path halving of p_c. The goal is to ensure that the unvisited part of τ is not connected to the unvisited part of p_c (say p') after path halving, moving it to the next phase. The remaining subtrees of c with p' will move to the next stage as a result of path halving of p_c.

Now, if at least one edge from τ is present on the upper half of p_c, we find the highest edge from τ to p_c (see Figure 2 (c)). Otherwise, we find the lowest edge from τ to p_c. Let it be (x, y), where $y \in p_c$ and $x \in \tau$. This ensures that on entering p_c through y, path halving would ensure that all the edges from τ to p_c are incident on the traversed part of p_c (say p).

We perform the traversal from r_c to x similar to the *disintegrating traversal* along $path(r_c, x)$, attaching it to T^*. Since none of the components of unvisited part of τ are connected to p', all the components formed would be of type $C1$ or $C2$ as described in Section 3.1. However, while finding the new root of each resulting component c', we also need to consider the lowest edge from the component on p. Further, since $\tau \notin \mathbb{T}_c$, size of each subtree in the resulting components is at most $n/2^i$. Thus, the resultant components of τ are moved to the next phase.

Remark. *If $r_c \in T(v_H)$, this traversal can also be performed on a $\tau \in \mathbb{T}_c$ getting a similar result. This is because each subtree in resultant components of τ will have size at most $n/2^i$ moving it to the next phase. However, if $r_c \notin T(v_H)$ we cannot use this traversal as the resultant component c' of type $C2$ formed can have a heavy subtree and a path $p_{c'}$ of arbitrary length. This is not permitted as it will move the component to some earlier stage in the same phase. Hence, in such a case we would process the component using heavy subtree traversal described as follows.*

3.4 Heavy Subtree Traversal

Consider a component c of type $C2$ with $r_c \in \tau$, where $\tau \in \mathbb{T}_c$. As described earlier, if $r_c = root(\tau)$ or $r_c \in T(v_H)$, the heavy subtree τ can be processed using disintegrating or disconnecting traversals respectively. Otherwise, we traverse it using one of three scenarios described as follows. Our algorithm checks each scenario in turn for its applicability to τ, eventually choosing a scenario to perform an l, p or r traversal (see Figure 3). This traversal ensures that it is followed by a *simpler* traversal described earlier, so that each component will either move to the next phase or the next stage. We shall also prove that these scenarios are indeed exhaustive, i.e., for any τ, one of these scenarios is indeed applicable. The following lemma describes the conditions for a scenario to be applicable. Refer to the full paper [23] for proofs of the lemmas described in this section.

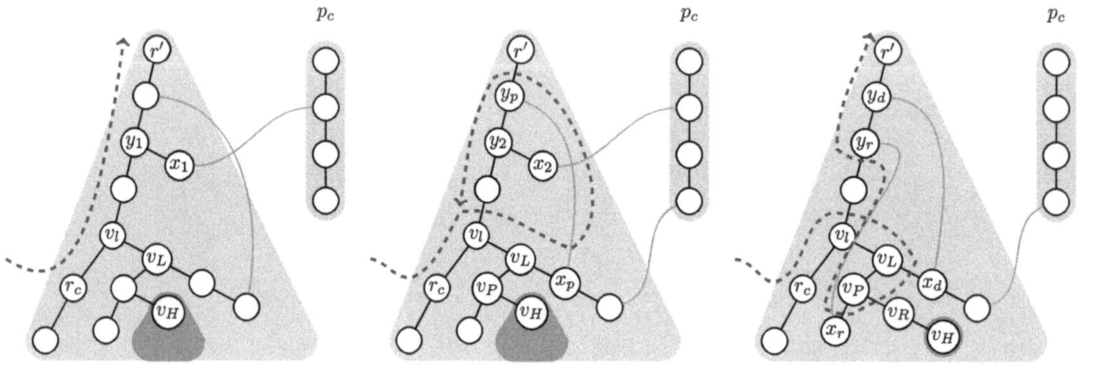

(a) (b) (c)

Figure 3: The three scenarios for Heavy Subtree Traversal (shown using blue dotted lines), (a) l traversal, (b) p traversal, and (c) r traversal.

Lemma 3.1 (Applicability Lemma). *After a traversal of path p^* in a subtree $\tau \in \mathbb{T}_c$, every component of unvisited part of c can be moved to the next phase/stage using a simpler traversal if*

- $\mathcal{A}_1$: *Traversal of p^* produces components of type C1 or C2 only,*
- $\mathcal{A}_2$: *The subtree $T(v_H)$ is connected to p_c (if in component of type C2),*
- $\mathcal{A}_3$: *The lowest edge on p^* from the component containing p_c is not a back edge from the subtree containing $T(v_H)$ with its end point outside $T(v_H)$.*

Remark. *Applicability lemma is employed when p^* does not traverse through $T(v_H)$. Otherwise, the unvisited component trivially moves to the next stage/phase This is because if p^* traverses through $T(v_H)$, the traversal preceding p^* was clearly applicable. Condition $\mathcal{A}_2$ ensures that the heavy subtree containing $T(v_H)$ does not form a component c' with arbitrary length of path $p_{c'}$, as this can move it to some previous stage which is not allowed. Because of the same reason* disconnecting *traversal is not used on such heavy subtrees.*

We now briefly describe the three scenarios, namely, l, p and r traversals and define a few notations related to them (shown in Figure 3). The l, p and r traversals follow the path shown in figure (using blue dotted lines) which shall henceforth be referred as p_L^*, p_P^* and p_R^* respectively. Both p and r traversals use a back edge during the traversal, denoted by (x_p, y_p) and (x_r, y_r) respectively. Further, we refer to the subtrees containing v_H that hangs from p_L^*, p_P^* and p_R^* as $T(v_L)$, $T(v_P)$ and $T(v_R)$ respectively. Any subtree hanging from the traversed path (p_L^*, p_P^* or p_R^*), shall be called an *eligible* subtree, if it has an edge to p_c. In each scenario we ensure $\mathcal{A}_1$ and $\mathcal{A}_2$ by construction, implying that the scenario will not be applicable only if $\mathcal{A}_3$ is violated. Thus, we only need to find the lowest edge on traversed path from the *eligible* subtrees, to determine the applicability of a scenario. Also, the edges (x_p, y_p) and (x_r, y_r) are chosen in such a way that if l and p traversals are not applicable, then r traversal always satisfies *applicability* lemma, with the lowest edge from component containing p_c being (x_d, y_d), where $x_d \in \tau_d \neq T(v_R)$.

Scenario 1: l traversal
Consider the traversal shown in Figure 3 (a), where $p_L^* = path(r_c, r')$. Since, this traversal does not create a new non-traversed path, $\mathcal{A}_1$ and $\mathcal{A}_2$ are implicitly satisfied. We find the lowest edge on p_L^* (highest edge on $path(r_c, r')$) from p_c and the *eligible* subtrees, say (x_1, y_1), where $y_1 \in p_L^*$. In case this edge satisfies $\mathcal{A}_3$, we perform the traversal otherwise move to the next scenario.

Remark. *This scenario is not applicable only if (x_1, y_1) is a back edge with $x_1 \in T(v_L)$ and $x_1 \notin T(v_H)$.*

Scenario 2: p traversal
Consider the traversal shown in Figure 3 (b), where $p_P^* = path(r_c, x_p) \cup (x_p, y_p) \cup path(y_p, par(v_l))$. To perform this traversal, we choose (x_p, y_p) along with (x_d, y_d) such that if p traversal using (x_p, y_p) is not applicable then r traversal using (x_d, y_d) is necessarily applicable. The presence of the back edge (x_1, y_1) (see remark of l traversal) can be used to show that (x_p, y_p) and (x_d, y_d) can be chosen satisfying the following properties Let τ_d and τ_p (if any), be the subtrees hanging from $path(v_L, v_H)$ containing x_d and x_p respectively.

Lemma 3.2. *The edge (x_p, y_p), which is a back edge, always exists and when used for p traversal satisfies $\mathcal{A}_1$ and $\mathcal{A}_2$.*

Lemma 3.3. *On performing r traversal using any edge (x_r, y_r), which satisfies (i) $x_r \in T(v_P) \cup \tau_p$ (if any), and (ii) the conditions $\mathcal{A}_1$ and $\mathcal{A}_2$, the r traversal is applicable with the lowest edge from* an eligible *subtree to p_R^* being (x_d, y_d) (from the* eligible *subtree τ_d), if either $\tau_d \neq \tau_p$ or τ_d is not traversed by p_R^*.*

Thus, Lemma 3.2 ensures that our traversal can follow p_P^* as shown in Figure 3 (b). To verify $\mathcal{A}_3$ we find the new root for the component having path p_c as follows. We find the lowest edge on p_P^* from p_c and the *eligible* subtrees hanging from p_P^*, say (x_2, y_2), where $y_2 \in p_P^*$. In case this edge satisfies $\mathcal{A}_3$, we perform the traversal otherwise move to the next scenario.

Remark. *This scenario is not applicable only if (x_2, y_2) is a back edge with $x_2 \in T(v_P)$ and $x_2 \notin T(v_H)$.*

Scenario 3: r traversal

Consider the traversal shown in Figure 3 (c), where $p_R^* = path(r_c, x_r) \cup (x_r, y_r) \cup path(y_r, r')$. We choose (x_2, y_2) as (x_r, y_r). However, while computing (x_2, y_2), τ_p (if exists) would have been partially traversed. Hence, if the lowest edge from τ_p to $path(r_c, r')$, say (x_2', y_2'), has y_2' lower than y_r on $path(r_c, r')$, τ_p would be connected to both p_c and $path(par(v_l), y_2) \setminus \{y_2\}$. This creates a component having p_c which is not of type C_1 or C_2 violating $\mathcal{A}_1$. In such a case we choose (x_2', y_2') as (x_r, y_r). The existence of back edge (x_2, y_2) (see remark of p traversal) implies the following property of (x_r, y_r).

Lemma 3.4. *The edge (x_r, y_r), which is a back edge, always exists and when used for r traversal satisfies $\mathcal{A}_1$ and $\mathcal{A}_2$.*

Thus, Lemma 3.4 ensures that our traversal can follow p_R^* as shown in Figure 3 (c). To verify $\mathcal{A}_3$ we find the new root for the component having path p_c as follows. We find the lowest edge on p_R^* from p_c and the *eligible* subtrees hanging from p_R^*, say (x_3, y_3), where $y_3 \in p_R^*$. In case this edge satisfies $\mathcal{A}_3$, we perform this traversal.

Using Lemma 3.3, we shall now describe the conditions when this edge satisfies the *applicability* lemma. The choice of (x_r, y_r) ensures that either $x_r \in T(v_P)$ (see remark in p traversal) or $x_r \in \tau_p$ (recall the computation of (x_2', y_2')). Further, using Lemma 3.4 our r traversal satisfies $\mathcal{A}_1$ and $\mathcal{A}_2$. Thus, using Lemma 3.3 the scenario is not applicable only in the *special case* where $\tau_d = \tau_p$ and p_R^* traverses τ_d.

We now present the conditions of the *special case* and present an overview of how it can be handled. Since $\tau_d = \tau_p$, p_R^* would traverse τ_d only if $x_r \in \tau_d = \tau_p$, i.e., $(x_r, y_r) = (x_2', y_2')$. Thus, both the lowest and the highest edges on $path(r_c, r')$, i.e., (x_p, y_p) and (x_r, y_r), from an eligible subtree hanging from $path(v_L, v_H)$ belong to τ_d. Moreover, since τ_d hangs from $path(v_L, v_H)$, it does not contain $T(v_H)$. This ensures that if modified r' traversal is performed ignoring τ_d, it can be followed by a disconnecting traversal of τ_d (see full paper [23] for details).

Correctness:

To prove the correctness of our algorithm, it is sufficient to prove two properties. *Firstly*, the components property is satisfied in each traversal mentioned above. *Secondly*, every component in a phase/stage, abides by the size constraints defining the phase/stage. By construction, we always choose the lowest edge from a component to the recently added path in T^* ensuring that the components property is satisfied. Furthermore, in different traversals we have clearly proved how each component progresses to the next stage/phase ensuring the size constraints. Thus, the final tree T^* returned by the algorithm is indeed a DFS tree of the updated graph.

Analysis

We now analyze a stage of the algorithm for processing a component c. In each stage, our algorithm performs at most $O(1)$ traversals of each type described above. Let us first consider the queries performed on the data structure $\mathcal{D}$. Every traversal described above performs $O(1)$ sets of these queries sequentially, where each set may have $O(|c|)$ parallel queries. Moreover, each of these sets is an *independent* set of parallel queries on $\mathcal{D}$ (recall the definition of *independent* queries in Section 2). This is because in each set of parallel queries, different queries are performed either on different untraversed subtrees of currently processed subtree or on the traversed path in the currently processed subtree. The remaining operations (excluding queries to $\mathcal{D}$) clearly requires only the knowledge of the current DFS tree T (and not whole G). Hence, they can be performed locally in the distributed and semi-streaming environment. Performing these operations efficiently in parallel shall be described in Section 4. Since our algorithm requires $\log n$ phases each having $\log n$ stages, we get the following theorem.

Theorem 3.5. *Given an undirected graph and its DFS tree T, any subtree τ of T can be rerooted at any vertex $r' \in \tau$ by sequentially performing $O(\log^2 n)$ sets of $O(|\tau|)$ independent queries on $\mathcal{D}$, in addition to local computation requiring only the subtree τ.*

4 IMPLEMENTATION ON EREW PRAM

We assign $|c|$ processors to process a component c, requiring overall n processors. We first present an efficient implementation of $\mathcal{D}$ and the operations on T used by our algorithm. These results are fairly simple or derived directly from classical results and hence may not be of independent interest (see full paper [23] for details).

Theorem 4.1. *The DFS tree T of a graph can be preprocessed to build a data structure $\mathcal{D}$ of size $O(m)$ in $O(\log n)$ time using m processors, such that a set of independent queries of types $Query(w, path(x, y))$, $Query(T(w), path(x, y))$ and $Query(path(v, w), path(x, y))$ on T can be answered simultaneously in $O(\log n)$ time using $1, |T(w)|$ and $|path(x, y)|$ processors respectively on an EREW PRAM.*

Remark. *Unlike the complicated $\mathcal{D}_0$ used by Baswana et al. [5], our data structure $\mathcal{D}$ is merely sorted adjacency lists of the graph according to the post order traversal of T.*

Theorem 4.2. *The DFS tree T of a graph can be preprocessed to build a data structure of size $O(n)$ in $O(\log n)$ time using n processors, such that the following queries can be answered in parallel in $O(\log n)$ time on an EREW PRAM*

- *LCA of two vertices, size of a subtree, testing if an edge is back edge and length of a path, using a single processor per query.*
- *Finding vertices on a path, subtrees hanging from a path, child subtree of a vertex containing a given vertex, highest/lowest edge among k edges, using k processors per query, where k is the size of the corresponding component.*

Using these data structures we can now analyze the time required by the *reduction* algorithm on an EREW PRAM. Since the queries on $\mathcal{D}$ and *LCA* queries on T can be answered in $O(\log n)$ time using n processors as described above, Theorem 2.2 reduces to the following theorem.

Theorem 4.3. *Given the DFS tree T of a graph and the data structure $\mathcal{D}$ built on it, any update on the graph can be reduced to independently rerooting disjoint subtrees of the DFS tree using n processors in $O(\log n)$ time on an EREW PRAM.*

Implementation details

Using Theorem 4.1 and Theorem 4.2, we can show that all operations required for each stage of our rerooting algorithm to reroot a subtree τ, can be performed in $O(\log n)$ time using $|\tau|$ processors. Both $root(\tau_c)$ and vertex v_H required by our algorithm while processing a component c, can be computed in parallel by comparing the size of each subtree using $|c|$ processors. Adding a path p to T^* essentially involves marking the corresponding edges as tree edges, which can be performed by informing the vertices on p. All the other operations of the rerooting algorithm are trivially reducible to the operations described in Theorem 4.2. Since our rerooting algorithm requires $\log n$ phases each having $\log n$ stages, we get the following theorem for rerooting disjoint subtrees using our rerooting algorithm.

Theorem 4.4. *Given an undirected graph with the data structure $\mathcal{D}$ build on its DFS tree, independently rerooting disjoint subtrees of the DFS tree can be performed in $O(\log^3 n)$ time using n processors on an EREW PRAM.*

Using Theorem 4.1 Theorem 4.3 and Theorem 4.4, we can prove our main result described as follows.

Theorem 1.1. *Given an undirected graph and its DFS tree, it can be preprocessed to build a data structure of size $O(m)$ in $O(\log n)$ time using m processors on an EREW PRAM, such that for any update in the graph, a DFS tree of the updated graph can be computed in $O(\log^3 n)$ time using n processors on an EREW PRAM.*

Now, in order to prove our result for Parallel Fully Dynamic DFS and Parallel Fault Tolerant DFS we need to first build the DFS tree of the original graph from scratch during the preprocessing stage. This can be done using the static DFS algorithm [37] or any advanced deterministic parallel algorithm [1, 17]. Thus, for processing any update we always have the current DFS tree built (either the original DFS tree built during preprocessing or the updated DFS tree built by our algorithm for the previous update). We can thus build the data structure $\mathcal{D}$ using Theorem 4.1 reducing Theorem 1.1 to the following theorem.

Theorem 4.5 (Parallel Fully Dynamic DFS). *Given an undirected graph, we can maintain its DFS tree under any arbitrary online sequence of vertex or edge updates in $O(\log^3 n)$ time per update using m processors on an EREW PRAM.*

However, if we limit the number of processors to n, our fully dynamic algorithm cannot update the DFS tree in $\tilde{O}(1)$ time, only because updating $\mathcal{D}$ in $\tilde{O}(1)$ time requires $O(m)$ processors (see Theorem 4.1). Thus, we build the data structure $\mathcal{D}$ using Theorem 4.1 during preprocessing itself, and attempt to use it to handle multiple updates.

Extending to multiple updates

Consider a sequence of k updates on graph, let T_i^* represent the DFS tree computed by our algorithm after i updates in the graph. We also denote the corresponding data structure $\mathcal{D}$ built on T_i^* as $\mathcal{D}_i$. Now, consider any stage of our algorithm while building the DFS tree T_i^*. For each component in parallel, $O(1)$ ancestor-descendant paths of T_{i-1}^* are added to T_i^*. Thus, any ancestor-descendant path p of T_i^*, is built by adding $O(\log^2 n)$ such paths of T_{i-1}^*, corresponding to $O(\log n)$ phases each having $O(\log n)$ stages. Hence, p is union of $O(\log^2 n)$ ancestor-descendant paths of T_{i-1}^*, say $p_1, ..., p_k$.

Using this reduction, it can be shown that a set of independent queries on path p in $\mathcal{D}_i$, can be reduced to $O(\log^2 n)$ sets of independent queries on corresponding $O(\log^2 n)$ paths $p_1, ..., p_k$ on $\mathcal{D}_{i-1}$ (see full paper [23] for details). Again, each of these paths $p_1, ..., p_k$, being an ancestor-descendant path of T_{i-1}^*, is a union of $O(\log^2 n)$ ancestor-descendant paths of T_{i-2}^*, and so on. Thus, any set of independent queries on $\mathcal{D}_i$ can be performed by $O(\log^{2(i-1)} n)$ sets of independent queries on $\mathcal{D}$, which takes $O(\log^{2i-1})$ time on an EREW PRAM using n processors when $k \leq \log n$ (see Theorem 4.1). The other data structures on T_{i-1}^* can be built in $O(\log n)$ time using n processors (see Theorem 4.2). This allows our algorithm to build the DFS tree T_i^* from T_{i-1}^* using $\mathcal{D}$ in $O(\log^{2i+1})$ time on an EREW PRAM using n processors (see Theorem 3.5). Thus, for a given set of k updates we build each T_i^* one by one using T_{i-1}^* and $\mathcal{D}$, to get the following theorem.

Theorem 4.6 (Parallel Fault Tolerant DFS). *Given an undirected graph, it can be preprocessed to build a data structure of size $O(m)$, such that for any set of k ($\leq \log n$) updates in the graph, a DFS tree of the updated graph can be computed in $O(k \log^{2k+1} n)$ time using n processors on an EREW PRAM.*

Remark. *For $k = 1$, our algorithm also gives an $O(n \log^3 n)$ time sequential algorithm for updating a DFS tree after a single update in the graph, achieving similar bounds as Baswana et al. [5]. However, our algorithm uses much simpler data structure $\mathcal{D}$ at the cost of a more complex algorithm.*

5 APPLICATIONS IN OTHER MODELS OF COMPUTATION

5.1 Semi-Streaming Setting

Our algorithm only stores the current DFS tree T and the partially built DFS tree T^* taking $O(n)$ space. Thus, all operations on T can be performed without any passes over the input graph. A set of independent queries on $\mathcal{D}$ is evaluated by performing a single pass over all the edges of the input graph using $O(n)$ space. This is because each set has $O(n)$ queries (see Theorem 2.2 and Theorem 3.5) and we are required to store only one edge per query (partial solution based on edges visited by the pass). Note that here the role of $\mathcal{D}$ is performed by a pass over the input graph. Hence, using Theorem 2.2 and Theorem 3.5 our algorithm requires $O(\log^2 n)$ passes per update proving our semi-streaming algorithm described as follows.

Theorem 5.1. *Given an undirected graph and its DFS tree, for any given update in the graph the updated DFS tree can be computed using $O(\log^2 n)$ passes over the input graph by a semi-streaming algorithm using $O(n)$ space.*

5.2 Distributed Setting

Our algorithm stores only the current DFS tree T and the partially built DFS tree T^* at each node. Thus, the operations on T are performed locally at each node and the distributed computation is only used to evaluate the queries on $\mathcal{D}$. Using Theorem 2.2 and Theorem 3.5, each update is performed by $O(\log^2 n)$ sequential sets of $O(n)$ independent queries on $\mathcal{D}$. Evaluation of a set of $O(n)$ independent queries on $\mathcal{D}$ can be essentially reduced to propagation of $O(n)$ words (partial solutions of n queries) throughout the network. Using the standard technique of pipelined broadcasts and convergecasts [30], we can propagate these $O(n)$ words in $O(D)$ rounds using messages of size $O(n/D)$. This proves our distributed algorithm described in Section 1.2. Refer to full paper [23] for details of implementation.

6 CONCLUSION

Our parallel dynamic algorithms take nearly optimal time on an EREW PRAM. However, the work efficiency of our fully dynamic algorithm is $\tilde{O}(m)$ whereas that of the best sequential algorithm [6] is $\tilde{O}(\sqrt{mn})$. Even though our fault tolerant algorithm is nearly work optimal, its only for constant number of updates. The primary reason behind these limitations is the difficulty in updating the data structure $\mathcal{D}$ using n processors. Our fault tolerant algorithm avoids this problem, by naively using the original $\mathcal{D}$ to simulate the queries of updated $\mathcal{D}$. It would be interesting to see if an algorithm can process significantly more updates using only n processors in $\tilde{O}(1)$ time (similar extension was performed by Baswana et al. [6] in the sequential setting). This may also lead to a fully dynamic algorithm that is nearly time optimal with better work efficiency.

Further, our distributed algorithm works only on a substantially restricted synchronous $CONGEST(n/D)$ model. Moreover, the number of messages passed during an update in the distributed algorithm is $O(nD\log^2 n + m)$, which is way worse than the number of messages required to compute a DFS from scratch when the message size is relaxed, i.e., $O(n)$. It would be interesting to see if dynamic DFS can be maintained in near optimal rounds in more stronger $CONGEST$ or $\mathcal{LOCAL}$ models.

ACKNOWLEDGMENTS

I am grateful to Christoph Lenzen for suggesting this problem. I would also like to express my sincere gratitude to my advisor Prof. Surender Baswana for valuable discussions and key insights that led to this paper. The idea of extending the parallel algorithm to the distributed setting was rooted in these discussions. Finally, I would like to thank the anonymous reviewers and my advisor whose critical assessment significantly helped me in refining the paper. This work is supported by Google India under the Google India PhD Fellowship Award.

REFERENCES

[1] Alok Aggarwal and Richard J. Anderson. 1988. A random NC algorithm for depth first search. *Combinatorica* 8, 1 (1988), 1–12.
[2] Alok Aggarwal, Richard J. Anderson, and Ming-Yang Kao. 1990. Parallel Depth-First Search in General Directed Graphs. *SIAM J. Comput.* 19, 2 (1990), 397–409.
[3] Sepehr Assadi, Sanjeev Khanna, Yang Li, and Grigory Yaroslavtsev. 2016. Maximum Matchings in Dynamic Graph Streams and the Simultaneous Communication Model. In *ACM-SIAM Symposium on Discrete Algorithms, SODA.* Society for Industrial and Applied Mathematics, Philadelphia, PA, USA, 1345–1364.
[4] Baruch Awerbuch, Israel Cidon, and Shay Kutten. 2008. Optimal maintenance of a spanning tree. *J. ACM* 55, 4, Article 18 (2008), 45 pages.
[5] Surender Baswana, Shreejit Ray Chaudhury, Keerti Choudhary, and Shahbaz Khan. 2015. Dynamic DFS Tree in Undirected Graphs: breaking the O(m) barrier, Full version of [6]. *CoRR* abs/1502.02481 (2015).
[6] Surender Baswana, Shreejit Ray Chaudhury, Keerti Choudhary, and Shahbaz Khan. 2016. Dynamic DFS in Undirected Graphs: breaking the $O(m)$ barrier. In *ACM-SIAM Symposium on Discrete Algorithms, SODA.* Society for Industrial and Applied Mathematics, Philadelphia, PA, USA, 730–739.
[7] Surender Baswana and Keerti Choudhary. 2015. On Dynamic DFS Tree in Directed Graphs. In *Mathematical Foundations of Computer Science, MFCS.* Springer Berlin Heidelberg, Berlin, Heidelberg, 102–114.
[8] Surender Baswana and Shahbaz Khan. 2014. Incremental Algorithm for Maintaining DFS Tree for Undirected Graphs. In *ICALP.* Springer Berlin Heidelberg, Berlin, Heidelberg, 138–149.
[9] E. Boros, K. Elbassioni, V. Gurvich, and L. Khachiyan. 2000. An efficient incremental algorithm for generating all maximal independent sets in hypergraphs of bounded dimension. *Parallel Processing Letters* 10 (2000), 253–266.
[10] Israel Cidon. 1988. Yet Another Distributed Depth-First-Search Algorithm. *Inf. Process. Lett.* 26, 6 (1988), 301–305.
[11] Shimon Even and Robert Endre Tarjan. 1975. Network Flow and Testing Graph Connectivity. *SIAM J. Comput.* 4, 4 (1975), 507–518.
[12] Martin Farach-Colton, Tsan-sheng Hsu, Meng Li, and Meng-Tsung Tsai. 2015. Finding Articulation Points of Large Graphs in Linear Time. In *Algorithms and Data Structures, WADS.* Springer International Publishing, Cham, 363–372.
[13] P. Ferragina. 1995. A Technique to Speed Up Parallel Fully Dynamic Algorithms for MST. *J. Parallel Distrib. Comput.* 31, 2 (Dec. 1995), 181–189.
[14] Paolo Giulio Franciosa, Giorgio Gambosi, and Umberto Nanni. 1997. The Incremental Maintenance of a Depth-First-Search Tree in Directed Acyclic Graphs. *Inf. Process. Lett.* 61, 2 (1997), 113–120.
[15] Jon Freeman. October 1991. Parallel Algorithms for Depth-First Search. *Technical Report, University of Pennsylvania* (October 1991).
[16] Ratan K. Ghosh and G. P. Bhattacharjee. 1984. A Parallel Search Algorithm for Directed Acyclic Graphs. *BIT* 24, 2 (1984), 134–150.
[17] Andrew V. Goldberg, Serge A. Plotkin, and Pravin M. Vaidya. 1993. Sublinear-Time Parallel Algorithms for Matching and Related Problems. *J. Algorithms* 14, 2 (1993), 180–213.
[18] Sudipto Guha, Andrew McGregor, and David Tench. 2015. Vertex and Hyperedge Connectivity in Dynamic Graph Streams. In *ACM Symposium on Principles of Database Systems, PODS.* ACM, New York, NY, USA, 241–247.
[19] Torben Hagerup. 1990. Planar Depth-First Search in O(log n) Parallel Time. *SIAM J. Comput.* 19, 4 (1990), 678–704.
[20] Monika Henzinger, Sebastian Krinninger, and Danupon Nanongkai. 2013. Sublinear-Time Maintenance of Breadth-First Spanning Tree in Partially Dynamic Networks. In *ICALP (2).* Springer-Verlag, Berlin, Heidelberg, 607–619.
[21] Zengfeng Huang and Pan Peng. 2016. Dynamic Graph Stream Algorithms in o(n) Space. In *43rd International Colloquium on Automata, Languages, and Programming (ICALP 2016).* Schloss Dagstuhl–Leibniz-Zentrum fuer Informatik, Dagstuhl, Germany, 18:1–18:16.
[22] Junting Jin, Xiaowei Shi, Cuiping Li, and Hong Chen. 2014. Fast Approximation of Shortest Path on Dynamic Information Networks. In *Web-Age Information Management WAIM.* Springer International Publishing, Cham, 272–276.
[23] Shahbaz Khan. 2017. Near Optimal Parallel Algorithms for Dynamic DFS in Undirected Graphs. *CoRR* abs/1705.03637 (2017).
[24] Valerie King, Shay Kutten, and Mikkel Thorup. 2015. Construction and Impromptu Repair of an MST in a Distributed Network with o(m) Communication. In *Proceedings of the 2015 ACM Symposium on Principles of Distributed Computing, PODC.* ACM, New York, NY, USA, 71–80.
[25] Devendra Kumar, S. Sitharama Iyengar, and Mohan B. Sharma. 1990. Corrigenda: Corrections to a Distributed Depth-First Search Algorithm. *Inf. Process. Lett.* 35, 1 (1990), 55–56.
[26] K. B. Lakshmanan, N. Meenakshi, and Krishnaiyan Thulasiraman. 1987. A Time-Optimal Message-Efficient Distributed Algorithm for Depth-First-Search. *Inf. Process. Lett.* 25, 2 (1987), 103–109.
[27] S. A. M. Makki and George Havas. 1996. Distributed Algorithms for Depth-First Search. *Inf. Process. Lett.* 60, 1 (1996), 7–12.
[28] Andrew McGregor. 2014. Graph Stream Algorithms: A Survey. *SIGMOD Rec.* 43, 1 (May 2014), 9–20.
[29] Thomas C. O'Connell. 2009. A Survey of Graph Algorithms Under Extended Streaming Models of Computation. In *Fundamental Problems in Computing: Essays in Honor of Professor Daniel J. Rosenkrantz*, S. S. Ravi and Sandeep K. Shukla (Eds.). Springer Netherlands, Dordrecht, 455–476.
[30] David Peleg. 2000. *Distributed Computing: A Locality-sensitive Approach.* Society for Industrial and Applied Mathematics, Philadelphia, PA, USA.
[31] John H. Reif. 1985. Depth-First Search is Inherently Sequential. *Inf. Process. Lett.* 20, 5 (1985), 229–234.
[32] Jan Matthias Ruhl. 2003. Efficient Algorithms for New Computational Models. *PhD Thesis* Department of Computer Science, MIT, Cambridge, MA (2003).
[33] Kirk Schloegel, George Karypis, and Vipin Kumar. 2002. Parallel static and dynamic multi-constraint graph partitioning. *Concurrency and Computation: Practice and Experience* 14, 3 (2002), 219–240.
[34] Mohan B. Sharma and S. Sitharama Iyengar. 1989. An Efficient Distributed Depth-First-Search Algorithm. *Inf. Process. Lett.* 32, 4 (1989), 183–186.
[35] Deepak D. Sherlekar, Shaunak Pawagi, and I. V. Ramakrishnan. 1985. O(1) Parallel Time Incremental Graph Algorithms. In *Foundations of Software Technology and Theoretical Computer Science.* Springer Berlin Heidelberg, Berlin, Heidelberg, 477–495.

[36] Bala Swaminathan and Kenneth J. Goldman. 1998. An Incremental Distributed Algorithm for Computing Biconnected Components in Dynamic Graphs. *Algorithmica* 22, 3 (1998), 305–329.
[37] Robert Endre Tarjan. 1972. Depth-First Search and Linear Graph Algorithms. *SIAM J. Comput.* 1, 2 (1972), 146–160.
[38] Robert Endre Tarjan. 1974. Finding Dominators in Directed Graphs. *SIAM J. Comput.* 3, 1 (1974), 62–89.
[39] Robert Endre Tarjan. 1976. Edge-Disjoint Spanning Trees and Depth-First Search. *Acta Inf.* 6 (1976), 171–185.
[40] Yung H. Tsin. 2002. Some remarks on distributed depth-first search. *Inf. Process. Lett.* 82, 4 (2002), 173–178.

A REDUCTION ALGORITHM

We now describe how updating a DFS tree after any kind of update in the graph is equivalent to a simple procedure, i.e., *rerooting* disjoint subtrees of the DFS tree. Note that similar reduction was also used by Baswana et al. [5] but we describe it here for the sake of completeness as follows (see Figure 4).

(1) **Deletion of an edge** (u, v):
If (u, v) is a back edge in T, simply delete it from the graph. Otherwise, let $u = par(v)$ in T. The algorithm finds the lowest edge (u', v') on the $path(u, r)$ from $T(v)$, where $v' \in T(v)$. The subtree $T(v)$ can then be rerooted to the new root v' and hanged from u' using (u', v') to get the final tree T^*.
(2) **Insertion of an edge** (u, v):
In case (u, v) is a back edge, simply insert it in the graph. Otherwise, let w be the LCA of u and v in T and v' be the child of w such that $v \in T(v')$. The subtree $T(v')$ can then be rerooted to the new root v and hanged from u using (u, v) to get the final tree T^*.
(3) **Deletion of a vertex** u:
Let $v_1, ..., v_c$ be the children of u in T. For each subtree $T(v_i)$, the algorithm finds the lowest edge (u_i', v_i') on the $path(par(u), r)$ from $T(v_i)$, where $v_i' \in T(v_i)$. Each subtree $T(v_i)$ can then be rerooted to the new root v_i' and hanged from u_i' using (u_i', v_i') to get the final tree T^*.
(4) **Insertion of a vertex** u:
Let $v_1, ..., v_c$ be the neighbors of u in the graph. Arbitrarily choose a neighbor v_j and make u the child of v_j in T^*. For each v_i, such that $v_i \notin path(v_j, r)$, let $T(v_i')$ be the subtree hanging from $path(v_j, r)$ such that $v_i \in T(v_i')$. Each subtree $T(v_i')$ can then be rerooted to the new root v_i and hanged from u using (u, v_i) to get the final tree T^*.

In case of a vertex update, multiple subtrees may be required to be rerooted by the algorithm. Let these subtrees be $T_1, ..., T_c$. Notice that each of these subtrees can be rerooted independent of each other, and hence in parallel. However, in order to perform the *reduction* algorithm efficiently in parallel, we require a structure to answer the following queries efficiently in parallel. (a) Finding LCA of two vertices in T. (b) Finding the highest edge from a subtree $T(v)$ to a path in T (a query on data structure $\mathcal{D}$). In addition to these we also require several other types of queries to be efficiently answered in parallel setting as testing if an edge is back edge, finding vertices on a path, child subtree of a vertex containing a given vertex etc. However, these can easily be answered using LCA queries (see full paper [23] for details). Thus, we have the following theorem.

Theorem 2.2. *Given an undirected graph G and its DFS tree T, any graph update can be reduced to independently rerooting disjoint subtrees of T by performing $O(1)$ sets of independent queries on the data structure $\mathcal{D}$ and $O(1)$ sets of LCA queries on T, where each set has at most n queries.*

Remark. *The implementation of reduction algorithm is simpler in distributed and semi-streaming environments, where any operation on the DFS tree T can be performed locally without any distributed computation or passes over the input graph respectively. Hence, for these environments the reduction algorithm requires only $O(1)$ sets of independent queries on the data structure $\mathcal{D}$.*

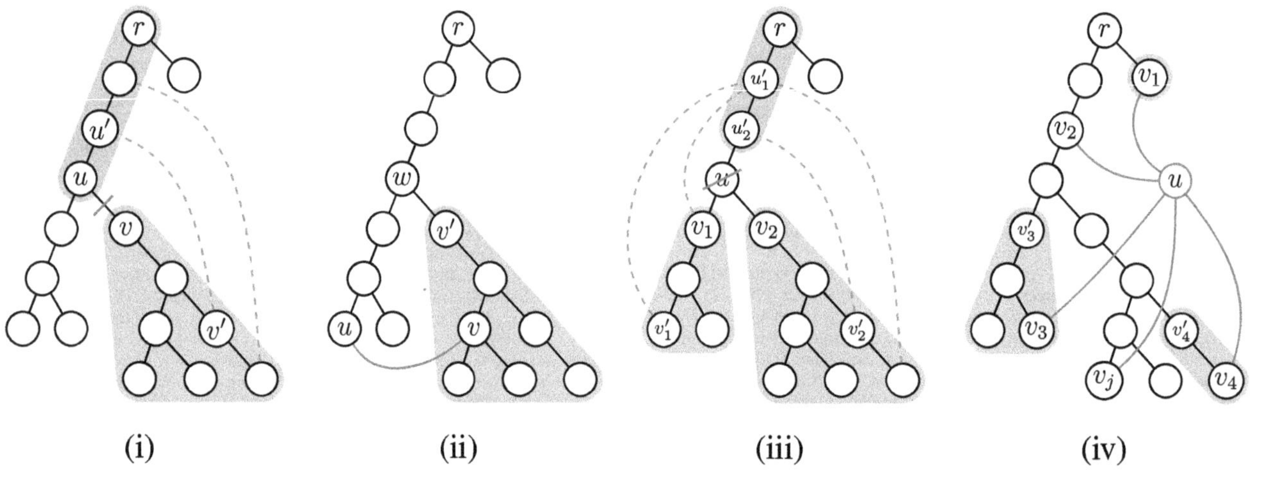

Figure 4: Updating the DFS tree after a single update: (i) deletion of an edge, (ii) insertion of an edge, (iii) deletion of a vertex, and (iv) insertion of a vertex. The reduction algorithm reroots the marked subtrees (shown in violet) and hangs it from the inserted edge (in case of insertion) or the lowest edge (in case of deletion) on the marked path (shown in blue) from the marked subtree (reproduced from [5]).

Julienne: A Framework for Parallel Graph Algorithms using Work-efficient Bucketing

Laxman Dhulipala
Carnegie Mellon University
ldhulipa@cs.cmu.edu

Guy Blelloch
Carnegie Mellon University
guyb@cs.cmu.edu

Julian Shun
UC Berkeley
jshun@eecs.berkeley.edu

ABSTRACT

Existing graph-processing frameworks let users develop efficient implementations for many graph problems, but none of them support efficiently bucketing vertices, which is needed for *bucketing-based* graph algorithms such as Δ-stepping and approximate set-cover. Motivated by the lack of simple, scalable, and efficient implementations of bucketing-based algorithms, we develop the Julienne framework, which extends a recent shared-memory graph processing framework called Ligra with an interface for maintaining a collection of buckets under vertex insertions and bucket deletions.

We provide a theoretically efficient parallel implementation of our bucketing interface and study several bucketing-based algorithms that make use of it (either bucketing by remaining degree or by distance) to improve performance: the peeling algorithm for k-core (coreness), Δ-stepping, weighted breadth-first search, and approximate set cover. The implementations are all simple and concise (under 100 lines of code). Using our interface, we develop the first work-efficient parallel algorithm for k-core in the literature with nontrivial parallelism.

We experimentally show that our bucketing implementation scales well and achieves high throughput on both synthetic and real-world workloads. Furthermore, the bucketing-based algorithms written in Julienne achieve up to 43x speedup on 72 cores with hyper-threading over well-tuned sequential baselines, significantly outperform existing work-inefficient implementations in Ligra, and either outperform or are competitive with existing special-purpose parallel codes for the same problem. We experimentally study our implementations on the largest publicly available graphs and show that they scale well in practice, processing real-world graphs with billions of edges in seconds, and hundreds of billions of edges in a few minutes. As far as we know, this is the first time that graphs at this scale have been analyzed in the main memory of a single multicore machine.

1 INTRODUCTION

Both the size and availability of real-world graphs has increased dramatically over the past decade. Due to the need to process this data quickly, many frameworks for processing massive graphs have been developed for both distributed-memory and shared-memory parallel machines such as Pregel [36], GraphLab [32, 33], PowerGraph [22], and Ligra [51]. Implementing algorithms using frameworks instead of as one-off programs enables users to easily take advantage of optimizations already implemented by the framework, such as direction-optimization, compression and parallelization over both the vertices and edges of a set of vertices [5, 55].

The performance of algorithms in these frameworks is often determined by the total amount of work performed. Unfortunately, the simplest algorithms to implement in existing frameworks are often work-inefficient, i.e., they perform asymptotically more work than the most efficient sequential algorithm. While work-inefficient algorithms can exhibit excellent self-relative speedup, their absolute performance can be an order of magnitude worse than the running time of the baseline sequential algorithm, even on a very large number of cores [38].

Many commonly implemented graph algorithms in existing frameworks are *frontier-based* algorithms. Frontier-based algorithms proceed in rounds, where each round performs some computation on vertices in the current frontier, and frontiers can change from round to round. For example, in breadth-first search (BFS), the frontier on round i is the set of vertices at distance i from the source of the search. In label propagation implementations of graph connectivity [22, 51], the frontier on each round consists of vertices whose labels changed in the previous round.

However, several fundamental graph algorithms cannot be expressed as frontier-based algorithms. These algorithms, which we call *bucketing-based* algorithms, maintain vertices in a set of ordered buckets. In each round, the algorithm extracts the vertices contained in the lowest (or highest) bucket and performs some computation on these vertices. It can then update the buckets containing either the extracted vertices or their neighbors. Frontier-based algorithms are a special case of bucketing-based algorithms, specifically they are bucketing-based algorithms that only use one bucket.

As an example, consider the weighted breadth-first search (wBFS) algorithm, which solves the single-source shortest path problem (SSSP) with nonnegative, integral edge weights in parallel [18]. Like BFS, wBFS processes vertices level by level, where level i contains all vertices at distance exactly i from *src*, the source vertex. The i'th round relaxes the neighbors of vertices in level i and updates any distances that change. Unlike a BFS, where the unvisited neighbors of the current level are in the next level, the neighbors of a level in wBFS can be spread across multiple levels. Because of this, wBFS maintains the levels in an ordered set of buckets. On round i, if a vertex v can decrease the distance to a neighbor u it places u in bucket $i+d(v,u)$. Finding the vertices in a given level can then easily be done using the bucket structure. We can show that the work of this algorithm is $O(r_{src} + |E|)$ and the depth is $O(r_{src} \log |V|)$ where r_{src} is the eccentricity from *src* (see Section 2). However, without

SPAA '17, , July 24-26, 2017, Washington DC, USA

ACM ISBN 978-1-4503-4593-4/17/07...$15.00
https://doi.org/10.1145/3087556.3087580

bucketing, the algorithm has to scan all vertices in each round to compute the current level, which makes it perform $O(r_{src}|V| + |E|)$ work and the same depth, which is not work-efficient.

In this paper, we study four bucketing-based graph algorithms—k-core[1], Δ-stepping, weighted breadth-first search (wBFS), and approximate set-cover. To provide simple and theoretically-efficient implementations of these algorithms, we design and implement a work-efficient interface for bucketing in the Ligra shared-memory graph processing framework [51]. Our extended framework, which we call ***Julienne***, enables us to write short (under 100 lines of code) implementations of the algorithms that are efficient and achieve good parallel speedup (up to 43x on 72 cores with two-way hyper-threading). Furthermore we are able to process the largest publicly-available real-world graph containing over 225 billion edges in the memory of a single multicore machine [39]. This graph must be compressed in order to be processed even on a machine with 1TB of main memory. Because Julienne supports the compression features of Ligra+, we were able to run our codes on this graph without extra modifications [55]. All of our implementations either outperform or are competitive with hand-optimized codes for the same problem. We summarize the cost bounds for the algorithms developed in this paper in Table 1.

Using our framework, we obtain the first work-efficient algorithm for k-core with nontrivial parallelism. The sequential requires performs $O(n + m)$ work [4], however the best prior parallel algorithms [16, 20, 41, 44, 51] require at least $O(k_{max}n+m)$ work where k_{max} is the largest core number in the graph—this is because these algorithms scan all remaining vertices when computing vertices in a particular core. By using bucketing, our algorithm only scans the edges of vertices with minimum degree, which makes it work-efficient. On a graph with 225B edges using 72 cores with two-way hyper-threading, our work-efficient implementation takes under 4 minutes to complete, whereas the work-inefficient implementation does not finish even after 3 hours.

Contributions. The main contributions of this paper are as follows.

1. A simple interface for dynamically maintaining sets of identifiers in buckets.
2. A theoretically efficient parallel algorithm that implements our bucketing interface, and four applications implemented using the interface.
3. The first work-efficient implementation of k-core with non-trivial parallelism.
4. Experimental results on the largest publicly available graphs, showing that our codes achieve high performance while remaining simple. To the best of our knowledge, this work is the first time graphs at the scale of billions of vertices and hundreds of billions of edges have been analyzed in minutes in the memory of a single shared-memory server.

[1]The definitions of k-core and coreness (see Secton 4.1) have been used interchangeably in the literature, however they are not the same problem, as pointed out in [46]. In this paper we use k-core to refer to the coreness problem. Note that computing a particular k-core from the coreness numbers requires finding the largest induced subgraph among vertices with coreness at least k, which can be done efficiently in parallel.

Algorithm	Work	Depth	Parameters
k-core	$O(\|E\| + \|V\|)$	$O(\rho \log \|V\|)$	ρ: peeling complexity, see Section 4.1.
wBFS	$O(r_{src} + \|E\|)$	$O(r_{src} \log \|V\|)$	r_{src}: eccentricity from the source vertex src, see Section 2.
Δ-stepping	$O(w_\Delta)$	$O(d_\Delta \log \|V\|)$	w_Δ, d_Δ: work and number of rounds of the original Δ-stepping algorithm.
Approximate Set Cover	$O(M)$	$O(\log^3 M)$	M: sum of the sizes of the sets.

Table 1: Cost bounds for the algorithms developed in this paper. The work bounds are in expectation and the depth bounds are with high probability.

2 PRELIMINARIES

We denote a directed unweighted graph by $G(V, E)$ where V is the set of vertices and E is the set of (directed) edges in the graph. A weighted graph is denoted by $G = (V, E, w)$, where w is a function which maps an edge to a real value (its weight). The number of vertices in a graph is $n = |V|$, and the number of edges is $m = |E|$. Vertices are assumed to be indexed from 0 to $n - 1$. For undirected graphs we use $N(v)$ to denote the neighbors of vertex v and $deg(v)$ to denote its degree. We use r_s to denote the eccentricity, or longest shortest path distance between a vertex s and any vertex v reachable from s. We assume that there are no self-edges or duplicate edges in the graph.

We analyze algorithms in the work-depth model, where the ***work*** is the number of operations used by the algorithm and the ***depth*** is the length of the longest sequential dependence in the computation [25]. We allow for concurrent reads and writes in the model. A ***compare-and-swap*** (CAS) is an atomic instruction that takes three arguments—a memory location (*loc*), an old value (*oldV*) and a new value (*newV*). If the value currently stored at *loc* is equal to *oldV* it atomically updates *newV* at *loc* and returns *true*. Otherwise, *loc* is not modified and the CAS returns *false*. A ***writeMin*** is an atomic instruction that takes two arguments—a memory location (*loc*) and an old value (*val*), and atomically updates the value stored at *loc* to be the minimum of the stored value and *val*, returning *true* if the stored value was atomically updated and *false* otherwise. We assume that both CAS and writeMin take $O(1)$ work and note that both primitives are very efficient in practice [52].

The following parallel procedures are used throughout the paper. ***Scan*** takes as input an array X of length n, an associative binary operator $\oplus$, and an identity element $\perp$ such that $\perp \oplus x = x$ for any x, and returns the array $(\perp, \perp\oplus X[0], \perp\oplus X[0]\oplus X[1], \ldots, \perp\oplus_{i=0}^{n-2} X[i])$ as well as the overall sum, $\perp \oplus_{i=0}^{n-1} X[i]$. Scan can be done in $O(n)$ work and $O(\log n)$ depth (assuming $\oplus$ takes $O(1)$ work) [25]. ***Reduce*** takes an array A and a binary associative function f and returns the "sum" of elements with respect to f. ***Filter*** takes an array A and a function f returning a boolean and returns a new array containing $e \in A$ for which $f(e)$ is true, in the same order as in A. Both reduce and filter can be done in $O(n)$ work and $O(\log n)$ depth (assuming f takes $O(1)$ work). A ***semisort*** takes an input array of elements, where each element has an associated key and reorders the elements so that elements with equal keys are contiguous, but elements with different keys are not necessarily ordered. The purpose is to collect equal keys together, rather than sort them. A semisort can be done in $O(n)$ expected work and $O(c \log n)$ depth with probability $1-1/n^c$ (i.e., ***with high probability (w.h.p.)***) [23].

2.1 Ligra Framework

In this section, we review the Ligra framework for shared-memory graph processing [51]. Ligra provides data structures for representing a graph $G = (V, E)$, and ***vertexSubsets*** (subsets of the vertices). It provides the functions VERTEXMAP, used for mapping over vertices, and EDGEMAP, used for mapping over edges. ***VERTEXMAP*** takes as input a vertexSubset U and a function F returning a boolean. It applies F to all vertices in U and returns a vertexSubset containing $U' \subseteq U$ where. $u \in U'$ if and only if $F(u) = true$. F can side-effect data structures associated with the vertices. ***EDGEMAP*** takes as input a graph $G(V, E)$, a vertexSubset U, and two functions F and C which both return a boolean. EDGEMAP applies F to $(u, v) \in E$ s.t. $u \in U$ and $C(v) = true$ (call this subset of edges E_a), and returns a vertexSubset U' where $u \in V$ if and only if $(u, v) \in E_a$ and $F(u, v) = true$. As in VERTEXMAP, F can side-effect data structures associated with the vertices.

Additional Primitives. We add several primitives to Julienne in addition to those provided by Ligra that simplify the expression of our algorithms. We include an option type MAYBE(T). We extend the vertexSubset data structure to allow vertices in the subset to have associated values. We denote a vertexSubset with associated value type **T** as ***vertexSubset***$_T$. A vertexSubset$_T$ can be supplied to any functions that accept a vertexSubset. We also add a function call operator to vertexSubset which returns a (vertex, data) pair.

We provide a new primitive, ***EDGEMAPREDUCE***, which takes a graph G, vertexSubset S, a map function $M : \mathbf{vtx} \rightarrow \mathbf{T}$, an associative and commutative reduce function $R : \mathbf{T} \times \mathbf{T} \rightarrow \mathbf{T}$, and an update function $U : \mathbf{vtx} \times \mathbf{T} \rightarrow$ MAYBE(**O**), and returns a vertexSubset$_O$. EDGEMAPREDUCE performs the following logic common to many graph algorithms: M is applied to each neighbor of S in parallel. The mapped values are reduced to a single value per neighbor using R (in an arbitrary ordering since R is associative and commutative). Finally, U is called on the neighboring vertex v and the reduced value for v. The output is a vertexSubset$_O$, where all vertices for which U returned NONE are filtered out. In our applications, we use ***EDGEMAPSUM***, which specializes M to 1 and R to SUM.

We provide a primitive, ***EDGEMAPFILTER***, which takes a graph G, vertexSubset U, and a predicate P, and outputs a vertexSubset$_{\mathbf{int}}$, where each vertex $u \in U$ has an associated count for the number of neighbors that satisfied P. EDGEMAPFILTER also takes an optional parameter PACK which lets applications remove edges to all neighbors that do not satisfy P by mutating G.

3 BUCKETING

The bucket structure maintains a dynamic mapping from identifiers to bucket_ids. The purpose of the structure is to provide efficient access to the inverse map—given a bucket_id, b, retrieve all identifiers currently mapped to b.

3.1 Interface

The bucket structure uses several types that we now define. An **identifier** is a unique integer representing a bucketed object. An identifier is mapped to a **bucket_id**, a unique integer for each bucket. The order that buckets are traversed in is given by the **bucket_order** type. **bucket_dest** is an opaque type representing where an identifier is moving inside of the structure. Once the structure is created, an object of type **buckets** is returned to the user.

The structure is created by calling MAKEBUCKETS and providing n, the number of identifiers, D, a function which maps identifiers to bucket_ids and O, a bucket_order. Initially, some identifiers may not be mapped to a bucket, so we add NULLBKT, a special bucket_id which lets D indicate this. Buckets in the structure are accessed monotonically in the order specified by O. While the interface can easily be modified to support random-access to buckets, we do not know of any algorithms that require it. Although we currently only use identifiers to represent vertices, our interface is not specific to storing and retrieving vertices, and may have applications other than graph algorithms. Even in the context of graphs, we envision algorithms where identifiers represent other objects such as edges, triangles, or graph motifs.

After the structure is created, NEXTBUCKET can be used to access the next non-empty bucket in non-decreasing (resp. non-increasing) order while UPDATEBUCKETS updates the bucket_ids for multiple identifiers. To iterate through the buckets, the structure internally maintains a variable CUR which stores the value of the current bucket being processed. Note that the CUR bucket can potentially be returned more than once by NEXTBUCKET if identifiers are inserted back into CUR. The GETBUCKET primitive is how users indicate that an identifier is moving buckets. We added this primitive to allow implementations to perform certain optimizations without extra involvement from the user. We describe these optimizations and present the rationale for the GETBUCKET primitive in Section 3.3.

The full list of functions is therefore:

- **MAKEBUCKETS**(n : *int*,
  D : identifier $\mapsto$ bucket_id
  O : bucket_order : buckets
  Creates a bucket structure containing n identifiers in the range $[0, n)$ where the bucket_id for identifier i is $D(i)$. The structure iterates over the buckets in order O which is either INCREASING or DECREASING.
- **NEXTBUCKET**() : (bucket_id, identifiers)
  Returns the bucket_id of the next non-empty bucket and the set of identifiers contained in it. When no identifiers are left in the bucket structure, the pair (NULLBKT, {}) is returned.
- **GETBUCKET**(PREV : bucket_id,
  NEXT : bucket_id) : bucket_dest
  Computes a bucket_dest for an identifier moving from bucket_id PREV to NEXT. Returns NULLBKT if the identifier does not need to be updated, or if NEXT< CUR.
- **UPDATEBUCKETS**(F : *int* $\mapsto$ (identifier, bucket_dest),
  k : *int*)
  Updates k identifiers in the bucket structure. The i'th identifier and its bucket_dest are given by $F(i)$.

3.2 Algorithms

We first discuss a sequential algorithm implementing the interface and analyze its cost. The sequential algorithm shares the same underlying ideas as the parallel algorithm, so we go through it in some detail. Both algorithms in this section represent buckets exactly and so the bucket_dest and bucket_id types are identical (in particular GETBUCKET just returns NEXT).

Sequential Bucketing. We represent each bucket using a dynamic array, and the set of buckets using a dynamic array B (B_i is the dynamic array for bucket i). For simplicity, we describe the algorithm in the case when buckets are processed in INCREASING order. The structure is initialized by computing the initial number of buckets by iterating over D and allocating a dynamic array of this size. Next, we iterate over the identifiers, inserting identifier i into bucket $B_{D(i)}$ if $D(i)$ is not NULLBKT, resizing if necessary. Updates are handled lazily. When UPDATEBUCKETS is called, we leave the identifier in B_{PREV} and just insert it into B_{NEXT}, opening new buckets if NEXT is outside the current range of buckets. As discussed in Section 3.1, buckets are extracted by maintaining a variable CUR which is initially the first bucket. When NEXTBUCKET is called, we check to see whether B_{CUR} is empty. If it is, we increment CUR and repeat. Otherwise, we compact B_{CUR}, only keeping identifiers $i \in B_{\text{CUR}}$ where $D(i) = \text{CUR}$, and return the resulting set of identifiers if it is nonempty, and repeat if it is empty.

We now discuss the total work done by the sequential algorithm. The work done by initialization is $O(n + T)$ work where T is the largest bucket used by the structure, as T is an upper bound on the number of buckets when the structure was initialized. Now, suppose the structure receives K calls to UPDATEBUCKETS after being initialized, each of which updates a set S_i of identifiers where $0 \leq i < K$. By amortizing the cost of creating new buckets against T, and noticing that each update that didn't create a new bucket can be done in $O(1)$ work, the total work across all calls to UPDATEBUCKETS is $O(T + \sum_{i=0}^{K} |S_i|)$.

We now argue that the total work done over all calls to NEXTBUCKET is also $O(T + \sum_{i=0}^{K} |S_i|)$. If CUR is empty, we increment it and repeat, which can happen at most T times. Otherwise, there are some number of identifiers $i \in A_{\text{CUR}}$. By charging each identifier, which can either be dead ($D(i) \neq \text{CUR}$) or live ($D(i) == \text{CUR}$), to the operation that inserted it into the current bucket, we obtain the bound. Summing the work for each primitive gives the following lemma.

LEMMA 3.1. *The total work performed by sequential bucketing when there are n identifiers, T total buckets and K calls to* UPDATEBUCKETS *each of which updates a set S_i of identifiers is $O(n + T + \sum_{i=0}^{K} |S_i|)$.*

As discussed in Section 3.1 a given bucket can be returned multiple times by NEXTBUCKET, and the same identifiers can be reinserted into the structure multiple times using UPDATEBUCKETS, so the total work of the bucket structure can potentially be much larger than $O(n)$. Some of our applications have the property that $\sum_{i=0}^{K} |S_i| = O(m)$, while also bounding T, the total number of buckets, as $O(n)$. For these applications, the cost of using the bucket-structure is $O(m + n)$.

Parallel Bucketing. In this section we describe a work-efficient parallel algorithm for our interface. The algorithm performs initialization, K calls to UPDATEBUCKETS, and L calls to NEXTBUCKET in the same work as the sequential algorithm and $O((K + L) \log n)$ depth w.h.p. As before, we maintain a dynamic array B of buckets. We initialize the structure by calculating the number of initial buckets in parallel using reduce in $O(n)$ work and $O(\log n)$ depth and allocating a dynamic array containing the initial number of buckets. Inserting identifiers into B can be done by then calling UPDATEBUCKETS(D, n). NEXTBUCKET performs a filter to keep $i \in A_{\text{CUR}}$ with $D(i) == \text{CUR}$ in parallel which can be done in $O(k)$ work and $O(\log k)$ depth on a bucket containing k identifiers.

We now describe our parallel implementation of UPDATEBUCKETS, which on a set of k updates inserts the identifiers into their new buckets in $O(k)$ expected work and $O(\log n)$ depth w.h.p. The key to achieving these bounds is a work-efficient parallel *semisort* (as described in Section 2).

Our algorithm first creates an array of (identifier, bucket_id) pairs and then calls the semisort routine, using bucket_ids as keys. The output of the semisort is an array of (identifier, bucket_id) pairs where all pairs with the same bucket_id are contiguous. Next, we map an indicator function over the semisorted pairs which outputs 1 if the index is the start of a distinct bucket_id and 0 otherwise. We then pack this mapped array to produce an array of indices corresponding to the start of each distinct bucket. Both steps can be done in $O(k)$ work and $O(\log k)$ depth. Using the offsets, we calculate the number of identifiers moving to each bucket and, in parallel, resize all buckets that have identifiers moving to them. Because all identifiers moving to a particular bucket are stored contiguously in the output of the semisort, we can simply copy them to the newly resized bucket in parallel.

Semisorting the pairs requires $O(k)$ expected work and $O(\log n)$ depth w.h.p. As in the sequential algorithm, the expected work done by K calls to UPDATEBUCKETS where the i'th call updates a set S_i of identifiers is $O(\sum_{i=0}^{K} |S_i|)$. Finally, because each substep of the routine requires at most $O(\log n)$ depth, each call to UPDATEBUCKETS runs in $O(\log n)$ depth w.h.p. As NEXTBUCKET also runs in $O(\log n)$ depth, we have that a total of K calls to UPDATEBUCKETS, and L calls to NEXTBUCKET runs in $O((K + L) \log n)$ depth w.h.p. This gives the following lemma.

LEMMA 3.2. *When there are n identifiers, T total buckets, K calls to* UPDATEBUCKETS, *each of which updates a set S_i of identifiers and L calls to* NEXTBUCKET *parallel bucketing takes $O(n + T + \sum_{i=0}^{K} |S_i|)$ expected work and $O((K + L) \log n)$ depth w.h.p.*

3.3 Optimizations

In practice, while many of our applications initialize the bucket structure with a large number of buckets (even $O(n)$ buckets), they only process a small fraction of them. In other applications like wBFS, the number of buckets needed by the algorithm is initially unknown. However, as the eccentricity of Web graphs and social networks tends to be small, few buckets are usually needed [58].

To make our code more efficient in situations where few buckets are being accessed, or identifiers are moved many times, we let the user specify a parameter n_B. We then only represent a range of n_B buckets (initially the first n_B buckets), and store identifiers in the remaining buckets in an 'overflow' bucket. We only move an identifier that is logically moving from its current bucket to a new bucket if its new bucket is in the current range, or if it is not yet in any bucket. This optimization is enabled by the GETBUCKET primitive, which has the user supply both the current bucket_id and next bucket_id for the identifier. Once the current range is finished, we remove identifiers in the overflow bucket and insert them back into the structure, where the n_B buckets are now used to represent the next range of n_B buckets in the algorithm.

The main benefit of this optimization is a potential reduction in the number of identifiers UPDATEBUCKETS must move as a small value of n_B can cause most of the movement to occur in the overflow bucket. We tried supporting this implementation strategy without requiring the GETBUCKET primitive by having the bucket structure maintain an extra internal mapping from identifiers to bucket_ids. However, we found that the cost of maintaining this array of size $O(n)$ was significant (about 30% more expensive) in our applications, due to the cost of an extra random-access read and write per identifier in UPDATEBUCKETS.

Additionally, while implementing UPDATEBUCKETS using a semisort is theoretically efficient, we found that it was slow in practice due to the extra data movement that occurs when shuffling the updates. Instead, our implementation of UPDATEBUCKETS directly writes identifiers to their destination buckets and avoids the shuffle phase. We first break the array of updates into n/M blocks of length M (we set M to 2048 in our implementation). Next, we count the number of identifiers going to each bucket in each block and store these per-block histograms in an array. We then scan the array with a stride of n_B to compute the total number of identifiers moving to each bucket and resize the buckets. Finally, we iterate over each block again, compute a unique offset into the target bucket using the scanned value, and insert the identifier into the target bucket at this location. The total depth of this implementation of UPDATEBUCKETS is $O(M + \log n)$ as each block is processed sequentially and the scan takes $O(\log n)$. For small values of n_B (our default value is 128), we found that this implementation is much faster than a semisort.

3.4 Performance

In this section we study the performance of our parallel implementation of bucketing on a synthetic workload designed to simulate how our applications use the bucket structure.

Experimental Setup. We run all of our experiments on a 72-core Dell PowerEdge R930 (with two-way hyper-threading) with 4 × 2.4GHz Intel 18-core E7-8867 v4 Xeon processors (with a 4800MHz bus and 45MB L3 cache) and 1TB of main memory. Our programs use Cilk Plus to express parallelism and are compiled with the g++ compiler (version 5.4.1) with the -O3 flag.

Microbenchmark. The microbenchmark simulates the behavior of a bucketing-based algorithm such as k-core and Δ-stepping. On each round, these applications extract a bucket containing a set S of identifiers (vertices), and update the buckets for identifiers in $N(S)$. The microbenchmark simulates this behavior on a degree-8 random graph. Given two inputs, b, the number of initial buckets, and n, the number of identifiers, it starts by bucketing the identifiers uniformly at random and iterating over the buckets in INCREASING order. On each round, it extracts a set S of identifiers and for each extracted identifier, it picks 8 randomly chosen neighbors $\{v_0, \ldots, v_7\}$, checks whether the bucket for v_i is greater than CUR, and if so updates its bucket to $\max(\text{CUR}, D(v_i)/2)$. If $D(v_i) \leq \text{CUR}$, it sets v_i's bucket to NULLBKT which ensures that identifiers extracted from the bucket structure are never reinserted.

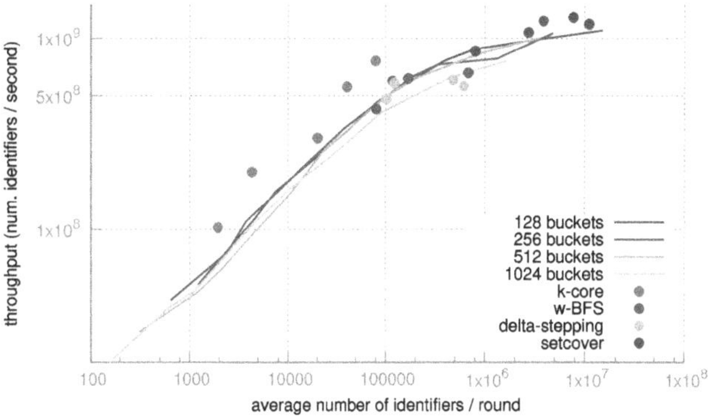

Figure 1: Log-log plot of throughput (billions of identifiers per second) vs. average number of identifiers processed per round.

We profile the performance of the bucket structure while varying b, the number of buckets. As our applications request at most about 1000 buckets, we run the microbenchmark to see how it performs when b is in the range $[128, 256, 512, 1024]$. For a given number of buckets, we vary the number of identifiers to generate different data points. The throughput of the bucket structure is calculated as the total number of identifiers extracted by NEXTBUCKET, plus the number of identifiers that move from their current bucket to a new bucket. Because identifiers moving to the NULLBKT-bucket are inexpensively handled by the bucket structure, (such requests are ignored by UPDATEBUCKETS and do not incur any random reads or writes) we exclude these requests from our total count.

We plot the throughput achieved by the structure vs. the average number of identifiers per round in Figure 1. The average number of identifiers per round is the total number of identifiers that are extracted and updated, divided by the number of rounds required to process all of the buckets. Using this data, we calculated the peak throughput supported by the bucket structure, and the half-performance length[2] which are approximately 1 billion identifiers per second, and an average of 500,000 identifiers per round, respectively.

Applications. We also plot points corresponding to the throughput and average number of identifiers per round achieved by our applications when run on our graphs in Figure 1. We observe that the benchmark throughput is a useful guideline for throughput achieved by our applications. We note that the average number of identifiers per round in k-core is noticeably lower than our other applications—this is because of the large number of rounds necessary to compute the coreness of each vertex using the peeling algorithm in our graphs (up to about 130,000). We discuss more details about our algorithms in Section 4 and their performance in Section 5.

[2]The number of identifiers when the system achieves half of its peak performance.

4 APPLICATIONS

In this section, we describe four bucketing-based algorithms and discuss how our framework can be used to produce theoretically efficient implementations of them.

4.1 k-core and Coreness

A k-core of an undirected graph G is a maximal connected subgraph where every vertex has induced-degree at least k. k-cores are widely studied in the context of data mining and social network analysis because participation in a large k-core is indicative of the importance of a node in the graph. The coreness problem is to compute for each $v \in V$ the maximum k-core v is in. We call this value the *coreness* of a vertex and denote it as $\lambda(v)$.

The notion of a k-core was introduced independently by Seidman [48], and by Matula and Beck [37] (who used the term k-linkage) and identifies the subgraphs of G that satisfy the induced degree property as the k-cores of G. Anderson and Mayr showed that the decision problem for k-core can be solved in NC for $k \leq 2$, but is P-complete[3] for $k \geq 3$ [3]. Since being defined, k-cores and coreness values have found many applications from graph mining, network visualization, fraud detection, and studying biological networks [2, 50, 60].

Matula and Beck give the first algorithm which computes all coreness values. Their algorithm bucket-sorts vertices by their degree, and then repeatedly deletes the minimum-degree vertex. The affected neighbors are then moved to a new bucket corresponding to their induced degree. The total work of their algorithm is $O(m + n)$. Batagelj and Zaversnik (BZ) give an implementation of the Matula-Beck algorithm that runs in the same time bounds [4].

While the sequential algorithm requires $O(m + n)$ work, all existing parallel algorithms with non-trivial parallelism take at least $O(m + k_{max}n)$ work where k_{max} is the largest core number in the graph [16, 20, 41, 44, 51]. This is because the implementations do not bucket the vertices and must scan all remaining vertices when computing each core number. Our parallel algorithm as well as some existing parallel algorithms are based on a peeling procedure, where on each iteration of the procedure, vertices below a certain degree are removed from the graph. The peeling process on random (hyper)graphs has been studied and it has been shown that $O(\log n)$ rounds of peeling suffices [1, 26], although for arbitrary graphs the number of rounds could be linear in the worst case. We note that computing a particular k-core from the coreness numbers requires finding the largest induced subgraph among vertices with coreness at least k, which can be done efficiently in parallel [14, 54].

The pseudocode for our implementation is shown in Algorithm 1. D holds the initial bucket for each vertex, which is initially its degree in G. The bucket structure is created on line 12 by supplying n, D and the INCREASING keyword, as lowest degree vertices are removed first. On line 14, the next non-empty bucket is extracted from the structure, with k updated to be the bucket id (this could be the same as the previous round if there are still vertices with that coreness number). The bucket contains all vertices with degree k. As these vertices now have their coreness set, we update *finished* with the number of vertices in the current bucket on line 15. We

Algorithm 1 Coreness

```
1: D = {deg(v_0), ..., deg(v_{n-1})}            ▷ initialized to initial degrees
2: k = 0                                         ▷ the core number being processed
3: procedure UPDATE(v, edgesRemoved)
4:     inducedD = D[v], newD = ∞
5:     if (inducedD > k) then
6:         newD = max(inducedD − edgesRemoved, k), D[v] = newD
7:         bkt = B.GET_BUCKET(inducedD, newD)
8:         if (bkt ≠ NULLBKT) then
9:             return SOME(bkt)
10:    return NONE
11: procedure CORENESS(G)
12:    B = MAKEBUCKETS(G.n, D, INCREASING), finished = 0
13:    while (finished < G.n) do
14:        (k, ids) = B.NEXTBUCKET()
15:        finished = finished + |ids|
16:        moved = EDGEMAPSUM(G, ids, UPDATE)
17:        B.UPDATEBUCKETS(moved, |moved|)
18:    return D
```

call EDGEMAPSUM on line 16, with the UPDATE function (lines 3–10) to count the number edges removed for each vertex. For a neighbor v, UPDATE updates $D[v]$. It returns a MAYBE(bucket_dest) by calling GETBUCKET on the previous induced-degree of v and the new induced-degree (if the new induced-degree falls below k, it will be set to k so that it can be placed in the current bucket). The result of EDGEMAPSUM is a vertexSubset$_{\text{bucket_dest}}$. On line 17 we update the buckets for vertices that have changed buckets, and repeat. The algorithm terminates once all of the vertices have been extracted from the bucket structure.

We now analyze the complexity of our algorithm by plugging in quantities into Lemma 3.2. We can bound $\sum_{i=0}^{K} |S_i| \leq 2m$, as in the worst case each removed edge will cause an independent request to the bucket structure. Furthermore, the total number of buckets, T is at most n, as vertices are initialized into a bucket corresponding to their degree. Plugging these quantities into Lemma 3.2 gives us $O(m+n)$ expected work, which makes our algorithm work-efficient.

To analyze the depth of our algorithm, we define ρ to be the ***peeling-complexity*** of a graph, or the number of steps needed to peel the graph completely. A step in the peeling process removes all vertices with minimum degree, decrements the degrees of all adjacent neighbors and repeats. On graphs with peeling-complexity ρ, our algorithm runs in $O(\rho \log n)$ depth w.h.p., as each peeling-step potentially requires a call to the bucket structure to update the buckets for affected neighbors. While ρ can be as large as n in the worst-case, in practice ρ is significantly smaller than n. Our algorithm is the first work-efficient algorithm for coreness with non-trivial parallelism. The bounds are summarized in the following theorem.

THEOREM 4.1. *Our algorithm for coreness requires $O(m + n)$ expected work and $O(\rho \log n)$ depth with high probability, where ρ is the peeling-complexity of the graph.*

Our serial implementation of coreness is based on an implementation of the BZ algorithm written in Khaouid et al. [28]. We re-wrote their code in C++ and integrated it into the Ligra+ framework (an extension of Ligra that supports graph compression) [55], which lets us run our implementation on our largest graphs.

[3] There is no polylogarithmic depth algorithm for this problem unless P = NC.

4.2 Δ-stepping and wBFS

The ***single-source shortest path (SSSP)*** problem takes as input a weighted graph $G = (V, E, w(E))$ and a source vertex *src*, and computes the shortest path distance from *src* to each vertex in V, with unreachable vertices having distance ∞. On graphs with non-negative edge weights, the problem can be solved in $O(m + n \log n)$ work by using Dijkstra's algorithm [19] with Fibonacci heaps [21]. While Dijkstra's algorithm cannot be used on graphs with negative edge-weights, the Bellman-Ford algorithm can, but at the cost of an increased worst-case work-bound of $O(mn)$ [15]. Bellman-Ford often performs very well in parallel, but is work-inefficient for graphs with only non-negative edge weights.

Both Dijkstra and Bellman-Ford work by relaxing vertices. We denote the shortest path to each vertex by *SP*. A relaxation occurs over a directed edge (u, v) when vertex u checks whether $SP(u) + w(u, v) < SP(v)$, updating $SP(v)$ to the smaller value if this is the case. In Dijkstra's algorithm, only the vertex, v, that is closest to the source is relaxed—as the graph is assumed to have non-negative edge-weights, we are guaranteed that $SP(v)$ is correct, and so each vertex only relaxes its outgoing edges once. In the simplest form of Bellman-Ford, all vertices relax their neighbors in each step, and so each step costs $O(m)$. The number of steps needed for Bellman-Ford to converge is proportional to the largest number of hops in a shortest path from *src* to any $v \in V$, which can be as large as $O(n)$.

Weighed breadth-first search (wBFS) is a version of Dijkstra's algorithm that works well for small integer edge weights and low-diameter graphs [18]. As described in Section 1, wBFS keeps a bucket for each possible distance and goes through them one by one from the lowest. Each bucket acts like a frontier as in BFS, but when we process a vertex v in a frontier i instead of placing its unvisited neighbors in the next frontier $i+1$ we place each neighbor u in the bucket $i + d(v, u)$. wBFS turns out to be a special case of Δ-stepping, and hence we return to it later.

The Δ-stepping algorithm provides a way to trade-off between the work-efficiency of Dijkstra's algorithm and the increased parallelism of Bellman-Ford [40]. In Δ-stepping, computation is broken up into a number of steps. On step i, vertices in the annulus at distance $[i\Delta, (i+1)\Delta)$ are relaxed until no further distances change. The algorithm then proceeds to the next annulus, repeating until the shortest-path distances for all reachable vertices are set. Note that when $\Delta = \infty$, this algorithm is equivalent to Bellman-Ford.

While Bellman-Ford is easy to implement in parallel, previous work has identified the difficulty in producing a scalable implementation of bucketing [24], which is required in the Δ-stepping algorithm [40]. Due to the difficulty of bucketing in parallel, many implementations of SSSP in graph-processing frameworks use the Bellman-Ford algorithm [22, 51]. Implementations of Δ-stepping do exist, but the algorithms are not easily expressed in existing frameworks, so they are either provided as primitives in a graph processing framework [42, 59] or are stand-alone implementations [6, 17, 24, 34, 35]. There are other parallel algorithms for SSSP, but for some of the algorithms, there is low parallelism [11, 43], and for others no parallel implementations exist [8, 13, 29, 49, 56]. Note that there is currently no parallel algorithm for single-source shortest paths with non-negative edge weights that matches the work of the sequential algorithm and has polylogarithmic depth. Our bucketing interface allows us to give a simple implementation of Δ-stepping with work matching that of the original algorithm [40].

Algorithm 2 Δ-stepping

```
1:  SP = {∞, . . . , ∞}                                   ▷ initialized to all ∞
2:  Fl = {0, . . . , 0}                                   ▷ initialized to all 0
3:  procedure GetBucketNum(i) return ⌊SP[i]/Δ⌋
4:  procedure Update(s, d, w)
5:      nDist = SP[s] + w,  oDist = SP[d],  res = None
6:      if (nDist < oDist) then
7:          if (CAS(&Fl[d], 0, 1) then
8:              res = Some(oDist)   ▷ the distance at the start of this round
9:          writeMin(&SP[d], nDist)
10:     return res
11: procedure Reset(v, oldDist)
12:     Fl[v] = 0,  newDist = SP[d]
13:     return B.get_bucket(⌊oldDist/Δ⌋, ⌊newDist/Δ⌋)
14: procedure Δ-stepping(G, Δ, src)
15:     SP[r] = 0
16:     B = makeBuckets(G.n, GetBucketNum, increasing)
17:     while ((id, ids) = B.nextBucket() and id ≠ nullbkt) do
18:         Moved = edgeMap(G, ids, Update)
19:         NewBuckets = vertexMap(Moved, Reset)
20:         B.updateBuckets(NewBuckets, |NewBuckets|)
21:     return SP
```

The pseudocode for our implementation is shown in Algorithm 2. Shortest-path distances are stored in an array *SP*, which are initially all ∞, except for the source, *src* which has an entry of 0. We also maintain an array of flags, *Fl*, which are used by edgeMap to remove duplicates. The bucket structure is created by specifying n, *SP*, and the keyword increasing (line 16). The i'th bucket represents the annulus of vertices between distance $[i\Delta, (i+1)\Delta)$ from the source. Each Δ-step processes the closest unfinished annulus and so the buckets are processed in increasing order. On line 17 we extract the next bucket, and terminate if it is nullbkt. Otherwise, we explore the outgoing edges of the set of vertices in the bucket using edgeMap. In the Update function passed to edgeMap (lines 4–10), a neighboring vertex, d, is visited over the edge (s, d, w). s checks whether it relaxes d, i.e., $SP[s] + w < SP[d]$. If it can, it first uses a CAS to test whether it is the unique neighbor of d that read its value before any modifications in this round (line 7) setting this distance to be the return value (line 8) if the CAS succeeds. s then uses an atomic writeMin operation to update the distance to d (line 9). Unsuccessful visitors return None, which signals that they did not capture the old value of d. The result of edgeMap is a vertexSubset where the value stored for each vertex is the distance before any modifications in this round.

Next, we call vertexMap (line 19), which calls the Reset function (lines 11–13) on each visited neighbor, v, that had its distance updated. Reset first resets the flag for v (line 12) to enable v to be correctly visited again on a future round. It then calculates the new bucket for v (line 13) and returns this value. The output is another vertexSubset called *NewBuckets* containing the neighbors and their new buckets. Finally, on line 20, we update the buckets containing each neighbor that had its distance lowered, by calling UpdateBuckets on the vertexSubset *NewBuckets*. We repeat these steps until the bucket structure is empty. While we describe visitors from the current frontier CAS'ing values in a separate array of flags, *Fl*, our actual implementation uses the highest-bit of *SP* to represent *Fl*, as this reduces the number of random-memory accesses and improves performance in practice.

The original description of Δ-stepping by Meyer and Sanders [40] separates edges into *light edges* and *heavy edges*, where light edges are of length at most Δ. Inside each annulus, light edges may be processed multiple times but heavy edges only need to be processed once, which reduces the amount of redundant work. We implemented this optimization but did not find a significant improvement in performance for our input graphs. Note that this optimization can fit into our framework by creating two graphs, one containing just the light edges and the other just the heavy edges. Light edges can be processed multiple times until the bucket number changes, at which point we relax the heavy edges once for the vertices in the bucket.

We will now argue that our implementation of Δ-stepping (with the light-heavy edge optimization) does the same amount of work as the original algorithm. The original algorithm takes at most $(d_c/\Delta)l_{\max}$ rounds to finish, where d_c is the maximum distance in the graph and $l_{\max}$ is the maximum number of light edges in a path with total weight at most Δ. Our implementation takes the same number of rounds to finish because we are relaxing exactly the same vertices as the original algorithm on each round. Using our work-efficient bucketing implementation, by Lemma 3.2 the work per round is linear in the number of vertices and outgoing edges processed, which matches that of the original algorithm. The depth of our algorithm is $O(\log n)$ times the number of rounds w.h.p.

When edge weights are integers, and $\Delta = 1$, Δ-stepping becomes wBFS. This is because there can only be one round within each step. In this case we have the following strong bound on work-efficiency.

THEOREM 4.2. *Our algorithm for wBFS (equivalent to Δ-stepping with integral weights and $\Delta = 1$) when run on a graph with m edges and eccentricity r_{src} from the source src, runs in $O(r_{src} + m)$ expected work and $O(r_{src} \log n)$ depth w.h.p.*

PROOF. The work follows directly from the fact we do no more work than the sequential algorithm, charging only $O(1)$ work per bucket insertion and removal, which is proportional to the number of edges (every edge does at most one insertion and is later removed). The depth comes from the number of rounds and the fact that each round takes $O(\log n)$ depth w.h.p. for the bucketing. □

4.3 Approximate Set Cover

The ***set cover*** problem takes as input a universe $\mathcal{U}$ of ground elements, $\mathcal{F}$ a collection of sets of $\mathcal{U}$ s.t. $\bigcup \mathcal{F} = \mathcal{U}$ and a cost function $c : \mathcal{F} \rightarrow \mathbb{R}_{+}$. The problem is to find the cheapest collection of sets $\mathcal{A} \subseteq \mathcal{F}$ that covers U, where the cost of a solution $\mathcal{A}$ is $c(\mathcal{A}) = \sum_{S \in \mathcal{A}} c(S)$. This problem can be modeled as a bipartite graph where sets and elements are vertices, with an edge connecting a set to an element if and only if the set covers that element. Finding the cheapest collection of sets is an NP-complete problem, and a sequential greedy algorithm [27] gives a H_n-approximation, where $H_n = \sum_{k=1}^{n} 1/k$, in $O(m)$ work for unweighted sets and $O(m \log m)$ work for weighted sets, where m is the sum of the sizes of the sets, or equivalently the number of edges in the bipartite graph. Parallel algorithms have been designed for approximating

Algorithm 3 Approximate Set Cover

```
El = {∞, . . . , ∞}                              ▷ initialized to all ∞
Fl = {0, . . . , 0}                               ▷ initialized to all 0
D = {deg(v_0), . . . , deg(v_{n-1})}     ▷ initialized to initial out-degrees
b                                                 ▷ the current bucket number
procedure BucketNum(s) return ⌊log_{1+ε} D[s]⌋
procedure ElmUncovered(e) return Fl[e] == 0
procedure UpdateD(s, d) D[s] = d
procedure AboveThreshold(s, d) return d >= ⌈(1 + ε)^{max(b,0)}⌉
procedure WonElm(s, e) return s == El[e]
procedure InCover(s) return D[s] == ∞
procedure VisitElms(s, e) writeMin(&El[e], s)
procedure WonEnough(s, elmsWon)
    threshold = ⌈(1 + ε)^{max(b-1,0)}⌉
    if (elmsWon > threshold) then
        D[s] = ∞                                  ▷ puts s in the set cover
procedure ResetElms(s, e)
    if (El[e] == s) then
        if (InCover(s)) then
            Fl[e] = 1                             ▷ e is covered by s
        else
            El[e] = ∞                             ▷ reset e
procedure SetCover(G = (S ∪ E, A))
    B = makeBuckets(|S|, BucketNum, decreasing)
    while ((b, Sets) = B.nextBucket() and b ≠ nullbkt) do
        SetsD = edgeMapFilter(G, Sets, ElmUncovered, Pack)
        vertexMap(SetsD, UpdateD)
        Active = vertexFilter(SetsD, AboveThreshold)
        edgeMap(G, Active, VisitElms, ElmUncovered)
        ActiveCts = edgeMapFilter(G, Active, WonElm)
        vertexMap(ActiveCts, WonEnough)
        edgeMap(G, Active, ResetElms)
        Rebucket = {(s, B.get_bucket(b, BucketNum(s)) |
                s ∈ Sets and not InCover(s)}
        B.updateBuckets(Rebucket, |Rebucket|)
    return {i | InCover(i) == true}
```

the set cover [7, 9, 10, 12, 30, 45, 57], and Blelloch et al. [9] present a work-efficient parallel algorithm for the problem, which takes $O(m)$ work and $O(\log^3 m)$ depth, and gives a $(1 + \epsilon)H_n$-approximation to the set cover problem. Blelloch et al. [10] later present a multicore implementation of the parallel set cover algorithm. Their code, however, is special-purpose, not being part of any general framework, and is not work-efficient. In this section, we give a work-efficient implementation of their algorithm using our bucketing interface, and we compare the performance of the codes in Section 5.

The Blelloch et al. algorithm works by first bucketing all sets based on their cost. In the weighted case, the algorithm first ensures that the ratio between the costliest set and cheapest set is polynomially bounded, so that the total number of buckets is kept logarithmic (see Lemma 4.2 of [10]). It does this by discarding sets that are costlier than a threshold, and including sets cheaper than another threshold in the cover. The remaining sets are bucketed based on their normalized cost (the cost per element). In order to guarantee polylogarithmic depth, only $O(\log m)$ buckets are maintained, with a set having cost C going into bucket $\lfloor \log_{1+\epsilon} C \rfloor$. The main loop of the algorithm iterates over the buckets from the least to most costly bucket. Each step invokes a subroutine to compute a maximal nearly-independent set (MaNIS) of sets in the current bucket. MaNIS computes a subset of the sets in the current bucket that are almost non-overlapping in the sense that each set chosen by MaNIS covers many elements that are not covered by any other chosen set. For sets not chosen by MaNIS, the number of uncovered elements they cover is shrunk by a constant factor w.h.p. We refer the reader to the original paper for proofs on both MaNIS and the set cover algorithm. We now describe our algorithm for unweighted set cover, and note that it can be easily modified for the weighted case as well.

The pseudocode for our implementation of the Blelloch et al. algorithm is shown in Algorithm 3. We assume that the set cover instance is represented as an undirected bipartite graph with sets and elements on opposite sides. The array *El* contains the set each element is assigned to. The array *Fl* specifies whether elements are covered ($Fl[e] = 0$ if and only if e is uncovered). Initially all elements are not covered (lines 1–2). The array D contains the number of remaining elements covered by each set (line 3). As sets are represented by vertices, each entry of D is initially just the degree of that vertex. b stores the current bucket id (line 4), which is updated on line 24 when we extract the next bucket. The bucket structure is created by specifying $n = |S|$, BUCKETNUM, and the keyword DECREASING (line 23), as we process sets in decreasing order based on the number of uncovered elements they cover.

Each round starts by extracting the next non-empty bucket (line 24). The degrees of sets are updated lazily, so the first phase of the algorithm packs out edges to covered elements and computes the sets that still cover enough elements to be active in this round. On line 25, we call EDGEMAPFILTER with the function ELMUNCOVERED and the option PACK, which packs out any covered elements in the sets' adjacency lists and updates their degrees. The return value of EDGEMAPFILTER is a $\text{vertexSubset}_{\text{int}}$ (*SetsD*), where the associated value with each set is its new degree. On line 26 we apply VERTEXMAP over *SetsD* with the function UPDATED, which updates D with the new degrees. Finally, we call VERTEXFILTER with the function ABOVETHRESHOLD to compute the vertexSubset, *Active*, which is the subset of *SetsD* that still have sufficient degree.

The next phase of the algorithm implements one step of MaNIS. Note that instead of implementing MaNIS as a separate subroutine, we implicitly compute it by fusing the loop that computes a MaNIS with the loop that iterates over the buckets. On line 28, active sets reserve uncovered elements using an EDGEMAP, breaking ties based on their IDs using writeMin. EDGEMAP checks whether a neighboring element is uncovered using ELMUNCOVERED (line 6), and if so calls VISITELMS (line 11), which uses a writeMin to atomically update the parent of e. Next, we compute a vertexSubset, *ActiveCts*, by calling EDGEMAPFILTER with the function WONELM (line 9). The value associated with each set in *ActiveCts* is the number of elements successfully reserved by it. We then apply VERTEXMAP over *ActiveCts* (line 30) with the function WONENOUGH (lines 12–15), which checks whether the number of elements reserved is above a threshold (line 13), and if so updates the set to be in the cover.

The last phase of the algorithm marks elements that are newly covered, resets elements whose sets did not make it into the cover, and finally reinserts sets that did not make it into the cover back into the bucket structure. On line 31, we call EDGEMAP with the supplied function RESETELMS (lines 16–21) which first checks that s is the set which reserved e (line 17). If s joined the cover, then we mark e as covered (line 19). Otherwise, we reset $El[e] = \infty$ (line 21) so that e can be correctly visited on future rounds. Finally, we compute *Rebucket*, a vertexSubset containing the sets that did not join the cover in this round, where the value associated with each set is its bucket_dest. The bucket structure is updated with the sets in *Rebucket* on line 33. Finally, after all rounds are over, we return the subset of sets whose ids are in the cover (line 34).

Input Graph	Num. Vertices	Num. Edges	ρ
com-Orkut	3,072,627	234,370,166	5,667
Twitter	41,652,231	1,468,365,182	-
Twitter-Sym	41,652,231	2,405,026,092	14,963
Friendster	124,836,180	3,612,134,270	10,034
Hyperlink2012-Host	101,717,775	2,043,203,933	-
Hyperlink2012-Host-Sym	101,717,775	3,880,015,728	19,063
Hyperlink2012	3,563,602,789	128,736,914,167	-
Hyperlink2012-Sym	3,563,602,789	225,840,663,232	58,710
Hyperlink2014	1,724,573,718	64,422,807,961	-
Hyperlink2014-Sym	1,724,573,718	124,141,874,032	130,728

Table 2: Graph inputs, including both vertices and edges.

5 EXPERIMENTS

All of our experiments are run on the same machine configuration as in Section 3.4. The input graph sizes and peeling-complexity (for undirected graphs) that we use are shown in Table 2. ***com-Orkut*** is an undirected graph of the Orkut social network. ***Twitter*** is a directed graph of the Twitter network, where edges represent the follower relationship [31]. ***Friendster*** is an undirected social-network graph. ***Hyperlink2012*** and ***Hyperlink2014*** are directed hyperlink graphs obtained from the WebDataCommons dataset where nodes represent web pages [39]. ***Hyperlink2012-Host*** is a directed hyperlink graph also from the WebDataCommons dataset where nodes represent a collection of web pages belonging to the same hostname. Unless mentioned otherwise, the input graph is assumed to be directed, with the symmetrized version of the graph denoted with the suffix ***Sym***.

We create weighted graphs for evaluating wBFS by selecting edge weights between $[1, \log n)$ uniformly at random. These graphs are not suitable for testing Δ-stepping, as we found that $\Delta = 1$ was always faster than a larger value of Δ. To understand the performance of our Δ-stepping implementation, we generate another family of weighted graphs with edge weights picked uniformly between $[1, 10^5)$. We successfully added edge-weights between $[1, \log n)$ to the Hyperlink2014 graph. However, due to space limitations on our machine, we were unable to store the Hyperlink2012 graph with edge-weights between $[1, \log n)$ and both the Hyperlink2012 and Hyperlink2014 graphs with edge-weights between $[1, 10^5)$. We use 'in parallel' to refer to running times using 144 hyper-threads.

k-core (coreness). Table 3 shows the running time of the work-efficient implementation of k-core from Julienne and the work-inefficient implementation of k-core from Ligra. Figure 2 shows the running time of both implementations as a function of thread count. We see that our work-efficient implementation achieves between 4-41x parallel speedup over the implementation running on a single thread. Our speedups are smaller on graphs where ρ is large while n and m are relatively small, such as com-Orkut and Twitter-Sym.

We also ran the Batagelj and Zaversnik (BZ) algorithm described in Section 4.1 and found that our single-thread times are always about 1.3x faster than that of the BZ algorithm. This is because on each round we move a vertex to a new bucket just once, even if many edges are deleted from it whereas the BZ algorithm will move that vertex many times. As our algorithm on a single thread is always faster than the BZ algorithm, we report self-relative speedup, which is a lower bound on speedup over the BZ algorithm.

Unfortunately, we were unable to obtain the code for the ParK algorithm [16], which is to the best of our knowledge the fastest existing parallel implementation of k-core. Instead, we used a similar work-inefficient implementation of k-core available in Ligra. In parallel, our work-efficient implementation is between 2.6–9.2x faster than the work-inefficient implementation from Ligra. On Hyperlink2012-Sym and Hyperlink2014-Sym, the work-inefficient implementation did not terminate in a reasonable amount of time, and so we only report times for our implementation in Julienne. A recent paper also reported experimental results for a different parallel algorithm for k-core that is not work-efficient [47]. On a similar configuration to their machine our implementation is about 10x faster on com-Orkut, the largest graph they test on.

wBFS and Δ-stepping. Table 3 shows the running time of the Δ-stepping and wBFS implementations from Julienne and the GAP benchmark suite, the priority-based Bellman-Ford implementation from Galois, the Bellman-Ford implementation from Ligra and the sequential solver from the DIMACS shortest path challenge [6, 42]. Figures 3 and 4 show the running time of the four parallel implementations as a function of thread count. To the best of our knowledge, we are not aware of any existing parallel implementations of wBFS, so we test wBFS against the same implementations as Δ-stepping, setting $\Delta = 1$. We see that our work-efficient implementation achieves between 22–43x parallel speedup over the implementation running on a single thread for wBFS and between 18–32.4x parallel speedup over our implementation running on a single thread for Δ-stepping. For Δ-stepping, we found that setting $\Delta = 32768$ performed best in our experiments.

Like our implementation, the SSSP implementation in GAP does not perform the light/heavy optimization described in the original Δ-stepping paper [40]. Instead of having shared buckets, it uses thread-local bins to represent buckets. The Galois algorithm is a version of Bellman-Ford that schedules nodes based on their distance from the source (closer vertices have higher priority). Because the Galois algorithm avoids synchronizing after each annulus, it achieves good speedup on graphs with large diameter, but where paths with few hops are also likely to be the shortest paths in the graph (such as road networks). On such graphs our algorithm performs poorly due to a large amount of synchronization.

All implementations achieve good speedup with an increased number of threads. On a single thread our implementation is usually faster than the single-thread times for other implementations. This is likely because of an optimization we implemented in our EDGEMAP routine, which allows traversals to only write to an amount of memory proportional to the size of the output frontier. In parallel, while the GAP implementation usually outperforms us by a small amount, we remain very competitive, being between 1.07-1.1x slower for wBFS, and between 1.1–1.7x faster for Δ-stepping. We are between 1.6–3.4x faster than the Galois implementation on wBFS and between 1.2–2.9x faster on Δ-stepping. Our implementation is between 1.2–3.9x faster for wBFS and 1.8–5.2x faster for Δ-stepping compared to the Bellman-Ford implementation in Ligra [51]. We note that there is recent work on another parallel algorithm for SSSP [35] and based on their speedups over the Δ-stepping implementation in Galois, our Julienne implementation seems competitive. We leave a detailed comparison for future work.

Approximate Set Cover. We generated bipartite graphs to use as set cover instances by having vertices represent both the sets and the elements. Table 3 shows the running time of the work-efficient implementation of approximate set cover from Julienne and the work-inefficient implementation of approximate set cover from the PBBS benchmark suite [53]. Figure 5 shows the running time of both implementations as a function of thread count. We set ϵ to be 0.01 for both implementations. We see that our work-efficient implementation achieves between 4–35x parallel speedup over the implementation running on a single thread. Both implementations achieve poor speedup on com-Orkut, due to the relatively large number of rounds compared to the graph size. Our implementation achieves between 17–35x parallel speedup on our other test graphs.

The PBBS implementation is from Blelloch et al. [10] and implements the same algorithm as us [9]. Both implementations compute the same covers. We note that the PBBS implementation is not work-efficient. Instead of rebucketing the sets that are not chosen in a given step by using a bucket structure, it carries them over to the next step. In parallel, our times are between 1.2x slower to 2x faster compared to the PBBS implementation. On graphs like Twitter-Sym, the PBBS implementation carries a large number of unchosen sets for many rounds. In these cases, our implementation achieves good speedup over the PBBS implementation because it rebuckets these sets instead of inspecting them on each round.

6 CONCLUSION

We have presented the Julienne framework which allows for simple and theoretically efficient implementations of bucketing-based graph algorithms. Using our framework, we obtain the first work-efficient k-core algorithm with non-trivial parallelism. Our implementations either outperform or are competitive with hand-optimized codes for the same applications, and can process graphs with hundreds of billions of edges in the order of minutes on a single machine.

ACKNOWLEDGMENTS

This research was supported in part by NSF grants CCF-1314590 and CCF-1533858, the Intel Science and Technology Center for Cloud Computing, and the Miller Institute for Basic Research in Science at UC Berkeley.

REFERENCES

[1] D. Achlioptas and M. Molloy. The solution space geometry of random linear equations. *Random Structures & Algorithms*, 46(2), 2015.

[2] J. I. Alvarez-Hamelin, L. Dall'asta, A. Barrat, and A. Vespignani. Large scale networks fingerprinting and visualization using the k-core decomposition. In *NIPS*. 2005.

[3] R. Anderson and E. W. Mayr. A P-complete problem and approximations to it. Technical report, 1984.

Application	com-Orkut			Twitter			Friendster			Hyperlink2012-Host			Hyperlink2012			Hyperlink2014		
	(1)	(72h)	(SU)	(1)	(72h)	(SU)	(1)	(72h)	(SU)	(1)	(72h)	(SU)	(1)	(72h)	(SU)	(1)	(72h)	(SU)
k-core (Julienne)	**5.43**	**1.3**	4.17	**74.6**	**6.37**	11.7	**182**	**7.7**	23.6	**118**	**8.7**	13.5	**8515**	**206**	41.3	**2820**	**97.2**	29.0
k-core (Ligra)	11.6	3.35	3.46	119	19.9	5.97	745	56	13.3	953	80.1	11.9	-	-	-	-	-	-
wBFS (Julienne)*	**2.01**	0.093	21.6	**22.8**	0.987	23.1	**73.9**	2.29	32.2	37.9	1.39	27.2	-	-	-	**392**	**9.02**	43.4
Bellman-Ford (Ligra)*	4.02	0.175	22.9	37.9	1.19	31.8	190	6.08	31.2	84.2	2.17	38.8	-	-	-	2610	35.5	73.5
wBFS (GAP)*	2.35	**0.083**	28.3	25.9	**0.919**	28.1	88.1	**2.14**	41.1	40.4	**1.26**	32.0	-	-	-	-	-	-
wBFS (Galois)*	3.46	0.319	10.8	31.9	1.59	20.06	87.6	4.49	19.5	45.5	2.85	15.9	-	-	-	-	-	-
wBFS (DIMACS)*	3.488	-	-	26.54	-	-	78.19	-	-	**35.38**	-	-	-	-	-	-	-	-
Δ-stepping (Julienne)†	**3.18**	**.167**	19.0	36.3	**2.01**	18.0	112	**3.45**	32.4	49.0	**2.09**	23.4	-	-	-	-	-	-
Bellman-Ford (Ligra)†	10.2	0.423	24.1	111	3.64	30.4	613	18.2	33.6	295	7.84	37.6	-	-	-	-	-	-
Δ-stepping (GAP)†	4.33	.294	14.7	67.6	2.39	28.2	175	4.23	41.3	57.9	2.33	24.8	-	-	-	-	-	-
Δ-stepping (Galois)†	5.1	.487	10.4	64.1	2.58	24.8	122	5.56	21.9	53.8	3.17	16.9	-	-	-	-	-	-
Δ-stepping (DIMACS)†	4.44	-	-	**35.7**	-	-	**105**	-	-	55.5	-	-	-	-	-	-	-	-
Set Cover (Julienne)	**3.66**	0.844	4.33	55.4	**3.23**	17.1	165	**6.6**	25.0	93.5	**4.83**	19.3	**3720**	**104**	35.7	**1070**	**45.1**	23.7
Set Cover (PBBS)	4.47	**0.665**	6.72	**48.4**	6.71	7.21	**137**	6.86	19.9	**71.6**	8.58	8.34	-	-	-	-	-	-

Table 3: Running times (in seconds) of our algorithms over various inputs on a 72-core machine (with hyper-threading) where (1) is the single-thread time, (72h) is the 72 core time using hyper-threading and (SU) is the speedup of the application (single-thread time divided by 72-core time). Applications marked with $*$ and † use graphs with weights uniformly distributed in $[1, \log n)$ and $[1, 10^5)$ respectively. We display the fastest sequential and parallel time for each problem in each column in bold.

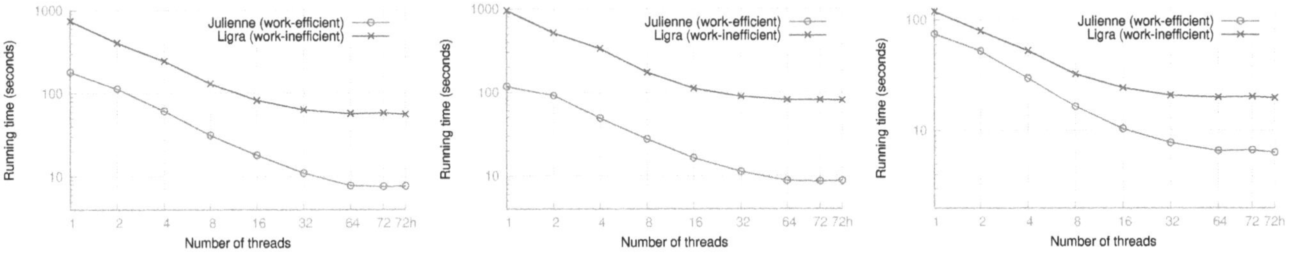

(a) Friendster (b) Hyperlink2012-Host-Sym (c) Twitter-Sym

Figure 2: Running time of k-core in seconds on a 72-core machine (with hyper-threading). "72h" refers to 144 hyper-threads.

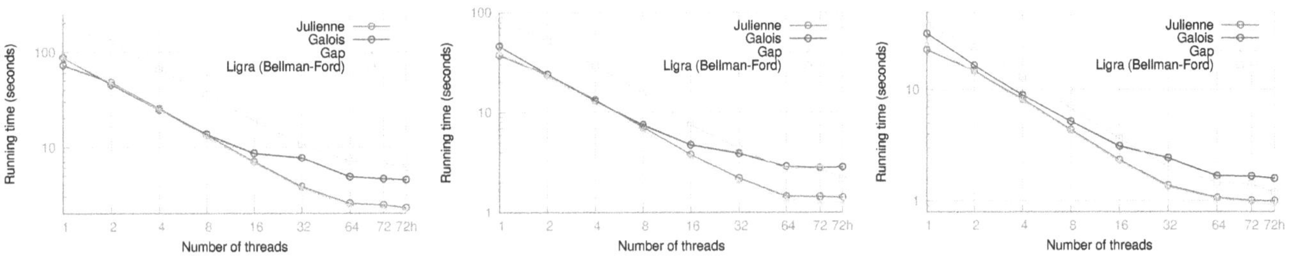

(a) Friendster (b) Hyperlink2012-Host-Sym (c) Twitter-Sym

Figure 3: Running time of wBFS in seconds on a 72-core machine (with hyper-threading). The graphs have edge weights that are uniformly distributed in $[1, \log n)$. "72h" refers to 144 hyper-threads.

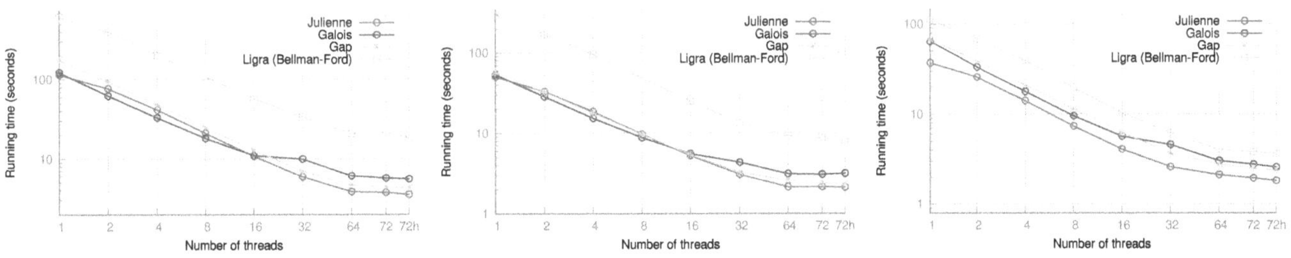

(a) Friendster (b) Hyperlink2012-Host-Sym (c) Twitter-Sym

Figure 4: Running time of Δ-stepping in seconds on a 72-core machine (with hyper-threading). The graphs have edge weights that are uniformly distributed in $[1, 10^5)$. "72h" refers to 144 hyper-threads.

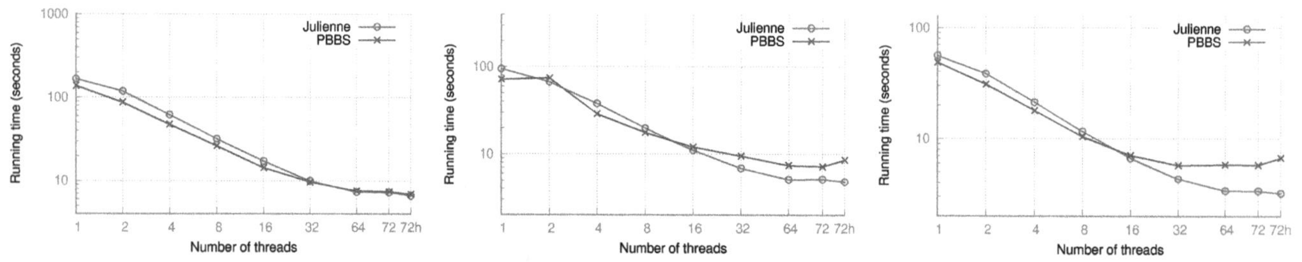

(a) Friendster (b) Hyperlink2012-Host-Sym (c) Twitter-Sym

Figure 5: Running time of set cover in seconds on a 72-core machine (with hyper-threading). "72h" refers to 144 hyper-threads.

[4] V. Batagelj and M. Zaversnik. An $O(m)$ algorithm for cores decomposition of networks. *CoRR*, cs.DS/0310049, 2003.

[5] S. Beamer, K. Asanović, and D. Patterson. Direction-optimizing breadth-first search. In *SC*, 2012.

[6] S. Beamer, K. Asanovic, and D. A. Patterson. The GAP benchmark suite. *CoRR*, abs/1508.03619, 2015.

[7] B. Berger, J. Rompel, and P. W. Shor. Efficient NC algorithms for set cover with applications to learning and geometry. *J. Comput. Syst. Sci.*, 49(3), Dec. 1994.

[8] G. E. Blelloch, Y. Gu, Y. Sun, and K. Tangwongsan. Parallel shortest paths using radius stepping. In *SPAA*, 2016.

[9] G. E. Blelloch, R. Peng, and K. Tangwongsan. Linear-work greedy parallel approximate set cover and variants. In *SPAA*, 2011.

[10] G. E. Blelloch, H. V. Simhadri, and K. Tangwongsan. Parallel and I/O efficient set covering algorithms. In *SPAA*, 2012.

[11] G. S. Brodal, J. L. Träff, and C. D. Zaroliagis. A parallel priority queue with constant time operations. *J. Parallel Distrib. Comput.*, 49(1), Feb. 1998.

[12] F. Chierichetti, R. Kumar, and A. Tomkins. Max-cover in map-reduce. In *WWW*, 2010.

[13] E. Cohen. Using selective path-doubling for parallel shortest-path computations. *J. Algorithms*, 22(1), Jan. 1997.

[14] R. Cole, P. N. Klein, and R. E. Tarjan. Finding minimum spanning forests in logarithmic time and linear work using random sampling. In *SPAA*, 1996.

[15] T. H. Cormen, C. E. Leiserson, R. L. Rivest, and C. Stein. *Introduction to Algorithms (3. ed.)*. MIT Press, 2009.

[16] N. S. Dasari, R. Desh, and M. Zubair. ParK: An efficient algorithm for k-core decomposition on multicore processors. In *Big Data*, 2014.

[17] A. A. Davidson, S. Baxter, M. Garland, and J. D. Owens. Work-efficient parallel GPU methods for single-source shortest paths. In *IPDPS*, 2014.

[18] R. B. Dial. Algorithm 360: Shortest-path forest with topological ordering [H]. *Commun. ACM*, 12(11), Nov. 1969.

[19] E. W. Dijkstra. A note on two problems in connexion with graphs. *Numer. Math.*, 1(1), Dec. 1959.

[20] B. Elser and A. Montresor. An evaluation study of bigdata frameworks for graph processing. In *Big Data*, 2013.

[21] M. L. Fredman and R. E. Tarjan. Fibonacci heaps and their uses in improved network optimization algorithms. *J. ACM*, 34(3), July 1987.

[22] J. E. Gonzalez, Y. Low, H. Gu, D. Bickson, and C. Guestrin. PowerGraph: Distributed graph-parallel computation on natural graphs. In *OSDI*, 2012.

[23] Y. Gu, J. Shun, Y. Sun, and G. E. Blelloch. A top-down parallel semisort. In *SPAA*, 2015.

[24] M. A. Hassaan, M. Burtscher, and K. Pingali. Ordered vs. unordered: A comparison of parallelism and work-efficiency in irregular algorithms. In *PPoPP*, 2011.

[25] J. Jaja. *Introduction to Parallel Algorithms*. Addison-Wesley Professional, 1992.

[26] J. Jiang, M. Mitzenmacher, and J. Thaler. Parallel peeling algorithms. *ACM Trans. Parallel Comput.*, 3(1), Jan. 2017.

[27] D. S. Johnson. Approximation algorithms for combinatorial problems. *J. Comput. Syst. Sci.*, 9(3), 1974.

[28] W. Khaouid, M. Barsky, V. Srinivasan, and A. Thomo. k-core decomposition of large networks on a single PC. *Proc. VLDB Endow.*, 9(1), Sept. 2015.

[29] P. N. Klein and S. Subramanian. A randomized parallel algorithm for single-source shortest paths. *J. Algorithms*, 25(2), Nov. 1997.

[30] R. Kumar, B. Moseley, S. Vassilvitskii, and A. Vattani. Fast greedy algorithms in mapreduce and streaming. *ACM Trans. Parallel Comput.*, 2(3), Sept. 2015.

[31] H. Kwak, C. Lee, H. Park, and S. Moon. What is twitter, a social network or a news media? In *WWW*, 2010.

[32] Y. Low, D. Bickson, J. Gonzalez, C. Guestrin, A. Kyrola, and J. M. Hellerstein. Distributed GraphLab: A framework for machine learning and data mining in the cloud. *Proc. VLDB Endow.*, 5(8), Apr. 2012.

[33] Y. Low, J. Gonzalez, A. Kyrola, D. Bickson, C. Guestrin, and J. M. Hellerstein. GraphLab: A new parallel framework for machine learning. In *UAI*, July 2010.

[34] K. Madduri, D. A. Bader, J. W. Berry, and J. R. Crobak. An experimental study of a parallel shortest path algorithm for solving large-scale graph instances. In *ALENEX*, 2007.

[35] S. Maleki, D. Nguyen, A. Lenharth, M. Garzarán, D. Padua, and K. Pingali. DSMR: A parallel algorithm for single-source shortest path problem. In *ICS*, 2016.

[36] G. Malewicz, M. H. Austern, A. J. Bik, J. C. Dehnert, I. Horn, N. Leiser, and G. Czajkowski. Pregel: A system for large-scale graph processing. In *SIGMOD*, 2010.

[37] D. W. Matula and L. L. Beck. Smallest-last ordering and clustering and graph coloring algorithms. *J. ACM*, 30(3), July 1983.

[38] F. McSherry, M. Isard, and D. G. Murray. Scalability! But at what COST? In *HotOS*, 2015.

[39] R. Meusel, S. Vigna, O. Lehmberg, and C. Bizer. The graph structure in the web–analyzed on different aggregation levels. *The Journal of Web Science*, 1(1), 2015.

[40] U. Meyer and P. Sanders. Δ-stepping: a parallelizable shortest path algorithm. *J. Algorithms*, 49(1), 2003.

[41] A. Montresor, F. D. Pellegrini, and D. Miorandi. Distributed k-core decomposition. *TPDS*, 24(2), 2013.

[42] D. Nguyen, A. Lenharth, and K. Pingali. A lightweight infrastructure for graph analytics. In *SOSP*, 2013.

[43] R. C. Paige and C. P. Kruskal. Parallel algorithms for shortest path problems. In *ICPP*, 1985.

[44] K. Pechlivanidou, D. Katsaros, and L. Tassiulas. MapReduce-based distributed k-shell decomposition for online social networks. In *SERVICES*, 2014.

[45] S. Rajagopalan and V. V. Vazirani. Primal-dual RNC approximation algorithms for set cover and covering integer programs. *SIAM J. Comput.*, 28(2), Feb. 1999.

[46] A. E. Sariyüce and A. Pinar. Fast hierarchy construction for dense subgraphs. *Proc. VLDB Endow.*, 10(3), Nov. 2016.

[47] A. E. Sariyuce, C. Seshadhri, and A. Pinar. Parallel local algorithms for core, truss, and nucleus decompositions. *arXiv preprint arXiv:1704.00386*, 2017.

[48] S. B. Seidman. Network structure and minimum degree. *Soc. Networks*, 5(3), 1983.

[49] H. Shi and T. H. Spencer. Time-work tradeoffs of the single-source shortest paths problem. *J. Algorithms*, 30(1), Jan. 1999.

[50] K. Shin, T. Eliassi-Rad, and C. Faloutsos. CoreScope: Graph mining using k-core analysis–patterns, anomalies and algorithms. In *ICDM*, 2016.

[51] J. Shun and G. E. Blelloch. Ligra: A lightweight graph processing framework for shared memory. In *PPoPP*, 2013.

[52] J. Shun, G. E. Blelloch, J. T. Fineman, and P. B. Gibbons. Reducing contention through priority updates. In *SPAA*, 2013.

[53] J. Shun, G. E. Blelloch, J. T. Fineman, P. B. Gibbons, A. Kyrola, H. V. Simhadri, and K. Tangwongsan. Brief announcement: the problem based benchmark suite. In *SPAA*, 2012.

[54] J. Shun, L. Dhulipala, and G. Blelloch. A simple and practical linear-work parallel algorithm for connectivity. In *SPAA*, 2014.

[55] J. Shun, L. Dhulipala, and G. Blelloch. Smaller and faster: Parallel processing of compressed graphs with Ligra+. In *DCC*, 2015.

[56] T. H. Spencer. Time-work tradeoffs for parallel algorithms. *J. ACM*, 44(5), Sept. 1997.

[57] S. Stergiou and K. Tsioutsiouliklis. Set cover at web scale. In *SIGKDD*, 2015.

[58] J. Ugander, B. Karrer, L. Backstrom, and C. Marlow. The anatomy of the facebook social graph. *arXiv preprint arXiv:1111.4503*, 2011.

[59] Y. Wang, A. A. Davidson, Y. Pan, Y. Wu, A. Riffel, and J. D. Owens. Gunrock: a high-performance graph processing library on the GPU. In *PPoPP*, 2016.

[60] S. Wuchty and E. Almaas. Peeling the yeast protein network. *Proteomics*, 5(2), 2005.

Improved Cover Time Bounds for the Coalescing-Branching Random Walk on Graphs

Colin Cooper
Dept Informatics, King's College London
London WC2R 2LS, U.K.
colin.cooper@kcl.ac.uk

Tomasz Radzik
Dept Informatics, King's College London
London WC2R 2LS, U.K.
tomasz.radzik@kcl.ac.uk

Nicolás Rivera
Dept Informatics, King's College London
London WC2R 2LS, U.K.
nicolas.rivera@kcl.ac.uk

ABSTRACT

We present improved bounds on the cover time of the *coalescing-branching random walk* process COBRA. The COBRA process, introduced in [Dutta et al., SPAA 2013], can be viewed as spreading a single item of information throughout an undirected graph in synchronised rounds. In each round, each vertex which has received the information in the previous round (possibly simultaneously from more than one neighbour and possibly not for the first time), 'pushes' the information to b randomly selected neighbours. The COBRA process is typically studied for integer branching rates $b \geq 2$ (with the case $b = 1$ corresponding to a random walk). The aim of the process is to propagate the information quickly, but with a limited number of transmissions per vertex per round.

The cover time of COBRA is defined as the expected number of rounds until each vertex has received the information at least once. Our main results are a bound of $O(m + (d_{\max})^2 \log n) = O(n^2 \log n)$ on the COBRA cover time for an arbitrary connected graph with n vertices, m edges and the maximum vertex degree $d_{\max}$, and a bound of $O((r^2+r/(1-\lambda)) \log n)$ for r-regular connected graphs with the second eigenvalue λ. Our bounds improve the $O(n^{11/4} \log n)$ and $O((r^4/\phi^2) \log^2 n)$ bounds shown in [Mitzenmacher et al., SPAA 2016], where ϕ is the conductance of the graph, and complement the $O((1/(1-\lambda))^3 \log n)$ bound shown in [Cooper et al., PODC 2016]. We obtain our bounds by analysing the process called *Biased Infection with Persistent Source* (BIPS), which was introduced in [Cooper et al., PODC 2016] as a dual process for COBRA .

CCS CONCEPTS

• **Theory of computation → Distributed algorithms; Random walks and Markov chains;** • **Mathematics of computing →** *Graph theory;*

KEYWORDS

Random processes on graphs; cover time; COBRA process; epidemic processes

SPAA '17, July 24-26, 2017, Washington DC, USA

ACM ISBN 978-1-4503-4593-4/17/07.
https://doi.org/10.1145/3087556.3087564

1 INTRODUCTION

Dutta et al. [5, 6] studied the following *coalescing-branching* random walk process for propagating information on a connected graph with n vertices and m edges. At the start of a round each vertex containing information 'pushes' this information to b randomly selected neighbours. It then stops passing the information until it receives the information again. At the end of a round if a vertex receives information from two or more vertices, then the information coalesces into one. Thus it does not help if a vertex receives the same information from more than one neighbour. The continuous act of coalescing and branching gives the name COBRA to this process.

A COBRA process can be modelled as a particle process. At the start of each round, each existing particle divides into b particles (the branching factor). These particles then move independently to random neighbours. At the end of each round any particles which meet at a vertex coalesce to form a single particle.

The aim of the COBRA process is to rapidly propagate information to all vertices but to limit the number of transmissions per vertex per round and without requiring that vertices store information for longer than one round. In the special case that $b = 1$, the COBRA process is a simple random walk, which achieves a low transmission rate but does not satisfy the fast propagation condition.

The main quantity of interest in information propagation processes is the time taken to inform (or visit) all vertices. By analogy with a random walk, this is referred to as the *cover time*. The w.h.p.[1] cover time results for the COBRA process obtained in [5, 6] for the case $b = 2$ include the following. (i) For the complete graph K_n all vertices are visited in $O(\log n)$ rounds. (ii) For regular constant-degree expanders, the cover time is $O(\log^2 n)$. (iii) For the D-dimensional grid, the cover time is $\widetilde{O}(n^{1/D})$, where $\widetilde{O}(.)$ indicates the presence of a poly-log n term. Improved bounds were shown later in [8]: an $O((r^4/\phi^2) \log^2 n)$ bound for r-regular graphs with conductance ϕ, an $O(D^2 n^{1/D})$ bound for D-dimensional grids, and an $O(n^{11/4} \log n)$ bound for general graphs.

Let Diam(G) denote the diameter of a graph G. Then $\max\{\log_2 n, \text{Diam}(G)\}$ is a lower bound on the number of rounds needed for the COBRA process with branching factor $b = 2$ to inform every vertex. This is the best possible, since the number of visited vertices at most doubles in each round. By comparison with the complete graph, and considering this lower bound, it might seem that the cover time of an r-regular expander by the COBRA process with

[1] *With high probability* (w.h.p.) means with probability at least $1 - n^{-c}$, for some positive constant c.

branching factor $b = 2$ should be $O(\log n)$ for any degree r between 3 and $n-1$. This is indeed the case as proven in [4]: the cover time is $O((1/(1-\lambda)^3 \log n)$ for r-regular graphs with the second eigenvalue λ, for any $3 \le r \le n-1$.

Our contributions. In this paper we show two new bounds on the cover time of the COBRA process for branching factor $b = 2$. For arbitrary connected graphs, we improve the $O(n^{11/4} \log n)$ bound given in [8] to $O(m + (d_{\max})^2 \log n) = O(n^2 \log n)$, where $d_{\max}$ is the maximum degreeof a vertex. For r-regular connected graphs, we show a bound of $O\left((r^2 + r/(1-\lambda)) \log n\right)$, which improves the $O((1/(1-\lambda)^3 \log n)$ bound given in [4] for the case when $1 - \lambda = o(1/\sqrt{r})$. Both bounds require that $1-\lambda > C\sqrt{(\log n)/n}$, for a suitably large constant C. Since $1 - \lambda \ge \phi^2/2$, our new bound for regular graphs improves also the $O((r^4/\phi^2) \log^2 n)$ bound given in [8]. As an example, consider the hypercube with $n = 2^d$ vertices, which has degree $r = \log n$ and both the conductance ϕ and the *eigenvalue gap* $1 - \lambda$ are $\Theta(1/\log n)$. The bounds presented in [8], [4] and in this paper give, respectively, the following cover-time bounds for the hypercube: $O(\log^8 n)$, $O(\log^4 n)$ and $O(\log^3 n)$.

We proceed with the formal definition of the COBRA process and the statement of our main results. Consider a graph $G = (V, E)$, an integer $b \ge 1$ and a subset of vertices $C \subseteq V$. The COBRA process with starting set C and branching factor b is the set process $(C_t)_{t\ge 0}$ with $C_0 = C$ and C_{t+1} generated as follows. Each vertex $v \in C_t$ independently chooses b neighbours uniformly at random with replacement and all the chosen vertices belong to C_{t+1}. For $C_0 = \{u\}$, let $\mathbf{cover}(u) = \min\{T : \bigcup_{t=0}^{T} C_t = V\}$ be the number of rounds needed for the COBRA process to visit all vertices of the graph starting from vertex u; and let $\text{COVER}(u) = \mathbf{E}(\mathbf{cover}(u))$. By analogy with the cover time of a random walk, which uses the worst case starting vertex, we let $\text{COVER}(G) = \max_{u\in V} \text{COVER}(u)$ be the cover time of the COBRA process on graph G. We derive asymptotic upper bounds on $\mathbf{cover}(u)$, which hold w.h.p. for each vertex $u \in V$ (Theorems 1.1 and 1.2). By the argument of 'restarting' the process from the current state in the low probability event that the graph has not been covered by the claimed bound, we conclude that the same asymptotic bounds apply also to the expectation $\text{COVER}(u)$, so to $\text{COVER}(G)$ as well.

THEOREM 1.1. *Let G be a connected graph with n vertices, m edges and the maximum vertex degree $d_{\max}$. For the COBRA process with branching factor $b = 2$, w.h.p. for each $u \in V$,* $\mathbf{cover}(u)$ *is*

$$O(m + (d_{\max})^2 \log n). \tag{1}$$

For a connected r-regular graph G with adjacency matrix $A(G)$, let $P = A(G)/r$ denote the transition matrix of the random-walk on G. Let $\lambda_1, \lambda_2, ..., \lambda_n$ be the eigenvalues of matrix P ordered in a non-increasing sequence. Thus $\lambda_1 = 1$ and $\lambda_n \ge -1$. Let $\lambda = \lambda(G) = \max_{i=2,...,n} |\lambda_i|$ be the second largest eigenvalue of (in absolute values). Our second result gives a bound on the cover time of COBRA for regular graphs in terms of the eigenvalue gap $1-\lambda$ and the vertex degree r. This bound assumes $1-\lambda > 0$, which holds if and only if the graph is connected and not bipartite. We note that the same bound can be derived for bipartite connected graphs, if we consider the 'lazy' COBRA process, which allows each vertex to also select itself with probability $1/2$.

THEOREM 1.2. *Let G be a connected r-regular n-vertex graph with $1 - \lambda > C\sqrt{(\log n)/n}$, for some suitably large constant C. For the COBRA process with branching factor $b = 2$, w.h.p. for each $u \in V$,* $\mathbf{cover}(u)$ *is*

$$O\left(\left(\frac{r}{1-\lambda} + r^2\right) \cdot \log n\right). \tag{2}$$

The COBRA process is a type of multiple random walk processes, so it is tempting to try to analyse it using techniques developed for such processes. Previous work on multiple random walks includes [1–3, 7], where cover times were analysed for various classes of graphs, assuming that the random walks are independent. The analyses of the COBRA process given in Dutta et al. [5, 6] and Mitzenmacher et al. [8] use a number of tools from multiple random walks, but applicability of those tools turns out to be limited because the random walks in COBRA are highly dependent. An alternative approach was proposed by Cooper et al. [4], who introduced and analysed a related epidemic process BIPS and showed that it is a dual (in some sense) of the COBRA process under time reversal.

Biased Infection with Persistent Source (BIPS). For a graph $G = (V, E)$, an integer $b \ge 1$ and a vertex v in G, which acts as the 'persistent' source of an infection, we consider the set process $(A_t)_{t\ge 0}$ defined by $A_0 = \{v\}$ and the following rule for generating A_{t+1} from A_t. Given A_t, each vertex $u \in V$, other than v, independently and uniformly with replacement selects b neighbours and becomes a member of A_{t+1} if and only if at least one of the selected neighbours is in A_t. Additionally, $v \in A_t$ for all $t \ge 0$. We call A_t the infected set at time t. Observe the source v is always infected, while other vertices can keep changing their status between infected and not infected.

For a subset $S \subseteq V$, let $\text{Infect}(S)$ denote the random set infected from S in one round: each vertex $u \in V$ selects independently uniformly with replacement two neighbours and becomes a member of $\text{Infect}(S)$, if and only if, at least one of the two selected neighbours is in S. Thus the BIPS process starts with $A_0 = \{v\}$ and $A_t = \text{Infect}(A_{t-1}) \cup \{v\}$, for each round $t \ge 1$.

The BIPS process is a discrete epidemic process of the Susceptible-Infected-Susceptible (SIS) type. The dynamics of such a process specifies how vertices get infected from their neighbours and how they lose infection (turn back into the susceptible state). In the BIPS process, the vertices (other than the source v) refresh their infected state at each round by contacting b randomly chosen neighbours. The presence of a persistent (or corrupted) source means that all vertices of the underlying graph eventually become infected. Our main reason for considering this particular BIPS process is that it is dual to the COBRA process. The BIPS process may however be also of independent interest since in the context of epidemics, certain viruses exhibit the property that a particular host can become persistently infected.

To avoid confusion between the BIPS process $(A_t)_{t\ge 0}$ and the COBRA process $(C_t)_{t\ge 0}$, we use the notation $\mathbf{P}(\cdot)$ for probabilities in the BIPS process, and $\widehat{\mathbf{P}}(\cdot)$ in the COBRA process. Let $\text{Hit}(w) = \min\{t : w \in C_t\}$, that is, the round in the COBRA process when vertex w gets a particle for the first time. We also write $\text{Hit}_C(w)$ and $\text{Hit}_u(w)$, if we want to indicate that $C_0 = C$ and $C_0 = \{u\}$, respectively. Our main results for COBRA follow from the duality between COBRA and BIPS introduced in [4] and expressed in the following theorem.

THEOREM 1.3. [4] *Let G be a connected graph and consider the COBRA and BIPS processes on G with the same parameter $b \geq 1$. For each $v \in V$ (the persistent source in BIPS), any set $\emptyset \neq C \subseteq V$ (the initial set with particles in COBRA) and $T \geq 0$, we have*

$$\widehat{\mathbf{P}}(\text{Hit}(v) > T | C_0 = C) = \mathbf{P}(C \cap A_T = \emptyset | A_0 = \{v\}).$$

This theorem says that the probability that a vertex v is not hit *by* round T in COBRA starting with particles at each vertex of set C is equal to the probability that none of the vertices in C is infected *at* round T in BIPS with the persistent source v. This theorem is formally proven in [4], so here we give only the underlying idea. Fix the sets of neighbours which the vertices select in rounds $1, 2, \ldots, T$: $\omega(u, t) \subseteq \mathcal{N}(u)$, for $u \in V$, $1 \leq t \leq T$, where $\mathcal{N}(u)$ denotes the set of neighbours of vertex u. Run the COBRA process for T rounds using these selections of neighbours, that is, if vertex u receives a particle in round $t - 1$, then it sends in round t one particle to each neighbour in $\omega(u, t)$. Run also the BIPS process using the same selections of neighbours but in the reverse time order, that is, the sets of neighbours $\omega(v, t)$, $v \in V$, are used in rounds $T + 1 - t$. It turns out that in the COBRA process vertex v is visited within these T rounds, if and only if, in the BIPS process at least one vertex in C is infected at round T. Crucially, the probability that the COBRA process selects exactly these sets $\omega(u, t)$ is equal to the probability that the BIPS process selects exactly the same sets in the reverse time order.

We define the infection time $\mathbf{infec}(v)$ as the first time when all vertices are infected by the BIPS process with the persistent source v. Proofs of the following two theorems about the BIPS process are the main new technical contribution of this paper.

THEOREM 1.4. *Let G be a connected graph with n vertices, m edges and the maximum vertex degree $d_{\max}$. For every $v \in V$, the infection time $\mathbf{infec}(v)$ of the BIPS process with $b = 2$ satisfies bound* (1) *with probability at least $1 - O(1/n^3)$.*

THEOREM 1.5. *Let G be a connected n-vertex r-regular graph with $1 - \lambda > C\sqrt{(\log n)/n}$, for some suitably large constant C. For every $v \in V$, the infection time $\mathbf{infec}(v)$ of the BIPS process with $b = 2$ satisfies bound* (2) *with probability at least $1 - O(1/n^3)$.*

Theorems 1.1 and 1.2 follow from Theorems 1.4 and 1.5, respectively, and from Theorem 1.3. For any two vertices $u, v \in V$ and any $T \geq 0$, applying Theorem 1.3 with $C = \{u\}$ gives

$$\begin{aligned}\widehat{\mathbf{P}}(\text{Hit}_u(v) > T) &= \mathbf{P}(u \notin A_T | A_0 = v)\\ &\leq \mathbf{P}(A_T \neq V | A_0 = v)\\ &= \mathbf{P}(\mathbf{infec}(v) > T).\end{aligned}$$

Theorem 1.4 says that there is a constant $c > 0$ such that for $T = c(m + (d_{\max})^2 \log n)$, $\mathbf{P}(\mathbf{infec}(v) > T) = O(1/n^3)$, implying $\widehat{\mathbf{P}}(\text{Hit}_u(v) > T) = O(1/n^3)$. We have $\mathbf{cover}(u) > T$, if and only if there is a vertex v such that $\text{Hit}_u(v) > T$. Thus, using the union bound, we conclude that $\mathbf{cover}(u)$ is greater than T with probability $O(1/n^2)$ and Theorem 1.1 follows. To see that the expected value of $\mathbf{cover}(u)$ is $O(T)$, consider restarting the COBRA process after T rounds from any vertex in C_T, if the graph has not yet been covered. We obtain Theorem 1.2 from the corresponding Theorem 1.5 in an analogous way.

COBRA process with branching factor less than 2. Theorems 1.1 and 1.2 are proved for a COBRA process with branching factor $b = 2$. However, it seems natural to ask if cover times of the same order can be obtained with less branching. Clearly $b = 1$ is not enough, since the cover time of any n vertex graph by a random walk is $\Omega(n \log n)$. Suppose that at the start of each round, each particle divides in two with probability ρ. This gives an expected branching factor of $b = 1 + \rho$. In the dual BIPS process, in each round each vertex u selects with probability ρ two random neighbours (with replacement) and with probability $1 - \rho$ only one random neighbour. Vertex u will be an infected vertex in the next iteration, if it has selected an infected neighbour in the current iteration. The duality Theorem 1.3 holds for any $b = 1 + \rho$. The bounds on the cover time and the infection time given in Theorems 1.1, 1.2, 1.4 and 1.5, hold for the COBRA and BIPS processes with parameter ρ, if $0 < \rho \leq 1$ is a constant.

In the remaining part of the paper, we prove Theorems 1.4 and 1.5, assuming from now on that $b = 2$, unless stated otherwise. Our analysis of the BIPS process presented in [4] was based on estimating the expected increase of the size of A_t in one round and relying on a strong concentration of this increase during the middle stage of the process. Separate care had to be given to the initial stage of the process when A_t is still relatively small and to the final stage when $V \setminus A_t$ becomes relatively small. The notion of 'relatively small' was quantified using the eigenvalue gap $1 - \lambda$.

In Theorem 1.4 we consider any graph, requiring only that it is connected. While we can still show a positive expected increase of the size of A_t in each round in this general case, the increase is too small to give any meaningful concentration, so we need a different approach.

Our proof of Theorem 1.4 is based on 'serialising' the BIPS process. All vertices which are to decide whether they will be included in the next infected set A_{t+1} make their decisions in one parallel 'global' step (round). In our analysis, however, we view this process as if the vertices were making decisions sequentially, one vertex after the other, according to an arbitrary, but fixed, order of all vertices. This serialisation is only an artifact of analysis and does not change the BIPS process in any way. To avoid potential confusion in terminology, the term *round* will refer to one 'global' parallel step of the BIPS process, and the term *step* will refer to the action of a single vertex in the serialisation of BIPS. It turs out that at this more granular level of such small steps, the process can be modelled as a martingale sequence.

The proof of Theorem 1.5 can be viewed as based on a combination of the above approach of serialising process BIPS and the approach used in [4] to provide more detailed analysis of the initial stage of the process, when the infected sets are relatively small.

2 PRELIMINARIES

The inequality given in Lemma 2.1 is a variant of the Azuma-Hoeffding inequality for super-martingales. The proof of this lemma is a straightforward adaptation of the proof of Theorem 3 from [9]. We will need in our analysis Corollary 2.2, which we derive from Lemma 2.1.

Lemma 2.1. *Let $Z_1, Z_2, \ldots$ be a sequence of discrete random variables such that for each $i \geq 1$, $|Z_i| \leq 1$ and*

$$\mathbf{E}(Z_i | Z_1, Z_2, \ldots, Z_{i-1}) \leq 0.$$

Then for any $\delta > 0$ and $q \geq 1$, with $S_q = \sum_{i=1}^{q} Z_i$,

$$\mathbf{P}(S_q > \delta q^{1/2}) \ < \ e^{-\delta^2/2}. \tag{3}$$

Proof. For a discrete random variable Z such that $|Z| \leq 1$ and $\mathbf{E}(Z) \leq 0$, and for any $\alpha > 0$, $\mathbf{E}(e^{\alpha Z}) < e^{\alpha^2/2}$. Because $f(x) = e^{\alpha x}$ is a convex function, for $x \in [-1, 1]$

$$\begin{aligned} e^{\alpha x} &\leq \frac{1-x}{2} e^{-\alpha} + \frac{1+x}{2} e^{\alpha} \\ &= \frac{1}{2}\left(e^{\alpha} + e^{-\alpha}\right) + \frac{x}{2}\left(e^{\alpha} - e^{-\alpha}\right). \end{aligned}$$

Thus

$$\begin{aligned} \mathbf{E}(e^{\alpha Z}) &\leq \frac{1}{2}\left(e^{\alpha} + e^{-\alpha}\right) + \frac{\mathbf{E}(Z)}{2}\left(e^{\alpha} - e^{-\alpha}\right) \\ &\leq \frac{1}{2}\left(e^{\alpha} + e^{-\alpha}\right) \leq e^{\alpha^2/2}. \end{aligned}$$

Using this bound we have for any $q \geq 1$,

$$\begin{aligned} \mathbf{E}(e^{\alpha S_q}) &= \mathbf{E}(e^{\alpha Z_q} e^{\alpha S_{q-1}}) \\ &= \mathbf{E}(\mathbf{E}(e^{\alpha Z_q} e^{\alpha S_{q-1}} \,|\, Z_1, Z_2, \ldots, Z_{q-1})) \\ &= \mathbf{E}(e^{\alpha S_{q-1}} \mathbf{E}(e^{\alpha Z_q} \,|\, Z_1, Z_2, \ldots, Z_{q-1})) \\ &< e^{\alpha^2/2} \cdot \mathbf{E}(e^{\alpha S_{q-1}}) \ \leq \ e^{\alpha^2 q/2}, \end{aligned}$$

where the last inequality follows by induction. Using Markov's inequality,

$$\begin{aligned} \mathbf{P}(S_q > \delta q^{1/2}) &= \mathbf{P}\left(e^{\alpha S_q} > e^{\alpha \delta q^{1/2}}\right) \\ &\leq e^{-\alpha \delta q^{1/2}} \cdot \mathbf{E}\left(e^{\alpha S_q}\right) \\ &< e^{-\alpha \delta q^{1/2} + \alpha^2 q/2} \ = \ e^{-\delta^2/2}, \end{aligned}$$

where the last equality holds by setting $\alpha = \delta / q^{1/2}$. □

Lemma 2.1 says that with high probability the sum S_q of random variables does not deviate too much from its expectation. In our analysis of the BIPS process, we will need high probability that the sums S_q for all $q \geq q_0$ do not deviate too much. The following corollary derived from Lemma 2.1 will work for us.

Corollary 2.2. *With the same setting as in Lemma 2.1, for any $\delta > 0$, $q \geq q_0 \geq 1$ and $0 < \alpha \leq 1$, we have*

$$\begin{aligned} &\mathbf{P}(\exists\, q \geq q_0 : \ S_q > \alpha(q - q_0) + \delta q_0^{1/2}) \\ &\qquad < \ q_0 e^{-\delta^2/4} + (16/\alpha^2) e^{-\alpha^2 q_0/4}. \end{aligned}$$

Proof.

$$\begin{aligned} &\mathbf{P}\left(\exists q \geq q_0 : \ S_q > \alpha(q - q_0) + \delta q_0^{1/2}\right) \\ &\leq \sum_{q \geq q_0} \mathbf{P}\left(S_q > \alpha(q - q_0) + \delta q_0^{1/2}\right) \\ &\leq \sum_{q=q_0}^{2q_0 - 1} \mathbf{P}\left(S_q > \delta q_0^{1/2}\right) + \sum_{q \geq 2q_0} \mathbf{P}\left(S_q > \alpha q/2\right) \\ &\leq \sum_{q=q_0}^{2q_0 - 1} \mathbf{P}\left(S_q > (\delta/2^{1/2}) q^{1/2}\right) \\ &\quad + \sum_{q \geq 2q_0} \mathbf{P}\left(S_q > (\alpha q^{1/2}/2) q^{1/2}\right) \\ &\leq q_0 e^{-\delta^2/4} + \sum_{q \geq 2q_0} e^{-\alpha^2 q/8} \qquad (4) \\ &\leq q_0 e^{-\delta^2/4} + (16/\alpha^2) e^{-\alpha^2 q_0/4}. \qquad (5) \end{aligned}$$

Inequality (4) follows from (3) applied to each term in both sums. Inequality (5) follows from the assumption that $0 < \alpha \leq 1$, so $e^{-\alpha^2/8} \leq 1 - \alpha^2/16$. □

3 INCREMENTAL NATURE OF BIPS ON ARBITRARY GRAPHS (THEOREM 4)

We consider in this section the BIPS process on any connected graph, not necessarily regular. We will be tracking the *degree* $d(A_t)$ of the infected set. For a subset of vertices $S \subseteq V$, its degree is defined as $d(S) = \sum_{u \in S} d(u)$, where $d(u)$ is the degree of vertex u.

We consider any round $t \geq 1$ such that $d(A_{t-1}) < 2m = d(V)$, that is, any round before the completion of the process (before the infected set becomes V). Let $A = A_{t-1}$ and $B = A_t$. We view the next infected set B as the disjoint union of sets B_{fix} and B_{rand}, where B_{fix} is the 'deterministic' part of B consisting of the vertices which have all neighbours in A, and $B_{\text{rand}} = B \setminus B_{\text{fix}}$ is the 'random' part of B. Note that according to this definition, the source v is in B_{fix}, if all its neighbours are in A, and in B_{rand} otherwise. Defining $\mathcal{N}(S) = \bigcup_{u \in S} \mathcal{N}(u)$, we can write

$$\begin{aligned} B_{\text{fix}} &= \{u \in V : \ \mathcal{N}(u) \subseteq A\}, \\ B_{\text{rand}} &\subseteq (\mathcal{N}(A) \cup \{v\}) \setminus B_{\text{fix}} \ \equiv \ C. \end{aligned} \tag{6}$$

The set $C = C_t$, which contains the candidates for inclusion in set B_{rand}, is never empty. If the source v is not in B_{fix}, then $v \in C$. If $v \in B_{\text{fix}}$, that is, v and all its neighbours are in A, then in a shortest path $(v, \ldots, u', u'', x)$ from the source v to a vertex in $V \setminus A$, vertex u'' is in C.

We have

$$d(A) - E(A, C) \ = \ d(B_{\text{fix}}) \ \leq \ d(A), \tag{7}$$

where for subsets $X, Y \subseteq V$, not necessarily disjoint,

$$E(X, Y) \ \equiv \ \sum_{u \in X} d_Y(u) \ = \ \sum_{u \in Y} d_X(u),$$

and $d_Y(u) \equiv |\mathcal{N}(u) \cap Y|$ is the number of the neighbours of vertex u which belong to set Y. We have the following lower bound for the expectation of $d(B_{\text{rand}})$.

$$\begin{aligned}
\mathbf{E}(d(B_{\text{rand}})) &= \\
&= 1_{v\in C}\cdot d(v) + \sum_{u\in C\setminus\{v\}} d(u)\left(1-\left(1-\frac{d_A(u)}{d(u)}\right)^2\right) \\
&= 1_{v\in C}\cdot d(v) + \sum_{u\in C\setminus\{v\}} d_A(u)\left(2-\frac{d_A(u)}{d(u)}\right) \\
&\ge \sum_{u\in C} d_A(u)\left(2-\frac{d_A(u)}{d(u)}\right) \ge \sum_{u\in C} d_A(u)\left(1+\frac{1}{d(u)}\right) \\
&\ge \left(1+\frac{1}{d_{\max}}\right)E(A,C). \qquad (8)
\end{aligned}$$

Using (7) and (8), we get the following lower bound on $\mathbf{E}(d(B))$.

$$\begin{aligned}
\mathbf{E}(d(B)) &= d(B_{\text{fix}}) + \mathbf{E}(d(B_{\text{rand}})) \qquad (9)\\
&= d(A) - E(A,C) + \mathbf{E}(d(B_{\text{rand}})) \\
&\ge d(A) + \frac{1}{d_{\max}}E(A,C). \qquad (10)
\end{aligned}$$

We write

$$d(B_{\text{rand}}) = \sum_{u\in C} d(u)X_u, \qquad (11)$$

where the binary random variable X_u is equal to 1 if, and only if, $v \in B_{\text{rand}}$. If C includes the source v, then $X_v \equiv 1$. Using (7) and (11), we have

$$\begin{aligned}
d(B) &= d(B_{\text{fix}}) + d(B_{\text{rand}}) \\
&= d(A) - E(A,C) + \sum_{u\in C} d(u)X_u \\
&= d(A) + \sum_{u\in C}(d(u)X_u - d_A(u)). \qquad (12)
\end{aligned}$$

For $1 \le \tau \le t \le T$, where T denotes the completion time of BIPS, the relation (12) for round τ can be written as

$$d(A_\tau) = d(A_{\tau-1}) + \sum_{u\in C_\tau}\left(d(u)X_{\tau,u} - d_{A_{\tau-1}}(u)\right). \qquad (13)$$

Summing (13) over rounds $\tau = 1, 2, \ldots, t$ gives

$$\begin{aligned}
d(A_t) &= d(v) + \sum_{\tau=1}^{t}\sum_{u\in C_\tau}(d(u)X_{\tau,u} - d_{A_{\tau-1}}(u)) \\
&\equiv d(v) + \sum_{l=1}^{\nu(t)} Y_l. \qquad (14)
\end{aligned}$$

Here $\nu(t) \equiv \sum_{\tau=1}^{t}|C_\tau|$ and

$$Y_{\nu(\tau-1)+i} \equiv d(u)X_{\tau,u} - d_{A_{\tau-1}}(u),$$

for $1 \le i \le |C_\tau|$, where u is the i-th smallest vertex of C_τ, according to some arbitrary but fixed ordering of the vertices in V. Since $C_\tau \ne \emptyset$, for each $1 \le \tau \le T$, we have

$$t \le \nu(t) \le \nu(t-1) + n, \qquad (15)$$

setting $\nu(0) = 0$. We say that round $t \le T$ consists of $|C_t|$ steps, with the random variable $Y_{\nu(t-1)+i}$ corresponding to step i of this round. Thus we can view the BIPS process as a sequence of steps $1, 2, \ldots, l, \ldots$, which are grouped into rounds.

While the BIPS process completes at round T, the sequence $(A_t)_{t\ge0}$ is defined in the natural way for all $t \ge 1$: $A_t = V$ and $d(A_t) = 2m$, for each $t > T$. The sequence (Y_l) is defined for $1 \le l \le \nu(T)$, that is, up till the completion of the BIPS process. For technical convenience, we set $Y_l = 1$ for all $l > \nu(T)$. The choice of the value 1 will become clear later. We note that (14) holds only for $t \le T$.

The random variables Y_l are not independent. The distribution of Y_l depends on the values of variables Y_i, $1 \le i \le l-1$. For any fixed $l \ge 1$ and any sequence of numbers $y_1, y_2, \ldots, y_{l-1}$, either this sequence of numbers is not a feasible sequence of values for the sequence of variables $Y_1, Y_2, \ldots, Y_{l-1}$, or it is feasible, shows in full the evolution of the BIPS process up till step $l-1$ and defines the distribution of the variable Y_l. Indeed, if $Y_1 = y_1, Y_2 = y_2, \ldots, Y_{l-1} = y_{l-1}$, then, starting from the known initial A_0 and C_1 and knowing that the vertices of C_1 are considered according to a fixed ordering of all vertices of V, we can keep tracking the values of $Y_1, Y_2, \ldots$ to identify the vertices in A_1 (this also gives the set C_2) then the vertices in A_2, and so on. Finally, either the process has completed before step l, so $Y_l \equiv 1$, or we identify the round t which includes step l, the set $A_{t-1} \subseteq V$ of the vertices infected in the previous round, and the vertex u considered in step l. In both cases, we get the distribution of the random variable Y_l.

Equation (14) implies that instead of analysing the sequence $d(A_t)$, $t \ge 1$, we can analyse the sequence of sums $R_q = \sum_{l=1}^{q} Y_l$, $q \ge 1$. There is a technical complication here because only for those $q = \nu(t)$ does the value of R_q correspond to the value of $d(A_t)$. This means that a large value of some R_q does not immediately imply a large value of $d(A_t)$. However, an appropriately long sequence $R_q, R_{q+1}, \ldots, R_{q'}$ of large values would imply a large value of some $d(A_t)$. More precisely, we have the following relation between the sequences $(d(A_t))_{t\ge1}$ and $(R_q)_{q\ge1}$. For each $1 \le k \le 2m - d(v)$ and each $t \ge 1$,

$$(d(A_t) < d(v) + k) \Rightarrow (\exists\, t \le q \le tn : R_q < k). \qquad (16)$$

Indeed, consider an execution of the BIPS process such that $d(A_t) < d(v) + k \le 2m$. From (14), $R_{\nu(t)} = \sum_{l=1}^{\nu(t)} Y_l < k$, and from (15), $t \le \nu(t) \le tn$. Thus $R_q < k$, for some $t \le q \le tn$.

We next derive a lower bound on the conditional expectation of Y_l given the values of the variables $Y_1, Y_2, \ldots, Y_{l-1}$. If these values show that the BIPS process has already completed (that is, $l > \nu(T)$), then $Y_l \equiv 1$ and $\mathbf{E}(Y_l|Y_1, Y_2, \ldots, Y_{l-1}) = 1$. Otherwise, let u denote the vertex corresponding to Y_l, let t denote the index of the current round (that is, the round which includes step l) and let $A = A_{t-1}$. As mentioned above, u, t and A_{t-1} are fully determined by the values of variables $Y_1, Y_2, \ldots, Y_{l-1}$. If $u = v$ (the source vertex), then $Y_l = d(v) - d_A(v)$ and $0 \le d_A(v) \le d(v) - 1$, so $Y_l \ge 1$. (In this case, $v \in C$, so $v \notin B_{\text{fix}}$ and $d_A(v) \le d(v) - 1$.) If $u \ne v$, then

$$\begin{aligned}
&\mathbf{E}(Y_l \mid Y_1, Y_2, \ldots, Y_{l-1}) \\
&= d(u)\left(1-\left(1-\frac{d_A(u)}{d(u)}\right)^2\right) - d_A(u) \\
&= d_A(u)\left(1-\frac{d_A(u)}{d(u)}\right) \ge 1 - \frac{1}{d(u)}. \qquad (17)
\end{aligned}$$

The inequality above holds because $u \in \mathcal{N}(A) \setminus B_{\text{fix}}$, so $1 \le d_A(u) \le d(u) - 1$. This also implies that $d(u) \ge 2$. Thus in all cases,

$$\mathbf{E}(Y_l | Y_1, Y_2, \ldots, Y_{l-1}) \ge \frac{1}{2}. \tag{18}$$

The proof of Theorem 1.4 follows from Lemma 3.1 (proved below) by choosing $k = 2m - d(v)$.

LEMMA 3.1. *Consider the BIPS process on a connected graph with n vertices, m edges and the maximum vertex degree $d_{\max}$. For any constant $C > 0$, there exists a constant $C' > 0$, such that for any $1 \le k \le 2m - d(v)$ and $t(k) = 4k + C'(d_{\max})^2 \log n$,*

$$\mathbf{P}\left(\exists\, t \ge t(k) : \ d(A_t) < d(v) + k\right) \le n^{-C}.$$

PROOF. For each $l \ge 1$, if the variable Y_l has the corresponding vertex u (that is, if $l \le v(T)$) and u is not the source v, then $Y_l \in \{-d_A(u), d(u) - d_A(u)\}$. If u is the source, then $Y_l = d(v) - d_A(v)$. If $l > v(T)$, then $Y_l = 1$. Thus in all cases $|Y_l| \le d_{\max} \equiv D$. We define $Z_l = (1/2 - Y_l)/D$, so that $|Z_l| \le 1$ and, from (18), $\mathbf{E}(Z_l | Z_1, Z_2, \ldots, Z_{l-1}) \le 0$. We will use Corollary 2.2 applied to the sum $\sum_{l=1}^{q} Z_l$.

For an arbitrary constant $C > 0$, let $\delta = \sqrt{4(C+4)\log n}$ and $C' = 16(C+4)$. These settings imply that for $q_0 = t(k) = 4k + C'D^2 \log n$, we have $q_0/2 - D\delta q_0^{1/2} \ge k$. Thus, using first the implication (16), then changing from variables Y_l to variables Z_l and using Corollary 2.2, we obtain

$$\begin{aligned}
&\mathbf{P}(\ \exists\, t \ge q_0 : \ d(A_t) < d(v) + k\ ) \\
&\le \mathbf{P}\left(\exists\, q \ge q_0 : \ \sum_{l=1}^{q} Y_l < k\right) \\
&= \mathbf{P}\left(\exists\, q \ge q_0 : \ \sum_{l=1}^{q} Z_l > \frac{q}{2D} - \frac{k}{D}\right) \\
&\le \mathbf{P}\left(\exists\, q \ge q_0 : \ \sum_{l=1}^{q} Z_l > \frac{q - q_0}{2D} + \delta q_0^{1/2}\right) \\
&\le q_0 e^{-\delta^2/4} + 64 D^2 e^{-q_0/(16D^2)} \qquad (19) \\
&\le n^3 e^{-\delta^2/4} + n^3 e^{-(C'/16)\log n)} \qquad (20) \\
&= n^{-(C+1)} + n^{-(C+1)} < n^{-C}. \qquad (21)
\end{aligned}$$

Inequality (19) follows from the inequality stated in Corollary 2.2, taking $\alpha = 1/(2D)$. Inequality (20) follows from the definition of q_0 and Equality (21) follows from our settings for δ and C'. □

4 BIPS ON REGULAR GRAPHS: KNOWN PROPERTIES

The analysis of the BIPS process on regular graphs given in [4] was broken into three phases. The first phase brings up the infection size from 1 to $\Omega(\log n/(1-\lambda)^2)$, the second phase increases it to $\Theta(n)$, and finally the third phase deals with comleting the infection of the whole graph. The first phase is the slow one, requiring $O(\log n/(1-\lambda)^3)$ time. The second and third phases require only $O(\log n/(1-\lambda))$ time and their joint performance is summarised in Lemma 4.3. All phases use Lemma 4.1, which gives a lower bound on the expected increase of infection in one round. Lemma 4.2 is the analog of Lemma 4.1 for branching factor $b = 1 + \rho$.

To improve the $O(\log n/(1-\lambda)^3)$ bound for small $1 - \lambda$, we will restructure the analysis presented in [4], but we will still refer directly to Lemmas 4.1, 4.2 and 4.3.

LEMMA 4.1. [4] *Let G be a connected r-regular graph on n vertices, with $\lambda < 1$, where λ is the absolute second eigenvalue of the random-walk transition matrix. Let A_t be the size of the infected set after round t of the BIPS process with $b = 2$, then*

$$\mathbf{E}(|A_{t+1}| \mid A_t = A) \ \ge\ |A|(1 + (1-\lambda^2)(1 - |A|/n)).$$

LEMMA 4.2. [4] *Let A_t be the size of the infected set after round t of the BIPS process with expected branching factor $b = 1 + \rho$, then*

$$\mathbf{E}(|A_{t+1}| \mid A_t = A) \ \ge\ |A|(1 + \rho(1-\lambda^2)(1 - |A|/n)).$$

LEMMA 4.3. [4] *Let G be a connected n-vertex r-regular graph and consider the BIPS process on G from some round $t > 0$. There exist constants C and K such that, if $1 - \lambda \ge C\sqrt{\log n/n}$ and $|A_t| \ge K \log n/(1-\lambda)^2$, then the whole graph is infected within $O(\log n/(1-\lambda))$ additional rounds with probability at least $1 - O(1/n^3)$.*

5 BIPS ON REGULAR GRAPHS: NEW ANALYSIS

In comparison with the analysis given in [4] and outlined in the previous section, our new analysis ends the first, initial phase earlier, more precisely as soon as the size of infection becomes (roughly) $\Omega(\log n/(1-\lambda))$. From that point we analyse in more detail how the size of infection increases until it reaches $\Theta(n)$. In this analysis we use and extend the methodology developed in Section 3. The analysis of the final phase, from infection of size $\Theta(n)$ to complete infection of the whole graph, is the same as in [4], so we simply refer to Lemma 4.3.

When considering regular graphs, for simplicity we track the size of the current infection set rather than the degree of this set. Applying Lemma 3.1 to r-regular graphs and substituting k with $(\kappa - 1)r$, we obtain the following corollary.

COROLLARY 5.1. *Consider the BIPS process on a connected r-regular graph with n vertices. For any constant $C > 0$, there exists a constant $C' > 0$, such that for any $1 \le \kappa \le n$ and $t(\kappa) = 4r\kappa + C'r^2 \log n$,*

$$\mathbf{P}(\exists\, t \ge t(\kappa) : \ |A_t| < \kappa) \le n^{-C}. \tag{22}$$

Consider r-regular graphs with the eigenvalue gap $1 - \lambda \ge C\sqrt{\log n/n}$, where C is the constant from Lemma 4.3. By applying Corollary 5.1 with $\kappa = K \log n/(1-\lambda)^2$ and then Lemma 4.3, we conclude that BIPS completes within $O((r/(1-\lambda)^2 + r^2)\log n)$ rounds, w.h.p. and in expectation. The constant K here is as needed in Lemma 4.3. In the remaining part of this section we extend our analysis to reduce this bound to $O((r/(1-\lambda) + r^2)\log n)$. To achieve this, we need to bridge the gap between the infection size $\Omega((\log n)/(1-\lambda))$ guaranteed by Corollary 5.1 after $O((r/(1-\lambda) + r^2)\log n)$ rounds, and the initial infection size $\Omega(\log n/(1-\lambda)^2)$ required by Lemma 4.3.

Corollary 5.1 with $\kappa = \Omega(r \log n)$ gives the size of infection $\Omega(\kappa)$ within $t(\kappa) = O(r\kappa)$ rounds. Thus the infection grows with the average rate of $\Omega(1/r)$ vertices per round. In the general case, that is, for any structure of regular graphs, we can show only this small rate of growth, because we can only guarantee that each set C_t (see (6)) contains at least one vertex. However, when the size of infection keeps increasing and passes through some appropriate thresholds, then, depending on the structure of the graph, the sizes of sets C_t also grow, gradually speeding up the rate of growth of infection. While there are various ways of lower bounding the size of C_t in terms of the size of A_t and the eigenvalue gap $1-\lambda$ of the graph, the following bound follows easily from the facts which we have already established.

Corollary 5.2. *For each round $t \geq 1$ of the BIPS process on an n-vertex r-regular graph, if $|A_{t-1}| \leq n/2$, then the size of the set C_t defined in (6) is at least $|A_{t-1}|(1-\lambda)/2$.*

Proof. We use the same notation as in Section 3: $A \equiv A_{t-1}$, $B \equiv A_t$ and $C \equiv C_t$. We have

$$\begin{aligned}|A| + |A|(1-\lambda)/2 &\leq \mathbf{E}(|B|) = |B_{\text{fix}}| + \mathbf{E}(|B_{\text{rand}}|)\\ &\leq |A| + \mathbf{E}(|B_{\text{rand}}|).\end{aligned}$$

The first inequality follows from Lemma 4.1 and the assumption that $|A| \leq n/2$. The middle equality is (9) divided by r, and the last inequality is (7) divided by r. Thus $\mathbf{E}(|B_{\text{rand}}|) \geq |A|(1-\lambda)/2$, while $|C|$ is an obvious upper bound on $\mathbf{E}(|B_{\text{rand}}|)$ because $B_{\text{rand}} \subseteq C$. □

We consider now the BIPS process from some round $t \geq 1$ and denote by $\tilde{Y}_l$ and $\tilde{R}_q$ the random variables Y_l and R_q from Section 3 divided by r. In this setting, (14) and (16) become

$$|A_{t+\Delta}| = |A_t| + \sum_{l=1}^{\nu(\Delta)} \tilde{Y}_l \equiv |A_t| + \tilde{R}_{\nu(\Delta)}, \tag{23}$$

$$(|A_{t+\Delta}| < |A_t| + \kappa) \Rightarrow (\exists\, \Delta \leq q < \Delta n : \tilde{R}_q < \kappa), \tag{24}$$

where $1 \leq \kappa \leq n - |A_t|$ and $\Delta \geq 1$. Generalising (24), we obtain the following implication, where $\alpha \geq 1$ is the threshold on the sizes of sets $C_{t+\tau}$ and $\mathcal{A}$ is an arbitrary event.

$$\begin{aligned}&((|A_{t+\Delta}| < |A_t| + \kappa) \wedge \mathcal{A})\\ &\quad\Rightarrow \left(\left(\exists\, \alpha\Delta \leq q < \Delta n : \tilde{R}_q < \kappa\right)\right)\\ &\quad\text{or } ((\exists\, 1 \leq \tau \leq \Delta : |C_{t+\tau}| < \alpha) \wedge \mathcal{A}).\end{aligned} \tag{25}$$

Indeed, if $|A_{t+\Delta}| < |A_t| + \kappa$ and $|C_{t+\tau}| \geq \alpha$ for each $1 \leq \tau \leq \Delta$ (that is, each round $\tau = t+1, t+2, \ldots, t+\Delta$ has at least α steps), then $\tilde{R}_{\nu(\Delta)} < \kappa$ and $\alpha\Delta \leq \nu(\Delta) < \Delta n$. Following the same argument as in the proof of Lemma 3.1 but for regular graphs and using (25) instead of (24), Corollary 5.1 becomes the following statement.

Corollary 5.3. *Consider the BIPS process on a connected r-regular graph with n vertices. For any constant $C > 0$, there exists a constant $C' > 0$, such that for any $\alpha \geq 1$, $t \geq 1$, infected set A_t ($v \in A_t \subset V$), $1 \leq \kappa \leq n - |A_t|$ and an event $\mathcal{A}$, defining*

$$\Delta(\kappa, \alpha) = (4r\kappa + C'r^2 \log n)/\alpha, \tag{26}$$

we have

$$\begin{aligned}&\mathbf{P}((\exists\, \Delta \geq \Delta(\kappa,\alpha) : |A_{t+\Delta}| < |A_t| + \kappa) \wedge \mathcal{A})\\ &\leq n^{-C} + \mathbf{P}((\exists\, 1 \leq \tau \leq \Delta(\kappa,\alpha) : |C_{t+\tau}| < \alpha) \wedge \mathcal{A}).\end{aligned}$$

Using Corollaries 5.1, 5.2 and 5.3, we obtain the following lemma.

Lemma 5.4. *Consider the BIPS process on a connected n-vertex r-regular graph G with eigenvalue gap $1-\lambda$. For any constant $C > 0$, there exists a constant C'' such that the probability that the size of infection is at least $n/4$ at some round $t \leq C''r(1/(1-\lambda) + r)\log n$ is at least $1 - n^{-C}$.*

Proof. Let $C > 0$ be an arbitrary constant and let $C' > 0$ be a constant which 'works' for the constant $C+2$ in both Corollaries 5.1 and 5.3. We first apply Corollary 5.1 with $k = \kappa_0$, where

$$\kappa_0 = \min\{1/(1-\lambda) + (C'r/4)\log n,\ n\},$$

and conclude that with probability at least $1 - n^{-(C+2)}$, the size of infection is at least κ_0 in each round $t \geq t_0 = 8r\kappa_0$. Reaching infection size κ_0 can be viewed as the first, initial phase of the BIPS process. If $\kappa_0 \geq n/4$, then we are done. Otherwise, we will be repeatedly doubling the target size of infection, that is, we will be analysing when the infection size is w.h.p. at least $\kappa_i = 2^i\kappa_0$, for $i = 1, 2, \ldots, j$, where $n/4 \leq 2^j\kappa_0 < n/2$.

Let $t_i = t_0 + 16ir/(1-\lambda)$ and let $\mathcal{A}$ be the event that $|A_t| < n/2$ for all $1 \leq t \leq t_j$. Observe that $t_{i+1} \geq t_i + \Delta(\kappa_i, \alpha_i)$, where $\Delta(\kappa, \alpha)$ is as defined in (26) and $\alpha_i = \kappa_i(1-\lambda)/2$. We prove by induction that for each $0 \leq i \leq j$,

$$\mathbf{P}((\exists\, t \geq t_i : |A_t| < \kappa_i) \wedge \mathcal{A}) < 3^i n^{-(C+2)}. \tag{27}$$

Observe that (27) with $i = j$ implies that the probability that $|A_t| < n/4 \leq \kappa_j$, for each $1 \leq t \leq t_j = O(r(1/(1-\lambda) + r)\log n)$, is at most $3^j n^{-(C+2)} < n^{-C}$, as claimed in the lemma. Thus it only remains to prove (27).

For $i = 0$, Inequality (27) is established in the first paragraph of the proof. Let $0 \leq i \leq j-1$ and consider (27) for $i+1$. We have, using the equivalent notation $A(t) \equiv A_t$,

$$\begin{aligned}&\mathbf{P}((\exists\, t \geq t_{i+1} : |A_t| < \kappa_{i+1}) \wedge \mathcal{A})\\ &\leq \mathbf{P}((\exists\, \Delta \geq \Delta(\kappa_i,\alpha_i) : |A(t_i+\Delta)| < \kappa_{i+1}) \wedge \mathcal{A})\\ &\leq \max\{\, \mathbf{P}((\exists\, \Delta \geq \Delta(\kappa_i,\alpha_i) : |A(t_i+\Delta)| < \kappa_{i+1}) \wedge \mathcal{A} \mid A_{t_i}) :\\ &\qquad v \in A(t_i) \subseteq V, |A(t_i)| \geq \kappa_i\}\\ &+ \mathbf{P}((|A(t_i)| < \kappa_i) \wedge \mathcal{A}).\end{aligned} \tag{28}$$

The induction hypothesis implies that

$$\mathbf{P}((|A(t_i)| < \kappa_i) \wedge \mathcal{A}) \leq 3^i n^{-(C+2)}. \tag{29}$$

If at the current round t we reduce the infection set A_t to $A'_t \subseteq A_t$, then for any $t' \geq t$, the distribution of $|A'_{t'}|$ stochastically dominates the distribution of $|A_{t'}|$. Thus, if $v \in A' \subseteq A'' \subseteq V$ and $|A'| = \kappa_i$, then

$$\begin{aligned}&\mathbf{P}((\exists\, \Delta \geq \Delta(\kappa_i,\alpha_i) : |A(t_i+\Delta)| < \kappa_{i+1}) \wedge \mathcal{A} \mid A(t_i) = A'')\\ &\leq \mathbf{P}((\exists\, \Delta \geq \Delta(\kappa_i,\alpha_i) : |A(t_i+\Delta)| < \kappa_{i+1}) \wedge \mathcal{A} \mid A(t_i) = A'),\end{aligned}$$

so it is enough to consider in 'max' in (28) only sets $A(t_i)$ of size κ_i. For any fixed $A(t_i)$ such that $v \in A(t_i) \subseteq V$ and $|A(t_i)| = \kappa_i$,

$$\begin{aligned}&\mathbf{P}((\exists\, \Delta \geq \Delta(\kappa_i,\alpha_i) : |A(t_i+\Delta)| < \kappa_{i+1}) \wedge \mathcal{A})\\ &= \mathbf{P}((\exists\, \Delta \geq \Delta(\kappa_i,\alpha_i) : |A(t_i+\Delta)| < |A_{t_i}| + \kappa_i) \wedge \mathcal{A})\\ &\leq \mathbf{P}((\exists\, 1 \leq \tau \leq \Delta(\kappa_i,\alpha_i) : |C(t_i+\tau)| < \alpha_i) \wedge \mathcal{A}),\\ &+ n^{-(C+2)}.\end{aligned} \tag{30}$$

The inequality above follows from Corollary 5.3.

$$\begin{aligned}
&\mathbf{P}((\exists\, 1 \le \tau \le \Delta(\kappa_i,\alpha_i): \ |C(t_i+\tau)| < \alpha_i) \wedge \mathcal{A}) \\
\le\ & \mathbf{P}((\exists\, t_i \le t \le t_{i+1}: \ |C_t| < \alpha_i) \wedge \mathcal{A}) \\
\le\ & \mathbf{P}((\exists\, t_i \le t \le t_{i+1}: \ (|A_t| < \kappa_i) \vee (|A_t| > n/2)) \wedge \mathcal{A}) \\
=\ & \mathbf{P}((\exists\, t_i \le t \le t_{i+1}: \ (|A_t| < \kappa_i)) \wedge \mathcal{A}) \\
\le\ & 3^i n^{-(C+2)}
\end{aligned} \tag{31}$$

The second inequality above follows from Corollary 5.2 and the last inequality follows from the induction hypothesis. Summarising, if we start from (28) and use (29)–(31), we obtain

$$\begin{aligned}
\mathbf{P}((\exists\, t \ge t_{i+1} : |A_t| < \kappa_{i+1}) \wedge \mathcal{A})& \\
&\le 2 \cdot 3^i n^{-(C+2)} + n^{-(C+2)} \\
&\le 3^{i+1} n^{-(C+2)}.
\end{aligned}$$

Thus (27) holds for $i+1$, so by induction, it holds for all $0 \le i \le j$. □

Proof of Theorem 1.5. Apply Lemma 5.4 to show that the size of infection is at least $n/4$ within $O(r(1/(1-\lambda)+r)\log n)$ rounds. Then apply Lemma 4.3 to show that the whole graph is infected after additional $O((\log n)/(1-\lambda))$ rounds. □

6 BIPS WITH BRANCHING FACTOR LESS THAN 2

The analysis of the BIPS process with branching factor $b = 1 + \rho$, for a constant $0 < \rho \le 1$, requires somewhat tedious but otherwise straightforward tracing of the analysis of the main case $b = 2$ and updating the probability that a vertex u catches infection in the current round. Denoting as before $A \equiv A_{t-1}$ and $B \equiv B_t$, if the branching factor is $b = 2$, then the probability that a vertex u gets infected in round t is equal to

$$\mathbf{P}_{(2)}(u \in B) = \left(1 - \left(1 - \frac{d_A(u)}{d(u)}\right)^2\right). \tag{32}$$

If the branching factor is $b = 1 + \rho \le 2$, then this probability is

$$\mathbf{P}_{(1+\rho)}(u \in B) = \left(1 - \left(1 - \frac{d_A(u)}{d(u)}\right)\left(1 - \rho\frac{d_A(u)}{d(u)}\right)\right). \tag{33}$$

We give a couple of examples of substituting (32) with (33) in the analysis. In Section 3, the probabilities of vertices becoming infected are used in (8) – (10) to obtain a lower bound on the expected size of infection in the next round. Adapting to the case $b = 1 + \rho \le 1$ gives:

$$\begin{aligned}
&\mathbf{E}(d(B_{\text{rand}})) = \\
&= 1_{v\in C}\cdot d(v) + \sum_{u\in C\setminus\{v\}} d(u)\left(1 - \left(1 - \frac{d_A(u)}{d(u)}\right)\left(1 - \rho\frac{d_A(u)}{d(u)}\right)\right) \\
&= 1_{v\in C}\cdot d(v) + \sum_{u\in C\setminus\{v\}} d_A(u)\left(1 + \rho - \rho\frac{d_A(u)}{d(u)}\right) \\
&\ge \sum_{u\in C} d_A(u)\left(1 + \rho - \rho\frac{d_A(u)}{d(u)}\right) \ge \left(1 + \frac{\rho}{d_{\max}}\right)E(A,C),
\end{aligned}$$

and

$$\mathbf{E}(d(B)) \ \ge\ d(A) + \frac{\rho}{d_{\max}}E(A,C).$$

Similarly (17) and (18) become:

$$\mathbf{E}(Y_l \mid Y_1, Y_2, \ldots, Y_{l-1}) \ge \rho\left(1 - \frac{1}{d(u)}\right),$$

and

$$\mathbf{E}(Y_l | Y_1, Y_2, \ldots, Y_{l-1}) \ \ge\ \frac{\rho}{2}.$$

The updates are also needed in Lemma 3.1 and Corollaries 5.1 and 5.3, where the number of rounds guaranteeing w.h.p. the increase of the size of infection (numbers $t(k)$, $t(\kappa)$ and $\Delta(\kappa,\alpha)$) should be multiplied by $1/\rho^2$.

7 CONCLUSIONS

The COBRA process was proposed for studies as a type of parallel random walks with relations to epidemics processes and potential applications in network algorithms [6, 8]. We have contributed to this studies by improving upper bounds on the cover time of the COBRA process. In particular we achieved a significant improvement of the general bound which applies to all connected graphs. We achieved this by exploiting the duality between COBRA and a related epidemics process.

The obvious open questions are about tightness of the existing bounds. For example, while our general bound of $O(n^2 \log n)$ is a significant improvement over the previous best bound of $O(n^{11/4} \log n)$, there are no known examples of the cover time $\omega(n \log n)$. It has actually been conjectured the worst-case cover time for any graph is $O(n \log n)$. Regarding cover time bounds for specific classes of graphs, the hypercube remains an interesting example, with the best known upper bound of $O(\log^3 n)$, implied by the results in this paper, and no good reason why it should be higher than $\Theta(\log n)$.

ACKNOWLEDGMENTS

This work was supported by EPSRC under Grant No.: EP/M005038/1 (Randomized algorithms for computer networks). Nicolás Rivera was also supported by funding from Becas CHILE.

REFERENCES

[1] N. Alon, C. Avin, M. Koucký, G. Kozma, Z. Lotker, and M. R. Tuttle. Many random walks are faster than one. *Combinatorics, Probability & Computing*, 20(4):481–502, 2011.
[2] A. Z. Broder, A. R. Karlin, P. Raghavan, and E. Upfal. Trading space for time in undirected s-t connectivity. In *STOC*, pages 543–549. ACM, 1989.
[3] C. Cooper, A. M. Frieze, and T. Radzik. Multiple random walks in random regular graphs. *SIAM J. Discrete Math.*, 23(4):1738–1761, 2009.
[4] C. Cooper, T. Radzik, N. Rivera. The Coalescing-Branching Random Walk on Expanders and the Dual Epidemic Process. PODC 2016: 461-467.
[5] C. Dutta, G. Pandurangan, R. Rajaraman, and S. Roche. Coalescing-branching random walks on graphs. In *Proceedings of the Twenty-fifth Annual ACM Symposium on Parallelism in Algorithms and Architectures*, SPAA '13, pages 176–185, New York, NY, USA, 2013. ACM.
[6] C. Dutta, G. Pandurangan, R. Rajaraman, and S. Roche. Coalescing-branching random walks on graphs. *ACM Trans. Parallel Comput.*, 2(3):20:1–20:29, Nov. 2015.
[7] R. Elsässer and T. Sauerwald. Tight bounds for the cover time of multiple random walks. In *Automata, Languages and Programming, 36th International Colloquium, ICALP 2009, Proceedings, Part I*, volume 5555 of *Lecture Notes in Computer Science*, pages 415–426. Springer, 2009.
[8] M. Mitzenmacher, R. Rajaraman, S. Roche. Better bounds for coalescing-branching random walks. In *Proceedings of the Twenty-eight Annual ACM Symposium on Parallelism in Algorithms and Architectures*, SPAA '16, pages 313–323, 2016. (see also http://arxiv.org/abs/1603.06109)
[9] E. Shamir and J. Spencer. Sharp concentration of the chromatic number on random graphs $G_{n,p}$. *Combinatorica*, March 1987, Volume 7, Issue 1, pp 121-129.

The Mobile Server Problem*

Björn Feldkord
Heinz Nixdorf Institut & Computer Science Dept.,
Paderborn University
Fürstenallee 11
Paderborn, Germany
bjoernf@mail.upb.de

Friedhelm Meyer auf der Heide
Heinz Nixdorf Institut & Computer Science Dept.,
Paderborn University
Fürstenallee 11
Paderborn, Germany
fmadh@upb.de

ABSTRACT

We introduce the mobile server problem, inspired by current trends to move computational tasks from cloud structures to multiple devices close to the end user. An example for this are embedded systems in autonomous cars that communicate in order to coordinate their actions.

Our model is a variant of the classical Page Migration Problem. More formally, we consider a mobile server holding a data page. The server can move in the Euclidean space (of arbitrary dimension). In every round, requests for data items from the page pop up at arbitrary points in the space. The requests are served, each at a cost of the distance from the requesting point and the server, and the mobile server may move, at a cost D times the distance traveled for some constant D. We assume a maximum distance m the server is allowed to move per round.

We show that no online algorithm can achieve a competitive ratio independent of the length of the input sequence in this setting. Hence we augment the maximum movement distance of the online algorithms to $(1 + \delta)$ times the maximum distance of the offline solution. We provide a deterministic algorithm which is simple to describe and works for multiple variants of our problem. The algorithm achieves almost tight competitive ratios independent of the length of the input sequence.

KEYWORDS

page migration; online algorithms; competitive analysis; resource augmentation

ACM Reference format:
Björn Feldkord and Friedhelm Meyer auf der Heide. 2017. The Mobile Server Problem. In *Proceedings of SPAA '17, Washington, DC, USA, July 24–26, 2017,* 7 pages.
https://doi.org/10.1145/3087556.3087575

*This work was partially supported by the German Research Foundation (DFG) within the Collaborative Research Centre "On-The-Fly Computing" (SFB 901).

ACM ISBN 978-1-4503-4593-4/17/07...$15.00
https://doi.org/10.1145/3087556.3087575

1 INTRODUCTION

Motivated by their large consumption of computational resources, a growing number of applications were shifted from a single machine at some end user to large computing centers. These centers may have networks of processors working on a common memory to execute some common computational task. This development has motivated lots of research problems regarding a static network of machines with some common resources such as memory and bandwidth of common communication channel (see [11] for a survey of scheduling problems for such networks).

Recently, another trend can be observed where the computation is shifting back to the user. This is commonly referred to as "edge computing" and involves a dynamic network with lots of (mobile) devices which are located close to the user. The machines may even be embedded systems such as in autonomous cars which need to share data in order to coordinate. As a result, the structure of the communication network might be much more complex in the sense that devices may join and leave the network and data may be shifted to nodes which are altering their physical location throughout the computation. For examples, see [1, 10].

The Page Migration Problem is a simple model for approaching the problem with shared memory in a cloud computing scenario. In the classical version of this problem we consider a memory page which is shared by multiple processors which are connected in a network. Only one processor can hold the page at a time. Processors request data from the page which incurs cost proportional to the distance within the network. In order to reduce these costs, the page may be moved to another processor; this however incurs cost proportional to the distance in the network times the size of the page.

In this paper, we present with the Mobile Server Problem a simple model which captures both the idea of Page Migration, namely modeling costs for accessing data items from an indivisible data page, and allowing mobility of data servers in order to improve the overall performance of the system.

Abstracting from specific network topologies, we replace the network graph with the Euclidean space, such that, at every step, an arbitrary (finite) number of requests for data items can appear anywhere in the space. In order to improve the overall performance, the mobile server holding the memory page can move to any point in the plane. For the purpose of bounding the time needed for a round, we limit the allowed distance the server can move in a step. The cost for a step is composed of the sum of the distances between the mobile server and the positions of the clients issuing the requests, plus the distance the server moves, weighted with a cost value D.

The Page Migration Problem is naturally often considered as an online problem as data requests may not be known at the start of a larger computation. This is especially true in our scenario where even the participating devices may not be known in advance. Hence, we also consider the Moving Server Problem as an online problem.

We mainly consider the variant where, in a step, a server may move knowing the position of the clients, but answer their requests afterwards. We also discuss other variants.

1.1 Related Work

The Page Migration Problem was first considered as an online problem by Black and Sleator [8] who gave 3-competitive algorithms for arbitrary trees and the complete graph. It was also shown that 3 is the best possible competitive ratio even if the given network just consists of two processors. This lower bound also holds for randomized algorithms against adaptive adversaries.

The first deterministic algorithm for general graphs was given by Westbrook in 1994 [15] which was called *Move-To-Min* as the strategy is to move to the optimal point in regards to the last D requests. The competitive ratio of this algorithm is 7.

For the randomized solutions, there is a simple 3-competitive algorithm called the *Coin-Flip Algorithm* which is simple to describe and also works against adaptive online adversaries. A more involved solution gives a 2.62-competitive algorithm against oblivious adversaries. These algorithms can be found in a paper by Westbrook [15].

An overview over these results including better results for the deterministic case can be found in a survey by Yair Bartal [3].

The Page Migration Problem belongs to the class of *relaxed task systems*. This was used to derive a deterministic solution for the problem with multiple copies of the page. The adaption within the framework is made from an online algorithm for the k-Server Problem [4].

The k-Server Problem can be formulated in terms of the Page Migration Problem with the restriction that requests which appear in the network must be satisfied by moving one of the k identical copies of the page to the location of the request. The competitive ratio of the problem is shown to be $\Omega(k)$. An overview of the most important results can be found in a survey by Elias Koutsoupias [14]. A recent paper by Böckenhauer et. al. also studied the advice complexity of the k-Server Problem where they design a $\frac{1}{1-2\sin(\frac{\pi}{2^b})}$-competitive algorithm reading b bits per time step [5].

In contrast to the k-Server model, Albers and Koga studied a variant with multiple different pages (only one copy per page) but where the processors only can hold one page at a time. The competitive ratio for this model can be bounded by a constant [2].

The Page Migration Problem has already been studied within the Manhattan and Euclidean plane, but without restricting the moving distance of the page in each time step [9, 13]. The Manhattan and Euclidean plane were also considered for the 3-Server Problem for which (almost) optimal online algorithms were given [6].

All the mentioned variants so far assumed a static network where the distances between the nodes do not change over time. Bienkowski et. al. considered a scenario where distances between nodes could change over time. The change in distance was done either by an adversary or determined by a stochastic process. In this scenario the competitive ratio depends both on the size of the page and the number of processors [7].

Since the competitive ratio for our problem does depend on the length of the input sequence, we analyze it using the concept of *resource augmentation*. This technique of giving the online algorithm slightly more power in some sense to get a bounded competitive ratio was first used by Kalyanasundaram and Pruhs for scheduling problems where the online algorithms were given slightly faster processors than the offline solution to improve from an unbounded ratio to a competitive ratio only dependent on the augmentation factor [12].

1.2 Our Contribution

We present the Mobile Server Problem introduced above (and formally described in Section 2). Our first results are lower bounds for the competitive ratio: We prove that no online algorithm can achieve a competitive ratio independent of the number of rounds for this problem.

We therefore consider the problem in a setting where the maximum distance a server may move is augmented by a factor of $(1+\delta)$ for the online algorithm. We show that a simple algorithm is sufficient to achieve a competitive ratio independent of the length of the input sequence for several variants of the problem.

In particular, we describe a deterministic algorithm which is $O(\frac{1}{\delta^{3/2}})$-competitive in the Euclidean Plane when the number of requests per round is fixed. We also briefly sketch how to modify our analysis to work for a varying number of requests per round and for a scenario where requests must be answered before the page can be moved.

To complement these results we show lower bounds for all of the variants which also hold for randomized algorithms against oblivious adversaries. Overall we get tight bounds for the 1-dimensional Euclidean space and almost tight bounds, up to a factor of $\frac{1}{\sqrt{\delta}}$, for arbitrary dimensions.

2 OUR MODEL

The model of the Moving Server Problem adapts some notation from the Page Migration Problem to allow for a better understanding and an easy comparison of the results.

We consider a mobile server holding a memory page, located at a point P_t in the Euclidean Plane at time t. Time is discrete and divided into steps. We refer to the length of an input sequence as the number of time steps denoted by T.

In each time step, clients can request data items from the page. Let r_t be the number of clients requesting data items in step t. These are represented by points $v_{t,1}, \ldots, v_{t,r_t}$ in the plane. The server can move in every time step by a distance of at most m, i.e. $d(P_t, P_{t+1}) \leq m$.

The cost for answering a request issued at position v when the server is located at position P is $d(P, v)$. Moving the server from position P_t to P_{t+1} induces cost $D \cdot d(P_t, P_{t+1})$ for some constant $D \geq 1$. An algorithm operating on an input sequence for the problem can decide in each step where to move the page under the given restriction of the distance.

The total costs of an algorithm *Alg* on a given input sequence are defined as follows:

$$C_{Alg} = \sum_{t=1}^{T} \left(D \cdot d(P_t, P_{t+1}) + \sum_{i=1}^{r_t} d(P_{t+1}, v_{t,i}) \right)$$

Note that in this definition, the page may be moved upon knowing the current requests. The requests are however served after the page has been moved, hence the costs are proportional to the distance to P_{t+1}.

We will discuss the implication of this definition in contrast to moving the page after serving the requests in the following section.

3 LOWER BOUNDS

In this section we show how the different parameters of our model influence the quality of the best possible approximation by an online algorithm.

In this paper we only present a deterministic online algorithm for the Mobile Server Problem, however we formulate the lower bounds for the expected competitive ratio of randomized online algorithms against oblivious adversaries. These lower bounds carry over to the deterministic case and to randomized online algorithms against stronger (adaptive) adversaries.

It should also be noted that these lower bounds hold in the Euclidean space for an arbitrary dimension.

For the lower bounds we use Yao's Min-Max Principle [16] which allows us to construct the lower bounds by generating a randomized sequence and examine the expected competitive ratio of a deterministic online algorithm.

First we show that without use of resource augmentation, there does not exist an online algorithm with a competitive ratio independent of T, even if there is only one request per time step.

THEOREM 3.1. *Every randomized online algorithm for the Mobile Server Problem has a competitive ratio of $\Omega(\sqrt{T}/D)$ against an oblivious adversary.*

PROOF. We consider a sequence of x time steps with one request each on the starting position of the server. Consider two opposite directions from the starting position which we will refer to as left and right. The adversary decides with probability $\frac{1}{2}$ at the beginning of the first step to either move its server a distance m to the left or to the right for the first x time steps. The cost for the adversary is at most $xDm + m \cdot \sum_{i=1}^{x} i \leq xDm + mx^2$ for these first x steps.

After these x steps, with probability $\frac{1}{2}$ the server of the online algorithm has a distance of at least xm to the server of the adversary.

For the remaining $T - x$ steps of the sequence the adversary issues requests on the position of its server and moves it a distance of m towards the same direction it already did during the first x steps. The costs for the adversary are $(T - x)Dm$ while the costs for the online algorithm are at least $(T - x) \cdot xm$ with probability $\frac{1}{2}$. By choosing $x = \sqrt{T}$ the expected competitive ratio is $\Omega(\frac{\sqrt{T}}{D})$. □

In order to have a chance to achieve a competitive ratio independent from T, we augment the maximum distance by which the server may move in every time step for the respective online algorithm.

We consider online algorithms which, in every round, can move their server by a distance of $(1 + \delta)m$ for some $\delta \in (0, 1]$. We do not consider bigger values for δ in this paper since 1 is a natural lower bound for all online problems. Hence asymptotically, for an online algorithm it is sufficient to utilize a distance of at most $2m$ to match the lower bound of $\frac{1}{\delta}$.

THEOREM 3.2. *Let R_{min} and R_{max} be the minimum and maximum number of requests per time step. Every randomized online algorithm using an augmented maximum moving distance of at most $(1 + \delta)m$ has an expected competitive ratio of $\Omega(\frac{1}{\delta} \cdot \frac{R_{max}}{R_{min}})$ against an oblivious adversary.*

PROOF. We use the same sequence as in the previous theorem to separate the servers of the adversary and the online algorithm:

For x time steps, there are R_{min} requests in every step on the starting position of the server. The adversary moves its server a distance m for x steps to the left or right with probability $\frac{1}{2}$ each, such that the distance between the two servers is at least xm with probability at least $\frac{1}{2}$ after these steps. The costs for the adversary are at most $Dxm + R_{min}mx^2$.

The adversary now issues R_{max} requests at the position of its server and moves it by a distance m in same direction as in the previous steps. This is done for exactly as many time steps as it would take the server of the online algorithm to "catch up" with the server of the adversary when it it is at least a distance xm away from the adversary's server and moves towards it with the maximum distance in each round. The necessary number of steps for that are $\frac{x}{\delta}$, since the distance between the two servers decreases by at most δm in every round.

The costs the online algorithm has to pay, in case the distance between the two servers is at least xm at the beginning of this phase, for serving the requests are minimized when the algorithm moves the server with a maximum distance towards the position of the adversary's server in every time step. The costs for the online algorithm are therefore at least

$$\begin{aligned} R_{max} \cdot \textstyle\sum_{i=1}^{\frac{x}{\delta}} (xm - i\delta m) &= R_{max} \left(\frac{mx^2}{2\delta} - \frac{mx}{2} \right) \\ &\geq \frac{1}{4} \frac{R_{max} mx^2}{\delta} \end{aligned}$$

with probability at least $\frac{1}{2}$ by choosing $x \geq 2\delta$. The adversary pays $\frac{x}{\delta} Dm$ in this phase.

By choosing x sufficiently large, the total costs of the adversary sum up to at most $3R_{min}mx^2$ over both described phases.

The adversary can now repeat the two phases in a circular way arbitrarily often. The costs can be analyzed as above since the one probabilistic choice the adversary does is made independently of the behavior of the online algorithm and its own former behavior. The resulting expected competitive ratio is $\Omega(\frac{R_{max}}{\delta R_{min}})$. □

We observe that as a special case, when $R_{max} = R_{min}$ the lower bound of the competitive ratio becomes independent of the number of requests in each round. In the following section we show that this is indeed possible to achieve in this scenario.

We finally address our decision to allow the algorithms to move the page before answering the requests. Consider the scenario in which an algorithm has to answer the requests before moving the server. It can be shown that the competitive ratio of such algorithms depend on the number of requests in each time step even if it is fixed throughout the whole sequence.

THEOREM 3.3. *If in every time step, requests must be answered before moving the server, every randomized algorithm has an expected competitive ratio of $\Omega(r/D)$ against an oblivious adversary if the number of requests in each time step is fixed to a constant r.*

PROOF. Consider the following two time steps: In the first step, r requests are issued at the common position of the servers. The adversary can now move the server to a position such that with probability at least $\frac{1}{2}$, the distance between the two servers is at least m. This can be done by throwing a fair coin and the moving to the left or right as in the previous theorems.

In the second step, r requests are issued at the position of the adversary's page. The two steps may be repeated in a cyclic manner since the random choice of the adversary does not depend on any former time steps.

The costs for the online algorithm for one repetition of these two steps are at least rm with probability at least $\frac{1}{2}$ while the costs of the adversary are at most Dm. □

4 A SIMPLE ALGORITHM

In this section we provide a simple algorithm which achieves an optimal competitive ratio on line segments and a near optimal competitive ratio for the Euclidean plane. We analyze the algorithm in detail only for the case of a fixed r since this is the most insightful case. The upper bounds for the other variants are briefly described in the next section.

The algorithm *Move-to-Center (MtC)* works as follows:

Assume the algorithm has its server located at a point P_{Alg} and receives requests $v_1, \ldots, v_r$. Let c be the point minimizing $\sum_{i=1}^{r} d(c, v_i)$. MtC moves the server towards c for a distance of $\min\{1, \frac{r}{D}\} \cdot d(P_{Alg}, c)$ if this distance is less than $(1+\delta)m$. Otherwise it moves the server a distance of $(1+\delta)m$ towards c.

The remainder of this chapter is devoted to prove the following theorem:

THEOREM 4.1. *MtC is $O(\frac{1}{\delta})$-competitive on the infinite line and $O(\frac{1}{\delta^{3/2}})$-competitive in the Euclidean plane using an augmented maximum moving distance of $(1+\delta)m$ for a fixed number r of requests per time step and some $\delta \in (0, 1]$.*

For the analysis, we use a potential function argument. Therefore we fix an arbitrary time step in the input sequence. First, we introduce some notation for this step.

By P_{Alg} and P'_{Alg}, we denote the position of the algorithm's server before and after moving it. P_{Opt} and P'_{Opt} will be used for the optimal server positions before and after moving respectively.

For the requests, we use $v_1, \ldots, v_r$ for the points and c as the point minimizing the sum of distances as above. For the rest of the analysis, we assume that there are r requests on c. This assumption only costs us an additive constant of 1 in the competitive ratio, which can be seen from the following estimation:

$$\begin{aligned}\sum_{i=1}^{r} d(P'_{Alg}, v_i) &\leq r \cdot d(P'_{Alg}, c) + \sum_{i=1}^{r} d(c, v_i)\\ &\leq r \cdot d(P'_{Alg}, c) + C_{Opt}\end{aligned}$$

where C_{Opt} are the optimal costs in the respective time step.

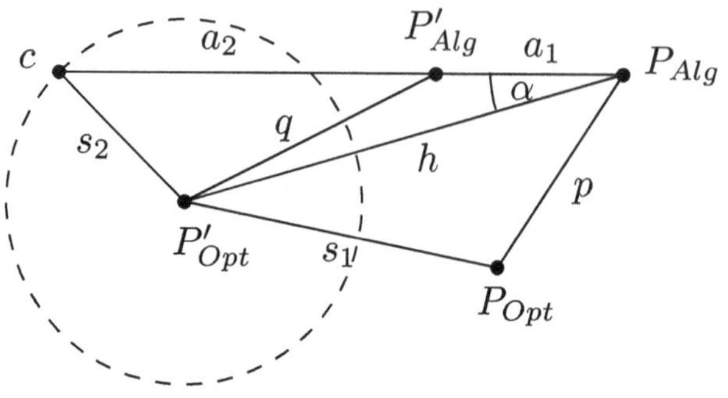

Figure 1: Illustration of relevant points and distances for estimating the potential difference. $h' = d(P_{Opt}, P'_{Alg})$ is omitted for better overview.

For better readability, we define the following abbreviations which we use for the distances and sometimes also for the lines as geometric objects:
$a_1 := d(P_{Alg}, P'_{Alg})$, $a_2 := d(P'_{Alg}, c)$, $s_1 := d(P_{Opt}, P_{Opt'})$, $s_2 := d(P'_{Opt}, c)$, $p := d(P_{Opt}, P_{Alg})$, $h := d(P'_{Opt}, P_{Alg})$, $h' := d(P_{Opt}, P'_{Alg})$ and $q := d(P'_{Opt}, P'_{Alg})$.
An illustration can be found in Figure 1.

Using this notation, the costs of the online algorithm are

$$C_{Alg} = Da_1 + ra_2$$

and the optimal costs are

$$C_{Opt} = Ds_1 + rs_2.$$

For the costs of the online algorithm, we often use the following estimation:

$$\begin{aligned}C_{Alg} &= Da_1 + ra_2\\ &\leq D(p + s_1 + q) + r(q + s_2)\end{aligned} \tag{1}$$

For server locations P_{Alg} and P_{Opt} of the online algorithm and the optimal solution respectively, the potential ϕ is defined as

$$\phi(P_{Opt}, P_{Alg}) := \begin{cases} 8\frac{r}{\delta m} \cdot d(P_{Opt}, P_{Alg})^2, & \text{for } d(P_{Opt}, P_{Alg}) > \delta \frac{Dm}{4r} \\ 2D \cdot d(P_{Opt}, P_{Alg}), & \text{otherwise} \end{cases}.$$

We start with an estimation of the difference $h - q$ which is essential for bounding the potential difference in the Euclidean space.

LEMMA 4.2. *If $s_2 \leq \frac{\sqrt{\delta}}{1+\frac{1}{2}\delta} a_2$, then $h - q \geq \frac{1+\frac{1}{2}\delta}{1+\delta} a_1$.*

PROOF. We want to get a lower bound for $h-q$ given fixed values for h, s_2 and a_1. q is maximized by choosing the angle α between a_1 and h as large as possible. This can be done by setting the angle between s_2 and a_2 to 90 degrees as shown in Figure 2.

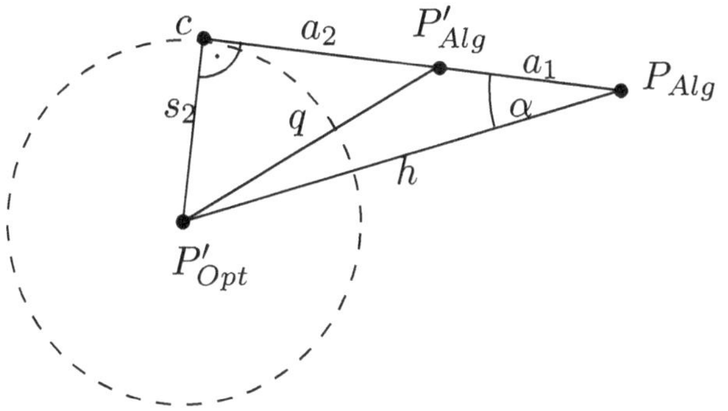

Figure 2: Setting where q is maximized given h, s_2 and a_1.

Making use of the 90 degree angle we get $h^2 = s_2^2 + (a_1 + a_2)^2$ and $q^2 = s_2^2 + a_2^2$. Let $s_2 = \epsilon \cdot a_2$. Then

$$\begin{aligned} h - q &= \sqrt{(\epsilon a_2)^2 + (a_1 + a_2)^2} - \sqrt{(\epsilon a_2)^2 + a_2^2} \\ &= \sqrt{(1+\epsilon^2)a_2^2 + 2a_1a_2 + a_1^2} - \sqrt{1+\epsilon^2}a_2 \\ &\geq \sqrt{(1+\epsilon^2)a_2^2 + 2\sqrt{1+\epsilon^2}a_2\frac{a_1}{\sqrt{1+\epsilon^2}} + \frac{a_1^2}{1+\epsilon^2}} \\ &\quad -\sqrt{1+\epsilon^2}a_2 \\ &= \frac{a_1}{\sqrt{1+\epsilon^2}}. \end{aligned}$$

It therefore holds

$$\epsilon \leq \sqrt{\frac{(1+\delta)^2}{(1+\frac{1}{2}\delta)^2} - 1} \Rightarrow h - q \geq \frac{1+\frac{1}{2}\delta}{1+\delta}a_1.$$

Since

$$\sqrt{\frac{(1+\delta)^2}{(1+\frac{1}{2}\delta)^2} - 1} = \frac{\sqrt{\delta + \frac{3}{4}\delta^2}}{1+\frac{1}{2}\delta} \geq \frac{\sqrt{\delta}}{1+\frac{1}{2}\delta}$$

this implies the lemma. □

4.1 Analysis for $r > D$

In the following, we analyze the algorithm for the case $r > D$ for both the line segment and the Euclidean plane. Most arguments apply to both cases, if there is a difference between the spaces it is stated explicitly in the respective case.

For each of the listed cases we bound the potential difference $\Delta\phi = \phi(P'_{Opt}, P'_{Alg}) - \phi(P_{Opt}, P_{Alg})$ and the costs of the online algorithm as expressions in C_{Opt}.

1. $p \leq \delta\frac{Dm}{4r} \leq \delta m$: The algorithm has the possibility to move its server to the same position as the optimal solution (or closer to c). Hence $a_2 \leq s_2$. If $q \leq \delta\frac{Dm}{4r}$ we have

$$\begin{aligned} \Delta\phi &= 2D(q-p) \\ &\leq 2r(s_2 + a_2) - 2Dp \\ &\leq 4C_{Opt} - 2Dp \end{aligned}$$

and

$$\begin{aligned} C_{Alg} &= Da_1 + ra_2 \\ &\leq D(p + s_1 + q) + ra_2 \\ &\leq D(p + s_1) + r(s_2 + 2a_2) \\ &\leq 3C_{Opt} + Dp. \end{aligned}$$

Otherwise it holds $q > \delta\frac{Dm}{4r} \geq p$ and we get

$$\begin{aligned} \Delta\phi &= 8\frac{r}{\delta m} \cdot q^2 - 2D \cdot p \\ &\leq 8\frac{r}{\delta m}(q^2 - p^2) \\ &= 8\frac{r}{\delta m}(q+p)(q-p) \\ &\leq 8\frac{r}{\delta m} \cdot 2 \cdot q \cdot (2+\delta)m \\ &\leq 48\frac{r}{\delta}(s_2 + a_2) \end{aligned}$$

and

$$\begin{aligned} C_{Alg} &= Da_1 + ra_2 \\ &\leq D(s_1 + 2(s_2 + a_2)) + ra_2 \\ &\leq 5C_{Opt}. \end{aligned}$$

2. $p > \delta\frac{Dm}{4r}$ and $q \leq \delta\frac{Dm}{4r}$: If $p < \delta m$, we have $a_2 \leq s_2$ as before. The potential difference can be estimated by

$$\begin{aligned} \Delta\phi &= 2Dq - 8\frac{r}{\delta m}p^2 \\ &\leq 2D(a_2 + s_2) - 2Dp \\ &\leq 4C_{Opt} - 2Dp \end{aligned}$$

and

$$\begin{aligned} C_{Alg} &= Da_1 + ra_2 \\ &\leq D(p + s_1 + q) + ra_2 \\ &\leq C_{Opt} + 2Dp. \end{aligned}$$

Else, we have

$$\begin{aligned} \Delta\phi &= 2Dq - 8\frac{r}{\delta m}p^2 \\ &\leq 2Dq - 8rp \\ &\leq -6rp \end{aligned}$$

and with (1) we get

$$C_{Alg} \leq C_{Opt} + 3rp.$$

In all of the following cases, we have $p > \delta\frac{Dm}{4r}$ and $q > \delta\frac{Dm}{4r}$.

3. $q - h \leq -(1+\frac{\delta}{2})m$ or $h' - p \leq -(1+\frac{\delta}{2})m$: Since $s_1 \leq m$, we have $q - p \leq -\frac{\delta}{2}m$. Therefore

$$\begin{aligned} \Delta\phi &\leq 8\frac{r}{\delta m}(q+p)(q-p) \\ &\leq 8\frac{r}{\delta m}(q+p)(-\frac{\delta}{2}m) \\ &\leq -4r(q+p) \end{aligned}$$

and (1) gives us

$$C_{Alg} \leq C_{Opt} + 2r(p+q).$$

4. $q - h > -(1+\frac{\delta}{2})m$ and $h' - p > -(1+\frac{\delta}{2})m$ and $p \geq 4m$: We estimate a_2 in two different ways: First assume our given space is the Euclidean plane. Since $\frac{1+\frac{\delta}{2}}{1+\delta}a_1 \geq (1+\frac{\delta}{2})m$ if $a_1 = (1+\delta)m$, we get $\sqrt{\delta}a_2 \leq s_2$ according to Lemma 4.2.

If the given space is a line segment, $a_1 = (1+\delta)m$ implies that the two algorithms must have moved their servers in opposite directions. This gives us $a_2 \leq s_2$.

For both cases, if $a_1 < (1+\delta)m$, then $a_2 = 0 \leq s_2$.

Now, if $\frac{1}{2}p \leq q$ we may estimate

$$\begin{aligned} \Delta\phi &\leq 8\frac{r}{\delta m}(q+p)(q-p) \\ &\leq 8\frac{r}{\delta m}(3q)(3m) \\ &\leq 72\frac{r}{\delta}(s_2 + a_2) \end{aligned}$$

and

$$\begin{aligned} C_{Alg} &= Da_1 + ra_2 \\ &\leq D(s_1 + 2(s_2 + a_2)) + ra_2 \\ &\leq \frac{5}{\sqrt{\delta}}C_{Opt}. \end{aligned}$$

Otherwise we use

$$\begin{aligned}\Delta\phi &\le 8\tfrac{r}{\delta m}(q+p)(q-p)\\ &\le 8\tfrac{r}{\delta m}(q+p)(-\tfrac{1}{2}p)\\ &\le -2\tfrac{r}{\delta}p\end{aligned}$$

and

$$\begin{aligned}C_{Alg} &= Da_1 + ra_2\\ &\le \tfrac{3}{\sqrt{\delta}}C_{Opt} + Dp.\end{aligned}$$

5. $q - h \le -(1+\frac{\delta}{2})m$ and $h' - p \le -(1+\frac{\delta}{2})m$ and $p < 4m$: We get $\sqrt{\delta}a_2 \le s_2$ and $a_2 \le s_2$ for the Euclidean plane and the line segment respectively as before. Since $q \le p + 3m$ we have

$$\begin{aligned}\Delta\phi &\le 8\tfrac{r}{\delta m}(q+p)(q-p)\\ &\le 8\tfrac{r}{\delta m}11m\cdot q - 8\tfrac{r}{\delta m}(q+p)\delta\tfrac{Dm}{4r}\\ &\le 88\tfrac{1}{\delta}(s_2+a_2) - 2D(q+p)\end{aligned}$$

and

$$\begin{aligned}C_{Alg} &= Da_1 + ra_2\\ &\le \tfrac{3}{\sqrt{\delta}}C_{Opt} + Dp.\end{aligned}$$

In all cases we have $C_{Alg} + \Delta\phi \le O(\frac{1}{\delta^{3/2}})\cdot C_{Opt}$.

4.2 Analysis for $r \le D$

For $r \le D$ we first give a detailed analysis for the Euclidean plane and then briefly describe how to modify the necessary parts to work for the line segment such that the competitive ratio becomes $O(\frac{1}{\delta})$.

1. Let $p \le \delta\frac{Dm}{4r}$ and $q \le \delta\frac{Dm}{4r}$. First we consider the case $s_2 \le \frac{\sqrt{\delta}}{1+\frac{\delta}{2}}a_2$. We bound the potential difference by

$$\begin{aligned}\Delta\phi &= 2D(q-p)\\ &\le 2D(q-h+h-p)\\ &\le -2D\tfrac{1+\frac{\delta}{2}}{1+\delta}a_1 + 2Ds_2.\end{aligned}$$

If $a_1 = \frac{r}{D}(a_1+a_2)$ then $\Delta\phi \le -2r(a_1+a_2)$. We have $C_{Alg} \le 2r(a_1+a_2)$.

Otherwise $a_1 = (1+\delta)m$ then $\Delta\phi \le -2D(1+\frac{\delta}{2})m$. In this case $p \le \delta\frac{Dm}{4r}$ can be used to bound C_{Alg}.

The second case is $s_2 > \frac{\sqrt{\delta}}{1+\frac{\delta}{2}}a_2$. Either $\frac{1}{2}p \le q$ immediately gives the desired bound or we have $\Delta\phi \le -Dp$.

We use the same argumentation for $p > \delta\frac{Dm}{4r}$ since in this case $-8\frac{r}{\delta m}p^2 \le -2Dp$.

2. $p > \delta\frac{Dm}{4r}$ and $q > \delta\frac{Dm}{4r}$: As before we start with the case that $s_2 \le \frac{\sqrt{\delta}}{1+\frac{\delta}{2}}a_2$. We have

$$\begin{aligned}\Delta\phi &= 8\tfrac{r}{\delta m}(q^2-p^2)\\ &\le 8\tfrac{r}{\delta m}(q+p)(q-p)\\ &\le 8\tfrac{r}{\delta m}(q+p)(-\tfrac{1+\frac{\delta}{2}}{1+\delta}a_1 + s_1).\end{aligned}$$

If $a_1 = (1+\delta)m$ then $\Delta\phi \le -4r(q+p)$ and $C_{Alg} \le 2r(a_1+a_2) \le 2C_{Opt} + 2r(p+q)$.

Else, $a_1 = \frac{r}{D}(a_1+a_2)$ and using $a_1 + a_2 \le 2\frac{Dm}{r}$ we get

$$\begin{aligned}\Delta\phi &\le 8\tfrac{r}{\delta m}(2(a_1+a_2) + 2s_2 + s_1)\\ &\quad\cdot(-\tfrac{3r}{4D}(a_1+a_2) + s_1)\\ &\le -6r(a_1+a_2) + 40\tfrac{D}{\delta}s_1 + 8\tfrac{r}{\delta}s_2.\end{aligned}$$

For the online algorithm we have $C_{Alg} \le 2r(a_1+a_2)$.

Now consider the case $s_2 > \frac{\sqrt{\delta}}{1+\frac{\delta}{2}}a_2$. If $\frac{1}{2}p \le q$ we use it to get

$$\begin{aligned}\Delta\phi &= 8\tfrac{r}{\delta m}(q+p)(q-p)\\ &\le 8\tfrac{r}{\delta m}(3q)(3m)\\ &= 216\tfrac{r}{\delta^{3/2}}s_2\end{aligned}$$

and

$$\begin{aligned}C_{Alg} &\le 2r(a_1+a_2)\\ &\le \tfrac{5}{\sqrt{\delta}}C_{Opt}.\end{aligned}$$

Otherwise we have

$$\begin{aligned}\Delta\phi &= 8\tfrac{r}{\delta m}(q+p)(q-p)\\ &\le 8\tfrac{r}{\delta m}(q+p)(-\tfrac{1}{2}p)\\ &= -D(q+p)\end{aligned}$$

and $C_{Alg} \le \frac{1}{\sqrt{\delta}}C_{Opt} + D(p+q)$.

Again, the arguments also apply to $q \le \delta\frac{Dm}{4r}$ due to $-2Dq \le -8\frac{r}{\delta m}q^2$.

To get the bound for the line segment, in each of the two big cases replace the distinction whether $s_2 \le \frac{\sqrt{\delta}}{1+\frac{\delta}{2}}a_2$ by $s_2 \le a_2$. Also the estimation of $q - h$ under the use of Lemma 4.2 may be replaced by $q - h \le -a_1$.

Again, in all cases we have $C_{Alg} + \Delta\phi \le O(\frac{1}{\delta^{3/2}})\cdot C_{Opt}$.

5 EXTENSIONS

In this section we briefly describe how to modify the analysis of our algorithm such that the resulting bounds match the lower bounds (up to a factor of $\frac{1}{\sqrt{\delta}}$) for the variants not covered in the previous chapter.

All results mentioned hold for the Euclidean plane (or any $\mathbb{R}^n$ with the Euclidean Distance as a metric) and therefore contain a factor of $\frac{1}{\delta^{3/2}}$. These results can also be applied to the 1-dimensional space where the factor is then reduced to $\frac{1}{\delta}$ by an easy modification of the proof from the previous chapter.

Corollary 5.1. *Let R_{min} and R_{max} be the minimum and maximum number of requests per time step. Algorithm MtC is $O(\frac{R_{max}}{\delta^{3/2}R_{min}})$-competitive utilizing a maximum moving distance of $(1+\delta)m$ if requests are served after the server is moved to a new position.*

Proof. We replace the fixed number of requests r in the potential function by the maximum number of requests R_{max}. In the cases where the potential is used to cancel out the costs of the algorithm this is then still possible. However if the potential difference is positive it may add a term which is $O(\frac{R_{max}}{R_{min}})$ times the optimal costs. □

Corollary 5.2. *Let $r \ge D$ be the fixed number of requests per time step. Algorithm MtC is $O(\frac{r}{D\cdot\delta^{3/2}})$-competitive utilizing a maximum moving distance of $(1+\delta)m$ if requests must be served before the server is moved to a new position.*

Proof. The only change in the proof comes from the fact that the costs of the algorithm now contain $r(a_1+a_2) \le r(p+s_1+q+a_2)$ for serving the requests where the term rs_1 produces the $\frac{r}{D}$ factor in the competitive ratio. □

6 CONCLUSION

We have seen that a simple, deterministic algorithm is sufficient to get an almost optimal competitive ratio in various versions of our model. For the Euclidean space of dimension 1, we have an asymptotically optimal competitive ratio which can not be beaten even by a randomized algorithm against an oblivious adversary.

For the Euclidean space of higher dimensions, we miss the optimal competitive ratio only by a factor of $\frac{1}{\sqrt{\delta}}$. We conjecture that this remaining gap between the upper and the lower bound can be closed towards the lower bound, but it remains an open problem to design an online algorithm and / or provide an analysis to achieve the better competitive ratio.

It seems an interesting question if the idea of limiting the movement of resources within a time slot also can be applied to other popular models such as the k-Server Problem (effectively turning it into the Page Migration Problem with multiple pages).

It may also be possible to extend existing online problems without a concept of movement by introducing a limited movement like in our model. In problems like the Online Facility Location Problem, this might give possibilities to the online algorithms to slightly improve upon decisions where to open a facility.

Furthermore the concept of allowing only a limited configuration change might be applicable to any problem which belongs to the class of Metrical Task Systems where in every step configurations may be changed to lower costs for answering a certain type of requests which have to be served by the system.

REFERENCES

[1] Arif Ahmed and Ejaz Ahmed. 2016. A Survey on Mobile Egde Computing. In *Proceedings of the 10th IEEE International Conference on Intelligent Systems and Control (ISCO)*. IEEE. https://doi.org/10.1109/ISCO.2016.7727082

[2] Susanne Albers and Hisashi Koga. 1995. Page Migration with Limited Local Memory Capacity. In *Proceedings of the 4th International Workshop on Algorithms and Data Structures (WADS)*. Springer, 147 – 158. https://doi.org/10.1007/3-540-60220-8_58

[3] Yair Bartal. 1998. Distributed Paging. In *Developments from a June 1996 Seminar on Online Algorithms: The State of the Art*. Springer, 97 – 117. http://dl.acm.org/citation.cfm?id=647371.723920

[4] Yair Bartal, Moses Charikar, and Piotr Indyk. 2001. On the Page Migration Problem and Other Relaxed Task Systems. *Theoretical Computer Science* 268, 1 (2001), 43 – 66. https://doi.org/10.1016/S0304-3975(00)00259-0

[5] Hans-Joachim Böckenhauer, Dennis Komm, Rastislav Královič, and Richard Královič. 2017. On the advice complexity of the k-server problem. *J. Comput. System Sci.* 86 (2017), 159 – 170. https://doi.org/10.1016/j.jcss.2017.01.001

[6] Wolfgang W. Bein, Marek Chrobak, and Lawrence L. Larmore. 2002. The 3-server problem in the plane. *Theoretical Computer Science* 289, 1 (2002), 335 – 354. https://doi.org/10.1016/S0304-3975(01)00305-X

[7] Marcin Bienkowski, Jaroslaw Byrka, Miroslaw Korzeniowski, and Friedhelm Meyer auf der Heide. 2009. Optimal algorithms for page migration in dynamic networks. *Journal of Discrete Algorithms* 7, 4 (2009), 545 – 569. https://doi.org/10.1016/j.jda.2008.07.006

[8] David L. Black and Daniel D. Sleator. 1989. *Competitive Algorithms for Replication and Migration Problems*. Technical Report CMU-CS-89-201. Department of Computer Science, Carnegie-Mellon University.

[9] Marek Chrobak, Lawrence L Larmore, Nick Reingold, and Jeffery Westbrook. 1997. Page Migration Algorithms Using Work Functions. *Journal of Algorithms* 24, 1 (1997), 124 – 157. https://doi.org/10.1006/jagm.1996.0853

[10] A. Davis, Jay Parikh, and William E. Weihl. 2004. Edgecomputing: Extending Enterprise Applications to the Edge of the Internet. In *Proceedings of the 13th International World Wide Web Conference on Alternate Track Papers & Posters*. ACM, 180 – 187. https://doi.org/10.1145/1013367.1013397

[11] Adam Janiak, Władysław Janiak, and Maciej Lichtenstein. 2007. Resource management in machine scheduling problems: a survey. *Decision Making in Manufacturing and Services* Vol. 1, no. 1-2 (2007), 59–89.

[12] Bala Kalyanasundaram and Kirk Pruhs. 1995. Speed is as Powerful as Clairvoyance. In *Proceedings of the 36th IEEE Annual Symposium Foundations of Computer Science (FOCS)*. IEEE, 214 – 221. https://doi.org/10.1145/347476.347479

[13] Amanj Khorramian and Akira Matsubayashi. 2016. Uniform Page Migration Problem in Euclidean Space. *Algorithms* 9, 3 (2016). https://doi.org/10.3390/a9030057

[14] Elias Koutsoupias. 2009. The k-server problem. *Computer Science Review* 3, 2 (2009), 105 – 118. https://doi.org/10.1016/j.cosrev.2009.04.002

[15] Jeffery Westbrook. 1994. Randomized Algorithms for Multiprocessor Page Migration. *SIAM J. Comput.* 23, 5 (1994), 951 – 965. https://doi.org/10.1137/S0097539791199796

[16] Andrew Chi-Chin Yao. 1977. Probabilistic computations: Toward a unified measure of complexity. In *Proceedings of the 18th IEEE Annual Symposium Foundations of Computer Science (FOCS)*. IEEE, 222 – 227. https://doi.org/10.1109/SFCS.1977.24

Brief Announcement: Efficient Best Response Computation for Strategic Network Formation under Attack

Tobias Friedrich, Sven Ihde, Christoph Keßler,
Pascal Lenzner, Stefan Neubert and David Schumann
Algorithm Engineering Group, Hasso Plattner Institute, Potsdam, Germany

ABSTRACT

Inspired by real world examples, e.g. the Internet, researchers have introduced an abundance of strategic games to study natural phenomena in networks. Unfortunately, almost all of these games have the conceptual drawback of being computationally intractable, i.e. computing a best response strategy or checking if an equilibrium is reached is NP-hard. Thus, a main challenge in the field is to find tractable realistic network formation models.

We address this challenge by establishing that the recently introduced model by Goyal et al. [WINE'16], which focuses on robust networks in the presence of a strong adversary, is a rare exception which is both realistic and computationally tractable. In particular, we sketch an efficient algorithm for computing a best response strategy, which implies that deciding whether the game has reached a Nash equilibrium can be done efficiently as well. Our algorithm essentially solves the problem of computing a minimal connection to a network which maximizes the reachability while hedging against severe attacks on the network infrastructure.

KEYWORDS

Strategic Network Formation, Best Response Computation, Network Robustness, Network Reachability

1 INTRODUCTION

Many of today's important networks, most prominently the Internet, are essentially the outcome of an unsupervised decentralized network formation process among many selfish entities [20]. Creating links in such networks yields a connectivity benefit but also harbors the risk of collateral damage if a neighbor is attacked.

Required features of any Internet-like communication network are reachability and robustness. Such networks have to ensure that even in case of cascading edge or node failures caused by technical defects or malicious attacks, e.g. DDoS-attacks or viruses, most participating nodes can still communicate. This focus on robustness has long been neglected and is now a very recent endeavor in the strategic network formation community, see e.g. [6, 14, 16, 18].

Our contribution is the proof that the recently introduced model by Goyal et al. [13, 14] is one of the few examples of a tractable realistic model for strategic network formation, which answers an open question by these authors. In particular, we provide an

efficient algorithm for computing a best response strategy for two variants of their model which enables large-scale simulations to analyze phenomena in real-world networks.

Related Work: The model by Goyal et al. [13, 14] essentially augments the well-known reachability model by Bala & Goyal [2] with robustness considerations. In particular, different types of adversaries are introduced which attack (and destroy) a node of the network. This attack then spreads virus-like to neighboring nodes and destroys them as well. Besides deciding which links to form, players also decide whether they want to buy immunization against eventual attacks. The model is the first model which incorporates network formation and immunization decisions at the same time.

On the one hand, the authors of [13, 14] provide beautiful structural results, e.g. they show that equilibrium networks are much more diverse than in the non-robust version, that the amount of edge overbuilding due to robustness concerns is small and that all equilibrium networks achieve very high social welfare. On the other hand, the authors raise the intriguing open problem of settling the complexity of computing a best response strategy in their model[1].

Computing a best response in network formation games can be done efficiently for the reachability model [2] and if the allowed strategy changes are simple [17]. However, these examples are exceptions. For almost all related network formation models, e.g. [4–6, 8, 10, 11, 15, 19], NP-hardness has been shown.

To the best of our knowledge, besides the model by Goyal et al. [13, 14] there are only a few other models which combine selfish network formation with robustness considerations and all of them consider a much weaker adversary. The earliest are models by Bala & Goyal [3] and Kliemann [16] and both augment the model [2] with single edge failures. Other related models are by Meirom et al. [18] and Chauhan et al. [6]. Both consider players striving for centrality but who at the same time want to protect themselves against single edge failures. The complexity status for computing a best response was only settled for the model by Chauhan et al. [6] where this problem was proven to be NP-hard.

Also vaccination games, e.g. [1, 7, 21], are related. There the network is fixed and the selfish nodes only have to decide if they want to immunize or not. Computing a best response in these models is trivial but pure Nash equilibria may not exist.

2 MODEL

We work with the strategic network formation model proposed by Goyal et al. [13, 14] and mostly use their notation. In this model the n nodes of a network $G = (V, E)$ correspond to individual players $v_1, \ldots, v_n$. The edge set E is determined by the players'

SPAA '17, July 24-26, 2017, Washington DC, USA
© 2017 Copyright held by the owner/author(s).
ACM ISBN 978-1-4503-4593-4/17/07.
https://doi.org/http://dx.doi.org/10.1145/3087556.3087594

---

[1] This question was raised in versions 1-4 of [13] and is replaced in later versions and in [14] with a reference to a preprint [12] of the present paper.

strategic behavior as follows. Each player $v_i \in V$ can decide to buy undirected edges to a subset of other players, paying $\alpha > 0$ per edge, where α is some fixed parameter of the model.

If player v_i decides to buy the edge to node v_j, then we say that the edge $\{v_i, v_j\}$ is owned and paid for by player v_i. Buying an undirected edge entails connectivity benefits and risks for both participating endpoints. In order to cope with these risks, each player can also decide to buy immunization against attacks at a cost of $\beta > 0$, which is also a fixed parameter. We call a player *immunized* if this player decides to buy immunization, and *vulnerable* otherwise.

The strategy $s_i = (x_i, y_i)$ of player v_i consists of the set $x_i \subseteq V \setminus \{v_i\}$ of the nodes to buy an edge to, and the immunization choice $y_i \in \{0, 1\}$, where $y_i = 1$ if and only if player v_i decides to immunize. The strategy profile $\mathbf{s} = (s_1, \ldots, s_n)$ of all players then induces an undirected graph $G(\mathbf{s}) = \left(V, \bigcup_{v_i \in V} \bigcup_{v_j \in x_i} \{v_i, v_j\}\right)$. The immunization choices $y_1, \ldots, y_n$ in $\mathbf{s}$ partition V into the set of immunized players $\mathcal{I} \subseteq V$ and vulnerable players $\mathcal{U} = V \setminus \mathcal{I}$. The components in the induced subgraph $G[\mathcal{U}]$ are called *vulnerable regions* and the set of those regions will be denoted by $\mathcal{R}_{\mathcal{U}}$. The vulnerable region of any vulnerable player $v_i \in \mathcal{U}$ is $\mathcal{R}_{\mathcal{U}}(v_i)$. *Immunized regions* $\mathcal{R}_{\mathcal{I}}$ are defined analogously as the components of the induced subgraph $G[\mathcal{I}]$.

After the network $G(\mathbf{s})$ is built, we assume that an adversary attacks one vulnerable player according to a strategy known to the players. We consider mostly the maximum carnage adversary [13, 14] which tries to destroy as many nodes of the network as possible. To achieve this, the adversary chooses a vulnerable region of maximum size and attacks some player in that region. If there is more than one such region with maximum size, then one of them is chosen uniformly at random. If a vulnerable player v_i is attacked, then v_i will be destroyed and the attack spreads to all vulnerable neighbors of v_i, eventually destroying all players in v_i's vulnerable region $\mathcal{R}_{\mathcal{U}}(v_i)$. Let $t_{max} = \max_{R \in \mathcal{R}_{\mathcal{U}}}\{|R|\}$ be the number of nodes in the vulnerable region of maximum size and $\mathcal{T} = \{v_i \in \mathcal{U} \mid |\mathcal{R}_{\mathcal{U}}(v_i)| = t_{max}\}$ is the corresponding set of nodes which may be targeted by the adversary. The set of targeted regions is $\mathcal{R}_{\mathcal{T}} = \{R \in \mathcal{R}_{\mathcal{U}} \mid |R| = t_{max}\}$, and $\mathcal{R}_{\mathcal{T}}(v_i)$ is the targeted region of a player $v_i \in \mathcal{T}$. Thus, if $v_i \in \mathcal{T}$ is attacked, then all players in the region $\mathcal{R}_{\mathcal{T}}(v_i)$ will be destroyed.

The *utility* of a player v_i in network $G(\mathbf{s})$ is defined as the expected number of nodes reachable by v_i after the adversarial attack on network $G(\mathbf{s})$ (zero in case v_i was destroyed) less v_i's expenditures for buying edges and immunization. More formally, let $CC_i(t)$ be the connected component of v_i after an attack to node $v_t \in \mathcal{T}$ and let $|CC_i(t)|$ denote its number of nodes. Then the utility (or profit) $u_i(\mathbf{s})$ of v_i in the strategy profile $\mathbf{s}$ is

$$u_i(\mathbf{s}) = \frac{1}{|\mathcal{T}|}\left(\sum_{v_t \in \mathcal{T}} |CC_i(t)|\right) - |x_i| \cdot \alpha - y_i \cdot \beta \ .$$

Fixing the strategies of all other players, the *best response* of a player v_i is a strategy $s_i^* = (x_i^*, y_i^*)$ which maximizes v_i's utility $u_i\left((s_1, \ldots, s_{i-1}, s_i^*, s_{i+1}, \ldots, s_n)\right)$. We will call the strategy change to s_i^* a best response for player v_i in the network $G(\mathbf{s})$, if changing from strategy $s_i \in \mathbf{s}$ to strategy s_i^* is the best possible strategy for player v_i if no other player changes her strategy.

A best response is calculated for one arbitrary but fixed player v_a, which we call the *active player*. Furthermore let C be the set of connected components which exist in $G(\mathbf{s}) \setminus v_a$. Let $C_{\mathcal{U}} = \{C \in C \mid C \cap \mathcal{I} = \emptyset\}$, $C_{\mathcal{I}} = C \setminus C_{\mathcal{U}}$ and $C_{inc} = \{C \in C \mid \exists u \in C : \{u, v\} \in E\}$, where $C_{\mathcal{U}}$ is the set of components in which all vertices are vulnerable, $C_{\mathcal{I}}$ is the set of components which contain at least one immunized vertex and C_{inc} is the set of components to which player v_a is connected via edges bought by some other player.

3 THE BEST RESPONSE ALGORITHM

A naive approach to calculate the best response for player v_a would consider all 2^n possible strategies and select one that yields the best utility. This is clearly infeasible for a larger number of players. Our algorithm exploits three observations to reduce the complexity from exponential to polynomial:

Observation 1: The network $G(\mathbf{s}) \setminus v_a$ may consist of several connected components that can be dealt with independently for most decisions. As long as the set of possible targets of the adversary does not change, the best response of v_a can be constructed by first choosing components to which a connection is profitable and then choosing for each of those components an optimal set of nodes within the respective component to build edges to.

Observation 2: Homogeneous components in $G(\mathbf{s}) \setminus v_a$, which consist of only vulnerable or only immunized nodes, provide the same benefit no matter whether v_a connects to them with one or with more than one edge. Thus the connection decision is a binary decision for those components.

Observation 3: Mixed components in $G(\mathbf{s}) \setminus v_a$, which contain both immunized and vulnerable nodes, consist of homogeneous regions that again have the property that at most one edge per homogeneous region can be profitable. Merging those regions into block nodes forms an auxilliary tree, called Meta Tree, which we use in an efficient dynamic programming algorithm to compute the most profitable subset of regions to connect with.

The Algorithm: Due to space constraints we introduce our algorithm, called BestResponseComputation, informally. A schematic overview can be found in Fig. 1. We refer to [12] for details.

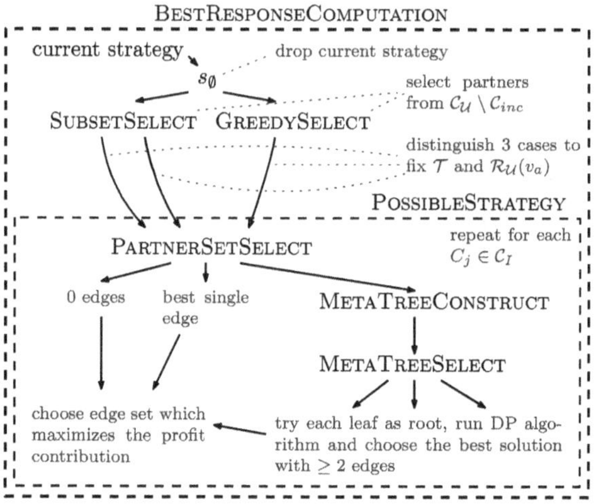

Figure 1: Schematic overview of the best response algorithm.

Our algorithm solves the problem of finding a best response strategy by considering both options of buying or not buying immunization and computing for both cases the best possible set of edges to buy. Thus, the first step of BestResponseComputation is to drop the current strategy of the active player v_a and to replace it with the empty strategy $s_\emptyset = (\emptyset, 0)$ in which player v_a does not buy any edge and does not buy immunization. Then the resulting strategy profile s' and the set of connected components $\mathcal{C}_\mathcal{U}$ and $\mathcal{C}_\mathcal{I}$ with respect to network $G(s') \setminus v_a$ is considered.

The subroutine SubsetSelect determines the optimal sets of components of $\mathcal{C}_\mathcal{U}$ to connect to if v_a does not immunize by solving an adjusted Knapsack problem which involes only small numbers. Two such sets of components are computed, depending on player v_a becoming targeted or not by connecting to these components. Additionally, GreedySelect computes a best possible subset of components of $\mathcal{C}_\mathcal{U}$ to connect to in case v_a buys immunization. It does so by greedily connecting to all profitable components in $\mathcal{C}_\mathcal{U}$.

The challenging part of the problem is to cope with the connected components in $\mathcal{C}_\mathcal{I}$ which also contain immunized nodes. For such components our algorithm detects and merges equivalent nodes and thereby simplifies these components. An auxiliary tree structure, which we call the Meta Tree, is constructed (see Fig. 2). This tree is

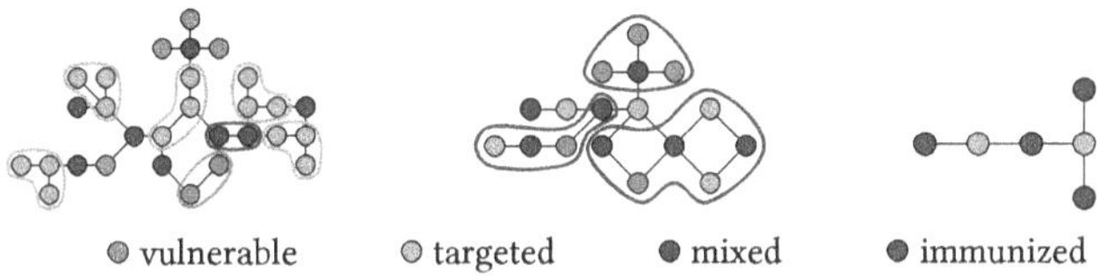

Figure 2: A mixed component; after merging the indicated nodes (middle); another merge yields the Meta Tree (right).

then used in a dynamic programming fashion to efficiently compute the best possible set of nodes to buy edges towards within the respective component. Thus, we handle components in $\mathcal{C}_\mathcal{I}$ by first performing a data-reduction similar to kernelization approaches in the realm of Parameterized Algorithmics [9] and then solving the reduced problem via dynamic programming.

The subroutine PossibleStrategy obtains the best set of nodes in components in $\mathcal{C}_\mathcal{I}$. As this set depends on the number of targeted regions, it has to be determined for several cases independently. These cases are v_a not being immunized and not being targeted, v_a not being immunized but being targeted, and v_a being immunized. For each case, the subroutine PossibleStrategy first chooses an arbitrary single edge to buy into the previously selected components from $\mathcal{C}_\mathcal{U}$. Then the best set of edges into components in $\mathcal{C}_\mathcal{I}$ to buy is computed independently for each component $C \in \mathcal{C}_\mathcal{I}$ via the subroutines PartnerSetSelect, MetaTreeConstruct and MetaTreeSelect. The union of the obtained sets is then returned. Finally, the algorithm compares the empty strategy and the individually obtained best possible strategies for the above mentioned cases and selects the one which maximizes player v_a's utility.

The run time of our best response algorithm heavily depends on the size of the largest obtained Meta Tree and we achieve a worst-case run time of $O(n^4 + k^5)$ for the maximum carnage adversary and $O(n^4 + nk^5)$ for the random attack adversary, where n is the number of nodes in the network and k is the number of blocks in the largest Meta Tree. This yields a run time in $O(n^5)$ and $O(n^6)$, respectively. To contrast this upper bound, we also provide empirical results showing that k is usually much smaller than n, which emphasizes the effectiveness of our data-reduction.

4 CONCLUSION

For most models of strategic network formation computing a utility maximizing strategy is known to be NP-hard. In this paper, we have proven that the model by Goyal et al. [13, 14] is a notable exception to this rule. The presented efficient algorithm for computing a best response for a player circumvents a combinatorial explosion essentially by simplifying the given network and thereby making it amenable to a dynamic programming approach. An efficient best response computation is the key ingredient for using the model in large scale simulations and for analyzing real world networks. Moreover, our algorithm can be adapted to a significantly stronger adversary and we are confident that further modifications for coping with other variants of the model are possible. One such variant is the directed version which would more accurately model the differences in risk and benefit which depend on the flow direction.

REFERENCES

[1] James Aspnes, Kevin Chang, and Aleksandr Yampolskiy. 2006. Inoculation strategies for victims of viruses and the sum-of-squares partition problem. *J. Comput. System Sci.* 72, 6 (2006), 1077–1093.
[2] Venkatesh Bala and Sanjeev Goyal. 2000. A Noncooperative Model of Network Formation. *Econometrica* 68, 5 (2000), 1181–1229.
[3] Venkatesh Bala and Sanjeev Goyal. 2003. A strategic analysis of network reliability. In *Networks and Groups*. Springer, 313–336.
[4] Davide Bilò, Luciano Gualà, Stefano Leucci, and Guido Proietti. 2014. Locality-based network creation games. In *SPAA'14*. 277–286.
[5] Davide Bilò, Luciano Gualà, and Guido Proietti. 2015. Bounded-Distance Network Creation Games. *ACM TEAC* 3, 3, Article 16 (2015), 20 pages.
[6] Ankit Chauhan, Pascal Lenzner, Anna Melnichenko, and Martin Münn. 2016. On Selfish Creation of Robust Networks. In *SAGT'16*. 141–152.
[7] Po-An Chen, Mary David, and David Kempe. 2010. Better vaccination strategies for better people. In *EC'10*. 179–188.
[8] Andreas Cord-Landwehr and Pascal Lenzner. 2015. Network Creation Games: Think Global - Act Local. In *MFCS'15*. 248–260.
[9] Rodney G. Downey and Michael R. Fellows. 2013. *Fundamentals of Parameterized Complexity*. Springer.
[10] Shayan Ehsani, Saber Shokat Fadaee, MohammadAmin Fazli, Abbas Mehrabian, Sina Sadeghian Sadeghabad, Mohammad Ali Safari, and Morteza Saghafian. 2015. A Bounded Budget Network Creation Game. *ACM TALG* 11, 4 (2015), 34.
[11] Alex Fabrikant, Ankur Luthra, Elitza N. Maneva, Christos H. Papadimitriou, and Scott Shenker. On a network creation game. In *PODC'03*. 347–351.
[12] Tobias Friedrich, Sven Ihde, Christoph Keßler, Pascal Lenzner, Stefan Neubert, and David Schumann. 2016. Efficient Best-Response Computation for Strategic Network Formation under Attack. *CoRR* abs/1610.01861 (2016). http://arxiv.org/abs/1610.01861
[13] Sanjeev Goyal, Shahin Jabbari, Michael Kearns, Sanjeev Khanna, and Jamie Morgenstern. 2015. Strategic Network Formation with Attack and Immunization. *CoRR* abs/1511.05196 (2015). http://arxiv.org/abs/1511.05196
[14] Sanjeev Goyal, Shahin Jabbari, Michael Kearns, Sanjeev Khanna, and Jamie Morgenstern. 2016. Strategic Network Formation with Attack and Immunization. In *WINE'16*. 429–443.
[15] Bernd Kawald and Pascal Lenzner. 2013. On dynamics in selfish network creation. In *SPAA'13*. 83–92.
[16] Lasse Kliemann. 2011. The Price of Anarchy for Network Formation in an Adversary Model. *Games* 2, 3 (2011), 302–332.
[17] Pascal Lenzner. Greedy Selfish Network Creation. In *WINE'12*. 142–155.
[18] Eli A. Meirom, Shie Mannor, and Ariel Orda. 2015. Formation games of reliable networks. In *INFOCOM'15*. 1760–1768.
[19] Matús Mihalák and Jan Christoph Schlegel. 2010. The Price of Anarchy in Network Creation Games Is (Mostly) Constant. In *SAGT'10*. 276–287.
[20] Christos H. Papadimitriou. 2001. Algorithms, games, and the internet. In *STOC'01*. 749–753.
[21] Sudip Saha, Abhijin Adiga, and Anil Kumar S Vullikanti. Equilibria in Epidemic Containment Games.. In *AAAI'14*. 777–783.

Brief Announcement: Complete Visibility for Oblivious Robots in Linear Time

Gokarna Sharma
Kent State University
Kent, OH
sharma@cs.kent.edu

Costas Busch
Louisiana State University
Baton Rouge, LA
busch@csc.lsu.edu

Supratik Mukhopadhyay
Louisiana State University
Baton Rouge, LA
supratik@csc.lsu.edu

ABSTRACT

We consider the distributed setting of N autonomous mobile robots that operate in *Look-Compute-Move* cycles following the well-celebrated *classic oblivious robots* model. We study the fundamental problem where starting from an arbitrary initial configuration, N autonomous robots reposition themselves to a convex hull formation on the plane where each robot is visible to all others (the COMPLETE VISIBILITY problem). We assume obstructed visibility, where a robot cannot see another robot if a third robot is positioned between them on the straight line connecting them. We provide the first $O(N)$ time algorithm for this problem in the fully synchronous setting. Our contribution is a significant improvement over the runtime of the only previously known algorithm for this problem which has a lower bound of $\Omega(N^2)$. Our proposed algorithm is collision-free – robots do not share positions and their paths do not cross.

CCS CONCEPTS

•**Theory of computation → Models of computation; Design and analysis of algorithms; Distributed algorithms;** •**Computing methodologies → Multi-agent systems; Intelligent agents; Mobile agents;**

KEYWORDS

Complete visibility; Obstruction; Collisions; Convex hull; Autonomous mobile robots; Oblivious Robots; Runtime

1 INTRODUCTION

The well-celebrated *classic oblivious model* of distributed computing by a finite team of autonomous mobile robots enjoys a long history of research [2]. In this model, the robots are points in a plane, which is also what we assume here. In a large spatial extent, robots can be seen as points relative to the spatial extent in which they operate and the solutions obtained for point robots form the building blocks for the robots that are not points (i.e., robots that occupy certain space such as an unit disk area). Moreover, many robot motion planning algorithms in $\mathbb{R}^2$ (such as bug algorithms [1]) have been studied for the point robots. Point robots are also interesting for exploring the computational efficiency of solving basic robot coordination tasks.

In this classic model, the point robots are: *autonomous* (no external control), *anonymous* (no unique identifiers), *indistinguishable* (no external identifiers), *oblivious* (do not remember their previous actions or the previous positions of the other robots), *silent* (no direct means of communication), and *disoriented* (no common coordinate system or unit of measure for the distances) [2]. Each robot executes the same algorithm and they all perform their actions following *Look-Compute-Move* (LCM) cycles, i.e., when a robot becomes active, it first observes the positions of other robots (*Look*), then computes a destination point based on that observation (*Compute*), and finally moves towards the destination (*Move*). Many fundamental distributed coordination problems, such as pattern formation, convergence, gathering, scattering, etc., were solved in this model [2].

The classic oblivious robots model makes one important assumption: All the robots in the system are visible to each other at all times. In other words, the visibility is *unobstructed* - three collinear robots are assumed to be mutually visible to each other [2]. The assumption of unobstructed visibility can be easily refuted because the view of the robots that are collinear is blocked in a real setting. Therefore, we remove this assumption which leads to the scenario of *obstructed visibility* under which a robot r_i can see another robot r_j if and only if there is no third robot in the line segment joining their positions. We assume that except the presence of robots, there is no other obstacle for a robot to see another robot. Therefore, we consider the variant of the classic model where robots have obstructed visibility.

Di Luna *et al.* [3] gave the first algorithm for classic oblivious robots to solve the fundamental COMPLETE VISIBILITY problem with obstructed visibility: Given a team of N mobile robots in arbitrary distinct positions in the Euclidean plane $\mathbb{R}^2$, all the robots reach a convex hull configuration in which each robot is in a distinct corner position from which it can see all other robots. Initially, some robots may be obstructed from the view of other robots, and the total number of robots, N, is known to the robots. The importance of solving the COMPLETE VISIBILITY problem is that it makes it possible to solve many other robot coordination problems, including gathering, shape formation, and leader election, under obstructed visibility.

Similar to Di Luna *et al.* [3], in our COMPLETE VISIBILITY solution the robots are arranged on corners of a convex polygon. Di Luna *et al.* [3] proved the correctness of their algorithm but gave no runtime analysis (except a proof of finite time termination). The goal of this work is to develop a fast runtime algorithm that solves COMPLETE VISIBILITY for classic oblivious robots.

SPAA'17, July 24–26, 2017, Washington, DC, USA.
© 2017 Copyright held by the owner/author(s).   978-1-4503-4593-4/17/07.
DOI: 10.1145/3087556.3087591

Contributions. We consider a distributed system of N robots (agents) from a set $Q = \{r_1, \ldots, r_N\}$. Each robot is a (dimensionless) point that can move in an infinite 2-dimensional real plane $\mathbb{R}^2$ following the classic oblivious robots model [2].

In this paper, we prove the following result which, to our knowledge, is the first algorithm for Complete Visibility that achieves linear runtime for classic oblivious robots with obstructed visibility. Time is measured in rounds. A *round* is the smallest number of LCM cycles within which each robot is guaranteed to be active at least once. Since we assume the $\mathcal{F}SYNCH$ setting, a round is a LCM cycle. This result assumes that a robot in motion cannot be stopped by an adversary, i.e., when a robot moves it stops only after it reaches to its destination point (also called *rigid* movements).

Theorem 1.1. *For any initial configuration of $N \geq 3$ classic oblivious robots being in distinct positions in a plane,* Complete Visibility *can be solved in $O(N)$ time without collisions in the fully synchronous setting.*

This is a significant improvement since it can be shown that the only previous algorithm of Di Luna *et al.* [3] for this problem has the time lower bound of $\Omega(N^2)$ in the fully synchronous setting.

The lower bound proof idea is to use an initial configuration where all N robots are on the points of two concentric circles, big and small, with distance between each robot and its two neighbors is the same. Moreover, the robots in the small circle are collinear with the robots in the big circle. Since the algorithm of Di Luna *et al.* [3] only moves the robots in the big circle inward, it can be shown, with appropriately chosen number of robots in the big and small circle, that the big circle does not coincide with the small circle even after executing the algorithm for at least $c \cdot N^2$ rounds, for some constant c. Moreover, collinear robots stay collinear during these rounds. The formal proof will be similar to [4, Theorem 4].

Technique. The main idea is to make robots move autonomously based on their local views (and without communicating with other robots) to become corners of a N-vertex convex hull. When all N robots become corners of a convex hull, the configuration naturally solves Complete Visibility.

Let H be a convex hull of the given N robots. Initially, the robots are either in the perimeter of H (i.e., corners and sides of H) or in its interior. The previous algorithm [3] asks robots in the corners of H to move inward to shrink the hull so that the existing corners of H remain as corners and the internal robots of H become new corners of H. The corners of H do not need to know completely H to move inward. It is sufficient for a corner robot r of H to determine all N robots are in a plane with angle $< 180°$ formed by r with the leftmost and the rightmost robot it sees. When a robot that was in the interior of H becomes a new corner of H, it starts moving inward causing other interior robots new corners of H. Since the robots know N, they eventually recognize the situation of all robots being in the corners of H and terminate, solving Complete Visibility. However, this approach has the time lower bound of $\Omega(N^2)$.

Our technique is to move internal robots in H outward towards the perimeter of H in addition to the moves of the corners of H inward used in [3]. This is challenging since internal robots in H may not know which direction is outward and which direction is inward (due to their weak capabilities). We indeed address this challenge and able to show that, in each round, at least an internal robot in H can correctly move outward towards the perimeter of H and becomes a new corner of H. We also show that our technique avoids collisions between robots. Solutions avoiding collisions are appealing since colliding of robots may endanger the robots themselves.

2 OVERVIEW OF THE ALGORITHM

In this section, we outline our $O(N)$ time algorithm for Complete Visibility. The algorithm consists of interior depletion (ID) and corner depletion (CD) procedures which work together to make robots reach a configuration where they are positioned in the corners of a N-vertex convex hull (polygon) H and terminate.

A special case in our algorithm is when initially all robots in Q are collinear. This situation can be detected when a robot r_i sees at most two other robots r_j, r_k, and r_i, r_j, r_k are collinear. If r_i sees two other robots r_j, r_k then r_i is not an endpoint robot of that line. Robot r_i then moves a small distance $\delta > 0$ directly perpendicular to the line $\overline{r_j r_k}$. For $N \geq 3$, we show that this move of r_i ensures that in the resulting configuration not all robots in Q are collinear. (The problem becomes trivial when $N \leq 2$.)

The Interior Depletion Procedure. The ID procedure makes the robots in the interior of H move outward toward the perimeter of H and the CD procedure makes the corner robots of H move inward in H. The robots in Q can easily determine whether they are corners of H or in its interior. If a robot r_i sees all robots in $C(r_i)$ (the positions of the robots in Q that r_i sees at any time $t \geq 0$) are within an angle of $< 180°$, r_i realizes that it is a corner robot of H and executes the CD procedure to move inward. If r_i does not see all robots in $C(r_i)$ within an angle of $< 180°$, it realizes that it is an interior robot and executes the ID procedure to move outward toward the perimeter of H. The robots which are already on the edges of H (angle exactly $= 180°$) perform no action until they become corners of H.

The Corner Depletion Procedure. The CD procedure for the corner robots of H is executed in such a way that they remain as corners of H and at least one robot that is not the corner of H (edge or interior) becomes a new corner of H. If there is at least one edge robot in H, it becomes a new corner of H immediately after all the corners of H move inward once. If there is no edge robot, at least a robot in the interior of H becomes a new corner of H due to the ID procedure executed by the interior robots (simultaneously with the corners of H). This all happens in a single round κ due to the $\mathcal{F}SYNCH$ setting. This is crucial since it allows us to guarantee the claimed runtime of $O(N)$ rounds. Fig. 2 shows how an internal robot r' in H become a new corner of H after r' moves to a point z' and the corner v_1 in H moves to point z''. A robot r_i terminates as soon as it sees N corners in $H(r_i)$, i.e., all N robots in Q are in the corners of $H(r_i)$ (r_i can do this decision since it knows N).

Formally, let v_1 be a corner robot of H and a, b be its left and right neighbors in the boundary of H, respectively. We need following definitions. Let $\Delta a v_1 b$ be the triangle formed by a, v_1, b. Let $\overline{xy}$ be a line parallel to $\overline{ab}$ passing through points $x = \text{length}(\overline{v_1 a})/8$ and $y = \text{length}(\overline{v_1 b})/8$ from v_1 in lines $\overline{v_1 a}$ and $\overline{v_1 b}$, respectively. We say line $\overline{xy}$ is the *triangle line segment* and denote it by TLS_{v_1}.

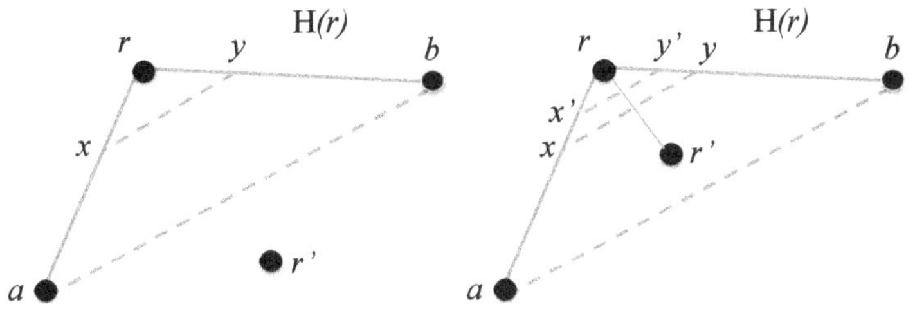

Figure 1: An illustration of (left) triangle line segment, where $\overline{xy}$ is TLS_r and (right) corner line segment, where $\overline{x'y'}$ is CLS_r for a corner robot r.

Let r' be a robot inside Δav_1b. Let z be the point in $\overline{v_1r'}$ at distance length($\overline{v_1r'}$)/8 from v_1. Let $\overline{x'y'}$ be a line parallel to $\overline{ab}$ (or $\overline{xy}$) passing through point z. We say line $\overline{x'y'}$ is the *corner line segment* and denote it by CLS_{v_1}. If there are many robots inside Δav_1b, let r' and r'' be the robots inside Δav_1b that are closest to $\overline{v_1a}$ and $\overline{v_1b}$, respectively. CLS_{v_1} is then computed based on r' or r'' that is closest to v_1. According to the definition of CLS_{v_1} and TLS_{v_1}, CLS_{v_1} is parallel to TLS_{v_1} and CLS_{v_1} is closer to the corner v_1 than TLS_{v_1} (Fig. 1).

Robot v_1 executes the CD procedure as follows.

- **No robot inside Δav_1b:** Robot v_1 moves to a position in the triangle line segment TLS_{v_1}.
- **Robots inside Δav_1b:** Robot v_1 moves to a position in the corner line segment CLS_{v_1}.

Simultaneously at the same round, an internal robot r' in the interior of H executes the ID procedure as follows.

- **Robot r' is not inside Δav_1b:** Robot r' moves to a position in the triangle line segment TLS_{v_1} (different than the one that will be occupied by v_1).
- **Robot r' is inside Δav_1b:** Robot r' moves to a position in the corner line segment CLS_{v_1} (different than the one that will be occupied by v_1).

We then prove that when both v_1 and r' move to either TLS_r or CLS_r, v_1 remains as a corner of H and r' becomes a new corner of H.

For r' to move outward toward v_1, $\overline{v_1a}$ and/or $\overline{v_1b}$ must be the closest edge to r' and r' is closest to v_1 than a and/or b. In situations where there are robots inside the triangular area divided by TLS_{v_1} or CLS_{v_1} towards v_1, r' may not become a new corner of H even after it moves to TLS_{v_1} or CLS_{v_1}. In this situation, we are able to show that some robot $\widehat{r'}$ inside that triangular area will become a new corner of H. Furthermore, r' may not be able to compute CLS_{v_1} when r' does not see b (or a). But, what we are able to guarantee is that CLS_{v_1} passes through the point that r' moves to and this is sufficient for our algorithm. Fig. 2 shows how a corner robot v_1 of H moves inward and a robot r' inside triangle $\Delta v_2v_1v_3$ moves outward toward v_1 and both get positioned in two distinct positions of CLS_{v_1} (shown as line segment $\overline{xy}$ in the figure). The figure also shows the positions z' and z'' that r' and v_1 occupy, respectively, in CLS_{v_1}. The point z' is at distance length($\overline{v_1r'}$)/8 from v_1 in line $\overline{v_1r'}$ and the point z'' is the midpoint of $\overline{z'y}$ with y being the intersection point of CLS_{v_1} and $\overline{v_1v_2}$. Note also that

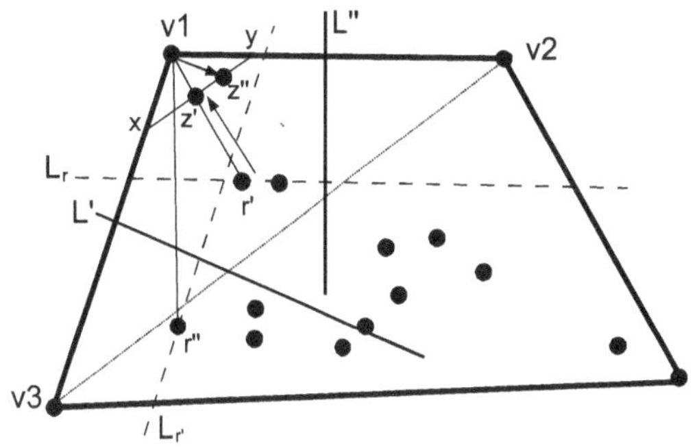

Figure 2: An illustration of how a corner robot $v_1 \in$ H moves inward and an internal robot $r' \in$ H moves outward toward v_1. Both v_1 and r' move to CLS_{v_1} (shown as $\overline{xy}$ in the figure) where the position of r' is the point z' at length($\overline{v_1r'}$)/8 from v_1 in line $\overline{v_1r'}$ and the position of v_1 is the point z'' that is midpoint of $\overline{z'y}$ with y being the point of intersection of CLS_{v_1} and $\overline{v_1v_2}$.

if two internal robots r', r'' closest to $\overline{v_1a}$ and $\overline{v_1b}$ move toward corner v_1, then our technique guarantees that at least one of r', r'' and v_1 are positioned in CLS_{v_1}.

Each robot $r_i \in Q$ works autonomously having only the information about C(r_i). If H(r_i) is not a line segment for each $r_i \in Q$, then the ID and CD procedures start immediately. However, if H(r_i) is a line segment, then in one round, the procedure we use for a collinear C_0 transforms C_0 into a non-collinear configuration. The ID and CD procedures then run until all robots of Q become corners of H.

Overview of the Analysis. The main goal is to show that in each round $\kappa \geq 0$, at least one robot either on any side of H or in the interior of H becomes a new corner of H. This will immediately give the claimed runtime of $O(N)$ for our algorithm. Since robots know N, after all robots in Q become corners of H, each robot can decide on its own (without communicating with other robots) Complete Visibility is solved and terminate its computation.

To prove the above claim, we first show that at least one robot in the interior of H moves outward toward H in each round $\kappa \geq 0$. We then prove that in the same round κ due to the moves of corner robots of H inward in H, a robot in any side of H or in the interior of H becomes a new corner of H. We also show that the corner robots of H remain as corners of H even after they have moved inward in H. We then prove that this indeed happens without collisions in every round κ. This altogether provides the $O(N)$ runtime for our algorithm avoiding collisions (Theorem 1.1).

REFERENCES

[1] Howie Choset, Kevin M. Lynch, Seth Hutchinson, George A Kantor, Wolfram Burgard, Lydia E. Kavraki, and Sebastian Thrun. 2005. *Principles of Robot Motion: Theory, Algorithms, and Implementations.* MIT Press, Cambridge, MA.

[2] Paola Flocchini, Giuseppe Prencipe, and Nicola Santoro. 2012. Distributed Computing by Oblivious Mobile Robots. *Synthesis Lectures on Distributed Computing Theory* 3, 2 (2012), 1–185.

[3] Giuseppe Antonio Di Luna, Paola Flocchini, Federico Poloni, Nicola Santoro, and Giovanni Viglietta. 2014. The Mutual Visibility Problem for Oblivious Robots. In *CCCG.*

[4] Gokarna Sharma, Costas Busch, and Supratik Mukhopadhyay. 2015. Bounds on Mutual Visibility Algorithms. In *CCCG.* 268–274.

Online Tree Caching*

Marcin Bienkowski
Institute of Computer Science
University of Wrocław
Poland

Jan Marcinkowski
Institute of Computer Science
University of Wrocław
Poland

Maciej Pacut
Institute of Computer Science
University of Wrocław
Poland

Stefan Schmid
Department of Computer Science
Aalborg University
Denmark

Aleksandra Spyra
Institute of Computer Science
University of Wrocław
Poland

ABSTRACT

We initiate the study of a natural and practically relevant new variant of online caching where the to-be-cached items can have dependencies. We assume that the universe is a tree T and items are tree nodes; we require that if a node v is cached then the whole subtree $T(v)$ rooted at v is cached as well. This theoretical problem finds an immediate application in the context of forwarding table optimization in IP routing and software-defined networks.

We present an elegant online deterministic algorithm TC for this problem, and rigorously prove that its competitive ratio is $O(\textsc{height}(T) \cdot k_{\text{ONL}}/(k_{\text{ONL}} - k_{\text{OPT}} + 1))$, where k_{ONL} and k_{OPT} denote the cache sizes of an online and the optimal offline algorithm, respectively. The result is optimal up to a factor of $O(\textsc{height}(T))$.

CCS CONCEPTS

• **Theory of computation → Online algorithms**; *Caching and paging algorithms*; • **Networks** → *Programmable networks*; Packet-switching networks;

KEYWORDS

online algorithms, competitive analysis, caching, routers, software-defined networking, forwarding information base

1 INTRODUCTION

In the classic online paging problem, items of some universe are requested by a processing entity (e.g., blocks of RAM are requested by the processor). To speed up the access, computers use a faster memory, called *cache*, capable of accommodating k such items. Upon a request to a non-cached item, the algorithm has to fetch it into the cache, paying a fixed cost, while a request to a cached item is free. If the cache is full, the algorithm has to free some space by evicting an arbitrary subset of items from the cache.

The paging problem is inherently online: the algorithm has to make decisions what to evict from the cache without the knowledge of future requests; its cost is compared to the cost of an optimal *offline* solution and the worst-case ratio of these two amounts is called *competitive ratio*. The first analysis of this basic problem in an online model was given over three decades ago by Sleator and Tarjan [30]. The problem was later considered in a variety of flavors. In particular, some papers considered a *bypassing model* [13, 17], where item fetching is optional: the requested item can be served without being in the cache, for another fixed cost (usually being at most the cost of item fetching).

In this paper, we introduce a natural extension of this fundamental problem, where items have inter-dependencies. More precisely, we assume that the universe is an arbitrary (not necessarily binary) rooted tree T and the requested items are its nodes. For any tree node v, $T(v) \subseteq T$ is a subtree rooted at v containing v and all its descendants. We require the following property: if a node v is in the cache, then all nodes of $T(v)$ are also cached. In other words, we require that *the cache is a subforest of* T, i.e., a union of disjoint subtrees of T. We call this problem *online tree caching*.

Furthermore, we assume a bypassing model and distinguish between two types of requests: a request can be either *positive* or *negative*. The positive requests correspond to "normal" requests known from caching problems: we pay 1 if the node is not cached; for a negative request, we pay 1 if the corresponding request is cached. After serving the request, we may reorganize our cache arbitrarily, but the resulting cache has to still be a subforest of T. We pay α for fetching or evicting any single node, where $\alpha \geq 1$ is an integer and a parameter of the problem. Our goal is to minimize the overall cost of maintaining the cache and serving the requests.

One interesting application for our model arises in the context of modern IP routers which need to store a rapidly increasing number of forwarding rules [1, 11]. In Section 2, we give a glimpse of this application, discussing how tree caching algorithms can be applied in existing systems to effectively reduce the memory requirements on IP routers.

1.1 Our Contributions and Paper Organization

We initiate the study of a natural new caching with bypassing problem which allows to account for tree-dependencies among

*Extended abstract. Full version of this paper is available at https://arxiv.org/abs/1602.08563. M. Pacut and A. Spyra were supported by Polish National Science Centre grant DEC-2013/09/B/ST6/01538, M. Bienkowski by Polish National Science Centre grant 2016/22/E/ST6/00499, and S. Schmid by Aalborg University's talent management program.

SPAA '17, July 24-26, 2017, Washington DC, USA

ACM ISBN 978-1-4503-4593-4/17/07...$15.00
https://doi.org/10.1145/3087556.3087558

items. The problem finds immediate applications, e.g., in IP routing and software-defined networking (see Section 2).

In particular, we consider the online tree caching problem within the resource augmentation paradigm: we assume that cache sizes of the online algorithm (k_{ONL}) and the optimal offline algorithm (k_{OPT}) may differ. We assume $k_{\text{ONL}} \geq k_{\text{OPT}}$ and let $R = k_{\text{ONL}}/(k_{\text{ONL}} - k_{\text{OPT}} + 1)$.

In Section 4, we present an elegant deterministic online algorithm TC for this problem. While our algorithm is simple, its analysis presented in Section 5 requires several non-trivial insights into the problem. In particular, we rigorously prove that TC is $O(h(T) \cdot R)$-competitive, where $h(T)$ is the height of tree T. That is, we show that there exists a constant β, such that $\text{TC}(I) \leq O(h(T) \cdot R) \cdot \text{OPT}(I) + \beta$ for any input I. Note that this result is optimal up to the factor $O(h(T))$: in Appendix C, we show that the lower bound R for the paging problem [30] implies an $\Omega(R)$ lower bound for our problem for any $\alpha \geq 1$. Finally, in Section 6, we show that TC can be implemented efficiently.

1.2 Related Work on Caching

Our formal model is a novel variant of competitive paging, a classic online problem. In the framework of the competitive analysis, the paging problem was first analyzed by Sleator and Tarjan [30], who showed that algorithms LEAST-RECENTLY-USED, FIRST-IN-FIRST-OUT and FLUSH-WHEN-FULL are $k_{\text{ONL}}/(k_{\text{ONL}} - k_{\text{OPT}} + 1)$-competitive and no deterministic algorithm can beat this ratio. In the non-augmented case when $k_{\text{ONL}} = k_{\text{OPT}} = k$, the competitive ratio is simply k.

The simple paging problem was later generalized to allow different fetching costs (weighted paging) [10, 34] and additionally different item sizes (file caching) [35], with the same competitive ratio. Asymptotically same results can be achieved when bypassing is allowed (see [13, 17] and references therein). With randomization, the competitive ratio can be reduced to $O(\log k)$ even for file caching [3]. The lower bound for randomized algorithms is $H_k = \Theta(\log k)$ [14] and is matched by known paging algorithms [2, 26].

To the best of our knowledge, the variant of caching, where fetching items to the cache is not allowed unless some other items are cached (e.g., because of tree dependencies) was not considered previously in the framework of competitive analysis. Note that there is a seemingly related problem called restricted caching [8] (there are also its variants called matroid caching [9] or companion caching [27]). Despite naming similarities, the restricted caching model is completely different from ours: there the restriction is that each item can be placed only in a restricted set of cache locations.

2 APPLICATION: MINIMIZING FORWARDING TABLES IN ROUTERS

Dependencies among to-be-cached items arise in numerous settings and are a natural refinement of many caching problems. To give a concrete example, one important application for our tree-based dependency model arises in the context of IP routers. In particular, the online tree caching problem we introduce in this paper is motivated by router memory constraints in IP-based networks. The material presented in this section serves for motivation, and is not necessary for understanding the remainder of the paper.

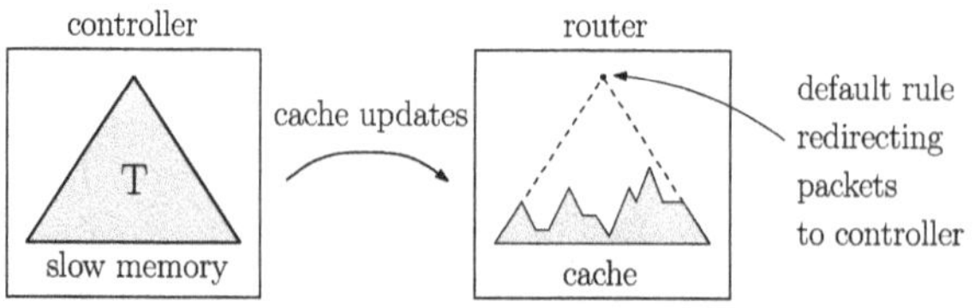

Figure 1: The router (*right*) caches only a subset of all rules, and rules that are not cached are answered by the controller (*left*) that keeps the whole tree of rules. Updates to the rules are passed by the controller to the router.

Nowadays, routers have to store an enormous number of forwarding rules: the number of rules has doubled in the last six years [1] and the superlinear growth is likely to be sustained [11]. This entails large costs for Internet Service Providers: fast router memory (usually Ternary Content Addressable Memory (TCAM)) is expensive and power-hungry [31]. Many routers currently either operate at (or beyond) the edge of their memory capacities. A solution, which could delay the need for expensive or impossible memory upgrades in routers, is to store only a subset of rules in the actual router and store all rules on a secondary device (for example a commodity server with a large but slow memory) [19–22, 29].

This solution is particularly attractive with the advent of Software-Defined Network (SDN) technology, which allows to manage the expensive memory using a software controller [19, 29]. In particular, our theoretical model can describe real-world architectures like [19, 29], that is, our model formalizes the underlying operational problems of such architectures. Our algorithm, when applied in the context of such architectures, can hence be used to prolong the lifetime of IP routers.

Setup, positive requests, fetches and evictions. The setup (see [29] for a more technical discussion) depicted in Figure 1 consists of two entities: the actual router (e.g., an OpenFlow switch) which caches only a subset of all forwarding rules, and the (SDN) controller, which keeps all rules in its less expensive and slower memory. During runtime, packets arrive at the router, and if an appropriate forwarding rule is found within the rules cached by the router, then the packet is forwarded accordingly, and the associated cost is zero. Otherwise, the packet has to be forwarded to the controller (where an appropriate forwarding rule exists); this indirection costs 1. Hence, the rules correspond to cacheable items and accesses to rules are modeled by positive requests to the corresponding items. At some chosen points in time, the caching algorithm run at the controller may decide to remove or add rules to the cache. Any such change entails a fixed cost α.[1]

Tree dependencies. Note that the technical feasibility of this solution heavily depends on the rule dependencies. In the most ubiquitous scenario, the rules are prefixes of IP addresses (they are bit strings). Whenever a packet arrives, the router follows a longest matching prefix (LMP) scheme: it searches for the rule that is a prefix of the destination IP of the packet and among matching rules it

[1]This cost corresponds to the transmission of a message from the controller to the router as well as the update of internal data structures of the router. Such an update of proprietary and vendor-dependent structures can be quite costly [16], but the empirical studies show it to be independent of the rule being updated [15].

chooses the longest one. In other words, if the prefixes corresponding to rules are stored in the tree[2], then the tree is traversed from the root downwards, and the last found rule is used. This explains why we require the cached nodes to form a subforest: leaving a less specific rule on the router while evicting a more specific one (i.e., keeping a tree node in cache while evicting its descendant) will result in a situation where packets will be forwarded according to the less specific rule, and hence potentially exit through the wrong port. The LMP scheme also ensures that the described approach is implementable: one could simply add an artificial rule at the tree root in the router (matching an empty prefix). This ensures that when no actual matching rule is found in the router (in the cache), the packet will be forwarded according to this artificial rule to the controller that stores all the rules and can handle all packets appropriately.

So far, the papers on IP rule caching avoided dependencies either assuming that rules do not overlap (a tree has a single level) [20] or by preprocessing the tree, so that the rules become non-overlapping [21, 22]. Unfortunately, this could lead to a large inflation of the routing table. A notable exception is a recent solution called CacheFlow [19]. The CacheFlow model supports dependencies even in the form of directed acyclic graphs. However, CacheFlow was evaluated only experimentally, and no worst-case guarantees were given on the overall cost of caching. Our work provides theoretical foundations for respecting tree dependencies.

Negative requests. Additionally, a rule may need to be updated. For example, due to a change communicated by a dynamic routing protocol (e.g., BGP) the action defined by a rule has to be modified. In either case, we have to update the rules at the controller: we assume that this cost is zero. (This cost is unavoidable for any algorithm, so such an assumption makes our problem only more difficult.) Furthermore, if the rule is also stored at the router, then we have to pay a fixed cost of α for updating the router (see the remark for the cost of fetches and evictions). Such penalties can be easily simulated in our model: we issue a sequence of α negative requests to the updated node. It is straightforward to show that the costs in these two models can differ by a factor of at most 2. For a formal argument, see Appendix B.

Implementability. Note that the whole input (fed to a tree caching algorithm) is created at the controller: positive requests are caused by cache misses (which redirect packet to the controller) and batches of α negative requests are caused by updates sent to the dynamic routing algorithm run at the controller. Therefore, the whole tree caching algorithm can be implemented in software in the controller only. Furthermore, our algorithm is a simple counter-based scheme, which can be implemented efficiently and also fine-tuned for speed, see Section 6.

Other work on forwarding table minimization. Other approaches for minimizing the number of stored rules were mostly based on *rules compression (aggregation)*, where the set of rules was replaced by another equivalent and smaller set. Optimal aggregation of a fixed routing table can be achieved by dynamic programming [12, 32], but the main challenge lies in balancing the achieved compression and the amount of changes to the routing table in the presence of *updates* to this table. While many practical heuristics have been devised by the networking community for this problem [18, 23–25, 28, 33, 36], worst-case analyses were presented only for some restricted scenarios [6, 7]. Combining rules compression and rules caching is so far an unexplored area.

[2]We do not have to assume that they are actually stored in a real tree; this tree is implicit in the LMP scheme.

3 PRELIMINARIES

We denote the height of T by $h(T)$. For any node v, $T(v)$ denotes the subtree of T rooted at v (containing v and all its descendants). A *tree cap* rooted at v is "an upper part" of $T(v)$, i.e., it contains v and if it contains node u, then it also contains all nodes on the path from u to v. If $A \subseteq B$ are both tree caps rooted at v, then we say that A is a tree cap of B.

We assume discrete time slotted into rounds, with round $t \geq 1$ corresponding to time interval $(t-1, t)$. In round t, the algorithm is given one (positive or negative) request to exactly one tree node and has to process it, i.e., pay associated costs (if any). Right after round t, at time t, the algorithm may arbitrarily reorganize its cache, (i) ensuring that the resulting cache is a subforest of T (i.e., if the cache contains node v, then it contains the entire $T(v)$) and (ii) preserving the cache capacity constraint. An algorithm pays α for a single node fetch or eviction. We denote the contents of the cache at round t by C_t. (As the cache changes contents only between rounds, C_t is well defined.) We assume that α is an even integer (this assumption may change costs at most by a constant factor). We assume that the algorithm starts with the empty cache.

We call a non-empty set X a *valid positive changeset* for cache C if $X \cap C = \emptyset$ and $C \cup X$ is a subforest of T, and a *valid negative changeset* if $X \subseteq C$ and $C \setminus X$ is a subforest of T. We call X a *valid changeset* if it is either valid positive or negative changeset. Note that the union of positive (negative) changesets is also a valid positive (negative) changeset. We say that the algorithm applies changeset X, if it fetches all nodes from X (for a positive changeset) and evicts all nodes from X (for a negative one). Note that not all valid changesets may be applied as the algorithm is also limited by its cache capacity (k_{ONL} for an online algorithm and k_{OPT} for the optimal offline one).

4 ALGORITHM

The algorithm Tree Caching (TC) presented in the following is a simple scheme that follows a *rent-or-buy paradigm*: it fetches (or evicts) a changeset X if the cost associated with requests at X reaches the cost of such fetch or eviction.

More concretely, TC operates in multiple phases. The first phase starts at time 0. TC starts each phase with the empty cache and proceeds as follows. Within a phase, every node keeps a counter, which is initially zero. If at round t it pays 1 for serving the request, it increments its counter. Whenever a node is fetched or evicted from the cache, its counter is reset to zero. Note that this implies that the counter of v is equal to the number of negative (positive) requests to v since its last fetching to the cache (eviction from the cache). For a set $A \subseteq T$, we denote the sum of all counters in A at time t by $\mathrm{cnt}_t(A)$. At time t, TC verifies whether there exists a valid changeset X, such that

- *(saturation property)* $\mathrm{cnt}_t(X) \geq |X| \cdot \alpha$ and

- *(maximality property)* $\text{cnt}_t(Y) < |Y| \cdot \alpha$ for any valid changeset $Y \supsetneq X$.

In this case, the algorithm modifies its cache applying X.

If, at time t, TC is supposed to fetch some set X, but by doing so it would exceed the cache capacity k_{ONL}, it evicts all nodes from the cache instead, and starts a new phase at time t. Such a *final eviction* might not be present in the last phase, in which case we call it *unfinished*.

In Lemma 5.1 (below), we show that at any time, all valid changesets satisfying both properties of TC are either all positive or all negative. Furthermore, right after the algorithm applies a changeset, no valid changeset satisfies saturation property.

5 ANALYSIS OF TC

Throughout the paper, we fix an input I, its partition into phases, and analyze both TC and OPT on a single fixed phase P. We denote the times at which P starts and ends by begin(P) and end(P), respectively, i.e., rounds in P are numbered from begin(P) + 1 to end(P). A proof of the following technical lemma follows by induction and is presented in Appendix A.

LEMMA 5.1. *Fix any time $t >$ begin(P). For any valid changeset X for C_t, it holds that $cnt_t(X) \leq |X| \cdot \alpha$. If a changeset X is applied at time t, the following properties hold:*

1. *X contains the node requested at round t,*
2. *$cnt_t(X) = |X| \cdot \alpha$,*
3. *$cnt_t(Y) < |Y| \cdot \alpha$ for any valid changeset Y for C_{t+1} (note that C_{t+1} is the cache state right after application of X),*
4. *X is a tree cap of a tree from C_{t+1} if X is positive and it is a tree cap of a tree from C_t if X is negative.*

In the following, we assume that no positive requests are given to nodes inside cache and no negative ones to nodes outside of it. (This does not change the behavior of TC and can only decrease the cost of OPT.)

For the sake of analysis, we assume that at time end(P), TC actually performs a cache fetch (exceeding the cache size limit) and then, at the same time instant, empties the cache. This replacement only increases the cost of TC. Let k_P denote the number of nodes in the cache of TC at end(P). In a finished phase, we measure it after the artificial fetch, but right before the final eviction, and thus $k_P \geq k_{\text{ONL}} + 1$; in an unfinished phase $k_P \leq k_{\text{ONL}}$.

The crucial part of our analysis that culminates in Section 5.2 is the technique of shifting requests. Namely, we modify the input sequence by shifting requests up or down the tree, so that the resulting input sequence (i) is not harder for OPT and (ii) is more structured: we may lower bound the cost of OPT on each node separately and relate it to the cost of TC.

5.1 Event Space and Fields

In our analysis, we look at a two-dimensional, discrete, spatial-temporal space, called the *event space*. The first dimension is indexed by tree nodes, whose order is an arbitrary extension of the partial order given by the tree. That is, the parent of a node v is always "above" v. The second dimension is indexed by round numbers of phase P. The space elements are called *slots*. Some slots are occupied by requests: a request at node v given at round t occupies slot (v, t).

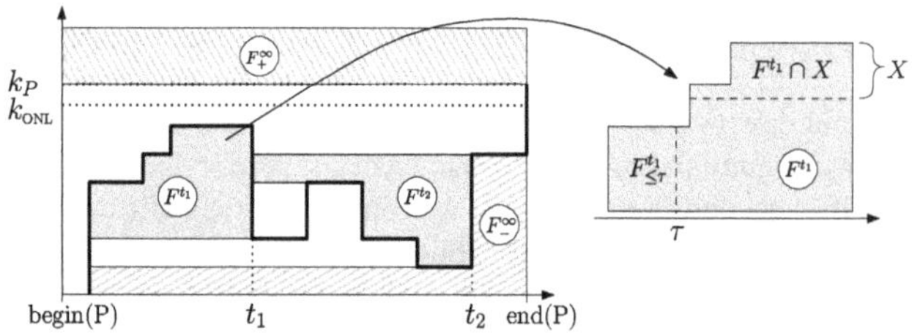

Figure 2: Partitioning of a single phase into fields for a line (a tree with no branches). The thick line represents cache contents. Possible final eviction at end(P) is not depicted. F^{t_1} is a negative field and F^{t_2} is a positive one. In the particular depicted example, nodes are ordered from the leaf (bottom) to the root (top of the picture). We emphasize that for a general, branched tree, some notions (in particular fields) no longer have nice geometric interpretations.

From now on, we will identify P with a set of requests occupying some slots in the event space.

We partition slots of the whole event space into disjoint parts, called *fields*, and we show how this partition is related to the costs of TC and OPT. For any node v and time t, $\text{last}_v(t)$ denotes the last time strictly before t, when node v changed state from cached to non-cached or vice versa; $\text{last}_v(t)$ = begin(P) if v did not change its state before t in phase P. For a changeset X_t applied by TC at time t, we define the field F^t as

$$F^t = \{ (v, r) : v \in X_t \wedge \text{last}_v(t) + 1 \leq r \leq t \}.$$

That is, field F^t contains all the requests that eventually trigger the application of X_t at time t. We say that F^t ends at t. We call field F^t *positive* (*negative*) if X_t is a positive (negative) changeset. An example of a partitioning into fields is given in Figure 2. We define $\text{req}(F^t)$ as the number of requests belonging to slots of F^t and let $\text{size}(F^t)$ be the number of involved nodes (note that $\text{size}(F^t) = |X_t|$). The observation below follows immediately by Lemma 5.1.

OBSERVATION 5.2. *For any field F, $req(F) = size(F) \cdot \alpha$. All these requests are positive (negative) if F is positive (negative).*

Finally, we call the rest of the event space defined by phase P *open field* and denote it by F^∞. The set of all fields except F^∞ is denoted by $\mathcal{F}$. Let $\text{size}(\mathcal{F}) = \sum_{F \in \mathcal{F}} \text{size}(F)$.

LEMMA 5.3. *For any phase P partitioned into a set of fields $\mathcal{F} \cup \{F^\infty\}$, it holds that $TC(P) \leq 2\alpha \cdot size(\mathcal{F}) + req(F^\infty) + k_P \cdot \alpha$.*

PROOF. By Observation 5.2, the cost associated with serving the requests from all fields from $\mathcal{F}$ is $\sum_{F \in \mathcal{F}} \alpha \cdot \text{size}(F) = \alpha \cdot \text{size}(\mathcal{F})$. The cost of the cache reorganization at the fields' ends is exactly the same. The term $\text{req}(F^\infty)$ represents the cost of serving the requests from F^∞ and $k_P \cdot \alpha$ upper-bounds the cost of the final eviction (not present in an unfinished phase). □

5.2 Shifting Requests

The actual challenge in the proof is to relate the structure of the fields to the cost of OPT. The rationale behind our construction is based on the following thought experiment. Assume that the phase is unfinished (for example, when the cache is so large that the whole input corresponds to a single phase). Recall that the number of requests in each field $F \in \mathcal{F}$ is equal to $\text{size}(F) \cdot \alpha$. Assume that these requests are evenly distributed among the nodes of F (each node from F receives α requests in the slots of F). Then, the history of any node v is alternating between periods spent in positive fields and periods spent in negative fields. By our even distribution assumption, each such a period contains exactly α requests. Hence, for any two consecutive periods of a single node, OPT has to pay at least α (either α for positive requests or α for negative ones, or α for changing the cached/non-cached state of v). Essentially, this shows that OPT has to pay an amount that can be easily related to $\alpha \cdot \text{size}(\mathcal{F})$.

Unfortunately, the requests may not be evenly distributed among the nodes. To alleviate this problem, we will modify the requests in phase P, so that the newly created phase P' is not harder for OPT and will "almost" have the even distribution property. In this construction, the time frame of P and its fields are fixed.

5.2.1 Legal Shifts.

We say that a request placed originally (in phase P) at slot (v, t) is *legally shifted* if its new slot is $(m(v), t)$, where (i) for a positive request, $m(v)$ is either equal to v or is one of its descendants and (ii) for a negative request, $m(v)$ is either equal to v or is one of its ancestors. For any fixed sequence of fetches and evictions within phase P, the associated cost may only decrease when these actions are replayed on the modified requests.

OBSERVATION 5.4. *If P' is created from P by legally shifting the requests, then $\text{OPT}(P') \leq \text{OPT}(P)$.*

The main difficulty is however in keeping the legally shifted requests within the field they originally belonged to. For example, a negative request from F shifted at round t from node u to its parent may fall out of F as the parent may still be outside the cache at round t. In effect, a careless shifting of requests may lead to a situation where, for a single node v, requests do not create interleaved periods of positive and negative requests, and hence we cannot argue that $\text{OPT}(P')$ is sufficiently large.

In the following subsections, we show that it is possible to legally shift the requests of any field $F \in \mathcal{F}$ (i.e., shift positive requests down and negative requests up), so that they remain within F, and they will be either exactly or approximately evenly distributed among nodes of F. This will create P' with appropriately large cost for OPT.

5.2.2 Notation.

We start with some general definitions and remarks. For any field F and set of nodes A, let $F \cap A = \{(v, t) \in F : v \in A\}$. Analogously, if L is a set of rounds, then let $F \cap L = \{(v, t) \in F : t \in L\}$. For any field F^t and time τ, we define

$$F^t_{\leq \tau} = F^t \cap \{t' : t' \leq \tau\}.$$

It is convenient to think that F^t evolves with time and $F^t_{\leq \tau}$ is the snapshot of F^t at time τ. Note that F^t may have some nodes not included in $F^t_{\leq \tau}$. These objects are depicted in Figure 2.

We may extend the notions of req and size to arbitrary subsets of fields in a natural way. For any subset $S \subseteq F$, we call it *over-requested* if $\text{req}(S) > \text{size}(S) \cdot \alpha$.

LEMMA 5.5. *Fix any field F^t, the corresponding changeset X_t, and any time τ.*

(1) *If F^t is negative, then for any tree cap D of X_t, the set $F^t_{\leq \tau} \cap D$ is not over-requested.*
(2) *If F^t is positive, then for any subtree $T' \subseteq T$, the set $F^t_{\leq \tau} \cap T'$ is not over-requested.*

PROOF. As the nodes from $F^t_{\leq \tau} \cap D$ form a valid changeset at time τ, Lemma 5.1 implies $\text{req}(F^t_{\leq \tau} \cap D) = \text{cnt}_\tau(F^t_{\leq \tau} \cap D) \leq |F^t_{\leq \tau} \cap D| \cdot \alpha$.

The proof of the second property is identical: As $F^t_{\leq \tau} \cap T'$ is also a valid changeset at time τ, by Lemma 5.1, $\text{req}(F^t_{\leq \tau} \cap T') = \text{cnt}_\tau(F^t_{\leq \tau} \cap T') \leq |F^t_{\leq \tau} \cap T'| \cdot \alpha$. □

By Lemma 5.5 applied at $\tau = t$ and Observation 5.2, we deduct the following corollary.

COROLLARY 5.6. *Fix any field F^t, the corresponding changeset X_t and any tree cap D of X_t.*

(1) *If F^t is positive, then $\text{req}(F^t \cap D) \geq \alpha \cdot |D|$.*
(2) *If F^t is negative, then $\text{req}(F^t \cap (X_t \setminus D)) \geq \alpha \cdot |X_t \setminus D|$.*

Informally speaking, the corollary above states that the average amount of requests in a positive field is *at least as large at the top of the field as at its bottom*. For a negative field this relation is reversed.

5.2.3 Shifting Negative Requests Up.

Fix a valid negative changeset X_t applied at time t and the corresponding field F^t. We call a tree cap $Y \subseteq X_t$ *proper* if

(1) $\text{req}(F^t \cap Y) = |Y| \cdot \alpha$ and
(2) $F^t_{\leq \tau} \cap D$ is not over-requested for any tree cap $D \subseteq Y$ and any time $\tau \leq t$.

The first property of Lemma 5.5 states that before we shift the requests of F_t, the set X_t is proper. We start with $Y = X_t$, and proceed in a bottom-up fashion, inductively using the lemma below. We take care of a single node of Y at a time and ensure that after the shift the number of requests at this node is exactly α and the remaining part of Y remains proper.

LEMMA 5.7. *Given a negative field F^t, the corresponding changeset X_t and a proper tree cap $Y \subseteq X_t$, it is possible to choose a leaf v and legally shift some requests inside Y, so that in result $\text{req}(v) = \alpha$ and $Y \setminus \{v\}$ is proper.*

PROOF. As $\text{req}(F^t \cap Y) = |Y| \cdot \alpha$, Corollary 5.6 implies that any leaf of Y was requested at least α times inside F^t. We pick an arbitrary leaf v, and let $r \geq \alpha$ be the number of requests to v in F^t.

We look at all the requests to v in F^t ordered by their round. Let s be the round when $(\alpha + 1)$-th of them arrives. We will now show that at round s, TC already has $p(v)$ in its cache. If it had not, $\{v\}$ would be a tree cap of $F^t_{\leq s}$, and by the first property of Lemma 5.5, it would contain at most α requests, which is a contradiction. Hence, if we shift the chronologically last $r - \alpha$ requests from v to $p(v)$, these requests stay within F^t.

It remains to show that $Y \setminus \{v\}$ is proper after such a shift. We choose any tree cap $D \subseteq Y$ and any time $\tau \leq t$. If D does not contain $p(v)$ or $\tau < s$, then the number of requests in $F^t_{\leq \tau} \cap D$ was not changed by the shift, and hence $F^t_{\leq \tau} \cap D$ is not over-requested. Otherwise, $D \cup \{v\}$ was a tree cap in Y and by the lemma assumption, $F^t_{\leq \tau} \cap (D \cup \{v\})$ was not over-requested. As $F^t_{\leq \tau} \cap D$ has now exactly α less requests than $F^t_{\leq \tau} \cap (D \cup \{v\})$ had, it is not over-requested, either. □

Corollary 5.8. *For any negative field F^t, it is possible to legally shift its requests up, so that they remain within F^t and after the modification each node is requested exactly α times.*

5.2.4 *Shifting Positive Requests Down.* We will now focus on the problem of shifting the positive requests down in a single positive field F^t, corresponding to a single fetch of TC at the time t. Our goal is to devise a shifting strategy, that will result in at least $\Omega(\text{size}(F^t)/h(T))$ nodes having $\alpha/2$ requests each. While this result may be suboptimal, deriving a shifting strategy for a positive field that would have the same equal distribution guarantee as the one provided by Corollary 5.8 is not possible (the details are presented in the full version of the paper).

First, we prove that from any node v in the field, we can shift down a constant fraction of its requests within the field, distributing them to different nodes.

Lemma 5.9. *Let F^t be a positive field and let X_t be the corresponding changeset fetched to the cache at time t. Fix any node $v \in X_t$ that has been requested at least $c \cdot (\alpha/2)$ times in F^t, where c is an integer. It is possible to shift down its requests to the nodes of $T(v) \cap X_t$, so that these requests remain inside F^t and $\lceil c/2 \rceil$ nodes of $T(v)$ get $\alpha/2$ requests each.*

Proof. We order the nodes $u_1, u_2, \ldots u_{|T(v) \cap X_t|}$ of $T(v) \cap X_t$, so that $\text{last}_{u_i}(t) \leq \text{last}_{u_{i+1}}(t)$ for all i. In case of a tie, we place nodes that are closer to v first. Note that this linear ordering is an extension of the partial order defined by the tree: the parent of a node cannot be evicted later than the node itself (otherwise the cache would cease to be a subforest of T). In particular, it holds that $u_1 = v$.

We number $c \cdot (\alpha/2)$ requests to v chronologically, starting from 1. For any $j \in \{1, \ldots, \lceil c/2 \rceil\}$ we look at round τ_j with the $((j-1) \cdot \alpha + 1)$-th request to v. When this request arrives, node u_j is already present in the cache. Otherwise, we would have at least $j \cdot \alpha + 1$ requests in $F^t_{\leq \tau_j} \cap \{u_1, \ldots, u_j\}$ (already in $F^t_{\leq \tau_j} \cap \{u_1\}$ alone), which would make it over-requested, and thus contradict the second property of Lemma 5.5. Hence, we may take requests numbered from $(j-1) \cdot \alpha + 1$ to $(j-1) \cdot \alpha + \alpha/2$, shift them down from v to u_j, and after such modification these requests are still inside F^t. Note that for $j = 1$ requests are not really shifted, as u_1 is v itself. We perform such shift for any $j \in \{1, \ldots, \lceil c/2 \rceil\}$, which yields the lemma. □

Lemma 5.10. *For any positive field F^t, it is possible to legally shift its requests down, so that they remain within F^t and after the modification at least $\text{size}(F^t)/(2h(T))$ nodes in F^t have at least $\alpha/2$ requests each.*

Proof. Let X_t be the changeset corresponding to field F^t, which is fetched to the cache at time t. By Observation 5.2, $\text{req}(F^t) = |X_t| \cdot \alpha$. We gather the requests at every node into groups of $\alpha/2$ consecutive requests. In every node at most $\alpha/2$ requests remain not grouped. Let $\overline{\text{req}}(X)$ denote the number of grouped requests in the set X. Clearly, $\overline{\text{req}}(F^t) \geq |X_t| \cdot \alpha/2$, i.e., there are at least $|X_t|$ groups of requests in set X_t.

Let $X_t = X_t^1 \sqcup X_t^2 \sqcup \cdots \sqcup X_t^{h(T)}$ be a partition of the nodes of the tree X_t into layers according to their distance to the root. By the pigeonhole principle, there is a layer X_t^i containing at least $\lceil |X_t|/h(T) \rceil$ groups of requests (each group has $\alpha/2$ requests).

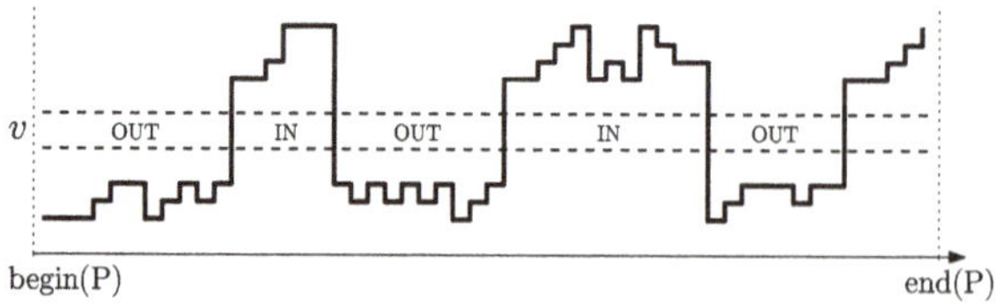

Figure 3: Partitioning of the phase into interleaving IN and OUT periods for node v. The thick line represents cache contents. The *leftover* OUT period (the last one) is present for node v as it has finished phase P inside TC's cache. The periods can be followed by requests contained in F^∞.

Nodes of X_t^i are independent, i.e., for $u, v \in X_t^i$ the trees $T(u)$ and $T(v)$ are disjoint. Therefore, we may use the shifting strategy described in Lemma 5.9 for each node of X_t^i separately. After such modification, at least $\lceil |X_t|/(2h(T)) \rceil \geq \text{size}(F_t)/(2h(T))$ nodes have at least $\alpha/2$ requests each. □

5.2.5 *Using Request Shifting for Bounding OPT.* Finally, we may use our request shifting to relate $\text{size}(\mathcal{F}) = \sum_{F \in \mathcal{F}} \text{size}(F)$ to the cost of Opt in a single phase P. Recall that k_P denotes the size of TC's cache at the end of P. We assume that Opt may start the phase with an arbitrary state of the cache.

Lemma 5.11. *For any phase P, $\text{Opt}(P) \geq (\text{size}(\mathcal{F})/(4h(T)) - k_P) \cdot \alpha/2$.*

Proof. We transform P using legal shifts that are described in Section 5.2.3 and Section 5.2.4. That is, we create a corresponding phase P' that satisfies both Corollary 5.8 and Lemma 5.10. By Observation 5.4, it is sufficient to show that $\text{Opt}(P') \geq (\text{size}(\mathcal{F})/(4h(T)) - k_P) \cdot \alpha/2$.

We focus on a single node v. We cut its history into interleaved periods: OUT *periods*, when v is outside the cache and receives positive requests, and IN *periods* when TC keeps v in the cache and v receives negative requests. A final (possibly empty) part corresponding to the time when v is in the F^∞ field is not accounted in OUT or IN periods, i.e., each IN or OUT period corresponds to some field $F \in \mathcal{F}$. Let p^{IN} and p^{OUT} denote the total number of IN and OUT periods (respectively) for all nodes during the phase. An example is given in Figure 3.

Recall that TC starts each phase with an empty cache, and hence each node starts with an OUT period. For k_P nodes that are in TC's cache at the end of the phase (and only for them) their history ends with an OUT period not followed by an IN period. We call them *leftover periods.* Thus, $p^{\text{OUT}} = p^{\text{IN}} + k_P$. The total number of periods $(p^{\text{IN}} + p^{\text{OUT}})$ is equal to the total size of all *fields*, $\text{size}(\mathcal{F})$, and thus $p^{\text{OUT}} \geq \text{size}(\mathcal{F})/2$.

We call a period *full* if it has at least $\alpha/2$ requests. The shifting strategies described in the previous section ensure that all IN periods are full and at least $1/(2h(T))$ of all OUT periods are full. Thus, there are at least $p^{\text{OUT}}/(2h(T)) - k_P$ full non-leftover OUT periods; each of them together with the following IN period constitutes a *full* OUT-IN *pair.*

Opt has to pay at least $\alpha/2$ for the node in the course of the history described by a full OUT-IN pair: it pays α either for changing the cached/non-cached state of a node, or $\alpha/2$ for all positive requests or $\alpha/2$ for all negative ones. Thus, $\text{OPT}(P') \geq (p^{\text{OUT}}/(2h(T)) - k_P) \cdot \alpha/2 \geq (\text{size}(\mathcal{F})/(4h(T)) - k_P) \cdot \alpha/2$. □

5.3 Competitive Ratio

To relate the cost of OPT to TC in a single phase P, we still need to upper-bound $\text{req}(F^\infty)$ and relate $k_P \cdot \alpha$ to the cost of OPT (i.e., compare the bounds on TC and OPT provided by Lemma 5.3 and Lemma 5.11, respectively).

For the next two lemmas, we define V_{OPT} as the set of all nodes that were in OPT cache at some time of P and let $V^c_{\text{OPT}} = T \setminus V_{\text{OPT}}$. Note that V_{OPT} is a union of subforests (nodes present in OPT's cache at consecutive times), and hence a subforest itself.

LEMMA 5.12. *For any phase P, it holds that $\text{req}(F^\infty) \leq 2 \cdot k_{\text{ONL}} \cdot \alpha + 2 \cdot \text{OPT}(P)$.*

PROOF. We assume first that P is a finished phase. Then, P ends with an artificial fetch of $X_{\text{end}(P)}$ at time $\text{end}(P)$ (followed by the final eviction). We split F^∞ into two disjoint parts (see Figure 2):

$$F^\infty_- = \{(v,t) : v \in C_{\text{end}(P)}, t \geq \text{last}_v(\text{end}(P))\},$$
$$F^\infty_+ = \{(v,t) : v \notin C_{\text{end}(P)} \sqcup X_{\text{end}(P)}, \ t \geq \text{last}_v(\text{end}(P))\}.$$

Note that F^∞_- contains only negative requests and F^∞_+ only positive ones. As $\text{req}(F^\infty) = \text{req}(F^\infty_-) + \text{req}(F^\infty_+ \cap V^c_{\text{OPT}}) + \text{req}(F^\infty_+ \cap V_{\text{OPT}})$, we estimate each of these summands separately.

- Nodes from F^∞_- are in the cache $C_{\text{end}(P)}$ and were not evicted from the cache. Thus, $\text{req}(F^\infty_-) \leq |C_{\text{end}(P)}| \cdot \alpha \leq k_{\text{ONL}} \cdot \alpha$.
- All the requests from V^c_{OPT} are paid by OPT, and hence $\text{req}(F^\infty_+ \cap V^c_{\text{OPT}}) \leq \text{req}(V^c_{\text{OPT}}) \leq \text{OPT}(P)$.
- F^∞_+ is a valid changeset for cache $C_{\text{end}(P)} \sqcup X_{\text{end}(P)}$. As V_{OPT} is a subforest of T, $F^\infty_+ \cap V_{\text{OPT}}$ is also a valid changeset for the cache $C_{\text{end}(P)} \sqcup X_{\text{end}(P)}$. Therefore, $\text{req}(F^\infty_+ \cap V_{\text{OPT}}) \leq \text{size}(F^\infty_+ \cap V_{\text{OPT}}) \cdot \alpha$, as otherwise the set fetched at time $\text{end}(P)$ would not be maximal. (TC could then fetch $X_{\text{end}(P)} \sqcup (F^\infty_+ \cap V_{\text{OPT}})$ instead of $X_{\text{end}(P)}$.) Thus, $\text{req}(F^\infty_+ \cap V_{\text{OPT}}) \leq |V_{\text{OPT}}| \cdot \alpha = k_{\text{OPT}} \cdot \alpha + (|V_{\text{OPT}}| - k_{\text{OPT}}) \cdot \alpha \leq k_{\text{ONL}} \cdot \alpha + \text{OPT}(P)$. The last inequality follows as — independently of the initial state — OPT needs to fetch at least $|V_{\text{OPT}}| - k_{\text{OPT}}$ nodes to the cache during P.

Hence, in total, $\text{req}(F^\infty) \leq 2 \cdot k_{\text{ONL}} \cdot \alpha + 2 \cdot \text{OPT}(P)$ for a finished phase P.

We note that if there was no cache change at $\text{end}(P)$, the analysis above would hold with $X_{\text{end}(P)} = \emptyset$ with virtually no change. Therefore, for an unfinished phase P ending with a fetch or ending without cache change at $\text{end}(P)$, the bound on $\text{req}(F^\infty)$ still holds. However, if an unfinished phase P ends with an eviction, then we look at the last eviction-free time τ of P. We now observe the evolution of field F^∞ from time τ till $\text{end}(P)$. At time τ, $\text{req}(F^\infty) \leq 2 \cdot k_{\text{ONL}} \cdot \alpha + 2 \cdot \text{OPT}(P)$. Furthermore, in subsequent times, it may only decrease: at any round F^∞ gets an additional request, but on eviction $\text{req}(F^\infty)$ decreases by α times the number of evicted nodes (i.e., at least by $\alpha \geq 1$). Hence, the value of $\text{req}(F^\infty)$ at $\text{end}(P)$ is also at most $2 \cdot k_{\text{ONL}} \cdot \alpha + 2 \cdot \text{OPT}(P)$. □

By combining Lemma 5.3, Lemma 5.11 and Lemma 5.12, we immediately obtain the following corollary (holding for both finished and unfinished phases).

COROLLARY 5.13. *For any phase P, it holds that $TC(P) \leq O(h(T)) \cdot \text{OPT}(P) + O(h(T) \cdot (k_P + k_{\text{ONL}}) \cdot \alpha)$.*

Using the corollary above, its remains to bound the value of k_P. This is easy for an unfinished phase, as $k_P \leq k_{\text{ONL}}$ there. For a finished phase, we provide another bound.

LEMMA 5.14. *For any finished phase P, it holds that $k_P \cdot \alpha \leq \text{OPT}(P) \cdot (k_{\text{ONL}} + 1)/(k_{\text{ONL}} + 1 - k_{\text{OPT}})$.*

PROOF. First, we compute the number of positive requests in V^c_{OPT}. Let $X_{t_1}, X_{t_2}, \ldots, X_{t_s}$ be all positive changesets applied by TC in P. For any t, let $X'_t = X_t \setminus V_{\text{OPT}}$. As X_t is some tree cap and V_{OPT} is a subforest of T, X'_t is a tree cap of X_t. By Corollary 5.6, the number of requests to nodes of X'_t in field F^t is at least $|X'_t| \cdot \alpha$. These requests for different changesets X_t are disjoint and they are all outside of V_{OPT}. Hence the total number of positive requests outside of V_{OPT} is at least $\sum_{i=1}^{s} |X'_{t_i}| \cdot \alpha$, where $\sum_{i=1}^{s} |X'_{t_i}| \geq |\bigcup_{i=1}^{s} X'_{t_i}| = |(\bigcup_{i=1}^{s} X_{t_i}) \setminus V_{\text{OPT}}| \geq |\bigcup_{i=1}^{s} X_{t_i}| - |V_{\text{OPT}}| \geq k_P - |V_{\text{OPT}}|$.

Now $\text{OPT}(P)$ can be split into the cost associated with nodes from V_{OPT} and V^c_{OPT}, respectively. For the former part, OPT has to pay at least $(|V_{\text{OPT}}| - k_{\text{OPT}}) \cdot \alpha$ for the fetches alone. For the latter part, it has to pay 1 for each of at least $(k_P - |V_{\text{OPT}}|) \cdot \alpha$ positive requests outside of V_{OPT}. Hence, $\text{OPT}(P) \geq (|V_{\text{OPT}}| - k_{\text{OPT}}) \cdot \alpha + (k_P - |V_{\text{OPT}}|) \cdot \alpha = (k_P - k_{\text{OPT}}) \cdot \alpha$. Then, $k_P \cdot \alpha \leq k_P \cdot \text{OPT}(P)/(k_P - k_{\text{OPT}})$. As the phase is finished, $k_P \geq k_{\text{ONL}} + 1$, and thus $k_P \cdot \alpha \leq (k_{\text{ONL}} + 1) \cdot \text{OPT}(P)/(k_{\text{ONL}} + 1 - k_{\text{OPT}})$. □

THEOREM 5.15. *The algorithm TC is $O(h(T) \cdot k_{\text{ONL}}/(k_{\text{ONL}} - k_{\text{OPT}} + 1))$-competitive.*

PROOF. Let $R = h(T) \cdot k_{\text{ONL}}/(k_{\text{ONL}} - k_{\text{OPT}} + 1)$. We split an input I into a sequence of finished phases followed by a single unfinished phase (which may not be present). For a finished phase P, we have $k_P > k_{\text{ONL}}$, and hence Corollary 5.13 and Lemma 5.14 imply that $TC(P) \leq O(R) \cdot \text{OPT}(P)$. For an unfinished phase $k_P \leq k_{\text{ONL}}$, and therefore, by Corollary 5.13, $TC(P) \leq O(h(T)) \cdot \text{OPT}(P) + O(h(T) \cdot k_{\text{ONL}} \cdot \alpha)$. Summing over all phases of I yields $TC(I) \leq O(R) \cdot \text{OPT}(I) + O(h(T) \cdot k_{\text{ONL}} \cdot \alpha)$. □

6 IMPLEMENTATION OF TC

Recall that at each time t, TC verifies the existence of a valid changeset that satisfies saturation and maximality properties (see the definition of TC in Section 4). Here, we show that this operation can be performed efficiently. In particular, in the following two subsections, we will prove the following theorem.

THEOREM 6.1. *TC can be implemented using $O(|T|)$ additional memory, so that to make a decision at time t, it performs $O(h(T) + \max\{h(T), deg(T)\} \cdot |X_t|)$ operations, where $deg(T)$ is a maximum node degree in T and X_t is the changeset applied at time t ($|X_t| = 0$ if no changeset is applied).*

Let v_t be the node requested at round t. Note that we may restrict our attention to requests that entail a cost for TC, as otherwise its counters remain unchanged and certainly TC does not change cache contents. We use Lemma 5.1 to restrict possible candidates for changesets that can be applied at time t. First, we note that if a node v_t requested at round t is outside the cache, then, at time t, TC may only fetch some changeset, and otherwise it may only evict some changeset. Therefore, we may construct two separate schemes, one governing fetches and one for evictions.

In Section 6.1, using Lemma 5.1, we show that after processing a positive request, TC needs to verify at most $h(T)$ possible positive changesets, each in constant time, using an auxiliary data structure. The cost of updating this structure at time t is $O(h(T) + h(T) \cdot |X_t|)$.

The situation for negative changesets is more complex as even after applying Lemma 5.1 there are still exponentially many valid negative changesets to consider. In Section 6.2, we construct an auxiliary data structure that returns a viable candidate in time $O(h(T) + \deg(T) \cdot |X_t|)$. The update of this structure at time t can be also done in $O(h(T) + \deg(T) \cdot |X_t|)$ operations.

6.1 Positive Requests and Fetches

At any time t and for any non-cached node u, we may define $P_t(u)$ as a tree cap rooted at u containing all non-cached nodes from $T(u)$. During an execution of TC, we maintain two values for each non-cached node u: $\text{cnt}_t(P_t(u))$ and $|P_t(u)|$. When a counter at node v_t is incremented, we update $\text{cnt}_t(P_t(u))$ for each ancestor u of v (at most $h(T)$ updated values). Furthermore, if a node v changes its state from cached to non-cached (or vice versa), we update the value of $|P_t(u)|$ for any ancestor u of v (at most $h(T)$ updates per each node that changes the state). Therefore, the total cost of updating these structures at time t is at most $O(h(T) + h(T) \cdot |X_t|)$.

By Lemma 5.1, a positive valid changeset fetched at time t has to contain v_t and is a single tree cap. Such a tree cap has to be equal to $P_t(u)$ for u being an ancestor of v_t. Hence, we may iterate over all ancestors u of v_t, starting from the tree root and ending at v_t, and we stop at the first node u, for which $P_t(u)$ is saturated (i.e., $\text{cnt}_t(P_t(u)) \geq |P_t(u)| \cdot \alpha$). If such a u is found, the corresponding set $P_t(u)$ satisfies also the maximality condition (cf. the definition of TC) as all valid changesets that are supersets of $P_t(u)$ were already verified to be non-saturated. Therefore, in such a case, TC fetches $P_t(u)$. Otherwise, if no saturated changeset is found, TC does nothing. Checking all ancestors of v_t can be performed in time $O(h(T))$.

6.2 Negative Requests and Evictions

Handling evictions is more complex. If the request to node v_t at round t was negative, Lemma 5.1 tells us only that the negative changeset evicted by TC has to be a tree cap rooted at u, where u is the root of the cached tree containing v_t. There are exponentially many such tree caps, and hence their naïve verification is intractable. To alleviate this problem, we introduce the following helper notion. For any set of cached nodes A and any time t, let

$$\text{val}_t(A) = \text{cnt}_t(A) - |A| \cdot \alpha + \frac{|A|}{|T| + 1}.$$

Note that for any non-empty set A, $\text{val}_t(A) \neq 0$ as the first two terms are integers and $|A|/(|T| + 1) \in (0, 1)$. Furthermore, val_t is additive: for two disjoint sets A and B, $\text{val}_t(A \sqcup B) = \text{val}_t(A) + \text{val}_t(B)$. For any time t and a cached node u, we define

$$H_t(u) = \arg\max_D \{\text{val}_t(D) : D \text{ is a non-empty tree cap rooted at } u\}.$$

Our scheme maintains the value $H_t(u)$ for any cached node u. To this end, we observe that $H_t(u)$ can be defined recursively as follows. Let $H'_t(u) = H_t(u)$ if $\text{val}_t(H_t(u)) > 0$ and $H'_t(u) = \emptyset$ otherwise. Then, for any node v and time t, by the additivity of val_t,

$$H_t(u) = \{u\} \sqcup \bigsqcup_{w \text{ is a child of } u} H'_t(w).$$

Each cached node u keeps the value $\text{val}_t(H_t(u))$. Note that set $H_t(u)$ itself can be recovered from this information: we iterate over all children of u (at most $\deg(T)$ of them) and for each child w, if $\text{val}_t(H_t(w)) > 0$, we recursively compute set $H_t(w)$. Thus, the total time for constructing $H_t(u)$ is $O(\deg(T) \cdot |H_t(u)|)$.

During an execution of TC, we update stored values accordingly. That is, whenever a counter at a cached node v_t is incremented, we update $\text{val}_t(H_t(u))$ values for each cached ancestor u of v_t, starting from $u = v_t$ and proceeding towards the cached tree root. Any such update can be performed in constant time, and the total time is thus $O(h(T))$. For a cache change, we process nodes from the changeset iteratively, starting with nodes closest to the root in case of an eviction and furthest from the root in case of a fetch. For any such node u, we appropriately stop or start maintaining the corresponding value of $\text{val}_t(H_t(u))$. The latter requires looking up the stored values at all its children. As u does not have cached ancestors, sets H_t (and hence also the stored values) at other nodes remain unchanged. In total, the cost of updating all H_t values at time t is at most $O(h(T) + \deg(T) \cdot |X_t|)$.

Finally, we show how to use sets H_t to quickly choose a valid changeset for eviction. Recall that for a negative request v_t, the changeset to be evicted has to be a tree cap rooted at u, where u is the root of a cached subtree containing v_t. For succinctness, we use H^u to denote $H_t(u)$. We show that if $\text{val}_t(H^u) < 0$, then there is no valid negative changeset that is saturated, and hence TC does not perform any action, and if $\text{val}_t(H^u) > 0$, then H^u is both saturated and maximal, and hence TC may evict H^u.

(1) First, assume that $\text{val}_t(H^u) < 0$. Then, for any tree cap X rooted at u, it holds that $\text{cnt}_t(X) - |X| \cdot \alpha < \text{val}_t(X) \leq \text{val}_t(H^u) < 0$, i.e., X is not saturated, and hence cannot be evicted by TC.

(2) Second, assume that $\text{val}_t(H^u) > 0$. As $\text{cnt}_t(H^u) - |H^u| \cdot \alpha$ is an integer and $|H^u|/(|T| + 1) < 1$, it holds that $\text{cnt}_t(H^u) - |H^u| \cdot \alpha \geq 0$, i.e., H^u is saturated. Moreover, by Lemma 5.1, $\text{cnt}_t(H^u) \leq |H^u| \cdot \alpha$, and therefore $\text{cnt}_t(H^u) - |H^u| \cdot \alpha = 0$, i.e., $\text{val}_t(H^u) = |H^u|/(|T| + 1)$. It remains to show that H^u is maximal, i.e., there is no valid saturated changeset $Y \supsetneq H^u$. By Lemma 5.1, Y has to be a tree cap rooted at u as well. If Y was saturated, $\text{val}_t(Y) = \text{cnt}_t(Y) - |Y| \cdot \alpha + |Y|/(|T| + 1) \geq |Y|/(|T| + 1) > |H^u|/(|T| + 1) = \text{val}_t(H^u)$, which would contradict the definition of H^u.

Note that node u can be found in time $O(h(T))$, and the actual set H^u (of size $|X_t|$) can be computed in time $O(\deg(T) \cdot |X_t|)$. Therefore the total time for finding set $|X_t|$ is $O(h(T) + \deg(T) \cdot |X_t|)$.

7 CONCLUSIONS

This paper defines a novel variant of online paging which finds applications in the context of IP routing networks where forwarding rules can be cached. We presented a deterministic online algorithm that achieves a provably competitive trade-off between the benefit of caching and update costs.

It is worth noting that, in the offline setting, choosing the best static cache in the presence of only positive requests is known as a *tree sparsity* problem and can be solved in $O(|T|^2)$ time [4].

We believe that our work opens interesting directions for future research. Most importantly, it will be interesting to study the optimality of the derived result; we conjecture that the true competitive ratio does not depend on the tree height. In particular, primal-dual approaches that were successfully applied for other caching problems [3, 5, 34] may turn out to be useful also for the considered variant.

ACKNOWLEDGEMENTS

The authors would like to thank Fred Baker from Cisco, Moti Medina from the Max-Planck-Institute and Paweł Gawrychowski from University of Wrocław for useful inputs.

REFERENCES

[1] BGP Statistics from Route-Views Data. http://bgp.potaroo.net/bgprpts/rva-index.html.

[2] Dimitris Achlioptas, Marek Chrobak, and John Noga. 2000. Competitive analysis of randomized paging algorithms. *Theoretical Computer Science* 234, 1–2 (2000), 203–218.

[3] Anna Adamaszek, Artur Czumaj, Matthias Englert, and Harald Räcke. 2012. An $O(\log k)$-competitive algorithm for generalized caching. In *23rd ACM-SIAM Symp. on Discrete Algorithms (SODA)*. 1681–1689.

[4] Arturs Backurs, Piotr Indyk, and Ludwig Schmidt. 2017. Better Approximations for Tree Sparsity in Nearly-Linear Time. In *Proc. 28th ACM-SIAM Symp. on Discrete Algorithms (SODA)*. 2215–2229.

[5] Nikhil Bansal, Niv Buchbinder, and Joseph Naor. 2012. Randomized Competitive Algorithms for Generalized Caching. *SIAM J. Comput.* 41, 2 (2012), 391–414.

[6] Marcin Bienkowski, Nadi Sarrar, Stefan Schmid, and Steve Uhlig. 2014. Competitive FIB Aggregation without Update Churn. In *Proc. 34th IEEE Int. Conf. on Distributed Computing Systems (ICDCS)*. 607–616.

[7] Marcin Bienkowski and Stefan Schmid. 2013. Competitive FIB Aggregation for Independent Prefixes: Online Ski Rental on the Trie. In *Proc. 20th Int. Colloq. on Structural Information and Communication Complexity (SIROCCO)*. 92–103.

[8] Mark Brehob, Richard J. Enbody, Eric Torng, and Stephen Wagner. 2003. On-line Restricted Caching. *Journal of Scheduling* 6, 2 (2003), 149–166.

[9] Niv Buchbinder, Shahar Chen, and Joseph Naor. 2014. Competitive Algorithms for Restricted Caching and Matroid Caching. In *Proc. 22th European Symp. on Algorithms (ESA)*. 209–221.

[10] Marek Chrobak, Howard J. Karloff, Thomas H. Payne, and Sundar Vishwanathan. 1991. New Results on Server Problems. *SIAM Journal on Discrete Mathematics* 4, 2 (1991), 172–181.

[11] Luca Cittadini, Wolfgang Muhlbauer, Steve Uhlig, Randy Bushy, Pierre Francois, and Olaf Maennel. 2010. Evolution of internet address space deaggregation: myths and reality. *IEEE J.Sel. A. Commun.* 28, 8 (2010), 1238–1249.

[12] Richard P. Draves, Christopher King, Srinivasan Venkatachary, and Brian D. Zill. 1999. Constructing optimal IP routing tables. In *Proc. 18th IEEE Int. Conf. on Computer Communications (INFOCOM)*. 88–97.

[13] Leah Epstein, Csanád Imreh, Asaf Levin, and Judit Nagy-György. 2015. Online File Caching with Rejection Penalties. *Algorithmica* 71, 2 (2015), 279–306.

[14] Amos Fiat, Richard M. Karp, Michael Luby, Lyle A. McGeoch, Daniel D. Sleator, and Neal E. Young. 1991. Competitive paging algorithms. *Journal of Algorithms* 12, 4 (1991), 685–699.

[15] Pierre François, Clarence Filsfils, John Evans, and Olivier Bonaventure. 2005. Achieving sub-second IGP convergence in large IP networks. *ACM SIGCOMM Computer Communication Review* 35, 3, 35–44.

[16] Danny Yuxing Huang, Ken Yocum, and Alex C. Snoeren. 2013. High-fidelity switch models for software-defined network emulation. In *Proc. 2ndACM SIGCOMM Workshop on Hot Topics in Software Defined Networking (HotSDN)*. 43–48.

[17] Sandy Irani. 2002. Page Replacement with Multi-Size Pages and Applications to Web Caching. *Algorithmica* 33, 3 (2002), 384–409.

[18] Elliott Karpilovsky, Matthew Caesar, Jennifer Rexford, Aman Shaikh, and Jacobus E. van der Merwe. 2012. Practical Network-Wide Compression of IP Routing Tables. *IEEE Transactions on Network and Service Management* 9, 4 (2012), 446–458.

[19] Naga Katta, Omid Alipourfard, Jennifer Rexford, and David Walker. 2016. CacheFlow: Dependency-Aware Rule-Caching for Software-Defined Networks. In *Proc. ACM Symposium on SDN Research (SOSR)*.

[20] Changhoon Kim, Matthew Caesar, Alexandre Gerber, and Jennifer Rexford. 2009. Revisiting Route Caching: The World Should Be Flat. In *Proc. 10th Int. Conf. on Passive and Active Network Measurement (PAM)*. 3–12.

[21] Huan Liu. 2001. Routing prefix caching in network processor design. In *Proc. 10th Int. Conf. on Computer Communications and Networks (ICCCN)*. 18–23.

[22] Yaoqing Liu, Vince Lehman, and Lan Wang. 2015. Efficient FIB caching using minimal non-overlapping prefixes. *Computer Networks* 83 (2015), 85–99.

[23] Yaoqing Liu, Beichuan Zhang, and Lan Wang. 2013. FIFA: Fast incremental FIB aggregation. In *Proc. 32nd IEEE Int. Conf. on Computer Communications (INFOCOM)*. 1213–1221.

[24] Yaoqing Liu, Xin Zhao, Kyuhan Nam, Lan Wang, and Beichuan Zhang. 2010. Incremental Forwarding Table Aggregation. In *Proc. Global Communications Conference (GLOBECOM)*. 1–6.

[25] Layong Luo, Gaogang Xie, Kavé Salamatian, Steve Uhlig, Laurent Mathy, and Yingke Xie. 2013. A trie merging approach with incremental updates for virtual routers. In *Proc. 32nd IEEE Int. Conf. on Computer Communications (INFOCOM)*. 1222–1230.

[26] Lyle A. McGeoch and Daniel D. Sleator. 1991. A Strongly Competitive Randomized Paging Algorithm. *Algorithmica* 6, 6 (1991), 816–825.

[27] Manor Mendel and Steven S. Seiden. 2004. Online companion caching. *Theoretical Computer Science* 324, 2–3 (2004), 183–200.

[28] Gábor Rétvári, János Tapolcai, Attila Korösi, András Majdán, and Zalán Heszberger. 2013. Compressing IP forwarding tables: towards entropy bounds and beyond. In *Proc. ACM SIGCOMM Conference*. 111–122.

[29] Nadi Sarrar, Steve Uhlig, Anja Feldmann, Rob Sherwood, and Xin Huang. 2012. Leveraging Zipf's law for traffic offloading. *ACM SIGCOMM Computer Communication Review* 42, 1 (2012), 16–22.

[30] Daniel D. Sleator and Robert E. Tarjan. 1985. Amortized efficiency of list update and paging rules. *Commun. ACM* 28, 2 (1985), 202–208.

[31] Ed Spitznagel, David E. Taylor, and Jonathan S. Turner. 2003. Packet Classification Using Extended TCAMs. In *Proc. 11th IEEE Int. Conf. on Network Protocols (ICNP)*. 120–131.

[32] Subhash Suri, Tuomas Sandholm, and Priyank Ramesh Warkhede. 2003. Compressing Two-Dimensional Routing Tables. *Algorithmica* 35, 4 (2003), 287–300.

[33] Zartash Afzal Uzmi, Markus E. Nebel, Ahsan Tariq, Sana Jawad, Ruichuan Chen, Aman Shaikh, Jia Wang, and Paul Francis. 2011. SMALTA: practical and near-optimal FIB aggregation. In *Proc. 7th Int. Conf. on Emerging Networking Experiments and Technologies (CoNEXT)*.

[34] Neal E. Young. 1994. The k-Server Dual and Loose Competitiveness for Paging. *Algorithmica* 11, 6 (1994), 525–541.

[35] Neal E. Young. 2002. On-Line File Caching. *Algorithmica* 33, 3 (2002), 371–383.

[36] Xin Zhao, Yaoqing Liu, Lan Wang, and Beichuan Zhang. 2010. On the aggregatability of router forwarding tables. In *Proc. 29th IEEE Int. Conf. on Computer Communications (INFOCOM)*. 848–856.

A PROOF OF LEMMA 5.1

Before proving Lemma 5.1, we present the following technical claim.

Claim A.1. *For any phase P, the following invariants hold for any time $t > begin(P)$:*

1. $cnt_{t-1}(X) < |X| \cdot \alpha$ *for a valid changeset X for* C_t,
2. $cnt_t(X) \leq |X| \cdot \alpha$ *for a valid changeset X for* C_t,
3. *any changeset X with property* $cnt_t(X) = |X| \cdot \alpha$ *contains the node requested at round t.*

Proof. First observe that Invariant 1 (for time t) along with the fact that round t contains only one request immediately implies that $\mathrm{cnt}_t(X) \leq \mathrm{cnt}_{t-1}(X) + 1 \leq (|X| \cdot \alpha - 1) + 1 = |X| \cdot \alpha$, i.e., Invariant 2 for time t. Furthermore the equality may hold only for changesets containing the node requested at round t, which implies Invariant 3 for time t.

It remains to show that Invariant 1 holds for any step $t >$ begin(P). It is trivially true for $t =$ begin$(P) + 1$ as $\text{cnt}_{t-1}(X) = 0$ then. Let $t + 1$ be the earliest time in phase P for which Invariant 1 does not hold; we will then show a contradiction with the definition of TC or a contradiction with other Invariants at time t. That is, we assume that there exists a positive changeset X for C_{t+1} such that $\text{cnt}_t(X) \geq |X| \cdot \alpha$ (the proof for a negative changeset is analogous). Note that TC must have performed an action (fetch or eviction) at time t as otherwise X would be also a changeset for $C_t = C_{t+1}$ with $\text{cnt}_t(X) \geq |X| \cdot \alpha$, which means that X should have been applied by TC at time t. We consider two cases.

If TC fetches a positive changeset Y at time t, $C_{t+1} = C_t \sqcup Y$ and $\text{cnt}_t(Y) = |Y| \cdot \alpha$. Then, $Y \sqcup X$ is a changeset for C_t, and $\text{cnt}_t(Y \sqcup X) \geq |Y \sqcup X| \cdot \alpha$. This contradicts the maximality property of set Y chosen at time t by TC.

If TC evicts a negative changeset Y at time t, $C_{t+1} = C_t \setminus Y$. Invariant 2 and the definition of TC implies $\text{cnt}_t(Y) = |Y| \cdot \alpha$, and thus, by Invariant 3, Y contains the node requested at round t. As $X \cap Y \subseteq C_t, X \cap Y$ does not have any positive requests at time t, and therefore $\text{cnt}_t(X \setminus Y) = \text{cnt}_t(X) \geq |X| \cdot \alpha \geq |X \setminus Y| \cdot \alpha$. By Invariant 2, $\text{cnt}_t(X \setminus Y) \leq |X \setminus Y| \cdot \alpha$, and hence $\text{cnt}_t(X \setminus Y) = |X \setminus Y| \cdot \alpha$. This contradicts Invariant 3 as $X \setminus Y$ cannot contain the node requested at round t (because Y contains this node). □

Proof of Lemma 5.1. The inequality $\text{cnt}_t(X) \leq |X| \cdot \alpha$ is equivalent to Invariant 2 of Claim A.1. Assume now that X is applied at time t. By the definition of TC, $\text{cnt}_t(X) \geq |X| \cdot \alpha$, and thus $\text{cnt}_t(X) = |X| \cdot \alpha$, i.e., Property 2 follows. Then, Invariant 3 of Claim A.1 implies Property 1. Finally, Invariant 1 of Claim A.1 for time $t + 1$ is equivalent to Property 3.

To show Property 4, observe that the changeset X applied at time t cannot be a disjoint union of two (or more) valid changesets X_1 and X_2. By Property 2, $|X| \cdot \alpha = \text{cnt}_t(X) = \text{cnt}_t(X_1) + \text{cnt}_t(X_2)$. If $\text{cnt}_t(X_1) < |X_1| \cdot \alpha$ or $\text{cnt}_t(X_2) < |X_2| \cdot \alpha$, then $\text{cnt}_t(X_1) + \text{cnt}_t(X_2) < (|X_1| + |X_2|) \cdot \alpha = |X| \cdot \alpha$, a contradiction. Therefore, $\text{cnt}_t(X_1) = |X_1| \cdot \alpha$ and $\text{cnt}_t(X_2) = |X_2| \cdot \alpha$. But then Invariant 3 of Claim A.1 would imply that both X_1 and X_2 contain a node requested at time t, which is a contradiction as they are disjoint.

Therefore, if X is a positive changeset applied at t, then X is a single tree cap of a tree from subforest C_{t+1}, and likewise if X is negative, then X is a single tree cap of a tree from subforest C_t. □

B MINIMIZING FORWARDING TABLES USING TREE CACHING

In this section, we present a formal argument showing why we can use any q-competitive online algorithm A_T for the tree caching problem to obtain a $2q$-competitive online algorithm A that minimizes forwarding tables.

Namely, we take any input I for the latter problem and create, in online fashion, an input I_T for the tree caching problem in a way described in Section 2. For any solution for I_T, we may replay its actions (fetches and evictions) on I and vice versa. However, there is one place, where these solutions may have different costs. Recall that an update of a rule stored at node v in I is mapped to a *chunk* of α negative requests to v in I_T. It is then possible that an algorithm for I_T modifies the cache *during* a chunk. An algorithm that never performs such an action is called *canonical*.

To alleviate this issue, we first note that any algorithm B for I_T can be transformed into a canonical solution B' by postponing all cache modifications that occur during some chunk to the time right after it. Such a transformation may increase the cost of a solution on a chunk at most by α and such an increase occurs only when B modifies a cache within this chunk. Hence, the additional cost of transformation can be mapped to the already existing cost of B, and thus the cost of B' is at most by a factor of 2 larger than that of B.

Furthermore, note that there is a natural cost-preserving bijection between solutions to I and canonical solutions to I_T (solutions perform same cache modifications). Hence, the algorithm A for I runs A_T on I_T, transforms it in an online manner into the canonical solution $A'_T(I_T)$, and replays its cache modification on I. Then, $A(I) = A'_T(I_T) \leq 2 \cdot A_T(I_T) \leq 2q \cdot \text{Opt}(I_T) \leq 2q \cdot \text{Opt}(I)$.

The second inequality follows immediately by the q-competitiveness of A_T. The third inequality follows by replaying cache modifications as well, but this time we take solution $\text{Opt}(I)$ and replay its actions on I_T, creating a canonical (not necessarily optimal) solution of the same cost.

C LOWER BOUND ON THE COMPETITIVE RATIO

Theorem C.1. *For any $\alpha \geq 1$, the competitive ratio of any deterministic online algorithm for the online tree caching problem is at least $\Omega(k_{\text{ONL}}/(k_{\text{ONL}} - k_{\text{OPT}} + 1))$*

Proof. We will assume that in the tree caching problem, evictions are free (this changes the cost by at most by a factor of two). We consider a tree whose leaves correspond to the set of all pages in the paging problem. The rest of the tree will be irrelevant.

For any input sequence I for the paging problem, we may create a sequence I_T for tree caching, where a request to a page is replaced by α requests to the corresponding leaf. Now, we claim that any solution A for I of cost c can be transformed, in online manner, into a solution A_T for I_T of cost $\Theta(\alpha \cdot c)$ and vice versa.

If upon a request r, an algorithm A fetches r to the cache and evicts some pages, then A_T bypasses α corresponding requests to leaf r, fetches r afterwards and evicts the corresponding leaves, paying $O(\alpha)$ times the cost of A. By doing it iteratively, A_T ensures that its cache is equivalent to that of A. In particular, a request free for A is also free for A_T.

Now take any algorithm A_T for I_T. It can be transformed to the algorithm A'_T that (i) keeps only leaves of the tree in the cache and (ii) performs actions only at times that are multiplicities of α (losing at most a constant factor in comparison to A_T). Then, fix any chunk of α requests to some leaf r' immediately followed by some fetches and evictions of A'_T leaves. Upon seeing the corresponding request r' in I, the algorithm A performs fetches and evictions on the corresponding pages. In effect, the cost of A is $O(1/\alpha)$ times the cost of A_T.

The bidirectional reduction described above preserves competitive ratios up to a constant factor. Hence, applying the adversarial strategy for the paging problem that enforces the competitive ratio $R = k_{\text{ONL}}/(k_{\text{ONL}} - k_{\text{OPT}} + 1)$ [30] immediately implies the lower bound of $\Omega(R)$ on the competitive ratio for the tree caching problem. □

Provably Efficient Scheduling of Cache-oblivious Wavefront Algorithms

Rezaul Chowdhury
Stony Brook University, Stony Brook, NY 11790
rezaul@cs.stonybrook.edu

Pramod Ganapathi
Stony Brook University, Stony Brook, NY 11790
pganapathi@cs.stonybrook.edu

Yuan Tang
School of Comp. Science, School of Software, Fudan Univ.
Shanghai Key Lab. of Intelligent Information Processing
State Key Lab. of Comp. Arch. ICT, CAS, China
yuantang@fudan.edu.cn

Jesmin Jahan Tithi
Intel Corporation
California, USA
jesmin.jahan.tithi@intel.com

ABSTRACT

Iterative wavefront algorithms for evaluating dynamic programming recurrences exploit optimal parallelism but show poor cache performance. Tiled-iterative wavefront algorithms achieve optimal cache complexity and high parallelism but are cache-aware and hence are not portable and not cache-adaptive. On the other hand, standard cache-oblivious recursive divide-and-conquer algorithms have optimal serial cache complexity but often have low parallelism due to artificial dependencies among subtasks.

Recently, we introduced cache-oblivious recursive wavefront (COW) algorithms, which do not have any artificial dependencies, but they are too complicated to develop, analyze, implement, and generalize. Though COW algorithms are based on fork-join primitives, they extensively use atomic operations for ensuring correctness, and as a result, performance guarantees (i.e., parallel running time and parallel cache complexity) provided by state-of-the-art schedulers (e.g., the randomized work-stealing scheduler) for programs with fork-join primitives do not apply. Also, extensive use of atomic locks may result in high overhead in implementation.

In this paper, we show how to systematically transform standard cache-oblivious recursive divide-and-conquer algorithms into recursive wavefront algorithms to achieve optimal parallel cache complexity and high parallelism under state-of-the-art schedulers for fork-join programs. Unlike COW algorithms these new algorithms do not use atomic operations. Instead, they use closed-form formulas to compute the time when each divide-and-conquer function must be launched in order to achieve high parallelism without losing cache performance. The resulting implementations are arguably much simpler than implementations of known COW algorithms. We present theoretical analyses and experimental performance and scalability results showing a superiority of these new algorithms over existing algorithms.

Keywords: wavefront; cache-oblivious; parallel; recursive; divide-and-conquer; dynamic programming; parallelism

SPAA '17, July 24-26, 2017, Washington DC, USA
© 2017 ACM. 978-1-4503-4593-4/17/07...$15.00
DOI: 10.1145/3087556.3087586

1 INTRODUCTION

Dynamic programming (DP) is a popular algorithm design technique to solve optimization problems that exhibit the properties of overlapping subproblems and optimal substructure. The process involves dividing a problem into smaller subproblems, solving them, storing their results in tables to avoid recomputations, and combining those solutions. DP is used in many real-world application areas, and extensively in computational biology [6, 22, 31, 52].

For good performance on a modern multicore machine with a cache hierarchy, algorithms must have good parallelism and should be able to use the caches efficiently at the same time. Iterative wavefront algorithms for solving DP problems have optimal parallelism but often suffer due to poor cache performance. On the other hand, though standard cache-oblivious [24] recursive divide-and-conquer DP algorithms have optimal serial cache complexity, they often have low parallelism. The tiled-iterative wavefront algorithms achieve optimality in cache complexity and achieve high parallelism but are cache-aware, and hence are not portable and do not adapt well when available cache space fluctuates during execution in a multiprogramming environment. Very recently, the *cache-oblivious wavefront (COW) algorithms* [46, 47] have been proposed that have optimal parallelism and optimal serial cache complexity. However, though those algorithms are based on fork-join primitives, they extensively use atomic operations for correctness. But, the current theory of scheduling nested parallel programs with fork-join primitives does not hold for such atomic operations. As a result, no bounds on parallel running time and parallel cache complexity could be proved for those algorithms. Those algorithms are also very difficult to implement since they require hacking into a parallel runtime system. Extensive use of atomic locks causes too much overhead for very large and higher dimensional DPs.

We present a provably efficient method for scheduling cache-oblivious recursive divide-and-conquer wavefront algorithms on a multicore machine which optimizes parallel cache complexity and achieves high parallelism. Our algorithms are based on fork-join primitives but do not use atomic operations. As a result, we are able to analyze their parallel running times and parallel cache complexities easily under the state-of-the-art schedulers for fork-join based parallel programs. Our algorithms are also much simpler to implement compared to COW algorithms.

Performance of a parallel program on multicores. We analyze the performance of a parallel program run on a shared-memory multicore machine using the *work-span* model [19]. The *work* of a multithreaded program, denoted by $T_1(n)$, where n is the input parameter, is the total number of CPU operations performed when run on a single processor[1]. The *span* (a.k.a. critical-path length or depth), denoted by $T_\infty(n)$, is the maximum number of operations performed on any processor when the program is run on an infinite number of processors. The *parallel running time* $T_p(n)$ of a program when scheduled by a greedy scheduler [11] on p processors is given by $T_p(n) = O\left(T_1(n)/p + T_\infty(n)\right)$. The *parallelism*, computed by the ratio of $T_1(n)$ and $T_\infty(n)$, is defined as the average amount of work done per step of the critical path. The notations and their meanings are summarized in Table 1.

Symb.	Meaning
n	Input parameter
n'	Switching point (to non-wavefront)
r	Parameter $\in [1, n]$
p	Number of processors
M	Cache size
B	Cache line size
T_1	Work or total #computations
T_∞	Span or critical-path length
T_p	Parallel running time
T_1/T_∞	Parallelism
Q_1	Serial cache complexity
Q_p	Parallel cache complexity
S_p	Extra-space complexity

Table 1: Standard notations used throughout the paper.

Cache complexity is a performance metric that counts the number of block transfers (or cache misses or I/O transfers or page faults) triggered by a program between adjacent levels of caches in a memory hierarchy. By Q_p we denote the total number of cache misses on a p-processor machine. So Q_1 is the *serial cache complexity*. We say that an algorithm has *spatial locality* provided each cache block it brings into a cache contains as much useful data as possible. We say that it has *temporal locality* provided it performs as much useful work as possible on each cache block it brings into a cache before the block gets evicted from the cache.

Iterative algorithms. Traditionally, DP algorithms are implemented using a series of (nested) loops and they can be parallelized easily. These algorithms often have good spatial locality, but no temporal locality and standard implementations may not have optimal parallelism either. For example, an iterative algorithm for the parenthesis problem [49] (shown in Figure 1 and explained in Section 2) has $T_\infty(n) = \Theta\left(n^2\right)$ and $Q_1(n) = \Theta\left(n^3\right)$.

Iterative algorithms are also implemented as tiled loops, in which case the entire DP table is blocked or tiled and the tiles are executed iteratively. For example, for a tiled iterative algorithm for the parenthesis problem with $r \times r$ tile size, where $r \in [2, n]$, we have $T_\infty(n) = \Theta\left((n/r)^2\right) \cdot \Theta\left(r^2\right) = \Theta\left(n^2\right)$, and $Q_1(n, r) = (n/r)^3 \cdot O\left(r^2/B + r\right) = O\left(n^3/(rB) + n^3/r^2\right)$.

Fastest iterative DP implementations have the following wavefront-like property. Let a single update on a cell x in the DP table needs to be applied by reading from cells $y_1, y_2, \ldots, y_s$. When the cells $y_1, y_2, \ldots, y_s$ are completely updated, then the cell x can immediately get updated, either partially or fully.

Recursive algorithms. Cache-oblivious parallel recursive divide-and-conquer DP algorithms can overcome many of the limitations of their iterative counterparts. While iterative algorithms often have poor or no temporal locality, recursive algorithms have excellent and often optimal temporal locality. One problem with recursive divide-and-conquer algorithms is that they trade off parallelism for cache optimality, and thus may end up with suboptimal parallelism.

[1]unless specified otherwise, we will use "processor" and "processing core" synonymously

```
PAR-LOOP-PARENTHESIS(C, n)
for t ← 2 to n − 1 do
  parallel for i ← 1 to n − t do
    j ← t + i
    for k ← i + 1 to j do
      C[i, j] ← min (C[i, j], C[i, k] + C[k, j] + w(i, k, j))
```

Figure 1: Parallel iterative algorithm for solving the parenthesis problem (a.k.a. the matrix-chain multiplication problem) which computes an optimal way to parenthesize a sequence of n matrices so that the cost of multiplying them is minimum.

For example, a 2-way recursive algorithm (where, each dimension of the subtask will be half the dimension of its parent task) for the parenthesis problem has $T_\infty(n) = \Theta\left(n^{\log_2 3}\right)$ and $Q_1(n) = \Theta\left(n^3/(B\sqrt{M})\right)$, that is, it has optimal serial cache complexity but suboptimal span [49]. For n-way recursive algorithm, $T_\infty(n) = \Theta(n \log n)$ and $Q_1(n) = O\left(n^3\right)$. This time, the span is almost linear in n but the serial cache complexity is the worst possible. Ideally, we want to have a balance between cache complexity and span by choosing r-way recursive algorithm in which case neither the span nor the parallel cache complexity will be the best possible, however, will have best practical performance.

Source of suboptimal parallelism in recursive algorithms. The suboptimal parallelism in 2-way recursive algorithms results from artificial dependencies among subproblems that are not implied by the underlying DP recurrence [47]. We use the 2-way recursive divide-and-conquer algorithm for the *Longest Common Subsequence* (LCS) problem as an example below.

For the LCS problem, each cell (i, j) in the DP table depends on a cell to its left $(i, j-1)$, a cell above $(i-1, j)$ and a cell on the diagonal $(i-1, j-1)$. The 2-way recursive divide-and-conquer algorithm for the LCS problem splits the DP table X into four equal quadrants: X_{11} (top-left), X_{12} (top-right), X_{21} (bottom-left), and X_{22} (bottom-right). It then recursively computes the quadrants in a way that respects the cell dependencies among the quadrants: first X_{11}, then X_{12} and X_{21} in parallel, and finally X_{22}. Notice that, the top-left quadrants of X_{12} and X_{21} i.e., $X_{12,11}$ and $X_{21,11}$, respectively, can only start executing when the execution of the bottom-right quadrant of X_{11} i.e., $X_{11,22}$ completes. These dependencies amomg subtasks are not implied by the DP recurrence but arise from the recursive structure of the algorithm. $X_{12,11}$ (resp. $X_{21,11}$) can start executing as soon as $X_{11,12}$ (resp. $X_{11,21}$) is done. We call these dependencies *artificial dependencies* and they appear at several different granularities. Most often, these artificial dependencies asymptotically increase the span, thereby reducing parallelism.

Recursive wavefront algorithms. By removing artificial dependencies from the recursive algorithms, it is possible to develop algorithms that simultaneously achieve parallel cache-optimality, near-optimal parallelism, and cache-obliviousness. Such algorithms are called *recursive wavefront* (or *cache-oblivious wavefront*) *algorithms*.

The recursive wavefront algorithms were introduced in [47]. However, those algorithms (also called COW algorithms) are too complicated to develop, analyze, implement, and generalize. Atomic

```
𝒜(X, X, X)
if X is a cell then 𝒜_cell(X, X, X)
else
  parallel: 𝒜(X11, X11, X11), 𝒜(X22, X22, X22)
  ℬ(X12, X11, X22)
```

```
ℬ(X, U, V)
if X is a cell then ℬ_cell(X, U, V)
else
  ℬ(X21, U22, V11)
  parallel: 𝒞(X11, U12, X21), 𝒞(X22, X21, V12)
  parallel: ℬ(X11, U11, V11), ℬ(X22, U22, V22)
  𝒞(X12, U12, X22)
  𝒞(X12, X11, V12)
  ℬ(X12, U11, V22)
```

```
𝒞(X, U, V)
if X is a cell then 𝒞_cell(X, U, V)
else
  parallel: 𝒞(X11, U11, V11), 𝒞(X12, U11, V12),
            𝒞(X21, U21, V11), 𝒞(X22, U21, V12)
  parallel: 𝒞(X11, U12, V21), 𝒞(X12, U12, V22),
            𝒞(X21, U22, V21), 𝒞(X22, U22, V22)
```

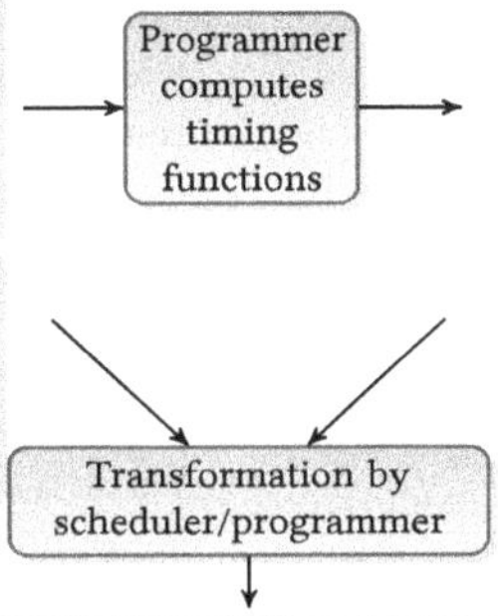


```
S_𝒜(X, X, X)
return ℭ(x_r, x_c)
```

```
S_ℬ(X, U, V)
return ℭ(x_r + n − 1, x_c)
```

```
S_𝒞(X, U, V)
m ← (x_r + n − 1 + x_c)/2; û ← u_c + n − 1
if u_c > m then return max {ℭ(u_r + n − 1, u_c), ℭ(u_c, x_c)} + 1
elif û < m then return max {ℭ(u_r + n − 1, û), ℭ(û, x_c)} + 1
else return
  (max {ℭ(u_r + n − 1, m), ℭ(m, x_c)} + 1).[u_c > (x_r + x_c)/2]
```

```
E_𝒜(X, X, X)
return ℭ(x_r, x_c+n−1)
```

```
E_ℬ(X, U, V)
return ℭ(x_r, x_c+n−1)
```

```
E_𝒞(X, U, V)
lval ← max {ℭ(u_r, u_c), ℭ(u_c, x_c + n − 1)}
rval ← max {ℭ(u_r, u_c + n − 1), ℭ(u_c + n − 1, x_c + n − 1)}
return (max {lval, rval} + 1).[u_c > (x_r + x_c)/2]
```

```
ℭ(i, j)
if (j − i) ≤ 1 then return (j − i) else return 2 × (j − i) − 1
```

```
RECURSIVE-WAVEFRONT-PARENTHESIS()
w ← 0
while w < ∞ do w ← 𝒜(G, G, G, w)
```

```
𝒜(X, X, X, w)
v_i ← ∞ for all i ∈ [1, 3]
if X is an n' × n' matrix then
  if w = S_𝒜(X, X, X) then 𝒜_chunk(X, X, X)
else
  ℱ_1..3 ← {𝒜, 𝒜, ℬ}
  arg_1..3 ← {(X11, X11, X11), (X22, X22, X22),
              (X12, X11, X22)}
  parallel: for i ← 1 to 3 do
    if w < S_ℱi(arg_i) then v_i ← S_ℱi(arg_i)
    elif w ≤ E_ℱi(arg_i) then v_i ← ℱ_i(arg_i, w)
  sync
return min v_i for all i ∈ [1, 3]
```

```
ℬ(X, U, V, w)
v_i ← ∞ for all i ∈ [1, 8]
if X is an n' × n' matrix then
  if w = S_ℬ(X, U, V) then ℬ_chunk(X, U, V)
else
  ℱ_1..8 ← {ℬ, 𝒞, 𝒞, ℬ, ℬ, 𝒞, 𝒞, ℬ}
  arg_1..8 ← {(X21, U22, V11), (X11, U12, X21),
              (X22, X21, V12), (X11, U11, V11),
              (X22, U22, V22), (X12, U12, X22),
              (X12, X11, V12), (X12, U11, V22)}
  parallel: for i ← 1 to 8 do
    if w < S_ℱi(arg_i) then v_i ← S_ℱi(arg_i)
    elif w ≤ E_ℱi(arg_i) then v_i ← ℱ_i(arg_i, w)
  sync
return min v_i for all i ∈ [1, 8]
```

```
𝒞(X, U, V, w)
v_i ← ∞ for all i ∈ [1, 8]
if X is an n' × n' matrix then
  if w = S_𝒞(X, U, V) then 𝒞_chunk(X, U, V)
else
  ℱ_1..8 ← {𝒞, 𝒞, 𝒞, 𝒞, 𝒞, 𝒞, 𝒞, 𝒞}
  arg_1..8 ← {(X11, U11, V11), (X12, U11, V12),
              (X21, U21, V11), (X22, U21, V12),
              (X11, U12, V21), (X12, U12, V22),
              (X21, U22, V21), (X22, U22, V22)}
  parallel: for i ← 1 to 8 do
    if w < S_ℱi(arg_i) then v_i ← S_ℱi(arg_i)
    elif w ≤ E_ℱi(arg_i) then v_i ← ℱ_i(arg_i, w)
  sync
return min v_i for all i ∈ [1, 8]
```

Figure 2: TOP: The programmer derives the timing functions (top-right) from a given standard 2-way recursive divide-and-conquer DP algorithm for the parenthesis problem (top-left). A region Z has its top-left corner at (z_r, z_c) and is of size $n \times n$. BOTTOM: A recursive divide-and-conquer wavefront algorithm is generated for the parenthesis problem. The programmer derives the algorithm if work-stealing scheduler (see Section 4.1) is used and the scheduler derives the algorithm if W-SB scheduler (see Section 4.2) is used. The algorithm makes use of the timing functions derived by the programmer.

operations were used to identify and launch ready tasks, and implementations required hacking into Cilk's runtime system. No bounds on parallel cache complexities of those algorithms are known.

In this paper, we present a generic method to schedule recursive wavefront algorithms based on timing functions. These algorithms have a structure similar to the standard recursive divide-and-conquer algorithms, but each recursive function call is annotated with start-time and end-time hints that are passed to the scheduler. The task scheduler will make sure that the algorithms are executed in a wavefront fashion using the timing functions. Indeed, the actions the scheduler is expected to take based on the timing functions is straightforward, and a programmer may choose to make some straightforward transformations of the code herself and use a scheduler that does not accept hints. The transformed code is still purely based on fork-join parallelism, and the performance bounds (e.g., parallel running time and parallel cache complexity) guaranteed by any scheduler supporting fork-join parallelism apply. The recursive wavefront algorithm for the parenthesis problem has $T_\infty(n) = \Theta(n \log n)$ and $Q_1(n) = O\left(n^3/(B\sqrt{M})\right)$. Bounds on T_p and Q_p can be obtained from scheduler guarantees.

Related work. The tiled iterative algorithms [20, 29, 37, 41, 43, 53] have been studied extensively as tiling is the traditional way of implementing dynamic programming and other matrix algorithms. There are several frameworks to automatically produce tiled codes such as PLuTo [10], Polly [30], and PoCC [38]. However, these software programs are not designed to generate efficient parallel tiled code for non-trivial DP recurrences. The major concerns with tiled programs are that they are cache-aware and sometimes processor-aware that sacrifices portability across machines. Another disadvantage of being cache-aware is that the algorithms are not cache-adaptive [7], i.e., the algorithms do not adapt to changes in available shared cache/memory space during execution and hence may run slower when multiple programs run concurrently in a shared-memory environment [14, 48]. Several existing systems such as Bellman's GAP compiler [28], semi-automatic synthesizer [39], EasyPDP [44], EasyHPS [21], pattern-based system [36], and parallelizing plugins [40] can be used to generate iterative and tiled loop programs. Parallel task graph execution systems such as Nabbit [5] and BDDT [50] execute DP tasks through unrolling, and lack cache efficiency.

The classic 2-way recursive divide-and-conquer algorithms having optimal serial cache complexity and good (but, not always optimal) parallelism have been developed, analyzed, and implemented in [16, 17, 49]. Hybrid r-way algorithms are considered in [16] but they are either cache- or processor-aware and complicated to program. Pochoir [45] is used to generate cache-oblivious implementations of stencil computations. However, the recursive algorithms often have low parallelism due to artificial dependencies among subtasks. Recently Aga et al. in [4] proposed a speculation approach to alleviate the concurrency constraints imposed by the artificial dependencies in standard parallel recursive divide-and-conquer programs and reported up to a 1.6× speedup over their baseline on 30 cores.

The recursive wavefront algorithms were introduced in [47] but they are complicated to develop, analyze, implement, and generalize. They make extensive use of atomic instructions, and standard analysis model of fork-join parallelism does not apply. In this paper, we try to address these issues.

Our contributions. Our major contributions are as follows:
(1) [**Algorithmic.**] We present a generic method to develop and schedule recursive wavefront algorithms based on timing functions. We present two approaches for scheduling a recursive wavefront algorithm: (*i*) the algorithm passes timing functions and space usage info to a hint-accepting space-bounded scheduler, and (*ii*) the programmer appropriately transforms the algorithm to use the timing functions, and uses a standard randomized work-stealing scheduler to run the program.
(2) [**Experimental.**] We present performance and scalability results of the presented algorithms on state-of-the-art multicore machines and show a comparative analysis with standard 2-way recursive divide-and-conquer and the original cache-oblivious wavefront (COW) algorithms from [47].

2 DERIVING RECURSIVE WAVEFRONT ALGORITHMS

In this section, we describe how to transform a standard recursive DP algorithm into a recursive wavefront algorithm. We have shown very recently that for a wide class of DP problems which includes the LCS problem, the parenthesis problem and Floyd-Warshall's all pair shortest path (APSP) problems among others, standard 2-way recursive DP algorithms can be generated automatically from simple iterative descriptions of the underlying DP recurrences [14, 33]. Our transformation [27] involves augmenting all recursive function calls with timing functions to launch them as early as possible without violating any dependency constraints implied by the DP recurrence. The timing functions are derived analytically and do not employ locks or atomic instructions.

Our transformation allows the updates to the DP table proceed in an order close to iterative wavefront, but from within the structure of a recursive divide-and-conquer algorithm. The goal is to reach the higher parallelism of an iterative wavefront algorithm while retaining the better cache performance (i.e., efficiency and adaptivity) and portability (i.e., cache- and processor-obliviousness) of a recursive algorithm [48, 49].

Wavefront Order. Let us first define the *wavefront order* of applying updates to a DP table. Each update writes to one DP table cell by reading values from other cells. We say that a cell is *fully updated* provided it is never updated in the future. An update becomes *ready* when all cells it reads from are fully updated. We assume that only ready updates can be applied and each such update can only be applied once. A wavefront order of updates proceeds in discrete timesteps. In each step, all ready updates to distinct cells are applied in parallel. However, if a cell has multiple ready updates only one of them is applied, and the rest are retained for future. A wavefront order does not have any artificial dependencies.

Transformation. It is completed in three major steps:
(1) [**Construct completion-time function.**] A closed-form formula is derived based on the original DP recurrence that gives the timestep at which each DP cell is fully updated in the wavefront order. See Section 2.1.
(2) [**Construct start- and end-time functions.**] Cell completion times are used to derive closed-form formulas that give the timesteps at which each recursive function call should start and end execution in the wavefront order. See Section 2.2.
(3) [**Derive the recursive wavefront algorithm.**] Each recursive function call in the standard recursive algorithm is augmented with its start- and end-time functions so that the algorithm can be used to apply the updates in any given timestep in wavefront order. We then use a variant of iterative deepening on top of this recursive algorithm to execute all timesteps efficiently. See Section 2.3.

We describe our transformation for arbitrary d-dimensional ($d \geq 1$) DP in which each dimension of the DP table is of the same length and is a power of 2.

Running example. We explain our transformation approach by applying it on a recursive algorithm for the parenthesis (a.k.a. matrix-chain multiplication) problem [12], which is defined as follows. Let $G[i, j]$ denote the minimum cost of parenthesizing $s_i \cdots s_j$. Then the 2D DP table $G[0 : n, 0 : n]$ is filled up as follows.

$$G[i,j] = \begin{cases} \infty & \text{if } 0 \leq i = j \leq n, \\ v_j & \text{if } 0 \leq i = j-1 < n, \\ \min\limits_{i \leq k \leq j} \left\{ \begin{array}{c} G[i,k] \\ +G[k,j] \\ +w(i,k,j) \end{array} \right\} & \text{if } 0 \leq i < j-1 < n; \end{cases} \quad (1)$$

where the v_j's and function $w(\cdot,\cdot,\cdot)$ are given. The recurrence is evaluated by the recursive algorithm [49] given at the top-left corner of Figure 2. Most simple DP examples (including LCS) do not consider multiple functions, or do not have race conditions, or do not portray all possible read-write constraints. We use the parenthesis problem because it is one of the simplest (and well-known) DP problems which covers most of the issues we would like to explain here. In the rest of the section, we show how a recursive wavefront algorithm (shown in Figure 2) can be derived from the given standard recursive algorithm.

Consider the standard 2-way recursive algorithm for the parenthesis problem given at the top-left corner of Figure 2. It has three functions that update the DP table. Initially, function $\mathcal{A}(G, G, G)$ is called, where G is the entire DP table. Then the computation progresses by recursively breaking the table into quadrants and calling functions $\mathcal{A}$, $\mathcal{B}$ and $\mathcal{C}$ on these smaller regions of G. At the base case (i.e., a 1×1 region of G), each function updates a cell. When x is a cell, function $\mathcal{A}(x, x, x)$ updates x by reading x itself which corresponds to the case $i = k = j$ in the recurrence. Similarly, $\mathcal{B}(x, u, v)$ updates cell x by reading x itself and two other cells u and v which correspond to cases $i = k \neq j$ and $i \neq k = j$. Finally, $\mathcal{C}(x, u, v)$ updates the cell x by reading the two cells u and v which corresponds to $i \neq k \neq j$.

The top part of Figure 3 shows how the standard 2-way recursive algorithm with 1×1 base case updates $G[1 : n, 1 : n]$ when $n = 8$. We use $\mathcal{F}_t$ in a cell to denote that function $\mathcal{F}$ updates the cell at timestep t, where $\mathcal{F} \in \{\mathcal{A}, \mathcal{B}, \mathcal{C}\}$. Using an unbounded number of processors the standard recursive algorithm updates the entire table in 31 timesteps. In contrast, the bottom part of Figure 3 shows that an iterative wavefront algorithm will update G in only 18 timesteps.

		Classic 2-way Recursive		Recursive Wavefront (this paper)	
Problem	Work (T_1)	Serial cache complexity (Q_1)	Span (T_∞)	Best serial cache complexity (Q_1)	Best span (T_∞)
Parenthesis problem [16]	$\Theta(n^3)$	$\Theta(n^3/(B\sqrt{M}))$	$\Theta(n^{\log_2 3})$	$\Theta(n^3/(B\sqrt{M}))$	$\Theta(n \log n)$
Floyd-Warshall's APSP 3-D [17]	$\Theta(n^3)$	$\Theta(n^3/B)$	$\Theta(n \log^2 n)$	$\Theta(n^3/B)$	$\Theta(n \log n)$
Floyd-Warshall's APSP 2-D [17]	$\Theta(n^3)$	$\Theta(n^3/(B\sqrt{M}))$	$\Theta(n \log^2 n)$	$\Theta(n^3/(B\sqrt{M}))$	$\Theta(n \log n)$
LCS / Edit distance [15]	$\Theta(n^2)$	$\Theta(n^2/(BM))$	$\Theta(n^{\log_2 3})$	$\Theta(n^2/(BM))$	$\Theta(n \log n)$
Gap problem [13]	$\Theta(n^3)$	$\Theta(n^3/(B\sqrt{M}))$	$\Theta(n^{\log_2 3})$	$\Theta(n^3/(B\sqrt{M}))$	$\Theta(n \log n)$
3-point stencil	$\Theta(n^2)$	$\Theta(n^2/(BM))$	$\Theta(n^{\log_2 3})$	$\Theta(n^3/(BM))$	$\Theta(n \log n)$
Protein accordion folding [49]	$\Theta(n^3)$	$\Theta(n^3/(B\sqrt{M}))$	$\Theta(n \log n)$	$\Theta(n^3/(B\sqrt{M}))$	$\Theta(n \log n)$
Spoken-word recognition [42]	$\Theta(n^2)$	$\Theta(n^2/(BM))$	$\Theta(n^{\log_2 3})$	$\Theta(n^2/(BM))$	$\Theta(n \log n)$
Function approximation	$\Theta(n^3)$	$\Theta(n^3/(B\sqrt{M}))$	$\Theta(n^{\log_2 3})$	$\Theta(n^3/(B\sqrt{M}))$	$\Theta(n \log n)$
Binomial coefficient [35]	$\Theta(n^2)$	$\Theta(n^2/(BM))$	$\Theta(n^{\log_2 3})$	$\Theta(n^2/(BM))$	$\Theta(n \log n)$
Bitonic traveling salesman [19]	$\Theta(n^2)$	$\Theta(n^2/(BM))$	$\Theta(n \log n)$	$\Theta(n^2/(BM))$	$\Theta(n \log n)$

Table 2: Work (T_1), serial cache complexity (Q_1), span (T_∞), and parallelism (T_1/T_∞) of classic 2-way recursive and recursive wavefront algorithms for several DP problems. Here, n = problem size, M = cache size, B = block size, and p = #cores. We assume that the DP table is too large to fit into the cache, and $M = \Omega(B^d)$ when $\Theta(n^d)$ is the size of the DP table. On p cores, the running time is $T_p = O(T_1/p + T_\infty)$. All algorithms have a parallel cache complexity of $Q_p = O(Q_1 + p(M/B)T_\infty)$ w.h.p. when run under the randomized work-stealing scheduler on a parallel machine with private caches. The recursive wavefront algorithms have a parallel cache complexity of $Q_p = O(Q_1)$ when run under the modified space-bounded scheduler of Section 4.2. For each recursive wavefront algorithm we have listed the best Q_1 and the best T_∞ it can achieve though it may not achieve both simultaneously (depends on base case size, i.e., value of n' chosen). In Section 4 we discuss how a cache-oblivious recursive wavefront algorithm can match the asymptotic Q_1 of the 2-way recursive non-wavefront algorithm while asymptotically improving over the T_∞ of that non-wavefront algorithm (and thus getting closer to the T_∞ of the iterative wavefront algorithm).

Our recursive wavefront algorithm (shown at the bottom of Figure 2) can be viewed as a hybrid between the pure iterative wavefront algorithm and standard 2-way recursive algorithm (assuming that the algorithm switches to standard 2-way recursive algorithm when it reaches a base case of size $n' \times n'$). Indeed, with a 1×1 base case our recursive wavefront algorithm will perform the updates in exactly the same order as the highly parallel iterative wavefront algorithm and terminate in 18 steps, and with an $n \times n$ base case it will reduce to the highly cache-efficient standard 2-way recursive algorithm. However, we are more interested in base case sizes that lie between these two extremes and results in useful tradeoffs between parallelism and cache performance.

2.1 Constructing completion-time function

This section defines completion-time, and shows how to compute it in $O(1)$ time for any cell.

*Definition 2.1 (**Completion-time**).* The completion-time $\mathfrak{C}(x)$ for cell x is the timestep in wavefront order at which x is fully updated. More formally, $\mathfrak{C}(x) = \max t \mid$ for all $\mathcal{F}_t(x, \ldots)$, where $\mathcal{F}_t(x, \ldots)$ means that cell x is updated by function $\mathcal{F}$ at timestep t.

Figure 3(a–b) show cell completion-times when the standard 2-way recursive algorithm (3(a)) and the iterative wavefront algorithm (3(b)) for solving the parenthesis problem are run on an 8×8 DP table. Observe that while all cells are updated in 31 steps in part 3(a), in part 3(b) they are completed in only 18 timesteps. Figure 3(c) shows cell update and completion times under the recursive wavefront algorithm using fractional timesteps. When $k > 0$, if multiple updates to a cell x are ready at integer time step t, this algorithm applies them one at a time at fractional timesteps $t.0, t.1, \ldots, t.(k-1)$ to avoid race conditions. Observe that the number of distinct fractional timesteps used is still exactly 18 as in the case of iterative wavefront algorithm (3(b)). Use of fractional timesteps makes completion times and update times easier to find which we explain below and in Section 2.2.

The completion-time function $\mathfrak{C}(x)$ will only return the integer part of the fractional timestep at which x is fully updated. The fractional part will be added back by the start-time and end-time functions of Section 2.2. We also assume that any cell x will be updated by a function of the form $\mathcal{F}(x, \ldots, y, \ldots)$ with $y = x$ at most once. We will call such an update a *self-update.*

Completion-time of a cell can be computed from the given DP recurrence as follows: $\mathfrak{C}(x) = smax(x) + su(x) + flag(x)$, where $smax(x)$ is the maximum completion time of the cells on which x directly depends, i.e., $smax(x) = \max_{\mathcal{F}(x,\ldots,y,\ldots) \wedge y \neq x} \mathfrak{C}(y)$; $su(x) = 1$ if x undergoes self-update, and 0 otherwise; and $flag(x) = 0$ if an update $\mathcal{F}(x, \ldots, y, \ldots)$ with $\mathfrak{C}(y) = smax(x)$ for some $y \neq x$ is a self-update for x, and 1 otherwise.

The completion-time for any cell (i, j) in the DP table for the parenthesis problem can be found as follows:

$$\mathfrak{C}(i,j) = \begin{cases} 0 & \text{if } i = j, \\ \mathfrak{C}(i, j-1) + 1 + 0 & \text{if } i = j - 1, \\ \mathfrak{C}(i, j-1) + 1 + 1 & \text{if } i < j - 1; \end{cases} \quad (2)$$

because $smax(i, j) = \mathfrak{C}(i, j-1) = \mathfrak{C}(i+1, j)$; for $i \leq j-1$, $su(i, j) = 1$ as cell (i, j) is updated by the self-update function $\mathcal{B}$, and $su(i, j) = 0$ otherwise; and for $i < j - 1$, $flag(i, j) = 1$ as function $\mathcal{B}$ does not read from a cell $y \neq (i, j)$ with $\mathfrak{C}(y) = smax(i, j)$, and $flag(i, j) = 0$ otherwise. Solving the recurrence (assuming that race will be avoided by fractional timing as explained in Section 2.2), we get the following: $\mathfrak{C}(i, j) = 0$ if $i = j$ and $\mathfrak{C}(i, j) = 2(j - i) - 1$ if $i < j$.

(a) top

$\mathcal{A}_0$	$\mathcal{B}_1$	$\mathcal{C}_3\mathcal{B}_4$	$\mathcal{C}_5\mathcal{C}_6\mathcal{B}_7$	$\mathcal{C}_{14}\mathcal{C}_{15}\mathcal{C}_{17}\mathcal{B}_{18}$	$\mathcal{C}_{14}\mathcal{C}_{15}\mathcal{C}_{19}\mathcal{C}_{20}\mathcal{B}_{21}$	$\mathcal{C}_{22}\mathcal{C}_{23}\mathcal{C}_{24}\mathcal{C}_{25}\mathcal{C}_{27}\mathcal{B}_{28}$	$\mathcal{C}_{22}\mathcal{C}_{23}\mathcal{C}_{24}\mathcal{C}_{25}\mathcal{C}_{29}\mathcal{C}_{30}\mathcal{B}_{31}$
–	$\mathcal{A}_0$	$\mathcal{B}_2$	$\mathcal{C}_3\mathcal{B}_4$	$\mathcal{C}_{14}\mathcal{C}_{15}\mathcal{B}_{16}$	$\mathcal{C}_{14}\mathcal{C}_{15}\mathcal{C}_{17}\mathcal{B}_{18}$	$\mathcal{C}_{22}\mathcal{C}_{23}\mathcal{C}_{24}\mathcal{C}_{25}\mathcal{B}_{26}$	$\mathcal{C}_{22}\mathcal{C}_{23}\mathcal{C}_{24}\mathcal{C}_{25}\mathcal{C}_{27}\mathcal{B}_{28}$
–	–	$\mathcal{A}_0$	$\mathcal{B}_1$	$\mathcal{C}_9\mathcal{B}_{10}$	$\mathcal{C}_{11}\mathcal{C}_{12}\mathcal{B}_{13}$	$\mathcal{C}_{14}\mathcal{C}_{15}\mathcal{C}_{17}\mathcal{B}_{18}$	$\mathcal{C}_{14}\mathcal{C}_{15}\mathcal{C}_{19}\mathcal{C}_{20}\mathcal{B}_{21}$
–	–	–	$\mathcal{A}_0$	$\mathcal{B}_8$	$\mathcal{C}_9\mathcal{B}_{10}$	$\mathcal{C}_{14}\mathcal{C}_{15}\mathcal{B}_{16}$	$\mathcal{C}_{14}\mathcal{C}_{15}\mathcal{C}_{17}\mathcal{B}_{18}$
–	–	–	–	$\mathcal{A}_0$	$\mathcal{B}_1$	$\mathcal{C}_3\mathcal{B}_4$	$\mathcal{C}_5\mathcal{C}_6\mathcal{B}_7$
–	–	–	–	–	$\mathcal{A}_0$	$\mathcal{B}_2$	$\mathcal{C}_3\mathcal{B}_4$
–	–	–	–	–	–	$\mathcal{A}_0$	$\mathcal{B}_1$
–	–	–	–	–	–	–	$\mathcal{A}_0$

0	1	4	7	18	21	28	31
–	0	2	4	16	18	26	28
–	–	0	1	10	13	18	21
–	–	–	0	8	10	16	18
–	–	–	–	0	1	4	7
–	–	–	–	–	0	2	4
–	–	–	–	–	–	0	1
–	–	–	–	–	–	–	0

(b) middle

$\mathcal{A}_0$	$\mathcal{B}_1$	$\mathcal{C}_2\mathcal{B}_3$	$\mathcal{C}_4\mathcal{C}_5\mathcal{B}_6$	$\mathcal{C}_4\mathcal{C}_7\mathcal{C}_8\mathcal{B}_9$	$\mathcal{C}_7\mathcal{C}_8\mathcal{C}_{10}\mathcal{C}_{11}\mathcal{B}_{12}$	$\mathcal{C}_7\mathcal{C}_{10}\mathcal{C}_{11}\mathcal{C}_{13}\mathcal{C}_{14}\mathcal{B}_{15}$	$\mathcal{C}_{10}\mathcal{C}_{11}\mathcal{C}_{13}\mathcal{C}_{14}\mathcal{C}_{16}\mathcal{C}_{17}\mathcal{B}_{18}$
–	$\mathcal{A}_0$	$\mathcal{B}_1$	$\mathcal{C}_2\mathcal{B}_3$	$\mathcal{C}_4\mathcal{C}_5\mathcal{B}_6$	$\mathcal{C}_4\mathcal{C}_7\mathcal{C}_8\mathcal{B}_9$	$\mathcal{C}_7\mathcal{C}_8\mathcal{C}_{10}\mathcal{C}_{11}\mathcal{B}_{12}$	$\mathcal{C}_7\mathcal{C}_{10}\mathcal{C}_{11}\mathcal{C}_{13}\mathcal{C}_{14}\mathcal{B}_{15}$
–	–	$\mathcal{A}_0$	$\mathcal{B}_1$	$\mathcal{C}_2\mathcal{B}_3$	$\mathcal{C}_4\mathcal{C}_5\mathcal{B}_6$	$\mathcal{C}_4\mathcal{C}_7\mathcal{C}_8\mathcal{B}_9$	$\mathcal{C}_7\mathcal{C}_8\mathcal{C}_{10}\mathcal{C}_{11}\mathcal{B}_{12}$
–	–	–	$\mathcal{A}_0$	$\mathcal{B}_1$	$\mathcal{C}_2\mathcal{B}_3$	$\mathcal{C}_4\mathcal{C}_5\mathcal{B}_6$	$\mathcal{C}_4\mathcal{C}_7\mathcal{C}_8\mathcal{B}_9$
–	–	–	–	$\mathcal{A}_0$	$\mathcal{B}_1$	$\mathcal{C}_2\mathcal{B}_3$	$\mathcal{C}_4\mathcal{C}_5\mathcal{B}_6$
–	–	–	–	–	$\mathcal{A}_0$	$\mathcal{B}_1$	$\mathcal{C}_2\mathcal{B}_3$
–	–	–	–	–	–	$\mathcal{A}_0$	$\mathcal{B}_1$
–	–	–	–	–	–	–	$\mathcal{A}_0$

0	1	3	6	9	12	15	18
–	0	1	3	6	9	12	15
–	–	0	1	3	6	9	12
–	–	–	0	1	3	6	9
–	–	–	–	0	1	3	6
–	–	–	–	–	0	1	3
–	–	–	–	–	–	0	1
–	–	–	–	–	–	–	0

(c) bottom

$\mathcal{A}_{0.0}$	$\mathcal{B}_{1.0}$	$\mathcal{C}_{2.0}\mathcal{B}_{3.0}$	$\mathcal{C}_{4.0}\mathcal{C}_{4.1}\mathcal{B}_{5.0}$	$\mathcal{C}_{4.0}\mathcal{C}_{6.0}\mathcal{C}_{6.1}\mathcal{B}_{7.0}$	$\mathcal{C}_{6.0}\mathcal{C}_{6.1}\mathcal{C}_{8.0}\mathcal{C}_{8.1}\mathcal{B}_{9.0}$	$\mathcal{C}_{6.0}\mathcal{C}_{8.0}\mathcal{C}_{8.1}\mathcal{C}_{10.0}\mathcal{C}_{10.1}\mathcal{B}_{11.0}$	$\mathcal{C}_{8.0}\mathcal{C}_{8.1}\mathcal{C}_{10.0}\mathcal{C}_{10.1}\mathcal{C}_{12.0}\mathcal{C}_{12.1}\mathcal{B}_{13.0}$
–	$\mathcal{A}_{0.0}$	$\mathcal{B}_{1.0}$	$\mathcal{C}_{2.0}\mathcal{B}_{3.0}$	$\mathcal{C}_{4.0}\mathcal{C}_{4.1}\mathcal{B}_{5.0}$	$\mathcal{C}_{4.0}\mathcal{C}_{6.0}\mathcal{C}_{6.1}\mathcal{B}_{7.0}$	$\mathcal{C}_{6.0}\mathcal{C}_{6.1}\mathcal{C}_{8.0}\mathcal{C}_{8.1}\mathcal{B}_{9.0}$	$\mathcal{C}_{6.0}\mathcal{C}_{8.0}\mathcal{C}_{8.1}\mathcal{C}_{10.0}\mathcal{C}_{10.1}\mathcal{B}_{11.0}$
–	–	$\mathcal{A}_{0.0}$	$\mathcal{B}_{1.0}$	$\mathcal{C}_{2.0}\mathcal{B}_{3.0}$	$\mathcal{C}_{4.0}\mathcal{C}_{4.1}\mathcal{B}_{5.0}$	$\mathcal{C}_{4.0}\mathcal{C}_{6.0}\mathcal{C}_{6.1}\mathcal{B}_{7.0}$	$\mathcal{C}_{6.0}\mathcal{C}_{6.1}\mathcal{C}_{8.0}\mathcal{C}_{8.1}\mathcal{B}_{9.0}$
–	–	–	$\mathcal{A}_{0.0}$	$\mathcal{B}_{1.0}$	$\mathcal{C}_{2.0}\mathcal{B}_{3.0}$	$\mathcal{C}_{4.0}\mathcal{C}_{4.1}\mathcal{B}_{5.0}$	$\mathcal{C}_{4.0}\mathcal{C}_{6.0}\mathcal{C}_{6.1}\mathcal{B}_{7.0}$
–	–	–	–	$\mathcal{A}_{0.0}$	$\mathcal{B}_{1.0}$	$\mathcal{C}_{2.0}\mathcal{B}_{3.0}$	$\mathcal{C}_{4.0}\mathcal{C}_{4.1}\mathcal{B}_{5.0}$
–	–	–	–	–	$\mathcal{A}_{0.0}$	$\mathcal{B}_{1.0}$	$\mathcal{C}_{2.0}\mathcal{B}_{3.0}$
–	–	–	–	–	–	$\mathcal{A}_{0.0}$	$\mathcal{B}_{1.0}$
–	–	–	–	–	–	–	$\mathcal{A}_{0.0}$

0	1	3	5	7	9	11	13
–	0	1	3	5	7	9	11
–	–	0	1	3	5	7	9
–	–	–	0	1	3	5	7
–	–	–	–	0	1	3	5
–	–	–	–	–	0	1	3
–	–	–	–	–	–	0	1
–	–	–	–	–	–	–	0

Figure 3: Timesteps at which each DP table cell is updated ($\mathcal{F}_t$ means function $\mathcal{F}$ updates at timestep t) and the timestep at which each cell becomes fully updated (on the right) for the parenthesis problem on a DP table of size 8×8 using (a) top: standard 2-way recursive algorithm, (b) middle: iterative wavefront algorithm, and (c) bottom: recursive wavefront algorithm with fractional timesteps. Observe that the number of fractional timesteps in the recursive wavefront algorithm (bottom part) is exactly the same as that in the iterative wavefront algorithm (middle part). Both recursive algorithms use a 1×1 base case. We assume that the number of processors is unbounded.

2.2 Constructing start-time and end-time functions

In this section, we define start-time and end-time for a recursive function call, and show how to derive them from completion-times.

*Definition 2.2 (**Start-time, end-time**).* The start-time (resp. end-time) of a recursive function call in a recursive wavefront algorithm is the earliest (resp. latest) timestep in the wavefront order at which one of the updates to be applied by that function call (either directly or through a recursive function call) becomes ready.

Let $\mathcal{F}(X, Y_1, \ldots, Y_s)$ be a function call that writes to a region X by reading from regions $Y_1, \ldots, Y_s$ of the DP table. Its start- and end-times, denoted by $\mathcal{S}_{\mathcal{F}}(X, Y_1, \ldots, Y_s)$ and $\mathcal{E}_{\mathcal{F}}(X, Y_1, \ldots, Y_s)$, respectively, are computed as follows.

$$\underbrace{\mathcal{S}_{\mathcal{F}}(X, Y_1, \ldots, Y_s)}_{X \in \{Y_1, \ldots, Y_s\}} = \begin{cases} ((\mathfrak{C}(X)).0 & \text{if } X \text{ is a cell,} \\ \min \mathcal{S}_{\mathcal{F}'}\left(X', Y'_1, \ldots, Y'_s\right) & \text{otherwise;} \end{cases}$$

$$\underbrace{\mathcal{S}_{\mathcal{F}}(X, Y_1, \ldots, Y_s)}_{X \notin \{Y_1, \ldots, Y_s\}} = \begin{cases} (\max_{1 \le i \le s}\{\mathfrak{C}(Y_i)\} + 1) & \\ .ra(X, Y_1, \ldots, Y_s) & \text{if } X \text{ is a cell,} \\ \min \mathcal{S}_{\mathcal{F}'}\left(X', Y'_1, \ldots, Y'_s\right) & \text{otherwise;} \end{cases}$$

$$\underbrace{\mathcal{E}_{\mathcal{F}}(X, Y_1, \ldots, Y_s)}_{X \in \{Y_1, \ldots, Y_s\}} = \begin{cases} ((\mathfrak{C}(X)).0 & \text{if } X \text{ is a cell,} \\ \max \mathcal{E}_{\mathcal{F}'}\left(X', Y'_1, \ldots, Y'_s\right) & \text{otherwise;} \end{cases}$$

$$\underbrace{\mathcal{E}_{\mathcal{F}}(X, Y_1, \ldots, Y_s)}_{X \notin \{Y_1, \ldots, Y_s\}} = \begin{cases} (\max_{1 \le i \le s}\{\mathfrak{C}(Y_i)\} + 1) & \\ .ra(X, Y_1, \ldots, Y_s) & \text{if } X \text{ is a cell,} \\ \max \mathcal{E}_{\mathcal{F}'}\left(X', Y'_1, \ldots, Y'_s\right) & \text{otherwise;} \end{cases}$$

where, in the non-cellular case, minimization/maximization is taken over all functions $\mathcal{F}'(X', Y'_1, \ldots, Y'_s)$ called by $\mathcal{F}(X, Y_1, \ldots, Y_s)$ recursively. Also, $ra(X, Y_1, \ldots, Y_s)$ is the problem-specific race avoidance condition used when two functions write to the same region. Though we use fractional timesteps for simplicity, the total number of distinct timesteps remain exactly the same as that in the iterative wavefront algorithm.

For the parenthesis problem, the start-times for the three functions $\mathcal{A}$, $\mathcal{B}$, and $\mathcal{C}$ are computed as below. Let (x_r, x_c), (u_r, u_c), and (v_r, v_c) denote the positions of the top-left cells of regions X, U and V, respectively. Then

$$\mathcal{S}_{\mathcal{A}}(X, X, X) = \begin{cases} (\mathfrak{C}(X)).0 & \text{if } X \text{ is a cell,} \\ \mathcal{S}_{\mathcal{A}}(X_{11}, X_{11}, X_{11}) & \text{otherwise;} \end{cases}$$

$$\mathcal{S}_{\mathcal{B}}(X, U, V) = \begin{cases} (\mathfrak{C}(X)).0 & \text{if } X \text{ is a cell,} \\ \mathcal{S}_{\mathcal{B}}(X_{21}, U_{22}, V_{11}) & \text{otherwise;} \end{cases}$$

$$\mathcal{S}_{\mathcal{C}}(X, U, V) = \begin{cases} (\max\{\mathfrak{C}(U), \mathfrak{C}(V)\} + 1) & \\ \cdot \left[u_c > \frac{x_r + x_c}{2}\right] & \text{if } X \text{ is a cell,} \\ \min \begin{Bmatrix} \mathcal{S}_{\mathcal{C}}(X_{21}, U_{21}, V_{11}), \\ \mathcal{S}_{\mathcal{C}}(X_{21}, U_{22}, V_{21}) \end{Bmatrix} & \text{otherwise;} \end{cases}$$

where [ ] is the *Iverson bracket* [34].

Both $\mathcal{A}$ and $\mathcal{B}$ read from and write to X, and hence their start-times follow directly from the first recurrence in Definition 2.2. In case of $\mathcal{B}$, X is updated by reading from pair $\langle U, X \rangle$ and also from $\langle X, V \rangle$. Function $\mathcal{C}$ follows the second recurrence from the definition. As $\mathcal{C}$ writes to the same region twice, there is a race and to avoid it we use the condition $[u_c > (x_r + x_c)/2]$ derived manually.

The end-times can be computed similarly. Solving the recurrences for the start-times and end-times, we obtain the timing functions shown in Figure 2.

2.3 Deriving a recursive wavefront algorithm

In this section, we describe how to use timing functions to derive a recursive wavefront algorithm from a given standard recursive divide-and-conquer DP algorithm. We use the parenthesis problem as an example.

A standard recursive algorithm for the parenthesis problem is shown at the top-left corner of Figure 2. We modify it as follows, and the modified algorithm is shown on the bottom part of the same figure.

First, we modify each function $\mathcal{F}$ to include a switching point $n' \ge 1$, and switch to the original non-wavefront recursive algorithm by calling $\mathcal{F}_{chunk}$ when the size of each input submatrix drops to $n' \times n'$ or below.

We augment each function to accept a timestep parameter w. We remove all serialization among recursive function calls by making sure that all functions that are called are launched in parallel. We do not launch a function unless w lies between its start-time and end-time which means that a function is not invoked if we know that it does not have an update to apply at timestep w in wavefront order. Observe that the function $\mathcal{F}_{chunk}$ at switching does not accept a timestep parameter, but if we reach it we know that it has an update to apply at timestep w. However, once we enter that function we do not stop until we apply all updates that function can apply at all timesteps $\geq w$.

Each function is also modified to return the smallest timestep above w for which it may have at least one update that is yet to be applied. It finds that timestep by checking the start-time of each function that was not launched because the start-time was larger than w, and the timestep returned by each recursive function that was launched and taking the smallest of all of them.

Finally, we add a loop (see RECURSIVE-WAVEFRONT-PARENTHESIS in Figure 2) to execute all timesteps of the wavefront using the modified functions. We start with timestep $w = 0$, and invoke the main function $\mathcal{A}(G, G, G, w)$ which applies all updates at timestep w and depending on the value chosen for n' possibly some updates above timestep w, and returns the smallest timestep above w for which there may still be some updates that are yet to be applied. We next call function $\mathcal{A}$ with that new timestep value, and keep iterating in the same fashion until we are able to exhaust all timesteps.

3 APPLICATIONS

In this section, we present the recursive wavefront algorithms for LCS, Floyd-Warshall's APSP, and gap problem [48]. We will only give the timing functions and not the entire recursive wavefront algorithm. We give references to the papers that present the standard (non-wavefront) recursive algorithms from which recursive wavefront algorithms can easily be derived by plugging in the timing functions as per Section 2.3.

Longest common subsequence (LCS). The LCS problem [15, 32] asks one to find the longest of all common subsequences [19] between two strings. In LCS DP, a cell depends on its three adjacent cells. Here, we are interested in finding only the length of the LCS.

We build on the recursive algorithm given in [15] which has only one function $\mathcal{A}$ (i.e., named LCS-OUTPUT-BOUNDARY in [15]). The timing functions are as follows.

$$\mathfrak{C}(i,j) = \begin{cases} 0 & \text{if } i < 0 \,||\, j < 0 \,||\, i = j = 0, \\ \max\begin{pmatrix} \mathfrak{C}(i-1,j), \mathfrak{C}(i,j-1), \\ \mathfrak{C}(i-1,j-1) \end{pmatrix} + 1 & \text{otherwise.} \end{cases}$$

$$\begin{aligned} &\mathcal{S}_{\mathcal{A}}(X) = \mathcal{E}_{\mathcal{A}}(X) = (\mathfrak{C}(X)).0 && \text{if } X \text{ is a cell,} \\ &\mathcal{S}_{\mathcal{A}}(X) = \mathcal{S}_{\mathcal{A}}(X_{11}) && \text{if } X \text{ is not a cell,} \\ &\mathcal{E}_{\mathcal{A}}(X) = \mathcal{E}_{\mathcal{A}}(X_{22}) && \text{if } X \text{ is not a cell.} \end{aligned}$$

Solving the recurrences, we have $\mathfrak{C}(i,j) = i+j$, $\mathcal{S}_{\mathcal{A}}(X) = \mathfrak{C}(x_r, x_c)$, and $\mathcal{E}_{\mathcal{A}}(X) = \mathfrak{C}(x_r+n-1, x_c+n-1)$, where, (x_r, x_c) is the top-left corner of X.

Gap problem. Sequence alignment with general gap penalty [25, 26, 49, 52] is a generalization of the edit distance problem. We build on the recursive algorithm given in [49]. The timing functions are as follows.

$$\mathfrak{C}(i,j) = \begin{cases} 0 & \text{if } i = -1 \,||\, j = -1 \,||\, i = j = 0, \\ \max(\mathfrak{C}(i-1,j), \mathfrak{C}(i,j-1)) + 2 & \text{otherwise.} \end{cases}$$

$$\mathcal{S}_{\mathcal{A}}(X,X) = \begin{cases} (\mathfrak{C}(X)).0 & \text{if } X \text{ is a cell,} \\ \mathcal{S}_{\mathcal{A}}(X_{11}, X_{11}) & \text{otherwise.} \end{cases}$$

$$\mathcal{S}_{\mathcal{B}}(X,U) = \begin{cases} (\mathfrak{C}(U)+1).0 & \text{if } X \text{ is a cell,} \\ \mathcal{S}_{\mathcal{B}}(X_{11}, U_{11}) & \text{otherwise.} \end{cases}$$

$$\mathcal{S}_{\mathcal{C}}(X,V) = \begin{cases} (\mathfrak{C}(V)+1).[x_c \geq 1] & \text{if } X \text{ is a cell,} \\ \mathcal{S}_{\mathcal{C}}(X_{11}, V_{11}) & \text{otherwise.} \end{cases}$$

Function $\mathcal{B}$ does not have races and hence its $ra(X,U) = 0$. But when we add function $\mathcal{C}$, there is a race condition with $\mathcal{B}$ when the completion-time of read cell of $\mathcal{C}$ is the same as the completion-time of one of the cells on the left of the write cell of $\mathcal{C}$. To avoid clashes with $\mathcal{B}$, we use $ra(X,V) = [x_c \geq 1]$. We can write similar recurrence for the end-times. Solving the recurrences, we have

$$\begin{aligned} &\mathfrak{C}(i,j) = 2(i+j), \\ &\mathcal{S}_{\mathcal{F}}(X,Y) = (\mathfrak{C}(y_r, y_c) + [X \neq Y]).ra(X,Y), \\ &\mathcal{E}_{\mathcal{F}}(X,Y) = (\mathfrak{C}(y_r+n-1, y_c+n-1) + [X \neq Y]).ra(X,Y); \end{aligned}$$

where, when $\mathcal{F}$ is $\mathcal{A}$ (resp. $\mathcal{B}$, $\mathcal{C}$), then Y is X (resp. U, V); (y_r, y_c) is the top-left corner of region Y; and $ra(X,Y) = [x_c \geq 1]$ for function $\mathcal{C}$, and $ra(X,Y) = 0$, otherwise.

Floyd-Warshall's all-pairs shortest path (APSP). We build on the recursive algorithm for Floyd-Warshall's APSP [23, 51] given in [17]. However, that algorithm violates our assumption that cells can only be updated using values from fully updated cells. That violation can be removed by performing the computation in cubic space instead of quadratic space as explained in [14, 19]. We find the timing functions the cubic space version which remain valid for the DP using quadratic space.

The recursive wavefront algorithm can be easily derived using the start- and end-time functions for the recursive algorithm given in [17]. The recursive algorithm must be modified slightly to account for the third dimension through the variable k. Then, the completion-time function for an (i,j,k)-cell can be found from the DP recurrence as:

$$\mathfrak{C}(i,j,k) = \begin{cases} -1 & \text{if } k = -1, \\ \max\begin{pmatrix} \mathfrak{C}(i,j,k-1), \mathfrak{C}(i,k,k-1), \\ \mathfrak{C}(k,j,k-1)) + 1 \end{pmatrix} & \text{otherwise.} \end{cases}$$

From Definition 2.1, we have $smax(i,j,k) = \max(\mathfrak{C}(i,j,k-1), \mathfrak{C}(i,k,k-1), \mathfrak{C}(k,j,k-1))$ and $su(i,j,k) = 0$. Similarly, the start- and end-time can be found as follows. When X is a cell, the start- and end-times of all functions is $\mathfrak{C}(x_r, x_c, x_h)$. The recurrences for start-times are as follows.

$$\mathcal{S}_{\mathcal{A}}(X) = \begin{cases} \mathfrak{C}(x_r, x_c, x_h) & \text{if } X \text{ is a cell,} \\ \mathcal{S}_{\mathcal{A}}(X_{111}) & \text{otherwise.} \end{cases}$$

$$\mathcal{S}_{\mathcal{B}}(X,U) = \begin{cases} \mathfrak{C}(x_r, x_c, x_h) & \text{if } X \text{ is a cell,} \\ \mathcal{S}_{\mathcal{B}}(X_{111}, U_{111}) & \text{otherwise.} \end{cases}$$

$$\mathcal{S}_{\mathcal{C}}(X,V) = \begin{cases} \mathfrak{C}(x_r, x_c, x_h) & \text{if } X \text{ is a cell,} \\ \mathcal{S}_{\mathcal{C}}(X_{111}, V_{111}) & \text{otherwise.} \end{cases}$$

$$\mathcal{S}_{\mathcal{D}}(X,U,V) = \begin{cases} \mathfrak{C}(x_r, x_c, x_h) & \text{if } X \text{ is a cell,} \\ \mathcal{S}_{\mathcal{D}}(X_{111}, U_{111}, V_{111}) & \text{otherwise.} \end{cases}$$

Similarly, recurrences can be written for the end-times as well. Solving the recurrences, we have

$$\mathfrak{C}(i,j,k) = 3k + [i \neq k] + [j \neq k],$$

where, [ ] is the Iversion bracket. Let (x_r, x_c, x_h) be the cell with the smallest coordinates in X. Then for each $\mathcal{F} \in \{\mathcal{A}, \mathcal{B}, \mathcal{C}, \mathcal{D}\}$,

$$\mathcal{S}_{\mathcal{F}}(X, \ldots) = \mathfrak{C}(x_r, x_c, x_h)$$

$$\text{and } \mathcal{E}_{\mathcal{F}}(X, \ldots) = \max \left\{ \begin{array}{c} \mathfrak{C}(x_r, x_c, x_h + n - 1), \\ \mathfrak{C}(x_r, x_c + n - 1, x_h + n - 1), \\ \mathfrak{C}(x_r + n - 1, x_c, x_h + n - 1), \\ \mathfrak{C}(x_r + n - 1, x_c + n - 1, x_h + n - 1) \end{array} \right\}$$

4 SCHEDULING RECURSIVE WAVEFRONT ALGORITHMS

In this section, we show how to schedule recursive wavefront algorithms to achieve provably good bounds (optimal or near-optimal) for both parallelism and cache performance.

Recall that our recursive wavefront algorithm switches to the original non-wavefront recursive algorithm when the input parameter n drops to a value $\leq n'$. While both recursive (wavefront and non-wavefront) algorithms have the same serial work complexity T_1, their spans are different. We use $T_\infty^R(n')$ to denote the span of the non-wavefront algorithm for a problem of size n'.

4.1 Using a work-stealing (WS) scheduler

In this section, we analyze the complexity of the hybrid recursive wavefront algorithms when scheduled using a randomized work-stealing (WS) scheduler [9].

THEOREM 4.1 (**WS COMPLEXITY**). *Suppose a DP recurrence is evaluated by the iterative wavefront algorithm in $N_\infty(n)$ parallel steps with an unbounded number of processors, where n is the size of each dimension of the DP table. When the recursive wavefront algorithm with switching point $n' \leq n$ evaluates the recurrence, we achieve the following bounds under a randomized work-stealing (WS) scheduler:*

(i) span, $T_\infty(n) = O\left(N_\infty(n/n') \times \left(\log n + T_\infty^R(n')\right)\right)$,
(ii) parallel time, $T_p(n) = O(T_1(n)/p + T_\infty(n))$ (w.h.p. in n),
(iii) parallel cache complexity, $Q_p(n) = O(Q_1(n) + p(M/B)T_\infty(n))$ (w.h.p. in n), and
(iv) extra space, $S_p(n) = O(p \log n)$.

We assume that $N_\infty(n)$ and $T_1(n)$ (work) are polynomials of n, and choose n' such that $T_1(n') = \Omega(\log n)$.

PROOF. Observe that the outer loop (e.g., the loop inside RECURSIVE-WAVEFRONT-PARENTHESIS of Figure 2) in the recursive wavefront algorithm will iterate $N_\infty(n/n')$ times.

With an unbounded number of processors reaching the switching point requires $O(\log(n/n'))$ time and the span below that point is $T_\infty^R(n')$. The bound for $T_\infty(n)$ follows.

We reach the switching point $T_1(n/n')$ times. So the total work is $\Theta(T_1(n/n')(T_1(n') + \log(n/n')))$. Since we assume $T_1(n)$ to be a polynomial function of n, we have $T_1(n/n') = \Theta(T_1(n)/T_1(n'))$. Then the total work remains $\Theta(T_1(n))$ assuming $T_1(n') = \Omega(\log n)$.

Let $T_1^{(i)}$, $T_\infty^{(i)}$ and $Q_1^{(i)}$ be the work, span and serial cache complexity, respectively, of the i-th iteration of the outer loop in the recursive wavefront algorithm. Then the parallel running time of that iteration under the WS scheduler is $O\left(1 + T_1^{(i)}(n)/p + T_\infty^{(i)}(n)\right)$ (w.h.p.). We sum up over all i, and obtain the claimed bound for $T_p(n)$.

The parallel cache complexity of the i-th iteration of the outer loop is $O\left(Q_1^{(i)}(n) + p(M/B)T_\infty^{(i)}(n)\right)$ (w.h.p.) under the WS scheduler. Summing up over all i gives us the claimed bound for $Q_p(n)$.

The bound on extra space comes from the observation that since we reduce n by a factor of 2 in each level of recursion the number of levels of recursion is $O(\log n)$. So each processor will require $O(\log n)$ stack space, and since there are p processors the bound on $S_p(n)$ follows. □

The following lemma gives a condition under which the recursive wavefront algorithm will have the same asymptotic serial cache complexity as the recursive non-wavefront algorithm.

LEMMA 4.2 (**WS COMPLEXITY**). *Suppose the original recursive non-wavefront algorithm has a serial cache complexity of $Q_1^R(n) = O(T_1(n)/f(M,B))$, where n is size of each dimension of the DP table, f is a function of cache size M and line size B, $T_1(n)$ is a polynomial of n, and the size of the DP table is $\Omega(M)$. Then if the recursive wavefront algorithm with switching point $n' = n^\alpha$ for some $\alpha \in (0,1]$ evaluates the recurrence, it will achieve a serial cache complexity of $Q_1(n) = \Theta\left(Q_1^R(n)\right)$ provided the size of the DP (sub-)table corresponding to n' is $\Omega(M)$.*

The proof of the lemma above follows directly from the observation that the recursive wavefront algorithm will reach the switching point $\Theta(T_1(n)/T_1(n'))$ times, and each time will incur $Q_1^R(n') = O(T_1(n')/f(M,B))$ serial cache misses. Thus its total serial cache complexity will be $\Theta(T_1(n)/T_1(n')) \times Q_1^R(n') = O(T_1(n)/f(M,B))$.

Hence, if the original recursive non-wavefront algorithm has optimal serial cache complexity, the recursive wavefront algorithm will also have the same under the conditions given above.

4.2 Using a modified space-bounded (W-SB) scheduler

In this section, we show how to modify a space-bounded scheduler [18] so that it can execute a recursive wavefront algorithm cache-optimally with parallelism higher than that of the corresponding recursive non-wavefront algorithm.

For each recursive function call, our W-SB scheduler accepts three hints: start-time, end-time and working set size (i.e., the total size of all regions in the DP table accessed by the function call). Given an implementation of a standard recursive algorithm with each function call annotated with those three hints, the W-SB can automatically generate a recursive wavefront implementation (similar to the one at the bottom of Figure 2). From the given start-times, the scheduler determines the lowest start-time and executes the tasks that can be executed at that lowest start-time. Since the scheduler knows all the cache sizes, as soon as the working set size of any function executing on a processor under a cache fits into that cache, the scheduler anchors the function to that cache in the sense that all recursive function calls made by that function and its descendants will only be executed by the processors under that anchored cache. This approach of limiting migration of tasks ensures cache-optimality [8, 18].

Theorem 4.3 (**W-SB complexity**). *Suppose a DP recurrence is evaluated by the iterative wavefront algorithm in $N_\infty(n)$ parallel steps with an unbounded number of processors, where n is the size of each dimension of the DP table. When the recursive wavefront algorithm with switching point $n' \le n$ evaluates the recurrence, we achieve the following bounds under the modified space-bounded (W-SB) scheduler:*

(*i*) *span*, $T_\infty(n) = O\left(N_\infty(n/n') \times \left(\log n + T_\infty^R(n')\right)\right)$,
(*ii*) *parallel cache complexity*, $Q_p(n) = O\left(Q_1(n)\right)$,
(*iii*) *extra space*, $S_p(n) = O\left(p \log n\right)$.

We assume that $N_\infty(n)$ and $N_1(n)$ (work) are polynomials of n, and choose n' such that $T_1^R(n') = \Omega(\log n)$.

Proof. The arguments for $T_\infty(n)$ and $S_p(n)$ are the same as those given in the proof of Theorem 4.1. The parallel cache complexity is found as follows.

When the working set size of a function call fits into a cache $\mathcal{M}$ the W-SB scheduler does not allow any recursive function calls made by that function or its descendants to migrate to other caches that are not a part of the subtree of caches rooted at $\mathcal{M}$. This implies the data is read completely and as much work as possible is done on this loaded cache data blocks in $\mathcal{M}$ before kicking them out of the cache. Hence, temporal cache locality is fully exploited at $\mathcal{M}$. As shown in [8, 18] being able to achieve cache-optimality for working set sizes that are smaller than the cache size by at most a constant factor guarantees $Q_p(n) = \Theta(Q_1(n))$ for our algorithms. □

Cache-optimality is achieved under conditions similar to those given in Lemma 4.2.

5 EXPERIMENTAL RESULTS

In this section, we present experimental results showing the performance of recursive wavefront algorithms for the LCS, Parenthesis and the 2D FW-APSP problems. We also compare the performance of those algorithms with the corresponding standard 2-way recursive divide-and-conquer and the original cache-oblivious wavefront (COW) algorithms [47].

We used C++ with Intel© Cilk™ Plus extension to implement all algorithms presented in this section. Therefore, all implementations used the work-stealing scheduler provided by Cilk™ runtime system. All programs were compiled with `-O3 -ip -parallel -AVX -xhost` optimization parameters. In order to reduce the overhead of recursion and to take advantage of vectorization all implementations switch to an iterative kernel when n is sufficiently small (e.g., 64 for Parenthesis and Floyd-Warshall's APSP, and 256 for LCS). To measure cache performance we used PAPI-5.3[2]. Table 3 lists the systems on which we ran our experiments.

Model	E5-2680	E5-4650	E5-2680
Cluster	Stampede [3]	Stampede [3]	Comet [1]
#Cores	2x8	4x8	2x12
Frequency	2.70GHz	2.70GHz	2.50GHz
L1	32K	32K	32K
L2	256K	256K	256K
L3	20480K	20480K	30720K
Cache-line size	64B	64B	64B
Memory	64GB	1TB	64GB
Compiler	15.0.2	15.0.2	15.2.164
OS	CentOS 6.6	CentOS 6.6	CentOS 6.6

Table 3: System specifications.

Projected parallelism. we have used the Intel© Cilkview scalability analyzer to compute the ideal parallelism and burdened span of the following implementations: (*i*) recursive wavefront algorithm that does not switch to the 2-way non-wavefront recursive algorithm and instead directly uses an iterative basecase (`wave`), (*ii*) recursive wavefront algorithm that switches to the 2-way recursive divide-and-conquer at some point (`wave-hybrid`), (*iii*) standard 2-way recursive divide-and-conquer algorithm (`CO_2Way`). For `wave-hybrid`, we have used $n' = \max\{256, \text{power of 2 closest to } n^{2/3}\}$.

Figure 5 shows the ideal parallelism reported by Cilkview for `wave-hybrid`, `wave` and `CO_2Way` algorithms for solving LCS, Parenthesis and Floyd-Warshall's APSP problems. These plots show that recursive wavefront algorithms scale much better than standard 2-way recursive divide-and-conquer algorithms. For example, when solving the parenthesis problem for a 16k×16k matrix, though `CO_2Way` scales up to 23 processors only, `wave` and `wave-hybrid` scale up to 1916 and 823 processors, respectively.

Running time and cache performance. Figure 4 shows performance of the following on a 16-core Sandy Bridge machine: (*i*) `wave`, (*ii*) `wave-hybrid`, (*iii*) `CO_2Way`, and (*iv*) the original cache-oblivious wavefront (COW) algorithms with atomic operations [47]. Since we have already shown in [14, 49] that `CO_2Way` outperforms parallel iterative and blocked iterative codes for the parenthesis and Floyd-Warshall's APSP problems, we have not repeated those results here.

For `wave-hybrid`, we have used $n' = \max\{256, \text{power of 2 closest to } n^{2/3}\}$. Figure 4 clearly shows that `wave` and `wave-hybrid` algorithms perform better than `CO_2Way` and the COW algorithms for all cases. For parenthesis problem, `wave` is 2.6×, and `wave-hybrid` is 2× faster than `CO_2Way`. Similarly, the number of cache misses of `CO_2Way` is slightly higher than that of both `wave` and `wave-hybrid`. For LCS `wave` is 1.5×, and `wave-hybrid` is 1.7× faster than `CO_2Way` and cache miss trends follow along. For Floyd-Warshall's APSP, `wave` is 18%, and `wave-hybrid` is 10% faster than `CO_2Way`. Therefore, even with 16 cores, the impact of improvements in parallelism and cache-misses is visible on the running time. On the other hand, though COW algorithms have excellent theoretical parallelism, their implementations heavily use atomic operations, which may have impacted their performance negatively for large n, especially for DP dimension $d > 1$.

Figures 6 and 7 show performance results on a 24-core Haswell machine. Values for n' and size of iterative kernels were determined in the same way as before. For FW-APSP, `wave` is 15% and `wave-hybrid` is 10% faster than `CO_2Way`. Although we see improvements in L1 and L2 cache misses, the number of L3 misses were worse here, probably due to increased parallelism. For LCS problem, `wave` is 57%, `wave-hybrid` is 60% and the original COW algorithm is 26% faster than the `CO_2Way` implementation. For parenthesis problem, `wave` is 16% and `wave-hybrid` is 18% faster than `CO_2Way`, and we see only improvement in L3 misses.

On a Stampede node with 32-core Sandy Bridge processors, `wave` for FW-APSP runs 73% faster and `wave-hybrid` runs 69% faster than `CO_2Way`. On the other hand, for the parenthesis problem, both `wave` and `wave-hybrid` are 2.1× faster than `CO_2Way`.

To summarize, recursive wavefront algorithms are faster and more scalable than standard recursive divde and conquer algorithms for DP problems.

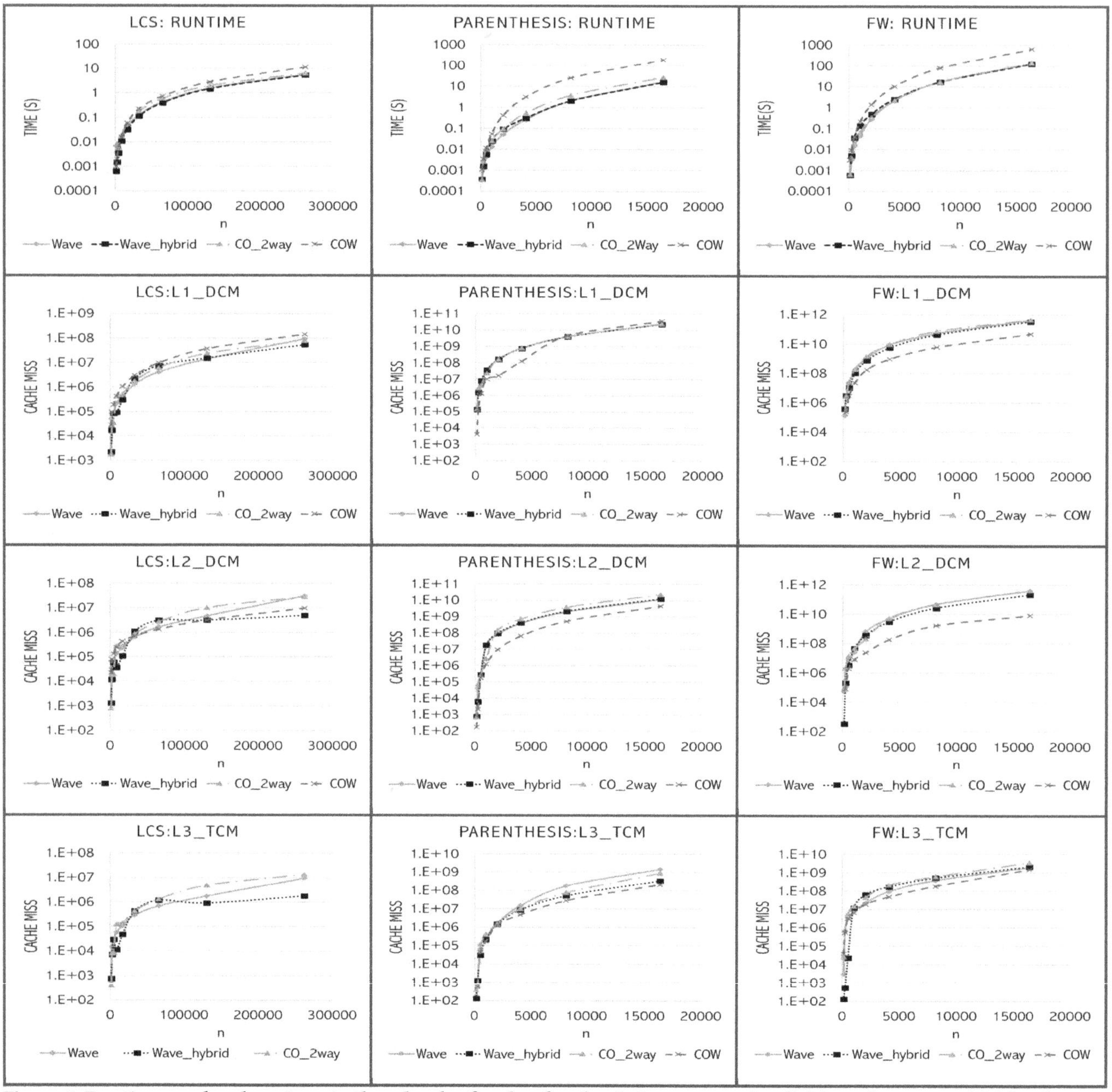

Figure 4: Runtimes and cache misses in three levels of caches for classic 2-way recursive divide-and-conquer, COW and recursive wavefront algorithms for LCS, Parenthesis and 2D FW-APSP Problems. All programs were run on 16 core machines in Stampede. All implementations used Cilk Plus's work-stealing scheduler.

6 CONCLUSION

We have presented a framework for designing recursive wavefront algorithms for dynamic programs which have excellent cache-complexity (i.e., temporal locality) and asymptotically more parallelism than standard 2-way recursive divide-and-conquer algorithms. The framework leads to theoretically fastest cache-oblivious parallel DP algorithms. Some open problems are as follows: (*i*) fully automate the framework, i.e., computation of timing functions and the race avoidance condition; (*ii*) investigate if recursive wavefront algorithms can achieve span asymptotically lower than $\Theta(n \log n)$; and (*iii*) extend the approach beyond DP problems.

ACKNOWLEDGMENTS

Chowdhury and Ganapathi were supported in part by NSF grants CCF-1439084 and CNS-1553510. Part of this work used the Extreme Science and Engineering Discovery Environment (XSEDE) which is supported by NSF grant ACI-1053575. The authors would like to thank anonymous reviewers for valuable comments and suggestions that have significantly improved the paper.

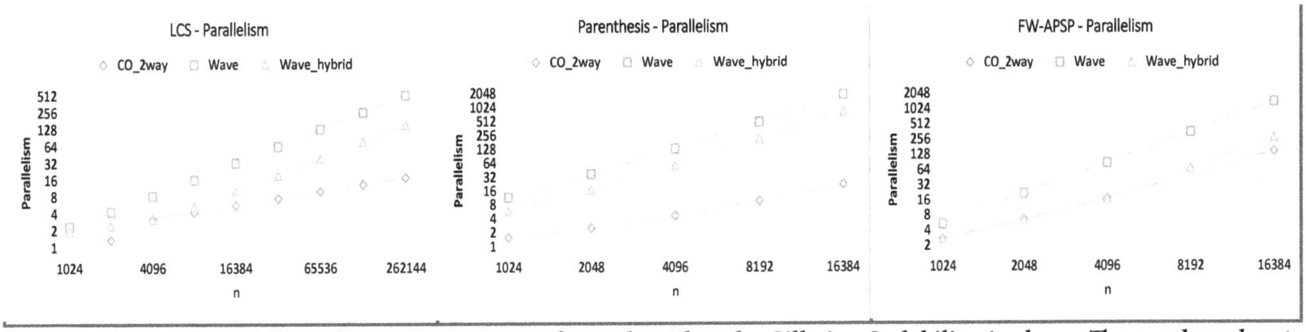

Figure 5: Projected scalability of new recursive wavefront algorithms by Cilkview Scalability Analyzer. The numbers denote till how many cores the implementation should scale linearly.

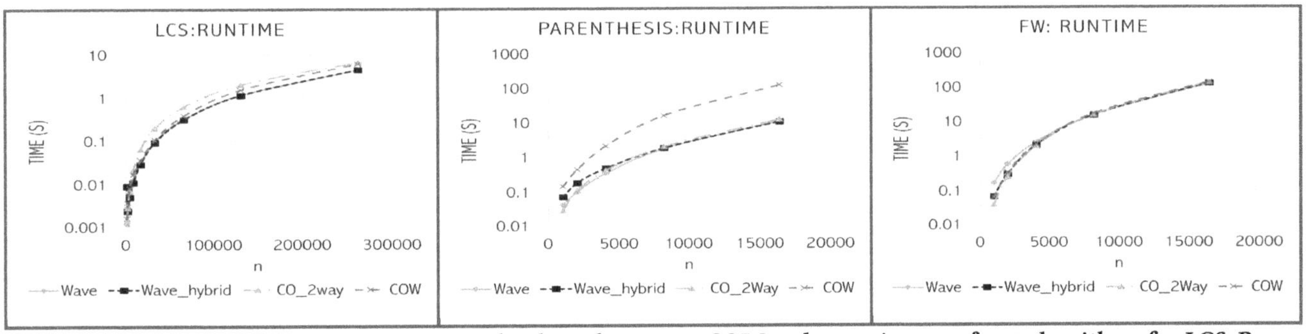

Figure 6: Runtimes for classic 2-way recursive divide-and-conquer, COW and recursive wavefront algorithms for LCS, Parenthesis and 2D FW-APSP. All programs were run on 24 core machines in Comet. All implementations used cilk plus's work-stealing scheduler.

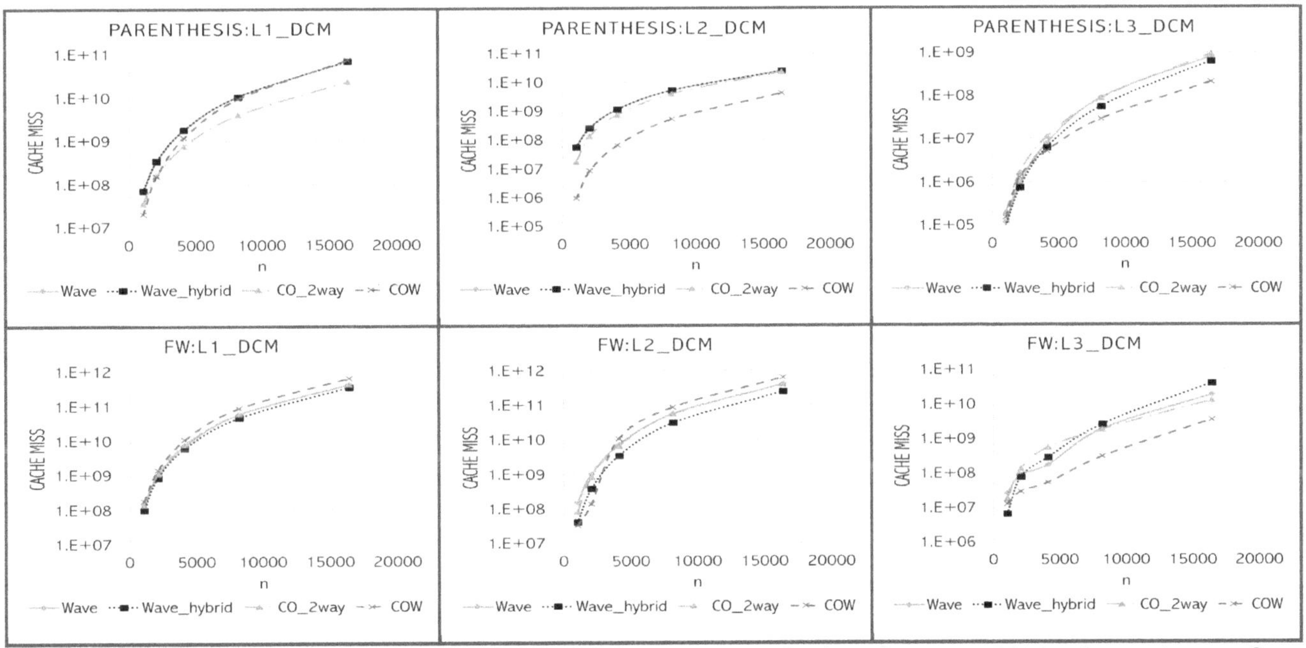

Figure 7: Cache misses in three levels of caches for classic 2-way recursive divide-and-conquer, COW and recursive wavefront algorithms for Parenthesis and 2D FW-APSP. All programs were run on 24 core machines in Comet. All implementations used cilk plus's work-stealing scheduler.

REFERENCES

[1] Comet Supercomputing Cluster. http://www.sdsc.edu/support/user_guides/comet.html. (2016).
[2] PAPI-5.3. http://icl.cs.utk.edu/papi/index.html. (2016).
[3] Stampede Supercomputing Cluster. https://www.tacc.utexas.edu/stampede/. (2016).
[4] Shaizeen Aga, Sriram Krishnamoorthy, and Satish Narayanasamy. 2015. CilkSpec: optimistic concurrency for Cilk. In *SC*. 83.
[5] Kunal Agrawal, Charles E Leiserson, and Jim Sukha. 2010. Executing task graphs using work-stealing. In *IPDPS*. 1–12.
[6] Vineet Bafna and Nathan Edwards. 2003. On de novo interpretation of tandem mass spectra for peptide identification. In *RECOMB*. 9–18.
[7] Michael A Bender, Roozbeh Ebrahimi, Jeremy T Fineman, Golnaz Ghasemiesfeh, Rob Johnson, and Samuel McCauley. 2014. Cache-adaptive algorithms. In *SODA*. 958–971.
[8] Guy E Blelloch, Jeremy T Fineman, Phillip B Gibbons, and Harsha Vardhan Simhadri. 2011. Scheduling irregular parallel computations on hierarchical caches. In *SPAA*. 355–366.
[9] Robert D Blumofe and Charles E Leiserson. 1999. Scheduling multithreaded computations by work stealing. *JACM* (1999), 46(5):720–748.
[10] Uday Bondhugula, Albert Hartono, Jagannathan Ramanujam, and Ponnuswamy Sadayappan. 2008. A practical automatic polyhedral parallelizer and locality optimizer. *ACM SIGPLAN Notices* (2008), 43(6):101–113.
[11] Richard Brent. 1974. The parallel evaluation of general arithmetic expressions. *JACM* (1974), 21:201–206.
[12] Cary Cherng and Richard E Ladner. 2005. Cache efficient simple dynamic programming. In *AofA DMTCS*. 49:58.
[13] Rezaul Chowdhury. 2007. *Cache-efficient Algorithms and Data Structures: Theory and Experimental Evaluation*. Ph.D. Dissertation. Department of Computer Sciences, The University of Texas at Austin.
[14] Rezaul Chowdhury, Pramod Ganapathi, Jesmin Jahan Tithi, Charles Bachmeier, Bradley C. Kuszmaul, Armando Solar-Lezama Charles E. Leiserson, and Yuan Tang. 2016. AutoGen: automatic discovery of cache-oblivious parallel recursive algorithms for solving dynamic programs. In *PPoPP*.
[15] Rezaul Chowdhury and Vijaya Ramachandran. 2006. Cache-oblivious dynamic programming. In *SODA*. 591–600.
[16] Rezaul Chowdhury and Vijaya Ramachandran. 2008. Cache-efficient dynamic programming algorithms for multicores. In *SPAA*. 207–216.
[17] Rezaul Chowdhury and Vijaya Ramachandran. 2010. The cache-oblivious Gaussian elimination paradigm: theoretical framework, parallelization and experimental evaluation. *Theory of Computing Systems* (2010), 47(4):878–919.
[18] Rezaul Chowdhury, Vijaya Ramachandran, Francesco Silvestri, and Brandon Blakeley. 2013. Oblivious algorithms for multicores and networks of processors. *J. Parallel and Distrib. Comput.* (2013), 73(7):911–925.
[19] Thomas Cormen, Charles Leiserson, Ronald Rivest, and Clifford Stein. 2009. *Introduction to Algorithms*. MIT press.
[20] Alain Darte, Georges-André Silber, and Frédéric Vivien. 1997. Combining retiming and scheduling techniques for loop parallelization and loop tiling. *Parallel Processing Letters* (1997), 7(4):379–392.
[21] Jun Du, Ce Yu, Jizhou Sun, Chao Sun, Shanjiang Tang, and Yanlong Yin. 2013. EasyHPS: a multilevel hybrid parallel system for dynamic programming. In *IPDPSW*. 630–639.
[22] Richard Durbin, Sean R. Eddy, Anders Krogh, and Graeme Mitchison. 1998. *Biological Sequence Analysis: Probabilistic Models of Proteins and Nucleic Acids*. Cambridge university press.
[23] Robert W Floyd. 1962. Algorithm 97: shortest path. *CACM* (1962), 5(6):345.
[24] Matteo Frigo, Charles E. Leiserson, Harald Prokop, and Sridhar Ramachandran. 1999. Cache-oblivious algorithms. In *40th FOCS*. 285–297.
[25] Zvi Galil and Raffaele Giancarlo. 1989. Speeding up dynamic programming with applications to molecular biology. *TCS* (1989), 64(1):107–118.
[26] Zvi Galil and Kunsoo Park. 1994. Parallel algorithms for dynamic programming recurrences with more than O (1) dependency. *JPDC* (1994), 21(2):213–222.
[27] Pramod Ganapathi. 2016. *Automatic Discovery of Efficient Divide-&-Conquer Algorithms for Dynamic Programming Problems*. Ph.D. Dissertation. Department of Computer Science, Stony Brook University.
[28] Robert Giegerich and Georg Sauthoff. 2011. Yield grammar analysis in the Bellman's GAP compiler. In *Workshop on language descriptions, tools & applications*.
[29] Georgios Goumas, Aristidis Sotiropoulos, and Nectarios Koziris. 2001. Minimizing completion time for loop tiling with computation and communication overlapping. In *IPDPS*. 10.
[30] Tobias Grosser, Armin Groesslinger, and Christian Lengauer. 2012. Polly-performing polyhedral optimizations on a low-level intermediate representation. *PPL* 22(04) (2012).
[31] Dan Gusfield. 1997. *Algorithms on Strings, Trees and Sequences: Computer Science and Computational Biology*. Cambridge University Press.
[32] Daniel S. Hirschberg. 1975. A linear space algorithm for computing maximal common subsequences. *CACM* (1975), 18(6):341–343.
[33] Shachar Itzhaky, Rohit Singh, Armando Solar-Lezama, Kuat Yessenov, Yongquan Lu, Charles Leiserson, and Rezaul Chowdhury. 2016. Deriving divide-and-conquer dynamic programming algorithms using solver-aided transformations. In *OOPSLA*. ACM, 145–164.
[34] Kenneth E. Iverson. 1962. *A Programming Language*. Wiley.
[35] Anany V Levitin. 2009. *Introduction to Design & Analysis of Algorithms: For Anna University, 2/e*. Pearson Education India.
[36] Weiguo Liu and Bertil Schmidt. 2004. A generic parallel pattern-based system for bioinformatics. In *Euro-Par*. 989–996.
[37] Preeti Ranjan Panda, Hiroshi Nakamura, Nikil D Dutt, and Alexandru Nicolau. 1999. Augmenting loop tiling with data alignment for improved cache performance. *Computers, IEEE Transactions on* (1999), 48(2):142–149.
[38] Louis-Noël Pouchet, Uday Bondhugula, Cédric Bastoul, Albert Cohen, J Ramanujam, and P Sadayappan. 2010. Combined iterative and model-driven optimization in an automatic parallelization framework. In *SC*. 1–11.
[39] Yewen Pu, Rastislav Bodik, and Saurabh Srivastava. 2011. Synthesis of first-order dynamic programming algorithms. In *ACM SIGPLAN Notices*. 46(10):83–98.
[40] Raphael Reitzig. 2012. *Automated Parallelisation of Dynamic Programming Recursions*. Master's thesis. University of Kaiserslautern.
[41] Lakshminarayanan Renganarayanan, Daegon Kim, Michelle Mills Strout, and Sanjay Rajopadhye. 2012. Parameterized loop tiling. *TOPLAS* (2012), 34(1):3.
[42] Hiroaki Sakoe and Seibi Chiba. 1978. Dynamic programming algorithm optimization for spoken word recognition. *Transactions on Acoustics, Speech and Signal Processing* (1978), 26(1):43–49.
[43] Vivek Sarkar and Nimrod Megiddo. 2000. An analytical model for loop tiling and its solution. In *ISPASS*. 146–153.
[44] Shanjiang Tang, Ce Yu, Jizhou Sun, Bu-Sung Lee, Tao Zhang, Zhen Xu, and Huabei Wu. 2012. EasyPDP: an efficient parallel dynamic programming runtime system for computational biology. *TPDS* (2012), 23(5):862–872.
[45] Yuan Tang, Rezaul Chowdhury, Bradley C Kuszmaul, Chi-Keung Luk, and Charles E Leiserson. 2011. The pochoir stencil compiler. In *SPAA*. 117–128.
[46] Yuan Tang, Ronghui You, Haibin Kan, Jesmin Jahan Tithi, Pramod Ganapathi, and Rezaul Chowdhury. 2014. Improving parallelism of recursive stencil computations without sacrificing cache performance. In *2nd WOSC*. 1–7.
[47] Yuan Tang, Ronghui You, Haibin Kan, Jesmin Jahan Tithi, Pramod Ganapathi, and Rezaul Chowdhury. 2015. Cache-oblivious wavefront: improving parallelism of recursive dynamic programming algorithms without losing cache-efficiency. In *PPoPP*. 205–214.
[48] Jesmin Jahan Tithi. 2015. *Engineering High-performance Parallel Algorithms with Applications to Bioinformatics*. Ph.D. Dissertation. State University of New York at Stony Brook, ProQuest Dissertations Publishing.
[49] Jesmin Jahan Tithi, Pramod Ganapathi, Aakrati Talati, Sonal Aggarwal, and Rezaul Chowdhury. 2015. High-performance energy-efficient recursive dynamic programming with matrix-multiplication-like flexible kernels. In *IPDPS*. 303–312.
[50] George Tzenakis, Angelos Papatriantafyllou, Hans Vandierendonck, Polyvios Pratikakis, and Dimitrios S Nikolopoulos. 2013. BDDT: block-level dynamic dependence analysis for task-based parallelism. In *APPT*. 17–31.
[51] Stephen Warshall. 1962. A theorem on boolean matrices. *JACM* (1962), 9(1):11–12.
[52] Michael S Waterman et al. 1995. *Introduction to Computational Biology: Maps, Sequences and Genomes*. Chapman & Hall Ltd.
[53] Michael Edward Wolf. 1992. *Improving Locality and Parallelism in Nested Loops*. Ph.D. Dissertation. Stanford University.

Bounding Cache Miss Costs of Multithreaded Computations Under General Schedulers

Richard Cole*
Courant Institute, New York University
New York, NY 10012
cole@cs.nyu.edu

Vijaya Ramachandran†
Department of Computer Science, UT-Austin
Austin, TX 78712
vlr@cs.utexas.edu

ABSTRACT

We analyze the caching overhead incurred by a class of multithreaded algorithms when scheduled by an arbitrary scheduler. We obtain bounds that match or improve upon the well-known $O(Q + S \cdot (M/B))$ caching cost for the randomized work stealing (RWS) scheduler, where S is the number of steals, Q is the sequential caching cost, and M and B are the cache size and block (or cache line) size respectively.

CCS CONCEPTS

•Theory of computation → Shared memory algorithms;

KEYWORDS

Fork-Join algorithms; cache oblivious; schedulers

ACM Reference format:
Richard Cole and Vijaya Ramachandran. 2017. Bounding Cache Miss Costs of Multithreaded Computations Under General Schedulers. In *Proceedings of SPAA '17, July 24-26, 2017, Washington DC, USA*, , 12 pages.
DOI: 10.1145/3087556.3087572

1 INTRODUCTION

The design and analysis of multithreaded cache-efficient parallel algorithms has been widely studied in recent years [6, 7, 11, 12, 17, 19]. Many of these algorithms are based on parallel divide and conquer (called variously *hierarchical divide and conquer* [6], *hierarchical balanced parallel (HBP) computations* [13, 14], etc.). The performance of these algorithms is usually analyzed for a specific scheduler, especially with regard to caching costs.

In this paper, we present general bounds on the cache miss cost for several algorithms, when scheduled using an arbitrary scheduler. Our bounds match the best bounds known for work stealing schedulers. The class of algorithms we consider includes efficient multithreaded algorithms for several fundamental problems such as matrix multiplication [19], the Gaussian Elimination Paradigm (GEP) [11], longest common subsequence (LCS) and related dynamic programming problems [9, 11], FFT [19], SPMS sorting [17], list ranking [12], and graph connectivity [12]. These are all well-known multithreaded algorithms that use parallel recursive divide and conquer. Our contribution here is to analyze their caching performance with a general scheduler, as a function of the number of parallel tasks scheduled across the processors (or *steals*), and to obtain bounds that match the current best bounds known only for work stealing schedulers.

We only consider multithreaded algorithms in this paper. As such, we do not directly deal with related work on parallel, cache-efficient algorithms designed for specific models such as the Multi-BSP, Parallel External Memory model, etc. [2–4, 22, 23], though all of the algorithms we consider can be scheduled and analyzed on these models.

1.1 Related Work

In a parallel execution of a multithreaded algorithm, the computation starts on one processor, and the scheduler moves parallel tasks to idle processors as needed. Each move of a parallel task from one processor to another is called a steal.

Let Q be the sequential caching cost of a multithreaded computation, and let $C(S)$ be the caching cost incurred in a parallel execution with S steals. Acar et al. [1] observed that an execution of a computation that incurs S steals when scheduled under randomized work-stealing (RWS) can be partitioned into $O(S)$ fragments, where each fragment runs on a single processor in this parallel execution, and represents a contiguous portion of the sequential execution of the computation. They then observed that the computation regains the state of the sequential execution after reading at most M/B distinct blocks, and therafter inherits the sequential cache complexity. Thus, $C(S)$ is bounded by $O(Q + S \cdot M/B)$.

Frigo and Strumpen [20] considered the above set-up for computations where any fragment of size r that occurs in a parallel execution incurs $O(f(r))$ cache misses, for some concave function f. They then showed that some of the known cache-efficient multithreaded algorithms have good concave functions f satisfying the above property and used this to refine the bound in [1]. If a multithreaded algorithm makes calls to different subroutines with different cache complexities, then the concave function will be at most as good as the least efficient of the caching bounds. Thus, the results in [20] are most effective for cache-efficient algorithms that recursively call only themselves, such as the matrix multiplication

*This work was supported in part by NSF grants CCF-1217989 and CCF-1527568.
†This work was supported in part by NSF Grant CCF-1320675.

SPAA '17, July 24-26, 2017, Washington DC, USA

DOI: 10.1145/3087556.3087572

HBP Algorithm	**Seq. Cache Bound Q**	**Cache miss bound with S steals, $C(S) = \min\{A,B\}$**	
		Bound A (Thm. 1)	**Bound B (Thm. 2)**
Scan, Prefix Sums	n/B	$Q + (M/B) \cdot S$	$Q + S$
Matrix Transpose	n/B	$Q + (M/B) \cdot S$	$Q + S \cdot B$
n^3 Matrix Multiply, GEP	$n^3/(B\sqrt{M})$	$Q + (M/B) \cdot S$	$Q + (n^2/B) \cdot S^{\frac{1}{3}} + S \cdot B$
Strassen Matrix Multiply	$n^\lambda/(BM^\gamma)$	$Q + (M/B) \cdot S$	$Q + (n^2/B) \cdot S^{1-\frac{2}{\lambda}} + S \cdot B$
FFT, SPMS, List Ranking	$\frac{n}{B} \cdot \log_M n$	$Q + (M/B) \cdot S$	$Q + \frac{n}{B} \cdot \frac{\log n}{\log[(n \log n)/S]} + S \cdot B$
Graph Connectivity	$\frac{n+m}{B} \cdot \log_M n$	$Q + (M/B) \cdot S$	$Q + \frac{n+m}{B} \cdot \frac{\log^2 n}{\log[((n+m)\log n)/S]} + S \cdot B$
Finding LCS sequence	$n^2/(BM)$	$Q + (M/B) \cdot S$	$Q + (n/B) \cdot \sqrt{S} + S \cdot B$

Table 1: Our upper bound for cache miss cost, $C(S)$, with S steals, for a general scheduler; $O(\cdot)$ is omitted. The sequential cache miss bound is Q, and a tall cache is assumed. Always, the new bound for a general scheduler matches or improves the bound in [1, 20] and matches the bound in [15]; all of these prior bounds held only for work stealing. For Strassen, $\lambda = \log_2 7$ and $\gamma = (\lambda/2) - 1$ [13, 19].

algorithm with depth n (Depth-n-MM), the Gaussian Elimination paradigm (IGEP) [11], and stencil computations. Further, even for these algorithms, the results in [20] apply only if parent stealing is used (i.e., if the node forking the two parallel tasks is placed on the task queue, as is the case in Intel CilkPlus). In [15] an example is given where the result in [20] for Depth-n-MM does not hold under child stealing (where the right child of the forking node is placed on the task queue, as in Intel TBB and Microsoft PPL).

The bounds in [20] were matched and also extended to a more general class of HBP computations for RWS under child stealing in [15]. The methodology in [15] is to charge the cost of the cache miss overhead to $O(S)$ disjoint tasks in the sequential computation, where each task is an HBP sub-computation, and then to bound the cost of the worst-case configuration of such a collection of $O(S)$ disjoint tasks.

These prior results were reported only for RWS, but the analysis holds for any work stealing scheduler. Work stealing is a natural and effective method for scheduling multithreaded algorithms, and is implemented in CilkPlus, TBB and PPL, as noted above. A key feature of work-stealing is that the task that an idle processor steals (i.e., moves) from another processor is the one at the head of the other processor's task queue. In other words, tasks are stolen from the task queue at any given processor in FIFO order. However, a multithreaded algorithm may be scheduled in environments where a work stealing scheduler is not available. In such a case, the system scheduler will be used to schedule the parallel tasks and this scheduler may not necessarily schedule tasks in FIFO order. For instance, SJF (Shortest Job First) is a commonly used scheduling policy, and this policy need not be FIFO at each processor. The Linux scheduler uses the Completely Fair Scheduler, and it is not clear if that scheduler uses the FIFO needed for work stealing.

Another reason for considering a general scheduler is to obtain 'oblivious' results as in sequential cache-oblivious algorithms [19], network-oblivious algorithms for distributed memory [5], and multicore-oblivious [12] and resource-oblivious [14, 17] algorithms for shared memory multicores. In all of these cases the desire is to have algorithms analyzed in a machine-independent manner so that bounds hold across diverse platforms. In that spirit our results give scheduler-independent results that extend across all types of schedulers as long as there is no preemption, duplication of tasks, or failures.

Further, one could consider future scenarios where new criteria such as power consumption may dictate the need for new types of schedulers. Our results show that there is not much degradation in the caching performance as a function of the number of parallel tasks scheduled even if such schedulers do not steal from the top of the dequeue.

If the scheduler does not steal in FIFO order, then the analysis used to derive the earlier results for caching overhead when using RWS is not valid. Thus, new techniques need to be developed in order to analyze caching costs with a general scheduler. This is the topic of this paper.

In this paper, we show that for a general class of multithreaded algorithms, including all those with series-parallel fork-join calls, the cache miss excess remains bounded by $O(Q + S \cdot M/B)$, and that for a class of well-structured HBP algorithms (including those listed in Table 1), the cache miss excess is bounded by the best bound currently known for work stealing schedulers.

We are able to achieve good bounds even when considering the worst-case effects of 'false-sharing' (fs misses) as long as we use the algorithms with the small modifications given in [14]; we omit discussing this in this extended abstract.

1.2 Overview of Our Results

We assume a tall cache ($M \geq B^2$), and we assume that a sequential execution that accesses r data items accesses $O((r/B) + \sqrt{r})$ blocks (see Sections 6.3, 6.4). Our main results are Theorems 2.1 and 2.5 in Section 2, and Table 1 lists the bounds we obtain for some well-known algorithms by applying these two theorems. All of these algorithms are well-known parallel multithreaded algorithms, and all have excellent sequential cache-oblivious caching bounds.

Consider a computation whose parallel execution incurs S steals. Previous analyses for the cache miss overhead all took the following approach: the sequential execution was partitioned into $O(S)$ consecutive pieces or fragments, which we call *task kernels*, with the property that in the parallel execution each task kernel was executed on a single processor. Then the analyses amounted to bounding the amount of data a task kernel uses that was used by an earlier task kernel in the sequential execution and which could have been available in the cache; this upper bounds the additional reloads due to steals. However, with a general scheduler, a partitioning with these properties in not possible in general, as we show in Example 4.3 in Section 4.2. Nonetheless, we are able to recover the simple $O(Q + S \cdot M/B)$ bound on $C(S)$, the number of cache misses with S steals. Further, with a more sophisticated analysis we achieve the results in Bound B in Table 1, bounds that match the earlier results in [15] which hold only for RWS, and which can be a strict improvement (depending on the value of S) over the $O(Q + S \cdot M/B)$ bound, as shown in Section 2.1 for FFT and SPMS sorting.

At a high level, our approach to establishing our bounds is similar to the one used in [15] for work stealing schedulers. It bounds the caching overhead for an HBP computation incurring S steals as being no more than the cost of reloading the cache for $O(S)$ HBP tasks in the computation. The final bound is obtained by considering the worst-case cost for a collection of $O(S)$ HBP tasks in the computation. However, within this high level approach, our current method differs from the one in [15], as described below.

In [15], the $O(S)$ tasks were required to be disjoint tasks (as was the case in [1, 20] as well), and this resulted in several different case analyses for different types of HBP computations. It also required rather strong balance conditions for the sizes of sibling recursive tasks because costs were being allocated from a steal-incurring subtask to a steal-free sibling. In our current analysis, we allow these $O(S)$ distinct HBP tasks to overlap, and we allocate the costs to the steal-incurring task itself. This allows us to unify the analysis for all HBP computations into a single argument.

Organization of the Paper. In Section 2 we state our two main theorems, and we describe the concrete results we obtain from our second theorem for specific algorithms. Section 3 gives basic background on work stealing and scheduling parallel tasks, and Section 4 describes our set-up for general schedulers. In Section 5 we define *task kernels* and give a proof of our first main theorem (Theorem 2.1). Finally, in Section 6 we present our refined analysis for BP and HBP computations, and establish our second main theorem. Some of the details and proofs are deferred to the full paper [16].

2 OUR MAIN THEOREMS

We consider a shared memory parallel environment comprising p processors, each with a private cache of size M. The p processors communicate through an arbitrarily large shared memory. Data is organized in blocks (or 'cache lines') of size B.

We will express parallelism through paired fork and join operations. A fork spawns two tasks that can execute in parallel. Its corresponding join is a synchronization point: both of the spawned tasks must complete before the computation can proceed beyond this join. For an overview of this model, see Chapter 27 in [18].

Our first theorem applies to the cache miss overhead under the scheduling of any series-parallel computation dag by a general scheduler, and it generalizes an earlier result in [1] that held only for RWS.

THEOREM 2.1. *Let $\mathcal{A}$ be a series-parallel algorithm and suppose it incurs S steals in a parallel execution using a general scheduler. Then the cache miss cost of this execution is $C(S) = O(Q + S \cdot M/B)$, where Q is the number of cache misses incurred by $\mathcal{A}$ in a sequential execution.*

Our second theorem improves on the above theorem for the following class of HBP algorithms, based on [13, 15]. Here, given a task τ, its *size*, $|\tau|$, is the number of distinct data items read or written by τ; this excludes any local variables declared by τ. A *balanced fork-join computation* consists of a fork tree followed by a join tree on a common set of leaves, where the sizes of the tasks decrease geometrically from parent to child in the fork tree.

Definition 2.2. **(HBP task)** A BP algorithm (or task) is a balanced binary fork-join computation on n leaves, where each fork, join and leaf node performs $O(1)$ computation.

A Type 1 HBP task comprises a sequence of $O(1)$ BP tasks.

A Type k HBP task, for $k \geq 2$, comprises a sequence of $O(1)$ *constituent* tasks. Each constituent task is either a BP task, a Type $h < k$ HBP task, or a *recursive constituent*, which is an ordered collection of one or more recursive instances of the Type k task. Each such ordered collection is initiated by a binary fork tree and ended by a complementary join tree.

In addition, certain requirements apply to data layout and data accesses as described in Section 6.2.

In order to bound the additional cache misses incurred due to steals, we now define $x(\tau)$, the *extended size* of τ, as follows.

Definition 2.3. **(Extended size)** Let τ be a task that calls $\tau_1, \tau_2, \ldots, \tau_l$, where each τ_i is a BP constituent task or an individual recursive task forked by a recursive constituent of τ. Then, τ's extended size $x(\tau)$ is given by $x(\tau) = |\tau| + \sum_{i=1}^{l} |\tau_i|$,

The extended size of a task τ incorporates τ's size, $|\tau|$, together with the sizes of individual tasks in its constituent tasks. The additional term over $|\tau|$ is the sum of the sizes of the tasks called by τ. This is done in order to account for the fact that a stolen sub-task of τ may need to read again some of this data, and τ can have several stolen sub-tasks. Also, there may be overlap in the data accessed by different tasks called recursively by τ. In general, in the extended size of τ the individual sizes of the tasks called by τ are added to the size of τ, possibly resulting in a value much larger than $|\tau|$. However, for all the algorithms we consider (see Table 1), the value of $x(\tau)$ remains $O(|\tau|)$.

We now state the constraints we impose on the algorithms we consider. To achieve the strongest cache miss bounds we need the algorithm to be cache-compliant, as defined next.

Definition 2.4. **(Cache-compliant task)** An HBP task $\mathcal{A}$ is *cache-compliant* if for each recursive task τ in $\mathcal{A}$ and for each recursive call τ' made by τ, there is a constant $\alpha < 1$ such that

- $|\tau'| \leq \alpha|\tau|$,
- $x(\tau') \leq \alpha \cdot x(\tau)$, and
- τ makes $O(|\tau|)$ recursive calls.

All the algorithms we consider are cache-compliant.

Our second theorem, given below, provides a refined bound for $C(S)$ for cache-compliant HBP algorithms (Table 1 gives a tighter result for Scan and Prefix Sums that does not follow directly from Theorem 2.5; that result is shown in Section 6.3).

THEOREM 2.5. *Suppose a cache-compliant Type k HBP algorithm $\mathcal{A}$ incurs S steals when executed using a general scheduler, and suppose that in a sequential execution $\mathcal{A}$ incurs Q cache misses.*
(i) If $k = 1$ then $C(S) = O(Q + S \cdot B)$.
(ii) If $k \geq 2$ then there is a collection $\tau_1, \tau_2, \ldots, \tau_l$ of distinct recursive tasks, with $l = O(S)$, where each of the τ_i is an h-HBP task for some $2 \leq h \leq k$, including possibly the whole computation, such that the cost, $C(S)$, of the cache misses incurred by this execution of $\mathcal{A}$ is bounded by

$$C(S) = O\left(Q + (\sum_{i=1}^{l} x(\tau_i)/B) + S \cdot B\right).$$

With the above bound in hand, it will suffice to bound $\sum_i x(\tau_i)/B$, where the sum is over all l tasks specified in Theorem 2.5. The result is a bound on $C(S)$ that is never worse than the earlier bound of $O(Q+S\cdot M/B)$, and in some cases improves on it, and which applies not only to work stealing schedulers but also to general schedulers.

As in [1, 8], we can incorporate the above bound for the overall cache miss cost $C(S)$ for any scheduler that steals S tasks into a bound on the overall time for the parallel execution as follows. Let b be the cost of a cache miss, and s the cost of a steal, i.e., s is the time taken by the scheduler to transfer a parallel task from its original processor to another processor that will execute it in parallel. Let T_1 be the sequential execution time for the computation, let T_∞ be the span (or critical path length) of the parallel computation, and let I be the total time spent by processors idling while not computing, stealing, or waiting on a cache miss. Then the time taken by this parallel execution is given by:

$$T_p = \frac{1}{p}(T_1 + b \cdot C(S) + s \cdot S + I) + b \cdot T_\infty.$$

In the above equation, S and I depend on the scheduler: A well-designed scheduler would steal as few tasks as it can while keeping all processors engaged in computation. Our contribution in this paper is to obtain a good bound for cache-compliant HBP computations for the term $C(S)$ in the above equation.

At a high level, our analysis proceeds as follows. It identifies $O(S)$ 'special' recursive tasks, some of which may be nested one in another, and assigns to these special tasks all the cache-miss costs apart from the sequential execution cost. In addition, each steal will be assigned to a special task (this task will be said to *own* the steal). Let τ_i be one of these special tasks and suppose it owns S_i steals; then the costs assigned to τ_i will be bounded by $O(x(\tau_i)/B + S_i \cdot B)$ as we will see later.

2.1 Analysis of Specific Algorithms

We apply Theorem 2.5 to several well-known algorithms, to obtain the results for bound B in Table 1. The GEP and LCS algorithms are presented in [10, 17], while the others are described in [14] (where their false sharing costs are analyzed). Here we obtain bound B for a couple of entries listed in Table 1. For the remaining entries in the table see [16].

$\log^2 n$-MM. This is a Type 2 HBP that has one recursive constituent that makes 8 recursive calls to $n/2\times n/2$ matrices, and a BP task that adds up the outputs of the recursive calls in pairs. Its sequential cache complexity is $O(n^3/(B\sqrt{M}))$. Applying Theorem 2.5 we see that the l largest HBP tasks are obtained by including all recursive tasks up to $j = (1/3)\log l$ levels of recursion. The sum of the sizes of these tasks is $O((n^2/4^j)\cdot 8^{(1/3)\log l}) = O(n^2 \cdot l^{1/3})$. Since $l = O(S)$, we obtain the overall cache miss cost with S steals as $O(Q + (n^2/B)\cdot S^{1/3} + S\cdot B)$.

FFT, SPMS Sort. The algorithms for both FFT [19] and SPMS sort [17] have the same structure, being Type 2 HBP algorithms that recursively call two collections of $O(\sqrt{n})$ parallel tasks of size $O(\sqrt{n})$, together with a constant number of calls to BP computations.

To bound $\sum_{i=1}^{O(S)} |v_i|/B$ for FFT, we observe that the total size of tasks of size r or larger is $O(n\log_r n)$, and there are $\Theta(\frac{n}{r}\log_r n)$ such tasks. Choosing r so that $S = \Theta(\frac{n}{r}\log_r n)$ we obtain $r\log r = \Theta(n\log n/S)$, so $\log r = \Theta(\log([n\log n/S])$. Thus $\max_C \sum_{v_i\in C}\frac{|v_i|}{B} = O(\frac{n}{B}\log_r n) = O(\frac{n}{B}\frac{\log n}{\log[(n\log n)/S]})$.

The analysis for SPMS is very similar, except that we need to handle two BP computations with somewhat irregular access patterns.

Observation. For FFT and SPMS, our refined bound is strictly better than the $O(Q + S\cdot M/B)$ bound since our overhead remains $O(Q)$ when $M^\epsilon = O((n\log n)/S$ for any constant $\epsilon > 0$, while the simple bound needs $M\log M = O((n\log n)/S)$ for Q to dominate $S\cdot M/B$.

3 SCHEDULING PARALLEL TASKS

The *computation dag* for a computation on a given input is the acyclic graph that results when we have a vertex (or node) for each unit (or constant) time computation, and a directed edge from a vertex u to a vertex v if vertex v can begin its computation immediately after u and v's other predecessors complete their computations, but not before. Since we consider multithreaded algorithms with binary forking, where the fork-joins are nested, the computation dag is a series-parallel graph.

During the execution of a computation dag on a given input, a parallel task is created each time a fork step f is executed. At this point the main computation proceeds with the left child of f, as in a standard sequential dfs computation, while the task τ at the right child r of the fork node is made available to be scheduled in parallel with the main computation. (This is *child stealing*, or the *help-first policy* [21]; one could also use the work-first policy where the main computation proceeds with the task spawned at the right child.) The parallel task τ consists of all of the computation starting at r and ending at the step before the join corresponding to the fork step f. A run-time scheduler determines if a forked task is to be moved to another processor for execution in parallel.

3.1 Caching Overhead Under Work-stealing

An important class of schedulers is the work-stealing scheduler. Each processor maintains a task queue on which it enqueues the parallel tasks it generates. When a processor is idle it attempts to steal, i.e., obtain a parallel task from the head of the task queue of another processor. The exact method for identifying the processor from which to obtain an available parallel task determines the type of work-stealing scheduler being used; however the stolen task is always the task at the head of the task queue of the chosen processor. The most popular type is randomized work-stealing (RWS, see e.g., [8]), where a processor picks a random processor and steals the task at the head of its task queue, if there is one. Otherwise, it continues to pick random processors and tries to find an available parallel task until it succeeds, or the computation completes. RWS has been widely analyzed and used, notably in Cilk. The following is a well-known fact about work stealing schedulers (see Figure 1).

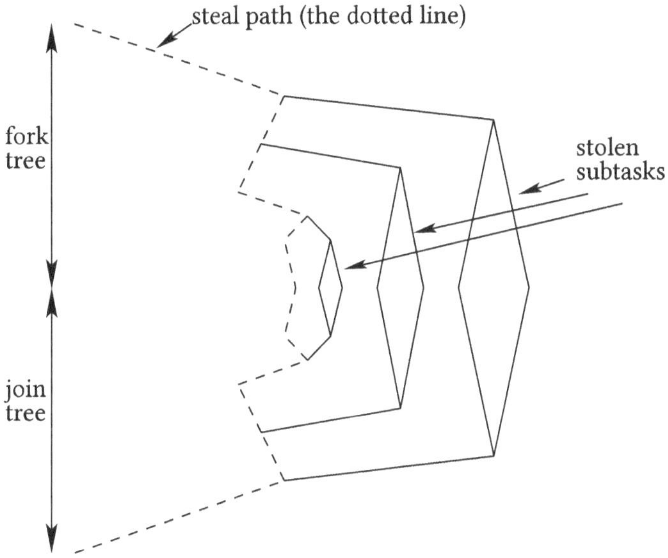

Figure 1: A steal path for a work-stealing scheduler with three stolen subtasks of a BP task.

Fact 1. **The Steal Path for Work-stealing Schedulers).** *Let τ be either the original task or a stolen subtask. Suppose that τ incurs steals of subtasks $\tau_1, \cdots, \tau_k$. Then there exists a path P_τ in τ's computation dag from its root to its final node such that the parent of every stolen task τ_i lies on P_τ, and every off-path right child of a fork node on P is the start node for a stolen subtask.*

We now review a well-known bound for RWS in Acar et al. [1] on $R(S)$, the caching overhead (over and above the sequential caching cost) in a parallel execution that incurs S steals. We will assume an optimal offline cache replacement policy (as in the sequential case). Let σ be the sequence of steps executed in a sequential execution. Now consider a parallel execution that incurs S steals. Partition σ into contiguous portions so that in the parallel execution each portion is executed in its sequential order on a single processor. Then, each processor can regain the state of the cache in the sequential execution once it has accessed M/B distinct blocks during its execution. Thus if there are K portions, then there will be $R(S) = O(K \cdot M/B)$ additional cache misses. (Actually, the justification of this claim requires the parallel analogue of the regularity assumption formulated in [19] to make it complete, see [17].)

It is shown in [1] that $K \leq 2S + 1$ for a work-stealing scheduler. This is readily seen from Fact 1. A steal creates three fragments within the sequential computation — (1) the sequential computation up to when the stolen task would start its computation, (2) the computation of the stolen task, which will occur on a different processor, and (3) the sequential computation following the stolen task. Each of these three fragments is computed sequentially. Each successive steal creates two additional fragments leading to the bound of $K \leq 2S + 1$ sequential fragments for a work stealing scheduler, and a bound of $R(S) = O(K \cdot M/B)$ additional cache misses. This implies $C(S) = O(Q + S \cdot (M/B))$.

4 GENERAL SCHEDULERS

In this paper, we consider the cache miss overhead for a general scheduler that is not necessarily work stealing. We will assume that there is no redundancy in the computation, and that each node in the computation dag is executed at exactly one processor. We will view the general scheduler as being similar to a work stealing scheduler, except that the task stolen from the chosen processor can be an arbitrary parallel task available for computation, not necessarily the task at the head of its task queue.

When a task other than the topmost task on a task queue is stolen, we call this a *deep* steal. More precisely, we have the following definition.

Definition 4.1. **(Deep steal)** Let σ be a task stolen from the task queue, Π, of τ, and suppose that σ is not the first task placed on Π. Let σ' be the task placed on Π immediately before σ. Then, this steal of σ is a *deep steal* if σ' is not stolen from Π.

In order to essentially maintain Fact 1 (the Steal Path Fact) we will treat all the tasks ahead of σ on the task queue Π as if they were 'pseudo-stolen' as per the following definition.

Definition 4.2. **(Pseudo-stolen task)** Consider the task queue Π for a task τ, and let σ be stolen from Π as a deep steal. Any task that was placed on Π before σ and which remains unstolen is a *pseudo-stolen* task.

We observe that in a computation that incurs deep steals, the steal path will contain not only the parent of every stolen task but also the parent of every pseudo-stolen task.

4.1 Execution Stacks

In order to obtain a tighter bound on the additional costs due to steals, we now take a closer look at how one stores variables that are generated during the execution of the algorithm. It is natural for the original task and each stolen task to each have an execution stack on which they store the variables declared by their residual task. But as we will see, in some circumstances, we may need more execution stacks. E_τ will denote the execution stack for a task τ if it has one. As is standard, each procedure and each fork node stores the variables it declares in a segment on the current top of the execution stack for the task to which it belongs, following the usual mode for a procedural language.

Execution Stack and Task Queue. The parallel tasks for a processor P are enqueued on its task queue in the order in which the segments for their parent fork nodes are created on P's execution stack. The task queue is a double-end queue, and P will remove an enqueued task σ from its task queue when it begins computing on σ's segment.

As noted in Section 3, work stealing is a popular scheduling strategy where a task that is stolen (i.e., transferred to another processor) is always the one that is at the head of the task queue in the processor from which it is stolen. However, with a general scheduler, an arbitrary task on the task queue can be stolen.

Cache Misses when Accessing an Execution Stack. Suppose that a subtask τ' is stolen from a task τ. Consider the join node v immediately following the node at which the computation of τ' terminates. Let P be the processor executing $\tau - \tau'$ when it reaches node v and let P' be the processor executing τ' at this point. To avoid unnecessary waiting, whichever processor (of P and P') reaches v second is the one that continues executing the remainder of τ. If this processor is P', we say that P' has *usurped* the computation of τ. The effect, in terms of cache misses, is that in order to access variables on E_τ, P' will incur cache misses that P might not. Even if P' does not usurp τ, P may have to read additional data when continuing the execution of τ beyond τ' (due to its having been first read by the stolen subtask). Our analysis of cache miss overhead in a parallel execution will use a single method to cover the costs in both cases. This analysis assumes that no data is in cache at the start of the execution of τ beyond τ', whether P or P' is performing this execution, and hence can only overestimate the necessary reloads of data.

Execution Stacks for a General Scheduler. We observe that when using a general scheduler, additional execution stacks may be needed. For suppose that processor P is executing a task τ from which a deep steal of subtask σ occurs. Let P' be the processor executing σ. Suppose that P is the first of P and P' to reach the join node at which the steal ends. Then P will leave the continuation of the execution of τ to P'. But P still needs to execute the parallel tasks remaining on its task queue, performing them in dfs order (i.e. from the rear of the queue). However, P cannot use the execution stack for τ to store the variables for these subtasks as (a) this would violate the standard practice in which the current variable order on the execution stack corresponds to the current path of open procedure calls, and (b) additional space on this stack may be needed for the execution by P' of the portion of τ following the join node. In these circumstances P will create a new execution stack for each such pseudo-stolen task on its task queue as and when it starts its execution. This is exactly what would happen were the task to be stolen. The difference is that this will not count as a steal. In fact, whether P reaches the join node first or not, it will need to execute the tasks remaining on its task queue, and it will use a new execution stack for each such pseudo-stolen task. P will continue to have a single task queue, however.

4.2 Caching Overhead for General Schedulers

We now give an example of an execution where a task could be fragmented into a sequence of several non-contiguous fragments of execution due to a single steal by a general scheduler, and hence the analysis in [1] for the cache miss excess bound of $R(S) = O(S \cdot M/B)$, which we saw earlier for work-stealing schedulers, does not immediately hold.

Example 4.3. See Figure 2. Let τ be a balanced fork-join task with n leaves, with unit-cost computation at each node. Suppose τ incurs one steal of a subtask τ_1, where the start of τ_1 is reached by traversing a path $\mathcal{P}$ of $k = (\frac{1}{2}\log n) - 1$ left child links followed by one right child link. Let $\mu_1, \mu_2, \ldots, \mu_k$ be the right subtasks of path $\mathcal{P}$, from top to bottom, preceding τ_1. Note that each of the tasks $\mu_1, \mu_2, \ldots, \mu_k$ is a pseudo-stolen task. Let $\overline{\mathcal{P}}$ be the path in the join tree complementary to $\mathcal{P}$ and suppose it comprises nodes $v_{k+1}, v_k, v_{k-1}, \ldots, v_1$ from bottom to top (v_1 is the root of the join tree and v_{k+1} is the join node that is the parent of the final node in the stolen subtask).

Let P be the processor executing τ initially and let P_1 be the processor executing stolen task τ_1. Suppose the timing is such that P_1 executes all the nodes on $\overline{\mathcal{P}}$. Then, P executes $k = \Theta(\log n)$ non-contiguous fragments of sequential computation, one for each μ_i. Likewise P_1 executes each of the v_i in turn, and these are also non-contiguous. Since $\Theta(\log n)$ fragments are created by one steal, the simple argument providing the $O(M/B)$ cache miss overhead per steal will not apply to general schedulers.

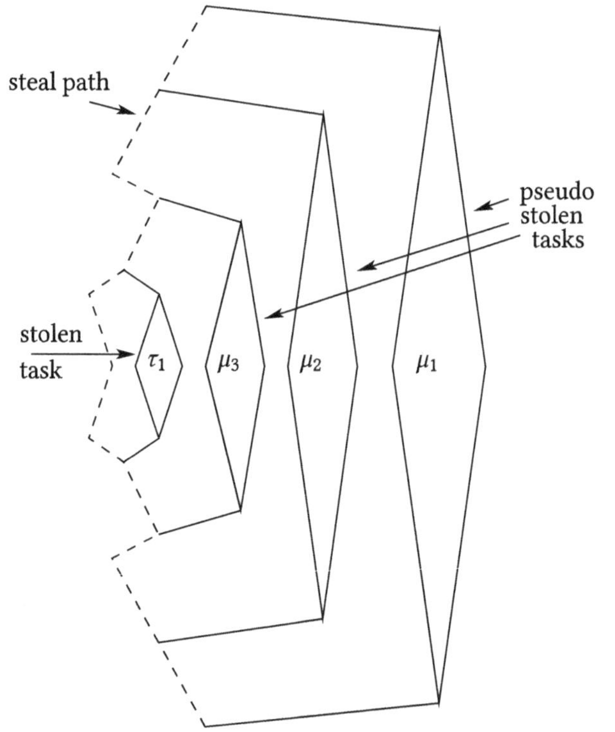

Figure 2: Illustrating Example 4.3. Here there are four stealable tasks to the right of the steal path, $\mu_1, \mu_2, \mu_3, \tau_1$. With a general scheduler, if the lowest such subtask, τ_1, were the only one that was stolen, this would be a deep steal inducing a pseudo task kernel consisting of the three other stealable tasks but not the portions of the steal path connecting them.

In the next section we recover the $R(S) = O(S \cdot M/B)$ bound for a general scheduler (for all series parallel computation dags) using a different analysis, and in Section 6 we present a further refined analysis for HBP algorithms.

5 THE NEW CACHE MISS ANALYSIS

We begin by specifying the partitioning of the computation into *task kernels* in Section 5.1. We follow this by demonstrating in Section 5.2 the simple $O(Q + S \cdot M/B)$ bound on the cache miss cost. We then outline our more sophisticated bound, analyzing in turn BP computations in Section 6.3 and HBP computations in Section 6.4.

5.1 Tasks and Task Kernels

Let τ be a task that incurs steals. Informally, a task kernel of τ is a maximal contiguous(or essentially contiguous) fragment of the computation that lies entirely within the unstolen portion of τ or entirely within a stolen task.

We now give the definition of the task kernels induced by the steals in a computation. This definition applies to any computation dag in which any given pair of forks and joins is either nested or disjoint, as for example in series-parallel dags, and this includes all HBP computations. Figure 3 gives examples of task kernels in a BP computation.

Definition 5.1. **(Task kernels.)** Consider a parallel execution of a computation C under a general scheduler, and suppose it incurs S steals, $\sigma_1, \sigma_2, \cdots, \sigma_S$, numbered in the order in which the stolen tasks are generated (i.e., the order in which the parent fork nodes are executed) in a sequential execution. In turn, we partition the computation dag into task kernels with respect to the sequence $\Sigma_i = \langle \sigma_1, \sigma_2, \ldots, \sigma_i \rangle$ to create the collection C_i. We let Σ_0 be the empty sequence and its associated partition C_0 be the single task kernel containing the entire computation dag. For each $i \geq 1$ the partition C_{i+1} is obtained from C_i as follows. Let τ be the task kernel in C_i that contains the fork node v_f at which steal σ_{i+1} is performed, and let v_j be the corresponding join node. Then, τ is partitioned into the following task kernels, each categorized as being of type *starting, finishing,* or *pseudo.* The initial task kernel in C_0 is given type starting.

1. τ_1, the stolen subtask created by σ_{i+1}. It is called a *starting task kernel.*

2. τ_2, the portion of τ preceding the stolen subtask in the sequential execution (this includes the portion of the computation descending from the left child of v_f that precedes v_j.) It is given the same type as τ.

3. If σ_{i+1} is a deep steal, let $\nu = \langle \mu_1, \mu_2, \ldots, \mu_k \rangle$ be the sequence of pseudo-stolen tasks forked from τ that are on the task queue for the processor executing τ at the time of this steal, with μ_k immediately preceding the subtask stolen by σ_{i+1}. Suppose that $\mu_{i_1}, \mu_{i_2}, \ldots, \mu_{i_j}$ (for $i_1 < i_2 < \cdots$) incur steals (note that any such steal would occur after σ_{i+1} in our ordering of steals). Then each of the collections $(\mu_1, \mu_2, \ldots, \mu_{i_1 - 1})$, $(\mu_{i_1}, \mu_{i_1+1}, \ldots, \mu_{i_2-1})$, …, $(\mu_{i_j}, \mu_{i_j+1}, \ldots, \mu_k)$ forms a *pseudo task kernel.*

4. τ_3, the portion of τ starting at v_j in the sequential execution but excluding the collection ν in part 3 above. This includes the join nodes following the pseudo-stolen tasks in ν. Then, $C_{i+1} = (C_i - \{\tau\}) \cup \{\tau_1, \tau_2, \tau_3\} \cup \{$pseudo task kernels formed in part 3, if any$\}$.

The final collection C_S is the collection of task kernels for this parallel execution of C.

In part 3 above, each pseudo task kernel comprises a maximal sequence of pseudo-stolen task kernels, which in execution order ends with a pseudo-stolen kernel that incurs a steal, with all the other pseudo-stolen task kernels in the sequence being steal-free. In part 4, the finishing task kernel μ_3 comprises the nodes descendant from v_j in the computation dag, including v_j itself. Note that in the sequential execution, both the finishing task kernel μ_3 and the pseudo task kernels in ν are executed after the stolen subtask, and they interleave in their execution. Some implications of this interleaving were explored in Example 4.3.

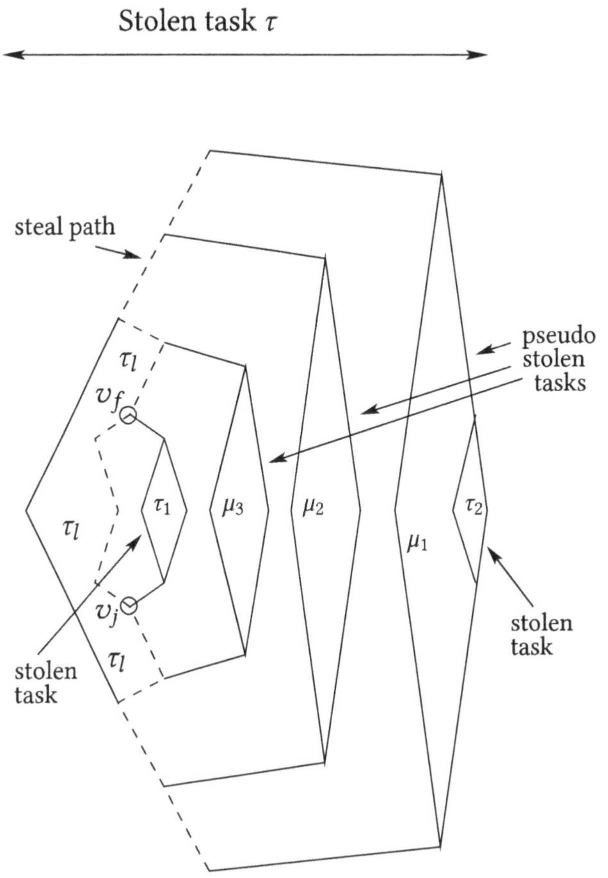

Figure 3: Task kernel types in a BP computation. Suppose a task τ undergoes a deep steal of subtask τ_1 at fork node v_f. Then τ_1 forms a starting task kernel. Also, τ_l, the portion of τ to the left of the steal path, plus the steal path up to but not including v_j, forms another starting task kernel. μ_1, μ_2, μ_3 are all pseudo stolen tasks; if μ_1 undergoes a steal but μ_2 and μ_3 do not, then $\mu_2 \cup \mu_3$ form a pseudo task kernel. Finally, the portion of the path of join nodes descending from v_j, and including v_j forms a finishing task kernel. (A finishing task kernel can incur a steal only in a Type k HBP, for $k > 1$.)

Lemma 5.2. *A series parallel computation with S steals has at most $4S + 1$ task kernels, of which at most $S + 1$ are starting kernels, S are finishing, and $2S$ are pseudo.*

Proof. In the absence of a deep steal, the number of task kernels is exactly $2S + 1$, since there is initially one task kernel, and each successive steal replaces a current task kernel with three new ones, according to parts 1, 2 and 4 in Definition 5.1, one finishing, one starting, and one of the previous type. This yields at most $S + 1$ starting and S finishing task kernels.

Now, let us consider the effect of part 3 in Definition 5.1, which creates $i_j + 1$ pseudo task kernels when i_j of the pseudo stolen tasks in v incur steals. We claim that we can bound the number of pseudo task kernels by $2S$ by charging at most two of them to each steal as follows. To each deep steal σ we assign the last pseudo task kernel $(\mu_{i_j+1}, \mu_{i_j+2}, \ldots, \mu_k)$ in its collection v (as defined in part 3 of Definition 5.1). We assign each of the remaining pseudo task kernels for σ to the earliest steal σ' (in our ordering) in the steal-incurring pseudo-stolen task kernel. Now consider σ'. It may be assigned another pseudo task kernel if it is itself a deep steal (in a different state of the execution stack). So σ' could be assigned two different pseudo task kernels. But it cannot be assigned a third one, since for any pseudo stolen task that contains v, the earliest steal in it is either σ or a steal earlier than σ. Thus, there are at most $2S$ additional task kernels created due to the pseudo task kernels, and this adds up to a total of at most $4S + 1$ task kernels. □

5.2 Proof of Theorem 1

Recall Example 4.3. Observe that the sequence $\langle \mu_k, v_k, \mu_{k-1}, v_{k-1}, \ldots, \mu_1, v_1 \rangle$ is contiguous. Thus each of P_1 and P executes a portion of the same contiguous sequence, and between them they execute all of it. Therefore their combined caching overhead is at most twice the sequential cost plus an additional M/B term for each of them. The proof of Theorem 2.1 will build on this insight to establish that in fact $C(S) = O(Q + S \cdot M/B)$ under a general scheduler for the entire class of series-parallel dags.

Proof of Theorem 2.1. For the purposes of this proof, we further refine the partitioning into task kernels as follows. Let μ be a pseudo task kernel that ends in a steal-incurring pseudo-stolen task. Let v_t be the terminal node in μ, i.e., the final node in μ in a sequential execution. Let v_j be the node following v_t in a sequential execution; then v_j is a join node and it lies in a finishing task kernel, which we will denote by v^μ. We split v^μ in two, where the initial portion v_1^μ contains the portion of v^μ up to, but not including v_j, and the latter portion v_2^μ contains the portion of v^μ starting at v_j. We then merge μ with v_1^μ to form a *super-finishing task kernel* μ-v (and we discard μ and v_1^μ). We repeatedly perform this split and merge into super-finishing task kernels at each steal-incurring pseudo task kernel.

The above process partitions the computation into at most $4S + 1$ task kernels, some of which may be super-finishing task kernels. Each of these task kernels has the useful property that it is executed contiguously in a sequential execution. Furthermore, at most two processors are used to execute each super-finishing task kernel, namely the processor starting the corresponding finishing kernel and the processor completing the corresponding pseudo task kernel. The other task kernels are all executed by a single processor.

Thus, as in the work-stealing case, for each of these $4S+1$ kernels there is a cost of $O(M/B)$ cache misses to restore the state that existed in the sequential execution, and as the execution of each of the at most S super-finishing kernels is shared among two processors, this at most doubles the cache miss cost of these portions of the computation, leading to a bound of at most $Q + (5S + 1) \cdot M/B$ additional cache misses due to the steals. This establishes the desired bound. □

6 THE HBP ANALYSIS

In this section we present an improved bound on the caching overhead of HBP algorithms under a general scheduler. Our approach to improving the bound in Theorem 2.1 is to carefully examine the features of HBP algorithms and tailor our analysis to algorithms in this class.

6.1 Reload Cost

We now define the notion of the reload cost of a sequence of steps executed within a sequential execution of a task τ.

Definition 6.1. **(Reload Cost)** Let μ be a sequence of steps within a task τ that are executed contiguously in a sequential execution of τ. The *reload cost of* μ is the number of distinct blocks accessed by μ during its execution, excluding blocks that contain variables declared during μ's computation.

In our analysis we will use the reload cost in place of the simple upper bound of M/B for the additional cache miss cost in executing a stolen task, or any task kernel that consists of the steps executed contiguously in a sequential execution (typically starting task kernels). We will use the following lemma in our analysis.

Lemma 6.2. *Let μ be a sequence of step within a task τ that are executed contiguously in a sequential execution of τ. Let Q be an upper bound on the number of cache misses incurred by τ during its execution of μ in a sequential execution. If μ is executed as a separate computation, then its cache miss cost is $O(Q+R)$, where R is its reload cost.*

Proof. Let us consider the additional cache miss cost in a separate execution of μ for reading in data that may have already resided in cache in an execution of μ within an execution of τ. Let us refer to the variables accessed by the execution of μ excluding variables declared during μ's computation as *new variables*, and the R blocks in memory in which they reside as *new blocks*. The only difference between a separate execution of μ and the execution of μ within a sequential execution of τ is that some of the R new blocks may already be in cache at the start of the latter execution, and hence the cost of reading these blocks is not included in Q. Now consider a separate execution of μ. If μ does not evict any of the R new blocks during its separate execution, then its cache miss cost is bounded by $O(Q + R)$ since the two executions only differ in the initial presence of these R blocks. On the other hand, any new block evicted by μ in its separate execution must also be evicted by τ in its execution of μ since both perform the same computation and both are assumed to use a given optimal cache replacement policy. Hence the number of cache misses in a separate execution of μ is bounded by $O(Q + R)$. □

The above proof does not address the 'block misalignment' cost [17] that arises from the fact that the block boundaries for data on an execution stack may be different in a parallel execution of a task from what they would be in a sequential execution. However, it is shown in [17] that its effect is bounded by a constant factor for HBP computations, if the cache miss bound is polynomial in M and B^1, so the bound in the above lemma holds even when accounting for block misalignment costs. In fact, this observation extends to the full analysis of the HPB algorithms in this paper.

6.2 Data Layout and Caching Costs

The caching cost of a computation, even in the sequential context, is highly dependent on the data layout and the pattern of accesses to the data during the computation. Since we are bounding the caching overhead for a class of algorithms, rather than for a specific algorithm, we now specify the type of data layouts that we allow in the algorithms we analyze, and the data access patterns. We focus mainly on BP computations, since that is where the most of variation in data layout occurs. An HBP computation may declare shared arrays which are accessed by BP computations within its recursive computations.

A BP computation will access access variables placed on the execution stack by its fork and join nodes as well as the shared data structures declared at the start of the computation. Recall that each BP node performs $O(1)$ computation. Here are the types of accesses we allow in the algorithms for which we bound the cache miss overhead.

Accesses to the Execution Stack. A BP or HBP node can access its $O(1)$ data, and it can also access data declared by its parent node.

Accesses to Shared Data. Consider a shared array where each data item is associated with a single node in the BP tree. Depending on the algorithm, a node may access just its associated data, or its data plus the data for some or all of its neighbors (children and parent). We will assume that the data in this array is laid out contiguously according to an *inorder* traversal of the BP fork tree. Our results will go through if preordering or postordering is used instead of the inorder traversal we assume. We choose to use inorder traversal because it aids in obtaining our false sharing results (false sharing is mentioned in the introduction, but is not included here).

Recall that we refer to the computation dag as a task, and any parallel task spawned by a fork node is also a task. We now define the notion of an extended task. Here we use the convention that a fork tree includes the non-fork leaf nodes that lie between it and the complementary join tree.

Definition 6.3. **(Extended task)** An *extended task* in a BP computation is any sequence of $r > 1$ consecutive nodes in the inorder traversal of its fork tree together with the complementary join nodes.

Any task is clearly also an extended task. From the definition of a starting task kernel, we can see that it is basically an extended task, except that some of the nodes on its steal path may not lie within this extended task kernel. Our cache miss analysis will separately analyze the costs due to the portion of the starting task kernel that forms an extended task, and the portion outside of this extended task.

We now define the *data dispersal* function $f(r)$ (previously called the cache friendliness function in [15]), which parameterizes the cost of accesses to the shared data structures.

[1]The polynomial dependence on M and B is implicit in the earlier work.

Definition 6.4. **(Data dispersal function $f(r)$ for BP computations)** A collection of r words is $f(r)$-dispersed if it is contained in $(r/B) + f(r)$ blocks. An extended task is $f(r)$-dispersed if the data its nodes access when executed is contained in $(r/B) + f(r)$ blocks. A BP computation is $f(r)$-dispersed if every extended task in it is $f(r)$-dispersed.

Notions similar to our use of $f(r)$ have been used in sequential caching analyses, though our set-up is more general, and this generality is needed to obtain bounds for the general class of BP and HBP computations, as opposed to analyzing a single algorithm.

Examples of data dispersal functions for algorithms for scans, prefix sums and matrix transpose are given in the full paper [16]. The algorithms in Table 1 (except for two procedures in SPMS sorting) are all $O(\sqrt{r})$-dispersed, and the ones for scans and prefix sums can be made $O(1)$-dispersed (for which we give an improved bound in Section 6.3). As a result they satisfy our assumption in Section 1.2 that a task that accesses r words will access $O((r/B) + \sqrt{r})$ blocks. We present this more general analysis here using $f(r)$ since it allows one to fully analyze the SPMS algorithm and other algorithms with complex data access patterns.

6.3 BP and Type 1 HBP Computations

Consider a BP computation τ. We begin with a high-level description of the structure of task kernels in a BP computation, which are also illustrated in Figure 3.

Starting task kernel. We first observe that in a BP computation, a starting task kernel will consist of a zig-zag path in the fork tree (the steal path) with subtasks comprising its off-path left subtrees, together with the complementary subtrees in the join tree, but not the complementary zig-zag path in the join tree, for it forms a finishing task kernel. Each left-going segment in the fork tree zig-zag path contains the parents of stolen or pseudo-stolen tasks, and the left subtrees in each right-going segment are part of the starting task kernel, as implicitly specified in Definition 5.1.

Pseudo task kernel. A pseudo task kernel comprises a sequence of one of more pseudo-stolen tasks, where each pseudo-stolen task is itself a (smaller) BP computation which returns to a parent node on the join path of the task from which it was "stolen." This join node is not part of the pseudo-stolen task or the pseudo task kernel. The topmost pseudo-stolen task in the pseudo task kernel may have incurred steals and as a result may have the same form as for a starting task kernel. The remaining pseudo-stolen tasks, if any, are steal-free.

Finishing task kernel. In a BP computation, a finishing task kernel is simply a path in the join tree that ends at a parent of a returning stolen task, or at the root.

Accessing the Shared Data Structures. We start by analyzing the cost of accesses to the shared data structures, and we first analyze this cost for finishing kernels. As noted above, in a BP computation, each finishing task kernel is simply a path in the join tree, and these paths are disjoint. As the computation at a node may also access the data for its parent, the accesses by a finishing task kernel may overlap those by other task kernels, but only at their end nodes.

We will bound the overall cache miss cost for all finishing task kernels, by separately analyzing the cost of accesses to nodes in the topmost $\log|\tau| - \log B$ levels in the join tree, and then to the nodes in the bottom $\log B$ levels. There are only $|\tau|/B$ nodes in total in the topmost $\log|\tau| - \log B$ levels, and each causes $O(1)$ cache misses and so collectively they have a cost of no more than $O(|\tau|/B)$ cache misses; this cost could be smaller if the $O(S)$ finishing task kernel join paths traverse fewer than $\Theta(|\tau|/B)$ nodes in this portion of the join tree. There are $O(\log B)$ accesses by each finishing task kernel to nodes in the bottom $\log B$ levels of the join tree; we simply charge these $O(\log B)$ accesses to each of these task kernels, which adds up to $O(S \cdot \log B)$ cache misses across all finishing task kernels. Hence the total cost of cache misses for finishing task kernels is $O(|\tau|/B + S \cdot \log B)$.

In the case that $f(r) = O(1)$ we can improve the $O(S \cdot \log B)$ term to $O(S)$. The reason is that the nodes in the subtree of height $\log B$ comprise $O(B)$ contiguous nodes in the inorder traversal and hence the data these B nodes access is stored in $O(1 + f(1)) = O(1)$ blocks. Clearly this bound also applies to the subset of $\log B$ nodes on the path in question. Consequently the execution of all these nodes, for each path, will incur $O(1)$ cache misses, or $O(S)$ cache misses when summed over all the finishing task kernels. This yields a total cost of $O(|\tau|/B + S)$ cache misses.

For a starting task kernel, the nodes on the zig-zag path in the fork tree which have off-path left children, plus their off-path subtrees, together with the complementary subtrees, are contiguous in inorder, and hence form an extended task. However, the accesses by the nodes on the remainder of the fork tree zig-zag path, namely the nodes with off-path right subtrees, will be non-contiguous. To bound this cost, we observe that the cost of the shared data structure accesses by these nodes is no larger than the bound for the finishing task kernels, as the complement of each fork tree zig-zag path is the union of one or more finishing task kernels. Hence we add in the charged cost to the complementary finishing task kernels. Clearly, each finishing task kernel is charged at most once.

In a pseudo task kernel μ, the data accesses are to the data for the nodes in the kernel plus the data for the parents of pseudo-stolen tasks forming μ, and this is a contiguous collection of nodes in the inorder traversal, aside any additional discontinuities caused by steals from μ, if any; any steals from the pseudo task kernel μ cause the same sort of discontinuities as the steals from a starting kernel, as discussed in the previous paragraph, and are bounded by a similar charging scheme.

Aside the accesses to the data for the portions of the fork tree zig-zag path nodes specified two paragraphs above, we see that every starting and pseudo task kernel is accessing a disjoint contiguous interval of nodes in inorder, hence by Definitions 6.1 and 6.4 and Lemma 6.2, the cache miss cost for these is bounded by $O(\sum_{i=1}^{k} r_i/B + f(r_i))$, where r_i is the number of nodes in the fork tree that are also in the i-th starting or pseudo kernel, $\sum_{i=1}^{k} r_i = n$, and there are $k = O(S)$ of these kernels in total. This sum totals $O(n/B + \sum_{i=1}^{k} f(r_i))$.

We now give tight upper bounds on this term for $f(r) = O(1)$ and $f(r) = O(\sqrt{r})$. Clearly, when $f(r) = O(1)$ this term is just $O(n/B + S)$. For $f(r) = O(\sqrt{r})$, the sum $\sum_{i=1}^{k} f(r_i)$ is maximized when the r_i are all equal, and contributes the term $O(S\sqrt{n/S}) = O(\sqrt{Sn})$. When $S \leq n/B^2$ this is $O(n/B)$ and when $S > n/B^2$, this is $O(S \cdot B)$. Thus it is always bounded by $O(n/B + S \cdot B)$.

Accessing the Execution Stacks. The overhead at execution stacks occurs when a stolen or pseudo-stolen task accesses the execution stack for its parent task when it returns from its computation, and when the subsequent finishing task kernel (in the case of a stolen task) has to reload the segments on the execution stack that it needs to access. This entails $O(1)$ accesses by each stolen task, $O(1)$ accesses by each pseudo-stolen task to the data segment for a distinct node in a finishing task kernel since each pseudo-stolen task is accessing its parent in the join tree, and $O(1)$ accesses by each node in each finishing task kernel, since each finishing task kernel accesses $O(1)$ data on the execution stack at each node on the join path that comprises the finishing task kernel. Since the segments for the nodes in each finishing task are consecutive on its execution stack, the cost for accessing a path of l nodes is $O(\lceil l/B \rceil)$ cache misses. Furthermore, each pseudo task kernel will be accessing a portion of a zig-zag path in the join tree, and it will be the only pseudo task kernel to access each of these nodes, aside from one finishing task kernel. Thus the cost of the accesses to the parent nodes in the join tree by each pseudo task kernel is no more that the cost for the corresponding finishing task kernel.

The total length of the paths for the finishing tasks is $O(|\tau|)$. Thus the cost of the accesses to the segments on the execution stack is bounded by $O(|\tau|/B + S)$; The $+S$ term is due to the rounding up of the term for each of the $O(S)$ paths, one path for each of the $O(S)$ finishing task kernels. Finally, the accesses by the stolen tasks add another $O(S)$ accesses to the total, which therefore sums to $O(|\tau|/B + S)$ cache misses. This bound for accesses to the execution stacks, together with the earlier bound for accesses by the task kernels, leads to the following lemma.

Lemma 6.5. *Consider a BP computation of size n. When scheduled with a general scheduler, it will incur $O((n/B) + S \cdot B)$ cache misses if $f(r) = O(\sqrt{r})$ and $O(n/B + S)$ cache misses if $f(r) = O(1)$, where S is the number of steals. In general, the number of cache misses will be bounded by $O(n/B + \max \sum_{i=1}^{3S+1} f(r_i))$ where $\sum_{i=1}^{3S+1} r_i = n$.*

Proof. The expression for the general bound arises because by Lemma 5.2, there are at most $3S + 1$ starting and pseudo kernels, each of which contributes to at most one of the $f(r_i)$ terms. □

This establishes part (i) of Theorem 2.5.

Note that it is only the accesses to the shared data structure that depend on the function $f(r)$. The bound for the accesses to the execution stacks is always $O(|\tau|/B + S)$. Other more irregular patterns of access to the shared data structure can arise and these would need to be analyzed separately.

Type 1 HBP Computations The one extra feature in a Type 1 HBP computation is that if one constituent μ of the computation incurs a steal then the finishing task kernel that emerges from μ may need to access variables previously accessed in the computation of μ (or earlier constituents, if any). But this entails $O(|\tau|/B)$ cache misses, and occurs at most once for each constituent (except the first), which is a total additional cost of $O(|\tau|/B)$ cache misses, as each Type 1 algorithm has $O(1)$ constituents by Definition 2.2 (and this is the reason for this restriction). This leads to the bound in Table 1 for Prefix Sums. Also, it turns out that a more careful analysis shows that the second prefix sums algorithm described earlier, which had $f(r) = O(\log(r/B))$, achieves the same bound as the algorithm with $f(r) = O(1)$. We omit the details here.

6.4 Outline of the HBP Analysis

We give here an overview of the HBP analysis. The full analysis is available in [16].

We start by defining the notions of fork tree ownership and local and remote steals.

Definition 6.6. An HBP task τ owns the fork trees for its constituent tasks. A steal in τ that occurs in a fork tree it owns is a *local steal* and is owned by τ. A steal in τ that occurs in a recursive task and not in a fork tree it owns is called a *remote steal.*

Our HBP analysis will proceed as follows.

1. Local Steals. We bound the costs of local steals by a straightforward extension of our previous analysis for BP computations. For this, we first extend the definition of $f(r)$-data dispersal to HBP tasks, and then we bound the cache miss costs for starting task kernels induced by local steals owned by an HBP task τ, to obtain the following lemma (See [16] for the proof.)

LEMMA 6.7. *Let τ be a recursive task owning h steals. Then the cache miss cost for executing τ is bounded by the sequential cost plus $(x(\tau)/B + h \cdot B)$, excluding the costs induced by remote steals.*

We can also bound the costs of the finishing and pseudo task kernels which are formed by local steals owned by τ and which are fully contained in τ. More precisely, a finishing or pseudo task kernel is analyzed under local steals only if both the steal at which the task kernel starts and the steal at which it ends are both local steals. Otherwise, the task kernel is considered to be formed from a remote steal, and its cache miss overhead is captured under the analysis for remote steals. The cost of a task kernel created by a remote steal will be assigned to τ only if the corresponding task kernel is completely contained in τ and is not contained in any task that is a proper descendant of τ.

2. Remote Steals. Consider a remote steal in an HBP task τ. This will be a local steal in some recursive task τ' within τ, but it may create a finishing task kernel and possibly a pseudo task kernel that contains a portion of $\tau - \tau'$. We bound the cost of remote steals in Section 6.4.1. There, we re-assign the cache miss cost of each finishing (and pseudo) task kernel v to one or two HBP tasks, resulting in $O(S)$ different HBP tasks being charged under this scheme. For a finishing task kernel, we will see that, in contrast to BP computations, in the Type k HBP for $k \geq 2$ it can be more complex than simply a join path, and can itself incur steals.

3. Overall Analysis. In Section 6.4.2, we bound the overall cache miss costs of all local and remote steals by performing a second level of reassignment of cache miss costs:. We define certain *special* HBP tasks and we show that we can re-assign the costs that were assigned to $O(S)$ HBP tasks in Section 6.4.1 to at most $4S - 1$ special tasks. We show that this leads to part (ii) of Theorem 2.5.

6.4.1 Analyzing Remote Steals.

We now give an overview of our analysis for remote steals. Suppose an HBP task $\tau = \tau_1$ incurs a remote steal in one of its recursive constituents, μ. Suppose the steal occurs in subtask τ_k, where τ_i calls τ_{i+1} recursively, for $1 \leq i < k$, and $\tau_2 - \tau_3, \ldots, \tau_{k-1} - \tau_k$ are all steal-free. This sequence of τ_i starts at τ_1, either because it is the root task for the whole computation, or because $\tau_1 - \tau_2$ is steal-incurring, and we will say that τ_1 *adopts* this remote steal and the finishing task kernel v created by this steal.

We consider the task kernels for which additional cache misses may occur due to the presence of this remote steal. As noted above, any starting kernel would be created by a steal in a fork-join tree owned by task τ_1, and hence would be created by a local steal and would be handled by the analysis for local steals. Thus the only task kernels that may incur new costs are pseudo task kernels and finishing task kernels. Our analysis will focus on the cost of finishing task kernels. The analysis of pseudo task kernels is similar.

The finishing task kernel, v, that emerges from τ_k will execute portions of $\tau_{k-1} - \tau_k, \tau_{k-2} - \tau_{k-1}, \ldots, \tau_2 - \tau_3, \tau_1 - \tau_2$, in turn. In each $\tau_i - \tau_{i+1}$, for $i > 1$, the execution of v starts with the traversal of a path in a join tree (the join tree complementary to the fork tree from which τ_{i+1} was forked) followed by the execution of the remaining constituent tasks in τ_i, if any. In $\tau_1 - \tau_2$, v will traverse a path in the join tree for μ (recall that μ is the recursive constituent of τ that contains v), and may execute other constituent tasks that follow μ in τ_1, depending on where the next steal in the computation occurs. We analyze separately the additional cache miss costs of v's access to the join paths, and v's execution of remaining constituent tasks in each τ_i.

In the analysis that follows, we apply a *charging* scheme. All of the cache miss costs incurred by the finishing task kernel v that emerges from a remote steal incurred by $\tau = \tau_1$ will be distributed as charges to τ_1 and τ_2, by exploiting the features of cache-compliant HBP algorithms, including the geometric decrease in the extended sizes of successive recursive tasks.

The charging scheme for finishing task kernels that end in τ. First, let us consider the finishing task kernel v described above, and let τ, μ, and the τ_i be as described above. We distribute the cache miss costs incurred by v as follows.

- **C1** The cache miss costs incurred by v in $\tau_1 - \tau_2$ are charged to τ_1.
- **C2** All of the remaining cache miss costs (i.e., the costs for the portions of v in $\tau_i - \tau_{i+1}$, for $i > 1$) are charged to τ_2.

We perform the above distribution for all finishing task kernels that start in μ and end in τ, and we obtain the following two bounds on these charges. The proofs of these two Lemmas are in [16].

LEMMA 6.8. *Let τ be an HBP task that incurs remote steals. Let the i-th constituent task of τ incur h_i steals in its fork tree, and let it incur remote steals in c_i of its collection of recursive tasks. Let $c = \sum_i c_i$ and $h = \sum_i h_i$. Across all steals, the C1 charge to τ is bounded by $O(x(\tau)/B + B + h + c)$ to τ.*

LEMMA 6.9. *Let $\tau_1, \cdots, \tau_k$ be HBP tasks as defined at the start of Section 6.4.1. There is a C2 charge of $O(x(\tau_2)/B + B)$ to τ_2 if $\tau_2 - \tau_3$ is steal free (otherwise $\tau_2 = \tau_k$, and there is no C2 charge to τ_2). Across all steals, this is the only C2 charge made to τ_2.*

6.4.2 Overall HBP Analysis. In Lemmas 6.7–6.9 we bounded the additional cache miss cost of local and remote steals by charging this cost to suitable recursive tasks (or the task that starts the computation). It remains to determine how many different (possibly overlapping) recursive tasks can be charged, and the amount charged to these tasks, as a function of their extended sizes. Once we have obtained good bounds for these, we will readily obtain the desired bound in part (ii) of Theorem 2.5.

There are at most S recursive tasks that incur a local steal, i.e., a steal in a fork tree they own. We call these *Type 1 special tasks.* It is convenient to make the root task, the task which starts the computation, Type 1 also. There are at most a further $S-1$ tasks which have steals in two or more of the recursive subtasks they call, while having no steals in their fork trees. We call these *Type 2 special tasks.* The Type 1 and Type 2 tasks correspond to the τ_1's in the analysis in Section 6.4.1; also, local steals occur only in Type 1 tasks. The remaining charged tasks, corresponding to the τ_2 when $k > 2$, must all be a child of a Type 1 or Type 2 task and further must have a descendant of Type 1 or 2 (corresponding to the τ_k). We call these *Type 3 special tasks.* Thus there are at most $2S-1$ of these, yielding a total of $4S-1$ special tasks. Note that only the special tasks have been charged.

We now perform one more round of redistribution of costs in order to remove the c term from Lemma 6.8. This will result in a charge to each special task that depends only on its extended size and the number of local steals.

LEMMA 6.10. *The charges to the special tasks for all steals can be redistributed so that a Type 1 task τ_1 that owns h steals receives a charge of $O(x(\tau_1)/B + B + h \cdot B)$, a Type 2 task τ_1' receives a charge of $O(x(\tau_1')/B + B)$ and a Type 3 task τ_2 receives a charge of $O(x(\tau_2)/B + B)$.*

Summing over all charged tasks, and noting that the number of special tasks is at most $4S-1$ (as shown above) yields a total charge of $O(\sum_{1\le i\le O(S)} x(\tau_i) + S \cdot B)$, where the τ_i are distinct recursive or BP tasks.

Together with the analysis of the costs due to pseudo task kernels, this proves the second claim in Theorem 2.5.

Acknowledgement. We thank Charles Leiserson for extensive discussions and helpful comments. We also thank Simon Peters and Emmett Witchel for their comments on schedulers used in practice.

REFERENCES

[1] U. A. Acar, G. E. Blelloch, and R. D. Blumofe. 2002. The Data Locality of Work Stealing. *Theory of Computing Systems* 35, 3 (2002). Springer.
[2] D. Ajwani, N. Sitchinava, and N. Zeh. 2010. Geometric algorithms for private-cache chip multiprocessors. In *Proc. Eur. Symp. Alg. (ESA).* 75–86.
[3] L. Arge, M. T. Goodrich, N. Nelson, and N. Sitchinava. 2008. Fundamental parallel algorithms for private-cache chip multiprocessors. In *ACM SPAA.* 197–206.
[4] L. Arge, M. T. Goodrich, and N. Sitchinava. 2010. Parallel external memory graph algorithms. In *IEEE IPDPS.*
[5] Gianfranco Bilardi, Andrea Pietracaprina, Geppino Pucci, Michele Scquizzato, and Francesco Silvestri. 2016. Network-Oblivious Algorithms. *JACM* 63 (2016), Article 3.
[6] G. Blelloch, R. A. Chowdhury, P. Gibbons, V. Ramachandran, S. Chen, and M. Kozuch. 2008. Provably Good Multicore Cache Performance for Divide-and-Conquer Algorithms. In *Proc. ACM-SIAM SODA.* 501–510.
[7] G. E. Blelloch, P. B. Gibbons, and H. V. Simhadri. 2010. Low depth cache-oblivious algorithms. In *Proc. ACM SPAA.* 189–199.
[8] R. Blumofe and C. E. Leiserson. 1999. Scheduling multithreaded computations by work stealing. *JACM* (1999), 720–748.
[9] R. Chowdhury, H. Le, and V. Ramachandran. 2010. Cache-oblivious dynamic programming for multicores. *IEEE/ACM Trans. Computational Biology (TCBB)* 7 (2010), 495–510.
[10] R. A. Chowdhury and V. Ramachandran. 2010. The Cache-oblivious Gaussian Elimination Paradigm: Theoretical Framework, Parallelization and Experimental Evaluation. *Theory of Computing Systems* 47, 1 (2010), 878–919.
[11] Rezaul Alam Chowdhury and Vijaya Ramachandran. 2008. Cache-efficient dynamic programming algorithms for multicores. In *Proc. ACM SPAA.* 207–216.
[12] Rezaul Alam Chowdhury, Vijaya Ramachandran, Francesco Silvestri, and Brandon Blakeley. 2013. Oblivious algorithms for multicores and network of processors. *Jour. Parallel and Distr. Computing* 23 (2013), 911–925.
[13] R. Cole and V. Ramachandran. 2011. Efficient Resource Oblivious Algorithms for Multicores. *CoRR* arXiv:1103.4071 [cs.DC] (2011).
[14] R. Cole and V. Ramachandran. 2012. Efficient Resource Oblivious Algorithms for Multicores with False Sharing. In *Proc. IEEE IPDPS.*
[15] R. Cole and V. Ramachandran. 2012. Revisiting the Cache Miss Analysis of Multithreaded Algorithms. In *Proc. LATIN'12.*
[16] R. Cole and V. Ramachandran. 2017. Bounding Cache Miss Costs of Multithreaded Computations Under General Schedulers. *CoRR* arXiv:1705.08350 [cs.DC] (2017).
[17] Richard Cole and Vijaya Ramachandran. 2017. Resource Oblivious Sorting on Multicores. *ACM Trans. on Parallel Computing (TOPC)* 3 (2017). Article 23.
[18] T. Cormen, C. E. Leiserson, R. L. Rivest, and C. Stein. 2009. *Introduction to Algorithms, Third Edition.* MIT Press.
[19] M. Frigo, C. E. Leiserson, H. Prokop, and S. Ramachandran. 2012. Cache-Oblivious Algorithms. *ACM Trans. Algor.* 4 (2012), 285–297.
[20] M. Frigo and V. Strumpen. 2009. The Cache Complexity of Multithreaded Cache Oblivious Algorithms. *Theory of Computing Systems* 45 (2009), 203–233.
[21] Y. Gao, I. Zhao, R. Barik, R. Raman, and V. Sarkar. 2009. Work-first and help-first scheduling policies for async-finish task parallelism. In *IEEE IPDPS.*
[22] N. Sitchinava and N. Zeh. 2012. A parallel buffer heap. In *ACM SPAA.* 214–223.
[23] Leslie G. Valiant. 2008. A Bridging Model for Multi-core Computing. In *Proc. Eur. Symp. Alg. (ESA).* 13–28.

Brief Announcement: Meeting the Challenges of Parallelizing Sequential Programs

Rohit Atre
Technische Universität Darmstadt
Darmstadt, Germany
atre@cs.tu-darmstadt.de

Ali Jannesari
University of California, Berkeley
Berkeley, USA
jannesari@berkeley.edu

Felix Wolf
Technische Universität Darmstadt
Darmstadt, Germany
wolf@cs.tu-darmstadt.de

ABSTRACT

Discovering which code sections in a sequential program can be made to run in parallel is the first step in parallelizing it, and programmers routinely struggle in this step. Most of the current parallelism discovery techniques focus on specific language constructs while trying to identify such code sections. In contrast, we propose to concentrate on the computations performed by a program. In our approach, a program is treated as a collection of computations communicating with one another using a number of variables. Each computation is represented as a Computational Unit (CU). A CU contains the inputs and outputs of a computation, and the three phases of a computation: read, compute, and write. Based on the notion of CU, We present a unified framework to identify both loop and task parallelism in sequential programs.

KEYWORDS

parallelism discovery; multicore architectures; static analysis; task parallelism; profiling;

1 INTRODUCTION

Millions of legacy programs are awaiting their parallelization. Programmers are required to solve a lot of problems while trying to parallelize a sequential program but "Which code sections to run in parallel?" is still one of the most difficult questions that needs to be answered first.

Until now, existing parallelism discovery techniques have been built on top of data-dependence analysis, performed either statically [6, 17] or dynamically [9, 16]. The idea of using data dependences to discover parallelism is based on Bernstein's conditions [4]: Let P_i and P_j be two program sections. I_i and O_i are the sets of input and output variables of P_i. Similarly, I_j and O_j are the sets of input and output variables of P_j. P_i and P_j can be executed in parallel if

$$I_j \cap O_i = \varnothing,$$
$$I_i \cap O_j = \varnothing,$$
$$O_i \cap O_j = \varnothing.$$

To discover parallelism, existing techniques check for the dependences that arise when one of these conditions is violated. However, these techniques do not strictly follow Bernstein's conditions. They do not necessarily distinguish between input and output variables of a code section. As a result, they end up applying data dependence analysis on all of the variables. This makes identifying parallelism unnecessarily complex, and it also leads to both false positives and false negatives in identified parallelism of a sequential program.

This paper discusses an approach to identify both loop and task parallelism in sequential programs following Bernstein's conditions. Our method treats a sequential program as a set of computations that communicate with each other. A computation is represented as a *Computational Unit* (CU). It contains three phases: read phase, compute phase, and write phase. Input and output variables of a CU are clearly distinguished and associated with the read phase and the write phase, respectively. A CU is also created in such a way that read phase is guaranteed to happen before write phase. Data dependences among CUs are obtained using dynamic dependence profiling. In the end, a sequential program is represented as a *CU graph*, in which vertices are CUs, and edges are data dependences.

Our approach targets both loop and task parallelism. A loop can easily be parallelized if there are no inter-iteration dependences in it. Such loops are called DOALL loops [12]. Loops that contain inter-iteration dependences and can still be parallelized are called DOACROSS [12] loops. In case of task parallelism, there are two different kinds of tasks: Tasks that are instances of the same code section but process different data (SPMD) [7], and tasks that execute completely different code sections performing unique computations (MPMD) [18]. Following Bernstein's conditions (BC) and with the help of CU graph, all the above kinds of parallelism can be easily identified. In the end, our method produces parallelization opportunities in sequential programs. A CU (or a set of CUs) provides us with the flexibility and versatility to create this framework. In it, a CU (or a set of CUs) can be used as task, an iteration of a loop, a stage in a pipeline, or other parallel constructs.

We have evaluated our approach by comparing the parallelization opportunities identified by our approach with the existing parallel versions. In addition, we also parallelized these opportunities as parallelizable but not parallelized in the parallel version of the benchmark applications. Our experiments on Barcelona OpenMP Tasks Suite (BOTS) [8], NAS parallel benchmarks [3], PARSEC [5] benchmark suite, and Starbench parallel benchmark suite [1] showed that all of the code sections identified as parallelizable by our approach are parallelized in existing parallel versions.

2 APPROACH

We firstly introduce computational unit, which is the most important concept in our method. Then CU graph, the graph we use to represent a sequential program, is introduced.

SPAA '17, July 24-26, 2017, Washington DC, USA
 978-1-4503-4593-4/17/07.
DOI: 10.1145/3087556.3087592

2.1 Computational Unit

A *computational unit* is a collection of instructions following the *read-compute-write* pattern: a set of variables is read by a collection of instructions and is used to perform a computation, then the result is written back to another set of variables. The two sets of variables are called *read set* and *write set*, respectively. These two sets do not necessarily have to be disjoint. Load instructions reading variables in the read set form the *read phase* of the CU, and store instructions writing variables in the write set form the *write phase* of the CU.

In practice, program tasks communicate with one another by reading and writing variables that are global to them, and computations are performed locally. A CU is defined by read-compute-write pattern for this reason. This is also why we require the variables in a CU's read set and the write set to be global to the CU. The variables local to the CU are part of the compute phase of the CU as they will not be used to communicate with other tasks during parallelization. We perform variable scope analysis to distinguish variables that are global to a code section. It is available in any ordinary compiler. Global variables in the read set and the write set do not have to be global to the whole program. They can be local to an encapsulating code section, but global to the target code section.

2.1.1 Cautious property. A code section is considered to be a CU only if it is *cautious*. Cautious property [15] was previously defined for operators in unordered algorithms. Ot states that an operator is said to be cautious if it reads all the elements of its neighbourhood before it modifies any of them. By adapting it to the CU, we make sure that a code section is cautious if every variable in its read set is read before it is written in the write phase of the CU.

Cautious property guarantees the read-compute-write pattern of the CU. It not only gives a clear way of separating read phase and write phase, but also after parallelism discovery, it allows multiple CUs to be executed speculatively without buffering updates or making backup copies of modified data. This is possible because all conflicts are detected during the read phase. Consequently, tasks extracted based on CUs also do not have any special requirement on runtime frameworks.

A computation may depend on data produced from other computations. To represent such dependences, we use a dynamic dependence profiler DiscoPoP[13]. DiscoPoP profiles detailed data dependences, gathers control-flow information, and identifies hotspots across the target program. We run the profiler multiple times using representative inputs to overcome the input sensitivity of the dynamic dependence analysis. Then we merge the dependence results obtained. These representative inputs are provided along with the benchmarks and they are of varying size and complexity. Next, we build a *CU graph*

2.2 CU Graph

A computation may depend on data produced from other computations. To represent such dependences, we use a dynamic dependence profiler DiscoPoP[13]. DiscoPoP profiles detailed data dependences, gathers control-flow information, and identifies hotspots across the target program. We run the profiler multiple times using representative inputs to overcome the input sensitivity of the dynamic dependence analysis. Then we merge the dependence results obtained. These representative inputs are provided along with the benchmarks and they are of varying size and complexity. Next, we build a *CU graph*, in which vertices are statically generated CUs and edges are dynamic data dependences. Hence, the CU graph combines static and dynamic information to help us discover parallelism. Data dependences in a CU graph are always among instructions in read phases and write phases. Dependences that are local to a CU are hidden because they do not prevent parallelism among CUs according to Bernstein's conditions. Moreover, since the number of global variables to a code section is usually far less than the number of local variables, a CU graph is much simpler than the traditional instruction-based dependence graph. This simplifies the parallelism discovery process. The CU graph is then expanded using runtime information to represent instances of tasks or loops, if necessary.

2.3 Parallelism discovery

There are two kinds of parallelism we can identify: parallelism among different computations, and parallelism among different instances of the same computation. Parallelism among different computations can be easily identified using CU graphs without instantiating these computations.

On the other hand, identifying parallelism among different instances of the same computation requires some additional effort. To discover such parallelism, a CU must be instantiated using real inputs passed into the computation and real outputs it produces. A CU graph consisting instantiated CUs is called an *expanded* CU graph.

2.3.1 ***Task parallelism.*** Task parallelism is discovered based on the following rules:

(1) A CU is instantiated into different instances using their real inputs and outputs with respect to the control flow. Two instances of the same computation can run in parallel if they are independent in the expanded CU graph (SPMD task parallelism).
(2) Two different computations can run in parallel if their corresponding CUs are independent in the CU graph (MPMD task parallelism).

Parallelism within a computation is not covered by our current approach. However, such parallelism can be detected by further applying techniques that track def-use chains [2] on compute phases of CUs. Nevertheless, in rare cases where a code section contains plenty of lines of code and complex computation (which is unlikely to be cautious), analyzing CUs built for it might provide opportunities to break the region down to smaller computations, leading to parallelism that is similar to OpenMP sections [14].

2.3.2 ***Loop parallelism.*** Loop parallelism is discovered based on the following rules:

- Iterations of a loop can run in parallel if for all CUs built for the loop, there are no inter-iteration *read-after-write* (RAW) dependences among the CUs or on a single CU (DOALL parallelism).
- If there are inter-iteration dependences in the loop, the loop may still be analyzed to check if it can be parallelized by using techniques e.g. reduction, privatization, pipeline etc. (DOACROSS parallelism).

DOALL parallelism: In case of DOALL loops, the iterations of loop are independent of each other. This means that the instances of CUs are also independent and as a result they satisfy Bernstein's conditions. However, it is not necessary to analyze all the instances of the CUs of a loop because loops have no parameters to be replaced, unlike function calls and their instances.

DOACROSS parallelism: It is possible to further analyze the dependence distances of the inter-iteration RAW dependences to discover DOACROSS [12] loops. A DOACROSS loop has inter-iteration dependences, but the dependence distance should not be as large as the distance between the first line of an iteration and the last line of the previous iteration. In other words, the first CU of the loop should not depend on the last CU of the loop. This raises the possibility that iterations of a DOACROSS loop can overlap, thus containing parallelism. Based on our CU graph, if the length of the longest dependence is smaller than the distance from the last CU to the first CU, we can classify such loops as candidates for DOACROSS parallelism. All the instances of CUs are not independent of each other in DOACROSS loops as there are inter-iteration dependences, unlike DOALL loops. But a subset of CUs in an iteration can be independent of another subset of CUs in the next iteration. Hence they satisfy Bernstein's conditions and can be run in parallel. Utilizing such parallelism is usually achieved by applying the pipeline pattern [11] [10].

3 CONCLUSION

This paper discusses an approach for discovery of parallelism by identifying code sections called computational units (CU) in sequential programs. A CU follows a read-compute-write pattern. CUs are detected statically from the source code using the cautious property. A CU graph is then created using the CUs and the dynamic dependences. This serves as the basis for parallelism detection. Bernstein's conditions are used to identify the tasks which can run in parallel to each other from a CU graph or an expanded CU graph

REFERENCES

[1] Michael Andersch, Ben Juurlink, and Chi Ching Chi. 2011. A Benchmark Suite for Evaluating Parallel Programming Models. In *Proceedings 24th Workshop on Parallel Systems and Algorithms (PARS '11)*. 7–17.

[2] Rohit Atre, Ali Jannesari, and Felix Wolf. 2015. The Basic Building Blocks of Parallel Tasks. In *Proceedings of the 2015 International Workshop on Code Optimisation for Multi and Many Cores (COSMIC '15)*. ACM, New York, NY, USA, Article 3, 11 pages.

[3] D. H. Bailey, E. Barszcz, J. T. Barton, D. S. Browning, R. L. Carter, R. A. Fatoohi, P. O. Frederickson, T. A. Lasinski, H. D. Simon, V. Venkatakrishnan, and S. K. Weeratunga. 1991. The NAS parallel benchmarks. *The International Journal of Supercomputer Applications* 5, 3 (1991), 63–73.

[4] Arthur Bernstein. 1966. {Analysis of programs for parallel processing}. *IEEE Transactions on Electronic Computers* 15, 5 (1966), 757–763.

[5] Christian Bienia, Sanjeev Kumar, Jaswinder Pal Singh, and Kai Li. 2008. The PARSEC Benchmark Suite: Characterization and Architectural Implications. In *Proceedings of the 17th International Conference on Parallel Architectures and Compilation Techniques (PACT '08)*. ACM, New York, NY, USA, 72–81. DOI: http://dx.doi.org/10.1145/1454115.1454128

[6] Michael Burke, Ron Cytron, Jeanne Ferrante, and Wilson Hsieh. 1989. Automatic generation of nested, fork-join parallelism. *The Journal of Supercomputing* 3, 2 (1989), 71–88. DOI: http://dx.doi.org/10.1007/BF00129843

[7] Frederica Darema. 2001. The spmd model: Past, present and future. In *Recent Advances in Parallel Virtual Machine and Message Passing Interface*. Springer, 1–1.

[8] Alejandro Duran, Xavier Teruel, Roger Ferrer, Xavier Martorell, and Eduard Ayguade. 2009. Barcelona openmp tasks suite: A set of benchmarks targeting the exploitation of task parallelism in openmp. In *Parallel Processing, 2009. ICPP'09. International Conference on*. IEEE, 124–131.

[9] Jialu Huang, Thomas B Jablin, Stephen R Beard, Nick P Johnson, and David I August. 2013. Automatically exploiting cross-invocation parallelism using runtime information. In *Code Generation and Optimization (CGO), 2013 IEEE/ACM International Symposium on*. IEEE, 1–11.

[10] Zia Ul Huda, Rohit Atre, Ali Jannesari, and Felix Wolf. 2016. Automatic Parallel Pattern Detection in the Algorithm Structure Design Space. In *Proc. of the 30th IEEE International Parallel and Distributed Processing Symposium (IPDPS), Chicago, USA*. IEEE Computer Society, 43–52. DOI: http://dx.doi.org/10.1109/IPDPS.2016.60

[11] Zia Ul Huda, Ali Jannesari, and Felix Wolf. 2015. Using Template Matching to Infer Parallel Design Patterns. *ACM Trans. Archit. Code Optim.* 11, 4, Article 64 (Jan. 2015), Article 64, 21 pages. DOI: http://dx.doi.org/10.1145/2688905

[12] Ken Kennedy and John R. Allen. 2002. *Optimizing Compilers for Modern Architectures: A Dependence-based Approach.* Morgan Kaufmann Publishers Inc., San Francisco, CA, USA.

[13] Zhen Li, Ali Jannesari, and Felix Wolf. 2015. An Efficient Data-Dependence Profiler for Sequential and Parallel Programs. In *Proceedings of the 29th IEEE International Parallel & Distributed Processing Symposium (IPDPS '15)*. 484–493.

[14] OpenMP Architecture Review Board. 2008. OpenMP Application Program Interface Version 3.0. (May 2008). http://www.openmp.org/mp-documents/spec30.pdf

[15] Keshav Pingali, Donald Nguyen, Milind Kulkarni, Martin Burtscher, M. Amber Hassaan, Rashid Kaleem, Tsung-Hsien Lee, Andrew Lenharth, Roman Manevich, Mario Méndez-Lojo, Dimitrios Prountzos, and Xin Sui. 2011. The Tao of Parallelism in Algorithms. *SIGPLAN Not.* 46, 6 (June 2011), 12–25. DOI: http://dx.doi.org/10.1145/1993316.1993501

[16] Sean Rul, Hans Vandierendonck, and Koen De Bosschere. 2010. A profile-based tool for finding pipeline parallelism in sequential programs. *Parallel Comput.* 36, 9 (2010), 531–551.

[17] Vivek Sarkar. 1991. Automatic partitioning of a program dependence graph into parallel tasks. *IBM Journal of Research and Development* 35, 5.6 (1991), 779–804.

[18] Barry Wilkinson and Michael Allen. 1999. *Parallel programming*. Vol. 999. Prentice hall New Jersey.

Brief Announcement: Hazard Eras - Non-Blocking Memory Reclamation

Pedro Ramalhete
Cisco Systems
pramalhe@gmail.com

Andreia Correia
Concurrency Freaks
andreiacraveiroramalhete@gmail.com

ABSTRACT

For non-blocking data-structures, only memory reclamation with pointer-based techniques can maintain non-blocking progress, but there can be high overhead associated to these techniques, with the most notable example being Hazard Pointers.

We present a new algorithm we named Hazard Eras, which allows for efficient lock-free or wait-free memory reclamation in concurrent data structures and can be used as drop-in replacement to Hazard Pointers. Results from our microbenchmark show that when applied to a lock-free linked list, Hazard Eras will match the throughput of Hazard Pointers in the worst-case, and can outperform Hazard Pointers by a factor of 5x. Hazard Eras provides the same progress conditions as Hazard Pointers and can equally be implemented with the C11/C++11 memory model and atomics, making it portable across multiple systems.

CCS CONCEPTS

• **Theory of computation → Concurrent algorithms**;

KEYWORDS

memory reclamation; hazard pointers; lock-free; wait-free; non-blocking; concurrent data structures

1 INTRODUCTION

Concurrent data structures are often measured on two vectors: the throughput they provide and the progress they guarantee. Data structures with lock-free progress are not that common, and with wait-free characteristics even less. To make things worse, the progress conditions of the memory reclamation technique can further reduce the progress of either *readers* (threads calling methods that de-reference pointers in the data structure) or *reclaimers* (threads calling methods that attempt to reclaim and delete an object/node in the data structure). Existing techniques for manual concurrent memory reclamation fall into one of three groups: *quiescence-based*, *reference counting*, and *pointer based*.

Quiescence-based techniques, like the Epoch-based by Fraser [3], Harris [5], or Userspace RCU [6], reclaim memory whenever readers pass though a *quiescent* state in which no reader holds a reference to a shared object. These techniques have light synchronization and can be wait-free for readers, but their throughput is significantly impacted by delays on readers, which can block the reaching of quiescent states, thus preventing any other thread from reclaiming memory [2]. Moreover, they can have an unbounded amount of unreclaimed memory, which can fatally exhaust all memory available to the application when there is a slow reader, or just because there is high oversubscription (more threads than cores to run them on).

Reference counting techniques [4] require expensive synchronization on the readers side [6], cause contention among readers and have several limitations as described in chapter 9.1 of [8].

Pointer-based techniques, such as Hazard Pointers [9], Pass The Buck [7], or Drop The Anchor [1], explicitly mark live objects (objects accessible by other threads) which can not be de-allocated. These techniques are wait-free for reclamation and it is possible to use them in a wait-free way for readers for some algorithms [11], but they are typically deployed lock-free.

SPAA '17, July 24-26, 2017, Washington DC, USA

ACM ISBN 978-1-4503-4593-4/17/07.
https://doi.org/10.1145/3087556.3087588

2 OVERALL DESIGN

Hazard Eras (HE) combines the low synchronization overhead of epoch-based techniques with the non-blocking properties of Hazard Pointers (HP) for both readers and reclaimers, while providing the same API as Hazard Pointers, specifically, the API that is currently being proposed to the C++ standard library [10].

In HE, the object's lifetime is tracked with a global monotonic clock, the `eraClock`. When an object is created, the current value of `eraClock` is stored in `object.newEra`, and when the object is retired, the current value of `eraClock` is stored in `object.delEra`, and subsequently the `eraClock` is atomically incremented. Every time an object's lifetime arrives at an end, the current era ends and a new era begins.

Unlike HP, where readers publish the pointer that they are using, in HE the reader publishes the *era* that was in `eraClock` at the point in time when the hazardous reference was read. One era must be published for each different pointer in use, just like on HP.

A reader that publishes an era with a value of x is guaranteeing that (after re-validation of `eraClock`) no object with a lifetime that encompasses x will be deleted. By definition, all objects currently in a *live* state are now protected from deletion, however, objects created after this era may be subsequently deleted, which is not possible in Epoch-based reclamation. In Epoch-based memory reclamation, all objects retired *after* a reader has started, will not be deleted unless the reader completes, because there is still an ongoing reader and it may be accessing those objects.

In HE, all objects created with a `newEra` greater than the highest of the published eras by all readers, can be retired and deleted. The algorithm guarantees that readers which published a precedent era can not have access to the objects of a higher era, and to be able to access those objects they will observe the era has changed and

Algorithm 1 Hazard Eras class

```
1  template<typename T> class HazardEras {
2
3  private:
4    static const uint64_t NONE = 0;
5    const int maxHEs;
6    const int maxThreads;
7    std::atomic<uint64_t> eraClock = { 1 };
8    std::atomic<uint64_t> he[MAX_THREADS][MAX_HES];
9    std::vector<T*> retiredList[MAX_THREADS];
10
11 public:
12   HazardEras(int maxHEs, int maxThreads) :
13           maxHEs{maxHEs}, maxThreads{maxThreads} {
14     for (int ith = 0; ith < MAX_THREADS; ith++) {
15       for (int ihe = 0; ihe < MAX_HES; ihe++) {
16         he[ith][ihe].store(NONE, std::memory_order_relaxed);
17       }
18     }
19   }
20
21   ~HazardEras() {
22     for (int ith = 0; ith < MAX_THREADS; ith++) {
23       for (auto i = 0; i < retiredList[ith].size(); i++) {
24         delete retiredList[ith][i];
25       }
26     }
27   }
```

Algorithm 2 Reader's API

```
28 T* get_protected(std::atomic<T*>& atom, int index, int tid) {
29   auto prevEra = he[tid][index].load(std::memory_order_relaxed);
30   while (true) {
31     T* ptr = atom.load();
32     auto era = eraClock.load(std::memory_order_acquire);
33     if (era == prevEra) return ptr;
34     he[tid][index].store(era);
35     prevEra = era;
36   }
37 }
38
39 void clear(const int tid) {
40   for (int ihe = 0; ihe < maxHEs; ihe++) {
41     he[tid][ihe].store(NONE, std::memory_order_release);
42   }
43 }
44
45 int64_t getEra() { return eraClock.load(); }
```

will be forced to re-read the atomic variable corresponding to the pointer and then re-publish the most recent era.

3 HAZARD ERAS ALGORITHM

In our implementation, the HazardEras class is composed of three objects, a global clock named `eraClock`, a bidimensional array of *eras* named `he`, and an array of lists named `retiredList`, as shown in Algorithm 1. The era timestamps are 64 bit integers so that they are large enough not to cause ABA issues and still be used atomically on recent CPUs. An instance of type `T` has two eras associated to it: the era of its birth `newEra`, which indicates the moment the instance was made visible to other threads, and the era of its death `delEra`, where `delEra+1` indicates the moment in time after which it is no longer visible for new accesses to objects on the data structure. The birth era of each object must be set on `newEra` before the object is made visible to other threads, i.e. inserted in the data structure, which can be easily done in the constructor of `T` or one of its base classes. The death era follows a reversed procedure, where the object is first removed from the data structure and only then is the `eraClock` read and its value stored in `delEra`.

Similarly to Hazard Pointers [10], in Hazard Eras we have three main APIs (`get_protected()`, `clear()`, `retire()`) plus one extra (`getEra()`). The method `retire()` is called during a reclamation operation, done by *reclaimers*, while the other three methods are called during a read operation, done by *readers*.

The method `get_protected()` in Algorithm 2 shows a lock-free loop for protecting an hazardous reference. There is a kind of *fast-path-slow-path* approach. When the `eraClock` has not changed from the previous published value (line 33), there is no need to publish again the same era value and pay the synchronization cost of doing a sequentially-consistent (seq-cst) store (line 34). By following this fast-path, the reader does two seq-cst loads instead of the two seq-cst loads and one seq-cst store that are needed for HP. This may seem a minor gain, however, seq-cst loads have an almost free cost on x86 architectures, having very little overhead, and therefore, providing high throughput for the readers. Even on non-x86 architectures, the price of doing a seq-cst load relative to a seq-cst store is much lower, thus providing higher throughput also on architectures like PowerPC and ARM. In the object's constructor or before inserting it in the data structure, the return value of `getEra()` must be placed in `object.newEra`.

The `retire()` method saves the current era in `object.delEra` and puts the object in the thread's `retiredList`. Then, to guarantee progress, it will advance the `eraClock` if another thread has not done so in the meantime (line 51), and scan the `retiredList` for objects that can be safely deleted. If there is at least one thread with a published era in the range `[newEra;delEra]` (line 68) the object can not be deleted yet.

A rarely mentioned advantage of HP is its low bound on memory usage. Quiescent-based techniques with *delegation* or *deferral* typically have no bound on memory usage. When using HP with an R factor of 1, there is the guarantee that there are at most MAX_THREADS × MAX_HPS objects in the retired list of each reclaimer, and therefore, there may be at most $\text{MAX\_THREADS}^2 \times \text{MAX\_HPS}$ retired objects waiting to be deleted.

Algorithm 3 Reclaimer's API

```
void retire(T* ptr, const int mytid) {
  auto currEra = eraClock.load();
  ptr->delEra = currEra;
  auto& rlist = retiredList[mytid*CLPAD];
  rlist.push_back(ptr);
  if (eraClock == currEra) eraClock.fetch_add(1);
  for (unsigned iret = 0; iret < rlist.size();) {
    auto obj = rlist[iret];
    if (canDelete(obj, mytid)) {
      rlist.erase(rlist.begin() + iret);
      delete obj;
      continue;
    }
    iret++;
  }
}

private:
bool canDelete(T* obj, const int mytid) {
  for (int tid = 0; tid < maxThreads; tid++) {
    for (int ihe = 0; ihe < maxHEs; ihe++) {
      const auto era = he[tid][ihe].load();
      if (era < obj->newEra || era > obj->delEra ||
          era == NONE) continue;
      return false;
    }
  }
  return true;
}
};
```

Hazard Eras' upper bound is limited to the number of objects that were in the data structure at a given clock era published in the hazard eras array, for all reader threads. At a given time t, the bound on the maximum number of unreclaimed objects is given by:

$$\#\left\{ \bigcup_{\substack{x \in X(t) \\ era \in \text{HEs(t)}}} x\colon x.\text{newEra} \leq era \leq x.\text{delEra} \right\} \tag{1}$$

where HEs(t) is the set of all clock eras published by readers at time t, X(t) is the set of objects created until `clockEra` at time t. By definition, the `delEra` of a live object is the highest possible value of `eraClock`.

The number of objects that can remain unreclaimed on each `era` becomes limited as soon as a memory reclamation event occurs (a call to `retire()`). Only the latest `era` can have an unbounded amount of live objects, and any unreclaimed objects are always on previous eras. As such, it is not possible for the program to allocate an unbounded number of objects in a single `era`, except on the latest `era` which only includes live objects. Depending on the number of such objects and the number of threads, the bound for HE may be higher, or lower than the bound for HP.

4 CONCLUSION

To the untrained eye, it may look as though there is little difference between an Epoch-based memory reclamation and Hazard Eras. However, in Epoch-based reclamation, each thread does one single publishing of the global epoch it saw per method call, causing it to have a small synchronization cost, but *unbounded* memory usage: a single sleeping or blocked reader is enough to prevent *any further memory reclamation*, even in variants of Epoch-based reclamation where the epoch is updated regularly by the readers. In Hazard Eras, each reader thread publishes the global era it saw, for each new pointer that is accessed, if and only if the era has changed, which incurs a small synchronization cost for each pointer. Furthermore, HE have *bounded* memory usage: a sleeping or blocked reader may prevent all currently allocated objects from being reclaimed, but newly allocated objects can be subsequently reclaimed.

Compared with Hazard Pointers, Hazard Eras have the same deployment complexity, with a lower synchronization cost for the readers, which gives HE up to 5x the throughput of HP. This increase in throughput comes with a price tag: higher memory usage. Unlike HP, HE requires each tracked object to have a `newEra` once created, a `delEra` once deleted, and the number of objects in memory which have been retired but not yet deleted, although finite, can be higher for HE than for HP.

Hazard Eras fall between Epoch-based and Hazard Pointers, providing the best characteristics of each: high throughput due to its low synchronization; non-blocking progress for readers and reclaimers; and a bound on memory usage.

REFERENCES

[1] Anastasia Braginsky, Alex Kogan, and Erez Petrank. 2013. Drop the anchor: lightweight memory management for non-blocking data structures. In *Proceedings of the twenty-fifth annual ACM symposium on Parallelism in algorithms and architectures*. ACM, 33–42.
[2] Dave Dice, Maurice Herlihy, and Alex Kogan. 2016. Fast non-intrusive memory reclamation for highly-concurrent data structures. In *Proceedings of the 2016 ACM SIGPLAN International Symposium on Memory Management*. ACM, 36–45.
[3] Keir Fraser. 2004. *Practical lock-freedom*. Ph.D. Dissertation. University of Cambridge.
[4] Anders Gidenstam, Marina Papatriantafilou, Håkan Sundell, and Philippas Tsigas. 2009. Efficient and reliable lock-free memory reclamation based on reference counting. *IEEE Transactions on Parallel and Distributed Systems* 20, 8 (2009), 1173–1187.
[5] Timothy L Harris. 2001. A pragmatic implementation of non-blocking linked-lists. In *Distributed Computing*. Springer, 300–314.
[6] Thomas E Hart, Paul E McKenney, Angela Demke Brown, and Jonathan Walpole. 2007. Performance of memory reclamation for lockless synchronization. *J. Parallel and Distrib. Comput.* 67, 12 (2007), 1270–1285.
[7] Maurice Herlihy, Victor Luchangco, and Mark Moir. 2002. The repeat offender problem: A mechanism for supporting dynamic-sized lock-free data structures. (2002).
[8] Paul E McKenney. 2011. Is parallel programming hard, and, if so, what can you do about it? *Linux Technology Center, IBM Beaverton* (2011).
[9] Maged M Michael. 2004. Hazard pointers: Safe memory reclamation for lock-free objects. *Parallel and Distributed Systems, IEEE Transactions on* 15, 6 (2004), 491–504.
[10] Maged M. Michael, Michael Wong, Paul McKenney, Arthur O'Dwyer, and David Hollman. 2017. Hazard Pointers - Safe Resource Reclamation for Optimistic Concurrency. http://www.open-std.org/jtc1/sc22/wg21/docs/papers/2017/p0233r3.pdf. (2017).
[11] Pedro Ramalhete and Andreia Correia. 2017. POSTER: A Wait-Free Queue with Wait-Free Memory Reclamation. In *Proceedings of the 22nd ACM SIGPLAN Symposium on Principles and Practice of Parallel Programming*. ACM, 453–454.

Brief Announcement: Extending Transactional Memory with Atomic Deferral

Tingzhe Zhou
Lehigh University
tiz214@lehigh.edu

Victor Luchangco
Oracle Labs
victor.luchangco@oracle.com

Michael Spear
Lehigh University
spear@lehigh.edu

ABSTRACT

Atomic deferral is a language-level mechanism for transactional memory (TM) that enables programmers to move output and long-running operations out of a transaction's body without sacrificing serializability: the deferred operation appears to execute as part of its parent transaction, even though it does not make use of TM.

We introduce the first implementation of atomic deferral, based on transaction-friendly locks; describe enhancements to its API; and demonstrate its effectiveness. Our experiments show that atomic deferral is useful for its original purpose of moving output operations out of transactions, and also for moving expensive library calls out of transactions. The result is a significant improvement in performance for the PARSEC dedup kernel, for both software and hardware TM systems.

CCS CONCEPTS

• **Computing methodologies → Parallel computing methodologies; Concurrent computing methodologies;**

KEYWORDS

Transactional Memory, Concurrency, Synchronization, I/O

ACM Reference format:

Tingzhe Zhou, Victor Luchangco, and Michael Spear. 2017. Brief Announcement: Extending Transactional Memory with Atomic Deferral. In *Proceedings of SPAA '17, Washington DC, USA, July 24-26, 2017*, 3 pages.
https://doi.org/10.1145/3087556.3087600

1 INTRODUCTION

Transactional memory (TM) [6] simplifies the task of writing correct, scalable code. With TM, a programmer designates code regions as "transactions". A run-time system, which employs custom hardware [8] (HTM) and/or compiler-generated software instrumentation [4, 7] (STM), monitors the low-level memory accesses of transactions, and allows concurrent transactions to execute simultaneously as long as their memory accesses do not conflict. If transactions conflict, the run-time system rolls back some subset of transactions and retries them. However, some operations (e.g., I/O) cannot be rolled back, and others are expensive, so that rolling them back wastes a lot of work (and increases the likelihood of conflict by extending the transaction). Programmers should avoid including such operations in transactions.

One approach for allowing long-running and I/O operations to be included in a transaction is to designate such a transaction as irrevocable [9, 10, 13], so that it cannot be aborted. When an irrevocable transaction runs, no other transaction may run. This ensures that the irrevocable transaction will not encounter a conflict, and thus will not abort. Consequently, it is safe for it to perform I/O, and the capacity constraints of HTM, and overheads of STM, need not apply.

As an alternative, a limited set of operations can be delayed until after a transaction commits [2, 9]. These "deferred" operations typically cannot access shared memory, and other threads might observe that the operations run *after* the transactions that requested them. By incorporating special "sentinel" locks into the operating system, Volos et al. [11] enabled broad support for transactional system calls, to include input and output. To perform output from a transaction, the operating system would lock the corresponding file descriptor, and make a copy of the data to write. When the transaction committed, the copied data would be written, and then the lock released. In this manner, the output would appear atomic with the transaction.

In a previous workshop paper, we introduced atomic deferral [14]. Atomic deferral is a language-supported mechanism for deferring output and other long-running operations. Like Volos's work, atomic deferral makes use of locks. However, the locks are a userspace construct, fully visible to the programmer. Programmers can associate one of these locks with any object, and then the compiler ensures that transactions who access those objects "subscribe" to the corresponding lock. To defer an operation, a transaction acquires the locks associated with the objects used by the operation. When the transaction commits, the locks will be held, and thus mutual exclusion is guaranteed for the deferred operation. After the deferred operation completes, the locks are released.

As a purely userspace construct, atomic deferral does not perform system calls during a transaction. Thus HTM transactions can use atomic deferral, whereas they cannot use sentinel locks. Furthermore, atomic deferral is not limited to system calls: it can be used by programmers to defer arbitrary operations, and it provides a path for programmers to avoid copying shared data before using it in deferred operations.

In this brief announcement, we describe our experience implementing atomic deferral and using it in the PARSEC dedup [1] kernel. The output operations in dedup are a known cause of serialization and poor scaling [12]. With atomic deferral, we moved these output operations out of transactions, resulting in a program with no mandatory irrevocability. However, the compression and decompression operations in dedup then become a bottleneck: they

SPAA '17, July 24-26, 2017, Washington DC, USA

ACM ISBN 978-1-4503-4593-4/17/07.
https://doi.org/10.1145/3087556.3087600

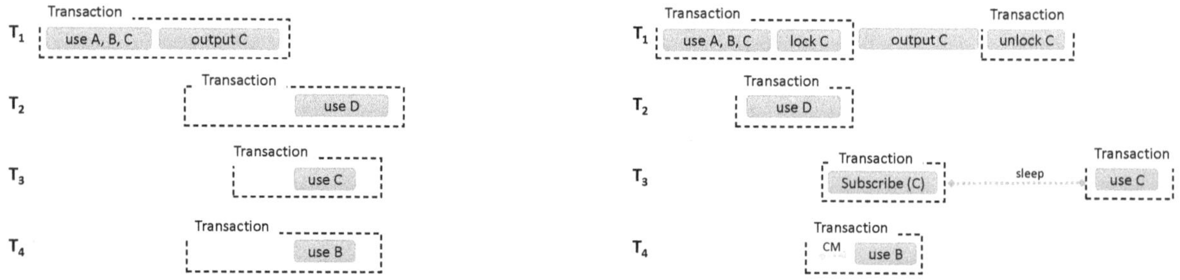

Figure 1: Motivation for atomic deferral. On the left, T_1's transaction outputs object C, which prevents other transactions, even unrelated ones, from making progress. On the right, C is locked, and then the output of C is deferred until after the transaction commits. The use of locking and deferral of the output of C enables the operations by threads T_2 and T_4 to progress more quickly, without violating serializability.

caused HTM transactions to exceed cache capacity, and STM transactions to incur instrumentation delays. Since atomic deferral is not limited to system calls, we also deferred these operations. After doing so, transactional dedup scaled well, performing on par with carefully tuned locks.

2 ATOMIC DEFERRAL

Atomic deferral makes use of special transaction-friendly spin locks (TxLocks), which, in turn, make use of retry-based condition synchronization [5]. TxLocks can be acquired from within transactions, and when an attempt to acquire a TxLock fails, the enclosing transaction aborts, rolls back, and does not try again until the TxLock is released. A transaction may access the data associated with a TxLock as long as the lock is not held. To do so, it *subscribes* to the lock. That is, before accessing the data, the transaction reads the lock to ensure that it is not held. If the lock is subsequently acquired, the subscribing transaction will automatically abort. If the lock is held by another thread when a transaction attempts to subscribe, the transaction will abort, and will not attempt to run again until the TxLock is released.

Armed with TxLocks, atomic defer is able to transform the behavior on the left side of Figure 1 to the behavior on the right side. In the figure, time flows from left to right. On the left side, the output of C causes the transaction by T_1 to become irrevocable. Due to irrevocability, the transaction by T_2 cannot start, even though it does not conflict with T_1's transaction. The transactions by threads T_3 and T_4 also must wait for the output to complete. However, these transactions have overlapping accesses with T_1's transaction, and might not be able to execute concurrently with T_1's transaction.

On the right side, T_1's transaction defers the output operation on object C. Before the transaction commits, it acquires C's TxLock. After committing, the output is performed, and then C is unlocked. Since the output is not performed within a transaction, T_1's transaction does not become irrevocable. Thus T_2's non-conflicting transaction does not delay. Similarly, T_4's transaction need only delay as long as is necessary for the contention manager to ensure that T_1 and T_4's transactions can both make progress. If both only read B, then T_4's transaction would not need to wait. T_3's transaction subscribes to the TxLock associated with C. When T_1's transaction acquires the lock, it causes T_3's transaction to abort, and T_3 to sleep until the lock is released. At that point, T_3 can wake and access C using a transaction.

Note that the execution remained serializable with atomic defer. On the right side of the figure, the result is equivalent to one in which T_1 completes, then T_2, and then T_3 and T_4 in either order. In particular, T_4 appears to complete after T_1, because it sees any updates to B; because it does not access C, it can run concurrently with the operations on C, yet order after T_1. If it had accessed C, then like the operation in T_3, it would have slept until T_1's transaction committed. In our extended API to atomic deferral, TxLocks are reentrant, and a request to defer an operation names all of the objects whose TxLocks must be held during the execution of the operation. In this manner, a thread may defer multiple operations, and yet still achieve serializability through two-phase locking [3]: All locks are acquired before a thread's transaction commits, and then no further locks are acquired; no locks are released until after the transaction commits; and after each deferred operation, only the corresponding locks are released, with reentrancy ensuring that they are not released too early.

In addition, we observe that there is no reason that the deferred operation on C must be an output operation. As long as the remainder of T_1's initial transaction does not access C, an arbitrary computation on C can be deferred without sacrificing atomicity.

3 PERFORMANCE EVALUATION

In their study of transactional condition synchronization [12], Wang et al. found that PARSEC's dedup kernel [1] ceased to scale when transactions replaced locks. Dedup is a pipeline application, where the final stage performs output while holding a lock; Wang's version replaces that lock with an irrevocable transaction. When the irrevocable transaction executes, it must serialize all concurrent transactions. We rewrote dedup's output operation to use atomic deferral. With the change, irrevocability ceased to cause performance degradation, but the benchmark still did not scale well.

The performance of dedup with this change appears in Figure 2, as the "+DeferIO" curves. The results were measured on a system with a 4-core/8-thread Intel Core i7-4770 CPU running at 3.40GHz. This CPU supports Intel's TSX extensions for HTM, includes 8 GB of RAM, and runs a Linux 4.3 kernel. Atomic defer was added to GCC 5.3.1. Results are the average of 5 trials.

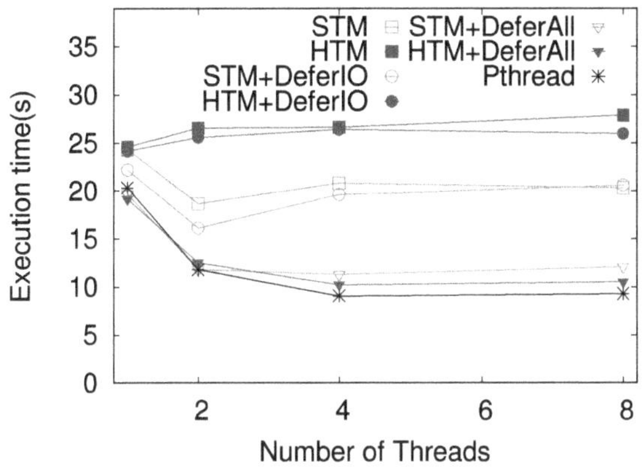

Figure 2: Using atomic deferral in PARSEC dedup

During profiling, we discovered that the `Compress` function was marked as `pure`, because it does not access any shared memory. Marking the function `pure` indicates to the compiler that the function can be run without instrumentation, lacks side effects, and can be run from a non-irrevocable context even when the compiler cannot prove that irrevocability is not needed. `Compress` is a long-running function, and in HTM, it accesses more memory than can be tracked by the HTM; the HTM execution serializes whenever a call to `Compress` exceeds the capacity of the hardware. In STM, a transaction executing `Compress` causes other transactions to delay in their commit operation. While the run-time behaviors are different, the consequence is the same: when one transaction calls `Compress`, other transactions cannot make progress.

`Compress` is amenable to atomic deferral, and the impact is profound. In HTM, the transaction ceases to overflow hardware capacity, and serialization is avoided. In STM, compression ceases to impede concurrent commits, and concurrent threads can make forward progress. In Figure 2, we see that the "+DeferAll" curves for both HTM and STM now compete with pthread locks, representing a 1.7x speedup for STM and 2.7x speedup for HTM. On a 36-thread multi-chip TSX machine (not shown), both HTM and STM performed equivalently to the baseline Pthread locks at all thread counts.

4 CONCLUSIONS AND FUTURE WORK

In this brief announcement, we presented our experience extending atomic deferral, implementing it, and using it on the PARSEC dedup kernel. In our experience, atomic deferral did not significantly complicate the program: the total lines of code changed in dedup were fewer than a dozen, and reasoning about what could and could not be deferred was straightforward. Using atomic deferral allowed transactions to perform output without serializing, and to move other long-running operations out of transactions. The result was a dramatic improvement in the performance of the transactional PARSEC dedup benchmark.

As future work, we are interested in tools for automatically transforming output operations into deferred operations, and studying the relationship between atomic deferral and nested transactions. We are also interested in crafting a more formal correctness argument, which may influence the use of transaction-friendly locks in a greater range of workloads.

Acknowledgments

We thank Dave Dice and Tim Harris for their advice and guidance during the conduct of this research. At Lehigh University, this work was supported in part by the National Science Foundation under Grant CAREER-1253362, and through financial support from Oracle. Any opinions, findings, and conclusions or recommendations expressed in this material are those of the authors and do not necessarily reflect the views of the National Science Foundation.

REFERENCES

[1] Christian Bienia, Sanjeev Kumar, Jaswinder Pal Singh, and Kai Li. 2008. The PARSEC Benchmark Suite: Characterization and Architectural Implications. In *Proceedings of the 17th International Conference on Parallel Architectures and Compilation Techniques.* Toronto, ON, Canada.
[2] Brian D. Carlstrom, Austen McDonald, Hassan Chafi, JaeWoong Chung, Chi Cao Minh, Christos Kozyrakis, and Kunle Olukotun. 2006. The Atomos Transactional Programming Language. In *Proceedings of the 27th ACM Conference on Programming Language Design and Implementation.*
[3] Kapali P. Eswaran, Jim Gray, Raymond A. Lorie, and Irving L. Traiger. 1976. The Notions of Consistency and Predicate Locks in a Database System. *Communications of the ACM* 19, 11 (1976), 624–633.
[4] Free Software Foundation. 2012. Transactional Memory in GCC. (2012). http://gcc.gnu.org/wiki/TransactionalMemory.
[5] Tim Harris, Simon Marlow, Simon Peyton Jones, and Maurice Herlihy. 2005. Composable Memory Transactions. In *Proceedings of the 10th ACM Symposium on Principles and Practice of Parallel Programming.* Chicago, IL.
[6] Maurice P. Herlihy and J. Eliot B. Moss. 1993. Transactional Memory: Architectural Support for Lock-Free Data Structures. In *Proceedings of the 20th International Symposium on Computer Architecture.* San Diego, CA.
[7] ISO/IEC JTC 1/SC 22/WG 21. 2015. Technical Specification for C++ Extensions for Transactional Memory. (May 2015). http://www.open-std.org/jtc1/sc22/wg21/docs/papers/2015/n4514.pdf
[8] Takuya Nakaike, Rei Odaira, Matthew Gaudet, Maged M. Michael, and Hisanobu Tomari. 2015. Quantitative Comparison of Hardware Transactional Memory for Blue Gene/Q, zEnterprise EC12, Intel Core, and POWER8. In *Proceedings of the 42nd Annual International Symposium on Computer Architecture.* Portland, OR.
[9] Yang Ni, Adam Welc, Ali-Reza Adl-Tabatabai, Moshe Bach, Sion Berkowits, James Cownie, Robert Geva, Sergey Kozhukow, Ravi Narayanaswamy, Jeffrey Olivier, Serguei Preis, Bratin Saha, Ady Tal, and Xinmin Tian. 2008. Design and Implementation of Transactional Constructs for C/C++. In *Proceedings of the 23rd ACM Conference on Object Oriented Programming, Systems, Languages, and Applications.* Nashville, TN, USA.
[10] Michael Spear, Michael Silverman, Luke Dalessandro, Maged M. Michael, and Michael L. Scott. 2008. Implementing and Exploiting Inevitability in Software Transactional Memory. In *Proceedings of the 37th International Conference on Parallel Processing.* Portland, OR.
[11] Haris Volos, Andres Jaan Tack, Neelam Goyal, Michael Swift, and Adam Welc. 2009. xCalls: Safe I/O in Memory Transactions. In *Proceedings of the EuroSys2009 Conference.* Nuremberg, Germany.
[12] Chao Wang, Yujie Liu, and Michael Spear. 2014. Transaction-Friendly Condition Variables. In *Proceedings of the 26th ACM Symposium on Parallelism in Algorithms and Architectures.* Prague, Czech Republic.
[13] Adam Welc, Bratin Saha, and Ali-Reza Adl-Tabatabai. 2008. Irrevocable Transactions and their Applications. In *Proceedings of the 20th ACM Symposium on Parallelism in Algorithms and Architectures.* Munich, Germany.
[14] Tingzhe Zhou and Michael Spear. 2016. The Mimir Approach to Transactional Output. In *Proceedings of the 11th ACM SIGPLAN Workshop on Transactional Computing.* Barcelona, Spain.

Brief Announcement: Hardware Transactional Storage Class Memory

Ellis Giles
Rice University
Houston, TX 77005, USA
erg@rice.edu

Kshitij Doshi
Intel Corporation
Chandler, AZ 85226, USA
kshitij.a.doshi@intel.com

Peter Varman
Rice University
Houston, TX 77005, USA
pjv@rice.edu

ABSTRACT

Emerging persistent memory technologies (generically referred to as Storage Class Memory or SCM) hold tremendous promise for accelerating popular data-management applications like in-memory databases. However, programmers now need to deal with ensuring the atomicity of transactions on SCM-resident data and maintaining consistency between the persistent and in-memory execution orders of concurrent transactions. The problem is specially challenging when high-performance isolation mechanisms like Hardware Transaction Memory (HTM) are used for concurrency control.

In this work we show how SCM-based HTM transactions can be ordered correctly using existing CPU instructions, without requiring any changes to existing processor cache hardware or HTM protocols. We describe a method that employs HTM for concurrency control and enforces atomic persistence and consistency with a novel software protocol and back-end external memory controller. In contrast, previous approaches require significant hardware changes to existing processor microarchitectures.

1 INTRODUCTION

Emerging storage class memory (SCM) technologies, such as Intel/Micron's 3DXPoint provide direct access to vast amounts of persistent memory through familiar byte/word grained LOAD and STORE instructions, hitherto employed to access the volatile memory hierarchy. This provides performance and programmability benefits by eliminating the I/O operations and bottlenecks common to many data management applications. It also raises problems of durability (power failures leaving pending updates in volatile buffers), atomicity, and consistency (power failures while SCM is partially updated with autonomous out-of-order cache evictions).

Existing SCM programming frameworks separate into categories based on the degree of change they require in the processor architecture for such problems. Pure software approaches (Mnemosyne [14], SoftWrap [7], ATLAS [3], REWIND [4], DUDETM [12]) work with existing processor capabilities. Approaches like Kiln [16], ATOM [10] and SPMS [11] require significant change to existing cache hardware and protocols in the processor microarchitecture, while solutions like WrAP [6], and NVM-Controller [5] only require external hardware controllers not affecting the processor core.

SPAA '17, July 24-26, 2017, Washington DC, USA
 978-1-4503-4593-4/17/07
DOI: http://dx.doi.org/10.1145/3087556.3087589

The solutions mentioned above either use two-phase locking protocols to isolate concurrent transactions or handle concurrency within the rubric of an STM [14]. PTM [15] proposes changes to processor caches while adding an on-chip scoreboard and global transaction id register to couple HTM with SCM. Recent work [1, 2, 12] has attempted to provide inter-transactional isolation by employing processor based Hardware Transactional Memory (HTM) [9, 13] mechanisms. However, these solutions all require changes to the existing HTM semantics and implementations. For instance, PHTM [2] and PHyTM [1] propose a new instruction called *TransparentFlush*, which can be used to flush a cache line from within an HTM transaction to SCM without causing transaction aborts. DUDETM [12] proposes allowing concurrent access to designated memory variables within an HTM without causing an abort. Selective and incremental changes to the clean isolation semantics of HTM are not to be undertaken lightly; understanding their impact on global system correctness and performance typically requires long gestation periods before processor manufacturers will embrace them.

In this paper we provide a new solution to obtain persistence consistency in NVM while using HTM for concurrency control. The solution does not alter the processor micro architecture, but leverages an external NVM memory controller along with a persistence protocol to supplement the existing HTM transaction semantics. The solution aims to achieve the concurrency benefits of HTM by allowing transactions to operate at the speed of in-memory volatile transactions, while using backend operations to guard against and recover to a consistent volatile state in the event of failure.

2 OVERVIEW

Consider transactions A and B of Listings 1 & 2 that update variables x, y and y, z respectively. The directives **HTMBegin** and **HTMEnd** demarcate code sections serialized by the HTM. Each transaction maintains the invariant $x + y + z = 1$ when executed by itself. When executed concurrently, the HTM aborts conflicting transactions to maintain the abstraction of isolated execution.

When x, y, z are persistent variables (*i.e.*, homed in SCM), additional correctness constraints arise. Suppose transaction A executes the HTM section; at **HTMEnd**, the new values of x and y become visible in the cache hierarchy but may or may not have been written to SCM. The subsequent code may use a sequence of CLWB instructions to force their write back from cache to SCM; however a crash that occurs before all the updates have been flushed can leave the SCM inconsistent. Furthermore, the cache itself may autonomously evict some of the updated variables due to cache pressure, resulting in loss of control over the precise state of the SCM at any time.

In [1, 2] the HTM semantics were changed to allow log records to be persisted to SCM from *within* an HTM transaction using a newly

Listing 1: Transaction A

```
A() {
  AtomicBegin();
  HTMBegin;
  x = 2;
  y = -1-z;
  HTMEnd;
  AtomicEnd();
}
```

Listing 2: Transaction B

```
B() {
  AtomicBegin();
  HTMBegin;
  y = -1- x;
  z =  2;
  HTMEnd;
  AtomicEnd();
}
```

proposed instruction *TransparentFlush*. With this mechanism, when a transaction completes *HTMEnd*, a log of all its writes would be persistent in SCM. Since the HTM mechanism isolates all writes and prevents the cached values from being evicted till *HTMEnd*, this ensures that there will be no spurious cache write backs till all the log records are persisted; should a subsequent crash occur, recovery proceeds from the persisted log records. There are two drawbacks to this solution: first, transactions are slowed down and complete only after its log records are written to the slower memory tier; and second, it is difficult to predict whether and when such intrusive hardware changes, which change established memory operation semantics, will be adopted by processor manufacturers.

Our solution to this problem is presented in the next section. The HTM transaction is enclosed within an atomic section demarcated by the primitives **AtomicBegin** and **AtomicEnd**. A transaction commits at **AtomicEnd** at which time its writes become durable (at least in a recoverable log). Logs are written to SCM *outside* the HTM transaction, and thus no change is required to HTM semantics or mechanisms. Non-conflicting transactions execute concurrently without waiting for a previous transaction to commit and their speed and ordering is determined solely by the HTM; logging operations continue in the background without slowing down the front-end HTM transactions.

3 OUR APPROACH

To couple persistence with HTM concurrency we need to solve three challenges: (a) Spurious Cache Evictions (b) Transaction Ordering and (c) Persisting the updates.

Cache Evictions: The HTM mechanism ensures that no updates will be evicted from the cache to SCM between **HTMBegin** and **HTMEnd**. However, cache evictions after **HTMEnd** and before the log is persisted can cause inconsistency in the SCM in case of a crash. We use the non-intrusive NVM controller proposed in [5] to address this problem. The controller implements a victim cache that holds evictions of SCM variables from the LLC until it is safe to update the SCM home locations of updated variables. A protocol for safely reclaiming entries from the victim cache while spilling the contents of the saved logs to the home locations was described in [5]. Here also we use the NVM controller to guard against spurious updates to SCM by cache evictions. However we need to modify the persistence protocol significantly: specifically, the conditions under which log retirements and victim cache deletions are triggered.

Transaction Ordering: To order transactions we use the platform-wide clock available on Intel architectures. Specifically, we use the platform timer read instruction RDTSCP to timestamp transactions. These timestamps will determine when and in what order the transactions are retired to SCM. Each transaction maintains two timestamps: a *start timestamp* (STS) that is set before the transaction executes **HTMBegin** and an *end timestamp* (ETS) that is set immediately before executing **HTMEnd**. The end timestamps will determine the transaction retirement order, so it is necessary that they correctly reflect transaction execution ordering in volatile memory. Specifically, if the HTM orders transaction A before a conflicting transaction B, then the end timestamp of A should be smaller than that of B. Since instruction delays are unpredictable, the instant that ETS is set must be correctly chosen. If two transactions have disjoint variable sets or are non-overlapping (the last invocation of one begins after the other's end), then any choice of the time stamping instant within their HTM sections will order them consistently. The tricky situation is when two transactions share variables and overlap their execution, but neither is aborted because the actual writes (or reads) to the shared variables in one transaction occur only after the second has completed its **HTMEnd**. In this case, if reading the timer is made the last instruction before the end of the HTM section, then we are guaranteed that the order of end timestamps will correctly reflect the consistency order [8].

We obtain the global system time stamp counter using the new Intel instruction RDTSCP or "read time stamp counter and processor ID". This instruction does not need to be preceded by a serializing CPUID instruction. However, later instructions may get reordered before RDTSCP; to prevent the reordering of an XEND before reading the timestamp counter into registers, we save the resulting time stamp into volatile memory, which, at the end of the HTM transaction after XEND, is guaranteed to instantly reflect all memory operations contained between XBEGIN and XEND.

Persisting Updates: After **HTMEnd**, a transaction writes its log records to SCM along with its end timestamp. The controller will retire the transactions in order of their ETS values. In retiring a transaction, the controller must persist the updates to the home locations of the variables, delete the log of the transaction, and reclaim any of these cache lines that may have spilled into the victim cache. To implement the retirement phase we employ two logical structures: a *blue* list and a *red* priority queue ordered by end timestamps. The structure can be implemented as a single lock-free data structure [8]. After setting its start timestamp, a new transaction places itself at the tail of the blue list of open transactions and executes **HTMBegin**. Just prior to completing its HTM section it sets the end timestamp. Following **HTMEnd**, the transaction persists its logs to SCM, inserts itself into the red priority queue in order of its end timestamp, and deletes itself from the blue list. A retirement thread retires the transaction at the head of the priority queue when it is safe: this occurs when all transactions in the blue list have start timestamps that are greater than its end timestamp. Since the head of the blue list has the earliest start timestamp, the retirement thread only needs to examine the head element.

A transaction can commit any time after being inserted into the priority queue. If it waits till retirement to commit then it is guaranteed durability of its updates. Otherwise, if a transaction with smaller ETS has not persisted its logs before a crash, its log may not be replayed on recovery. The application can choose between early commit versus guaranteed durability. In any case, SCM will be restored to a consistent previous state on recovery.

Algorithm 1: Transaction Wrapper Library and Controller

```
Wrap Library:
OpenWrapC ()
    wrapId = OpenWrap(); // Triggers HandleOpenWrap
    Initialize write set ws; // For logging the updates
    memory fence;
    HTMBegin(); // HTM Begin call XBEGIN
    On abort call AbortWrap;
wrapStore (addrVar, Value)
    Add {addrVar, Value} to ws;
    Normal store of Value to addrVar;
CloseWrapC ()
    t = RDTSCP(); // Set end time stamp in volatile memory
    HTMEnd(); // XEND
    PublishRTC(wrapId, t); // Triggers HandlePublishedRTC
    for ({addrVar, Value} in ws)
        Add ({addrVar, Value} to SCM log;
    memory fence;
    CloseWrap(wrapId); // Triggers HandleCloseWrap
Controller:
HandleOpenWrap (wrapId w)
    Mark w with start timestamp = RDTSCP();
    Add w to tail of Blue List;
HandlePublishedRTC (wrapId w, time endTime)
    Add w to Red Priority Queue with endTime value;
    Remove w from Blue List;
HandleCloseWrap (wrapId w)
    Mark w in Red Priority Queue as complete;
```

3.1 Algorithm

The controller catches cache evictions of SCM variables and holds them in a volatile victim cache till their home locations have been updated by transaction retirements. It tracks the set of open transactions in a bit vector and uses it to tag evicted cache lines with a dependency set. When a transaction retires it is removed from all dependency sets. When the dependency set of a cache line is empty it can be deleted from the victim cache. For details see [5].

Algorithm 1 shows the controller actions and the software wrapper to invoke its functions. We refer to an HTM transaction and the associated logging and retirement operations as a *wrap*.

OpenWrapC opens a wrap, which triggers HandleOpenWrap. It then opens an HTM transaction with HTMBegin (instruction XBEGIN). The HTM transaction detects concurrency conflicts in the transaction. On an HTM abort, the HTM transaction can be re-attempted with exponential back-off or revert to a global fallback lock after several attempts. Additionally, if an HTM transaction is aborted, the associated wrap is also aborted.

wrapStore is a normal write, but also records the address and value of the store to an in-cache memory log to be saved to SCM on successful HTM end. Not every write within the HTM transaction needs to be wrapped. Only the final write to a variable needs to create a log record. However, creating multiple log records for a variable will not affect correctness.

CloseWrapC sets the end timestamp of the transaction using RDTSCP. Following a successful end of the HTM section it moves the wrap to the appropriate place in the priority queue based on its end timestamp, persists the log, and then marks the entry in the priority queue as ready for retirement.

The SCM Controller retires logs in order of end timestamps provided all prior opened transactions have completed. **HandlePublishedRTC** moves a wrap from the Blue list to the Red Priority Queue with priority of the end timestamp. **HandleCloseWrap** simply marks the wrap, which is in the Red Priority Queue, as complete.

For retirement, the head of the Red Priority Queue is examined. If the head element is marked as complete and its end timestamp is less than the start timestamp of all transactions in the Blue list then the head element in the Red Queue may be removed and variables in the wrap retired. Retiring the wrap simply reads the log, copies values safely to home locations, and after all variables are safely committed, removes the log.

3.2 Recovery

The Red Priority Queue and Blue list are not saved in persistent SCM. However, the transaction start timestamp, end timestamp, and log completion flag are stored in the log in persistent memory. This allows for easy reconstruction of the state of the queues during recovery following a failure.

For recovery, we read all logs and rebuild the Blue list and Red Queue. We then process the completed transactions starting from the head of the Red queue that have end timestamps that are less than the smallest start timestamp in the Blue list. This brings the system back into the closest possible point for in-memory consistency.

3.3 NVM Controller Variant

The NVM controller presented in [5] retires transactions directly from transaction logs and removes elements from the victim cache when the dependency set becomes empty. In a variant on the NVM controller, we can instead propagate elements directly from the victim cache to the backend SCM when the dependency set of a cache line in the victim cache becomes empty and use logs only for recovery. A number of alternative implementations are possible in this approach *e.g.* explicitly evict transaction values from the processor caches using CLWB instructions after a transaction ends its concurrency section and periodic fence instructions (which guarantee durability of the flushed values in recent Intel architectures) to allow saved logs to be deleted. The details are deferred to the full paper.

3.4 Example

Figure 1a shows example transactions A and B from Listings 1 and 2 using the Wrap Library functions from Algorithm 1. Variables *x,y* and *y,z* are updated using *wrapStore* within *OpenWrapC()* and *CloseWrapC()* bounds.

Figure 1b shows an example set of four transactions, T1-T4, happening concurrently. The Table shown in Figure 1c illustrates the contents of the Blue list and Red priority queue at each time step indicated in Figure 1b.

```
A() {
    OpenWrapC();
    wrapStore(x, 2);
    wrapStore(y, -1-z);
    CloseWrapC();
}


B() {
    OpenWrapC();
    wrapStore(y,   -1- x);
    wrapStore(z, 2);
    CloseWrapC();
}
```

(a) Example Wrapped Transactions A & B

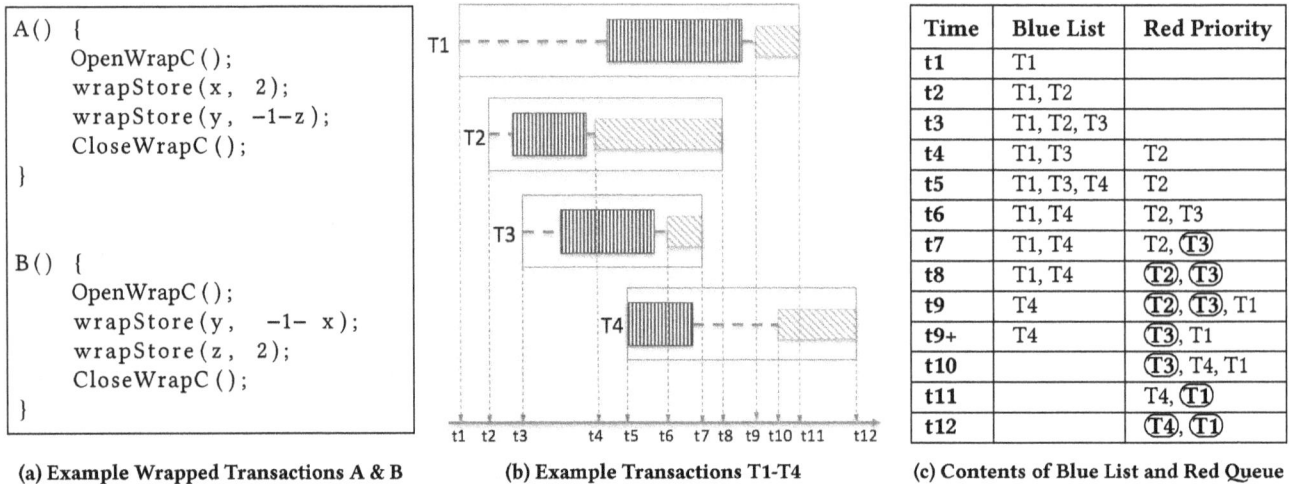

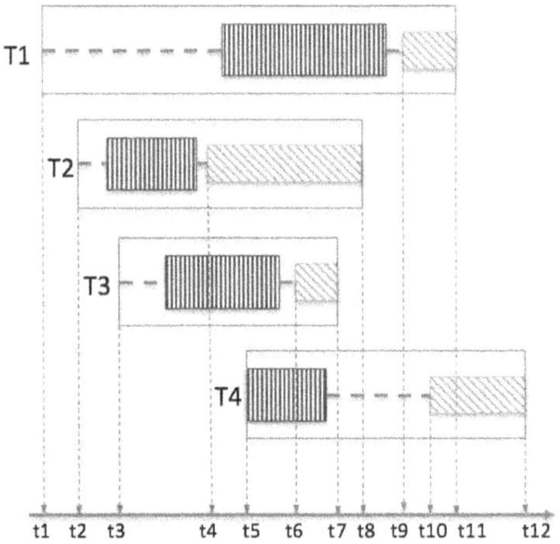

(b) Example Transactions T1-T4

Time	Blue List	Red Priority
t1	T1	
t2	T1, T2	
t3	T1, T2, T3	
t4	T1, T3	T2
t5	T1, T3, T4	T2
t6	T1, T4	T2, T3
t7	T1, T4	T2, **(T3)**
t8	T1, T4	**(T2)**, **(T3)**
t9	T4	**(T2)**, **(T3)**, T1
t9+	T4	**(T3)**, T1
t10		**(T3)**, T4, T1
t11		T4, **(T1)**
t12		**(T4)**, **(T1)**

(c) Contents of Blue List and Red Queue

Figure 1: Example Transactions and Contents of Blue List and Red Priority Queue

First, at time $t1$, T1 opens and places itself with its start timestamp at the end of the Blue list. At times $t2$ and $t3$, transactions T2 and T3 are added to the end of the Blue list with their start timestamps. T2 then completes its concurrency section and publishes its end timestamp at time $t4$ and begins writing its logs, moving from Blue to Red. Transaction T4 starts at time $t5$ and is added to the Blue list. T3 completes its concurrency section and publishes its end timestamp at $t6$, moving from the Blue to Red queue.

At time $t7$, transaction T3 has completed writing its logs and is marked completed in the Red queue, denoted by a bold and circled entry. However, T3 cannot be retired since it is not the head of the Red queue and T1, the head of the Blue list, has a smaller start timestamp, which could potentially place it near the front of the Red queue. When T2 completes writing of logs at time $t8$, it is marked as complete in the Red queue, but also has a later completion time than T1, the head of the Blue list.

When T1 finally completes its concurrency section and publishes its end timestamp at $t9$, T1 is moved from the Blue list to the Red queue and T2 is retired. At time $t9+$, T3, the new head of the Red priority queue, is complete with a published end timestamp and log. However, at this time, T3 cannot be retired since it is waiting on T4, which hasn't yet published its end time and had started before T3 completed.

At time $t10$, T4 publishes its end timestamp and moves from the Blue List to Red Queue. Note that T4 has an ending time before T1, so it is placed **before** T1 in the Red Priority Queue. T1 completes log writing at $t11$ and is marked ready for retirement, but is behind T4, which hasn't yet finished writing its logs. At time $t12$, T4 completes writing its logs and both T4 and T1 can be retired in order.

ACKNOWLEDGMENTS

Supported by NSF Grant CCF 1439075 and Intel SSG.

REFERENCES

[1] Hillel Avni and Trevor Brown. 2016. PHyTM: Persistent Hybrid Transactional Memory. *Proceedings of the VLDB Endowment* 10, 4 (2016), 409–420.

[2] Hillel Avni, Eliezer Levy, and Avi Mendelson. 2015. Hardware transactions in nonvolatile memory. In *International Symposium on Distributed Computing*. Springer, 617–630.

[3] Dhruva R. Chakrabarti, Hans-J. Boehm, and Kumud Bhandari. 2014. Atlas: Leveraging Locks for Non-volatile Memory Consistency. In *Proceedings of the 2014 ACM International Conference on Object Oriented Programming Systems Languages & Applications (OOPSLA '14)*. ACM, New York, NY, USA, 433–452. https://doi.org/10.1145/2660193.2660224

[4] Andreas Chatzistergiou, Marcelo Cintra, and Stratis D Viglas. 2015. Rewind: Recovery write-ahead system for in-memory non-volatile data-structures. *Proceedings of the VLDB Endowment* 8, 5 (2015), 497–508.

[5] Kshitij Doshi, Ellis Giles, and Peter Varman. 2016. Atomic Persistence for SCM with a Non-intrusive Backend Controller. In *The 22nd International Symposium on High-Performance Computer Architecture*. IEEE. Early version in Comp. Arch. Letters, Vol. 15 Issue 1.

[6] Ellis Giles, Kshitij Doshi, and Peter Varman. 2013. Bridging the programming gap between persistent and volatile memory using WrAP. In *Proceedings of the ACM International Conference on Computing Frontiers*. ACM, 30. Early version in MeAOW 2012.

[7] Ellis Giles, Kshitij Doshi, and Peter Varman. 2015. SoftWrAP: A lightweight framework for transactional support of storage class memory. In *Mass Storage Systems and Technologies (MSST), 2015 31st Symposium on*. 1–14. https://doi.org/10.1109/MSST.2015.7208276 Early version in MeAOW 2013.

[8] Ellis Giles, Kshitij Doshi, and Peter Varman. 2017. Continuous Checkpointing of HTM Transactions in NVM. In *Proceedings of the 2017 International Symposium on Memory Management (ISMM '17)*. ACM, New York, NY, USA.

[9] Maurice Herlihy and J Eliot B Moss. 1993. *Transactional memory: Architectural support for lock-free data structures*. Vol. 21,2. ACM.

[10] Arpit Joshi, Vijay Nagarajan, Stratis Viglas, and Marcelo Cintra. 2017. ATOM: Atomic Durability in Non-volatile Memory through Hardware Logging. In *2017 IEEE International Symposium on High Performance Computer Architecture*.

[11] Shuo Li, Peng Wang, Nong Xiao, Guangyu Sun, and Fang Liu. 2017. SPMS: Strand Based Persistent Memory System. In *2017 Design, Automation & Test in Europe Conference & Exhibition (DATE)*. IEEE, 622–625.

[12] Mengxing Liu, Mingxing Zhang, Kang Chen, Xuehai Qian, Yongwei Wu, and Jinglei Ren. 2017. DUDETM: Building Durable Transactions with Decoupling for Persistent Memory. In *To Appear: ASPLOS 2017*.

[13] Ravi Rajwar and James R Goodman. 2001. Speculative lock elision: Enabling highly concurrent multithreaded execution. In *Proceedings of the 34th annual ACM/IEEE international symposium on Microarchitecture*. IEEE Computer Society, 294–305.

[14] H. Volos, A. J. Tack, and M. Swift. 2011. Mnemosyne: Lightweight Persistent Memory. In *Proceedings of 16th International Conference on Architectural Support for Programming Languages and Operating Systems*. ACM Press, 91–104.

[15] Zhaoguo Wang, Han Yi, Ran Liu, Mingkai Dong, and Haibo Chen. 2015. Persistent transactional memory. *IEEE Computer Architecture Letters* 14, 1 (2015), 58–61.

[16] Jishen Zhao, Sheng Li, Doe Hyun Yoon, Yuan Xie, and Norman P. Jouppi. 2013. Kiln: Closing the Performance Gap Between Systems with and Without Persistence Support. In *Proceedings of the 46th Annual IEEE/ACM International Symposium on Microarchitecture (MICRO-46)*. ACM, New York, NY, USA, 421–432. https://doi.org/10.1145/2540708.2540744

Author Index

NOTES